FRENCH
DICTIONARY

D0591784

Published by Collins
An imprint of HarperCollins Publishers
Westerhill Road
Bishopbriggs
Glasgow G64 2QT

Twelfth Edition 2016

10 9 8 7 6 5 4 3

© William Collins Sons & Co. Ltd
1979, 1988
© HarperCollins Publishers 1993, 1997,
2000, 2001, 2003, 2005, 2006, 2009,
2012, 2016

ISBN 978-0-00-814187-5

Collins® and Collins Gem®
are registered trademarks of
HarperCollins Publishers Limited

www.collinsdictionary.com

Typeset by Davidson Publishing
Solutions, Glasgow

Printed in Italy by Grafica Veneta S.p.A.

The contents of this publication are
believed correct at the time of printing.
Nevertheless the Publisher can accept
no responsibility for errors or omissions,
changes in the detail given or for any
expense or loss thereby caused.

HarperCollins does not warrant that
any website mentioned in this title will
be provided uninterrupted, that any
website will be error free, that defects
will be corrected, or that the website or
the server that makes it available are
free of viruses or bugs. For full terms
and conditions please refer to the site
terms provided on the website.

A catalogue record for this book is
available from the British Library.

If you would like to comment on any
aspect of this book, please contact us
at the given address or online.
E-mail: dictionaries@harpercollins.co.uk
 facebook.com/collinsdictionary
 @collinsdict

Acknowledgements
We would like to thank those authors
and publishers who kindly gave
permission for copyright material to be
used in the Collins Corpus. We would
also like to thank Times Newspapers
Ltd for providing valuable data.

TABLE DES MATIÈRES   CONTENTS

EDITOR
Susie Beattie

CONTRIBUTORS
Laurence Larroche
Sabine Citron
Cordelia Lilly
Jean-François Allan
Cécile Aubinière-Robb
Wendy Lee
Catherine Love

FOR THE PUBLISHER
Janice McNeillie
Hannah Dove
Sheena Shanks

Based on the first edition
of the Collins Gem French
Dictionary under the direction
of Pierre-Henri Cousin.

INTRODUCTION

Nous sommes très heureux que vous ayez choisi ce dictionnaire et espérons que vous aimerez l'utiliser et que vous en tirerez profit au lycée, à la maison, en vacances ou au travail.

Cette introduction a pour but de vous donner quelques conseils sur la façon d'utiliser au mieux votre dictionnaire, en vous référant non seulement à son importante nomenclature mais aussi aux informations contenues dans chaque entrée. Ceci vous aidera à lire et à comprendre, mais aussi à communiquer et à vous exprimer en anglais contemporain.

Au début du dictionnaire, vous trouverez la liste des abréviations utilisées dans le texte et celle de la transcription des sons par des symboles phonétiques. Vous y trouverez également la liste des verbes irréguliers en anglais, suivis d'une section finale sur les nombres et sur les expressions de temps.

COMMENT UTILISER VOTRE DICTIONNAIRE

Ce dictionnaire offre une richesse d'informations et utilise diverses formes et tailles de caractères, symboles, abréviations, parenthèses et crochets. Les conventions et symboles utilisés sont expliqués dans les sections qui suivent.

ENTRÉES

Les mots que vous cherchez dans le dictionnaire – les entrées – sont classés par ordre alphabétique. Ils sont imprimés en **gras** pour pouvoir être repérés rapidement. Les entrées figurant en haut de page indiquent le premier (sur la page de gauche) et le dernier mot (sur la page de droite) des deux pages en question.

Des informations sur l'usage ou sur la forme de certaines entrées sont données entre parenthèses, après la transcription phonétique. Ces indications apparaissent sous forme abrégée et en italiques (par ex. (*fam*), (*Comm*)).

Pour plus de facilité, les mots de la même famille sont regroupés sous la même entrée (**ronger, rongeur ; accept, acceptance**) et apparaissent également en gras, ainsi que les expressions courantes dans lesquelles apparaît l'entrée (par exemple **retard** [...] **avoir du ~**).

TRANSCRIPTION PHONÉTIQUE
La transcription phonétique de chaque entrée (indiquant sa prononciation) est présentée entre crochets immédiatement après l'entrée (par ex. **fumer** [fyme] ; **knee** [niː]). La liste des symboles phonétiques figure aux pages xii et xiii.

TRADUCTIONS
Les traductions des entrées apparaissent en caractères ordinaires ; lorsque plusieurs sens ou usages coexistent, ces traductions sont séparées par un point-virgule. Vous trouverez des synonymes de l'entrée en italique entre parenthèses avant les traductions (par ex. **poser** (*installer: moquette, carrelage*)) ou des mots qui fournissent le contexte dans lequel l'entrée est susceptible d'être utilisée (par ex. **poser** (*question*)).

MOTS-CLÉS
Une importance particulière est accordée à certains mots français et anglais qui sont considérés comme des « mots-clés » dans chacune des langues. Cela peut être dû à leur utilisation très fréquente ou au fait qu'ils ont divers types d'usage (par ex. **vouloir, plus** ; **get, that**). L'utilisation de triangles et de chiffres aide à distinguer différentes catégories grammaticales et différents sens. D'autres renseignements utiles apparaissent en italique et entre parenthèses dans la langue de l'utilisateur.

DONNÉES GRAMMATICALES

Les catégories grammaticales sont données sous forme abrégée et en italique après la transcription phonétique (par ex. *vt, adv, conj*). Les genres des noms français sont indiqués de la manière suivante : *nm* pour un nom masculin et *nf* pour un nom féminin. Le féminin et le pluriel irréguliers de certains noms sont également indiqués (par ex. **directeur, -trice** ; **cheval, -aux**).

Le masculin et le féminin des adjectifs sont indiqués lorsque ces deux formes sont différentes (par ex. **noir, e**). Lorsque l'adjectif a un féminin ou un pluriel irrégulier, ces formes sont clairement indiquées (par ex. **net, nette**). Les pluriels irréguliers des noms et les formes irrégulières des verbes anglais sont indiqués entre parenthèses, avant la catégorie grammaticale (par ex. **man** (*pl* **men**) *n* ; **give** (*pt* **gave**; *pp* **given**) *vt*).

INTRODUCTION

We are delighted that you have chosen this dictionary and hope you will enjoy and benefit from using it at school, at home, on holiday or at work.

This introduction gives you a few tips on how to get the most out of your dictionary – not simply from its comprehensive wordlist but also from the information provided in each entry. This will help you to read and understand modern French, as well as communicate and express yourself in the language.

This dictionary begins by listing the abbreviations used in the text and illustrating the sounds shown by the phonetic symbols. You will also find French verb tables, followed by a final section on numbers and time expressions.

USING YOUR DICTIONARY

A wealth of information is presented in the dictionary, using various typefaces, sizes of type, symbols, abbreviations and brackets. The various conventions and symbols used are explained in the following sections.

HEADWORDS

The words you look up in a dictionary – 'headwords' – are listed alphabetically. They are printed in **bold** for rapid identification. The headwords appearing at the top of each page indicate the first (if it appears on a left-hand page) and last word (if it appears on a right-hand page) dealt with on the page in question.

Information about the usage or form of certain headwords is given in brackets after the phonetic spelling. This usually appears in abbreviated form and in italics (e.g. (*inf*), (*Comm*)).

Where appropriate, words related to headwords are grouped in the same entry (**ronger, rongeur; accept, acceptance**) and are also in bold, as are common expressions in which the headword appears (e.g. **enquire** [...] **to enquire ~ about**).

PHONETIC SPELLINGS

The phonetic spelling of each headword (indicating its pronunciation) is given in square brackets immediately after the headword (e.g. **fumer** [fyme]; **knee** [niː]). A list of these symbols is given on pages xii and xiii.

TRANSLATIONS

Headword translations are given in ordinary type and, where more than one meaning or usage exists, these are separated by a semi-colon. You will often find other words in italics in brackets before the translations. These offer suggested contexts in which the headword might appear (e.g. **rough** (*voice*) [...] (*plan*)) or provide synonyms (e.g. **rough** (*manner: coarse*)). The gender of the translation also appears in italics immediately following the key element of the translation.

KEYWORDS

Special status is given to certain French and English words which are considered as 'keywords' in each language. They may, for example, occur very frequently or have several types of usage (e.g. **vouloir, plus**; **get, that**). A combination of triangles and numbers helps you to distinguish different parts of speech and different meanings. Further helpful information is provided in brackets and italics.

GRAMMATICAL INFORMATION

Parts of speech are given in abbreviated form in italics after the phonetic spellings of headwords (e.g. *vt, adv, conj*). Genders of French nouns are indicated as follows: *nm* for a masculine noun and *nf* for a feminine noun. Feminine and irregular plural forms of nouns are also shown (**directeur, -trice**; **cheval, -aux**).

Adjectives are given in both masculine and feminine forms where these forms are different (e.g. **noir, e**). Clear information is provided where adjectives have an irregular feminine or plural form (e.g. **net, nette**).

ABRÉVIATIONS

ABBREVIATIONS

abréviation	*ab(b)r*	abbreviation
adjectif, locution adjectivale	*adj*	adjective, adjectival phrase
administration	*Admin*	administration
adverbe, locution adverbiale	*adv*	adverb, adverbial phrase
agriculture	*Agr*	agriculture
anatomie	*Anat*	anatomy
architecture	*Archit*	architecture
article défini	*art déf*	definite article
article indéfini	*art indéf*	indefinite article
automobile	*Aut(o)*	automobiles
aviation, voyages aériens	*Aviat*	flying, air travel
biologie	*Bio(l)*	biology
botanique	*Bot*	botany
anglais britannique	*BRIT*	British English
chimie	*Chem*	chemistry
commerce, finance, banque	*Comm*	commerce, finance, banking
informatique	*Comput*	computing
conjonction	*conj*	conjunction
construction	*Constr*	building
nom utilisé comme adjectif	*cpd*	compound element
cuisine	*Culin*	cookery
article défini	*def art*	definite article
économie	*Écon, Econ*	economics
électricité, électronique	*Élec, Elec*	electricity, electronics
en particulier	*esp*	especially
exclamation, interjection	*excl*	exclamation, interjection
féminin	*f*	feminine
langue familière (! emploi vulgaire)	*fam(!)*	colloquial usage (! particularly offensive)
emploi figuré	*fig*	figurative use
(verbe anglais) dont la particule est inséparable	*fus*	(phrasal verb) where the particle is inseparable
généralement	*gén, gen*	generally
géographie, géologie	*Géo, Geo*	geography, geology
géométrie	*Géom, Geom*	geometry
article indéfini	*indef art*	indefinite article
langue familière (! emploi vulgaire)	*inf(!)*	colloquial usage (! particularly offensive)
infinitif	*infin*	infinitive
informatique	*Inform*	computing
invariable	*inv*	invariable
irrégulier	*irreg*	irregular
domaine juridique	*Jur*	law

ABRÉVIATIONS		ABBREVIATIONS
grammaire, linguistique	*Ling*	grammar, linguistics
masculin	*m*	masculine
mathématiques, algèbre	*Math*	mathematics, calculus
médecine	*Méd, Med*	medical term, medicine
masculin ou féminin	*m/f*	masculine or feminine
domaine militaire, armée	*Mil*	military matters
musique	*Mus*	music
nom	*n*	noun
navigation, nautisme	*Navig, Naut*	sailing, navigation
nom ou adjectif numéral	*num*	numeral noun or adjective
	o.s.	oneself
péjoratif	*péj, pej*	derogatory, pejorative
photographie	*Phot(o)*	photography
physiologie	*Physiol*	physiology
pluriel	*pl*	plural
politique	*Pol*	politics
participe passé	*pp*	past participle
préposition	*prép, prep*	preposition
pronom	*pron*	pronoun
psychologie, psychiatrie	*Psych*	psychology, psychiatry
temps du passé	*pt*	past tense
quelque chose	*qch*	
quelqu'un	*qn*	
religion, domaine ecclésiastique	*Rel*	religion
	sb	somebody
enseignement, système scolaire et universitaire	*Scol*	schooling, schools and universities
singulier	*sg*	singular
	sth	something
subjonctif	*sub*	subjunctive
sujet (grammatical)	*subj*	(grammatical) subject
techniques, technologie	*Tech*	technical term, technology
télécommunications	*Tél, Tel*	telecommunications
télévision	*TV*	television
typographie	*Typ(o)*	typography, printing
anglais des États-Unis	*US*	American English
verbe (auxiliaire)	*vb (aux)*	(auxiliary) verb
verbe intransitif	*vi*	intransitive verb
verbe transitif	*vt*	transitive verb
zoologie	*Zool*	zoology
marque déposée	®	registered trademark
indique une équivalence culturelle	≈	indicates a cultural equivalent

TRANSCRIPTION PHONÉTIQUE

CONSONNES		**CONSONANTS**
NB. **p, b, t, d, k, g** sont suivis d'une aspiration en anglais.		NB. **p, b, t, d, k, g** are not aspirated in French.
pou**p**ée	p	**p**u**pp**y
bom**b**e	b	**b**a**b**y
ten**t**e **th**ermal	t	**t**en**t**
din**d**e	d	**d**a**dd**y
co**q** **q**ui **k**épi	k	**c**or**k** **k**iss **ch**ord
ga**g**e ba**gu**e	g	**g**a**g** **gu**ess
sale **c**e na**t**ion	s	**s**o ri**c**e ki**ss**
zéro ro**s**e	z	**c**ou**s**in bu**zz**
ta**ch**e **ch**at	ʃ	**sh**eep **s**ugar
gi**l**et **j**uge	ʒ	plea**s**ure bei**g**e
	tʃ	**ch**urch
	dʒ	**j**udge **g**eneral
fer **ph**are	f	**f**arm ra**ff**le
ver**v**eine	v	**v**ery re**v**el
	θ	**th**in ma**th**s
	ð	**th**at o**th**er
lent sa**ll**e	l	**l**ittle ba**ll**
rare **r**ent**r**er	R	
	r	**r**at **r**are
ma**m**an fe**mm**e	m	**m**u**mm**y co**mb**
non bo**nn**e	n	**n**o ra**n**
a**gn**eau vi**gn**e	ɲ	**ch**urch
	ŋ	si**ng**ing ba**n**k
	h	**h**at re**h**earse
yeux pa**ill**e p**i**ed	j	**y**et
n**ou**er **ou**i	w	**w**all **w**ail
h**ui**le l**ui**	ɥ	
	x	lo**ch**
DIVERS		**MISCELLANEOUS**
pour l'anglais : le **r** final se prononce en liaison devant une voyelle	r	in English transcription: final **r** can be pronounced before a vowel
pour l'anglais : précède la syllabe accentuée	'	in French wordlist: no liaison before aspirate **h** and **y**

En règle générale, la prononciation est donnée entre crochets après chaque entrée. Toutefois, du côté anglais-français et dans le cas des expressions composées de deux ou plusieurs mots non réunis par un trait d'union et faisant l'objet d'une entrée séparée, la prononciation doit être cherchée sous chacun des mots constitutifs de l'expression en question.

PHONETIC TRANSCRIPTION

VOYELLES

NB. La mise en équivalence de certains sons n'indique qu'une ressemblance approximative.

VOWELS

NB. The pairing of some vowel sounds only indicates approximate equivalence.

ici vie lyrique	i iː	heel bead
	ɪ	hit pity
jouer été	e	
lait jouet merci	ɛ	set tent
plat amour	a æ	bat apple
bas pâte	ɑ ɑː	after car calm
	ʌ	fun cousin
le premier	ə	over above
beurre peur	œ	
peu deux	ø əː	urgent fern work
or homme	ɔ	wash pot
mot eau gauche	o ɔː	born cork
genou roue	u	full hook
	uː	boom shoe
rue urne	y	

DIPHTONGUES

DIPHTHONGS

	ɪə	beer tier
	ɛə	tear fair there
	eɪ	date plaice day
	aɪ	life buy cry
	aʊ	owl foul now
	əʊ	low no
	ɔɪ	boil boy oily
	ʊə	poor tour

NASALES

NASAL VOWELS

matin plein	ɛ̃
brun	œ̃
sang an dans	ɑ̃
non pont	ɔ̃

In general, we give the pronunciation of each entry in square brackets after the word in question. However, on the English-French side, where the entry is composed of two or more unhyphenated words, each of which is given elsewhere in this dictionary, you will find the pronunciation of each word in its alphabetical position.

FRENCH VERB FORMS

a Present participle **b** Past participle **c** Present **d** Imperfect **e** Future
f Conditional **g** Present subjunctive

1 ARRIVER a arrivant **b** arrivé **c** arrive, arrives, arrive, arrivons, arrivez, arrivent **d** arrivais **e** arriverai **f** arriverais **g** arrive

2 FINIR a finissant **b** fini **c** finis, finit, finissons, finissez, finissent **d** finissais **e** finirai **f** finirais **g** finisse

3 PLACER a plaçant **b** placé **c** place, places, place, plaçons, placez, placent **d** plaçais, plaçais, plaçait, placions, placiez, plaçaient **e** placerai, placeras, placera, placerons, placerez, placeront **f** placerais, placerais, placerait, placerions, placeriez, placeraient **g** place

3 BOUGER a bougeant **b** bougé **c** bouge, bougeons **d** bougeais, bougions **e** bougerai **f** bougerais **g** bouge

4 appeler a appelant **b** appelé **c** appelle, appelons **d** appelais **e** appellerai **f** appellerais **g** appelle

4 jeter a jetant **b** jeté **c** jette, jetons **d** jetais **e** jetterai **f** jetterais **g** jette

5 geler a gelant **b** gelé **c** gèle, gelons **d** gelais **e** gèlerai **f** gèlerais **g** gèle

6 CÉDER a cédant **b** cédé **c** cède, cèdes, cède, cédons, cédez, cèdent **d** cédais, cédais, cédait, cédions, cédiez, cédaient **e** céderai, céderas, cédera, céderons, céderez, céderont **f** céderais, céderais, céderait, céderions, céderiez, céderaient **g** cède

7 épier a épiant **b** épié **c** épie, épies, épie, épions **d** épiais **e** épierai **g** épie

8 noyer a noyant **b** noyé **c** noie, noyons **d** noyais **e** noierai **f** noierais **g** noie

9 ALLER a allant **b** allé **c** vais, vas, va, allons, allez, vont **d** allais **e** irai **f** irais **g** aille

10 HAÏR a haïssant **b** haï **c** hais, hais, hait, haïssons, haïssez, haïssent **d** haïssais, haïssais, haïssait, haïssions, haïssiez, haïssaient **e** haïrai, haïras, haïra, haïrons, haïrez, haïront **f** haïrais, haïrais, haïrait, haïrions, haïriez, haïraient **g** haïsse

11 courir a courant **b** couru **c** cours, courons **d** courais **e** courrai **g** coure

12 cueillir a cueillant **b** cueilli **c** cueille, cueillons **d** cueillais **e** cueillerai **g** cueille

13 assaillir – a assaillant **b** assailli **c** assaille, assaillons **d** assaillais **e** assaillirai **g** assaille

14 servir a servant **b** servi **c** sers, servons **d** servais **g** serve

15 bouillir a bouillant **b** bouilli **c** bous, bouillons **d** bouillais **g** bouille

16 partir a partant **b** parti **c** pars, partons **d** partais **g** parte

17 fuir a fuyant **b** fui **c** fuis, fuyons,

fuient d fuyais g fuie

18 couvrir a couvrant b couvert
c couvre, couvrons d couvrais
g couvre

19 mourir a mourant b mort
c meurs, mourons, meurent
d mourais e mourrai g meure

20 vêtir a vêtant b vêtu c vêts,
vêtons d vêtais e vêtirai g vête

21 acquérir a acquérant b acquis
c acquiers, acquérons,
acquièrent d acquérais
e acquerrai g acquière

22 venir a venant b venu c viens,
venons, viennent d venais
e viendrai g vienne

23 pleuvoir a pleuvant b plu c pleut,
pleuvent d pleuvait e pleuvra
g pleuve

24 prévoir *like* voir e prévoirai

25 pourvoir a pourvoyant b pourvu
c pourvois, pourvoyons,
pourvoient d pourvoyais
g pourvoie

26 asseoir a asseyant b assis
c assieds, asseyons, asseyez,
asseyent d asseyais e asseiérai
g asseye

27 MOUVOIR a mouvant b mû
c meus, meus, meut, mouvons,
mouvez, meuvent d mouvais
e mouvrai f mouvrais g meuve,
meuves, meuve, mouvions,
mouviez, meuvent

28 RECEVOIR a recevant b reçu
c reçois, reçois, reçoit, recevons,
recevez, reçoivent d recevais
e recevrai f recevrais g reçoive

29 valoir a valant b valu c vaux,

vaut, valons d valais e vaudrai
g vaille

30 voir a voyant b vu c vois, voyons,
voient d voyais e verrai g voie

31 vouloir a voulant b voulu c veux,
veut, voulons, veulent d voulais
e voudrai g veuille ; *impératif*
veuillez !

32 savoir a sachant b su c sais,
savons, savent d savais e saurai
g sache *impératif* sache ! sachons !
sachez !

33 pouvoir a pouvant b pu c peux,
peut, pouvons, peuvent
d pouvais e pourrai g puisse

34 AVOIR a ayant b eu c ai, as, a,
avons, avez, ont d avais e aurai
f aurais g aie, aies, ait, ayons,
ayez, aient

35 conclure a concluant b conclu
c conclus, concluons d concluais
g conclue

36 rire a riant b ri c ris, rions d riais
g rie

37 dire a disant b dit c dis, disons,
dites, disent d disais g dise

38 nuire a nuisant b nui c nuis,
nuisons d nuisais e nuirai f nuirais
g nuise

39 écrire a écrivant b écrit c écris,
écrivons d écrivais g écrive

40 suivre a suivant b suivi c suis,
suivons d suivais g suive

41 RENDRE a rendant b rendu
c rends, rends, rend, rendons,
rendez, rendent d rendais
e rendrai f rendrais g rende

42 vaincre a vainquant b vaincu
c vaincs, vainc, vainquons

d vainquais g vainque

43 lire a lisant b lu c lis, lisons
d lisais g lise

44 croire a croyant b cru c crois,
croyons, croient d croyais g croie

45 CLORE a closant b clos c clos,
clos, clôt, closent e clorai, cloras,
clora, clorons, clorez, cloront
f clorais, clorais, clorait, clorions,
cloriez, cloraient

46 vivre a vivant b vécu c vis, vivons
d vivais g vive

47 MOUDRE a moulant b moulu
c mouds, mouds, moud,
moulons, moulez, moulent
d moulais, moulais, moulait,
moulions, mouliez, moulaient
e moudrai, moudras, moudra,
moudrons, moudrez, moudront
f moudrais, moudrais, moudrait,
moudrions, moudriez,
moudraient g moule

48 coudre a cousant b cousu
c couds, cousons, cousez,
cousent d cousais g couse

49 joindre a joignant b joint c joins,
joignons d joignais g joigne

50 TRAIRE a trayant b trait c trais,
trais, trait, trayons, trayez,
traient d trayais b trayais, trayait,
trayions, trayiez, trayaient
e trairai, trairas, traira, trairons,
trairez, trairont f trairais,
trairais, trairait, trairions,
trairiez, trairaient g traie

51 ABSOUDRE a absolvant
b absous c absous, absous,

absout, absolvons, absolvez,
absolvent d absolvais, absolvais,
absolvait, absolvions, absolviez,
absolvaient e absoudrai,
absoudras, absoudra,
absoudrons, absoudrez,
absoudront f absoudrais,
absoudrais, absoudrait,
absoudrions, absoudriez,
absoudraient g absolve

52 craindre a craignant b craint
c crains, craignons d craignais
g craigne

53 boire a buvant b bu c bois,
buvons, boivent d buvais g boive

54 plaire a plaisant b plu c plais,
plaît, plaisons d plaisais g plaise

55 croître a croissant b crû c croîs,
croissons d croissais g croisse

56 mettre a mettant b mis c mets,
mettons d mettais g mette

57 CONNAÎTRE a connaissant
b connu c connais, connaît,
connaissons d connaissais
g connaisse

58 prendre a prenant b pris
c prends, prenons, prennent
d prenais g prenne

59 naître a naissant b né c nais,
naît, naissons d naissais g naisse

60 FAIRE a faisant b fait c fais, fais,
fait, faisons, faites, font d faisais
e ferai f ferais g fasse

61 ÊTRE a étant b été c suis, es,
est, sommes, êtes, sont d étais
e serai f serais g sois, sois, soit,
soyons, soyez, soient

VERBES IRRÉGULIERS ANGLAIS

PRÉSENT	PASSÉ	PARTICIPE	PRÉSENT	PASSÉ	PARTICIPE
arise	arose	arisen	**fall**	fell	fallen
awake	awoke	awoken	**feed**	fed	fed
be	was, were	been	**feel**	felt	felt
(am, is, are; being)			**fight**	fought	fought
bear	bore	born(e)	**flee**	fled	fled
beat	beat	beaten	**fling**	flung	flung
become	became	become	**fly**	flew	flown
begin	began	begun	**forbid**	forbad(e)	forbidden
bend	bent	bent	**forecast**	forecast	forecast
bet	bet,	bet,	**forget**	forgot	forgotten
	betted	betted	**forgive**	forgave	forgiven
bid (at auction,	bid	bid	**forsake**	forsook	forsaken
cards)			**freeze**	froze	frozen
bid (say)	bade	bidden	**get**	got	got,
bind	bound	bound			(us) gotten
bite	bit	bitten	**give**	gave	given
bleed	bled	bled	**go** (goes)	went	gone
blow	blew	blown	**grind**	ground	ground
break	broke	broken	**grow**	grew	grown
breed	bred	bred	**hang**	hung	hung
bring	brought	brought	**hang** (execute)	hanged	hanged
build	built	built	**have**	had	had
burn	burnt,	burnt,	**hear**	heard	heard
	burned	burned	**hide**	hid	hidden
burst	burst	burst	**hit**	hit	hit
buy	bought	bought	**hold**	held	held
can	could	(been able)	**hurt**	hurt	hurt
cast	cast	cast	**keep**	kept	kept
catch	caught	caught	**kneel**	knelt,	knelt,
choose	chose	chosen		kneeled	kneeled
cling	clung	clung	**know**	knew	known
come	came	come	**lay**	laid	laid
cost	cost	cost	**lead**	led	led
cost (work	costed	costed	**lean**	leant,	leant,
out price of)				leaned	leaned
creep	crept	crept	**leap**	leapt,	leapt,
cut	cut	cut		leaped	leaped
deal	dealt	dealt	**learn**	learnt,	learnt,
dig	dug	dug		learned	learned
do (does)	did	done	**leave**	left	left
draw	drew	drawn	**lend**	lent	lent
dream	dreamed,	dreamed,	**let**	let	let
	dreamt	dreamt	**lie** (lying)	lay	lain
drink	drank	drunk	**light**	lit,	lit,
drive	drove	driven		lighted	lighted
dwell	dwelt	dwelt	**lose**	lost	lost
eat	ate	eaten	**make**	made	made

PRÉSENT	PASSÉ	PARTICIPE	PRÉSENT	PASSÉ	PARTICIPE
may	might	–	speed	sped,	sped,
mean	meant	meant		speeded	speeded
meet	met	met	spell	spelt,	spelt,
mistake	mistook	mistaken		spelled	spelled
mow	mowed	mown,	spend	spent	spent
		mowed	spill	spilt,	spilt,
must	(had to)	(had to)		spilled	spilled
pay	paid	paid	spin	spun	spun
put	put	put	spit	spat	spat
quit	quit,	quit,	spoil	spoiled,	spoiled,
	quitted	quitted		spoilt	spoilt
read	read	read	spread	spread	spread
rid	rid	rid	spring	sprang	sprung
ride	rode	ridden	stand	stood	stood
ring	rang	rung	steal	stole	stolen
rise	rose	risen	stick	stuck	stuck
run	ran	run	sting	stung	stung
saw	sawed	sawed,	stink	stank	stunk
		sawn	stride	strode	stridden
say	said	said	strike	struck	struck
see	saw	seen	strive	strove	striven
seek	sought	sought	swear	swore	sworn
sell	sold	sold	sweep	swept	swept
send	sent	sent	swell	swelled	swollen,
set	set	set			swelled
sew	sewed	sewn	swim	swam	swum
shake	shook	shaken	swing	swung	swung
shear	sheared	shorn,	take	took	taken
		sheared	teach	taught	taught
shed	shed	shed	tear	tore	torn
shine	shone	shone	tell	told	told
shoot	shot	shot	think	thought	thought
show	showed	shown	throw	threw	thrown
shrink	shrank	shrunk	thrust	thrust	thrust
shut	shut	shut	tread	trod	trodden
sing	sang	sung	wake	woke,	woken,
sink	sank	sunk		waked	waked
sit	sat	sat	wear	wore	worn
slay	slew	slain	weave	wove	woven
sleep	slept	slept	weave (wind)	weaved	weaved
slide	slid	slid	wed	wedded,	wedded,
sling	slung	slung		wed	wed
slit	slit	slit	weep	wept	wept
smell	smelt,	smelt,	win	won	won
	smelled	smelled	wind	wound	wound
sow	sowed	sown,	wring	wrung	wrung
		sowed	write	wrote	written
speak	spoke	spoken			

LES NOMBRES

un (une)	1	one
deux	2	two
trois	3	three
quatre	4	four
cinq	5	five
six	6	six
sept	7	seven
huit	8	eight
neuf	9	nine
dix	10	ten
onze	11	eleven
douze	12	twelve
treize	13	thirteen
quatorze	14	fourteen
quinze	15	fifteen
seize	16	sixteen
dix-sept	17	seventeen
dix-huit	18	eighteen
dix-neuf	19	nineteen
vingt	20	twenty
vingt et un (une)	21	twenty-one
vingt-deux	22	twenty-two
trente	30	thirty
quarante	40	forty
cinquante	50	fifty
soixante	60	sixty
soixante-dix	70	seventy
soixante-et-onze	71	seventy-one
soixante-douze	72	seventy-two
quatre-vingts	80	eighty
quatre-vingt-un (-une)	81	eighty-one
quatre-vingt-dix	90	ninety
cent	100	a hundred, one hundred
cent un (une)	101	a hundred and one
deux cents	200	two hundred
deux cent un (une)	201	two hundred and one
quatre cents	400	four hundred
mille	1000	a thousand
cinq mille	5000	five thousand
un million	1000000	a million

LES NOMBRES

premier (première), 1er (1ère)
deuxième, 2e or 2ème
troisième, 3e or 3ème
quatrième, 4e or 4ème
cinquième, 5e or 5ème
sixième, 6e or 6ème
septième
huitième
neuvième
dixième
onzième
douzième
treizième
quartorzième
quinzième
seizième
dix-septième
dix-huitième
dix-neuvième
vingtième
vingt-et-unième
vingt-deuxième
trentième
centième
cent-unième
millième

NUMBERS

first, 1st
second, 2nd
third, 3rd
fourth, 4th
fifth, 5th
sixth, 6th
seventh
eighth
ninth
tenth
eleventh
twelfth
thirteenth
fourteenth
fifteenth
sixteenth
seventeenth
eighteenth
nineteenth
twentieth
twenty-first
twenty-second
thirtieth
hundredth
hundred-and-first
thousandth

LES FRACTIONS ETC.

un demi
un tiers
un quart
un cinquième
zéro virgule cinq, 0,5
trois virgule quatre, 3,4
dix pour cent
cent pour cent

FRACTIONS ETC.

a half
a third
a quarter
a fifth
(nought) point five, 0.5
three point four, 3.4
ten per cent
a hundred per cent

EXEMPLES

elle habite au septième (étage)
il habite au sept
au chapitre/à la page sept
il est arrivé (le) septième

EXAMPLES

she lives on the 7th floor
he lives at number 7
chapter/page 7
he came in 7th

XX

L'HEURE	THE TIME
quelle heure est-il ?	*what time is it?*
il est …	*it's ou it is …*
minuit	midnight, twelve p.m.
une heure (du matin)	one o'clock (in the morning), one (a.m.)
une heure cinq	five past one
une heure dix	ten past one
une heure et quart	a quarter past one, one fifteen
une heure vingt-cinq	twenty-five past one, one twenty-five
une heure et demie, une heure trente	half-past one, one thirty
deux heures moins vingt-cinq, une heure trente-cinq	twenty-five to two, one thirty-five
deux heures moins vingt, une heure quarante	twenty to two, one forty
deux heures moins le quart, une heure quarante-cinq	a quarter to two, one forty-five
deux heures moins dix, une heure cinquante	ten to two, one fifty
midi	twelve o'clock, midday, noon
deux heures (de l'après-midi), quatorze heures	two o'clock (in the afternoon), two (p.m.)
sept heures (du soir), dix-neuf heures	seven o'clock (in the evening), seven (p.m.)
à quelle heure ?	*(at) what time?*
à minuit	at midnight
à sept heures	at seven o'clock
dans vingt minutes	in twenty minutes
il y a un quart d'heure	fifteen minutes ago

Français – Anglais

French – English

a [a] *vb voir* **avoir**

○ **MOT-CLÉ**

à [a] (*à + le* = **au**, *à + les* = **aux**) *prép* **1** (*endroit, situation*) at, in; **être à Paris/au Portugal** to be in Paris/Portugal; **être à la maison/à l'école** to be at home/at school; **à la campagne** in the country; **c'est à 10 m/km/à 20 minutes (d'ici)** it's 10 m/km/20 minutes away

2 (*direction*) to; **aller à Paris/au Portugal** to go to Paris/Portugal; **aller à la maison/à l'école** to go home/to school; **à la campagne** to the country

3 (*temps*): **à 3 heures/minuit** at 3 o'clock/midnight; **au printemps** in the spring; **au mois de juin** in June; **à Noël/Pâques** at Christmas/Easter; **à demain/la semaine prochaine!** see you tomorrow/next week!

4 (*attribution, appartenance*) to; **le livre est à Paul/à lui/à nous** this book is Paul's/his/yours; **donner qch à qn** to give sth to sb; **un ami à moi** a friend of mine

5 (*moyen*) with; **se chauffer au gaz** to have gas heating; **à bicyclette** on a ou by bicycle; **à pied** on foot; **à la main/machine** by hand/machine

6 (*provenance*) from; **boire à la bouteille** to drink from the bottle

7 (*caractérisation, manière*): **l'homme aux yeux bleus** the man with the blue eyes; **à la russe** the Russian way

8 (*but, destination*): **tasse à café** coffee cup; **maison à vendre** house for sale; **je n'ai rien à lire** I don't have anything to read; **à bien réfléchir** ... thinking about it ..., on reflection ...

9 (*rapport, évaluation, distribution*): **100 km/unités à l'heure** 100 km/units per ou an hour; **payé à l'heure** paid by the hour; **cinq à six** five to six

10 (*conséquence, résultat*): **à ce qu'il prétend** according to him; **à leur grande surprise** much to their surprise; **à nous trois nous n'avons pas su le faire** we couldn't do it even between the three of us; **ils sont arrivés à quatre** four of them arrived (together)

abaisser [abese] /1/ *vt* to lower, bring down; (*manette*) to pull down; **s'abaisser** *vi* to go down; (*fig*) to demean o.s.

abandon [abādɔ̃] *nm* abandoning; giving up; withdrawal; **être à l'~** to be in a state of neglect; **laisser à l'~** to abandon

abandonner [abādɔne] /1/ *vt* (*personne*) to leave, abandon, desert; (*projet, activité*) to abandon, give up; (*Sport*) to retire ou withdraw from; (*céder*) to surrender; **s'~ à** (*paresse, plaisirs*) to give o.s. up to

abat-jour [abaʒuʀ] *nm inv* lampshade

abats [aba] *nmpl* (*de bœuf, porc*) offal *sg*; (*de volaille*) giblets

abattement [abatmɑ̃] *nm*: **~ fiscal** ≈ tax allowance

abattoir [abatwaʀ] *nm* slaughterhouse

abattre [abatʀ] /41/ *vt* (*arbre*) to cut down, fell; (*mur, maison*) to pull down; (*avion, personne*) to shoot down; (*animal*) to shoot, kill; (*fig*) to wear out, tire out; to demoralize; **s'abattre** *vi* to crash down: **ne pas se laisser ~** to keep one's spirits up, not to let things get one down; **s'~ sur** to beat down on; (*coups, injures*) to rain down on; **~ du travail** ou **de la besogne** to get through a lot of work

abbaye [abei] *nf* abbey

abbé [abe] *nm* priest; (*d'abbaye*) abbot

abcès [apsɛ] *nm* abscess

abdiquer [abdike] /1/ *vt* to abdicate

abdominal, e, -aux [abdɔminal, -o] *adj* abdominal; **abdominaux** *nmpl*: **faire des abdominaux** to do sit-ups

abeille [abɛj] *nf* bee

aberrant, e [abeʀɑ̃, -ɑ̃t] *adj* absurd

aberration [abeʀasjɔ̃] *nf* aberration

abîme [abim] *nm* abyss, gulf

abîmer [abime] /1/ *vt* to spoil, damage; **s'abîmer** *vi* to get spoilt ou damaged

aboiement [abwamɑ̃] *nm* bark, barking *no pl*

abolir [abɔliʀ] /2/ *vt* to abolish

abominable [abɔminabl] *adj* abominable

abondance [abɔ̃dɑ̃s] *nf* abundance

abondant, e [abɔ̃dɑ̃, -ɑ̃t] *adj* plentiful, abundant, copious; **abonder** /1/ *vi* to abound, be plentiful; **abonder dans le sens de qn** to concur with sb

abonné, e [abɔne] *nm/f* subscriber; season ticket holder

abonnement [abɔnmɑ̃] *nm*

subscription; (*pour transports en commun, concerts*) season ticket

abonner [abɔne] /1/ *vt*: **s'abonner à** to subscribe to, take out a subscription to; **s'~ aux tweets de qn sur Twitter** to follow sb on Twitter

abord [abɔʀ] *nm*: **abords** *nmpl* (*environs*) surroundings; **d'~** first; **au premier ~** at first sight, initially

abordable [abɔʀdabl] *adj* (*personne*) approachable; (*prix*) reasonable

aborder [abɔʀde] /1/ *vi* to land ▷ *vt* (*sujet, difficulté*) to tackle; (*personne*) to approach; (*rivage etc*) to reach

aboutir [abutiʀ] /2/ *vi* (*négociations etc*) to succeed; **~ à/dans/sur** to end up at/in/on; **n'~ à rien** to come to nothing

aboyer [abwaje] /8/ *vi* to bark

abréger [abʀeʒe] /3, 6/ *vt* to shorten

abreuver [abʀœve] /1/: **s'abreuver** *vi* to drink; **abreuvoir** *nm* watering place

abréviation [abʀevjasjɔ̃] *nf* abbreviation

abri [abʀi] *nm* shelter; **être à l'~** to be under cover; **se mettre à l'~** to shelter; **à l'~ de** sheltered from; (*danger*) safe from

abricot [abʀiko] *nm* apricot

abriter [abʀite] /1/ *vt* to shelter; **s'abriter** *vi* to shelter, take cover

abrupt, e [abʀypt] *adj* sheer, steep; (*ton*) abrupt

abruti, e [abʀyti] *adj* stunned, dazed ▷ *nm/f* (*fam*) idiot; **~ de travail** overworked

absence [apsɑ̃s] *nf* absence; (*Méd*) blackout; **en l'~ de** in the absence of; **avoir des ~s** to have mental blanks

absent, e [apsɑ̃, -ɑ̃t] *adj* absent ▷ *nm/f* absentee; **absenter** /1/: **s'absenter** *vi* to take time off work; (*sortir*) to leave, go out

absolu, e [apsɔly] *adj* absolute; **absolument** *adv* absolutely

absorbant, e [apsɔʀbɑ̃, -ɑ̃t] *adj* absorbent

absorber [apsɔʀbe] /1/ vt to absorb; (gén, Méd: manger, boire) to take

abstenir [apstəniʀ] /22/: **s'abstenir** vi: **s'~ de qch/de faire** to refrain from sth/from doing

abstrait, e [apstʀɛ, -ɛt] adj abstract

absurde [apsyʀd] adj absurd

abus [aby] nm abuse; **~ de confiance** breach of trust; **il y a de l'~!** (fam) that's a bit much!; **abuser** /1/ vi to go too far, overstep the mark; **s'abuser** vi (se méprendre) to be mistaken; **abuser de** (violer, duper) to take advantage of; **abusif, -ive** adj exorbitant; (punition) excessive

académie [akademi] nf academy; (Scol: circonscription) ≈ regional education authority; see note "**Académie française**"

* **ACADÉMIE FRANÇAISE**
*
* The Académie française was founded
* by Cardinal Richelieu in 1635,
* during the reign of Louis XIII. It is
* made up of forty elected scholars
* and writers who are known as 'les
* Quarante' or 'les Immortels'. One
* of the Académie's functions is to
* keep an eye on the development
* of the French language, and its
* recommendations are frequently
* the subject of lively public debate.
* It has produced several editions
* of its famous dictionary and also
* awards various literary prizes.

acajou [akaʒu] nm mahogany

acariâtre [akaʀjɑtʀ] adj cantankerous

accablant, e [akɑblɑ̃, -ɑ̃t] adj (chaleur) oppressive; (témoignage, preuve) overwhelming

accabler [akɑble] /1/ vt to overwhelm, overcome; **~ qn d'injures** to heap on shower abuse on sb; **~ qn de travail** to overwork sb

accalmie [akalmi] nf lull

accaparer [akapaʀe] /1/ vt to monopolize; (travail etc) to take up (all) the time ou attention of

accéder [aksede] /6/: **~ à** (lieu) to reach; (accorder: requête) to grant, accede to

accélérateur [akseleʀatœʀ] nm accelerator

accélérer [akseleʀe] /6/ vt to speed up ▷ vi to accelerate

accent [aksɑ̃] nm accent; (Phonétique, fig) stress; **mettre l'~ sur** (fig) to stress; **~ aigu/grave/circonflexe** acute/grave/circumflex accent; **accentuer** /1/ vt (Ling) to accent; (fig) to accentuate, emphasize; **s'accentuer** vi to become more marked ou pronounced

acceptation [akseptasjɔ̃] nf acceptance

accepter [aksepte] /1/ vt to accept; **~ faire** to agree to do

accès [aksɛ] nm (à un lieu) access; (Méd: de toux) fit; (: de fièvre) bout; **d'~ facile/malaisé** easily/not easily accessible; **facile d'~** easy to get to; **~ de colère** fit of anger; **accessible** adj accessible; (livre, sujet): **accessible à qn** within the reach of sb

accessoire [akseswaʀ] adj secondary; (frais) incidental ▷ nm accessory; (Théât) prop

accident [aksidɑ̃] nm accident; **par~** by chance; **~ de la route** road accident; **accidenté, e** adj damaged ou injured (in an accident); (relief, terrain) uneven; hilly; **accidentel, le** adj accidental

acclamer [aklame] /1/ vt to cheer, acclaim

acclimater [aklimate] /1/: **s'acclimater** vi to become acclimatized

accolade [akɔlad] nf (amicale) embrace; (signe) brace

accommoder [akɔmɔde] /1/ vt (Culin) to prepare; **s'accommoder**

de to put up with; (se contenter de) to make do with

accompagnateur, -trice [akɔ̃paɲatœʀ, -tʀis] nm/f (Mus) accompanist; (de voyage) guide; (de voyage organisé) courier

accompagner [akɔ̃paɲe] /1/ vt to accompany, be ou go ou come with; (Mus) to accompany

accompli, e [akɔ̃pli] adj accomplished

accomplir [akɔ̃pliʀ] /2/ vt (tâche, projet) to carry out; (souhait) to fulfil; **s'accomplir** vi to be fulfilled

accord [akɔʀ] nm agreement; (entre des styles, tons etc) harmony; (Mus) chord; **se mettre d'~** to come to an agreement (with each other); **être d'~ to agree; d'~! OK!**

accordéon [akɔʀdeɔ̃] nm (Mus) accordion

accorder [akɔʀde] /1/ vt (faveur, délai) to grant; **~ de l'importance/de la valeur à qch** to attach importance/ value to sth; (harmoniser) to match; (Mus) to tune

accoster [akɔste] /1/ vt (Navig) to draw alongside ▷ vi to berth

accouchement [akuʃmɑ̃] nm delivery, (child)birth; labour

accoucher [akuʃe] /1/ vi to give birth, have a baby; **~ d'un garçon** to give birth to a boy

accouder [akude] /1/: **s'accouder** vi: **s'~ à/contre/sur** to rest one's elbows on/against/on; **accoudoir** nm armrest

accoupler [akuple] /1/ vt to couple; (pour la reproduction) to mate; **s'accoupler** vi to mate

accourir [akuʀiʀ] /11/ vi to rush ou run up

accoutumance [akutymɑ̃s] nf (gén) adaptation; (Méd) addiction

accoutumé, e [akutyme] adj (habituel) customary, usual

accoutumer [akutyme] /1/ vt: **s'accoutumer à** to get accustomed ou used to

accroc [akʀo] nm (déchirure) tear; (fig) hitch, snag

accrochage [akʀɔʃaʒ] nm (Auto) (minor) collision; (dispute) clash, brush

accrocher [akʀɔʃe] /1/ vt (suspendre) to hang; (fig) to catch, attract; **s'accrocher** (se disputer) to have a clash ou brush; **~ qch à** (suspendre) to hang sth (up) on; (attacher: remorque) to hitch sth (up) to; (déchirer) to catch sth (on); **il a accroché ma voiture** he bumped into my car; **s'~ à** (rester pris à) to catch on; (agripper, fig) to hang on ou cling to

accroissement [akʀwasmɑ̃] nm increase

accroître [akʀwatʀ] /55/ vt: **s'accroître** vi to increase

accroupir [akʀupiʀ] /2/: **s'accroupir** vi to squat, crouch (down)

accru, e [akʀy] pp de **accroître**

accueil [akœj] nm welcome; **comité/centre d'~** reception committee/centre; **accueillir** /12/ vt to welcome; (aller chercher) to meet, collect

accumuler [akymyle] /1/ vt to accumulate, amass; **s'accumuler** vi to accumulate; to pile up

accusation [akyzasjɔ̃] nf (gén) accusation; (Jur) charge; (partie): **l'~** the prosecution

accusé, e [akyze] nm/f accused; (prévenu(e)) defendant ▷ nm: **~ de réception** acknowledgement of receipt

accuser [akyze] /1/ vt to accuse; (fig) to emphasize, bring out; (: montrer) to show; **~ qn de** to accuse sb of; **~ qn de qch** to charge sb with; **~ réception de** to acknowledge receipt of

acéré, e [asere] adj sharp

acharné, e [aʃaʀne] adj (lutte, adversaire) fierce, bitter; (travail) relentless

acharner [aʃaʀne] /1/: **s'acharner** vi: **s'~ sur** to go at fiercely; **s'~ contre**

to set o.s. against; (*malchance*) to hound; **s'~ à faire** to try doggedly to do; to persist in doing

achat [aʃa] nm purchase; **faire l'~ de** to buy; **faire des ~s** to do some shopping

acheter [aʃte] /5/ vt to buy, purchase; (*soudoyer*) to buy; **~ qch à** (*marchand*) to buy ou purchase sth from; (*ami etc: offrir*) to buy sth for; **acheteur, -euse** nm/f buyer; shopper; (*Comm*) buyer

achever [aʃ(ə)ve] /5/ vt to complete, finish; (*blessé*) to finish off; **s'achever** vi to end

acide [asid] adj sour, sharp; (*Chimie*) acid(ic) ▷ nm acid; **acidulé, e** adj slightly acid; **bonbons acidulés** acid drops

acier [asje] nm steel; **aciérie** nf steelworks sg

acné [akne] nf acne

acompte [akɔ̃t] nm deposit

à-côté [akote] nm side-issue; (*argent*) extra

à-coup [aku] nm: **par ~s** by fits and starts

acoustique [akustik] nf (*d'une salle*) acoustics pl

acquéreur [akerœʀ] nm buyer, purchaser

acquérir [akeʀiʀ] /21/ vt to acquire

acquis, e [aki, -iz] pp de **acquérir** ▷ nm (*accumulated*) experience; **son aide nous est ~e** we can count on ou be sure of his help

acquitter [akite] /1/ vt (*Jur*) to acquit; (*facture*) to pay, settle; **s'~ de** to discharge; (*promesse, tâche*) to fulfil

âcre [akʀ] adj acrid, pungent

acrobate [akʀɔbat] nm/f acrobat; **acrobatie** nf acrobatics sg

acte [akt] nm act, action; (*Théât*) act; **prendre ~ de** to take note of; **faire ~ de présence** to put in an appearance; **faire ~ de candidature** to submit an application; **~ de**

mariage/naissance marriage/birth certificate

acteur [aktœʀ] nm actor

actif, -ive [aktif, -iv] adj active ▷ nm (*Comm*) assets pl; (*fig*): **avoir à son ~** to have to one's credit; **population active** working population

action [aksjɔ̃] nf (*gén*) action; (*Comm*) share; **une bonne/mauvaise ~** a good/an unkind deed; **actionnaire** nm/f shareholder; **actionner** /1/ vt (*mécanisme*) to activate; (*machine*) to operate

activer [aktive] /1/ vt to speed up; **s'activer** vi to bustle about; (*se hâter*) to hurry up

activité [aktivite] nf activity; **en ~** (*volcan*) active; (*fonctionnaire*) in active life

actrice [aktʀis] nf actress

actualité [aktÿalite] nf (*d'un problème*) topicality; (*événements*): **l'~** current events; **les ~s** (*Ciné, TV*) the news; **d'~** topical

actuel, le [aktÿɛl] adj (*présent*) present; (*d'actualité*) topical; **à l'heure ~le** at this moment in time; **actuellement** [aktÿɛlmɑ̃] adv at present, at the present time

> Attention à ne pas traduire
> *actuellement* par *actually*.

acupuncture [akypɔ̃ktyʀ] nf acupuncture

adaptateur, -trice [adaptatœʀ, -tʀis] nm/f adapter

adapter [adapte] /1/ vt to adapt; **s'~ (à)** (*personne*) to adapt (to); **~ qch à** (*approprier*) to adapt sth to (fit); **~ qch sur/dans/à** (*fixer*) to fit sth on/into/to

addition [adisjɔ̃] nf addition; (*au café*) bill; **additionner** /1/ vt to add (up)

adepte [adɛpt] nm/f follower

adéquat, e [adekwa(t), -at] adj appropriate, suitable

adhérent, e [adeʀɑ̃, -ɑ̃t] nm/f member

adhérer [adere] /6/: **~ à** (coller) to adhere ou stick to; (se rallier à: parti, club) to join; **adhésif, -ive** adj adhesive, sticky; **ruban adhésif** sticky ou adhesive tape

adieu, x [adjø] excl goodbye ▷ nm farewell

adjectif [adʒɛktif] nm adjective

adjoint, e [adʒwɛ̃ -wɛ̃t] nm/f assistant; **~ au maire** deputy mayor; **directeur ~** assistant manager

admettre [admɛtR] /56/ vt (visiteur) to admit; (candidat: Scol) to pass; (tolérer) to allow, accept; (reconnaître) to admit, acknowledge

administrateur, -trice [administratœR, -tRis] nm/f (Comm) director; (Admin) administrator

administration [administRasjɔ̃] nf administration; **l'A~** = the Civil Service

administrer [administRe] /1/ vt (firme) to manage, run; (biens, remède, sacrement etc) to administer

admirable [admiRabl] adj admirable, wonderful

admirateur, -trice [admiRatœR, -tRis] nm/f admirer

admiration [admiRasjɔ̃] nf admiration

admirer [admiRe] /1/ vt to admire

admis, e [admi, -iz] pp de **admettre**

admissible [admisibl] adj (candidat) eligible; (comportement) admissible, acceptable

ADN sigle m (= acide désoxyribonucléique) DNA

ado [ado] (fam) nm/f teen

adolescence [adolesɑ̃s] nf adolescence

adolescent, e [adolesɑ̃ -ɑ̃t] nm/f adolescent, teenager

adopter [adɔpte] /1/ vt to adopt; **adoptif, -ive** adj (parents) adoptive; (fils, patrie) adopted

adorable [adɔRabl] adj adorable

adorer [adɔRe] /1/ vt to adore; (Rel) to worship

adosser [adose] /1/ vt: **~ qch à** ou **contre** to stand sth against; **s'~ à** ou **contre** to lean with one's back against

adoucir [adusiR] /2/ vt (goût, température) to make milder; (avec du sucre) to sweeten; (peau, voix, eau) to soften; **s'adoucir** vi (caractère) to mellow

adresse [adRɛs] nf skill, dexterity; (domicile) address; **~ électronique** email address

adresser [adRese] /1/ vt (lettre: expédier) to send; (: écrire l'adresse sur) to address; (injure, compliments) to address; **s'adresser à** (parler à) to speak to, address; (s'informer auprès de) to go and see; (: bureau) to enquire at; (livre, conseil) to be aimed at; **~ la parole à qn** to speak to ou address sb

adroit, e [adRwa, -wat] adj skilled

ADSL sigle m (= asymmetrical digital subscriber line) ADSL, broadband

adulte [adylt] nm/f adult, grown-up ▷ adj (personne, attitude) adult, grown-up; (chien, arbre) fully-grown, mature

adverbe [adverb] nm adverb

adversaire [adveRsɛR] nm/f (Sport, gén) opponent, adversary

aération [aeRasjɔ̃] nf airing; (circulation de l'air) ventilation

aérer [aeRe] /6/ vt to air; (fig) to lighten

aérien, ne [aeRjɛ̃, -ɛn] adj (Aviat) air cpd, aerial; (câble, métro) overhead; (fig) light; **compagnie ~ne** airline (company)

aéro: aérobic nf aerobics sg; **aérogare** nf airport (buildings); (en ville) air terminal; **aéroglisseur** nm hovercraft; **aérophagie** nf (Méd) wind, aerophagia (Méd); **aéroport** nm airport; **aérosol** nm aerosol

affaiblir [afeblir] /2/: **s'affaiblir** vi to weaken

affaire [afɛR] nf (problème, question) matter; (criminelle, judiciaire) case; (scandaleuse etc) affair; (entreprise) business; *(marché, transaction)* (business) deal, (piece of) business *no pl*; *(occasion intéressante)* good deal; **affaires** *nfpl* affairs; *(activité commerciale)* business *sg*; *(effets personnels)* things, belongings; **~s de sport** sports gear; **tirer qn/se tirer d'~** to get sb/o.s. out of trouble; **ceci fera l'~** this will do (nicely); **avoir ~ à** *(en contact)* to be dealing with; **ce sont mes ~s** *(cela me concerne)* that's my business; **occupe-toi de tes ~s!** mind your own business!; **les ~s étrangères** *(Pol)* foreign affairs;

affairer /1/: **s'affairer** *vi* to busy o.s., bustle about

affamé, e [afame] *adj* starving

affecter [afɛkte] /1/ *vt* to affect; **~ qch à** to allocate *ou* allot sth to; **~ qn à** to appoint sb to; *(diplomate)* to post sb to

affectif, -ive [afɛktif, -iv] *adj* emotional

affection [afɛksjɔ̃] *nf* affection; *(mal)* ailment; **affectionner** /1/ *vt* to be fond of; **affectueux, -euse** *adj* affectionate

affichage [afiʃaʒ] *nm* billposting; *(électronique)* display; **"~ interdit"** "stick no bills"; **~ à cristaux liquides** liquid crystal display, LCD

affiche [afiʃ] *nf* poster; *(officielle)* (public) notice; *(Théât)* bill; **être à l'~** to be on

afficher [afiʃe] /1/ *vt* *(affiche)* to put up; *(réunion)* to put up a notice about; *(électroniquement)* to display; *(fig)* to exhibit, display; *(péj)* to flaunt o.s.; *(électroniquement)* to be displayed; **"défense d'~"** "no bill posters"

affilée [afile]: **d'~** *adv* at a stretch

affirmatif, -ive [afirmatif, -iv] *adj* affirmative

affirmer [afirme] /1/ *vt* to assert

affligé, e [afliʒe] *adj* distressed, grieved; **~ de** *(maladie, tare)* afflicted with

affliger [afliʒe] /3/ *vt* *(peiner)* to distress, grieve

affluence [aflyɑ̃s] *nf* crowds *pl*; **heures d'~** rush hour *sg*; **jours d'~** busiest days

affluent [aflyɑ̃] *nm* tributary

affolement [afɔlmɑ̃] *nm* panic

affoler [afɔle] /1/ *vt* to throw into a panic; **s'affoler** *vi* to panic

affranchir [afrɑ̃ʃir] /2/ *vt* to put a stamp *ou* stamps on; *(à la machine)* to frank *(BRIT)*, meter *(US)*; *(fig)* to free, liberate; **affranchissement** *nm* postage

affreux, -euse [afrø, -øz] *adj* dreadful, awful

affront [afrɔ̃] *nm* affront; **affrontement** *nm* clash, confrontation

affronter [afrɔ̃te] /1/ *vt* to confront, face

affût [afy] *nm*: **à l'~ (de)** *(gibier)* lying in wait (for); *(fig)* on the look-out (for)

Afghanistan [afganistɑ̃] *nm*: **l'~** Afghanistan

afin [afɛ̃]: **~ que** *conj* so that, in order that; **~ de faire** in order to do, so as to do

africain, e [afrikɛ̃, -ɛn] *adj* African ▷ *nm/f*: **A~, e** African

Afrique [afrik] *nf*: **l'~** Africa; **l'~ australe/du Nord/du Sud** southern/North/South Africa

agacer [agase] /3/ *vt* to irritate

âge [aʒ] *nm* age; **quel ~ as-tu?** how old are you?; **prendre de l'~** to be getting on (in years); **le troisième ~** *(personnes âgées)* senior citizens; *(période)* retirement; **âgé, e** *adj* old, elderly; **âgé de 10 ans** 10 years old

agence [aʒɑ̃s] *nf* agency, office; *(succursale)* branch; **~ immobilière** estate agent's (office) *(BRIT)*, real estate office *(US)*; **~ de voyages** travel agency

agenda [aʒɛ̃da] *nm* diary; **~ électronique** PDA

Attention à ne pas traduire *agenda* par le mot anglais *agenda*.

agenouiller [aʒ(ə)nuje] /1/: **s'agenouiller** vi to kneel (down)

agent, e [aʒɑ̃, ɑ̃t] nm/f (aussi: **~(e) de police**) policeman (policewoman); (Admin) official, officer; **~ immobilier** estate agent (BRIT), realtor (US)

agglomération [aglɔmeʀasjɔ̃] nf town; (Auto) built-up area; **l'~ parisienne** the urban area of Paris

aggraver [agʀave] /1/: **s'aggraver** vi to worsen

agile [aʒil] adj agile, nimble

agir [aʒiʀ] /2/ vi to act; **il s'agit de**: it's a matter ou question of; (ça traite de) it is about; **il s'agit de faire** we (ou you etc) must do; **de quoi s'agit-il?** what is it about?

agitation [aʒitasjɔ̃] nf (hustle and) bustle; (trouble) agitation, excitement; (politique) unrest, agitation

agité, e [aʒite] adj fidgety, restless; (troublé) agitated, perturbed; (mer) rough

agiter [aʒite] /1/ vt (bouteille, chiffon) to shake; (bras, mains) to wave; (préoccuper, exciter) to trouble

agneau, x [aɲo] nm lamb

agonie [agɔni] nf mortal agony, death pangs pl; (fig) death throes pl

agrafe [agʀaf] nf (de vêtement) hook, fastener; (de bureau) staple; **agrafer** /1/ vt to fasten; to staple; **agrafeuse** [agʀaføz] nf stapler

agrandir [agʀɑ̃diʀ] /2/ vt to extend; **s'agrandir** vi (ville, famille) to grow, expand; (trou, écart) to get bigger; **agrandissement** nm (photographie) enlargement

agréable [agʀeabl] adj pleasant, nice

agréé, e [agʀee] adj: **concessionnaire ~** registered dealer

agréer [agʀee] /1/ vt (requête) to accept; **~ à** to please, suit; **veuillez ~, Monsieur/Madame,**

mes salutations distinguées (personne nommée) yours sincerely; (personne non nommée) yours faithfully

agrégation [agʀegasjɔ̃] nf highest teaching diploma in France; **agrégé, e** nm/f holder of the agrégation

agrément [agʀemɑ̃] nm (accord) consent, approval; (attraits) charm, attractiveness; (plaisir) pleasure

agresser [agʀese] /1/ vt to attack; **agresseur** nm aggressor, attacker; (Pol, Mil) aggressor; **agressif, -ive** adj aggressive

agricole [agʀikɔl] adj agricultural; **agriculteur, -trice** nm/f farmer; **agriculture** nf agriculture; farming

agripper [agʀipe] /1/ vt to grab, clutch; **s'~ à** to cling (on) to, clutch, grip

agroalimentaire [agʀɔalimɑ̃tɛʀ] nm farm-produce industry

agrumes [agʀym] nmpl citrus fruit(s)

aguets [agɛ]: **aux ~** adv; **être aux ~** to be on the look-out

ai [ɛ] vb voir **avoir**

aide [ɛd] nm/f assistant ▷ nf assistance, help; (secours financier) aid; **à l'~ de** with the help ou aid of; **appeler (qn) à l'~** to call for help (from sb); **à l'~!** help!; **~ judiciaire** legal aid; **~ ménagère** nf = home help (BRIT) ou helper (US); **aide-mémoire** nm inv memoranda pages pl; (key facts) handbook

aider [ede] /1/ vt to help; **~ à qch** to help (towards) sth; **~ qn à faire qch** to help sb to do sth; **s'~ de** (se servir de) to use, make use of

aide-soignant, e [ɛdswaɲɑ̃, -ɑ̃t] nm/f auxiliary nurse

aie etc [ɛ] vb voir **avoir**

aïe [aj] excl ouch!

aigle [ɛgl] nm eagle

aigre [ɛgʀ] adj sour, sharp; (fig) sharp, cutting; **aigre-doux, -douce** adj (sauce) sweet and sour; **aigreur** nf sourness; sharpness

aigu, ë [egy] *adj (objet, arête)* sharp; *(son, voix)* high-pitched, shrill; *(note)* high(-pitched)

aiguille [eguij] *nf* needle; *(de montre)* hand; **~ à tricoter** knitting needle

aiguiser [egize] /1/ *vt* to sharpen; *(fig)* to stimulate (*: sens*) to excite

ail [aj] *nm* garlic

aile [ɛl] *nf* wing; **aileron** *nm (de requin)* fin; **ailier** *nm* winger

aille *etc* [aj] *vb voir* **aller**

ailleurs [ajœʀ] *adv* elsewhere, somewhere else; **partout/nulle part ~** everywhere/nowhere else; **d'~** *(du reste)* moreover, besides; **par ~** *(d'autre part)* moreover, furthermore

aimable [ɛmabl] *adj* kind, nice

aimant [ɛmɑ̃] *nm* magnet

aimer [eme] /1/ *vt* to love; *(d'amitié, affection, par goût)* to like; **j'aimerais ...** *(souhait)* I would like ...; **j'aime faire du ski** I love skiing; **je t'aime** I love you; **bien ~ qn/qch** to like sb/sth; **j'aime mieux Paul (que Pierre)** I prefer Paul (to Pierre); **j'aimerais autant** *ou* **mieux y aller maintenant** I'd sooner *ou* rather go now

aine [ɛn] *nf* groin

aîné, e [ene] *adj* elder, older; *(le plus âgé)* eldest, oldest > *nm/f* oldest child *ou* one, oldest boy *ou* son/girl *ou* daughter

ainsi [ɛ̃si] *adv (de cette façon)* like this, in this way, thus; *(ce faisant)* thus > *conj* thus, so; **~ que** *(comme)* (just) as; *(et aussi)* as well as; **pour ~ dire** so to speak; **et ~ de suite** and so on (and so forth)

air [ɛʀ] *nm* air; *(mélodie)* tune; *(expression)* look, air; **paroles/menaces en l'~** empty words/threats; **prendre l'~** to get some (fresh) air; **avoir l'~** *(sembler)* to look, appear; **avoir l'~ triste** to look *ou* seem sad; **avoir l'~ de qch** to look like sth; **avoir l'~ de faire** to look as though one is doing

airbag [ɛʀbag] *nm* airbag

aisance [ɛzɑ̃s] *nf* ease; *(richesse)* affluence

aise [ɛz] *nf* comfort; **être à l'~** *ou* **à son ~** to be comfortable; *(pas embarrassé)* to be at ease; *(financièrement)* to be comfortably off; **se mettre à l'~** to make o.s. comfortable; **être mal à l'~** *ou* **à son ~** to be uncomfortable; *(gêné)* to be ill at ease; **en faire à son ~** to do as one likes; **aisé, e** *adj* easy; *(assez riche)* well-to-do, well-off

aisselle [ɛsɛl] *nf* armpit

ait [ɛ] *vb voir* **avoir**

ajonc [aʒɔ̃] *nm* gorse *no pl*

ajourner [aʒuʀne] /1/ *vt (réunion)* to adjourn; *(décision)* to defer, postpone

ajouter [aʒute] /1/ *vt* to add

alarme [alaʀm] *nf* alarm; **donner l'~** to give *ou* raise the alarm; **alarmer** /1/ *vt* to alarm; **s'alarmer** *vi* to become alarmed

Albanie [albani] *nf*: **l'~** Albania

album [albɔm] *nm* album

alcool [alkɔl] *nm*: **l'~** alcohol; **un ~** a spirit, a brandy; **bière sans ~** non-alcoholic *ou* alcohol-free beer; **~ à brûler** methylated spirits *(BRIT)*, wood alcohol *(US)*; **~ à 90°** surgical spirit; **alcoolique** *adj, nm/f* alcoholic; **alcoolisé, e** *adj* alcoholic; **une boisson non alcoolisée** a soft drink; **alcoolisme** *nm* alcoholism; **alco(o)test®** *nm* Breathalyser®; *(test)* breath-test

aléatoire [aleatwaʀ] *adj* uncertain; *(Inform, Statistique)* random

alentour [alɑ̃tuʀ] *adv* around (about); **alentours** *nmpl* surroundings; **aux ~s de** in the vicinity *ou* neighbourhood of, around about; *(temps)* around about

alerte [alɛʀt] *adj* agile, nimble; *(style)* brisk, lively > *nf* alert; warning; **~ à la bombe** bomb scare; **alerter** /1/ *vt* to alert

algèbre [alʒɛbʀ] *nf* algebra

Alger [alʒe] n Algiers

Algérie [alʒeʀi] nf: **l'~** Algeria; **algérien, ne** adj Algerian ▷ nm/f: **Algérien, ne** Algerian

algue [alg] nf seaweed no pl; (Bot) alga

alibi [alibi] nm alibi

aligner [aliɲe] /1/ vt to align, line up; (idées, chiffres) to string together; (adapter): **~ qch sur** to bring sth into alignment with; **s'aligner** (soldats etc) to line up; **s'~ sur** (Pol) to align o.s. with

aliment [alimɑ̃] nm food; **alimentation** nf (en eau etc, de moteur) supplying; (commerce) food trade; (régime) diet; (Inform) feed; **alimentation (générale)** grocer's; **alimenter** /1/ vt to feed; (Tech): **alimenter (en)** to supply (with), feed (with); (fig) to sustain, keep going

allaiter [alete] /1/ vt to (breast-)feed, nurse; (animal) to suckle

allécher [aleʃe] /6/ vt: **~ qn** to make sb's mouth water; to tempt sb, entice sb

allée [ale] nf (de jardin) path; (en ville) avenue, drive; **~s et venues** comings and goings

allégé, e [aleʒe] adj (yaourt etc) low-fat

alléger [aleʒe] /3, 6/ vt (voiture) to make lighter; (chargement) to lighten; (souffrance) to alleviate, soothe

Allemagne [alman] nf: **l'~** Germany; **allemand, e** adj German ▷ nm (Ling) German ▷ nm/f: **Allemand, e** German

aller [ale] /9/ nm (trajet) outward journey; (billet) single (BRIT) ou one-way ticket (US) ▷ vi (gén) to go; **~ simple** (billet) single (BRIT) ou one-way ticket; **~ (et) retour (AR)** return trip ou journey (BRIT), round trip (US); (billet) return (BRIT) ou round-trip (US) ticket; **~ (convenir)** to suit; (forme, pointure etc) to fit;

~ avec (couleurs, style etc) to go (well) with; **je vais le faire/me fâcher** I'm going to do it/to get angry; **~ voir/chercher qn** to go and see/look for sb; **comment allez-vous?** how are you?; **comment ça va?** how are you?; (affaires etc) how are things?; **il va bien/mal** he's well/ not well, he's fine/ill; **ça va bien/mal** (affaires etc) it's going well/not going well; **~ mieux** to be better; **allez!** come on!; **allons!** come now!

allergie [alerʒi] nf allergy

allergique [alerʒik] adj: **~ à** allergic to

alliance [aljɑ̃s] nf (Mil, Pol) alliance; (bague) wedding ring

allier [alje] /7/ vt (Pol, gén) to ally; (fig) to combine; **s'allier** to become allies; (éléments, caractéristiques) to combine

allô [alo] excl hullo, hallo

allocation [alɔkasjɔ̃] nf allowance; **~ (de) chômage** unemployment benefit; **~s familiales** = child benefit

allonger [alɔ̃ʒe] /3/ vt to lengthen, make longer; (étendre: bras, jambe) to stretch (out); **s'allonger** vi to get longer; (se coucher) to lie down, stretch out; **~ le pas** to hasten one's step(s)

allumage [alymaʒ] nm (Auto) ignition

allume-cigare [alymsigaʀ] nm inv cigar lighter

allumer [alyme] /1/ vt (lampe, phare, radio) to put ou switch on; (pièce) to put ou switch the light(s) on in; (feu, bougie, cigare, pipe, gaz) to light; **s'allumer** vi (lumière, lampe) to come ou go on

allumette [alymɛt] nf match

allure [alyʀ] nf (vitesse) speed; (: à pied) pace; (démarche) walk; (aspect, air) look; **avoir de l'~** to have style; **à toute ~** at full speed

allusion [a(l)lyzjɔ̃] nf allusion; (sous-entendu) hint; **faire ~ à** to allude ou refer to; to hint at

○ **MOT-CLÉ**

alors [alɔʀ] *adv* **1** *(à ce moment-là)* then, at that time; **il habitait alors à Paris** he lived in Paris at that time **2** *(par conséquent)* then; **tu as fini?** alors je m'en vais have you finished? I'm going then

3: **et alors?** so (what)?

▸ *conj*: **alors que** *(au moment où)* when, as; **il est arrivé alors que je partais** he arrived as I was leaving; *(tandis que)* whereas, while; **alors que son frère travaillait dur, lui se reposait** while his brother was working hard, HE would rest; *(bien que)* even though; **il a été puni alors qu'il n'a rien fait** he was punished, even though he had done nothing

alourdir [aluʀdiʀ] /2/ *vt* to weigh down, make heavy

Alpes [alp] *nfpl*: **les ~** the Alps

alphabet [alfabɛ] *nm* alphabet; *(livre)* ABC (book)

alpinisme [alpinism] *nm* mountaineering, climbing

Alsace [alzas] *nf* Alsace; **alsacien, ne** *adj* Alsatian ▸ *nm/f*: **Alsacien, ne** Alsatian

altermondialisme [altɛʀmɔ̃djalism] *nm* anti-globalism; **altermondialiste** *adj, nm/f* anti-globalist

alternatif, -ive [altɛʀnatif, -iv] *adj* alternating ▸ *nf* alternative; **alternative** *nf (choix)* alternative; **alterner** /1/ *vt* to alternate

altitude [altityd] *nf* altitude, height

alto [alto] *nm (instrument)* viola

aluminium [alyminjɔm] *nm* aluminium (BRIT), aluminum (US)

amabilité [amabilite] *nf* kindness

amaigrissant, e [amegʀisɑ̃, -ɑ̃t] *adj*: **régime ~** slimming (BRIT) ou weight-reduction (US) diet

amande [amɑ̃d] *nf (de l'amandier)* almond; **amandier** *nm* almond (tree)

amant [amɑ̃] *nm* lover

amas [amɑ] *nm* heap, pile; **amasser** /1/ *vt* to amass

amateur [amatœʀ] *nm* amateur; **en ~** *(péj)* amateurishly; **~ de musique/sport** *etc* music/sport *etc* lover

ambassade [ɑ̃basad] *nf* embassy; **l'~ de France** the French Embassy; **ambassadeur, -drice** *nm/f* ambassador/ambassadress

ambiance [ɑ̃bjɑ̃s] *nf* atmosphere; **il y a de l'~** everyone's having a good time

ambigu, ë [ɑ̃bigy] *adj* ambiguous

ambitieux, -euse [ɑ̃bisjø, -jøz] *adj* ambitious

ambition [ɑ̃bisjɔ̃] *nf* ambition

ambulance [ɑ̃bylɑ̃s] *nf* ambulance; **ambulancier, -ière** *nm/f* ambulanceman/woman (BRIT), paramedic (US)

âme [ɑm] *nf* soul; **~ sœur** kindred spirit

amélioration [ameljɔʀasjɔ̃] *nf* improvement

améliorer [ameljɔʀe] /1/ *vt* to improve; **s'améliorer** *vi* to improve, get better

aménager [amenaʒe] /3/ *vt* *(agencer)* to fit out; *(: terrain)* to lay out; *(: quartier, territoire)* to develop; *(installer)* to fix up, put in; **ferme aménagée** converted farmhouse

amende [amɑ̃d] *nf* fine; **faire ~ honorable** to make amends

amener [am(ə)ne] /5/ *vt* to bring; *(causer)* to bring about; **s'amener** *vi* (fam) to show up, turn up; **~ qn à qch/à faire** to lead sb to sth/to do

amer, amère [amɛʀ] *adj* bitter

américain, e [ameʀikɛ̃, -ɛn] *adj* American ▸ *nm/f*: **A~, e** American

Amérique [ameʀik] *nf* America; **l'~ centrale** Central America; **l'~ latine** Latin America; **l'~ du Nord** North America; **l'~ du Sud** South America

amertume [amɛʀtym] *nf* bitterness

ameublement [amœbləmɑ̃] nm
furnishing; (meubles) furniture

ami, e [ami] nm/f friend; (amant/
maîtresse) boyfriend/girlfriend ▷ adj:
pays/groupe ~ friendly country/
group; **petit ~/petite ~e** boyfriend/
girlfriend

amiable [amjabl]: **à l'~** adv (Jur) out
of court; (gén) amicably

amiante [amjɑ̃t] nm asbestos

amical, e, -aux [amikal, -o] adj
friendly; **amicalement** adv in a
friendly way; (formule épistolaire)
regards

amincir [amɛ̃siʀ] /2/ vt: **~ qn**
to make sb thinner ou slimmer;
(vêtement) to make sb look slimmer

amincissant, e [amɛ̃sisɑ̃, -ɑ̃t] adj
slimming; **régime ~** diet; **crème ~e**
slimming cream

amiral, -aux [amiʀal, -o] nm
admiral

amitié [amitje] nf friendship;
prendre en ~ to take a liking to;
faire ou présenter ses ~s à qn
to send sb one's best wishes; **~s**
(formule épistolaire) (with) best wishes

amonceler [amɔ̃s(ə)le] /4/ vt to pile
ou heap up; **s'amonceler** to pile ou
heap up; (fig) to accumulate

amont [amɔ̃]: **en ~** adv upstream

amorce [amɔʀs] nf (sur un hameçon)
bait; (explosif) cap; (tube) primer
(: contenu) priming; (fig: début)
beginning(s), start

amortir [amɔʀtiʀ] /2/ vt (atténuer:
choc) to absorb, cushion; (: bruit,
douleur) to deaden; (Comm: dette)
to pay off; **~ un abonnement**
to make a season ticket pay (for itself);
amortisseur nm shock absorber

amour [amuʀ] nm love; **faire l'~** to
make love; **amoureux, -euse** adj
(regard, tempérament) amorous; (vie,
problèmes) love cpd; (personne): **être
amoureux (de qn)** to be in love
(with sb) ▷ nmpl courting couple(s);
amour-propre nm self-esteem, pride

ampère [ɑ̃pɛʀ] nm amp(ere)

amphithéâtre [ɑ̃fiteɑtʀ] nm
amphitheatre; (d'université) lecture
hall ou theatre

ample [ɑ̃pl] adj (vêtement) roomy,
ample; (gestes, mouvement) broad;
(ressources) ample; **amplement**
adv: **amplement suffisant** more
than enough; **ampleur** nf (de dégâts,
problème) extent

amplificateur [ɑ̃plifikatœʀ] nm
amplifier

amplifier [ɑ̃plifje] /7/ vt (fig) to
expand, increase

ampoule [ɑ̃pul] nf (électrique) bulb;
(de médicament) phial; (aux mains,
pieds) blister

amusant, e [amyzɑ̃, -ɑ̃t] adj
(divertissant, spirituel) entertaining,
amusing; (comique) funny, amusing

amuse-gueule [amyzgœl] nm inv
appetizer, snack

amusement [amyzmɑ̃] nm (voir
amusé) amusement; (jeu etc) pastime,
diversion

amuser [amyze] /1/ vt (divertir) to
entertain, amuse; (égayer, faire rire) to
amuse; **s'amuser** vi (jouer) to amuse
o.s.; (se divertir) to enjoy o.s., have
fun; (fig) to mess around

amygdale [amidal] nf tonsil

an [ɑ̃] nm year; **être âgé de ou avoir
3 ans** to be 3 (years old); **le jour de
l'an, le premier de l'an, le nouvel
an** New Year's Day

analphabète [analfabɛt] nm/f
illiterate

analyse [analiz] nf analysis; (Méd)
test; **analyser** /1/ vt to analyse;
(Méd) to test

ananas [anana(s)] nm pineapple

anatomie [anatɔmi] nf anatomy

ancêtre [ɑ̃sɛtʀ] nm/f ancestor

anchois [ɑ̃ʃwa] nm anchovy

ancien, ne [ɑ̃sjɛ̃, -jɛn] adj old; (de
jadis, de l'antiquité) ancient; (précédent,
ex-) former, old; (par l'expérience)
senior ▷ nm/f (dans une tribu etc) elder;

ancienneté nf (Admin) (length of) service; (privilèges obtenus) seniority

ancre [ɑ̃kʀ] nf anchor; **jeter/lever l'~** to cast/weigh anchor; **ancrer** /1/ vt (Constr: câble etc) to anchor; (fig) to fix firmly

Andorre [ɑ̃dɔʀ] nf Andorra

andouille [ɑ̃duj] nf (Culin) sausage made of chitterlings; (fam) clot, nit

âne [ɑn] nm donkey, ass; (péj) dunce

anéantir [aneɑ̃tiʀ] /2/ vt to annihilate, wipe out; (fig) to obliterate, destroy

anémie [anemi] nf anaemia; **anémique** adj anaemic

anesthésie [anestezi] nf anaesthesia; **~ générale/locale** general/local anaesthetic; **faire une ~ locale à qn** to give sb a local anaesthetic

ange [ɑ̃ʒ] nm angel; **être aux ~s** to be over the moon

angine [ɑ̃ʒin] nf throat infection; **~ de poitrine** angina (pectoris)

anglais, e [ɑ̃glɛ, -ɛz] adj English ▷ nm (Ling) English ▷ nm/f: **A~, e** Englishman/woman; **les A~** the English; **filer à l'~e** to take French leave

angle [ɑ̃gl] nm angle; (coin) corner

Angleterre [ɑ̃glətɛʀ] nf: **l'~** England

anglo... [ɑ̃glo] préfixe Anglo-, anglo(-); **anglophone** adj English-speaking

angoisse [ɑ̃gwas] nf: **l'~** anguish no pl; **angoissé, e** adj (personne) distressed

anguille [ɑ̃gij] nf eel

animal, e, -aux [animal, -o] adj, nm animal

animateur, -trice [animatœʀ, -tʀis] nm/f (de télévision) host; (de groupe) leader, organizer

animation [animɑsjɔ̃] nf (voir animé) busyness; liveliness; (Ciné: technique) animation

animé, e [anime] adj (rue, lieu) busy, lively; (conversation, réunion) lively, animated

animer [anime] /1/ vt (ville, soirée) to liven up; (mettre en mouvement) to drive

anis [ani(s)] nm (Culin) aniseed; (Bot) anise

ankyloser [ɑ̃kiloze] /1/: **s'ankyloser** vi to get stiff

anneau, x [ano] nm (de rideau, bague) ring; (de chaîne) link

année [ane] nf year

annexe [anɛks] adj (problème) related; (document) appended; (salle) adjoining ▷ nf (bâtiment) annex(e); (jointe à une lettre, un dossier) enclosure

anniversaire [anivɛʀsɛʀ] nm birthday; (d'un événement, bâtiment) anniversary

annonce [anɔ̃s] nf announcement; (signe, indice) sign; (aussi: **~ publicitaire**) advertisement; **les petites ~s** the small ou classified ads

annoncer [anɔ̃se] /3/ vt to announce; (être le signe de) to herald; **s'annoncer bien/difficile** to look promising/difficult

annuaire [anɥɛʀ] nm yearbook, annual; **~ téléphonique** (telephone) directory, phone book

annuel, le [anɥɛl] adj annual, yearly

annulation [anylɑsjɔ̃] nf cancellation

annuler [anyle] /1/ vt (rendez-vous, voyage) to cancel, call off; (jugement) to quash (BRIT), repeal (US); (Math, Physique) to cancel out

anonymat [anɔnima] nm anonymity; **garder l'~** to remain anonymous

anonyme [anɔnim] adj anonymous; (fig) impersonal

anorak [anɔʀak] nm anorak

anorexie [anɔʀɛksi] nf anorexia

anormal, e, -aux [anɔʀmal, -o] adj abnormal

ANPE sigle f (= Agence nationale pour l'emploi) national employment agency (functions include job creation)

antarctique [ɑ̃taʀktik] *adj* Antarctic
▷ *nm*: **l'A~** the Antarctic

antenne [ɑ̃tɛn] *nf* (*de radio, télévision*)
aerial; (*d'insecte*) antenna, feeler;
(*poste avancé*) outpost; (*petite succursale*) sub-branch; (*petite succursale*) sub-branch; **passer à/avoir l'~** to go/be on the air;
~ parabolique satellite dish

antérieur, e [ɑ̃teʀjœʀ] *adj* (*d'avant*)
previous, earlier; (*de devant*) front

anti... [ɑ̃ti] *préfixe* anti...;
antialcoolique *adj* anti-alcohol;
antibiotique *nm* antibiotic;
antibrouillard *adj*: **phare antibrouillard** fog lamp

anticipation [ɑ̃tisipasjɔ̃] *nf*: **livre/ film d'~** science fiction book/film

anticipé, e [ɑ̃tisipe] *adj*: **avec mes remerciements ~s** thanking you in advance *ou* anticipation

anticiper [ɑ̃tisipe] /1/ *vt* (*événement, coup*) to anticipate, foresee

anti: anticorps *nm* antibody;
antidote *nm* antidote; **antigel** *nm*
antifreeze; **antihistaminique** *nm*
antihistamine

antillais, e [ɑ̃tijɛ, -ɛz] *adj* West
Indian, Caribbean ▷ *nm/f*: **A~, e** West
Indian, Caribbean

Antilles [ɑ̃tij] *nfpl*: **les ~** the West
Indies; **les Grandes/Petites ~** the
Greater/Lesser Antilles

antilope [ɑ̃tilɔp] *nf* antelope

anti: antimite(s) *adj, nm*: **(produit) antimite(s)** mothproofer, moth
repellent; **antimondialisation** *nf*
anti-globalization; **antipathique** *adj* unpleasant, disagreeable;
antipelliculaire *adj* anti-dandruff

antiquaire [ɑ̃tikɛʀ] *nm/f* antique
dealer

antique [ɑ̃tik] *adj* antique; (*très vieux*) ancient, antiquated; **antiquité** *nf* (*objet*) antique; **l'Antiquité** Antiquity; **magasin/marchand d'antiquités** antique shop/dealer

anti: antirabique *adj* rabies *cpd*;
antirouille *adj inv* anti-rust *cpd*;

antisémite *adj* anti-Semitic;

antiseptique *adj, nm* antiseptic;

antivirus *nm* (*Inform*) antivirus
(program); **antivol** *adj, nm*:
(dispositif) antivol antitheft device

anxieux, -euse [ɑ̃ksjø, -jøz] *adj*
anxious, worried

AOC *sigle f* (= *Appellation d'origine contrôlée*) guarantee of quality of wine

août [u(t)] *nm* August

apaiser [apeze] /1/ *vt* (*colère*) to calm;
(*douleur*) to soothe; (*personne*) to calm
(down), pacify; **s'apaiser** *vi* (*tempête, bruit*) to die down, subside; (*personne*)
to calm down

apercevoir [apɛʀsəvwaʀ] /28/ *vt* to
see; **s'apercevoir de** *vt* to notice; **s'~ que** to notice that

aperçu [apɛʀsy] *nm* (*vue d'ensemble*)
general survey

apéritif, -ive [apeʀitif, -iv] *adj*
which stimulates the appetite ▷ *nm*
(*boisson*) aperitif; (*réunion*) (pre-lunch
ou -dinner) drinks *pl*

à-peu-près [apøpʀɛ] *nm inv* (*péj*)
vague approximation

apeuré, e [apœʀe] *adj* frightened,
scared

aphte [aft] *nm* mouth ulcer

apitoyer [apitwaje] /8/ *vt* to move
to pity; **s'~ (sur qn/qch)** to feel pity
ou compassion (for sb/over sth)

aplatir [aplatir] /2/ *vt* to flatten;
s'aplatir *vi* to become flatter; (*écrasé*)
to be flattened

aplomb [aplɔ̃] *nm* (*équilibre*) balance,
equilibrium; (*fig*) self-assurance
nerve; **d'~** steady

apostrophe [apɔstʀɔf] *nf* (*signe*)
apostrophe

apparaître [apaʀɛtʀ] /57/ *vi* to
appear

appareil [apaʀɛj] *nm* (*outil, machine*)
piece of apparatus, device; (*électrique etc*) appliance; (*avion*) (aero)plane ,
aircraft *inv*; (*téléphonique*) telephone;
(*dentier*) brace (BRIT), braces (US); **qui est à l'~?** who's speaking?; **dans le**

plus simple ~ in one's birthday suit;
~ **(photo)** camera; ~ **numérique**
digital camera; ~ (Navig) to cast off, get under way ▷ vt
(assortir) to match up

apparemment [aparamɑ̃] adv
apparently

apparence [aparɑ̃s] nf appearance;
en ~ apparently

apparent, e [aparɑ̃, -ɑ̃t] adj
visible; (évident) obvious; (superficiel)
apparent

apparenté, e [aparɑ̃te] adj: ~ **à**
related to; (fig) similar to

apparition [aparisjɔ̃] nf
appearance; (surnaturelle) apparition

appartement [apartəmɑ̃] nm flat
(BRIT), apartment (US)

appartenir [apartənir] /22/: ~ **à** vt
to belong to; **il lui appartient de** it
is up to him to

apparu, e [apary] pp de **apparaître**

appât [apɑ] nm (Pêche) bait; (fig)
lure, bait

appel [apel] nm call; (nominal) roll call
(: Scol) register; (Mil: recrutement) call-
up; **faire** ~ **à** (invoquer) to appeal to;
(avoir recours à) to call on; (nécessiter)
to call for, require; **faire ou interjeter**
~ (Jur) to appeal; **faire l'**~ to call the
roll; (Scol) to call the register; **sans** ~
(fig) final, irrevocable; ~ **d'offres**
(Comm) invitation to tender; **faire un**
~ **de phares** to flash one's headlights;
~ **(téléphonique)** (tele)phone call

appelé [ap(ə)le] nm (Mil) conscript

appeler [ap(ə)le] /4/ vt to call; (faire
venir: médecin etc) to call, send for;
s'appeler vi: **elle s'appelle Gabrielle**
her name is Gabrielle, she's called
Gabrielle; **comment vous appelez-
vous?** what's your name?; **comment
ça s'appelle?** what's that called?

appendicite [apɑ̃disit] nf
appendicitis

appesantir [apəzɑ̃tir] /2/:
s'appesantir vi to grow heavier; **s'**~
sur (fig) to dwell at length on

appétissant, e [apetisɑ̃, -ɑ̃t] adj
appetizing, mouth-watering

appétit [apeti] nm appetite; **bon** ~!
enjoy your meal!

applaudir [aplodir] /2/ vt to
applaud ▷ vi to applaud, clap;
applaudissements nmpl applause
sg, clapping sg

appli [apli] nf app

application [aplikasjɔ̃] nf
application

appliquer [aplike] /1/ vt to apply;
(loi) to enforce; **s'appliquer** vi (élève
etc) to apply o.s.; **s'**~ **à** to apply to

appoint [apwɛ̃] nm (extra)
contribution ou help; **avoir/faire**
l'~ to have/give the right change ou
money; **chauffage d'**~ extra heating

apporter [aporte] /1/ vt to bring

appréciable [apresjabl] adj
appreciable

apprécier [apresje] /7/ vt to
appreciate; (évaluer) to estimate,
assess

appréhender [apreɑ̃de] /1/ vt
(craindre) to dread; (arrêter) to
apprehend

apprendre [aprɑ̃dr] /58/ vt to
learn; (événement, résultats) to learn
of, hear of; ~ **qch à qn** (informer) to
tell sb (of) sth; (enseigner) to teach sb
sth; ~ **à faire qch** to learn to do sth;
~ **à qn à faire qch** to teach sb to do
sth; **apprenti, e** nm/f apprentice;
apprentissage nm learning; (Comm,
Scol: période) apprenticeship

apprêter [aprete] /1/: **s'apprêter** vi:
s'~ **à qch/à faire qch** to prepare for
sth/for doing sth

appris, e [apri, -iz] pp de **apprendre**

apprivoiser [aprivwaze] /1/ vt
to tame

approbation [aprobasjɔ̃] nf
approval

approcher [aprɔʃe] /1/ vi to
approach, come near ▷ vt to
approach; (rapprocher) ~ **qch (de**
qch) to bring ou put ou move sth near

(to sth); **s'approcher de** to approach, go ou come ou move near to; **~ de** (lieu, but) to draw near to; (quantité, moment) to approach

approfondir [apʀɔfɔdiʀ]/2/ vt to deepen; (question) to go further into

approprié, e [apʀɔpʀije] adj: **~ (à)** appropriate (to), suited (to)

approprier [apʀɔpʀije]/7/: **s'approprier** vt to appropriate, take over; **s'~ en** to stock up with

approuver [apʀuve] /1/ vt to agree with; (trouver louable) to approve of

approvisionner [apʀɔvizjɔne] /1/ vt to supply; (compte bancaire) to pay funds into; **s'~ en** to stock up with

approximatif, -ive [apʀɔksimatif, -iv] adj approximate, rough; (imprécis) vague

appt abr = **appartement**

appui [apɥi] nm support; **prendre ~ sur** to lean on; (objet) to rest on; **l'~ de la fenêtre** the windowsill, the window ledge

appuyer [apɥije] /8/ vt (poser, soutenir: personne, demande) to support, back (up) ▷ vi: **~ sur** (bouton) to press, push; (mot, détail) to stress, emphasize; **s'appuyer sur** vt to lean on; (compter sur) to rely on; **~ qch sur/contre/à** to lean ou rest sth on/ against/on; **~ sur le frein** to brake, to apply the brakes

après [apʀɛ] prép after ▷ adv afterwards; **deux heures ~** two hours later; **~ qu'il est parti/avoir fait** after he left/having done; **courir ~ qn** to run after sb; **crier ~ qn** to shout at sb; **être toujours ~ qn** (critiquer etc) to be always on at sb; **~ quoi** after which; **d'~ (selon)** according to; **~ coup** after the event, afterwards; **~ tout** (au fond) after all; **et (puis) ~?** so what?; **après-demain** adv the day after tomorrow; **après-midi** [apʀɛmidi] nm ou f inv afternoon; **après-rasage** nm inv after-shave; **après-shampooing**

nm inv conditioner; **après-ski** nm inv snow boot

après-soleil [apʀɛsɔlɛj] adj inv after-sun cpd ▷ nm after-sun cream ou lotion

apte [apt] adj: **~ à qch/faire qch** capable of sth/doing sth; **~ (au service)** (Mil) fit (for service)

aquarelle [akwaʀɛl] nf watercolour

aquarium [akwaʀjɔm] nm aquarium

arabe [aʀab] adj Arabic; (désert, cheval) Arabian; (nation, peuple) Arab ▷ nm (Ling) Arabic ▷ nm/f: **A~** Arab

Arabie [aʀabi] nf: **~ Saoudite** ou **Séoudite** Saudi Arabia

arachide [aʀaʃid] nf groundnut (plant); (graine) peanut, groundnut

araignée [aʀeɲe] nf spider

arbitraire [aʀbitʀɛʀ] adj arbitrary

arbitre [aʀbitʀ] nm (Sport) referee (: Tennis, Cricket) umpire; (fig) arbiter, judge; (Jur) arbitrator; **arbitrer** /1/ vt to referee; to umpire; to arbitrate

arbre [aʀbʀ] nm tree; (Tech) shaft

arbuste [aʀbyst] nm small shrub

arc [aʀk] nm (arme) bow; (Géom) arc; (Archit) arch; **en ~ de cercle** semi-circular

arcade [aʀkad] nf arch(way); **~s** arcade sg, arches

arc-en-ciel [aʀkɑ̃sjɛl] nf rainbow

arche [aʀʃ] nf arch; **~ de Noé** Noah's Ark

archéologie [aʀkeɔlɔʒi] nf arch(a)eology; **archéologue** nm/f arch(a)eologist

archet [aʀʃɛ] nm bow

archipel [aʀʃipɛl] nm archipelago

architecte [aʀʃitɛkt] nm architect

architecture [aʀʃitɛktyʀ] nf architecture

archives [aʀʃiv] nfpl (collection) archives

arctique [aʀktik] adj Arctic ▷ nm: **l'A~** the Arctic

ardent, e [aʀdɑ̃, -ɑ̃t] adj (soleil) blazing; (amour) ardent, passionate; (prière) fervent

ardoise [ardwaz] nf slate

ardu, e [ardy] adj (travail) arduous; (problème) difficult

arène [aren] nf arena; **arènes** nfpl bull-ring sg

arête [aret] nf (de poisson) bone; (d'une montagne) ridge

argent [arʒã] nm (métal) silver; (monnaie) money; **~ de poche** pocket money; **~ liquide** ready money, (ready) cash; **argenterie** nf silverware

argentin, e [arʒãtɛ̃, -in] adj Argentinian ▷ nm/f: **A~, e** Argentinian

Argentine [arʒãtin] nf: **l'~** Argentina

argentique [arʒãtik] adj (appareil photo) film cpd

argile [arʒil] nf clay

argot [argo] nm slang; **argotique** adj slang cpd; (très familier) slangy

argument [argymã] nm argument

argumenter [argymãte] /1/ vi to argue

aride [arid] adj arid

aristocratie [aristɔkrasi] nf aristocracy; **aristocratique** adj aristocratic

arithmétique [aritmetik] adj arithmetic(al) ▷ nf arithmetic

arme [arm] nf weapon; **armes** nfpl weapons, arms; (blason) (coat of) arms; **~ à feu** firearm; **~s de destruction massive** weapons of mass destruction

armée [arme] nf army; **~ de l'air** Air Force; **~ de terre** Army

armer [arme] /1/ vt to arm; (arme à feu) to cock; (appareil photo) to wind on; **s'armer vi: s'~ de** to arm o.s. with; **~ qch de** to reinforce sth with

armistice [armistis] nm armistice; **l'A~** = Remembrance (BRIT) ou. Veterans (US) Day

armoire [armwar] nf (tall) cupboard; (penderie) wardrobe (BRIT), closet (US)

armure [armyr] nf armour no pl, suit of armour; **armurier** nm gunsmith

arnaque [arnak] (fam) nf swindling; **c'est de l'~** it's daylight robbery; **arnaquer** /1/ (fam) vt to do (fam)

arobase [arobaz] nf (Inform) 'at' symbol; **"paul ~ société point fr"** "paul at société dot fr"

aromates [aromat] nmpl seasoning sg, herbs (and spices)

aromathérapie [aromaterapi] nf aromatherapy

aromatisé, e [aromatize] adj flavoured

arôme [arom] nm aroma

arracher [araʃe] /1/ vt to pull out; (page etc) to tear off, tear out; (légume, herbe, souche) to pull up; (bras etc) to tear off; **s'arracher** vt (article très recherché) to fight over; **~ qch à qn** to snatch sth from sb; (fig) to wring sth out of sb

arrangement [arãʒmã] nm arrangement

arranger [arãʒe] /3/ vt to arrange; (réparer) to fix, put right; (régler) to settle, sort out; (convenir à) to suit, be convenient for; **cela m'arrange** that suits me (fine); **s'arranger** vi (se mettre d'accord) to come to an agreement ou arrangement; **je vais m'~** I'll manage; **ça va s'~** it'll sort itself out

arrestation [arestasjɔ̃] nf arrest

arrêt [are] nm stopping; (de bus etc) stop; (Jur) judgment, decision; **être à l'~** to be stopped; **rester ou tomber en ~ devant** to stop short in front of; **sans ~** non-stop; (fréquemment) continually; **~ de travail** stoppage (of work)

arrêter [arete] /1/ vt to stop; (chauffage etc) to turn off, switch off; (fixer: date etc) to appoint, decide on; (criminel, suspect) to arrest; **s'arrêter** vi to stop; **~ de faire** to stop doing

arrhes [ar] nfpl deposit sg

arrière [arjer] nm back; (Sport) fullback ▷ adj inv: **siège/roue**

~ back ou rear seat/wheel; **à l'~** behind, at the back; **en ~** behind; (*regarder*) back, behind; (*tomber, aller*) backwards; **arrière-goût** nm aftertaste; **arrière-grand-mère** nf great-grandmother; **arrière-grand-père** nm great-grandfather; **arrière-pays** nm inv hinterland; **arrière-pensée** nf ulterior motive; (*doute*) mental reservation; **arrière-plan** nm background; **à l'arrière-plan** in the background; **arrière-saison** nf late autumn

arrimer [aʀime] /1/ vt (*cargaison*) to stow; (*fixer*) to secure

arrivage [aʀivaʒ] nm consignment

arrivée [aʀive] nf arrival; (*ligne d'arrivée*) finish

arriver [aʀive] /1/ vi to arrive; (*survenir*) to happen, occur; **il arrive à Paris à 8 h** he gets to ou arrives in Paris at 8; **~ à** (*atteindre*) to reach; **~ à (faire) qch** to manage (to do) sth; **en ~ à faire ...** to end up doing ...; **il arrive que ...** it happens that ...; **il lui arrive de faire ...** he sometimes does ...

arrobase [aʀɔbaz] nf (*Inform*) 'at' symbol

arrogance [aʀɔgɑ̃s] nf arrogance

arrogant, e [aʀɔgɑ̃, -ɑ̃t] adj arrogant

arrondissement [aʀɔ̃dismɑ̃] nm (*Admin*) ≈ district

arroser [aʀoze] /1/ vt to water; (*victoire etc*) to celebrate (over a drink); (*Culin*) to baste; **arrosoir** nm watering can

arsenal, -aux [aʀsənal, -o] nm (*Navig*) naval dockyard; (*Mil*) arsenal; (*fig*) gear, paraphernalia

art [aʀ] nm art

artère [aʀtɛʀ] nf (*Anat*) artery; (*rue*) main road

arthrite [aʀtʀit] nf arthritis

artichaut [aʀtiʃo] nm artichoke

article [aʀtikl] nm article; (*Comm*) item, article; **à l'~ de la mort** at the point of death

articulation [aʀtikylasjɔ̃] nf articulation; (*Anat*) joint

articuler [aʀtikyle] /1/ vt to articulate

artificiel, le [aʀtifisjɛl] adj artificial

artisan [aʀtizɑ̃] nm artisan, (self-employed) craftsman; **artisanal, e, -aux** [aʀtizanal, -o] adj of ou made by craftsmen; (*péj*) cottage industry cpd; **de fabrication artisanale** home-made; **artisanat** [aʀtizana] nm arts and crafts pl

artiste [aʀtist] nm/f artist; (*Théât, Mus*) performer; (*de variétés*) entertainer; **artistique** adj artistic

as vb [a]; voir **avoir** ▷ nm [ɑs] ace

ascenseur [asɑ̃sœʀ] nm lift (BRIT), elevator (US)

ascension [asɑ̃sjɔ̃] nf ascent; (*de montagne*) climb; **l'A~** (*Rel*) the Ascension

◆ **L'ASCENSION**

- The *fête de l'Ascension* is a public
- holiday in France. It always falls on
- a Thursday, usually in May. Many
- French people take the following
- Friday off work too and enjoy a long
- weekend.

asiatique [azjatik] adj Asian, Asiatic ▷ nm/f: **A~** Asian

Asie [azi] nf: **l'~** Asia

asile [azil] nm (*refuge*) refuge, sanctuary; **droit d'~** (*Pol*) (political) asylum

aspect [aspɛ] nm appearance, look; (*fig*) aspect, side; **à l'~ de** at the sight of

asperge [aspɛʀʒ] nf asparagus no pl

asperger [aspɛʀʒe] /3/ vt to spray, sprinkle

asphalte [asfalt] nm asphalt

asphyxier [asfiksje] /7/ vt to suffocate, asphyxiate; (*fig*) to stifle

aspirateur [aspiʀatœʀ] nm vacuum cleaner; **passer l'~** to vacuum

aspirer [aspire] /1/ vt (air) to inhale; (liquide) to suck (up); (appareil) to suck ou draw up; **~ à** to aspire to

aspirine [aspiʀin] nf aspirin

assagir [asaʒiʀ] /2/ vt, **s'assagir** vi to quieten down, settle down

assaillir [asajiʀ] /13/ vt to assail, attack

assaisonnement [asɛzɔnmã] nm seasoning

assaisonner [asɛzɔne] /1/ vt to season

assassin [asasɛ̃] nm murderer; assassin; **assassiner** /1/ vt to murder; (Pol) to assassinate

assaut [aso] nm assault, attack; **prendre d'~** to (take by) storm, assault; **donner l'~ (à)** to attack

assécher [aseʃe] /6/ vt to drain

assemblage [asãblaʒ] nm (action) assembling; **un ~ de** (fig) a collection of

assemblée [asãble] nf (réunion) meeting; (public, assistance) gathering; (Pol) assembly; **l'A- nationale (AN)** (the French) National Assembly

assembler [asãble] /1/ vt (joindre, monter) to assemble, put together; (amasser) to gather (together), collect (together); **s'assembler** vi to gather together

asseoir [aswaʀ] /26/ vt (malade, bébé) to sit up; (personne debout) to sit down; (autorité, réputation) to establish; **s'asseoir** vi to sit (o.s.) down

assez [ase] adv (suffisamment) enough, sufficiently; (passablement) rather, quite, fairly; **~ de pain/ livres** enough ou sufficient bread/ books; **vous en avez ~?** have you got enough?; **j'en ai ~!** I've had enough!

assidu, e [asidy] adj assiduous, painstaking; (régulier) regular

assied etc [asje] vb voir **asseoir**

assiérai etc [asjeʀe] vb voir **asseoir**

assiette [asjɛt] nf plate; (contenu) plate(ful); **il n'est pas dans son ~** he's not feeling quite himself; **~ à dessert** dessert ou side plate; **~ anglaise** assorted cold meats; **~ creuse** (soup) dish, soup plate; **~ plate** (dinner) plate

assimiler [asimile] /1/ vt to assimilate, absorb; (comparer): **~ qch/qn à** to liken ou compare sth/ sb to; **s'assimiler** vi (s'intégrer) to be assimilated ou absorbed

assis, e [asi, -iz] pp de **asseoir** ▷ adj sitting (down), seated

assistance [asistãs] nf (public) audience; (aide) assistance; **enfant de l'A- (publique)** child in care

assistant, e [asistã, -ãt] nm/f assistant; (d'université) probationary lecturer; **~e sociale** social worker

assisté, e [asiste] adj (Auto) power-assisted; **~ par ordinateur** computer-assisted; **direction ~e** power steering

assister [asiste] /1/ vt to assist; **~ à** (scène, événement) to witness; (conférence) to attend, be (present) at; (spectacle, match) to be at, see

association [asɔsjasjɔ̃] nf association

associé, e [asɔsje] nm/f associate; (Comm) partner

associer [asɔsje] /7/ vt to associate; **~ qn à** (profits) to give sb a share of; (affaire) to make sb a partner in; (joie, triomphe) to include sb in; **~ qch à** (joindre, allier) to combine sth with; **s'associer** vi to join together; **s'~ à** (couleurs, qualités) to be combined with; (opinions, joie de qn) to share in; **s'~ à** ou **avec qn pour faire** to join (forces) with to join together with sb to do

assoiffé, e [aswafe] adj thirsty

assommer [asɔme] /1/ vt (étourdir, abrutir) to knock out, stun

Assomption [asɔ̃psjɔ̃] nf: **l'~** the Assumption

● **L'ASSOMPTION**

The fête de l'Assomption, more
commonly known as "le 15 août"
is a national holiday in France.
Traditionally, large numbers of
holidaymakers leave home on
15 August, frequently causing
chaos on the roads.

assorti, e [asɔʀti] adj matched,
matching; **fromages/légumes**
~s assorted cheeses/vegetables;
~ à matching; **assortiment** nm
assortment, selection
assortir [asɔʀtiʀ] /2/ vt to match;
~ qch à to match sth with; **~ qch de**
to accompany sth with
assouplir [asupliʀ] /2/ vt to make
supple, (fig) to relax; **assouplissant**
nm (fabric) softener
assumer [asyme] /1/ vt (fonction,
emploi) to assume, take on
assurance [asyʀɑ̃s] nf (certitude)
assurance; (confiance en soi) (self-)
confidence; (contrat) insurance
(policy); (secteur commercial) insurance;
~ au tiers third party insurance;
~ maladie (AM) health insurance;
~ tous risques (Auto) comprehensive
insurance; **~s sociales (AS)** ≈
National Security (BRIT), ≈ Social
Security (US); **assurance-vie** nf life
assurance ou insurance
assuré, e [asyʀe] adj (réussite, échec,
victoire etc) certain, sure; (démarche,
voix) assured; (pas) steady ▷ nm/f
insured (person); **assurément** adv
assuredly, most certainly
assurer [asyʀe] /1/ vt (Comm)
to insure; (victoire etc) to ensure;
(frontières, pouvoir) to make secure;
(service, garde) to provide, operate;
s'assurer (contre) (Comm) to insure
o.s. (against); **~ à qn que** to assure sb
that; **~ qn de** to assure sb of; **s'~ de/**
que (vérifier) to make sure of/that;
s'~ (de) (aide de qn) to secure

asthmatique [asmatik] adj, nm/f
asthmatic
asthme [asm] nm asthma
asticot [astiko] nm maggot
astre [astʀ] nm star
astrologie [astʀɔlɔʒi] nf astrology
astronaute [astʀonot] nm/f
astronaut
astronomie [astʀɔnɔmi] nf
astronomy
astuce [astys] nf shrewdness,
astuteness; (truc) trick, clever way;
astucieux, -euse adj clever
atelier [atəlje] nm workshop; (de
peintre) studio
athée [ate] adj atheistic ▷ nm/f
atheist
Athènes [atɛn] n Athens
athlète [atlɛt] nm/f (Sport) athlete;
athlétisme nm athletics sg
atlantique [atlɑ̃tik] adj Atlantic
▷ nm: **l'(océan) A~** the Atlantic
(Ocean)
atlas [atlɑs] nm atlas
atmosphère [atmɔsfɛʀ] nf
atmosphere
atome [atom] nm atom; **atomique**
adj atomic; nuclear
atomiseur [atɔmizœʀ] nm atomizer
atout [atu] nm trump; (fig) asset
atroce [atʀɔs] adj atrocious
attachant, e [ataʃɑ̃, -ɑ̃t] adj
engaging, likeable
attache [ataʃ] nf clip, fastener; (fig) tie
attacher [ataʃe] /1/ vt to tie up;
(étiquette) to attach, tie on; (ceinture)
to fasten; (souliers) to do up ▷ vi (poêle,
riz) to stick; **s'~ à** (par affection) to
become attached to; **~ qch à** to tie ou
fasten ou attach sth to
attaque [atak] nf attack; (cérébrale)
stroke; (d'épilepsie) fit
attaquer [atake] /1/ vt to attack;
(en justice) to sue ▷ vi to attack;
s'attaquer à vt (personne) to attack;
(épidémie, misère) to tackle
attarder [ataʀde] /1/: **s'attarder**
vi to linger

atteindre [atɛdʀ] /49/ vt to reach; (blesser) to hit; (émouvoir) to affect; **atteint, e** adj (Méd): **être atteint de** to be suffering from ▷ nf attack; **hors d'atteinte** out of reach; **porter atteinte à** to strike a blow at

attendant [atɑdɑ]: **en ~** adv meanwhile, in the meantime

attendre [atɑdʀ] /41/ vt to wait for; (être destiné ou réservé à) to await, be in store for ▷ vi to wait; **s'~ (à ce que)** to expect (that); **attendez-moi, s'il vous plaît** wait for me, please; **~ un enfant** to be expecting a baby; **~ de faire/d'être** to wait until one does/is; **attendez qu'il vienne** wait until he comes; **~ qch de** to expect sth of

| Attention à ne pas traduire *attendre* par *to attend*.

attendrir [atɑdʀiʀ] /2/ vt to move (to pity); (viande) to tenderize

attendu, e [atɑdy] adj (événement) long-awaited; (prévu) expected; **~ que** considering that, since

attentat [atɑta] nm assassination attempt; **~ à la pudeur** indecent assault no pl; **~ suicide** suicide bombing

attente [atɑt] nf wait; (espérance) expectation

attenter [atɑte] /1/: **~ à** vt (liberté) to violate; **~ à la vie de qn** to make an attempt on sb's life

attentif, -ive [atɑtif, -iv] adj (auditeur) attentive; (travail) careful; **~ à** paying attention to

attention [atɑsjɔ] nf attention; (prévenance) thoughtfulness no pl; **à l'~ de** for the attention of; **faire ~ (à)** to be careful (of); **faire ~ (à ce) que** to be ou make sure that; **~! careful!**, watch out!; **~ à la voiture!** watch out for that car!; **attentionné, e** [atɑsjɔne] adj thoughtful, considerate

atténuer [atenye] /1/ vt (douleur) to alleviate, ease; (couleurs) to soften;

s'atténuer vi to ease; (violence etc) to abate

atterrir [ateʀiʀ] /2/ vi to land; **atterrissage** nm landing

attestation nf certificate

attirant, e [atiʀɑ, -ɑt] adj attractive, appealing

attirer [atiʀe] /1/ vt to attract; (appâter) to lure, entice; **~ qn dans un coin/vers soi** to draw sb into a corner/towards one; **~ l'attention de qn** to attract sb's attention; **~ l'attention de qn sur qch** to draw sb's attention to sth; **s'~ des ennuis** to bring trouble upon o.s., get into trouble

attitude [atityd] nf attitude; (position du corps) bearing

attraction [atʀaksjɔ] nf attraction; (de cabaret, cirque) number

attrait [atʀɛ] nm appeal, attraction

attraper [atʀape] /1/ vt (catch); (habitude, amende) to get, pick up; (fam: duper) to con; **se faire ~ (fam)** to be told off

attrayant, e [atʀɛjɑ, -ɑt] adj attractive

attribuer [atʀibɥe] /1/ vt (prix) to award; (rôle, tâche) to allocate, assign; (imputer): **~ qch à** to attribute sth to; **s'attribuer** vt (s'approprier) to claim for o.s.

attrister [atʀiste] /1/ vt to sadden

attroupement [atʀupmɑ] nm crowd

attrouper [atʀupe] /1/: **s'attrouper** vi to gather

au [o] prép voir **à**

aubaine [obɛn] nf godsend

aube [ob] nf dawn, daybreak; **à l'~** at dawn ou daybreak

aubépine [obepin] nf hawthorn

auberge [obɛʀʒ] nf inn; **~ de jeunesse** youth hostel

aubergine [obɛʀʒin] nf aubergine

aucun, e [okœ̃, -yn] adj, pron no; (positif) any ▷ pron none; (positif) any(one); **sans ~ doute** without any doubt; **plus qu'~ autre** more than any other; **il le ferait mieux qu'~ de nous** he'll do it better than any of us; **~ des deux** neither of the two; **~ d'entre eux** none of them

audace [odas] *nf* daring, boldness; (*péj*) audacity; **audacieux, -euse** *adj* daring, bold

au-delà [od(ə)la] *adv* beyond ▷ *nm*: **l'~** the hereafter; **~ de** beyond

au-dessous [odsu] *adv* underneath; below; **~ de** under(neath); below; (*limite, somme etc*) below, under; (*dignité, condition*) below

au-dessus [odsy] *adv* above; **~ de** above

au-devant [od(ə)vɑ̃]: **~ de** *prép*: **aller ~ de** (*personne, danger*) to go (out) and meet; (*souhaits de qn*) to anticipate

audience [odjɑ̃s] *nf* audience; (*Jur: séance*) hearing

audio-visuel, le [odjovizɥɛl] *adj* audio-visual

audition [odisjɔ̃] *nf* (*ouïe, écoute*) hearing; (*Jur: de témoins*) examination; (*Mus, Théât: épreuve*) audition

auditoire [oditwar] *nm* audience

augmentation [ɔgmɑ̃tasjɔ̃] *nf* increase; **~ (de salaire)** rise (*in salary*) (BRIT), (pay) raise (us)

augmenter [ɔgmɑ̃te] /1/ *vt* to increase; (*salaire, prix*) to increase, raise, put up; (*employé*) to increase the salary of ▷ *vi* to increase

augure [ogyr] *nm*: **de bon/mauvais ~** of good/ill omen

aujourd'hui [oʒurdɥi] *adv* today

aumône [omon] *nf* alms *sg* (*pl inv*); **aumônier** *nm* chaplain

auparavant [oparavɑ̃] *adv* before(hand)

auprès [oprɛ]: **~ de** *prép* next to, close to; (*recourir, s'adresser*) to; (*en comparaison de*) compared with

auquel [okɛl] *pron voir* **lequel**

aurai *etc* [ɔrɛ] *vb voir* **avoir**

aurons *etc* [ɔrɔ̃] *vb voir* **avoir**

aurore [ɔrɔr] *nf* dawn, daybreak

ausculter [ɔskylte] /1/ *vt* to sound

aussi [osi] *adv* (*également*) also, too; (*de comparaison*) as ▷ *conj* therefore, consequently; **~ fort que** as strong as; **moi ~** me too

aussitôt [osito] *adv* straight away, immediately; **~ que** as soon as

austère [ɔstɛr] *adj* austere

austral, e [ɔstral] *adj* southern

Australie [ɔstrali] *nf*: **l'~** Australia; **australien, ne** *adj* Australian ▷ *nm/f*: **Australien, ne** Australian

autant [otɑ̃] *adv* so much; **je ne savais pas que tu la détestais ~ !** I didn't know you hated her so much; (*comparatif*): **~ (que)** as much (as); (*nombre*) as many (as); **~ (de)** so much (ou many); as many (ou many); **~ partir** we (ou you etc) may as well leave; **~ dire que ...** one might as well say that ...; **pour ~** for all that; **d'~ plus/mieux (que)** all the more/the better (since)

autel [otɛl] *nm* altar

auteur [otœr] *nm* author

authentique [otɑ̃tik] *adj* authentic, genuine

auto [oto] *nf* car; **autobiographie** *nf* autobiography; **autobronzant** *nm* self-tanning cream (*or lotion etc*); **autobus** *nm* bus; **autocar** *nm* coach

autochtone [ɔtɔkton] *nm/f* native

auto-: autocollant, e *adj* self-adhesive; (*enveloppe*) self-seal ▷ *nm* sticker; **autocuiseur** *nm* pressure cooker; **autodéfense** *nf* self-defence; **autodidacte** *nm/f* self-taught person; **auto-école** *nf* driving school; **autographe** *nm* autograph

automate [ɔtɔmat] *nm* (*machine*) (automatic) machine

automatique [ɔtɔmatik] *adj* automatic ▷ *nm*: **l'~** = direct dialling

automne [ɔtɔn] *nm* autumn (BRIT), fall (us)

automobile [ɔtɔmɔbil] *adj* motor *cpd* ▷ *nf* (motor) car; **automobiliste** *nm/f* motorist

automutiler [otomytile] /1/:
s'**automutiler** vr to self-harm
autonome [otɔnɔm] adj
autonomous; **autonomie** nf
autonomy; (Pol) self-government
autopsie [otɔpsi] nf post-mortem
(examination), autopsy
autoradio [otoʀadjo] nf car radio
autorisation [otɔʀizasjɔ̃] nf
authorization; (papiers) permit
autorisé, e [otɔʀize] adj (opinion,
sources) authoritative
autoriser [otɔʀize] /1/ vt to give
permission for, authorize; (fig) to
allow (of)
autoritaire [otɔʀitɛʀ] adj
authoritarian
autorité [otɔʀite] nf authority; **faire
~** to be authoritative
autoroute [otoʀut] nf motorway
(BRIT), expressway (US); **~ de
l'information** (Inform) information
superhighway

AUTOROUTE

- Motorways in France, indicated
- by blue road signs with the letter
- A followed by a number, are toll
- roads. The speed limit is 130 km/h
- (110 km/h when it is raining). At the
- tollgate, the lanes marked 'réservé'
- and with an orange 't' are reserved
- for people who subscribe to
- 'télépéage', an electronic payment
- system.

auto-stop [otostɔp] nm: **faire de
l'~** to hitch-hike; **prendre qn en ~**
to give sb a lift; **auto-stoppeur, -euse**
nm/f hitch-hiker
autour [otuʀ] adv around; **~ de**
around; **tout ~** all around

○ **MOT-CLÉ**

autre [otʀ] adj **1** (différent) other,
different; **je préférerais un**

autre verre I'd prefer another ou a
different glass
2 (supplémentaire) other; **je
voudrais un autre verre d'eau** I'd
like another glass of water
3: **autre chose** something else;
autre part somewhere else;
d'autre part on the other hand
▶ pron: **un autre** another (one);
nous/vous autres us/you;
d'autres others; **l'autre** the other
(one); **les autres** the others; (autrui)
others; **l'un et l'autre** both of
them; **se détester l'un l'autre/les
uns les autres** to hate each other
ou one another; **d'une semaine/
minute à l'autre** from one week/
minute ou moment to the next;
(incessamment) any week/minute
ou moment now; **entre autres**
(personnes) among others; (choses)
among other things

autrefois [otʀəfwa] adv in the past
autrement [otʀəmɑ̃] adv differently;
(d'une manière différente) in another
way; (sinon) otherwise; **~ dit** in
other words
Autriche [otʀiʃ] nf: **l'~** Austria;
autrichien, ne adj Austrian ▷ nm/f:
Autrichien, ne Austrian
autruche [otʀyʃ] nf ostrich
aux [o] prép voir **à**
auxiliaire [oksiljɛʀ] adj, nm/f
auxiliary
auxquels, auxquelles [okɛl] pron
voir **lequel**
avalanche [avalɑ̃ʃ] nf avalanche
avaler [avale] /1/ vt to swallow
avance [avɑ̃s] nf (de troupes etc)
advance; (progrès) progress; (d'argent)
advance; (opposé à retard) lead;
avances nfpl (amoureuses) advances;
(être) en ~ to be early; (sur un
programme) (to be) ahead of schedule;
d'~, à l'~ in advance
avancé, e [avɑ̃se] adj advanced;
(travail etc) well on, well under way

avancement [avɑ̃smɑ̃] *nm* (professionnel) promotion

avancer [avɑ̃se] /3/ *vi* to move forward, advance; (projet, travail) to make progress; (montre, réveil) to be fast ▷ *vt* to move forward, advance; (argent) to advance; (montre, pendule) to put forward; **s'avancer** *vi* to move forward, advance; (fig) to commit o.s.

avant [avɑ̃] *prép* before ▷ *adj inv*: **siège/roue** ~ front seat/wheel ▷ *nm* (d'un véhicule, bâtiment) front; (Sport: joueur) forward; ~ **qu'il parte/de partir** before he leaves/ leaving; ~ **tout** (surtout) above all; **à l'** ~ (dans un véhicule) in the front; **en** ~ (se pencher, tomber) forward(s); **partir en** ~ to go on ahead; **en** ~ **de** in front of

avantage [avɑ̃taʒ] *nm* advantage; ~**s sociaux** fringe benefits; **avantager** /3/ *vt* (favoriser) to favour; (embellir) to flatter; **avantageux, -euse** *adj* (prix) attractive

avant: **avant-bras** *nm inv* forearm; **avant-coureur** *adj inv*: **signe avant-coureur** advance indication ou sign; **avant-dernier, -ière** *adj, nm/f* next to last, last but one; **avant-goût** *nm* foretaste; **avant-hier** *adv* the day before yesterday; **avant-première** *nf* (de film) preview; **avant-veille** *nf*: **l'avant-veille** two days before

avare [avaʁ] *adj* miserly, avaricious ▷ *nmf* miser; ~ **de compliments** stingy ou sparing with one's compliments

avec [avɛk] *prép* with; (à l'égard de) to(wards), with; **et** ~ **ça?** (dans un magasin) anything ou something else?

avenir [avniʁ] *nm*: **l'** ~ the future; **à l'** ~ in future; **carrière/politicien d'** ~ career/politician with prospects ou a future

aventure [avɑ̃tyʁ] *nf*: **l'** ~ adventure; **une** ~ (amoureuse) an affair;

aventureux, -euse *adj* adventurous, venturesome; (projet) risky, chancy

avenue [avny] *nf* avenue

avérer [aveʁe] /6/: **s'avérer** *vr*: **s'** ~ **faux/coûteux** to prove (to be) wrong/expensive

averse [avɛʁs] *nf* shower

averti, e [avɛʁti] *adj* (well-) informed

avertir [avɛʁtiʁ] /2/ *vt*: ~ **qn (de qch/que)** to warn sb (of sth/that); (renseigner) to inform sb (of sth/ that); **avertissement** *nm* warning; **avertisseur** *nm* horn, siren

aveu, x [avø] *nm* confession

aveugle [avœgl] *adj* blind ▷ *nm/f* blind person

aviation [avjasjɔ̃] *nf* aviation; (sport, métier de pilote) flying; (Mil) air force

avide [avid] *adj* eager; (péj) greedy, grasping

avion [avjɔ̃] *nm* (aero)plane (BRIT), (air)plane (US); **aller (quelque part) en** ~ to go (somewhere) by plane, fly (somewhere); **par** ~ by airmail; ~ **à réaction** jet (plane)

aviron [aviʁɔ̃] *nm* oar; (sport): **l'** ~ rowing

avis [avi] *nm* opinion; (notification) notice; **à mon** ~ in my opinion; **changer d'** ~ to change one's mind; **jusqu'à nouvel** ~ until further notice

aviser [avize] /1/ *vt* (informer): ~ **qn de/que** to advise ou inform ou notify sb of/that ▷ *vi* to think about things, assess the situation; **nous aviserons sur place** we'll work something out once we're there; **s'** ~ **de qch/que** to become suddenly aware of sth/ that; **s'** ~ **de faire** to take it into one's head to do

avocat, e [avɔka, -at] *nm/f* (Jur) = barrister (BRIT), lawyer ▷ *nm* (Culin) avocado (pear); **l'** ~ **de la défense/partie civile** the counsel for the defence/plaintiff; ~ **général** assistant public prosecutor

avoine [avwan] *nf* oats pl

◯ **MOT-CLÉ**

avoir [avwaʀ] /34/ *vt* **1** (*posséder*)
to have; **elle a deux enfants/une
belle maison** she has (got) two
children/a lovely house; **il a les yeux
bleus** he has (got) blue eyes; **vous
avez du sel?** do you have any salt?;
avoir du courage/de la patience to
be brave/patient
2 (*éprouver*): **avoir de la peine** to be
ou feel sad; **voir aussi faim, peur**
3 (*âge, dimensions*) to be: **il a 3 ans** he
is 3 (years old); **le mur a 3 mètres de
haut** the wall is 3 metres high
4 (*fam: duper*) to have; **on vous a
eu!** you've been done *ou* had!; (*fait une
plaisanterie*) we *ou* they had you there
5: **en avoir contre qn** to have a
grudge against sb; **en avoir assez**
to be fed up; **j'en ai pour une demi-
heure** it'll take me half an hour
6 (*obtenir, attraper*) to get; **j'ai réussi
à avoir mon train** I managed to
get *ou* catch my train; **j'ai réussi à
avoir le renseignement qu'il me
fallait** I managed to get (hold of) the
information I needed
▶ *vb aux* **1** to have; **avoir mangé/
dormi** to have eaten/slept
2 (*avoir +à +infinitif*): **avoir à faire
qch** to have to do sth; **vous n'avez
qu'à lui demander** you only have
to ask him
▶ *vb impers* **1**: **il y a** (+ *singulier*)
there is; (+ *pluriel*) there are; **il y
avait du café/des gâteaux** there
was coffee/there were cakes; **qu'y
a-t-il?, qu'est-ce qu'il y a?** what's
the matter?, what is it?; **il doit y
avoir une explication** there must
be an explanation; **il n'y a qu'à ...**
we (*ou* you *etc*) will just have to ...; **il
ne peut y en avoir qu'un** there can
only be one
2: **il y a** (*temporel*): **il y a 10 ans**
10 years ago; **il y a 10 ans/
longtemps que je le connais** I've

known him for 10 years/a long time;
il y a 10 ans qu'il est arrivé it's 10
years since he arrived
▶ *nm* assets *pl*, resources *pl*; (*Comm*)
credit

avortement [avɔʀtəmɑ̃] *nm*
abortion

avouer [avwe] /1/ *vt* (*crime, défaut*)
to confess (to); **~ avoir fait/que** to
admit *ou* confess to having done/that

avril [avʀil] *nm* April

axe [aks] *nm* axis (*pl* axes); (*de roue etc*)
axle; (*fig*) main line; **~ routier** trunk
road (BRIT), main road, highway (US)

ayons *etc* [ɛjɔ̃] *vb voir* **avoir**

bâbord [babɔʀ] nm: **à** ou **par ~ to** port, on the port side

baby-foot [babifut] nm inv table football

baby-sitting [babisitiŋ] nm baby-sitting; **faire du ~** to baby-sit

bac [bak] nm (récipient) tub

baccalauréat [bakalɔʀea] nm ≈ high school diploma

bâcler [bakle] /1/ vt to botch (up)

baffe [baf] nf (fam) slap, clout

bafouiller [bafuje] /1/ vi, vt to stammer

bagage [bagaʒ] nm: **~s** luggage sg; (connaissances) background, knowledge; **~s à main** hand-luggage

bagarre [bagaʀ] nf fight, brawl; **bagarrer** /1/: **se bagarrer** vi to (have a) fight

bagnole [baɲɔl] nf (fam) car

bague [bag] nf ring; **~ de fiançailles** engagement ring

baguette [baget] nf stick; (cuisine chinoise) chopstick; (de chef d'orchestre) baton; (pain) stick of (French) bread; **~ magique** magic wand

baie [bɛ] nf (Géo) bay; (fruit) berry; **~ (vitrée)** picture window

baignade [beɲad] nf bathing; "**~ interdite**" "no bathing"

baigner [beɲe] /1/ vt (bébé) to bath; **se baigner** vi to go swimming ou bathing; **baignoire** nf bath(tub)

bail (pl **baux**) [baj, bo] nm lease

bâiller [baje] /1/ vi to yawn; (être ouvert) to gape

bain [bɛ̃] nm bath; **prendre un ~** to have a bath; **se mettre dans le ~** (fig) to get into (the way of) it ou things; **~ de bouche** mouthwash; **~ moussant** bubble bath; **~ de soleil: prendre un ~ de soleil** to sunbathe; **bain-marie** nm: **faire chauffer au bain-marie** (boîte etc) to immerse in boiling water

baiser [beze] /1/ nm kiss ▷ vt (main, front) to kiss; (fam!) to screw (!)

baisse [bɛs] nf fall, drop; **en ~** falling

baisser [bese] /1/ vt to lower; (radio, chauffage) to turn down ▷ vi to fall, drop, go down; (vue, santé) to fail, dwindle; **se baisser** vi to bend down

bal [bal] nm dance; (grande soirée) ball; **~ costumé/masqué** fancy-dress/masked ball

balade [balad] (fam) nf (à pied) walk, stroll; (en voiture) drive; **balader** /1/ (fam): **se balader** vi to go for a walk ou stroll; to go for a drive; **baladeur** [baladœʀ] nm personal stereo, Walkman®

balai [balɛ] nm broom, brush

balance [balɑ̃s] nf scales pl; (signe): **la B~** Libra; **~ commerciale** balance of trade

balancer [balɑ̃se] /3/ vt to swing; (lancer) to fling, chuck; (renvoyer, jeter) to chuck out; **se balancer** vi to swing; to rock; **se ~ de qch** (fam) not to give a toss about sth; **balançoire** nf swing; (sur pivot) seesaw

balayer [baleje] /7/ vt (feuilles etc) to sweep up, brush up; (pièce, cour) to sweep; (chasser) to sweep away ou aside; (radar) to scan; **balayeur, -euse** [balejœr, -øz] nm/f road sweeper ▷ nf (engin) road sweeper

balbutier [balbysje] /7/ vi, vt to stammer

balcon [balkɔ̃] nm balcony; (Théât) dress circle

Bâle [bɑl] n Basle ou Basel

Baléares [baleaʀ] nfpl: **les ~** the Balearic Islands, the Balearics

baleine [balɛn] nf whale

balise [baliz] nf (Navig) beacon, (marker) buoy; (Aviat) runway light, beacon; (Auto, Ski) sign, marker; **baliser** /1/ vt to mark out (with beacons ou lights etc)

balle [bal] nf (de fusil) bullet; (de sport) ball; (fam: franc) franc

ballerine [bal(ə)ʀin] nf (danseuse) ballet dancer; (chaussure) pump, ballet shoe

ballet [balɛ] nm ballet

ballon [balɔ̃] nm (de sport) ball; (jouet, Aviat) balloon; **~ de football** football; **~ d'oxygène** oxygen bottle

balnéaire [balneɛʀ] adj seaside cpd; **station ~** seaside resort

balustrade [balystʀad] nf railings pl, handrail

bambin [bɑ̃bɛ̃] nm little child

bambou [bɑ̃bu] nm bamboo

banal, e [banal] adj banal, commonplace; (péj) trite; **banalité** nf banality

banane [banan] nf banana; (sac) waist-bag, bum-bag

banc [bɑ̃] nm seat, bench; (de poissons) shoal; **~ d'essai** (fig) testing ground

bancaire [bɑ̃kɛʀ] adj banking; (chèque, carte) bank cpd

bancal, e [bɑ̃kal] adj wobbly

bandage [bɑ̃daʒ] nm bandage

bande [bɑ̃d] nf (de tissu etc) strip; (Méd) bandage; (motif, dessin) stripe; (groupe) band; (péj): **une ~ de** a bunch ou crowd of; **faire ~ à part** to keep to o.s.; **~ dessinée (BD)** comic strip; **~ magnétique** magnetic tape; **~ sonore** sound track

bande-annonce [bɑ̃danɔ̃s] nf trailer

bandeau, x [bɑ̃do] nm headband; (sur les yeux) blindfold

bander [bɑ̃de] /1/ vt (blessure) to bandage; **~ les yeux à qn** to blindfold sb

bandit [bɑ̃di] nm bandit

bandoulière [bɑ̃duljɛʀ] nf: **en ~** (slung ou worn) across the shoulder

Bangladesh [bɑ̃ɡladɛʃ] nm: **le ~** Bangladesh

banlieue [bɑ̃ljø] nf suburbs pl; **quartiers de ~** suburban areas; **trains de ~** commuter trains

bannir [baniʀ] /2/ vt to banish

banque [bɑ̃k] nf bank; (activités) banking; **~ de données** data bank

banquet [bɑ̃kɛ] nm dinner; (d'apparat) banquet

banquette [bɑ̃kɛt] nf seat

banquier [bɑ̃kje] nm banker

banquise [bɑ̃kiz] nf ice field

baptême [batɛm] nm christening; baptism; **~ de l'air** first flight

baptiser [batize] /1/ vt to christen; to baptize

bar [baʀ] nm bar

baraque [baʀak] nf shed; (fam) house; **~ foraine** fairground stand; **baraqué, e** (fam) adj well-built, hefty

barbant, e [baʀbɑ̃, -ɑ̃t] adj (fam) deadly (boring)

barbare [baʀbaʀ] adj barbaric

barbe [baʀb] nf beard; **(au nez et) à la ~ de qn** (fig) under sb's very nose; **la ~!** (fam) damn it!; **quelle ~!** (fam) what a drag ou bore!; **~ à papa** candy-floss (BRIT), cotton candy (US)

barbelé [baʀbəle] adj, nm: **(fil de fer) ~** barbed wire no pl

barbiturique [baʀbityʀik] *nm* barbiturate

barbouiller [baʀbuje] /1/ *vt* to daub; **avoir l'estomac barbouillé** to feel queasy *ou* sick

barbu, e [baʀby] *adj* bearded

barder [baʀde] /1/ *vi* (*fam*): **ça va ~** sparks will fly

barème [baʀɛm] *nm* (*Scol*) scale; (*liste*) table

baril [baʀi(l)] *nm* barrel; (*de poudre*) keg

bariolé, e [baʀjɔle] *adj* many-coloured, rainbow-coloured

baromètre [baʀɔmɛtʀ] *nm* barometer

baron [baʀɔ̃] *nm* baron

baronne [baʀɔn] *nf* baroness

baroque [baʀɔk] *adj* (*Art*) baroque; (*fig*) weird

barque [baʀk] *nf* small boat

barquette [baʀkɛt] *nf* small boat-shaped tart; (*récipient: en aluminium*) tub; (: *en bois*) basket; (*pour repas*) tray; (*pour frites*) punnet

barrage [baʀaʒ] *nm* dam; (*sur route*) roadblock, barricade

barre [baʀ] *nf* (*de fer etc*) rod; (*Navig*) helm; (*écrite*) line, stroke

barreau, x [baʀo] *nm* bar; (*Jur*): **le ~** the Bar

barrer [baʀe] /1/ *vt* (*route etc*) to block; (*mot*) to cross out; (*chèque*) to cross (*BRIT*); (*Navig*) to steer; **se barrer** *vi* (*fam*) to clear off

barrette [baʀɛt] *nf* (*pour cheveux*) (hair) slide (*BRIT*), barrette (*US*)

barricader [baʀikade] /1/: **se barricader** *vi*: **se ~ chez soi** to lock o.s. in

barrière [baʀjɛʀ] *nf* fence; (*obstacle*) barrier; (*porte*) gate

barrique [baʀik] *nf* barrel, cask

bar-tabac [baʀtaba] *nm* bar (*which sells tobacco and stamps*)

bas, basse [bɑ, bɑs] *adj* low; (*vêtement*) stocking; (*partie inférieure*): **le ~ de** the lower part *ou* foot *ou* bottom of ▷ *adv* low; (*parler*) softly; **au ~ mot** at the lowest estimate; **enfant en ~ âge** young child; **en ~** down below; (*d'une liste, d'un mur etc*) at (*ou* to) the bottom; (*dans une maison*) downstairs; **en ~ de** at the bottom of; **à ~ la dictature!** down with dictatorship!

bas-côté [bɑkote] *nm* (*de route*) verge (*BRIT*), shoulder (*US*)

basculer [baskyle] /1/ *vi* to fall over, topple (over); (*benne*) to tip up ▷ *vt* (*contenu*) to tip out; (*benne*) tip up

base [bɑz] *nf* base; (*fondement, principe*) basis (*pl* bases); **la ~** (*Pol*) the rank and file; **de ~** basic; **à ~ de café etc** coffee etc -based; **~ de données** database; **baser** /1/ *vt*: **baser qch sur** to base sth on; **se baser sur** (*données, preuves*) to base one's argument on

bas-fond [bɑfɔ̃] *nm* (*Navig*) shallow; **bas-fonds** *nmpl* (*fig*) dregs

basilic [bazilik] *nm* (*Culin*) basil

basket [baskɛt] *nm* basketball

baskets [baskɛt] *nfpl* trainers (*BRIT*), sneakers (*US*)

basque [bask] *adj* Basque ▷ *nm/f*: **B~** Basque; **le Pays ~** the Basque country

basse [bɑs] *adj voir* **bas** ▷ *nf* (*Mus*) bass; **basse-cour** *nf* farmyard

bassin [basɛ̃] *nm* (*pièce d'eau*) pond, pool; (*de fontaine, Géo*) basin; (*Anat*) pelvis; (*portuaire*) dock

bassine [basin] *nf* basin; (*contenu*) bowl, bowlful

basson [basɔ̃] *nm* bassoon

bat [ba] *vb voir* **battre**

bataille [bataj] *nf* battle; (*rixe*) fight; **elle avait les cheveux en ~** her hair was a mess

bateau, x [bato] *nm* boat; ship; **bateau-mouche** *nm* (*passenger*) pleasure boat (*on the Seine*)

bâti, e [bati] *adj* (*terrain*) developed; **bien ~** well-built

bâtiment [batimɑ̃] *nm* building; (*Navig*) ship, vessel; (*industrie*): **le ~** the building trade

bâtir [batiʀ] /2/ vt to build

bâtisse [batis] nf building

bâton [batɔ̃] nm stick; **parler à ~s rompus** to chat about this and that

bats [ba] vb voir **battre**

battement [batmɑ̃] nm (de cœur) beat; (intervalle) interval (between classes, trains etc); **10 minutes de ~** 10 minutes to spare

batterie [batʀi] nf (Mil, Élec) battery; (Mus) drums pl, drum kit; **~ de cuisine** kitchen utensils pl; (casseroles etc) pots and pans pl

batteur [batœʀ] nm (Mus) drummer; (appareil) whisk

battre [batʀ] /41/ vt to beat; (blé) to thresh; (cartes) to shuffle; (passer au peigne fin) to scour ▷ vi (cœur) to beat; (volets etc) to bang, rattle; **se battre** vi to fight; **~ la mesure** to beat time; **~ son plein** to be at its height, be going full swing; **~ des mains** to clap one's hands

baume [bom] nm balm

bavard, e [bavaʀ, -aʀd] adj (very) talkative; gossipy; **bavarder** /1/ vi to chatter; (indiscrètement) to gossip; (révéler un secret) to blab

baver [bave] /1/ vi to dribble; (chien) to slobber, slaver; **en ~** (fam) to have a hard time (of it)

bavoir [bavwaʀ] nm bib

bavure [bavyʀ] nf smudge; (fig) hitch; (policière etc) blunder

bazar [bazaʀ] nm general store; (fam) jumble; **bazarder** /1/ vt (fam) to chuck out

BCBG sigle adj (= bon chic bon genre) smart and trendy, ≈ preppy

BD sigle f = **bande dessinée**

bd abr = **boulevard**

béant, e [beɑ̃, -ɑ̃t] adj gaping

beau (bel), belle, beaux [bo, bɛl] adj beautiful, lovely; (homme) handsome ▷ adv: **il fait ~** the weather's fine ▷ nm: **un ~ jour** one (fine) day; **de plus belle** more than ever, even more; **bel et bien** well

and truly; **le plus ~ c'est que ...** the best of it is that ...; **on a ~ essayer** however hard ou no matter how hard we try; **faire le ~** (chien) to sit up and beg

MOT-CLÉ

beaucoup [buku] adv **1** a lot; **il boit beaucoup** he drinks a lot; **il ne boit pas beaucoup** he doesn't drink much ou a lot

2 (suivi de plus, trop etc) much, a lot; **il est beaucoup plus grand** he is much ou a lot taller; **c'est beaucoup plus cher** it's a lot ou much more expensive; **il a beaucoup plus de temps que moi** he has much ou a lot more time than me; **il y a beaucoup plus de touristes ici** there are a lot ou many more tourists here; **beaucoup trop vite** much too fast; **il fume beaucoup trop** he smokes far too much

3: **beaucoup de** (nombre) many, a lot of; (quantité) a lot of; **beaucoup d'étudiants/de touristes** a lot of ou many students/tourists; **beaucoup de courage** a lot of courage; **il n'a pas beaucoup d'argent** he hasn't got much ou a lot of money

4: **de beaucoup** by far

beau: beau-fils nm son-in-law; (remariage) stepson; **beau-frère** nm brother-in-law; **beau-père** nm father-in-law; (remariage) stepfather

beauté [bote] nf beauty; **de toute ~** beautiful; **finir qch en ~** to complete sth brilliantly

beaux-arts [bozaʀ] nmpl fine arts

beaux-parents [bopaʀɑ̃] nmpl wife's/husband's family, in-laws pl

bébé [bebe] nm baby

bec [bɛk] nm beak, bill; (de cafetière etc) spout; (de casserole etc) lip; (fam) mouth; **~ de gaz** (street) gaslamp

bêche [bɛʃ] nf spade; **bêcher** /1/ vt to dig

bedaine [bədɛn] nf paunch

bedonnant, e [bədɔnɑ̃, -ɑ̃t] adj potbellied

bée [be] adj: **bouche** ~ gaping

bégayer [begeje] /8/ vt, vi to stammer

beige [bɛʒ] adj beige

beignet [bɛɲɛ] nm fritter

bel [bɛl] adj m voir **beau**

bêler [bele] /1/ vi to bleat

belette [bəlɛt] nf weasel

belge [bɛlʒ] adj Belgian ▷ nm/f: **B**~ Belgian

Belgique [bɛlʒik] nf: **la** ~ Belgium

bélier [belje] nm ram; (signe): **le B**~ Aries

belle [bɛl] adj voir **beau** ▷ nf (Sport): **la** ~ the decider; **belle-fille** nf daughter-in-law; (remariage) stepdaughter; **belle-mère** nf mother-in-law; (remariage) stepmother; **belle-sœur** nf sister-in-law

belvédère [bɛlvedɛʀ] nm panoramic viewpoint (or small building there)

bémol [bemɔl] nm (Mus) flat

bénédiction [benediksjɔ̃] nf blessing

bénéfice [benefis] nm (Comm) profit; (avantage) benefit; **bénéficier** /7/ vi: **bénéficier de** to enjoy; (profiter) to benefit by ou from; **bénéfique** adj beneficial

Benelux [benelyks] nm: **le** ~ Benelux, the Benelux countries

bénévole [benevɔl] adj voluntary, unpaid

bénin, -igne [benɛ̃, -iɲ] adj minor, mild; (tumeur) benign

bénir [beniʀ] /2/ vt to bless; **bénit, e** adj consecrated; **eau bénite** holy water

benne [bɛn] nf skip; (de téléphérique) (cable) car; **à ordures** (amovible) skip

béquille [bekij] nf crutch; (de bicyclette) stand

berceau, x [bɛʀso] nm cradle, crib

bercer [bɛʀse] /3/ vt to rock, cradle; (musique etc) to lull; ~ **qn de** (promesses etc) to delude sb with; **berceuse** nf lullaby

béret [beʀɛ] nm (aussi: ~ **basque**) beret

berge [bɛʀʒ] nf bank

berger, -ère [bɛʀʒe, -ɛʀ] nm/f shepherd/shepherdess; ~ **allemand** alsatian (dog) (BRIT), German shepherd (dog) (US)

Berlin [bɛʀlɛ̃] n Berlin

Bermudes [bɛʀmyd] nfpl: **les (îles)** ~ Bermuda

Berne [bɛʀn] n Bern

berner [bɛʀne] /1/ vt to fool

besogne [bəzɔɲ] nf work no pl, job

besoin [bəzwɛ̃] nm need; (pauvreté): **le** ~ need, want; **faire ses** ~**s** to relieve o.s.; **avoir** ~ **de qch/faire qch** to need sth/to do sth; **au** ~ if need be; **être dans le** ~ to be in need ou want

bestiole [bɛstjɔl] nf (tiny) creature

bétail [betaj] nm livestock, cattle pl

bête [bɛt] nf animal; (bestiole) insect, creature ▷ adj stupid, silly; **chercher la petite** ~ to nit-pick; ~ **noire** pet hate; ~ **sauvage** wild beast

bêtise [betiz] nf stupidity; (action, remarque) stupid thing (to say ou do)

béton [betɔ̃] nm concrete; **(en)** ~ (fig: alibi, argument) cast iron; ~ **armé** reinforced concrete

betterave [bɛtʀav] nf beetroot (BRIT), beet (US); ~ **sucrière** sugar beet

Beur [bœʀ] nm/f see note **"Beur"**

BEUR

Beur is a term used to refer to a person born in France of North African immigrant parents. It is not racist and is often used by the media, anti-racist groups and second-generation North Africans themselves. The word itself comes from back slang or 'verlan'.

beurre [bœʀ] nm butter; **beurrer** /1/ vt to butter; **beurrier** nm butter dish

biais [bjɛ] nm (moyen) device, expedient; (aspect) angle; **en ~, de ~** (obliquement) at an angle; **par le ~ de** by means of

bibelot [biblo] nm trinket, curio

biberon [bibʀɔ̃] nm (feeding) bottle; **nourrir au ~** to bottle-feed

bible [bibl] nf bible

bibliobus [biblijobys] nm mobile library van

bibliothécaire nm/f librarian

bibliothèque nf library; (meuble) bookcase

bic® [bik] nm Biro®

bicarbonate [bikaʀbɔnat] nm: **~ (de soude)** bicarbonate of soda

biceps [bisɛps] nm biceps

biche [biʃ] nf doe

bicolore [bikɔlɔʀ] adj two-coloured

bicoque [bikɔk] nf (péj) shack

bicyclette [bisiklɛt] nf bicycle

bidet [bidɛ] nm bidet

bidon [bidɔ̃] nm can ▸ adj inv (fam) phoney

bidonville [bidɔ̃vil] nm shanty town

bidule [bidyl] nm (fam) thingamajig

○ **MOT-CLÉ**

bien [bjɛ̃] nm 1 (avantage, profit): **faire du bien à qn** to do sb good; **dire du bien de** to speak well of; **c'est pour son bien** it's for his own good 2 (possession, patrimoine) possession, property; **son bien le plus précieux** his most treasured possession; **avoir du bien** to have property; **biens (de consommation** etc) (consumer etc) goods 3 (moral): **le bien** good; **distinguer le bien du mal** to tell good from evil ▸ adv 1 (de façon satisfaisante) well; **elle travaille/mange bien** she works/eats well; **croyant bien faire, je/il ...** thinking I/he was doing the right thing, I/he ...; **tiens-toi bien!** (assieds-toi correctement)

sit up straight!; (debout) stand up straight!; (sois sage) behave yourself!; (prépare-toi) wait for it! 2 (valeur intensive) quite; **bien jeune** quite young; **bien assez** quite enough; **bien mieux** (very) much better; **bien du temps/des gens** quite a time/a number of people; **j'espère bien y aller** I do hope to go; **je veux bien le faire** (concession) I'm quite willing to do it; **il faut bien le faire** it has to be done; **cela fait bien deux ans que je ne l'ai pas vu** I haven't seen him for at least ou a good two years; **Paul est bien venu, n'est-ce pas?** Paul HAS come, hasn't he?; **où peut-il bien être passé?** where on earth can he have got to? ▸ excl right!, OK!, fine!; (c'est) bien **fait!** it serves you (ou him etc) right!; **bien sûr!** certainly! ▸ adj inv 1 (en bonne forme, à l'aise): **je me sens bien** I feel fine; **je ne me sens pas bien** I don't feel well; **on est bien dans ce fauteuil** this chair is very comfortable 2 (joli, beau) good-looking; **tu es bien dans cette robe** you look good in that dress 3 (satisfaisant) good; **elle est bien, cette maison/secrétaire** it's a good house/she's a good secretary; **c'est très bien (comme ça)** it's fine (like that); **c'est bien?** is that all right? 4 (moralement) right; (personne) good, nice; (respectable) respectable; **ce n'est pas bien de ...** it's not right to ...; **elle est bien, cette femme** she's a nice woman, she's a nice sort; **des gens bien** respectable people 5 (en bons termes): **être bien avec qn** to be on good terms with sb; **bien-aimé, e** adj, nm/f beloved; **bien-être** nm well-being; **bienfaisance** nf charity; **bienfait** nm act of generosity, benefaction; (de la science etc) benefit; **bienfaiteur, -trice**

bientôt [bjɛ̃to] adv soon; **à ~** see you soon

bienveillant, e [bjɛ̃vɛjɑ̃, -ɑ̃t] adj kindly

bienvenu, e [bjɛ̃vny] adj welcome ▷ nf: **souhaiter la ~e à** to welcome; **~e à** welcome to

bière [bjɛʀ] nf (boisson) beer; (cercueil) bier; **~ blonde** lager; **~ brune** brown ale (BRIT), dark beer (US); **~ (à la) pression** draught beer

bifteck [biftɛk] nm steak

bigoudi [bigudi] nm curler

bijou, x [biʒu] nm jewel; **bijouterie** nf jeweller's (shop); **bijoutier, -ière** nm/f jeweller

bikini [bikini] nm bikini

bilan [bilɑ̃] nm (Comm) balance sheet(s); (fig) (net) outcome (: de victimes) toll; **faire le ~ de** to assess; to review; **déposer son ~** to file a bankruptcy statement; **~ de santé** check-up

bile [bil] nf bile; **se faire de la ~** (fam) to worry o.s. sick

bilieux, -euse [biljø, -øz] adj bilious; (fig: colérique) testy

bilingue [bilɛ̃g] adj bilingual

billard [bijaʀ] nm billiards sg; (table) billiard table

bille [bij] nf ball; (du jeu de billes) marble

billet [bijɛ] nm (aussi: **~ de banque**) (bank)note; (de cinéma, de bus etc) ticket; (courte lettre) note; **~ électronique** e-ticket; **billetterie** nf ticket office; (distributeur) ticket dispenser; (Banque) cash dispenser

billion [biljɔ̃] nm billion (BRIT), trillion (US)

bimensuel, le [bimɑ̃sɥɛl] adj bimonthly

bio [bjo] adj organic

bio... [bjo] préfixe bio...;

biocarburant [bjokaʀbyʀɑ̃] nm biofuel; **biochimie** nf biochemistry; **biodiesel** nm biodiesel; **biogazole** nm biodiesel; **biographie** nf biography; **biologie** nf biology; **biologique** adj biological; **biométrie** nf biometrics; **biotechnologie** nf biotechnology; **bioterrorisme** nm bioterrorism

bipolaire [bipɔlɛʀ] adj bipolar

Birmanie [biʀmani] nf Burma

bis¹, e [bi, biz] adj (couleur) greyish brown ▷ nf (baiser) kiss; (vent) North wind; **faire une** ou **la ~ à qn** to kiss sb; **grosses ~es (de)** (sur lettre) love and kisses (from)

bis² [bis] adv: **12 ~ 12a** ou A ▷ excl, nm encore

bise [biz] nf voir **bis²**

bisexuel, le [bisɛksɥɛl] adj bisexual

bisou [bizu] nm (fam) kiss

bissextile [bisɛkstil] adj: **année ~** leap year

bistro(t) [bistʀo] nm bistro, café

bitume [bitym] nm asphalt

bizarre [bizaʀ] adj strange, odd

blague [blag] nf (propos) joke; (farce) trick; **sans ~!** no kidding!; **blaguer** /1/ vi to joke

blaireau, x [blɛʀo] nm (Zool) badger; (brosse) shaving brush

blâme [blɑm] nm blame; (sanction) reprimand; **blâmer** /1/ vt to blame

blanc, blanche [blɑ̃, blɑ̃ʃ] adj white; (non imprimé) blank ▷ nm/f white; white man/woman ▷ nm (couleur) white; (espace non écrit) blank; (aussi: **~ d'œuf**) (egg-)white; (aussi: **~ de poulet**) breast meat; (aussi: **vin ~**) white wine ▷ nf (Mus) minim (BRIT), half note (US); **chèque en ~** blank cheque; **à ~** (chauffer) white-hot; (tirer, charger) with blanks; **~ cassé** off-white; **blancheur** nf whiteness

blanchir [blɑ̃ʃiʀ] /2/ vt (gén) to whiten; (linge) to launder; (Culin) to blanch; (fig: disculper) to clear ▷ vi (cheveux) to go white; **blanchisserie** nf laundry

blason [blazɔ̃] nm coat of arms

blasphème [blasfɛm] nm blasphemy

blazer [blazɛʀ] nm blazer

blé [ble] nm wheat

bled [blɛd] nm (péj) hole

blême [blɛm] adj pale

blessé, e [blese] adj injured ▷ nm/f injured person, casualty

blesser [blese] /1/ vt to injure; (délibérément) to wound; (offenser) to hurt; **se ~ au pied** etc to injure one's foot etc; **blessure** nf (accidentelle) injury; (intentionnelle) wound

bleu, e [blø] adj blue; (bifteck) very rare ▷ nm (couleur) blue; (contusion) bruise; (vêtement: aussi: **~s**) overalls pl; **fromage ~** blue cheese; **~ marine/ nuit/roi** navy/midnight/royal blue; **bleuet** nm cornflower

bloc [blɔk] nm (de pierre etc) block; (de papier à lettres) pad; (ensemble) group, block; **serré à ~** tightened right down; **en ~** as a whole; **~ opératoire** operating ou theatre block; **blocage** nm (des prix) freezing; (Psych) hangup; **bloc-notes** nm note pad

blog [blɔg] nm blog; **blogosphère** nf blogosphere; **bloguer** /1/ vi to blog

blond, e [blɔ̃, -ɔ̃d] adj fair; blond; (sable, blés) golden

bloquer [blɔke] /1/ vt (passage) to block; (pièce mobile) to jam; (crédits, compte) to freeze

blottir [blɔtiʀ] /2/: **se blottir** vi to huddle up

blouse [bluz] nf overall

blouson [bluzɔ̃] nm blouson (jacket); **~ noir** (fig) ≈ rocker

bluff [blœf] nm bluff

bobine [bɔbin] nf reel; (Élec) coil

bobo [bobo] sigle m/f (= bourgeois bohème) boho

bocal, -aux [bɔkal, -o] nm jar

bock [bɔk] nm glass of beer

bœuf [bœf] (pl **bœufs**) [bœf, bø] nm ox; (Culin) beef

bof [bɔf] excl (fam: indifférence) don't care!; (pas terrible) nothing special

bohémien, ne [bɔemjɛ̃, -ɛn] nm/f gipsy

boire [bwaʀ] /53/ vt to drink; (s'imprégner de) to soak up; **un coup** to have a drink

bois [bwɑ] nm wood; **de ~, en ~** wooden; **boisé, e** adj woody, wooded

boisson [bwasɔ̃] nf drink

boîte [bwat] nf box; (fam: entreprise) firm; **aliments en ~** canned ou tinned (BRIT) foods; **~ à gants** glove compartment; **~ à ordures** dustbin (BRIT), trash can (US); **~ aux lettres** letter box; **~ d'allumettes** box of matches; (vide) matchbox; **~ de conserves** can ou tin (BRIT) (of food); **~ de nuit** night club; **~ de vitesses** gear box; **~ postale (BP)** PO box; **~ vocale** voice mail

boiter [bwate] /1/ vi to limp; (fig: raisonnement) to be shaky

boîtier [bwatje] nm case

boive etc [bwav] vb voir **boire**

bol [bɔl] nm bowl; **un ~ d'air** a breath of fresh air; **en avoir ras le ~** (fam) to have had a bellyful; **avoir du ~** (fam) to be lucky

bombarder [bɔ̃baʀde] /1/ vt to bomb; **~ qn de** (cailloux, lettres) to bombard sb with

bombe [bɔ̃b] nf bomb; (atomiseur) (aerosol) spray

MOT-CLÉ

bon, bonne [bɔ̃, bɔn] adj **1** (agréable, satisfaisant) good; **un bon repas/ restaurant** a good meal/restaurant; **être bon en maths** to be good at maths

2 (charitable): **être bon (envers)** to be good (to)
3 (correct) right; **le bon numéro/moment** the right number/moment
4 (souhaits): **bon anniversaire!** happy birthday!; **bon courage!** good luck!; **bon séjour!** enjoy your stay!; **bon voyage!** have a good trip!; **bonne année!** happy New Year!; **bonne chance!** good luck!; **bonne fête!** happy holiday!; **bonne nuit!** good night!
5 (approprié): **bon à/pour** fit to/for; **à quoi bon (...)?** what's the point ou use of (...)?
6: **bon enfant** adj inv accommodating, easy-going; **bonne femme** (péj) woman; **bonne heure** early; **bon marché** cheap; **bon mot** witticism; **bon sens** common sense; **bon vivant** jovial chap; **bonnes œuvres** charitable works, charities
▶ nm **1** (billet) voucher; (aussi: **bon cadeau**) gift voucher; **bon d'essence** petrol coupon; **bon du Trésor** Treasury bond
2: **avoir du bon** to have its good points; **pour de bon** for good
▶ adv: **il fait bon** ou the weather is fine; **sentir bon** to smell good; **tenir bon** to stand firm
▶ excl good!; **ah bon?** really?; **bon, je reste** right, I'll stay; voir aussi **bonne**

bonbon [bɔ̃bɔ̃] nm (boiled) sweet
bond [bɔ̃] nm leap; **faire un ~** to leap in the air
bondé, e [bɔ̃de] adj packed (full)
bondir [bɔ̃diʁ] /2/ vi to leap
bonheur [bɔnœʁ] nm happiness; **porter ~ (à qn)** to bring (sb) luck; **au petit ~** haphazardly; **par ~** fortunately
bonhomme [bɔnɔm] (pl **bonshommes**) nm fellow; **~ de neige** snowman

bonjour [bɔ̃ʒuʁ] excl, nm hello; (selon l'heure) good morning (ou afternoon); **c'est simple comme ~!** it's easy as pie!
bonne [bɔn] adj f voir **bon** ▷ nf (domestique) maid
bonnet [bɔnɛ] nm hat; (de soutien-gorge) cup; **~ de bain** bathing cap
bonsoir [bɔ̃swaʁ] excl nm good evening
bonté [bɔ̃te] nf kindness no pl
bonus [bɔnys] nm (Assurances) no-claims bonus; (de DVD) extras pl
bord [bɔʁ] nm (de table, verre, falaise) edge; (de rivière, lac) bank; (de route) side; (monter) **à ~** (to go) on board; **jeter par-dessus ~** to throw overboard; **le commandant de ~/les hommes du ~** the ship's master/crew; **au ~ de la mer/route** at the seaside/roadside; **être au ~ des larmes** to be on the verge of tears
bordeaux [bɔʁdo] nm Bordeaux ▷ adj inv maroon
bordel [bɔʁdɛl] nm brothel; (fam!) bloody (BRIT) ou goddamn (US) mess (!)
border [bɔʁde] /1/ vt (être le long de) to line, border; (qn dans son lit) to tuck up; **~ qch de** (garnir) to trim sth with
bordure [bɔʁdyʁ] nf border; **en ~ de** on the edge of
borne [bɔʁn] nf boundary stone; (aussi: **~ kilométrique**) kilometre-marker; = milestone; **bornes** nfpl (fig) limits; **dépasser les ~s** to go too far
borné, e [bɔʁne] adj (personne) narrow-minded
borner [bɔʁne] /1/ vt: **se ~ à faire** (se contenter de) to content o.s. with doing; (se limiter à) to limit o.s. to doing
bosniaque [bɔznjak] adj Bosnian ▷ nm/f: **B~** Bosnian
Bosnie-Herzégovine [bɔsnieʁzegɔvin] nf Bosnia-Herzegovina
bosquet [bɔskɛ] nm grove

bosse [bos] nf (de terrain etc) bump; (enflure) lump; (du bossu, du chameau) hump; **avoir la ~ des maths** etc (fam) to have a gift for maths etc; **il a roulé sa ~** (fam) he's been around

bosser [bose] /1/ vi (fam) to work; (: dur) to slave (away)

bossu, e [bosy] nm/f hunchback

botanique [botanik] nf botany ▷ adj botanic(al)

botte [bot] nf (soulier) (high) boot; (gerbe): **~ de paille** bundle of straw; **~ de radis/d'asperges** bunch of radishes/asparagus; **~s de caoutchouc** wellington boots

bottine [botin] nf ankle boot

bouc [buk] nm goat; (barbe) goatee; **~ émissaire** scapegoat

boucan [bukɑ̃] nm din, racket

bouche [buʃ] nf mouth; **faire du ~ à ~ à qn** to give sb the kiss of life (BRIT), give sb mouth-to-mouth resuscitation; **rester ~ bée** to stand open-mouthed; **~ d'égout** manhole; **~ d'incendie** fire hydrant; **~ de métro** métro entrance

bouché, e [buʃe] adj (flacon etc) stoppered; (temps, ciel) overcast; (péj: personne) thick; **avoir le nez ~** to have a blocked(-up) nose; **c'est un secteur ~** there's no future in that area; **l'évier est ~** the sink's blocked

bouchée [buʃe] nf mouthful; **~s à la reine** chicken vol-au-vents

boucher [buʃe] /1/ nm butcher ▷ vt (pour colmater) to stop up; (trou) to fill up; (obstruer) to block (up); **se boucher** vi (tuyau etc) to block up, get blocked up; **j'ai le nez bouché** my nose is blocked; **se ~ le nez** to hold one's nose

bouchère [buʃɛʀ] nf butcher

boucherie nf butcher's (shop); (fig) slaughter

bouchon [buʃɔ̃] nm (en liège) cork; (autre matière) stopper; (de tube) top; (fig: embouteillage) holdup; (Pêche) float

boucle [bukl] nf (forme, figure) loop; (objet) buckle; **~ (de cheveux)** curl; **~ d'oreille** earring

bouclé, e [bukle] adj (cheveux) curly

boucler [bukle] /1/ vt (fermer: ceinture etc) to fasten; (terminer) to finish off; (enfermer) to shut away; (quartier) to seal off ▷ vi to curl

bouder [bude] /1/ vi to sulk ▷ vt (personne) to refuse to have anything to do with

boudin [budɛ̃] nm: **~ (noir)** black pudding; **~ blanc** white pudding

boue [bu] nf mud

bouée [bwe] nf buoy; **~ (de sauvetage)** lifebuoy

boueux, -euse [bwø, -øz] adj muddy

bouffe [buf] nf (fam) grub, food

bouffée [bufe] nf (de cigarette) puff; **une ~ d'air pur** a breath of fresh air; **~ de chaleur** hot flush (BRIT) ou flash (US)

bouffer [bufe] /1/ vi (fam) to eat

bouffi, e [bufi] adj swollen

bouger [buʒe] /3/ vi to move; (dent etc) to be loose; (s'activer) to get moving ▷ vt to move; **les prix/les couleurs n'ont pas bougé** prices/colours haven't changed

bougie [buʒi] nf candle; (Auto) spark(ing) plug

bouillabaisse [bujabɛs] nf type of fish soup

bouillant, e [bujɑ̃, -ɑ̃t] adj (qui bout) boiling; (très chaud) boiling (hot)

bouillie [buji] nf (de bébé) cereal; **en ~ (fig)** crushed

bouillir [bujiʀ] /15/ vi to boil ▷ vt to boil; **~ de colère** etc to seethe with anger etc

bouilloire [bujwaʀ] nf kettle

bouillon [bujɔ̃] nm (Culin) stock no pl; **bouillonner** /1/ vi to bubble; (fig: idées) to bubble up

bouillotte [bujɔt] nf hot-water bottle

boulanger, -ère [bulɑ̃ʒe, -ɛʀ] nm/f baker; **boulangerie** nf bakery

boule [bul] *nf* (*gén*) ball; (*de pétanque*) bowl; **~ de neige** snowball

boulette [bulɛt] *nf* (*de viande*) meatball

boulevard [bulvar] *nm* boulevard

bouleversement [bulvɛrsəmɑ̃] *nm* upheaval

bouleverser [bulvɛrse] /1/ *vt* (*émouvoir*) to overwhelm; (*causer du chagrin à*) to distress; (*pays, vie*) to disrupt; (*papiers, objets*) to turn upside down

boulimie [bulimi] *nf* bulimia

boulimique [bulimik] *adj* bulimic

boulon [bulɔ̃] *nm* bolt

boulot[1] [bulo] *nm* (*fam: travail*) work

boulot[2], te [bulo, -ɔt] *adj* plump, tubby

boum [bum] *nm* bang ▷ *nf* (*fam*) party

bouquet [bukɛ] *nm* (*de fleurs*) bunch (of flowers), bouquet; (*de persil etc*) bunch; **c'est le ~!** that's the last straw!

bouquin [bukɛ̃] *nm* (*fam*) book; **bouquiner** /1/ *vi* (*fam*) to read

bourdon [burdɔ̃] *nm* bumblebee

bourg [bur] *nm* small market town (*ou village*)

bourgeois, e [burʒwa, -waz] *adj* ≈ (upper) middle class; **bourgeoisie** *nf* ≈ upper middle classes *pl*

bourgeon [burʒɔ̃] *nm* bud

Bourgogne [burɡɔɲ] *nf*: **la ~** Burgundy ▷ *nm*: **b~** Burgundy (wine)

bourguignon, ne [burɡiɲɔ̃, -ɔn] *adj* of *ou* from Burgundy, Burgundian

bourrasque [burask] *nf* squall

bourratif, -ive [buratif, -iv] (*fam*) *adj* filling, stodgy

bourré, e [bure] *adj* (*rempli*): **~ de** crammed full of; (*fam: ivre*) pickled, plastered

bourrer [bure] /1/ *vt* to fill; (*poêle*) to pack; (*pipe*) to cram full; (*valise*) to cram (full)

bourru, e [bury] *adj* surly, gruff

bourse [burs] *nf* (*subvention*) grant; (*porte-monnaie*) purse; **la B~** the Stock Exchange

bous [bu] *vb voir* **bouillir**

bousculade [buskylad] *nf* (*hâte*) rush; (*poussée*) crush; **bousculer** /1/ *vt* (*heurter*) to knock into; (*fig*) to push, rush

boussole [busɔl] *nf* compass

bout [bu] *vb voir* **bouillir** ▷ *nm* bit; (*d'un bâton etc*) tip; (*d'une ficelle, table, rue, période*) end; **au ~ de** at the end of, after; **pousser qn à ~** to push sb to the limit (of his patience); **venir à ~ de** to manage to finish (off) *ou* overcome; **à ~ portant** at point-blank range

bouteille [butɛj] *nf* bottle; (*de gaz butane*) cylinder

boutique [butik] *nf* shop

bouton [butɔ̃] *nm* button; (*Bot*) bud; (*sur la peau*) spot; **boutonner** /1/ *vt* to button up; **boutonnière** *nf* buttonhole; **bouton-pression** *nm* press stud

bovin, e [bovɛ̃, -in] *adj* bovine ▷ *nm*: **~s** cattle *pl*

bowling [boliŋ] *nm* (*tenpin*) bowling; (*salle*) bowling alley

boxe [bɔks] *nf* boxing

BP *sigle f* = **boîte postale**

bracelet [braslɛ] *nm* bracelet

braconnier [brakɔnje] *nm* poacher

brader [brade] /1/ *vt* to sell off; **braderie** *nf* cut-price (*BRIT*) *ou* cut-rate (*US*) stall

braguette [bragɛt] *nf* fly, flies *pl* (*BRIT*), zipper (*US*)

braise [brɛz] *nf* embers *pl*

brancard [brɑ̃kar] *nm* (*civière*) stretcher; **brancardier** *nm* stretcher-bearer

branche [brɑ̃ʃ] *nf* branch

branché, e [brɑ̃ʃe] *adj* (*fam*) trendy

brancher [brɑ̃ʃe] /1/ *vt* to connect (up); (*en mettant la prise*) to plug in

brandir [brɑ̃dir] /2/ *vt* to brandish

braquer [brake] /1/ *vi* (*Auto*) to turn (the wheel) ▷ *vt* (*revolver etc*): **~ qch sur** to aim sth at, point sth at; (*mettre en colère*): **~ qn** to antagonize sb

bras [bʀɑ] nm arm; **~ dessus ~ dessous** arm in arm; **se retrouver avec qch sur les ~** (fam) to be landed with sth; **~ droit** (fig) right hand man

brassard [bʀasaʀ] nm armband

brasse [bʀas] nf (nage) breast-stroke; **~ papillon** butterfly(-stroke)

brassée [bʀase] nf armful

brasser [bʀase] /1/ vt to mix; **~ l'argent/les affaires** to handle a lot of money/ business

brasserie [bʀasʀi] nf (restaurant) bar (selling food); (usine) brewery

brave [bʀav] adj (courageux) brave; (bon, gentil) good, kind

braver [bʀave] /1/ vt to defy

bravo [bʀavo] excl bravo! ▷ nm cheer

bravoure [bʀavuʀ] nf bravery

break [bʀɛk] nm (Auto) estate car

brebis [bʀabi] nf ewe; **~ galeuse** black sheep

bredouiller [bʀaduje] /1/ vi, vt to mumble, stammer

bref, brève [bʀɛf, bʀɛv] adj short, brief ▷ adv in short; **d'un ton ~** sharply, curtly; **en ~** in short, in brief

Brésil [bʀezil] nm: **le ~** Brazil

Bretagne [bʀataɲ] nf: **la ~** Brittany

bretelle [bʀatɛl] nf (de vêtement) strap; (d'autoroute) slip road (BRIT), entrance ou exit ramp (US); **bretelles** nfpl (pour pantalon) braces (BRIT), suspenders (US)

breton, ne [bʀatɔ̃, -ɔn] adj Breton ▷ nm/f: **B~, ne** Breton

brève [bʀɛv] adj f voir **bref**

brevet [bʀave] nm diploma, certificate; **~ (des collèges)** school certificate, taken at approx. 16 years; **~ (d'invention)** patent; **breveté, e** adj patented

bricolage [bʀikɔlaʒ] nm: **le ~** do-it-yourself (jobs)

bricoler [bʀikɔle] /1/ vi (en amateur) to do DIY jobs; (passe-temps) to potter about ▷ vt (réparer) to fix up; **bricoleur, -euse** nm/f handyman/woman, DIY enthusiast

bridge [bʀidʒ] nm (Cartes) bridge

brièvement [bʀijɛvmɑ̃] adv briefly

brigade [bʀigad] nf (Police) squad; (Mil) brigade; **brigadier** nm ≈ sergeant

brillamment [bʀijamɑ̃] adv brilliantly

brillant, e [bʀijɑ̃, -ɑ̃t] adj (remarquable) bright; (luisant) shiny, shining

briller [bʀije] /1/ vi to shine

brin [bʀɛ̃] nm (de laine, ficelle etc) strand; (fig): **un ~ de** a bit of

brindille [bʀɛ̃dij] nf twig

brioche [bʀijɔʃ] nf brioche (bun); (fam: ventre) paunch

brique [bʀik] nf brick; (de lait) carton ▷ adj inv brick red

briquet [bʀikɛ] nm (cigarette) lighter

brise [bʀiz] nf breeze

briser [bʀize] /1/ vt to break; **se briser** vi to break

britannique [bʀitanik] adj British ▷ nm/f: **B~** Briton, British person; **les B~s** the British

brocante [bʀɔkɑ̃t] nf (objets) secondhand goods pl, junk; **brocanteur, -euse** nm/f junk shop owner; junk dealer

broche [bʀɔʃ] nf brooch; (Culin) spit; (Méd) pin; **à la ~** spit-roasted

broché, e [bʀɔʃe] adj (livre) paper-backed

brochet [bʀɔʃɛ] nm pike inv

brochette [bʀɔʃɛt] nf (ustensile) skewer; (plat) kebab

brochure [bʀɔʃyʀ] nf pamphlet, brochure, booklet

broder [bʀɔde] /1/ vt to embroider ▷ vi: **(sur des faits ou une histoire)** to embroider the facts; **broderie** nf embroidery

bronches [bʀɔ̃ʃ] nfpl bronchial tubes; **bronchite** nf bronchitis

bronze [bʀɔ̃z] nm bronze

bronzer [bʀɔ̃ze] /1/ vi to get a tan; **se bronzer** to sunbathe

brosse [bʀɔs] nf brush; **coiffé en ~** with a crewcut; **~ à cheveux**

hairbrush; **~ à dents** toothbrush; **~ à habits** clothesbrush; **brosser** /1/ vt (nettoyer) to brush; (fig: tableau etc) to paint; **se brosser les dents** to brush one's teeth

brouette [bʀuɛt] nf wheelbarrow

brouhaha [bʀuaa] nm hubbub

brouillard [bʀujaʀ] nm fog

brouiller [bʀuje] /1/ vt (œufs, message) to scramble; (idées) to mix up; (rendre trouble) to cloud; (désunir: amis) to set at odds; **se brouiller** vi (ciel, vue) to cloud over; **se ~ (avec)** to fall out (with)

brouillon, ne [bʀujɔ̃, -ɔn] adj (sans soin) untidy; (qui manque d'organisation) disorganized ▷ nm (first) draft; **(papier) ~** rough paper

broussailles [bʀusaj] nfpl undergrowth sg; **broussailleux, -euse** adj bushy

brousse [bʀus] nf: **la ~** the bush

brouter [bʀute] /1/ vi to graze

brugnon [bʀyɲɔ̃] nm nectarine

bruiner [bʀɥine] /1/ vb impers: **il bruine** it's drizzling, there's a drizzle

bruit [bʀɥi] nm: **un ~** a noise, a sound; (fig: rumeur) a rumour; **le ~ noise; sans ~** without a sound, noiselessly; **~ de fond** background noise

brûlant, e [bʀylɑ̃, -ɑ̃t] adj burning (hot); (liquide) boiling (hot)

brûlé, e [bʀyle] adj (fig: démasqué) blown ▷ nm: **odeur de ~** smell of burning

brûler [bʀyle] /1/ vt to burn; (eau bouillante) to scald; (consommer: électricité, essence) to use; (: feu rouge, signal) to go through (without stopping) ▷ vi to burn; **se brûler** to burn o.s.; (s'ébouillanter) to scald o.s.; **tu brûles** (jeu) you're getting warm ou hot

brûlure [bʀylyʀ] nf (lésion) burn; **~s d'estomac** heartburn sg

brume [bʀym] nf mist

brumeux, -euse [bʀymø, -øz] adj misty

brun, e [bʀœ̃, -yn] adj (gén, bière) brown; (cheveux, personne, tabac) dark; **elle est ~** she's got dark hair

brunch [bʀœntʃ] nm brunch

brushing [bʀœʃiŋ] nm blow-dry

brusque [bʀysk] adj abrupt

brut, e [bʀyt] adj (diamant) uncut; (soie, minéral) raw; (Comm) gross; **(pétrole) ~** crude (oil)

brutal, e, -aux [bʀytal, -o] adj brutal

Bruxelles [bʀysɛl] n Brussels

bruyamment [bʀɥijamɑ̃] adv noisily

bruyant, e [bʀɥijɑ̃, -ɑ̃t] adj noisy

bruyère [bʀɥijɛʀ] nf heather

BTS sigle m (= Brevet de technicien supérieur) vocational training certificate taken at end of two-year higher education course

bu, e [by] pp de **boire**

buccal, e, -aux [bykal, -o] adj: **par voie ~e** orally

bûche [byʃ] nf log; **prendre une ~** (fig) to come a cropper (BRIT), fall flat on one's face; **~ de Noël** Yule log

bûcher [byʃe] /1/ nm (funéraire) pyre; (supplice) stake ▷ vi (fam) to swot, slave (away) ▷ vt to swot up, slave away at

budget [bydʒɛ] nm budget

buée [bɥe] nf (sur une vitre) mist

buffet [byfɛ] nm (meuble) sideboard; (de réception) buffet; **~ (de gare)** (station) buffet, snack bar

buis [bɥi] nm box tree; (bois) box(wood)

buisson [bɥisɔ̃] nm bush

bulbe [bylb] nm (Bot, Anat) bulb

Bulgarie [bylgaʀi] nf: **la ~** Bulgaria

bulle [byl] nf bubble

bulletin [byltɛ̃] nm (communiqué, journal) bulletin; (Scol) report; **~ d'informations** news bulletin; **~ (de vote)** ballot paper; **~ météorologique** weather report

bureau, x [byʀo] nm (meuble) desk; (pièce, service) office; (Inform) desktop; **~ de change** (foreign) exchange office *ou* bureau; **~ de poste** post office; **~ de tabac** tobacconist's (shop); **bureaucratie** [byʀokʀasi] *nf* bureaucracy

bus¹ *vb* [by] *voir* **boire**

bus² *nm* [bys] *(véhicule)* bus

buste [byst] *nm (Anat)* chest (*: de femme*) bust

but [by] *vb voir* **boire** ▷ *nm (cible)* target; *(fig)* goal, aim; *(Football etc)* goal; **de ~ en blanc** point-blank; **avoir pour ~ de faire** to aim to do; **dans le ~ de** with the intention of

butane [bytan] *nm* butane; *(domestique)* calor gas® (BRIT), butane

butiner [bytine] /1/ *vi (abeilles)* to gather nectar

buvais *etc* [byvɛ] *vb voir* **boire**

buvard [byvaʀ] *nm* blotter

buvette [byvɛt] *nf* bar

C

c' [s] *pron voir* **ce**

ça [sa] *pron (pour désigner)* this (*: plus loin*) that; *(comme sujet indéfini)* it; **ça m'étonne que** it surprises me that; **ça va?** how are you?; how are things?; *(d'accord?)* OK?, all right?; **où ça?** where's that?; **pourquoi ça?** why's that?; **qui ça?** who's that?; **ça alors!** *(désapprobation)* well!, really!; **c'est ça** that's right; **ça y est** that's it

cabane [kaban] *nf* hut, cabin

cabaret [kabaʀɛ] *nm* night club

cabillaud [kabijo] *nm* cod *inv*

cabine [kabin] *nf (de bateau)* cabin; *(de piscine etc)* cubicle; *(de camion, train)* cab; *(d'avion)* cockpit; **~ d'essayage** fitting room; **~ (téléphonique)** call *ou* (tele) phone box

cabinet [kabinɛ] *nm (petite pièce)* closet; *(de médecin)* surgery (BRIT), office (US); *(de notaire etc)* office (*: clientèle*) practice; *(Pol)* cabinet;

cabinets nmpl (w.-c.) toilet sg; **~ de toilette** toilet

câble [kabl] nm cable; **le ~** (TV) cable television, cablevision (us)

cacahuète [kakaɥɛt] nf peanut

cacao [kakao] nm cocoa

cache [kaʃ] nm mask, card (for masking)

cache-cache [kaʃkaʃ] nm: **jouer à ~** to play hide-and-seek

cachemire [kaʃmir] nm cashmere

cacher [kaʃe] /1/ vt to hide, conceal; **~ qch à qn** to hide ou conceal sth from sb; **se cacher** vi (volontairement) to hide; (être caché) to be hidden ou concealed

cachet [kaʃe] nm (comprimé) tablet; (de la poste) postmark; (rétribution) fee; (fig) style, character

cachette [kaʃɛt] nf hiding place; **en ~** on the sly, secretly

cactus [kaktys] nm cactus

cadavre [kadavr] nm corpse, (dead) body

Caddie® [kadi] nm (supermarket) trolley (BRIT), (grocery) cart (US)

cadeau, x [kado] nm present, gift; **faire un ~ à qn** to give sb a present ou gift; **faire ~ de qch à qn** to give sb sth as a present ou give sth to sb as a present

cadenas [kadna] nm padlock

cadet, te [kadɛ, -ɛt] adj younger; (le plus jeune) youngest ▷ nm/f youngest child ou one

cadran [kadrɑ̃] nm dial; **~ solaire** sundial

cadre [kadr] nm frame; (environnement) surroundings pl ▷ nm/f (Admin) managerial employee, executive; **dans le ~ de** (fig) within the framework ou context of

cafard [kafar] nm cockroach; **avoir le ~** to be down in the dumps

café [kafe] nm coffee; (bistro) café ▷ adj inv coffee(-coloured); **~ au lait** white coffee; **~ noir** black coffee; **café-tabac** nm tobacconist's or newsagent's

also serving coffee and spirits; **cafétéria** [kafeterja] nf cafeteria; **cafetière** nf (pot) coffee-pot

cage [kaʒ] nf cage; **~ d'escalier** (stair) well; **~ thoracique** rib cage

cageot [kaʒo] nm crate

cagoule [kagul] nf (passe-montagne) balaclava

cahier [kaje] nm notebook; **~ de brouillons** rough book, jotter; **~ d'exercices** exercise book

caille [kaj] nf quail

caillou, x [kaju] nm (little) stone; **caillouteux, -euse** adj stony

Caire [kɛr] nm: **le ~** Cairo

caisse [kɛs] nf box; (où l'on met la recette) till; (où l'on paye) cash desk (BRIT), checkout counter; (: au supermarché) checkout; (de banque) cashier's desk; **~ enregistreuse** cash register; **~ d'épargne (CE)** savings bank; **~ de retraite** pension fund; **caissier, -ière** nm/f cashier

cake [kɛk] nm fruit cake

calandre [kalɑ̃dr] nf radiator grill

calcaire [kalkɛr] nm limestone ▷ adj (eau) hard; (Géo) limestone cpd

calcul [kalkyl] nm calculation; **le ~** (Scol) arithmetic; **~ (biliaire)** (gall) stone; **calculateur** nm, **calculatrice** nf calculator; **calculer** /1/ vt to calculate, work out; **calculette** nf (pocket) calculator

cale [kal] nf (de bateau) hold; (en bois) wedge

calé, e [kale] adj (fam) clever, bright

caleçon [kalsɔ̃] nm (d'homme) boxer shorts; (de femme) leggings

calendrier [kalɑ̃drije] nm calendar; (fig) timetable

calepin [kalpɛ̃] nm notebook

caler [kale] /1/ vt to wedge ▷ vi (moteur, véhicule) to stall

calibre [kalibr] nm calibre

câlin, e [kalɛ̃, -in] adj cuddly, cuddlesome; (regard, voix) tender

calmant [kalmɑ̃] nm tranquillizer, sedative; (contre la douleur) painkiller

calme [kalm] *adj* calm, quiet ▷ *nm* calm(ness), quietness; **sans perdre son ~** without losing one's cool *ou* calmness; **calmer** /1/ *vt* to calm (down); (*douleur, inquiétude*) to ease, soothe; **se calmer** *vi* to calm down

calorie [kaloʀi] *nf* calorie

camarade [kamaʀad] *nm/f* friend, pal; (*Pol*) comrade

Cambodge [kɑ̃bɔdʒ] *nm*: **le ~** Cambodia

cambriolage [kɑ̃bʀijɔlaʒ] *nm* burglary; **cambrioler** /1/ *vt* to burgle (*BRIT*), burglarize (*US*); **cambrioleur, -euse** *nm/f* burglar

camelote [kamlɔt] (*fam*) *nf* rubbish, trash, junk

caméra [kameʀa] *nf* (*Ciné, TV*) camera; (*d'amateur*) cine-camera

Cameroun [kamʀun] *nm*: **le ~** Cameroon

caméscope® [kameskɔp] *nm* camcorder

camion [kamjɔ̃] *nm* lorry (*BRIT*), truck; **~ de dépannage** breakdown (*BRIT*) *ou* tow (*US*) truck; **camionnette** *nf* (small) van; **camionneur** *nm* (*entrepreneur*) haulage contractor (*BRIT*), trucker (*US*); (*chauffeur*) lorry (*BRIT*) *ou* truck driver

camomille [kamɔmij] *nf* camomile; (*boisson*) camomile tea

camp [kɑ̃] *nm* camp; (*fig*) side

campagnard, e [kɑ̃paɲaʀ, -aʀd] *adj* country *cpd*

campagne [kɑ̃paɲ] *nf* country, countryside; (*Mil, Pol, Comm*) campaign; **à la ~** in/to the country

camper [kɑ̃pe] /1/ *vi* to camp ▷ *vt* to sketch; **se ~ devant** to plant o.s. in front of; **campeur, -euse** *nm/f* camper

camping [kɑ̃piŋ] *nm* camping; **(terrain de) ~** campsite, camping site; **faire du ~** to go camping; **camping-car** *nm* camper, motorhome (*US*); **camping-gaz®** *nm inv* camp(ing) stove

Canada [kanada] *nm*: **le ~** Canada; **canadien, ne** *adj* Canadian ▷ *nm/f*: **Canadien, ne** Canadian ▷ *nf* (*veste*) fur-lined jacket

canal, -aux [kanal, -o] *nm* canal; (*naturel, TV*) channel; **canalisation** *nf* (*tuyau*) pipe

canapé [kanape] *nm* settee, sofa

canard [kanaʀ] *nm* duck; (*fam: journal*) rag

cancer [kɑ̃seʀ] *nm* cancer; (*signe*): **le C~** Cancer

cancre [kɑ̃kʀ] *nm* dunce

candidat, e [kɑ̃dida, -at] *nm/f* candidate; (*à un poste*) applicant, candidate; **candidature** *nf* (*Pol*) candidature; (*à poste*) application; **poser sa candidature à un poste** to apply for a job

cane [kan] *nf* (*female*) duck

canette [kanɛt] *nf* (*de bière*) (flip-top) bottle

canevas [kanva] *nm* (*Couture*) canvas (for tapestry work)

caniche [kaniʃ] *nm* poodle

canicule [kanikyl] *nf* scorching heat

canif [kanif] *nm* penknife, pocket knife

canne [kan] *nf* (*walking*) stick; **~ à pêche** fishing rod; **~ à sucre** sugar cane

cannelle [kanɛl] *nf* cinnamon

canoë [kanɔe] *nm* canoe; (*sport*) canoeing; **~ (kayak)** kayak

canot [kano] *nm* ding(h)y; **~ pneumatique** rubber *ou* inflatable ding(h)y; **~ de sauvetage** lifeboat

cantatrice [kɑ̃tatʀis] *nf* (*opera*) singer

cantine [kɑ̃tin] *nf* canteen

canton [kɑ̃tɔ̃] *nm* district (*consisting of several communes*); (*en Suisse*) canton

caoutchouc [kautʃu] *nm* rubber; **~ mousse** foam rubber; **en ~** rubber *cpd*

CAP *sigle m* (= *Certificat d'aptitude professionnelle*) vocational training certificate taken at secondary school

cap [kap] nm (Géo) cape; (promontoire) headland; (fig: tournant) watershed; (Navig): **changer de ~** to change course; **mettre le ~ sur** to head for

capable [kapabl] adj able, capable; **~ de qch/faire** capable of sth/doing

capacité [kapasite] nf ability; (Jur, Inform, d'un récipient) capacity

cape [kap] nf cape, cloak; **rire sous ~** to laugh up one's sleeve

CAPES [kapes] sigle m (= Certificat d'aptitude au professorat de l'enseignement du second degré) secondary teaching diploma

capitaine [kapiten] nm captain

capital, e, -aux [kapital, -o] adj (œuvre) major; (question, rôle) fundamental ▷ nm capital; (fig) stock ▷ nf (ville) capital; (lettre) capital (letter); **d'une importance ~e** of capital importance; **capitaux** nmpl (fonds) capital sg; **~ (social)** authorized capital; **~ d'exploitation** working capital; **capitalisme** nm capitalism; **capitaliste** adj, nm/f capitalist

caporal, -aux [kapoʀal, -o] nm lance corporal

capot [kapo] nm (Auto) bonnet (BRIT), hood (US)

câpre [kɑpʀ] nf caper

caprice [kapʀis] nm whim, caprice; **faire des ~s** to be temperamental; **capricieux, -euse** adj (fantasque) capricious; whimsical; (enfant) temperamental

Capricorne [kapʀikɔʀn] nm: **le ~** Capricorn

capsule [kapsyl] nf (de bouteille) cap; (Bot etc, spatiale) capsule

capter [kapte] /1/ vt (ondes radio) to pick up; (fig) to win, capture

captivant, e [kaptivɑ̃, -ɑ̃t] adj captivating

capture [kaptyʀ] nf (action) capture; **~ d'écran** (Inform) screenshot

capturer [kaptyʀe] /1/ vt to capture

capuche [kapyʃ] nf hood

capuchon [kapyʃɔ̃] nm hood; (de stylo) cap, top

car [kaʀ] nm coach (BRIT), bus ▷ conj because, for

carabine [kaʀabin] nf rifle

caractère [kaʀaktɛʀ] nm (gén) character; **en ~s gras** in bold type; **en petits ~s** in small print; **en ~s d'imprimerie** in block capitals; **avoir bon/mauvais ~** to be good-/ill-natured ou tempered

caractériser [kaʀakteʀize] /1/ vt to characterize; **se ~ par** to be characterized ou distinguished by

caractéristique [kaʀakteʀistik] adj, nf characteristic

carafe [kaʀaf] nf decanter; (pour eau, vin ordinaire) carafe

caraïbe [kaʀaib] adj Caribbean; **les Caraïbes** nfpl the Caribbean (Islands)

carambolage [kaʀɑ̃bolaʒ] nm multiple crash, pileup

caramel [kaʀamɛl] nm (bonbon) caramel, toffee; (substance) caramel

caravane [kaʀavan] nf caravan; **caravaning** nm caravanning

carbone [kaʀbon] nm carbon; (double) carbon (copy)

carbonique [kaʀbonik] adj: **gaz ~** carbon dioxide; **neige ~** dry ice

carbonisé, e [kaʀbonize] adj charred

carburant [kaʀbyʀɑ̃] nm (motor) fuel

carburateur [kaʀbyʀatœʀ] nm carburettor

cardiaque [kaʀdjak] adj cardiac, heart cpd ▷ nm/f heart patient; **être ~** to have a heart condition

cardigan [kaʀdigɑ̃] nm cardigan

cardiologue [kaʀdjolɔɡ] nm/f cardiologist, heart specialist

Carême [kaʀɛm] nm: **le ~** Lent

carence [kaʀɑ̃s] nf (manque) deficiency

caresse [kaʀɛs] nf caress

caresser [kaʀese] /1/ vt to caress; (animal) to stroke

cargaison [kaʀgɛzõ] nf cargo, freight

cargo [kaʀgo] nm freighter

caricature [kaʀikatyʀ] nf caricature

carie [kaʀi] nf: **la ~ (dentaire)** tooth decay; **une ~** a bad tooth

carnaval [kaʀnaval] nm carnival

carnet [kaʀnɛ] nm (calepin) book; (de tickets, timbres etc) book; **~ de chèques** cheque book

carotte [kaʀɔt] nf carrot

carré, e [kaʀe] adj square; (fig: franc) straightforward ▶ nm (Math) square; **kilomètre ~** square kilometre

carreau, x [kaʀo] nm (en faïence etc) (floor) tile; (au mur) (wall) tile; (de fenêtre) (window) pane; (motif) check, square; (Cartes: couleur) diamonds pl; **tissu à ~x** checked fabric

carrefour [kaʀfuʀ] nm crossroads sg

carrelage [kaʀlaʒ] nm (sol) (tiled) floor

carrelet [kaʀlɛ] nm (poisson) plaice

carrément [kaʀemɑ̃] adv (franchement) straight out, bluntly; (sans détours, sans hésiter) straight; (intensif) completely; **c'est ~ impossible** it's completely impossible

carrière [kaʀjɛʀ] nf (de roches) quarry; (métier) career; **militaire de ~** professional soldier

carrosserie [kaʀɔsʀi] nf body, bodywork no pl (BRIT)

carrure [kaʀyʀ] nf build; (fig) calibre

cartable [kaʀtabl] nm satchel, (school)bag

carte [kaʀt] nf (de géographie) map; (marine, du ciel) chart; (de fichier, d'abonnement etc, à jouer) card; (au restaurant) menu; (aussi: **~ postale**) (post)card; (aussi: **~ de visite**) (visiting) card; **avoir/ donner ~ blanche** to have/give carte blanche ou a free hand; **à la ~** (au restaurant) à la carte; **~ à puce** smart card; **~ bancaire** cash card; **C~ Bleue®** debit card; **~ de crédit** credit card; **~ de fidélité** loyalty card; **~ d'identité** identity card; **la**

~ grise (Auto) ≈ the (car) registration document; **~ mémoire** (d'appareil photo numérique) memory card; **~ routière** road map; **~ de séjour** residence permit; **~ SIM** SIM card; **~ téléphonique** phonecard

carter [kaʀtɛʀ] nm sump

carton [kaʀtõ] nm (matériau) cardboard; (boîte) (cardboard) box; **faire un ~** to score a hit; (à dessin) portfolio

cartouche [kaʀtuʃ] nf cartridge; (de cigarettes) carton

cas [kɑ] nm case; **ne faire aucun ~ de** to take no notice of; **en aucun ~** on no account; **au ~ où** in case; **en ~ de** in case of, in the event of; **en ~ de besoin** if need be; **en tout ~** in any case, at any rate

cascade [kaskad] nf waterfall, cascade

case [kɑz] nf (hutte) hut; (compartiment) compartment; (sur un formulaire, de mots croisés) square

caser [kaze] /1/ (fam) vt (mettre) to put; (loger) to put up; **se caser** vi (se marier) to settle down; (trouver un emploi) to find a (steady) job

caserne [kazɛʀn] nf barracks

casier [kazje] nm (case) compartment; (pour courrier) pigeonhole; (à clef) locker; **~ judiciaire** police record

casino [kazino] nm casino

casque [kask] nm helmet; (chez le coiffeur) (hair-)dryer; (pour audition) (head-)phones pl, headset

casquette [kaskɛt] nf cap

casse-croûte nm inv snack

casse-noisettes, casse-noix nm inv nutcrackers pl

casse-pieds nm/f inv (fam): **il est ~, c'est un ~** he's a pain (in the neck)

casser [kɑse] /1/ vt to break; (Jur) to quash; **se casser** vi, vt to break; **~ les pieds à qn** (fam: irriter) to get on sb's nerves; **se ~ la tête** (fam) to go to a lot of trouble

casserole [kasʀɔl] nf saucepan

casse-tête [kastɛt] nm inv (difficultés) headache (fig)

cassette [kasɛt] nf (bande magnétique) cassette; (coffret) casket

cassis [kasis] nm blackcurrant

cassoulet [kasulɛ] nm sausage and bean hotpot

catalogue [katalɔg] nm catalogue

catalytique [katalitik] adj: **pot ~** catalytic converter

catastrophe [katastrɔf] nf catastrophe, disaster

catéchisme [kateʃism] nm catechism

catégorie [kategɔʀi] nf category; **catégorique** adj categorical

cathédrale [katedʀal] nf cathedral

catholique [katɔlik] adj, nm/f (Roman) Catholic; **pas très ~** a bit shady ou fishy

cauchemar [koʃmaʀ] nm nightmare

cause [koz] nf cause; (Jur) lawsuit, case; **à ~ de** because of, owing to; **pour ~ de** on account of; **(et) pour ~** and for (a very) good reason; **être en ~** to be at stake; **remettre en ~** to challenge; **causer** /1/ vt to cause ▷ vi to chat, talk

caution [kosjɔ̃] nf guarantee, security; (Jur) bail (bond); (fig) backing, support; **libéré sous ~** released on bail

cavalier, -ière [kavalje, -jɛʀ] adj (désinvolte) offhand ▷ nm/f rider; (au bal) partner ▷ nm (Échecs) knight

cave [kav] nf cellar

caverne [kavɛʀn] nf cave

CD sigle m (= compact disc) CD

CDD sigle m (= contrat à durée déterminée) fixed-term contract

CDI sigle m (= centre de documentation et d'information) school library; (= contrat à durée indéterminée) permanent ou open-ended contract

CD-ROM [sederɔm] nm inv CD-Rom

 MOT-CLÉ

ce, cette [sə, sɛt] (devant nm **cet** + voyelle ou h aspiré; pl **ces**) adj dém

(proximité) this; these pl; (non-proximité) that; those pl; **cette maison(-ci/là)** this/that house; **cette nuit** (qui vient) tonight; (passée) last night
▶ pron 1: **c'est** it's, it is; **c'est un peintre** he's ou he is a painter; **ce sont des peintres** they're ou they are painters; **c'est le facteur** etc (à la porte) it's the postman etc; **qui est-ce?** who is it?; (en désignant) who is he/she?; **qu'est-ce?** what is it?; **c'est toi qui lui as parlé** it was you who spoke to him
2: **c'est ça** (correct) that's right
3: **ce qui, ce que** what; **ce qui me plaît, c'est sa franchise** what I like about him ou her is his ou her frankness; **il est bête, ce qui me chagrine** he's stupid, which saddens me; **tout ce qui bouge** everything that ou which moves; **tout ce que je sais** all I know; **ce dont j'ai parlé** what I talked about; **ce que c'est grand!** it's so big!; voir aussi **c'est-à-dire; -ci; est-ce que; n'est-ce pas**

ceci [səsi] pron this

céder [sede] /6/ vt to give up ▷ vi (pont, barrage) to give way; (personne) to give in; **~ à** to yield to, give in to

cédérom [sederɔm] nm CD-ROM

CEDEX [sedɛks] sigle m (= courrier d'entreprise à distribution exceptionnelle) accelerated postal service for bulk users

cédille [sedij] nf cedilla

ceinture [sɛ̃tyʀ] nf belt; (taille) waist; **~ de sécurité** safety ou seat belt

cela [s(ə)la] pron that; (comme sujet indéfini) it; **~ m'étonne que** it surprises me that; **quand/où ~?** when/where (was that)?

célèbre [selɛbʀ] adj famous; **célébrer** /6/ vt to celebrate

céleri [sɛlʀi] nm: **~-(rave)** celeriac; **~ (en branche)** celery

célibataire [selibatɛʀ] adj single, unmarried ▷ nm/f bachelor/

unmarried ou single woman; **mère ~** single ou unmarried mother

celle, celles [sɛl] pron voir **celui**

cellule [selyl] nf (gén) cell; **~ souche** stem cell

cellulite [selylit] nf cellulite

⬤ **MOT-CLÉ**

celui, celle [səlɥi, sɛl] (mpl **ceux**, fpl **celles**) [səlɥi, sɛl] pron **1** : **celui-ci/là, celle-ci/là** this one/that one; **celui-ci, celles-ci** these (ones); **ceux-là, celles-là** those (ones); **celui de mon frère** my brother's; **celui du salon/ du dessous** the one in (ou from) the lounge/below

2 (+ relatif): **celui qui bouge** the one which ou that moves; (personne) the one who moves; **celui que je vois** the one (which ou that) I see; (personne) the one (whom) I see; **celui dont je parle** the one I'm talking about

3 (valeur indéfinie): **celui qui veut** whoever wants

cendre [sɑ̃dʀ] nf ash; **~s** (d'un défunt) ashes; **sous la ~** (Culin) in (the) embers; **cendrier** nm ashtray

censé, e [sɑ̃se] adj: **être ~ faire** to be supposed to do

censeur [sɑ̃sœʀ] nm (Scol) deputy head (BRIT), vice-principal (US)

censure [sɑ̃syʀ] nf censorship; **censurer** /1/ vt (Ciné, Presse) to censor; (Pol) to censure

cent [sɑ̃] num a hundred, one hundred (US, Canada, partie de l'euro etc) cent; **centaine** nf: **une centaine (de)** about a hundred, a hundred or so; **des centaines (de)** hundreds (of); **centenaire** adj hundred-year-old ▷ nm (anniversaire) centenary; (monnaie) cent; **centième** num hundredth; **centigrade** nm centigrade; **centilitre** nm centilitre; **centime** nm centime; **centime**

d'euro euro cent, cent; **centimètre** nm centimetre; (ruban) measuring tape

central, e, -aux [sɑ̃tʀal, -o] adj central ▷ nm: **~ (télép...** (telephone) exchange; **~e** station; **~e électrique/n...** electric/nuclear power sta...

centre [sɑ̃tʀ] nm centre; **~ commercial/sportif/cultu...** shopping/sports/arts centre; **~ d'appels** call centre; **centre-v...** town centre (BRIT) ou center (US

cèpe [sɛp] nm (edible) boletus

cependant [s(ə)pɑ̃dɑ̃] adv howeve... nevertheless

céramique [seʀamik] nf ceramics nf ce...

cercle [sɛʀkl] nm circle; **~ vicieux** vicious circle

cercueil [sɛʀkœj] nm coffin

céréale [seʀeal] nf cereal

cérémonie [seʀemɔni] nf ceremony; **sans ~** (inviter, manger) informally

cerf [sɛʀ] nm stag

cerf-volant [sɛʀvɔlɑ̃] nm kite

cerise [s(ə)ʀiz] nf cherry; **cerisier** nm cherry (tree)

cerner [sɛʀne] /1/ vt (Mil etc) to surround; (fig: problème) to delimit, define

certain, e [sɛʀtɛ̃, -ɛn] adj certain; **~ (de/que)** certain ou sure (of/that); **d'un ~ âge** past one's prime, not so young; **un ~ temps** (quite) some time; **sûr et ~** absolutely certain; **un ~ Georges** someone called Georges; **~s** pron some; **certainement** adv (probablement) most probably ou likely; (bien sûr) certainly, of course

certes [sɛʀt] adv (sans doute) admittedly; (bien sûr) of course; indeed (yes)

certificat [sɛʀtifika] nm certificate

certifier [sɛʀtifje] /7/ vt: **~ qch à qn** to guarantee sth to sb

certitude [sɛʀtityd] nf certainty

cerveau, x [sɛʀvo] nm brain

cervelas [sɛʀvəla] nm savely

elle [sɛrvɛl] nf (Anat) brain; **~(in)** brain(s)

sigle m (= Collège d'enseignement **ondaire**) ≈ (junior) secondary school **s** [se] pl dém voir **ce**

sse [sɛs]: **sans ~** adv (tout le **temps**) continually, constantly; (sans **interruption**) continuously; **il n'avait de ~ que** he would not rest until; **cesser** /1/ vt to stop ▷ vi to stop, cease; **cesser de faire** to stop doing; **cessez-le-feu** nm inv ceasefire

c'est-à-dire [sɛtadir] adv that is (to say)

cet [sɛt] adj dém voir **ce**

ceux [sø] pron voir **celui**

chacun, e [ʃakœ̃, -yn] pron each; (indéfini) everyone, everybody

chagrin, e [ʃagrɛ̃, -in] adj morose ▷ nm grief, sorrow; **avoir du ~** to be grieved ou sorrowful

chahut [ʃay] nm uproar; **chahuter** /1/ vt to rag, bait ▷ vi to make an uproar

chaîne [ʃɛn] nf chain; (Radio, TV: stations) channel; **travail à la ~** production line work; **réactions en ~** chain reactions; **~ (haute-fidélité** ou **hi-fi)** hi-fi system; **~ (de montagnes)** (mountain) range

chair [ʃɛr] nf flesh; **avoir la ~ de poule** to have goose pimples ou goose flesh; **bien en ~** plump, well-padded; **en ~ et en os** in the flesh; **~ à saucisse** sausage meat

chaise [ʃɛz] nf chair; **~ longue** deckchair

châle [ʃal] nm shawl

chaleur [ʃalœr] nf heat; (fig: d'accueil) warmth; **chaleureux, -euse** adj warm

chamailler [ʃamɑje] /1/: **se chamailler** vi to squabble, bicker

chambre [ʃɑ̃br] nf bedroom; (Pol) chamber; (Comm) chamber; **faire ~ à part** to sleep in separate rooms; **~ à un lit/deux lits** single/twin-bedded room; **~ à air** (de pneu) (inner) tube; **~ d'amis** spare ou guest room; **~ à**

coucher bedroom; **~ d'hôte** ≈ bed and breakfast (in private home); **~ meublée** bedsit(ter) (BRIT), furnished room; **~ noire** (Photo) dark room

chameau, x [ʃamo] nm camel

chamois [ʃamwa] nm chamois

champ [ʃɑ̃] nm field; **~ de bataille** battlefield; **~ de courses** racecourse

champagne [ʃɑ̃paɲ] nm champagne

champignon [ʃɑ̃piɲɔ̃] nm mushroom; (terme générique) fungus; **~ de couche** ou **de Paris** button mushroom

champion, ne [ʃɑ̃pjɔ̃, -ɔn] adj, nm/f champion; **championnat** nm championship

chance [ʃɑ̃s] nf: **la ~** luck; **chances** nfpl (probabilités) chances; **~ avoir de la ~** to be lucky; **il a des ~s de gagner** he has a chance of winning; **bonne ~!** good luck!

change [ʃɑ̃ʒ] nm (Comm) exchange

changement [ʃɑ̃ʒmɑ̃] nm change; **~ climatique** climate change; **~ de vitesse** gears pl; (action) gear change

changer [ʃɑ̃ʒe] /3/ vt (modifier) to change, alter; (remplacer, Comm) to change ▷ vi to change, alter; **se changer** vi to change (o.s.); (remplacer: adresse, nom, voiture etc) to change one's; **~ de train** to change trains; **~ d'avis, ~ d'idée** to change one's mind; **~ de vitesse** to change gear; **~ qn/qch de place** to move sb/sth to another place

chanson [ʃɑ̃sɔ̃] nf song

chant [ʃɑ̃] nm song; (art vocal) singing; (d'église) hymn

chantage [ʃɑ̃taʒ] nm blackmail; **faire du ~** to use blackmail

chanter [ʃɑ̃te] /1/ vt, vi to sing; **si cela lui chante** (fam) if he feels like it ou fancies it; **chanteur, -euse** nm/f singer

chantier [ʃɑ̃tje] nm (building) site; (sur une route) roadworks pl; **mettre en ~** to start work on; **~ naval** shipyard

chantilly [ʃɑ̃tiji] *nm voir* **crème**

chantonner [ʃɑ̃tɔne] /1/ *vi, vt* to sing to oneself, hum

chapeau, x [ʃapo] *nm* hat; ~! well done!

chapelle [ʃapɛl] *nf* chapel

chapitre [ʃapitʀ] *nm* chapter

chaque [ʃak] *adj* each, every; (*indéfini*) every

char [ʃaʀ] *nm*: ~ **(d'assaut)** tank; ~ **à voile** sand yacht

charbon [ʃaʀbɔ̃] *nm* coal; ~ **de bois** charcoal

charcuterie [ʃaʀkytʀi] *nf* (*magasin*) pork butcher's shop and delicatessen; (*produits*) cooked pork meats *pl*; **charcutier, -ière** *nm/f* pork butcher

chardon [ʃaʀdɔ̃] *nm* thistle

charge [ʃaʀʒ] *nf* (*fardeau*) load; (*Élec, Mil, Jur*) charge; (*rôle, mission*) responsibility; **charges** *nfpl* (*du loyer*) service charges; **à la ~ de** (*dépendant de*) dependent upon; (*aux frais de*) chargeable to; **prendre en ~** to take charge of; (*véhicule*) to take on; (*dépenses*) to take care of; **~s sociales** social security contributions

chargement [ʃaʀʒəmɑ̃] *nm* (*objets*) load

charger [ʃaʀʒe] /3/ *vt* (*voiture, fusil, caméra*) to load; (*batterie*) to charge ▷ *vi* (*Mil etc*) to charge; **se ~ de** to see to, take care of

chargeur [ʃaʀʒœʀ] *nm* (*de batterie*) charger

chariot [ʃaʀjo] *nm* trolley; (*charrette*) waggon

charité [ʃaʀite] *nf* charity; **faire la ~ à** to give (something) to

charmant, e [ʃaʀmɑ̃, -ɑ̃t] *adj* charming

charme [ʃaʀm] *nm* charm; **charmer** /1/ *vt* to charm

charpente [ʃaʀpɑ̃t] *nf* frame(work); **charpentier** *nm* carpenter

charrette [ʃaʀɛt] *nf* cart

charter [tʃaʀtœʀ] *nm* (*vol*) charter flight

chasse [ʃas] *nf* hunting; (*au fusil*) shooting; (*poursuite*) chase; (*aussi:* ~ **d'eau**) flush; **prendre en** ~ to give chase to; **tirer la ~ (d'eau)** to flush the toilet, pull the chain; ~ **à courre** hunting; **chasse-neige** *nm inv* snowplough (BRIT), snowplow (US)

chasser /1/ *vt* to hunt; (*expulser*) to chase away ou out, drive away ou out; **chasseur, -euse** *nm/f* hunter ▷ *nm* (*avion*) fighter

chat¹ [ʃa] *nm* cat

chat² [tʃat] *nm* (*Internet: salon*) chat room; (: *conversation*) chat

châtaigne [ʃatɛɲ] *nf* chestnut

châtain [ʃatɛ̃] *adj inv* chestnut (brown); (*personne*) chestnut-haired

château, x [ʃato] *nm* (*forteresse*) castle; (*résidence royale*) palace; (*manoir*) mansion; ~ **d'eau** water tower; ~ **fort** stronghold, fortified castle

châtiment [ʃatimɑ̃] *nm* punishment

chaton [ʃatɔ̃] *nm* (*Zool*) kitten

chatouiller [ʃatuje] /1/ *vt* to tickle; **chatouilleux, -euse** [ʃatujø, -øz] *adj* ticklish; (*fig*) touchy, over-sensitive

chatte [ʃat] *nf* (she-)cat

chatter [tʃate] /1/ *vi* (*Internet*) to chat

chaud, e [ʃo, -od] *adj* (*gén*) warm; (*très chaud*) hot ▷ *nm*: **il fait ~** it's warm; it's hot; **avoir ~** to be warm; to be hot; **ça me tient ~** it keeps me warm; **rester au ~** to stay in the warm

chaudière [ʃodjɛʀ] *nf* boiler

chauffage [ʃofaʒ] *nm* heating; ~ **central** central heating

chauffe-eau [ʃofo] *nm inv* water heater

chauffer [ʃofe] /1/ *vt* to heat ▷ *vi* to heat up, warm up; (*trop chauffer: moteur*) to overheat; **se chauffer** *vi* (*au soleil*) to warm o.s.

chauffeur [ʃofœʀ] *nm* driver; (*privé*) chauffeur

chaumière [ʃomjɛʀ] *nf* (*thatched*) cottage

chaussée [ʃose] *nf* road(way)

chausser [ʃose] /1/ vt (bottes, skis) to put on; (enfant) to put shoes on; **~ du 38/42** to take size 38/42

chaussette [ʃosɛt] nf sock

chausson [ʃosɔ̃] nm slipper; (de bébé) bootee; **~ (aux pommes)** (apple) turnover

chaussure [ʃosyR] nf shoe; **~s basses** flat shoes; **~s montantes** ankle boots; **~ de ski** ski boots

chauve [ʃov] adj bald; **chauve-souris** nf bat

chauvin, e [ʃovɛ̃, -in] adj chauvinistic

chaux [ʃo] nf lime; **blanchi à la ~** whitewashed

chef [ʃɛf] nm head, leader; (de cuisine) chef; **général/commandant en ~** general-/commander-in-chief; **~ d'accusation** charge; **~ d'entreprise** company head; **~ d'état** head of state; **~ de famille** head of the family; **~ de file** (de parti etc) leader; **~ de gare** station master; **~ d'orchestre** conductor; **chef-d'œuvre** nm masterpiece; **chef-lieu** nm county town

chelou, e [ʃəlu] (fam) adj sketchy, dodgy

chemin [ʃəmɛ̃] nm path; (itinéraire, direction, trajet) way; **en ~** on the way; **~ de fer** railway (BRIT), railroad (US)

cheminée [ʃəmine] nf chimney; (à l'intérieur) chimney piece, fireplace; (de bateau) funnel

chemise [ʃəmiz] nf shirt; (dossier) folder; **~ de nuit** nightdress

chemisier [ʃəmizje] nm blouse

chêne [ʃɛn] nm oak (tree); (bois) oak

chenil [ʃənil] nm kennels pl

chenille [ʃənij] nf (Zool) caterpillar

chèque [ʃɛk] nm cheque (BRIT), check (US); **faire/toucher un ~** to write/cash a cheque; **par ~** by cheque; **~ barré/sans provision** crossed (BRIT) /bad cheque; **~ de voyage** traveller's cheque; **chéquier** [ʃekje] nm cheque book

cher, -ère [ʃɛR] adj (aimé) dear; (coûteux) expensive, dear ▷ adv: **cela coûte ~** it's expensive

chercher [ʃɛRʃe] /1/ vt to look for; (gloire etc) to seek; **aller ~** to go for, go and fetch; **~ à faire** to try to do; **chercheur, -euse** nm/f researcher

chéri, e [ʃeRi] adj beloved, dear; **(mon) ~** darling

cheval, -aux [ʃəval, -o] nm horse; (Auto): **~ (vapeur)** horsepower no pl; **faire du ~** to ride; **à ~** on horseback; **à ~ sur** astride; (fig) overlapping; **~ de course** race horse

chevalier [ʃəvalje] nm knight

chevaux [ʃəvo] nmpl voir **cheval**

chevet [ʃəvɛ] nm: **au ~ de qn** at sb's bedside; **lampe de ~** bedside lamp

cheveu, x [ʃəvø] nm hair ▷ nmpl (chevelure) hair sg; **avoir les ~x courts/en brosse** to have short hair/a crew cut

cheville [ʃəvij] nf (Anat) ankle; (de bois) peg; (pour enfoncer une vis) plug

chèvre [ʃɛvR] nf (she-)goat

chèvrefeuille [ʃɛvRəfœj] nm honeysuckle

chevreuil [ʃəvRœj] nm roe deer inv; (Culin) venison

MOT-CLÉ

chez [ʃe] prép **1** (à la demeure de) at; (: direction) to; **chez qn/à** to sb's house ou place; **je suis chez moi** I'm at home; **je rentre chez moi** I'm going home; **allons chez Nathalie** let's go to Nathalie's

2 (+profession) at; (: direction) to; **chez le boulanger/dentiste** at ou to the baker's/dentist's

3 (dans le caractère, l'œuvre de) in; **chez ce poète** in this poet's work; **c'est ce que je préfère chez lui** that's what I like best about him

chic [ʃik] adj inv chic, smart; (généreux) nice, decent ▷ nm stylishness; **avoir**

le ~ **de** ou **pour** to have the knack of ou for; **~!** great!

chicorée [ʃikɔʀe] *nf* (*café*) chicory; (*salade*) endive

chien [ʃjɛ̃] *nm* dog; (*de pistolet*) hammer; **~ d'aveugle** guide dog; **~ de garde** guard dog

chienne [ʃjɛn] *nf* (she-)dog, bitch

chiffon [ʃifɔ̃] *nm* (piece of) rag; **chiffonner** /1/ *vt* to crumple; (*tracasser*) to concern

chiffre [ʃifʀ] *nm* (*représentant un nombre*) figure; numeral; (*montant, total*) total, sum; **en ~s ronds** in round figures; **~ d'affaires (CA)** turnover; **chiffrer** /1/ *vt* (*dépense*) to (en)code, cipher ▷ *vi*: **chiffrer à, se chiffrer à** to add up to

chignon [ʃiɲɔ̃] *nm* chignon, bun

Chili [ʃili] *nm*: **le ~** Chile; **chilien, ne** *adj* Chilean ▷ *nm/f*: **Chilien, ne** Chilean

chimie [ʃimi] *nf* chemistry; **chimiothérapie** [ʃimjɔteʀapi] *nf* chemotherapy; **chimique** *adj* chemical; **produits chimiques** chemicals

chimpanzé [ʃɛ̃pɑ̃ze] *nm* chimpanzee

Chine [ʃin] *nf*: **la ~** China; **chinois, e** *adj* Chinese ▷ *nm* (*Ling*) Chinese ▷ *nm/f*: **Chinois, e** Chinese

chiot [ʃjo] *nm* pup(py)

chips [ʃips] *nfpl* crisps (BRIT), (potato) chips (US)

chirurgie [ʃiʀyʀʒi] *nf* surgery; **~ esthétique** cosmetic ou plastic surgery; **chirurgien, ne** *nm/f* surgeon

chlore [klɔʀ] *nm* chlorine

choc [ʃɔk] *nm* (*heurt*) impact; shock; (*collision*) crash; (*moral*) shock; (*affrontement*) clash

chocolat [ʃɔkɔla] *nm* chocolate; **~ au lait** milk chocolate

chœur [kœʀ] *nm* (*chorale*) choir; (*Opéra, Théât*) chorus; **en ~** in chorus

choisir [ʃwaziʀ] /2/ *vt* to choose, select

choix [ʃwa] *nm* choice; selection; **avoir le ~** to have the choice; **de premier ~** (*Comm*) class ou grade one; **de ~** selected; **au ~** as you wish ou prefer

chômage [ʃomaʒ] *nm* unemployment; **mettre au ~** to make redundant, put out of work; **être au ~** to be unemployed ou out of work; **chômeur, -euse** *nm/f* unemployed person

chope [ʃɔp] *nf* tankard

choquer [ʃɔke] /1/ *vt* (*offenser*) to shock; (*commotionner*) to shake (up)

chorale [kɔʀal] *nf* choir

chose [ʃoz] *nf* thing; **c'est peu de ~** it's nothing much

chou, x [ʃu] *nm* cabbage; **mon petit ~** (my) sweetheart; **~ à la crème** cream bun (*made of choux pastry*); **~ de Bruxelles** Brussels sprout; **choucroute** *nf* sauerkraut

chouette [ʃwɛt] *nf* owl ▷ *adj* (*fam*) great, smashing

chou-fleur [ʃuflœʀ] *nm* cauliflower

chrétien, ne [kʀetjɛ̃, -ɛn] *adj, nm/f* Christian

Christ [kʀist] *nm*: **le ~** Christ; **christianisme** *nm* Christianity

chronique [kʀɔnik] *adj* chronic ▷ *nf* (*de journal*) column, page; (*historique*) chronicle; (*Radio, TV*): **la ~ sportive/théâtrale** the sports/theatre review

chronologique [kʀɔnɔlɔʒik] *adj* chronological

chronomètre [kʀɔnɔmɛtʀ] *nm* stopwatch; **chronométrer** /6/ *vt* to time

chrysanthème [kʀizɑ̃tɛm] *nm* chrysanthemum

- **CHRYSANTHÈME**
- Chrysanthemums are strongly
- associated with funerals in France,
- and therefore should not be given
- as gifts.

chuchotement [ʃyʃɔtmɑ̃] *nm*
whisper

chuchoter [ʃyʃɔte] /1/ *vt, vi* to
whisper

chut *excl* [ʃyt] sh!

chute [ʃyt] *nf* fall; (*déchet*) scrap;
faire une ~ (de 10 m) to fall (10 m);
~s de pluie/neige rain/snowfalls;
~ (d'eau) waterfall; **~ libre** free fall

Chypre [ʃipʀ] *nf* Cyprus

-ci [si] *adv voir par* ▷ *adj dém*: **ce
garçon~/-là** this/that boy; **ces
femmes~/-là** these/those women

cible [sibl] *nf* target

cicatrice [sikatʀis] *nf* scar;
cicatriser /1/ *vt* to heal

ci-contre [sikɔ̃tʀ] *adv* opposite

ci-dessous [sidəsu] *adv* below

ci-dessus [sidəsy] *adv* above

cidre [sidʀ] *nm* cider

Cie *abr* (= *compagnie*) Co

ciel [sjɛl] *nm* sky; (*Rel*) heaven

cieux [sjø] *nmpl voir* **ciel**

cigale [sigal] *nf* cicada

cigare [sigaʀ] *nm* cigar

cigarette [sigaʀɛt] *nf* cigarette;
~ électronique e-cigarette

ci-inclus, e [siɛ̃kly, -yz] *adj, adv*
enclosed

ci-joint, e [siʒwɛ̃, -ɛ̃t] *adj, adv*
enclosed

cil [sil] *nm* (eye)lash

cime [sim] *nf* top; (*montagne*) peak

ciment [simɑ̃] *nm* cement

cimetière [simtjɛʀ] *nm* cemetery;
(*d'église*) churchyard

cinéaste [sineast] *nm/f* film-maker

cinéma [sinema] *nm* cinema

cinq [sɛ̃k] *num* five; **cinquante**
nf: **une cinquantaine (de)** about
fifty; **avoir la cinquantaine** (*âge*) to
be around fifty; **cinquante** *num* fifty;
cinquantenaire *adj, nf/f* fifty-year-
old; **cinquième** *num* fifth ▷ *nf* (*Scol*)
year 8 (*BRIT*), seventh grade (*US*)

cintre [sɛ̃tʀ] *nm* coat-hanger

cintré, e [sɛ̃tʀe] *adj* (*chemise*) fitted

cirage [siʀaʒ] *nm* (shoe) polish

circonflexe [siʀkɔ̃flɛks] *adj*: **accent
~** circumflex accent

circonstance [siʀkɔ̃stɑ̃s] *nf*
circumstance; (*occasion*) occasion;
~s atténuantes mitigating
circumstances

circuit [siʀkɥi] *nm* (*trajet*) tour,
(round) trip; (*Élec, Tech*) circuit

circulaire [siʀkylɛʀ] *adj, nf* circular

circulation [siʀkylasjɔ̃] *nf*
circulation; (*Auto*): **la ~** (the) traffic

circuler [siʀkyle] /1/ *vi* (*véhicules*)
to drive (along); (*passants*) to walk
along; (*train etc*) to run; (*sang, devises*)
to circulate; **faire ~** (*nouvelle*) to
spread (about), circulate; (*badauds*)
to move on

cire [siʀ] *nf* wax; **ciré** *nm* oilskin; **cirer**
[siʀe] /1/ *vt* to wax, polish

cirque [siʀk] *nm* circus; (*fig*) chaos,
bedlam; **quel ~!** what a carry-on!

ciseau, x [sizo] *nm*: **~ (à bois)** chisel
▷ *nmpl* (*paire de ciseaux*) (pair of) scissors

citadin, e [sitadɛ̃, -in] *nm/f* city dweller

citation [sitasjɔ̃] *nf* (*d'auteur*)
quotation; (*Jur*) summons *sg*

cité [site] *nf* town; (*plus grande*)
city; **~ universitaire** students'
residences *pl*

citer [site] /1/ *vt* (*un auteur*) to quote
(from); (*nommer*) to name; (*Jur*) to
summon

citoyen, ne [sitwajɛ̃, -ɛn] *nm/f*
citizen

citron [sitʀɔ̃] *nm* lemon; **~ pressé**
(fresh) lemon juice; **~ vert** lime;
citronnade *nf* still lemonade

citrouille [sitʀuj] *nf* pumpkin

civet [sivɛ] *nm*: **~ de lapin** rabbit stew

civière [sivjɛʀ] *nf* stretcher

civil, e [sivil] *adj* (*Jur, Admin, poli*) civil;
(*non militaire*) civilian; **en ~** in civilian
clothes; **dans la ~** in civilian life
civilisation [sivilizasjɔ̃] *nf*
civilization

clair, e [klɛʀ] *adj* light; (*chambre*)
light, bright; (*eau, son, fig*) clear ▷ *adv*:
voir ~ to see clearly ▷ *nm*: **mettre au ~**

(notes etc) to tidy up; **tirer qch au ~** to clear sth up, clarify sth; **~ de lune** moonlight; **clairement** adv clearly

clairière [klɛʀjɛʀ] nf clearing

clandestin, e [klɑ̃dɛstɛ̃, -in] adj clandestine, covert; (Pol) underground, clandestine; (travailleur, immigration) illegal; **passager ~** stowaway

claque [klak] nf (gifle) slap; **claquer** /1/ vi (porte) to bang, slam; (fam: mourir) to snuff it ⊳ vt (porte) to slam, bang; (doigts) to snap; (fam: dépenser) to blow; **elle claquait des dents** her teeth were chattering; **être claqué** (fam) to be dead tired; **se claquer un muscle** to pull ou strain a muscle; **claquettes** nfpl tap-dancing sg; (chaussures) flip-flops

clarinette [klaʀinɛt] nf clarinet

classe [klas] nf class; (Scol: local) class(room); (: leçon) class; (: élèves) class; **aller en ~** to go to school; **classement** nm (rang: Scol) place; (: Sport) placing; (liste: Scol) class list (in order of merit); (: Sport) placings pl

classer [klase] /1/ vt (idées, livres) to classify; (papiers) to file; (candidat, concurrent) to grade; (Jur: affaire) to close; **se ~ premier/dernier** to come first/last; (Sport) to finish first/last; **classeur** nm (cahier) file

classique [klasik] adj (sobre, coupe etc) classic(al), classical; (habituel) standard, classic

clavicule [klavikyl] nf collarbone

clavier [klavje] nm keyboard; (de portable) keypad

clé [kle] nf key; (Mus) clef; (de mécanicien) spanner (BRIT), wrench (US); **prix ~s en main** (d'une voiture) on-the-road price; **; ~ de contact** ignition key; **~ USB** USB key

clergé [klɛʀʒe] nm clergy

clic [klik] nm (Inform) click

cliché [kliʃe] nm (fig) cliché; (Photo) negative; print; (Typo) (printing) plate; (Ling) cliché

client, e [klijɑ̃, -ɑ̃t] nm/f (acheteur) customer, client; (d'hôtel) guest, patron; (du docteur) patient; (de l'avocat) client; **clientèle** nf (du magasin) customers pl, clientèle; (du docteur, de l'avocat) practice

cligner [kliɲe] /1/ vi: **~ des yeux** to blink (one's eyes); **~ de l'œil** to wink; **clignotant** nm (Auto) indicator; **clignoter** /1/ vi (étoiles etc) to twinkle; (lumière) to flicker

climat [klima] nm climate

climatisation [klimatizasjɔ̃] nf air conditioning; **climatisé, e** adj air-conditioned

clin d'œil [klɛ̃dœj] nm wink; **en un ~** in a flash

clinique [klinik] nf (private) clinic

clip [klip] nm (pince) clip; (boucle d'oreille) clip-on; (vidéo) ~ pop (ou promotional) video

cliquer [klike] /1/ vi (Inform) to click; **~ deux fois** to double-click ⊳ vi to click; **~ sur** to click on

clochard, e [klɔʃaʀ, -aʀd] nm/f tramp

cloche [klɔʃ] nf (d'église) bell; (fam) clot; **clocher** /1/ nm church tower; (en pointe) steeple ⊳ vi (fam) to be ou go wrong; **de clocher** (péj) parochial

cloison [klwazɔ̃] nf partition (wall)

clonage [klɔnaʒ] nm cloning

cloner [klɔne] /1/ vt to clone

cloque [klɔk] nf blister

clore [klɔʀ] /45/ vt to close

clôture [klotyʀ] nf closure; (barrière) enclosure

clou [klu] nm nail; **clous** nmpl = **passage clouté**; **pneus à ~s** studded tyres; **le ~ du spectacle** the highlight of the show; **~ de girofle** clove

clown [klun] nm clown

club [klœb] nm club

coaguler [kɔagyle] /1/ vi, vt, **se coaguler** vi (sang) to coagulate

cobaye [kɔbaj] nm guinea-pig

coca® [kɔka] nm Coke®

cocaïne [kɔkain] nf cocaine

coccinelle [kɔksinɛl] nf ladybird (BRIT), ladybug (US)

cocher [kɔʃe] /1/ vt to tick off

cochon, ne [kɔʃɔ̃, -ɔn] nm pig ▷ adj (fam) dirty, smutty; **~ d'Inde** guinea-pig; **cochonnerie** nf (fam: saleté) filth; (marchandises) rubbish, trash

cocktail [kɔktɛl] nm cocktail; (réception) cocktail party

cocorico [kɔkɔriko] excl, nm cock-a-doodle-doo

cocotte [kɔkɔt] nf (en fonte) casserole; **ma ~** (fam) sweetie (pie); **~ (minute)**® pressure cooker

code [kɔd] nm code ▷ adj: **phares ~s** dipped lights; **se mettre en ~(s)** to dip (BRIT) ou dim (US) one's (head) lights; **~ à barres** bar code; **~ civil** Common Law; **~ pénal** penal code; **~ postal** (numéro) postcode (BRIT), zip code (US); **~ de la route** highway code; **~ secret** cipher

cœur [kœʀ] nm heart; (Cartes: couleur) hearts pl; (: carte) heart; **avoir bon ~** to be kind-hearted; **avoir mal au ~** to feel sick; **par ~** by heart; **de bon ~** willingly; **cela lui tient à ~** that's (very) close to his heart

coffre [kɔfʀ] nm (meuble) chest; (d'auto) boot (BRIT), trunk (US); **coffre-fort** nm safe; **coffret** nm casket

cognac [kɔɲak] nm brandy, cognac

cogner [kɔɲe] /1/ vi to knock; **se ~ contre** to knock ou bump into; **se ~ la tête** to bang one's head

cohérent, e [kɔeʀɑ̃, -ɑ̃t] adj coherent, consistent

coiffé, e [kwafe] adj: **bien/mal ~** with tidy/untidy hair; **~ d'un béret** wearing a beret

coiffer [kwafe] /1/ vt (fig: surmonter) to cover, top; **~ qn** to do sb's hair; **se**

coiffer vi to do one's hair; **coiffeur, -euse** nm/f hairdresser ▷ nf (table) dressing table; **coiffure** nf (cheveux) hairstyle, hairdo; (art): **la coiffure** hairdressing

coin [kwɛ̃] nm corner; (pour coincer) wedge; **l'épicerie du ~** the local grocer; **dans le ~** (aux alentours) in the area, around about; (habiter) locally; **je ne suis pas du ~** I'm not from here; **au ~ du feu** by the fireside; **regard en ~** side/queasy glance

coincé, e [kwɛ̃se] adj stuck, jammed; (fig: inhibé) inhibited, with hang-ups

coïncidence [kɔɛ̃sidɑ̃s] nf coincidence

coing [kwɛ̃] nm quince

col [kɔl] nm (de chemise) collar; (encolure, cou) neck; (de montagne) pass; **~ roulé** polo-neck; **~ de l'utérus** cervix

colère [kɔlɛʀ] nf anger; **une ~** a fit of anger; **être en ~ (contre qn)** to be angry (with sb); **mettre qn en ~** to make sb angry; **se mettre en ~ contre qn** to get angry with sb; **se mettre en ~** to get angry; **coléreux, -euse, colérique** adj quick-tempered, irascible

colin [kɔlɛ̃] nm hake

colique [kɔlik] nf diarrhoea

colis [kɔli] nm parcel

collaborer [kɔ(l)labɔʀe] /1/ vi to collaborate; **~ à** to collaborate on; (revue) to contribute to

collant, e [kɔlɑ̃, -ɑ̃t] adj sticky; (robe etc) clinging, skintight; (péj) clinging ▷ nm (bas) tights pl; (de danseur) leotard

colle [kɔl] nf glue; (à papiers peints) (wallpaper) paste; (devinette) teaser, riddle; (Scol: fam) detention

collecte [kɔlɛkt] nf collection; **collectif, -ive** adj collective; (visite, billet etc) group cpd

collection [kɔlɛksjɔ̃] nf collection; (Édition) series; **collectionner** /1/ vt (tableaux, timbres) to

collect; **collectionneur, -euse**
[kɔlɛksjɔnœʀ, -øz] nm/f collector
collectivité [kɔlɛktivite] nf group;
les ~s locales local authorities
collège [kɔlɛʒ] nm (école) (secondary)
school; (assemblée) body; **collégien,
ne** nm/f secondary school pupil
(BRIT), high school student (US)
collègue [kɔ(l)lɛg] nm/f colleague
coller [kɔle] /1/ vt (papier, timbre)
to stick (on); (affiche) to stick up;
(enveloppe) to stick down; (morceaux)
to paste; (fam: mettre, fourrer) to stick,
shove; (Scol: candidat) to keep in ▷ vi
(être collant) to be sticky; (adhérer) to
stick; **~ à** to stick to; **être collé à un
examen** (fam) to fail an exam
collier [kɔlje] nm (bijou) necklace; (de
chien, Tech) collar
colline [kɔlin] nf hill
collision [kɔlizjɔ̃] nf collision, crash;
entrer en ~ (avec) to collide (with)
collyre [kɔliʀ] nm eye lotion
colombe [kɔlɔ̃b] nf dove
Colombie [kɔlɔ̃bi] nf: **la ~** Colombia
colonie [kɔlɔni] nf colony; **~ de
vacances** holiday camp (for children)
colonne [kɔlɔn] nf column; **se
mettre en ~ par deux/quatre** to
get into twos/fours; **~ (vertébrale)**
spine, spinal column
colorant [kɔlɔʀɑ̃] nm colouring
colorer [kɔlɔʀe] /1/ vt to colour
colorier [kɔlɔʀje] /7/ vt to colour (in)
coloris [kɔlɔʀi] nm colour, shade
colza [kɔlza] nm rape(seed)
coma [kɔma] nm coma; **être dans le
~** to be in a coma
combat [kɔ̃ba] nm fight; fighting
no pl; **~ de boxe** boxing match;
combattant nm: **ancien
combattant** war veteran;
combattre /41/ vt to fight; (épidémie,
ignorance) to combat, fight against
combien [kɔ̃bjɛ̃] adv (quantité) how
much; (nombre) how many; **~ de**
how much; (nombre) how many;

~ de temps how long; **~ coûte/
pèse ceci?** how much does this cost/
weigh?; **on est le ~ aujourd'hui?**
(fam) what's the date today?
combinaison [kɔ̃binɛzɔ̃] nf
combination; (astuce) scheme; (de
femme) slip; (de plongée) wetsuit; (bleu
de travail) boilersuit (BRIT), coveralls
pl (US)
combiné [kɔ̃bine] nm (aussi:
~ téléphonique) receiver
comble [kɔ̃bl] adj (salle) packed
(full) ▷ nm (du bonheur, plaisir) height;
combles nmpl (Constr) attic sg, loft sg;
c'est le ~! that beats everything!
combler [kɔ̃ble] /1/ vt (trou) to fill in;
(besoin, lacune) to fill; (déficit) to make
good; (satisfaire) fulfil
comédie [kɔmedi] nf comedy; (fig)
playacting no pl; **faire une ~** (fig) to
make a fuss; **~ musicale** musical;
comédien, ne nm/f actor/actress
comestible [kɔmɛstibl] adj edible
comique [kɔmik] adj (drôle) comical;
(Théât) comic ▷ nm (artiste) comic,
comedian
commandant [kɔmɑ̃dɑ̃] nm (gén)
commander, commandant; (Navig)
captain
commande [kɔmɑ̃d] nf (Comm)
order; **commandes** nfpl (Aviat etc)
controls; **sur ~** to order; **commander**
/1/ vt (Comm) to order; (diriger,
ordonner) to command; **commander
à qn de faire** to command ou order
sb to do

⊙ **MOT-CLÉ**

comme [kɔm] prép **1** (comparaison)
like; **tout comme son père** just like
his father; **fort comme un bœuf** as
strong as an ox; **joli comme tout**
ever so pretty
2 (manière) like; **faites-le comme ça**
do it like this, do it this way; **comme
ci, comme ça** so-so, middling
3 (en tant que) as a; **donner comme**

prix to give as a prize; **travailler comme secrétaire** to work as a secretary

4: **comme il faut** adv properly
▶ conj **1** (ainsi que) as; **elle écrit comme elle parle** she writes as she talks; **comme si** as if
2 (au moment où, alors que) as; **il est parti comme j'arrivais** he left as I arrived
3 (parce que, puisque) as; **comme il était en retard, il ... as** he was late, he ...
▶ adv: **comme il est fort/c'est bon!** he's so strong/it's so good!

commencement [kɔmɑ̃smɑ̃] nm beginning, start

commencer [kɔmɑ̃se] /3/ vt, vi to begin, start; **~ à** ou **de faire** to begin ou start doing

comment [kɔmɑ̃] adv how; **~?** (que dites-vous?) (I beg your) pardon?; **et ~!** and how!

commentaire [kɔmɑ̃tɛʀ] nm comment; remark; **~ (de texte)** commentary

commerçant, e [kɔmɛʀsɑ̃, -ɑ̃t] nm/f shopkeeper, trader

commerce [kɔmɛʀs] nm (activité) trade, commerce; (boutique) business; **~ électronique** e-commerce; **~ équitable** fair trade; **commercial, e, -aux** adj commercial, trading; (péj) commercial; **commercialiser** /1/ vt to market

commettre [kɔmɛtʀ] /56/ vt to commit

commissaire [kɔmisɛʀ] nm (de police) ≈ (police) superintendent; **~ aux comptes** (Admin) auditor; **commissariat** nm police station

commission [kɔmisjɔ̃] nf (comité, pourcentage) commission; (message) message; (course) errand; **commissions** nfpl (achats) shopping sg

commode [kɔmɔd] adj (pratique) convenient, handy; (facile) easy; (personne) **pas ~** awkward (to deal with) ▷ nf chest of drawers

commun, e [kɔmœ̃, -yn] adj common; (pièce) communal, shared; (réunion, effort) joint ▷ nf (Admin) commune, ≈ district (▷ urbaine) ≈ borough; **communs** nmpl (bâtiments) outbuildings; **cela sort du ~** it's out of the ordinary; **le ~ des mortels** the common run of people; **en ~** (faire) jointly; **mettre en ~** to pool, share; **d'un ~ accord** of one accord

communauté [kɔmynote] nf community

commune [kɔmyn] adj f, nf voir **commun**

communication [kɔmynikasjɔ̃] nf communication

communier [kɔmynje] /7/ vi (Rel) to receive communion

communion [kɔmynjɔ̃] nf communion

communiquer [kɔmynike] /1/ vt (nouvelle, dossier) to pass on, convey; (peur etc) to communicate ▷ vi to communicate; **se ~ à** (se propager) to spread to

communisme [kɔmynism] nm communism; **communiste** adj, nm/f communist

commutateur [kɔmytatœʀ] nm (Élec) (change-over) switch, commutator

compact, e [kɔ̃pakt] adj (dense) dense; (appareil) compact

compagne [kɔ̃paɲ] nf companion

compagnie [kɔ̃paɲi] nf (firme, Mil) company; **tenir ~ à qn** to keep sb company; **fausser ~ à qn** to give sb the slip, slip ou sneak away from sb; **~ aérienne** airline (company)

compagnon [kɔ̃paɲɔ̃] nm companion

comparable [kɔ̃paʀabl] adj: **~ (à)** comparable (to)

comparaison [kɔ̃paʀɛzɔ̃] nf
comparison

comparer [kɔ̃paʀe] /1/ vt to
compare; **~ qch/qn à** ou **et** (pour
choisir) to compare sth/sb with ou
and; (pour établir une similitude) to
compare sth/sb to ou and

compartiment [kɔ̃paʀtimɑ̃] nm
compartment

compas [kɔ̃pa] nm (Géom) (pair of)
compasses pl; (Navig) compass

compatible [kɔ̃patibl] adj
compatible

compatriote [kɔ̃patʀijɔt] nm/f
compatriot

compensation [kɔ̃pɑ̃sasjɔ̃] nf
compensation

compenser [kɔ̃pɑ̃se] /1/ vt to
compensate for, make up for

compétence [kɔ̃petɑ̃s] nf
competence

compétent, e [kɔ̃petɑ̃, -ɑ̃t] adj (apte)
competent, capable

compétition [kɔ̃petisjɔ̃] nf (gén)
competition; (Sport: épreuve) event; **la
~ automobile** motor racing

complément [kɔ̃plemɑ̃] nm
complement; (reste) remainder;
~ d'information (Admin)
supplementary ou further
information; **complémentaire**
adj complementary; (additionnel)
supplementary

complet, -ète [kɔ̃plɛ, -ɛt] adj
complete; (plein: hôtel etc) full ▷ nm
(aussi: **~-veston**) suit; **pain ~**
wholemeal bread; **complètement**
adv completely; **compléter** /6/
vt (porter à la quantité voulue) to
complete; (augmenter: connaissances,
études) to complement, supplement;
(: garde-robe) to add to

complexe [kɔ̃plɛks] adj complex
▷ nm: **~ hospitalier/industriel**
hospital/industrial complex;
complexé, e adj mixed-up, hung-up

complication [kɔ̃plikasjɔ̃] nf
complexity, intricacy; (difficulté, ennui)

complication; **complications** nfpl
(Méd) complications

complice [kɔ̃plis] nm accomplice

compliment [kɔ̃plimɑ̃]
nm (louange) compliment;
compliments nmpl (félicitations)
congratulations

compliqué, e [kɔ̃plike] adj
complicated, complex; (personne)
complicated

comportement [kɔ̃pɔʀtəmɑ̃] nm
behaviour

comporter [kɔ̃pɔʀte] /1/ vt (consister
en) to consist of, comprise; (être
équipé de) to have; **se comporter** vi
to behave

composer [kɔ̃poze] /1/ vt (musique,
texte) to compose; (mélange, équipe) to
make up; (faire partie de) to make up,
form ▷ vi (transiger) to come to terms;
se ~ de to be composed of, be made
up of; **~ un numéro** (au téléphone) to
dial a number; **compositeur, -trice**
nm/f (Mus) composer; **composition**
nf composition; (Scol) test

composter [kɔ̃pɔste] /1/ vt (billet)
to punch

• **COMPOSTER**

• In France you have to punch your
• ticket on the platform to validate it
• before getting onto the train.

compote [kɔ̃pɔt] nf stewed fruit no
pl; **~ de pommes** stewed apples

compréhensible [kɔ̃pʀeɑ̃sibl]
adj comprehensible; (attitude)
understandable

compréhensif, -ive [kɔ̃pʀeɑ̃sif, -iv]
adj understanding
▌ Attention à ne pas traduire
compréhensif par comprehensive.

comprendre [kɔ̃pʀɑ̃dʀ] /58/ vt
to understand; (se composer de) to
comprise, consist of

compresse [kɔ̃pʀɛs] nf compress

comprimé [kɔ̃pʀime] nm tablet

compris, e [kɔ̃pʀi, -iz] *pp de* **comprendre** ▷ *adj (inclus)* included; **~ entre** *(situé)* contained between; **la maison ~e/non ~e**, **y/non ~e la maison** including/excluding the house; **100 euros tout ~** 100 euros all inclusive *ou* all in

comptabilité [kɔ̃tabilite] *nf (activité, technique)* accounting, accountancy; *accounts pl*, books *pl*; *(service)* accounts office *ou* department

comptable [kɔ̃tabl] *nm/f* accountant

comptant [kɔ̃tɑ̃] *adv*: **payer ~** to pay cash; **acheter ~** to buy for cash

compte [kɔ̃t] *nm* count; *(total, montant)* count, (right) number; *(bancaire, facture)* account; **comptes** *nmpl* accounts, books; *(fig)* explanation *sg*; **s'en tirer à bon ~** to get off lightly; **pour le ~ de** on behalf of; **pour son propre ~** for one's own benefit; **travailler à son ~** to work for oneself; **régler un ~** *(s'acquitter de qch)* to settle an account; *(se venger)* to get one's own back; **rendre des ~s à qn** *(fig)* to be answerable to sb; **tenir ~ de qch** to take sth into account; **~ courant (CC)** current account; **à rebours** countdown; **~ rendu** account, report; *(de film, livre)* review; *voir aussi* **rendre**; **compte-gouttes** *nm inv* dropper

compter [kɔ̃te] /1/ *vt* to count; *(facturer)* to charge for; *(avoir à son actif, comporter)* to have; *(prévoir)* to allow, reckon; *(penser, espérer)*: **~ réussir/revenir** to expect to succeed/return ▷ *vi* to count; *(être économe)* to economize; *(figurer)*: **~ parmi** to rank among; **~ sur** to count (up)on; **~ avec qch/qn** to reckon with *ou* take account of sth/sb; **sans ~ que** besides which

compteur [kɔ̃tœʀ] *nm* meter; **~ de vitesse** speedometer

comptine [kɔ̃tin] *nf* nursery rhyme

comptoir [kɔ̃twaʀ] *nm (de magasin)* counter; *(de café)* counter, bar

con, ne [kɔ̃, kɔn] *adj (fam!)* bloody *(BRIT!)* *ou* damned stupid

concentrer [kɔ̃sɑ̃tʀe] /1/ *vt* to concentrate; **se concentrer** *vi* to concentrate

concerner [kɔ̃sɛʀne] /1/ *vt* to concern; **en ce qui me concerne** as far as I am concerned

concert [kɔ̃sɛʀ] *nm* concert; **de ~** *(décider)* unanimously

concessionnaire [kɔ̃sesjɔnɛʀ] *nm/f* agent, dealer

concevoir [kɔ̃s(ə)vwaʀ] /28/ *vt (idée, projet)* to conceive (of); *(comprendre)* to understand; *(enfant)* to conceive; **maison bien/mal conçue** well-/badly-designed *ou* -planned house

concierge [kɔ̃sjɛʀʒ] *nm/f* caretaker

concis, e [kɔ̃si, -iz] *adj* concise

conclure [kɔ̃klyʀ] /35/ *vt* to conclude; **conclusion** *nf* conclusion

conçois [kɔ̃swa] *vb voir* **concevoir**

concombre [kɔ̃kɔ̃bʀ] *nm* cucumber

concours [kɔ̃kuʀ] *nm* competition; *(Scol)* competitive examination; *(assistance)* aid, help; **~ de circonstances** combination of circumstances; **~ hippique** horse show; *voir* **'hors-concours'**

concret, -ète [kɔ̃kʀe, -ɛt] *adj* concrete

conçu, e [kɔ̃sy] *pp de* **concevoir**

concubinage [kɔ̃kybinaʒ] *nm (Jur)* cohabitation

concurrence [kɔ̃kyʀɑ̃s] *nf* competition; **jusqu'à ~ de** up to; **faire ~ à** to be in competition with

concurrent, e [kɔ̃kyʀɑ̃, -ɑ̃t] *nm/f* *(Sport, Écon etc)* competitor; *(Scol)* candidate

condamner [kɔ̃dɑne] /1/ *vt (blâmer)* to condemn; *(Jur)* to sentence; *(porte, ouverture)* to fill in, block up; **~ qn à deux ans de prison** to sentence sb to two years' imprisonment

condensation [kɔ̃dɑ̃sasjɔ̃] nf condensation

condition [kɔ̃disjɔ̃] nf condition; **conditions** nfpl (tarif, prix) terms; (circonstances) conditions; **sans ~** unconditionally; **à ~ de** ou **que** provided that; **conditionnel, le** nm conditional (tense)

conditionnement [kɔ̃disjɔnmɑ̃] nm (emballage) packaging

condoléances [kɔ̃dɔleɑ̃s] nfpl condolences

conducteur, -trice [kɔ̃dyktœʀ, -tʀis] nm/f driver ⊳ nm (Élec etc) conductor

conduire [kɔ̃dɥiʀ] /38/ vt to drive; (délégation, troupeau) to lead; **se conduire** vi to behave; **~ vers/à** to lead towards/to; **~ qn quelque part** to take sb somewhere; **to drive sb somewhere**

conduite [kɔ̃dɥit] nf (comportement) behaviour; (d'eau, de gaz) pipe; **sous la ~ de** led by

confection [kɔ̃fɛksjɔ̃] nf (fabrication) making; (Couture): **la ~** the clothing industry

conférence [kɔ̃feʀɑ̃s] nf (exposé) lecture; (pourparlers) conference; **~ de presse** press conference

confesser [kɔ̃fese] /1/ vt to confess; **confession** nf confession; (culte: catholique etc) denomination

confetti [kɔ̃feti] nm confetti no pl

confiance [kɔ̃fjɑ̃s] nf (en l'honnêteté de qn) confidence, trust; (en la valeur de qch) faith, trust; **avoir ~ en** to have confidence ou faith in, trust; **faire ~ à** to trust; **mettre qn en ~** to win sb's trust; **~ en soi** self-confidence; voir **question**

confiant, e [kɔ̃fjɑ̃, -ɑ̃t] adj confident; trusting

confidence [kɔ̃fidɑ̃s] nf confidence; **confidentiel, le** adj confidential

confier [kɔ̃fje] /7/ vt: **~ à qn** (objet en dépôt, travail etc) to entrust to sb; (secret, pensée) to confide to sb; **se ~ à qn** to confide in sb

confirmation [kɔ̃fiʀmasjɔ̃] nf confirmation

confirmer [kɔ̃fiʀme] /1/ vt to confirm

confiserie [kɔ̃fizʀi] nf (magasin) confectioner's ou sweet shop; **confiseries** nfpl (bonbons) confectionery sg

confisquer [kɔ̃fiske] /1/ vt to confiscate

confit, e [kɔ̃fi, -it] adj: **fruits ~s** crystallized fruits ⊳ nm: **~ d'oie** potted goose

confiture [kɔ̃fityʀ] nf jam

conflit [kɔ̃fli] nm conflict

confondre [kɔ̃fɔ̃dʀ] /41/ vt (jumeaux, faits) to confuse, mix up; (témoin, menteur) to confound; **se confondre** vi to merge; **se ~ en excuses** to offer profuse apologies

conforme [kɔ̃fɔʀm] adj: **~ à** (en accord avec: loi, règle) in accordance with; **conformément** adv: **conformément à** in accordance with; **conformer** /1/ vt: **se conformer à** to conform to

confort [kɔ̃fɔʀ] nm comfort; **tout ~** (Comm) with all mod cons (BRIT) ou modern conveniences; **confortable** adj comfortable

confronter [kɔ̃fʀɔ̃te] /1/ vt to confront

confus, e [kɔ̃fy, -yz] adj (vague) confused; (embarrassé) embarrassed; **confusion** nf (voir confus) confusion; embarrassment; (voir confondre) confusion; mixing up

congé [kɔ̃ʒe] nm (vacances) holiday; **en ~** on holiday; **semaine/jour de ~** week/day off; **prendre ~ de qn** to take one's leave of sb; **donner son ~ à** to hand ou give in one's notice to; **~ de maladie** sick leave; **~ de maternité** maternity leave; **~s payés** paid holiday pay

congédier [kɔ̃ʒedje] /7/ vt to dismiss

congélateur [kɔ̃ʒelatœʀ] nm freezer

congeler [kɔ̃ʒ(ə)le] /5/ vt to freeze; **les produits congelés** frozen foods; **se congeler** vi to freeze

congestion [kɔ̃ʒɛstjɔ̃] nf congestion

Congo [kɔ̃ɡo] nm: **le ~** the Congo

congrès [kɔ̃ɡʀɛ] nm congress

conifère [kɔnifɛʀ] nm conifer

conjoint, e [kɔ̃ʒwɛ̃, -wɛ̃t] adj joint
  ▷ nm/f spouse

conjonctivite [kɔ̃ʒɔ̃ktivit] nf conjunctivitis

conjoncture [kɔ̃ʒɔ̃ktyʀ] nf circumstances pl; **la ~ (économique)** the economic climate ou situation

conjugaison [kɔ̃ʒyɡɛzɔ̃] nf (Ling) conjugation

connaissance [kɔnɛsɑ̃s] nf (savoir) knowledge no pl; (personne connue) acquaintance; **être sans ~** to be unconscious; **perdre/reprendre ~** to lose/regain consciousness; **à ma/sa ~** to (the best of) my/his knowledge; **faire ~ avec qn** ou **la ~ de qn** to meet sb

connaisseur, -euse [kɔnɛsœʀ, -øz] nm/f connoisseur

connaître [kɔnɛtʀ] /57/ vt to know; (éprouver) to experience; (avoir: succès) to have; to enjoy; **~ de nom/vue** to know by name/sight; **ils se sont connus à Genève** they (first) met in Geneva; **s'y ~ en qch** to know about sth

connecter [kɔnɛkte] /1/ vt to connect; **se ~ à Internet** to log onto the Internet

connerie [kɔnʀi] nf (fam) (bloody) stupid (BRIT) ou damn-fool (US) thing to do ou say

connexion [kɔnɛksjɔ̃] nf connection

connu, e [kɔny] adj (célèbre) well-known

conquérir [kɔ̃keʀiʀ] /21/ vt to conquer; **conquête** [kɔ̃kɛt] nf conquest

consacrer [kɔ̃sakʀe] /1/ vt (Rel) to consecrate; **~ qch à** (employer) to devote ou dedicate sth to; **se ~ à**
qch/faire to dedicate ou devote o.s. to sth/to doing

conscience [kɔ̃sjɑ̃s] nf conscience; **avoir/prendre ~ de** to be/become aware of; **perdre/reprendre ~** to lose/regain consciousness; **avoir bonne/mauvaise ~** to have a clear, guilty conscience; **consciencieux, -euse** adj conscientious; **conscient adj** conscious

consécutif, -ive [kɔ̃sekytif, -iv] adj consecutive; **~ à** following upon

conseil [kɔ̃sɛj] nm (avis) piece of advice; (assemblée) council; **donner un ~** ou **des ~s à qn** to give sb (a piece of) advice; **prendre ~ (auprès de qn)** to take advice (from sb); **~ d'administration (CA)** board (of directors); **~ général** regional council; **le ~ des ministres** ≈ the Cabinet; **~ municipal (CM)** town council

conseiller¹ [kɔ̃seje] vt (personne) to advise; (méthode, action) to recommend, advise; **~ à qn de faire qch** to advise sb to do sth

conseiller², -ière [kɔ̃seje, -ɛʀ] nm/f adviser; **~ d'orientation** (Scol) careers adviser (BRIT), (school) counselor (US)

consentement [kɔ̃sɑ̃tmɑ̃] nm consent

consentir [kɔ̃sɑ̃tiʀ] /16/ vt: **~ (à qch/faire)** to agree ou consent (to sth/to doing)

conséquence [kɔ̃sekɑ̃s] nf consequence; **en ~** (donc) consequently; (de façon appropriée) accordingly; **conséquent, e** adj logical, rational; (fam: important) substantial; **par conséquent** consequently

conservateur, -trice [kɔ̃sɛʀvatœʀ -tʀis] nm/f (Pol) conservative; (de musée) curator ▷ nm (pour aliments) preservative

conservatoire [kɔ̃sɛʀvatwaʀ] nm academy

conserve [kɔ̃sɛʀv] nf (gén pl) canned ou tinned (BRIT); **en ~** canned, tinned (BRIT)

conserver [kɔ̃sɛʀve] /1/ vt (faculté) to retain, keep; (amis, livres) to keep; (préserver, Culin) to preserve

considérable [kɔ̃sideʀabl] adj considerable, significant, extensive

considération [kɔ̃sideʀasjɔ̃] nf consideration; (estime) esteem

considérer [kɔ̃sideʀe] /6/ vt to consider; **~ qch comme** to regard sth as

consigne [kɔ̃siɲ] nf (de gare) left luggage (office) (BRIT), checkroom (US); (ordre, instruction) instructions pl; **~ automatique** left-luggage locker

consister [kɔ̃siste] /1/ vi: **~ en/dans/à faire** to consist of/in/in doing

consoler [kɔ̃sɔle] /1/ vt to console

consommateur, -trice [kɔ̃sɔmatœʀ, -tʀis] nm/f (Écon) consumer; (dans un café) customer

consommation [kɔ̃sɔmasjɔ̃] nf (Écon) consumption; (boisson) drink; **de ~** (biens, société) consumer cpd

consommer [kɔ̃sɔme] /1/ vt (personne) to eat ou drink, consume; (voiture, usine, poêle) to use, consume; (Jur: mariage) to consummate ▷ vi (dans un café) to (have a) drink

consonne [kɔ̃sɔn] nf consonant

constamment [kɔ̃stamɑ̃] adv constantly

constant, e [kɔ̃stɑ̃, -ɑ̃t] adj constant; (personne) steadfast

constat [kɔ̃sta] nm (de police) report; **~ (à l'amiable)** (jointly agreed) statement for insurance purposes; **~ d'échec** acknowledgement of failure

constatation [kɔ̃statasjɔ̃] nf (remarque) observation

constater [kɔ̃state] /1/ vt (remarquer) to note; (Admin, Jur: attester) to certify

consterner [kɔ̃stɛʀne] /1/ vt to dismay

constipé, e [kɔ̃stipe] adj constipated

constitué, e [kɔ̃stitɥe] adj: **~ de** made up ou composed of

constituer [kɔ̃stitɥe] /1/ vt (comité, équipe) to set up; (dossier, collection) to put together; (éléments, parties: composer) to make up, constitute; (: représenter, être) to constitute; **se ~ prisonnier** to give o.s. up

constructeur [kɔ̃stʀyktœʀ] nm/f manufacturer, builder

constructif, -ive [kɔ̃stʀyktif, -iv] adj constructive

construction [kɔ̃stʀyksjɔ̃] nf construction, building

construire [kɔ̃stʀɥiʀ] /38/ vt to build, construct

consul [kɔ̃syl] nm consul; **consulat** nm consulate

consultant, e adj, nm consultant

consultation [kɔ̃syltasjɔ̃] nf consultation; **heures de ~** (Méd) surgery (BRIT) ou office (US) hours

consulter [kɔ̃sylte] /1/ vt to consult ▷ vi (médecin) to hold surgery (BRIT), be in (the office) (US)

contact [kɔ̃takt] nm contact; **au ~ de** (air, peau) on contact with; (gens) through contact with; **mettre/couper le ~** (Auto) to switch on/off the ignition; **entrer en ~** to come into contact; **prendre ~ avec** to get in touch ou contact with; **contacter** /1/ vt to contact, get in touch with

contagieux, -euse [kɔ̃taʒjø, -øz] adj infectious; (par le contact) contagious

contaminer [kɔ̃tamine] /1/ vt to contaminate

conte [kɔ̃t] nm tale; **~ de fées** fairy tale

contempler [kɔ̃tɑ̃ple] /1/ vt to contemplate, gaze at

contemporain, e [kɔ̃tɑ̃pɔʀɛ̃, -ɛn] adj, nm/f contemporary

contenir [kɔ̃t(ə)niʀ] /22/ vt to contain; (avoir une capacité de) to hold

content, e [kɔ̃tɑ̃, -ɑ̃t] *adj* pleased, glad; **~ de** pleased with; **contenter** /1/ *vt* to satisfy, please; **se contenter de** to content o.s. with

contenu, e [kɔ̃t(ə)ny] *nm* (*d'un bol*) contents *pl*; (*d'un texte*) content

conter [kɔ̃te] /1/ *vt* to recount, relate

conteste [kɔ̃tɛst]: **sans ~** *adv* unquestionably, indisputably; **contester** /1/ *vt* to question ▷ *vi* (*Pol, gén*) to rebel (against established authority)

contexte [kɔ̃tɛkst] *nm* context

continent [kɔ̃tinɑ̃] *nm* continent

continu, e [kɔ̃tiny] *adj* continuous; **faire la journée ~e** to work without taking a full lunch break; **(courant) ~** direct current, DC

continuel, le [kɔ̃tinɥɛl] *adj* (*qui se répète*) constant, continual; (*continu*) continuous

continuer [kɔ̃tinɥe] /1/ *vt* (*travail, voyage etc*) to continue (with), carry on (with), go on with; (*prolonger: alignement, rue*) to continue ▷ *vi* (*pluie, vie, bruit*) to continue, go on; **~ à** *ou* **de faire** to go on *ou* continue doing

contourner [kɔ̃turne] /1/ *vt* to bypass, walk *ou* drive round; (*difficulté*) to get round

contraceptif, -ive [kɔ̃trasɛptif, -iv] *adj, nm* contraceptive; **contraception** *nf* contraception

contracté, e [kɔ̃trakte] *adj* tense

contracter [kɔ̃trakte] /1/ *vt* (*muscle etc*) to tense, contract; (*maladie, dette, obligation*) to contract; (*assurance*) to take out; **se contracter** *vi* (*métal, muscles*) to contract

contractuel, le [kɔ̃traktɥɛl] *nm/f* (*agent*) traffic warden

contradiction [kɔ̃tradiksjɔ̃] *nf* contradiction; **contradictoire** *adj* contradictory, conflicting

contraignant, e [kɔ̃trɛɲɑ̃, -ɑ̃t] *adj* restricting

contraindre [kɔ̃trɛ̃dr] /52/ *vt*: **~ qn à faire** to force *ou* compel sb to do

contraint, e *pp de* **contraindre** ▷ *nf* constraint

contraire [kɔ̃trɛr] *adj, nm* opposite; **~ à** contrary to; **au ~** on the contrary

contrarier [kɔ̃trarje] /7/ *vt* (*personne*) to annoy; (*projets*) to thwart, frustrate; **contrariété** [kɔ̃trarjete] *nf* annoyance

contraste [kɔ̃trast] *nm* contrast

contrat [kɔ̃tra] *nm* contract

contravention [kɔ̃travɑ̃sjɔ̃] *nf* parking ticket

contre [kɔ̃tr] *prép* against; (*en échange*) (in exchange) for; **par ~** on the other hand

contrebande [kɔ̃trəbɑ̃d] *nf* (*trafic*) contraband, smuggling; (*marchandise*) contraband, smuggled goods *pl*; **faire la ~ de** to smuggle

contrebas [kɔ̃trəba]: **en ~** *adv* (down) below

contrebasse [kɔ̃trəbas] *nf* (double) bass

contre...: **contrecoup** *nm* repercussions *pl*; **contredire** /37/ *vt* (*personne*) to contradict; (*témoignage, assertion, faits*) to refute

contrefaçon [kɔ̃trəfasɔ̃] *nf* forgery

contre...: **contre-indication** (*pl* **contre-indications**) *nf* (*Méd*) contra indication; **"contre-indication en cas d'eczéma"** "should not be used by people with eczema"; **contre-indiqué, e** *adj* (*Méd*) contraindicated; (*déconseillé*) unadvisable, ill-advised

contremaître [kɔ̃trəmɛtr] *nm* foreman

contre-plaqué [kɔ̃trəplake] *nm* plywood

contresens [kɔ̃trəsɑ̃s] *nm* (*erreur*) misinterpretation; (*mauvaise traduction*) mistranslation; **à ~** the wrong way

contretemps [kɔ̃trətɑ̃] *nm* hitch; **à ~** (*fig*) at an inopportune moment

contribuer [kɔ̃tribɥe] /1/: **~ à** to contribute towards; **contribution** *nf* contribution;

mettre à contribution to call upon; **contributions directes/indirectes** direct/indirect taxation

contrôle [kɔ̃tʀol] nm checking no pl, check; monitoring; (test) examination; **perdre le ~ de son véhicule** to lose control of one's vehicle; **~ continu** (Scol) continuous assessment; **~ d'identité** identity check

contrôler [kɔ̃tʀole] /1/ vt (vérifier) to check; (surveiller: opérations) to supervise; (: prix) to monitor, control; (maîtriser, Comm: firme) to control; **contrôleur, -euse** nm/f (de train) (ticket) inspector; (de bus) (bus) conductor/tress

controversé, e [kɔ̃tʀovɛʀse] adj (personnage, question) controversial

contusion [kɔ̃tyzjɔ̃] nf bruise, contusion

convaincre [kɔ̃vɛ̃kʀ] /42/ vt: **~ qn (de qch)** to convince sb (of sth); **~ qn (de faire)** to persuade sb (to do)

convalescence [kɔ̃valesɑ̃s] nf convalescence

convenable [kɔ̃vnabl] adj suitable; (assez bon) decent

convenir [kɔ̃vniʀ] /22/ vi to be suitable; **~ à** to suit; **~ de** (bien-fondé de qch) to admit (to), acknowledge; (date, somme etc) to agree upon; **~ que** (admettre) to admit that; **~ de faire qch** to agree to do sth

convention [kɔ̃vɑ̃sjɔ̃] nf convention; **conventions** nfpl (convenances) convention sg; **~ collective** (Écon) collective agreement; **conventionné, e** adj (Admin) applying charges laid down by the state

convenu, e [kɔ̃vny] pp de **convenir** ▷ adj agreed

conversation [kɔ̃vɛʀsasjɔ̃] nf conversation

convertir [kɔ̃vɛʀtiʀ] /2/ vt: **~ qn (à)** to convert sb (to); **~ qch en** to convert sth into; **se ~ (à)** to be converted (to)

conviction [kɔ̃viksjɔ̃] nf conviction

convienne etc [kɔ̃vjɛn] vb voir **convenir**

convivial, e [kɔ̃vivjal] adj (Inform) user-friendly

convocation [kɔ̃vɔkasjɔ̃] nf (document) notification to attend; (Jur) summons sg

convoquer [kɔ̃vɔke] /1/ vt (assemblée) to convene; (subordonné, témoin) to summon; (candidat) to ask to attend

coopération [kɔɔpeʀasjɔ̃] nf co-operation; (Admin): **la C~** ≈ Voluntary Service Overseas (BRIT) ou the Peace Corps (US: done as alternative to military service)

coopérer [kɔɔpeʀe] /6/ vi: **~ (à)** to co-operate (in)

coordonné, e [kɔɔʀdɔne] adj coordinated; **coordonnées** nfpl (détails personnels) address, phone number, schedule etc

coordonner [kɔɔʀdɔne] /1/ vt to coordinate

copain, copine nm/f pal; (petit ami) boyfriend; (petite amie) girlfriend

copie [kɔpi] nf copy; (Scol) script, paper; **copier** /7/ vt, vi to copy; **copier coller** (Inform) copy and paste; **copier sur** to copy from; **copieur** nm (photo)copier

copieux, -euse [kɔpjø, -øz] adj copious

copine [kɔpin] nf voir **copain**

coq [kɔk] nm cockerel

coque [kɔk] nf (de noix, mollusque) shell; (de bateau) hull; **à la ~** (Culin) (soft-)boiled

coquelicot [kɔkliko] nm poppy

coqueluche [kɔklyʃ] nf whooping-cough

coquet, te [kɔkɛ, -ɛt] adj appearance-conscious; (logement) smart, charming

coquetier [kɔk(ə)tje] nm egg-cup

coquillage [kɔkijaʒ] nm (mollusque) shellfish inv; (coquille) shell

coquille [kɔkij] nf shell; (Typo)
misprint; **~ St Jacques** scallop

coquin, e [kɔkɛ̃, -in] adj mischievous,
roguish; (polisson) naughty

cor [kɔr] nm (Mus) horn; (Méd): **~ (au
pied)** corn

corail, -aux [kɔraj, -o] nm coral no pl

Coran [kɔrɑ̃] nm: **le ~** the Koran

corbeau, x [kɔrbo] nm crow

corbeille [kɔrbɛj] nf basket; (Inform)
recycle bin; **~ à papier** waste paper
basket ou bin

corde [kɔrd] nf rope; (de violon,
raquette, d'arc) string; **usé jusqu'à
la ~** threadbare; **~ à linge** washing
ou clothes line; **~ à sauter** skipping
rope; **~s vocales** vocal cords

cordée [kɔrde] nf (d'alpinistes) rope,
roped party

cordialement [kɔrdjalmɑ̃] adv
(formule épistolaire) (kind) regards

cordon [kɔrdɔ̃] nm cord, string;
~ sanitaire/de police sanitary/
police cordon; **~ ombilical** umbilical
cord

cordonnerie [kɔrdɔnri] nf shoe
repairer's ou mender's (shop);
cordonnier nm shoe repairer ou
mender

Corée [kɔre] nf: **la ~ du Sud/du
Nord** South/North Korea

coriace [kɔrjas] adj tough

corne [kɔrn] nf horn; (de cerf) antler

cornée [kɔrne] nf cornea

corneille [kɔrnɛj] nf crow

cornemuse [kɔrnəmyz] nf
bagpipes pl

cornet [kɔrnɛ] nm (paper) cone; (de
glace) cornet, cone

corniche [kɔrniʃ] nf (route) coast road

cornichon [kɔrniʃɔ̃] nm gherkin

Cornouailles [kɔrnwaj] fpl Cornwall

corporel, le [kɔrpɔrɛl] adj bodily;
(punition) corporal

corps [kɔr] nm body; **à ~ perdu**
headlong; **prendre ~** to take shape;
le ~ électoral the electorate; **le ~
enseignant** the teaching profession

correct, e [kɔrɛkt] adj correct;
correcteur, -trice nm/f (Scol)
examiner; **correction** nf (voir corriger)
correction; (voir correct) correctness;
(coups) thrashing

correspondance [kɔrɛspɔ̃dɑ̃s]
nf correspondence; (de train,
d'avion) connection; **cours par ~**
correspondence course; **vente par ~**
mail-order business

correspondant, e [kɔrɛspɔ̃dɑ̃,
-ɑ̃t] nm/f correspondent; (Tél) person
phoning (ou being phoned)

correspondre [kɔrɛspɔ̃dr] /41/ vi te
correspond, tally; **~ à** to correspond
to; **~ avec qn** to correspond with sb

corrida [kɔrida] nf bullfight

corridor [kɔridɔr] nm corridor

corrigé [kɔriʒe] nm (Scol: d'exercice)
correct version

corriger [kɔriʒe] /3/ vt (devoir) to
correct; (punir) to thrash; **~ qn de
(défaut)** to cure sb of

corrompre [kɔrɔ̃pr] /41/ vt to
corrupt; (acheter: témoin etc) to bribe

corruption [kɔrypsjɔ̃] nf corruptio
(de témoins) bribery

corse [kɔrs] adj Corsican ▷ nm/f: **C~**
Corsican ▷ nf: **la C~** Corsica

corsé, e [kɔrse] adj (café etc) full-
flavoured (BRIT) ou -flavored (US);
(sauce) spicy; (problème) tough

cortège [kɔrtɛʒ] nm procession

cortisone [kɔrtizon] nf cortisone

corvée [kɔrve] nf chore, drudgery
no pl

cosmétique [kɔsmetik] nm beaut
care product

cosmopolite [kɔsmɔpɔlit] adj
cosmopolitan

costaud, e [kɔsto, -od] adj strong,
sturdy

costume [kɔstym] nm (d'homme)
suit; (de théâtre) costume; **costumé
adj** dressed up

cote [kɔt] nf (en Bourse etc) quotatio
~ d'alerte danger ou flood level; **~ d
popularité** popularity rating

côte [kot] *nf (rivage)* coast(line); *(pente)* hill; *(Anat)* rib; *(d'un tricot, tissu)* rib, ribbing *no pl*; **~ à ~** side by side; **la C~ (d'Azur)** the (French) Riviera

côté [kote] *nm (gén)* side; *(direction)* way, direction; *(de)* on each side of; **de tous les ~s** from all directions; **de quel ~ est-il parti?** which way or in which direction did he go?; **de ce/de l'autre ~** this/the other way; **du ~ de** *(provenance)* from; *(direction)* towards; **du ~ de Lyon** *(proximité)* near Lyons; **de ~** *(regarder)* sideways; **mettre de ~** to put aside, put on one side; **mettre de l'argent ~** to save some money; **à ~** *(right)* nearby; *(voisins)* next door; **à ~ de** beside; next to; *(fig)* in comparison to; **être aux ~s de** to be by the side of

Côte d'Ivoire [kotdivwaʀ] *nf*: **la ~** Côte d'Ivoire, the Ivory Coast

côtelette [kotlɛt] *nf* chop

côtier, -ière [kotje, -jɛʀ] *adj* coastal

cotisation [kotizasjɔ̃] *nf* subscription, dues *pl*; *(pour une pension)* contributions *pl*

cotiser [kotize] */ʌ/ vi*: **~ (à)** to pay contributions (to); **se cotiser** *vi* to club together

coton [kotɔ̃] *nm* cotton; **~ hydrophile** cotton wool *(BRIT)*, absorbent cotton *(US)*

Coton-Tige® *nm* cotton bud

cou [ku] *nm* neck

couchant [kuʃɑ̃] *adj*: **soleil ~** setting sun

couche [kuʃ] *nf* layer; *(de peinture, vernis)* coat; *(de bébé)* nappy *(BRIT)*, diaper *(US)*; **~s sociales** social levels *ou* strata

couché, e [kuʃe] *adj* lying down; *(au lit)* in bed

coucher [kuʃe] */ʌ/ vt (personne)* to put to bed; *(: loger)* to put up; *(objet)* to lay on its side ▷ *vi* to sleep; **~ avec qn** to sleep with sb; **se coucher** *vi (pour dormir)* to go to bed; *(pour se reposer)*

to lie down; *(soleil)* to set; **~ de soleil** sunset

couchette [kuʃɛt] *nf* couchette; *(pour voyageur, sur bateau)* berth

coucou [kuku] *nm* cuckoo

coude [kud] *nm (Anat)* elbow; *(de tuyau, de la route)* bend; **~ à ~** shoulder to shoulder, side by side

coudre [kudʀ] */48/ vt (bouton)* to sew on ▷ *vi* to sew

couette [kwɛt] *nf* duvet; **couettes** *nfpl (cheveux)* bunches

couffin [kufɛ̃] *nm* Moses basket

couler [kule] */ʌ/ vi* to flow, run; *(fuir: stylo, récipient)* to leak; *(: nez)* to run; *(sombrer: bateau)* to sink ▷ *vt (cloche, sculpture)* to cast; *(bateau)* to sink; *(faire échouer: personne)* to bring down, ruin

couleur [kulœʀ] *nf* colour *(BRIT)*, color *(US)*; *(Cartes)* suit; **en ~s** *(film)* in colo(u)r; **télévision en ~s** colo(u)r television; **de ~** *(homme, femme: vieilli)* colo(u)red

couleuvre [kulœvʀ] *nf* grass snake

coulisse [kulis] *nf (Tech)* runner; **coulisses** *nfpl (Théât)* wings; *(fig)*: **dans les ~s** behind the scenes

couloir [kulwaʀ] *nm* corridor, passage; *(d'avion)* aisle; *(de bus)* gangway; **~ aérien** air corridor *ou* lane; **~ de navigation** shipping lane

coup [ku] *nm (heurt, choc)* knock; *(affectif)* blow, shock; *(agressif)* blow; *(avec arme à feu)* shot; *(de l'horloge)* stroke; *(Sport: golf)* stroke; *(: tennis)* shot; *(fam: fois)* time; **~ de coude/genou** nudge (with the elbow)/with the knee; **donner un ~ de balai** to give the floor a sweep; **être dans le/hors du ~** to be/not to be in on it; *(à la page)* to be hip *ou* trendy; **du ~** as a result; **d'un seul ~** *(subitement)* suddenly; *(à la fois)* at one go; **du premier ~** first time *ou* go; **du même ~** at the same time; **à ~ ~ sûr** definitely, without fail; **après ~** afterwards; **~ sur ~** in quick succession; **sur le ~**

outright; **sous le ~ de** (*surprise etc*) under the influence of; **à tous les ~s** every time; **tenir le ~** to hold out; **~ de chance** stroke of luck; **~ de couteau** stab (of a knife); **~ d'envoi** kick-off; **~ d'essai** first attempt; **~ d'état** coup d'état; **~ de feu** shot; **~ de filet** (*Police*) haul; **~ de foudre** (*fig*) love at first sight; **~ franc** free kick; **~ de frein** (sharp) braking *no pl*; **~ de grâce** coup de grâce; **~ de main**: **donner un ~ de main à qn** to give sb a (helping) hand; **~ d'œil** glance; **~ de pied** kick; **~ de poing** punch; **~ de soleil** sunburn *no pl*; **~ de sonnette** ring of the bell; **~ de téléphone** phone call; **~ de tête** (*fig*) (sudden) impulse; **~ de théâtre** (*fig*) dramatic turn of events; **~ de tonnerre** clap of thunder; **~ de vent** gust of wind; **en ~ de vent** (*rapidement*) in a tearing hurry

coupable [kupabl] *adj* guilty ▷ *nm/f* (*gén*) culprit; (*Jur*) guilty party

coupe [kup] *nf* (*verre*) goblet; (*à fruits*) dish; (*Sport*) cup; (*de cheveux, de vêtement*) cut; (*graphique, plan*) (cross) section

couper [kupe] /1/ *vt* to cut; (*retrancher*) to cut (out); (*route, courant*) to cut off; (*appétit*) to take away; (*vin, cidre: à table*) to dilute (with water) ▷ *vi* to cut; (*prendre un raccourci*) to take a short-cut; **se couper** *vi* (*se blesser*) to cut o.s.; **~ la parole à qn** to cut sb short; **nous avons été coupés** we've been cut off

couple [kupl] *nm* couple

couplet [kuplɛ] *nm* verse

coupole [kupɔl] *nf* dome

coupon [kupɔ̃] *nm* (*ticket*) coupon; (*de tissu*) remnant

coupure [kupyʀ] *nf* cut; (*billet de banque*) note; (*de journal*) cutting; **~ de courant** power cut

cour [kuʀ] *nf* (*de ferme, jardin*) (court) yard; (*d'immeuble*) back yard; (*Jur,*

royale) court; **faire la ~ à qn** to court sb; **~ d'assises** court of assizes; **~ de récréation** playground

courage [kuʀaʒ] *nm* courage, bravery; **courageux, -euse** *adj* brave, courageous

couramment [kuʀamɑ̃] *adv* commonly; (*parler*) fluently

courant, e [kuʀɑ̃, -ɑ̃t] *adj* (*fréquent*) common; (*Comm, gén: normal*) standard; (*en cours*) current ▷ *nm* current; (*fig*) movement; (*: d'opinion*) trend; **être au ~ (de)** (*fait, nouvelle*) to know (about); **mettre qn au ~ (de)** to tell sb (about); (*nouveau travail etc*) to teach sb the basics (of); **se tenir au ~ (de)** (*techniques etc*) to keep o.s. up-to-date (on); **dans le ~ de** (*pendant*) in the course of; **le 10 ~** (*Comm*) the 10th inst.; **~ d'air** draught; **~ électrique** (electric) current, power

courbature [kuʀbatyʀ] *nf* ache

courbe [kuʀb] *adj* curved ▷ *nf* curve

coureur, -euse [kuʀœʀ, -øz] *nm/f* (*Sport*) runner (*ou* driver); (*péj*) womanizer/manhunter

courge [kuʀʒ] *nf* (*Culin*) marrow; **courgette** *nf* courgette (BRIT), zucchini (US)

courir [kuʀiʀ] /11/ *vi* to run ▷ *vt* (*Sport: épreuve*) to compete in; (*: risque*) to run; (*: danger*) to face; **~ les cafés/bals** to do the rounds of the cafés/dances; **le bruit court que** the rumour is going round that

couronne [kuʀɔn] *nf* crown; (*de fleurs*) wreath, circlet

couronns [kuʀɔ̃] *vb voir* **courir**

courriel [kuʀjɛl] *nm* email

courrier [kuʀje] *nm* mail, post; (*lettres à écrire*) letters *pl*; **est-ce que j'ai du ~?** are there any letters for me?; **~ électronique** email

⚠ Attention à ne pas traduire *courrier* par le mot anglais *courier*

courroie [kuʀwa] *nf* strap; (*Tech*) be

courrons *etc* [kuʀɔ̃] *vb voir* **courir**

cours [kuʀ] nm (leçon) class (: particulier) lesson; (série de leçons) course; (écoulement) flow; (Comm: de devises) rate; (: de denrées) price; **donner libre ~ à** to give free expression to; **avoir ~** (Scol) to have a class ou lecture; **en ~** (année) current; (travaux) in progress; **en ~ de route** on the way; **au ~ de** in the course of; during; **le ~ du change** the exchange rate; **~ d'eau** waterway; **~ du soir** night school

course [kuʀs] nf running; (Sport: épreuve) race; (d'un taxi, autocar) journey, trip; (petite mission) errand; **courses** nfpl (achats) shopping sg; **faire les** ou **ses ~s** to go shopping

court, e [kuʀ, kuʀt] adj short ▷ adv short ▷ nm: **~ (de tennis)** (tennis) court; **à ~ de** short of; **prendre qn de ~** to catch sb unawares; **court-circuit** nm short-circuit

courtoisie [kuʀtwazi] nf courtesy

couru, e [kuʀy] pp de courir

cousais etc [kuze] vb voir coudre

couscous [kuskus] nm couscous

cousin, e [kuzɛ̃, -in] nm/f cousin

coussin [kusɛ̃] nm cushion

cousu, e [kuzy] pp de coudre

coût [ku] nm cost; **le ~ de la vie** the cost of living

couteau, x [kuto] nm knife

coûter [kute] /1/ vt to cost ▷ vi to cost; **~ cher** to be expensive; **combien ça coûte?** how much is it?, what does it cost?; **coûte que coûte** at all costs; **coûteux, -euse** adj costly, expensive

coutume [kutym] nf custom

couture [kutyʀ] nf sewing; (profession) dress-making; (points) seam; **couturier** nm fashion designer; **couturière** nf dressmaker

couvent [kuvɑ̃] nm (de sœurs) convent; (de frères) monastery

couver [kuve] /1/ vt to hatch; (maladie) to be sickening for ▷ vi (feu) to smoulder; (révolte) to be brewing

couvercle [kuvɛʀkl] nm lid; (de bombe aérosol etc, qui se visse) cap, top

couvert, e [kuvɛʀ, -ɛʀt] pp de couvrir ▷ adj (ciel) overcast ▷ nm place setting; (place à table) place; **couverts** nmpl (ustensiles) cutlery sg; **~ de** covered with ou in; **mettre le ~** to lay the table

couverture [kuvɛʀtyʀ] nf blanket; (de livre, fig, Assurances) cover; (Presse) coverage

couvre-lit [kuvʀəli] nm bedspread

couvrir [kuvʀiʀ] /18/ vt to cover; **se couvrir** vi (ciel) to cloud over; (s'habiller) to cover up; (se coiffer) to put on one's hat

cow-boy [koboj] nm cowboy

crabe [kʀab] nm crab

cracher [kʀaʃe] /1/ vi to spit ▷ vt to spit out

crachin [kʀaʃɛ̃] nm drizzle

craie [kʀɛ] nf chalk

craindre [kʀɛ̃dʀ] /52/ vt to fear, be afraid of; (être sensible à: chaleur, froid) to be easily damaged by

crainte [kʀɛ̃t] nf fear; **de ~ de/que** for fear of/that; **craintif, -ive** adj timid

crampe [kʀɑ̃p] nf cramp; **j'ai une ~ à la jambe** I've got cramp in my leg

cramponner [kʀɑ̃pɔne] /1/: **se cramponner** vi: **se ~ (à)** to hang ou cling on (to)

cran [kʀɑ̃] nm (entaille) notch; (de courroie) hole; (courage) guts pl

crâne [kʀɑn] nm skull

crapaud [kʀapo] nm toad

craquement [kʀakmɑ̃] nm crack, snap; (du plancher) creak, creaking no pl

craquer [kʀake] /1/ vi (bois, plancher) to creak; (fil, branche) to snap; (couture) to come apart; (fig: accusé) to break down, fall apart ▷ vt: **une allumette** to strike a match; **j'ai craqué** (fam) I couldn't resist it

crasse [kʀas] nf grime, filth; **crasseux, -euse** adj filthy

cravache [kʀavaʃ] *nf* (riding) crop

cravate [kʀavat] *nf* tie

crawl [kʀol] *nm* crawl; **dos ~é** backstroke

crayon [kʀɛjɔ̃] *nm* pencil; **~ à bille** ball-point pen; **~ de couleur** crayon; **crayon-feutre** (*pl* **crayons-feutres**) *nm* felt(-tip) pen

création [kʀeasjɔ̃] *nf* creation

crèche [kʀɛʃ] *nf* (*de Noël*) crib; (*garderie*) crèche, day nursery

crédit [kʀedi] *nm* (*gén*) credit; **crédits** *nmpl* funds; **acheter à ~** to buy on credit *ou* on easy terms; **faire ~ à qn** to give sb credit; **créditer** /1/ *vt*: **créditer un compte (de)** to credit an account (with)

créer [kʀee] /1/ *vt* to create

crémaillère [kʀemajɛʀ] *nf*: **pendre la ~** to have a house-warming party

crème [kʀɛm] *nf* cream; (*entremets*) cream dessert ▷ *adj inv* cream; **un (café) ~** ≈ a white coffee; **~ anglaise** (egg) custard; **~ chantilly** whipped cream; **~ à raser** shaving cream; **~ solaire** sun cream

créneau, x [kʀeno] *nm* (*de fortification*) crenel(le); (*fig. aussi Comm*) gap, slot; (*Auto*): **faire un ~** to reverse into a parking space (*between cars alongside the kerb*)

crêpe [kʀɛp] *nf* (*galette*) pancake ▷ *nm* (*tissu*) crêpe; **crêperie** *nf* pancake shop *ou* restaurant

crépuscule [kʀepyskyl] *nm* twilight, dusk

cresson [kʀesɔ̃] *nm* watercress

creuser [kʀøze] /1/ *vt* (*trou, tunnel*) to dig; (*sol*) to dig a hole in; (*fig*) to go (deeply) into; **ça creuse** that gives you a real appetite; **se ~ (la cervelle)** to rack one's brains

creux, -euse [kʀø, -øz] *adj* hollow ▷ *nm* hollow; **heures creuses** slack periods; (*électricité, téléphone*) off-peak periods; **avoir un ~** (*fam*) to be hungry

crevaison [kʀəvɛzɔ̃] *nf* puncture

crevé, e [kʀəve] *adj* (*fam: fatigué*) shattered (BRIT), exhausted

crever [kʀəve] /5/ *vt* (*tambour, ballon*) to burst ▷ *vi* (*pneu*) to burst; (*automobiliste*) to have a puncture (BRIT) *ou* a flat (tire) (US); (*fam*) to die

crevette [kʀəvɛt] *nf*: **~ (rose)** prawn; **~ grise** shrimp

cri [kʀi] *nm* cry, shout; (*d'animal: spécifique*) cry, call; **c'est le dernier ~** (*fig*) it's the latest fashion

criard, e [kʀijaʀ, -aʀd] *adj* (*couleur*) garish, loud; (*voix*) yelling

cric [kʀik] *nm* (*Auto*) jack

crier [kʀije] /7/ *vi* (*pour appeler*) to shout, cry (out); (*de peur, de douleur etc*) to scream, yell ▷ *vt* (*ordre, injure*) to shout (out), yell (out)

crime [kʀim] *nm* crime; (*meurtre*) murder; **criminel, le** *nm/f* criminal; murderer

crin [kʀɛ̃] *nm* (*de cheval*) hair *no pl*

crinière [kʀinjɛʀ] *nf* mane

crique [kʀik] *nf* creek, inlet

criquet [kʀikɛ] *nm* grasshopper

crise [kʀiz] *nf* crisis (*pl* crises); (*Méd*) attack (*: d'épilepsie*) fit; **~ cardiaque** heart attack; **avoir une ~ de foie** to have really bad indigestion; **piquer une ~ de nerfs** to go hysterical

cristal, -aux [kʀistal, -o] *nm* crystal

critère [kʀitɛʀ] *nm* criterion (*pl* criteria

critiquable [kʀitikabl] *adj* open to criticism

critique [kʀitik] *adj* critical ▷ *nm/f* (*de théâtre, musique*) critic ▷ *nf* criticism; (*Théât etc article*) review

critiquer [kʀitike] /1/ *vt* (*dénigrer*) to criticize; (*évaluer, juger*) to assess, examine (critically)

croate [kʀɔat] *adj* Croatian ▷ *nm* (*Ling*) Croat, Croatian ▷ *nm/f*: **C~** Croat, Croatian

Croatie [kʀɔasi] *nf*: **la ~** Croatia

crochet [kʀɔʃɛ] *nm* hook; (*détour*) detour; (*Tricot: aiguille*) crochet hook; (*: technique*) crochet; **vivre aux ~s de qn** to live *ou* sponge off sb

crocodile [kʀɔkɔdil] nm crocodile

croire [kʀwaʀ] /44/ vt to believe; **se ~ fort** to think one is strong; **~ que** to believe ou think that; **~ à, ~ en** to believe in

croisade [kʀwazad] nf crusade

croisement [kʀwazmɑ̃] nm (carrefour) crossroads sg; (Bio) crossing (: résultat) crossbreed

croiser [kʀwaze] /1/ vt (personne, voiture) to pass; (route) to cross, cut across; (Bio) to cross; **se croiser** vi (personnes, véhicules) to pass each other; (routes) to cross; (regards) to meet; **se ~ les bras** (fig) to fold one's arms, to twiddle one's thumbs

croisière [kʀwazjɛʀ] nf cruise

croissance [kʀwasɑ̃s] nf growth

croissant, e [kʀwasɑ̃, -ɑ̃t] adj growing ▷ nm (à manger) croissant; (motif) crescent

croître [kʀwatʀ] /55/ vi to grow

croix [kʀwa] nf cross; **la C~ Rouge** the Red Cross

croque-madame [kʀɔkmadam] nm inv toasted cheese sandwich with a fried egg on top

croque-monsieur [kʀɔkməsjø] nm inv toasted ham and cheese sandwich

croquer [kʀɔke] /1/ vt (manger) to crunch (: fruit) to munch; (dessiner) to sketch; **chocolat à ~** plain dessert chocolate

croquis [kʀɔki] nm sketch

crotte [kʀɔt] nf droppings pl; **crottin** [kʀɔtɛ̃] nm dung, manure; (fromage) (small round) cheese (made of goat's milk)

croustillant, e [kʀustijɑ̃, -ɑ̃t] adj crisp

croûte [kʀut] nf crust; (du fromage) rind; (Méd) scab; **en ~** (Culin) in pastry

croûton [kʀutɔ̃] nm (Culin) crouton; (bout du pain) crust, heel

croyant, e [kʀwajɑ̃, -ɑ̃t] nm/f believer

CRS sigle fpl (= Compagnies républicaines de sécurité) state security police force ▷ sigle m member of the CRS

cru, e [kʀy] pp de **croire** ▷ adj (non cuit) raw; (lumière, couleur) harsh; (paroles, langage) crude ▷ nm (vignoble) vineyard; (vin) wine; **un grand ~** a great vintage; **jambon ~** Parma ham

crû [kʀy] pp de **croître**

cruauté [kʀyote] nf cruelty

cruche [kʀyʃ] nf pitcher, (earthenware) jug

crucifix [kʀysifi] nm crucifix

crudité [kʀydite] nf crudeness no pl; **crudités** nfpl (Culin) selection of raw vegetables

crue [kʀy] nf (inondation) flood; voir aussi **cru**

cruel, le [kʀyɛl] adj cruel

crus, crûs etc [kʀy] vb voir **croire**; **croître**

crustacés [kʀystase] nmpl shellfish

Cuba [kyba] nm Cuba; **cubain, e** adj Cuban ▷ nm/f: **Cubain, e** Cuban

cube [kyb] nm cube; (jouet) brick; **mètre ~** cubic metre; **2 au ~ = 8** 2 cubed is 8

cueillette [kœjɛt] nf picking, (quantité) crop, harvest

cueillir [kœjiʀ] /12/ vt (fruits, fleurs) to pick, gather; (fig) to catch

cuiller, cuillère [kɥijɛʀ] nf spoon; **~ à café** coffee spoon; (Culin) = teaspoonful; **~ à soupe** soup spoon; (Culin) = tablespoonful; **cuillerée** nf spoonful

cuir [kɥiʀ] nm leather; (avant tannage) hide; **~ chevelu** scalp

cuire [kɥiʀ] /38/ vt: (aliments) to cook; (au four) to bake ▷ vi to cook; **bien cuit** (viande) well done; **trop cuit** overdone

cuisine [kɥizin] nf (pièce) kitchen; (art culinaire) cookery, cooking; (nourriture) cooking, food; **faire la ~** to cook; **cuisiné, e** adj: **plat cuisiné** ready-made meal ou dish; **cuisiner** /1/ vt to cook; (fam) to grill ▷ vi to cook; **cuisinier, -ière** nm/f cook ▷ nf (poêle) cooker

cuisse [kɥis] nf thigh; (Culin) leg

cuisson [kɥisɔ̃] nf cooking
cuit, e [kɥi, -it] pp de **cuire**
cuivre [kɥivʀ] nm copper; **les ~s**
  (Mus) the brass
cul [ky] nm (fam!) arse (!)
culminant, e [kylminã, -ãt] adj:
  point ~ highest point
culot [kylo] (fam) nm (effronterie) cheek
culotte [kylɔt] nf (de femme) panties
  pl, knickers pl (BRIT)
culte [kylt] nm (religion) religion;
  (hommage, vénération) worship;
  (protestant) service
cultivateur, -trice [kyltivatœʀ,
  -tʀis] nm/f farmer
cultivé, e [kyltive] adj (personne)
  cultured, cultivated
cultiver [kyltive] /1/ vt to cultivate;
  (légumes) to grow, cultivate
culture [kyltyʀ] nf cultivation;
  (connaissances etc) culture; **les ~s**
  intensives intensive farming;
  ~ OGM GM crop; **~ physique** physical
  training; **culturel, le** adj cultural
cumin [kymɛ̃] nm cumin
cure [kyʀ] nf (Méd) course of
  treatment; **~ d'amaigrissement**
  slimming course; **~ de repos** rest
  cure
curé [kyʀe] nm parish priest
cure-dent [kyʀdã] nm toothpick
curieux, -euse [kyʀjø, -øz] adj
  (étrange) strange, curious; (indiscret)
  curious, inquisitive ▷ nmpl (badauds)
  onlookers; **curiosité** nf curiosity;
  (site) unusual feature ou sight
curriculum vitae [kyʀikylɔmvite]
  nm inv curriculum vitae
curseur [kyʀsœʀ] nm (Inform) cursor;
  (de règle) slide; (de fermeture-éclair)
  slider
cutané, e [kytane] adj skin cpd
cuve [kyv] nf (à mazout etc) tank
cuvée [kyve] nf vintage
cuvette [kyvɛt] nf (récipient) bowl,
  basin; (Géo) basin
CV sigle m (Auto): = **cheval (vapeur)**;
  (Admin) = **curriculum vitae**

cybercafé [sibɛʀkafe] nm Internet
  café
cyberespace [sibɛʀɛspas] nm
  cyberspace
cybernaute [sibɛʀnot] nm/f
  Internet user
cyclable [siklabl] adj: **piste ~**
  cycle track
cycle [sikl] nm cycle; **cyclisme**
  [siklism] nm cycling; **cycliste**
  [siklist] nm/f cyclist ▷ adj cycle cpd;
  coureur cycliste racing cyclist
cyclomoteur [siklomɔtœʀ] nm
  moped
cyclone [siklon] nm hurricane
cygne [siɲ] nm swan
cylindre [silɛ̃dʀ] nm cylinder;
  cylindrée nf (Auto) (cubic) capacity;
  une (voiture de) grosse cylindrée a
  big-engined car
cymbale [sɛ̃bal] nf cymbal
cynique [sinik] adj cynical
cystite [sistit] nf cystitis

d

MOT-CLÉ

dans [dã] *prép* **1** *(position)* in; (: *à l'intérieur de*) inside; **c'est dans le tiroir/le salon** it's in the drawer/ lounge; **dans la boîte** in ou inside the box; **marcher dans la ville/la rue** to walk about the town/along the street; **je l'ai lu dans le journal** I read it in the newspaper

2 *(direction)* into; **elle a couru dans le salon** she ran into the lounge; **monter dans une voiture/le bus** to get into a car/on to the bus

3 *(provenance)* out of, from; **je l'ai pris dans le tiroir/salon** I took it out of ou from the drawer/lounge; **boire dans un verre** to drink out of ou from a glass

4 *(temps)* in; **dans deux mois** in two months, in two months' time

5 *(approximation)* about; **dans les 20 euros** about 20 euros

danse [dãs] *nf*: **la ~** dancing; *(classique)* (ballet) dancing; **une ~** a dance; **danser** /1 *vi*, *vt* to dance; **danseur, -euse** *nm/f* ballet dancer; *(au bal etc)* dancer (: *cavalier*) partner

date [dat] *nf* date; **de longue ~** longstanding; **~ de naissance** date of birth; **~ limite** deadline; **dater** /1/ *vt*, *vi* to date; **dater de** to date from; **à dater de** (as) from

datte [dat] *nf* date

dauphin [dofɛ̃] *nm* *(Zool)* dolphin

davantage [davãtaʒ] *adv* more; *(plus longtemps)* longer; **~ de** more

MOT-CLÉ

de, d' [də, d] *(de + le =* **du**, *de + les =* **des**) *prép* **1** *(appartenance)* of; **le toit de la maison** the roof of the house; **la voiture d'Elisabeth/de mes parents** Elizabeth's/my parents' car

2 *(provenance)* from; **il vient de Londres** he comes from London; **elle**

---

dactylo [daktilo] *nf* (aussi: **~graphe**) typist; (aussi: **~graphie**) typing

dada [dada] *nm* hobby-horse

daim [dɛ̃] *nm* (fallow) deer *inv*; *(cuir suédé)* suede

daltonien, ne [daltɔnjɛ̃, -ɛn] *adj* colour-blind

dame [dam] *nf* lady; *(Cartes, Échecs)* queen; **dames** *nfpl* *(jeu)* draughts *sg* (BRIT), checkers *sg* (US)

Danemark [danmark] *nm*: **le ~** Denmark

danger [dãʒe] *nm* danger; **mettre en ~** *(personne)* to put in danger; *(projet, carrière)* to jeopardize; **être en ~** *(personne)* to be in danger; **être en ~ de mort** to be in peril of one's life; **être hors de ~** to be out of danger; **dangereux, -euse** *adj* dangerous

danois, e [danwa, -waz] *adj* Danish ▷ *nm* *(Ling)* Danish ▷ *nm/f*: **D~, e** Dane

est sortie du cinéma she came out of the cinema

3 (moyen) with; **je l'ai fait de mes propres mains** I did it with my own two hands

4 (caractérisation, mesure): **un mur de brique/bureau d'acajou** a brick wall/mahogany desk; **un billet de 10 euros** a 10 euro note; **une pièce de 2 m de large** ou **large de 2 m** a room 2 m wide, a 2m-wide room; **un bébé de 10 mois** a 10-month-old baby; **12 mois de crédit/travail** 12 months' credit/work; **elle est payée 20 euros de l'heure** she's paid 20 euros an hour ou per hour; **augmenter de 10 euros** to increase by 10 euros

5 (rapport) from; **de quatre à six** from four to six

6 (cause): **mourir de faim** to die of hunger; **rouge de colère** red with fury

7 (vb + de + infin) to; **il m'a dit de rester** he told me to stay

▶ **art 1** (phrases affirmatives) some (souvent omis); **du vin, de l'eau, des pommes** (some) wine, (some) water, (some) apples; **des enfants sont venus** some children came; **pendant des mois** for months

2 (phrases interrogatives et négatives) any; **a-t-il du vin?** has he got any wine?; **il n'a pas de pommes/d'enfants** he hasn't (got) any apples/children, he has no apples/children

dé [de] nm (à jouer) die ou dice; (aussi: **dé à coudre**) thimble

déballer [debale] /1/ vt to unpack

débarcadère [debaʀkadɛʀ] nm wharf

débardeur [debaʀdœʀ] nm (pour femme) vest top; (pour homme) sleeveless top

débarquer [debaʀke] /1/ vt to unload, land ▷ vi to disembark; (fig) to turn up

débarras [debaʀa] nm (pièce) lumber room; (placard) junk cupboard; **bon ~!** good riddance!; **débarrasser** /1/ vt

to clear ▷ vi (enlever le couvert) to clear away; **se débarrasser de** vt to get rid of; **débarrasser qn de** (vêtements, paquets) to relieve sb of

débat [deba] nm discussion, debate; **débattre** /41/ vt to discuss, debate; **se débattre** vi to struggle

débit [debi] nm (d'un liquide, fleuve) (rate of) flow; (d'un magasin) turnover (of goods); (élocution) delivery; (bancaire) debit; **~ de boissons** drinking establishment; **~ de tabac** tobacconist's (shop)

déblayer [debleje] /8/ vt to clear

débloquer [debloke] /1/ vt (frein, fonds) to release; (prix, crédits) to free ▷ vi (fam) to talk rubbish

déboîter [debwate] /1/ vt (Auto) to pull out; **se ~ le genou** etc to dislocate one's knee etc

débordé, e [debɔʀde] adj: **être ~** (de travail, demandes) to be snowed under with

déborder [debɔʀde] /1/ vi to overflow; (lait etc) to boil over; **~ (de) qch** (dépasser) to extend beyond sth; **~ de** (joie, zèle) to be brimming over with ou bursting with

débouché [debuʃe] nm (pour vendre) outlet; (perspective d'emploi) opening

déboucher [debuʃe] /1/ vt (évier, tuyau etc) to unblock; (bouteille) to uncork ▷ vi: **~ de** to emerge from; **~ sur** (études) to lead on to

debout [dəbu] adv: **être ~** (personne) to be standing, stand; (levé, éveillé) to be up (and about); **se mettre ~** to get up (on one's feet); **se tenir ~** to stand; **~!** stand up!; (du lit) get up!; **cette histoire ne tient pas ~** this story doesn't hold water

déboutonner [debutɔne] /1/ vt to undo, unbutton

débraillé, e [debʀaje] adj slovenly, untidy

débrancher [debʀɑ̃ʃe] /1/ vt (appareil électrique) to unplug; (téléphone, courant électrique) to disconnect

débrayage [debʀɛjaʒ] nm (Auto) clutch; **débrayer** /8/ vi (Auto) to declutch; (cesser le travail) to stop work

débris [debʀi] nm fragment ▷ nmpl: **des ~ de verre** bits of glass

débrouillard, e [debʀujaʀ, -aʀd] adj smart, resourceful

débrouiller [debʀuje] /1/ vt to disentangle, untangle; **se débrouiller** vi to manage; **débrouillez-vous** you'll have to sort things out yourself

début [deby] nm beginning, start; **débuts** nmpl (de carrière) début sg; **~ juin** in early June; **débutant, e** nm/f beginner, novice; **débuter** /1/ vi to begin, start; (faire ses débuts) to start out

décaféiné, e [dekafeine] adj decaffeinated

décalage [dekalaʒ] nm gap; **~ horaire** time difference (between time zones), time-lag

décaler [dekale] /1/ vt to shift forward ou back

décapotable [dekapotabl] adj convertible

décapsuleur [dekapsylœʀ] nm bottle-opener

décédé, e [desede] adj deceased

décéder [desede] /6/ vi to die

décembre [desɑ̃bʀ] nm December

décennie [deseni] nf decade

décent, e [desɑ̃, -ɑ̃t] adj decent

déception [desɛpsjɔ̃] nf disappointment

décès [desɛ] nm death

décevoir [des(ə)vwaʀ] /28/ vt to disappoint

décharge [deʃaʀʒ] nf (dépôt d'ordures) rubbish tip ou dump; (électrique) electrical discharge; **décharger** /3/ vt (marchandise, véhicule) to unload; (faire feu) to discharge, fire; **décharger qn de** (responsabilité) to relieve sb of, release sb from

déchausser [deʃose] /1/ vt (skis) to take off; **se déchausser** vi to take

off one's shoes; (dent) to come ou work loose

déchet [deʃɛ] nm (de bois, tissu etc) scrap; **déchets** nmpl (ordures) refuse sg, rubbish sg; **~s nucléaires** nuclear waste

déchiffrer [deʃifʀe] /1/ vt to decipher

déchirant, e [deʃiʀɑ̃, -ɑ̃t] adj heart-rending

déchirement [deʃiʀmɑ̃] nm (chagrin) wrench, heartbreak; (gén pl: conflit) rift, split

déchirer [deʃiʀe] /1/ vt to tear; (mettre en morceaux) to tear up; (arracher) to tear out; (fig) to tear apart; **se déchirer** vi to tear, rip; **se ~ un muscle/tendon** to tear a muscle/tendon

déchirure [deʃiʀyʀ] nf (accroc) tear, rip; **~ musculaire** torn muscle

décidé, e [deside] adj (personne, air) determined; **c'est ~** it's decided; **décidément** adv really

décider [deside] /1/ vt: **~ qch** to decide on sth; **~ de faire/que** to decide to do/that; **~ qn (à faire qch)** to persuade ou induce sb (to do sth); **se ~ à faire** to decide ou make up one's mind to do; **se ~ pour qch** to decide on ou in favour of sth

décimal, e, -aux [desimal, -o] adj decimal

décimètre [desimɛtʀ] nm decimetre

décisif, -ive [desizif, -iv] adj decisive

décision [desizjɔ̃] nf decision

déclaration [deklaʀasjɔ̃] nf declaration; (discours: Pol etc) statement; **~ d'impôts** = tax return; **~ de revenus** statement of income; **faire une ~ de vol** to report a theft

déclarer [deklaʀe] /1/ vt to declare; (décès, naissance) to register; **se déclarer** vi (feu, maladie) to break out

déclencher [deklɑ̃ʃe] /1/ vt (mécanisme etc) to release; (sonnerie) to set off; (attaque, grève) to launch; (provoquer) to trigger off; **se déclencher** vi (sonnerie) to go off

décliner [dekline] /1/ vi to decline
▷ vt (invitation) to decline; (nom,
adresse) to state

décoiffer [dekwafe] /1/ vt: ~ qn
to mess up sb's hair; **je suis toute
décoiffée** my hair is in a real mess

déçois etc [deswa] vb voir **décevoir**

décollage [dekɔlaʒ] nm (Aviat, Écon)
takeoff

décoller [dekɔle] /1/ vt to unstick ▷ vi
(avion) to take off; **se décoller** vi to
come unstuck

décolleté, e [dekɔlte] adj low-cut
▷ nm low neck(line); (plongeant)
cleavage

décolorer [dekɔlɔre] /1/: **se
décolorer** vi to fade; **se ~ les
cheveux** to have one's hair bleached

décommander [dekɔmɑ̃de] /1/
vt to cancel; **se décommander** vi
to cancel

déconcerter [dekɔ̃sɛrte] /1/ vt to
disconcert, confound

décongeler [dekɔ̃ʒ(ə)le] /5/ vt to
thaw (out)

déconner [dekɔne] /1/ vi (fam!)
to talk (a load of) rubbish (BRIT) ou
garbage (US)

déconseiller [dekɔ̃seje] /1/ vt: ~ **qch
(à qn)** to advise (sb) against sth;
c'est déconseillé it's not advised ou
advisable

décontracté, e [dekɔ̃trakte] adj
relaxed, laid-back (fam)

décontracter [dekɔ̃trakte] /1/: **se
décontracter** vi to relax

décor [dekɔr] nm décor; (paysage)
scenery; **décorateur, -trice** nm/f
(interior) decorator; **décoration**
nf decoration; **décorer** /1/ vt to
decorate

décortiquer [dekɔrtike] /1/ vt to
shell; (fig: texte) to dissect

découdre /48/: **se découdre** vi to
come unstitched

découper [dekupe] /1/ vt (papier,
tissu etc) to cut up; (volaille, viande) to
carve; (manche, article) to cut out

décourager [dekuraʒe] /3/ vt to
discourage; **se décourager** vi to lose
heart, become discouraged

décousu, e [dekuzy] adj unstitched;
(fig) disjointed, disconnected

découvert, e [dekuvɛr, -ɛrt] adj
(tête) bare, uncovered; (lieu) open,
exposed ▷ nm (bancaire) overdraft
▷ nf discovery; **faire la ~e de** to
discover

découvrir [dekuvrir] /18/ vt to
discover; (enlever ce qui couvre ou
protège) to uncover; (montrer, dévoiler)
to reveal; **se découvrir** vi (chapeau)
to take off one's hat; (se déshabiller) to
take something off; (ciel) to clear

décrire [dekrir] /39/ vt to describe

décrocher [dekrɔʃe] /1/ vt (dépendre)
to take down; (téléphone) to take
off the hook; (: pour répondre): ~ **(le
téléphone)** to pick up ou lift the
receiver; (fig: contrat etc) to get, land
▷ vi (fam: abandonner) to drop out;
(: cesser d'écouter) to switch off

déçu, e [desy] pp de **décevoir**

dédaigner [dedɛɲe] /1/ vt to
despise, scorn; (négliger) to disregard,
spurn; **dédaigneux, -euse** adj
scornful, disdainful; **dédain** nm
scorn, disdain

dedans [dədɑ̃] adv inside; (pas en
plein air) indoors, inside ▷ nm inside;
au ~ inside

dédicacer [dedikase] /3/ vt: ~ **(à qn)**
to sign (for sb), autograph (for sb)

dédier [dedje] /7/ vt: ~ **à** to dedicate
to

dédommagement [dedɔmaʒmɑ̃]
nm compensation

dédommager [dedɔmaʒe] /3/ vt:
~ **qn (de)** to compensate sb (for)

dédouaner [dedwane] /1/ vt to clear
through customs

déduire [deduir] /38/ vt: ~ **qch (de)**
(ôter) to deduct sth (from); (conclure)
to deduce ou infer sth (from)

défaillance [defajɑ̃s] nf (syncope)
blackout; (fatigue) (sudden) weakness

no pl; (technique) fault, failure; **~ cardiaque** heart failure

défaire [defɛʀ] /60/ vt (installation, échafaudage) to take down, dismantle; (paquet etc, nœud, vêtement) to undo; **se ~ de** to come undone; **se ~ de** to get rid of

défait, e [defɛ, -ɛt] adj (visage) haggard, ravaged ▷ vb défaire

défaut [defo] nm (moral) fault, failing, defect; (d'étoffe, métal) fault, flaw; (manque, carence) **~ de** shortage of; **prendre qn en ~** to catch sb out; **faire ~** (manquer) to be lacking; **à ~ de** for lack ou want of

défavorable [defavɔʀabl] adj unfavourable (BRIT), unfavorable (US)

défavoriser [defavɔʀize] /1/ vt to put at a disadvantage

défectueux, -euse [defɛktɥø, -øz] adj faulty, defective

défendre [defɑ̃dʀ] /41/ vt to defend; (interdire) to forbid; **se défendre** vi to defend o.s.; **~ à qn qch/de faire** to forbid sb sth/to do; **il se défend** (fig) he can hold his own; **se ~ de/contre** to protect o.s. from/against; **se ~ de** (se garder de) to refrain from

défense [defɑ̃s] nf defence; (d'éléphant etc) tusk; **ministre de la ~** Minister of Defence (BRIT), Defence Secretary; **"~ de fumer/cracher"** "no smoking/spitting"

défi [defi] nm challenge; **lancer un ~ à qn** to challenge sb; **sur un ton de ~** defiantly

déficit [defisit] nm (Comm) deficit

défier [defje] /7/ vt (provoquer) to challenge; (fig) to defy; **~ qn de faire** to challenge ou defy sb to do

défigurer [defigyʀe] /1/ vt to disfigure

défilé [defile] nm (Géo) (narrow) gorge ou pass; (soldats) parade; (manifestants) procession, march

défiler [defile] /1/ vi (troupes) to march past; (sportifs) to parade; (manifestants) to march; (visiteurs) to pour, stream; **faire ~ un document** (Inform) to scroll a document; **se défiler** vi: **il s'est défilé** (fam) he wriggled out of it

définir [definiʀ] /2/ vt to define

définitif, -ive [definitif, -iv] adj (final) final, definitive; (pour longtemps) permanent, definitive; (sans appel) definite ▷ nf: **en définitive** eventually; (somme toute) when all is said and done; **définitivement** adv permanently

déformer [defɔʀme] /1/ vt to put out of shape; (pensée, fait) to distort; **se déformer** vi to lose its shape

défouler [defule] /1/: **se défouler** vi to unwind, let off steam

défunt, e [defɛ̃, -ɛ̃t] adj: **son ~ père** his late father ▷ nm/f deceased

dégagé, e [degaʒe] adj (route, ciel) clear; **sur un ton ~** casually

dégager [degaʒe] /3/ vt (exhaler) to give off; (délivrer) to free, extricate; (désencombrer) to clear; (isoler, mettre en valeur) to bring out; **se dégager** vi (passage, ciel) to clear; **~ qn de** (engagement, parole etc) to release ou free sb from

dégâts [dega] nmpl damage sg; **faire des ~** to damage

dégel [deʒɛl] nm thaw; **dégeler** /5/ vt to thaw (out)

dégivrer [deʒivʀe] /1/ vt (frigo) to defrost; (vitres) to de-ice

dégonflé, e [degɔ̃fle] adj (pneu) flat

dégonfler [degɔ̃fle] /1/ vt (pneu, ballon) to let down, deflate; **se dégonfler** vi (fam) to chicken out

dégouliner [deguline] /1/ vi to trickle, drip

dégourdi, e [deguʀdi] adj smart, resourceful

dégourdir [deguʀdiʀ] /2/ vt: **se ~ (les jambes)** to stretch one's legs

dégoût [degu] nm disgust, distaste; **dégoûtant, e** adj disgusting; **dégoûté, e** adj disgusted; **dégoûté**

de sick of; **dégoûter** /1/ vt to disgust;
dégoûter qn de qch to put sb off sth
dégrader [degʀade] /1/ vt (Mil:
officier) to degrade; (abîmer) to
damage, deface; **se dégrader** vi
(relations, situation) to deteriorate
degré [dəgʀe] nm degree
dégressif, -ive [degʀesif, -iv] adj on
a decreasing scale
dégringoler [degʀɛ̃gɔle] /1/ vi to
tumble (down)
déguisement [degizmɑ̃] nm (pour
s'amuser) fancy dress
déguiser [degize] /1/: **se déguiser
(en)** vi (se costumer) to dress up (as);
(pour tromper) to disguise o.s. (as);
dégustation [degystasjɔ̃] nf (de
fromages etc) sampling; **~ de vin(s)**
wine-tasting
déguster [degyste] /1/ vt (vins)
to taste; (fromages etc) to sample;
(savourer) to enjoy
dehors [dəɔʀ] adv outside; (en plein
air) outdoors ▷ nm outside ▷ nmpl
(apparences) appearances; **mettre** ou
jeter ~ to throw out; **au ~** outside;
au ~ de outside; **en ~ de** apart from
déjà [deʒa] adv already; (auparavant)
before, already
déjeuner [deʒœne] /1/ vi to (have)
lunch; (le matin) to have breakfast
▷ nm lunch
delà [dəla] adv: **en ~ (de), au ~ (de)**
beyond
délacer [delase] /3/ vt (chaussures) to
undo, unlace
délai [delɛ] nm (attente) waiting period;
(sursis) extension (of time); (temps
accordé) time limit; **sans ~** without
delay; **dans les ~s** within the time limit
délaisser [delese] /1/ vt to abandon,
desert
délasser [delɑse] /1/ vt to relax; **se
délasser** vi to relax
délavé, e [delave] adj faded
délayer [deleje] /8/ vt (Culin) to
mix (with water etc); (peinture) to
thin down

delco® [dɛlko] nm (Auto) distributor
délégué, e [delege] nm/f
representative
déléguer [delege] /6/ vt to delegate
délibéré, e [delibeʀe] adj (conscient)
deliberate
délicat, e [delika, -at] adj delicate;
(plein de tact) tactful; (attentionné)
thoughtful; **délicatement** adv
delicately; (avec douceur) gently
délice [delis] nm delight
délicieux, -euse [delisjø, -øz]
adj (au goût) delicious; (sensation,
impression) delightful
délimiter [delimite] /1/ vt (terrain) to
delimit, demarcate
délinquant, e [delɛ̃kɑ̃, -ɑ̃t] adj, nm/f
delinquent
délirer [deliʀe] /1/ vi to be delirious;
tu délires! (fam) you're crazy!
délit [deli] nm (criminal) offence
délivrer [delivʀe] /1/ vt (prisonnier)
to (set) free, release; (passeport,
certificat) to issue
deltaplane® [dɛltaplan] nm
hang-glider
déluge [delyʒ] nm (biblique) Flood;
(grosse pluie) downpour
demain [d(ə)mɛ̃] adv tomorrow;
~ matin/soir tomorrow morning/
evening
demande [d(ə)mɑ̃d] nf (requête)
request; (revendication) demand;
(formulaire) application; (Écon): **la ~**
demand; **"~s d'emploi"** situations
wanted'
demandé, e [d(ə)mɑ̃de] adj
(article etc): **très ~** (very) much in
demand
demander [d(ə)mɑ̃de] /1/ vt to
ask for; (date, heure, chemin) to
ask; (requérir, nécessiter) to require,
demand; **~ qch à qn** to ask sb for sth;
~ à qn de faire to ask sb to do; **se ~
si/pourquoi** etc to wonder if/why
etc; **je ne demande pas mieux** I'm
asking nothing more; **demandeur,
-euse** nm/f: **demandeur d'asile**

asylum-seeker; **demandeur d'emploi** job-seeker

démangeaison [demãʒεzɔ̃] nf itching; **avoir des ~s** to be itching

démanger [demãʒe] /3/ vi to itch

démaquillant [demakijã] nm make-up remover

démaquiller [demakije] /1/ vt: **se démaquiller** to remove one's make-up

démarche [demaʁʃ] nf (allure) gait, walk; (intervention) step; (fig: intellectuelle) thought processes pl; **faire les ~s nécessaires (pour obtenir qch)** to take the necessary steps (to obtain sth)

démarrage [demaʁaʒ] nm start

démarrer [demaʁe] /1/ vi (conducteur) to start (up); (véhicule) to move off; (travaux, affaire) to get moving; **démarreur** nm (Auto) starter

démêlant, e [demɛlã, -ãt] adj: **crème ~e** (hair) conditioner ▷ nm conditioner

démêler [demele] /1/ vt to untangle; **démêlés** nmpl problems

déménagement [demenaʒmã] nm move; **entreprise/camion de ~** removal (BRIT) ou moving (US) firm/van

déménager [demenaʒe] /3/ vt (meubles) to (re)move ▷ vi to move (house); **déménageur** nm removal man

démerder [demɛʁde] /1/: **se démerder** vi (fam!) to bloody well manage for o.s.

démettre [demɛtʁ] /56/ vt: **~ qn de** (fonction, poste) to dismiss sb from; **se ~ l'épaule** etc to dislocate one's shoulder etc

demeurer [d(ə)mœʁe] /1/ vi (habiter) to live; (rester) to remain

demi, e [dəmi] /62/ half; **et ~: trois heures/bouteilles et ~es** three and a half hours/bottles ▷ nm (bière: ≈ 0.25 litre) ≈ half-pint; **il est 2 heures et ~e** it's half past 2; **il est midi et ~** it's

half past 12; **à ~** half-; **à la ~e** (heure) on the half-hour; **demi-douzaine** nf half-dozen, half a dozen; **demi-finale** nf semifinal; **demi-frère** nm half-brother; **demi-heure** nf: **une demi-heure** a half-hour, half an hour; **demi-journée** nf half-day, half a day; **demi-litre** nm half-litre (BRIT), half a litre (US), half a litre ou liter; **demi-livre** nf half-pound, half a pound; **demi-pension** nf half-board; **demi-pensionnaire** nm/f: **être demi-pensionnaire** to take school lunches

démis, e [demi] adj (épaule etc) dislocated

demi-sœur [dəmisœʁ] nf half-sister

démission [demisjɔ̃] nf resignation; **donner sa ~** to give ou hand in one's notice; **démissionner** /1/ vi to resign

demi-tarif [dəmitaʁif] nm half-price; (Transports) half-fare; **voyager à ~** to travel half-fare

demi-tour [dəmituʁ] nm about-turn; **faire ~** to turn (and go) back

démocratie [demokʁasi] nf democracy; **démocratique** adj democratic

démodé, e [demɔde] adj old-fashioned

demoiselle [d(ə)mwazɛl] nf (jeune fille) young lady; (célibataire) single lady, maiden lady; **~ d'honneur** bridesmaid

démolir [demɔliʁ] /2/ vt to demolish

démon [demɔ̃] nm (enfant turbulent) devil, demon; **le D~** the Devil

démonstration [demɔ̃stʁasjɔ̃] nf demonstration

démonter [demɔ̃te] /1/ vt (machine etc) to take down, dismantle; **se démonter** vi (meuble) to be dismantled, be taken to pieces; (personne) to lose countenance

démontrer [demɔ̃tʁe] /1/ vt to demonstrate

démouler [demule] /1/ vt to turn out

démuni, e [demyni] adj (sans argent) impoverished; **~ de** without

d

dénicher [denife] /1/ vt (fam: objet) to unearth; (: restaurant etc) to discover

dénier [denje] /7/ vt to deny

dénivellation [denivelasjɔ̃] nf (pente) ramp

dénombrer [denɔ̃bʀe] /1/ vt to count

dénomination [denɔminasjɔ̃] nf designation, appellation

dénoncer [denɔ̃se] /3/ vt to denounce; **se dénoncer** to give o.s. up, come forward

dénouement [denumɑ̃] nm outcome

dénouer [denwe] /1/ vt to unknot, undo

denrée [dɑ̃ʀe] nf (aussi: **~ alimentaire**) food(stuff)

dense [dɑ̃s] adj dense; **densité** nf density

dent [dɑ̃] nf tooth; **~ de lait/sagesse** milk/wisdom tooth; **dentaire** adj dental; **cabinet dentaire** dental surgery

dentelle [dɑ̃tɛl] nf lace no pl

dentier [dɑ̃tje] nm denture

dentifrice [dɑ̃tifʀis] nm: (**pâte**) **~** toothpaste

dentiste nm/f dentist

dentition [dɑ̃tisjɔ̃] nf teeth pl

dénué, e [denɥe] adj: **~ de** devoid of

déodorant [deɔdɔʀɑ̃] nm deodorant

déontologie [deɔ̃tɔlɔʒi] nf (professional) code of practice

dépannage [depanaʒ] nm: **service/camion de ~** (Auto) breakdown service/truck

dépanner [depane] /1/ vt (voiture, télévision) to fix, repair; (fig) to bail out, help out; **dépanneuse** nf breakdown lorry (BRIT), tow truck (US)

dépareillé, e [depaʀeje] adj (collection, service) incomplete; (gant, volume, objet) odd

départ [depaʀ] nm departure; (Sport) start; **au ~** at the start; **la veille de son ~** the day before he leaves/left

département [depaʀtəmɑ̃] nm department

○ **DÉPARTEMENTS**

○ France is divided into 96
○ administrative units called
○ *départements*. These local
○ government divisions are headed
○ by a state-appointed 'préfet',
○ and administered by an elected
○ 'Conseil général'. *Départements* are
○ usually named after prominent
○ geographical features such as
○ rivers or mountain ranges.

dépassé, e [depase] adj superseded, outmoded; (fig) out of one's depth

dépasser [depase] /1/ vt (véhicule, concurrent) to overtake; (endroit) to pass, go past; (somme, limite) to exceed; (fig: en beauté etc) to surpass, outshine ▷ vi (jupon) to show; **se dépasser** to excel o.s.

dépaysé, e [depeize] adj disoriented

dépaysement [depeizmɑ̃] nm change of scenery

dépêcher [depeʃe] /1/: **se dépêcher** vi to hurry

dépendance [depɑ̃dɑ̃s] nf dependence no pl; (bâtiment) outbuilding

dépendre [depɑ̃dʀ] /41/ vt: **~ de** vt to depend on, to be dependent on; **ça dépend** it depends

dépens [depɑ̃] nmpl: **aux ~ de** at the expense of

dépense [depɑ̃s] nf spending no pl, expense, expenditure no pl; **dépenser** /1/ vt to spend; (fig) to expend, use up; **se dépenser** vi to exert o.s.

dépeupler [depœple] /1/: **se dépeupler** vi to become depopulated

dépilatoire [depilatwaʀ] adj: **crème ~** hair-removing ou depilatory cream

dépister [depiste] /1/ vt to detect; (voleur) to track down

dépit [depi] *nm* vexation, frustration; **en ~ de** in spite of; **en ~ du bon sens** contrary to all good sense; **dépité, e** *adj* vexed, frustrated

déplacé, e [deplase] *adj (propos)* out of place, uncalled-for

déplacement [deplasmã] *nm (voyage)* trip, travelling *no pl*; **en ~** away (on a trip)

déplacer [deplase] /3/ *vt (table, voiture)* to move, shift; **se déplacer** *vi* to move; *(voyager)* to travel; **se ~ une vertèbre** to slip a disc

déplaire [depleʀ] /54/ *vi*: **ceci me déplaît** I don't like this, I dislike this; **se ~ quelque part** to dislike it *ou* be unhappy somewhere; **déplaisant, e** *adj* disagreeable

dépliant [deplijã] *nm* leaflet

déplier [deplije] /7/ *vt* to unfold

déposer [depoze] /1/ *vt (gén: mettre, poser)* to lay down, put down; *(à la banque, à la consigne)* to deposit; *(passager)* to drop (off), set down; *(roi)* to depose; *(marque)* to register; *(plainte)* to lodge; **se déposer** *vi* to settle; **dépositaire** *nm/f (Comm)* agent; **déposition** *nf* statement

dépôt [depo] *nm (à la banque, sédiment)* deposit; *(entrepôt, réserve)* warehouse, store

dépourvu, e [depuʀvy] *adj* ~ **de** lacking in, without; **prendre qn au ~** to catch sb unawares

dépression *nf* depression; **~ (nerveuse)** (nervous) breakdown

déprimant, e [depʀimã, -ãt] *adj* depressing

déprimer [depʀime] /1/ *vt* to depress

MOT-CLÉ

depuis [depɥi] *prép* **1** *(point de départ dans le temps)* since; **il habite Paris depuis 1983/l'an dernier** he has been living in Paris since 1983/last year; **depuis quand?** since when?;

depuis quand le connaissez-vous? how long have you known him?
2 *(temps écoulé)* for; **il habite Paris depuis cinq ans** he has been living in Paris for five years; **je le connais depuis trois ans** I've known him for three years
3 *(lieu)*: **il a plu depuis Metz** it's been raining since Metz; **elle a téléphoné depuis Valence** she rang from Valence
4 *(quantité, rang)* from; **depuis les plus petits jusqu'aux plus grands** from the youngest to the oldest
▶ *adv (temps)* since (then); **je ne lui ai pas parlé depuis** I haven't spoken to him since (then); **depuis que** *conj* (ever) since; **depuis qu'il m'a dit ça** (ever) since he said that to me

député, e [depyte] *nm/f (Pol)* ≈ Member of Parliament (BRIT), ≈ Congressman/woman (US)

dérangement [deʀãʒmã] *nm (gêne, déplacement)* trouble; *(gastrique etc)* disorder; **en ~** *(téléphone)* out of order

déranger [deʀãʒe] /3/ *vt (personne)* to trouble, bother; *(projets)* to disrupt, upset; *(objets, vêtements)* to disarrange; **se déranger** *vi*: **surtout ne vous dérangez pas pour moi** please don't put yourself out on my account; **est-ce que cela vous dérange si ...?** do you mind if ...?

déraper [deʀape] /1/ *vi (voiture)* to skid; *(personne, semelles, couteau)* to slip

dérégler [deʀegle] /6/ *vt (mécanisme)* to put out of order; *(estomac)* to upset

dérisoire [deʀizwaʀ] *adj* derisory

dérive [deʀiv] *nf*: **aller à la ~** *(Navig, fig)* to drift

dérivé, e [deʀive] *nm (Tech)* by-product

dermatologue [deʀmatɔlɔg] *nm/f* dermatologist

dernier, -ière [deʀnje, -jeʀ] *adj* last; *(le plus récent: gén avant n)* latest, last; **lundi/le mois ~** last Monday/month; **le ~ cri** the last word (in fashion); **en ~** last; **ce ~, cette dernière** the latter; **dernièrement** adv recently

dérogation [deʀɔgasjɔ̃] nf (special) dispensation

dérouiller [deʀuje] /1/ vt: **se ~ les jambes** to stretch one's legs (fig)

déroulement [deʀulmɑ̃] nm (d'une opération etc) progress

dérouler [deʀule] /1/ vt (ficelle) to unwind; **se dérouler** vi (avoir lieu) to take place; (se passer) to go; **tout s'est déroulé comme prévu** everything went as planned

dérouter [deʀute] /1/ vt (avion, train) to reroute, divert; (étonner) to disconcert, throw (out)

derrière [deʀjɛʀ] adv, prép behind ▷ nm (d'une maison) back; (postérieur) behind, bottom; **les pattes de ~** the back legs, the hind legs; **par ~** from behind; (fig) behind one's back

des [de] art voir **de**

dès [dɛ] prép from; **~ que** as soon as; **~ son retour** as soon as he was (ou is) back

désaccord [dezakɔʀ] nm disagreement

désagréable [dezagreabl] adj unpleasant

désagrément [dezagremɑ̃] nm annoyance, trouble no pl

désaltérer [dezaltere] /6/ vt: **se désaltérer** to quench one's thirst

désapprobateur, -trice [dezapʀɔbatœʀ, -tʀis] adj disapproving

désapprouver [dezapʀuve] /1/ vt to disapprove of

désarmant, e [dezaʀmɑ̃, -ɑ̃t] adj disarming

désastre [dezastʀ] nm disaster; **désastreux, -euse** adj disastrous

désavantage [dezavɑ̃taʒ] nm disadvantage; **désavantager** /3/ vt to put at a disadvantage

descendre [desɑ̃dʀ] /41/ vt (escalier, montagne) to go (ou come) down; (valise, paquet) to take ou get down; (étagère etc) to lower; (fam: abattre) to shoot down ▷ vi to go (ou come) down; (passager: s'arrêter) to get out, alight; **~ à pied/en voiture** to walk/drive down; **~ de** (famille) to be descended from; **~ du train** to get out of ou off the train; **~ d'un arbre** to climb down from a tree; **~ de cheval** to dismount; **~ à l'hôtel** to stay at a hotel

descente [desɑ̃t] nf descent, going down; (chemin) way down; (Ski) downhill (race); **au milieu de la ~** halfway down; **~ de lit** bedside rug; **~ (de police)** raid

description [dɛskʀipsjɔ̃] nf description

déséquilibre [dezekilibʀ] nm (position): **être en ~** to be unsteady; (fig: des forces, du budget) imbalance

désert, e [dezɛʀ, -ɛʀt] adj deserted ▷ nm desert; **désertique** adj desert cpd

désespéré, e [dezɛspeʀe] adj desperate

désespérer [dezɛspeʀe] /6/ vi: **~ de** to despair of; **désespoir** nm despair; **en désespoir de cause** in desperation

déshabiller [dezabije] /1/ vt to undress; **se déshabiller** vi to undress (o.s.)

déshydraté, e [dezidʀate] adj dehydrated

désigner [dezine] /1/ vt (montrer) to point out, indicate; (dénommer) to denote; (candidat etc) to name

désinfectant, e [dezɛ̃fɛktɑ̃, -ɑ̃t] adj, nm disinfectant

désinfecter [dezɛ̃fɛkte] /1/ vt to disinfect

désintéressé, e [dezɛ̃teʀese] adj disinterested, unselfish

désintéresser [dezɛ̃teʀese] /1/ vt: **se désintéresser (de)** to lose interest (in)

désintoxication [dezɛ̃tɔksikasjɔ̃]
nf: **faire une cure de ~** to have ou
undergo treatment for alcoholism (ou
drug addiction)

désinvolte [dezɛ̃vɔlt] adj casual,
off-hand

désir [deziʀ] nm wish; (fort, sensuel)
desire; **désirer** /1/ vt to want, wish
for; (sexuellement) to desire; **je désire
...** (formule de politesse) I would like ...

désister [deziste] /1/: **se désister** vi
to stand down, withdraw

désobéir [dezɔbeiʀ] /2/ vi:
~ (à qn/qch) to disobey (sb/sth);
désobéissant, e adj disobedient

désodorisant [dezɔdɔʀizɑ̃] nm air
freshener, deodorizer

désolé, e [dezɔle] adj (paysage)
desolate; **je suis ~** I'm sorry

désordonné, e [dezɔʀdɔne] adj
untidy

désordre [dezɔʀdʀ] nm
disorder(liness), untidiness; (anarchie)
disorder; **en ~** in a mess, untidy

désormais [dezɔʀmɛ] adv from
now on

desquels, desquelles [dekɛl]
voir **lequel**

dessécher [deseʃe] /6/: **se
dessécher** vi to dry out

desserrer [deseʀe] /1/ vt to loosen;
(frein) to release

dessert [desɛʀ] nm dessert, pudding

desservir [desɛʀviʀ] /14/ vt (ville,
quartier) to serve; (débarrasser): **~ (la
table)** to clear the table

dessin [desɛ̃] nm (œuvre, art) drawing;
(motif) pattern, design; **~ animé**
cartoon (film); **~ humoristique**
cartoon; **dessinateur, -trice**
nm/f drawer; (de bandes dessinées)
cartoonist; (industriel) draughtsman
(BRIT), draftsman (US); **dessiner**
/1/ vt to draw; (concevoir) to design; **se
dessiner** vi (forme) to be outlined; (fig:
solution) to emerge

dessous [d(ə)su] adv underneath,
beneath ▷ nm underside; **les voisins
du ~** the downstairs neighbours
▷ nmpl (sous-vêtements) underwear
sg; **en ~** underneath; below; **par ~**
underneath; below; **avoir le ~** to get
the worst of it; **dessous-de-plat** nm
inv tablemat

dessus [d(ə)sy] adv on top;
(collé, écrit) on it ▷ nm top; **les
voisins/l'appartement du ~** the
upstairs neighbours/flat; **en ~** above;
par ~ adv over it; prép over; **au-**
above; **avoir/prendre le ~** to have/
get the upper hand; **sens ~ dessous**
upside down; **dessus-de-lit** nm inv
bedspread

destin [dɛstɛ̃] nm fate; (avenir) destiny

destinataire [dɛstinatɛʀ] nm/f
(Postes) addressee; (d'un colis)
consignee

destination [dɛstinasjɔ̃] nf (lieu)
destination; (usage) purpose; **à ~ de**
bound for; travelling to

destiner [dɛstine] /1/ vt:
(envisager de donner) to intend sb to
have sth; (adresser) to intend sth for
sb; **se ~ à l'enseignement** to intend
to become a teacher; **être destiné à**
(usage) to be intended ou meant for

détachant [detaʃɑ̃] nm stain remover

détacher [detaʃe] /1/ vt (enlever)
to detach, remove; (délier) to untie;
(Admin): **~ qn (auprès de ou à)**
to post sb (to); **se détacher** vi
(se séparer) to come off; (page) to
come out; (se défaire) to come
undone; **se ~ sur** to stand out
against; **se ~ de** (se désintéresser) to
grow away from

détail [detaj] nm detail; (Comm): **le
~** retail; **au ~** (Comm) retail; **en ~** in
detail; **détaillant, e** nm/f retailer;
détaillé, e adj (récit, plan, explications)
detailed; (facture) itemized; **détailler**
/1/ vt (expliquer) to explain in detail

détecter [detɛkte] /1/ vt to detect

détective [detɛktiv] nm detective;
~ (privé) private detective ou
investigator

déteindre [detɛ̃dʀ] /52/ vi to fade; (au lavage) to run; ~ **sur** (vêtement) to run into; (fig) to rub off on

détendre [detɑ̃dʀ] /41/ vt (personne, atmosphère, corps, esprit) to relax; **se détendre** vi (ressort) to lose its tension; (personne) to relax

détenir [det(ə)niʀ] /22/ vt (fortune, objet, secret) to be in possession of; (prisonnier) to detain; (record) to hold; ~ **le pouvoir** to be in power

détente [detɑ̃t] nf relaxation

détention [detɑ̃sjɔ̃] nf (de fortune, objet, secret) possession; (captivité) detention; ~ **préventive** (pre-trial) custody

détenu, e [det(ə)ny] nm/f prisoner
▷ nm/f prisoner

détergent [deteʀʒɑ̃] nm detergent

détériorer [deterjɔʀe] /1/ vt to damage; **se détériorer** vi to deteriorate

déterminé, e [detɛʀmine] adj (résolu) determined; (précis) specific, definite

déterminer [detɛʀmine] /1/ vt (fixer) to determine; ~ **qn à faire** to decide sb to do; **se ~ à faire** to make up one's mind to do

détester [detɛste] /1/ vt to hate, detest

détour [detuʀ] nm detour; (tournant) bend, curve; **ça vaut le ~** it's worth the trip; **sans ~** (fig) plainly

détourné, e [detuʀne] adj (sentier, chemin, moyen) roundabout

détourner [detuʀne] /1/ vt to divert; (par la force) to hijack; (yeux, tête) to turn away; (de l'argent) to embezzle; **se détourner** vi to turn away

détraquer [detʀake] /1/ vt to put out of order; (estomac) to upset; **se détraquer** vi to go wrong

détrimen [detʀimɑ̃] nm: **au ~ de** to the detriment of

détroit [detʀwa] nm strait

détruire [detʀɥiʀ] /38/ vt to destroy

dette [dɛt] nf debt

DEUG [dœg] sigle m = **Diplôme d'études universitaires générales**

● **DEUG**
●
● French students sit their DEUG
● ('diplôme d'études universitaires
● générales') after two years at
● university. They can then choose to
● leave university altogether, or go
● on to study for their 'licence'. The
● certificate specifies the student's
● major subject and may be awarded
● with distinction.

deuil [dœj] nm (perte) bereavement; (période) mourning; **prendre le/être en ~** to go into/be in mourning

deux [dø] num two; **les ~** both; **ses ~ mains** both his hands, his two hands; à **~ fois** twice; **deuxième** num second; **deuxième** adv secondly; **deux-pièces** nm inv (tailleur) two-piece (suit); (de bain) two-piece (swimsuit); (appartement (US); **deux-points** nm inv colon sg; **deux-roues** nm inv two-wheeled vehicle

devais etc [dəvɛ] vb voir **devoir**

dévaluation [devalɥasjɔ̃] nf devaluation

devancer [d(ə)vɑ̃se] /3/ vt to get ahead of; (arriver avant) to arrive before; (prévenir) to anticipate

devant [d(ə)vɑ̃] adv in front; (à distance: en avant) ahead ▷ prép in front of; (en avant) ahead ▷ nm front; (avec mouvement: passer) past; (fig) before, in front of (: vis-à-vis) in front; **prendre les ~s** to make the first move; **les pattes de ~** the front legs, the forelegs; **par ~** (boutonner) at the front; (entrer) the front way; **aller au-~ de qn** to go out to meet sb; **aller au-~ de** (désirs de qn) to anticipate

devanture [d(ə)vɑ̃tyʀ] nf (étalage) display; (vitrine) (shop) window

développement [dev(ə)lɔpmɑ̃]
nm development; **pays en voie de
~** developing countries; **~ durable**
sustainable development
développer [dev(ə)lɔpe] /1/ *vt* to
develop; **se développer** *vi* to develop
devenir [dəv(ə)niʀ] /22/ *vi* to
become; **que sont-ils devenus?**
what has become of them?
devez [dəve] *vb voir* **devoir**
déviation [devjasjɔ̃] *nf* (*Auto*)
diversion (*BRIT*), detour (*US*)
devienne *etc* [dəvjɛn] *vb voir* **devenir**
deviner [d(ə)vine] /1/ *vt* to guess;
(*apercevoir*) to distinguish; **devinette**
nf riddle
devis [d(ə)vi] *nm* estimate, quotation
devise [dəviz] *nf* (*formule*) motto,
watchword; **devises** *nfpl* (*argent*)
currency *sg*
dévisser [devise] /1/ *vt* to unscrew,
undo; **se dévisser** *vi* to come
unscrewed
devoir [d(ə)vwaʀ] /28/ *nm* duty;
(*Scol*) homework *no pl* (: *en classe*)
exercise ▷ *vt* (*argent*, *respect*): **~ qch
(à qn)** to owe (sb) sth; **combien
est-ce que je vous dois?** how
much do I owe you?; **il doit le faire**
(*obligation*) he has to do it, he must
do it; **cela devait arriver un jour**
it was bound to happen; **il doit
partir demain** (*intention*) he is due
to leave tomorrow; **il doit être tard**
(*probabilité*) it must be late
dévorer [devɔʀe] /1/ *vt* to devour;
(*feu*, *soucis*) to consume; **~ qn/qch
des yeux** *ou* **du regard** (*convoitise*) to
eye sb/sth greedily
dévoué, e [devwe] *adj* devoted
dévouer [devwe] /1/: **se dévouer** *vi*
(*se sacrifier*): **se ~ (pour)** to sacrifice
o.s. (for); (*se consacrer*): **se ~ à** to
devote ou dedicate o.s. to
devrai *etc* [dəvʀe] *vb voir* **devoir**
dézipper [dezipe] /1/ *vt* to unzip
diabète [djabɛt] *nm* diabetes *sg*;
diabétique *nm/f* diabetic

diable [djabl] *nm* devil
diabolo [djabɔlo] *nm* (*boisson*)
lemonade and fruit cordial
diagnostic [djagnɔstik] *nm*
diagnosis *sg*; **diagnostiquer** /1/ *vt*
to diagnose
diagonal, e, -aux [djagɔnal, -o]
adj, nf diagonal; **en ~** diagonally
diagramme [djagʀam] *nm* chart,
graph
dialecte [djalɛkt] *nm* dialect
dialogue [djalɔg] *nm* dialogue
diamant [djamɑ̃] *nm* diamond
diamètre [djamɛtʀ] *nm* diameter
diapo [djapo], **diapositive**
[djapozitiv] *nf* transparency, slide
diarrhée [djaʀe] *nf* diarrhoea
dictateur [diktatœʀ] *nm* dictator;
dictature [diktatyʀ] *nf* dictatorship
dictée [dikte] *nf* dictation
dicter [dikte] /1/ *vt* to dictate
dictionnaire [diksjɔnɛʀ] *nm*
dictionary
dièse [djɛz] *nm* sharp
diesel [djezɛl] *nm, adj inv* diesel
diète [djɛt] *nf* (*jeûne*) starvation
diet; (*régime*) diet; **diététique** *adj*:
magasin diététique health food
shop (*BRIT*) ou store (*US*)
dieu, x [djø] *nm* god; **D~** God; **mon
D~!** good heavens!
différemment [difeʀamɑ̃] *adv*
differently
différence [difeʀɑ̃s] *nf* difference; **à
la ~ de** unlike; **différencier** /7/ *vt* to
differentiate
différent, e [difeʀɑ̃, -ɑ̃t] *adj*
(*dissemblable*) different; **~ de** different
from; **~s objets** different ou various
objects
différer [difeʀe] /6/ *vt* to postpone,
put off ▷ *vi*: **~ (de)** to differ (from)
difficile [difisil] *adj* difficult;
(*exigeant*) hard to please;
difficilement *adv* with difficulty
difficulté [difikylte] *nf* difficulty;
en ~ (*bateau*, *alpiniste*) in trouble ou
difficulties

diffuser [difyze] /1/ vt (chaleur, bruit, lumière) to diffuse; (émission, musique) to broadcast; (nouvelle, idée) to circulate; (Comm) to distribute

digérer [diʒere] /6/ vt to digest; (fig: accepter) to stomach, put up with; **digestif, -ive** nm (after-dinner) liqueur; **digestion** nf digestion

digne [diɲ] adj dignified; **~ de** worthy of; **~ de foi** trustworthy; **dignité** nf dignity

digue [dig] nf dike, dyke

dilemme [dilɛm] nm dilemma

diligence [diliʒɑ̃s] nf stagecoach

diluer [dilɥe] /1/ vt to dilute

dimanche [dimɑ̃ʃ] nm Sunday

dimension [dimɑ̃sjɔ̃] nf (grandeur) size; (dimensions) dimensions

diminuer [diminɥe] /1/ vt to reduce, decrease; (ardeur etc) to lessen; (dénigrer) to belittle ▷ vi to decrease, diminish; **diminutif** /1/ vt (surnom) pet name

dinde [dɛ̃d] nf turkey

dindon [dɛ̃dɔ̃] nm turkey

dîner [dine] /1/ vi to have dinner ▷ nm to have dinner

dingue [dɛ̃g] adj (fam) crazy

dinosaure [dinozɔʀ] nm dinosaur

diplomate [diplɔmat] adj diplomatic ▷ nm diplomat; (fig) diplomatist; **diplomatie** nf diplomacy

diplôme [diplom] nm diploma certificate; **avoir des ~s** to have qualifications; **diplômé, e** adj qualified

dire [diʀ] /37/ vt to say; (secret, mensonge) to tell; **se dire** (à soi-même) to say to oneself ▷ nm: **au ~ de** according to; **~ qch à qn** to tell sb sth; **~ à qn qu'il fasse** ou **de faire** to tell sb to do; **on dit que** they say that; **on dirait que** it looks (ou sounds etc) as though; **que dites-vous de** (penser) what do you think of; **si cela lui dit** if he fancies it; **dis donc!**, **dites donc!** (pour attirer l'attention)

hey!; (au fait) by the way; **ceci** ou **cela dit** that being said; **ça ne se dit pas** (impoli) you shouldn't say that; (pas en usage) you don't say that

direct, e [diʀɛkt] adj direct ▷ nm: **en ~** (émission) live; **directement** adv directly

directeur, -trice [diʀɛktœʀ, -tʀis] nm/f (d'entreprise) director; (de service) manager/eress; (d'école) head(teacher) (BRIT), principal (US)

direction [diʀɛksjɔ̃] nf (d'entreprise) management; (Auto) steering; (sens) direction; **"toutes ~s"** "all routes"

dirent [diʀ] vb voir **dire**

dirigeant, e [diʀiʒɑ̃, -ɑ̃t] adj (classes) ruling ▷ nm/f (d'un parti) leader

diriger [diʀiʒe] /3/ vt (entreprise) to manage, run; (véhicule) to steer; (orchestre) to conduct; (recherches, travaux) to supervise; (arme): **~ sur** to point ou level ou aim at; **se diriger** vi (s'orienter) to find one's way; **~ son regard sur** to look in the direction of; **se ~ vers** ou **sur** to make ou head for

dis [di] vb voir **dire**

discerner [diseʀne] /1/ vt to discern, make out

discipline [disiplin] nf discipline; **discipliner** /1/ vt to discipline

discontinu, e [diskɔ̃tiny] adj intermittent

discontinuer [diskɔ̃tinɥe] /1/ vi: **sans ~** without stopping, without a break

discothèque [diskɔtek] nf (boîte de nuit) disco(thèque)

discours [diskuʀ] nm speech

discret, -ète [diskʀɛ, -ɛt] adj discreet; (fig: musique, style, maquillage) unobtrusive; **discrétion** nf discretion; **à discrétion** as much as one wants

discrimination nf discrimination; **sans ~** indiscriminately

discussion [diskysjɔ̃] nf discussion

discutable [diskytabl] adj debatable

discuter [diskyte] /1/ vt (contester) to question, dispute; (débattre: prix) to discuss ▷ vi to talk; (protester) to argue; **~ de** to discuss

dise etc [diz] vb voir **dire**

disjoncteur [disʒɔ̃ktœʀ] nm (Élec) circuit breaker

disloquer [disbke] /1/: **se disloquer** vi (parti, empire) to break up; (meuble) to come apart; **se~l'épaule** to dislocate one's shoulder

disons etc [dizɔ̃] vb voir **dire**

disparaître [disparetr] /57/ vi to disappear; (se perdre: traditions etc) to die out; (personne: mourir) to die; **faire ~** (objet, tache, trace) to remove; (personne, douleur) to get rid of

disparition [disparisjɔ̃] nf disappearance; **espèce en voie de ~** endangered species

disparu, e [dispary] nm/f missing person; **être porté ~** to be reported missing

dispensaire [dispɑ̃sɛʀ] nm community clinic

dispenser [dispɑ̃se] /1/ vt: **~ qn de** to exempt sb from

disperser [disperse] /1/ vt to scatter; **se disperser** vi to scatter

disponible [disponibl] adj available

disposé, e [dispoze] adj: **bien/mal ~** (humeur) in a good/bad mood; **~ à** (prêt à) willing ou prepared to

disposer [dispoze] /1/ vt to arrange ▷ vi: **vous pouvez ~** you may leave; **~ de** to have (at one's disposal); **se ~ à faire** to prepare to do, be about to do

dispositif [dispozitif] nm device; (fig) system, plan of action

disposition [dispozisjɔ̃] nf (arrangement) arrangement, layout; (humeur) mood; **prendre ses ~s** to make arrangements; **avoir des ~s pour la musique** etc to have a special aptitude for music etc; **à la ~ de qn** at sb's disposal; **je suis à votre ~** I am at your service

disproportionné, e [disproporsjone] adj disproportionate, out of all proportion

dispute [dispyt] nf quarrel, argument; **disputer** /1/ vt (match) to play; (combat) to fight; **se disputer** vi to quarrel

disqualifier [diskalifje] /7/ vt to disqualify

disque [disk] nm (Mus) record; (forme, pièce) disc; (Sport) discus; **~ compact** compact disc; **~ dur** hard disk; **disquette** nf floppy disc, diskette

dissertation [disɛʀtasjɔ̃] nf (Scol) essay

dissimuler [disimyle] /1/ vt to conceal

dissipé, e [disipe] adj (indiscipliné) unruly

dissolvant [disɔlvɑ̃] nm nail polish remover

dissuader [disɥade] /1/ vt: **~ qn de faire/de qch** to dissuade sb from doing/from sth

distance [distɑ̃s] nf distance; (fig: écart) gap; **à ~** at ou from a distance; **distancer** /3/ vt to outdistance

distant, e [distɑ̃, -ɑ̃t] adj (réservé) distant; **~ de** (lieu) far away ou a long way from

distillerie [distilʀi] nf distillery

distinct, e [distɛ̃(kt), distɛ̃kt] adj distinct; **distinctement** [distɛ̃ktəmɑ̃] adv distinctly; **distinctif, -ive** adj distinctive

distingué, e [distɛ̃ge] adj distinguished

distinguer [distɛ̃ge] /1/ vt to distinguish; **se distinguer** vi: **se ~ (de)** to distinguish o.s. ou be distinguished (from)

distraction [distraksjɔ̃] nf (manque d'attention) absent-mindedness; (passe-temps) distraction, entertainment

distraire [distrɛʀ] /50/ vt (déranger) to distract; (divertir) to entertain, divert; **se distraire** vi to amuse ou enjoy o.s.; **distrait, e** [distʀɛ, -ɛt] pp de **distraire** ⊳ adj absent-minded

distrayant, e [distʀɛjɑ̃, -ɑ̃t] adj entertaining

distribuer [distʀibɥe] /1/ vt to distribute; to hand out; (Cartes) to deal (out); (courrier) to deliver; **distributeur** nm (Auto, Comm) distributor; (automatique) (vending) machine; **distributeur de billets** cash dispenser

dit, e [di, dit] pp de **dire** ⊳ adj (fixé): **le jour ~** the arranged day; (surnommé): **X, ~ Pierrot** X, known as ou called Pierrot

dites [dit] vb voir **dire**

divan [divɑ̃] nm divan

divers, es [divɛʀ, -ɛʀs] adj (varié) diverse, varied; (différent) different, various; **~es** personnes various ou several people

diversité [divɛʀsite] nf diversity, variety

divertir [divɛʀtiʀ] /2/: **se divertir** vi to amuse ou enjoy o.s.; **divertissement** nm entertainment

diviser [divize] /1/ vt to divide; **division** nf division

divorce [divɔʀs] nm divorce; **divorcé, e** nm/f divorcee; **divorcer** /3/ vi to get a divorce, get divorced; **divorcer de** ou **d'avec qn** to divorce sb

divulguer [divylge] /1/ vt to disclose

dix [di, dis, diz] num ten; **dix-huit** num eighteen; **dix-huitième** num eighteenth; **dixième** num tenth; **dix-neuf** num nineteen; **dix-neuvième** num nineteenth; **dix-sept** num seventeen; **dix-septième** num seventeenth

dizaine [dizɛn] nf: **une ~ (de)** about ten, ten or so

do [do] nm (note) C; (en chantant la gamme) do(h)

docile [dɔsil] adj docile

dock [dɔk] nm dock; **docker** nm docker

docteur, e [dɔktœʀ] nm/f doctor; **doctorat** nm: **doctorat (d'Université)** ≈ doctorate

doctrine [dɔktʀin] nf doctrine

document [dɔkymɑ̃] nm document; **documentaire** adj, nm documentary; **documentation** nf documentation, literature; **documenter** /1/ vt: **se documenter (sur)** to gather information ou material (on ou about)

dodo [dodo] nm: **aller faire ~** to go to beddy-byes

dogue [dɔg] nm mastiff

doigt [dwa] nm finger; **à deux ~s de** within an ace (BRIT) ou an inch of; **un ~ de lait/whisky** a drop of milk/ whisky; **~ de pied** toe

doit etc [dwa] vb voir **devoir**

dollar [dɔlaʀ] nm dollar

domaine [dɔmɛn] nm estate, property; (fig) domain, field

domestique [dɔmɛstik] adj domestic ▷ nm/f servant, domestic

domicile [dɔmisil] nm home, place of residence; **à ~** at home; **livrer à ~** to deliver; **domicilié, e** adj: **être domicilié à** to have one's home in ou at

dominant, e [dɔminɑ̃, -ɑ̃t] adj (opinion) predominant

dominer [dɔmine] /1/ vt to dominate; (sujet) to master; (surpasser) to outclass, surpass; (surplomber) to tower above, dominate ▷ vi to be in the dominant position; **se dominer** vt to control o.s.

domino [dɔmino] nm domino; **dominos** nmpl (jeu) dominoes sg

dommage [dɔmaʒ] nm: **~s (dégâts, pertes)** damage no pl; **c'est ~ de faire/que** it's a shame ou pity to do/ that; **quel ~!, c'est ~!** what a pity ou shame!

dompter [dɔ̃(p)te] /1/ vt to tame; **dompteur, -euse** nm/f trainer

DOM-ROM [dɔmʀɔm] sigle m(pl) (= Département(s) et Régions/

Territoire(s) d'outre-mer French overseas departments and regions

don [dɔ̃] nm gift; (charité) donation; **avoir des ~s pour** to have a gift ou talent for; **elle a le ~ de m'énerver** she's got a knack of getting on my nerves

donc [dɔ̃k] conj therefore, so; (après une digression) so, then

dongle [dɔ̃gl] nm dongle

donné, e [dɔne] adj (convenu: lieu, heure) given; (pas cher) very cheap; **données** nfpl data; **c'est ~** it's a gift; **étant ~ que ...** given that ...

donner [dɔne] /1/ vt to give; (vieux habits etc) to give away; (spectacle) to put on; **~ qch à qn** to give sb sth, give sth to sb; **~ sur** (fenêtre, chambre) to look (out) onto; **ça donne soif/faim** it makes you (feel) thirsty/hungry; **se ~ à fond (à son travail)** to give one's all (to one's work); **se ~ du mal ou de la peine (pour faire qch)** to go to a lot of trouble (to do sth); **s'en ~ à cœur joie** (fam) to have a great time (of it)

⊘ **MOT-CLÉ**

dont [dɔ̃] pron relatif **1** (appartenance: objets) whose, of which; (: êtres animés) whose; **la maison dont le toit est rouge** the house the roof of which is red, the house whose roof is red; **l'homme dont je connais la sœur** the man whose sister I know **2** (parmi lesquel(le)s: **deux livres, dont l'un est ...** two books, one of which is ...; **il y avait plusieurs personnes, dont Gabrielle** there were several people, among them Gabrielle; **10 blessés, dont 2 grièvement** 10 injured, 2 of them seriously **3** (complément d'adjectif, de verbe): **le fils dont il est si fier** the son he's so proud of; **le pays dont il est originaire** the country he's from; **ce**

dont je parle what I'm talking about; **la façon dont il l'a fait** the way (in which) he did it

dopage [dɔpaʒ] nm (Sport) drug use; (de cheval) doping

doré, e [dɔre] adj golden; (avec dorure) gilded, gilt

dorénavant [dɔrenavɑ̃] adv henceforth

dorer [dɔre] /1/ vt to gild; **(faire) ~** (Culin) to brown

dorloter [dɔrlɔte] /1/ vt to pamper

dormir [dɔrmir] /16/ vi to sleep; (être endormi) to be asleep

dortoir [dɔrtwar] nm dormitory

dos [do] nm back; (de livre) spine; **"voir au ~"** "see over"; **de ~** from the back

dosage [dozaʒ] nm mixture

dose [doz] nf dose; **doser** /1/ vt to measure out; **il faut savoir doser ses efforts** you have to be able to pace yourself

dossier [dosje] nm (renseignements, fichier) file; (de chaise) back; (Presse) feature; (Inform) folder; **un ~ scolaire** a school report

douane [dwan] nf customs pl; **douanier, -ière** adj customs cpd ▷ nm customs officer

double [dubl] adj, adv double ▷ nm (autre exemplaire) duplicate, copy; (sosie) double; (Tennis) doubles sg; (2 fois plus): **le ~ (de)** twice as much (ou many) (as); **en ~ (exemplaire)** in duplicate; **faire ~ emploi** to be redundant; **double-cliquer** /1/ vi (Inform) to double-click

doubler [duble] /1/ vt (multiplier par 2) to double; (vêtement) to line; (dépasser) to overtake, pass; (film) to dub; (acteur) to stand in for ▷ vi to double

doublure [dublyr] nf lining; (Ciné) stand-in

douce [dus] adj f voir **doux**; **douceâtre** adj sickly sweet;

doucement adv gently; (lentement) slowly; **douceur** nf softness; (de climat) mildness; (de quelqu'un) gentleness

douche [duʃ] nf shower; **prendre une ~** to have ou take a shower; **doucher** /1/: **se doucher** vi to have ou take a shower

doué, e [dwe] adj gifted, talented; **être ~ pour** to have a gift for

douille [duj] nf (Élec) socket

douillet, te [dujɛ, -ɛt] adj cosy; (péj: à la douleur) soft

douleur [dulœʀ] nf pain; (chagrin) grief, distress; **douloureux, -euse** adj painful

doute [dut] nm doubt; **sans ~** no doubt; (probablement) probably; **sans nul ou aucun ~** without (a) doubt; **douter** /1/ vt to doubt; **douter de** (allié, sincérité de qn) to have (one's) doubts about, doubt; (résultat, réussite) to be doubtful of; **douter que** to doubt whether ou if; **se douter de qch/que** to suspect sth/that; **je m'en doutais** I suspected as much; **douteux, -euse** adj (incertain) doubtful; (péj) dubious-looking

Douvres [duvʀ] n Dover

doux, douce [du, dus] adj soft; (sucré, agréable) sweet; (peu fort: moutarde etc, clément: climat) mild; (pas brusque) gentle

douzaine [duzɛn] nf (12) dozen; (environ 12): **une ~ (de)** a dozen or so

douze [duz] num twelve; **douzième** num twelfth

dragée [dʀaʒe] nf sugared almond

draguer [dʀage] /1/ vt (rivière) to dredge; (fam) to try and pick up

dramatique [dʀamatik] adj dramatic; (tragique) tragic ⊳ nf (TV) (television) drama

drame [dʀam] nm drama

drap [dʀa] nm (de lit) sheet; (tissu) woollen fabric

drapeau, x [dʀapo] nm flag

drap-housse [dʀaus] nm fitted sheet

dresser [dʀese] /1/ vt (mettre vertical, monter) to put up, erect; (liste, bilan, contrat) to draw up; (animal) to train; **se dresser** vi (falaise, obstacle) to stand; (personne) to draw o.s. up; **~ l'oreille** to prick up one's ears; **~ qn contre qn d'autre** to set sb against sb else

drogue [dʀɔg] nf drug; **la ~** drugs pl; **drogué, e** nm/f drug addict; **droguer** /1/ vt (victime) to drug; **se droguer** vi (aux stupéfiants) to take drugs; (péj: de médicaments) to dose o.s. up; **droguerie** nf ≈ hardware shop (BRIT) ou store (US); **droguiste** nm ≈ keeper (ou owner) of a hardware shop ou store

droit, e [dʀwa, dʀwat] adj (non courbe) straight; (vertical) upright, straight; (fig: loyal, franc) upright, straight(forward); (opposé à gauche) right, right-hand ⊳ adv straight ⊳ nm (prérogative) right; (taxe) duty, tax; (: d'inscription) fee; (lois, branche): **le ~** law ⊳ nf (Pol) right (wing); **avoir le ~ de** to be allowed to; **avoir ~ à** to be entitled to; **être dans son ~** to be within one's rights; **à ~e** on the right; (direction) (to the) right; **~s d'auteur** royalties; **~s d'inscription** enrolment ou registration fees; **droitier, -ière** adj right-handed

drôle [dʀol] adj (amusant) funny, amusing; (bizarre) funny, peculiar; **un ~ de…** (bizarre) a strange ou funny…; (intensif) an incredible…, a terrific…

dromadaire [dʀɔmadɛʀ] nm dromedary

du [dy] art voir **de**

dû, due [dy] pp de **devoir** ⊳ adj (somme) owing, owed; (causé par): **dû à** due to ⊳ nm due

dune [dyn] nf dune

duplex [dyplɛks] nm (appartement) split-level apartment, duplex

duquel [dykɛl] voir **lequel**

dur, e [dyʀ] *adj (pierre, siège, travail, problème)* hard; *(lumière, voix, climat)* harsh; *(sévère)* hard, harsh; *(cruel)* hard(-hearted); *(porte, col)* stiff; *(viande)* tough ▷ *adv* hard ▷ *nm (fam: meneur)* tough nut; **~ d'oreille** hard of hearing

durant [dyʀɑ̃] *prép (au cours de)* during; *(pendant)* for; **des mois ~** for months

durcir [dyʀsiʀ] /2/ *vt*, *vi* to harden; **se durcir** *vi* to harden

durée [dyʀe] *nf* length; *(d'une pile etc)* life; **de courte ~** *(séjour, répit)* brief

durement [dyʀmɑ̃] *adv* harshly

durer [dyʀe] /1/ *vi* to last

dureté [dyʀte] *nf* hardness; harshness; stiffness; toughness

durit® [dyʀit] *nf (car radiator)* hose

duvet [dyvɛ] *nm* down

DVD *sigle m (= digital versatile disc)* DVD

dynamique [dinamik] *adj* dynamic; **dynamisme** *nm* dynamism

dynamo [dinamo] *nf* dynamo

dyslexie [disleksi] *nf* dyslexia, word blindness

e

eau, x [o] *nf* water ▷ *nfpl (Méd)* waters; **prendre l'~** to leak, let in water; **tomber à l'~** *(fig)* to fall through; **~ de Cologne** eau de Cologne; **~ courante** running water; **~ douce** fresh water; **~ gazeuse** sparkling (mineral) water; **~ de Javel** bleach; **~ minérale** mineral water; **~ plate** still water; **~ salée** salt water; **~ de toilette** toilet water; **eau-de-vie** *nf* brandy

ébène [ebɛn] *nf* ebony; **ébéniste** [ebenist] *nm* cabinetmaker

éblouir [ebluiʀ] /2/ *vt* to dazzle

éboueur [ebwœʀ] *nm* dustman *(BRIT)*, garbage man *(US)*

ébouillanter [ebujɑ̃te] /1/ *vt* to scald; *(Culin)* to blanch

éboulement [ebulmɑ̃] *nm* rock fall

ébranler [ebʀɑ̃le] /1/ *vt* to shake; *(rendre instable)* to weaken; **s'ébranler** *vi (partir)* to move off

ébullition [ebylisjɔ̃] *nf* boiling point; **en ~** boiling

écaille [ekaj] *nf (de poisson)* scale; *(matière)* tortoiseshell; **écailler** /1/ *vt (poisson)* to scale; **s'écailler** *vi* to flake ou peel (off)

écart [ekar] *nm* gap; **à l'~** out of the way; **à l'~ de** away from; **faire un ~** *(voiture)* to swerve

écarté, e [ekarte] *adj (lieu)* out-of-the-way, remote; *(ouvert):* **les jambes ~es** legs apart; **les bras ~s** arms outstretched

écarter [ekarte] /1/ *vt (séparer)* to move apart, separate; *(éloigner)* to push back, move away; *(ouvrir: bras, jambes)* to spread, open; *(: rideau)* to draw (back); *(éliminer: candidat, possibilité)* to dismiss; **s'écarter** *vi* to part; *(personne)* to move away; **s'~ de** to wander from

échafaudage [eʃafodaʒ] *nm* scaffolding

échalote [eʃalɔt] *nf* shallot

échange [eʃɑ̃ʒ] *nm* exchange; **en ~ de** in exchange ou return for; **échanger** /3/ *vt:* **échanger qch (contre)** to exchange sth for

échantillon [eʃɑ̃tijɔ̃] *nm* sample

échapper [eʃape] /1/: **~ à** *vt (gardien)* to escape (from); *(punition, péril)* to escape; **~ à qn** *(détail, sens)* to escape sb; *(objet qu'on tient)* to slip out of sb's hands; **laisser ~** *(cri etc)* to let out; **l'~ belle** to have a narrow escape

écharde [eʃard] *nf* splinter (of wood)

écharpe [eʃarp] *nf* scarf; **avoir le bras en ~** to have one's arm in a sling

échauffer [eʃofe] /1/ *vt (métal, moteur)* to overheat; **s'échauffer** *vi (Sport)* to warm up; *(discussion)* to become heated

échéance [eʃeɑ̃s] *nf (d'un paiement: date)* settlement date; *(fig)* deadline; **à brève/longue ~** in the short/long term

échéant [eʃeɑ̃]: **le cas ~** *adv* if the case arises

échec [eʃɛk] *nm* failure; *(Échecs):* **~ et mat/au roi** checkmate/check;

échecs *nmpl (jeu)* chess *sg*; **tenir en ~** to hold in check

échelle [eʃɛl] *nf* ladder; *(fig, d'une carte)* scale

échelon [eʃ(ə)lɔ̃] *nm (d'échelle)* rung; *(Admin)* grade; **échelonner** /1/ *vt* to space out, spread out

échiquier [eʃikje] *nm* chessboard

écho [eko] *nm* echo; **échographie** *nf:* **passer une échographie** to have a scan

échouer [eʃwe] /1/ *vi* to fail; **s'échouer** *vi* to run aground

éclabousser [eklabuse] /1/ *vt* to splash

éclair [eklɛr] *nm (d'orage)* flash of lightning, lightning *no pl; (gâteau)* éclair

éclairage [eklɛraʒ] *nm* lighting

éclaircie [eklɛrsi] *nf* bright ou sunny interval

éclaircir [eklɛrsir] /2/ *vt* to lighten; *(fig: mystère)* to clear up; *(point)* to clarify; **s'éclaircir** *vi (ciel)* to brighten up; **s'~ la voix** to clear one's throat; **éclaircissement** *nm* clarification

éclairer [eklɛre] /1/ *vt (lieu)* to light (up); *(personne: avec une lampe de poche etc)* to light the way for; *(fig: rendre compréhensible)* to shed light on ▸ *vi:* **~ mal/bien** to give a poor/good light; **s'~ à la bougie/l'électricité** to use candlelight/have electric lighting

éclat [ekla] *nm (de bombe, de verre)* fragment; *(du soleil, d'une couleur etc)* brightness, brilliance; *(d'une cérémonie)* splendour; *(scandale):* **faire un ~** to cause a commotion; **~ de rire** burst ou roar of laughter; **~ de voix** shout

éclatant, e [eklatɑ̃, -ɑ̃t] *adj* brilliant

éclater [eklate] /1/ *vi (pneu)* to burst; *(bombe)* to explode; *(guerre, épidémie)* to break out; *(groupe, parti)* to break up; **~ de rire/en sanglots** to burst out laughing/sobbing

écluse [eklyz] *nf* lock

écœurant, e [ekœrɑ̃, -ɑ̃t] *adj* sickening; *(gâteau etc)* sickly

écœurer [ekœre] vt: ~ **qn** (nourriture) to make sb feel sick; (fig: conduite, personne) to disgust sb

école [ekɔl] nf school; **aller à l'~** to go to school; ~ **maternelle** nursery school; ~ **primaire** primary (BRIT) ou grade (US) school; ~ **secondaire** secondary (BRIT) ou high (US) school; **écolier, -ière** nm/f schoolboy/girl

écologie [ekɔlɔʒi] nf ecology; **écologique** adj environment-friendly; **écologiste** nm/f ecologist

économe [ekɔnɔm] adj thrifty ▷ nm/f (de lycée etc) bursar (BRIT), treasurer (US)

économie [ekɔnɔmi] nf economy; (gain: d'argent, de temps etc) saving; (science) economics sg; **économies** nfpl (pécule) savings; **économique** adj (avantageux) economical; (Écon) economic; **économiser** /1/ vt, vi to save

écorce [ekɔrs] nf bark; (de fruit) peel

écorcher [ekɔrʃe] /1/ vt: **s'~ le genou** etc to scrape ou graze one's knee etc; **écorchure** nf graze

écossais, e [ekɔsɛ, -ɛz] adj Scottish ▷ nm/f: **É~, -e** Scot

Écosse [ekɔs] nf: **l'~** Scotland

écotaxe [ekɔtaks] nf green tax

écouter [ekute] /1/ vt to listen to; **s'écouter** vi (malade) to be a bit of a hypochondriac; **si je m'écoutais** if I followed my instincts; **écouteur** nm (Tél) receiver; **écouteurs** nmpl (casque) headphones, headset sg

écran [ekrɑ̃] nm screen; **le petit ~** television; ~ **tactile** touchscreen; ~ **total** sunblock

écrasant, e [ekrazɑ̃, -ɑ̃t] adj overwhelming

écraser [ekraze] /1/ vt to crush; (piéton) to run over; **s'~ (au sol)** vi to crash; **s'~ contre** to crash into

écrémé, e [ekreme] adj (lait) skimmed

écrevisse [ekrəvis] nf crayfish inv

écrire [ekrir] /39/ vt, vi to write; **s'écrire** vi to write to one another;

ça s'écrit comment? how is it spelt?; **écrit** nm (examen) written paper; **par écrit** in writing

écriteau, x [ekrito] nm notice, sign

écriture [ekrityr] nf writing; **écritures** nfpl (Comm) accounts, books; **l'É~ (sainte), les É~s** the Scriptures

écrivain [ekrivɛ̃] nm writer

écrou [ekru] nm nut

écrouler [ekrule] /1/: **s'écrouler** vi to collapse

écru, e [ekry] adj off-white, écru

écume [ekym] nf foam

écureuil [ekyrœj] nm squirrel

écurie [ekyri] nf stable

eczéma [egzema] nm eczema

EDF sigle f (= Électricité de France) national electricity company

Édimbourg [edɛ̃buʀ] n Edinburgh

éditer [edite] /1/ vt (publier) to publish; (annoter) to edit; **éditeur, -trice** nm/f publisher; **édition** nf edition; **l'édition** publishing

édredon [edrədɔ̃] nm eiderdown

éducateur, -trice [edykatœr, -tris] nm/f teacher; (en école spécialisée) instructor

éducatif, -ive [edykatif, -iv] adj educational

éducation [edykasjɔ̃] nf education; (familiale) upbringing; (manières) (good) manners pl

édulcorant [edylkɔrɑ̃] nm sweetener

éduquer [edyke] /1/ vt to educate; (élever) to bring up

effacer [efase] /3/ vt to erase, rub out; **s'effacer** vi (inscription etc) to wear off; (pour laisser passer) to step aside

effarant, e [efarɑ̃, -ɑ̃t] adj alarming

effectif, -ive [efɛktif, -iv] adj real ▷ nm (Scol) total number of pupils; (Comm) manpower sg; **effectivement** adv (réellement) actually, really; (en effet) indeed

effectuer [efɛktɥe] /1/ vt (opération, mission) to carry out; (déplacement, trajet) to make

effervescent, e [efɛʀvesɑ̃, -ɑ̃t] adj effervescent

effet [efɛ] nm effect; (impression) impression; **effets** nmpl (vêtements etc) things; **faire ~** (médicament) to take effect; **faire de l'~** (impressionner) to make an impression; **faire bon/mauvais ~ sur qn** to make a good/bad impression on sb; **en ~** indeed; **~ de serre** greenhouse effect

efficace [efikas] adj (personne) efficient; (action, médicament) effective; **efficacité** nf efficiency; effectiveness

effondrer [efɔ̃dʀe] /1/: **s'effondrer** vi to collapse

efforcer [efɔʀse] /3/: **s'efforcer de** vt: **s'~ de faire** to try hard to do

effort [efɔʀ] nm effort

effrayant, e [efʀɛjɑ̃, -ɑ̃t] adj frightening

effrayer [efʀeje] /8/ vt to frighten, scare; **s'effrayer (de)** to be frightened ou scared (by)

effréné, e [efʀene] adj wild

effronté, e [efʀɔ̃te] adj insolent

effroyable [efʀwajabl] adj horrifying, appalling

égal, e, -aux [egal, -o] adj equal; (constant: vitesse) steady ⊳ nm/f equal; **être ~ à** (prix, nombre) to be equal to; **ça m'est ~** it's all the same to me, I don't mind; **sans ~** matchless, unequalled; **d'~ à ~** as equals; **également** adv equally; (aussi) too, as well; **égaler** /1/ vt to equal; **égaliser** /1/ vt (sol, salaires) to level (out); (chances) to equalize ⊳ vi (Sport) to equalize; **égalité** nf equality; **être à égalité (de points)** to be level

égard [egaʀ] nm: **égards** nmpl consideration sg; **à cet ~** in this respect; **par ~ pour** out of consideration for; **à l'~ de** towards

égarer [egaʀe] /1/ vt to mislay; **s'égarer** vi to get lost, lose one's way; (objet) to go astray

églefin [egləfɛ̃] nm haddock

église [egliz] nf church; **aller à l'~** to go to church

égoïsme [egoism] nm selfishness; **égoïste** adj selfish

égout [egu] nm sewer

égoutter [egute] /1/ vi to drip; **s'égoutter** vi to drip; **égouttoir** nm draining board; (mobile) draining rack

égratignure [egʀatiɲyʀ] nf scratch

Égypte [eʒipt] nf: **l'~** Egypt; **égyptien, ne** adj Egyptian ⊳ nm/f: **Égyptien, ne** Egyptian

eh [e] excl hey!; **eh bien** well

élaborer [elabɔʀe] /1/ vt to elaborate; (projet, stratégie) to work out; (rapport) to draft

élan [elɑ̃] nm (Zool) elk, moose; (Sport) run up; (fig: de tendresse etc) surge; **prendre son ~/de l'~** to take a run up/gather speed

élancer [elɑ̃se] /3/: **s'élancer** vi to dash, hurl o.s.

élargir [elaʀʒiʀ] /2/ vt to widen; **s'élargir** vi to widen; (vêtement) to stretch

élastique [elastik] adj elastic ⊳ nm (de bureau) rubber band; (pour la couture) elastic no pl

élection [elɛksjɔ̃] nf election

électricien, ne [elɛktʀisjɛ̃, -ɛn] nm/f electrician

électricité [elɛktʀisite] nf electricity; **allumer/éteindre l'~** to put on/off the light

électrique [elɛktʀik] adj electric(al)

électrocuter [elɛktʀɔkyte] /1/ vt to electrocute

électroménager [elɛktʀomenaʒe] adj: **appareils ~s** domestic (electrical) appliances ⊳ nm: **l'~** household appliances

électronique [elɛktʀɔnik] adj electronic ⊳ nf electronics sg

élégance [elegɑ̃s] nf elegance

élégant, e [elegɑ̃, -ɑ̃t] adj elegant

élément [elemã] nm element; (pièce) component, part; **élémentaire** adj elementary

éléphant [elefã] nm elephant

élevage [el(ə)vaʒ] nm breeding; (de bovins) cattle breeding ou rearing; **truite d'~** farmed trout

élevé, e [el(ə)ve] adj high; **bien/mal ~** well-/ill-mannered

élève [elev] nm/f pupil

élever [el(ə)ve] /5/ vt (enfant) to bring up, raise; (bétail, volaille) to breed; (hausser: taux, niveau) to raise; (édifier: monument) to put up, erect; **s'élever** vi (avion, alpiniste) to go up; (niveau, température, aussi) to rise; **s'~ à** (frais, dégâts) to amount to, add up to; **s'~ contre** to rise up against; **~ la voix** to raise one's voice; **éleveur, -euse** nm/f stock breeder

éliminatoire [eliminatwaʀ] nf (Sport) heat

éliminer [elimine] /1/ vt to eliminate

élire [eliʀ] /43/ vt to elect

elle [ɛl] pron (sujet: personne) she; (: chose) it; (complément) her; it; **~s** (sujet) they; (complément) them; **~-même** herself; itself; **~s-mêmes** themselves; voir **il**

éloigné, e [elwaɲe] adj distant, far-off; (parent) distant

éloigner [elwaɲe] /1/ vt (échéance) to put off, postpone; (soupçons, danger) to ward off; **~ qch (de)** to move ou take sth away (from); **s'éloigner (de)** (personne) to go away (from); (véhicule) to move away (from); (affectivement) to become estranged (from); **~ qn (de)** to take sb away ou remove sb (from)

élu, e [ely] pp de **élire** ⊳ nm/f (Pol) elected representative

Élysée [elize] nm: **le palais de l'~** the Élysée palace

émail, -aux [emaj, -o] nm enamel

e-mail [imel] nm email; **envoyer qch par ~** to email sth

émanciper [emãsipe] /1/: **s'émanciper** vi (fig) to become emancipated ou liberated

emballage [ãbalaʒ] nm (papier) wrapping; (carton) packaging

emballer [ãbale] /1/ vt to wrap (up); (dans un carton) to pack (up); (fig: fam) to thrill (to bits); **s'emballer** vi (moteur) to race; (cheval) to bolt; (fig: personne) to get carried away

embarcadère [ãbaʀkadɛʀ] nm landing stage (BRIT), pier

embarquement [ãbaʀkəmã] nm embarkation; (de marchandises) loading; (de passagers) boarding

embarquer [ãbaʀke] /1/ vt (personne) to embark; (marchandise) to load; (fam) to cart off ⊳ vi (passager) to board; **s'embarquer** vi to board; **s'~ dans** (affaire, aventure) to embark upon

embarras [ãbaʀa] nm (confusion) embarrassment; **être dans l'~** to be in a predicament ou an awkward position; **vous n'avez que l'~ du choix** the only problem is choosing

embarrassant, e [ãbaʀasã, -ãt] adj embarrassing

embarrasser [ãbaʀase] /1/ vt (encombrer) to clutter (up); (gêner) to hinder, hamper; to put in an awkward position; **s'embarrasser de** to burden o.s. with

embaucher [ãboʃe] /1/ vt to take on, hire

embêtant, e [ãbɛtã, -ãt] adj annoying

embêter [ãbete] /1/ vt to bother; **s'embêter** vi (s'ennuyer) to be bored

emblée [ãble]: **d'~** adv straightaway

embouchure [ãbuʃyʀ] nf (Géo) mouth

embourber [ãbuʀbe] /1/: **s'embourber** vi to get stuck in the mud

embouteillage [ãbutejaʒ] nm traffic jam, (traffic) holdup (BRIT)

embranchement [ɑ̃bʀɑ̃ʃmɑ̃] nm (routier) junction

embrasser [ɑ̃bʀase] /1/ vt to kiss; (sujet, période) to embrace, encompass

embrayage [ɑ̃bʀejaʒ] nm clutch

embrouiller [ɑ̃bʀuje] /1/ vt (fils) to tangle (up); (fiches, idées, personne) to muddle up; **s'embrouiller** vi to get in a muddle

embruns [ɑ̃bʀœ̃] nmpl sea spray sg

embué, e [ɑ̃bɥe] adj misted up

émeraude [em(ə)ʀod] nf emerald

émerger [emɛʀʒe] /3/ vi to emerge; (faire saillie, aussi fig) to stand out

émeri [em(ə)ʀi] nm: **toile** ou **papier ~** emery paper

émerveiller [emɛʀveje] /1/ vt to fill with wonder; **s'émerveiller de** to marvel at

émettre [emɛtʀ] /56/ vt (son, lumière) to give out, emit; (message etc: Radio) to transmit; (billet, timbre, emprunt, chèque) to issue; (hypothèse, avis) to voice, put forward ▷ vi to broadcast

émeus etc [emø] vb voir **émouvoir**

émeute [emøt] nf riot

émigrer [emigʀe] /1/ vi to emigrate

émincer [emɛ̃se] /3/ vt to slice thinly

émission [emisjɔ̃] nf (voir émettre) emission; (d'un message) transmission; (de billet, timbre, emprunt, chèque) issue; (Radio, TV) programme, broadcast

emmêler [ɑ̃mele] /1/ vt to tangle (up); (fig) to muddle up; **s'emmêler** vi to get into a tangle

emménager [ɑ̃menaʒe] /3/ vi to move in; **~ dans** to move into

emmener [ɑ̃m(ə)ne] /5/ vt to take (with one); (comme otage, capture) to take away; **~ qn au cinéma** to take sb to the cinema

emmerder [ɑ̃mɛʀde] /1/ (!) vt to bug, bother; **s'emmerder** vi to be bored stiff

émoticone [emotikon] nm smiley

émotif, -ive [emotif, -iv] adj emotional

émotion [emosjɔ̃] nf emotion

émouvoir [emuvwaʀ] /27/ vt to move; **s'émouvoir** vi to be moved; to be roused

empaqueter [ɑ̃pakte] /4/ vt to pack up

emparer [ɑ̃paʀe] /1/: **s'emparer de** vt (objet) to seize, grab; (comme otage, Mil) to seize; (peur etc) to take hold of

empêchement [ɑ̃pɛʃmɑ̃] nm (unexpected) obstacle, hitch

empêcher [ɑ̃peʃe] /1/ vt to prevent; **~ qn de faire** to prevent ou stop sb (from) doing; **il n'empêche que** nevertheless; **il n'a pas pu s'~ de rire** he couldn't help laughing

empereur [ɑ̃pʀœʀ] nm emperor

empiffrer [ɑ̃pifʀe] /1/: **s'empiffrer** vi (péj) to stuff o.s.

empiler [ɑ̃pile] /1/ vt to pile (up)

empire [ɑ̃piʀ] nm empire; (fig) influence

empirer [ɑ̃piʀe] /1/ vi to worsen, deteriorate

emplacement [ɑ̃plasmɑ̃] nm site

emploi [ɑ̃plwa] nm use; (poste) job, situation; (Comm, Écon) employment; **mode d'~** directions for use; **~ du temps** timetable, schedule

employé, e [ɑ̃plwaje] nm/f employee; **~ de bureau/banque** office/bank employee ou clerk

employer [ɑ̃plwaje] /8/ vt to use; (ouvrier, main-d'œuvre) to employ; **s'~ à qch/à faire** to apply ou devote o.s. to sth/to doing; **employeur, -euse** nm/f employer

empoigner [ɑ̃pwaɲe] /1/ vt to grab

empoisonner [ɑ̃pwazɔne] /1/ vt to poison; (empester: air, pièce) to stink out; (fam): **~ qn** to drive sb mad

emporter [ɑ̃pɔʀte] /1/ vt to take (with one); (en dérobant ou enlevant, emmener: blessés, voyageurs) to take away; (entraîner) to carry away ou along; (rivière, vent) to carry away; **s'emporter** vi (de colère) to fly into a rage; **l'~ (sur)** to get the upper hand (of); **plats à ~** take-away meals

empreint, e [ɑ̃pʀɛ̃, -ɛt] adj: **~ de** marked with ▷ **nf** (de pied, main) print; **~e** (digitale) fingerprint; **~e écologique** carbon footprint

empressé, e [ɑ̃pʀese] adj attentive

empresser [ɑ̃pʀese] /1/: **s'empresser** vi: **s'~ auprès de qn** to surround sb with attentions; **s'~ de faire** to hasten to do

emprisonner [ɑ̃pʀizɔne] /1/ vt to imprison

emprunt [ɑ̃pʀœ̃] nm loan (from debtor's point of view)

emprunter [ɑ̃pʀœ̃te] /1/ vt to borrow; (itinéraire) to take, follow

ému, e [emy] pp de **émouvoir** ▷ adj (gratitude) touched; (compassion) moved

MOT-CLÉ

en [ɑ̃] prép 1 (endroit, pays) in; (: direction) to; **habiter en France/ ville** to live in France/town; **aller en France/ville** to go to France/town

2 (moment, temps) in; **en été/juin** in summer/June; **en 3 jours/20 ans** in 3 days/20 years

3 (moyen) by; **en avion/taxi** by plane/taxi

4 (composition) made of; **c'est en verre/coton/laine** it's (made of) glass/cotton/wool; **un collier en argent** a silver necklace

5 (description, état): **une femme (habillée) en rouge** a woman (dressed) in red; **peindre qch en rouge** to paint sth red; **en T/étoile** T-/star- shaped; **en chemise/chaussettes** in one's shirt sleeves/socks; **en soldat** as a soldier; **cassé en plusieurs morceaux** broken into several pieces; **en réparation** being repaired, under repair; **en vacances** on holiday; **en deuil** in mourning; **le même en plus grand** the same but ou bigger

6 (avec gérondif) while; on; **en dormant** while sleeping, as one

sleeps; **en sortant** on going out, as he etc went out; **sortir en courant** to run out

7: **en tant que** as; **je te parle en ami** I'm talking to you as a friend

▷ pron 1 (indéfini): **j'en ai/veux** I have/want some; **en as-tu?** have you got any?; **je n'en veux pas** I don't want any; **j'en ai deux** I've got two; **combien y en a-t-il?** how many (of them) are there?; **j'en ai assez** I've got enough (of it ou them); (j'en ai marre) I've had enough

2 (provenance) from there; **j'en viens** I've come from there

3 (cause): **il en est malade/perd le sommeil** he is ill/can't sleep because of it

4 (complément de nom, d'adjectif, de verbe): **j'en connais les dangers** I know its ou the dangers; **j'en suis fier/ai besoin** I am proud of it/need it

encadrer [ɑ̃kɑdʀe] /1/ vt (tableau, image) to frame; (fig: entourer) to surround; (personnel, soldats etc) to train

encaisser [ɑ̃kese] /1/ vt (chèque) to cash; (argent) to collect; (fig: coup, défaite) to take

en-cas [ɑ̃kɑ] nm inv snack

enceinte [ɑ̃sɛ̃t] adj f: **~ (de six mois)** (six months) pregnant ▷ nf (mur) wall; (espace) enclosure; **~ (acoustique)** speaker

encens [ɑ̃sɑ̃] nm incense

encercler [ɑ̃sɛʀkle] /1/ vt to surround

enchaîner [ɑ̃ʃene] /1/ vt to chain up; (mouvements, séquences) to link (together) ▷ vi to carry on

enchanté, e [ɑ̃ʃɑ̃te] adj (ravi) delighted; (ensorcelé) enchanted; **~ (de faire votre connaissance)** pleased to meet you

enchère [ɑ̃ʃɛʀ] nf bid; **mettre/ vendre aux ~s** to put up for (sale by)/ sell by auction

enclencher [ɑ̃klɑ̃ʃe] /1/ vt
(*mécanisme*): to engage; **s'enclencher**
vi to engage

encombrant, e [ɑ̃kɔ̃brɑ̃, -ɑ̃t] adj
cumbersome, bulky

encombrement [ɑ̃kɔ̃brəmɑ̃] nm:
être pris dans un ~ to be stuck in a
traffic jam

encombrer [ɑ̃kɔ̃bre] /1/ vt to clutter
(up); (*gêner*) to hamper; **s'encombrer
de** (*bagages etc*) to load ou burden
o.s. with

○ **MOT-CLÉ**

encore [ɑ̃kɔr] adv **1** (*continuation*)
still; **il y travaille encore** he's still
working on it; **pas encore** not yet
2 (*de nouveau*) again; **j'irai encore
demain** I'll go again tomorrow;
encore une fois (once) again
3 (*en plus*) more; **encore un peu de
viande?** a little more meat?; **encore
deux jours** two more days
4 (*intensif*) even, still; **encore plus
fort/mieux** even louder/better,
louder/better still; **quoi encore?**
what now?
5 (*restriction*) even so ou then, only;
encore pourrais-je le faire si ...
even so, I might be able to do it if ...; **s'il
encore** if only

encourager [ɑ̃kuraʒe] /3/ vt to
encourage; **~ qn à faire qch** to
encourage sb to do sth
encourir [ɑ̃kurir] /11/ vt to incur
encre [ɑ̃kr] nf ink; **~ de Chine**
Indian ink
encyclopédie [ɑ̃siklɔpedi] nf
encyclopaedia
endetter [ɑ̃dete] /1/: **s'endetter**
vi to get into debt
endive [ɑ̃div] nf chicory no pl
endormi, e [ɑ̃dɔrmi] adj asleep
endormir [ɑ̃dɔrmir] /16/ vt to put
to sleep; (*chaleur etc*) to send to sleep;
(*Méd: dent, nerf*) to anaesthetize; (*fig:*
soupçons) to allay; **s'endormir** vi to
fall asleep, go to sleep

endroit [ɑ̃drwa] nm place; (*opposé à
l'envers*) right side; **à l'~** (*vêtement*)
the right way out; (*objet posé*) the right
way round
endurance [ɑ̃dyrɑ̃s] nf endurance
endurant, e [ɑ̃dyrɑ̃, -ɑ̃t] adj tough,
hardy
endurcir [ɑ̃dyrsir] /2/: **s'endurcir**
vi (*physiquement*) to become tougher;
(*moralement*) to become hardened
endurer [ɑ̃dyre] /1/ vt to endure,
bear
énergétique [enɛrʒetik] adj
(*aliment*) energizing
énergie [enɛrʒi] nf (*Physique*) energy;
(*Tech*) power; (*morale*) vigour, spirit;
énergique adj energetic; vigorous;
(*mesures*) drastic, stringent
énervant, e [enɛrvɑ̃, -ɑ̃t] adj
irritating, annoying
énerver [enɛrve] /1/ vt to irritate,
annoy; **s'énerver** vi to get excited,
get worked up
enfance [ɑ̃fɑ̃s] nf childhood
enfant [ɑ̃fɑ̃] nm/f child; **enfantin, e**
adj childlike; (*langage*) children's cpd
enfer [ɑ̃fɛr] nm hell
enfermer [ɑ̃fɛrme] /1/ vt to shut up;
(*à clef, interner*) to lock up; **s'enfermer**
to shut o.s. away
enfiler [ɑ̃file] /1/ vt (*vêtement*): to
slip on; (*perles*) to string; (*aiguille*) to
thread; **~ un tee-shirt** to slip into
a T-shirt
enfin [ɑ̃fɛ̃] adv at last; (*en énumérant*)
lastly; (*de restriction, résignation*) still;
(*pour conclure*) in a word; (*somme*
toute) after all
enflammer [ɑ̃flame] /1/:
s'enflammer vi to catch fire; (*Méd*) to
become inflamed
enflé, e [ɑ̃fle] adj swollen
enfler [ɑ̃fle] /1/ vi to swell (up)
enfoncer [ɑ̃fɔ̃se] /3/ vt (*clou*) to drive
in; (*faire pénétrer*): **~ qch dans** to push
(ou drive) sth into; (*forcer: porte*) to

break open; **s'enfoncer** vi to sink;
s' ~ dans to sink into; (forêt, ville) to
disappear into

enfouir [ãfwiʀ] /2/ vt (dans le sol) to
bury; (dans un tiroir etc) to tuck away

enfuir [ãfɥiʀ] /17/: **s'enfuir** vi to run
away ou off

engagement [ãɡaʒmã] nm
commitment; **sans ~** without
obligation

engager [ãɡaʒe] /3/ vt (embaucher)
to take on; (: artiste) to engage;
(commencer) to start; (lier) to bind,
commit; (impliquer, entraîner) to
involve; (investir) to invest, lay out;
(introduire, clé) to insert; (inciter):
~ qn à faire to urge sb to do;
s'engager vi (Mil) to enlist; (promettre)
to commit o.s.; (débuter: conversation etc)
to start (up); **s' ~ à faire** to undertake
to do; **s' ~ dans** (rue, passage) to turn
into; (fig: affaire, discussion) to enter
into, embark on

engelures [ãʒlyʀ] nfpl chilblains

engin [ãʒɛ̃] nm machine; (outil)
instrument; (Auto) vehicle; (Aviat)
aircraft inv

⬛ Attention à ne pas traduire engin
par le mot anglais engine.

engloutir [ãɡlutiʀ] /2/ vt to
swallow up

engouement [ãɡumã] nm (sudden)
passion

engouffrer [ãɡufʀe] /1/ vt to
swallow up, devour; **s'engouffrer
dans** to rush into

engourdir [ãɡuʀdiʀ] /2/ vt to numb;
(fig) to dull, blunt; **s'engourdir** vi to
go numb

engrais [ãɡʀɛ] nm manure;
~ (chimique) (chemical) fertilizer

engraisser [ãɡʀese] /1/ vt to
fatten (up)

engrenage [ãɡʀənaʒ] nm gears pl,
gearing; (fig) chain

engueuler [ãɡœle] /1/ vt (fam) to
bawl at ou out

enhardir [ãaʀdiʀ] /2/: **s'enhardir** vi
to grow bolder

énigme [eniɡm] nf riddle

enivrer [ãnivʀe] /1/ vt: **s'enivrer** to
get drunk

enjamber [ãʒãbe] /1/ vt to stride over

enjeu, x [ãʒø] nm stakes pl

enjoué, e [ãʒwe] adj playful

enlaidir [ãlediʀ] /2/ vt to make ugly
▷ vi to become ugly

enlèvement [ãlɛvmã] nm (rapt)
abduction, kidnapping

enlever [ãl(ə)ve] /5/ vt (ôter: gén)
to remove; (: vêtement, lunettes) to
take off; (emporter: ordures etc) to
collect; (kidnapper) to abduct, kidnap;
(obtenir: prix, contrat) to win; (prendre):
~ qch à qn to take sth (away) from sb

enliser [ãlize] /1/: **s'enliser** vi to sink,
get stuck

enneigé, e [ãneʒe] adj snowy

ennemi, e [ɛnmi] adj hostile; (Mil)
enemy cpd ▷ nm/f enemy

ennui [ãnɥi] nm (lassitude) boredom;
(difficulté) trouble no pl; **avoir des
~s** to have problems; **ennuyer**
/8/ vt (agacer) to annoy; (lasser) to bore;
s'ennuyer vi to be bored; **si cela ne
vous ennuie pas** if it's no trouble to
you; **ennuyeux, -euse** adj boring,
tedious; (agaçant) annoying

énorme [enɔʀm] adj enormous,
huge; **énormément** adv enormously;
énormément de neige/gens an
enormous amount of snow/number
of people

enquête [ãkɛt] nf (de journaliste,
de police) investigation; (judiciaire,
administrative) inquiry; (sondage
d'opinion) survey; **enquêter** /1/ vi to
investigate; **enquêter (sur)** to do a
survey (on)

enragé, e [ãʀaʒe] adj (Méd) rabid,
with rabies; (fig) fanatical

enrageant, e [ãʀaʒã, -ãt] adj
infuriating

enrager [ãʀaʒe] /3/ vi to be furious

enregistrement [ãʀ(ə)ʒistʀəmã]
nm recording; **~ des bagages**
baggage check-in

enregistrer [ɑ̃ʀ(ə)ʒistʀe] /1/ vt (Mus) to record; (fig: mémoriser) to make a mental note of; (bagages: à l'aéroport) to check in

enrhumer [ɑ̃ʀyme] /1/: **s'enrhumer** vi to catch a cold

enrichir [ɑ̃ʀiʃiʀ] /2/ vt to make rich(er); (fig) to enrich; **s'enrichir** vi to get rich(er)

enrouer [ɑ̃ʀwe] /1/: **s'enrouer** vi to go hoarse

enrouler [ɑ̃ʀule] /1/ vt (fil, corde) to wind (up); **s'enrouler** to coil up; **~ qch autour de** to wind sth (a)round

enseignant, e [ɑ̃sɛɲɑ̃, -ɑ̃t] nm/f teacher

enseignement [ɑ̃sɛɲ(ə)mɑ̃] nm teaching; (Admin) education

enseigner [ɑ̃sɛɲe] /1/ vt, vi to teach; **~ qch à qn/à qn que** to teach sb sth/sb that

ensemble [ɑ̃sɑ̃bl] adv together ▷ nm (assemblage) set; (vêtements) outfit; (unité, harmonie) unity; **l'~ du/de la** (totalité) the whole ou entire; **impression/idée d'~** overall ou general impression/idea; **dans l'~** (en gros) on the whole

ensoleillé, e [ɑ̃soleje] adj sunny

ensuite [ɑ̃sɥit] adv then, next; (plus tard) afterwards, later

entamer [ɑ̃tame] /1/ vt (pain, bouteille) to start; (hostilités, pourparlers) to open

entasser [ɑ̃tase] /1/ vt (empiler) to pile up, heap up; **s'entasser** vi (s'amonceler) to pile up; **s'~ dans** to cram into

entendre [ɑ̃tɑ̃dʀ] /41/ vt to hear; (comprendre) to understand; (vouloir dire) to mean; **s'entendre** vi (sympathiser) to get on; (se mettre d'accord) to agree; **j'ai entendu dire que** I've heard (it said) that; **~ parler de** to hear of

entendu, e [ɑ̃tɑ̃dy] adj (réglé) agreed; (au courant: air) knowing; **(c'est) ~** all right, agreed; **bien ~** of course

entente [ɑ̃tɑ̃t] nf understanding; (accord, traité) agreement; **à double ~** (sens) with a double meaning

enterrement [ɑ̃tɛʀmɑ̃] nm (cérémonie) funeral, burial

enterrer [ɑ̃teʀe] /1/ vt to bury

entêtant, e [ɑ̃tɛtɑ̃, -ɑ̃t] adj heady

en-tête [ɑ̃tɛt] nm heading; **papier à ~** headed notepaper

entêté, e [ɑ̃tete] adj stubborn

entêter [ɑ̃tete] /1/: **s'entêter** vi: **s'~ (à faire)** to persist (in doing)

enthousiasme [ɑ̃tuzjasm] nm enthusiasm; **enthousiasmer** /1/ vt to fill with enthusiasm; **s'enthousiasmer (pour qch)** to get enthusiastic (about sth); **enthousiaste** adj enthusiastic

entier, -ière [ɑ̃tje, -jɛʀ] adj (total, complet: satisfaction etc) whole; complete; (fig: caractère) unbending ▷ nm (Math) whole; **en ~** totally; **lait ~** full-cream milk; **entièrement** adv entirely, wholly

entonnoir [ɑ̃tɔnwaʀ] nm funnel

entorse [ɑ̃tɔʀs] nf (Méd) sprain; (fig): **à la loi/au règlement** infringement of the law/rule

entourage [ɑ̃tuʀaʒ] nm circle; (famille) family (circle); (ce qui enclôt) surround

entourer [ɑ̃tuʀe] /1/ vt to surround; (apporter son soutien à) to rally round; **~ de** to surround with; **s'entourer de** to surround o.s. with

entracte [ɑ̃tʀakt] nm interval

entraide [ɑ̃tʀɛd] nf mutual aid ou assistance

entrain [ɑ̃tʀɛ̃] nm spirit; **avec ~** energetically; **faire qch sans ~** to do sth half-heartedly ou without enthusiasm

entraînement [ɑ̃tʀɛnmɑ̃] nm training

entraîner [ɑ̃tʀene] /1/ vt (charrier) to carry ou drag along; (Tech) to drive; (emmener: personne) to take (off); (mener à l'assaut, influencer) to lead;

(Sport) to train; (impliquer) to entail; **~ qn à faire** (inciter) to lead sb to do; **s'entraîner** vi (Sport) to train; **s'~ à qch/à faire** to train o.s. for sth/to do; **entraîneur** nm/f (Sport) coach, trainer ▷ nm (Hippisme) jockey

entre [ɑ̃tʀ] prép (parmi) among(st); **l'un d'~ eux/nous** one of them/us; **~ autres (choses)** among other things; **ils se battent ~ eux** they are fighting among(st) themselves; **entrecôte** nf entrecote ou rib steak

entrée [ɑ̃tʀe] nf entrance; (accès: au cinéma etc) admission; (billet) (admission) ticket; (Culin) first course

entre: entrefilet nm (article) paragraph, short report; **entremets** nm (cream) dessert

entrepôt [ɑ̃tʀəpo] nm warehouse

entreprendre [ɑ̃tʀəpʀɑ̃dʀ]/58/ vt (se lancer dans) to undertake; (commencer) to begin ou start (upon)

entrepreneur, -euse [ɑ̃tʀəpʀənœʀ, -øz] nm/f: **~ (en bâtiment)** (building) contractor

entrepris, e [ɑ̃tʀəpʀi, -iz] pp de **entreprendre** ▷ nf (société) firm, business; (action) undertaking, venture

entrer [ɑ̃tʀe] /1/ vi to go (ou come) in, enter ▷ vt (Inform) to input, enter; **~ dans** (gén) to enter; (pièce) to go (ou come) into, enter; (club) to join; (heurter) to run into; **(faire) ~ qch dans** to get sth into; **~ à l'hôpital** to go into hospital; **faire ~** (visiteur) to show in

entre-temps [ɑ̃tʀətɑ̃] adv meanwhile

entretenir [ɑ̃tʀət(ə)niʀ]/22/ vt to maintain; (famille, maîtresse) to support, keep; **~ qn (de)** to speak to sb (about)

entretien [ɑ̃tʀətjɛ̃] nm maintenance; (discussion) discussion, talk; (pour un emploi) interview

entrevoir [ɑ̃tʀəvwaʀ] /30/ vt (à peine) to make out; (brièvement) to catch a glimpse of

entrevu, e [ɑ̃tʀəvy] pp de **entrevoir** ▷ nf (audience) interview

entrouvert, e [ɑ̃tʀuvɛʀ, -ɛʀt] adj half-open

énumérer [enymeʀe] /6/ vt to list

envahir [ɑ̃vaiʀ] /2/ vt to invade; (inquiétude, peur) to come over; **envahissant, e** adj (péj: personne) intrusive

enveloppe [ɑ̃v(ə)lɔp] nf (de lettre) envelope; (crédits) budget; **envelopper** /1/ vt to wrap; (fig) to envelop, shroud

enverrai etc [ɑ̃veʀe] vb voir **envoyer**

envers [ɑ̃vɛʀ] prép towards, to ▷ nm other side; (d'une étoffe) wrong side; **à l'~** (verticalement) upside down; (pull) back to front; (vêtement) inside out

envie [ɑ̃vi] nf (sentiment) envy; (souhait) desire, wish; **avoir ~ de** to feel like; (désir plus fort) to want; **avoir ~ de faire** to feel like doing; to want to do; **avoir ~ que** to wish that; **cette glace me fait ~** I fancy some of that ice cream; **envier** /7/ vt to envy; **envieux, -euse** adj envious

environ [ɑ̃viʀɔ̃] adv: **~ 3 h/2 km** (around) about 3 o'clock/2 km; voir aussi **environs**

environnant, e [ɑ̃viʀɔnɑ̃, -ɑ̃t] adj surrounding

environnement [ɑ̃viʀɔnmɑ̃] nm environment

environs [ɑ̃viʀɔ̃] nmpl surroundings; **aux ~ de** around

envisager [ɑ̃vizaʒe] /3/ vt to contemplate; (avoir en vue) to envisage; **~ de faire** to consider doing

envoler [ɑ̃vɔle] /1/: **s'envoler** vi (oiseau) to fly away ou off; (avion) to take off; (papier, feuille) to blow away; (fig) to vanish (into thin air)

envoyé, e [ɑ̃vwaje] nm/f (Pol) envoy; (Presse) correspondent; **~ spécial** special correspondent

envoyer [ɑ̃vwaje] /8/ vt to send; (lancer) to hurl, throw; **~ chercher**

to send for; ~ **promener qn** (fam) to send sb packing

éolien, ne [eɔljɛ̃, -ɛn] adj wind ▷ nf wind turbine

épagneul, e [epaɲœl] nm/f spaniel

épais, se [epɛ, -ɛs] adj thick; **épaisseur** nf thickness

épanouir [epanwiʁ] /2/: **s'épanouir** vi (fleur) to bloom, open out; (visage) to light up; (se développer) to blossom (out)

épargne [epaʁɲ] nf saving

épargner [epaʁɲe] /1/ vt to save; (ne pas tuer ou endommager) to spare ▷ vi to save; ~ **qch à qn** to spare sb sth

éparpiller [epaʁpije] /1/ vt to scatter; **s'éparpiller** vi to scatter; (fig) to dissipate one's efforts

épatant, e [epatã, -ãt] adj (fam) super

épater [epate] /1/ vt (fam) to amaze; (: impressionner) to impress

épaule [epol] nf shoulder

épave [epav] nf wreck

épée [epe] nf sword

épeler [ep(ə)le] /4/ vt to spell

éperon [epʁɔ̃] nm spur

épervier [epɛʁvje] nm sparrowhawk

épi [epi] nm (de blé, d'orge) ear; (de maïs) cob

épice [epis] nf spice

épicé, e [epise] adj spicy

épicer [epise] /3/ vt to spice

épicerie [episʁi] nf grocer's shop; (denrées) groceries pl; ~ **fine** delicatessen shop; **épicier, -ière** nm/f grocer

épidémie [epidemi] nf epidemic

épiderme [epidɛʁm] nm skin

épier [epje] /7/ vt to spy on, watch closely

épilepsie [epilɛpsi] nf epilepsy

épiler [epile] /1/ vt (jambes) to remove the hair from; (sourcils) to pluck

épinards [epinaʁ] nmpl spinach sg

épine [epin] nf thorn, prickle; (d'oursin etc) spine

épingle [epɛ̃gl] nf pin; ~ **de nourrice** ou **de sûreté** ou **double** safety pin

épisode [epizɔd] nm episode; **film/ roman à ~s** serial; **épisodique** adj occasional

épluche-légumes [eplyʃlegym] nm inv potato peeler

éplucher [eplyʃe] /1/ vt (fruit, légumes) to peel; (comptes, dossier) to go over with a fine-tooth comb; **épluchures** nfpl peelings

éponge [epɔ̃ʒ] nf sponge; **éponger** /3/ vt (liquide) to mop ou sponge up; (surface) to sponge; (fig: déficit) to soak up

époque [epɔk] nf (de l'histoire) age, era; (de l'année, la vie) time; **d'~** (meuble) period cpd

épouse [epuz] nf wife; **épouser** /1/ vt to marry

épousseter [epuste] /4/ vt to dust

épouvantable [epuvɑ̃tabl] adj appalling, dreadful

épouvantail [epuvɑ̃taj] nm scarecrow

épouvante [epuvɑ̃t] nf terror; **film d'~** horror film; **épouvanter** /1/ vt to terrify

époux [epu] nm husband ▷ nmpl: **les ~** the (married) couple

épreuve [epʁœv] nf (d'examen) test; (malheur, difficulté) trial, ordeal; (Photo) print; (Typo) proof; (Sport) event; **à toute ~** unfailing; **mettre à l'~** to put to the test

éprouver [epʁuve] /1/ vt (tester) to test; to afflict, distress; (ressentir) to experience

EPS sigle f (= Éducation physique et sportive) = PE

épuisé, e [epɥize] adj exhausted; (livre) out of print; **épuisement** nm exhaustion

épuiser [epɥize] /1/ vt (fatiguer) to exhaust, wear ou tire out; (stock, sujet) to exhaust; **s'épuiser** vi to wear ou tire o.s. out, exhaust o.s.

épuisette [epɥizɛt] nf shrimping net

équateur [ekwatœʁ] nm equator; **(la république de) l'É~** Ecuador

équation [ekwasjɔ̃] nf equation

équerre [ekɛʀ] nf (à dessin) (set) square

équilibre [ekilibʀ] nm balance;
garder/perdre l'~ to keep/lose one's
balance; **être en ~** to be balanced;
équilibré, e adj well-balanced;
équilibrer /1/ vt to balance;
s'équilibrer vi to balance

équipage [ekipaʒ] nm crew

équipe [ekip] nf team; **travailler en
~** to work as a team

équipé, e [ekipe] adj: **bien/mal ~**
well-/poorly-equipped

équipement [ekipmɑ̃] nm
equipment

équiper [ekipe] vt to equip; **~ qn/
qch de** to equip sb/sth with

équipier, -ière [ekipje, -jɛʀ] nm/f
team member

équitation [ekitasjɔ̃] nf (horse-)
riding; **faire de l'~** to go (horse-)riding

équivalent, e [ekivalɑ̃, -ɑ̃t] adj, nm
equivalent

équivaloir [ekivalwaʀ] /29/ : **~ à** vt
to be equivalent to

érable [eʀabl] nm maple

érafler [eʀafle] /1/ vt to scratch;
éraflure nf scratch

ère [ɛʀ] nf era; **en l'an 1050 de notre
~** in the year 1050 A.D.

érection [eʀɛksjɔ̃] nf erection

éroder [eʀɔde] /1/ vt to erode

érotique [eʀɔtik] adj erotic

errer [eʀe] /1/ vi to wander

erreur [eʀœʀ] nf mistake, error; **par
~** by mistake; **faire ~** to be mistaken

éruption [eʀypsjɔ̃] nf eruption;
(boutons) rash

es [ɛ] vb voir **être**

ès [ɛs] prép: **licencié ès lettres/
sciences** ≈ Bachelor of Arts/Science

ESB sigle f (= encéphalopathie
spongiforme bovine) BSE

escabeau, x [ɛskabo] nm (tabouret)
stool; (échelle) stepladder

escalade [ɛskalad] nf climbing no
pl; (Pol etc) escalation; **escalader** /1/
vt to climb

escale [ɛskal] nf (Navig: durée) call;
(: port) port of call; (Aviat) stop(over);
faire ~ à (Navig) to put in at; (Aviat)
to stop over at; **vol sans ~** nonstop
flight

escalier [ɛskalje] nm stairs pl;
dans l'~ ou **les ~s** on the stairs;
~ mécanique ou **roulant** escalator

escapade [ɛskapad] nf: **faire une
~** to go on a jaunt; (s'enfuir) to run
away ou off

escargot [ɛskaʀgo] nm snail

escarpé, e [ɛskaʀpe] adj steep

esclavage [ɛsklavaʒ] nm slavery

esclave [ɛsklav] nm/f slave

escompte [ɛskɔ̃t] nm discount

escrime [ɛskʀim] nf fencing

escroc [ɛskʀo] nm swindler, con-
man; **escroquer** /1/ vt: **~ qn (de qch)/qch à qn** to swindle
sb (out of sth)/sth out of sb;
escroquerie
[ɛskʀɔkʀi] nf swindle

espace [ɛspas] nm space; **espacer**
/3/ vt to space out; **s'espacer** vi
(visites etc) to become less frequent

espadon [ɛspadɔ̃] nm swordfish inv

espadrille [ɛspadʀij] nf rope-soled
sandal

Espagne [ɛspaɲ] nf: **l'~** Spain;
espagnol, e adj Spanish ▷ nm
(Ling) Spanish ▷ nm/f: **Espagnol, e**
Spaniard

espèce [ɛspɛs] nf (Bio, Bot, Zool)
species inv; (gén: sorte) sort, kind,
type; (péj): **~ de maladroit/de
brute!** you clumsy oaf/you brute!;
espèces nfpl (Comm) cash sg; **payer
en ~s** to pay (in) cash

espérance [ɛspeʀɑ̃s] nf hope; **~ de
vie** life expectancy

espérer [ɛspeʀe] /6/ vt to hope for;
j'espère (bien) I hope so; **~ que/
faire** to hope that/to do

espiègle [ɛspjɛgl] adj mischievous

espion, ne [ɛspjɔ̃, -ɔn] nm/f spy;
espionnage nm espionage, spying;
espionner /1/ vt to spy (up)on

espoir [ɛspwaʀ] nm hope; **dans l'~ de/que** in the hope of/that; **reprendre ~** not to lose hope

esprit [ɛspʀi] nm (pensée, intellect) mind; (humour, ironie) wit; (mentalité, d'une loi etc, fantôme etc) spirit; **faire de l'~** to try to be witty; **reprendre ses ~s** to come to; **perdre l'~** to lose one's mind

esquimau, de, x [ɛskimo, -od] adj Eskimo ▷ nm: **E-® ice** lolly (BRIT), popsicle (US) ▷ nm/f: **E-, de** Eskimo

essai [ese] nm (tentative) attempt, try; (de produit) testing; (Rugby) try; (Littérature) essay; **à l'~** on a trial basis; **mettre à l'~** to put to the test

essaim [esɛ̃] nm swarm

essayer [eseje] /8/ vt to try; (vêtement, chaussures) to try on; (restaurant, méthode, voiture) to try (out) ▷ vi to try; **~ de faire** to try to attempt to do

essence [esɑ̃s] nf (de voiture) petrol (BRIT), gas(oline) (US); (extrait de plante) essence; (espèce d'arbre) species inv

essentiel, le [esɑ̃sjɛl] adj essential; **c'est l'~** (ce qui importe) that's the main thing; **l'~ de** the main part of

essieu, x [esjø] nm axle

essor [esɔʀ] nm (de l'économie etc) rapid expansion

essorer [esɔʀe] /1/ vt (en tordant) to wring (out); (par la force centrifuge) to spin-dry; **essoreuse** nf spin-dryer

essouffler [esufle] /1/: **s'essouffler** vi to get out of breath

essuie-glace [esɥiglas] nm windscreen (BRIT) ou windshield (US) wiper

essuyer [esɥije] /8/ vt to wipe; (fig: subir) to suffer; **s'essuyer** (après le bain) to dry o.s.; **~ la vaisselle** to dry up

est vb [ɛ] voir **être** ▷ nm [ɛst]: **l'~** the east ▷ adj inv [ɛst] east; (région) east(ern); **à l'~** in the east; (direction) to the east, east(wards); **à l'~ de** (to the) east of

est-ce que [ɛskə] adv: **~ c'est cher/c'était bon?** is it expensive/ was it good?; **quand est-ce qu'il part?** when does he leave?, when is he leaving?; voir aussi **que**

esthéticienne [ɛstetisjɛn] nf beautician

esthétique [ɛstetik] adj attractive

estimation [ɛstimasjɔ̃] nf valuation; (chiffre) estimate

estime [ɛstim] nf esteem, regard; **estimer** /1/ vt (respecter) to esteem; (expertiser: bijou) to value; (évaluer: coût etc) to assess, estimate; (penser): **estimer que/être** to consider that/o.s. to be

estival, e, -aux [ɛstival, -o] adj summer cpd

estivant, e [ɛstivɑ̃, -ɑ̃t] nm/f (summer) holiday-maker

estomac [ɛstoma] nm stomach

estragon [ɛstʀagɔ̃] nm tarragon

estuaire [ɛstɥɛʀ] nm estuary

et [e] conj and; **et lui?** what about him?; **et alors?** so what?

étable [etabl] nf cowshed

établi, e [etabli] nm (work)bench

établir [etabliʀ] /2/ vt (papiers d'identité, facture) to make out; (liste, programme) to draw up; (gouvernement, artisan etc) to set up; (réputation, usage, fait, culpabilité, relations) to establish; **s'établir** vi to be established; **s'~** (à son compte) to set up in business; **s'~ à/près de** to settle in/near

établissement [etablismɑ̃] nm (entreprise, institution) establishment; **~ scolaire** school, educational establishment

étage [etaʒ] nm (d'immeuble) storey, floor; **au 2ème** on the 2nd (BRIT) ou 3rd (US) floor; **à l'~** upstairs; **c'est à quel ~?** what floor is it on?

étagère [etaʒɛʀ] nf (rayon) shelf; (meuble) shelves pl

étai [etɛ] nm stay, prop

étain [etɛ̃] nm pewter no pl

étais etc [etɛ] vb voir **être**

étaler [etale] /1/ vt (carte, nappe) to spread (out); (peinture, liquide) to spread; (échelonner: paiements, dates, vacances) to spread, stagger; (marchandises) to display; (richesses, connaissances) to parade; **s'étaler** vi (liquide) to spread out; (fam) to fall flat on one's face; **s'~ sur** (paiements etc) to be spread over

étalon [etalɔ̃] nm (cheval) stallion

étanche [etɑ̃ʃ] adj (récipient) watertight; (montre, vêtement) waterproof

étang [etɑ̃] nm pond

étant [etɑ̃] vb voir **être**; **donné**

étape [etap] nf stage; (lieu d'arrivée) stopping place; (: Cyclisme) staging point

état [eta] nm (Pol, condition) state; **en bon/mauvais ~** in good/poor condition; **en ~ (de marche)** in (working) order; **remettre en ~** to repair; **hors d'~** out of order; **être en ~/hors d' ~ de faire** to be in a state/in no fit state to do; **être dans tous ses ~s** to be in a state; **faire ~ de** (alléguer) to put forward; **l'É~** the State; **~ civil** civil status; **~ des lieux** inventory of fixtures; **États-Unis** nmpl: **les États-Unis (d'Amérique)** the United States (of America)

et cætera, et cetera, etc. [ɛtsetera] adv etc

été [ete] pp de **être** ▷ nm summer

éteindre [etɛ̃dʀ] /52/ vt (lampe, lumière, radio, chauffage) to turn on switch off; (cigarette, incendie, bougie) to put out, extinguish; **s'éteindre** vi (feu, lumière) to go out; (mourir) to pass away; **éteint, e** adj (fig) lacklustre, dull; (volcan) extinct

étendre [etɑ̃dʀ] /41/ vt (pâte, liquide) to spread; (carte etc) to spread out; (lessive, linge) to hang up ou out; (bras, jambes) to stretch out; (fig: agrandir) to extend; **s'étendre** vi (augmenter, se propager) to spread; (terrain, forêt

etc): **s'~ jusqu'à/de ...à** to stretch as far as/from ... to; **s'~ sur** (se coucher) to lie down (on); (fig: expliquer) to elaborate ou enlarge (upon)

étendu, e [etɑ̃dy] adj extensive

éternel, le [etɛʀnɛl] adj eternal

éternité [etɛʀnite] nf eternity; **ça a duré une ~** it lasted for ages

éternuement [etɛʀnymɑ̃] nm sneeze

éternuer [etɛʀnɥe] /1/ vi to sneeze

êtes [ɛt(z)] vb voir **être**

Éthiopie [etjɔpi] nf: **l'~** Ethiopia

étiez [etje] vb voir **être**

étinceler [etɛ̃s(ə)le] /4/ vi to sparkle

étincelle [etɛ̃sɛl] nf spark

étiquette [etikɛt] nf label; (protocole): **l'~** etiquette

étirer [etiʀe] /1/ vt to stretch out; **s'étirer** vi (personne) to stretch; (convoi, route): **s'~ sur** to stretch out over

étoile [etwal] nf star; **à la belle ~** (out) in the open; **~ filante** shooting star; **~ de mer** starfish; **étoilé, e** adj starry

étonnant, e [etɔnɑ̃, -ɑ̃t] adj surprising

étonnement [etɔnmɑ̃] nm surprise, amazing

étonner [etɔne] /1/ vt to surprise, amaze; **s'étonner que/de** to be surprised that/at; **cela m'~ait (que)** (j'en doute) I'd be (very) surprised (if)

étouffer [etufe] /1/ vt to suffocate; (bruit) to muffle; (scandale) to hush up ▷ vi to suffocate; **s'étouffer** vi (en mangeant etc) to choke; **on étouffe** it's stifling

étourderie [eturdəri] nf (caractère) absent-mindedness no pl; (faute) thoughtless blunder

étourdi, e [eturdi] adj (distrait) scatterbrained, heedless

étourdir [eturdir] /2/ vt (assommer) to stun, daze; (griser) to make dizzy ou giddy; **étourdissement** nm dizzy spell

étrange [etʀɑ̃ʒ] adj strange

étranger, -ère [etʀɑ̃ʒe, -ɛʀ] adj
foreign; (pas de la famille, non familier)
strange ▷ nm/f foreigner; stranger
▷ nm: **à l'~** abroad

étrangler [etʀɑ̃gle] /1/ vt to
strangle; **s'étrangler** vi (en mangeant
etc) to choke

O **MOT-CLÉ**

être [ɛtʀ] /61/ nm being; **être
humain** human being
▶ vb copule 1 (état, description) to
be; **il est instituteur** he is ou he's
a teacher; **vous êtes grand/
intelligent/fatigué** you are ou you're
tall/clever/tired
2 (+à: appartenir) to be; **le livre est
à Paul** the book is Paul's ou belongs
to Paul; **c'est à moi/eux** it is ou it's
mine/theirs
3 (+de: provenance): **il est de Paris** he
is from Paris; (: appartenance): **il est
des nôtres** he is one of us
4 (date): **nous sommes le 10 janvier**
it's the 10th of January (today)
▶ vi to be; **je ne serai pas ici demain**
I won't be there tomorrow
▶ vb aux 1 to have; to be; **être arrivé/
allé** to have arrived/gone; **il est
parti** he has left, he has gone
2 (forme passive) to be; **être fait par**
to be made by; **il a été promu** he has
been promoted
3 (+à +inf. obligation, but): **c'est à
réparer** it needs repairing; **c'est
à essayer** it should be tried; **il est
à espérer que ...** it is ou it's to be
hoped that ...
▶ vb impers 1: **il est** (+adj) it is; **il est
impossible de le faire** it's impossible
to do it
2: (heure, date): **il est 10 heures**
it is ou it's 10 o'clock
3 (emphatique): **c'est moi** it's me;
c'est à lui de le faire it's up to him
to do it

étrennes [etʀɛn] nfpl ≈ Christmas
box sg

étrier [etʀije] nm stirrup

étroit, e [etʀwa, -wat] adj
narrow; (vêtement) tight; (fig: liens,
collaboration) close; **à l'~** cramped;
~ d'esprit narrow-minded

étude [etyd] nf studying; (ouvrage,
rapport) study; (Scol: salle de travail)
study room; **études** nfpl (Scol)
studies; **être à l'~** (projet etc) to be
under consideration; **faire des ~s
(de droit/médecine)** to study (law/
medicine)

étudiant, e [etydjɑ̃, -ɑ̃t] nm/f student

étudier [etydje] /7/ vt, vi to study

étui [etɥi] nm case

eu, eue [y] pp de **avoir**

euh [ø] excl er

euro [øʀo] nm euro

Europe [øʀɔp] nf: **l'~** Europe;
européen, ne adj European ▷ nm/f:
Européen, ne European

eus etc [y] vb voir **avoir**

eux [ø] pron (sujet) they; (objet) them

évacuer [evakɥe] /1/ vt to evacuate

évader [evade] /1/: **s'évader** vi to
escape

évaluer [evalɥe] /1/ vt (expertiser)
to assess, evaluate; (juger
approximativement) to estimate

évangile [evɑ̃ʒil] nm gospel; **É~**
Gospel

évanouir [evanwiʀ] /2/: **s'évanouir**
vi to faint; (disparaître) to vanish,
disappear; **évanouissement** nm
(syncope) fainting fit

évaporer [evapɔʀe] /1/: **s'évaporer**
vi to evaporate

évasion [evazjɔ̃] nf escape

éveillé, e [eveje] adj awake; (vif)
alert, sharp; **éveiller** /1/ vt to (a)
waken; (soupçons etc) to arouse;
s'éveiller vi to (a)waken; (fig) to be
aroused

événement [evɛnmɑ̃] nm event

éventail [evɑ̃taj] nm fan; (choix)
range

éventualité [evɑ̃tɥalite] nf
eventuality; possibility; **dans l'~ de**
in the event of

éventuel, le [evɑ̃tɥɛl] adj possible
⚠ Attention à ne pas traduire
éventuel par eventual.

éventuellement [evɑ̃tɥɛlmɑ̃] adv
possibly
⚠ Attention à ne pas traduire
éventuellement par eventually.

évêque [evɛk] nm bishop

évidemment [evidamɑ̃] adv
(bien sûr) of course; (certainement)
obviously

évidence [evidɑ̃s] nf obviousness;
(fait) obvious fact; **de toute ~** quite
obviously ou evidently; **être en ~** to
be clearly visible; **mettre en ~**
(fait) to highlight; **évident, e** adj obvious,
evident; **ce n'est pas évident** it's not
as simple as all that

évier [evje] nm (kitchen) sink

éviter [evite] /1/ vt to avoid; **~ de
faire/que** to avoid doing/sth happening; **~ qch à qn** to
spare sb sth

évoluer [evɔlɥe] /1/ vi (enfant,
maladie) to develop; (situation,
moralement) to evolve, develop; (aller
et venir) to move about; **évolution** nf
development; evolution

évoquer [evɔke] /1/ vt to call to
mind, evoke; (mentionner) to mention

ex- [ɛks] préfixe ex-; **son ~mari** her ex-
husband; **son ~femme** his ex-wife

exact, e [ɛgza(kt), ɛgzakt] adj exact;
(correct) correct; (ponctuel) punctual;
l'heure ~e the right ou exact time;
exactement adv exactly

ex aequo [ɛgzeko] adj equally placed;
arriver ~ to finish neck and neck

exagéré, e [ɛgzaʒere] adj (prix etc)
excessive

exagérer [ɛgzaʒere] /6/ vt to
exaggerate ▷ vi (abuser) to go too far;
(déformer les faits) to exaggerate

examen [ɛgzamɛ̃] nm examination;
(Scol) exam, examination; **à l'~** under

consideration; **~ médical** (medical)
examination; (analyse) test

examinateur, -trice
[ɛgzaminatœʀ, -tʀis] nm/f examiner

examiner [ɛgzamine] /1/ vt to
examine

exaspérant, e [ɛgzasperɑ̃, -ɑ̃t] adj
exasperating

exaspérer [ɛgzaspere] /6/ vt to
exasperate

exaucer [ɛgzose] /3/ vt (vœu) to grant

excéder [ɛksede] /6/ vt (dépasser) to
exceed; (agacer) to exasperate

excellent, e [ɛksɛlɑ̃, -ɑ̃t] adj
excellent

excentrique [ɛksɑ̃tʀik] adj
eccentric

excepté, e [ɛksɛpte] adj, prép: **les
élèves ~s, ~ les élèves** except ou
apart from the pupils

exception [ɛksɛpsjɔ̃] nf exception;
à l'~ de except for, with the
exception of; **d'~** (mesure, loi) special,
exceptional; **exceptionnel, le** adj
exceptional; **exceptionnellement**
adv exceptionally

excès [ɛksɛ] nm surplus ▷ nmpl
excesses; **faire des ~** to overindulge;
~ de vitesse speeding no pl; **excessif,
-ive** adj excessive

excitant, e [ɛksitɑ̃, -ɑ̃t] adj exciting
▷ nm stimulant; **excitation** nf (état)
excitement

exciter [ɛksite] /1/ vt to excite; (café
etc) to stimulate; **s'exciter** vi to get
excited

exclamer [ɛksklame] /1/:
s'exclamer vi to exclaim

exclu, e [ɛkskly] adj: **il est/n'est pas
~ que ...** it's out of the question/not
impossible that ...

exclure [ɛksklyʀ] /35/ vt (faire sortir)
to expel; (ne pas compter) to exclude,
leave out; (rendre impossible) to
exclude, rule out; **exclusif, -ive** adj
exclusive; **exclusion** nf expulsion; **à
l'exclusion de** with the exclusion ou
exception of; **exclusivité** nf (Comm)

exclusive rights pl; **film passant en exclusivité** à film showing only at

excursion [ɛkskyʀsjɔ̃] nf (en autocar) excursion, trip; (à pied) walk, hike

excuse [ɛkskyz] nf excuse; **excuses** nfpl (regret) apology sg, apologies;

excuser /1/ vt to excuse; **s'excuser (de)** to apologize (for); **"excusez-moi"** "I'm sorry"; (pour attirer l'attention) "excuse me"

exécuter [ɛgzekyte] /1/ vt (prisonnier) to execute; (tâche etc) to execute, carry out; (Mus: jouer) to perform, execute; **s'exécuter** vi to comply

exemplaire [ɛgzɑ̃plɛʀ] nm copy

exemple [ɛgzɑ̃pl] nm example; **par ~** for instance, for example; **donner l'~** to set an example

exercer [ɛgzɛʀse] /3/ vt (pratiquer) to exercise, practise; (influence, contrôle, pression) to exert; (former) to exercise, train; **s'exercer** vi (médecin) to be in practice; (sportif, musicien) to practise

exercice [ɛgzɛʀsis] nm exercise

exhiber [ɛgzibe] /1/ vt (montrer: papiers, certificat) to present, produce; (péj) to display, flaunt; **s'exhiber** vi to parade; (exhibitionniste) to expose o.s.; **exhibitionniste** nm/f exhibitionist

exigeant, e [ɛgziʒɑ̃, -ɑ̃t] adj demanding; (péj) hard to please

exiger [ɛgziʒe] /3/ vt to demand, require

exil [ɛgzil] nm exile; **exiler** /1/ vt to exile; **s'exiler** vi to go into exile

existence [ɛgzistɑ̃s] nf existence

exister [ɛgziste] /1/ vi to exist; **il existe un/des** there is a/are (some)

exorbitant, e [ɛgzɔʀbitɑ̃, -ɑ̃t] adj exorbitant

exotique [ɛgzɔtik] adj exotic; **yaourt aux fruits ~s** tropical fruit yoghurt

expédier [ɛkspedje] /7/ vt (lettre, paquet) to send; (troupes, renfort) to dispatch; (péj: travail etc) to dispose of, dispatch; **expéditeur, -trice**

nm/f sender; **expédition** nf sending; (scientifique, sportive, Mil) expedition

expérience [ɛkspeʀjɑ̃s] nf (de la vie, des choses) experience; (scientifique) experiment

expérimenté, e [ɛkspeʀimɑ̃te] adj experienced

expérimenter [ɛkspeʀimɑ̃te] /1/ vt to test out, experiment with

expert, e [ɛkspɛʀ, -ɛʀt] adj ⊳ nm expert; **~ en assurances** insurance valuer; **expert-comptable** nm ≈ chartered accountant (BRIT) ou certified public (US) accountant

expirer [ɛkspiʀe] /1/ vi (prendre fin, lit: mourir) to expire; (respirer) to breathe out

explication [ɛksplikasjɔ̃] nf explanation; (discussion) discussion; (dispute) argument

explicite [ɛksplisit] adj explicit

expliquer [ɛksplike] /1/ vt to explain; **s'expliquer** to explain o.s.; **s'~ avec qn** (discuter) to have it o.s. in to sb

exploit [ɛksplwa] nm exploit, feat; **exploitant, e** nm/f: **exploitant (agricole)** farmer; **exploitation** nf exploitation; (d'une entreprise) running;

exploitation agricole farming concern; **exploiter** /1/ vt (personne, don) to exploit; (entreprise, ferme) to run, operate; (mine) to exploit, work

explorer [ɛksplɔʀe] /1/ vt to explore

exploser [ɛksploze] /1/ vi to explode, blow up; (engin explosif) to go off; (personne: de colère) to explode; **explosif, -ive** adj, nm explosive; **explosion** nf explosion; **explosion de joie/colère** outburst of joy/rage

exportateur, -trice [ɛkspɔʀtatœʀ, -tʀis] adj export cpd, exporting ⊳ nm exporter

exportation [ɛkspɔʀtasjɔ̃] nf (action) exportation; (produit) export

exporter [ɛkspɔʀte] /1/ vt to export

exposant [ɛkspozɑ̃] nm exhibitor

exposé, e [ɛkspoze] nm talk ▷ adj: **~ au sud** facing south

exposer [ɛkspoze] /1/ vt (marchandise) to display; (peinture) to exhibit, show; (parler de) to explain, set out; (mettre en danger, orienter, Photo) to expose; **s'exposer à** (soleil, danger) to expose o.s. to; **exposition** nf (manifestation) exhibition; (Photo) exposure

exprès¹ [ɛksprɛ] adv (délibérément) on purpose; (spécialement) specially; **faire ~ de faire qch** to do sth on purpose

exprès², -esse [ɛksprɛs] adj inv (Postes: lettre, colis) express

express [ɛksprɛs] adj, nm: **(café) ~** espresso; **(train) ~** fast train

expressif, -ive [ɛkspresif, -iv] adj expressive

expression [ɛkspresjɔ̃] nf expression

exprimer [ɛksprime] /1/ vt (sentiment, idée) to express; (jus, liquide) to press out; **s'exprimer** vi (personne) to express o.s.

expulser [ɛkspylse] /1/ vt to expel; (locataire) to evict; (Football) to send off

exquis, e [ɛkski, -iz] adj exquisite

extasier [ɛkstazje] /7/: **s'~ sur** to go into raptures over

exténuer [ɛkstenɥe] /1/ vt to exhaust

extérieur, e [ɛksterjœr] adj (porte, mur etc) outer, outside; (commerce, politique) foreign; (influences, pressions) external; (apparent: calme, gaieté etc) outer ▷ nm (d'une maison, d'un récipient etc) outside, exterior; (apparence) exterior; **à l'~** outside; (à l'étranger) abroad

externat [ɛksterna] nm day school

externe [ɛkstern] adj external, outer ▷ nm/f (Méd) non-resident medical student, extern (us); (Scol) day pupil

extincteur [ɛkstɛ̃ktœr] nm (fire) extinguisher

extinction [ɛkstɛ̃ksjɔ̃] nf: **~ de voix** loss of voice

extra [ɛkstra] adj inv first-rate; (fam) fantastic ▷ nm inv extra help

extraire [ɛkstrɛr] /50/ vt to extract; **~ qch de** to extract sth from; **extrait** nm extract; **extrait de naissance** birth certificate

extraordinaire [ɛkstraɔrdinɛr] adj extraordinary; (Pol, Admin: mesures etc) special

extravagant, e [ɛkstravagɑ̃, -ɑ̃t] adj extravagant

extraverti, e [ɛkstraverti] adj extrovert

extrême [ɛkstrɛm] adj, nm extreme; **d'un ~ à l'autre** from one extreme to another; **extrêmement** adv extremely; **Extrême-Orient** nm: **l'Extrême-Orient** the Far East

extrémité [ɛkstremite] nf end; (situation) straits pl, plight; (geste désespéré) extreme action; **extrémités** nfpl (pieds et mains) extremities

exubérant, e [ɛgzyberɑ̃, -ɑ̃t] adj exuberant

F *abr* (= franc) fr.; (*appartement*): **un F2/F3** a 2-/3-roomed flat (BRIT) ou apartment (US)

fa [fa] *nm inv* (Mus) F; (*en chantant la gamme*) fa

fabricant, e [fabrikɑ̃, -ɑ̃t] *nm/f* manufacturer

fabrication [fabrikasjɔ̃] *nf* manufacture

fabrique [fabrik] *nf* factory; **fabriquer** [fabrike] /1/ *vt* to make; (*industriellement*) to manufacture; (*fam*): **qu'est-ce qu'il fabrique?** what is he up to?

fac [fak] *nf* (*fam: Scol*) (= *faculté*) Uni (BRIT *fam*), = college (US)

façade [fasad] *nf* front, façade

face [fas] *nf* face; (*fig: aspect*) side ▷ *adj*: **le côté ~** heads; **en ~ de** opposite; (*fig*) in front of; **de ~** face on; **~ à** facing; (*fig*) faced with, in the face of; **faire ~ à** to face; **~ à** *adv* facing each other; **face-à-face** *nm inv* encounter

fâché, e [faʃe] *adj* angry; (*désolé*) sorry

fâcher [faʃe] /1/ *vt* to anger; **se fâcher** *vi* to get angry; **se ~ avec** (*se brouiller*) to fall out with

facile [fasil] *adj* easy; (*caractère*) easy-going; **facilement** *adv* easily; **facilité** *nf* easiness; (*disposition, don*) aptitude; **facilités** *nfpl* (*possibilités*) facilities; (*Comm*) terms; **faciliter** /1/ *vt* to make easier

façon [fasɔ̃] *nf* (*manière*) way; (*d'une robe etc*) making-up; cut; **façons** *nfpl* (*péj*) fuss *sg*; **sans ~** *adv* without fuss; **non merci, sans ~** no thanks, honestly; **de ~ à** so as to; **de ~ à ce que** so that; **de toute ~** anyway, in any case

facteur, -trice [faktœʀ, -tʀis] *nm/f* postman/woman (BRIT), mailman/woman (US) ▷ *nm* (Math, gén: *élément*) factor

facture [faktyʀ] *nf* (*à payer: gén*) bill; (: *Comm*) invoice

facultatif, -ive [fakyltatif, -iv] *adj* optional

faculté [fakylte] *nf* (*intellectuelle, d'université*) faculty; (*pouvoir, possibilité*) power

fade [fad] *adj* insipid

faible [fɛbl] *adj* weak; (*voix, lumière, vent*) faint; (*rendement, intensité, revenu etc*) low ▷ *nm* (*pour quelqu'un*) weakness, soft spot; **faiblesse** *nf* weakness; **faiblir** [feblir] /2/ *vi* to weaken; (*lumière*) to dim; (*vent*) to drop

faïence [fajɑ̃s] *nf* earthenware *no pl*

faillir [fajiʀ] /2/ *vi*: **j'ai failli tomber/lui dire** I almost ou nearly fell/told him

faillite [fajit] *nf* bankruptcy; **faire ~** to go bankrupt

faim [fɛ̃] *nf* hunger; **avoir ~** to be hungry; **rester sur sa ~** (*aussi fig*) to be left wanting more

fainéant, e [fɛneɑ̃, -ɑ̃t] *nm/f* idler, loafer

MOT-CLÉ

faire [fɛʀ] /60/ vt **1** (*fabriquer, être l'auteur de*) to make; **faire du vin/une offre/un film** to make wine/an offer/a film; **faire du bruit** to make a noise

2 (*effectuer: travail, opération*) to do; **que faites-vous?** (*quel métier etc*) what do you do?; (*quelle activité: au moment de la question*) what are you doing?; **faire la lessive/le ménage** to do the washing/the housework

3 (*études*) to do; (*sport, musique*) to play; **faire du droit/du français** to do law/French; **faire du rugby/piano** to play rugby/the piano

4 (*visiter*): **faire les magasins** to go shopping; **faire l'Europe** to tour *ou* do Europe

5 (*distance*): **faire 50 (à l'heure)** to do 50 (km an hour); **nous avons fait 1000 km in 2 jours** we did *ou* covered 1000 km in 2 days

6 (*simuler*): **faire le malade/l'ignorant** to act the invalid/the fool

7 (*transformer, avoir un effet sur*): **faire de qn un frustré/avocat** to make sb frustrated/a lawyer; **ça ne me fait rien** (*m'est égal*) I don't care *ou* mind; (*me laisse froid*) it has no effect on me; **ça ne fait rien** it doesn't matter; **faire que** (*impliquer*) to mean that

8 (*calculs, prix, mesures*): **deux et deux font quatre** two and two are *ou* make four; **ça fait 10 m/15 euros** it's 10 m/15 euros; **je vous le fais 10 euros** I'll let you have it for 10 euros; **je fais du 40** I take a size 40

9: **qu'a-t-il fait de sa valise/de sa sœur?** what has he done with his case/his sister?

10: **ne faire que**: **il ne fait que critiquer** (*sans cesse*) all he (ever) does is criticize; (*seulement*) he's only criticizing

11 (*dire*) to say; **vraiment? fit-il** really? he said

12 (*maladie*) to have; **faire du diabète/de la tension** to have diabetes *ou* high blood pressure

▶ vi **1** (*agir, s'y prendre*) to act, do; **il faut faire vite** we (*ou* you etc) must act quickly; **comment a-t-il fait pour?** how did he manage to?; **faites comme chez vous** make yourself at home

2 (*paraître*) to look; **faire vieux/démodé** to look old/old-fashioned; **ça fait bien** it looks good

3 (*remplaçant un autre verbe*) to do; **ne le casse pas comme je l'ai fait** don't break it as I did; **je peux le voir?** — **faites!** can I see it? — please do!

▶ vb impers **1**: **il fait beau** *etc* the weather is fine *etc*; voir aussi **froid; jour** *etc*

2 (*temps écoulé, durée*): **ça fait deux ans qu'il est parti** it's two years since he left; **ça fait deux ans qu'il y est** he's been there for two years

▶ vb aux **1**: **faire** (+*infinitif: action directe*) to make; **faire tomber/bouger qch** to make sth fall/move; **faire démarrer un moteur/chauffer de l'eau** to start up an engine/heat some water; **cela fait dormir** it makes you sleep; **faire travailler les enfants** to make the children work *ou* get the children to work; **il m'a fait traverser la rue** he helped me to cross the road

2: **faire** (+*infinitif: indirectement, par un intermédiaire*) to have; **faire réparer qch** to get *ou* have sth repaired; **faire punir les enfants** to have the children punished

se faire vr **1** (*vin, fromage*) to mature

2 (*être convenable*): **cela se fait beaucoup/ne se fait pas** it's done a lot/not done

3 (+*nom ou pron*): **se faire une jupe** to make o.s. a skirt; **se faire des amis** to make friends; **se faire du souci** to worry; **il ne s'en fait pas** he doesn't worry

4 (+adj: devenir): **se faire vieux** to be getting old; (: délibérément): **se faire beau** to do o.s. up
5: **se faire à** (s'habituer) to get used to; **je n'arrive pas à me faire à la nourriture/au climat** I can't get used to the food/climate
6 (: +infinitif): **se faire examiner la vue/opérer** to have one's eyes tested/have an operation; **se faire couper les cheveux** to get one's hair cut; **il va se faire tuer/punir** he's going to get himself killed/punished (himself); **il s'est fait aider** he got somebody to help him; **il s'est fait aider par Simon** he got Simon to help him; **se faire faire un vêtement** to get a garment made for o.s.
7 (impersonnel): **comment se fait-il/faisait-il que?** how is it/was it that?

faire-part [fɛʀpaʀ] nm inv announcement (of birth, marriage etc)
faisan, e [fəzɑ̃, -an] nm/f pheasant
faisons etc [fəzɔ̃] vb voir **faire**
fait[1] [fɛ] nm (événement) event, occurrence; (réalité, donnée) fact; **être au ~ (de)** to be informed (of); **au ~** (à propos) by the way; **en venir au ~** to get to the point; **du ~ de ceci/qu'il a menti** because of ou on account of this/his having lied; **de ce ~** for this reason; **en ~** in fact; **prendre qn sur le ~** to catch sb in the act; **~ divers** (short) news item
fait[2]**, e** [fɛ, fɛt] adj (mûr: fromage, melon) ripe; **c'est bien ~ (pour lui ou eux etc)** it serves him (ou them etc) right
faites [fɛt] vb voir **faire**
falaise [falɛz] nf cliff
falloir [falwaʀ] /29/ vb impers: **il faut faire les lits** we (ou you etc) have to ou must make the beds; **il faut que je fasse les lits** I have to ou must make the beds; **il a fallu qu'il parte** he had to leave; **il faudrait**

qu'elle rentre she should come ou go back, she ought to come ou go back; **il faut faire attention** you have to be careful; **il me faudrait 100 euros** I would need 100 euros; **il vous faut tourner à gauche après l'église** you have to turn left past the church; **nous avons ce qu'il (nous) faut** we have what we need; **il ne fallait pas** you shouldn't have (done); **s'en falloir** vi: **il s'en est fallu de 10 euros/5 minutes** we (ou they etc) were 10 euros short/5 minutes late (ou early); **il s'en est fait de beaucoup qu'il soit …** he is far from being …; **il s'en est fallu de peu que cela n'arrive** it very nearly happened; **comme il faut** adj proper; adv properly

famé, e [fame] adj: **mal ~** disreputable, of ill repute
fameux, -euse [famø, -øz] adj (illustre) famous; (bon: repas, plat etc) first-rate, first-class; (intensif) **un ~ problème** etc a real problem etc
familial, e, -aux [familjal, -o] adj family cpd
familiarité [familjaʀite] nf familiarity
familier, -ière [familje, -jɛʀ] adj (connu, impertinent) familiar; (atmosphère) informal, friendly; (Ling) informal, colloquial ▷ nm regular (visitor)
famille [famij] nf family; **il a de la ~ à Paris** he has relatives in Paris
famine [famin] nf famine
fana [fana] adj, nm/f (fam) =**fanatique**
fanatique [fanatik] adj: **~ (de)** fanatical (about) ▷ nm/f fanatic
faner [fane] /1/: **se faner** vi to fade
fanfare [fɑ̃faʀ] nf (orchestre) brass band; (musique) fanfare
fantaisie [fɑ̃tezi] nf (spontanéité) fancy, imagination; (caprice) whim ▷ adj: **bijou (de) ~** (piece of) costume jewellery (BRIT) ou jewelry (US)

fantasme [fɑ̃tasm] nm fantasy

fantastique [fɑ̃tastik] adj fantastic

fantôme [fɑ̃tom] nm ghost, phantom

faon [fɑ̃] nm fawn (deer)

FAQ sigle f (= foire aux questions) FAQ pl

farce [faʀs] nf (viande) stuffing; (blague) (practical) joke; (Théât) farce; **farcir** /2/ vt (viande) to stuff

farder [faʀde] /1/: **se farder** vi to make o.s. up

farine [faʀin] nf flour

farouche [faʀuʃ] adj shy, timid

fart [faʀt] nm (ski) wax

fascination [fasinasjɔ̃] nf fascination

fasciner [fasine] /1/ vt to fascinate

fascisme [faʃism] nm fascism

fasse etc [fas] vb voir **faire**

fastidieux, -euse [fastidjø, -øz] adj tedious, tiresome

fatal, e [fatal] adj fatal; (inévitable) inevitable; **fatalité** nf (destin) fate; (coïncidence) fateful coincidence

fatidique [fatidik] adj fateful

fatigant, e [fatigɑ̃, -ɑ̃t] adj tiring; (agaçant) tiresome

fatigue [fatig] nf tiredness, fatigue; **fatigué, e** adj tired; **fatiguer** /1/ vt to tire, make tired; (fig: agacer) to annoy ▷ vi (moteur) to labour, strain; **se fatiguer** to get tired

fauché, e [foʃe] adj (fam) broke

faucher [foʃe] /1/ vt (herbe) to cut; (champs, blés) to reap; (véhicule) to mow down; (fam: voler) to pinch

faucon [fokɔ̃] nm falcon, hawk

faudra etc [fodʀa] vb voir **falloir**

faufiler [fofile] /1/: **se faufiler** vi: **se ~ dans** to edge one's way into; **se ~ parmi/entre** to thread one's way among/between

faune [fon] nf (Zool) wildlife, fauna

fausse [fos] adj f voir **faux²**;
faussement adv (accuser) wrongly, wrongfully; (croire) falsely

fausser [fose] /1/ vt (objet) to bend, buckle; (fig) to distort; **~ compagnie à qn** to give sb the slip

faut [fo] vb voir **falloir**

faute [fot] nf (erreur) mistake, error; (péché, manquement) misdemeanour; (Football etc) offence; (Tennis) fault; **c'est de sa/ma ~** it's his/my fault; **être en ~** to be in the wrong; **~ de** (temps, argent) for ou through lack of; **sans ~** without fail; **~ de frappe** typing error; **~ professionnelle** professional misconduct no pl

fauteuil [fotœj] nm armchair; **~ d'orchestre** seat in the front stalls (Brit) ou the orchestra (US); **~ roulant** wheelchair

fautif, -ive [fotif, -iv] adj (incorrect) incorrect, inaccurate; (responsable) at fault, in the wrong; **il se sentait ~** he felt guilty

fauve [fov] nm wildcat ▷ adj (couleur) fawn

faux¹ [fo] nf scythe

faux², fausse [fo, fos] adj (inexact) wrong; (piano, voix) out of tune; (billet) fake, forged; (sournois, postiche) false ▷ adv (Mus) out of tune ▷ nf (copie) fake, forgery; **faire ~ bond à qn** to let sb down; **~ frais** nm pl extras, incidental expenses; **~ mouvement** awkward movement; **faire un ~ pas** to trip; (fig) to make a faux pas; **~ témoignage** (délit) perjury; **fausse alerte** false alarm; **fausse couche** miscarriage; **fausse note** wrong note; **faux-filet** nm sirloin

faveur [favœʀ] nf favour; **traitement de ~** preferential treatment; **en ~ de** in favo(u)r of

favorable [favoʀabl] adj favo(u)rable

favori, te [favoʀi, -it] adj, nm/f favo(u)rite

favoriser [favoʀize] /1/ vt to favour

fax [faks] nm fax

fécond, e [fekɔ̃, -ɔ̃d] adj fertile; **féconder** /1/ vt to fertilize

féculent [fekylɑ̃] nm starchy food

fédéral, e, -aux [fedeʀal, -o] adj federal

fée [fe] nf fairy

feignant, e [fɛɲɑ̃, -ɑ̃t] nm/f
= **fainéant**

feindre [fɛ̃dʀ] /52/ vt to feign; **~ de
faire** to pretend to do

fêler [fele] /1/ vt to crack

félicitations [felisitasjɔ̃] nfpl
congratulations

féliciter [felisite] /1/ vt: **~ qn (de)** to
congratulate sb (on)

félin, e [felɛ̃, -in] nm (big) cat

femelle [fəmɛl] adj, nf female

féminin, e [feminɛ̃, -in] adj
feminine; (sexe) female; (équipe,
vêtements etc) women's ▷ nm (Ling)
feminine; **féministe** adj feminist

femme [fam] nf woman; (épouse)
wife; **~ de chambre** chambermaid;
~ au foyer housewife; **~ de ménage**
cleaning lady

fémur [femyʀ] nm femur, thighbone

fendre [fɑ̃dʀ] /41/ vt (couper en deux)
to split; (fissurer) to crack; (traverser)
to cut through; **se fendre** vi to crack

fenêtre [f(ə)nɛtʀ] nf window

fenouil [fənuj] nm fennel

fente [fɑ̃t] nf (fissure) crack; (de boîte à
lettres etc) slit

fer [fɛʀ] nm iron; **~ à cheval** horseshoe;
~ forgé wrought iron; **~ à friser**
curling tongs; **~ (à repasser)** iron

ferai etc [fəʀe] vb voir **faire**

fer-blanc [fɛʀblɑ̃] nm tin(plate)

férié, e [feʀje] adj: **jour ~** public
holiday

ferions etc [fəʀjɔ̃] vb voir **faire**

ferme [fɛʀm] adj firm ▷ adv (travailler
etc) hard ▷ nf (exploitation) farm;
(maison) farmhouse

fermé, e [fɛʀme] adj closed, shut;
(gaz, eau etc) off; (fig: milieu) exclusive

fermenter [fɛʀmɑ̃te] /1/ vi to ferment

fermer [fɛʀme] /1/ vt to close, shut;
(cesser l'exploitation de) to close
down, shut down; (eau, lumière, électricité,
robinet) to turn off; (aéroport, route)
to close ▷ vi to close, shut; (magasin:
définitivement) to close down, shut

down; **se fermer** vi to close, shut; **~
à clef** to lock

fermeté [fɛʀməte] nf firmness

fermeture [fɛʀmətyʀ] nf closing;
(dispositif) catch; **heure de ~** closing
time; **~-éclair®** ou **à glissière** zip
(fastener) (BRIT), zipper (US)

fermier, -ière [fɛʀmje, -jɛʀ] nm/f
farmer

féroce [feʀɔs] adj ferocious, fierce

ferons etc [fəʀɔ̃] vb voir **faire**

ferrer [feʀe] /1/ vt (cheval) to shoe

ferroviaire [feʀɔvjɛʀ] adj rail cpd,
railway cpd (BRIT), railroad cpd (US)

ferry(-boat) [feʀe(bot)] nm ferry

fertile [fɛʀtil] adj fertile; **~ en
incidents** eventful, packed with
incidents

fervent, e [fɛʀvɑ̃, -ɑ̃t] adj fervent

fesse [fɛs] nf buttock; **fessée** nf
spanking

festin [fɛstɛ̃] nm feast

festival [fɛstival] nm festival

festivités [fɛstivite] nfpl festivities

fêtard, e [fɛtaʀ, -aʀd] (fam) nm/f (péj)
high liver, merrymaker

fête [fɛt] nf (religieuse) feast; (publique)
holiday; (réception) party; (kermesse)
fête, fair; (du nom) feast day, name
day; **faire la ~** to live it up; **faire ~
à qn** to give sb a warm welcome;
les ~s (de fin d'année) the festive
season; **la salle/le comité des ~s**
the village hall/festival committee;
la ~ des Mères/Pères Mother's/
Father's Day; **la ~ foraine** (fun)fair; **la
~ de la musique**; see note **"fête de la
musique"**; **fêter** /1/ vt to celebrate;
(personne) to have a celebration for

● **FÊTE DE LA MUSIQUE**

● The *Fête de la Musique* is a music
● festival which has taken place
● every year since 1981. On 21 June
● throughout France local musicians
● perform free of charge in parks,
● streets and squares.

feu, x [fø] nm (gén) fire; (signal lumineux) light; (de cuisinière) ring; **feux** nmpl (Auto) (traffic) lights; **au ~!** (incendie) fire!; **à ~ doux/vif** over a slow/brisk heat; **à petit ~** (Culin) over a gentle heat; (fig) slowly; **faire ~** to fire; **ne pas faire long ~** not to last long; **prendre ~** to catch fire; **mettre le ~ à** to set fire to; **faire du ~** to make a fire; **avez-vous du ~?** (pour cigarette) have you (got) a light?; **~ rouge/ vert/orange** red/green/amber (BRIT) ou yellow (US) light; **~ arrière** rear light; **~ d'artifice** firework; (spectacle) fireworks pl; **~ de joie** bonfire; **~x de brouillard** fog lights ou lamps; **~x de croisement** dipped (BRIT) ou dimmed (US) headlights; **~x de position** sidelights; **~x de route** (Auto) headlights (on full (BRIT) ou high (US) beam)

feuillage [fœjaʒ] nm foliage, leaves pl

feuille [fœj] nf (d'arbre) leaf; **~ (de papier)** sheet (of paper); **~ de calcul** spreadsheet; **~ d'impôts** tax form; **~ de maladie** medical expenses claim form; **~ de paye** pay slip

feuillet [fœjɛ] nm leaf

feuilleté, e [fœjte] adj: **pâte ~** flaky pastry

feuilleter [fœjte] /4/ vt (livre) to leaf through

feuilleton [fœjtɔ̃] nm serial

feutre [føtʀ] nm felt; (chapeau) felt hat; (stylo) felt-tip(ped pen); **feutré, e** adj (pas, voix, atmosphère) muffled

fève [fɛv] nf broad bean

février [fevʀije] nm February

fiable [fjabl] adj reliable

fiançailles [fjɑ̃saj] nfpl engagement sg

fiancé, e [fjɑ̃se] nm/f fiancé (fiancée) ⊳ adj: **être ~ (à)** to be engaged (to)

fibre [fibʀ] nf fibre; **~ de verre** fibreglass

ficeler [fis(ə)le] /4/ vt to tie up

ficelle [fisɛl] nf string no pl; (morceau) piece ou length of string

fiche [fiʃ] nf (carte) (index) card; (formulaire) form; (Élec) plug; **~ de paye** pay slip

ficher [fiʃe] /1/ vt (dans un fichier) to file; (: Police) to put on file; (fam: faire) to do; (: donner) to give; (: mettre) to stick ou shove; **fiche(-moi) le camp** (fam) clear off; **fiche-moi la paix** (fam) leave me alone; **se ~ de** (fam: rire de) to make fun of; (: être indifférent à) not to care about

fichier [fiʃje] nm file; **~ joint** (Inform) attachment

fichu, e [fiʃy] pp de **ficher** ⊳ adj (fam: fini, inutilisable) bust, done for; (: intensif) wretched, damned ⊳ nm (foulard) (head)scarf; **mal ~** feeling lousy

fictif, -ive [fiktif, -iv] adj fictitious

fiction [fiksjɔ̃] nf fiction; (fait imaginé) invention

fidèle [fidɛl] adj: **~ (à)** faithful (to) ⊳ nm/f (Rel): **les ~s** (à l'église) the congregation; **fidélité** nf (d'un conjoint) fidelity, faithfulness; (d'un ami, client) loyalty

fier¹ [fje]: **se ~ à** vt to trust

fier², fière [fjɛʀ] adj proud; **~ de** proud of; **fierté** nf pride

fièvre [fjɛvʀ] nf fever; **avoir de la ~/39 de ~** to have a high temperature/a temperature of 39°C; **fiévreux, -euse** adj feverish

figer [fiʒe] /3/: **se figer** vi to congeal; (personne) to freeze

fignoler [fiɲɔle] /1/ vt to put the finishing touches to

figue [fig] nf fig; **figuier** nm fig tree

figurant, e [figyʀɑ̃, -ɑ̃t] nm/f (Théât) walk-on; (Ciné) extra

figure [figyʀ] nf (visage) face; (image, tracé, forme, personnage) figure; (illustration) picture, diagram

figuré, e [figyʀe] adj (sens) figurative

figurer [figyʀe] /1/ vi to appear ⊳ vt to represent; **se ~ que** to imagine that

fil [fil] nm (brin, fig: d'une histoire) thread; (d'un couteau) edge; **au ~ des**

années with the passing of the years; **au ~ de l'eau** with the stream *ou* current; **coup de ~** (*fam*) phone call; **donner/recevoir un coup de ~** to make/get a phone call; **~ électrique** electric wire; **~ de fer** wire; **~ de fer barbelé** barbed wire

file [fil] *nf* line; (*d'un* **~ (d'attente)** queue (BRIT), line (US); **à la ~** (*d'affilée*) in succession; **à la** *ou* **en ~ indienne** in single file

filer [file] /1/ *vt* (tissu, toile, verre) to spin; (prendre en filature) to shadow, tail; (fam: donner): **~ qch à qn** to slip sb sth ⊳ *vi* (bas, maille, liquide, pâte) to run; (aller vite) to fly past *ou* by; (fam: partir) to make off; **~ doux** to behave o.s.

filet [file] *nm* net; (Culin) fillet; (d'eau, de sang) trickle; **~ (à provisions)** string bag

filial, e, -aux [filjal, -o] *adj* filial ⊳ *nf* (Comm) subsidiary

filière [filjɛʀ] *nf* (carrière) path; **suivre la ~** to work one's way up (through the hierarchy)

fille [fij] *nf* girl; (opposé à fils) daughter; **vieille ~** old maid; **fillette** *nf* (little) girl

filleul, e [fijœl] *nm/f* godchild, godson (goddaughter)

film [film] *nm* (pour photo) (roll of) film; (œuvre) film, picture, movie

fils [fis] *nm* son; **~ à papa** (péj) daddy's boy

filtre [filtʀ] *nm* filter; **filtrer** /1/ *vt* to filter; (fig: candidats, visiteurs) to screen

fin¹ [fɛ̃] *nf* end; **fins** *nfpl* (but) ends; **~ mai** at the end of May; **prendre ~** to come to an end; **mettre ~ à** to put an end to; **à la ~** in the end, eventually; **en ~ de compte** in the end; **sans ~** endless

fin², e [fɛ̃, fin] *adj* (papier, couche, fil) thin; (cheveux, poudre, pointe, visage) fine; (taille) neat, slim; (esprit, remarque) subtle ⊳ *adv* (moudre, couper) finely; **~ prêt/soûl** quite ready/drunk; **avoir la vue/l'ouïe ~e** to have keen eyesight/hearing; **or/linge/vin ~** fine gold/linen/wine; **~es herbes** mixed herbs

final, e [final] *adj, nf* final; **~e** *nm* (Mus) finale; **quarts de ~e** quarter-finals; **finalement** *adv* finally, in the end; (après tout) after all

finance [finɑ̃s] *nf* finance; **finances** *nfpl* (situation financière) finances; (activités financières) finance *sg*; **moyennant ~** for a fee *ou* consideration; **financer** /3/ *vt* to finance; **financier, -ière** *adj* financial

finesse [fines] *nf* thinness; (raffinement) fineness; (subtilité) subtlety

fini, e [fini] *adj* finished; (Math) finite ⊳ *nm* (d'un objet manufacturé) finish

finir [finiʀ] /2/ *vt* to finish, end; **~ de faire** to finish doing; (cesser) to stop doing; **~ par faire** to end *ou* finish up doing; **il finit par m'agacer** he's beginning to get on my nerves; **en ~ avec** to be *ou* have done with; **il va mal ~** he will come to a bad end

finition [finisjɔ̃] *nf* (résultat) finish

finlandais, e [fɛ̃lɑ̃dɛ, -ez] *adj* Finnish ⊳ *nm/f*: **F~, e** Finn

Finlande [fɛ̃lɑ̃d] *nf*: **la ~** Finland

finnois, e [finwa, -waz] *adj* Finnish ⊳ *nm* (Ling) Finnish

fioul [fjul] *nm* fuel oil

firme [fiʀm] *nf* firm

fis [fi] *vb voir* **faire**

fisc [fisk] *nm* tax authorities *pl*; **fiscal, e, -aux** *adj* tax *cpd*, fiscal; **fiscalité** *nf* tax system

fissure [fisyʀ] *nf* crack; **fissurer** /1/ *vt* to crack; **se fissurer** *vi* to crack

fit [fi] *vb voir* **faire**

fixation [fiksasjɔ̃] *nf* (attache) fastening; (Psych) fixation

fixe [fiks] *adj* fixed; (emploi) steady, regular ⊳ *nm* (salaire) basic salary; (téléphone) landline; **à heure ~** at a set time; **menu à prix ~** set menu

fixé, e [fikse] adj: **être ~ (sur)** (savoir à quoi s'en tenir) to have made up one's mind (about)

fixer [fikse] /1/ vt (attacher): **~ qch (à/sur)** to fix ou fasten sth (to/onto); (déterminer) to fix, set; (poser son regard sur) to stare at; **se fixer** (s'établir) to settle down; **se ~ sur** (attention) to focus on

flacon [flakɔ̃] nm bottle

flageolet [flaʒɔlɛ] nm (Culin) dwarf kidney bean

flagrant, e [flagrɑ̃, -ɑ̃t] adj flagrant, blatant; **en ~ délit** = to be in the act

flair [flɛʀ] nm sense of smell; (fig) intuition; **flairer** /1/ vt (humer) to sniff (at); (détecter) to scent

flamand, e [flamɑ̃, -ɑ̃d] adj Flemish ▷ nm (Ling) Flemish ▷ nm/f: **F~, e** Fleming

flamant [flamɑ̃] nm flamingo

flambant [flɑ̃bɑ̃] adv: **~ neuf** brand new

flambé, e [flɑ̃be] adj (Culin) flambé

flambée [flɑ̃be] nf blaze; **~ des prix** (sudden) shooting up of prices

flamber [flɑ̃be] /1/ vi to blaze (up)

flamboyer [flɑ̃bwaje] /8/ vi to blaze (up)

flamme [flam] nf flame; (fig) fire, fervour; **en ~s** on fire, ablaze

flan [flɑ̃] nm (Culin) custard tart ou pie

flanc [flɑ̃] nm side; (Mil) flank

flancher [flɑ̃ʃe] /1/ vi to fail, pack up

flanelle [flanɛl] nf flannel

flâner [flane] /1/ vi to stroll

flanquer [flɑ̃ke] /1/ vt to flank; (fam: mettre) to chuck, shove; **~ par terre/à la porte** (jeter) to fling to the ground/chuck out

flaque [flak] nf (d'eau) puddle; (d'huile, de sang etc) pool

flash [flaʃ] (pl flashes) nm (Photo) flash; **~ (d'information)** newsflash

flatter [flate] /1/ vt to flatter; **se ~ de qch** to pride o.s. on sth; **flatteur, -euse** adj flattering

flèche [flɛʃ] nf arrow; (de clocher) spire; **monter en ~** (fig) to soar, rocket; **partir en ~** to be off like a shot; **fléchette** nf dart

flétrir [fletʀiʀ] /2/: **se flétrir** vi to wither

fleur [flœʀ] nf flower; (d'un arbre) blossom; **être en ~** (arbre) to be in blossom; **tissu à ~s** flowered ou flowery fabric

fleuri, e [flœʀi] adj (jardin) in flower ou bloom; (style, tissu, papier) flowery; (teint) glowing

fleurir [flœʀiʀ] /2/ vi (rose) to flower; (arbre) to blossom; (fig) to flourish ▷ vt (tombe) to put flowers on; (chambre) to decorate with flowers

fleuriste [flœʀist] nm/f florist

fleuve [flœv] nm river

flexible [flɛksibl] adj flexible

flic [flik] nm (fam: péj) cop

flipper [flipœʀ] nm pinball (machine)

flirter [flœʀte] /1/ vi to flirt

flocon [flɔkɔ̃] nm flake

flore [flɔʀ] nf flora

florissant, e [flɔʀisɑ̃, -ɑ̃t] adj (économie) flourishing

flot [flo] nm flood, stream; **flots** nmpl (de la mer) waves; **être à ~** (Navig) to be afloat; **entrer à ~s** to stream ou pour in

flottant, e [flɔtɑ̃, -ɑ̃t] adj (vêtement) loose(-fitting)

flotte [flɔt] nf (Navig) fleet; (fam: eau) water; (: pluie) rain

flotter [flɔte] /1/ vi to float; (nuage, odeur) to drift; (drapeau) to fly; (vêtements) to hang loose ▷ vb impers (fam: pleuvoir): **il flotte** it's raining; **faire ~** to float; **flotteur** nm float

flou, e [flu] adj fuzzy, blurred; (fig) woolly (BRIT), vague

fluide [flyid] adj fluid; (circulation etc) flowing freely ▷ nm fluid

fluor [flyɔʀ] nm: **dentifrice au ~** fluoride toothpaste

fluorescent, e [flyɔʀesɑ̃, -ɑ̃t] adj fluorescent

flûte [flyt] *nf* (*aussi*: **~ traversière**) flute; (*verre*) flute glass; (*pain*) (thin) baguette; **~I** drat it!; **~ (à bec)** recorder

flux [fly] *nm* incoming tide; (*écoulement*) flow; **le ~ et le re~** the ebb and flow

foc [fɔk] *nm* jib

foi [fwa] *nf* faith; **digne de ~** reliable; **être de bonne/mauvaise ~** to be in good faith/not to be in good faith

foie [fwa] *nm* liver; **crise de ~** stomach upset

foin [fwɛ̃] *nm* hay; **faire du ~** (*fam*) to kick up a row

foire [fwar] *nf* fair; (*fête foraine*) (fun) fair; **~ aux questions** (*Internet*) frequently asked questions; **faire la ~** to whoop it up; **~ (exposition)** trade fair

fois [fwa] *nf* time; **une/deux ~** once/twice; **deux ~ deux** twice two; **une ~ (passé)** once; (*futur*) sometime; **une (bonne) ~ pour toutes** once and for all; **une ~ que c'est fait** once it's done; **des ~ (parfois)** sometimes; **à la ~ (ensemble)** (all) at once

fol [fɔl] *adj m voir* **fou**

folie [fɔli] *nf* (*d'une décision, d'un acte*) madness, folly; (*état*) madness, insanity; **la ~ des grandeurs** delusions of grandeur; **faire des ~s (en dépenses)** to be extravagant

folklorique [fɔlklɔrik] *adj* folk *cpd*; (*fam*) weird

folle [fɔl] *adj f, nf voir* **fou**; **follement** *adv* (*très*) madly, wildly

foncé, e [fɔ̃se] *adj* dark

foncer [fɔ̃se] /3/ *vi* to go darker; (*fam*: *aller vite*) to tear ou belt along; **~ sur** to charge at

fonction [fɔ̃ksjɔ̃] *nf* function; (*emploi, poste*) post, position; **fonctions** *nfpl* (*professionnelles*) duties; **voiture de ~** company car; **en ~ de** (*par rapport à*) according to; **faire ~ de** to serve as; **la ~ publique** the state ou civil (BRIT) service; **fonctionnaire** *nm/f*

state employee ou official; (*dans l'administration*) ≈ civil servant; **fonctionner** /1/ *vi* to work, function

fond [fɔ̃] *nm voir aussi* **fonds**; (*d'un récipient, trou*) bottom; (*d'une salle, scène*) back; (*d'un tableau, décor*) background; (*opposé à la forme*) content; (*Sport*): **le ~** long distance (running); **au ~ de** at the bottom of; at the back of; **à ~ (connaître, soutenir)** thoroughly; (*appuyer, visser*) right down ou home; **à ~ (de train)** (*fam*) full tilt; **dans le ~, au ~ (en somme)** basically, really; **de ~ en comble** from top to bottom; **~ de teint** foundation

fondamental, e, -aux [fɔ̃damɑ̃tal, -o] *adj* fundamental

fondant, e [fɔ̃dɑ̃, -ɑ̃t] *adj* (*neige*) melting; (*poire*) that melts in the mouth

fondation [fɔ̃dasjɔ̃] *nf* founding; (*établissement*) foundation; **fondations** *nfpl* (*d'une maison*) foundations

fondé, e [fɔ̃de] *adj* (*accusation etc*) well-founded; **être ~ à croire** to have grounds for believing ou good reason to believe

fondement [fɔ̃dmɑ̃] *nm*: **sans ~** (*rumeur etc*) groundless, unfounded

fonder [fɔ̃de] /1/ *vt* to found; (*fig*): **~ qch sur** to base sth on; **se ~ sur** (*personne*) to base o.s. on

fonderie [fɔ̃dri] *nf* smelting works *sg*

fondre [fɔ̃dr] /41/ *vt* (*aussi*: **faire ~**) to melt; (*dans l'eau*) to dissolve; (*fig*: *mélanger*) to merge, blend ▷ *vi* (*à la chaleur*) to melt; to dissolve; (*fig*) to melt away; (*se précipiter*): **~ sur** to swoop down on; **~ en larmes** to dissolve into tears

fonds [fɔ̃] *nm* (*Comm*): **~ (de commerce)** business ▷ *nmpl* (*argent*) funds

fondu, e [fɔ̃dy] *adj* (*beurre, neige*) melted; (*métal*) molten ▷ *nf* (*Culin*) fondue

font [fɔ̃] vb voir **faire**

fontaine [fɔ̃tɛn] nf fountain; (source) spring

fonte [fɔ̃t] nf melting; (métal) cast iron; **la ~ des neiges** (the spring) thaw

foot [fut], **football** [futbol] nm football, soccer; **footballeur, -euse** nm/f footballer (BRIT), football ou soccer player

footing [futiŋ] nm jogging; **faire du ~** to go jogging

forain, e [fɔrɛ̃, -ɛn] adj fairground cpd ▷ nm (marchand) stallholder; (acteur etc) fairground entertainer

forçat [fɔrsa] nm convict

force [fɔrs] nf strength; (Physique, Mécanique) force; **forces** nfpl (physiques) strength sg; (Mil) forces; **à ~ de faire** by dint of doing; **de ~** forcibly, by force; **dans la ~ de l'âge** in the prime of life; **les ~s de l'ordre** the police

forcé, e [fɔrse] adj forced; **c'est ~!** it's inevitable!; **forcément** adv inevitably; **pas forcément** not necessarily

forcer [fɔrse] /3/ vt to force; (moteur, voix) to strain ▷ vi (Sport) to overtax o.s.; **se ~ à faire qch** to force o.s. to do sth; **~ la dose/l'allure** to overdo it/increase the pace

forestier, -ière [fɔrɛstje, -jɛr] adj forest cpd

forêt [fɔrɛ] nf forest

forfait [fɔrfɛ] nm (Comm) all-in deal ou price; **déclarer ~** to withdraw; **forfaitaire** adj inclusive

forge [fɔrʒ] nf forge, smithy; **forgeron** nm (black)smith

formaliser [fɔrmalize] /1/: **se formaliser** vi: **se ~ (de)** to take offence (at)

formalité [fɔrmalite] nf formality; **simple ~** mere formality

format [fɔrma] nm size; **formater** /1/ vt (disque) to format

formation [fɔrmasjɔ̃] nf forming; training; **la ~ permanente** ou

continue continuing education; **la ~ professionnelle** vocational training

forme [fɔrm] nf (gén) form; (d'un objet) shape, form; **formes** nfpl (bonnes manières) proprieties; (d'une femme) figure sg; **en ~ de poire** pear-shaped, in the shape of a pear; **être ~ (en)** ou **pleine)** ~ (Sport etc) to be on form; **en bonne et due ~** in due form

formel, le [fɔrmɛl] adj (preuve, décision) definite, positive; **formellement** adv (interdit) strictly; (absolument) positively

former [fɔrme] /1/ vt to form; (éduquer) to train; **se former** vi to form

formidable [fɔrmidabl] adj tremendous

formulaire [fɔrmylɛr] nm form

formule [fɔrmyl] nf (gén) formula; (expression) phrase; **~ de politesse** polite phrase; (en fin de lettre) letter ending

fort, e [fɔr, fɔrt] adj strong; (intensité, rendement) high, great; (corpulent) large; (doué): **être ~ (en)** to be good (at) ▷ adv (empoigner, serrer) hard; (sonner) loud(ly); (beaucoup) greatly, very much; (très) very ▷ nm (édifice) fort; (point fort) strong point, forte; **~e tête** rebel; **forteresse** nf fortress

fortifiant [fɔrtifjɑ̃] nm tonic

fortune [fɔrtyn] nf fortune; **faire ~** to make one's fortune; **de ~** makeshift; **fortuné, e** adj wealthy

forum [fɔrɔm] nm forum; **~ de discussion** (Internet) message board

fosse [fos] nf (grand trou) pit; (tombe) grave

fossé [fose] nm ditch; (fig) gulf, gap

fossette [fosɛt] nf dimple

fossile [fosil] nm fossil ▷ adj fossilized, fossil cpd

fou (fol), folle [fu, fɔl] adj mad; (déréglé etc) wild, erratic; (fam: extrême, très grand) terrific, tremendous ▷ nm/f madman/woman ▷ nm (du

roi) jester; **être ~ de** to be mad ou
crazy about; **avoir le ~ rire** to have
the giggles

foudre [fudʀ] nf: **la ~** lightning

foudroyant, e [fudʀwajɑ̃, -ɑ̃t]
adj (progrès) lightning cpd; (succès)
stunning; (maladie, poison) violent

fouet [fwɛ] nm whip; (Culin) whisk;
de plein ~ adv (se heurter) head on;
fouetter /1/ vt to whip; (crème)
to whisk

fougère [fuʒɛʀ] nf fern

fougue [fug] nf ardour, spirit;
fougueux, -euse adj fiery

fouille [fuj] nf search; **fouilles** nfpl
(archéologiques) excavations; **fouiller**
/1/ vt to search; (creuser) to dig ▷ vi:
fouiller dans/parmi to rummage in/
among; **fouillis** nm jumble, muddle

foulard [fulaʀ] nm scarf

foule [ful] nf crowd; **la ~** crowds pl;
une ~ de masses of

foulée [fule] nf stride

fouler [fule] /1/ vt to press; (sol) to tread
upon; **se ~ la cheville** to sprain one's
ankle; **il ne se foule pas** he doesn't
overexert o.s.; **il ne se foule pas** he doesn't put
himself out; **foulure** nf sprain

four [fuʀ] nm oven; (de potier) kiln;
(Théât: échec) flop

fourche [fuʀʃ] nf pitchfork

fourchette [fuʀʃɛt] nf fork;
(Statistique) bracket, margin

fourgon [fuʀgɔ̃] nm van; (Rail)
wag(g)on; **fourgonnette** nf
(delivery) van

fourmi [fuʀmi] nf ant; **avoir des
~s dans les jambes/mains** to have
pins and needles in one's legs/hands;
fourmilière nf ant-hill; **fourmiller**
/1/ vi to swarm

fourneau, x [fuʀno] nm stove

fourni, e [fuʀni] adj (barbe, cheveux)
thick; (magasin): **bien ~ (en)** well
stocked (with)

fournir [fuʀniʀ] /2/ vt to supply;
(preuve, exemple) to provide, supply;
(effort) to put in; **~ qch à qn** to

supply sth to sb, supply ou provide sb
with sth; **fournisseur, -euse** nm/f
supplier; **fournisseur d'accès à
Internet** (Internet) service provider,
ISP; **fourniture** nf supply(ing);
fournitures scolaires school
stationery

fourrage [fuʀaʒ] nm fodder

fourré, e [fuʀe] adj (bonbon, chocolat)
filled; (manteau, botte) fur-lined ▷ nm
thicket

fourrer [fuʀe] /1/ vt (fam) to stick,
shove; **se ~ dans/sous** to get into/
under

fourrière [fuʀjɛʀ] nf pound

fourrure [fuʀyʀ] nf fur; (pelage) coat

foutre [futʀ] /1/ vt (fam!) = **ficher**;
foutu, e adj (fam!) = **fichu**

foyer [fwaje] nm (de cheminée) hearth;
(famille) family; (domicile) home; (local
de réunion) social club; (résidence)
hostel; (salon) foyer; **lunettes à
double ~** bi-focal glasses

fracassant, e [fʀakasɑ̃, -ɑ̃t] adj
(succès) staggering

fraction [fʀaksjɔ̃] nf fraction;
fracturation nf: **~
hydraulique** fracking

fracture [fʀaktyʀ] nf fracture; **~ du
crâne** fractured skull; **fracturer** /1/
vt (coffre, serrure) to break open; (os,
membre) to fracture; **se fracturer le
crâne** to fracture one's skull

fragile [fʀaʒil] adj fragile, delicate;
(fig) frail; **fragilité** nf fragility

fragment [fʀagmɑ̃] nm (d'un objet)
fragment, piece

fraîche [fʀɛʃ] adj f voir **frais**;
fraîcheur nf coolness; (d'un aliment)
freshness; voir **frais**; **fraîchir** /2/ vi
to get cooler; (vent) to freshen

frais, fraîche [fʀɛ, fʀɛʃ] adj (air,
eau, accueil) cool; (petit pois, œufs,
nouvelles, couleur, troupes) fresh ▷ adv
(récemment) newly, fresh(ly) ▷ nm:
mettre au ~ to put in a cool place;
prendre le ~ to take a breath of cool
air ▷ nmpl (débours) expenses; (Comm)

costs; **il fait ~** it's cool; **servir ~** serve chilled; **faire des ~** to go to a lot of expense; **~ généraux** overheads; **~ de scolarité** school fees (BRIT), tuition (US)

fraise [fʀɛz] *nf* strawberry; **~ des bois** wild strawberry

framboise [fʀɑ̃bwaz] *nf* raspberry

franc, franche [fʀɑ̃, fʀɑ̃ʃ] *adj* (*personne*) frank, straightforward; (*visage*) open; (*net: refus, couleur*) clear; (*: coupure*) clean; (*intensif*) downright ▷ *nm* franc

français, e [fʀɑ̃sɛ, -ɛz] *adj* French ▷ *nm* (*Ling*) French ▷ *nm/f*: **F~, e** Frenchman/woman

France [fʀɑ̃s] *nf*: **la ~** France; **~ 2, ~ 3** public-sector television channels

■ **FRANCE TÉLÉVISION**

● *France 2* and *France 3* are public-
● sector television channels, *France*
● *2* is a national general interest and
● entertainment channel; *France*
● *3* provides regional news and
● information as well as programmes
● for the national network.

franche [fʀɑ̃ʃ] *adj f voir* **franc**; **franchement** [fʀɑ̃ʃmɑ̃] *adv* frankly; clearly; (*nettement*) definitely; (*tout à fait*) downright

franchir [fʀɑ̃fiʀ] /2/ *vt* (*obstacle*) to clear, get over; (*seuil, ligne, rivière*) to cross; (*distance*) to cover

franchise [fʀɑ̃ʃiz] *nf* frankness; (*douanière*) exemption; (*Assurances*) excess

franc-maçon [fʀɑ̃masɔ̃] *nm* Freemason

franco [fʀɑ̃ko] *adv* (*Comm*): **~ (de port)** postage paid

francophone [fʀɑ̃kɔfɔn] *adj* French-speaking

franc-parler [fʀɑ̃paʀle] *nm inv* outspokenness; **avoir son ~** to speak one's mind

frange [fʀɑ̃ʒ] *nf* fringe

frangipane [fʀɑ̃ʒipan] *nf* almond paste

frappant, e [fʀapɑ̃, -ɑ̃t] *adj* striking

frappé, e [fʀape] *adj* iced

frapper [fʀape] /1/ *vt* to hit, strike; (*étonner*) to strike; **~ dans ses mains** to clap one's hands; **frappé de stupeur** dumbfounded

fraternel, le [fʀatɛʀnɛl] *adj* brotherly, fraternal; **fraternité** *nf* brotherhood

fraude [fʀod] *nf* fraud; (*Scol*) cheating; **passer qch en ~** to smuggle sth in (*ou* out); **~ fiscale** tax evasion

frayeur [fʀɛjœʀ] *nf* fright

fredonner [fʀədɔne] /1/ *vt* to hum

freezer [fʀizœʀ] *nm* freezing compartment

frein [fʀɛ̃] *nm* brake; **mettre un ~ à** (*fig*) to put a brake on, check; **~ à main** handbrake; **freiner** /1/ *vi* to slow down ▷ *vt* (*progrès etc*) to check

frêle [fʀɛl] *adj* frail, fragile

frelon [fʀəlɔ̃] *nm* hornet

frémir [fʀemiʀ] /2/ *vi* (*de froid, de peur*) to shudder; (*de colère*) to shake; (*de joie, feuillage*) to quiver

frêne [fʀɛn] *nm* ash (tree)

fréquemment [fʀekamɑ̃] *adv* frequently

fréquent, e [fʀekɑ̃, -ɑ̃t] *adj* frequent

fréquentation [fʀekɑ̃tasjɔ̃] *nf* frequenting; **fréquentations** *nfpl* (*relations*) company *sg*; **avoir de mauvaises ~s** to be with the wrong crowd, keep bad company

fréquenté, e [fʀekɑ̃te] *adj*: **très ~** (very) busy; **mal ~** patronized by disreputable elements

fréquenter [fʀekɑ̃te] /1/ *vt* (*lieu*) to frequent; (*personne*) to see; **se fréquenter** to see a lot of each other

frère [fʀɛʀ] *nm* brother

fresque [fʀɛsk] *nf* (*Art*) fresco

fret [fʀɛ(t)] *nm* freight

friand, e [fʀijɑ̃, -ɑ̃d] *adj*: ~ **de** very fond of ▷ *nm*: ~ **au fromage** cheese puff

friandise [fʀijɑ̃diz] *nf* sweet

fric [fʀik] *nm (fam)* cash, bread

friche [fʀiʃ]: **en** ~ *adj, adv* (lying) fallow

friction [fʀiksjɔ̃] *nf (massage)* rub, rub-down; *(Tech, fig)* friction

frigidaire® [fʀiʒidɛʀ] *nm* refrigerator

frigo [fʀigo] *nm* fridge

frigorifique [fʀigoʀifik] *adj* refrigerating

frileux, -euse [fʀilø, -øz] *adj* sensitive to (the) cold

frimer [fʀime] /1/ *vi (fam)* to show off

fringale [fʀɛ̃gal] *nf (fam)*: **avoir la** ~ to be ravenous

fringues [fʀɛ̃g] *nfpl (fam)* clothes

fripé, e [fʀipe] *adj* crumpled

frire [fʀiʀ] *vt* to fry ▷ *vi* to fry

frisé, e [fʀize] *adj (cheveux)* curly; *(personne)* curly-haired

frisson [fʀisɔ̃] *nm (de froid)* shiver; *(de peur)* shudder; **frissonner** /1/ *vi (de fièvre, froid)* to shiver; *(d'horreur)* to shudder

frit, e [fʀi, fʀit] *pp de* **frire** ▷ *nf*: **(pommes) ~es** chips (BRIT), French fries; **friteuse** *nf* deep fryer, chip pan (BRIT); **friture** *nf (huile)* (deep) fat; *(plat)*: **friture (de poissons)** fried fish

froid, e [fʀwa, fʀwad] *adj* ▷ *nm* cold; **il fait** ~ it's cold; **avoir** ~ to be cold; **prendre** ~ to catch a chill ou cold; **être en** ~ **avec** to be on bad terms with; **froidement** *adv (accueillir)* coldly; *(décider)* coolly

froisser [fʀwase] /1/ *vt* to crumple (up), crease; *(fig)* to hurt, offend; **se froisser** *vi* to crumple, crease; *(personne)* to take offence (BRIT) ou offense (US); **se** ~ **un muscle** to strain a muscle

frôler [fʀole] /1/ *vt* to brush against; *(projectile)* to skim past; *(fig)* to come

very close to, come within a hair's breadth of

fromage [fʀɔmaʒ] *nm* cheese; ~ **blanc** soft white cheese

froment [fʀɔmɑ̃] *nm* wheat

froncer [fʀɔ̃se] /3/ *vt* to gather; ~ **les sourcils** to frown

front [fʀɔ̃] *nm* forehead, brow; *(Mil, Météorologie, Pol)* front; **de** ~ *(se heurter)* head-on; *(rouler)* together (2 or 3 abreast); *(simultanément)* at once; **faire** ~ **à** to face up to

frontalier, -ière [fʀɔ̃talje, -jɛʀ] *adj* border *cpd*, frontier *cpd* ▷ **(travailleurs) ~s** commuters from across the border

frontière [fʀɔ̃tjɛʀ] *nf* frontier, border

frotter [fʀɔte] /1/ *vi* to rub, scrape ▷ *vt* to rub; *(pommes de terre, plancher)* to scrub; ~ **une allumette** to strike a match

fruit [fʀɥi] *nm* fruit *no pl*; ~**s de mer** seafood *sg*; ~**s secs** dried fruit *sg*; **fruité, e** [fʀɥite] *adj* fruity; **fruitier, -ière** *adj*: **arbre fruitier** fruit tree

frustrer [fʀystʀe] /1/ *vt* to frustrate

fuel(-oil) [fjul(ɔjl)] *nm* fuel oil; *(pour chauffer)* heating oil

fugace [fygas] *adj* fleeting

fugitif, -ive [fyʒitif, -iv] *adj (lueur, amour)* fleeting ▷ *nm/f* fugitive

fugue [fyg] *nf*: **faire une** ~ to run away, abscond

fuir [fɥiʀ] /17/ *vt* to flee from; *(éviter)* to shun ▷ *vi* to run away; *(gaz, robinet)* to leak

fuite [fɥit] *nf* flight; *(divulgation)* leak; **être en** ~ to be on the run; **mettre en** ~ to put to flight

fulgurant, e [fylgyʀɑ̃, -ɑ̃t] *adj* lightning *cpd*, dazzling

fumé, e [fyme] *adj (Culin)* smoked; *(verre)* tinted ▷ *nf* smoke

fumer [fyme] /1/ *vi* to smoke; *(liquide)* to steam ▷ *vt* to smoke

fûmes [fym] *vb voir* **être**

fumeur, -euse [fymœʀ, -øz] *nm/f* smoker

fumier [fymje] *nm* manure

funérailles [fyneʀɑj] *nfpl* funeral *sg*

fur [fyʀ]: **au ~ et à mesure** *adv* as one goes along; **au ~ et à mesure que** as

furet [fyʀɛ] *nm* ferret

fureter [fyʀ(ə)te] /5/ *vi* (*péj*) to nose about

fureur [fyʀœʀ] *nf* fury; **être en ~** to be infuriated; **faire ~** to be all the rage

furie [fyʀi] *nf* fury; (*femme*) shrew, vixen; **en ~** (*mer*) raging; **furieux, -euse** *adj* furious

furoncle [fyʀɔ̃kl] *nm* boil

furtif, -ive [fyʀtif, -iv] *adj* furtive

fus [fy] *vb voir* **être**

fusain [fyzɛ̃] *nm* (*Art*) charcoal

fuseau, x [fyzo] *nm* (*pantalon*) (ski-)pants *pl*; (*pour filer*) spindle; **~ horaire** time zone

fusée [fyze] *nf* rocket

fusible [fyzibl] *nm* (*Élec*: *fil*) fuse wire; (: *fiche*) fuse

fusil [fyzi] *nm* (*de guerre, à canon rayé*) rifle, gun; (*de chasse, à canon lisse*) shotgun, gun; **fusillade** *nf* gunfire *no pl*, shooting *no pl*; **fusiller** /1/ *vt* to shoot; **fusiller qn du regard** to look daggers at sb

fusionner [fyzjɔne] /1/ *vi* to merge

fût [fy] *vb voir* **être** ▷ *nm* (*tonneau*) barrel, cask

futé, e [fyte] *adj* crafty; **Bison ~®** *TV and radio traffic monitoring service*

futile [fytil] *adj* futile; (*frivole*) frivolous

futur, e [fytyʀ] *adj*, *nm* future

fuyard, e [fɥijaʀ, -aʀd] *nm/f* runaway

Gabon [ɡabɔ̃] *nm*: **le ~** Gabon

gâcher [ɡɑʃe] /1/ *vt* (*gâter*) to spoil; (*gaspiller*) to waste; **gâchis** *nm* waste *no pl*

gaffe [ɡaf] *nf* blunder; **faire ~** (*fam*) to watch out

gage [ɡaʒ] *nm* (*dans un jeu*) forfeit; (*fig: de fidélité*) token; **gages** *nmpl* (*salaire*) wages; **mettre en ~** to pawn

gagnant, e [ɡaɲɑ̃, -ɑ̃t] *adj*: **billet/ numéro ~** winning ticket/number ▷ *nm/f* winner

gagne-pain [ɡaɲpɛ̃] *nm inv* job

gagner [ɡaɲe] /1/ *vt* to win; (*somme d'argent, revenu*) to earn; (*aller vers, atteindre*) to reach; (*s'emparer de*) to overcome; (*envahir*) to spread to ▷ *vi* to win; (*fig*) to gain; **~ du temps/ de la place** to gain time/save space; **~ sa vie** to earn one's living

gai, e [ɡe] *adj* cheerful; (*un peu ivre*) merry; **gaiement** *adv* cheerfully;

gaieté *nf* cheerfulness; **de gaieté de cœur** with a light heart

gain [gɛ̃] *nm* (*revenu*) earnings *pl*; (*bénéfice: gén pl*) profits *pl*

gala [gala] *nm* official reception; **soirée de ~** gala evening

galant, e [galɑ̃, -ɑ̃t] *adj* (*courtois*) courteous, gentlemanly; (*entreprenant*) flirtatious, gallant; (*scène, rendez-vous*) romantic

galerie [galʀi] *nf* gallery; (*Théât*) circle; (*de voiture*) roof rack; (*fig: spectateurs*) audience; **~ marchande** shopping mall; **~ de peinture** (*private*) art gallery

galet [galɛ] *nm* pebble

galette [galɛt] *nf* flat pastry cake; **la ~ des Rois** *cake traditionally eaten on Twelfth Night*

■ **GALETTE DES ROIS**

● A *galette des Rois* is a cake eaten
● on Twelfth Night containing a
● figurine. The person who finds it
● is the king (or queen) and gets a
● paper crown. They then choose
● someone else to be their queen
● (or king).

galipette [galipɛt] *nf* somersault

Galles [gal] *nfpl*: **le pays de ~** Wales; **gallois, e** *adj* Welsh ▷ *nm* (*Ling*) Welsh ▷ *nm/f*: **Gallois, e** Welshman(-woman)

galocher [galɔʃe] (*fam*) *vt* to French kiss

galon [galɔ̃] *nm* (*Mil*) stripe; (*décoratif*) piece of braid

galop [galo] *nm* gallop; **galoper** /1/ *vi* to gallop

gambader [gɑ̃bade] /1/ *vi* (*animal, enfant*) to leap about

gamin, e [gamɛ̃, -in] *nm/f* kid ▷ *adj* mischievous

gamme [gam] *nf* (*Mus*) scale; (*fig*) range

gang [gɑ̃g] *nm* (*de criminels*) gang

gant [gɑ̃] *nm* glove; **~ de toilette** (*face*) flannel (*BRIT*), face cloth

garage [gaʀaʒ] *nm* garage; **garagiste** *nm/f* garage owner; (*mécanicien*) garage mechanic

garantie [gaʀɑ̃ti] *nf* guarantee; **(bon de) ~** guarantee *ou* warranty slip

garantir /2/ *vt* to guarantee; **je vous garantis que** I can assure you that

garçon [gaʀsɔ̃] *nm* boy; (*aussi*: **~ de café**) waiter; **vieux ~** (*célibataire*) bachelor; **~ de courses** messenger

garde [gaʀd] *nm* (*de prisonnier*) guard; (*de domaine etc*) warden; (*soldat, sentinelle*) guardsman ▷ *nf* (*soldats*) guard; **de ~** on duty; **monter la ~** to stand guard; **mettre en ~** to warn; **prendre ~ (à)** to take care (of); **~ champêtre** *nm* rural policeman; **~ du corps** *nm* bodyguard; **~ à vue** *nf* (*Jur*) = police custody; **garde-boue** *nm inv* mudguard; **garde-chasse** *nm* gamekeeper

garder [gaʀde] /1/ *vt* (*conserver*) to keep; (*surveiller: enfants*) to look after; (*: immeuble, lieu, prisonnier*) to guard; **se garder** *vi* (*aliment: se conserver*) to keep; **se ~ de faire** to be careful not to do; **~ le lit/la chambre** to stay in bed/indoors; **pêche/chasse gardée** private fishing/hunting (ground)

garderie [gaʀdəʀi] *nf* day nursery, crèche

garde-robe [gaʀdəʀɔb] *nf* wardrobe

gardien, ne [gaʀdjɛ̃, -ɛn] *nm/f* (*garde*) guard; (*de prison*) warder; (*de domaine, réserve*) warden; (*de musée etc*) attendant; (*de phare, cimetière*) keeper; (*d'immeuble*) caretaker; (*fig*) guardian; **~ de but** goalkeeper; **~ de nuit** night watchman; **~ de la paix** policeman

gare [gaʀ] *nf* (*railway*) station ▷ *excl*: **~ à ...** mind ...!; **~ à toi!** watch out!; **~ routière** bus station

garer [gaʀe] /1/ *vt* to park; **se garer** *vi* to park

garni, e [gaʀni] *adj* (*plat*) served with vegetables (*and chips, pasta or rice*)

garniture [garnityr] nf (Culin)
vegetables pl; **~ de frein** brake lining

gars [ga] nm guy

Gascogne [gaskɔɲ] nf: **la ~** Gascony;
le golfe de ~ the Bay of Biscay

gas-oil [gazɔjl] nm diesel oil

gaspiller [gaspije] /1/ vt to waste

gastronome [gastrɔnɔm] nm/f
gourmet; **gastronomique** adj
gastronomic

gâteau, x [gato] nm cake; **~ sec**
biscuit

gâter [gate] /1/ vt to spoil; **se gâter**
vi (dent, fruit) to go bad; (temps,
situation) to change for the worse

gâteux, -euse [gatø, -øz] adj senile

gauche [goʃ] adj left, left-hand;
(maladroit) awkward, clumsy ▷ nf
(Pol) left (wing); **le bras ~** the left
arm; **le côté ~** the left-hand side;
à ~ on the left; (direction) to the
left; **gaucher, -ère** adj left-handed;
gauchiste nm/f leftist

gaufre [gofr] nf waffle

gaufrette [gofrɛt] nf wafer

gaulois, e [golwa, -waz] adj Gallic
▷ nm/f: **G~, e** Gaul

gaz [gaz] nm inv gas; **ça sent le ~** I can
smell gas, there's a smell of gas

gaze [gaz] nf gauze

gazette [gazɛt] nf news sheet

gazeux, -euse [gazø, -øz] adj (eau)
sparkling; (boisson) fizzy

gazoduc [gazodyk] nm gas pipeline

gazon [gazɔ̃] nm (herbe) grass;
(pelouse) lawn

géant, e [ʒeɑ̃, -ɑ̃t] adj gigantic;
(Comm) giant-size ▷ nm/f giant

geindre [ʒɛ̃dr] /52/ vi to groan, moan

gel [ʒɛl] nm frost; **~ douche** shower
gel

gélatine [ʒelatin] nf gelatine

gelé, e [ʒ(ə)le] adj frozen ▷ nf jelly;
(gel) frost

geler [ʒ(ə)le] /5/ vt, vi to freeze; **il**
gèle it's freezing

gélule [ʒelyl] nf (Méd) capsule

Gémeaux [ʒemo] nmpl: **les ~** Gemini

gémir [ʒemir] /2/ vi to groan, moan

gênant, e [ʒɛnɑ̃, -ɑ̃t] adj (objet) in the
way; (histoire, personne) embarrassing

gencive [ʒɑ̃siv] nf gum

gendarme [ʒɑ̃darm] nm gendarme;
gendarmerie nf military police force in
countryside and small towns; their police
station or barracks

gendre [ʒɑ̃dr] nm son-in-law

gêné, e [ʒene] adj embarrassed

gêner [ʒene] /1/ vt (incommoder) to
bother; (encombrer) to be in the way
of; (embarrasser): **~ qn** to make sb feel
ill-at-ease; **se gêner** to put o.s. out;
ne vous gênez pas! don't mind me!

général, e, -aux [ʒeneral, -o] adj,
nm general; **en ~** usually, in general;
généralement adv generally;
généraliser /1/ vt, vi to generalize;
se généraliser vi to become
widespread; **généraliste** nm/f
general practitioner, GP

génération [ʒenerasjɔ̃] nf generation

généreux, -euse [ʒenerø, -øz] adj
generous

générique [ʒenerik] nm (Ciné, TV)
credits pl

générosité [ʒenerozite] nf
generosity

genêt [ʒ(ə)nɛ] nm (Bot) broom no pl

génétique [ʒenetik] adj genetic

Genève [ʒ(ə)nɛv] n Geneva

génial, e, -aux [ʒenjal, -o] adj of
genius; (fam: formidable) fantastic,
brilliant

génie [ʒeni] nm genius; (Mil): **le**
~ ≈ the Engineers pl; **~ civil** civil
engineering

genièvre [ʒənjɛvr] nm juniper (tree)

génisse [ʒenis] nf heifer

génital, e, -aux [ʒenital, -o] adj
genital; **les parties ~es** the genitals

génois, e [ʒenwa, -waz] adj Genoese
▷ nf (gâteau) ≈ sponge cake

génome [ʒenɔm] nm genome

genou, x [ʒ(ə)nu] nm knee; **à ~x**
on one's knees; **se mettre à ~x** to
kneel down

genre [ʒɑ̃R] nm kind, type, sort; (Ling) gender; **avoir bon ~** to look a nice sort; **avoir mauvais ~** to be coarse-looking; **ce n'est pas son ~** it's not like him

gens [ʒɑ̃] nmpl (f in some phrases) people pl

gentil, le [ʒɑ̃ti, -ij] adj kind; (enfant: sage) good; (sympathique: endroit etc) nice; **gentillesse** nf kindness; **gentiment** adv kindly

géographie [ʒeɔgRafi] nf geography

géologie [ʒeɔlɔʒi] nf geology

géomètre [ʒeɔmɛtR] nm: **(arpenteur-)~** (land) surveyor

géométrie [ʒeɔmetRi] nf geometry; **géométrique** adj geometric

géranium [ʒeRanjɔm] nm geranium

gérant, e [ʒeRɑ̃, -ɑ̃t] nm/f manager/ manageress; **~ d'immeuble** managing agent

gerbe [ʒɛRb] nf (de fleurs, d'eau) spray; (de blé) sheaf

gercé, e [ʒɛRse] adj chapped

gerçure [ʒɛRsyR] nf crack

gérer [ʒeRe] /6/ vt to manage

germain, e [ʒɛRmɛ̃, -ɛn] adj: **cousin ~** first cousin

germe [ʒɛRm] nm germ; **germer** /1/ vi to sprout; (semence) to germinate

geste [ʒɛst] nm gesture

gestion [ʒɛstjɔ̃] nf management

Ghana [gana] nm: **le ~** Ghana

gibier [ʒibje] nm (animaux) game

gicler [ʒikle] /1/ vi to spurt, squirt

gifle [ʒifl] nf slap (in the face); **gifler** /1/ vt to slap (in the face)

gigantesque [ʒigɑ̃tɛsk] adj gigantic

gigot [ʒigo] nm leg (of mutton ou lamb)

gigoter [ʒigɔte] /1/ vi to wriggle (about)

gilet [ʒile] nm waistcoat; (pull) cardigan; **~ de sauvetage** life jacket

gin [dʒin] nm gin; **~-tonic** gin and tonic

gingembre [ʒɛ̃ʒɑ̃bR] nm ginger

girafe [ʒiRaf] nf giraffe

giratoire [ʒiRatwaR] adj: **sens ~** roundabout

girofle [ʒiRɔfl] nm: **clou de ~** clove

girouette [ʒiRwɛt] nf weather vane ou cock

gitan, e [ʒitɑ̃, -an] nm/f gipsy

gîte [ʒit] nm (maison) home; (abri) shelter; **~ (rural)** (country) holiday cottage ou apartment, gîte (self-catering accommodation in the country)

givre [ʒivR] nm (hoar) frost; **givré, e** adj covered in frost; (fam: fou) nuts; **citron givré/orange givrée** lemon/orange sorbet (served in fruit skin)

glace [glas] nf (eau; crème glacée) ice cream; (miroir) mirror; (de voiture) window

glacé, e [glase] adj (mains, vent, pluie) freezing; (lac) frozen; (boisson) iced

glacer [glase] /3/ vt to freeze; (gâteau) to ice; **~ qn** (intimider) to chill sb; (fig) to make sb's blood run cold

glacial, e [glasjal] adj icy

glacier [glasje] nm (Géo) glacier; (marchand) ice-cream maker

glacière [glasjɛR] nf icebox

glaçon [glasɔ̃] nm icicle; (pour boisson) ice cube

glaïeul [glajœl] nm gladiola

glaise [glɛz] nf clay

gland [glɑ̃] nm acorn; (décoration) tassel

glande [glɑ̃d] nf gland

glissade [glisad] nf (par jeu) slide; (chute) slip; **faire des ~s** to slide

glissant, e [glisɑ̃, -ɑ̃t] adj slippery

glissement [glismɑ̃] nm: **~ de terrain** landslide

glisser [glise] /1/ vi (avancer) to glide ou slide along; (coulisser, tomber) to slide; (déraper) to slip; (être glissant) to be slippery ▷ vt to slip; **se ~ dans/entre** to slip into/between

global, e, -aux [glɔbal, -o] adj overall

globe [glɔb] nm globe

globule [glɔbyl] nm (du sang): **~ blanc/rouge** white/red corpuscle

gloire [glwar] nf glory

glousser [gluse] /1/ vi to cluck; (rire) to chuckle

glouton, ne [glutɔ̃, -ɔn] adj gluttonous

gluant, e [glyɑ̃, -ɑ̃t] adj sticky, gummy

glucose [glykoz] nm glucose

glycine [glisin] nf wisteria

GO sigle fpl (= grandes ondes) LW

goal [gol] nm goalkeeper

gobelet [gɔblɛ] nm (en métal) tumbler; (en plastique) beaker; (à dés) cup

goéland [gɔelɑ̃] nm (sea)gull

goélette [gɔelɛt] nf schooner

goinfre [gwɛ̃fʀ] nm glutton

golf [gɔlf] nm golf; (terrain) golf course; **~ miniature** crazy ou miniature golf

golfe [gɔlf] nm gulf; (petit) bay

gomme [gɔm] nf (à effacer) rubber (BRIT), eraser; **gommer** /1/ vt to rub out (BRIT), erase

gonflé, e [gɔ̃fle] adj swollen; **il est ~** (fam: courageux) he's got some nerve; (: impertinent) he's got a nerve

gonfler [gɔ̃fle] /1/ vt (pneu, ballon) to inflate, blow up; (nombre, importance) to inflate ▷ vi to swell (up); (Culin: pâte) to rise

gonzesse [gɔ̃zɛs] nf (fam) chick, bird (BRIT)

googler [gugle] /1/ vt to google

gorge [gɔʀʒ] nf (Anat) throat; (Géo) gorge

gorgé, e [gɔʀʒe] adj: **~ de** filled with ▷ nf (petite) sip; (grande) gulp

gorille [gɔʀij] nm gorilla; (fam) bodyguard

gosse [gɔs] nm/f kid

goudron [gudʀɔ̃] nm tar; **goudronner** /1/ vt to tar(mac) (BRIT), asphalt (US)

gouffre [gufʀ] nm abyss, gulf

goulot [gulo] nm neck; **boire au ~** to drink from the bottle

goulu, e [guly] adj greedy

gourde [gurd] nf (récipient) flask; (fam) (clumsy) clot ou oaf ▷ adj oafish

gourdin [gurdɛ̃] nm club, bludgeon

gourmand, e [gurmɑ̃, -ɑ̃d] adj greedy; **gourmandise** nf greed; (bonbon) sweet

gousse [gus] nf: **~ d'ail** clove of garlic

goût [gu] nm taste; **de bon ~** tasteful; **de mauvais ~** tasteless; **avoir bon/mauvais ~** to taste nice/nasty; **prendre ~ à** to develop a taste ou a liking for

goûter [gute] /1/ vt (essayer) to taste; (apprécier) to enjoy ▷ vi to have (afternoon) tea ▷ nm (afternoon) tea; **je peux ~?** can I have a taste?

goutte [gut] nf drop; (Méd) gout; (alcool) nip of brandy, drop (US); **tomber ~ à ~** to drip; **goutte-à-goutte** nm inv (Méd) drip

gouttière [gutjɛʀ] nf gutter

gouvernail [guvɛʀnaj] nm rudder; (barre) helm, tiller

gouvernement [guvɛʀnəmɑ̃] nm government

gouverner [guvɛʀne] /1/ vt to govern

grâce [gʀas] nf (charme, Rel) grace; (faveur) favour; (Jur) pardon; **faire ~ à qn de qch** to spare sb sth; **demander ~** to beg for mercy; **~ à** thanks to; **gracieux, -euse** adj graceful

grade [gʀad] nm rank; **monter en ~** to be promoted

gradin [gʀadɛ̃] nm tier; (de stade) step; **gradins** nmpl (de stade) terracing no pl

gradué, e [gʀadɥe] adj: **verre ~** measuring jug

graduel, le [gʀadɥɛl] adj gradual

graduer [gʀadɥe] /1/ vt (effort etc) to increase gradually; (règle, verre) to graduate

graffiti [gʀafiti] nmpl graffiti

grain [gʀɛ̃] nm (gén) grain; (Navig) squall; **~ de beauté** beauty spot; **~ de café** coffee bean; **~ de poivre** peppercorn

graine [gʀɛn] nf seed

graissage [gʀɛsaʒ] nm lubrication, greasing

graisse [gʀɛs] nf fat; (lubrifiant) grease; **graisser** /1/ vt to lubricate, grease; (tacher) to make greasy; **graisseux, -euse** adj greasy

grammaire [gʀamɛʀ] nf grammar

gramme [gʀam] nm gramme

grand, e [gʀɑ̃, gʀɑ̃d] adj (haut) tall; (gros, vaste, large) big, large; (long) long; (plus âgé) big; (adulte) grown-up; (important, brillant) great ▷ adv: **~ ouvert** wide open; **au ~ air** in the open (air); **les ~s blessés/brûlés** the severely injured/burned; **~ ensemble** housing scheme; **~ magasin** department store; **~e personne** grown-up; **~ surface** hypermarket; **~es écoles** prestige university-level colleges with competitive entrance examinations; **~es lignes** (Rail) main lines; **~es vacances** summer holidays (BRIT) ou vacation (US); **grand-chose** nm/f inv: **pas grand-chose** not much; **Grande-Bretagne** nf: **la Grande-Bretagne** (Great) Britain; **grandeur** nf (dimension) size; **grandeur nature** life-size; **grandiose** adj imposing; **grandir** /2/ vi to grow; grow ▷ vt: **grandir qn** (vêtement, chaussure) to make sb look taller; **grand-mère** nf grandmother; **grand-peine**: **à grand-peine** adv with (great) difficulty; **grand-père** nm grandfather; **grands-parents** nmpl grandparents

grange [gʀɑ̃ʒ] nf barn

granit [gʀanit] nm granite

graphique [gʀafik] adj graphic ▷ nm graph

grappe [gʀap] nf cluster; **~ de raisin** bunch of grapes

gras, se [gʀɑ, gʀɑs] adj (viande, soupe) fatty; (personne) fat; (surface, main, cheveux) greasy; (plaisanterie) coarse; (Typo) bold ▷ nm (Culin) fat; **faire la ~e matinée** to have a lie-in

(BRIT), sleep late; **grassement** adv: **grassement payé** handsomely paid

gratifiant, e [gʀatifjɑ̃, -ɑ̃t] adj gratifying, rewarding

gratin [gʀatɛ̃] nm (Culin) cheese- (ou crumb-)topped dish; (: croûte) topping; **tout le ~ parisien** all the best people of Paris; **gratiné** adj (Culin) au gratin

gratis [gʀatis] adv free

gratitude [gʀatityd] nf gratitude

gratte-ciel [gʀatsjɛl] nm inv skyscraper

gratter [gʀate] /1/ vt (frotter) to scrape; (avec un ongle) to scratch; (enlever: avec un outil) to scrape off; (: avec un ongle) to scratch off ▷ vi (irriter) to be scratchy; (démanger) to itch; **se gratter** to scratch o.s.

gratuit, e [gʀatɥi, -ɥit] adj (entrée) free; (fig) gratuitous

grave [gʀav] adj (maladie, accident) serious, bad; (sujet, problème) serious, grave; (personne, air) grave, solemn; (voix, son) deep, low-pitched; **gravement** adv seriously; (parler, regarder) gravely

graver [gʀave] /1/ vt (plaque, nom) to engrave; (CD, DVD) to burn

graveur [gʀavœʀ] nm engraver; **~ de CD/DVD** CD/DVD burner or writer

gravier [gʀavje] nm (loose) gravel no pl; **gravillons** nmpl gravel sg

gravir [gʀaviʀ] /2/ vt to climb (up)

gravité [gʀavite] nf (de maladie, d'accident) seriousness; (de sujet, problème) gravity

graviter [gʀavite] /1/ vi to revolve

gravure [gʀavyʀ] nf engraving; (reproduction) print

gré [gʀe] nm: **à son ~** to his liking; **contre le ~ de qn** against sb's will; **de son (plein) ~** of one's own free will; **de ~ ou de force** whether one likes it or not; **de bon ~** willingly; **bon ~ mal ~** like it or not; **savoir (bien) ~ à qn de qch** to be (most) grateful to sb for sth

grec, grecque [gʀɛk] *adj* Greek ; *(classique: vase etc)* Grecian ▷ *nm (Ling)* Greek ▷ *nm/f:* **Grec, Grecque** Greek

Grèce [gʀɛs] *nf:* **la ~** Greece

greffe [gʀɛf] *nf (Bot, Méd: de tissu)* graft ; *(Méd: d'organe)* transplant ; **greffer** /1/ *vt (Bot, Méd: tissu)* to graft ; *(Méd: organe)* to transplant

grêle [gʀɛl] *adj* (very) thin ▷ *nf* hail ; **grêler** /1/ *vb impers:* **il grêle** it's hailing ; **grêlon** *nm* hailstone

grelot [gʀəlo] *nm* little bell

grelotter [gʀəlɔte] /1/ *vi* to shiver

grenade [gʀənad] *nf (explosive)* grenade ; *(Bot)* pomegranate ; **grenadine** *nf* grenadine

grenier [gʀənje] *nm* attic ; *(de ferme)* loft

grenouille [gʀənuj] *nf* frog

grès [gʀɛ] *nm* sandstone ; *(poterie)* stoneware

grève [gʀɛv] *nf (d'ouvriers)* strike ; *(plage)* shore ; **se mettre en/faire ~** to go on/be on strike ; **~ de la faim** hunger strike ; **~ sauvage** wildcat strike

gréviste [gʀevist] *nm/f* striker

grièvement [gʀijɛvmɑ̃] *adv* seriously

griffe [gʀif] *nf* claw ; *(d'un couturier, parfumeur)* label ; **griffer** /1/ *vt* to scratch

grignoter [gʀiɲɔte] /1/ *vt (personne)* to nibble at ; *(souris)* to gnaw at ▷ *vi* to nibble

gril [gʀil] *nm* steak *ou* grill pan ; **grillade** *nf* grill

grillage [gʀijaʒ] *nm (treillis)* wire netting ; *(clôture)* wire fencing

grille [gʀij] *nf (portail)* (metal) gate ; *(clôture)* railings *pl* ; *(d'égout)* (metal) grate ; grid

grille-pain [gʀijpɛ̃] *nm inv* toaster

griller [gʀije] /1/ *vt (aussi:* **faire ~**) *(pain)* to toast ; *(viande)* to grill ; *(châtaignes)* to roast ; *(fig: ampoule etc)* to burn out ; **~ un feu rouge** to jump the lights

grillon [gʀijɔ̃] *nm* cricket

grimace [gʀimas] *nf* grimace ; *(pour faire rire):* **faire des ~s** to pull *ou* make faces

grimper [gʀɛ̃pe] /1/ *vi, vt* to climb

grincer [gʀɛ̃se] /3/ *vi (porte, roue)* to grate ; *(plancher)* to creak ; **~ des dents** to grind one's teeth

grincheux, -euse [gʀɛ̃ʃø, -øz] *adj* grumpy

grippe [gʀip] *nf* flu, influenza ; **~ A** swine flu ; **~ aviaire** bird flu ; **grippé, e** *adj:* **être grippé** to have (the) flu

gris, e [gʀi, gʀiz] *adj* grey ; *(ivre)* tipsy

grisaille [gʀizaj] *nf* greyness, dullness

griser [gʀize] /1/ *vt* to intoxicate

grive [gʀiv] *nf* thrush

Groenland [gʀɔɛnlɑ̃d] *nm:* **le ~** Greenland

grogner [gʀɔɲe] /1/ *vi* to growl ; *(fig)* to grumble ; **grognon, ne** *adj* grumpy

grommeler [gʀɔmle] /4/ *vi* to mutter to o.s.

gronder [gʀɔ̃de] /1/ *vi* to rumble ; *(fig: révolte)* to be brewing ▷ *vt* to scold ; **se faire ~** to get a telling-off

gros, se [gʀo, gʀos] *adj* big, large ; *(obèse)* fat ; *(travaux, dégâts)* extensive ; *(large)* thick ; *(rhume, averse)* heavy ▷ *adv:* **risquer/gagner ~** to risk/win a lot ▷ *nm (Comm)* fat man/woman ▷ *nm (Comm):* **le ~** the wholesale business ; **prix de ~** wholesale price ; **par ~ temps/~ se mer** in rough weather/ heavy seas ; **le ~ de** the bulk of ; **en ~** roughly ; *(Comm)* wholesale ; **~ lot** jackpot ; **~ mot** swearword ; **~ plan** *(Photo)* close-up ; **~ sel** cooking salt ; **~ titre** headline ; **~se caisse** big drum

groseille [gʀozɛj] *nf:* **~ (rouge)/ (blanche)** red/white currant ; **~ à maquereau** gooseberry

grosse [gʀos] *adj f voir* **gros** ; **grossesse** *nf* pregnancy ; **grosseur** *nf* size ; *(tumeur)* lump

grossier, -ière [gʀosje, -jɛʀ] *adj* coarse ; *(insolent)* rude ; *(dessin)* rough; (travail) roughly done; (imitation, instrument) crude; (évident: erreur) gross; **grossièrement** adv (vulgairement) coarsely; (sommairement) roughly; (en gros) roughly; **grossièreté** nf rudeness; (mot): **dire des grossièretés** to use coarse language

grossir [gʀosiʀ] /2/ vi (personne) to put on weight ▷ vt (exagérer) to exaggerate; (au microscope) to magnify; (vêtement): **~ qn** to make sb look fatter

grossiste [gʀosist] nm/f wholesaler

grotesque [gʀɔtɛsk] adj (extravagant) grotesque; (ridicule) ludicrous

grotte [gʀɔt] nf cave

groupe [gʀup] nm group; **~ de parole** support group; **~ sanguin** blood group; **~ scolaire** school complex; **grouper** /1/ vt to group; **se grouper** vi to get together

grue [gʀy] nf crane

GSM [ʒeɛsɛm] nm, adj GSM

guenon [gənɔ̃] nf female monkey

guépard [ɡepaʀ] nm cheetah

guêpe [ɡɛp] nf wasp

guère [ɡɛʀ] adv (avec adjectif, adverbe): **ne ... ~** hardly; (avec verbe: pas beaucoup): **ne ... ~** (tournure négative) much; (pas souvent) hardly ever; (tournure négative) (very) long; **il n'y a ~ que/de** there's hardly anybody (ou anything) but/hardly any; **ce n'est ~ difficile** it's hardly difficult; **nous n'avons ~ de temps** we have hardly any time

guérilla [ɡeʀija] nf guerrilla warfare

guérillero [ɡeʀijeʀo] nm guerrilla

guérir [ɡeʀiʀ] /2/ vt (personne, maladie) to cure; (membre, plaie) to heal ▷ vi (personne, malade) to recover, be cured; (maladie) to be cured; (plaie, chagrin, blessure) to heal; **guérison** nf (de maladie) curing; (de membre, plaie) healing; (de malade) recovery; **guérisseur, -euse** nm/f healer

guerre [ɡɛʀ] nf war; **en ~** at war; **faire la ~ à** to wage war against; **~ civile/mondiale** civil/world war; **guerrier, -ière** adj warlike ▷ nm/f warrior

guet [ɡɛ] nm: **faire le ~** to be on the watch ou look-out; **guet-apens** [ɡetapɑ̃] nm ambush; **guetter** /1/ vt (épier) to watch (intently); (attendre) to watch (out) for; (: pour surprendre) to be lying in wait for

gueule [ɡœl] nf (d'animal) mouth; (fam: visage) mug; (: bouche) gob (!), mouth; **ta ~!** (fam) shut up!; **avoir la ~ de bois** (fam) to have a hangover, be hung over; **gueuler** /1/ vi to bawl

gui [ɡi] nm mistletoe

guichet [ɡiʃɛ] nm (de bureau, banque) counter; **les ~s** (à la gare, au théâtre) the ticket office

guide [ɡid] nm (personne) guide; (livre) guide(book) ▷ nf (fille scout) (girl) guide; **guider** /1/ vt to guide

guidon [ɡidɔ̃] nm handlebars pl

guignol [ɡiɲɔl] nm ≈ Punch and Judy show; (fig) clown

guillemets [ɡijmɛ] nmpl: **entre ~** in inverted commas ou quotation marks

guindé, e [ɡɛ̃de] adj (personne, air) stiff, starchy; (style) stilted

Guinée [ɡine] nf: **la (République de) ~** (the Republic of) Guinea

guirlande [ɡiʀlɑ̃d] nf (fleurs) garland; **~ de Noël** tinsel no pl

guise [ɡiz] nf: **à votre ~** as you wish ou please; **en ~ de** by way of

guitare [ɡitaʀ] nf guitar

Guyane [ɡɥijan] nf: **la ~ (française)** (French) Guiana

gym [ʒim] nf (exercices) gym; **gymnase** nm gym(nasium); **gymnaste** nm/f gymnast; **gymnastique** nf gymnastics sg; (au réveil etc) keep-fit exercises pl

gynécologie [ʒinekɔlɔʒi] nf gynaecology; **gynécologique** adj gynaecological; **gynécologue** nm/f gynaecologist

h

habile [abil] *adj* skilful; (*malin*) clever; **habileté** [abilte] *nf* skill, skilfulness; cleverness

habillé, e [abije] *adj* dressed; (*chic*) dressy

habiller [abije] /1/ *vt* to dress; (*fournir en vêtements*) to clothe; (*couvrir*) to cover; **s'habiller** *vi* to dress (o.s.); (*se déguiser, mettre des vêtements chic*) to dress up

habit [abi] *nm* outfit; **habits** *nmpl* (*vêtements*) clothes; ~ **(de soirée)** evening dress; (*pour homme*) tails *pl*

habitant, e [abitã, -ãt] *nm/f* inhabitant; (*d'une maison*) occupant; **loger chez l'~** to stay with the locals

habitation [abitasjɔ̃] *nf* house; **~s à loyer modéré (HLM)** ≈ council flats

habiter [abite] /1/ *vt* to live in *ou* at; *vi*: **~ à/dans** to live in *ou* at

habitude [abityd] *nf* habit; **avoir l'~ de faire** to be in the habit of doing; (*expérience*) to be used to doing;

avoir l'~ des enfants to be used to children; **d'~** usually; **comme d'~** as usual

habitué, e [abitчe] *nm/f* (*de maison*) regular visitor; (*client*) regular (customer)

habituel, le [abitчɛl] *adj* usual

habituer [abitчe] /1/ *vt*: **~ qn à** to get sb used to; **s'habituer à** to get used to

'hache ['aʃ] *nf* axe

'hacher ['aʃe] /1/ *vt* (*viande*) to mince; (*persil*) to chop; **'hachis** *nm* mince *no pl*; **hachis Parmentier** ≈ shepherd's pie

'haie ['ɛ] *nf* hedge; (*Sport*) hurdle

'haillons ['ajɔ̃] *nmpl* rags

'haine ['ɛn] *nf* hatred

'haïr ['aiʀ] /10/ *vt* to detest, hate

'hâlé, e ['ale] *adj* (*sun*)tanned, sunburnt

haleine [alɛn] *nf* breath; **hors d'~** out of breath; **tenir en ~** (*attention*) to hold spellbound; (*en attente*) to keep in suspense; **de longue ~** long-term

'haleter ['alte] /5/ *vi* to pant

'hall ['ol] *nm* hall

'halle ['al] *nf* (*covered*) market; **'halles** *nfpl* (*d'une grande ville*) central food market *sg*

hallucination [alysinasjɔ̃] *nf* hallucination

'halte ['alt] *nf* stop, break; (*escale*) stopping place ▷ *excl* stop!; **faire ~** to stop

haltère [altɛʀ] *nm* dumbbell, barbell; **(poids et) ~s** (*activité*) weightlifting *sg*; **haltérophilie** *nf* weightlifting

'hamac ['amak] *nm* hammock

'hamburger ['ãbuʀgœʀ] *nm* hamburger

'hameau, x ['amo] *nm* hamlet

hameçon [amsɔ̃] *nm* (fish) hook

'hamster ['amstɛʀ] *nm* hamster

'hanche ['ãʃ] *nf* hip

'hand-ball ['ãdbal] *nm* handball

'handicapé, e ['ɑ̃dikape] adj disabled ▷ nm/f person with a disability; **~ mental/physique** person with learning difficulties/a disability; **~ moteur** person with a movement disorder

'hangar ['ɑ̃gar] nm shed; (Aviat) hangar

'hanneton ['antɔ̃] nm cockchafer

'hanter ['ɑ̃te] /1/ vt to haunt

'hantise ['ɑ̃tiz] nf obsessive fear

'harceler ['arsəle] /5/ vt to harass; **~ qn de questions** to plague sb with questions

'hardi, e ['ardi] adj bold, daring

'hareng ['arɑ̃] nm herring; **~ saur** kipper, smoked herring

'hargne ['arɲ] nf aggressivity, aggressiveness; **'hargneux, -euse** adj aggressive

'haricot ['ariko] nm bean; **~ blanc/rouge** haricot/kidney bean; **~ vert** French (BRIT) ou green bean

harmonica [armonika] nm mouth organ

harmonie [armoni] nf harmony; **harmonieux, -euse** adj harmonious; (couleurs, couple) well-matched

harpe ['arp] nf harp

'hasard ['azar] nm: **le ~** chance, fate; **un ~** a coincidence; **au ~** (sans but) aimlessly; (à l'aveuglette) at random; **par ~** by chance; **à tout ~** (en espérant trouver ce qu'on cherche) on the off chance; (en cas de besoin) just in case

'hâte ['ɑt] nf haste; **à la ~** hurriedly, hastily; **en ~** posthaste, with all possible speed; **avoir ~ de** to be eager ou anxious to; **hâter** /1/ vt to hasten; **se hâter** to hurry; **hâtif, -ive** adj (travail) hurried; (décision) hasty

'hausse ['os] nf rise, increase; **être en ~** to be going up; **hausser** /1/ vt to raise; **hausser les épaules** to shrug (one's shoulders)

'haut, e ['o, 'ot] adj high; (grand) tall ▷ adv high ▷ nm top (part); **de 3 m de ~**

3 m high, 3 m in height; **en ~ lieu** in high places; **à ~ e voix, (tout) ~** aloud, out loud; **des ~ s et des bas** ups and downs; **du ~ de** from the top of; **de ~ en bas** from top to bottom; **plus ~** higher up, further up; (dans un texte) above; (parler) louder; **en ~** (être/aller) at (ou to) the top; (dans une maison) upstairs; **en ~ de** at the top of; **~ débit** broadband

'hautain, e ['otɛ̃, -ɛn] adj haughty

'hautbois ['obwa] nm oboe

'hauteur ['otœr] nf height; **à la ~ de** (sur la même ligne) level with; (fig: tâche, situation) equal to; **à la ~** (fig) up to it

'haut-parleur ['oparlœr] nm (loud) speaker

Hawaï [awai] n Hawaii; **les îles ~** the Hawaiian Islands

'Haye ['ɛ] n: **la ~** the Hague

hebdomadaire [ɛbdɔmadɛr] adj, nm weekly

hébergement [ebɛrʒəmɑ̃] nm accommodation

héberger [ebɛrʒe] /3/ vt (touristes) to accommodate, lodge; (amis) to put up; (réfugiés) to take in

hébergeur [ebɛrʒœr] nm (Internet) host

hébreu, x [ebrø] adj m, nm Hebrew

Hébrides [ebrid] nf: **les ~** the Hebrides

hectare [ɛktar] nm hectare

'hein ['ɛ̃] excl eh?

'hélas ['elas] excl alas! ▷ adv unfortunately

'héler ['ele] /6/ vt to hail

hélice [elis] nf propeller

hélicoptère [elikɔptɛr] nm helicopter

helvétique [ɛlvetik] adj Swiss

hématome [ematom] nm haematoma

hémisphère [emisfɛr] nm: **~ nord/sud** northern/southern hemisphere

hémorragie [emɔraʒi] nf bleeding no pl, haemorrhage

hémorroïdes [emɔʀɔid] *nfpl* piles, haemorrhoids

'hennir ['eniʀ] /2/ *vi* to neigh, whinny

hépatite [epatit] *nf* hepatitis

herbe [ɛʀb] *nf* grass; (*Culin, Méd*) herb; **~s de Provence** mixed herbs; **en ~** unripe; (*fig*) budding; **herbicide** *nm* weed-killer; **herboriste** *nm/f* herbalist

héréditaire [eʀeditɛʀ] *adj* hereditary

hérisson ['eʀisɔ̃] *nm* hedgehog

héritage [eʀitaʒ] *nm* inheritance; (*coutumes, système*) heritage; legacy

hériter [eʀite] /1/ *vi*: **~ de qch (de qn)** to inherit sth (from sb); **héritier, -ière** *nm/f* heir/heiress

hermétique [ɛʀmetik] *adj* airtight; (*à l'eau*) watertight; (*fig: écrivain, style*) abstruse; (*visage*) impenetrable

hermine [ɛʀmin] *nf* ermine

'hernie ['ɛʀni] *nf* hernia

héroïne [eʀɔin] *nf* heroine; (*drogue*) heroin

héroïque [eʀɔik] *adj* heroic

'héron ['eʀɔ̃] *nm* heron

'héros ['eʀo] *nm* hero

hésitant, e [ezitɑ̃, -ɑ̃t] *adj* hesitant

hésitation [ezitasjɔ̃] *nf* hesitation

hésiter [ezite] /1/ *vi*: **~ (à faire)** to hesitate (to do)

hétérosexuel, le [eteʀɔsɛkɥɛl] *adj* heterosexual

'hêtre ['ɛtʀ] *nm* beech

heure ['œʀ] *nf* hour; (*Scol*) period; (*moment, moment fixé*) time; **c'est l'~** it's time; **quelle ~ est-il?** what time is it?; **2 ~s (du matin)** 2 o'clock (in the morning); **être à l'~** to be on time; (*montre*) to be right; **mettre à l'~** to set right; **à toute ~** at any time; **24 ~s sur 24** round the clock, 24 hours a day; **à l'~ qu'il est** at this time (of day); (*fig*) now; **à l'~ actuelle** at the present time; **sur l'~** at once; **à une ~ avancée (de la nuit)** at a late hour (of the night); **de bonne ~** early; **~ de pointe** rush hour; (*téléphone*) peak period; **~s de bureau** office hours; **~s supplémentaires** overtime *sg*

heureusement [œʀøzmɑ̃] *adv* (*par bonheur*) fortunately, luckily

heureux, -euse [œʀø, -øz] *adj* happy; (*chanceux*) lucky, fortunate

'heurt ['œʀ] *nm* (*choc*) collision

'heurter ['œʀte] /1/ *vt* (*mur*) to strike, hit; (*personne*) to collide with

hexagone [ɛgzagɔn] *nm* hexagon; **l'H~** (*la France*) France (*because of its roughly hexagonal shape*)

hiberner [ibɛʀne] /1/ *vi* to hibernate

'hibou, x ['ibu] *nm* owl

'hideux, -euse ['idø, -øz] *adj* hideous

hier [jɛʀ] *adv* yesterday; **~ matin/ soir/midi** yesterday morning/ evening/lunchtime; **toute la journée d'~** all day yesterday; **toute la matinée d'~** all yesterday morning

'hiérarchie ['jeʀaʀʃi] *nf* hierarchy

hindou, e [ɛ̃du] *adj* Hindu ▷ *nm/f*: **H~, e** Hindu; (*Indien*) Indian

hippique [ipik] *adj* equestrian, horse *cpd*; **un club ~** a riding centre; **un concours ~** a horse show; **hippisme** [ipism] *nm* (horse-)riding

hippodrome [ipɔdʀom] *nm* racecourse

hippopotame [ipɔpɔtam] *nm* hippopotamus

hirondelle [iʀɔ̃dɛl] *nf* swallow

'hisser ['ise] /1/ *vt* to hoist, haul up

histoire [istwaʀ] *nf* (*science, événements*) history; (*anecdote, récit, mensonge*) story; (*affaire*) business *no pl*; (*chichis: gén*) fuss *no pl*; **histoires** *nfpl* (*ennuis*) trouble *sg*; **~ géo** humanities *pl*; **historique** *adj* historical; (*important*) historic ▷ *nm*: **faire l'historique de** to give the background to

'hit-parade ['itpaʀad] *nm*: **le ~** the charts

hiver [ivɛʀ] *nm* winter; **hivernal, e, -aux** *adj* winter *cpd*; (*comme en hiver*) wintry; **hiverner** /1/ *vi* to winter

HLM sigle m ou f (= habitations à loyer modéré) low-rent, state-owned housing; **un(e)** ~ = a council flat (ou house)

'**hobby** ['ɔbi] nm hobby

'**hocher** ['ɔʃe] /1/ vt: ~ **la tête** to nod; (signe négatif ou dubitatif) to shake one's head

'**hockey** ['ɔkɛ] nm: ~ **(sur glace/gazon)** (ice/field) hockey

'**hold-up** ['ɔldœp] nm inv hold-up

'**hollandais, e** ['ɔlɑ̃dɛ, -ɛz] adj Dutch ▷ nm (Ling) Dutch ▷ nm/f: **H~, e** Dutchman/woman

'**Hollande** ['ɔlɑ̃d] nf: **la ~** Holland

'**homard** ['ɔmaʀ] nm lobster

homéopathique [ɔmeɔpatik] adj homoeopathic

homicide [ɔmisid] nm murder; ~ **involontaire** manslaughter

hommage [ɔmaʒ] nm tribute; **rendre ~ à** to pay tribute to

homme [ɔm] nm man; ~ **d'affaires** businessman; ~ **d'État** statesman; ~ **de main** hired man; ~ **de paille** stooge; ~ **politique** politician; **l'~ de la rue** the man in the street

homogène adj homogeneous

homologue nm/f counterpart

homologué, e adj (Sport) ratified; (tarif) authorized

homonyme nm (Ling) homonym; (d'une personne) namesake

homoparental, e, -aux [ɔmɔpaʀɑ̃tal, o] adj (famille) same-sex

homosexuel, le adj homosexual

Hong-Kong ['ɔ̃gkɔ̃g] n Hong Kong

Hongrie ['ɔ̃gʀi] nf: **la ~** Hungary; '**hongrois, e** adj Hungarian ▷ nm (Ling) Hungarian ▷ nm/f: **Hongrois, e** Hungarian

honnête [ɔnɛt] adj (intègre) honest; (juste, satisfaisant) fair; **honnêteté** adv honestly; **honnêteté** nf honesty

honneur [ɔnœʀ] nm honour; (mérite): **l'~ lui revient** the credit is his; **en l'~ de** (personne) in honour of;

(événement) on the occasion of; **faire ~ à** (engagements) to honour; (famille, professeur) to be a credit to; (fig: repas etc) to do justice to

honorable [ɔnɔʀabl] adj worthy, honourable; (suffisant) decent

honoraire [ɔnɔʀɛʀ] adj honorary; **honoraires** nmpl fees; **professeur ~** professor emeritus

honorer [ɔnɔʀe] /1/ vt to honour; (estimer) to hold in high regard; (faire honneur à) to be a credit to

honte [ɔ̃t] nf shame; **avoir ~ de** to be ashamed of; **faire ~ à qn** to make sb (feel) ashamed; **honteux, -euse** adj ashamed; (conduite, acte) shameful, disgraceful

hôpital, -aux [ɔpital, -o] nm hospital; **où est l'~ le plus proche?** where is the nearest hospital?

'**hoquet** ['ɔkɛ] nm: **avoir le ~** to have (the) hiccups

horaire [ɔʀɛʀ] adj hourly ▷ nm timetable, schedule; **horaires** nmpl (heures de travail) hours; ~ **flexible** ou **mobile** ou **à la carte** ou **souple** flex(i)time

horizon [ɔʀizɔ̃] nm horizon

horizontal, e, -aux adj horizontal

horloge [ɔʀlɔʒ] nf clock; **l'~ parlante** the speaking clock; **horloger, -ère** nm/f watchmaker; clockmaker

hormis ['ɔʀmi] prép save

horoscope [ɔʀɔskɔp] nm horoscope

horreur [ɔʀœʀ] nf horror; **quelle ~!** how awful!; **avoir ~ de** to loathe ou detest; **horrible** adj horrible; **horrifier** /7/ vt to horrify

'**hors** ['ɔʀ] prép: ~ **de** out of; ~ **pair** outstanding; ~ **de propos** inopportune; ~ **service (HS)**, ~ **d'usage** out of service; **être ~ de soi** to be beside o.s.; '**hors-bord** nm inv speedboat (with outboard motor); '**hors-d'œuvre** nm inv hors d'œuvre; '**hors-la-loi** nm inv outlaw; '**hors-taxe** adj duty-free

hortensia [ɔʀtɑ̃sja] nm hydrangea

hospice [ɔspis] *nm (de vieillards)* home

hospitalier, -ière [ɔspitalje, -jɛʀ] *adj (accueillant)* hospitable; *(Méd: service, centre)* hospital *cpd*

hospitaliser [ɔspitalize] */1/ vt* to take *(ou* send) to hospital, hospitalize

hospitalité [ɔspitalite] *nf* hospitality

hostie [ɔsti] *nf* host

hostile [ɔstil] *adj* hostile; **hostilité** *nf* hostility

hôte [ot] *nm (maître de maison)* host ▷ *nm/f (invité)* guest

hôtel [otɛl] *nm* hotel; **aller à l'~** to stay in a hotel; **~ (particulier)** (private) mansion; **~ de ville** town hall; *see note "hôtels"*; **hôtellerie** [otɛlʀi] *nf* hotel business

▪ HÔTELS

- There are six categories of hotel
- in France, from zero ('non classé')
- to four stars and luxury four
- stars ('quatre étoiles luxe'). Prices
- include VAT but not breakfast. In
- some towns, guests pay a small
- additional tourist tax, the 'taxe
- de séjour'.

hôtesse [otɛs] *nf* hostess; **~ de l'air** flight attendant

houblon ['ublɔ̃] *nm (Bot)* hop; *(pour la bière)* hops *pl*

houille ['uj] *nf* coal; **~ blanche** hydroelectric power

houle ['ul] *nf* swell; **houleux, -euse** *adj* stormy

hourra ['uʀa] *excl* hurrah!

housse ['us] *nf* cover

houx ['u] *nm* holly

hovercraft [ɔvœʀkʀaft] *nm* hovercraft

hublot ['yblo] *nm* porthole

huche ['yʃ] *nf*: **huche à pain** bread bin

huer ['ɥe] */1/ vt* to boo

huile [ɥil] *nf* oil

huissier [ɥisje] *nm* usher; *(Jur)* ≈ bailiff

huit ['ɥi(t)] *num* eight; **samedi en ~** a week on Saturday; **dans ~ jours** in a week('s time); **huitaine** ['ɥiten] *nf*: **une huitaine de jours** a week or so; **huitième** *num* eighth

huître [ɥitʀ] *nf* oyster

humain, e [ymɛ̃, -ɛn] *adj* human; *(compatissant)* humane ▷ *nm* human (being); **humanitaire** *adj* humanitarian; **humanité** *nf* humanity

humble [œ̃bl] *adj* humble

humer ['yme] */1/ vt (parfum)* to inhale; *(pour sentir)* to smell

humeur [ymœʀ] *nf* mood; **de bonne/mauvaise ~** in a good/ bad mood

humide [ymid] *adj* damp; *(main, yeux)* moist; *(climat, chaleur)* humid; *(saison, route)* wet

humilier [ymilje] */7/ vt* to humiliate

humilité [ymilite] *nf* humility, humbleness

humoristique [ymɔʀistik] *adj* humorous

humour [ymuʀ] *nm* humour; **avoir de l'~** to have a sense of humour; **~ noir** sick humour

huppé, e ['ype] *adj (fam)* posh

hurlement ['yʀləmɑ̃] *nm* howling *no pl*, howl; yelling *no pl*, yell

hurler ['yʀle] */1/ vi* to howl, yell

hutte ['yt] *nf* hut

hydratant, e [idʀatɑ̃, -ɑ̃t] *adj (crème)* moisturising

hydraulique [idʀolik] *adj* hydraulic

hydravion [idʀavjɔ̃] *nm* seaplane

hydrogène [idʀɔʒɛn] *nm* hydrogen

hydroglisseur [idʀɔglisœʀ] *nm* hydroplane

hyène [jɛn] *nf* hyena

hygiène [iʒjɛn] *nf* hygiene

hygiénique [iʒenik] *adj* hygienic

hymne [imn] *nm* hymn

hyperlien [ipɛʀljɛ̃] *nm* hyperlink

hypermarché [ipɛʀmaʀʃe] *nm* hypermarket

hypermétrope [ipɛʀmetʀɔp] *adj* long-sighted

hypertension [ipɛʀtɑ̃sjɔ̃] *nf* high blood pressure

hypnose [ipnoz] *nf* hypnosis; **hypnotiser** /1/ *vt* to hypnotize

hypocrisie [ipɔkʀizi] *nf* hypocrisy; **hypocrite** *adj* hypocritical

hypothèque [ipɔtɛk] *nf* mortgage

hypothèse [ipɔtɛz] *nf* hypothesis

hystérique [isteʀik] *adj* hysterical

iceberg [isbɛʀg] *nm* iceberg

ici [isi] *adv* here; **jusqu'~** as far as this; (*temporel*) until now; **d'~ là** by then; **d'~ demain** by tomorrow; in the meantime; **d'~ peu** before long

icône [ikon] *nf* icon

idéal, e, -aux [ideal, -o] *adj* ideal ▷ *nm* ideal; **idéaliste** *adj* idealistic ▷ *nm/f* idealist

idée [ide] *nf* idea; **se faire des ~s** to imagine things, get ideas into one's head; **avoir dans l'~ que** to have an idea that; **~s noires** black *ou* dark thoughts; **~s reçues** accepted ideas *ou* wisdom

identifier [idɑ̃tifje] /7/ *vt* to identify; **s'identifier** *vi*: **s'~ avec** *ou* **à qn/qch** (*héros etc*) to identify with sb/sth

identique [idɑ̃tik] *adj*: **~ (à)** identical (to)

identité [idɑ̃tite] *nf* identity

idiot, e [idjo, idjɔt] *adj* idiotic ▷ *nm/f* idiot

idole [idɔl] nf idol

if [if] nm yew

ignoble [iɲɔbl] adj vile

ignorant, e [iɲɔʀɑ̃, -ɑ̃t] adj ignorant; **~ de** ignorant of, not aware of

ignorer [iɲɔʀe] /1/ vt not to know; (personne) to ignore

il [il] pron he; (animal, chose, en tournure impersonnelle) it; **il neige** it's snowing; **Pierre est-il arrivé?** has Pierre arrived?; **il a gagné** he won; voir aussi **avoir**

île [il] nf island; **l'~ Maurice** Mauritius; **les ~s anglo-normandes** the Channel Islands; **les ~s Britanniques** the British Isles

illégal, e, -aux [ilegal, -o] adj illegal

illimité, e [ilimite] adj unlimited

illisible [ilizibl] adj illegible; (roman) unreadable

illogique [ilɔʒik] adj illogical

illuminer [ilymine] /1/ vt to light up; (monument, rue: pour une fête) to illuminate; (: au moyen de projecteurs) floodlight

illusion [ilyzjɔ̃] nf illusion; **se faire des ~s** to delude o.s.; **faire ~** to delude ou fool people

illustration [ilystʀasjɔ̃] nf illustration

illustré, e [ilystʀe] adj illustrated ▷ nm comic

illustrer [ilystʀe] /1/ vt to illustrate; **s'illustrer** to become famous, win fame

ils [il] pron they

image [imaʒ] nf (gén) picture; (comparaison, ressemblance) image; **~ de marque** brand image; (d'une personne) (public) image; **imagé, e** adj (texte) full of imagery; (langage) colourful

imaginaire [imaʒinɛʀ] adj imaginary

imagination [imaʒinasjɔ̃] nf imagination; **avoir de l'~** to be imaginative

imaginer [imaʒine] /1/ vt to imagine; (inventer: expédient, mesure)

to devise, think up; **s'imaginer** vt (se figurer: scène etc) to imagine, picture; **s'~ que** to imagine that

imam [imam] nm imam

imbécile [ɛ̃besil] adj idiotic ▷ nm/f idiot

imbu, e [ɛ̃by] adj: **~ de** full of

imitateur, -trice [imitatœʀ, -tʀis] nm/f (gén) imitator; (Music-Hall) impersonator

imitation [imitasjɔ̃] nf imitation; (de personalité) impersonation

imiter [imite] /1/ vt to imitate; (contrefaire) to forge; (ressembler à) to look like

immangeable [ɛ̃mɑ̃ʒabl] adj inedible

immatriculation [imatʀikylasjɔ̃] nf registration

> **IMMATRICULATION**
>
> The last two numbers on vehicle licence plates used to show which 'département' of France the vehicle was registered in. For example, a car registered in Paris had the number 75 on its licence plates. In 2009, a new alphanumeric system was introduced, in which the 'département' number no longer features. Displaying this number to the right of the plate is now optional.

immatriculer [imatʀikyle] /1/ vt to register; **faire/se faire ~** to register

immédiat, e [imedja, -at] adj immediate ▷ nm: **dans l'~** for the time being; **immédiatement** adv immediately

immense [imɑ̃s] adj immense

immerger [imɛʀʒe] /3/ vt to immerse, submerge

immeuble [imœbl] nm building; **~ locatif** block of rented flats

immigration [imigʀasjɔ̃] nf immigration

immigré, e [imigʀe] nm/f immigrant

imminent, e [iminɑ̃, -ɑ̃t] adj imminent

immobile [imɔbil] adj still, motionless

immobilier, -ière [imɔbilje, -jɛʀ] adj property cpd ▷ nm: **l'~** the property ou the real estate business

immobiliser [imɔbilize] /1/ vt (gén) to immobilize; (circulation, véhicule, affaires) to bring to a standstill; **s'immobiliser** (personne) to stand still; (machine, véhicule) to come to a halt ou a standstill

immoral, e, -aux [imɔʀal, -o] adj immoral

immortel, le [imɔʀtɛl] adj immortal

immunisé, e [im(m)ynize] adj: **~ contre** immune to

immunité [imynite] nf immunity

impact [ɛ̃pakt] nm impact

impair, e [ɛ̃pɛʀ] adj odd ▷ nm faux pas, blunder

impardonnable [ɛ̃paʀdɔnabl] adj unpardonable, unforgivable

imparfait, e [ɛ̃paʀfɛ, -ɛt] adj imperfect

impartial, e, -aux [ɛ̃paʀsjal, -o] adj impartial, unbiased

impasse [ɛ̃pas] nf dead-end, cul-de-sac; (fig) deadlock

impassible [ɛ̃pasibl] adj impassive

impatience [ɛ̃pasjɑ̃s] nf impatience

impatient, e [ɛ̃pasjɑ̃, -ɑ̃t] adj impatient; **impatienter** /1/: **s'impatienter** vi to get impatient

impeccable [ɛ̃pekabl] adj faultless; (propre) spotlessly clean; (fam) smashing

impensable [ɛ̃pɑ̃sabl] adj (événement hypothétique) unthinkable; (événement qui a eu lieu) unbelievable

impératif, -ive [ɛ̃peʀatif, -iv] adj imperative ▷ nm (Ling) imperative; **impératifs** nmpl (exigences: d'une fonction, d'une charge) requirements; (: de la mode) demands

impératrice [ɛ̃peʀatʀis] nf empress

imperceptible [ɛ̃pɛʀseptibl] adj imperceptible

impérial, e, -aux [ɛ̃peʀjal, -o] adj imperial

impérieux, -euse [ɛ̃peʀjø, -øz] adj (caractère, ton) imperious; (obligation, besoin) pressing, urgent

impérissable [ɛ̃peʀisabl] adj undying

imperméable [ɛ̃pɛʀmeabl] adj waterproof; (fig): **~ à** impervious to ▷ nm raincoat

impertinent, e [ɛ̃pɛʀtinɑ̃, -ɑ̃t] adj impertinent

impitoyable [ɛ̃pitwajabl] adj pitiless, merciless

implanter [ɛ̃plɑ̃te] /1/: **s'implanter dans** vi to be established in

impliquer [ɛ̃plike] /1/ vt to imply; **~ qn (dans)** to implicate sb (in)

impoli, e [ɛ̃pɔli] adj impolite, rude

impopulaire [ɛ̃pɔpylɛʀ] adj unpopular

importance [ɛ̃pɔʀtɑ̃s] nf importance; (de somme) size; **sans ~** unimportant

important, e [ɛ̃pɔʀtɑ̃, -ɑ̃t] adj important; (en quantité: somme, retard) considerable, sizeable; (: gamme, dégâts) extensive; (péj: airs, ton) self-important ▷ nm: **l'~** the important thing

importateur, -trice [ɛ̃pɔʀtatœʀ, -tʀis] nm/f importer

importation [ɛ̃pɔʀtasjɔ̃] nf (produit) import

importer [ɛ̃pɔʀte] /1/ vt (Comm) to import; (maladies, plantes) to introduce ▷ vi (être important) to matter; **il importe qu'il fasse** it is important that he should do; **peu m'importe** (je n'ai pas de préférence) I don't mind; (je m'en moque) I don't care; **peu importe (que)** it doesn't matter (if); voir aussi **n'importe**

importun, e [ɛ̃pɔʀtœ̃, -yn] adj irksome, importunate; (arrivée, visite)

inopportune, ill-timed ▷ nm intruder;
importuner /1/ vt to bother
imposant, e [ɛ̃pozɑ̃, -ɑ̃t] adj
imposing
imposer [ɛ̃poze] /1/ vt (taxer) to
tax; ~ **qch à qn** to impose sth on
sb; **s'imposer** (être nécessaire) to be
imperative; **en ~ à** to impress; **s'~
comme** to emerge as; **s'~ par** to win
recognition through
impossible [ɛ̃posibl] adj impossible;
il m'est ~ de le faire it is impossible
for me to do it, I can't possibly do
it; **faire l'~ (pour que)** to do one's
utmost (so that)
imposteur [ɛ̃postœʀ] nm impostor
impôt [ɛ̃po] nm tax; ~ **sur le chiffre
d'affaires** corporation (BRIT) ou
corporate (US) tax; ~ **foncier** land
tax; ~ **sur le revenu** income tax;
~**s locaux** rates, local taxes (US), ≈
council tax (BRIT)
impotent, e [ɛ̃potɑ̃, -ɑ̃t] adj
disabled
impraticable [ɛ̃pʀatikabl] adj
(projet) impracticable, unworkable;
(piste) impassable
imprécis, e [ɛ̃pʀesi, -iz] adj
imprecise
imprégner [ɛ̃pʀeɲe] /6/ vt: ~ **(de)**
(tissu, tampon) to soak ou impregnate
(with); (lieu, air) to fill (with);
s'imprégner de (fig) to absorb
imprenable [ɛ̃pʀənabl] adj
(forteresse) impregnable; **vue ~**
unimpeded outlook
impression [ɛ̃pʀesjɔ̃] nf
impression; (d'un ouvrage, tissu)
printing; **faire bonne/mauvaise
~** to make a good/bad impression;
impressionnant, e adj (imposant)
impressive; (bouleversant) upsetting;
impressionner /1/ vt (frapper) to
impress; (troubler) to upset
imprévisible [ɛ̃pʀevizibl] adj
unforeseeable
imprévu, e [ɛ̃pʀevy] adj unforeseen,
unexpected ▷ nm (incident)

unexpected incident; **des vacances
pleines d'~** holidays full of surprises;
en cas d'~ if anything unexpected
happens; **sauf ~** unless anything
unexpected crops up
imprimante [ɛ̃pʀimɑ̃t] nf printer;
~ **à laser** laser printer
imprimé [ɛ̃pʀime] nm (formulaire)
printed form; (Postes) printed matter
no pl; (tissu) printed fabric; **un ~ à
fleurs/pois** (tissu) a floral-/polka-
dot print
imprimer [ɛ̃pʀime] /1/ vt to print;
(publier) to publish; **imprimerie** nf
printing; (établissement) printing
works sg; **imprimeur** nm printer
impropre [ɛ̃pʀopʀ] adj
inappropriate; ~ **à** unsuitable for
improviser [ɛ̃pʀovize] /1/ vt, vi to
improvize
improviste [ɛ̃pʀovist]: **à l'~** adv
unexpectedly, without warning
imprudence [ɛ̃pʀydɑ̃s] nf (d'une
personne, d'une action) carelessness no
pl; (d'une remarque) imprudence no pl;
commettre une ~ to do something
foolish
imprudent, e [ɛ̃pʀydɑ̃, -ɑ̃t] adj
(conducteur, geste, action) careless;
(remarque) unwise, imprudent;
(projet) foolhardy
impuissant, e [ɛ̃pɥisɑ̃, -ɑ̃t] adj
helpless; (sans effet) ineffectual;
(sexuellement) impotent
impulsif, -ive [ɛ̃pylsif, -iv] adj
impulsive
impulsion [ɛ̃pylsjɔ̃] nf (Élec, instinct)
impulse; (élan, influence) impetus
inabordable [inabordabl] adj (cher)
prohibitive
inacceptable [inaksɛptabl] adj
unacceptable
inaccessible [inaksesibl] adj
inaccessible; ~ **à** impervious to
inachevé, e [inaʃve] adj unfinished
inactif, -ive [inaktif, -iv] adj
inactive; (remède) ineffective; (Bourse:
marché) slack

inadapté, e [inadapte] adj (Psych)
maladjusted; **~ à** not adapted to,
unsuited to

inadéquat, e [inadekwa, -wat] adj
inadequate

inadmissible [inadmisibl] adj
inadmissible

inadvertance [inadvɛrtɑ̃s]: **par ~**
adv inadvertently

inanimé, e [inanime] adj (matière)
inanimate; (évanoui) unconscious;
(sans vie) lifeless

inanition [inanisjɔ̃] nf: **tomber d'~**
to faint with hunger (and exhaustion)

inaperçu, e [inapɛrsy] adj: **passer
~** to go unnoticed

inapte [inapt] adj: **~ à** incapable of;
(Mil) unfit for

inattendu, e [inatɑ̃dy] adj
unexpected

inattentif, -ive [inatɑ̃tif, -iv] adj
inattentive; **~ à** (dangers, détails)
heedless of; **inattention** nf
inattention; **faute d'inattention**
careless mistake

inaugurer [inɔgyre] /1/ vt
(monument) to unveil; (exposition,
usine) to open; (fig) to inaugurate

inavouable [inavwabl] adj
(bénéfices) undisclosable; (honteux)
shameful

incalculable [ɛ̃kalkylabl] adj
incalculable

incapable [ɛ̃kapabl] adj incapable;
~ de faire incapable of doing;
(empêché) unable to do

incapacité [ɛ̃kapasite] nf
(incompétence) incapability;
(impossibilité) incapacity; **être dans
l'~ de faire** to be unable to do

incarcérer [ɛ̃karsere] /6/ vt to
incarcerate, imprison

incassable [ɛ̃kasabl] adj unbreakable

incendie [ɛ̃sɑ̃di] nm fire; **~ criminel**
arson no pl; **~ de forêt** forest fire;
incendier /7/ vt (mettre le feu à)
to set fire to, set alight; (brûler
complètement) to burn down

incertain, e [ɛ̃sɛrtɛ̃, -ɛn] adj
uncertain; (temps) unsettled;
(imprécis: contours) indistinct, blurred;
incertitude nf uncertainty

incessamment [ɛ̃sesamɑ̃] adv
very shortly

incident [ɛ̃sidɑ̃] nm incident; **~ de
parcours** minor hitch ou setback;
~ technique technical difficulties pl

incinérer [ɛ̃sinere] /6/ vt (ordures) to
incinerate; (mort) to cremate

incisif, -ive [ɛ̃sizif, -iv] adj incisive
▷ nf incisor

inciter [ɛ̃site] /1/ vt: **~ qn à (faire)
qch** to prompt ou encourage sb to
do sth; (à la révolte etc) to incite sb
to do sth

incivilité [ɛ̃sivilite] nf (grossièreté)
incivility; **incivilités** nfpl antisocial
behaviour s

inclinable [ɛ̃klinabl] adj: **siège à
dossier ~** reclining seat

inclinaison [ɛ̃klinɛzɔ̃] nf (pente) slope

inclination [ɛ̃klinasjɔ̃] nf (penchant)
inclination

incliner [ɛ̃kline] /1/ vt (bouteille) to
tilt ▷ vi: **~ à qch/à faire** to incline
towards sth/doing; **s'incliner** vi
(route) to slope; **s'~ (devant)** to bow
(before)

inclure [ɛ̃klyr] /35/ vt to include;
(joindre à un envoi) to enclose

inclus, e [ɛ̃kly, -yz] pp de **inclure**
▷ adj included; (joint à un envoi)
enclosed; (compris: frais, dépense)
included; **jusqu'au 10 mars ~** until
10th March inclusive

incognito [ɛ̃kɔɲito] adv incognito
▷ nm: **garder l'~** to remain incognito

incohérent, e [ɛ̃kɔerɑ̃, -ɑ̃t] adj
(comportement) inconsistent; (geste,
langage, texte) incoherent

incollable [ɛ̃kɔlabl] adj (riz) that
does not stick; (fam): **il est ~** he's got
all the answers

incolore [ɛ̃kɔlɔr] adj colourless

incommoder [ɛ̃kɔmɔde] /1/ vt:
~ qn (chaleur, odeur) to bother ou
inconvenience sb

incomparable [ɛ̃kɔ̃paʀabl] adj
incomparable

incompatible [ɛ̃kɔ̃patibl] adj
incompatible

incompétent, e [ɛ̃kɔ̃petɑ̃, -ɑ̃t] adj
incompetent

incomplet, -ète [ɛ̃kɔ̃plɛ, -ɛt] adj
incomplete

incompréhensible [ɛ̃kɔ̃pʀeɑ̃sibl]
adj incomprehensible

incompris, e [ɛ̃kɔ̃pʀi, -iz] adj
misunderstood

inconcevable [ɛ̃kɔ̃svabl] adj
inconceivable

inconfortable [ɛ̃kɔ̃fɔʀtabl] adj
uncomfortable

incongru, e [ɛ̃kɔ̃gʀy] adj unseemly

inconnu, e [ɛ̃kɔny] adj unknown
▷ nm/f stranger ▷ nm: **l'~** the
unknown ▷ nf unknown factor

inconsciemment [ɛ̃kɔ̃sjamɑ̃] adv
unconsciously

inconscient, e [ɛ̃kɔ̃sjɑ̃, -ɑ̃t] adj
unconscious; (irréfléchi) thoughtless,
reckless; (sentiment) subconscious
▷ nm (Psych): **l'~** the unconscious;
~ de unaware of

inconsidéré, e [ɛ̃kɔ̃sideʀe] adj
ill-considered

inconsistant, e [ɛ̃kɔ̃sistɑ̃, -ɑ̃t] adj
flimsy, weak

inconsolable [ɛ̃kɔ̃sɔlabl] adj
inconsolable

incontestable [ɛ̃kɔ̃tɛstabl] adj
indisputable

incontinent, e [ɛ̃kɔ̃tinɑ̃, -ɑ̃t] adj
incontinent

incontournable [ɛ̃kɔ̃tuʀnabl] adj
unavoidable

incontrôlable [ɛ̃kɔ̃tʀolabl]
adj unverifiable; (irrépressible)
uncontrollable

inconvénient [ɛ̃kɔ̃venjɑ̃] nm
disadvantage, drawback; **si vous
n'y voyez pas d'~** if you have no
objections

incorporer [ɛ̃kɔʀpɔʀe] /1/ vt: **~ (à)**
to mix in (with); **~ (dans)** (paragraphe

etc) to incorporate (in); (Mil: appeler)
to recruit (into); **il a très bien su s'~
à notre groupe** he was very easily
incorporated into our group

incorrect, e [ɛ̃kɔʀɛkt] adj (impropre,
inconvenant) improper; (défectueux)
faulty; (inexact) incorrect; (impoli)
impolite; (déloyal) underhand

incorrigible [ɛ̃kɔʀiʒibl] adj
incorrigible

incrédule [ɛ̃kʀedyl] adj incredulous;
(Rel) unbelieving

incroyable [ɛ̃kʀwajabl] adj incredible

incruster [ɛ̃kʀyste] /1/ vt:
s'incruster vi (invité) to take root;
~ qch dans/qch de (Art) to inlay sth
into/sth with

inculpé, e [ɛ̃kylpe] nm/f accused

inculper [ɛ̃kylpe] /1/ vt: **~ (de)** to
charge (with)

inculquer [ɛ̃kylke] /1/ vt: **~ qch à** to
inculcate sth in, instil sth into

Inde [ɛ̃d] nf: **l'~** India

indécent, e [ɛ̃desɑ̃, -ɑ̃t] adj indecent

indécis, e [ɛ̃desi, -iz] adj (par nature)
indecisive; (perplexe) undecided

indéfendable [ɛ̃defɑ̃dabl] adj
indefensible

indéfini, e [ɛ̃defini] adj (imprécis,
incertain) undefined; (illimité, Ling)
indefinite; **indéfiniment** adv
indefinitely; **indéfinissable** adj
indefinable

indélébile [ɛ̃delebil] adj indelible

indélicat, e [ɛ̃delika, -at] adj tactless

indemne [ɛ̃dɛmn] adj unharmed;
indemniser /1/ vt: **indemniser qn
(de)** to compensate sb (for)

indemnité [ɛ̃dɛmnite] nf
(dédommagement) compensation
no pl; (allocation) allowance; **~ de
licenciement** redundancy payment

indépendamment [ɛ̃depɑ̃damɑ̃]
adv independently; **~ de** (abstraction
faite de) irrespective of; (en plus de)
over and above

indépendance [ɛ̃depɑ̃dɑ̃s] nf
independence

indépendant, e [ɛ̃depɑ̃dɑ̃, -ɑ̃t] *adj*
independent; **~ de** independent of;
travailleur ~ self-employed worker
indescriptible [ɛ̃dɛskʁiptibl] *adj*
indescribable
indésirable [ɛ̃dezirabl] *adj*
undesirable
indestructible [ɛ̃dɛstʁyktibl] *adj*
indestructible
indéterminé, e [ɛ̃detɛʁmine] *adj*
(date, cause, nature) unspecified;
(forme, longueur, quantité)
indeterminate
index [ɛ̃dɛks] *nm (doigt)* index finger;
(d'un livre etc) index; **mettre à l'~** to
blacklist
indicateur [ɛ̃dikatœʀ] *nm (Police)*
informer; *(Tech)* gauge; indicator
▷ *adj:* **poteau ~** signpost; **~ des
chemins de fer** railway timetable;
~ de rues street directory
indicatif, -ive [ɛ̃dikatif, -iv] *adj:* **à
titre ~** for (your) information ▷ *nm
(Ling)* indicative; *(d'une émission)*
theme *ou* signature tune; *(Tél)* dialling
code *(BRIT)*, area code *(US)*; **quel est
l'~ de ...** what's the code for ...?
indication [ɛ̃dikasjɔ̃] *nf* indication;
(renseignement) information *no
pl*; **indications** *nfpl (directives)*
instructions
indice [ɛ̃dis] *nm (marque, signe)*
indication, sign; *(Police: lors d'une
enquête)* clue; *(Jur: présomption)*
piece of evidence; *(Science, Écon,
Tech)* index; **~ de protection** (sun
protection) factor
indicible [ɛ̃disibl] *adj* inexpressible
indien, ne [ɛ̃djɛ̃, -ɛn] *adj* Indian
▷ *nm/f:* **I~, ne** Indian
indifféremment [ɛ̃difeʀamɑ̃] *adv
(sans distinction)* equally
indifférence [ɛ̃difeʀɑ̃s] *nf* indifference
indifférent, e [ɛ̃difeʀɑ̃, -ɑ̃t] *adj
(peu intéressé)* indifferent; **ça m'est
~ (que ...)** it doesn't matter to me
(whether ...); **elle m'est ~e** I am
indifferent to her

indigène [ɛ̃diʒɛn] *adj* native,
indigenous; *(de la région)* local ▷ *nm/f*
native
indigeste [ɛ̃diʒɛst] *adj* indigestible
indigestion [ɛ̃diʒɛstjɔ̃] *nf*
indigestion *no pl;* **avoir une ~** to have
indigestion
indigne [ɛ̃diɲ] *adj:* **~ (de)** unworthy
(of)
indigner [ɛ̃diɲe] /1/ *vt:* **s'indigner
(de/contre)** to be (*ou* become)
indignant (at)
indiqué, e [ɛ̃dike] *adj (date, lieu)*
given; *(adéquat)* appropriate;
(conseillé) advisable
indiquer [ɛ̃dike] /1/ *vt:* **~ qch/qn
à qn** to point sth/sb out to sb; *(faire
connaître: médecin, lieu, restaurant)*
to tell sb of sth/sb; *(pendule, aiguille)*
to show; *(étiquette, plan)* to show,
indicate; *(renseigner sur)* to point
out, tell; *(déterminer: date, lieu)* to
give, state; *(dénoter)* to indicate,
point to; **pourriez-vous m'~ les
toilettes/l'heure?** could you direct
me to the toilets/tell me the time?
indiscipliné, e [ɛ̃disipline] *adj*
undisciplined
indiscret, -ète [ɛ̃diskʀɛ, -ɛt] *adj*
indiscreet
indiscutable [ɛ̃diskytabl] *adj*
indisputable
indispensable [ɛ̃dispɑ̃sabl] *adj*
indispensable, essential
indisposé, e [ɛ̃dispoze] *adj*
indisposed
indistinct, e [ɛ̃distɛ̃, -ɛkt] *adj*
indistinct; **indistinctement** *adv
(voir, prononcer)* indistinctly; *(sans
distinction)* indiscriminately
individu [ɛ̃dividy] *nm* individual;
individuel, le *(gén)* individual;
(opinion, livret, contrôle, avantages)
personal; **chambre individuelle**
single room; **maison individuelle**
detached house; **propriété
individuelle** personal *ou* private
property

indolore [ɛ̃dɔlɔʀ] adj painless

Indonésie [ɛ̃dɔnezi] nf: **l'~** Indonesia

indu, e [ɛ̃dy] adj: **à une heure ~e** at some ungodly hour

indulgent, e [ɛ̃dylʒɑ̃, -ɑ̃t] adj (parent, regard) indulgent; (juge, examinateur) lenient

industrialisé, e [ɛ̃dystʀijalize] adj industrialized

industrie [ɛ̃dystʀi] nf industry; **industriel, le** adj industrial ▷ nm industrialist

inébranlable [inebʀɑ̃labl] adj (masse, colonne) solid; (personne, certitude, foi) unwavering

inédit, e [inedi, -it] adj (correspondance etc) (hitherto) unpublished; (spectacle, moyen) novel, original; (film) unreleased

inefficace [inefikas] adj (remède, moyen) ineffective; (machine, employé) inefficient

inégal, e, -aux [inegal, -o] adj unequal; (irrégulier) uneven; **inégalable** adj matchless; **inégalé, e** adj (record) unequalled; (beauté) unrivalled; **inégalité** nf inequality

inépuisable [inepɥizabl] adj inexhaustible

inerte [inɛʀt] adj (immobile) lifeless; (apathique) passive

inespéré, e [inɛspeʀe] adj unhoped-for, unexpected

inestimable [inɛstimabl] adj priceless; (fig: bienfait) invaluable

inévitable [inevitabl] adj unavoidable; (fatal, habituel) inevitable

inexact, e [inɛgzakt] adj inaccurate

inexcusable [inɛkskyzabl] adj unforgivable

inexplicable [inɛksplikabl] adj inexplicable

in extremis [inɛkstʀemis] adv at the last minute ▷ adj last-minute

infaillible [ɛ̃fajibl] adj infallible

infarctus [ɛ̃faʀktys] nm: **~ (du myocarde)** coronary (thrombosis)

infatigable [ɛ̃fatigabl] adj tireless

infect, e [ɛ̃fɛkt] adj revolting; (repas, vin) revolting, foul; (personne) obnoxious; (temps) foul

infecter [ɛ̃fɛkte] /1/ vt (atmosphère, eau) to contaminate; (Méd) to infect; **s'infecter** to become infected ou septic; **infection** nf infection; (puanteur) stench

inférieur, e [ɛ̃feʀjœʀ] adj lower; (en qualité, intelligence) inferior ▷ nm/f inferior; **~ à** (somme, quantité) less ou smaller than; (moins bon que) inferior to

infernal, e, -aux [ɛ̃fɛʀnal, -o] adj (insupportable: chaleur, rythme) infernal; (: enfant) horrid; (méchanceté, complot) diabolical

infidèle [ɛ̃fidɛl] adj unfaithful

infiltrer [ɛ̃filtʀe] /1/: **s'infiltrer** vi: **s'~ dans** to penetrate into; (liquide) to seep into; (fig: noyauter) to infiltrate

infime [ɛ̃fim] adj minute, tiny

infini, e [ɛ̃fini] adj infinite ▷ nm infinity; **à l'~** endlessly; **infiniment** adv infinitely; **infinité** nf: **une infinité de** an infinite number of

infinitif, -ive [ɛ̃finitif, -iv] nm infinitive

infirme [ɛ̃fiʀm] adj disabled ▷ nm/f person with a disability

infirmerie [ɛ̃fiʀməʀi] nf sick bay

infirmier, -ière [ɛ̃fiʀmje, -jɛʀ] nm/f nurse; **infirmière chef** sister

infirmité [ɛ̃fiʀmite] nf disability

inflammable [ɛ̃flamabl] adj (in)flammable

inflation [ɛ̃flasjɔ̃] nf inflation

influençable [ɛ̃flyɑ̃sabl] adj easily influenced

influence [ɛ̃flyɑ̃s] nf influence; **influencer** /3/ vt to influence; **influent, e** adj influential

informaticien, ne [ɛ̃fɔʀmatisjɛ̃, -ɛn] nm/f computer scientist

information [ɛ̃fɔʀmasjɔ̃] nf (renseignement) piece of information; (Presse, TV: nouvelle) item of news; (*diffusion de renseignements, Inform*) information; (*Jur*) inquiry, investigation; **informations** *nfpl* (*TV*) news *sg*

informatique [ɛ̃fɔʀmatik] *nf* (*technique*) data processing; (*science*) computer science ▷ *adj* computer *cpd*; **informatiser** /1/ *vt* to computerize

informer [ɛ̃fɔʀme] /1/ *vt*: ~ **qn (de)** to inform sb (of); **s'informer (sur)** to inform o.s. (about); **s'~ (de qch/si)** to inquire ou find out (about sth/whether ou if)

infos [ɛ̃fo] *nfpl* (= *informations*) news

infraction [ɛ̃fʀaksjɔ̃] *nf* offence; ~ **à** violation ou breach of; **être en ~** to be in breach of the law

infranchissable [ɛ̃fʀɑ̃ʃisabl] *adj* impassable; (*fig*) insuperable

infrarouge [ɛ̃fʀaʀuʒ] *adj* infrared

infrastructure [ɛ̃fʀastʀyktyʀ] *nf* (*Aviat, Mil*) ground installations *pl*; (*Écon: touristique etc*) facilities *pl*

infuser [ɛ̃fyze] /1/ *vt* (*thé*) to brew; (*tisane*) to infuse ▷ *vi* to brew; **infusion** *nf* (*tisane*) herb tea

ingénier [ɛ̃ʒenje] /7/: **s'~ à faire** vi: to strive to do

ingénierie [ɛ̃ʒeniʀi] *nf* engineering

ingénieur [ɛ̃ʒenjœʀ] *nm* engineer; ~ **du son** sound engineer

ingénieux, -euse [ɛ̃ʒenjø, -øz] *adj* ingenious, clever

ingrat, e [ɛ̃gʀa, -at] *adj* (*personne*) ungrateful; (*travail, sujet*) thankless; (*visage*) unprepossessing

ingrédient [ɛ̃gʀedjɑ̃] *nm* ingredient

inhabité, e [inabite] *adj* uninhabited

inhabituel, le [inabituɛl] *adj* unusual

inhibition [inibisjɔ̃] *nf* inhibition

inhumain, e [inymɛ̃, -ɛn] *adj* inhuman

inimaginable [inimaʒinabl] *adj* unimaginable

ininterrompu, e [inɛ̃teʀɔ̃py] *adj* (*file, série*) unbroken; (*flot, vacarme*)

uninterrupted, non-stop; (*effort*) unremitting, continuous; (*suite, ligne*) unbroken

initial, e, -aux [inisjal, -o] *adj* initial; **initiales** *nfpl* initials

initiation [inisjasjɔ̃] *nf*: ~ **à** introduction to

initiative [inisjativ] *nf* initiative

initier [inisje] /7/ *vt*: ~ **qn à** to initiate sb into; (*faire découvrir: art, jeu*) to introduce sb to

injecter [ɛ̃ʒɛkte] /1/ *vt* to inject; **injection** *nf* injection; **à injection** (*Auto*) fuel injection *cpd*

injure [ɛ̃ʒyʀ] *nf* insult, abuse *no pl*; **injurier** /7/ *vt* to insult, abuse; **injurieux, -euse** *adj* abusive, insulting

injuste [ɛ̃ʒyst] *adj* unjust, unfair; **injustice** [ɛ̃ʒystis] *nf* injustice

inlassable [ɛ̃lɑsabl] *adj* tireless

inné, e [ine] *adj* innate, inborn

innocent, e [inɔsɑ̃, -ɑ̃t] *adj* innocent; **innocenter** /1/ *vt* to clear, prove innocent

innombrable [inɔ̃bʀabl] *adj* innumerable

innover [inɔve] /1/ *vi*: ~ **en matière d'art** to break new ground in the field of art

inoccupé, e [inɔkype] *adj* unoccupied

inodore [inɔdɔʀ] *adj* (*gaz*) odourless; (*fleur*) scentless

inoffensif, -ive [inɔfɑ̃sif, -iv] *adj* harmless, innocuous

inondation [inɔ̃dasjɔ̃] *nf* flood

inonder [inɔ̃de] /1/ *vt* to flood; **~ de** to flood ou swamp with

inopportun, e [inɔpɔʀtœ̃, -yn] *adj* ill-timed, untimely

inoubliable [inublijabl] *adj* unforgettable

inouï, e [inwi] *adj* unheard-of, extraordinary

inox [inɔks] *nm* stainless (steel)

inquiet, -ète [ɛ̃kjɛ, -ɛt] *adj* anxious; **inquiétant, e** *adj* worrying, disturbing; **inquiéter** /6/ vt to worry; **s'inquiéter** to worry; **s'inquiéter de** to worry about; (: *s'enquérir de*) to inquire about; **inquiétude** nf anxiety

insaisissable [ɛ̃sezisabl] adj (fugitif, ennemi) elusive; (différence, nuance) imperceptible

insalubre [ɛ̃salybʁ] adj insalubrious

insatisfait, e [ɛ̃satisfɛ, -ɛt] adj (non comblé) unsatisfied; (mécontent) dissatisfied

inscription [ɛ̃skʁipsjɔ̃] nf inscription; (à une institution) enrolment

inscrire [ɛ̃skʁiʁ] /39/ vt (marquer: sur son calepin etc) to note ou write down; (: sur un mur, une affiche etc) to write; (: dans la pierre, le métal) to inscribe; (mettre: sur une liste, un budget etc) to put down; ~ **qn** à (club, école etc) to enrol sb at; **s'inscrire** (pour une excursion etc) to put one's name down; **s'~ (à)** (club, parti) to join; (université) to register or enrol (at); (examen, concours) to register ou enter (for)

insecte [ɛ̃sɛkt] nm insect; **insecticide** nm insecticide

insensé, e [ɛ̃sɑ̃se] adj mad

insensible [ɛ̃sɑ̃sibl] adj (nerf, membre) numb; (dur, indifférent) insensitive

inséparable [ɛ̃sepaʁabl] adj: ~ **(de)** inseparable (from) ▷ nmpl: ~s (oiseaux) lovebirds

insigne [ɛ̃siɲ] nm (d'un parti, club) badge ▷ adj distinguished; **insignes** nmpl (d'une fonction) insignia pl

insignifiant, e [ɛ̃siɲifjɑ̃, -ɑ̃t] adj insignificant; trivial

insinuer [ɛ̃sinɥe] /1/ vt to insinuate; **s'insinuer dans** (fig) to worm one's way into

insipide [ɛ̃sipid] adj insipid

insister [ɛ̃siste] /1/ vi to insist; (s'obstiner) to keep on; ~ **sur** (détail, note) to stress

insolation [ɛ̃sɔlasjɔ̃] nf (Méd) sunstroke no pl

insolent, e [ɛ̃sɔlɑ̃, -ɑ̃t] adj insolent

insolite [ɛ̃sɔlit] adj strange, unusual

insomnie [ɛ̃sɔmni] nf insomnia no pl; **avoir des ~s** to sleep badly

insouciant, e [ɛ̃susjɑ̃, -ɑ̃t] adj carefree; ~ **du danger** heedless of (the) danger

insoupçonnable [ɛ̃supsɔnabl] adj unsuspected; (personne) above suspicion

insoupçonné, e [ɛ̃supsɔne] adj unsuspected

insoutenable [ɛ̃sutnabl] adj (argument) untenable; (chaleur) unbearable

inspecter [ɛ̃spɛkte] /1/ vt to inspect; **inspecteur, -trice** nm/f inspector; **inspecteur d'Académie** (regional) director of education; **inspecteur des finances** = tax inspector (BRIT), ≈ Internal Revenue Service agent (US); **inspecteur (de police)** (police) inspector; **inspection** nf inspection

inspirer [ɛ̃spiʁe] /1/ vt (gén) to inspire ▷ vi (aspirer) to breathe in; **s'inspirer de** to be inspired by

instable [ɛ̃stabl] adj (meuble, équilibre) unsteady; (population, temps) unsettled; (paix, régime, caractère) unstable

installation [ɛ̃stalasjɔ̃] nf (mise en place) installation; **installations** nfpl (industrielles) plant sg; (de sport, dans un camping) facilities; **l'~ électrique** wiring

installer [ɛ̃stale] /1/ vt to put; (meuble) to put in; (rideau, étagère, tente) to put up; (appartement) to fit out; **s'installer** (s'établir: artisan, dentiste etc) to set o.s. up; (emménager) to settle in; (sur un siège, d'un emplacement) to settle (down); (fig: maladie, grève) to take a firm hold ou grip; **s'~ à l'hôtel/chez qn** to move into a hotel/in with sb

instance [ɛ̃stɑ̃s] nf (Admin: autorité) authority; **affaire en ~** matter pending; **être en ~ de divorce** to be awaiting a divorce

instant [ɛ̃stɑ̃] nm moment, instant; **dans un ~** in a moment; **à l'~** this instant; **je l'ai vu à l'~** I've just this minute seen him, I saw him a moment ago; **pour l'~** for the moment, for the time being

instantané, e [ɛ̃stɑ̃tane] adj (lait, café) instant; (explosion, mort) instantaneous ▷ nm snapshot

instar [ɛ̃staʀ]: **à l'~ de** prép following the example of, like

instaurer [ɛ̃stɔʀe] /1/ vt to institute; (couvre-feu) to impose; **s'instaurer** vi (collaboration, paix etc) to be established; (doute) to set in

instinct [ɛ̃stɛ̃] nm instinct; **instinctivement** adv instinctively

instituer [ɛ̃stitɥe] /1/ vt to establish

institut [ɛ̃stity] nm institute; **~ de beauté** beauty salon; **I~ universitaire de technologie (IUT)** ≈ Institute of technology

instituteur, -trice [ɛ̃stitytœʀ, -tʀis] nm/f (primary (BRIT) ou grade (US) school) teacher

institution [ɛ̃stitysjɔ̃] nf institution; (collège) private school; **institutions** nfpl (structures politiques et sociales) institutions

instructif, -ive [ɛ̃stʀyktif, -iv] adj instructive

instruction [ɛ̃stʀyksjɔ̃] nf (enseignement, savoir) education; (Jur) (preliminary) investigation and hearing; **instructions** nfpl (mode d'emploi) instructions; **~ civique** civics sg

instruire [ɛ̃stʀɥiʀ] /38/ vt (élèves) to teach; (recrues) to train; (Jur: affaire) to conduct the investigation for; **s'instruire** to educate o.s.; **instruit, e** adj educated

instrument [ɛ̃stʀymɑ̃] nm instrument; **~ à cordes/vent** stringed/wind instrument; **~ de mesure** measuring instrument; **~ de musique** musical instrument; **~ de travail** (working) tool

insu [ɛ̃sy] nm: **à l'~ de qn** without sb knowing

insuffisant, e [ɛ̃syfizɑ̃, -ɑ̃t] adj (en quantité) insufficient; (en qualité) inadequate; (sur une copie) poor

insulaire [ɛ̃sylɛʀ] adj island cpd; (attitude) insular

insuline [ɛ̃sylin] nf insulin

insulte [ɛ̃sylt] nf insult; **insulter** /1/ vt to insult

insupportable [ɛ̃sypɔʀtabl] adj unbearable

insurmontable [ɛ̃syʀmɔ̃tabl] adj (difficulté) insuperable; (aversion) unconquerable

intact, e [ɛ̃takt] adj intact

intarissable [ɛ̃taʀisabl] adj inexhaustible

intégral, e, -aux [ɛ̃tegʀal, -o] adj complete; **texte ~** unabridged version; **bronzage ~** all-over suntan; **intégralement** adv in full; **intégralité** nf whole (ou full) amount; **dans son intégralité** in its entirety; **intégrant, e** adj: **faire partie intégrante de** to be an integral part of

intègre [ɛ̃tegʀ] adj upright

intégrer [ɛ̃tegʀe] /6/: **s'intégrer** vr: **s'~ à** ou **dans** to become integrated into; **bien s'~** to fit in

intégrisme [ɛ̃tegʀism] nm fundamentalism

intellectuel, le [ɛ̃telɛktɥel] adj, nm/f intellectual; (péj) highbrow

intelligence [ɛ̃teliʒɑ̃s] nf intelligence; (compréhension): **l'~ de** the understanding of; (complicité): **regard d'~** glance of complicity; (accord): **vivre en bonne ~ avec qn** to be on good terms with sb

intelligent, e [ɛ̃teliʒɑ̃, -ɑ̃t] adj intelligent

intelligible [ɛ̃teliʒibl] adj intelligible

intempéries [ɛ̃tɑ̃peʀi] nfpl bad weather sg

intenable [ɛ̃tnabl] adj unbearable

intendant, e [ɛ̃tɑ̃dɑ̃, -ɑ̃t] nm/f (Mil) quartermaster; (Scol) bursar

intense [ɛ̃tɑ̃s] adj intense; **intensif, -ive** adj intensive; **cours intensif** crash course

intenter [ɛ̃tɑ̃te] /1/ vt: **~ un procès contre** ou **à qn** to start proceedings against sb

intention [ɛ̃tɑ̃sjɔ̃] nf intention; (Jur) intent; **avoir l'~ de faire** to intend to do; **à l'~ de** for; (renseignement) for the benefit ou information of; (film, ouvrage) aimed at; **à cette ~** with this aim in view; **intentionné, e** adj: **bien intentionné** well-meaning ou -intentioned; **mal intentionné** ill-intentioned

interactif, -ive [ɛ̃teraktif, -iv] adj (aussi Inform) interactive

intercepter [ɛ̃tɛrsɛpte] /1/ vt to intercept; (lumière, chaleur) to cut off

interchangeable [ɛ̃tɛrʃɑ̃ʒabl] adj interchangeable

interdiction [ɛ̃tɛrdiksjɔ̃] nf ban; **~ de fumer** no smoking

interdire [ɛ̃tɛrdir] /37/ vt to forbid; (Admin) to ban, prohibit; (: journal, livre) to ban; **~ à qn de faire** to forbid sb to do; (empêchement) to prevent ou preclude sb from doing

interdit, e [ɛ̃tɛrdi, -it] pp de **interdire** ▷ adj (stupéfait) taken aback; **film ~ aux moins de 18/12 ans** ≈ 18-/12A-rated film; **stationnement ~** no parking

intéressant, e [ɛ̃teresɑ̃, -ɑ̃t] adj interesting; (avantageux) attractive

intéressé, e [ɛ̃terese] adj (parties) involved, concerned; (amitié, motifs) self-interested

intéresser [ɛ̃terese] /1/ vt (captiver) to interest; (toucher) to be of interest ou concern to; (Admin: concerner) to affect, concern; **s'intéresser à** vi to take an interest in

intérêt [ɛ̃terɛ] nm interest; (égoïsme) self-interest; **tu as ~ à accepter** it's in your interest to accept; **tu as ~ à te dépêcher** you'd better hurry

intérieur, e [ɛ̃terjœr] adj (mur, escalier, poche) inside; (commerce, politique) domestic; (cour, calme, vie) inner; (navigation) inland ▷ nm (d'une maison, d'un récipient etc) inside; (d'un pays, aussi décor, mobilier) interior; **l'I~** (the Department of) the Interior, ≈ the Home Office (BRIT); **à l'~ (de)** inside; **intérieurement** adv inwardly

intérim [ɛ̃terim] nm interim period; **assurer l'~ (de)** to deputize (for); **président par ~** interim president; **faire de l'~** to temp

intérimaire [ɛ̃terimɛr] adj (directeur, ministre) acting; (secrétaire, personnel) temporary ▷ nm/f (secrétaire etc) temporary, temp (BRIT)

interlocuteur, -trice [ɛ̃tɛrlɔkytœr, -tris] nm/f speaker; **son ~** the person he ou she was speaking to

intermédiaire [ɛ̃tɛrmedjɛr] adj intermediate; (solution) temporary ▷ nm/f intermediary; (Comm) middleman; **sans ~** directly; **par l'~ de** through

interminable [ɛ̃tɛrminabl] adj never-ending

intermittence [ɛ̃tɛrmitɑ̃s] nf: **par ~** intermittently, sporadically

internat [ɛ̃tɛrna] nm boarding school

international, e, -aux [ɛ̃tɛrnasjɔnal, -o] adj, nm/f international

internaute [ɛ̃tɛrnot] nm/f Internet user

interne [ɛ̃tɛrn] adj internal ▷ nm/f (Scol) boarder; (Méd) houseman

Internet [ɛ̃tɛrnɛt] nm: **l'~** the Internet

interpeller [ɛ̃tɛrpele] /1/ vt (appeler) to call out to; (apostropher) to shout at; (Police) to take in for questioning; (Pol) to question; (concerner) to concern

interphone [ɛ̃tɛrfɔn] nm intercom; (d'immeuble) entry phone

i

interposer [ɛ̃tɛʀpoze] /1/ vt; **s'interposer** to intervene; **par personnes interposées** through a third party

interprète [ɛ̃tɛʀpʀɛt] nm/f interpreter; (porte-parole) spokesman

interpréter [ɛ̃tɛʀpʀete] /6/ vt to interpret; (jouer) to play; (chanter) to sing

interrogatif, -ive [ɛ̃teʀɔgatif, -iv] adj (Ling) interrogative

interrogation [ɛ̃teʀɔgasjɔ̃] nf question; (Scol) (written ou oral) test

interrogatoire [ɛ̃teʀɔgatwaʀ] nm (Police) questioning no pl; (Jur, aussi fig) cross-examination

interroger [ɛ̃teʀɔʒe] /3/ vt to question; (Inform) to search; (Scol) to test

interrompre [ɛ̃teʀɔ̃pʀ] /41/ vt (gén) to interrupt; (négociations) to break off; (match) to stop; **s'interrompre** to break off; **interrupteur** nm switch; **interruption** nf interruption; (pause) break; **sans interruption** without a break; **interruption volontaire de grossesse** abortion

intersection [ɛ̃tɛʀsɛksjɔ̃] nf intersection

intervalle [ɛ̃tɛʀval] nm (espace) space; (de temps) interval; **dans l'~** in the meantime; **à deux jours d'~** two days apart

intervenir [ɛ̃tɛʀvəniʀ] /22/ vi (gén) to intervene; **~ auprès de/en faveur de qn** to intervene with/on behalf of sb; **intervention** nf intervention; (discours) speech; **intervention (chirurgicale)** operation

interview [ɛ̃tɛʀvju] nf interview

intestin, e [ɛ̃tɛstɛ̃, -in] adj internal ▷ nm intestine

intime [ɛ̃tim] adj intimate; (vie, journal) private; (convictions) inmost; (dîner, cérémonie) quiet ▷ nm/f close friend; **un journal ~** a diary

intimider [ɛ̃timide] /1/ vt to intimidate

intimité [ɛ̃timite] nf: **dans l'~** in private; (sans formalités) with only a few friends, quietly

intolérable [ɛ̃tɔleʀabl] adj intolerable

intox [ɛ̃tɔks] (fam) nf brainwashing

intoxication [ɛ̃tɔksikasjɔ̃] nf: **~ alimentaire** food poisoning

intoxiquer [ɛ̃tɔksike] /1/ vt to poison; (fig) to brainwash

intraitable [ɛ̃tʀɛtabl] adj inflexible, uncompromising

intransigeant, e [ɛ̃tʀɑ̃ziʒɑ̃, -ɑ̃t] adj intransigent

intrépide [ɛ̃tʀepid] adj dauntless

intrigue [ɛ̃tʀig] nf (scénario) plot; **intriguer** /1/ vt to puzzle, intrigue

introduction [ɛ̃tʀɔdyksjɔ̃] nf introduction

introduire [ɛ̃tʀɔduiʀ] /38/ vt to introduce; (visiteur) to show in; (aiguille, clef): **~ qch dans** to insert ou introduce sth into; **s'introduire** vi (techniques, usages) to be introduced; **s'~ dans** to gain entry into; (dans un groupe) to get o.s. accepted into

introuvable [ɛ̃tʀuvabl] adj which cannot be found; (Comm) unobtainable

intrus, e [ɛ̃tʀy, -yz] nm/f intruder

intuition [ɛ̃tɥisjɔ̃] nf intuition

inusable [inyzabl] adj hard-wearing

inutile [inytil] adj useless; (superflu) unnecessary; **inutilement** adv needlessly; **inutilisable** adj unusable

invalide [ɛ̃valid] adj disabled ▷ nm/f: **~ de guerre** disabled ex-serviceman

invariable [ɛ̃vaʀjabl] adj invariable

invasion [ɛ̃vazjɔ̃] nf invasion

inventaire [ɛ̃vɑ̃tɛʀ] nm inventory; (Comm: liste) stocklist; (: opération) stocktaking no pl

inventer [ɛ̃vɑ̃te] /1/ vt to invent; (subterfuge) to devise, invent; (histoire, excuse) to make up, invent; **inventeur, -trice** nm/f inventor; **inventif, -ive** adj inventive; **invention** nf invention

inverse [ɛ̃vɛʀs] *adj* opposite ▷ *nm* inverse; **l'~** the opposite; **dans l'ordre ~** in the reverse order; **dans le sens ~ des aiguilles d'une montre** anti-clockwise; **en sens ~** in (*ou* from) the opposite direction; **inversement** *adv* conversely; **inverser** /1/ *vt* to reverse, invert; (*Élec*) to reverse

investir [ɛ̃vɛstiʀ] /2/ *vt* to invest; **~ qn de** (*d'une fonction, d'un pouvoir*) to vest *ou* invest sb with; **s'investir** *vi* (*Psych*) to involve o.s.; **s'~ dans** to put a lot into; **investissement** *nm* investment

invisible [ɛ̃vizibl] *adj* invisible

invitation [ɛ̃vitasjɔ̃] *nf* invitation

invité, e [ɛ̃vite] *nm/f* guest

inviter [ɛ̃vite] /1/ *vt* to invite; **~ qn à faire qch** to invite sb to do sth

invivable [ɛ̃vivabl] *adj* unbearable

involontaire [ɛ̃vɔlɔ̃tɛʀ] *adj* (*mouvement*) involuntary; (*insulte*) unintentional; (*complice*) unwitting

invoquer [ɛ̃vɔke] /1/ *vt* (*Dieu, muse*) to call upon, invoke; (*prétexte*) to put forward (as an excuse); (*loi, texte*) to refer to

invraisemblable [ɛ̃vʀɛsɑ̃blabl] *adj* (*fait, nouvelle*) unlikely, improbable; (*bizarre*) incredible

iode [jɔd] *nm* iodine

irai *etc* [iʀe] *vb voir* **aller**

Irak [iʀak] *nm*: **l'~** Iraq *ou* Irak; **irakien, ne** *adj* Iraqi ▷ *nm/f*: **Irakien, ne** Iraqi

Iran [iʀɑ̃] *nm*: **l'~** Iran; **iranien, ne** *adj* Iranian ▷ *nm/f*: **Iranien, ne** Iranian

irions *etc* [iʀjɔ̃] *vb voir* **aller**

iris [iʀis] *nm* iris

irlandais, e [iʀlɑ̃dɛ, -ɛz] *adj* Irish ▷ *nm/f*: **I~, e** Irishman/woman

Irlande [iʀlɑ̃d] *nf*: **l'~** Ireland; **la République d'~** the Irish Republic; **~ du Nord** Northern Ireland; **la mer d'~** the Irish Sea

ironie [iʀɔni] *nf* irony; **ironique** *adj* ironical; **ironiser** /1/ *vi* to be ironical

irons *etc* [iʀɔ̃] *vb voir* **aller**

irradier [iʀadje] /7/ *vt* to irradiate

irraisonné, e [iʀɛzɔne] *adj* irrational

irrationnel, le [iʀasjɔnɛl] *adj* irrational

irréalisable [iʀealizabl] *adj* unrealizable; (*projet*) impracticable

irrécupérable [iʀekypeʀabl] *adj* beyond repair; (*personne*) beyond redemption *ou* recall

irréel, le [iʀeɛl] *adj* unreal

irréfléchi, e [iʀefleʃi] *adj* thoughtless

irrégularité [iʀegylaʀite] *nf* irregularity; (*de travail, d'effort, de qualité*) unevenness *no pl*

irrégulier, ière [iʀegylje, -jɛʀ] *adj* irregular; (*travail, effort, qualité*) uneven; (*élève, athlète*) erratic

irrémédiable [iʀemedjabl] *adj* irreparable

irremplaçable [iʀɑ̃plasabl] *adj* irreplaceable

irréparable [iʀepaʀabl] *adj* beyond repair; (*fig*) irreparable

irréprochable [iʀepʀɔʃabl] *adj* irreproachable, beyond reproach; (*tenue, toilette*) impeccable

irrésistible [iʀezistibl] *adj* irresistible; (*preuve, logique*) compelling; (*amusant*) hilarious

irrésolu, e [iʀezɔly] *adj* irresolute

irrespectueux, -euse [iʀɛspɛktɥø, -øz] *adj* disrespectful

irresponsable [iʀɛspɔ̃sabl] *adj* irresponsible

irriguer [iʀige] /1/ *vt* to irrigate

irritable [iʀitabl] *adj* irritable

irriter [iʀite] /1/ *vt* to irritate

irruption [iʀypsjɔ̃] *nf*: **faire ~ chez qn** to burst in on sb

Islam [islam] *nm*: **l'~** Islam; **islamique** *adj* Islamic; **islamophobie** *nf* Islamophobia

Islande [islɑ̃d] *nf*: **l'~** Iceland

isolant, e [izɔlɑ̃, -ɑ̃t] *adj* insulating; (*insonorisant*) soundproofing

isolation [izɔlasjɔ̃] *nf* insulation; **~ acoustique** soundproofing

isolé, e [izɔle] *adj* isolated; (*contre le froid*) insulated

isoler [izɔle] /1/ *vt* to isolate; (*prisonnier*) to put in solitary confinement; (*ville*) to cut off, isolate; (*contre le froid*) to insulate; **s'isoler** *vi* to isolate o.s.

Israël [israɛl] *nm*: **l'~** Israel; **israélien, ne** *adj* Israeli ▷ *nm/f*: **Israélien, ne** Israeli; **israélite** *adj* Jewish ▷ *nm/f*: **Israélite** Jew/Jewess

issu, e [isy] *adj*: **~ de** (*né de*) descended from; (*résultant de*) stemming from ▷ *nf* (*ouverture, sortie*) exit; (*solution*) way out, solution; (*dénouement*) outcome; **à l'~e de** at the conclusion *ou* close of; **voie sans ~e** dead end; **~e de secours** emergency exit

Italie [itali] *nf*: **l'~** Italy; **italien, ne** *adj* Italian ▷ *nm* (*Ling*) Italian ▷ *nm/f*: **Italien, ne** Italian

italique [italik] *nm*: **en ~(s)** in italics

itinéraire [itineʀɛʀ] *nm* itinerary, route; **~ bis** alternative route

IUT *sigle m* = **Institut universitaire de technologie**

IVG *sigle f* (= interruption volontaire de grossesse) abortion

ivoire [ivwaʀ] *nm* ivory

ivre [ivʀ] *adj* drunk; **~ de** (*colère*) wild with; **ivrogne** *nm/f* drunkard

j' [ʒ] *pron voir* **je**

jacinthe [ʒasɛ̃t] *nf* hyacinth

jadis [ʒadis] *adv* formerly

jaillir [ʒajiʀ] /2/ *vi* (*liquide*) to spurt out; (*cris, réponses*) to burst out

jais [ʒɛ] *nm* jet; (**d'un noir) de ~** jet-black

jalousie [ʒaluzi] *nf* jealousy; (*store*) (venetian) blind

jaloux, -ouse [ʒalu, -uz] *adj* jealous; **être ~ de qn/qch** to be jealous of sb/sth

jamaïquain, e [ʒamaikɛ̃, -ɛn] *adj* Jamaican ▷ *nm/f*: **J~, e** Jamaican

Jamaïque [ʒamaik] *nf*: **la ~** Jamaica

jamais [ʒamɛ] *adv* never; (*sans négation*) ever; **ne ... ~** never; **si ~ ...** if ever ...; **je ne suis ~ allé en Espagne** I've never been to Spain

jambe [ʒɑ̃b] *nf* leg

jambon [ʒɑ̃bɔ̃] *nm* ham

jante [ʒɑ̃t] *nf* (*wheel*) rim

janvier [ʒɑ̃vje] *nm* January

Japon [ʒapɔ̃] *nm*: **le ~** Japan;
japonais, e *adj* Japanese ▷ *nm* (Ling)
Japanese ▷ *nm/f*: **japonais, e** Japanese

jardin [ʒaʀdɛ̃] *nm* garden; **~
d'enfants** nursery school; **jardinage**
nm gardening; **jardiner** /1/ *vi*
to garden; **jardinier, -ière** *nm/f*
gardener ▷ *nf* (de fenêtre) window
box; **jardinière (de légumes)** (Culin)
mixed vegetables

jargon [ʒaʀɡɔ̃] *nm* (charabia)
gibberish; (publicitaire, scientifique
etc) jargon

jarret [ʒaʀɛ] *nm* back of knee; (Culin)
knuckle, shin

jauge [ʒoʒ] *nf* (instrument) gauge;
~ (de niveau) d'huile (Auto) dipstick

jaune [ʒon] *adj* yellow ▷ *adv*
(fam): **rire ~** to laugh on the other
side of one's face; **~ d'œuf** (egg)
yolk; **jaunir** /2/ *vi, vt* to turn yellow;
jaunisse *nf* jaundice

Javel [ʒavɛl] *nf voir* **eau**

javelot [ʒavlo] *nm* javelin

j.-C. *sigle m* = **Jésus-Christ**

je, j' [ʒə, ʒ] *pron* I

jean [dʒin] *nm* jeans *pl*

Jésus-Christ [ʒezykri(st)] *n* Jesus
Christ; **600 avant/après ~** 600
B.C./A.D.

jet [ʒɛ] *nm* (lancer: action) throwing
no pl; (: résultat) throw; (jaillissement:
d'eau) jet; (: de sang) spurt; **~ d'eau**
spray

jetable [ʒətabl] *adj* disposable

jetée [ʒəte] *nf* jetty; (grande) pier

jeter [ʒəte] /4/ *vt* (gén) to throw;
(se défaire de) to throw away ou out;
~ qch à qn to throw sth to sb; (de
façon agressive) to throw sth at sb;
~ un coup d'œil (à) to take a look
(at); **~ un sort à qn** to cast a spell on
sb; **se ~ sur** to throw o.s. onto; **se ~
dans** (fleuve) to flow into

jeton [ʒətɔ̃] *nm* (au jeu) counter

jette *etc* [ʒɛt] *vb voir* **jeter**

jeu, x [ʒø] *nm* (divertissement, Tech:
d'une pièce) play; (Tennis: partie,

Football etc: façon de jouer) game;
(Théât etc) acting; (série d'objets, jouet)
set; (Cartes) hand; (au casino): **le ~**
gambling; **en ~** at stake; **remettre
en ~** to throw in; **entrer/mettre en ~**
to come/bring into play; **~ de cartes**
pack of cards; **~ d'échecs** chess set;
~ de hasard game of chance; **~ de
mots** pun; **~ de société** board game;
~ télévisé television quiz; **~ vidéo**
video game

jeudi [ʒødi] *nm* Thursday

jeun [ʒœ̃]: **à ~** *adv* on an empty
stomach; **être à ~** to have eaten
nothing; **rester à ~** not to eat
anything

jeune [ʒœn] *adj* young; **les ~s** young
people; **~ fille** girl; **~ homme** young
man; **~s gens** young people

jeûne [ʒøn] *nm* fast

jeunesse [ʒœnɛs] *nf* youth; (aspect)
youthfulness

joaillier, -ière [ʒɔaje, -jɛʀ] *nm/f*
jeweller

jogging [dʒɔɡin] *nm* jogging;
(survêtement) tracksuit; **faire du ~**
to go jogging

joie [ʒwa] *nf* joy

joindre [ʒwɛ̃dʀ] /49/ *vt* to join;
(contacter) to contact, get in touch
with; **~ qch à** (à une lettre) to enclose
sth with; **~ un fichier à un mail**
(Inform) to attach a file to an email;
se ~ à qn to join sb; **se ~ à qch** to
join in sth

joint, e [ʒwɛ̃, -ɛt] *adj*: **~ (à)** (lettre,
paquet) attached (to), enclosed
(with) ▷ *nm* (ligne) join; (articulation)
pièce ~e (de lettre) enclosure; (de mail)
attachment; **~ de culasse** cylinder
head gasket

joli, e [ʒɔli] *adj* pretty, attractive; **une
~e somme/situation** a nice little
sum/situation; **c'est du ~!** (ironique)
that's very nice!; **tout ça, c'est bien
~ mais …** that's all very well but …

jonc [ʒɔ̃] *nm* (bul)rush

jonction [ʒɔ̃ksjɔ̃] *nf* junction

jongleur, -euse [ʒɔ̃glœʀ, -øz] nm/f
juggler

jonquille [ʒɔ̃kij] nf daffodil

Jordanie [ʒɔʀdani] nf: **la ~** Jordan

joue [ʒu] nf cheek

jouer [ʒwe] /1/ vt to play; (somme
d'argent, réputation) to stake, wager;
(simuler: sentiment) to affect, feign
▷ vi to play; (Théât, Ciné) to act; (au
casino) to gamble; (bois, porte: se
voiler) to warp; (clef, pièce: avoir du jeu)
to be loose; **~ sur** (miser) to gamble
on; **~ de** (Mus) to play; **à** (jeu, sport,
roulette) to play; **~ un tour à qn** to
play a trick on sb; **~ la comédie** to
put on an act; **~ serré** to play a close
game; **à toi/nous de ~** it's your/our
go ou turn; **bien joué!** well done!; **on
joue Hamlet au théâtre X** Hamlet is
on at the X theatre

jouet [ʒwɛ] nm toy; **être le ~ de**
(illusion etc) to be the victim of

joueur, -euse [ʒwœʀ, -øz] nm/f
player; **être beau/mauvais ~** to be a
good/bad loser

jouir [ʒwiʀ] /2/ vi (sexe: fam) to come
▷ vt: **~ de** to enjoy

jour [ʒuʀ] nm day; (opposé à la nuit)
day, daytime; (clarté) daylight; (fig:
aspect, ouverture) opening; **sous un ~
favorable/nouveau** in a favourable/
new light; **de ~** (crème, service) day cpd;
travailler de ~ to work during the
day; **voyager de ~** to travel by day; **au
~ le ~** from day to day; **de nos ~s** these
days; **du ~ au lendemain** overnight;
il fait ~ it's daylight; **au grand ~** (fig)
in the open; **mettre au ~** to disclose;
mettre à ~ to bring up to date;
donner le ~ à to give birth to; **voir le
~** to be born; **~ férié** public holiday; **le
~ J** D-day; **~ ouvrable** working day

journal, -aux [ʒuʀnal, -o] nm
(news)paper; (personnel) journal;
(intime) diary; **~ de bord** log; **~ parlé/
télévisé** radio/television news sg

journalier, -ière [ʒuʀnalje, -jɛʀ] adj
daily; (banal) everyday

journalisme [ʒuʀnalism] nm
journalism; **journaliste** [ʒuʀnalist] nm/f
journalist

journée [ʒuʀne] nf day; **la ~
continue** the 9 to 5 working day
(with short lunch break)

joyau, x [ʒwajo] nm gem, jewel

joyeux, -euse [ʒwajø, -øz] adj joyful,
merry; **~ Noël!** Merry ou Happy
Christmas!; **~ anniversaire!** many
happy returns!

jubiler [ʒybile] /1/ vi to be jubilant,
exult

judas [ʒyda] nm (trou) spy-hole

judiciaire [ʒydisjɛʀ] adj judicial

judicieux, -euse [ʒydisjø, -øz] adj
judicious

judo [ʒydo] nm judo

juge [ʒyʒ] nm judge; **~ d'instruction**
examining (BRIT) ou committing
(US) magistrate; **~ de paix** justice
of the peace

jugé [ʒyʒe]: **au ~** adv by guesswork

jugement [ʒyʒmɑ̃] nm judgment;
(Jur: au pénal) sentence; (: au civil)
decision

juger [ʒyʒe] /3/ vt to judge;
(estimer) to consider; **~ qn/qch
satisfaisant** to consider sb/sth (to
be) satisfactory; **~ bon de faire** to
consider it a good idea to do

juif, -ive [ʒɥif, -iv] adj Jewish
▷ nm/f: **J~, -ive** Jewish man/woman
ou Jew

juillet [ʒɥijɛ] nm July

LE 14 JUILLET

- Le 14 juillet is a national holiday in
- France and commemorates the
- storming of the Bastille during the
- French Revolution. Throughout
- the country there are celebrations,
- which feature parades, music,
- dancing and firework displays. In
- Paris a military parade along the
- Champs-Élysées is attended by the
- President.

juin [ʒɥɛ̃] nm June

jumeau, -elle, x [ʒymo, -ɛl] adj, nm/f twin

jumeler [ʒymle] /4/ vt to twin

jumelle [ʒymɛl] adj f, nf voir **jumeau**

jument [ʒymɑ̃] nf mare

jungle [ʒɔ̃gl] nf jungle

jupe [ʒyp] nf skirt

jupon [ʒypɔ̃] nm waist slip ou petticoat

juré, e [ʒyʀe] nm/f juror ▷ adj: **ennemi ~** sworn ou avowed enemy

jurer [ʒyʀe] /1/ vt (obéissance etc) to swear, vow ▷ vi (dire des jurons) to swear, curse; (dissoner): **~ (avec)** to clash (with); **~ de faire/que** to swear ou vow to do/that; **~ de qch** (s'en porter garant) to swear to sth

juridique [ʒyʀidik] adj legal

juron [ʒyʀɔ̃] nm curse, swearword

jury [ʒyʀi] nm jury; (Art, Sport) panel of judges; (Scol) board (of examiners), jury

jus [ʒy] nm juice; (de viande) gravy, (meat) juice; **~ de fruits** fruit juice

jusque [ʒysk]: **jusqu'à** prép (endroit) as far as, (up) to; (moment) until, till; (limite) up to; **~ sur/dans** up to; (y compris) even on/in; **jusqu'à ce que** until; **jusqu'à présent** ou **maintenant** so far; **jusqu'où?** how far?

justaucorps [ʒystokɔʀ] nm inv leotard

juste [ʒyst] adj (équitable) just, fair; (légitime) just; (exact, vrai) right; (pertinent) apt; (étroit) tight; (insuffisant) on the short side ▷ adv right; (chanter) in tune; (seulement) just; **~ assez/au-dessus** just enough/above; **pouvoir tout ~ faire** to be only just able to do; **au ~ exactly; le ~ milieu** the happy medium; **c'était ~** it was a close thing; **justement** adv justly; (précisément) just, precisely; **justesse** nf (précision) accuracy; (d'une remarque) aptness; (d'une opinion) soundness; **de justesse** only just

justice [ʒystis] nf (équité) fairness, justice; (Admin) justice; **rendre ~ à qn** to do sb justice

justificatif, -ive [ʒystifikatif, -iv] adj (document etc) supporting; **pièce justificative** written proof

justifier [ʒystifje] /7/ vt to justify; **~ de** to prove

juteux, -euse [ʒytø, -øz] adj juicy

juvénile [ʒyvenil] adj youthful

j

kit [kit] nm kit; **~ piéton** ou **mains libres** hands-free kit; **en ~** in kit form

kiwi [kiwi] nm kiwi

klaxon [klaksɔn] nm horn;

klaxonner /1/ vi, vt to hoot (BRIT), honk (one's horn) (US)

km abr (= kilomètre) km

km/h abr (= kilomètres/heure) km/h, kph

K.-O. adj inv shattered, knackered

Kosovo [kɔsɔvo] nm: **le ~** Kosovo

Koweit, Kuweit [kɔwɛt] nm: **le ~** Kuwait

k-way® [kawɛ] nm (lightweight nylon) cagoule

kyste [kist] nm cyst

K [ka] nm inv K

kaki [kaki] adj inv khaki

kangourou [kɑ̃guʀu] nm kangaroo

karaté [kaʀate] nm karate

kascher [kaʃɛʀ] adj inv kosher

kayak [kajak] nm kayak; **faire du ~** to go kayaking

képi [kepi] nm kepi

kermesse [kɛʀmɛs] nf bazaar, (charity) fête; village fair

kidnapper [kidnape] /1/ vt to kidnap

kilo [kilo] nm kilo; **kilogramme** nm kilogramme; **kilométrage** nm number of kilometres travelled, ≈ mileage; **kilomètre** nm kilometre; **kilométrique** adj (distance) in kilometres

kinésithérapeute [kineziteʀapøt] nm/f physiotherapist

kiosque [kjɔsk] nm kiosk, stall

kir [kiʀ] nm kir (white wine with blackcurrant liqueur)

l' [l] art déf voir **le**

la [la] art déf voir **le** ▷ nm (Mus) A; (en chantant la gamme) la

là [la] adv there; (ici) here; (dans le temps) then; **elle n'est pas là** she isn't here; **c'est là que** this is where; **là où** where; **de là** (fig) hence; **par là** (fig) by that; voir aussi **-ci**; **celui**; **là-bas** adv there

labo [labo] nm (= laboratoire) lab

laboratoire [labɔratwaʀ] nm laboratory; **~ de langues/d'analyses** language/(medical) analysis laboratory

laborieux, -euse [labɔʀjø, -øz] adj (tâche) laborious

labourer /1/ vt to plough

labyrinthe [labiʀɛ̃t] nm labyrinth, maze

lac [lak] nm lake

lacet [lasɛ] nm (de chaussure) lace; (de route) sharp bend; (piège) snare

lâche [lɑʃ] adj (poltron) cowardly; (desserré) loose, slack ▷ nm/f coward

lâcher [lɑʃe] /1/ vt to let go of; (ce qui tombe, abandonner) to drop; (oiseau, animal: libérer) to release, set free; (fig: mot, remarque) to let slip, come out with ▷ vi (freins) to fail; **~ les amarres** (Navig) to cast off (the moorings); **~ prise** to let go

lacrymogène [lakʀimɔʒɛn] adj: **grenade/gaz ~** tear gas grenade/tear gas

lacune [lakyn] nf gap

là-dedans [ladədɑ̃] adv inside (there), in it; (fig) in that

là-dessous [ladsu] adv underneath, under there; (fig) behind that

là-dessus [ladsy] adv on there; (fig: sur ces mots) at that point; (: à ce sujet) about that

ladite [ladit] adj f voir **ledit**

lagune [lagyn] nf lagoon

là-haut [lao] adv up there

laid, e [lɛ, lɛd] adj ugly; **laideur** nf ugliness no pl

lainage [lɛnaʒ] nm (vêtement) woollen garment; (étoffe) woollen material

laine [lɛn] nf wool

laïque [laik] adj lay, civil; (Scol) state cpd (as opposed to private and Roman Catholic) ▷ nm/f layman(-woman)

laisse [lɛs] nf (de chien) lead, leash; **tenir en ~** to keep on a lead ou leash

laisser [lese] /1/ vt to leave ▷ vb aux: **~ qn faire** to let sb do; **se ~ aller** to let o.s. go; **laisse-toi faire** let me (ou him) do it; **laisser-aller** nm carelessness, slovenliness; **laissez-passer** nm inv pass

lait [lɛ] nm milk; **frère/sœur de ~** foster brother/sister; **~ écrémé/entier/concentré/condensé** skimmed/full/concentrated/condensed/evaporated milk; **laitage** nm dairy product; **laiterie** nf dairy; **laitier, -ière** adj dairy cpd ▷ nm/f milkman (dairywoman)

laiton [letɔ̃] nm brass

laitue [lety] nf lettuce

lambeau, x [lãbo] *nm* scrap; **en ~x** in tatters, tattered

lame [lam] *nf* blade; (*vague*) wave; (*lamelle*) strip; **~ de fond** ground swell *no pl*; **~ de rasoir** razor blade; **lamelle** *nf* small blade

lamentable [lamãtabl] *adj* appalling

lamenter [lamãte] /1/: **se lamenter** *vi*: **se ~ (sur)** to moan (over)

lampadaire [lãpadɛʀ] *nm* (*de salon*) standard lamp; (*dans la rue*) street lamp

lampe [lãp] *nf* lamp; (*Tech*) valve; **~ à pétrole** oil lamp; **~ à bronzer** sunlamp; **~ de poche** torch (BRIT), flashlight (US); **~ halogène** halogen lamp

lance [lãs] *nf* spear; **~ d'incendie** fire hose

lancée [lãse] *nf*: **être/continuer sur sa ~** to be under way/keep going

lancement [lãsmã] *nm* launching *no pl*

lance-pierres [lãspjɛʀ] *nm inv* catapult

lancer [lãse] /3/ *nm* (*Sport*) throwing *no pl*, throw ▷ *vt* to throw; (*émettre, projeter*) to throw out, send out; (*produit, fusée, bateau, artiste*) to launch; (*injure*) to hurl, fling; **se lancer** *vi* (*prendre de l'élan*) to build up speed; (*se précipiter*): **se ~ sur** *ou* **contre** to rush at; **~ du poids** putting the shot; **se ~ qch à qn** to throw sth to sb; (*de façon agressive*) to throw sth at sb; **~ un cri** *ou* **un appel** to shout *ou* call out; **se ~ dans** (*discussion*) to launch into; (*aventure*) to embark on

landau [lãdo] *nm* pram (BRIT), baby carriage (US)

lande [lãd] *nf* moor

langage [lãgaʒ] *nm* language

langouste [lãgust] *nf* crayfish inv; **langoustine** *nf* Dublin Bay prawn

langue [lãg] *nf* (*Anat, Culin*) tongue; (*Ling*) language; **tirer la ~ (à)** to stick out one's tongue (at); **de ~ française** French-speaking; **~ maternelle** native language, mother tongue; **~s vivantes** modern languages

langueur [lãgœʀ] *nf* languidness

languir [lãgiʀ] /2/ *vi* to languish; (*conversation*) to flag; **faire ~ qn** to keep sb waiting

lanière [lanjɛʀ] *nf* (*de fouet*) lash; (*de valise, bretelle*) strap

lanterne [lãtɛʀn] *nf* (*portable*) lantern; (*électrique*) light, lamp; (*de voiture*) (side)light

laper [lape] /1/ *vt* to lap up

lapidaire [lapidɛʀ] *adj* (*fig*) terse

lapin [lapɛ̃] *nm* rabbit; (*fourrure*) rabbitskin; (*fourrure*) cony; **poser un ~ à qn** to stand sb up

Laponie [laponi] *nf*: **la ~** Lapland

laps [laps] *nm*: **~ de temps** space of time, time *no pl*

laque [lak] *nf* (*vernis*) lacquer; (*pour cheveux*) hair spray

laquelle [lakɛl] *pron voir* **lequel**

larcin [laʀsɛ̃] *nm* theft

lard [laʀ] *nm* (*graisse*) fat; (*bacon*) (streaky) bacon

lardon [laʀdɔ̃] *nm* piece of chopped bacon

large [laʀʒ] *adj* wide; broad; (*fig*) generous ▷ *adv*: **calculer/voir ~** to allow extra/think big ▷ *nm* (*largeur*): **5 m de ~** 5 m wide *ou* in width; (*mer*): **le ~** the open sea; **au ~ de** off; **~ d'esprit** broad-minded; **largement** *adv* widely; (*de loin*) greatly; (*amplement, au minimum*) easily; (*donner etc*) generously; **c'est largement suffisant** that's ample; **largesse** *nf* generosity; **largesses** *nfpl* (*dons*) liberalities; **largeur** *nf* (*qu'on mesure*) width; (*impression visuelle*) wideness, width; (*d'esprit*) broadness

larguer [laʀge] /1/ *vt* to drop; **~ les amarres** to cast off (the moorings)

larme [laʀm] *nf* tear; (*fig*): **une ~ de** a drop of; **en ~s** in tears; **larmoyer** /8/ *vi* (*yeux*) to water; (*se plaindre*) to whimper

larvé, e [laʀve] adj (fig) latent
laryngite [laʀeʒit] nf laryngitis
las, lasse [lɑ, lɑs] adj weary
laser [lazeʀ] nm: **(rayon) ~** laser (beam); **chaîne** ou **platine ~** compact disc (player); **disque ~** compact disc
lasse [lɑs] adj f voir **las**
lasser [lɑse] /1/ vt to weary, tire
latéral, e, -aux [lateʀal, -o] adj side cpd, lateral
latin, e [latɛ̃, -in] adj Latin ▷ nm (Ling) Latin ▷ nm/f: **L~, e** Latin
latitude [latityd] nf latitude
lauréat, e [lɔʀea, -at] nm/f winner
laurier [lɔʀje] nm (Bot) laurel; (Culin) bay leaves pl
lavable [lavabl] adj washable
lavabo [lavabo] nm washbasin; **lavabos** nmpl toilet sg
lavage [lavaʒ] nm washing no pl, wash; **~ de cerveau** brainwashing no pl
lavande [lavɑ̃d] nf lavender
lave [lav] nf lava no pl
lave-linge [lavlɛ̃ʒ] nm inv washing machine
laver [lave] /1/ vt to wash; (tache) to wash off; **se laver** vi to have a wash, wash; **se ~ les mains/dents** to wash one's hands/clean one's teeth; **~ la vaisselle/le linge** to wash the dishes/clothes; **~ qn de** (accusation) to clear sb of; **laverie** nf: **laverie (automatique)** Launderette® (BRIT), Laundromat® (US); **lavette** nf dish cloth; (fam) drip; **laveur, -euse** nm/f cleaner; **lave-vaisselle** nm inv dishwasher; **lavoir** nm wash house; (évier) sink
laxatif, -ive [laksatif, -iv] adj, nm laxative
layette [lɛjɛt] nf layette

MOT-CLÉ

le, la, l' [lə, la, l] (pl **les**) art déf **1** the; **le livre/la pomme/l'arbre**
the book/the apple/the tree; **les étudiants** the students
2 (noms abstraits): **le courage/ l'amour/la jeunesse** courage/ love/youth
3 (indiquant la possession): **se casser la jambe** etc to break one's leg etc; **levez la main** put your hand up; **avoir les yeux gris/le nez rouge** to have grey eyes/a red nose
4 (temps): **le matin/soir** in the morning/evening; mornings/ evenings; **le jeudi** etc (d'habitude) on Thursdays etc; (ce jeudi-là etc) on (the) Thursday
5 (distribution, évaluation) a, an; **trois euros le mètre/kilo** three euros a ou per metre/kilo; **le tiers/quart de** a third/quarter of
▷ pron **1** (personne: mâle) him; (: femelle) her; (: pluriel) them; **je le/ la/les vois** I can see him/her/them
2 (animal, chose: singulier) it; (: pluriel) them; **je le (ou la) vois** I can see it; **je les vois** I can see them
3 (remplaçant une phrase): **je ne le savais pas** I didn't know (about it); **il était riche et ne l'est plus** he was once rich but no longer is

lécher [leʃe] /6/ vt to lick; (laper: lait, eau) to lick ou lap up; **se ~ les doigts/lèvres** to lick one's fingers/ lips; **lèche-vitrines** nm inv: **faire du lèche-vitrines** to go window-shopping
leçon [ləsɔ̃] nf lesson; **faire la ~ à** (fig) to give a lecture to; **~s de conduite** driving lessons; **~s particulières** private lessons ou tuition sg (BRIT)
lecteur, -trice [lɛktœʀ, -tʀis] nm/f reader; (d'université) (foreign language) assistant ▷ nm (Tech): **~ de cassettes** cassette player; **~ de disquette(s)** disk drive; **~ de CD/DVD** CD/DVD player; **~ MP3** MP3 player
lecture [lɛktyʀ] nf reading

■ Attention à ne pas traduire *lecture*
par le mot anglais *lecture*.

ledit, ladite [lədit, ladit] (*mpl*
lesdits, *fpl* **lesdites**) *adj* the aforesaid

légal, e, -aux [legal, -o] *adj* legal;
légaliser /v/ *vt* to legalize; **légalité**
nf legality

légendaire [leʒɑ̃dɛʀ] *adj* legendary

légende [leʒɑ̃d] *nf* (*mythe*) legend; (*de
carte, plan*) key; (*de dessin*) caption

léger, -ère [leʒe, -ɛʀ] *adj* light; (*bruit,
retard*) slight; (*superficiel*) thoughtless;
(*volage*) free and easy; **à la légère**
(*parler, agir*) rashly, thoughtlessly;
légèrement *adv* (*s'habiller, bouger*)
lightly; **légèrement plus grand**
slightly bigger; **manger légèrement**
to eat a light meal; **légèreté** *nf*
lightness; (*d'une remarque*) flippancy

législatif, -ive [leʒislatif, -iv] *adj*
legislative; **législatives** *nfpl* general
election *sg*

légitime [leʒitim] *adj* (*Jur*) lawful,
legitimate; (*fig*) rightful, legitimate;
en état de ~ défense in self-defence

legs [lɛg] *nm* legacy

léguer [lege] /6/ *vt*: **~ qch à qn** (*Jur*)
to bequeath sth to sb

légume [legym] *nm* vegetable; **~s
verts** green vegetables; **~s secs**
pulses

lendemain [lɑ̃dmɛ̃] *nm*: **le ~ the**
next *ou* following day; **le ~ matin/
soir** the next *ou* following morning/
evening; **le ~ de** the day after

lent, e [lɑ̃, lɑ̃t] *adj* slow; **lentement**
adv slowly; **lenteur** *nf* slowness *no pl*

lentille [lɑ̃tij] *nf* (*Optique*) lens *sg*;
(*Bot*) lentil; **~s de contact** contact
lenses

léopard [leɔpaʀ] *nm* leopard

lèpre [lɛpʀ] *nf* leprosy

● **MOT-CLÉ**

lequel, laquelle [ləkɛl, lakɛl] (*mpl*
lesquels, *fpl* **lesquelles**) (*à + lequel*
= auquel, *de + lequel* = **duquel** *etc*)
pron **1** (*interrogatif*) which, which one;
lequel des deux? which one?
2 (*relatif: personne: sujet*) who; (: *objet,
après préposition*) whom; (: *chose*)
which
▶ *adj*: **auquel cas** in which case

les [le] *art déf, pron voir* **le**

lesbienne [lɛsbjɛn] *nf* lesbian

lesdits, lesdites [ledi, ledit] *adj*
pl voir **ledit**

léser [leze] /6/ *vt* to wrong

lésiner [lezine] /1/ *vi*: **ne pas ~ sur
les moyens** (*pour mariage etc*) to push
the boat out

lésion [lezjɔ̃] *nf* lesion, damage *no pl*

lessive [lesiv] *nf* (*poudre*) washing
powder; (*linge*) washing, wash;
lessiver /1/ *vt* to wash; (*fam: fatiguer*)
to tire out, exhaust

lest [lɛst] *nm* ballast

leste [lɛst] *adj* sprightly, nimble

lettre [lɛtʀ] *nf* letter; **lettres** *nfpl*
(*étude, culture*) literature *sg*; (*Scol*) arts
(subjects); **à la ~** literally; **en toutes
~s** in full; **~ piégée** letter bomb

leucémie [løsemi] *nf* leukaemia

● **MOT-CLÉ**

leur [lœʀ] *adj poss* their; **leur maison**
their house; **leurs amis** their friends
▶ *pron* **1** (*objet indirect*) (to) them; **je
leur ai dit la vérité** I told them the
truth; **je le leur ai donné** I gave it to
them, I gave them it
2 (*possessif*): **le (la) leur, les leurs**
theirs

levain [ləvɛ̃] *nm* leaven

levé, e [ləve] *adj*: **être ~** to be up;
levée *nf* (*Postes*) collection

lever [ləve] /5/ *vt* (*vitre, bras etc*) to
raise; (*soulever de terre, supprimer:
interdiction, siège*) to lift; (*impôts,
armée*) to levy ▶ *vi* to rise ▶ *nm*: **au
~** on getting up; **se lever** *vi* to get
up; (*soleil*) to rise; (*jour*) to break;

(brouillard) to lift; **ça va se ~** (temps) it's going to clear up; **~ du jour** daybreak; **~ de soleil** sunrise

levier [ləvje] nm lever

lèvre [lɛvʀ] nf lip

lévrier [levʀije] nm greyhound

levure [ləvyʀ] nf yeast; **~ chimique** baking powder

lexique [lɛksik] nm vocabulary, lexicon; (glossaire) vocabulary

lézard [lezaʀ] nm lizard

lézarde [lezaʀd] nf crack

liaison [ljɛzɔ̃] nf (rapport) connection; (Rail, Aviat etc) link; (amoureuse) affair; (Culin, Phonétique) liaison; **entrer/être en ~ avec** to get/be in contact with

liane [ljan] nf creeper

liasse [ljas] nf wad, bundle

Liban [libɑ̃] nm: **le ~** (the) Lebanon

libeller [libele] /1/ vt (chèque, mandat): **~ (au nom de)** to make out (to); (lettre) to word

libellule [libelyl] nf dragonfly

libéral, e, -aux [liberal, -o] adj, nm/f liberal; **les professions ~es** liberal professions

libérer [libeʀe] /6/ vt (délivrer) to free, liberate (Psych) to liberate; (relâcher: prisonnier) to discharge, release; (gaz, cran d'arrêt) to release; **se libérer** vi (de rendez-vous) to get out of previous engagements

liberté [libɛʀte] nf freedom; (loisir) free time, **libertés** nfpl (privautés) liberties; **mettre/être en ~** to set/be free; **en ~ provisoire/surveillée/conditionnelle** on bail/probation/parole

libraire [libʀɛʀ] nm/f bookseller

librairie [libʀɛʀi] nf bookshop

Attention ne pas traduire librairie par library.

libre [libʀ] adj free; (route) clear; (place etc) free; (poste) not engaged; (Scol) non-state; **~ de qch/de faire** free from sth/to do; **~ arbitre** free will; **libre-échange** nm free trade; **libre-service** nm inv self-service store

Libye [libi] nf: **la ~** Libya

licence [lisɑ̃s] nf (permis) permit; (diplôme) (first) degree; (liberté) liberty, freedom; (Sport) permit; **licencié, e** nm/f (Scol): **licencié ès lettres/en droit ≈** Bachelor of Arts/Law

licenciement [lisɑ̃simɑ̃] nm redundancy

licencier [lisɑ̃sje] /7/ vt (renvoyer) to dismiss; (débaucher) to make redundant

licite [lisit] adj lawful

lie [li] nf dregs pl, sediment

lié, e [lje] adj: **très ~ avec** very friendly with ou close to

Liechtenstein [liʃtɛnʃtajn] nm: **le ~** Liechtenstein

liège [ljɛʒ] nm cork

lien [ljɛ̃] nm (corde, fig: affectif, culturel) bond; (rapport) link, connection; **~ de parenté** family tie; **~ hypertexte** hyperlink

lier [lje] /7/ vt (attacher) to link up; (joindre) to bind; (fig: unir, engager) to bind; **~ conversation (avec)** to strike up a conversation (with); **~ connaissance avec** to get to know

lierre [ljɛʀ] nm ivy

lieu, x [ljø] nm place; **lieux** nmpl (locaux) premises; (endroit: d'un accident etc) scene sg; **arriver/être sur les ~x** to arrive/be on the scene; **en premier ~** in the first place; **en dernier ~** lastly; **avoir ~** to take place; **tenir ~ de** to serve as; **donner ~ à** to give rise to; **au ~ de** instead of; **~ commun** commonplace; **lieu-dit** (pl **lieux-dits**) nm locality

lieutenant [ljøtnɑ̃] nm lieutenant

lièvre [ljɛvʀ] nm hare

ligament [ligamɑ̃] nm ligament

ligne [liɲ] nf (gén) line; (Transports: liaison) service; (: trajet) route; (silhouette) figure; **garder la ~** to keep one's figure; **en ~** (Inform) online; **entrer en ~ de compte** to be taken into account; **~ fixe** (Tél) landline

ligné, e [liɲe] *adj*: **papier ~** ruled paper ▷ *nf* line, lineage

ligoter [ligɔte] /1/ *vt* to tie up

ligue [lig] *nf* league

lilas [lila] *nm* lilac

limace [limas] *nf* slug

limande [limãd] *nf* dab

lime [lim] *nf* file; **~ à ongles** nail file; **limer** /1/ *vt* to file

limitation [limitasjɔ̃] *nf*: **~ de vitesse** speed limit

limite [limit] *nf* (*de terrain*) boundary; (*partie ou point extrême*) limit; **à la ~** (*au pire*) if the worst comes (*ou* came) to the worst; **vitesse/charge ~** maximum speed/load; **cas ~** borderline case; **date ~** deadline; **date ~ de vente/consommation** sell-by/best-before date; **limiter** /1/ *vt* (*restreindre*) to limit, restrict; (*délimiter*) to border; **limitrophe** *adj* border *cpd*

limoger [limɔʒe] /3/ *vt* to dismiss

limon [limɔ̃] *nm* silt

limonade [limɔnad] *nf* lemonade

lin [lɛ̃] *nm* (*tissu, toile*) linen

linceul [lɛ̃sœl] *nm* shroud

linge [lɛ̃ʒ] *nm* (*serviettes etc*) linen; (*aussi*: **~ de corps**) underwear; (*lessive*) washing; **lingerie** *nf* lingerie, underwear

lingot [lɛ̃go] *nm* ingot

linguistique [lɛ̃gɥistik] *adj* linguistic ▷ *nf* linguistics *sg*

lion, ne [ljɔ̃, ljɔn] *nm/f* lion (lioness); (*signe*): **le L~** Leo; **lionceau, x** *nm* lion cub

liqueur [likœʀ] *nf* liqueur

liquidation [likidasjɔ̃] *nf* (*vente*) sale, liquidation; (*Comm*) clearance (sale)

liquide [likid] *adj* liquid ▷ *nm* liquid; (*Comm*): **en ~** in ready money *ou* cash; **je n'ai pas de ~** I haven't got any cash; **liquider** /1/ *vt* to liquidate; (*Comm*: *articles*) to clear, sell off

lire [liʀ] /43/ *vt* (*monnaie*) lira ▷ *vt*, *vi* to read

lis *vb* [li] *voir* **lire** ▷ *nm* [lis] = **lys**

Lisbonne [lizbɔn] *n* Lisbon

liseuse [lizøz] *nf* e-reader

lisible [lizibl] *adj* legible

lisière [lizjɛʀ] *nf* (*de forêt*) edge

lisons [lizɔ̃] *vb voir* **lire**

lisse [lis] *adj* smooth

lisseur [lisœʀ] *nm* straighteners

liste [list] *nf* list; **faire la ~** de to list; **~ électorale** electoral roll; **~ de mariage** wedding (present) list; **listing** *nm* (*Inform*) printout

lit [li] *nm* bed; **petit ~, ~ à une place** single bed; **grand ~, ~ à deux places** double bed; **faire son ~** to make one's bed; **aller/se mettre au ~** to go to/get into bed; **~ de camp** camp bed; **~ d'enfant** cot (BRIT), crib (US)

literie [litʀi] *nf* bedding, bedclothes *pl*

litige [litiʒ] *nm* dispute

litre [litʀ] *nm* litre

littéraire [literɛʀ] *adj* literary ▷ *nm/f* arts student; **elle est très ~** she's very literary

littéral, e, -aux [literal, -o] *adj* literal

littérature [literatyʀ] *nf* literature

littoral, e, -aux [litɔral, -o] *nm* coast

livide [livid] *adj* livid, pallid

livraison [livʀɛzɔ̃] *nf* delivery

livre [livʀ] *nm* book ▷ *nf* (*poids, monnaie*) pound; **~ numérique** e-book; **~ de poche** paperback

livré, e [livʀe] *adj*: **~ à soi-même** left to oneself *ou* one's own devices

livrer [livʀe] /1/ *vt* (*Comm*) to deliver; (*otage, coupable*) to hand over; (*secret, information*) to give away; **se ~ à** (*se rendre*) to give o.s. up to; (*faire: pratiques, actes*) to indulge in; (*enquête*) to carry out

livret [livʀɛ] *nm* booklet; (*d'opéra*) libretto; **~ de caisse d'épargne** (savings) bank-book; **~ de famille** (official) family record book; **~ scolaire** (school) report book

livreur, -euse [livʀœʀ, -øz] nm/f delivery boy ou man/girl ou woman

local, e, -aux [lɔkal, -o] adj local ▷ nm (salle) premises pl ▷ nmpl premises; **localité** nf locality

locataire [lɔkatɛʀ] nm/f tenant; (de chambre) lodger

location [lɔkasjɔ̃] nf (par le locataire) renting; (par le propriétaire) renting out, letting; (bureau) booking office; "~ de voitures" "car hire (BRIT) ou rental (US)"; **habiter en ~** to live in rented accommodation; **prendre une ~ (pour les vacances)** to rent a house etc (for the holidays)

⚠ Attention à ne pas traduire location par le mot anglais location.

locomotive [lɔkɔmɔtiv] nf locomotive, engine

locution [lɔkysjɔ̃] nf phrase

loge [lɔʒ] nf (Théât: d'artiste) dressing room; (: de spectateurs) box; (de concierge, franc-maçon) lodge

logement [lɔʒmɑ̃] nm flat (BRIT), apartment (US); accommodation no pl (BRIT), accommodations pl (US); (Pol, Admin): **le ~** housing

loger [lɔʒe] /1/ vt to accommodate ▷ vi to live; **se loger** vr: **trouver à se ~** to find accommodation; **se ~ dans** (balle, flèche) to lodge itself in; **être logé, nourri** to have board and lodging; **logeur, -euse** nm/f landlord/landlady

logiciel [lɔʒisjɛl] nm piece of software

logique [lɔʒik] adj logical ▷ nf logic

logo [lɔgo] nm logo

loi [lwa] nf law; **faire la ~** to lay down the law

loin [lwɛ̃] adv far; (dans le temps: futur) a long way off; (: passé) a long time ago; **plus ~** further; **~ de** far from; **~ d'ici** a long way from here; **au ~** far off; **de ~** from a distance; (fig: de beaucoup) by far

lointain, e [lwɛ̃tɛ̃, -ɛn] adj faraway, distant; (dans le futur, passé) distant; (cause, parent) remote, distant ▷ nm: **dans le ~** in the distance

loir [lwaʀ] nm dormouse

Loire [lwaʀ] nf: **la ~** the Loire

loisir [lwaziʀ] nm: **heures de ~** spare time; **loisirs** nmpl (temps libre) leisure sg; (activités) leisure activities; **avoir le ~ de faire** to have the time ou opportunity to do; **(tout) à ~** at leisure

londonien, ne [lɔ̃dɔnjɛ̃, -ɛn] adj London cpd, of London ▷ nm/f: **L~, ne** Londoner

Londres [lɔ̃dʀ] n London

long, longue [lɔ̃, lɔ̃g] adj long ▷ adv: **en savoir ~** to know a great deal ▷ nm: **de 3 m de ~** 3 m long, 3 m in length; **ne pas faire ~ feu** not to last long; **(tout) le ~ de** (all) along; **tout au ~ de** (année, vie) throughout; **de ~ en large** (marcher) to and fro, up and down

longer [lɔ̃ʒe] /3/ vt to go (ou walk ou drive) along(side); (mur, route) to border

longiligne [lɔ̃ʒiliɲ] adj long-limbed

longitude [lɔ̃ʒityd] nf longitude

longtemps [lɔ̃tɑ̃] adv (for) a long time, (for) long; **avant ~** before long; **pour/pendant ~** for a long time; **mettre ~ à faire** to take a long time to do; **il en a pour ~** he'll be a long time

longue [lɔ̃g] adj f voir **long** ▷ nf: **à la ~** in the end; **longuement** adv (longtemps) for a long time; (en détail) at length

longueur [lɔ̃gœʀ] nf length; **longueurs** nfpl (fig: d'un film etc) tedious parts; **en ~** lengthwise; **tirer en ~** to drag on; **à ~ de journée** all day long

loquet [lɔkɛ] nm latch

lorgner [lɔʀɲe] /1/ vt to eye; (fig) to have one's eye on

lors [lɔʀ]: **~ de** prép (au moment de) at the time of; (pendant) during; **~ même que** even though

lorsque [lɔʀsk] *conj* when, as

losange [lɔzɑ̃ʒ] *nm* diamond

lot [lo] *nm* (*part*) share; (*de loterie*) prize; (*fig: destin*) fate, lot; (*Comm, Inform*) batch; **le gros ~** the jackpot

loterie [lɔtʀi] *nf* lottery

lotion [losjɔ̃] *nf* lotion; **~ après rasage** after-shave (lotion)

lotissement [lɔtismɑ̃] *nm* housing development; (*parcelle*) (building) plot, lot

loto [lɔto] *nm* lotto

lotte [lɔt] *nf* monkfish

louange [lwɑ̃ʒ] *nf* **à la ~ de** in praise of; **louanges** *nfpl* praise *sg*

loubar(d) [lubaʀ] *nm* (*fam*) lout

louche [luʃ] *adj* shady, fishy, dubious ▷ *nf* ladle; **loucher** /1/ *vi* to squint

louer [lwe] /1/ *vt* (*maison: propriétaire*) to let, rent (out); (: *locataire*) to rent; (*voiture etc: entreprise*) to hire out (BRIT), rent (out); (: *locataire*) to hire (BRIT), rent (out); (*réserver*) to book; (*faire l'éloge de*) to praise; **"à ~"** "to let" (BRIT), **"for rent"** (US)

loup [lu] *nm* wolf; **jeune ~** young go-getter

loupe [lup] *nf* magnifying glass; **à la ~** in minute detail

louper [lupe] /1/ *vt* (*fam: manquer*) to miss; (*examen*) to flunk

lourd, e [luʀ, luʀd] *adj* heavy; (*chaleur, temps*) sultry; **~ de** (*menaces*) charged with; (*conséquences*) fraught with; **lourdaud, e** *adj* clumsy; **lourdement** *adv* heavily

loutre [lutʀ] *nf* otter

louveteau, x [luvto] *nm* wolf-cub; (*scout*) cub (scout)

louvoyer [luvwaje] /8/ *vi* (*fig*) to hedge, evade the issue

loyal, e, -aux [lwajal, -o] *adj* (*fidèle*) loyal, faithful; (*fair-play*) fair; **loyauté** *nf* loyalty, faithfulness; fairness

loyer [lwaje] *nm* rent

lu, e [ly] *pp de* **lire**

lubie [lybi] *nf* whim, craze

lubrifiant [lybʀifjɑ̃] *nm* lubricant

lubrifier [lybʀifje] /7/ *vt* to lubricate

lubrique [lybʀik] *adj* lecherous

lucarne [lykaʀn] *nf* skylight

lucide [lysid] *adj* lucid; (*accidenté*) conscious

lucratif, -ive [lykʀatif, -iv] *adj* lucrative; profitable; **à but non ~** non profit-making

lueur [lɥœʀ] *nf* (*chatoyante*) glimmer *no pl*; (*pâle*) (faint) light; (*fig*) glimmer, gleam

luge [lyʒ] *nf* sledge (BRIT), sled (US)

lugubre [lygybʀ] *adj* gloomy; dismal

MOT-CLÉ

lui [lɥi] *pron* **1** (*objet indirect: mâle*) (to) him; (: *femelle*) (to) her; (: *chose, animal*) (to) it; **je lui ai parlé** I have spoken to him (ou to her); **il lui a offert un cadeau** he gave him (ou her) a present

2 (*après préposition, comparatif: personne*) him; (: *chose, animal*) it; **elle est contente de lui** she is pleased with him; **je la connais mieux que lui** I know her better than he does; I know her better than him; **cette voiture est à lui** this car belongs to him, this is HIS car; **c'est à lui de jouer** it's his turn *ou* go

3 (*sujet, forme emphatique*) he; **lui, il est à Paris** HE is in Paris; **c'est lui qui l'a fait** HE did it

4 (*objet, forme emphatique*) him; **c'est lui que j'attends** I'm waiting for HIM

5: **lui-même** himself; itself

luire [lɥiʀ] /38/ *vi* to shine; (*reflets chauds, cuivrés*) to glow

lumière [lymjɛʀ] *nf* light; **mettre en ~** (*fig*) to highlight; **~ du jour/soleil** day/sunlight

luminaire [lyminɛʀ] *nm* lamp, light

lumineux, -euse [lyminø, -øz] *adj* luminous; (*éclairé*) illuminated; (*ciel, journée, couleur*) bright; (*rayon etc*) of light, light *cpd*; (*fig: regard*) radiant

lunatique [lynatik] *adj* whimsical, temperamental

lundi [lœdi] *nm* Monday; **on est ~** it's Monday; **le(s) ~(s)** on Mondays; **à ~!** see you (on) Monday!; **~ de Pâques** Easter Monday

lune [lyn] *nf* moon; **~ de miel** honeymoon

lunette [lynɛt] *nf*: **~s** glasses, spectacles; (*protectrices*) goggles; **~ arrière** (*Auto*) rear window; **~s noires** dark glasses; **~s de soleil** sunglasses

lustre [lystʀ] *nm* (*de plafond*) chandelier; (*fig: éclat*) lustre; **lustrer** /1/ *vt*: **lustrer qch** to make sth shine

luth [lyt] *nm* lute

lutin [lytɛ̃] *nm* imp, goblin

lutte [lyt] *nf* (*conflit*) struggle; (*Sport*): **la ~** wrestling; **lutter** /1/ *vi* to fight, struggle

luxe [lyks] *nm* luxury; **de ~** luxury *cpd*

Luxembourg [lyksɑ̃buʀ] *nm*: **le ~** Luxembourg

luxer [lykse] /1/ *vt*: **se ~ l'épaule** to dislocate one's shoulder

luxueux, -euse [lyksɥø, -øz] *adj* luxurious

lycée [lise] *nm* (state) secondary (*BRIT*) ou high (*US*) school; **lycéen, ne** *nm/f* secondary school pupil

Lyon [ljɔ̃] *n* Lyons

lyophilisé, e [ljofilize] *adj* (*café*) freeze-dried

lyrique [liʀik] *adj* lyrical; (*Opéra*) lyric; **artiste ~** opera singer

lys [lis] *nm* lily

M *abr* = **Monsieur**

m' [m] *pron voir* **me**

ma [ma] *adj poss voir* **mon**

macaron [makaʀɔ̃] *nm* (*gâteau*) macaroon; (*insigne*) (round) badge

macaroni(s) [makaʀɔni] *nm (pl)* macaroni *sg*; **~ au gratin** macaroni cheese (*BRIT*), macaroni and cheese (*US*)

Macédoine [masedwan] *nf* Macedonia

macédoine [masedwan] *nf*: **~ de fruits** fruit salad; **~ de légumes** mixed vegetables *pl*

macérer [maseʀe] /6/ *vi*, *vt* to macerate; (*dans du vinaigre*) to pickle

mâcher [mɑʃe] /1/ *vt* to chew; **ne pas ~ ses mots** not to mince one's words

machin [maʃɛ̃] *nm* (*fam*) thingamajig; (*personne*): **M~(e)** what's-his-(*ou* her)-name

machinal, e, -aux [maʃinal, -o] *adj* mechanical, automatic

machination [maʃinasjɔ̃] *nf* frame-up

machine [maʃin] *nf* machine; (*locomotive*) engine; **~ à laver/coudre/tricoter** washing/sewing/knitting machine; **~ à sous** fruit machine

mâchoire [mɑʃwar] *nf* jaw

mâchonner [mɑʃɔne] /1/ *vt* to chew (at)

maçon [masɔ̃] *nm* bricklayer; (*constructeur*) builder; **maçonnerie** *nf* (*murs*) brickwork; (: *de pierre*) masonry, stonework

Madagascar [madagaskar] *nf* Madagascar

Madame [madam] (*pl* **Mesdames**) *nf*: **~ X** Mrs X; **occupez-vous de ~/Monsieur/Mademoiselle** please serve this lady/gentleman; (*young*) lady; **bonjour ~/Monsieur/Mademoiselle** good morning; (*ton déféren*t) good morning Madam/Sir/Madam; (*le nom est connu*) good morning Mrs X/Mr X/Miss X; **~/Monsieur/Mademoiselle!** (*pour appeler*) excuse me!; **~/Monsieur/Mademoiselle** (*sur lettre*) Dear Madam/Sir/Madam; **chère Madame/cher Monsieur/chère Mademoiselle** Dear Mrs X/Mr X/Miss X; **Mesdames** Ladies; **mesdames, mesdemoiselles, messieurs** ladies and gentlemen

madeleine [madlɛn] *nf* madeleine, ≈ sponge finger cake

Mademoiselle [madmwazɛl] (*pl* **Mesdemoiselles**) *nf* Miss; *voir aussi* **Madame**

Madère [madɛr] *nf* Madeira ▷ *nm*: **madère** Madeira (wine)

Madrid [madrid] *n* Madrid

magasin [magazɛ̃] *nm* (*boutique*) shop; (*entrepôt*) warehouse; **en ~** (*Comm*) in stock

MAGASINS

French shops are usually open from 9am to noon and from 2pm to 7pm. Most shops are closed on Sunday and some do not open on Monday. In bigger towns and shopping centres, most shops are open throughout the day.

magazine [magazin] *nm* magazine

Maghreb [magrɛb] *nm*: **le ~** North(-West) Africa; **maghrébin, e** *adj* North African ▷ *nm/f*: **Maghrébin, e** North African

magicien, ne [maʒisjɛ̃, -ɛn] *nm/f* magician

magie [maʒi] *nf* magic; **magique** *adj* magic; (*fig*) magical

magistral, e, -aux [maʒistral, -o] *adj* (*œuvre, adresse*) masterly; (*ton*) authoritative; **cours ~** lecture

magistrat [maʒistra] *nm* magistrate

magnétique [maɲetik] *adj* magnetic

magnétophone [maɲetɔfɔn] *nm* tape recorder; **~ à cassettes** cassette recorder

magnétoscope [maɲetɔskɔp] *nm*: **~ (à cassette)** video (recorder)

magnifique [maɲifik] *adj* magnificent

magret [magrɛ] *nm*: **~ de canard** duck breast

mai [mɛ] *nm* May; *voir aussi* **juillet**

LE PREMIER MAI

Le premier mai is a public holiday in France and commemorates the trades union demonstrations in the United States in 1886 when workers demanded the right to an eight-hour working day. Sprigs of lily of the valley are traditionally exchanged. *Le 8 mai* is also a public holiday and

• commemorates the surrender of
the German army to Eisenhower
on 7 May, 1945. It is marked by
parades of ex-servicemen and
ex-servicewomen in most towns.
• The social upheavals of May
and June 1968, with their student
demonstrations, workers' strikes
and general rioting, are usually
referred to as 'les événements de
mai 68'. De Gaulle's Government
survived, but reforms in
education and a move towards
decentralization ensued.

maigre [mɛgʀ] *adj* (very) thin,
skinny; (*viande*) lean; (*fromage*)
low-fat; (*végétation*) thin, sparse; (*fig*)
poor, meagre, skimpy; **jours ~s** days
of abstinence, fish days; **maigreur**
nf thinness; **maigrir** /2/ *vi* to get
thinner, lose weight; **maigrir de 2
kilos** to lose 2 kilos

mail [mɛl] *nm* email

maille [maj] *nf* stitch; **~ à
l'endroit/à l'envers** plain/purl stitch

maillet [majɛ] *nm* mallet

maillon [majɔ̃] *nm* link

maillot [majo] *nm* (*aussi:* **~ de
corps**) vest; (*de sportif*) jersey; **~ de
bain** swimming *ou* bathing (BRIT)
costume, swimsuit; (*d'homme*)
(swimming *ou* bathing (BRIT))
trunks *pl*

main [mɛ̃] *nf* hand; **à la ~** (*tenir, avoir*)
in one's hand; (*faire, tricoter etc*) by
hand; **se donner la ~** to hold hands;
donner *ou* **tendre la ~ à qn** to hold
out one's hand to sb; **se serrer la
~** to shake hands; **serrer la ~ à qn**
to shake hands with sb; **sous la ~**
to *ou* at hand; **haut les ~s!** hands
up!; **attaque à ~ armée** armed
attack; **à remettre en ~s propres**
to be delivered personally; **mettre
la dernière ~ à** to put the finishing
touches to; **se faire/perdre la ~** to
get one's hand in/lose one's touch;

avoir qch bien en ~ to have got
the hang of sth; **main-d'œuvre** *nf*
manpower, labour; **mainmise** *nf*
(*fig*): **avoir la mainmise sur** to have a
grip *ou* stranglehold on

mains-libres [mɛ̃libʀ] *adj inv*
(*téléphone, kit*) hands-free

maint, e [mɛ̃, mɛ̃t] *adj* many a; **~s**
many; **à ~es reprises** time and
(time) again

maintenant [mɛ̃tnɑ̃] *adv* now;
(*actuellement*) nowadays

maintenir [mɛ̃tniʀ] /22/ *vt* (*retenir,
soutenir*) to support; (*contenir: foule
etc*) to keep in check; (*conserver*) to
maintain; **se maintenir** *vi* (*prix*) to
keep steady; (*préjugé*) to persist

maintien [mɛ̃tjɛ̃] *nm* maintaining;
(*attitude*) bearing

maire [mɛʀ] *nm* mayor; **mairie**
nf (*bâtiment*) town hall; (*administration*)
town council

mais [mɛ] *conj* but; **~ non!** of
course not!; **~ enfin** but after all!;
(*indignation*) look here!

maïs [mais] *nm* maize (BRIT),
corn (US)

maison [mɛzɔ̃] *nf* house; (*chez-soi*)
home; (*Comm*) firm ▷ *adj inv* (*Culin*)
home-made; (*Comm*) in-house, own;
à la ~ at home; (*direction*) home;
~ close brothel; **~ des jeunes** = youth
club; **~ mère** parent company; **~ de
passe** = **maison close**; **~ de repos**
convalescent home; **~ de retraite**
old people's home; **~ de santé**
psychiatric facility

maître, -esse [mɛtʀ, mɛtʀɛs] *nm/f*
master (mistress); (*Scol*) teacher,
schoolmaster/-mistress ▷ *nm* (*peintre
etc*) master; (*titre*): **M~ (M~)** Maître
(*term of address for lawyers etc*) ▷ *adj*
(*principal, essentiel*) main; **être ~
de** (*soi-même, situation*) to be in
control of; **une maîtresse femme**
a forceful woman; **~ chanteur**
blackmailer; **~/maîtresse d'école**
schoolmaster/-mistress; **~ d'hôtel**

(domestique) butler; (d'hôtel) head waiter; **~ nageur** lifeguard; **maîtresse de maison** hostess; (ménagère) housewife

maîtrise [metriz] nf (aussi: **~ de soi**) self-control, self-possession; (habileté) skill, mastery; (suprématie) mastery, command; (diplôme) ≈ master's degree; **maîtriser** /1/ vt (cheval, incendie) to (bring under) control; (sujet) to master; (émotion) to control, master; **se maîtriser** to control o.s.

majestueux, -euse [maʒestɥø, -øz] adj majestic

majeur, e [maʒœʀ] adj (important) major; (Jur) of age ▷ nm (doigt) middle finger; **en ~e partie** for the most part; **la ~e partie de** most of

majorer [maʒɔʀe] /1/ vt to increase

majoritaire [maʒɔʀitɛʀ] adj cpd majority

majorité [maʒɔʀite] nf (gén) majority; (parti) party in power; **en ~** (composé etc) mainly; **avoir la ~** to have the majority

majuscule [maʒyskyl] adj, nf: **(lettre)** ~ capital (letter)

mal (pl **maux**) [mal, mo] nm (opposé au bien) evil; (tort, dommage) harm; (douleur physique) pain, ache; (maladie) illness, sickness no pl ▷ adv badly ▷ adj: **être ~ (à l'aise)** to be uncomfortable; **être ~ avec qn** to be on bad terms with sb; **il a ~ compris** he misunderstood; **se sentir** ou **se trouver ~** to feel ill ou unwell; **dire/penser du ~ de** to speak/think ill of; **avoir du ~ à faire qch** to have trouble doing sth; **se donner du ~ pour faire qch** to go to a lot of trouble to do sth; **ne voir aucun ~ à** to see no harm in, see nothing wrong in; **faire du ~ à qn** to hurt sb; **se faire ~** to hurt o.s.; **ça fait ~** it hurts; **j'ai ~ au dos** my back aches; **avoir ~ à la tête/à la gorge** to have a headache/a sore throat; **avoir ~ aux**

dents/à l'oreille to have toothache/earache; **avoir le ~ du pays** to be homesick; **~ de mer** seasickness; **~ en point** in a bad state; voir aussi **cœur**

malade [malad] adj ill, sick; (poitrine, jambe) bad; (plante) diseased ▷ nm/f invalid, sick person; (à l'hôpital) patient; **tomber ~** to fall ill; **être ~ du cœur** to have heart trouble ou a bad heart; **~ mental** mentally ill person; **maladie** nf (spécifique) disease, illness; (mauvaise santé) illness, sickness; **maladif, -ive** adj sickly; (curiosité, besoin) pathological

maladresse [maladʀɛs] nf clumsiness no pl; (gaffe) blunder

maladroit, e [maladʀwa, -wat] adj clumsy

malaise [malɛz] nm (Méd) feeling of faintness; (fig) uneasiness, malaise; **avoir un ~** to feel faint ou dizzy

Malaisie [malezi] nf: **la ~** Malaysia

malaria [malaʀja] nf malaria

malaxer [malakse] /1/ vt (pétrir) to knead; (mêler) to mix

malbouffe [malbuf] nf (fam): **la ~** junk food

malchance [malʃɑ̃s] nf misfortune, ill luck no pl; **par ~** unfortunately; **malchanceux, -euse** adj unlucky

mâle [mɑl] adj (Élec, Tech) male; (viril: voix, traits) manly ▷ nm male

malédiction [malediksjɔ̃] nf curse

mal: **malentendant, e** nm/f: **les malentendants** the hard of hearing; **malentendu** nm misunderstanding; **il y a eu un malentendu** there's been a misunderstanding; **malfaçon** nf fault; **malfaisant, e** adj evil, harmful; **malfaiteur** nm lawbreaker, criminal; (voleur) burglar, thief; **malfamé, e** adj disreputable

malgache [malgaʃ] adj Malagasy, Madagascan ▷ nm (Ling) Malagasy ▷ nm/f: **M~** Malagasy, Madagascan

malgré [malgʀe] prép in spite of, despite; **~ tout** in spite of everything

malheur [malœʀ] nm (situation) adversity, misfortune; (événement) misfortune (: plus fort) disaster, tragedy; **faire un ~** to be a smash hit; **malheureusement** adv unfortunately; **malheureux, -euse** adj (triste) unhappy, miserable; (infortuné, regrettable) unfortunate; (malchanceux) unlucky; (insignifiant) wretched ▷ nm/f poor soul

malhonnête [malɔnɛt] adj dishonest; **malhonnêteté** nf dishonesty

malice [malis] nf mischievousness; (méchanceté): **par ~** out of malice ou spite; **sans ~** guileless; **malicieux, -euse** adj
Attention à ne pas traduire malicieux par malicious.

malin, -igne [malɛ̃, -iɲ] adj (futé) (f gén **maline**) smart, shrewd; (Méd) malignant

malingre [malɛ̃gʀ] adj puny

malle [mal] nf trunk; **mallette** nf (small) suitcase; (pour documents) attaché case

malmener [malməne] /5/ vt to manhandle; (fig) to give a rough ride to

malodorant, e [malɔdɔʀɑ̃, -ɑ̃t] adj foul-smelling

malpoli, e [malpɔli] adj impolite

malsain, e [malsɛ̃, -ɛn] adj unhealthy

malt [malt] nm malt

Malte [malt] nf Malta

maltraiter [maltʀɛte] /1/ vt to manhandle, ill-treat

malveillance [malvɛjɑ̃s] nf (animosité) ill will; (intention de nuire) malevolence

malversation [malvɛʀsasjɔ̃] nf embezzlement

maman [mamɑ̃] nf mum(my)

mamelle [mamɛl] nf teat

mamelon [mamlɔ̃] nm (Anat) nipple

mamie [mami] nf (fam) granny

mammifère [mamifɛʀ] nm mammal

mammouth [mamut] nm mammoth

manche [mɑ̃ʃ] nf (de vêtement) sleeve; (d'un jeu, tournoi) round; (Géo): **la M~** the (English) Channel ▷ nm (d'outil, casserole) handle; (de pelle, pioche etc) shaft; **à ~s courtes/ longues** short-/long-sleeved; **~ à balai** broomstick; (Aviat, Inform) joystick nm inv

manchette [mɑ̃ʃɛt] nf (de chemise) cuff; (coup) forearm blow; (titre) headline

manchot [mɑ̃ʃo] nm one-armed man; armless man; (Zool) penguin

mandarine [mɑ̃daʀin] nf mandarin (orange), tangerine

mandat [mɑ̃da] nm (postal) postal ou money order; (d'un député etc) mandate; (procuration) power of attorney, proxy; (Police) warrant; **~ d'arrêt** warrant for arrest; **~ de perquisition** search warrant; **mandataire** nm/f (représentant, délégué) representative; (Jur) proxy

manège [manɛʒ] nm riding school; (à la foire) roundabout (BRIT), merry-go-round; (fig) game, ploy

manette [manɛt] nf lever, tap; **~ de jeu** joystick

mangeable [mɑ̃ʒabl] adj edible, eatable

mangeoire [mɑ̃ʒwaʀ] nf trough, manger

manger [mɑ̃ʒe] /3/ vt to eat; (ronger: rouille etc) to eat into ou away ▷ vi to eat; **donner à ~ à** (enfant) to feed

mangue [mɑ̃g] nf mango

maniable [manjabl] adj (outil) handy; (voiture, voilier) easy to handle

maniaque [manjak] adj finicky, fussy ▷ nm/f (méticuleux) fusspot; (fou) maniac

manie [mani] nf mania; (tic) odd habit; **avoir la ~ de** to be obsessive about

manier [manje] /7/ vt to handle

maniéré, e [manjeʀe] adj affected

m

manière [manjɛʀ] nf *(façon)* way, manner; **manières** nfpl *(attitude)* manners; *(chichis)* fuss sg; **de ~ à** so as to; **de cette ~** in this way ou manner; **d'une ~ générale** generally speaking, as a general rule; **de toute ~** in any case; **d'une certaine ~** in a (certain) way

manifestant, e [manifɛstɑ̃, -ɑ̃t] nm/f demonstrator

manifestation [manifɛstasjɔ̃] nf *(de joie, mécontentement)* expression, demonstration; *(symptôme)* outward sign; *(fête etc)* event; *(Pol)* demonstration

manifeste [manifɛst] adj obvious, evident ▷ nm manifesto; **manifester** /1/ vt *(volonté, intentions)* to show, indicate; *(joie, peur)* to express, show ▷ vi to demonstrate; **se manifester** vi *(émotion)* to show ou express itself; *(difficultés)* to arise; *(symptômes)* to appear

manigancer [manigɑ̃se] /3/ vt to plot

manipulation [manipylasjɔ̃] nf handling; *(Pol, génétique)* manipulation

manipuler [manipyle] /1/ vt to handle; *(fig)* to manipulate

manivelle [manivɛl] nf crank

mannequin [mankɛ̃] nm *(Couture)* dummy; *(Mode)* model

manœuvre [manœvʀ] nf *(gén)* manoeuvre *(BRIT)*, maneuver *(US)* ▷ nm labourer; **manœuvrer** /1/ vt to manoeuvre *(BRIT)*, maneuver *(US)*; *(levier, machine)* to operate ▷ vi to manoeuvre ou maneuver

manoir [manwaʀ] nm manor ou country house

manque [mɑ̃k] nm *(insuffisance, vide)* emptiness, gap; *(Méd)* withdrawal; **~ de** lack of; **être en état de ~** to suffer withdrawal symptoms

manqué [mɑ̃ke] adj failed; **garçon ~** tomboy

manquer [mɑ̃ke] /1/ vi *(faire défaut)* to be lacking; *(être absent)* to be missing; *(échouer)* to fail ▷ vt to miss ▷ vb impers: **il (nous) manque encore 10 euros** we are still 10 euros short; **il manque des pages (au livre)** there are some pages missing ou some pages are missing (from the book); **à qn** *(absent etc)*: **il/cela me manque** I miss him/that; **~ à** *(règles etc)* to be in breach of, fail to observe; **~ de** to lack; **ne pas ~ de faire: je ne manquerai pas de le lui dire** I'll be sure to tell him; **il a manqué (de) se tuer** he very nearly got killed

mansarde [mɑ̃saʀd] nf attic; **mansardé, e** adj: **chambre mansardée** attic room

manteau, x [mɑ̃to] nm coat

manucure [manykyʀ] nf manicurist

manuel, le [manɥɛl] adj manual ▷ nm *(ouvrage)* manual, handbook

manufacture [manyfaktyʀ] nf factory; **manufacturé, e** adj manufactured

manuscrit, e [manyskʀi, -it] adj handwritten ▷ nm manuscript

manutention [manytɑ̃sjɔ̃] nf *(Comm)* handling

mappemonde [mapmɔ̃d] nf *(plane)* map of the world; *(sphère)* globe

maquereau, x [makʀo] nm *(Zool)* mackerel inv; *(fam)* pimp

maquette [makɛt] nf *(d'un décor, bâtiment, véhicule)* (scale) model

maquillage [makijaʒ] nm making up; *(produits)* make-up

maquiller [makije] /1/ vt *(personne, visage)* to make up; *(truquer: passeport, statistique)* to fake; *(: voiture volée)* to do over *(respray etc)*; **se maquiller** vi to make o.s. up

maquis [maki] nm *(Géo)* scrub; *(Mil)* maquis, underground fighting no pl

maraîcher, -ère [maʀeʃe, maʀeʃɛʀ] adj: **cultures maraîchères** market gardening sg ▷ nm/f market gardener

marais [maʀɛ] nm marsh, swamp

marasme [maʀasm] nm stagnation, sluggishness

marathon [maratɔ̃] nm marathon

marbre [maʀbʀ] nm marble

marc [maʀ] nm (de raisin, pommes) marc

marchand, e [maʀʃɑ̃, -ɑ̃d] nm/f shopkeeper, tradesman/-woman; (au marché) stallholder; **~ de charbon/vins** coal/wine merchant ⊳ adj: **prix/valeur ~(e)** market price/value; **~/e de fruits** fruiterer (BRIT), fruit seller (US); **~/e de journaux** newsagent; **~/e de légumes** greengrocer (BRIT), produce dealer (US); **~/e de poisson** fishmonger (BRIT), fish seller (US); **marchander** /1/ vi to bargain, haggle; **marchandise** nf goods pl, merchandise no pl

marche [maʀʃ] nf (d'escalier) step; (activité) walking; (promenade, trajet, allure) walk; (démarche) walk, gait; (Mil, Mus) march; (fonctionnement) running; (des événements) course; **dans le sens de la ~** (Rail) facing the engine; **en ~** (monter etc) while the vehicle is moving ou in motion; **mettre en ~** to start; **se mettre en ~** (personne) to get moving; (machine) to start; **être en état de ~** to be in working order; **faire ~ arrière** to reverse (gear); **faire ~ arrière** reverse (gear); (fig) to backtrack, back-pedal; **~ à suivre** (correct) procedure

marché [maʀʃe] nm market; (transaction) bargain, deal; **faire du ~ noir** to buy and sell on the black market; **~ aux puces** flea market

marcher [maʀʃe] /1/ vi to walk; (Mil) to march; (aller: voiture, train, affaires) to go; (prospérer) to go well; (fonctionner) to work, run; (fam: consentir) to go along, agree; (: croire naïvement) to be taken in; **faire ~ qn** (pour rire) to pull sb's leg; (pour tromper) to lead sb up the garden path; **marcheur, -euse** nm/f walker

mardi [maʀdi] nm Tuesday; **M~ gras** Shrove Tuesday

mare [maʀ] nf pond; (flaque) pool

marécage [maʀekaʒ] nm marsh, swamp; **marécageux, -euse** adj marshy

maréchal, -aux [maʀeʃal, -o] nm marshal

marée [maʀe] nf tide; (poissons) fresh (sea) fish; **~ haute/basse** high/low tide; **~ noire** oil slick

marelle [maʀɛl] nf: **(jouer à) la ~** (to play) hopscotch

margarine [maʀgaʀin] nf margarine

marge [maʀʒ] nf margin; **en ~ de** (fig) on the fringe of; **~ bénéficiaire** profit margin

marginal, e, -aux [maʀʒinal, -o] nm/f (original) eccentric; (déshérité) dropout

marguerite [maʀgəʀit] nf marguerite, (oxeye) daisy; (d'imprimante) daisy-wheel

mari [maʀi] nm husband

mariage [maʀjaʒ] nm marriage; (noce) wedding; **~ civil/religieux** registry office (BRIT) ou civil/church wedding

marié, e [maʀje] adj married ⊳ nm/f (bride)groom/bride; **les ~s** the bride and groom; **les (jeunes) ~s** the newly-weds

marier [maʀje] /7/ vt to marry; (fig) to blend; **se ~ (avec)** to marry, get married (to)

marin, e [maʀɛ̃, -in] adj sea cpd, marine ⊳ nm sailor ⊳ nf navy; **~e marchande** merchant navy

marine [maʀin] adj voir **marin** ⊳ adj inv navy (blue) ⊳ nm (Mil) marine

mariner [maʀine] /1/ vt to marinate

marionnette [maʀjɔnɛt] nf puppet

maritalement [maʀitalmã] adv: **vivre ~** to live together (as husband and wife)

maritime [maʀitim] adj sea cpd, maritime

mark [maʀk] nm mark

m

marmelade [marməlad] nf stewed fruit, compote; **~ d'oranges** (orange) marmalade

marmite [marmit] nf (cooking-) pot

marmonner [marmɔne] /1/ vt, vi to mumble, mutter

marmotte [marmɔt] nf marmot

marmotter [marmɔte] /1/ vt to mumble

Maroc [marɔk] nm: **le ~** Morocco; **marocain, e** [marɔkɛ̃, -ɛn] adj Moroccan ▷ nm/f: **Marocain, e** Moroccan

maroquinerie [marɔkinri] nf (commerce) leather shop; (articles) fine leather goods pl

marquant, e [markɑ̃, -ɑ̃t] adj outstanding

marque [mark] nf mark; (Comm: de nourriture) brand; (: de voiture, produits manufacturés) make; (: de disques) label; **de ~** high-class; (personnage, hôte) distinguished; **~ déposée** registered trademark; **~ de fabrique** trademark; **une grande ~ de vin** a well-known brand of wine

marquer [marke] /1/ vt to mark; (inscrire) to write down; (bétail) to brand; (Sport: but etc) to score; (: joueur) to mark; (accentuer: taille etc) to emphasize; (manifester: refus, intérêt) to show ▷ vi (événement, personnalité) to stand out, be outstanding; (Sport) to score; **~ les points** to keep the score

marqueterie [markɛtri] nf inlaid work, marquetry

marquis, e [marki, -iz] nm/f marquis ou marquess (marchioness)

marraine [marɛn] nf godmother

marrant, e [marɑ̃, -ɑ̃t] adj (fam) funny

marre [mar] adv (fam): **en avoir ~ de** to be fed up with

marrer [mare] /1/: **se marrer** vi (fam) to have a (good) laugh

marron, ne [marɔ̃, -ɔn] nm (fruit) chestnut ▷ adj inv brown ▷ adj (péj) crooked; **~s glacés** marrons glacés;

marronnier nm chestnut (tree)

mars [mars] nm March

Marseille [marsɛj] n Marseilles

marteau, x [marto] nm hammer; **être ~** (fam) to be nuts; **marteau-piqueur** nm pneumatic drill

marteler [martəle] /5/ vt to hammer

martien, ne [marsjɛ̃, -ɛn] adj Martian, of ou from Mars

martyr, e [martir] nm/f martyr ▷ adj martyred; **enfants ~s** battered children; **martyre** nm martyrdom; (fig: sens affaibli) agony, torture; **martyriser** /1/ vt (Rel) to martyr; (fig) to bully (: enfant) to batter

marxiste [marksist] adj, nm/f Marxist

mascara [maskara] nm mascara

masculin, e [maskylɛ̃, -in] adj masculine; (sexe, population) male; (équipe, vêtements) men's; (viril) manly ▷ nm masculine

masochiste [mazɔʃist] adj masochistic

masque [mask] nm mask; **~ de beauté** face pack; **~ de plongée** diving mask; **masquer** /1/ vt (cacher: porte, goût) to hide, conceal; (dissimuler: vérité, projet) to mask, obscure

massacre [masakr] nm massacre, slaughter; **massacrer** /1/ vt to massacre, slaughter; (texte etc) to murder

massage [masaʒ] nm massage

masse [mas] nf mass; (Élec) earth; (maillet) sledgehammer; **une ~ de** (fam) masses ou loads of; **la ~** (péj) the masses; **en ~** (adv: en bloc) in bulk; (en foule) en masse; adj: exécutions, production) mass cpd

masser [mase] /1/ vt (assembler: gens) to gather; (pétrir) to massage; **se masser** vi (foule) to gather; **masseur, -euse** nm/f (personne) masseur/masseuse; nm (appareil) massager ▷ nf (appareil) vibro-massage (-euse)

massif, -ive [masif, -iv] adj (porte) solid, massive; (visage) heavy, large;

(*bois, or*) solid; (*dose*) massive; (*déportations etc*) mass *cpd* ▷ *nm* (*montagneux*) massif; (*de fleurs*) clump, bank; **le M~ Central** the Massif Central

massue [masy] *nf* club, bludgeon

mastic [mastik] *nm* (*pour vitres*) putty; (*pour fentes*) filler

mastiquer [mastike] /1/ *vt* (*aliment*) to chew, masticate

mat, e [mat] *adj* (*couleur, métal*) mat(t); (*bruit, son*) dull ▷ *adj inv* (*Échecs*): **être ~** to be checkmate

mât [mɑ] *nm* (*Navig*) mast; (*poteau*) pole, post

match [matʃ] *nm* match; **faire ~ nul** to draw; **~ aller** first leg; **~ retour** second leg, return match

matelas [matlɑ] *nm* mattress; **~ pneumatique** air bed ou mattress

matelot [matlo] *nm* sailor, seaman

mater [mate] /1/ *vt* (*personne*) to bring to heel, subdue; (*révolte*) to put down

matérialiser [materjalize] /1/: **se matérialiser** *vi* to materialize

matérialiste [materjalist] *adj* materialistic

matériau, x [materjo] *nm* material; **matériaux** *nmpl* material(s)

matériel, le [materjɛl] *adj* material ▷ *nm* equipment *no pl*; (*de camping etc*) gear *no pl*; (*Inform*) hardware

maternel, le [matɛrnɛl] *adj* (*amour, geste*) motherly, maternal; (*grand-père, oncle*) maternal ▷ *nf* (*aussi*: **école maternelle**) (state) nursery school

maternité [matɛrnite] *nf* (*établissement*) maternity hospital; (*état de mère*) motherhood, maternity; (*grossesse*) pregnancy; **congé de ~** maternity leave

mathématique [matematik] *adj* mathematical; **mathématiques** *nfpl* mathematics *sg*

maths [mat] *nfpl* maths

matière [matjɛr] *nf* matter; (*Comm, Tech*) material; matter *no pl*; (*fig: d'un* livre *etc*) subject matter, material; (*Scol*) subject; **en ~ de** as regards; **~s grasses** fat (content) *sg*; **~s premières** raw materials

Matignon [matiɲɔ̃] *nm*: **(l'hôtel) ~** the French Prime Minister's residence

matin [matɛ̃] *nm, adv* morning; **le ~** (*pendant le matin*) in the morning; **demain/hier/dimanche ~** tomorrow/yesterday/Sunday morning; **tous les ~s** every morning; **du ~ au soir** from morning till night; **une heure du ~** one o'clock in the morning; **de grand** ou **bon ~** early in the morning

matinal, e, -aux [matinal, -o] *adj* (*toilette, gymnastique*) morning *cpd*; **être matinal** (*personne*) to be up early; (*habituellement*) to be an early riser; **matinée** *nf* morning; (*spectacle*) matinée

matou [matu] *nm* tom(cat)

matraque [matrak] *nf* (*de policier*) truncheon (BRIT), billy (US)

matricule [matrikyl] *nm* (*Mil*) regimental number; (*Admin*) reference number

matrimonial, e, -aux [matrimɔnjal, -o] *adj* marital, marriage *cpd*

maudit, e [modi, -it] *adj* (*fam: satané*) blasted, confounded

maugréer [mogree] /1/ *vi* to grumble

maussade [mosad] *adj* sullen; (*ciel, temps*) gloomy

mauvais, e [mɔvɛ, -ɛz] *adj* bad; (*méchant, malveillant*) malicious, spiteful; (*faux*): **le ~ numéro** the wrong number ▷ *adv*: **il fait ~** the weather is bad; **sentir ~** to have a nasty smell, smell bad ou nasty; **la mer est ~e** the sea is rough; **~e plaisanterie** nasty trick; **~ joueur** bad loser; **~e herbe** weed; **~e langue** gossip, scandalmonger (BRIT)

mauve [mov] *adj* mauve

maux [mo] *nmpl voir* **mal**

maximum [maksimɔm] *adj, nm*
maximum; **au ~** (*le plus possible*) as
much as one can; (*tout au plus*) at
the (very) most *ou* maximum; **faire le ~**
to do one's level best

mayonnaise [majɔnɛz] *nf*
mayonnaise

mazout [mazut] *nm* (fuel) oil

me, m' [mə, m] *pron* (*direct: téléphoner,*
attendre etc) me; (*indirect: parler, donner*
etc) (to) me; (*réfléchi*) myself

mec [mɛk] *nm* (*fam*) guy, bloke (BRIT)

mécanicien, ne [mekanisjɛ̃,
-ɛn] *nm/f* mechanic; (*Rail*) (train ou
engine) driver

mécanique [mekanik] *adj*
mechanical ▷ *nf* (*science*) mechanics
sg; (*mécanisme*) mechanism; **ennui ~**
engine trouble *no pl*

mécanisme [mekanism] *nm*
mechanism

méchamment [meʃamɑ̃] *adv*
nastily, maliciously; spitefully

méchanceté [meʃɑ̃te] *nf* nastiness,
maliciousness; **dire des ~s à qn** to
say spiteful things to sb

méchant, e [meʃɑ̃, -ɑ̃t] *adj* nasty,
malicious, spiteful; (*enfant: pas sage*)
naughty; (*animal*) vicious

mèche [mɛʃ] *nf* (*de lampe, bougie*)
wick; (*d'un explosif*) fuse; (*de cheveux*)
lock; **se faire faire des ~s** to have
highlights put in one's hair; **de ~ avec**
in league with

méchoui [meʃwi] *nm* whole sheep
barbecue

méconnaissable [mekɔnɛsabl] *adj*
unrecognizable

méconnaître [mekɔnɛtʀ] /57/
vt (*ignorer*) to be unaware of;
(*mésestimer*) to misjudge

mécontent, e [mekɔ̃tɑ̃, -ɑ̃t]
adj: **~ (de)** discontented *ou*
dissatisfied *ou* displeased
(with); (*contrarié*) annoyed
(at); **mécontentement** *nm*
dissatisfaction, discontent,
displeasure; (*irritation*) annoyance

Mecque [mɛk] *nf*: **la ~** Mecca

médaille [medaj] *nf* medal

médaillon [medajɔ̃] *nm* (*bijou*) locket

médecin [medsɛ̃] *nm* doctor

médecine [medsin] *nf* medicine

média [medja] *nmpl*: **les ~** the
media; **médiatique** *adj* media *cpd*

médical, e, -aux [medikal, -o] *adj*
medical; **passer une visite ~e** to
have a medical

médicament [medikamɑ̃] *nm*
medicine, drug

médiéval, e, -aux [medjeval, -o]
adj medieval

médiocre [medjɔkʀ] *adj* mediocre,
poor

méditer [medite] /1/ *vi* to meditate

Méditerranée [mediteʀane]
nf: **la (mer) ~** the Mediterranean
(Sea); **méditerranéen, ne**
adj Mediterranean ▷ *nm/f*:
Méditerranéen, ne Mediterranean

méduse [medyz] *nf* jellyfish

méfait [mefɛ] *nm* (*faute*)
misdemeanour, wrongdoing;
méfaits *nmpl* (*ravages*) ravages,
damage *sg*

méfiance [mefjɑ̃s] *nf* mistrust,
distrust

méfiant, e [mefjɑ̃, -ɑ̃t] *adj*
mistrustful, distrustful

méfier [mefje] /7/: **se méfier** *vi* to be
wary; (*faire attention*) to be careful; **se**
~ de to mistrust, distrust, be wary of

méga-octet [megaɔktɛ] *nm*
megabyte

mégarde [megaʀd] *nf*: **par ~**
(*accidentellement*) accidentally; (*par*
erreur) by mistake

mégère [meʒɛʀ] *nf* shrew

mégot [mego] *nm* cigarette end
ou butt

meilleur, e [mɛjœʀ] *adj, adv* better
▷ *nm*: **le ~** the best; **le ~ des deux** the
better of the two; **il fait ~ qu'hier**
it's better weather than yesterday;
~ marché cheaper

mél [mɛl] *nm* email ▷

mélancolie [melãkɔli] nf melancholy, gloom; **mélancolique** adj melancholy

mélange [melãʒ] nm mixture; **mélanger** /3/ vt to mix; (vins, couleurs) to blend; (mettre en désordre, confondre) to mix up, muddle (up)

mêlée [mele] nf mêlée, scramble; (Rugby) scrum(mage)

mêler [mele] /1/ vt (substances, odeurs, races) to mix; (embrouiller) to muddle (up), mix up; **se mêler** vi to mix; **se ~ à** (personne) to join; (s'associer à) to mix with; **se ~ de** (personne) to meddle with, interfere in; **mêle-toi de tes affaires!** mind your own business!

mélodie [melɔdi] nf melody; **mélodieux, -euse** adj melodious

melon [m(ə)lɔ̃] nm (Bot) (honeydew) melon; (aussi: **chapeau ~**) bowler (hat)

membre [mãbʀ] nm (Anat) limb; (personne, pays, élément) member ▷ adj member cpd

mémé [meme] nf (fam) granny

🔵 **MOT-CLÉ**

même [mɛm] adj **1** (avant le nom) same; **en même temps** at the same time; **ils ont les mêmes goûts** they have the same ou similar tastes
2 (après le nom, renforcement): **il est la loyauté même** he is loyalty itself; **ce sont ses paroles/celles-là même** they are his very words/the very ones
▶ pron: **le (la) même** the same one
▶ adv **1** (renforcement): **il n'a même pas pleuré** he didn't even cry; **même lui l'a dit** even HE said it; **ici même** in this very place; **même si** even if
2: **à même: à même la bouteille** straight from the bottle; **à même la peau** next to the skin; **être à même de faire** to be in a position to do, be able to do
3: **de même** likewise; **faire de même** to do likewise ou the same; **lui de même** so does (ou did ou is) he; **de même que** just as; **il en va de même pour** the same goes for

mémoire [memwaʀ] nf memory ▷ nm (Scol) dissertation, paper; **à la ~ de** to the ou in memory of; **de ~** from memory; **~ morte** read-only memory, ROM; **~ vive** random access memory, RAM

mémoires [memwaʀ] nmpl memoirs

mémorable [memɔʀabl] adj memorable

menace [mənas] nf threat; **menacer** /3/ vt to threaten

ménage [menaʒ] nm (travail) housework; (couple) (married) couple; (famille, Admin) household; **faire le ~** to do the housework; **ménagement** nm care and attention

ménager¹ [menaʒe] vt (traiter avec mesure) to handle with tact; (utiliser) to use sparingly; (prendre soin de) to take (great) care of, look after; (organiser) to arrange

ménager², -ère [menaʒe, -ɛʀ] adj household cpd, domestic ▷ nf housewife

mendiant, e [mãdjã, -ãt] nm/f beggar

mendier [mãdje] /7/ vi to beg ▷ vt to beg (for)

mener [məne] /5/ vt to lead; (enquête) to conduct; (affaires) to manage ▷ vi: **~ à/dans** (emmener) to take to/into; **~ qch à bonne fin** ou **à terme** ou **à bien** to see sth through (to a successful conclusion), complete sth successfully

meneur, -euse [mənœʀ, -øz] nm/f leader; (péj) ringleader

méningite [menẽʒit] nf meningitis no pl

ménopause [menopoz] nf menopause

menotte [mənɔt] nf (langage enfantin) handie; **menottes** nfpl handcuffs

mensonge [mɑ̃sɔ̃ʒ] nm: **le ~** lying no pl; **un ~** a lie; **mensonger, -ère** adj false

mensualité [mɑ̃sɥalite] nf (somme payée) monthly payment

mensuel, le [mɑ̃sɥɛl] adj monthly

mensurations [mɑ̃syʀasjɔ̃] nfpl measurements

mental, e, -aux [mɑ̃tal, -o] adj mental; **mentalité** nf mentality

menteur, -euse [mɑ̃tœʀ, -øz] nm/f liar

menthe [mɑ̃t] nf mint

mention [mɑ̃sjɔ̃] nf (note) note, comment; (Scol): **~ (très) bien/ passable** (very) good/satisfactory pass; "**rayer la ~ inutile**" "delete as appropriate"; **mentionner** /1/ vt to mention

mentir [mɑ̃tiʀ] /16/ vi to lie

menton [mɑ̃tɔ̃] nm chin

menu, e [məny] adj (mince) slim, slight; (frais, difficulté) minor ▷ adv (couper, hacher) very fine ▷ nm menu; **~ touristique** popular ou tourist menu

menuiserie [mənɥizʀi] nf (travail) joinery, carpentry; (d'amateur) woodwork; **menuisier** nm joiner, carpenter

méprendre [mepʀɑ̃dʀ] /58/: **se méprendre** vi: **se ~ sur** to be mistaken about

mépris, e [mepʀi, -iz] pp de **méprendre** ▷ nm (dédain) contempt, scorn; **au ~ de** regardless of, in defiance of; **méprisable** adj contemptible, despicable; **méprisant, e** adj scornful; **méprise** nf mistake, error; **mépriser** /1/ vt to scorn, despise; (gloire, danger) to scorn, spurn

mer [mɛʀ] nf sea; (marée) tide; **en ~** at sea; **en haute** ou **pleine ~** off shore, on the open sea; **la ~ Morte** the Dead Sea; **la ~ Noire** the Black Sea; **la ~ du Nord** the North Sea; **la ~ Rouge** the Red Sea

mercenaire [mɛʀsənɛʀ] nm mercenary, hired soldier

mercerie [mɛʀsəʀi] nf (boutique) haberdasher's (shop) (BRIT), notions store (US)

merci [mɛʀsi] excl thank you ▷ nf: **à la ~ de qn/qch** at sb's mercy/the mercy of sth; **~ beaucoup** thank you very much; **~ de** ou **pour** thank you for; **sans ~** merciless; mercilessly

mercredi [mɛʀkʀədi] nm Wednesday; **~ des Cendres** Ash Wednesday; voir aussi **lundi**

mercure [mɛʀkyʀ] nm mercury

merde [mɛʀd] (!) nf shit (!) ▷ excl (bloody) hell (!)

mère [mɛʀ] nf mother ▷ adj inv mother cpd; **~ célibataire** single parent, unmarried mother; **~ de famille** housewife, mother

merguez [mɛʀɡɛz] nf spicy North African sausage

méridional, e, -aux [meʀidjɔnal, -o] adj southern ▷ nm/f Southerner

meringue [məʀɛ̃ɡ] nf meringue

mérite [meʀit] nm merit; **avoir du ~ (à faire qch)** to deserve credit (for doing sth); **mériter** /1/ vt to deserve

merle [mɛʀl] nm blackbird

merveille [mɛʀvɛj] nf marvel, wonder; **faire** ou **des ~s** to work wonders; **à ~** perfectly, wonderfully; **merveilleux, -euse** adj marvellous, wonderful

mes [me] adj poss voir **mon**

mésange [mezɑ̃ʒ] nf tit (mouse)

mésaventure [mezavɑ̃tyʀ] nf misadventure, misfortune

Mesdames [medam] nfpl voir **Madame**

Mesdemoiselles [medmwazɛl] nfpl voir **Mademoiselle**

mesquin, e [mɛskɛ̃, -in] adj mean, petty; **mesquinerie** nf meanness no pl; (procédé) mean trick

message [mesaʒ] nm message; **~ SMS** text message; **messager, -ère** nm/f messenger; **messagerie** nf

(*Internet*): **messagerie électronique** email; **messagerie instantanée** instant messenger; **messagerie vocale** voice mail

messe [mɛs] *nf* mass; **aller à la ~** to go to mass

Messieurs [mesjø] *nmpl voir* **Monsieur**

mesure [məzyʀ] *nf* (*évaluation, dimension*) measurement; (*étalon, récipient, contenu*) measure; (*Mus: cadence*) time, tempo; (: *division*) bar; (*retenue*) moderation; (*disposition*) measure, step; **sur ~** (*costume*) made-to-measure; **dans la ~ où** insofar as, inasmuch as; **dans une certaine ~** to some *ou* a certain extent; **à ~ que** as; **être en ~ de** to be in a position to

mesurer [məzyʀe] /1/ *vt* to measure; (*juger*) to weigh up, assess; (*modérer: ses paroles etc*) to moderate

métal, -aux [metal, -o] *nm* metal; **métallique** *adj* metallic

météo [meteo] *nf* (*bulletin*) (weather) forecast

météorologie [meteɔʀɔlɔʒi] *nf* meteorology

méthode [metɔd] *nf* method; (*livre, ouvrage*) manual, tutor

méticuleux, -euse [metikylø, -øz] *adj* meticulous

métier [metje] *nm* (*profession: gén*) job; (: *manuel*) trade; (: *artisanal*) craft; (*technique, expérience*) (acquired) skill *ou* technique; (*aussi:* **~ à tisser**) (weaving) loom

métrage [metʀaʒ] *nm*: **long/ moyen/court ~** feature *ou* full-length/medium-length/short film

mètre [mɛtʀ] *nm* metre; (*règle*) metre rule; (*ruban*) tape measure; **métrique** *adj* metric

métro [metʀo] *nm* underground (*BRIT*), subway (*US*)

métropole [metʀɔpɔl] *nf* (*capitale*) metropolis; (*pays*) home country

mets [mɛ] *nm* dish

metteur [metœʀ] *nm*: **~ en scène** (*Théât*) producer; (*Ciné*) director

○ **MOT-CLÉ**

mettre [mɛtʀ] /56/ *vt* 1 (*placer*) to put; **mettre en bouteille/en sac** to bottle/put in bags *ou* sacks

2 (*vêtements: revêtir*) to put on; (: *porter*) to wear; **mets ton gilet** put your cardigan on; **je ne mets plus mon manteau** I no longer wear my coat

3 (*faire fonctionner: chauffage, électricité*) to put on; (: *réveil, minuteur*) to set; (*installer: gaz, eau*) to put in, lay on; **mettre en marche** to start up

4 (*consacrer*): **mettre du temps/ deux heures à faire qch** to take time/two hours to do sth; **y mettre du sien** to pull one's weight

5 (*noter, écrire*) to say, put (down); **qu'est-ce qu'il a mis sur la carte?** what did he say *ou* write on the card?; **mettez au pluriel ...** put ... into the plural

6 (*supposer*): **mettons que ...** let's suppose *ou* say that ...

se mettre *vr* 1 (*se placer*): **vous pouvez vous mettre là** you can sit (*ou* stand) there; **où ça se met?** where does it go?; **se mettre au lit** to get into bed; **se mettre au piano** to sit down at the piano; **se mettre de l'encre sur les doigts** to get ink on one's fingers

2 (*s'habiller*): **se mettre en maillot de bain** to get into *ou* put on a swimsuit; **n'avoir rien à se mettre** to have nothing to wear

3: **se mettre à** to begin, start; **se mettre à faire** to begin *ou* start doing *ou* to do; **se mettre au piano** to start learning the piano; **se mettre au régime** to go on a diet; **se mettre au travail/à l'étude** to get down to work/one's studies

meuble [mœbl] *nm* piece of furniture; (*ameublement*) furniture *no pl*; **meublé** *nm* furnished flat (BRIT) *ou* apartment (US); **meubler** /1/ *vt* to furnish; **se meubler** to furnish one's house

meuf [mœf] *nf* (*fam*) woman

meugler [møgle] /1/ *vi* to low, moo

meule [møl] *nf* (*de foin, blé*) stack; (*de fromage*) round

meunier, -ière [mønje, -jɛʀ] *nm* miller ▷ *nf* miller's wife

meurs *etc* [mœʀ] *vb voir* **mourir**

meurtre [mœʀtʀ] *nm* murder; **meurtrier, -ière** *adj* (*arme, épidémie, combat*) deadly; (*fureur, instincts*) murderous ▷ *nm/f* murderer(-ess)

meurtrir [mœʀtʀiʀ] /2/ *vt* to bruise; (*fig*) to wound

meus *etc* [mœ] *vb voir* **mouvoir**

meute [møt] *nf* pack

mexicain, e [mɛksikɛ̃, -ɛn] *adj* Mexican ▷ *nm/f*: **M~, e** Mexican

Mexico [mɛksiko] *n* Mexico City

Mexique [mɛksik] *nm*: **le ~** Mexico

mi [mi] *nm* (Mus) E; (*en chantant la gamme*) mi

mi... [mi] *préfixe* half/-, mid-; **à la mi-janvier** in mid-January; **à mi-jambes/-corps** (up *ou* down) to the knees/waist; **à mi-hauteur/-chemin** halfway up (*ou* down)/up (*ou* down) the hill

miauler [mjole] /1/ *vi* to miaow

miche [miʃ] *nf* round *ou* cob loaf

mi-chemin [miʃmɛ̃]: **à ~** *adv* halfway, midway

mi-clos, e [miklo, -kloz] *adj* half-closed

micro [mikʀo] *nm* mike, microphone; (*Inform*) micro

microbe [mikʀɔb] *nm* germ, microbe

micro: **micro-onde** *nf*: **four à micro-ondes** microwave oven; **micro-ordinateur** *nm* microcomputer; **microscope** *nm* microscope; **microscopique** *adj* microscopic

midi [midi] *nm* midday, noon; (*moment du déjeuner*) lunchtime; (*sud*) south; **le M~** the South (of France), the Midi; **à ~** at 12 (o'clock) *ou* midday *ou* noon

mie [mi] *nf* inside (of the loaf)

miel [mjɛl] *nm* honey; **mielleux, -euse** *adj* (*personne*) sugary, syrupy

mien, ne [mjɛ̃, mjɛn] *pron*: **le (la) ~(ne), les ~s** mine; **les ~s** my family

miette [mjɛt] *nf* (*de pain, gâteau*) crumb; (*fig: de la conversation etc*) scrap; **en ~s** in pieces *ou* bits

MOT-CLÉ

mieux [mjø] *adv* **1** (*d'une meilleure façon*): **mieux (que)** better (than); **elle travaille/mange mieux** she works/eats better; **aimer mieux** to prefer; **elle va mieux** she is better; **de mieux en mieux** better and better
2 (*de la meilleure façon*) best; **ce que je sais le mieux** what I know best; **les livres les mieux faits** the best made books
▷ *adj inv* **1** (*plus à l'aise, en meilleure forme*) better; **se sentir mieux** to feel better
2 (*plus satisfaisant*) better; **c'est mieux ainsi** it's better like this; **c'est le mieux des deux** it's the better of the two; **le/la mieux, les mieux** the best; **demandez-lui, c'est le mieux** ask him, it's the best thing
3 (*plus joli*) better-looking; **il est mieux que son frère** (*plus beau*) he's better-looking than his brother; (*plus gentil*) he's nicer than his brother; **il est mieux sans moustache** he looks better without a moustache
4: **au mieux** at best; **au mieux avec** on the best of terms with; **pour le mieux** for the best
▷ *nm* **1** (*progrès*) improvement
2: **de mon/ton mieux** as best I/you can (*ou* could); **faire de son mieux** to do one's best

mignon, ne [miɲɔ̃, -ɔn] *adj* sweet, cute

migraine [migʀɛn] *nf* headache; (*Méd*) migraine

mijoter [miʒɔte] /1/ *vt* to simmer; (*préparer avec soin*) to cook lovingly; (*affaire, projet*) to plot, cook up ▷ *vi* to simmer

milieu, x [miljø] *nm* (*centre*) middle; (*aussi:* **juste ~**) happy medium; (*Bio, Géo*) environment; (*entourage social*) milieu; (*familial*) background; (*pègre*) **le ~** the underworld; **au ~ de** in the middle of; **au beau ou en plein ~ (de)** right in the middle (of)

militaire [militɛʀ] *adj* military, army *cpd* ▷ *nm* serviceman

militant, e [militɑ̃, -ɑ̃t] *adj, nm/f* militant

militer [milite] /1/ *vi* to be a militant

mille [mil] *num a* ou one thousand ▷ *nm* (*mesure*): **~ (marin)** nautical mile; **mettre dans le ~** (*fig*) to be bang on (target); **millefeuille** *nm* cream ou vanilla slice; **millénaire** ▷ *nm* millennium ▷ *adj* thousand-year-old; (*fig*) ancient; **mille-pattes** *nm inv* centipede

millet [mijɛ] *nm* millet

milliard [miljaʀ] *nm* milliard, thousand million (*BRIT*), billion (*US*); **milliardaire** *nm/f* multimillionaire (*BRIT*), billionaire (*US*)

millier [milje] *nm* thousand; **un ~ (de)** a thousand or so, about a thousand; **par ~s** in (their) thousands, by the thousand

milligramme [miligʀam] *nm* milligramme

millimètre [milimɛtʀ] *nm* millimetre

million [miljɔ̃] *nm* million; **deux ~s de** two million; **millionnaire** *nm/f* millionaire

mime [mim] *nm/f* (*acteur*) mime(r) ▷ *nm* (*art*) mime, miming; **mimer** /1/ *vt* to mime; (*singer*) to mimic, take off

minable [minabl] *adj* (*personne*) shabby(-looking); (*travail*) pathetic

mince [mɛ̃s] *adj* thin; (*personne, taille*) slim, slender; (*fig: profit, connaissances*) slight, small; (: *prétexte*) weak ▷ *excl*: **~ (alors)!** darn it!; **minceur** *nf* thinness; (*d'une personne*) slimness, slenderness;

mincir /2/ *vi* to get slimmer ou thinner

mine [min] *nf* (*physionomie*) expression, look; (*extérieur*) exterior, appearance; (*de crayon*) lead; (*gisement, exploitation, explosif*) mine; **avoir bonne ~** (*personne*) to look well; (*ironique*) to look an utter idiot; **avoir mauvaise ~** to look unwell; **faire ~ de faire** to make a pretence of doing; **~ de rien** although you wouldn't think so

miner [mine] /1/ *vt* (*saper*) to undermine, erode; (*Mil*) to mine

minerai [minʀɛ] *nm* ore

minéral, e, -aux [mineʀal, -o] *adj* mineral

minéralogique [mineʀalɔʒik] *adj*: **plaque ~** number (*BRIT*) ou license (*US*) plate; **numéro ~** registration (*BRIT*) ou license (*US*) number

minet, te [minɛ, -ɛt] *nm/f* (*chat*) pussy-cat; (*péj*) young trendy

mineur, e [minœʀ] *adj* minor ▷ *nm/f* (*Jur*) minor ▷ *nm* (*travailleur*) miner

miniature [minjatyʀ] *adj, nf* miniature

minibus [minibys] *nm* minibus

minier, -ière [minje, -jɛʀ] *adj* mining

mini-jupe [miniʒyp] *nf* mini-skirt

minime [minim] *adj* minor, minimal

minimiser [minimize] /1/ *vt* to minimize; (*fig*) to play down

minimum [minimɔm] *adj, nm* minimum; **au ~** at the very least

ministère [ministɛʀ] *nm* (*cabinet*) government; (*département*) ministry; (*Rel*) ministry

ministre [ministʀ] *nm* minister (*BRIT*), secretary; (*Rel*) minister; **~ d'État** senior minister ou secretary

Minitel® [minitɛl] nm (former)
videotext terminal and service

minoritaire [minɔritɛr] adj
minority cpd

minorité [minɔrite] nf minority;
être en ~ to be in the ou a minority

minuit [minɥi] nm midnight

minuscule [minyskyl] adj minute,
tiny ▷ nf: (lettre) **~** small letter

minute [minyt] nf minute; **à la
~** (just) this instant; (passé) there
and then; **minuter** /1/ vt to time;
minuterie nf time switch

minutieux, -euse [minysjø, -øz]
adj (personne) meticulous; (travail)
requiring painstaking attention
to detail

mirabelle [mirabɛl] nf (cherry) plum

miracle [mirakl] nm miracle

mirage [miraʒ] nm mirage

mire [mir] nf: **point de ~** (fig) focal
point

miroir [mirwar] nm mirror

miroiter [mirwate] /1/ vi to sparkle,
shimmer; **faire ~ qch à qn** to paint
sth in glowing colours for sb, dangle
sth in front of sb's eyes

mis, e [mi, miz] pp de **mettre** ▷ adj:
bien ~ well dressed ▷ nf (argent: au
jeu) stake; (tenue) clothing; attire;
être de ~e to be acceptable ou in
season; **~e de fonds** capital outlay;
~e à jour update; **~e en plis** set; **~e
au point** (fig) clarification; **~e en
scène** production

miser [mize] /1/ vt (enjeu) to stake,
bet; **~ sur** (cheval, numéro) to bet on;
(fig) to bank ou count on

misérable [mizerabl] adj
(lamentable, malheureux) pitiful,
wretched; (pauvre) poverty-stricken;
(insignifiant, mesquin) miserable
▷ nm/f wretch

misère [mizɛr] nf (extreme) poverty,
destitution; **misères** nfpl (malheurs)
woes, miseries; (ennuis) little troubles;
salaire de ~ starvation wage

missile [misil] nm missile

mission [misjɔ̃] nf mission; **partir
en ~** (Admin, Pol) to go on an
assignment; **missionnaire** nm/f
missionary

mité, e [mite] adj moth-eaten

mi-temps [mitɑ̃] nf inv (Sport: période)
half; (: pause) half-time; **à ~** part-time

miteux, -euse [mitø, -øz] adj seedy

mitigé, e [mitiʒe] adj (sentiments)
mixed

mitoyen, ne [mitwajɛ̃, -ɛn] adj
(mur) common, party (car); **maisons
~nes** semi-detached houses; (plus
de deux) terraced (BRIT) ou row (US)
houses

mitrailler [mitraje] /1/ vt to
machine-gun; (fig: photographier)
to snap away at; **~ qn de** to pelt ou
bombard sb with; **mitraillette** nf
submachine gun; **mitrailleuse** nf
machine gun

mi-voix [mivwa]: **à ~** adv in a low ou
hushed voice

mixage [miksaʒ] nm (Ciné) (sound)
mixing

mixer [miksɛr] nm (food) mixer

mixte [mikst] adj (gén) mixed; (Scol)
mixed, coeducational; **cuisinière ~**
combined gas and electric cooker

mixture [mikstyr] nf mixture; (fig)
concoction

Mlle (pl **Mlles**) abr = **Mademoiselle**

MM abr = **Messieurs**

Mme (pl **Mmes**) abr = **Madame**

mobile [mɔbil] adj mobile; (pièce de
machine) moving ▷ nm (motif) motive;
(œuvre d'art) mobile; (téléphone) **~**
mobile (phone)

mobilier, -ière [mɔbilje, -jɛr] nf
furniture

mobiliser [mɔbilize] /1/ vt to mobilize

mobylette® [mɔbilɛt] nf moped

mocassin [mɔkasɛ̃] nm moccasin

moche [mɔʃ] adj (fam: laid) ugly;
(mauvais, méprisable) rotten

modalité [mɔdalite] nf form, mode

mode [mɔd] nf fashion ▷ nm (manière)
form, mode; (Ling) mood; (Inform,

Mus) mode; **à la ~** fashionable, in fashion; **~ d'emploi** directions *pl* (for use); **~ de paiement** method of payment; **~ de vie** way of life

modèle [mɔdɛl] *adj* ▶ *nm* model; (*qui pose: de peintre*) sitter; **~ déposé** registered design; **~ réduit** small-scale model; **modeler** /5/ *vt* to model

modem [mɔdɛm] *nm* modem

modéré, e [mɔdeʀe] *adj*, *nm/f* moderate

modérer [mɔdeʀe] /6/ *vt* to moderate; **se modérer** *vi* to restrain o.s

moderne [mɔdɛʀn] *adj* modern ▶ *nm* (*Art*) modern style; (*ameublement*) modern furniture; **moderniser** /1/ *vt* to modernize

modeste [mɔdɛst] *adj* modest; **modestie** *nf* modesty

modifier [mɔdifje] /7/ *vt* to modify, alter; **se modifier** *vi* to alter

modique [mɔdik] *adj* modest

module [mɔdyl] *nm* module

moelle [mwal] *nf* marrow

moelleux, -euse [mwalø, -øz] *adj* soft; (*gâteau*) light and moist

mœurs [mœʀ] *nfpl* (*conduite*) morals; (*manières*) manners; (*pratiques sociales*) habits

moi [mwa] *pron* me; (*emphatique*): **~, je ...** for my part, I ..., I myself ...; **c'est ~ qui l'ai fait** I did it, it was me who did it; **apporte-le-~** bring it to me; **à ~** mine; (*dans un jeu*) my turn; **moi-même** *pron* myself; (*emphatique*) I myself

moindre [mwɛ̃dʀ] *adj* lesser; lower; **le (la) ~, les ~s** the least; the slightest; **c'est la ~ des choses** it's nothing at all

moine [mwan] *nm* monk, friar

moineau, x [mwano] *nm* sparrow

 MOT-CLÉ

moins [mwɛ̃] *adv* **1** (*comparatif*): **moins (que)** less (than); **moins**

grand que less tall than, not as tall as; **il a trois ans de moins que moi** he's three years younger than me; **moins je travaille, mieux je me porte** the less I work, the better I feel

2 (*superlatif*): **le moins** (the) least; **c'est ce que j'aime le moins** it's what I like (the) least; **le (la) moins doué(e)** the least gifted; **au moins, du moins** at least; **pour le moins** at the very least

3: **moins de** (*quantité*) less (than); (*nombre*) fewer (than); **moins de sable/d'eau** less sand/water; **moins de livres/gens** fewer books/people; **moins de deux ans** less than two years; **moins de midi** not yet midday

4: **de moins, en moins**: **100 euros/ 3 jours de moins** 100 euros/3 days less; **trois livres en moins** three books fewer; three books too few; **de l'argent en moins** less money; **le soleil en moins** but for the sun, minus the sun; **de moins en moins** less and less

5: **à moins de, à moins que** unless; **à moins de faire** unless we do (*ou* he does *etc*); **à moins que tu ne fasses** unless you do; **à moins d'un accident** barring any accident

▶ *prép*: **quatre moins deux** four minus two; **dix heures moins cinq** five to ten; **il fait moins cinq** it's five (degrees) below (freezing), it's minus five; **il est moins cinq** it's five to

mois [mwa] *nm* month

moisi [mwazi] *nm* mould, mildew; **odeur de ~** musty smell; **moisir** /2/ *vi* to go mouldy; **moisissure** *nf* mould *no pl*

moisson [mwasɔ̃] *nf* harvest; **moissonner** /1/ *vt* to harvest, reap; **moissonneuse** *nf* (*machine*) harvester

moite [mwat] *adj* sweaty, sticky

moitié [mwatje] *nf* half; **la ~** half; **la ~ de** half (of); **la ~ du temps/des gens** half the time/the people; **à la ~ de** halfway through; **à ~** half *(avant le verbe)*, half- *(avant l'adjectif)*; **à ~ prix** (at) half price

molaire [mɔlɛʀ] *nf* molar

molester [mɔlɛste] */1/ vt* to manhandle, maul (about)

molle [mɔl] *adj f voir* **mou**; **mollement** *adv (péj: travailler)* sluggishly; *(protester)* feebly

mollet [mɔlɛ] *nm* calf ▷ *adj m*: **œuf ~** soft-boiled egg

molletonné, e [mɔltɔne] *adj* fleece-lined

mollir [mɔliʀ] */2/ vi (personne)* to relent; *(substance)* to go soft

mollusque [mɔlysk] *nm* mollusc

môme [mom] *nm/f (fam: enfant)* brat

moment [mɔmɑ̃] *nm* moment; **ce n'est pas le ~** this is not the right time; **au même ~** at the same time; *(instant)* at the same moment; **pour un bon ~** for a good while; **pour le ~** for the moment, for the time being; **au ~ de** at the time of; **au ~ où** as; **à tout ~** at any time *ou* moment; *(continuellement)* constantly, continually; **en ce ~** at the moment; *(aujourd'hui)* at present; **sur le ~** at the time; **par ~s** now and then, at times; **d'un ~ à l'autre** any time (now); **du ~ où** *ou* **que** seeing that, since; **momentané, e** *adj* temporary, momentary; **momentanément** *adv* for a while

momie [mɔmi] *nf* mummy

mon, ma *(pl* **mes**) [mɔ̃, ma, me] *adj poss* my

Monaco [mɔnako] *nm*: **le ~** Monaco

monarchie [mɔnaʀʃi] *nf* monarchy

monastère [mɔnastɛʀ] *nm* monastery

mondain, e [mɔ̃dɛ̃, -ɛn] *adj (soirée, vie)* society *cpd*

monde [mɔ̃d] *nm* world; **le ~** *(personnes mondaines)* (high) society; **il**

y a du ~ *(beaucoup de gens)* there are a lot of people; *(quelques personnes)* there are some people; **beaucoup/peu de ~** many/few people; **mettre au ~** to bring into the world; **pas le moins du ~** not in the least; **mondial, e, -aux** *adj (population)* world *cpd*; *(influence)* world-wide; **mondialement** *adv* throughout the world; **mondialisation** *nf* globalization

monégasque [mɔnegask] *adj* Monegasque, of *ou* from Monaco ▷ *nm/f*: **M~** Monegasque

monétaire [mɔnetɛʀ] *adj* monetary

moniteur, -trice [mɔnitœʀ, -tʀis] *nm/f (Sport)* instructor *(instructrice)*; *(de colonie de vacances)* supervisor ▷ *nm (écran)* monitor

monnaie [mɔnɛ] *nf (Écon: moyen d'échange)* currency; *(petites pièces)*: **avoir de la ~** to have (some) change; **faire de la ~** to get (some) change; **avoir/faire la ~ de 20 euros** to have change of/get change for 20 euros; **rendre à qn la ~ (sur 20 euros)** to give sb the change (from *ou* out of 20 euros)

monologue [mɔnɔlɔg] *nm* monologue, soliloquy; **monologuer** */1/ vi* to soliloquize

monopole [mɔnɔpɔl] *nm* monopoly

monotone [mɔnɔtɔn] *adj* monotonous

Monsieur *(pl* **Messieurs**) [məsjø, mesjø] *nm (titre)* Mr; **un/le monsieur** *(homme quelconque)* a/the gentleman; **~, ...** *(en tête de lettre)* Dear Sir, ...; *voir aussi* **Madame**

monstre [mɔ̃stʀ] *nm* monster ▷ *adj (fam: effet, publicité)* massive; **un travail ~** a fantastic amount of work; **monstrueux, -euse** *adj* monstrous

mont [mɔ̃] *nm*: **par ~s et par vaux** up hill and down dale; **le M~ Blanc** Mont Blanc

montage [mɔ̃taʒ] *nm (d'une machine etc)* assembly; *(Photo)* photomontage; *(Ciné)* editing

montagnard, e [mɔ̃taɲaʀ, -aʀd] adj mountain cpd ▷ nm/f mountain-dweller

montagne [mɔ̃taɲ] nf (cime) mountain; (région): **la ~** the mountains pl; **~s russes** big dipper sg, switchback sg; **montagneux, -euse** adj mountainous; (basse montagne) hilly

montant, e [mɔ̃tɑ̃, -ɑ̃t] adj rising; (robe, corsage) high-necked ▷ nm (somme, total) (sum) total, (total) amount; (de fenêtre) upright; (de lit) post

monte-charge [mɔ̃tʃaʀʒ] nm inv goods lift, hoist

montée [mɔ̃te] nf rise; (escalade) climb; (côte) hill; **au milieu de la ~** halfway up

monter [mɔ̃te] /1/ vt (escalier, côte) to go (ou come) up; (valise, paquet) to take (ou bring) up; (étagère) to raise; (tente, échafaudage) to put up; (machine) to assemble; (Ciné) to edit; (Théât) to put on, stage; (société, coup etc) to set up ▷ vi to go (ou come) up; (chemin, niveau, température, voix, prix) to go up, rise; (passager) to get on; **~ à cheval** (faire du cheval) to ride a horse); **~ sur** to climb upon; **~ sur ou à un arbre/une échelle** to climb (up) a tree/ladder; **se ~** (frais etc) to add up to, come to

montgolfière [mɔ̃ɡɔlfjɛʀ] nf hot-air balloon

montre [mɔ̃tʀ] nf watch; **contre la ~** (Sport) against the clock

Montréal [mɔ̃ʀeal] n Montreal

montrer [mɔ̃tʀe] /1/ vt to show; **~ qch à qn** to show sb sth

monture [mɔ̃tyʀ] nf (bête) mount; (d'une bague) setting; (de lunettes) frame

monument [mɔnymɑ̃] nm monument; **~ aux morts** war memorial

moquer [mɔke] /1/: **se ~ de** vt to make fun of, laugh at; (fam: se

désintéresser de) not to care about; (tromper): **se ~ de qn** to take sb for a ride

moquette [mɔkɛt] nf fitted carpet

moqueur, -euse [mɔkœʀ, -øz] adj mocking

moral, e, -aux [mɔʀal, -o] adj moral ▷ nm morale ▷ nf (conduite) morals pl (règles); (valeurs) moral standards pl, morality; (d'une fable etc) moral; **faire la ~e à** to lecture, preach at; **moralité** nf morality; (conclusion, enseignement) moral

morceau, x [mɔʀso] nm piece, bit; (d'une œuvre) passage, extract; (Mus) piece; (Culin: de viande) cut; (: de sucre) lump; **mettre en ~x** to pull to pieces ou bits; **manger un ~** to have a bite (to eat)

morceler [mɔʀsəle] /4/ vt to break up, divide up

mordant, e [mɔʀdɑ̃, -ɑ̃t] adj (ton, remarque) scathing, cutting; (froid) biting ▷ nm (fougue) bite, punch

mordiller [mɔʀdije] /1/ vt to nibble at, chew at

mordre [mɔʀdʀ] /41/ vt to bite ▷ vi (poisson) to bite; **~ sur** (fig) to go over into, overlap into; **~ à l'hameçon** to bite, rise to the bait

mordu, e [mɔʀdy] nm/f enthusiast; **un ~ du jazz/de la voile** a jazz/sailing fanatic ou buff

morfondre [mɔʀfɔ̃dʀ] /41/: **se ~** vi to mope

morgue [mɔʀɡ] nf (arrogance) haughtiness; (lieu: de la police) morgue; (: à l'hôpital) mortuary

morne [mɔʀn] adj dismal, dreary

morose [mɔʀoz] adj sullen, morose

mors [mɔʀ] nm bit

morse [mɔʀs] nm (Zool) walrus; (Tél) Morse (code)

morsure [mɔʀsyʀ] nf bite

mort¹ [mɔʀ] nf death

mort², e [mɔʀ, mɔʀt] pp de **mourir** ▷ adj dead ▷ nm/f (défunt) dead man/woman; (victime): **il y a eu plusieurs**

m

~s several people were killed; **~ de peur/fatigue** frightened to death/dead tired

mortalité [mɔʀtalite] nf mortality, death rate

mortel, le [mɔʀtɛl] adj (poison etc) deadly, lethal; (accident, blessure) fatal; (silence, ennemi) deadly; (danger, frayeur, péché) mortal; (ennui, soirée) deadly (boring)

mort-né, e [mɔʀne] adj (enfant) stillborn

mortuaire [mɔʀtɥɛʀ] adj: **avis ~s** death announcements

morue [mɔʀy] nf (Zool) cod inv

mosaïque [mɔzaik] nf mosaic

Moscou [mɔsku] n Moscow

mosquée [mɔske] nf mosque

mot [mo] nm word; (message) line, note; **~ à ~** word for word; **~ de passe** password; **~s croisés** crossword (puzzle) sg

motard [mɔtaʀ] nm biker; (policier) motorcycle cop

mot-dièse nm (Inform: Twitter) hashtag

motel [mɔtɛl] nm motel

moteur, -trice [mɔtœʀ, -tʀis] adj (Anat, Physiol) motor; (Tech) driving; (Auto): **à 4 roues motrices** 4-wheel drive ▷ nm engine, motor; **à ~** power-driven, motor cpd; **~ de recherche** search engine

motif [mɔtif] nm (cause) motive; (décoratif) design, pattern, motif; **sans ~** groundless

motivation [mɔtivasjɔ̃] nf motivation

motiver [mɔtive] /1/ vt (justifier) to justify, account for; (Admin, Jur, Psych) to motivate

moto [mɔto] nf (motor)bike; **motocycliste** nm/f motorcyclist

motorisé, e [mɔtɔʀize] adj (personne) having one's own transport

motrice [mɔtʀis] adj f voir **moteur**

motte [mɔt] nf: **~ de terre** lump of earth, clod (of earth); **~ de beurre** lump of butter

mou (mol), molle [mu, mɔl] adj soft; (personne) sluggish; (résistance, protestations) feeble ▷ nm: **avoir du ~** to be slack

mouche [muʃ] nf fly

moucher [muʃe] /1/: **se moucher** vi to blow one's nose

moucheron [muʃʀɔ̃] nm midge

mouchoir [muʃwaʀ] nm handkerchief, hanky; **~ en papier** tissue, paper hanky

moudre [mudʀ] /47/ vt to grind

moue [mu] nf pout; **faire la ~** to pout; (fig) to pull a face

mouette [mwɛt] nf (sea)gull

moufle [mufl] nf (gant) mitt(en)

mouillé, e [muje] adj wet

mouiller [muje] /1/ vt (humecter) to wet, moisten; (tremper): **~ qn/qch** to make sb/sth wet ▷ vi (Navig) to lie ou be at anchor; **se mouiller** to get wet; (fam: prendre des risques) to commit o.s

moulant, e [mulɑ̃, -ɑ̃t] adj figure-hugging

moule [mul] nf mussel ▷ nm (Culin) mould; **~ à gâteau** nm cake tin (BRIT) ou pan (US)

mouler [mule] /1/ vt (vêtement) to hug, fit closely round

moulin [mulɛ̃] nm mill; **~ à café** coffee mill; **~ à eau** watermill; **~ à légumes** (vegetable) shredder; **~ à paroles** (fig) chatterbox; **~ à poivre** pepper mill; **~ à vent** windmill

moulinet [muline] nm (de canne à pêche) reel; (mouvement): **faire des ~s avec qch** to whirl sth around

moulinette® [mulinɛt] nf (vegetable) shredder

moulu, e [muly] pp de **moudre**

mourant, e [muʀɑ̃, -ɑ̃t] adj dying

mourir [muʀiʀ] /1/ vi to die; (civilisation) to die out; **~ de froid/faim/vieillesse** to die of exposure/hunger/old age; **~ de faim/d'ennui** (fig) to be starving/be bored to death; **~ d'envie de faire** to be dying to do

mousse [mus] *nf* (Bot) moss; (de savon) lather; (écume: sur eau, bière) froth, foam; (Culin) mousse ⊳ *nm* (Navig) ship's boy; **~ à raser** shaving foam

mousseline [muslin] *nf* muslin; **pommes ~** creamed potatoes

mousser [muse] /1/ *vi* (bière, détergent) to foam; (savon) to lather; **mousseux, -euse** *adj* frothy ⊳ *nm*: **(vin) mousseux** sparkling wine

mousson [musɔ̃] *nf* monsoon

moustache [mustaʃ] *nf* moustache; **moustaches** *nfpl* (d'animal) whiskers *pl*; **moustachu, e** *adj* with a moustache

moustiquaire [mustikɛʀ] *nf* mosquito net

moustique [mustik] *nm* mosquito

moutarde [mutaʀd] *nf* mustard

mouton [mutɔ̃] *nm* sheep *inv*; (peau) sheepskin; (Culin) mutton

mouvement [muvmɑ̃] *nm* movement; (geste) gesture; **avoir un bon ~** to make a nice gesture; **en ~** in motion; on the move; **mouvementé, e** *adj* (vie, poursuite) eventful; (réunion) turbulent

mouvoir [muvwaʀ] /27/: **se mouvoir** *vi* to move

moyen, ne [mwajɛ̃, -ɛn] *adj* average; (tailles, prix) medium; (de grandeur moyenne) medium-sized ⊳ *nm* (façon) means *sg*, way ⊳ *nf* average; (Statistique) mean; (Scol: à l'examen) pass mark; **moyens** *nmpl* (capacités) means; **très ~** (résultats) pretty poor; **je n'en ai pas les ~** I can't afford it; **au ~ de** by means of; **par tous les ~s** by every possible means, every possible way; **par ses propres ~s** all by oneself; **~ âge** Middle Ages; **~ de transport** means of transport; **~ne d'âge** average age; **~ne entreprise** (Comm) medium-sized firm

moyennant [mwajɛnɑ̃] *prép* (somme) for; (service, conditions) in return for; (travail, effort) with

Moyen-Orient [mwajɛnɔʀjɑ̃] *nm*: **le ~** the Middle East

moyeu, x [mwajø] *nm* hub

MST *sigle f* (= maladie sexuellement transmissible) STD

mû, mue [my] *pp de* **mouvoir**

muer [mɥe] /1/ *vi* (oiseau, mammifère) to moult; (serpent) to slough (its skin); (jeune garçon): **il mue** his voice is breaking

muet, te [mɥɛ, -ɛt] *adj* (fig): **~ d'admiration** *etc* speechless with admiration *etc*; (Ciné) silent

mufle [myfl] *nm* muzzle; (goujat) boor

mugir [myʒiʀ] /2/ *vi* (bœuf) to bellow; (vache) to low; (fig) to howl

muguet [mygɛ] *nm* lily of the valley

mule [myl] *nf* (Zool) (she-)mule

mulet [mylɛ] *nm* (Zool) (he-)mule; (poisson) mullet

multinational, e, -aux [myltinasjɔnal, -o] *adj, nf* multinational

multiple [myltipl] *adj* multiple, numerous; (varié) many, manifold; **multiplication** *nf* multiplication; **multiplier** /7/ *vt* to multiply; **se multiplier** *vi* to multiply

municipal, e, -aux [mynisipal, -o] *adj* (élections, stade) municipal; (conseil) town *cpd*; **piscine/ bibliothèque ~e** public swimming pool/library; **municipalité** *nf* (corps municipal) town council; (commune) municipality

munir [myniʀ] /2/ *vt*: **~ qn/qch de** to equip sb/sth with; **se ~ de** to provide o.s. with

munitions [mynisjɔ̃] *nfpl* ammunition *sg*

mur [myʀ] *nm* wall; (Inform) paywall; **~ du son** sound barrier

mûr, e [myʀ] *adj* ripe; (personne) mature

muraille [myʀaj] *nf* (high) wall

mural, e, -aux [myʀal, -o] *adj* wall *cpd* ⊳ *nm* (Art) mural

m

mûre [myʀ] *nf* blackberry

muret [myʀɛ] *nm* low wall

mûrir [myʀiʀ] /2/ *vi (fruit, blé)* to ripen; *(abcès, furoncle)* to come to a head; *(fig: idée, personne)* to mature ▷ *vt (personne)* to (make) mature; *(pensée, projet)* to nurture

murmure [myʀmyʀ] *nm* murmur; **murmurer** /1/ *vi* to murmur

muscade [myskad] *nf (aussi:* **noix (de) ~)** nutmeg

muscat [myska] *nm (raisin)* muscat grape; *(vin)* muscatel (wine)

muscle [myskl] *nm* muscle; **musclé, e** *adj* muscular; *(fig)* strong-arm *cpd*

museau, x [myzo] *nm* muzzle; *(Culin)* brawn

musée [myze] *nm* museum; *(de peinture)* art gallery

museler [myzle] /4/ *vt* to muzzle; **muselière** *nf* muzzle

musette [myzɛt] *nf (sac)* lunch bag

musical, e, -aux [myzikal, -o] *adj* musical

music-hall [myzikol] *nm (salle)* variety theatre; *(genre)* variety

musicien, ne [myzisjɛ̃, -ɛn] *adj* musical ▷ *nm/f* musician

musique [myzik] *nf* music

musulman, e [myzylmɑ̃, -an] *adj, nm/f* Moslem, Muslim

mutation [mytasjɔ̃] *nf (Admin)* transfer

muter [myte] /1/ *vt* to transfer, move

mutilé, e [mytile] *nm/f* person with a disability *(through loss of limbs)*

mutiler [mytile] /1/ *vt* to mutilate, maim

mutin, e [mytɛ̃, -in] *adj (enfant, air, ton)* mischievous, impish ▷ *nm/f (Mil, Navig)* mutineer; **mutinerie** *nf* mutiny

mutisme [mytism] *nm* silence

mutuel, le [mytɥɛl] *adj* mutual ▷ *nf* mutual benefit society

myope [mjɔp] *adj* short-sighted

myosotis [mjɔzɔtis] *nm* forget-me-not

myrtille [miʀtij] *nf* blueberry

mystère [mistɛʀ] *nm* mystery; **mystérieux, -euse** *adj* mysterious

mystifier [mistifje] /7/ *vt* to fool

mythe [mit] *nm* myth

mythologie [mitɔlɔʒi] *nf* mythology

n

n' [n] *adv voir* ne

nacre [nakʀ] *nf* mother-of-pearl

nage [naʒ] *nf* swimming; *(manière)* style of swimming, stroke; **traverser/s'éloigner à la ~** to swim across/away; **en ~** bathed in sweat; **nageoire** *nf* fin; **nager** /3/ *vi* to swim; **nageur, -euse** *nm/f* swimmer

naïf, -ïve [naif, naiv] *adj* naive

nain, e [nɛ̃, nɛn] *nm/f* dwarf (!)

naissance [nɛsɑ̃s] *nf* birth; **donner ~ à** to give birth to; *(fig)* to give rise to; **lieu de ~** place of birth

naître [nɛtʀ] /59/ *vi* to be born; *(conflit, complications)*: **~ de** to arise from, be born out of; **je suis né en 1960** I was born in 1960; **faire ~** *(fig)* to give rise to, arouse

naïveté [naivte] *nf* naivety

nana [nana] *nf (fam: fille)* bird (BRIT), chick

nappe [nap] *nf* tablecloth; *(de pétrole, gaz)* layer; **napperon** *nm* table-mat

narguer [naʀge] /1/ *vt* to taunt

narine [naʀin] *nf* nostril

natal, e [natal] *adj* native; **natalité** *nf* birth rate

natation [natasjɔ̃] *nf* swimming

natif, -ive [natif, -iv] *adj* native

nation [nasjɔ̃] *nf* nation; **national, e, -aux** *adj* national ▷ *nf*: **(route) nationale** ≈ A road (BRIT), ≈ state highway (US); **nationaliser** /1/ *vt* to nationalize; **nationalisme** *nm* nationalism; **nationalité** *nf* nationality

natte [nat] *nf (tapis)* mat; *(cheveux)* plait

naturaliser [natyʀalize] /1/ *vt* to naturalize

nature [natyʀ] *nf* nature ▷ *adj, adv* *(Culin)* plain, without seasoning or sweetening; *(café, thé)* black; without sugar; *(yaourt)* natural; **payer en ~** to pay in kind; **~ morte** still-life; **naturel, le** *adj* natural ▷ *nm* naturalness; *(caractère)* disposition, nature; **naturellement** *adv* naturally; *(bien sûr)* of course

naufrage [nofʀaʒ] *nm* (ship)wreck; **faire ~** to be shipwrecked

nausée [noze] *nf* nausea; **avoir la ~** to feel sick

nautique [notik] *adj* nautical, water *cpd*; **sports ~s** water sports

naval, e [naval] *adj* naval; *(industrie)* shipbuilding

navet [navɛ] *nm* turnip; *(péj: film)* third-rate film

navette [navɛt] *nf* shuttle; **faire la ~ (entre)** to go to and fro (between)

navigateur [navigatœʀ] *nm (Navig)* seafarer; *(Inform)* browser

navigation [navigasjɔ̃] *nf* navigation, sailing

naviguer [navige] /1/ *vi* to navigate, sail; **~ sur Internet** to browse the Internet

navire [naviʀ] *nm* ship

navrer [navʀe] /1/ *vt* to upset, distress; **je suis navré (de/de faire/que)** I'm so sorry (for/for doing/that)

ne, n' [nə, n] *adv voir* **pas¹; plus²;**
jamais *etc*; *(sans valeur négative, non*
traduit): **c'est plus loin que je ne le**
croyais it's further than I thought
né, e [ne] *pp de* **naître; né en 1960**
born in 1960; **née Scott** née Scott
néanmoins [neãmwɛ̃] *adv*
nevertheless
néant [neã] *nm* nothingness;
réduire à ~ to bring to nought;
(espoir) to dash
nécessaire [nesesɛʀ] *adj* necessary
▷ *nm* necessary; *(sac)* kit; **faire le ~**
to do the necessary; **~ de couture**
sewing kit; **~ de toilette** toilet bag;
nécessité *nf* necessity; **nécessiter**
/1/ *vt* to require
nectar [nɛktaʀ] *nm* nectar
néerlandais, e [neɛʀlɑ̃dɛ, -ez]
adj Dutch
nef [nɛf] *nf (d'église)* nave
néfaste [nefast] *adj (nuisible)*
harmful; *(funeste)* ill-fated
négatif, -ive [negatif, -iv] *adj*
negative ▷ *nm (Photo)* negative
négligé, e [negliʒe] *adj (en désordre)*
slovenly ▷ *nm (tenue)* negligee
négligeable [negliʒabl] *adj*
negligible
négligent, e [negliʒã, -ãt] *adj*
careless; negligent
négliger [negliʒe] /3/ *vt (épouse,*
jardin) to neglect; *(tenue)* to be
careless about; *(avis, précautions)* to
disregard; **~ de faire** to fail to do, not
bother to do
négociant, e [negɔsjã, -jãt] *nm/f*
merchant '
négociation [negɔsjasjɔ̃] *nf*
negotiation
négocier [negɔsje] /7/ *vi, vt* to
negotiate
nègre [nɛgʀ] *nm (péj)* Negro (!);
(écrivain) ghost writer
neige [nɛʒ] *nf* snow; **neiger** /3/ *vi*
to snow
nénuphar [nenyfaʀ] *nm* water-lily
néon [neɔ̃] *nm* neon

néo-zélandais, e [neozelãdɛ, -ez]
adj New Zealand *cpd* ▷ *nm/f*: **N~, e**
New Zealander
Népal [nepal] *nm*: **le ~** Nepal
nerf [nɛʀ] *nm* nerve; **être** *ou* **vivre**
sur les ~s to live on one's nerves;
nerveux, -euse *adj* nervous;
(irritable) touchy, nervy; *(voiture)*
nippy, responsive; **nervosité** *nf*
excitability, tenseness
n'est-ce pas [nɛspa] *adv* isn't it?,
won't you? *etc (selon le verbe qui*
précède)
net, nette [nɛt] *adj (sans équivoque,*
distinct) clear; *(amélioration, différence)*
marked, distinct; *(propre)* neat,
clean; *(Comm: prix, salaire, poids)* net
▷ *adv (refuser)* flatly ▷ *nm*: **mettre**
au ~ to copy out; **s'arrêter ~** to
stop dead; **nettement** *adv* clearly;
(incontestablement) decidedly;
netteté *nf* clearness
nettoyage [netwajaʒ] *nm* cleaning;
~ à sec dry cleaning
nettoyer [netwaje] /8/ *vt* to clean
neuf¹ [nœf] *num* nine
neuf², neuve [nœf, nœv] *adj* new;
remettre à ~ to do up (as good as
new), refurbish; **quoi de ~?** what's
new?
neutre [nøtʀ] *adj (Ling)* neuter
neuve [nœv] *adj f voir* **neuf²**
neuvième [nœvjɛm] *num* ninth
neveu, x [nəvø] *nm* nephew
New York [njujɔʀk] *n* New York
nez [ne] *nm* nose; **avoir du ~** to have
flair; **~ à ~ avec** face to face with
ni [ni] *conj*: **ni ... ni** neither ... nor;
je n'aime ni les lentilles ni les
épinards I like neither lentils nor
spinach; **il n'a dit ni oui ni non** he
didn't say either yes or no; **elles ne**
sont venues ni l'une ni l'autre
neither of them came; **il n'a rien**
vu ni entendu he didn't see or hear
anything
niche [niʃ] *nf (du chien)* kennel; *(de mur)*
recess, niche; **nicher** /1/ *vi* to nest

nid [ni] nm nest; **~ de poule** pothole

nièce [njɛs] nf niece

nier [nje] /7/ vt to deny

Nil [nil] nm: **le ~** the Nile

n'importe [nɛ̃pɔʀt] adv: **~ qui/ quoi/où** anybody/anything/ anywhere; **~ quand** any time; **~ quel/quelle** any; **~ lequel/laquelle** any (one); **~ comment** (sans soin) carelessly

niveau, x [nivo] nm level; (des élèves, études) standard; **~ de vie** standard of living

niveler [nivle] /4/ vt to level

noble [nɔbl] adj noble; **noblesse** nf nobility; (d'une action etc) nobleness

noce [nɔs] nf wedding; (gens) wedding party (ou guests pl); **faire la ~** (fam) to go on a binge; **~s d'or/d'argent/de diamant** golden/ silver/diamond wedding

nocif, -ive [nɔsif, -iv] adj harmful

nocturne [nɔktyʀn] adj nocturnal ▷ nf late opening

Noël [nɔɛl] nm Christmas

nœud [nø] nm knot; (ruban) bow; **~ papillon** bow tie

noir, e [nwaʀ] adj black; (obscur, sombre) dark ▷ nm/f black man/ woman ▷ nm: **dans le ~** in the dark ▷ nf (Mus) crotchet (BRIT), quarter note (US); **travailler au ~** to work on the side; **noircir** /2/ vt, vi to blacken

noisette [nwazɛt] nf hazelnut

noix [nwa] nf walnut; (Culin): **une ~ de beurre** a knob of butter; **à la ~** (fam) worthless; **~ de cajou** cashew nut; **~ de coco** coconut; **~ muscade** nutmeg

nom [nɔ̃] nm name; (Ling) noun; **~ de famille** surname; **~ de jeune fille** maiden name; **~ d'utilisateur** username

nomade [nɔmad] nm/f nomad

nombre [nɔ̃bʀ] nm number; **venir en ~** to come in large numbers; **depuis ~ d'années** for many years; **au ~ de mes amis** among

my friends; **nombreux, -euse** adj many, numerous; (avec nom sg: foule etc) large; **peu nombreux** few; **de nombreux cas** many cases

nombril [nɔ̃bʀi(l)] nm navel

nommer [nɔme] /1/ vt to name; (élire) to appoint, nominate; **se nommer** vr: **il se nomme Pascal** his name's Pascal, he's called Pascal

non [nɔ̃] adv (réponse) no; (suivi d'un adjectif, adverbe) not; **Paul est venu, ~?** Paul came, didn't he?; **~ pas que** not that; **moi ~ plus** neither do I, I don't either; **je pense que ~** I don't think so; **~ alcoolisé** non-alcoholic

nonchalant, e [nɔ̃ʃalɑ̃, -ɑ̃t] adj nonchalant

non-fumeur, -euse [nɔ̃fymœʀ, -øz] nm/f non-smoker

non-sens [nɔ̃sɑ̃s] nm absurdity

nord [nɔʀ] nm North ▷ adj northern; north; **au ~** (situation) in the north; (direction) to the north; **au ~ de** to the north of; **nord-africain, e** adj North African ▷ nm/f: **N~-Africain, e** North African; **nord-est** nm North-East; **nord-ouest** nm North-West

normal, e, -aux [nɔʀmal, -o] adj normal ▷ nf: **la ~e** the norm, the average; **c'est tout à fait ~** it's perfectly natural; **vous trouvez ça ~?** does it seem right to you?; **normalement** adv (en général) normally

normand, e [nɔʀmɑ̃, -ɑ̃d] adj Norman ▷ nm/f: **N~, e** (de Normandie) Norman

Normandie [nɔʀmɑ̃di] nf: **la ~** Normandy

norme [nɔʀm] nf norm; (Tech) standard

Norvège [nɔʀvɛʒ] nf: **la ~** Norway; **norvégien, ne** adj Norwegian ▷ nm (Ling) Norwegian ▷ nm/f: **Norvégien, ne** Norwegian

nos [no] adj pl voir **notre**

nostalgie [nɔstalʒi] nf nostalgia; **nostalgique** adj nostalgic

notable [nɔtabl] *adj* notable,
noteworthy; *(marqué)* noticeable,
marked ▷ *nm* prominent citizen

notaire [nɔtɛʀ] *nm* solicitor

notamment [nɔtamɑ̃] *adv* in
particular, among others

note [nɔt] *nf (écrite, Mus)* note; *(Scol)*
mark *(BRIT)*, grade; *(facture)* bill; **~ de
service** memorandum

noter [nɔte] */1/ vt (écrire)* to write
down; *(remarquer)* to note, notice;
(devoir) to mark, give a grade to

notice [nɔtis] *nf* summary, short
article; *(brochure)*: **~ explicative**
explanatory leaflet, instruction
booklet

notifier [nɔtifje] */7/ vt*: **~ qch à qn** to
notify sb of sth, notify sth to sb

notion [nɔsjɔ̃] *nf* notion, idea

notoire [nɔtwaʀ] *adj* widely known;
(en mal) notorious

notre (*pl* **nos**) [nɔtʀ(ə), no] *adj poss* our

nôtre [nɔtʀ] *adj* ours ▷ *pron*: **le/la ~**
ours; **les ~s** ours; *(alliés etc)* our own
people; **soyez des ~s** join us

nouer [nwe] */1/ vt* to tie, knot; *(fig:
alliance etc)* to strike up

noueux, -euse [nwø, -øz] *adj*
gnarled

nourrice [nuʀis] *nf* ≈ child-minder

nourrir [nuʀiʀ] */2/ vt* to feed;
(fig: espoir) to harbour, nurse;
nourrissant, e *adj* nutritious;
nourrisson *nm* (unweaned) infant;
nourriture *nf* food

nous [nu] *pron (sujet)* we; *(objet)* us;
nous-mêmes *pron* ourselves

nouveau (nouvel), -elle, x [nuvo,
-ɛl] *adj* new ▷ *nm/f* new pupil *(ou
employee)* ▷ *nm*: **il y a du ~** there's
something new ▷ *nf (piece of)* news
sg; *(Littérature)* short story; **nouvelles**
nfpl (Presse, TV) news; **de ~, à ~** again;
je suis sans nouvelles de lui I
haven't heard from him; **Nouvel An**
New Year; **venu, nouvelle venue**
newcomer; **~x mariés** newly-weds;
nouveau-né, e *nm/f* newborn

(baby); **nouveauté** *nf* novelty; *(chose
nouvelle)* something new

nouvelle: **Nouvelle-Calédonie**
[nuvɛlkaledɔni] *nf*: **la Nouvelle-
Calédonie** New Caledonia;
Nouvelle-Zélande [nuvɛlzelɑ̃d] *nf*:
la Nouvelle-Zélande New Zealand

novembre [nɔvɑ̃bʀ] *nm* November;
voir aussi **juillet**

LE 11 NOVEMBRE

Le 11 novembre is a public holiday
in France and commemorates
the signing of the armistice, near
Compiègne, at the end of the First
World War.

noyade [nwajad] *nf* drowning *no pl*

noyau, x [nwajo] *nm (de fruit)*
stone; *(Bio, Physique)* nucleus; *(fig:
centre)* core

noyer [nwaje] */8/ nm* walnut (tree);
(bois) walnut ▷ *vt* to drown; *(moteur)*
to flood; **se noyer** to be drowned,
drown; *(suicide)* to drown o.s.

nu, e [ny] *adj* naked; *(membres)* naked,
bare; *(chambre, fil, plaine)* bare ▷ *nm*
(Art) nude; **tout nu** stark naked; **se
mettre nu** to strip

nuage [nɥaʒ] *nm (aussi Inform)* cloud;
informatique en ~ cloud computing;
nuageux, -euse *adj* cloudy

nuance [nɥɑ̃s] *nf (de couleur, sens)*
shade; **il y a une ~ (entre)** there's a
slight difference (between); **nuancer**
/3/ vt (pensée, opinion) to qualify

nucléaire [nykleɛʀ] *adj* nuclear
▷ *nm*: **le ~** nuclear power

nudiste [nydist] *nm/f* nudist

nuée [nɥe] *nf*: **une ~ de** a cloud *ou*
host *ou* swarm of

nuire [nɥiʀ] */38/ vi* to be harmful;
~ à to harm, do damage to; **nuisible**
[nɥizibl] *adj* harmful; **(animal)**
nuisible pest

nuit [nɥi] *nf* night; **il fait ~** it's dark;
cette ~ *(hier)* last night; *(aujourd'hui*

tonight; **de ~** (vol, service) night cpd;
~ blanche sleepless night
nul, nulle [nyl] adj (aucun) no;
(minime) nil, non-existent; (non
valable) null; (péj) useless, hopeless
▷ pron none, no one; **résultat ~,**
match ~ draw; **nulle part** nowhere;
nullement adv by no means
numérique [nymeʀik] adj
numerical; (affichage, son, télévision)
digital
numéro [nymeʀo] nm number;
(spectacle) act, turn; (Presse) issue,
number; **~ de téléphone** (tele)phone
number; **~ vert** ≈ Freefone® number
(BRIT), ≈ toll-free number (US);
numéroter /1/ vt to number
nuque [nyk] nf nape of the neck
nu-tête [nytɛt] adj inv bareheaded
nutritif, -ive [nytʀitif, -iv] adj
(besoins, valeur) nutritional; (aliment)
nutritious, nourishing
nylon [nilɔ̃] nm nylon

O

oasis [ɔazis] nm ou f oasis
obéir [ɔbeiʀ] /2/ vi to obey; **~ à** to
obey; **obéissance** nf obedience;
obéissant, e adj obedient
obèse [ɔbɛz] adj obese; **obésité** nf
obesity
objecter [ɔbʒɛkte] /1/ vt: **~ (à qn)**
que to object (to sb) that; **objecteur**
nm: **objecteur de conscience**
conscientious objector
objectif, -ive [ɔbʒɛktif, -iv] adj
objective ▷ nm (Optique, Photo) lens
sg; (Mil, fig) objective
objection [ɔbʒɛksjɔ̃] nf objection
objectivité [ɔbʒɛktivite] nf
objectivity
objet [ɔbʒɛ] nm object; (d'une
discussion, recherche) subject; **être**
ou faire l'~ de (discussion) to be the
subject of; (soins) to be given ou
shown; **sans ~** purposeless; (sans
fondement) groundless; **~ d'art** objet
d'art; **~s personnels** personal items;

~s trouvés lost property sg (BRIT), lost-and-found sg (US); **~s de valeur** valuables

obligation [ɔbligasjɔ̃] nf obligation; (Comm) bond, debenture; **obligatoire** adj compulsory, obligatory; **obligatoirement** adv necessarily; (fam: sans aucun doute) inevitably

obliger [ɔbliʒe] /3/ vt (contraindre): **~ qn à faire** to force ou oblige sb to do; **je suis bien obligé (de le faire)** I have to (do it)

oblique [ɔblik] adj oblique; **en ~** diagonally

oblitérer [ɔblitere] /6/ vt (timbre-poste) to cancel

obnubiler [ɔbnybile] /1/ vt to obsess

obscène [ɔpsɛn] adj obscene

obscur, e [ɔpskyr] adj dark; (raisons) obscure; **obscurcir** /2/ vt to darken; (fig) to obscure; **s'obscurcir** vi to grow dark; **obscurité** nf darkness; **dans l'obscurité** in the dark, in darkness

obsédé, e [ɔpsede] nm/f fanatic; **~(e) sexuel(le)** sex maniac

obséder [ɔpsede] /6/ vt to obsess, haunt

obsèques [ɔpsɛk] nfpl funeral sg

observateur, -trice [ɔpsɛrvatœr, -tris] adj observant, perceptive ▷ nm/f observer

observation [ɔpsɛrvasjɔ̃] nf observation; (d'un règlement etc) observance; (reproche) reproof; **en ~** (Méd) under observation

observatoire [ɔpsɛrvatwar] nm observatory

observer [ɔpsɛrve] /1/ vt (regarder) to observe, watch; (scientifiquement, aussi: règlement, jeûne etc) to observe; (surveiller) to watch; (remarquer) to observe, notice; **faire ~ qch à qn** (dire) to point out sth to sb

obsession [ɔpsesjɔ̃] nf obsession

obstacle [ɔpstakl] nm obstacle; (Équitation) jump, hurdle; **faire ~ à**

(projet) to hinder, put obstacles in the path of

obstiné, e [ɔpstine] adj obstinate

obstiner [ɔpstine] /1/: **s'obstiner** vi to insist, dig one's heels in; **s'~ à faire** to persist (obstinately) in doing

obstruer [ɔpstrye] /1/ vt to block, obstruct

obtenir [ɔptənir] /22/ vt to obtain, get; (résultat) to achieve, obtain; **~ de pouvoir faire** to obtain permission to do

obturateur [ɔptyratœr] nm (Photo) shutter

obus [ɔby] nm shell

occasion [ɔkazjɔ̃] nf (aubaine, possibilité) opportunity; (circonstance) occasion; (Comm: article non neuf) secondhand buy; (: acquisition avantageuse) bargain; **à plusieurs ~s** on several occasions; **à l'~** sometimes, on occasions; **d'~** secondhand; **occasionnel, le** adj occasional

occasionner [ɔkazjɔne] /1/ vt to cause

occident [ɔksidɑ̃] nm: **l'O~** the West; **occidental, e, -aux** adj western; (Pol) Western ▷ nm/f Westerner

occupation [ɔkypasjɔ̃] nf occupation

occupé, e [ɔkype] adj (Mil, Pol) occupied; (personne) busy; (place, sièges) taken; (toilettes) engaged; **la ligne est ~e** the line's engaged (BRIT) ou busy (US)

occuper [ɔkype] /1/ vt to occupy; (poste, fonction) to hold; **s'~ (à qch)** to occupy o.s ou keep o.s. busy (with sth); **s'~ de** (être responsable de) to be in charge of; (se charger de: affaire) to take charge of, deal with; (: clients etc) to attend to

occurrence [ɔkyrɑ̃s] nf: **en l'~** in this case

océan [ɔseɑ̃] nm ocean

octet [ɔktɛ] nm byte

octobre [ɔktɔbr] nm October

oral, e, -aux [ɔʀal, -o] adj oral; (Méd):
par voie ~e orally ▷ nm oral

orange [ɔʀɑ̃ʒ] adj inv, nf orange;
orangé, e adj orangey, orange-
coloured; **orangeade** nf orangeade;
oranger nm orange tree

orateur [ɔʀatœʀ] nm speaker

orbite [ɔʀbit] nf (Anat) (eye-)socket;
(Physique) orbit

Orcades [ɔʀkad] nfpl: **les ~** the
Orkneys, the Orkney Islands

orchestre [ɔʀkɛstʀ] nm orchestra;
(de jazz, danse) band; (places) stalls pl
(BRIT), orchestra (US)

orchidée [ɔʀkide] nf orchid

ordinaire [ɔʀdinɛʀ] adj ordinary;
(modèle, qualité) standard; (péj:
commun) common ▷ nm ordinary;
(menus) everyday fare ▷ nf (essence)
≈ two-star (petrol) (BRIT), ≈ regular
(gas) (US); **d'~** usually, normally;
comme à l'~ as usual

ordinateur [ɔʀdinatœʀ] nm
computer; **~ individuel** ou
personnel personal computer;
~ portable laptop (computer)

ordonnance [ɔʀdɔnɑ̃s] nf (Méd)
prescription; (Mil) orderly, batman
(BRIT)

ordonné, e [ɔʀdɔne] adj tidy, orderly

ordonner [ɔʀdɔne] /1/ vt (agencer) to
organize, arrange; (donner un ordre):
~ à qn de faire to order sb to do; (Rel)
to ordain; (Méd) to prescribe

ordre [ɔʀdʀ] nm order; (propreté et
soin) orderliness, tidiness; **à l'~ de**
payable to; (nature): **d'~ pratique** of
a practical nature; **ordres** nmpl (Rel)
holy orders; **mettre en ~** to tidy (up),
put in order; **par ~ alphabétique/
d'importance** in alphabetical order/
in order of importance; **être aux
~s de qn/sous les ~s de qn** to be at
sb's disposal/under sb's command;
jusqu'à nouvel ~ until further notice;
de premier ~ first-rate; **~ du jour**
(d'une réunion) agenda; **à l'~ du jour**
(fig) topical; **~ public** law and order

ordure [ɔʀdyʀ] nf filth no pl; **ordures**
nfpl (balayures, déchets) rubbish sg,
refuse sg; **~s ménagères** household
refuse

oreille [ɔʀɛj] nf ear; **avoir de l'~**
to have a good ear (for music)

oreiller [ɔʀeje] nm pillow

oreillons [ɔʀejɔ̃] nmpl mumps sg

ores [ɔʀ]: **d'~ et déjà** adv already

orfèvrerie [ɔʀfɛvʀəʀi] nf
goldsmith's (ou silversmith's) trade;
(ouvrage) (silver ou gold) plate

organe [ɔʀgan] nm organ; (porte-
parole) representative, mouthpiece

organigramme [ɔʀganigʀam] nm
(hiérarchique, structure) organization
chart; (des opérations) flow chart

organique [ɔʀganik] adj organic

organisateur, -trice
[ɔʀganizatœʀ, -tʀis] nm/f organizer

organisation [ɔʀganizasjɔ̃] nf
organization; **O~ des Nations
unies (ONU)** United Nations
(Organization) (UN(O))

organiser [ɔʀganize] /1/ vt to
organize; (mettre sur pied: service
etc) to set up; **s'organiser** to get
organized

organisme [ɔʀganism] nm (Bio)
organism; (corps humain) body;
(Admin, Pol etc) body

organiste [ɔʀganist] nm/f organist

orgasme [ɔʀgasm] nm orgasm, climax

orge [ɔʀʒ] nf barley

orgue [ɔʀg] nm organ

orgueil [ɔʀgœj] nm pride;
orgueilleux, -euse adj proud

oriental, e, -aux [ɔʀjɑ̃tal, -o] adj
(langue, produit) oriental; (frontière)
eastern

orientation [ɔʀjɑ̃tasjɔ̃] nf (de
recherches) orientation; (d'une maison
etc) aspect; (d'un journal) leanings pl;
avoir le sens de l'~ to have a (good)
sense of direction; **~ professionnelle**
careers advisory service

orienté, e [ɔʀjɑ̃te] adj (fig: article,
journal) slanted; **bien/mal ~**

(appartement) well/badly positioned;
~ au sud facing south, with a
southern aspect

orienter [ɔʀjɑ̃te] /1/ vt (tourner:
antenne) to direct, turn; (: voyageur,
touriste, recherches) to direct; (fig:
élève) to orientate; **s'orienter**
(se repérer) to find one's bearings; **s'~
vers** (fig) to turn towards

origan [ɔʀigɑ̃] nm oregano

originaire [ɔʀiʒinɛʀ] adj: **être ~ de**
to be a native of

original, e, -aux [ɔʀiʒinal, -o] adj
original; (bizarre) eccentric ▷ nm/f
eccentric ▷ nm (document etc, Art)
original

origine [ɔʀiʒin] nf origin; **origines**
nfpl (d'une personne) origins; **d'~
(pays)** of origin; (pneus etc) original;
d'~ française of French origin; **à l'~**
originally; **originel, le** adj original

orme [ɔʀm] nm elm

ornement [ɔʀnəmɑ̃] nm ornament

orner [ɔʀne] /1/ vt to decorate,
adorn

ornière [ɔʀnjɛʀ] nf rut

orphelin, e [ɔʀfəlɛ̃, -in] adj
orphan(ed) ▷ nm/f orphan; **~ de
père/mère** fatherless/motherless;
orphelinat nm orphanage

orteil [ɔʀtɛj] nm toe; **gros ~** big toe

orthographe [ɔʀtɔgʀaf] nf spelling

ortie [ɔʀti] nf (stinging) nettle

os [ɔs] nm bone; **os à moelle**
marrowbone

osciller [ɔsile] /1/ vi (au vent etc)
to rock; (fig): **~ entre** to waver ou
fluctuate between

osé, e [oze] adj daring, bold

oseille [ozɛj] nf sorrel

oser [oze] /1/ vi, vt to dare; **~ faire**
to dare (to) do

osier [ozje] nm willow; **d'~, en ~**
wicker(work) cpd

osseux, -euse [ɔsø, -øz] adj bony;
(tissu, maladie, greffe) bone cpd

otage [ɔtaʒ] nm hostage; **prendre
qn comme ~** to take sb hostage

OTAN sigle f (= Organisation du traité de
l'Atlantique Nord) NATO

otarie [ɔtaʀi] nf sea-lion

ôter [ote] /1/ vt to remove; (soustraire)
to take away; **~ qch à qn** to take sth
(away) from sb; **~ qch de** to remove
sth from

otite [ɔtit] nf ear infection

ou [u] conj or; **ou ... ou** either ... or;
ou bien or (else)

MOT-CLÉ

où [u] pron relatif **1** (position, situation)
where, that; (souvent omis) **la
chambre où il était** the room (that)
he was in, the room where he was; **la
ville où je l'ai rencontré** the town
where I met him; **la pièce d'où il
est sorti** the room he came out of;
le village d'où je viens the village
I come from; **les villes par où il est
passé** the towns where he went through
2 (temps, état) that; (souvent omis): **le
jour où il est parti** the day (that) he
left; **au prix où c'est** at the price it is
▷ adv **1** (interrogation) where; **où est-
il/va-t-il?** where is he/is he going?;
par où? which way?; **d'où vient
que ...?** how come ...?
2 (position) where; **je sais où il est**
I know where he is; **où que l'on aille**
wherever you go

ouate [wat] nf cotton wool (BRIT),
cotton (US)

oubli [ubli] nm (acte): **l'~ de**
forgetting; (trou de mémoire) lapse
of memory; (négligence) omission,
oversight; **tomber dans l'~** to sink
into oblivion

oublier [ublije] /7/ vt to forget; (ne pas
voir: erreurs etc) to miss; (laisser quelque
part: chapeau etc) to leave behind

ouest [wɛst] nm west ▷ adj inv west;
(région) western; **à l'~** in the west;
(direction) (to the) west, westwards;
à l'~ de (to the) west of

ouf [uf] *excl* phew!

oui [wi] *adv* yes

oui-dire ['widiʀ]: **par ~** *adv* by hearsay

ouïe [wi] *nf* hearing; **ouïes** *nfpl* (*de poisson*) gills

ouragan [uʀagã] *nm* hurricane

ourlet [uʀlɛ] *nm* hem

ours [uʀs] *nm* bear; **~ brun/blanc** brown/polar bear; **~ (en peluche)** teddy (bear)

oursin [uʀsɛ̃] *nm* sea urchin

ourson [uʀsɔ̃] *nm* (bear-)cub

ouste [ust] *excl* hop it!

outil [uti] *nm* tool; **outiller** /1/ *vt* to equip

outrage [utʀaʒ] *nm* insult; **~ à la pudeur** indecent behaviour *no pl*

outrance [utʀɑ̃s]: **à ~** *adv* excessively, to excess

outre [utʀ] *prép* besides ▷ *adv*: **passer ~ à** to disregard, take no notice of; **en ~** besides, moreover; **~ mesure** to excess; (*manger, boire*) immoderately; **outre-Atlantique** *adv* across the Atlantic; **outre-mer** *adv* overseas

ouvert, e [uvɛʀ, -ɛʀt] *pp de* **ouvrir** ▷ *adj* open; (*robinet, gaz etc*) on; **ouvertement** *adv* openly; **ouverture** *nf* opening; (*Mus*) overture; **ouverture d'esprit** open-mindedness; **heures d'ouverture** (*Comm*) opening hours

ouvrable [uvʀabl] *adj*: **jour ~** working day, weekday

ouvrage [uvʀaʒ] *nm* (*tâche, de tricot etc*) work *no pl*; (*texte, livre*) work

ouvre-boîte(s) [uvʀəbwat] *nm inv* tin (BRIT) ou can opener

ouvre-bouteille(s) [uvʀəbutɛj] *nm inv* bottle-opener

ouvreuse [uvʀøz] *nf* usherette

ouvrier, -ière [uvʀije, -jɛʀ] *nm/f* worker ▷ *adj* working-class; (*problèmes, conflit*) industrial; (*mouvement*) labour *cpd*; **classe ouvrière** working class

ouvrir [uvʀiʀ] /18/ *vt* (*gén*) to open; (*brèche, passage*) to open up; (*commencer l'exploitation de, créer*) to open (up); (*eau, électricité, chauffage, robinet*) to turn on; (*Méd: abcès*) to open up, cut open ▷ *vi* to open; to open up; **s'ouvrir** *vi* to open; **s'~ à qn (de qch)** to open one's heart to sb (about sth); **~ l'appétit à qn** to whet sb's appetite

ovaire [ovɛʀ] *nm* ovary

ovale [oval] *adj* oval

OVNI [ovni] *sigle m* (= *objet volant non identifié*) UFO

oxyder [okside] /1/: **s'oxyder** *vi* to become oxidized

oxygéné, e [oksiʒene] *adj*: **eau ~e** hydrogen peroxide

oxygène [oksiʒɛn] *nm* oxygen

ozone [ozon] *nm* ozone; **trou dans la couche d'~** hole in the ozone layer

O

P

pacifique [pasifik] *adj* peaceful ▷ *nm*: **le P~, l'océan P~** the Pacific (Ocean)

pack [pak] *nm* pack

pacotille [pakɔtij] *nf* cheap junk sg

PACS *sigle m* (= *pacte civil de solidarité*) ≈ civil partnership; **se pacser** *vi* to form a civil partnership

pacte [pakt] *nm* pact, treaty

pagaille [pagaj] *nf* mess, shambles sg

page [paʒ] *nf* page ▷ *nm* page (boy); **à la ~** (*fig*) up-to-date; **~ d'accueil** (*Inform*) home page; **~ Web** (*Inform*) web page

païen, ne [pajɛ̃, -ɛn] *adj, nm/f* pagan, heathen

paillasson [pajasɔ̃] *nm* doormat

paille [paj] *nf* straw

pain [pɛ̃] *nm* (*substance*) bread; (*unité*) loaf (of bread); (*morceau*): **~ de cire** *etc* bar of wax *etc*; **~ bis/complet** brown/wholemeal (BRIT) ou wholewheat (US) bread; **~ d'épice** ≈ gingerbread; **~ grillé** toast; **~ de**

mie sandwich loaf; **~ au chocolat** pain au chocolat; **~ aux raisins** currant pastry

pair, e [pɛʀ] *adj* (*nombre*) even ▷ *nm* peer; **aller de ~ (avec)** to go hand in hand *ou* together (with); **jeune fille au ~** au pair; **paire** *nf* pair

paisible [pezibl] *adj* peaceful, quiet

paix [pɛ] *nf* peace; **faire la ~ avec** to make peace with; **fiche-lui la ~!** (*fam*) leave him alone!

Pakistan [pakistɑ̃] *nm*: **le ~** Pakistan

palais [palɛ] *nm* palace; (*Anat*) palate

pâle [pɑl] *adj* pale; **bleu ~** pale blue

Palestine [palɛstin] *nf*: **la ~** Palestine

palette [palɛt] *nf* (*de peintre*) palette; (*de produits*) range

pâleur [pɑlœʀ] *nf* paleness

palier [palje] *nm* (*d'escalier*) landing; (*fig*) level, plateau; **par ~s** in stages

pâlir [pɑliʀ] /2/ *vi* to turn *ou* go pale; (*couleur*) to fade

pallier [palje] /7/ *vt*: **~ à** to offset, make up for

palme [palm] *nf* (*de plongeur*) flipper; **palmé, e** [palme] *adj* (*pattes*) webbed

palmier [palmje] *nm* palm tree; (*gâteau*) heart-shaped biscuit made of flaky pastry

pâlot, te [pɑlo, -ɔt] *adj* pale, peaky

palourde [paluʀd] *nf* clam

palper [palpe] /1/ *vt* to feel, finger

palpitant, e [palpitɑ̃, -ɑ̃t] *adj* thrilling

palpiter [palpite] /1/ *vi* (*cœur, pouls*) to beat (: *plus fort*) to pound, throb

paludisme [palydism] *nm* malaria

pamphlet [pɑ̃flɛ] *nm* lampoon, satirical tract

pamplemousse [pɑ̃pləmus] *nm* grapefruit

pan [pɑ̃] *nm* section, piece ▷ *excl* bang!

panache [panaʃ] *nm* plume; (*fig*) spirit, panache

panaché, e [panaʃe] *nm* (*bière*) shandy; **glace ~e** mixed ice cream

pancarte [pɑ̃kaʁt] nf sign, notice

pancréas [pɑ̃kʁeas] nm pancreas

pandémie [pɑ̃demi] nf pandemic

pané, e [pane] adj fried in breadcrumbs

panier [panje] nm basket; **mettre au ~** to chuck away; **~ à provisions** shopping basket; **panier-repas** nm packed lunch

panique [panik] adj panicky ▷ nf panic; **paniquer** /1/ vi to panic

panne [pan] nf breakdown; **être/ tomber en ~** to have broken down/ break down; **être en ~ d'essence** ou **en ~ sèche** to have run out of petrol (BRIT) ou gas (US); **~ d'électricité** ou **de courant** power ou electrical failure

panneau, x [pano] nm (écriteau) sign, notice; **~ d'affichage** notice (BRIT) ou bulletin (US) board; **~ indicateur** signpost; **~ de signalisation** roadsign

panoplie [panɔpli] nf (jouet) outfit; (d'armes) display; (fig) array

panorama [panɔʁama] nm panorama

panse [pɑ̃s] nf paunch

pansement [pɑ̃smɑ̃] nm dressing, bandage; **~ adhésif** sticking plaster

pantacourt [pɑ̃takuʁ] nm cropped trousers pl

pantalon [pɑ̃talɔ̃] nm trousers pl (BRIT), pants pl (US), pair of trousers ou pants; **~ de ski** ski pants pl

panthère [pɑ̃tɛʁ] nf panther

pantin [pɑ̃tɛ̃] nm puppet

pantoufle [pɑ̃tufl] nf slipper

paon [pɑ̃] nm peacock

papa [papa] nm dad(dy)

pape [pap] nm pope

paperasse [papʁas] nf (péj) bumf no pl, papers pl; **paperasserie** nf (péj) red tape no pl; paperwork no pl

papeterie [papetʁi] nf (magasin) stationer's (shop)

papi [papi] nm (fam) granddad

papier [papje] nm paper; (article) article; **papiers** nmpl (aussi: **~s**

d'identité) (identity) papers; **~ (d') aluminium** aluminium (BRIT) ou aluminum (US) foil, tinfoil; **~ calque** tracing paper; **~ hygiénique** ou **(de) toilette** toilet paper; **~ journal** newspaper; **~ à lettres** writing paper, notepaper; **~ peint** wallpaper; **~ de verre** sandpaper

papillon [papijɔ̃] nm butterfly; (fam: contravention) (parking) ticket; **~ de nuit** moth

papillote [papijɔt] nf **~** cooked in tinfoil

papoter [papote] /1/ vi to chatter

paquebot [pakbo] nm liner

pâquerette [pakʁɛt] nf daisy

Pâques [pɑk] nm, nfpl Easter

> **PÂQUES**
>
> In France, Easter eggs are said to
> be brought by the Easter bells or
> cloches de Pâques which fly from
> Rome and drop them in people's
> gardens.

paquet [pakɛ] nm packet; (colis) parcel; (fig: tas): **~ de** pile ou heap of; **paquet-cadeau** nm gift-wrapped parcel

par [paʁ] prép by; **finir** etc **~** to end etc with; **~ amour** out of love; **passer ~ Lyon/la côte** to go via ou through Lyons/along by the coast; **~ la fenêtre** (jeter, regarder) out of the window; **trois ~ jour/personne** three a ou per day/head; **deux ~ deux** in twos; **~ ici** this way; (dans le coin) round here; **~-ci, ~-là** here and there; **~ temps de pluie** in wet weather

parabolique [paʁabɔlik] adj: **antenne ~** satellite dish

parachute [paʁaʃyt] nm parachute; **parachutiste** [paʁaʃytist] nm/f parachutist; (Mil) paratrooper

parade [paʁad] nf (spectacle, défilé) parade; (Escrime, Boxe) parry

paradis [paradi] nm heaven, paradise

paradoxe [paradɔks] nm paradox

paraffine [parafin] nf paraffin

parages [paraʒ] nmpl: **dans les ~ (de)** in the area ou vicinity (of)

paragraphe [paragraf] nm paragraph

paraître [parɛtr] /57/ vb copule to seem, look, appear ▷ vi to appear; (être visible) to show; (Presse, Édition) to be published, come out, appear ▷ vb impers: **il paraît que** it seems ou appears that

parallèle [paralɛl] adj parallel; (police, marché) unofficial ▷ nm (comparaison): **faire un ~ entre** to draw a parallel between ou nf parallel (line)

paralyser [paralize] /1/ vt to paralyze

paramédical, e, -aux [paramedikal, -o] adj: **personnel ~** paramedics pl, paramedical workers pl

paraphrase [parafraz] nf paraphrase

parapluie [paraplɥi] nm umbrella

parasite [parazit] nm parasite; **parasites** nmpl (Tél) interference sg

parasol [parasɔl] nm parasol, sunshade

paratonnerre [paratɔnɛr] nm lightning conductor

parc [park] nm (public) park, gardens pl; (de château etc) grounds pl; (d'enfant) playpen; **~ d'attractions** amusement park; **~ éolien** wind farm; **~ de stationnement** car park; **~ à thème** theme park

parcelle [parsɛl] nf fragment, scrap; (de terrain) plot, parcel

parce que [parskə] conj because

parchemin [parʃəmɛ̃] nm parchment

parc(o)mètre [park(ɔ)mɛtr] nm parking meter

parcourir [parkurir] /11/ vt (trajet, distance) to cover; (article, livre) to skim ou glance through; (lieu) to go

all over, travel up and down; (frisson, vibration) to run through

parcours [parkur] nm (trajet) journey; (itinéraire) route

par-dessous [pardəsu] prép, adv under(neath)

pardessus [pardəsy] nm overcoat

par-dessus [pardəsy] prép over (the top of) ▷ adv over (the top); **~ le marché** on top of it all; **~ tout** above all; **en avoir ~ la tête** to have had enough

par-devant [pardəvɑ̃] adv (passer) round the front

pardon [pardɔ̃] nm forgiveness no pl ▷ excl (I'm) sorry; (pour interpeller etc) excuse me; **demander ~ à qn (de)** to apologize to sb (for); **je vous demande ~** I'm sorry; (pour interpeller) excuse me; **pardonner** /1/ vt to forgive; **pardonner qch à qn** to forgive sb for sth

pare: pare-brise nm inv windscreen (Brit), windshield (US); **pare-chocs** nm inv bumper; **pare-feu** nm inv (de foyer) fireguard; (Inform) firewall ▷ adj inv

pareil, le adj (identique) the same, alike; (similaire) similar; (tel): **un courage/livre ~** such courage/a book, courage/a book like this; **de ~s livres** such books; **faire ~** to do the same (thing); **~ à** the same as; similar to; **sans ~** unparalleled, unequalled

parent, e [parɑ̃, -ɑ̃t] nm/f: **un/une ~/e** a relative ou relation; **parents** nmpl (père et mère) parents; **parenté** nf (lien) relationship

parenthèse [parɑ̃tɛz] nf (ponctuation) bracket, parenthesis; (digression) parenthesis, digression; **entre ~s** in brackets; (fig) incidentally

paresse [parɛs] nf laziness; **paresseux, -euse** adj lazy

parfait, e [parfɛ, -ɛt] adj perfect ▷ nm (Ling) perfect (tense); **parfaitement** adv perfectly ▷ excl (most) certainly

parfois [paʁfwa] adv sometimes

parfum [paʁfœ̃] nm (produit) perfume, scent; (odeur: de fleur) scent, fragrance; (goût) flavour ; **parfumé, e** adj (fleur, fruit) fragrant; (femme) perfumed; **parfumé au café** coffee-flavoured (BRIT) ou -flavored (US);
parfumer /1/ vt (odeur, bouquet) to perfume; (crème, gâteau) to flavour ;
parfumerie nf (produits) perfumes; (boutique) perfume shop (BRIT) ou store (US)

pari [paʁi] nm bet; **parier** /7/ vt to bet

Paris [paʁi] n Paris; **parisien, ne** adj Parisian; (Géo, Admin) Paris cpd ▷ nm/f: **Parisien, ne** Parisian

parité [paʁite] nf: ~ **hommes-femmes** (Pol) balanced representation of men and women

parjure [paʁʒyʁ] nm perjury

parking [paʁkiŋ] nm (lieu) car park (BRIT), parking lot (US)

⚠ Attention à ne pas traduire *parking* par le mot anglais *parking*.

parlant, e [paʁlɑ̃, -ɑ̃t] adj (comparaison, preuve) eloquent; (Ciné) talking

parlement [paʁləmɑ̃] nm parliament; **parlementaire** adj parliamentary ▷ nm/f ≈ Member of Parliament (BRIT) ou Congress (US)

parler [paʁle] /1/ vi to speak, talk; (avouer) to talk; **~ (à qn) de** to talk ou speak (to sb) about; **~ le/en français** to speak French/in French; **~ affaires** to talk business; **sans ~ de** (fig) not to mention, to say nothing of; **tu parles!** (bien sûr) you bet!

parloir [paʁlwaʁ] nm (d'une prison, d'un hôpital) visiting room

parmi [paʁmi] prép among(st)

paroi [paʁwa] nf wall; (cloison) partition

paroisse [paʁwas] nf parish

parole [paʁɔl] nf (mot, promesse) word; (faculté): **la ~** speech; **paroles** nfpl (Mus) words, lyrics; **tenir ~** to keep one's word; **prendre la ~** to speak; **demander la ~** to ask for permission to speak; **je le crois sur ~** I'll take his word for it

parquet [paʁkɛ] nm (parquet) floor; (Jur) public prosecutor's office; **le ~ (général)** ≈ the Bench

parrain [paʁɛ̃] nm godfather; **parrainer** /1/ vt (nouvel adhérent) to sponsor

pars [paʁ] vb voir **partir**

parsemer [paʁsəme] /5/ vt (feuilles, papiers) to be scattered over; **~ qch de** to scatter sth with

part [paʁ] nf (qui revient à qn) share; (fraction, partie) part; **prendre ~ à** (débat etc) to take part in; (soucis, douleur de qn) to share in; **faire ~ de qch à qn** to announce sth to sb, inform sb of sth; **pour ma ~** as for me, as far as I'm concerned; **à ~ entière** full; **de la ~ de** (au nom de) on behalf of; (donné par) from; **de toute(s) ~s** from all sides ou quarters; **de ~ et d'autre** on both sides, on either side; **d'une ~ ... d'autre ~** on the one hand ... on the other hand; **d'autre ~** (de plus) moreover; **à ~** adv separately; (de côté) aside; prép apart from, except for; **faire la ~ des choses** to make allowances

partage [paʁtaʒ] nm sharing (out) no pl, share-out; dividing up

partager [paʁtaʒe] /3/ vt to share; (distribuer, répartir) to share (out); (morceler, diviser) to divide (up); **se partager** (héritage etc) to share between themselves (ou ourselves etc)

partenaire [paʁtənɛʁ] nm/f partner

parterre [paʁtɛʁ] nm (de fleurs) (flower) bed; (Théât) stalls pl

parti [paʁti] nm (Pol) party; (décision) course of action; (personne à marier) match; **tirer ~ de** to take advantage of, turn to good account; **prendre ~ (pour/contre)** to take sides ou a stand (for/against); **~ pris** bias

P

partial, e, -aux [paʀsjal, -o] *adj* biased, partial

participant, e [paʀtisipɑ̃, -ɑ̃t] *nm/f* participant; (*à un concours*) entrant

participation [paʀtisipasjɔ̃] *nf* participation; (*financière*) contribution

participer [paʀtisipe] /1/: ~ **à** *vt* (*course, réunion*) to take part in; (*frais etc*) to contribute to; (*chagrin, succès de qn*) to share (in)

particularité [paʀtikylaʀite] *nf* (*distinctive*) characteristic

particulier, ière [paʀtikylje, -jeʀ] *adj* (*personnel, privé*) private; (*étrange*) peculiar, odd; (*spécial*) special, particular; (*spécifique*) particular ▷ *nm* (*individu: Admin*) private individual; ~ **à** peculiar to; **en** ~ (*surtout*) in particular, particularly; (*en privé*) in private; **particulièrement** *adv* particularly

partie [paʀti] *nf* (*gén*) part; (*Jur etc: protagonistes*) party; (*de cartes, tennis etc*) game; (*de campagne, de pêche*) an outing in the country/a fishing party ou trip; **en** ~ partly, in part; **faire** ~ **de** (*chose*) to be part of; **prendre qn à** ~ to take sb to task; **en grande** ~ largely, in the main; ~ **civile** (*Jur*) party claiming damages in a criminal case

partiel, le [paʀsjɛl] *adj* partial ▷ *nm* (*Scol*) class exam

partir [paʀtiʀ] /16/ *vi* (*gén*) to go; (*quitter*) to go, leave; (*tache*) to go, come out; ~ **de** (*lieu: quitter*) to leave; (*commencer à*) to start from; ~ **pour/à** (*lieu, pays etc*) to leave for ou go off to; **à** ~ **de** from

partisan, e [paʀtizɑ̃, -an] *nm/f* partisan; **être** ~ **de qch/faire** to be in favour (BRIT) ou favor (US) of sth/doing

partition [paʀtisjɔ̃] *nf* (*Mus*) score

partout [paʀtu] *adv* everywhere; ~ **où il allait** everywhere ou wherever he went

paru [paʀy] *pp de* **paraître**

parution [paʀysjɔ̃] *nf* publication

parvenir [paʀvəniʀ] /22/: ~ **à** (*atteindre*) to reach; (*réussir*): ~ **à faire** to manage to do, succeed in doing; **faire** ~ **qch à qn** to have sth sent to sb

---

MOT-CLÉ

pas¹ [pɑ] *adv* 1 (*en corrélation avec ne, non etc*) not; **il ne pleure pas** (*habituellement*) he does not ou doesn't cry; (*maintenant*) he's not ou isn't crying; **il n'a pas pleuré/ne pleurera pas** he did not ou didn't/ will not ou won't cry; **ils n'ont pas de voiture/d'enfants** they haven't got a car/any children; **il m'a dit de ne pas le faire** he told me not to do it; **non pas que** ... not that ..

2 (*employé sans ne etc*): **pas moi** not me, I don't (*ou* can't *etc*); **elle travaille, (mais) lui pas** *ou* **pas lui** she works but he doesn't ou does not; **une pomme mûre** an apple which isn't ripe; **pas du tout** not at all; **pas de sucre, merci** no sugar, thanks; **ceci est à vous ou pas?** is this yours or not?, is this yours or isn't it?

3: **pas mal** (*joli: personne, maison*) not bad; **pas mal fait** not badly ou made; **comment ça va? — pas mal** how are things? — not bad; **pas mal de** quite a lot of

pas² [pɑ] *nm* (*enjambée, Danse*) step; (*bruit*) (foot)step; (*trace*) footprint; (*allure, mesure*) pace; ~ **à** ~ step by step; **au** ~ at a walking pace; **marcher à grands** ~ to stride along; **à** ~ **de loup** stealthily; **faire les cent** ~ to pace up and down; **faire les premiers** ~ to make the first move; **sur le** ~ **de la porte** on the doorstep

passage [pasaʒ] *nm* (*fait de passer*): *voir* **passer**; (*lieu, prix de la traversée, extrait de livre etc*) passage; (*chemin*) way; **de ~** (*touristes*) passing through; **~ clouté** pedestrian crossing; **"~ interdit"** "no entry"; **~ à niveau** level (BRIT) ou grade (US) crossing; **~ souterrain** subway (BRIT), underpass

passager, -ère [pɑsaʒe, -ɛʀ] *adj* passing ▷ *nm/f* passenger

passant, e [pɑsɑ̃, -ɑ̃t] *adj* (*rue, endroit*) busy ▷ *nm/f* passer-by; **remarquer qch en ~** to notice sth in passing

passe [pɑs] *nf* (*Sport*) pass; (*Navig*) channel; **être en ~ de faire** to be on the way to doing; **être dans une mauvaise ~** to be going through a bad patch

passé, e [pɑse] *adj* (*événement, temps*) past; (*dernier: semaine etc*) last; (*couleur, tapisserie*) faded ▷ *prép* after ▷ *nm* past; (*Ling*) past (tense); **~ de mode** out of fashion; **~ composé** perfect (tense); **~ simple** past historic

passe-partout [pɑspaʀtu] *nm inv* master ou skeleton key ▷ *adj inv* all-purpose

passeport [pɑspɔʀ] *nm* passport

passer [pɑse] /1/ *vi* (*se rendre, aller*) to go to; (*voiture, piétons: défiler*) to pass (by), go by; (*facteur, laitier etc*) to come, call; (*pour rendre visite*) to call ou drop in on; (*film, émission*) to be on; (*temps, jours*) to go by, pass; (*couleur, papier*) to fade; (*mode*) to die out; (*douleur*) to pass, go away; (*Scol*): **~ dans la classe supérieure** to go up (to the next class) ▷ *vt* (*frontière, rivière etc*) to cross; (*douane*) to go through; (*examen*) to sit, take; (*visite médicale etc*) to have; (*journée, temps*) to spend; **~ qch à qn** (*sel etc*) to pass sth to sb; (*prêter*) to lend sb sth; (*lettre, message*) to pass sth on to sb; (*tolérer*) to let sb get away with sth; (*enfiler: vêtement*) to slip on; (*film, pièce*) to show, put on; (*disque*) to play, put on; (*commande*) to place; (*marché,*

accord) to agree to; **se passer** *vi* (*avoir lieu: scène, action*) to take place; (*se dérouler: entretien etc*) to go; (*arriver*) **que s'est-il passé?** what happened?; (*s'écouler: semaine etc*) to pass, go by; **se ~** to go to go ou do without; **~ par** to go through; **~ avant qch/qn** (*fig*) to come before sth/sb; **~ un coup de fil à qn** (*fam*) to give sb a ring; **laisser ~** (*air, lumière, personne*) to let through; (*occasion*) to let slip, miss; (*erreur*) to overlook; **~ à la radio/télévision** to be on the radio/on television; **~ à table** to sit down to eat; **~ au salon** to go through to ou into the sitting room; **~ son tour** to miss one's turn; **~ la seconde** (*Auto*) to change into second; **~ le balai/l'aspirateur** to sweep up/hoover; **je vous passe M. Dupont** (*je vous mets en communication avec lui*) I'm putting you through to Mr Dupont; (*je lui passe l'appareil*) here is Mr Dupont, I'll hand you over to Mr Dupont

passerelle [pɑsʀɛl] *nf* footbridge; (*de navire, avion*) gangway

passe-temps [pɑstɑ̃] *nm inv* pastime

passif, -ive [pɑsif, -iv] *adj* passive

passion [pɑsjɔ̃] *nf* passion; **passionnant, e** *adj* fascinating; **passionné, e** *adj* (*personne, tempérament*) passionate; (*description, récit*) impassioned; **être passionné de** ou **pour qch** to have a passion for sth; **passionner** /1/ *vt* (*personne*) to fascinate, grip

passoire [pɑswaʀ] *nf* sieve; (*à légumes*) colander; (*à thé*) strainer

pastèque [pɑstɛk] *nf* watermelon

pasteur [pɑstœʀ] *nm* (*protestant*) minister, pastor

pastille [pɑstij] *nf* (*à sucer*) lozenge, pastille

patate [patat] *nf* spud; **~ douce** sweet potato

patauger [patoʒe] /3/ *vi* to splash about

P

pâte [pat] *nf (à tarte)* pastry; *(à pain)* dough; *(à frire)* batter; **pâtes** *nfpl (macaroni etc)* pasta *sg;* ~ **d'amandes** almond paste, marzipan; ~ **brisée** shortcrust (BRIT) *ou* pie crust (US) pastry; ~ **à choux/feuilletée** choux/ puff *ou* flaky (BRIT) pastry; ~ **de fruits** crystallized fruit *no pl;* ~ **à modeler** modelling clay, Plasticine® (BRIT)

pâté [pate] *nm (charcuterie)* pâté; *(tache)* ink blot; *(de sable)* sandpie; ~ **(en croûte)** = meat pie; ~ **de maisons** block of houses

pâtée [pate] *nf* mash, feed

patente [patɑ̃t] *nf (Comm)* trading licence (BRIT) *ou* license (US)

paternel, le [patɛʀnɛl] *adj (amour, soins)* fatherly; *(ligne, autorité)* paternal

pâteux, -euse [patø, -øz] *adj* pasty; **avoir la bouche** *ou* **langue pâteuse** to have a furred (BRIT) *ou* coated tongue

pathétique [patetik] *adj* moving

patience [pasjɑ̃s] *nf* patience

patient, e [pasjɑ̃, -ɑ̃t] *adj, nm/f* patient; **patienter** /1/ *vi* to wait

patin [patɛ̃] *nm* skate; *(sport)* skating; ~**s (à glace)** (ice) skates; ~**s à roulettes** roller skates

patinage [patinaʒ] *nm* skating

patiner [patine] /1/ *vi* to skate; *(roue, voiture)* to spin; **se patiner** *vi (meuble, cuir)* to acquire a sheen; **patineur, -euse** *nm/f* skater; **patinoire** *nf* skating rink, (ice) rink

pâtir [patiʀ] /2/: ~ **de** *vt* to suffer because of

pâtisserie [patisʀi] *nf (boutique)* cake shop; *(à la maison)* baking *ou* cake-making, baking; **pâtisseries** *nfpl (gâteaux)* pastries; cakes; **pâtissier, -ière** *nf/f* pastrycook

patois [patwa] *nm* dialect, patois

patrie [patʀi] *nf* homeland

patrimoine [patʀimwan] *nm (culture)* heritage

○ **JOURNÉES DU PATRIMOINE**
○
○ Once a year, important public
○ buildings are opened to the public
○ for a weekend. During these
○ *Journées du Patrimoine*, there are
○ guided visits and talks based on a
○ particular theme.

patriotique [patʀijɔtik] *adj* patriotic

patron, ne [patʀɔ̃, -ɔn] *nm/f* boss; *(Rel)* patron saint ▷ *nm (Couture)* pattern; **patronat** *nm* employers *pl;* **patronner** /1/ *vt* to sponsor, support

patrouille [patʀuj] *nf* patrol

patte [pat] *nf (jambe)* leg; *(pied: de chien, chat)* paw; *(: d'oiseau)* foot

pâturage [patyʀaʒ] *nm* pasture

paume [pom] *nf* palm

paumé, e [pome] *nm/f (fam)* drop-out

paupière [popjɛʀ] *nf* eyelid

pause [poz] *nf (arrêt)* break; *(en parlant, Mus)* pause; ~ **de midi** lunch break

pauvre [povʀ] *adj* poor; **les ~s** the poor; **pauvreté** *nf (état)* poverty

pavé, e [pave] *adj (cour)* paved; *(rue)* cobbled ▷ *nm (bloc)* paving stone; cobblestone; ~ **numérique** keypad

pavillon [pavijɔ̃] *nm (de banlieue)* small (detached) house; pavilion; *(Navig)* flag

payant, e [pejɑ̃, -ɑ̃t] *adj (spectateurs etc)* paying; *(fig: entreprise)* profitable; *(effort)* which pays off; **c'est ~** you have to pay, there is a charge

paye [pɛj] *nf* pay, wages *pl*

payer [peje] /8/ *vt (créancier, employé, loyer)* to pay; *(achat, réparations, faute)* to pay for ▷ *vi (achat)* to pay; *(métier)* to be well-paid; *(effort, tactique etc)* to pay off; **il me l'a fait ~ 10 euros** he charged me 10 euros for it; ~ **qch à qn** to buy sth for sb, buy sb sth; **se ~ la tête de qn** to take the mickey out of sb (BRIT)

pays [pei] nm country; (région) region; **du ~** local

paysage [peiza3] nm landscape

paysan, ne [peizɑ̃, -an] nm/f farmer; (péj) peasant ▷ adj (rural) country cpd; (agricole) farming

Pays-Bas [peiba] nmpl: **les ~** the Netherlands

PC sigle m (Inform: = personal computer) PC; = **permis de construire**; (= **prêt conventionné**) type of loan for house purchase

PDA sigle m (= personal digital assistant) PDA

PDG sigle m = **président directeur général**

péage [pea3] nm toll; (endroit) tollgate

peau, x [po] nf skin; **gants de ~** leather gloves; **être bien/mal dans sa ~** to be at ease/ill-at-ease; **~ de chamois** (chiffon) chamois leather, shammy

péché [peʃe] nm sin

pêche [pɛʃ] nf (sport, activité) fishing; (poissons pêchés) catch; (fruit) peach; **~ à la ligne** (en rivière) angling

pécher [peʃe] /6/ vi (Rel) to sin

pêcher [peʃe] /1/ vi to go fishing ▷ vt (attraper) to catch; (chercher) to fish for ▷ nm peach tree

pécheur, -eresse [peʃœʀ, peʃʀɛs] nm/f sinner

pêcheur [peʃœʀ] nm voir **pêcher** fisherman; (à la ligne) angler

pédagogie [pedagoʒi] nf educational methods pl, pedagogy; **pédagogique** adj educational

pédale [pedal] nf pedal

pédalo [pedalo] nm pedal-boat

pédant, e [pedɑ̃, -ɑ̃t] adj (péj) pedantic ▷ nm/f pedant

pédestre [pedɛstʀ] adj: **randonnée ~** ramble; **sentier ~** pedestrian footpath

pédiatre [pedjatʀ] nm/f paediatrician, child specialist

pédicure [pedikyʀ] nm/f chiropodist

pègre [pɛgʀ] nf underworld

peigne [pɛɲ] nm comb; **peigner** /1/ vt to comb (the hair of); **se peigner** vi to comb one's hair; **peignoir** nm dressing gown; **peignoir de bain** bathrobe

peindre [pɛ̃dʀ] /52/ vt to paint; (fig) to portray, depict

peine [pɛn] nf (affliction) sorrow, sadness no pl; (mal, effort) trouble no pl, effort; (difficulté) difficulty; (jur) sentence; **faire de la ~ à qn** to distress ou upset sb; **prendre la ~ de faire** to go to the trouble of doing; **se donner de la ~** to make an effort; **ce n'est pas la ~ de faire** there's no point in doing, it's not worth doing; **avoir de la ~ à faire** to struggle; **à ~** scarcely, barely; **à ~ ... que** hardly ... than, no sooner ... than; **~ capitale** capital punishment; **~ de mort** death sentence ou penalty; **peiner** [pɛne] /1/ vi to work hard; to struggle; (moteur, voiture) to labour (BRIT), labor (us) ▷ vt to grieve, sadden

peintre [pɛ̃tʀ] nm painter; **~ en bâtiment** painter and decorator

peinture [pɛ̃tyʀ] nf painting; (couche de peinture, couleur) paint; (surfaces peintes: aussi: **~s**) paintwork; **"~ fraîche"** "wet paint"

péjoratif, -ive [peʒɔʀatif, -iv] adj pejorative, derogatory

Pékin [pekɛ̃] n Beijing

pêle-mêle [pɛlmɛl] adv higgledy-piggledy

peler [pəle] /5/ vt, vi to peel

pèlerin [pɛlʀɛ̃] nm pilgrim

pèlerinage [pɛlʀinaʒ] nm pilgrimage

pelle [pɛl] nf shovel; (d'enfant, de terrassier) spade

pellicule [pelikyl] nf film; **pellicules** nfpl (Méd) dandruff sg

pelote [pəlɔt] nf (de fil, laine) ball; **~ basque** pelota

peloton [pəlɔtɔ̃] nm group; squad; (Sport) pack

pelotonner [pəlɔtɔne] /1/: **se pelotonner** vi to curl (o.s.) up

pelouse [pəluz] nf lawn

peluche [pəlyʃ] nf: **animal en ~** soft toy, fluffy animal; **chien/lapin en ~** fluffy dog/rabbit

pelure [pəlyr] nf peeling, peel no pl

pénal, e, -aux [penal, -o] adj penal; **pénalité** nf penalty

penchant [pɑ̃ʃɑ̃] nm: **un ~ à faire/à qch** a tendency to do/to sth; **un ~ pour qch** a liking or fondness for sth

pencher [pɑ̃ʃe] /1/ vi to tilt, lean over ▷ vt to tilt; **se pencher** vi to lean over; (se baisser) to bend down; **se ~ sur** (fig: problème) to look into; **~ pour** to be inclined to favour (BRIT) ou favor (US)

pendant, e [pɑ̃dɑ̃, -ɑ̃t] adj hanging (out) ▷ prép (au cours de) during; (indiquant la durée) for; **~ que** while

pendentif [pɑ̃dɑ̃tif] nm pendant

penderie [pɑ̃dri] nf wardrobe

pendre [pɑ̃dr] /41/ vt, vi to hang; **se ~ (à)** (se suicider) to hang o.s. (on); **~ qch à** (mur) to hang sth (up) on; (plafond) to hang sth (up) from

pendule [pɑ̃dyl] nf clock ▷ nm pendulum

pénétrer [penetre] /6/ vi to come ou get in ▷ vt to penetrate; **~ dans** to enter

pénible [penibl] adj (astreignant) hard; (affligeant) painful; (personne, caractère) tiresome; **péniblement** adv with difficulty

péniche [peniʃ] nf barge

pénicilline [penisilin] nf penicillin

péninsule [penɛ̃syl] nf peninsula

pénis [penis] nm penis

pénitence [penitɑ̃s] nf (repentir) penitence; (peine) penance; **pénitencier** nm penitentiary (US)

pénombre [penɔ̃br] nf (faible clarté) half-light; (obscurité) darkness

pensée [pɑ̃se] nf thought; (démarche, doctrine) thinking no pl; (Bot) pansy; **en ~** in one's mind

penser [pɑ̃se] /1/ vi to think ▷ vt to think; **~ à** (prévoir) to think of; (ami,

vacances) to think of ou about; **~ faire qch** to be thinking of doing sth, intend to do sth; **faire ~ à** to remind one of; **pensif, -ive** adj pensive, thoughtful

pension [pɑ̃sjɔ̃] nf (allocation) pension; (prix du logement) board and lodging, bed and board; (école) boarding school; **~ alimentaire** (de divorcée) maintenance allowance; alimony; **~ complète** full board; **~ de famille** boarding house, guesthouse; **pensionnaire** nm/f (Scol) boarder; **pensionnat** nm boarding school

pente [pɑ̃t] nf slope; **en ~** sloping

Pentecôte [pɑ̃tkot] nf: **la ~** Whitsun (BRIT), Pentecost

pénurie [penyri] nf shortage

pépé [pepe] nm (fam) grandad

pépin [pepɛ̃] nm (Bot: graine) pip; (fam: ennui) snag, hitch

pépinière [pepinjɛr] nf nursery

perçant, e [pɛrsɑ̃, -ɑ̃t] adj (vue, regard, yeux) sharp; (cri, voix) piercing, shrill

perce-neige [pɛrsənɛʒ] nm ou f inv snowdrop

percepteur, -trice [pɛrsɛptœr, -tris] nm/f tax collector

perception [pɛrsɛpsjɔ̃] nf perception; (bureau) tax (collector's) office

percer [pɛrse] /3/ vt to pierce; (ouverture etc) to make; (mystère, énigme) to penetrate ▷ vi to break through; **perceuse** nf drill

percevoir [pɛrsəvwar] /28/ vt (distinguer) to perceive, detect; (taxe, impôt) to collect; (revenu, indemnité) to receive

perche [pɛrʃ] nf (bâton) pole

percher [pɛrʃe] /1/ vt to perch; **se percher** vi to perch; **perchoir** nm perch

perçois etc [pɛrswa] vb voir **percevoir**

perçu, e [pɛrsy] pp de **percevoir**

percussion [pɛrkysjɔ̃] nf percussion

oculiste [ɔkylist] *nm/f* eye specialist
odeur [ɔdœʀ] *nf* smell
odieux, -euse [ɔdjø, -øz] *adj* hateful
odorant, e [ɔdɔʀɑ̃, -ɑ̃t] *adj* sweet-smelling, fragrant
odorat [ɔdɔʀa] *nm* (sense of) smell
œil [œj] (*pl* **yeux**) *nm* eye; **avoir un ~ poché** *ou* **au beurre noir** to have a black eye; **à l'~** (*fam*) for free; **à l'~ nu** with the naked eye; **fermer les yeux (sur)** (*fig*) to turn a blind eye (to); **les yeux fermés** (*aussi fig*) with one's eyes shut; **ouvrir l'~** (*fig*) to keep one's eyes open *ou* an eye out
œillères [œjɛʀ] *nfpl* blinkers (BRIT), blinders (US)
œillet [œjɛ] *nm* (*Bot*) carnation
œuf [œf] *nm* egg; **~ à la coque/dur/mollet** boiled/hard-boiled/soft-boiled egg; **~ au plat/poché** fried/poached egg; **~s brouillés** scrambled eggs; **~ de Pâques** Easter egg
œuvre [œvʀ] *nf* (*tâche*) task, undertaking; (*ouvrage achevé, livre, tableau etc*) work; (*ensemble de la production artistique*) works *pl* ▷ *nm* (*Constr*): **le gros ~** the shell; **mettre en ~** (*moyens*) to make use of; **~ d'art** work of art; **~s de bienfaisance** charitable works
offense [ɔfɑ̃s] *nf* insult; **offenser** /1/ *vt* to offend, hurt; **s'offenser de** *vi* to take offence (BRIT) *ou* offense (US) at
offert, e [ɔfɛʀ, -ɛʀt] *pp de* **offrir**
office [ɔfis] *nm* (*agence*) bureau, agency; (*Rel*) service ▷ *nm ou f* (*pièce*) pantry; **faire ~ de** to act as; **d'~** automatically; **~ du tourisme** tourist office
officiel, le [ɔfisjɛl] *adj, nm/f* official
officier [ɔfisje] /7/ *nm* officer
officieux, -euse [ɔfisjø, -øz] *adj* unofficial
offrande [ɔfʀɑ̃d] *nf* offering
offre [ɔfʀ] *nf* offer; (*aux enchères*) bid; (*Admin: soumission*) tender; (*Écon*): **l'~ et la demande** supply and demand; **~ d'emploi** job advertised; **"~s d'emploi"** "situations vacant"; **~ publique d'achat (OPA)** takeover bid
offrir [ɔfʀiʀ] /18/ *vt*: **~ (à qn)** to offer (to sb); (*faire cadeau*) to give to (sb); **s'offrir**, *vt* (*vacances, voiture*) to treat o.s. to; **~ (à qn) de faire qch** to offer to do sth (for sb); **~ à boire à qn** (*chez soi*) to offer sb a drink; **je vous offre un verre** I'll buy you a drink
OGM *sigle m* (= *organisme génétiquement modifié*) GMO
oie [wa] *nf* (*Zool*) goose
oignon [ɔɲɔ̃] *nm* onion; (*de tulipe etc*) bulb
oiseau, x [wazo] *nm* bird; **~ de proie** bird of prey
oisif, -ive [wazif, -iv] *adj* idle
oléoduc [ɔleɔdyk] *nm* (oil) pipeline
olive [ɔliv] *nf* (*Bot*) olive; **olivier** *nm* olive (tree)
OLP *sigle f* (= *Organisation de libération de la Palestine*) PLO
olympique [ɔlɛ̃pik] *adj* Olympic
ombragé, e [ɔ̃bʀaʒe] *adj* shaded, shady
ombre [ɔ̃bʀ] *nf* (*espace non ensoleillé*) shade; (*ombre portée, tache*) shadow; **à l'~** in the shade; **dans l'~** (*fig*) in the dark; **~ à paupières** eye shadow
omelette [ɔmlɛt] *nf* omelette; **~ norvégienne** baked Alaska
omettre [ɔmɛtʀ] /56/ *vt* to omit, leave out
omoplate [ɔmɔplat] *nf* shoulder blade

MOT-CLÉ

on [ɔ̃] *pron* **1** (*indéterminé*) you, one; **on peut le faire ainsi** you *ou* one can do it like this, it can be done like this
2 (*quelqu'un*): **on les a attaqués** they were attacked; **on vous demande au téléphone** there's a phone call for you, you're wanted on the phone
3 (*nous*) we; **on va y aller demain** we're going tomorrow

4 (*les gens*) they; **autrefois, on croyait …** they used to believe ..
5: **on ne peut plus** *adv*: **on ne peut plus stupide** as stupid as can be

oncle [ɔ̃kl] *nm* uncle

onctueux, -euse [ɔ̃ktɥø, -øz] *adj* creamy; smooth

onde [ɔ̃d] *nf* wave; **~s courtes (OC)** short wave *sg*; **~s moyennes (OM)** medium wave *sg*; **grandes ~s (GO), ~s longues (OL)** long wave *sg*

ondée [ɔ̃de] *nf* shower

on-dit [ɔ̃di] *nm inv* rumour

onduler [ɔ̃dyle] /1/ *vi* to undulate; (*cheveux*) to wave

onéreux, -euse [ɔnerø, -øz] *adj* costly

ongle [ɔ̃gl] *nm* nail

ont [ɔ̃] *vb voir* **avoir**

ONU *sigle f* (= *Organisation des Nations unies*) UN(O)

onze [ɔ̃z] *num* eleven; **onzième** *num* eleventh

OPA *sigle f* = **offre publique d'achat**

opaque [ɔpak] *adj* opaque

opéra [ɔpera] *nm* opera; (*édifice*) opera house

opérateur, -trice [ɔperatœr, -tris] *nm/f* operator; **~ (de prise de vues)** cameraman

opération [ɔperasjɔ̃] *nf* operation; (*Comm*) dealing

opératoire [ɔperatwar] *adj* (*choc etc*) post-operative

opérer [ɔpere] /6/ *vt* (*Méd*) to operate on; (*faire, exécuter*) to carry out, make ▷ *vi* (*remède: faire effet*) to act, work; (*Méd*) to operate; **s'opérer** *vi* (*avoir lieu*) to occur, take place; **se faire ~** to have an operation

opérette [ɔperet] *nf* operetta, light opera

opinion [ɔpinjɔ̃] *nf* opinion; **l'~ (publique)** public opinion

opportun, e [ɔpɔrtœ̃, -yn] *adj* timely, opportune; **opportuniste** [ɔpɔrtynist] *nm/f* opportunist

opposant, e [ɔpozɑ̃, -ɑ̃t] *nm/f* opponent

opposé, e [ɔpoze] *adj* (*direction, rive*) opposite; (*faction*) opposing; (*opinions, intérêts*) conflicting; (*contre*): **~ à** opposed to, against ▷ *nm*: **l'~** the other *ou* opposite side (*ou* direction); (*contraire*) the opposite; **à l'~** (*fig*) on the other hand; **à l'~ de** (*fig*) contrary to, unlike

opposer [ɔpoze] /1/ *vt* (*personnes, armées, équipes*) to oppose; (*couleurs, termes, tons*) to contrast; **~ qch à** (*comme obstacle, défense*) to set sth against; (*comme objection*) to put sth forward against; **s'opposer** *vi* (*équipes*) to confront each other; (*opinions*) to conflict; (*couleurs, styles*) to contrast; **s'~ à** (*interdire, empêcher*) to oppose

opposition [ɔpozisjɔ̃] *nf* opposition; **par ~ à** as opposed to; **entrer en ~ avec** to come into conflict with; **faire ~ à un chèque** to stop a cheque

oppressant, e [ɔpresɑ̃, -ɑ̃t] *adj* oppressive

oppresser [ɔprese] /1/ *vt* to oppress; **oppression** *nf* oppression

opprimer [ɔprime] /1/ *vt* to oppress

opter [ɔpte] /1/ *vi*: **~ pour** to opt for; **~ entre** to choose between

opticien, ne [ɔptisjɛ̃, -ɛn] *nm/f* optician

optimisme [ɔptimism] *nm* optimism; **optimiste** [ɔptimist] *adj* optimistic ▷ *nm/f* optimist

option [ɔpsjɔ̃] *nf* option; **matière à ~** (*Scol*) optional subject

optique [ɔptik] *adj* (*nerf*) optic; (*verres*) optical ▷ *nf* (*fig: manière de voir*) perspective

or [ɔr] *nm* gold ▷ *conj* now, but; **en** *ou* **or** *cpd*; **une affaire en or** a real bargain; **il croyait gagner or il a perdu** he was sure he would win and yet he lost

orage [ɔraʒ] *nm* (thunder)storm; **orageux, -euse** *adj* stormy

oral, e, -aux [ɔʀal, -o] *adj* oral; (*Méd*): **par voie ~e** orally, ▷ *nm* oral

orange [ɔʀɑ̃ʒ] *adj inv*, *nf* orange; **orangé, e** *adj* orange, orange-coloured; **orangeade** *nf* orangeade; **oranger** *nm* orange tree

orateur [ɔʀatœʀ] *nm* speaker

orbite [ɔʀbit] *nf* (*Anat*) (eye-)socket; (*Physique*) orbit

Orcades [ɔʀkad] *nfpl*: **les ~** the Orkneys, the Orkney Islands

orchestre [ɔʀkɛstʀ] *nm* orchestra; (*de jazz, danse*) band; (*places*) stalls *pl* (*BRIT*), orchestra (*US*)

orchidée [ɔʀkide] *nf* orchid

ordinaire [ɔʀdinɛʀ] *adj* ordinary; (*modèle, qualité*) standard; (*péj: commun*) common ▷ *nm* ordinary; (*menus*) everyday fare ▷ *nf* (*essence*) ≈ two-star (petrol) (*BRIT*), ≈ regular (gas) (*US*); **d'~** usually, normally; **comme à l'~** as usual

ordinateur [ɔʀdinatœʀ] *nm* computer; **~ individuel** *ou* **personnel** personal computer; **~ portable** laptop computer

ordonnance [ɔʀdɔnɑ̃s] *nf* (*Méd*) prescription; (*Mil*) orderly, batman (*BRIT*)

ordonné, e [ɔʀdɔne] *adj* tidy, orderly

ordonner [ɔʀdɔne] /1/ *vt* (*agencer*) to organize, arrange; (*donner un ordre*): **~ à qn de faire** to order sb to do; (*Rel*) to ordain; (*Méd*) to prescribe

ordre [ɔʀdʀ] *nm* order; (*propreté et soin*) orderliness, tidiness; **à l'~ de** payable to; (*nature*): **d'~ pratique** of a practical nature; **ordres** *nmpl* (*Rel*) holy orders; **mettre en ~** to tidy (up), put in order; **par ~ alphabétique/d'importance** in alphabetical order/in order of importance; **être aux ~s de qn/sous les ~s de qn** to be at sb's disposal/under sb's command; **jusqu'à nouvel ~** until further notice; **de premier ~** first-rate; **~ du jour** (*d'une réunion*) agenda; **à l'~ du jour** (*fig*) topical; **~ public** law and order

ordure [ɔʀdyʀ] *nf* filth *no pl*; **ordures** *nfpl* (*balayures, déchets*) rubbish *sg*, refuse *sg*; **~s ménagères** household refuse

oreille [ɔʀɛj] *nf* ear; **avoir de l'~** to have a good ear (for music)

oreiller [ɔʀeje] *nm* pillow

oreillons [ɔʀejɔ̃] *nm* mumps *sg*

ores [ɔʀ]: **d'~ et déjà** *adv* already

orfèvrerie [ɔʀfɛvʀəʀi] *nf* goldsmith's (*ou* silversmith's) trade; (*ouvrage*) (silver *ou* gold) plate

organe [ɔʀgan] *nm* organ; (*porte-parole*) representative, mouthpiece

organigramme [ɔʀganigʀam] *nm* (*hiérarchique, structure*) organization chart; (*des opérations*) flow chart

organique [ɔʀganik] *adj* organic

organisateur, -trice [ɔʀganizatœʀ, -tʀis] *nm/f* organizer

organisation [ɔʀganizasjɔ̃] *nf* organization; **O~ des Nations unies (ONU)** United Nations (Organization) UN(O))

organiser [ɔʀganize] /1/ *vt* to organize; (*mettre sur pied: service etc*) to set up; **s'organiser** to get organized

organisme [ɔʀganism] *nm* (*Bio*) organism; (*corps humain*) body; (*Admin, Pol etc*) body

organiste [ɔʀganist] *nm/f* organist

orgasme [ɔʀgasm] *nm* orgasm, climax

orge [ɔʀʒ] *nf* barley

orgue [ɔʀg] *nm* organ

orgueil [ɔʀgœj] *nm* pride; **orgueilleux, -euse** *adj* proud

oriental, e, -aux [ɔʀjɑ̃tal, -o] *adj* (*langue, produit*) oriental; (*frontière*) eastern

orientation [ɔʀjɑ̃tasjɔ̃] *nf* (*de recherches*) orientation; (*d'une maison etc*) aspect; (*d'un journal*) leanings *pl*; **avoir le sens de l'~** to have a (good) sense of direction; **~ professionnelle** careers advisory service

orienté, e [ɔʀjɑ̃te] *adj* (*fig: article, journal*) slanted; **bien/mal ~**

(*appartement*) well/badly positioned; **~ au sud** facing south, with a southern aspect

orienter [ɔʀjɑ̃te] /1/ vt (*tourner: antenne*) to direct, turn; (: *voyageur, touriste, recherches*) to direct; (*fig: élève*) to orientate; **s'orienter** (*se repérer*) to find one's bearings; **s'~ vers** (*fig*) to turn towards

origan [ɔʀiɡɑ̃] nm oregano

originaire [ɔʀiʒinɛʀ] adj: **être ~ de** to be a native of

original, e, -aux [ɔʀiʒinal, -o] adj original; (*bizarre*) eccentric ▷ nm/f eccentric ▷ nm (*document etc, Art*) original

origine [ɔʀiʒin] nf origin; **origines** nfpl (*d'une personne*) origins; **d'~** (*pays*) of origin; (*pneus etc*) original; **d'~ française** of French origin; **à l'~** originally; **originel, le** adj original

orme [ɔʀm] nm elm

ornement [ɔʀnəmɑ̃] nm ornament

orner [ɔʀne] /1/ vt to decorate, adorn

ornière [ɔʀnjɛʀ] nf rut

orphelin, e [ɔʀfəlɛ̃, -in] adj orphan(ed) ▷ nm/f orphan; **~ de père/mère** fatherless/motherless; **orphelinat** nm orphanage

orteil [ɔʀtɛj] nm toe; **gros ~** big toe

orthographe [ɔʀtɔɡʀaf] nf spelling

ortie [ɔʀti] nf (*stinging*) nettle

os [ɔs] nm bone; **os à moelle** marrowbone

osciller [ɔsile] /1/ vi (*au vent etc*) to rock; (*fig*): **~ entre** to waver ou fluctuate between

osé, e [oze] adj daring, bold

oseille [ozɛj] nf sorrel

oser [oze] /1/ vi, vt to dare; **~ faire** to dare (to) do

osier [ozje] nm willow; **d'~, en ~** wicker(work) cpd

osseux, -euse [ɔsø, -øz] adj bony; (*tissu, maladie, greffe*) bone cpd

otage [ɔtaʒ] nm hostage; **prendre qn comme ~** to take sb hostage

OTAN sigle f (= *Organisation du traité de l'Atlantique Nord*) NATO

otarie [ɔtaʀi] nf sea-lion

ôter [ote] /1/ vt to remove; (*soustraire*) to take away; **~ qch à qn** to take sth (away) from sb; **~ qch de** to remove sth from

otite [ɔtit] nf ear infection

ou [u] conj or; **ou ... ou** either ... or; **ou bien** or (else)

MOT-CLÉ

où [u] pron relatif **1** (*position, situation*) where, that (*souvent omis*); **la chambre où il était** the room (that) he was in, the room where he was; **la ville où je l'ai rencontré** the town where I met him; **la pièce d'où il est sorti** the room he came out of; **le village d'où je viens** the village I come from; **les villes par où il est passé** the towns he went through **2** (*temps, état*) that (*souvent omis*); **le jour où il est parti** the day (that) he left; **au prix où c'est** at the price it is
▷ adv **1** (*interrogation*) where; **où est-il/va-t-il?** where is he/is he going?; **par où?** which way?; **d'où vient que ...?** how come ...?
2 (*position*) where; **je sais où il est** I know where he is; **où que l'on aille** wherever you go

ouate [wat] nf cotton wool (BRIT), cotton (US)

oubli [ubli] nm (*acte*): **l'~ de** forgetting; (*trou de mémoire*) lapse of memory; (*négligence*) omission, oversight; **tomber dans l'~** to sink into oblivion

oublier [ublije] /7/ vt to forget; (*ne pas voir: erreurs etc*) to miss; (*laisser quelque part: chapeau etc*) to leave behind

ouest [wɛst] nm west ▷ adj inv west; (*région*) western; **à l'~** in the west; (*direction*) (to the) west, westwards; **à l'~ de** (to the) west of

ouf [uf] *excl* phew!

oui [wi] *adv* yes

ouï-dire ['widiʀ]: **par ~** *adv* by hearsay

ouïe [wi] *nf* hearing; **ouïes** *nfpl* (*de poisson*) gills

ouragan [uʀagɑ̃] *nm* hurricane

ourlet [uʀlɛ] *nm* hem

ours [uʀs] *nm* bear; **~ brun/blanc** brown/polar bear; **~ (en peluche)** teddy (bear)

oursin [uʀsɛ̃] *nm* sea urchin

ourson [uʀsɔ̃] *nm* (bear-)cub

ouste [ust] *excl* hop it!

outil [uti] *nm* tool; **outiller** /1/ *vt* to equip

outrage [utʀaʒ] *nm* insult; **~ à la pudeur** indecent behaviour *no pl*

outrance [utʀɑ̃s]: **à ~** *adv* excessively, to excess

outre [utʀ] *prép* besides ▷ *adv*: **passer ~ à** to disregard, take no notice of; **en ~** besides, moreover; **~ mesure** to excess; (*manger, boire*) immoderately; **outre-Atlantique** *adv* across the Atlantic; **outre-mer** *adv* overseas

ouvert, e [uvɛʀ, -ɛʀt] *pp de* **ouvrir** ▷ *adj* open; (*robinet, gaz etc*) on; **ouvertement** *adv* openly; **ouverture** *nf* opening; (*Mus*) overture; **ouverture d'esprit** open-mindedness; **heures d'ouverture** (*Comm*) opening hours

ouvrable [uvʀabl] *adj*: **jour ~** working day, weekday

ouvrage [uvʀaʒ] *nm* (*tâche, de tricot etc*) work *no pl*; (*texte, livre*) work

ouvre-boîte(s) [uvʀəbwat] *nm inv* tin (BRIT) ou can opener

ouvre-bouteille(s) [uvʀəbutɛj] *nm inv* bottle-opener

ouvreuse [uvʀøz] *nf* usherette

ouvrier, -ière [uvʀije, -jɛʀ] *nm/f* worker ▷ *adj* working-class; (*problèmes, conflit*) industrial; (*mouvement*) labour *cpd*; **classe ouvrière** working class

ouvrir [uvʀiʀ] /18/ *vt* (*gén*) to open; (*brèche, passage*) to open up; (*commencer l'exploitation de, créer*) to open (up); (*eau, électricité, chauffage, robinet*) to turn on; (*Méd: abcès*) to open up, cut open ▷ *vi* to open; to open up; **s'ouvrir** *vi* to open; **s'~ à qn (de qch)** to open one's heart to sb (about sth); **~ l'appétit à qn** to whet sb's appetite

ovaire [ɔvɛʀ] *nm* ovary

ovale [ɔval] *adj* oval

OVNI [ɔvni] *sigle m* (= *objet volant non identifié*) UFO

oxyder [ɔkside] /1/: **s'oxyder** *vi* to become oxidized

oxygéné, e [ɔksiʒene] *adj*: **eau ~e** hydrogen peroxide

oxygène [ɔksiʒɛn] *nm* oxygen

ozone [ozon] *nm* ozone; **trou dans la couche d'~** hole in the ozone layer

o

p

pacifique [pasifik] *adj* peaceful ▷ *nm*: **le P~**, **l'océan P~** the Pacific (Ocean)

pack [pak] *nm* pack

pacotille [pakɔtij] *nf* cheap junk *pl*

PACS *sigle m* (= *pacte civil de solidarité*) ≈ civil partnership; **pacser** /1/: **se pacser** *vi* ≈ to form a civil partnership

pacte [pakt] *nm* pact, treaty

pagaille [pagaj] *nf* mess, shambles *sg*

page [paʒ] *nf* page ▷ *nm* page (boy); **à la ~** (*fig*) up-to-date; **~ d'accueil** (*Inform*) home page; **~ Web** (*Inform*) web page

païen, ne [pajɛ̃, -ɛn] *adj, nm/f* pagan, heathen

paillasson [pajasɔ̃] *nm* doormat

paille [paj] *nf* straw

pain [pɛ̃] *nm* (*substance*) bread; (*unité*) loaf (of bread); (*morceau*): **~ de cire** *etc* bar of wax *etc*; **~ bis/complet** brown/wholemeal (*BRIT*) *ou* wholewheat (*US*) bread; **~ d'épice** ≈ gingerbread; **~ grillé** toast; **~ de mie** sandwich loaf; **~ au chocolat** pain au chocolat; **~ aux raisins** currant pastry

pair, e [pɛʀ] *adj* (*nombre*) even ▷ *nm* peer; **aller de ~ (avec)** to go hand in hand *ou* together (with); **jeune fille au ~** au pair; **paire** *nf* pair

paisible [pezibl] *adj* peaceful, quiet

paix [pɛ] *nf* peace; **faire la ~ avec** to make peace with; **fiche-lui la ~!** (*fam*) leave him alone!

Pakistan [pakistɑ̃] *nm*: **le ~** Pakistan

palais [palɛ] *nm* palace; (*Anat*) palate

pâle [pɑl] *adj* pale; **bleu ~** pale blue

Palestine [palɛstin] *nf*: **la ~** Palestine

palette [palɛt] *nf* (*de peintre*) palette; (*de produits*) range

pâleur [pɑlœʀ] *nf* paleness

palier [palje] *nm* (*d'escalier*) landing; (*fig*) level, plateau; **par ~s** in stages

pâlir [paliʀ] /2/ *vi* to turn *ou* go pale; (*couleur*) to fade

pallier [palje] /7/ *vt*: **~ à** to offset, make up for

palme [palm] *nf* (*de plongeur*) flipper; **palmé, e** [palme] *adj* (*pattes*) webbed

palmier [palmje] *nm* palm tree; (*gâteau*) heart-shaped biscuit made of flaky pastry

pâlot, te [pɑlo, -ɔt] *adj* pale, peaky

palourde [paluʀd] *nf* clam

palper [palpe] /1/ *vt* to feel, finger

palpitant, e [palpitɑ̃, -ɑ̃t] *adj* thrilling

palpiter [palpite] /1/ *vi* (*cœur, pouls*) to beat; (*plus fort*) to pound, throb

paludisme [palydism] *nm* malaria

pamphlet [pɑ̃flɛ] *nm* lampoon, satirical tract

pamplemousse [pɑ̃pləmus] *nm* grapefruit

pan [pɑ̃] *nm* section, piece ▷ *excl* bang!

panache [panaʃ] *nm* plume; (*fig*) spirit, panache

panaché, e [panaʃe] *adj* (*bière*) shandy; **glace ~e** mixed ice cream

pancarte [pɑ̃kaʀt] nf sign, notice

pancréas [pɑ̃kʀeas] nm pancreas

pandémie [pɑ̃demi] nf pandemic

pané, e [pane] adj fried in breadcrumbs

panier [panje] nm basket; **mettre au ~** to chuck away; **~ à provisions** shopping basket; **panier-repas** nm packed lunch

panique [panik] adj panicky ▷ nf panic; **paniquer** /1/ vi to panic

panne [pan] nf breakdown; **être/tomber en ~** to have broken down/break down; **être en ~ d'essence** ou **en ~ sèche** to have run out of petrol (BRIT) ou gas (US); **~ d'électricité** ou **de courant** power ou electrical failure

panneau, x [pano] nm (écriteau) sign, notice; **~ d'affichage** notice (BRIT) ou bulletin (US) board; **~ indicateur** signpost; **~ de signalisation** roadsign

panoplie [panɔpli] nf (jouet) outfit; (d'armes) display; (fig) array

panorama [panɔʀama] nm panorama

panse [pɑ̃s] nf paunch

pansement [pɑ̃smɑ̃] nm dressing, bandage; **~ adhésif** sticking plaster

pantacourt [pɑ̃takuʀ] nm cropped trousers pl

pantalon [pɑ̃talɔ̃] nm trousers pl (BRIT), pants pl (US), pair of trousers ou pants; **~ de ski** ski pants pl

panthère [pɑ̃tɛʀ] nf panther

pantin [pɑ̃tɛ̃] nm puppet

pantoufle [pɑ̃tufl] nf slipper

paon [pɑ̃] nm peacock

papa [papa] nm dad(dy)

pape [pap] nm pope

paperasse [papʀas] nf (péj) bumf no pl, papers pl; **paperasserie** nf (péj) red tape no pl; paperwork no pl

papeterie [papɛtʀi] nf (magasin) stationer's (shop) (BRIT)

papi [papi] nm (fam) granddad

papier [papje] nm paper; (article) article; **papiers** nmpl (aussi: **~s**

d'identité) (identity) papers; **~ (d') aluminium** aluminium (BRIT) ou aluminum (US) foil, tinfoil; **~ calque** tracing paper; **~ hygiénique** ou **(de) toilette** toilet paper; **~ journal** newspaper; **~ à lettres** writing paper, notepaper; **~ peint** wallpaper; **~ de verre** sandpaper

papillon [papijɔ̃] nm butterfly; (fam: contravention) (parking) ticket; **~ de nuit** moth

papillote [papijɔt] nf: **en ~** cooked in tinfoil

papoter [papɔte] /1/ vi to chatter

paquebot [pakbo] nm liner

pâquerette [pakʀɛt] nf daisy

Pâques [pak] nm, nfpl Easter

◦ **PÂQUES**
◦
◦ In France, Easter eggs are said to
◦ be brought by the Easter bells or
◦ cloches de Pâques which fly from
◦ Rome and drop them in people's
◦ gardens.

paquet [pakɛ] nm packet; (colis) parcel; (fig: tas) ~ **de** pile ou heap of; **paquet-cadeau** nm gift-wrapped parcel

par [paʀ] prép by; **finir** etc ~ to end etc with; ~ **amour** out of love; **passer** ~ **Lyon/la côte** to go via ou through Lyons/along by the coast; ~ **la fenêtre** (jeter, regarder) out of the window; **trois** ~ **jour/personne** three a ou per day/head; **deux** ~ **deux** in twos; ~ **ici** this way; (dans le coin) round here; ~**-ci, par**~**-là** here and there; ~ **temps de pluie** in wet weather

parabolique [paʀabɔlik] adj: **antenne** ~ satellite dish

parachute [paʀaʃyt] nm parachute; **parachutiste** [paʀaʃytist] nm/f parachutist; (Mil) paratrooper

parade [paʀad] nf (spectacle, défilé) parade; (Escrime, Boxe) parry

paradis [paradi] nm heaven, paradise
paradoxe [paradɔks] nm paradox
paraffine [parafin] nf paraffin
parages [paraʒ] nmpl: **dans les ~ (de)** in the area ou vicinity (of)
paragraphe [paragraf] nm paragraph
paraître [paretr] /57/ vb copule to seem, look, appear ▷ vi to appear; (être visible) to show; (Presse, Édition) to be published, come out, appear ▷ vb impers: **il paraît que** it seems ou appears that
parallèle [paralel] adj parallel; (police, marché) unofficial ▷ nm (comparaison): **faire un ~ entre** to draw a parallel between ▷ nf parallel (line)
paralyser [paralize] /1/ vt to paralyze
paramédical, e, -aux [paramedikal, -o] adj: **personnel ~** paramedics pl, paramedical workers pl
paraphrase [parafraz] nf paraphrase
parapluie [paraplyi] nm umbrella
parasite [parazit] nm parasite; **parasites** nmpl (Tél) interference sg
parasol [parasɔl] nm parasol, sunshade
paratonnerre [paratɔnɛr] nm lightning conductor
parc [park] nm (public) park, gardens pl; (de château etc) grounds pl; (d'enfant) playpen; **~ d'attractions** amusement park; **~ éolien** wind farm; **~ de stationnement** car park; **~ à thème** theme park
parcelle [parsel] nf fragment, scrap; (de terrain) plot, parcel
parce que [parskə] conj because
parchemin [parʃəmɛ̃] nm parchment
parc(o)mètre [park(o)mɛtr] nm parking meter
parcourir [parkurir] /11/ vt (trajet, distance) to cover; (article, livre) to skim ou glance through; (lieu) to go

all over, travel up and down; (frisson, vibration) to run through
parcours [parkur] nm (trajet) journey; (itinéraire) route
par-dessous [pardəsu] prép, adv under(neath)
pardessus [pardəsy] nm overcoat
par-dessus [pardəsy] prép over (the top of) ▷ adv over (the top); **~ le marché** on top of it all; **~ tout** above all; **en avoir ~ la tête** to have had enough
par-devant [pardəvɑ̃] adv (passer) round the front
pardon [pardɔ̃] nm forgiveness no pl ▷ excl (I'm) sorry; (pour interpeller etc) excuse me; **demander ~ à qn (de)** to apologize to sb (for); **je vous demande ~** I'm sorry; (pour interpeller) excuse me; **pardonner** /1/ vt to forgive; **pardonner qch à qn** to forgive sb for sth
pare: **pare-brise** nm inv windscreen (BRIT), windshield (US); **pare-chocs** nm inv bumper; **pare-feu** nm inv (de foyer) fireguard; (Inform) firewall ▷ adj inv
pareil, le [parɛj] adj (identique) the same, alike; (similaire) similar; (tel): **un courage/livre ~** such courage/a book, courage/a book like this; **de ~s livres** such books; **faire ~** to do the same (thing); **~ à** the same as; similar to; **sans ~** unparalleled, unequal
parent, e [parɑ̃, -ɑ̃t] nm/f: **un/une ~/e** a relative ou relation; **parents** nmpl (père et mère) parents; **parenté** nf (lien) relationship
parenthèse [parɑ̃tɛz] nf (ponctuation) bracket, parenthesis; (digression) parenthesis, digression; **entre ~s** in brackets; (fig) incidentally
paresse [parɛs] nf laziness; **paresseux, -euse** adj lazy
parfait, e [parfɛ, -ɛt] adj perfect ▷ nm (Ling) perfect (tense); **parfaitement** adv perfectly ▷ excl (most) certainly

parfois [paʀfwa] adv sometimes
parfum [paʀfœ̃] nm (produit) perfume, scent; (odeur: de fleur) scent, fragrance; (goût) flavour; **parfumé, e** adj (fleur, fruit) fragrant; (femme) perfumed; **parfumé au café** coffee-flavoured (BRIT) ou -flavored (US)
parfumer /1/ vt (odeur, bouquet) to perfume; (crème, gâteau) to flavour; **parfumerie** nf (produits) perfumes; (boutique) perfume shop (BRIT) ou store (US)
pari [paʀi] nm bet; **parier** /7/ vt to bet
Paris [paʀi] n Paris; **parisien, ne** adj Parisian; (Géo, Admin) Paris cpd
▷ nm/f: **Parisien, ne** Parisian
parité [paʀite] nf: ~ **hommes-femmes** (Pol) balanced representation of men and women
parjure [paʀʒyʀ] nm perjury
parking [paʀkiŋ] nm (lieu) car park (BRIT), parking lot (US)

> Attention à ne pas traduire *parking* par le mot anglais *parking*.

parlant, e [paʀlɑ̃, -ɑ̃t] adj (comparaison, preuve) eloquent; (Ciné) talking
parlement [paʀləmɑ̃] nm parliament; **parlementaire** adj parliamentary ▷ nm/f ≈ Member of Parliament (BRIT) ou Congress (US)
parler [paʀle] /1/ vi to speak, talk; (avouer) to speak (to sb) about; **~ (à qn) de** to talk ou speak (to sb) about; **~ le/en français** to speak French/in French; **~ affaires** to talk business; **sans ~ de** (fig) not to mention, to say nothing of; **tu parles!** (bien sûr) you bet!
parloir [paʀlwaʀ] nm (d'une prison, d'un hôpital) visiting room
parmi [paʀmi] prép among(st)
paroi [paʀwa] nf wall; (cloison) partition
paroisse [paʀwas] nf parish
parole [paʀɔl] nf (mot, promesse) word; (faculté): **la ~** speech; **paroles** nfpl (Mus) words, lyrics; **tenir ~** to

keep one's word; **prendre la ~** to speak; **demander la ~** to ask for permission to speak; **je le crois sur ~** I'll take his word for it
parquet [paʀkɛ] nm (parquet) floor; (Jur) public prosecutor's office; **le ~ (général)** ≈ the Bench
parrain [paʀɛ̃] nm godfather; **parrainer** /1/ vt (nouvel adhérent) to sponsor
pars [paʀ] vb voir **partir**
parsemer [paʀsəme] /5/ vt (feuilles, papiers) to be scattered over; **~ qch de** to scatter sth with
part [paʀ] nf (qui revient à qn) share; (fraction, partie) part; **prendre ~ à** (débat etc) to take part in; (soucis, douleur de qn) to share in; **faire ~ de qch à qn** to announce sth to sb, inform sb of sth; **pour ma ~** as for me, as far as I'm concerned; **à ~ entière** full; **de la ~ de** (au nom de) on behalf of; (donné par) from; **de toute(s) ~(s)** from all sides ou quarters; **de ~ et d'autre** on both sides, on either side; **d'une ~ ... d'autre ~** on the one hand ... on the other hand; **d'autre ~** (de plus) moreover; **à ~** adv separately; (de côté) aside; prép apart from, except for; **faire la ~ des choses** to make allowances
partage [paʀtaʒ] nm sharing (out) no pl, share-out; dividing up
partager [paʀtaʒe] /3/ vt to share; (distribuer, répartir) to share (out); (morceler, diviser) to divide (up); **se partager** vt (héritage etc) to share between themselves (ou ourselves etc)
partenaire [paʀtənɛʀ] nm/f partner
parterre [paʀtɛʀ] nm (de fleurs) (flower) bed; (Théât) stalls pl
parti [paʀti] nm (Pol) party; (décision) course of action; (personne à marier) match; **tirer ~ de** to take advantage of, turn to good account; **prendre ~ (pour/contre)** to take sides ou a stand (for/against); **~ pris** bias

partial, e, -aux [paʀsjal, -o] *adj*
biased, partial

participant, e [paʀtisipɑ̃, -ɑ̃t] *nm/f*
participant; (*à un concours*) entrant

participation
nf participation; (*financière*)
contribution [paʀtisipasjɔ̃]

participer [paʀtisipe] /1/: ~ **à** *vt*
(*course, réunion*) to take part in; (*frais
etc*) to contribute to; (*chagrin, succès
de qn*) to share (in)

particularité [paʀtikylaʀite] *nf*
(*distinctive*) characteristic

particulier, -ière [paʀtikylje, -jεʀ]
adj (*personnel, privé*) private; (*étrange*)
peculiar, odd; (*spécial*) special,
particular; (*spécifique*) particular ▷ *nm*
(*individu*: Admin) private individual;
~ **à** peculiar to; **en ~** (*surtout*) in
particular, particularly; (*en privé*)
in private; **particulièrement** *adv*
particularly

partie [paʀti] *nf* (*gén*) part; (*Jur etc*:
protagonistes) party; (*de cartes, tennis
etc*) game; **une ~ de campagne/de
pêche** an outing in the country/a
fishing party *ou* trip; **en ~** partly, in
part; **faire ~ de** (*chose*) to be part of;
prendre qn à ~ to take sb to task;
en grande ~ largely, in the main;
~ **civile** (*Jur*) party claiming damages in
a criminal case

partiel, le [paʀsjεl] *adj* partial ▷ *nm*
(*Scol*) class exam

partir [paʀtiʀ] /16/ *vi* (*gén*) to go;
(*quitter*) to go, leave; (*tache*) to go,
come out; ~ **de** (*lieu*) (*quitter*) to leave;
(*commencer à*) to start from; ~ **pour/à**
(*lieu, pays etc*) to leave for/go off to;
à ~ de from

partisan, e [paʀtizɑ̃, -an] *nm/f*
partisan; **être ~ de qch/faire** to
be in favour of sth/doing (*ou* want (*us*) of
sth/doing [BRIT]

partition [paʀtisjɔ̃] *nf* (*Mus*) score

partout [paʀtu] *adv* everywhere;
~ **où il allait** everywhere *ou* wherever
he went

paru [paʀy] *pp de* **paraître**

parution [paʀysjɔ̃] *nf* publication

parvenir [paʀvəniʀ] /22/: ~ **à** *vt*
(*atteindre*) to reach; (*réussir*): ~ **à
faire qch** to manage to do, succeed in doing;
faire ~ qch à qn to have sth sent to sb

MOT-CLÉ

pas¹ [pɑ] *adv* **1** (*en corrélation avec
ne, non etc*) not; **il ne pleure pas**
(*habituellement*) he does not *ou*
doesn't cry; (*maintenant*) he's not *ou*
isn't crying; **il n'a pas pleuré/ne
pleurera pas** he did not *ou* didn't/
will not *ou* won't cry; **ils n'ont pas de
voiture/d'enfants** they haven't got
a car/any children; **il m'a dit de ne
pas le faire** he told me not to do it;
non pas que ... not that ..
2 (*employé sans ne etc*): **pas moi**
not me, I don't (*ou can't etc*); **elle
travaille, (mais) lui pas** *ou* **pas lui**
she works but he doesn't *ou* does
not; **une pomme pas mûre** an
apple which isn't ripe; **pas du tout**
not at all; **pas de sucre, merci** no
sugar, thanks; **ceci est à vous *ou*
pas?** is this yours or not?, is this yours
or isn't it?
3: **pas mal** (*joli: personne, maison*) not
bad; **pas mal fait** not badly done *ou*
made; **comment ça va? — pas mal**
how are things? — not bad; **pas mal
de** quite a lot of

pas² [pɑ] *nm* (*enjambée, Danse*) step;
(*bruit*) (foot)step; (*trace*) footprint;
(*allure, mesure*) pace; ~ **à ~** step
by step; **au ~** at a walking pace;
marcher à grands ~ to stride along;
à ~ de loup stealthily; **faire les cent
~** to pace up and down; **faire les
premiers ~** to make the first move;
sur le ~ de la porte on the doorstep

passage [pɑsaʒ] *nm* (*fait de passer*);
voir **passer**; (*lieu, prix de la traversée,
extrait de livre etc*) passage; (*chemin*

way; **de ~** (touristes) passing through; **~ clouté** pedestrian crossing; **"~ interdit"** "no entry"; **~ à niveau** level (BRIT) ou grade (US) crossing; **~ souterrain** subway (BRIT), underpass

passager, -ère [pɑsaʒe, -ɛʀ] adj passing ▷ nm/f passenger

passant, e [pɑsɑ̃, -ɑ̃t] adj (rue, endroit) busy ▷ nm/f passer-by; **remarquer qch en ~** to notice sth in passing

passe [pɑs] nf (Sport) pass; (Navig) channel; **être en ~ de faire** to be on the way to doing; **être dans une mauvaise ~** to be going through a bad patch

passé, e [pɑse] adj (événement, temps) last; (dernier: semaine etc) last; (couleur, tapisserie) faded ▷ prép after ▷ nm past; (Ling) past (tense); **~ de mode** out of fashion; **~ composé** perfect (tense); **~ simple** past historic

passe-partout [pɑspaʀtu] nm inv master ou skeleton key ▷ adj inv all-purpose

passeport [pɑspɔʀ] nm passport

passer [pɑse] /1/ vi (se rendre, aller) to go; (voiture, piétons: défiler) to pass (by), go by; (facteur, laitier etc) to come, call; (pour rendre visite) to call ou pop in (film, émission) to be on; (temps, jours) to pass, go by; (couleur, papier) to fade; (mode) to die out; (douleur) to go away; (Scol): **~ dans la classe supérieure** to go up (to the next class) ▷ vt (frontière, rivière etc) to cross; (douane) to go through; (examen) to sit, take; (visite médicale etc) to have; (journée, temps) to spend; **~ qch à qn** (sel etc) to pass sth to sb; (prêter) to lend sth to sb; (lettre, message) to pass sth on to sb; (tolérer) to let sb get away with sth; (enfiler: vêtement) to slip on; (film, pièce) to show, put on; (disque) to play, put on; (commande) to place; (marché,

accord) to agree on; **se passer** vi (avoir lieu: scène, action) to take place; (se dérouler: entretien etc) to go; (arriver): **que s'est-il passé?** what happened?; (s'écouler: semaine etc) to pass, go by; **se ~ de** to go ou do without; **~ par** to go through; **~ avant qch/qn** (fig) to come before sth/sb; **un coup de fil à qn** (fam) to give sb a ring; **laisser ~** (air, lumière, personne) to let through; (occasion) to let slip, miss; (erreur) to overlook; **~ à la radio/télévision** to be on the radio/on television; **~ à table** to sit down to eat; **~ au salon** to go through to ou into the sitting room; **~ son tour** to miss one's turn; **~ la seconde** (Auto) to change into second; **~ le balai/l'aspirateur** to sweep up/hoover; **je vous passe M. Dupont** (je vous mets en communication avec lui) I'm putting you through to Mr Dupont; (je lui passe l'appareil) here is Mr Dupont, I'll hand you over to Mr Dupont

passerelle [pɑsʀɛl] nf footbridge; (de navire, avion) gangway

passe-temps [pɑstɑ̃] nm inv pastime

passif, -ive [pasif, -iv] adj passive

passion [pɑsjɔ̃] nf passion; **passionnant, e** adj fascinating; **passionné, e** adj (personne, tempérament) passionate; (description, récit) impassioned; **être passionné de** ou **pour qch** to have a passion for sth; **passionner** /1/ vt (personne) to fascinate, grip

passoire [pɑswaʀ] nf sieve; (à légumes) colander; (à thé) strainer

pastèque [pastɛk] nf watermelon

pasteur [pastœʀ] nm (protestant) minister, pastor

pastille [pɑstij] nf (à sucer) lozenge, pastille

patate [patat] nf spud; **~ douce** sweet potato

patauger [patoʒe] /3/ vi to splash about

p

pâte [pɑt] nf (à tarte) pastry; (à pain) dough; (à frire) batter; **pâtes** nfpl (macaroni etc) pasta sg; **~ d'amandes** almond paste, marzipan; **~ brisée** shortcrust (BRIT) ou pie crust (US) pastry; **~ à choux/feuilletée** choux/ puff ou flaky (BRIT) pastry; **~ de fruits** crystallized fruit no pl; **~ à modeler** modelling clay, Plasticine® (BRIT)

pâté [pɑte] nm (charcuterie) pâté; (tache) ink blot; (de sable) sandpie; **~ (en croûte)** = meat pie; **~ de maisons** block (of houses)

pâtée [pɑte] nf mash, feed

patente [pɑtɑ̃t] nf (Comm) trading licence (BRIT) ou license (US)

paternel, le [paternεl] adj (amour, soins) fatherly; (ligne, autorité) paternal

pâteux, -euse [pɑtø, -øz] adj pasty; **avoir la bouche** ou **langue pâteuse** to have a furred (BRIT) ou coated tongue

pathétique [patetik] adj moving

patience [pasjɑ̃s] nf patience

patient, e [pasjɑ̃, -ɑ̃t] adj, nm/f patient; **patienter** /1/ vi to wait

patin [patɛ̃] nm skate; (sport) skating; **~s (à glace)** (ice) skates; **~s à roulettes** roller skates

patinage [patinaʒ] nm skating

patiner [patine] /1/ vi to skate; (roue, voiture) to spin; **se patiner** vi (meuble, cuir) to acquire a sheen; **patineur, -euse** nm/f skater; **patinoire** nf skating rink, (ice) rink

pâtir [pɑtir] /2/: **~ de** vt to suffer because of

pâtisserie [pɑtisri] nf (boutique) cake shop; (à la maison) pastry- ou cake-making, baking; **pâtisseries** nfpl (gâteaux) pastries, cakes; **pâtissier, -ière** nf f pastrycook

patois [patwa] nm dialect, patois

patrie [patri] nf homeland

patrimoine [patrimwan] nm (culture) heritage

● **JOURNÉES DU PATRIMOINE**
●
● Once a year, important public
● buildings are open to the public
● for a weekend. During these
● *Journées du Patrimoine*, there are
● guided visits and talks based on a
● particular theme.

patriotique [patrijɔtik] adj patriotic

patron, ne [patrɔ̃, -ɔn] nm/f boss; (Rel) patron saint ▷ nm (Couture) pattern; **patronat** nm employers pl; **patronner** /1/ vt to sponsor, support

patrouille [patruj] nf patrol

patte [pat] nf (jambe) leg; (pied: de chien, chat) paw; (: d'oiseau) foot

pâturage [pɑtyraʒ] nm pasture

paume [pom] nf palm

paumé, e [pome] nm/f (fam) drop-out

paupière [popjɛr] nf eyelid

pause [poz] nf (arrêt) break; (en parlant, Mus) pause; **~ de midi** lunch break

pauvre [povr] adj poor; **les ~s** the poor; **pauvreté** nf (état) poverty

pavé, e [pave] adj (cour) paved; (rue) cobbled ▷ nm (bloc) paving stone; cobblestone; **~ numérique** keypad

pavillon [pavijɔ̃] nm (de banlieue) small (detached) house; pavilion; (Navig) flag

payant, e [pεjɑ̃, -ɑ̃t] adj (spectateurs etc) paying; (fig: entreprise) profitable; (effort) which pays off; **c'est ~** you have to pay, there is a charge

paye [pεj] nf pay, wages pl

payer [peje] /8/ vt (créancier, employé, loyer) to pay; (achat, réparations, faute) to pay for ▷ vi to pay; (métier) to be well-paid; (effort, tactique etc) to pay off; **il me l'a fait ~ 10 euros** he charged me 10 euros for it; **~ qch à qn** to buy sth for sb, buy sb sth; **se ~ la tête de qn** to take the mickey out of sb (BRIT)

pétrin [petʀɛ̃] nm (fig): **dans le ~** in a jam ou fix

pétrir [petʀiʀ] /2/ vt to knead

pétrole [petʀɔl] nm oil; (pour lampe, réchaud etc) paraffin; **pétrolier, -ière** nm oil tanker

⚠ Attention à ne pas traduire pétrole par le mot anglais petrol.

○ MOT-CLÉ

peu [pø] adv **1** (modifiant verbe, adjectif, adverbe): **il boit peu** he doesn't drink (very) much; **il est peu bavard** he's not very talkative; **peu avant/après** shortly before/afterwards

2 (modifiant nom): **peu de: peu de gens/d'arbres** few ou not (very) many people/trees; **il a peu d'espoir** he hasn't (got) much hope, he has little hope; **pour peu de temps** for (only) a short while

3: peu à peu little by little; **à peu près** just about, more or less; **à peu près 10 kg/10 euros** approximately 10 kg/10 euros

▸ nm **1: le peu de gens qui** the few people who; **le peu de sable qui** what little sand, the little sand which

2: un peu a little; **un petit peu** a little bit; **un peu d'espoir** a little hope; **elle est un peu bavarde** she's rather talkative; **un peu plus de** slightly more than; **un peu moins de** slightly less than; (avec pluriel) slightly fewer than

▸ pron: **peu le savent** few know (it); **de peu** (only) just

peuple [pœpl] nm people; **peupler** /1/ vt (pays, région) to populate; (étang) to stock; (hommes, poissons) to inhabit

peuplier [pøplije] nm poplar (tree)

peur [pœʀ] nf fear; **avoir ~ (de/ de faire/que)** to be frightened ou afraid (of/of doing/that); **faire ~ à** to frighten; **de ~ de/que** for fear of/

that; **peureux, -euse** adj fearful, timorous

peut [pø] vb voir **pouvoir**

peut-être [pøtɛtʀ] adv perhaps, maybe; **~ que** perhaps, maybe; **~ bien qu'il fera/est** he may well do/be

phare [faʀ] nm (en mer) lighthouse; (de véhicule) headlight

pharmacie [faʀmasi] nf (magasin) chemist's (BRIT), pharmacy; (armoire) medicine chest ou cupboard; **pharmacien, ne** nm/f pharmacist, chemist (BRIT)

phénomène [fenɔmɛn] nm phenomenon

philosophe [filozof] nm/f philosopher ▷ adj philosophical

philosophie [filozofi] nf philosophy

phobie [fɔbi] nf phobia

phoque [fɔk] nm seal

phosphorescent, e [fɔsfɔʀesɑ̃, -ɑ̃t] adj luminous

photo [foto] nf photo; **prendre en ~** to take a photo of; **aimer la/ faire de la ~** to like taking/take photos; **~ d'identité** passport photo; **photocopie** nf (photocopy); **photocopier** /7/ vt to photocopy

photocopieur [fotokɔpjœʀ] nm, **photocopieuse** [fotokɔpjøz] nf (photo)copier

photo: photographe nm/f photographer; **photographie** nf (procédé, technique) photography; (cliché) photograph; **photographier** /7/ vt to photograph

phrase [fʀɑz] nf sentence

physicien, ne [fizisjɛ̃, -ɛn] nm/f physicist

physique [fizik] adj physical ▷ nf physique ▷ nf physics sg; **au ~** physically; **physiquement** adv physically

pianiste [pjanist] nm/f pianist

piano [pjano] nm piano; **pianoter** /1/ vi to tinkle away (at the piano)

pic [pik] nm (instrument) pick(axe); (montagne) peak; (Zool) woodpecker;

à ~ vertically; (fig: tomber, arriver) just at the right time

pichet [piʃɛ] nm jug

picorer [pikɔʀe] /1/ vt to peck

pie [pi] nf magpie

pièce [pjɛs] nf (d'un logement) room; (Théât) play; (de mécanisme, machine) part; (de monnaie) coin; (document) document; (de drap, fragment, d'une collection) piece; **deux euros ~** two euros each; **vendre à la ~** to sell separately ou individually; **travailler/payer à la ~** to do piecework/pay piece rate; **un maillot une ~** a one-piece swimsuit; **un deux-~s cuisine** a two-room(ed) flat (BRIT) ou apartment (US) with kitchen; **~ à conviction** exhibit; **~ d'eau** ornamental lake ou pond; **~ d'identité: avez-vous une ~ d'identité?** have you got any (means of) identification?; **~ jointe** (Inform) attachment; **~ montée** tiered cake; **~ de rechange** spare (part); **~s détachées** spares, (spare) parts; **~s justificatives** supporting documents

pied [pje] nm foot; (de table) leg; (de lampe) base; **~s nus** barefoot; **à ~** on foot; **au ~ de la lettre** literally; **avoir ~** to be able to touch the bottom, not to be out of one's depth; **avoir le ~ marin** to be a good sailor; **sur ~** (debout, rétabli) up and about; **mettre sur ~** (entreprise) to set up; **c'est le ~!** (fam) it's brilliant!; **mettre les ~s dans le plat** (fam) to put one's foot in it; **il se débrouille comme un ~** (fam) he's completely useless; **pied-noir** nm Algerian-born Frenchman

piège [pjɛʒ] nm trap; **prendre au ~** to trap; **piéger** /3, 6/ vt (avec une bombe) to booby-trap; **lettre/voiture piégée** letter-/car-bomb

piercing [pjɛʀsiŋ] nm piercing

pierre [pjɛʀ] nf stone; **~ tombale** tombstone; **pierreries** nfpl gems, precious stones

piétiner [pjetine] /1/ vi (trépigner) to stamp (one's foot); (fig) to be at a standstill ▷ vt to trample on

piéton, ne [pjetɔ̃, -ɔn] nm/f pedestrian; **piétonnier, -ière** adj pedestrian cpd

pieu, x [pjø] nm post; (pointu) stake

pieuvre [pjœvʀ] nf octopus

pieux, -euse [pjø, -øz] adj pious

pigeon [piʒɔ̃] nm pigeon

piger [piʒe] /3/ vi (fam) to get it ▷ vt (fam) to get

pigiste [piʒist] nm/f freelance journalist (paid by the line)

pignon [piɲɔ̃] nm (de mur) gable

pile [pil] nf (tas, pileot) pile; (Élec) battery ▷ adv (net, brusquement) dead; **à deux heures ~** at two on the dot; **jouer à ~ ou face** to toss up (for it); **~ ou face?** heads or tails?

piler [pile] /1/ vt to crush, pound

pilier [pilje] nm pillar

piller [pije] /1/ vt to pillage, plunder, loot

pilote [pilɔt] nm pilot; (de char, voiture) driver ▷ adj pilot cpd; **~ de chasse/d'essai/de ligne** fighter/test/airline pilot; **~ de course** racing driver; **piloter** /1/ vt (navire) to pilot; (avion) to fly; (automobile) to drive

pilule [pilyl] nf pill; **prendre la ~** to be on the pill

piment [pimɑ̃] nm (Bot) pepper, capsicum; (fig) spice, piquancy; **~ rouge** (Culin) chilli; **pimenté, e** adj (plat) hot and spicy

pin [pɛ̃] nm pine (tree)

pinard [pinaʀ] nm (fam) (cheap) wine, plonk (BRIT)

pince [pɛ̃s] nf (d'outil) pliers pl; (de homard, crabe) pincer, claw; (Couture: pli) dart; **~ à épiler** tweezers pl; **~ à linge** clothes peg (BRIT) ou pin (US)

pincé, e [pɛ̃se] adj (air) stiff

pinceau, x [pɛ̃so] nm (paint)brush

pincer [pɛ̃se] /3/ vt to pinch; (fam) to nab

pinède [pinɛd] nf pinewood, pine forest

pingouin [pɛ̃gwɛ̃] nm penguin

ping-pong [piŋpɔ̃g] nm table tennis

pinson [pɛ̃sɔ̃] nm chaffinch

pintade [pɛ̃tad] nf guinea-fowl

pion, ne [pjɔ̃, pjɔn] nm/f (Scol: péj) student paid to supervise schoolchildren ▷ nm (Échecs) pawn; (Dames) piece

pionnier [pjɔnje] nm pioneer

pipe [pip] nf pipe; **fumer la** ou **une ~** to smoke a pipe

piquant, e [pikã, -ãt] adj (barbe, rosier etc) prickly; (saveur, sauce) hot, pungent; (fig: détail) titillating; (: mordant, caustique) biting ▷ nm (épine) thorn, prickle; (fig) spiciness, spice

pique [pik] nf pike; (fig): **envoyer** ou **lancer des ~s à qn** to make cutting remarks to sb ▷ nm (Cartes) spades pl

pique-nique [piknik] nm picnic; **pique-niquer** /1/ vi to (have a) picnic

piquer [pike] /1/ vt (percer) to prick; (Méd) to give an injection to; (: animal blessé etc) to put to sleep; (insecte, fumée, ortie) to sting; (moustique) to bite; (froid) to bite; (intérêt etc) to arouse; (fam: voler) to pinch ▷ vi (oiseau, avion) to go into a dive

piquet [pikɛ] nm (pieu) post, stake; (de tente) peg

piqûre [pikyR] nf (d'épingle) prick; (d'ortie) sting; (de moustique) bite; (Méd) injection, shot (us); **faire une ~ à qn** to give sb an injection

pirate [piRat] adj ▷ nm pirate; **~ de l'air** hijacker

pire [piR] adj worse; (superlatif): **le (la) ~ ... the worst ...** ▷ nm: **le ~ (de)** the worst (of); **au ~** at (the very) worst

pis [pi] nm (de vache) udder ▷ adj, adv worse; **de mal en ~** from bad to worse

piscine [pisin] nf (swimming) pool; **~ couverte** indoor (swimming) pool

pissenlit [pisãli] nm dandelion

pistache [pistaʃ] nf pistachio (nut)

piste [pist] nf (d'un animal, sentier) track, trail; (indice) lead; (de stade, de cassette/magnétophone) track; (de cirque) ring; (de danse) floor; (de patinage) rink; (de ski) run; (Aviat) runway; **~ cyclable** cycle track

pistolet [pistɔlɛ] nm (arme) pistol, gun; (à peinture) spray gun; **pistolet-mitrailleur** nm submachine gun

piston [pistɔ̃] nm (Tech) piston; **avoir du ~** (fam) to have friends in the right places; **pistonner** /1/ vt (candidat) to pull strings for

piteux, -euse [pitø, -øz] adj pitiful, sorry (avant le nom); **en ~ état** in a sorry state

pitié [pitje] nf pity; **il me fait ~** I feel sorry for him; **avoir ~ de** (compassion) to pity, feel sorry for; (merci) to have pity ou mercy on

pitoyable [pitwajabl] adj pitiful

pittoresque [pitɔRɛsk] adj picturesque

pizza [pidza] nf pizza

PJ sigle f (= police judiciaire) ≈ CID (BRIT), ≈ FBI (US)

placard [plakaR] nm (armoire) cupboard; (affiche) poster, notice

place [plas] nf (emplacement, situation, classement) place; (de ville, village) square; (espace libre) room, space; (de parking) space; (siège: de train, cinéma, voiture) seat; (emploi) job; **en ~** (mettre) in its place; **sur ~** on the spot; **faire ~ à** to give way to; **ça prend de la ~** it takes up a lot of room ou space; **à la ~ de** in place of, instead of; **à votre ~ ...** if I were you ...; **se mettre à la ~ de qn** to put o.s. in sb's place ou in sb's shoes

placé, e [plase] adj: (Hippisme): **être bien/mal ~** to be well/badly placed; (spectateur) to have a good/bad seat; **il est bien ~ pour le savoir** he is in a position to know

placement [plasmã] nm (Finance) investment; **agence** ou **bureau de ~** employment agency

P

placer [plase] /3/ vt to place; (convive, spectateur) to seat; (capital, argent) to place, invest; **se ~ au premier rang** to go and stand out (ou sit) in the first row

plafond [plafɔ̃] nm ceiling

plage [plaʒ] nf beach; **~ arrière** (Auto) parcel ou back shelf

plaider [plede] /1/ vi (avocat) to plead ▷ vt to plead; **~ pour** (fig) to speak for; **plaidoyer** nm (Jur) speech for the defence (BRIT) ou defense (US); (fig) plea

plaie [plɛ] nf wound

plaignant, e [plɛɲɑ̃, -ɑ̃t] nm/f plaintiff

plaindre [plɛ̃dʀ] /52/ vt to pity, feel sorry for; **se plaindre** vi (gémir) to moan; (protester, rouspéter) **se ~ (à qn) (de)** to complain (to sb) (about); **se ~ de** (souffrir) to complain of

plaine [plɛn] nf plain

plain-pied [plɛ̃pje] adv: **de ~ (avec)** on the same level (as)

plaint, e [plɛ̃, -ɛ̃t] pp de **plaindre** ▷ nf (gémissement) moan, groan; (doléance) complaint; **porter ~e** to lodge a complaint

plaire [plɛʀ] /54/ vi to be a success, be successful; **cela me plaît** I like it; **ça plaît beaucoup aux jeunes** it's very popular with young people; **se ~ quelque part** to like being somewhere; **s'il vous plaît, s'il te plaît** please

plaisance [plɛzɑ̃s] nf (aussi: **navigation de ~**) (pleasure) sailing, yachting

plaisant, e [plɛzɑ̃, -ɑ̃t] adj pleasant; (histoire, anecdote) amusing

plaisanter [plɛzɑ̃te] /1/ vi to joke; **plaisanterie** nf joke

plaisir [plɛziʀ] nm pleasure; **faire ~ à qn** (délibérément) to be nice to sb, please sb; **ça me fait ~** I'm delighted ou very pleased with this; **j'espère que ça te fera ~** I hope you'll like it; **pour le** ou **pour son** ou **par ~** for pleasure

plaît [plɛ] vb voir **plaire**

plan, e [plɑ̃, -an] adj flat ▷ nm plan; (fig) level, plane; (Ciné) shot; **au premier/second ~** in the foreground/ middle distance; **à l'arrière ~** in the background; **~ d'eau** lake

planche [plɑ̃ʃ] nf (pièce de bois) plank, (wooden) board; (illustration) plate; **~ à repasser** ironing board; **~ (à roulettes)** skateboard; **~ à voile** (sport) windsurfing

plancher [plɑ̃ʃe] /1/ nm floor; (planches) floorboards pl ▷ vi to work hard

planer [plane] /1/ vi to glide; (fam: rêveur) to have one's head in the clouds; **~ sur** (danger) to hang over

planète [planɛt] nf planet

planeur [planœʀ] nm glider

planifier [planifje] /7/ vt to plan

planning [planiŋ] nm programme, schedule; **~ familial** family planning

plant [plɑ̃] nm seedling, young plant

plante [plɑ̃t] nf plant;
~ d'appartement house ou pot plant; **~ du pied** sole (of the foot); **~ verte** house plant

planter [plɑ̃te] /1/ vt (plante) to plant; (enfoncer) to hammer ou drive in; (tente) to put up, pitch; (fam: mettre) to dump; **se planter** vi (fam: se tromper) to get it wrong; (: ordinateur) to crash

plaque [plak] nf (de tôle, de verglas, d'eczéma) patch; (avec inscription) plaque; **~ chauffante** hotplate; **~ de chocolat** bar of chocolate; **~ tournante** (fig) centre

plaqué, e [plake] adj: **~ or/argent** gold-/silver-plated

plaquer [plake] /1/ vt (Rugby) to bring down; (fam: laisser tomber) to drop

plaquette [plakɛt] nf (de chocolat) bar; (de beurre) packet; **~ de frein** brake pad

plastique [plastik] adj ▷ nm plastic ▷ nf plastic arts pl; (d'une statue) modelling; **plastiquer** /1/ vt to blow up

plat, e [pla, -at] adj flat; (style) flat, dull ▷ nm (récipient, Culin) dish; (d'un repas) course; **à ~ ventre** face down; **à ~** (pneu, batterie) flat; (fam: fatigué) dead beat; **~ cuisiné** pre-cooked meal (ou dish); **~ du jour** dish of the day; **~ principal** ou **de résistance** main course

platane [platan] nm plane tree

plateau, x [plato] nm (support) tray; (Géo) plateau; (Ciné) set; **à ~ fromages** cheeseboard

plate-bande [platbɑ̃d] nf flower bed

plate-forme [platfɔʀm] nf platform; **~ de forage/pétrolière** drilling/oil rig

platine [platin] nm platinum ▷ nf (d'un tourne-disque) turntable; **~ laser** ou **compact-disc** compact disc (player)

plâtre [plɑtʀ] nm (matériau) plaster; (statue) plaster statue; (Méd) (plaster) cast; **avoir un bras dans le ~** to have an arm in plaster

plein, e [plɛ̃, -ɛn] adj full ▷ nm: **faire le ~ (d'essence)** to fill up (with petrol (BRIT) ou gas (US)); **à ~es mains** (ramasser) in handfuls; **à ~ temps** full-time; **en ~ air** in the open air; **en ~ soleil** in direct sunlight; **en ~e nuit/rue** in the middle of the night/street; **en ~ jour** in broad daylight

pleurer [plœʀe] /1/ vi to cry; (yeux) to water ▷ vt to mourn (for); **~ sur** to lament (for), bemoan

pleurnicher [plœʀniʃe] /1/ vi to snivel, whine

pleurs [plœʀ] nmpl: **en ~** in tears

pleut [plø] vb voir **pleuvoir**

pleuvoir [pløvwaʀ] /23/ vb impers to rain ▷ vi (coups) to rain down; (critiques, invitations) to shower down; **il pleut** it's raining; **il pleut des cordes** ou **à verse** ou **à torrents** it's pouring (down), it's raining cats and dogs

pli [pli] nm fold; (de jupe) pleat; (de pantalon) crease

pliant, e [plijɑ̃, -ɑ̃t] adj folding

plier [plije] /7/ vt to fold; (pour ranger) to fold up; (genou, bras) to bend ▷ vi to bend; (fig) to yield; **se ~ à** to submit to

plisser [plise] /1/ vt (yeux) to screw up; (front) to furrow; (jupe) to put pleats in

plomb [plɔ̃] nm (métal) lead; (d'une cartouche) (lead) shot; (Pêche) sinker; (Élec) fuse; **sans ~** (essence) unleaded

plomberie [plɔ̃bʀi] nf plumbing

plombier [plɔ̃bje] nm plumber

plonge [plɔ̃ʒ] nf: **faire la ~** to be a washer-up (BRIT) ou dishwasher (person)

plongeant, e [plɔ̃ʒɑ̃, -ɑ̃t] adj (vue) from above; (tir, décolleté) plunging

plongée [plɔ̃ʒe] nf (Sport) diving no pl; (: sans scaphandre) skin diving; **~ sous-marine** diving

plongeoir [plɔ̃ʒwaʀ] nm diving board

plongeon [plɔ̃ʒɔ̃] nm dive

plonger [plɔ̃ʒe] /3/ vi to dive ▷ vt: **~ qch dans** to plunge sth into; **se ~ dans** (études, lecture) to bury ou immerse o.s. in; **plongeur, -euse** [plɔ̃ʒœʀ, -øz] nm/f diver

plu [ply] pp de **plaire**, **pleuvoir**

pluie [plɥi] nf rain

plume [plym] nf feather; (pour écrire) (pen) nib; (fig) pen

plupart [plypaʀ]: **la ~** pron the majority, most (of them); **la ~ des** most, the majority of; **la ~ du temps/d'entre nous** most of the time/of us; **pour la ~** for the most part, mostly

pluriel [plyʀjɛl] nm plural

plus¹ [ply] vb voir **plaire**

○ **MOT-CLÉ**

plus² [ply] adv **1** (forme négative): **ne ... plus** no more, no longer; **je n'ai plus d'argent** I've got no more money ou no money left; **il ne travaille plus** he's no longer working, he doesn't work any more

2 [ply, plyz + *voyelle*] (*comparatif*) more, ...+er; (*superlatif*): **le plus** the most, the ...+est; **plus grand/ intelligent (que)** bigger/more intelligent (than); **le plus grand/ intelligent** the biggest/most intelligent; **tout au plus** at the very most

3 [plys, plyz + *voyelle*] (*davantage*) more; **il travaille plus (que)** he works more (than); **plus il travaille, plus il est heureux** the more he works, the happier he is; **plus de 10 personnes/trois heures/quatre kilos** more than ou over 10 people/ three hours/four kilos; **trois heures de plus que** three hours more than; **de plus** what's more, moreover; **il a trois ans de plus que moi** he's three years older than me; **trois kilos en plus** three kilos more; **en plus** in addition to; **de plus en plus** more and more; **plus ou moins** more or less; **ni plus ni moins** no more, no less

▶ *prép* [plys]: **quatre plus deux** four plus two

plusieurs [plyzjœʀ] *adj, pron* several; **ils sont ~** there are several of them

plus-value [plyvaly] *nf* (*bénéfice*) capital gain

plutôt [plyto] *adv* rather; **je ferais ~ ceci** I'd rather ou sooner do this; **~ que (de) faire** rather than ou instead of doing

pluvieux, -euse [plyvjø, -øz] *adj* rainy, wet

PME *sigle fpl* (= *petites et moyennes entreprises*) small businesses

PMU *sigle m* (= *pari mutuel urbain*) (*dans un café*) betting agency

PNB *sigle m* (= *produit national brut*) GNP

pneu [pnø] *nm* tyre (BRIT), tire (US)

pneumonie [pnømɔni] *nf* pneumonia

poche [pɔʃ] *nf* pocket; (*sous les yeux*) bag, pouch; **argent de ~** pocket money

pochette [pɔʃɛt] *nf* (*d'aiguilles etc*) case; (*de femme*) clutch bag; (*mouchoir*) breast pocket handkerchief; **~ de disque** record sleeve

podcast [pɔdkast] *nm* podcast; **podcaster** /1/ *vi* to podcast

poêle [pwal] *nm* stove ▶ *nf*: **~ (à frire)** frying pan

poème [pɔɛm] *nm* poem

poésie [pɔezi] *nf* (*poème*) poem; (*art*): **la ~** poetry

poète [pɔɛt] *nm* poet

poids [pwa] *nm* weight; (*Sport*) shot; **vendre au ~** to sell by weight; **perdre/prendre du ~** to lose/put on weight; **~ lourd** (*camion*) (big) lorry (BRIT), truck (US)

poignant, e [pwaɲɑ̃, -ɑ̃t] *adj* poignant

poignard [pwaɲaʀ] *nm* dagger; **poignarder** /1/ *vt* to stab, knife

poigne [pwaɲ] *nf* grip; **avoir de la ~** (*fig*) to rule with a firm hand

poignée [pwaɲe] *nf* (*de sel etc, fig*) handful; (*de couvercle, porte*) handle; **~ de main** handshake

poignet [pwaɲɛ] *nm* (*Anat*) wrist; (*de chemise*) cuff

poil [pwal] *nm* (*Anat*) hair; (*de pinceau, brosse*) bristle; (*de tapis, tissu*) strand; (*pelage*) coat; **à ~** (*fam*) starkers; **au ~** (*fam*) hunky-dory; **poilu, e** *adj* hairy

poinçonner [pwɛ̃sɔne] /1/ *vt* (*bijou etc*) to hallmark; (*billet, ticket*) to punch

poing [pwɛ̃] *nm* fist; **coup de ~** punch

point [pwɛ̃] *nm* dot; (*de ponctuation*) full stop, period (US); (*Couture, Tricot*) stitch ▶ *adv* = **pas¹**; **faire le ~** (*fig*) to take stock (of the situation); **sur le ~ de faire** (just) about to do; **à ~** much so that; **mettre au ~** (*mécanisme, procédé*) to develop;

(affaire) to settle; **à ~** (Culin: viande) medium; **à ~ (nommé)** just at the right time; **deux ~s** colon; **~ (de côté)** stitch (pain); **~ d'exclamation** exclamation mark; **~ faible** weak spot; **~ final** full stop, period (us); **~ d'interrogation** question mark; **~ mort; au ~ mort** (Auto) in neutral; **~ de repère** landmark; (dans le temps) point of reference; **~ de vente** retail outlet; **~ de vue** point of view; (fig: opinion) point of view; **~s cardinaux** cardinal points; **~s de suspension** suspension points

pointe [pwɛ̃t] nf point; (clou) tack; **une ~ d'ail/d'accent** a touch ou hint of garlic/of an accent; **être à la ~ de** (fig) to be in the forefront of; **sur la ~ des pieds** on tiptoe; **en ~** adj pointed, tapered; **de ~** (technique etc) leading; **heures/jours de ~** peak hours/days

pointer [pwɛte] /1/ vt (diriger: canon, longue-vue, doigt): **~ vers qch, ~ sur qch** to point to sth ▷ vi (employé) to clock in ou on

pointeur, -euse [pwɛtœʀ, -øz] nf timeclock ▷ nm (Inform) cursor

pointillé [pwɛtije] nm (trait) dotted line

pointilleux, -euse [pwɛtijø, -øz] adj particular, pernickety

pointu, e [pwɛty] adj pointed; (voix) shrill; (analyse) precise

pointure [pwɛtyʀ] nf size

point-virgule [pwɛviʀgyl] nm semi-colon

poire [pwaʀ] nf pear; (fam, péj) mug

poireau, x [pwaʀo] nm leek

poirier [pwaʀje] nm pear tree

pois [pwa] nm (Bot) pea; (sur une étoffe) dot, spot; **à ~** (cravate etc) spotted, polka-dot cpd; **~ chiche** chickpea

poison [pwazɔ̃] nm poison

poisseux, -euse [pwasø, -øz] adj sticky

poisson [pwasɔ̃] nm fish gén inv; **les P~s** (Astrologie: signe) Pisces; **~ d'avril**

April fool; (blague) April fool's day trick; see note **"poisson d'avril"**; **~ rouge** goldfish; **poissonnerie** nf fishmonger's; **poissonnier, -ière** nm/f fishmonger; (BRIT), fish merchant (us)

○ **POISSON D'AVRIL**
●
● The traditional April Fools'
● Day prank in France involves
● attaching a cut-out paper fish,
● known as a 'poisson d'avril', to the
● back of one's victim, without being
● caught.

poitrine [pwatʀin] nf chest; (seins) bust, bosom; (Culin) breast

poivre [pwavʀ] nm pepper

poivron [pwavʀɔ̃] nm pepper, capsicum

polaire [pɔlɛʀ] adj polar

pôle [pol] nm (Géo, Élec) pole; **le ~ Nord/Sud** the North/South Pole

poli, e [pɔli] adj polite; (lisse) smooth

police [pɔlis] nf police; **~ judiciaire (PJ)** = Criminal Investigation Department (CID) (BRIT), = Federal Bureau of Investigation (FBI) (us); **~ secours** = emergency services pl (BRIT), = paramedics pl (us); **policier, -ière** adj police cpd ▷ nm policeman; (aussi: **roman policier**) detective novel

polir [pɔliʀ] /2/ vt to polish

politesse [pɔlites] nf politeness

politicien, ne [pɔlitisjɛ̃, -ɛn] nm/f (péj) politician

politique [pɔlitik] adj political ▷ nf politics sg; (principes, tactique) policies pl

politiquement [pɔlitikmɑ̃] adv politically; **~ correct** politically correct

pollen [pɔlɛn] nm pollen

polluant, e [pɔlɥɑ̃, -ɑ̃t] adj polluting ▷ nm pollutant; **non-** non-polluting

polluer [pɔlɥe] /1/ vt to pollute;
pollution nf pollution
polo [pɔlo] nm (tricot) polo shirt
Pologne [pɔlɔɲ] nf: la ~ Poland;
polonais, e adj Polish ▷ nm (Ling)
Polish ▷ nm/f: **Polonais, e** Pole
poltron, ne [pɔltrɔ̃, -ɔn] adj
cowardly
polycopier [pɔlikɔpje] /7/ vt to
duplicate
Polynésie [pɔlinezi] nf: la ~ Polynesia;
la ~ française French Polynesia
polyvalent, e [pɔlivalɑ̃, -ɑ̃t] adj
(rôle) varied; (salle) multi-purpose
pommade [pɔmad] nf ointment,
cream
pomme [pɔm] nf apple; **tomber
dans les ~s** (fam) to pass out;
~ **d'Adam** Adam's apple; ~ **de pin**
pine ou fir cone; ~ **de terre** potato; **~s
vapeur** boiled potatoes
pommette [pɔmɛt] nf cheekbone
pommier [pɔmje] nm apple tree
pompe [pɔ̃p] nf pump; (faste)
pomp (and ceremony); ~ **à eau/
essence** water/petrol pump; **~s
funèbres** undertaker's sg, funeral
parlour sg; **pomper** /1/ vt to pump;
(aspirer) to pump up; (absorber) to
soak up
pompeux, -euse [pɔ̃pø, -øz] adj
pompous
pompier [pɔ̃pje] nm fireman
pompiste [pɔ̃pist] nm/f petrol (BRIT)
ou gas (US) pump attendant
poncer [pɔ̃se] /3/ vt to sand (down)
ponctuation [pɔ̃ktɥasjɔ̃] nf
punctuation
ponctuel, le [pɔ̃ktɥɛl] adj punctual
pondéré, e [pɔ̃dere] adj level-
headed, composed
pondre [pɔ̃dr] /41/ vt to lay
poney [pɔnɛ] nm pony
pont [pɔ̃] nm bridge; (Navig) deck;
faire le ~ to take the extra day off;
see note **"faire le pont"**; ~ **suspendu**
suspension bridge; **pont-levis** nm
drawbridge

○ **FAIRE LE PONT**
○
○ The expression 'faire le pont' refers
○ to the practice of taking a Monday
○ or Friday off to make a long
○ weekend if a public holiday falls on
○ a Tuesday or Thursday. The French
○ commonly take an extra day off
○ work to give four consecutive days'
○ holiday at 'l'Ascension', 'le 14 juillet'
○ and 'le 15 août'.

pop [pɔp] adj inv pop
populaire [pɔpylɛr] adj popular;
(manifestation) mass cpd; (milieux,
clientèle) working-class; (mot etc) used
by the lower classes (of society)
popularité [pɔpylarite] nf
popularity
population [pɔpylasjɔ̃] nf population
populeux, -euse [pɔpylø, -øz] adj
densely populated
porc [pɔr] nm pig; (Culin) pork
porcelaine [pɔrsəlɛn] nf porcelain,
china; (objet) piece of china(ware)
porc-épic [pɔrkepik] nm porcupine
porche [pɔrʃ] nm porch
porcherie [pɔrʃəri] nf pigsty
pore [pɔr] nm pore
porno [pɔrno] adj porno ▷ nm porn
port [pɔr] nm harbour, port; (ville)
port; (de l'uniforme etc) wearing;
(pour lettre) postage; (pour colis,
aussi: posture) carriage; ~ **d'arme**
(Jur) carrying of a firearm; ~ **payé**
postage paid
portable [pɔrtabl] adj (portatif)
portable; (téléphone) mobile
▷ nm (inform) laptop (computer);
(téléphone) mobile (phone)
portail [pɔrtaj] nm gate
portant, e [pɔrtɑ̃, -ɑ̃t] adj: **bien/
mal ~** in good/poor health
portatif, -ive [pɔrtatif, -iv] adj
portable
porte [pɔrt] nf door; (de ville,
forteresse) gate; **mettre à la ~** to
throw out; ~ **d'entrée** front door

porté, e [pɔʀte] adj: **être ~ à faire qch** to be inclined to do sth; **être ~ sur qch** to be partial to sth

porte: **porte-avions** nm inv aircraft carrier; **porte-bagages** nm inv luggage rack (ou basket etc); **porte-bonheur** nm inv lucky charm; **porte-clefs** nm inv key ring; **porte-documents** nm inv attaché ou document case

portée [pɔʀte] nf (d'une arme) range; (fig: importance) impact, import; (: capacités) scope, capabilities; (de chatte etc) litter; (Mus) stave, staff; **à/ hors de ~ (de)** within/out of reach (of); **à ~ de (la) main** within (arm's) reach; **à la ~ de qn** (fig) at sb's level, within sb's capabilities

porte: **portefeuille** nm wallet; **portemanteau, x** nm coat rack; (cintre) coat hanger; **porte-monnaie** nm inv purse; **porte-parole** nm inv spokesperson

porter [pɔʀte] /1/ vt to carry; (sur soi: vêtement, barbe, bague) to wear; (fig: responsabilité etc) to bear, carry; (inscription, marque, titre, patronyme, fruits, fleurs) to bear; (coup) to deal; (attention) to turn; (apporter): **~ qch quelque part/à qn** to take sth somewhere/to sb ▷ vi to carry; (coup, argument) to hit home; **se porter** vi (se sentir): **se ~ bien/mal** to be well/unwell; **~ sur** (conférence etc) to concern; **se faire ~ malade** to report sick

porteur, -euse [pɔʀtœʀ, -øz] nm/f ▷ nm (de bagages) porter; (de chèque) bearer

porte-voix [pɔʀtəvwa] nm inv megaphone

portier [pɔʀtje] nm doorman

portière [pɔʀtjɛʀ] nf door

portion [pɔʀsjɔ̃] nf (part) portion, share; (partie) portion, section

porto [pɔʀto] nm (vin) port (wine)

portrait [pɔʀtʀɛ] nm portrait; (photographie) photograph; **portrait-robot** nm Identikit® ou Photo-fit® (BRIT) picture

portuaire [pɔʀtɥɛʀ] adj port cpd, harbour cpd

portugais, e [pɔʀtygɛ, -ɛz] adj Portuguese ▷ nm (Ling) Portuguese ▷ nm/f: **P~, e** Portuguese

Portugal [pɔʀtygal] nm: **le ~** Portugal

pose [poz] nf (de moquette) laying; (attitude, d'un modèle) pose; (Photo) exposure

posé, e [poze] adj calm

poser [poze] /1/ vt (place) to put down, to put; (déposer, installer: moquette, carrelage) to lay; (rideaux, papier peint) to hang; (question) to ask; (principe, conditions) to lay ou set down; (problème) to formulate; (difficulté) to pose ▷ vi (modèle) to pose; **se poser** vi (oiseau, avion) to land; (question) to arise; **~ qch (sur)** to put sth down (on); **~ qn à** to drop sb at; **~ qch sur qch/quelque part** to put sth on sth/somewhere; **~ sa candidature à un poste** to apply for a post

positif, -ive [pozitif, -iv] adj positive

position [pozisjɔ̃] nf position; **prendre ~** (fig) to take a stand

posologie [pozɔlɔʒi] nf dosage

posséder [posede] /6/ vt to own, possess; (qualité, talent) to have, possess; (sexuellement) to possess

possession nf ownership no pl; possession; **être en possession de qch** to be in possession of sth; **prendre possession de qch** to take possession of sth

possibilité [posibilite] nf possibility; **possibilités** nfpl potential sg

possible [posibl] adj possible; (projet, entreprise) feasible ▷ nm: **faire son ~** to do all one can, do one's utmost; **le plus/moins de livres ~** as many/ few books as possible; **le plus vite ~** as quickly as possible; **dès que ~** as soon as possible

postal, e, -aux [pɔstal, -o] *adj* postal
poste¹ [pɔst] *nf* (*service*) post, postal
service; (*administration, bureau*)
post office; **mettre à la ~** to post;
~ restante (BRIT), general delivery (US)
poste² [pɔst] *nm* (*fonction, Mil*)
post; (*Tél*) extension; **~ de radio** *etc*
set; **~ d'incendie** fire point; **~
de pilotage** cockpit, flight deck; **~
(de police)** police station; **~ de secours** first-
aid post
poster /1/ *vt* [pɔste] to post ▷ *nm*
[pɔstɛʀ] poster
postérieur, e [pɔsteʀjœʀ] *adj* (*date*)
later; (*partie*) back ▷ *nm* (*fam*) behind
postuler [pɔstyle] /1/ *vi*: **~ à** *ou* **pour
un emploi** to apply for a job
pot [po] *nm* (*en verre*) jar; (*en terre*)
pot; (*en plastique, carton*) carton; (*en
métal*) tin; (*fam: chance*) luck; **avoir
du ~** to be lucky; **boire** *ou* **prendre
un ~** (*fam*) to have a drink; **petit
~** (*pour bébé*) jar of baby food;
~ catalytique catalytic converter;
~ d'échappement exhaust pipe
potable [pɔtabl] *adj*: **eau (non) ~**
(not) drinking water
potage [pɔtaʒ] *nm* soup; **potager,
-ère** *adj*: (*jardin*) **potager** kitchen *ou*
vegetable garden
pot-au-feu [pɔtofø] *nm inv* (*beef*)
stew
pot-de-vin [pɔdvɛ̃] *nm* bribe
pote [pɔt] *nm* (*fam*) pal
poteau, x [pɔto] *nm* post;
~ indicateur signpost
potelé, e [pɔtle] *adj* plump, chubby
potentiel, le [pɔtɑ̃sjɛl] *adj, nm*
potential
poterie [pɔtʀi] *nf* pottery; (*objet*)
piece of pottery
potier, -ière [pɔtje, -jɛʀ] *nm/f*
potter
potiron [pɔtiʀɔ̃] *nm* pumpkin
pou, x [pu] *nm* louse
poubelle [pubɛl] *nf* (dust)bin

pouce [pus] *nm* thumb
poudre [pudʀ] *nf* powder; (*fard:
(face) powder*); (*explosif*) gunpowder;
en ~: café en ~ instant coffee; **lait en
~** dried *ou* powdered milk
poudreux, -euse [pudʀø, -øz] *adj*
dusty; (*neige*) powder *cpd*
poudrier [pudʀije] *nm*
(powder) compact
pouffer [pufe] /1/ *vi*: **~ (de rire)** to
burst out laughing
poulailler [pulaje] *nm* henhouse
poulain [pulɛ̃] *nm* foal; (*fig*) protégé
poule [pul] *nf* hen; (*Culin*) (boiling)
fowl; **~ mouillée** coward
poulet [pulɛ] *nm* chicken; (*fam*) cop
poulie [puli] *nf* pulley
pouls [pu] *nm* pulse; **prendre le ~ de
qn** to take sb's pulse
poumon [pumɔ̃] *nm* lung
poupée [pupe] *nf* doll
pour [puʀ] *prép* for ▷ *nm*: **le ~ et le
contre** the pros and cons; **~ faire**
(so as) to do, in order to do; **~ avoir
fait** for having done; **~ que** so that,
in order that; **fermé ~ (cause de)
travaux** closed for refurbishment *ou*
alterations; **c'est ~ ça que ...** that's
why ...; **~ quoi faire?** what for?; **~ 20
euros d'essence** 20 euros' worth
of petrol; **~ cent** per cent; **~ ce qui
est de** as for as
pourboire [puʀbwaʀ] *nm* tip
pourcentage [puʀsɑ̃taʒ] *nm*
percentage
pourchasser [puʀʃase] /1/ *vt* to
pursue
pourparlers [puʀpaʀle] *nmpl* talks,
negotiations
pourpre [puʀpʀ] *adj* crimson
pourquoi [puʀkwa] *adv, conj*
why ▷ *nm inv*: **le ~ (de)** the reason
(for)
pourrai *etc* [puʀe] *vb voir* **pouvoir**
pourri, e [puʀi] *adj* rotten
pourrir [puʀiʀ] /2/ *vi* to rot; (*fruit*) to
go rotten *ou* bad ▷ *vt* to rot; (*fig*) to
spoil thoroughly; **pourriture** *nf* rot

poursuite [puʀsɥit] nf pursuit, chase; **poursuites** nfpl (Jur) legal proceedings

poursuivre [puʀsɥivʀ] /40/ vt to pursue, chase (after); (obséder) to haunt; (Jur) to bring proceedings against, prosecute (: au civil) to sue; (but) to strive towards; (voyage, études) to carry on with, continue; **se poursuivre** vi to go on, continue

pourtant [puʀtɑ̃] adv yet; **c'est ~ facile** (and) yet it's easy

pourtour [puʀtuʀ] nm perimeter

pourvoir [puʀvwaʀ] /25/ vt : ~ qch/ qn de to equip sth/sb with ▷ vi : ~ à to provide for; **pourvu, e** adj: **pourvu de** equipped with; **pourvu que** (si) provided that, so long as; (espérons que) let's hope (that)

pousse [pus] nf growth; (bourgeon) shoot

poussée [puse] nf thrust; (d'acné) eruption; (fig: prix) upsurge

pousser [puse] /1/ vt to push; (émettre: cri etc) to give; (stimuler: élève) to urge on; (poursuivre: études, discussion) to carry on ▷ vi to push; (croître) to grow; **se pousser** vi to move over; ~ **qn à faire qch** (inciter) to urge ou press sb to do sth; **faire ~** (plante) to grow

poussette [puset] nf pushchair (BRIT), stroller (US)

poussière [pusjɛʀ] nf dust; **poussiéreux, -euse** adj dusty

poussin [pusɛ̃] nm chick

poutre [putʀ] nf beam

MOT-CLÉ

pouvoir [puvwaʀ] /33/ nm power; (dirigeants): **le pouvoir** those in power; **les pouvoirs publics** the authorities; **pouvoir d'achat** purchasing power

▷ vb aux **1** (être en état de) can, be able to; **je ne peux pas le réparer** I can't ou I am not able to repair it; **déçu de ne pas pouvoir le faire** disappointed

not to be able to do it

2 (avoir la permission) can, may, be allowed to; **vous pouvez aller au cinéma** you can ou may go to the pictures

3 (probabilité, hypothèse) may, might, could; **il a pu avoir un accident** he may ou might ou could have had an accident; **il aurait pu le dire!** he might ou could have said (so)!

▷ vb impers may, might, could; **il peut arriver que** it may ou might ou could happen that; **il pourrait pleuvoir** it might rain

▷ vt can, be able to; **j'ai fait tout ce que j'ai pu** I did all I could; **je n'en peux plus** (épuisé) I'm exhausted; (à bout) I can't take any more

se pouvoir vi: **il se peut que** it may ou might be that; **cela se pourrait** that's quite possible

prairie [pʀeʀi] nf meadow

praline [pʀalin] nf sugared almond

praticable [pʀatikabl] adj passable; practicable

pratiquant, e [pʀatikɑ̃, -ɑ̃t] nm/f (regular) churchgoer

pratique [pʀatik] nf practice ▷ adj practical; **pratiquement** adv (pour ainsi dire) practically, virtually;

pratiquer /1/ vt to practise; (l'équitation, la pêche) to go in for; (le golf, football) to play; (intervention, opération) to carry out

pré [pʀe] nm meadow

préalable [pʀealabl] adj preliminary; **au ~** beforehand

préambule [pʀeɑ̃byl] nm preamble; (fig) prelude; **sans ~** straight away

préau, x [pʀeo] nm (d'une cour d'école) covered playground

préavis [pʀeavi] nm notice

précaution [pʀekosjɔ̃] nf precaution; **avec ~** cautiously; **par ~** as a precaution

précédemment [pʀesedamɑ̃] adv before, previously

précédent, e [presedã, -ãt] *adj*
previous ▷ *nm* precedent; **sans ~**
unprecedented; **le jour ~** the day
before, the previous day

précéder [presede] /6/ *vt* to precede

prêcher [pʀeʃe] /1/ *vt* to preach

précieux, -euse [pʀesjø, -øz] *adj*
precious; (*collaborateur, conseils*)
invaluable

précipice [pʀesipis] *nm* drop, chasm

précipitamment [pʀesipitamã]
adv hurriedly, hastily

précipitation [pʀesipitasjɔ̃] *nf*
(*hâte*) haste

précipité, e [pʀesipite] *adj* hurried;
hasty

précipiter [pʀesipite] /1/ *vt* (*hâter:
départ*) to hasten; **se précipiter** to
speed up; **~ qn/qch du haut de**
(*faire tomber*) to throw ou hurl sb/sth
off ou from; **se ~ sur/vers** to rush
at/towards

précis, e [pʀesi, -iz] *adj* precise;
(*tir, mesures*) accurate, precise; **à
4 heures ~es** at 4 o'clock sharp;
précisément *adv* precisely; **préciser**
/1/ *vt* (*expliquer*) to be more specific
about, clarify; (*spécifier*) to state,
specify; **se préciser** *vi* to become
clear(er); **précision** *nf* precision;
(*détail*) point ou detail (*made clear ou
to be clarified*)

précoce [pʀekɔs] *adj* early; (*enfant*)
precocious

préconçu, e [pʀekɔ̃sy] *adj*
preconceived

préconiser [pʀekɔnize] /1/ *vt* to
advocate

prédécesseur [pʀedesesœʀ] *nm*
predecessor

prédilection [pʀedilɛksjɔ̃] *nf*: **avoir
une ~ pour** to be partial to

prédire [pʀediʀ] /37/ *vt* to predict

prédominer [pʀedɔmine] /1/ *vi* to
predominate

préface [pʀefas] *nf* preface

préfecture [pʀefɛktyʀ] *nf* prefecture;
~ de police police headquarters

préférable [pʀefeʀabl] *adj*
preferable

préféré, e [pʀefeʀe] *adj, nm/f*
favourite

préférence [pʀefeʀɑ̃s] *nf*
preference; **de ~** preferably

préférer [pʀefeʀe] /6/ *vt*: **~ qn/qch
(à)** to prefer sb/sth (to), like sb/sth
better (than); **~ faire** to prefer to do;
je préférerais du thé I would rather
have tea, I'd prefer tea

préfet [pʀefɛ] *nm* prefect

préhistorique [pʀeistɔʀik] *adj*
prehistoric

préjudice [pʀeʒydis] *nm* (*matériel*)
loss; (*moral*) harm *no pl*; **porter ~ à** to
harm, be detrimental to; **au ~ de** at
the expense of

préjugé [pʀeʒyʒe] *nm* prejudice;
avoir un ~ contre to be prejudiced
against

prélasser [pʀelase] /1/: **se prélasser**
vi to lounge

prélèvement [pʀelɛvmã] *nm*
(*montant*) deduction; **faire un ~ de
sang** to take a blood sample

prélever [pʀelve] /5/ *vt* (*échantillon*)
to take; **~ (sur)** (*argent*) to deduct
(from); (*sur son compte*) to withdraw
(from)

prématuré, e [pʀematyʀe] *adj*
premature ▷ *nm* premature baby

premier, -ière [pʀəmje, -jɛʀ] *adj*
first; (*rang*) front; (*fig: fondamental*)
basic ▷ *nf* (*Rail, Aviat etc*) first
class; (*Scol*) year 12 (*BRIT*), eleventh
grade (*US*); **de ~ ordre** first-rate;
le ~ venu the first person to come
along; **P~ Ministre** Prime Minister;
**première ** *adv* firstly

prémonition [pʀemɔnisjɔ̃] *nf*
premonition

prenant, e [pʀənã, -ãt] *adj*
absorbing, engrossing

prénatal, e [pʀenatal] *adj* (*Méd*)
antenatal

prendre [pʀɑ̃dʀ] /58/ *vt* to take;
(*repas*) to have; (*aller chercher*) to

get; (malfaiteur, poisson) to catch; (passager) to pick up; (personnel) to take on; (traiter: enfant, problème) to handle; (voix, ton) to put on; (ôter): ~ **qch à** to take sth from; (coincer) to get; **~ les doigts dans** to get one's fingers caught in ▸ vi (liquide, ciment) to set; (greffe, vaccin) to take; (feu: foyer) to go; (se diriger): **~ à gauche** to turn (to the) left; **~ froid** to catch cold; **se ~ pour** to think one is; **s'en ~ à** to attack; **se ~ d'amitié/d'affection pour** to befriend/become fond of; **s'y ~** (procéder) to set about it

preneur [pʁənœʁ] nm: **être ~** to be willing to buy; **trouver ~** to find a buyer

prénom [pʁenɔ̃] nm first name

préoccupation [pʁeɔkypasjɔ̃] nf (souci) concern; (idée fixe) preoccupation

préoccuper [pʁeɔkype] /1/ vt (tourmenter, tracasser) to concern; (absorber, obséder) to preoccupy; **se ~ de qch** to be concerned about sth

préparatifs [pʁepaʁatif] nmpl preparations

préparation [pʁepaʁasjɔ̃] nf preparation

préparer [pʁepaʁe] /1/ vt to prepare; (café, repas) to make; (examen) to prepare for; (voyage, entreprise) to plan; **se préparer** vi (orage, tragédie) to brew, be in the air; **se ~ (à qch/à faire)** to prepare (o.s.) ou get ready (for sth/to do); **~ qch à qn** (surprise etc) to have sth in store for sb

prépondérant, e [pʁepɔ̃deʁɑ̃, -ɑ̃t] adj major, dominating

préposé, e [pʁepoze] nm/f employee; (facteur) postman/woman

préposition [pʁepozisjɔ̃] nf preposition

près [pʁɛ] adv near, close; **~ de** near (to), close to; (environ) nearly, almost; **de ~** closely; **à cinq kg ~** to within about five kg; **il n'est pas à 10 minutes ~** he can spare 10 minutes

présage [pʁezaʒ] nm omen

presbyte [pʁɛsbit] adj long-sighted

presbytère [pʁɛsbitɛʁ] nm presbytery

prescription [pʁɛskʁipsjɔ̃] nf prescription

prescrire [pʁɛskʁiʁ] /39/ vt to prescribe

présence [pʁezɑ̃s] nf presence; (au bureau etc) attendance

présent, e [pʁezɑ̃, -ɑ̃t] adj, nm present; **à ~ que** now that

présentation [pʁezɑ̃tasjɔ̃] nf presentation; (de nouveau venu) introduction; (allure) appearance; **faire les ~s** to do the introductions

présenter [pʁezɑ̃te] /1/ vt to present; (invité, candidat) to introduce; (félicitations, condoléances) to offer; **~ qn à** to introduce sb to ▸ vi: **~ mal/bien** to have an unattractive/a pleasing appearance; **se présenter** vi (à une élection) to stand; (occasion) to arise; **se ~ à un examen** to sit an exam; **je vous présente Nadine** this is Nadine

préservatif [pʁezɛʁvatif] nm condom, sheath

préserver [pʁezɛʁve] /1/ vt: **~ de** (protéger) to protect from

président [pʁezidɑ̃] nm (Pol) president; (d'une assemblée, Comm) chairman; **~ directeur général** chairman and managing director

présidentiel, le [pʁezidɑ̃sjɛl] adj presidential; **présidentielles** nfpl presidential election(s)

présider [pʁezide] /1/ vt to preside over; (dîner) to be the guest of honour (BRIT) ou honor (US) at

presque [pʁɛsk] adv almost, nearly; **~ rien** hardly anything; **~ pas** hardly (at all); **~ pas de** hardly any; **personne, ou ~** next to nobody, hardly anyone

presqu'île [pʁɛskil] nf peninsula

pressant, e [pʁɛsɑ̃, -ɑ̃t] adj urgent

presse [pʁɛs] nf press; (affluence): **heures de ~** busy times

pressé, e [pʀese] *adj* in a hurry;
(*besogne*) urgent; **orange ~e** freshly
squeezed orange juice

pressentiment [pʀesɑ̃timɑ̃] *nm*
foreboding, premonition

pressentir [pʀesɑ̃tiʀ] /16/ *vt* to
sense

presse-papiers [pʀɛspapje] *nm inv*
paperweight

presser [pʀese] /1/ *vt* (*fruit, éponge*)
to squeeze; (*interrupteur, bouton*) to
press; (*allure, affaire*) to speed up;
(*inciter*): **~ qn de faire** to urge ou press
sb to do ▷ *vi* to be urgent; **se presser**
vi (*se hâter*) to hurry (up); **rien ne
presse** there's no hurry; **se ~ contre
qn** to squeeze up against sb; **le
temps presse** there's not much time

pressing [pʀesiŋ] *nm* (*magasin*)
dry-cleaner's

pression [pʀesjɔ̃] *nf* pressure;
(*bouton*) press stud (BRIT), snap
fastener (US); (*fam: bière*) draught
beer; **faire ~ sur** to put pressure on;
sous ~ pressurized, under pressure;
(*fig*) keyed up; **~ artérielle** blood
pressure

prestataire [pʀestatɛʀ] *nm/f* person
receiving benefits; **~ de services**
provider of services

prestation [pʀestasjɔ̃] *nf* (*allocation*)
benefit; (*d'une entreprise*) service
provided; (*d'un joueur, artiste*)
performance

prestidigitateur, -trice
[pʀestidiʒitatœʀ, -tʀis] *nm/f*
conjurer

prestige [pʀestiʒ] *nm* prestige;
prestigieux, -euse *adj* prestigious

présumer [pʀezyme] /1/ *vt*: **~ que** to
presume ou assume that

prêt, e [pʀɛ, pʀɛt] *adj* ready ▷ *nm*
(*somme prêtée*) loan; **prêt-à-porter**
nm ready-to-wear ou off-the-peg
(BRIT) clothes *pl*

prétendre [pʀetɑ̃dʀ] /41/ *vt*
(*affirmer*): **~ que** to claim that; **~ faire
qch** (*avoir l'intention de*) to mean ou

intend to do sth; **prétendu, e** *adj*
(*supposé*) so-called

▎ Attention à ne pas traduire
prétendre par *to pretend*.

prétentieux, -euse [pʀetɑ̃sjø, -øz]
adj pretentious

prétention [pʀetɑ̃sjɔ̃] *nf*
pretentiousness; (*exigence, ambition*)
claim

prêter [pʀete] /1/ *vt*: (*livres, argent*) to lend sth to sb;
(*caractère, propos*) to attribute sth
to sb

prétexte [pʀetɛkst] *nm* pretext,
excuse; **sous aucun ~** on no account;
prétexter [pʀetɛkste] /1/ *vt* to give
as a pretext ou an excuse

prêtre [pʀɛtʀ] *nm* priest

preuve [pʀœv] *nf* proof; (*indice*)
proof, evidence *no pl*; **faire ~ de**
to show; **faire ses ~s** to prove o.s.
(*ou itself*)

prévaloir [pʀevalwaʀ] /29/ *vi* to
prevail

prévenant, e [pʀevnɑ̃, -ɑ̃t] *adj*
thoughtful, kind

prévenir [pʀevniʀ] /22/ *vt* (*éviter:
catastrophe etc*) to avoid, prevent;
(*anticiper: désirs, besoins*) to
anticipate; **~ qn (de)** (*avertir*) to warn
sb (about); (*informer*) to tell ou inform
sb (about)

préventif, -ive [pʀevɑ̃tif, -iv] *adj*
preventive

prévention [pʀevɑ̃sjɔ̃] *nf*
prevention; **~ routière** road safety

prévenu, e [pʀevny] *nm/f* (Jur)
defendant, accused

prévision [pʀevizjɔ̃] *nf*: **~s**
predictions; (*météorologiques,
économiques*) forecast *sg*; **en
~ de** in anticipation of; **~s
météorologiques** *ou* **du temps**
weather forecast *sg*

prévoir [pʀevwaʀ] /24/ *vt* (*deviner*)
to foresee; (*s'attendre à*) to expect,
reckon on; (*organiser: voyage etc*)
to plan; (*préparer, réserver*) to

allow; **comme prévu** as planned; **prévoyant, e** *adj* gifted with (*ou* showing) foresight; **prévu, e** *pp de* **prévoir**

prier [prije] /7/ *vi* to pray ▷ *vt* (*Dieu*) to pray to; (*implorer*) to beg; (*demander*): **~ qn de faire** to ask sb to do; **se faire ~** to need coaxing *ou* persuading; **je vous en prie** (*allez-y*) please do; (*de rien*) don't mention it; **prière** *nf* prayer; **"prière de faire ..."** "please do ..."

primaire [primɛʀ] *adj* primary ▷ *nm* (*Scol*) primary education

prime [prim] *nf* (*bonification*) bonus; (*subside*) allowance; (*Comm: cadeau*) free gift; (*Assurances, Bourse*) premium ▷ *adj*: **de ~ abord** at first glance; **primer** /1/ *vt* (*récompenser*) to award a prize to ▷ *vi* to dominate

primevère [primvɛʀ] *nf* primrose

primitif, -ive [primitif, -iv] *adj* primitive; (*originel*) original

prince [prɛ̃s] *nm* prince; **princesse** *nf* princess

principal, e, -aux [prɛ̃sipal, -o] *adj* principal, main ▷ *nm* (*Scol*) head (teacher) (BRIT), principal (US); (*essentiel*) main thing

principe [prɛ̃sip] *nm* principle; **par ~** on principle; **en ~** (*habituellement*) as a rule; (*théoriquement*) in principle

printemps [prɛ̃tɑ̃] *nm* spring

priorité [prijorite] *nf* priority; (*Auto*): **à droite** right of way to vehicles coming from the right

pris, e [pri, priz] *pp de* **prendre** ▷ *adj* (*place*) taken; (*journée, mains*) full; (*personne*) busy; **avoir le nez/ la gorge ~(e)** to have a stuffy nose/a bad throat; **être ~ de peur/de fatigue/de panique** to be stricken with fear/overcome with fatigue/ panic-stricken

prise [priz] *nf* (*d'une ville*) capture; (*Pêche, Chasse*) catch; (*point d'appui ou pour empoigner*) hold; (*Élec: fiche*) plug; (*: femelle*) socket; **être aux ~s avec**

to be grappling with; **~ de courant** power point; **~ multiple** adaptor; **~ de sang** blood test

priser [prize] /1/ *vt* (*estimer*) to prize, value

prison [prizɔ̃] *nf* prison; **aller/être en ~** to go to/be in prison *ou* jail; **prisonnier, -ière** *nm/f* prisoner ▷ *adj* captive

privé, e [prive] *adj* private; (*en punition*): **tu es ~ de télé!** no TV for you! ▷ *nm* (*Comm*) private sector; **en ~ in private**

priver [prive] /1/ *vt*: **~ qn de** to deprive sb of; **se ~ de** to go ou do without

privilège [privilɛʒ] *nm* privilege

prix [pri] *nm* price; (*récompense, Scol*) prize; **hors de ~** exorbitantly priced; **à aucun ~** not at any price; **à tout ~** at all costs

probable [probabl] *adj* likely, probable; **probablement** *adv* probably

problème [problɛm] *nm* problem

procédé [prosede] *nm* (*méthode*) process; (*comportement*) behaviour *no pl*

procéder [prosede] /6/ *vi* to proceed; (*moralement*) to behave; **~ à** to carry out

procès [prosɛ] *nm* trial (*poursuites*) proceedings *pl*; **être en ~ avec** to be involved in a lawsuit with

processus [prosesys] *nm* process

procès-verbal, -aux [prosevɛrbal, -o] *nm* (*de réunion*) minutes *pl*; (*aussi*: **PV**): **avoir un ~** to get a parking ticket

prochain, e [prɔʃɛ̃, -ɛn] *adj* next; (*proche: départ, arrivée*) impending ▷ *nm* fellow man; **la ~e fois/semaine ~e** next time/week; **prochainement** *adv* soon, shortly

proche [prɔʃ] *adj* nearby; (*dans le temps*) imminent; (*parent, ami*) close; **proches** *nmpl* (*parents*) close relatives; **être ~ (de)** to be near, be close (to)

proclamer [prɔklame] /1/ vt to proclaim

procuration [prɔkyrasjɔ̃] nf proxy

procurer [prɔkyre] /1/ vt (fournir): **~ qch à qn** (obtenir) to get ou obtain sth for sb; (plaisir etc) to bring ou give sb sth; **se procurer** vt to get; **procureur** nm public prosecutor

prodige [prɔdiʒ] nm marvel, wonder; (personne) prodigy; **prodiguer** /1/ vt (soins, attentions): **prodiguer qch à qn** to lavish sth on sb

producteur, -trice [prɔdyktœr, -tris] nm/f producer

productif, -ive [prɔdyktif, -iv] adj productive

production [prɔdyksjɔ̃] nf production; (rendement) output

productivité [prɔdyktivite] nf productivity

produire [prɔdɥir] /38/ vt to produce; **se produire** vi (acteur) to perform, appear; (événement) to happen, occur

produit, e [prɔdɥi, -it] nm product; **~ chimique** chemical; **~ d'entretien** cleaning product; **~s agricoles** farm produce sg; **~s de beauté** beauty products, cosmetics

prof [prɔf] nm (fam) teacher

proférer [prɔfere] /6/ vt to utter

professeur, e [prɔfesœr] nm/f teacher; (titulaire d'une chaire) professor; **~ (de faculté)** (university) lecturer

profession [prɔfesjɔ̃] nf (libérale) profession; (gén) occupation; **"sans ~"** "unemployed"; **professionnel, le** adj, nm/f professional

profil [prɔfil] nm profile; **de ~** in profile

profit [prɔfi] nm (avantage) benefit, advantage; (Comm, Finance) profit; **au ~ de** in aid of; **tirer ou retirer ~ de** to profit from; **profitable** adj (utile) beneficial; (lucratif) profitable; **profiter** /1/ vi: **profiter de** (situation, occasion) to take advantage of; (vacances, jeunesse etc) to make the most of

profond, e [prɔfɔ̃, -ɔ̃d] adj deep; (méditation, mépris) profound; **profondément** adv deeply; **il dort profondément** he is sound asleep; **profondeur** nf depth; **l'eau a quelle profondeur?** how deep is the water?

programme [prɔgram] nm programme; (Scol) syllabus, curriculum; (Inform) program; **programmer** /1/ vt (organiser, prévoir: émission) to schedule; (Inform) to program; **programmeur, -euse** nm/f (computer) programmer

progrès [prɔgrɛ] nm progress no pl; **faire des/être en ~** to make/ be making progress; **progresser** /1/ vi to progress; **progressif, -ive** adj progressive

proie [prwa] nf prey no pl

projecteur [prɔʒektœr] nm projector; (de théâtre, cirque) spotlight

projectile [prɔʒektil] nm missile

projection [prɔʒeksjɔ̃] nf projection; (séance) showing

projet [prɔʒɛ] nm plan; (ébauche) draft; **~ de loi** bill; **projeter** /4/ vt (envisager) to plan; (film, photos) to project; (ombre, lueur) to throw, cast; (jeter) to throw up (ou off ou out)

prolétaire [prɔletɛr] adj, nm/f proletarian

prolongement [prɔlɔ̃ʒmɑ̃] nm extension; **dans le ~ de** running on from

prolonger [prɔlɔ̃ʒe] /3/ vt (débat, séjour) to prolong; (délai, billet, rue) to extend; **se prolonger** vi to go on

promenade [prɔmnad] nf walk (ou drive ou ride); **faire une ~** to go for a walk; **une ~ (à pied)/en voiture/à vélo** a walk/drive/(bicycle) ride

promener [prɔmne] /5/ vt (personne, chien) to take out for a walk; (doigts, regard): **~ qch sur** to run sth over; **se promener** vi to go for (ou be out for) a walk

promesse [prɔmɛs] nf promise

promettre [pʀɔmɛtʀ] /56/ vt to promise ▷ vi to look promising; **~ à qn de faire** to promise sb that one will do

promiscuité [pʀɔmiskɥite] nf lack of privacy

promontoire [pʀɔmɔ̃twaʀ] nm headland

promoteur, -trice [pʀɔmɔtœʀ, -tʀis] nm/f: **~ (immobilier)** property developer (BRIT), real estate promoter (US)

promotion [pʀɔmosjɔ̃] nf promotion; **en ~** on (special) offer

promouvoir [pʀɔmuvwaʀ] /27/ vt to promote

prompt, e [pʀɔ̃, pʀɔ̃t] adj swift, rapid

prôner [pʀone] /1/ vt (préconiser) to advocate

pronom [pʀɔnɔ̃] nm pronoun

prononcer [pʀɔnɔ̃se] /3/ vt to pronounce; (dire) to utter; (discours) to deliver; **se prononcer** vi to be pronounced; **se ~ (sur)** (se décider) to reach a decision (on ou about), give a verdict (on); **ça se prononce comment?** how do you pronounce this? **prononciation** nf pronunciation

pronostic [pʀɔnɔstik] nm (Méd) prognosis; (fig: aussi: **~s**) forecast

propagande [pʀɔpagɑ̃d] nf propaganda

propager [pʀɔpaʒe] /3/ vt to spread; **se propager** vi to spread

prophète, prophétesse [pʀɔfɛt, pʀɔfetɛs] nm/f prophet(ess)

prophétie [pʀɔfesi] nf prophecy

propice [pʀɔpis] adj favourable

proportion [pʀɔpɔʀsjɔ̃] nf proportion; **toute(s) ~(s) gardée(s)** making due allowance(s)

propos [pʀɔpo] nm (paroles) talk no pl, remark; (intention, but) intention, aim; (sujet): **à quel ~?** what about?; **à ~ de** about, regarding; **à tout ~** for no reason at all; **à ~** by the way; (opportunément) (just) at the right moment

proposer [pʀɔpoze] /1/ vt to propose; **~ qch (à qn)/de faire** (suggérer) to suggest sth (to sb)/ doing, propose sth (to sb)/(to) do; (offrir) to offer (sb) sth/to do; **se ~ (pour faire)** to offer one's services (to do); **proposition** nf suggestion; proposal; (Ling) clause

propre [pʀɔpʀ] adj clean; (net) neat, tidy; (possessif) own; (sens) literal; (particulier): **~ à** peculiar to; (approprié): **~ à** suitable ou appropriate for ▷ nm: **recopier au ~** to make a fair copy of; **proprement** adv (avec propreté) cleanly; **à proprement parler** strictly speaking; **le village proprement dit** the village itself; **propreté** nf cleanliness

propriétaire [pʀɔpʀijetɛʀ] nm/f owner; (pour le locataire) landlord(-lady)

propriété [pʀɔpʀijete] nf (droit) ownership; (objet, immeuble etc) property

propulser [pʀɔpylse] /1/ vt to propel

prose [pʀoz] nf prose (style)

prospecter [pʀɔspɛkte] /1/ vt to prospect; (Comm) to canvass

prospectus [pʀɔspɛktys] nm leaflet

prospère [pʀɔspɛʀ] adj prosperous; **prospérer** /6/ vi to thrive

prosterner [pʀɔstɛʀne] /1/: **se prosterner** vi to bow low, prostrate o.s.

prostituée [pʀɔstitɥe] nf prostitute

prostitution [pʀɔstitɥsjɔ̃] nf prostitution

protecteur, -trice [pʀɔtɛktœʀ, -tʀis] adj protective; (air, ton: péj) patronizing ▷ nm/f protector

protection [pʀɔtɛksjɔ̃] nf protection; (d'un personnage influent: aide) patronage

protéger [pʀɔteʒe] /6, 3/ vt to protect; **se ~ de/contre** to protect o.s. from

protège-slip [pʀɔtɛʒslip] nm panty liner

protéine [pʀɔtein] nf protein

protestant, e [pʀɔtɛstɑ̃, -ɑ̃t] adj, nm/f Protestant

protestation [pʀɔtɛstasjɔ̃] nf (plainte) protest

protester [pʀɔtɛste] /1/ vi: **~ (contre)** to protest (against ou about); **~ de** (son innocence, sa loyauté) to protest

prothèse [pʀɔtɛz] nf: **~ dentaire** denture

protocole [pʀɔtɔkɔl] nm (fig) etiquette

proue [pʀu] nf bow(s pl), prow

prouesse [pʀuɛs] nf feat

prouver [pʀuve] /1/ vt to prove

provenance [pʀɔvnɑ̃s] nf origin; **avion en ~ de** plane (arriving) from

provenir [pʀɔvniʀ] /22/: **~ de** vt to come from

proverbe [pʀɔvɛʀb] nm proverb

province [pʀɔvɛ̃s] nf province

proviseur [pʀɔvizœʀ] ≈ nm head (teacher) (BRIT), ≈ principal (US)

provision [pʀɔvizjɔ̃] nf (réserve) stock, supply; **provisions** nfpl (vivres) provisions, food no pl

provisoire [pʀɔvizwaʀ] adj temporary; **provisoirement** adv temporarily

provocant, e [pʀɔvɔkɑ̃, -ɑ̃t] adj provocative

provoquer [pʀɔvɔke] /1/ vt (défier) to provoke; (causer) to cause, bring about; (inciter): **~ qn à** to incite sb to

proxénète [pʀɔksenɛt] nm procurer

proximité [pʀɔksimite] nf nearness, closeness; (dans le temps) imminence, closeness; **à ~** near ou close by; **à ~ de** near (to), close to

prudemment [pʀydamɑ̃] adv carefully; wisely, sensibly

prudence [pʀydɑ̃s] nf carefulness; **avec ~** carefully; **par (mesure de) ~** as a precaution

prudent, e [pʀydɑ̃, -ɑ̃t] adj (pas téméraire) careful; (: en général) safety-conscious; (sage, conseillé) wise, sensible; **c'est plus ~** it's wiser

prune [pʀyn] nf plum

pruneau, x [pʀyno] nm prune

prunier [pʀynje] nm plum tree

PS sigle m = **parti socialiste**; (= post-scriptum) PS

pseudonyme [psødɔnim] nm (gén) fictitious name; (d'écrivain) pseudonym, pen name

psychanalyse [psikanaliz] nf psychoanalysis

psychiatre [psikjatʀ] nm/f psychiatrist; **psychiatrique** adj psychiatric

psychique [psiʃik] adj psychological

psychologie [psikɔlɔʒi] nf psychology; **psychologique** adj psychological; **psychologue** nm/f psychologist

pu [py] pp de **pouvoir**

puanteur [pɥɑ̃tœʀ] nf stink, stench

pub [pyb] nf (fam) = **publicité**; **la ~** advertising

public, -ique [pyblik] adj public; (école, instruction) state cpd ▷ nm public; (assistance) audience; **en ~** in public

publicitaire [pyblisitɛʀ] adj advertising cpd; (film, voiture) publicity cpd

publicité [pyblisite] nf (méthode, profession) advertising; (annonce) advertisement; (révélations) publicity

publier [pyblije] /7/ vt to publish

publipostage [pyblipɔstaʒ] nm (mass) mailing

publique [pyblik] adj f voir **public**

puce [pys] nf flea; (Inform) chip; **carte à ~** smart card; **(marché aux) ~s** flea market sg

pudeur [pydœʀ] nf modesty; **pudique** adj (chaste) modest; (discret) discreet

puer [pɥe] /1/ (péj) vi to stink

puéricultrice [pɥeʀikyltʀis] nf ≈ paediatric nurse

puéril, e [pɥeʀil] adj childish

puis [pɥi] vb voir **pouvoir** ▷ adv then

puiser [pɥize] /1/ vt: **~ (dans)** to draw (from)

puisque [pɥisk] conj since

puissance [pɥisɑ̃s] nf power; **en ~** adj potential

puissant, e [pɥisɑ̃, -ɑ̃t] adj powerful

puits [pɥi] nm well

pull(-over) [pyl(ɔvœʀ)] nm sweater

pulluler [pylyle] /1/ vi to swarm

pulpe [pylp] nf pulp

pulvériser [pylveʀize] /1/ vt to pulverize; (liquide) to spray

punaise [pynez] nf (Zool) bug; (clou) drawing pin (BRIT), thumb tack (US)

punch [pɔ̃ʃ] nm (boisson) punch

punir [pyniʀ] /2/ vt to punish; **punition** nf punishment

pupille [pypij] nf (Anat) pupil ▷ nm/f (enfant) ward

pupitre [pypitʀ] nm (Scol) desk

pur, e [pyʀ] adj pure; (vin) undiluted; (whisky) neat; **en ~e perte** to no avail; **c'est de la folie ~e** it's sheer madness

purée [pyʀe] nf: **~ de pommes de terre** ≈ mashed potatoes pl; **~ de marrons** chestnut purée

purement [pyʀmɑ̃] adv purely

purgatoire [pyʀgatwaʀ] nm purgatory

purger [pyʀʒe] /3/ vt (Méd, Pol) to purge; (Jur: peine) to serve

pur-sang [pyʀsɑ̃] nm inv thoroughbred

pus [py] nm pus

putain [pytɛ̃] nf (!) whore (!)

puzzle [pœzl] nm jigsaw (puzzle)

PV sigle m = **procès-verbal**

pyjama [piʒama] nm pyjamas pl (BRIT), pajamas pl (US)

pyramide [piʀamid] nf pyramid

Pyrénées [piʀene] nfpl: **les ~** the Pyrenees

q

QI sigle m (= quotient intellectuel) IQ

quadragénaire [kadʀaʒenɛʀ] nm/f man/woman in his/her forties

quadruple [k(w)adʀypl] nm: **le ~ de** four times as much as

quai [ke] nm (de port) quay; (de gare) platform; **être à ~** (navire) to be alongside

qualification [kalifikasjɔ̃] nf qualification

qualifier [kalifje] /1/ vt to qualify; **~ qch/qn de** to describe sth/sb as; **se qualifier** vi to qualify

qualité [kalite] nf quality

quand [kɑ̃] conj, adv when; **je serai riche** when I'm rich; **~ même** all the same; **~ même, il exagère!** really, he overdoes it!; **~ bien même** even though

quant [kɑ̃]: **~ à** prép (pour ce qui est de) as for, as to; (au sujet de) regarding

quantité [kɑ̃tite] nf quantity, amount; **une ou des ~(s) de** (grand nombre) a great deal of

quarantaine [kaʀɑ̃tɛn] *nf*
(*isolement*) quarantine; **une ~ (de)**
forty or so, about forty; **avoir la ~
(âge)** to be around forty

quarante [kaʀɑ̃t] *num* forty

quart [kaʀ] *nm* (*fraction*) quarter;
(*surveillance*) watch; **un ~ de vin** a
quarter litre of wine; **le ~ de** a quarter
of; **~ d'heure** quarter of an hour; **~s
de finale** quarter finals

quartier [kaʀtje] *nm* (*de ville*) district,
area; (*de bœuf, de la lune*) piece;
(*de fruit, fromage*) piece; **cinéma/
salle de ~** local cinema/hall; **avoir
~ libre** to be free; **~ général (QG)**
headquarters (HQ)

quartz [kwaʀts] *nm* quartz

quasi [kazi] *adv* almost, nearly;
quasiment *adv* almost, (*very*) nearly;
quasiment jamais hardly ever

quatorze [katɔʀz] *num* fourteen

quatorzième [katɔʀzjɛm] *num*
fourteenth

quatre [katʀ] *num* four; **à ~ pattes**
on all fours; **se mettre en ~ pour
qn** to go out of one's way for sb; **~s
~ à ~ (monter, descendre)** four at
a time; **quatre-vingt-dix** *num*
ninety; **quatre-vingts** *num* eighty;
quatrième *num* fourth ▷ *nf* (*Scol*)
year 9 (BRIT), eighth grade (US)

quatuor [kwatɥɔʀ] *nm* quartet(te)

MOT-CLÉ

que [kə] *conj* **1** (*introduisant complétive*)
that; **il sait que tu es là** he knows
(that) you're here; **je veux que tu
acceptes** I want you to accept; **il
a dit que oui** he said he would (*ou*
it was) *etc*

2 (*reprise d'autres conjonctions*): **quand
il rentrera et qu'il aura mangé**
when he gets back and (when) he has
eaten; **si tu y vas ou que vous
...** if you go there or if you ...

3 (*en tête de phrase, hypothèse, souhait
etc*): **qu'il le veuille ou non** whether

he likes it or not; **qu'il fasse ce qu'il
voudra!** let him do as he pleases!

4 (*but*): **tenez-le qu'il ne tombe pas**
hold it so (that) it doesn't fall

5 (*après comparatif*) than, as; *voir aussi*
plus², **aussi**, **autant** *etc*

6 (*seulement*): **ne ... que** only; **il ne
boit que de l'eau** he only drinks
water

7 (*temps*): **il y a quatre ans qu'il est
parti** it is four years since he left, he
left four years ago

▷ *adv* (*exclamation*): **qu'il ou qu'est-ce
qu'il est bête/court vite!** he's so
silly!/he runs so fast!; **que de livres!**
what a lot of books!

▷ *pron* **1** (*relatif: personne*) whom;
(: *chose*) that, which; **l'homme que
je vois** the man (whom) I see; **le livre
que tu vois** the book (that *ou* which)
you see; **un jour que j'étais ...** a day
when I was ...

2 (*interrogatif*): **que fais-tu?**,
qu'est-ce que tu fais? what are you
doing?; **qu'est-ce que c'est?** what
is it?, what's that?; **que faire?** what
can one do?

Québec [kebɛk] *nm*: **le ~** Quebec
(Province)

québécois, e *adj* Quebec *cpd* ▷ *nm*
(*Ling*) Quebec French ▷ *nm/f*: **Q~, e**
Quebecois, Quebec(k)er

MOT-CLÉ

quel, quelle [kɛl] *adj* **1** (*interrogatif:
personne*) who; (: *chose*) what; **quel
est cet homme?** who is this man?;
quel est ce livre? what is this
book?; **quel livre/homme?** what
book/man?; (*parmi un certain choix*)
which book/man?; **quels acteurs
préférez-vous?** which actors do you
prefer?; **dans quels pays êtes-vous
allé?** which *ou* what countries did
you go to?

2 (*exclamatif*): **quelle surprise/**

**coïncidence! what a surprise/
coincidence!**

3: quel que soit le coupable
whoever is guilty; **quel que soit
votre avis** whatever your opinion
(may be)

quelconque [kɛlkɔ̃k] adj (médiocre:
repas) indifferent, poor; (sans attrait)
ordinary, plain; (indéfini): **un ami/
prétexte ~** some friend/pretext
or other

○ **MOT-CLÉ**

quelque [kɛlk] adj **1** (au singulier)
some; (au pluriel) a few, some;
(tournure interrogative) any; **quelque
espoir** some hope; **il a quelques
amis** he has a few ou some friends;
a-t-il quelques amis? does he have
any friends?; **les quelques livres
qui** the few books which; **20 kg et
quelque(s)** a bit over 20 kg
2: quelque ... que: quelque
livre qu'il choisisse whatever (ou
whichever) book he chooses
quelque chose something;
(tournure interrogative) anything;
quelque chose d'autre something
else; anything else; **quelque part**
somewhere; anywhere; **en quelque
sorte** as it were
▶ adv **1** (environ): **quelque 100
mètres** some 100 metres
2: quelque peu rather, somewhat

quelquefois [kɛlkəfwa] adv
sometimes

quelques-uns, -unes [kɛlkəzœ̃,
-yn] pron some, a few

quelqu'un [kɛlkœ̃] pron someone,
somebody; (+ tournure interrogative
ou négative) anyone, anybody; **~
d'autre** someone ou somebody else;
anybody else

qu'en dira-t-on [kɑ̃diratɔ̃] nm inv:
le ~ gossip, what people say

querelle [kəʀɛl] nf quarrel; **quereller**
/1/: **se quereller** vi to quarrel

qu'est-ce que [kɛskə] voir **que**

qu'est-ce qui [kɛski] voir **qui**

question [kɛstjɔ̃] nf question;
(fig) matter; issue; **il a été ~** we
(ou they) spoke about; **de quoi
est-il ~?** what is it about?; **il n'en
est pas ~** there's no question of
it; **en ~** in question; **hors de ~** out
of the question; **(re)mettre en ~**
to question; **questionnaire** nm
questionnaire; **questionner** /1/ vt
to question

quête [kɛt] nf collection; (recherche)
quest, search; **faire la ~** (à l'église) to
take the collection; (artiste) to pass
the hat round

quetsche [kwɛtʃ] nf damson

queue [kø] nf tail; (fig: du classement)
bottom; (: de poêle) handle; (: de fruit,
feuille) stalk; (: de train, colonne, file)
rear; **faire la ~** to queue (up) (BRIT),
line up (US); **~ de cheval** ponytail; **~
de poisson: faire une ~ de poisson
à qn** (Auto) to cut in front of sb

○ **MOT-CLÉ**

qui [ki] pron **1** (interrogatif: personne)
who; (: chose): **qu'est-ce qui est
sur la table?** what is on the table?;
qui est-ce qui? who?; **qui est-ce
que?** who?; **à qui est ce sac?** whose
bag is this?; **à qui parlais-tu?** who
were you talking to?, to whom were
you talking?; **chez qui allez-vous?**
whose house are you going to?
2 (relatif: personne) who; (+ prép)
whom; **l'ami de qui je vous ai parlé**
the friend I told you about; **la dame
chez qui je suis allé** the lady whose
house I went to
3 (sans antécédent): **amenez qui vous
voulez** bring who you like; **qui que
ce soit** whoever it may be

quiche [kiʃ] nf quiche

quiconque [kikɔ̃k] *pron (celui qui)* whoever, anyone who; *(n'importe qui, personne)* anyone, anybody

quille [kij] *nf:* **(jeu de) ~s** skittles *sg* (BRIT), bowling (us)

quincaillerie [kɛ̃kajʀi] *nf (ustensiles)* hardware; *(magasin)* hardware shop ou store (us)

quinquagénaire [kɛ̃kaʒenɛʀ] *nm/f* man/woman in his/her fifties

quinquennat [kɛ̃kena] *nm* five year term of office (of French President)

quinte [kɛ̃t] *nf:* **~ (de toux)** coughing fit

quintuple [kɛ̃typl] *nm:* **le ~ de** five times as much as

quinzaine [kɛ̃zɛn] *nf:* **une ~ (de)** about fifteen, fifteen or so; **une ~ (de jours)** a fortnight (BRIT), two weeks

quinze [kɛ̃z] *num* fifteen; **dans ~ jours** in a fortnight('s time) (BRIT), in two weeks('time)

quinzième [kɛ̃zjɛm] *num* fifteenth

quittance [kitɑ̃s] *nf (reçu)* receipt

quitte [kit] *adj:* **être ~ envers qn** to be no longer in sb's debt; *(fig)* to be quits with sb; **~ à faire** even if it means doing

quitter [kite] */1/ vt* to leave; *(vêtement)* to take off; **se quitter** *vi (couples, interlocuteurs)* to part; **ne quittez pas** *(au téléphone)* hold the line

qui-vive [kiviv] *nm inv:* **être sur le ~** to be on the alert

MOT-CLÉ

quoi [kwa] *pron interrog* **1** what; **~ de neuf?** what's new?; **~?** *(qu'est-ce que tu dis?)* what?
2 *(avec prép):* **à ~ tu penses?** what are you thinking about?; **de ~ parlez-vous?** what are you talking about?; **à ~ bon?** what's the use?
▶ *pron relatif:* **as-tu de ~ écrire?** do you have anything to write with?; **il n'y a pas de ~** *(please)* don't mention

it; **il n'y a pas de ~ rire** there's nothing to laugh about
▶ *pron (locutions):* **~ qu'il arrive** whatever happens; **~ qu'il en soit** be that as it may; **~ que ce soit** anything at all
▶ *excl* what!

quoique [kwak] *conj* (al)though

quotidien, ne [kɔtidjɛ̃, -ɛn] *adj* daily; *(banal)* everyday ▷ *nm (journal)* daily (paper); **quotidiennement** *adv* daily, every day

r

R, r abr = **route; rue**

rab [Rab] nm (fam: nourriture) extra; **est-ce qu'il y a du ~?** are there any seconds?

rabâcher [Rabɑʃe] /1/ vt to keep on repeating

rabais [Rabɛ] nm reduction, discount; **rabaisser** /1/ vt (rabattre: prix) to reduce; (dénigrer) to belittle

Rabat [Raba(t)] n Rabat

rabattre [RabatR] /41/ vt (couvercle, siège) to pull down; (déduire) to reduce; **se rabattre** vi (bords, couvercle) to fall shut; (véhicule, coureur) to cut in; **se ~ sur** to fall back on

rabbin [Rabɛ̃] nm rabbi

rabougri, e [Rabugri] adj stunted

raccommoder [Rakɔmɔde] /1/ vt to mend, repair

raccompagner [Rakɔ̃paɲe] /1/ vt to take ou see back

raccord [RakɔR] nm link; (retouche) touch-up; **raccorder** /1/ vt to join (up), link up; (pont etc) to connect, link

raccourci [Rakursi] nm short cut

raccourcir [RakursiR] /2/ vt to shorten ▷ vi (jours) to grow shorter, draw in

raccrocher [RakRɔʃe] /1/ vt (tableau, vêtement) to hang back up; (récepteur) to put down ▷ vi (Tél) to hang up, ring off

race [Ras] nf race; (d'animaux, fig) breed; **de ~** purebred, pedigree

rachat [Raʃa] nm buying; (du même objet) buying back

racheter [Raʃte] /5/ vt (article perdu) to buy another; (davantage) to buy more; (après avoir vendu) to buy back; (d'occasion) to buy; (Comm: part, firme) to buy up; **se racheter** (gén) to make amends; **~ du lait/trois œufs** to buy more milk/another three eggs

racial, e, -aux [Rasjal, -o] adj racial

racine [Rasin] nf root; **~ carrée/cubique** square/cube root

racisme [Rasism] nm racism

raciste [Rasist] adj, nm/f racist

racket [Rakɛt] nm racketeering no pl

raclée [Rɑkle] nf (fam) hiding, thrashing

racler [Rɑkle] /1/ vt (os, plat) to scrape; **se ~ la gorge** to clear one's throat

racontars [Rakɔ̃taR] nmpl stories, gossip sg

raconter [Rakɔ̃te] /1/ vt: **~ (à qn)** (décrire) to relate (to sb), tell (sb) about; (dire) to tell (sb); **~ une histoire** to tell a story

radar [RadaR] nm radar; **~ (automatique)** (Auto) speed camera

rade [Rad] nf (natural) harbour; **rester en ~** (fig) to be left stranded

radeau, x [Rado] nm raft

radiateur [RadjatœR] nm radiator, heater; (Auto) radiator; **~ électrique/à gaz** electric/gas heater ou fire

radiation [Radjasjɔ̃] nf (Physique) radiation

radical, e, -aux [Radikal, -o] adj radical

radieux, -euse [Radjø, -øz] adj
radiant

radin, e [Radɛ̃, -in] adj (fam) stingy

radio [Radjo] nf radio; (Méd) X-ray
▷ nm radio operator; **à la ~** on
the radio; **radioactif, -ive** adj
radioactive; **radiocassette** nf
cassette radio; **radiographie**
nf radiography; (photo) X-ray
photograph; **radiophonique** adj
radio cpd; **radio-réveil** (pl **radios-
réveils**) nm radio alarm (clock)

radis [Radi] nm radish

radoter [Radɔte] /1/ vi to ramble on

radoucir [Radusir] /2/: **se radoucir**
vi (se réchauffer) to become milder; (se
calmer) to calm down

rafale [Rafal] nf (vent) gust of wind);
(de balles, d'applaudissements) burst

raffermir [Rafɛrmir] /2/ vt, **se
raffermir** vi to firm up

raffiner [Rafine] /1/ vt to refine;
raffinerie nf refinery

raffoler [Rafɔle] /1/: ~ **de** vt to be
very keen on

rafle [Rafl] nf (de police) raid; **rafler** /1/
vt (fam) to swipe, nick

rafraîchir [Rafʀɛʃir] /2/ vt
(atmosphère, température) to cool
(down); (boisson) to chill; (fig: rénover)
to brighten up; **se rafraîchir** vi to
grow cooler; (en se lavant) to freshen
up; (en buvant etc) to refresh o.s.;
rafraîchissant, e adj refreshing;
rafraîchissement nm (boisson)
cool drink; **rafraîchissements** nmpl
(boissons, fruits etc) refreshments

rage [Raʒ] nf (Méd): **la ~** rabies; (fureur)
rage, fury; **faire ~** to rage; **~ de dents**
(raging) toothache

ragot [Rago] nm (fam) malicious
gossip no pl

ragoût [Ragu] nm stew

raide [Rɛd] adj (tendu) taut, tight;
(escarpé) steep; (droit: cheveux)
straight; (ankylosé, dur, guindé) stiff;
(fam: sans argent) flat broke; (osé,
licencieux) daring ▷ adv (en pente)

steeply; **~ mort** stone dead; **raideur**
nf (rigidité) stiffness; **avec raideur**
(répondre) stiffly, abruptly; **raidir** /2/
vt (muscles) to stiffen; **se raidir** vi to
stiffen; (personne) to tense up; (: se
préparer moralement) to brace o.s.; (fig:
devenir intransigeant) to harden

raie [Rɛ] nf (Zool) skate, ray; (rayure)
stripe; (des cheveux) parting

raifort [Rɛfɔr] nm horseradish

rail [Raj] nm rail; (chemins de fer)
railways pl; **par ~** by rail

railler [Raje] /1/ vt to scoff at, jeer at

rainure [Renyr] nf groove

raisin [Rezɛ̃] nm (aussi: **~s**) grapes pl;
~ secs raisins

raison [Rezɔ̃] nf reason; **avoir ~** to be
right; **donner ~ à qn** to agree with
sb; (fait) to prove sb right; **se faire
une ~** to learn to live with it; **perdre
la ~** to become insane; **~ de plus** all
the more reason; **à plus forte ~** all
the more so; **sans ~** for no reason;
en ~ de because of; **à ~ de** at the
rate of; **~ sociale** corporate name;
raisonnable adj reasonable, sensible

raisonnement [Rezɔnmɑ̃] nm
reasoning; argument

raisonner [Rezɔne] /1/ vi (penser) to
reason; (argumenter, discuter) to argue
▷ vt (personne) to reason with

rajeunir [Raʒœnir] /2/ vt (en
recrutant) to inject new blood into
▷ vi to become (ou look) younger; **~
qn** (coiffure, robe) to make sb look
younger

rajouter [Raʒute] /1/ vt to add

rajuster [Raʒyste] /1/ vt (vêtement) to
straighten, tidy; (salaires) to adjust

ralenti [Ralɑ̃ti] nm: **au ~** (fig) at a
slower pace; **tourner au ~** (Auto) to
tick over, idle

ralentir [Ralɑ̃tir] /2/ vt, vi, **se
ralentir** vi to slow down

râler [Rɑle] /1/ vi to groan; (fam) to
grouse, moan (and groan)

rallier [Ralje] /1/ vt (rejoindre) to
rejoin; (gagner à sa cause) to win over

rallonge [Ralɔ̃ʒ] *nf* (*de table*) (extra) leaf

rallonger [Ralɔ̃ʒe] /3/ *vt* to lengthen

rallye [Rali] *nm* rally; (*Pol*) march

ramassage [Ramasaʒ] *nm*: ~ **scolaire** school bus service

ramasser [Ramase] /1/ *vt* (*objet tombé ou par terre*) to pick up; (*recueillir*: copies, ordures) to collect; (*récolter*) to gather; **ramassis** *nm* (*péj*: *de voyous*) bunch; (*de choses*) jumble

rambarde [Rãbard] *nf* guardrail

rame [Ram] *nf* (*aviron*) oar; (*de métro*) train; (*de papier*) ream

rameau, x [Ramo] *nm* (small) branch; **les R~x** (*Rel*) Palm Sunday *sg*

ramener [Ramne] /5/ *vt* to bring back; (*reconduire*) to take back; ~ **qch à** (*réduire à*) to reduce sth to

ramer [Rame] /1/ *vi* to row

ramollir [Ramolir] /2/ *vt* to soften; **se ramollir** *vi* to get (ou go) soft

rampe [Rãp] *nf* (*d'escalier*) banister(s *pl*); (*dans un garage, d'un terrain*) ramp; **la ~** (*Théât*) the footlights *pl*; **~ de lancement** launching pad

ramper [Rãpe] /1/ *vi* to crawl

rancard [Rãkar] *nm* (*fam*) date

rancart [Rãkar] *nm*: **mettre au ~** to scrap

rance [Rãs] *adj* rancid

rancœur [Rãkœr] *nf* rancour

rançon [Rãsɔ̃] *nf* ransom

rancune [Rãkyn] *nf* grudge, rancour; **garder ~ à qn (de qch)** to bear sb a grudge (for sth); **sans ~!** no hard feelings!; **rancunier, -ière** *adj* vindictive, spiteful

randonnée [Rãdɔne] *nf* ride; (*à pied*) walk, ramble; (*en montagne*) hike, hiking *no pl*; **la ~** (*activité*) hiking, walking; **une ~ à cheval** a pony trek

rang [Rã] *nm* (*rangée*) row; (*grade, condition sociale, classement*) rank; **rangs** *nmpl* (*Mil*) ranks; **se mettre en ~s/sur un ~** to get into ou form rows/a line; **au premier ~** in the first row; (*fig*) ranking first

rangé, e [Rãʒe] *adj* (*vie*) well-ordered; (*sérieux: personne*) steady

rangée [Rãʒe] *nf* row

ranger [Rãʒe] /3/ *vt* (*classer, grouper*) to order, arrange; (*mettre à sa place*) to put away; (*mettre de l'ordre dans*) to tidy up; (*fig: classer*): ~ **qn/qch parmi** to rank sb/sth among; **se ranger** *vi* (*véhicule, conducteur*) to pull over or in; (*piéton*) to step aside; (*s'assagir*) to settle down; **se ~** (*à*: *avis*) to come round to

ranimer [Ranime] /1/ *vt* (*personne évanouie*) to bring round; (*douleur, souvenir*) to revive; (*feu*) to rekindle

rapace [Rapas] *nm* bird of prey

râpe [Rɑp] *nf* (*Culin*) grater; **râper** /1/ *vt* (*Culin*) to grate

rapide [Rapid] *adj* fast; (*prompt: intelligence, coup d'œil, mouvement*) quick ▷ *nm* express (train); (*de cours d'eau*) rapid; **rapidement** *adv* fast; quickly

rapiécer [Rapjese] /3, 6/ *vt* to patch

rappel [Rapel] *nm* (*Théât*) curtain call; (*Méd: vaccination*) booster; (*d'une aventure, d'un nom*) reminder; **rappeler** /4/ *vt* to call back; (*ambassadeur, Mil*) to recall; (*faire se souvenir*): **rappeler qch à qn** to remind sb of sth; **se rappeler** *vt* (*se souvenir de*) to remember, recall

rapport [Rapor] *nm* (*compte rendu*) report; (*profit*) yield, return; (*lien, analogie*) relationship; (*corrélation*) connection; **rapports** *nmpl* (*entre personnes, pays*) relations; **avoir ~ à** to have something to do with; **être/se mettre en ~ avec qn** to get/be in touch with sb; **par ~ à** in relation to; **~s (sexuels)** (sexual) intercourse *sg*; **~ qualité-prix** value (for money)

rapporter [Raporte] /1/ *vt* (*rendre, ramener*) to bring back; (*investissement*) to yield; (*relater*) to report ▷ *vi* (*investissement*) to give a good return ou yield; (*activité*) to be very profitable; **se ~ à** to relate to

rapprochement [ʀapʀɔʃmɑ̃] nm (de nations, familles) reconciliation; (analogie, rapport) parallel

rapprocher [ʀapʀɔʃe] /1/ vt (deux objets) to bring closer together; (ennemis, partis etc) to bring together; (comparer) to establish a parallel between; (chaise d'une table): ~ qch (de) to bring sth closer (to); se rapprocher vi to draw closer ou nearer; se ~ de to come closer to; (présenter une analogie avec) to be close to

raquette [ʀakɛt] nf (de tennis) racket; (de ping-pong) bat

rare [ʀɑʀ] adj rare; se faire ~ to become scarce; **rarement** adv rarely, seldom

ras, e [ʀɑ, ʀɑz] adj (tête, cheveux) close-cropped; (poil, herbe) short ▷ adv short; **en ~e campagne** in open country; **à ~ bords** to the brim; **en avoir ~ le bol** (fam) to be fed up

raser [ʀaze] /1/ vt (barbe, cheveux) to shave off; (menton, personne) to shave; (fam: ennuyer) to bore; (démolir) to raze (to the ground); (frôler) to graze, skim; **se raser** vi to shave; (fam) to be bored (to tears); **rasoir** nm razor

rassasier [ʀasazje] /7/ vt: **être rassasié** to be sated

rassemblement [ʀasɑ̃bləmɑ̃] nm (groupe) gathering, (Pol) union

rassembler [ʀasɑ̃ble] /1/ vt (réunir) to assemble, gather; (documents, notes) to gather together, collect; **se rassembler** vi to gather

rassurer [ʀasyʀe] /1/ vt to reassure; **se rassurer** vi to be reassured; **rassure-toi** don't worry

rat [ʀa] nm rat

rate [ʀat] nf spleen

raté, e [ʀate] adj (tentative) unsuccessful, failed ▷ nm/f (fam: personne) failure

râteau, x [ʀɑto] nm rake

rater [ʀate] /1/ vi (affaire, projet etc) to go wrong, fail ▷ vt (cible, train,

occasion) to miss; (démonstration, plat) to spoil; (examen) to fail

ration [ʀasjɔ̃] nf ration

RATP sigle f (= Régie autonome des transports parisiens) Paris transport authority

rattacher [ʀataʃe] /1/ vt (animal, cheveux) to tie up again; ~ **qch à** (relier) to link sth with

rattraper [ʀatʀape] /1/ vt (fugitif) to recapture; (retenir, empêcher de tomber) to catch (hold of); (atteindre, rejoindre) to catch up with; (réparer: erreur) to make up for; **se rattraper** vi to make up for it; **se ~ (à)** (se raccrocher) to stop o.s. falling (by catching hold of)

rature [ʀatyʀ] nf deletion, erasure

rauque [ʀok] adj (voix) hoarse

ravages [ʀavaʒ] nmpl: **faire des ~** to wreak havoc

ravi, e [ʀavi] adj: **être ~ de/que** to be delighted with/that

ravin [ʀavɛ̃] nm gully, ravine

ravir [ʀaviʀ] /2/ vt (enchanter) to delight; **à ~** adv beautifully

raviser [ʀavize] /1/: **se raviser** vi to change one's mind

ravissant, e [ʀavisɑ̃, -ɑ̃t] adj delightful

ravisseur, -euse [ʀavisœʀ, -øz] nm/f abductor, kidnapper

ravitailler [ʀavitaje] /1/ vt (en vivres, munitions) to provide with fresh supplies; (véhicule) to refuel; **se ravitailler** vi to get fresh supplies

raviver [ʀavive] /1/ vt (feu) to rekindle; (douleur) to revive; (couleurs) to brighten up

rayé, e [ʀeje] adj (à rayures) striped

rayer [ʀeje] /8/ vt (érafler) to scratch; (barrer) to cross out ou score out; (d'une liste) to cross out ou strike off

rayon [ʀejɔ̃] nm (de soleil etc) ray; (Géom) radius; (de roue) spoke; (étagère) shelf; (de grand magasin) department; **dans un ~ de** within a radius of; ~ **de soleil** sunbeam; ~s **X** X-rays

rayonnement [ʀɛjɔnmã] nm (d'une culture) influence

rayonner [ʀɛjɔne] /1/ vi (fig) to shine forth; (: visage, personne) to be radiant; (touriste) to go touring (from one base)

rayure [ʀɛjyʀ] nf (motif) stripe; (éraflure) scratch; **à ~s** striped

raz-de-marée [ʀɑdmaʀe] nm inv tidal wave

ré [ʀe] nm (Mus) D; (en chantant la gamme) re

réaction [ʀeaksjɔ̃] nf reaction

réadapter [ʀeadapte] /1/: **se ~ (à)** vi to readjust (to)

réagir [ʀeaʒiʀ] /2/ vi to react

réalisateur, -trice [ʀealizatœʀ, -tʀis] nm/f (TV, Ciné) director

réalisation [ʀealizasjɔ̃] nf realization; (Ciné) production; **en cours de ~** under way

réaliser [ʀealize] /1/ vt (projet, opération) to carry out, realize; (rêve, souhait) to realize, fulfil; (exploit) to achieve; (film) to produce; (se rendre compte de) to realize; **se réaliser** vi to be realized

réaliste [ʀealist] adj realistic

réalité [ʀealite] nf reality; **en ~** in (actual) fact; **dans la ~** in reality

réanimation [ʀeanimasjɔ̃] nf resuscitation; **service de ~** intensive care unit

rébarbatif, -ive [ʀebaʀbatif, -iv] adj forbidding

rebattu, e [ʀəbaty] adj hackneyed

rebelle [ʀəbɛl] nm/f rebel ▷ adj (troupes) rebel; (enfant) rebellious; (mèche etc) unruly

rebeller [ʀəbele] /1/: **se rebeller** vi to rebel

rebondir [ʀəbɔ̃diʀ] /2/ vi (ballon: au sol) to bounce; (: contre un mur) to rebound; (fig) to get moving again

rebord [ʀəbɔʀ] nm edge; **le ~ de la fenêtre** the windowsill

rebours [ʀəbuʀ]: **à ~** adv the wrong way

rebrousser [ʀəbʀuse] /1/ vt: **~ chemin** to turn back

rebuter [ʀəbyte] /1/ vt to put off

récalcitrant, e [ʀekalsitʀã, -ãt] adj refractory

récapituler [ʀekapityle] /1/ vt to recapitulate; to sum up

receler [ʀəsəle] /5/ vt (produit d'un vol) to receive; (fig) to conceal; **receleur, -euse** nm/f receiver

récemment [ʀesamã] adv recently

recensement [ʀəsãsmã] nm census

recenser [ʀəsãse] /1/ vt (population) to take a census of; (dénombrer) to list

récent, e [ʀesã, -ãt] adj recent

récépissé [ʀesepise] nm receipt

récepteur, -trice [ʀeseptœʀ, -tʀis] adj receiving ▷ nm receiver

réception [ʀesepsjɔ̃] nf receiving no pl; (accueil) reception, welcome; (bureau) reception (desk); (réunion mondaine) reception, party; **réceptionniste** nm/f receptionist

recette [ʀəsɛt] nf recipe; (Comm) takings pl; **recettes** nfpl (Comm: rentrées) receipts; **faire ~** (spectacle, exposition) to be a winner

recevoir [ʀəsəvwaʀ] /28/ vt to receive; (client, patient, représentant) to see; **être reçu** (à un examen) to pass

rechange [ʀəʃãʒ]: **de ~** adj (pièces, roue) spare; (fig: solution) alternative; **des vêtements de ~** a change of clothes

recharge [ʀəʃaʀʒ] nf refill; **rechargeable** adj (stylo etc) refillable; **recharger** /3/ vt (briquet, stylo) to refill; (batterie) to recharge

réchaud [ʀeʃo] nm (portable) stove

réchauffement [ʀeʃofmã] nm warming (up); **le ~ de la planète** global warming

réchauffer [ʀeʃofe] /1/ vt (plat) to reheat; (mains, personne) to warm; **se réchauffer** vi (température) to get warmer; (personne) to warm o.s. (up)

rêche [ʀɛʃ] adj rough

recherche [ʀəʃɛʀʃ] nf (action): **la ~ de** the search for; (raffinement) studied elegance; (scientifique etc): **la ~** research; **recherches** nfpl (de la police) investigations; (scientifiques) research sg; **être/se mettre à la ~ de** to go in search of

recherché, e [ʀəʃɛʀʃe] adj (rare, demandé) much sought-after; (raffiné) affected; (tenue) elegant

rechercher [ʀəʃɛʀʃe] /1/ vt (objet égaré, personne) to look for; (causes d'un phénomène, nouveau procédé) to try to find; (bonheur etc, l'amitié de qn) to seek

rechute [ʀəʃyt] nf (Méd) relapse

récidiver [residive] /1/ vi to commit a second (ou subsequent) offence; (fig) to do it again

récif [ʀesif] nm reef

récipient [ʀesipjã] nm container

réciproque [ʀesipʀɔk] adj reciprocal

récit [ʀesi] nm story; **récital** nm recital; **réciter** /1/ vt to recite

réclamation [ʀeklamasjõ] nf complaint; **réclamations** nfpl complaints department sg

réclame [ʀeklam] nf: **une ~** ad(vertisement), an advert (BRIT); **article en ~** special offer; **réclamer** /1/ vt to ask for; (revendiquer) to claim, demand ▸ vi to complain

réclusion [ʀeklyzjõ] nf imprisonment

recoin [ʀəkwɛ̃] nm nook, corner

reçois etc [ʀəswa] vb voir **recevoir**

récolte [ʀekɔlt] nf harvesting, gathering; (produits) harvest, crop; **récolter** /1/ vt to harvest, gather (in); (fig) to get

recommandé [ʀəkɔmɑ̃de] nm (Postes): **en ~** by registered mail

recommander [ʀəkɔmɑ̃de] /1/ vt to recommend; (Postes) to register

recommencer [ʀəkɔmɑ̃se] /3/ vt (reprendre: lutte, séance) to resume, start again; (refaire: travail, explications) to start afresh, start (over) again ▸ vi to start again; (récidiver) to do it again

récompense [ʀekõpɑ̃s] nf reward; (prix) award; **récompenser** /1/ vt: **récompenser qn (de** ou **pour)** to reward sb (for)

réconcilier [ʀekõsilje] /7/ vt to reconcile; **se réconcilier (avec)** to be reconciled (with)

reconduire [ʀəkõdɥiʀ] /38/ vt (raccompagner) to take ou see back; (renouveler) to renew

réconfort [ʀekõfɔʀ] nm comfort; **réconforter** /1/ vt (consoler) to comfort

reconnaissance [ʀəkɔnɛsɑ̃s] nf (action de reconnaître) recognition; (gratitude) gratitude, gratefulness; (Mil) reconnaissance, recce; **reconnaissant, e** adj grateful; **je vous serais reconnaissant de bien vouloir** I should be most grateful if you would (kindly)

reconnaître [ʀəkɔnɛtʀ] /57/ vt to recognize; (Mil: lieu) to reconnoitre; (Jur: enfant, dette, droit) to acknowledge; (erreur) to admit ou acknowledge that; **~ que** to admit ou acknowledge that; **~ qn/qch à** (l'identifier grâce à) to recognize sb/sth by; **reconnu, e** adj (indiscute, connu) recognized

reconstituer [ʀəkõstitɥe] /1/ vt (fresque, vase brisé) to piece together, reconstitute; (événement, accident) to reconstruct

reconstruire [ʀəkõstʀɥiʀ] /38/ vt to rebuild

reconvertir [ʀəkõvɛʀtiʀ] /2/ vt to reconvert; **se ~ dans** (un métier, une branche) to move into

record [ʀəkɔʀ] nm, adj record

recoupement [ʀəkupmɑ̃] nm: **par ~** cross-checking

recouper [ʀəkupe] /1/: **se recouper** vi (témoignages) to match up

recourber [ʀəkuʀbe] /1/: **se recourber** vi to curve (up), bend (up)

recourir [ʀəkuʀiʀ] /11/: **~ à** vt (ami, agence) to turn ou appeal to; (force, ruse, emprunt) to resort to

recours [RəkuR] *nm*: **avoir ~ à**
= **recourir à**; **en dernier ~** as a last
resort

recouvrer [RəkuvRe] /1/ *vt* (*vue*,
santé etc) to recover, regain

recouvrir [RəkuvRiR] /18/ *vt* (*couvrir
à nouveau*) to re-cover; (*couvrir
entièrement, aussi fig*) to cover

récréation [RekReasjɔ̃] *nf* (*Scol*)
break

recroqueviller [RəkRɔkvije] /1/:
se recroqueviller *vi* (*personne*) to
huddle up

recrudescence [RəkRydesɑ̃s] *nf*
fresh outbreak

recruter [RəkRyte] /1/ *vt* to recruit

rectangle [Rεktɑ̃gl] *nm* rectangle;
rectangulaire *adj* rectangular

rectificatif, -ive [Rεktifikatif, -iv]
adj corrected ▷ *nm* correction

rectifier [Rεktifje] /7/ *vt* (*calcul,
adresse*) to correct; (*erreur, faute*)
to rectify

rectiligne [Rεktiliɲ] *adj* straight

recto [Rεkto] *nm* front (*of a sheet
of paper*); **~ verso** on both sides of
the page)

reçu, e [Rəsy] *pp de* **recevoir** ▷ *adj*
(*candidat*) successful; (*admis, consacré*)
accepted ▷ *nm* (*Comm*) receipt

recueil [Rəkœj] *nm* collection;
recueillir /12/ *vt* to collect; (*voix,
suffrages*) to win; (*accueillir: réfugiés,
chat*) to take in; **se recueillir** *vi* to
gather one's thoughts; to meditate

recul [Rəkyl] *nm* (*déclin*) decline;
(*éloignement*) distance; **avoir un
mouvement de ~** to recoil; **prendre
du ~** to stand back; **être en ~** to be on
the decline; **avec le ~** in retrospect;
reculé, e *adj* remote; **reculer** /1/ *vi*
to move back, back away; (*Auto*) to
reverse, back up; (*fig*) to (be on the)
decline ▷ *vt* to move back; (*véhicule*)
to reverse, back (up); (*date, décision*)
to postpone; **reculer devant** (*danger,
difficulté*) to shrink from; **reculons: à
reculons** *adv* backwards

récupérer [RekypeRe] /6/ *vt* to
recover, get back; (*déchets etc*) to
salvage (for reprocessing); (*journée,
heures de travail*) to make up ▷ *vi* to
recover

récurer [RekyRe] /1/ *vt* to scour;
poudre à ~ scouring powder

reçus *etc* [Rəsy] *vb voir* **recevoir**

recycler [Rəsikle] /1/ *vt* (*matériau*) to
recycle; (*personne*) to retrain

rédacteur, -trice [RedaktœR, -tRis]
nm/f (*journaliste*) writer; subeditor;
(*d'ouvrage de référence*) editor,
compiler

rédaction [Redaksjɔ̃] *nf* writing;
(*rédacteurs*) editorial staff; (*Scol:
devoir*) essay, composition

redescendre [Rədesɑ̃dR] /41/ *vi*
to go back down ▷ *vt* (*pente etc*) to
go down

rédiger [Rediʒe] /3/ *vt* to write;
(*contrat*) to draw up

redire [RədiR] /37/ *vt* to repeat;
trouver à ~ à to find fault with

redoubler [Rəduble] /1/ *vi* (*tempête,
violence*) to intensify; (*Scol*) to repeat a
year; **~ de patience/prudence** to be
doubly patient/careful

redoutable [Rədutabl] *adj*
formidable, fearsome

redouter [Rədute] /1/ *vt* to dread

redressement [RədRεsmɑ̃] *nm*
(*économique*) recovery

redresser [RədRese] /1/ *vt* (*arbre,
mât*) to set upright; (*pièce tordue*) to
straighten out; (*situation, économie*)
to put right; **se redresser** *vi* (*personne*)
to sit (*ou* stand) up; (*pays, situation*)
to recover

réduction [Redyksjɔ̃] *nf* reduction

réduire [RedyiR] /38/ *vt* to reduce;
(*prix, dépenses*) to cut; reduce; **réduit**
nm tiny room

rééducation [Reedykasjɔ̃] *nf* (*d'un
membre*) re-education; (*de délinquants,
d'un blessé*) rehabilitation

réel, le [Reεl] *adj* real; **réellement**
adv really

réexpédier [ʀeɛkspedje] /7/ vt
(à l'envoyeur) to return, send back;
(au destinataire) to send on, forward

refaire [ʀəfɛʀ] /60/ vt to do again;
(sport) to take up again; (réparer,
restaurer) to do up

réfectoire [ʀefɛktwaʀ] nm refectory

référence [ʀefeʀɑ̃s] nf reference;
références nfpl (recommandations)
reference ⊳ sg

référer [ʀefeʀe] /6/: **se ~ à** vt to
refer to

refermer [ʀəfɛʀme] /1/ vt to close
again, shut again; **se refermer** vi
(porte) to close ou shut (again)

refiler [ʀəfile] /1/ vt (fam): **~ qch à qn**
to palm (BRIT) ou fob sth off on sb

réfléchi, e [ʀefleʃi] adj (caractère)
thoughtful; (action) well-thought-
out; (Ling) reflexive; **c'est tout ~** my
mind's made up

réfléchir [ʀefleʃiʀ] /2/ vt to reflect
⊳ vi to think; **~ à ou sur** to think about

reflet [ʀəflɛ] nm reflection; (sur
l'eau etc) sheen no pl, glint; **refléter**
/6/ vt to reflect; **se refléter** vi to be
reflected

réflexe [ʀeflɛks] adj, nm reflex

réflexion [ʀeflɛksjɔ̃] nf (de la
lumière etc) reflection; (fait de penser)
thought; (remarque) remark; **~ faite,
à la ~** on reflection; **délai de ~**
cooling-off period; **groupe de ~**
think tank

réflexologie [ʀeflɛksɔlɔʒi] nf
reflexology

réforme [ʀefɔʀm] nf reform; (Rel):
la R~ the Reformation; **réformer**
/1/ vt to reform; (Mil) to declare unfit
for service

refouler [ʀəfule] /1/ vt (envahisseurs)
to drive back; (liquide, larmes) to force
back; (désir, colère) to repress

refrain [ʀəfʀɛ̃] nm refrain, chorus

refréner, réfréner [ʀəfʀene, ʀefʀene]
/6/ vt to curb, check

réfrigérateur [ʀefʀiʒeʀatœʀ] nm
refrigerator

refroidir [ʀəfʀwadiʀ] /2/ vt to
cool; (personne) to put off ⊳ vi to cool
(down); **se refroidir** vi (temps) to get
cooler ou colder; (fig: ardeur) to cool
(off); **refroidissement** nm (grippe
etc) chill

refuge [ʀəfyʒ] nm refuge; **réfugié,
e** adj, nm/f refugee; **réfugier** /7/: **se
réfugier** vi to take refuge

refus [ʀəfy] nm refusal; **ce n'est pas
de ~** I won't say no, it's very welcome;
refuser /1/ vt to refuse; (Scol:
candidat) to fail; **refuser qch à qn/de
faire** to refuse sb sth/to do; **refuser
du monde** to have to turn people
away; **se refuser à qch** ou **à faire
qch** to refuse to do sth

regagner [ʀəgaɲe] /1/ vt (argent,
faveur) to win back; (lieu) to get back to

régal [ʀegal] nm treat; **régaler** /1/
vt: **régaler qn de** to treat sb to; **se
régaler** vi to have a delicious meal;
(fig) to enjoy o.s.

regard [ʀəgaʀ] nm (coup d'œil) look,
glance; (expression) look (in one's eye);
au ~ de (loi, morale) from the point of
view of; **en ~ de** in comparison with

regardant, e [ʀəgaʀdɑ̃, -ɑ̃t] adj:
très/peu ~ (sur) quite fussy/very
free (about); (économe) very tight-
fisted/quite generous (with)

regarder [ʀəgaʀde] /1/ vt to look
at; (film, télévision, match) to watch;
(concerner) to concern ⊳ vi to look;
ne pas ~ à la dépense to spare no
expense; **~ qn/qch comme** to regard
sb/sth as

régie [ʀeʒi] nf (Comm, Industrie)
state-owned company; (Théât, Ciné)
production; (Radio, TV) control room

régime [ʀeʒim] nm (Pol) régime;
(Admin: carcéral, fiscal etc) system;
(Méd) diet; (de bananes, dattes) bunch;
se mettre au/suivre un ~ to go on/
be on a diet

régiment [ʀeʒimɑ̃] nm regiment

région [ʀeʒjɔ̃] nf region; **régional, e,
-aux** adj regional

régir [ʀeʒiʀ] /2/ vt to govern

régisseur [ʀeʒisœʀ] nm (d'un domaine) steward; (Ciné, TV) assistant director; (Théât) stage manager

registre [ʀaʒistʀ] nm register

réglage [ʀeglaʒ] nm adjustment

réglé, e [ʀegle] adj well-ordered; (arrangé) settled

règle [ʀɛgl] nf (instrument) ruler; (loi, prescription) rule; **règles** nfpl (Physiol) period sg; **en ~** (papiers d'identité) in order; **en ~ générale** as a (general) rule

règlement [ʀɛgləmɑ̃] nm (paiement) settlement; (arrêté) regulation; (règles, statuts) regulations pl, rules pl, **réglementaire** adj conforming to the regulations; (tenue, uniforme) regulation cpd; **réglementation** nf (règlements) regulations pl; **réglementer** /1/ vt to regulate

régler [ʀegle] /6/ vt (mécanisme, machine) to regulate, adjust; (thermostat etc) to set, adjust; (question, conflit, facture, dette) to settle; (fournisseur) to settle up with

réglisse [ʀeglis] nm ou f liquorice

règne [ʀɛɲ] nm (d'un roi etc, fig) reign; **le ~ végétal/animal** the vegetable/ animal kingdom; **régner** /6/ vi (roi) to rule, reign; (fig) to reign

regorger [ʀəgɔʀʒe] /3/ vi: **~ de** to overflow with, be bursting with

regret [ʀəgʀɛ] nm regret; **à ~** with regret; **sans ~** with no regrets; **regrettable** adj regrettable; **regretter** /1/ vt (personne) to miss; **non, je regrette** no, I'm sorry

regrouper [ʀəgʀupe] /1/ vt (grouper) to group together; (contenir) to include, comprise; **se regrouper** vi to gather (together)

régulier, -ière [ʀegylje, -jɛʀ] adj (gén) regular; (vitesse, qualité) steady; (répartition, pression) even; (Transports: ligne, service) scheduled, regular; (légal, réglementaire) lawful,

in order; (fam: correct) straight, on the level; **régulièrement** adv regularly; evenly

rehausser [ʀəose] /1/ vt (relever) to heighten, raise; (fig: souligner) to set off, enhance

rein [ʀɛ̃] nm kidney; **reins** nmpl (dos) back sg

reine [ʀɛn] nf queen

reine-claude [ʀɛnklod] nf greengage

réinscriptible [ʀeɛ̃skʀiptibl] adj (CD, DVD) rewritable

réinsertion [ʀeɛ̃sɛʀsjɔ̃] nf (de délinquant) reintegration, rehabilitation

réintégrer [ʀeɛ̃tegʀe] /6/ vt (lieu) to return to; (fonctionnaire) to reinstate

rejaillir [ʀəʒajiʀ] /2/ vi to splash up; **~ sur** (fig) (scandale) to rebound on; (gloire) to be reflected on

rejet [ʀəʒɛ] nm rejection; **rejeter** /4/ vt (relancer) to throw back; (vomir) to bring ou throw up; (écarter) to reject; (déverser) to throw out, discharge; **rejeter la responsabilité de qch sur qn** to lay the responsibility for sth at sb's door

rejoindre [ʀəʒwɛ̃dʀ] /49/ vt (famille, régiment) to rejoin, return to; (lieu) to get (back) to; (route etc) to meet, join; (rattraper) to catch up (with); **se rejoindre** vi to meet; **je te rejoins au café** I'll see ou meet you at the café

réjouir [ʀeʒwiʀ] /2/ vt to delight; **se ~ de qch/de faire** to be delighted about sth/to do; **réjouissances** nfpl (fête) festivities

relâche [ʀəlɑʃ]: **sans ~** adv without respite ou a break; **relâché, e** adj loose, lax; **relâcher** /1/ vt (ressort, prisonnier) to release; (étreinte, cordes) to loosen; **se relâcher** vi (discipline) to become slack ou lax; (élève etc) to slacken off

relais [ʀəlɛ] nm (Sport): **(course de) ~** relay (race); **prendre le ~ (de)** to take

over (from); **~ routier** = transport
café (BRIT); = truck stop (US)

relancer [ʀəlɑ̃se] /3/ vt (balle)
to throw back (again); (moteur)
to restart; (fig) to boost, revive;
(personne): **~ qn** to pester sb

relatif, -ive [ʀəlatif, -iv] adj relative

relation [ʀəlɑsjɔ̃] nf (rapport)
relation(ship); (connaissance)
acquaintance; **relations** nfpl
(rapports) relations; (connaissances)
connections; **être/entrer en ~(s)
avec** to be in contact ou be dealing/
get in contact with

relaxer [ʀəlakse] /1/: **se relaxer**
vi to relax

relayer [ʀəleje] /8/ vt (collaborateur,
coureur etc) to relieve; **se relayer** vi
(dans une activité) to take it in turns

reléguer [ʀəlege] /6/ vt to relegate

relevé, e [ʀəlve] adj (manches) rolled-
up; (sauce) highly-seasoned ▷ nm
(lecture) reading; **~ bancaire** ou **de
compte** bank statement

relève [ʀəlɛv] nf (personne) relief;
prendre la ~ to take over

relever [ʀəlve] /5/ vt (statue, meuble)
to stand up again; (personne tombée)
to help up; (vitre, plafond, niveau de
vie) to raise; (col) to turn up; (style,
conversation) to elevate; (plat, sauce) to
season; (sentinelle, équipe) to relieve;
(fautes, points) to pick out; (défi) to
accept, take up; (noter: adresse etc) to
take down, note; (: plan) to sketch;
(compteur) to read; (ramasser: cahiers,
copies) to collect, take in ▷ vi: **~ de**
(maladie) to be recovering from; (être
du ressort de) to be a matter for; (fig)
to pertain to; **se relever** vi (se remettre
debout) to get up; **~ qn de** (fonctions)
to relieve sb of; **~ la tête** to look up

relief [ʀəljɛf] nm relief; **mettre en ~**
(fig) to bring out, highlight

relier [ʀəlje] /7/ vt to link up; (livre) to
bind; **~ qch à** to link sth to

religieux, -euse [ʀəliʒjø, -øz] adj
religious ▷ nm monk

religion [ʀəliʒjɔ̃] nf religion

relire [ʀəliʀ] /43/ vt (à nouveau)
to reread, read again; (vérifier) to
read over

reluire [ʀəluiʀ] /38/ vi to gleam

remanier [ʀəmanje] /7/ vt to
reshape, recast; (Pol) to reshuffle

remarquable [ʀəmaʀkabl] adj
remarkable

remarque [ʀəmaʀk] nf remark;
(écrite) note

remarquer [ʀəmaʀke] /1/ vt (voir)
to notice; **se remarquer** vi to
be noticeable; **se faire ~** to draw
attention to o.s.; **faire ~ (à qn) que**
to point out (to sb) that; **faire ~
qch (à qn)** to point sth out (to sb);
remarquez, ... mind you, ...

rembourrer [ʀɑ̃buʀe] /1/ vt to stuff

remboursement [ʀɑ̃buʀsəmɑ̃]
nm (de dette, d'emprunt) repayment;
(de frais) refund; **rembourser** /1/ vt
to pay back, repay; (frais, billet etc)
to refund; **se faire rembourser** to
get a refund

remède [ʀəmɛd] nm (médicament)
medicine; (traitement, fig) remedy,
cure

remémorer [ʀəmemɔʀe] /1/: **se
remémorer** vt to recall, recollect

remerciements [ʀəmɛʀsimɑ̃] nmpl
thanks; **(avec) tous mes ~** (with)
grateful ou many thanks

remercier [ʀəmɛʀsje] /7/ vt to
thank; (congédier) to dismiss; **~ qn
de/d'avoir fait** to thank sb for/for
having done

remettre [ʀəmɛtʀ] /56/ vt
(vêtement): **~ qch** to put sth back on;
(replacer): **~ qch quelque part** to
put sth back somewhere; (ajouter):
~ du sel/un sucre to add more salt/
another lump of sugar; (ajourner):
~ qch (à) to postpone sth ou put sth off
(until); **se remettre** vi to get better;
~ qch à qn (donner) to hand over sth
to sb; (prix, décoration) to present sb
with sth; **se ~ de** to recover from;

s'en ~ à to leave it (up) to; **se ~ à faire/qch** to start doing/sth again

remis, e [Rəmi, -iz] pp de **remettre** ▷ nf (rabais) discount; (local) shed; **~e en cause/question** calling into question/challenging; **~e en jeu** (Football) throw-in; **~e de peine** remission of sentence; **~e des prix** prize-giving

remontant [Rəmɔ̃tɑ̃] nm tonic, pick-me-up

remonte-pente [Rəmɔ̃tpɑ̃t] nm ski lift

remonter [Rəmɔ̃te] /1/ vi to go back up; (prix, température) to go up again; (en voiture) to get back in ▷ vt (pente) to go up; (fleuve) to sail (ou swim etc) up; (manches, pantalon) to roll up; (fam) to wind up; (niveau, limite) to raise; (personne) to buck up; (moteur, meuble) to put back together, reassemble; (montre, mécanisme) to wind up; **~ le moral à qn** to raise sb's spirits; **~ à** (dater de) to date ou go back to

remords [Rəmɔʀ] nm remorse no pl; **avoir des ~** to feel remorse

remorque [Rəmɔʀk] nf trailer; **remorquer** /1/ vt to tow; **remorqueur** nm tug(boat)

remous [Rəmu] nm (d'un navire) (back)wash no pl; (de rivière) swirl, eddy pl; (fig) stir sg

remparts [Rɑ̃paʀ] nmpl walls, ramparts

remplaçant, e [Rɑ̃plasɑ̃, -ɑ̃t] nm/f replacement, stand-in; (Scol) supply (BRIT) ou substitute (US) teacher

remplacement [Rɑ̃plasmɑ̃] nm replacement; **faire des ~s** (professeur) to do supply ou substitute teaching; (secrétaire) to temp

remplacer [Rɑ̃plase] /3/ vt to replace; **~ qch/qn par** to replace sth/sb with

rempli, e [Rɑ̃pli] adj (emploi du temps) full, busy; **~ de** full of, filled with

remplir [Rɑ̃pliʀ] /2/ vt to fill (up); (questionnaire) to fill out ou up; (obligations, fonction, condition) to fulfil; **se remplir** vi to fill up

remporter [Rɑ̃pɔʀte] /1/ vt (marchandise) to take away; (fig) to win, achieve

remuant, e [Rəmɥɑ̃, -ɑ̃t] adj restless

remue-ménage [Rəmymenaʒ] nm inv commotion

remuer [Rəmɥe] /1/ vt to move; (café, sauce) to stir ▷ vi to move; **se remuer** vi to move; (fam: s'activer) to get a move on

rémunérer [Remyneʀe] /6/ vt to remunerate

renard [Rənaʀ] nm fox

renchérir [Rɑ̃ʃeʀiʀ] /2/ vi (fig): **~ (sur)** (en paroles) to add something (to)

rencontre [Rɑ̃kɔ̃tʀ] nf meeting; (imprévue) encounter; **aller à la ~ de qn** to go and meet sb; **rencontrer** /1/ vt to meet; (mot, expression) to come across; (difficultés) to meet with; **se rencontrer** vi to meet

rendement [Rɑ̃dmɑ̃] nm (d'un travailleur, d'une machine) output; (d'une culture, d'un champ) yield

rendez-vous [Rɑ̃devu] nm appointment; (d'amoureux) date; (lieu) meeting place; **donner ~ à qn** to arrange to meet sb; **avoir/prendre ~ (avec)** to have/make an appointment (with)

rendre [Rɑ̃dʀ] /41/ vt (livre, argent etc) to give back, return; (otages, visite, politesse, invitation) to return; (sang, aliments) to bring up; (exprimer, traduire) to render; (faire devenir): **~ qn célèbre/qch possible** to make sb famous/sth possible; **se rendre** vi (capituler) to surrender, give o.s. up; (aller): **se ~ quelque part** to go somewhere; **se ~ compte de qch** to realize sth; **~ la monnaie** to give change

rênes [Rɛn] nfpl reins

renfermé, e [ʀɑ̃fɛʀme] *adj* (*fig*) withdrawn ▷ *nm*: **sentir le ~** to smell stuffy

renfermer [ʀɑ̃fɛʀme] /1/ *vt* to contain

renforcer [ʀɑ̃fɔʀse] /3/ *vt* to reinforce; **renfort** *nm*: **renforts** *nmpl* reinforcements; **à grand renfort de** with a great deal of

renfrogné, e [ʀɑ̃fʀɔɲe] *adj* sullen, scowling

renier [ʀənje] /7/ *vt* (*parents*) to disown, repudiate; (*foi*) to renounce

renifler [ʀənifle] /1/ *vi* to sniff ▷ *vt* (*odeur*) to sniff

renne [ʀɛn] *nm* reindeer *inv*

renom [ʀənɔ̃] *nm* reputation; (*célébrité*) renown; **renommé, e** *adj* celebrated, renowned ▷ *nf* fame

renoncer [ʀənɔ̃se] /3/: **~ à** *vt* to give up; **~ à faire** to give up the idea of doing

renouer [ʀənwe] /1/ *vt*: **~ avec** (*habitude*) to take up again

renouvelable [ʀ(ə)nuvlabl] *adj* (*contrat, bail, énergie*) renewable

renouveler [ʀənuvle] /4/ *vt* to renew; (*exploit, méfait*) to repeat; **se renouveler** *vi* (*incident*) to recur, happen again; **renouvellement** *nm* renewal

rénover [ʀenɔve] /1/ *vt* (*immeuble*) to renovate, do up; (*quartier*) to redevelop

renseignement [ʀɑ̃sɛɲmɑ̃] *nm* information *no pl*, piece of information; (**guichet des**) **~s** information desk; (**service des**) **~s** (*Tél*) directory inquiries (*BRIT*), information (*US*)

renseigner [ʀɑ̃seɲe] /1/ *vt*: **~ qn (sur)** to give information to sb (about); **se renseigner** *vi* to ask for information, make inquiries

rentabilité [ʀɑ̃tabilite] *nf* profitability

rentable [ʀɑ̃tabl] *adj* profitable

rente [ʀɑ̃t] *nf* income; (*pension*) pension

rentrée [ʀɑ̃tʀe] *nf*: **~ (d'argent)** cash *no pl* coming in; **la ~ (des classes** *ou* **scolaire)** the start of the new school year

rentrer [ʀɑ̃tʀe] /1/ *vi* (*entrer de nouveau*) to go (*ou* come) back in; (*entrer*) to go (*ou* come) in; (*revenir chez soi*) to go (*ou* come) (back) home; (*air, clou: pénétrer*) to go in; (*revenu, argent*) to come in ▷ *vt* to bring in; (*véhicule*) to put away; (*chemise dans pantalon etc*) to tuck in; (*griffes*) to draw in; **~ le ventre** to pull in one's stomach; **~ dans** (*heurter*) to crash into; **~ dans l'ordre** to get back to normal; **~ dans ses frais** to recover one's expenses (*ou* initial outlay)

renverse [ʀɑ̃vɛʀs]: **à la ~** *adv* backwards

renverser [ʀɑ̃vɛʀse] /1/ *vt* (*faire tomber: chaise, verre*) to knock over, overturn; (*: piéton*) to knock down; (*: liquide, contenu*) to spill, upset; (*retourner*) to turn upside down; (*: ordre des mots etc*) to reverse; (*fig: gouvernement etc*) to overthrow; (*stupéfier*) to bowl over; **se renverser** *vi* (*verre, vase*) to fall over; (*contenu*) to spill

renvoi [ʀɑ̃vwa] *nm* (*d'employé*) dismissal; (*d'élève*) expulsion; (*référence*) cross-reference; (*éructation*) belch; **renvoyer** /8/ *vt* to send back; (*congédier*) to dismiss; (*élève: définitivement*) to expel; (*lumière*) to reflect; (*ajourner*): **renvoyer qch (à)** to postpone sth (until)

repaire [ʀəpɛʀ] *nm* den

répandre [ʀepɑ̃dʀ] /41/ *vt* (*renverser*) to spill; (*étaler, diffuser*) to spread; (*chaleur, odeur*) to give off; **se répandre** *vi* to spill; to spread; **répandu, e** *adj* (*opinion, usage*) widespread

réparateur, -trice [ʀepaʀatœʀ, -tʀis] *nm/f* repairer

réparation [ʀepaʀasjɔ̃] *nf* repair

réparer [ʀepaʀe] /1/ vt to repair; (fig: offense) to make up for, atone for; (: oubli, erreur) to put right

repartie [ʀəpaʀti] nf retort; **avoir de la ~** to be quick at repartee

repartir [ʀəpaʀtiʀ] /16/ vi to set off again; (voyageur) to leave again; (fig) to get going again; **~ à zéro** to start from scratch (again)

répartir [ʀepaʀtiʀ] /2/ vt (pour attribuer) to share out; (pour disperser, disposer) to divide up; (poids, chaleur) to distribute; **se répartir** vt (travail, rôles) to share out between themselves; **répartition** nf (des richesses etc) distribution

repas [ʀəpa] nm meal

repassage [ʀəpasaʒ] nm ironing

repasser [ʀəpase] /1/ vi to come (ou go) back ▷ vt (vêtement, tissu) to iron; (examen) to retake, resit; (film) to show again; (leçon, rôle: revoir) to go over (again)

repentir [ʀəpɑ̃tiʀ] /16/ nm repentance; **se repentir** vi to repent; **se ~ d'avoir fait qch** (regretter) to regret having done sth

répercussions [ʀepeʀkysjɔ̃] nfpl repercussions

répercuter [ʀepeʀkyte] /1/: **se répercuter** vi (bruit) to reverberate; (fig): **se ~ sur** to have repercussions on

repère [ʀəpeʀ] nm mark; (monument etc) landmark

repérer [ʀəpeʀe] /6/ vt (erreur, connaissance) to spot; (abri, ennemi) to locate; **se repérer** vi to get one's bearings

répertoire [ʀepeʀtwaʀ] nm (liste) (alphabetical) list; (carnet) index notebook; (Inform) directory; (d'un théâtre, artiste) repertoire

répéter [ʀepete] /6/ vt to repeat; (préparer: leçon) to learn, go over; (Théât) to rehearse; **se répéter** (redire) to repeat o.s.; (se reproduire) to be repeated, recur

répétition [ʀepetisjɔ̃] nf repetition; (Théât) rehearsal; **~ générale** final dress rehearsal

répit [ʀepi] nm respite; **sans ~** without letting up

replier [ʀəplije] /7/ vt (rabattre) to fold down ou over; **se replier** vi (armée) to withdraw, fall back; **se ~ sur soi-même** to withdraw into oneself

réplique [ʀeplik] nf (repartie, fig) reply; (Théât) line; (copie) replica; **répliquer** /1/ vi to reply; (riposter) to retaliate

répondeur [ʀepɔ̃dœʀ] nm: **~ (automatique)** (Tél) answering machine

répondre [ʀepɔ̃dʀ] /41/ vi to answer, reply; (freins, mécanisme) to respond; **~ à** to reply to; answer; (affection, salut) to return; (provocation) to respond to; (correspondre à: besoin) to answer; (conditions) to meet; (description) to match; **~ à qn** (avec impertinence) to answer sb back; **~ de** to answer for

réponse [ʀepɔ̃s] nf answer, reply; **en ~ à** in reply to

reportage [ʀəpɔʀtaʒ] nm report

reporter[1] [ʀəpɔʀtɛʀ] nm reporter

reporter[2] [ʀəpɔʀte] vt (ajourner): **~ qch (à)** to postpone sth (until); (transférer): **~ qch sur** to transfer sth to; **se ~ à** (époque) to think back to; (document) to refer to

repos [ʀəpo] nm rest; (fig) peace (and quiet); (Mil): **~!** (stand at) ease!; **ce n'est pas de tout ~!** it's no picnic!

reposant, e [ʀ(ə)pozɑ̃, -ɑ̃t] adj restful

reposer [ʀəpoze] /1/ vt (verre, livre) to put down; (délasser) to rest ▷ vi: **laisser ~** (pâte) to leave to stand

repoussant, e [ʀəpusɑ̃, -ɑ̃t] adj repulsive

repousser [ʀəpuse] /1/ vi to grow again ▷ vt to repel, repulse; (offre) to

turn down, reject; (*tiroir, personne*) to push back; (*différer*) to alter
reprendre [ʁəpʁɑ̃dʁ] /58/ *vt* (*prisonnier, ville*) to recapture; (*firme, entreprise*) to take over; (*emprunter: argument, idée*) to take up; (*refaire: article etc*) to go over again; (*jupe etc*) to alter; (*réprimander*) to tell off; (*corriger*) to correct; (*travail, promenade*) to resume; (*chercher*): **je viendrai te ~ à 4 h** I'll come and fetch you *ou* I'll come back for you at 4; (*se resservir de*): **~ du pain/un œuf** to take (*ou* eat) more bread/another egg ▷ *vi* (*classes, pluie*) to start (up) again; (*activités, travaux, combats*) to resume, start (up) again; (*affaires, industrie*) to pick up; (*dire*): **reprit-il** he went on; **~ des forces** to recover one's strength; **~ courage** to take new heart; **~ la route** to resume one's journey, set off again; **~ haleine** *ou* **son souffle** to get one's breath back
représentant, e [ʁəpʁezɑ̃tɑ̃, -ɑ̃t] *nm/f* representative
représentation [ʁəpʁezɑ̃tasjɔ̃] *nf* representation; (*spectacle*) performance
représenter [ʁəpʁezɑ̃te] /1/ *vt* to represent; (*donner: pièce, opéra*) to perform; **se représenter** *vt* (*se figurer*) to imagine
répression [ʁepʁesjɔ̃] *nf* repression
réprimer [ʁepʁime] /1/ *vt* (*émotions*) to suppress; (*peuple etc*) repress
repris, e [ʁəpʁi, -iz] *pp de* **reprendre** ▷ *nm*: **~ de justice** ex-prisoner, ex-convict
reprise [ʁəpʁiz] *nf* (*recommencement*) resumption; (*économique*) recovery; (*TV*) repeat; (*Comm*) trade-in, part exchange; (*raccommodage*) mend; **à plusieurs ~s** on several occasions
repriser [ʁəpʁize] /1/ *vt* (*chaussette, lainage*) to darn; (*tissu*) to mend
reproche [ʁəpʁɔʃ] *nm* (*remontrance*) reproach; **faire des ~s à qn** to reproach sb; **sans ~(s)** beyond *ou* above reproach; **reprocher** /1/ *vt*: **reprocher qch à qn** to reproach *ou* blame sb for sth; **reprocher qch à** (*machine, théorie*) to have sth against
reproduction [ʁəpʁɔdyksjɔ̃] *nf* reproduction
reproduire [ʁəpʁɔdɥiʁ] /38/ *vt* to reproduce; **se reproduire** *vi* (*Bio*) to reproduce; (*recommencer*) to recur, re-occur
reptile [ʁɛptil] *nm* reptile
république [ʁepyblik] *nf* republic
répugnant, e [ʁepyɲɑ̃, -ɑ̃t] *adj* repulsive
répugner [ʁepyɲe] /1/: **~ à** *vt*: **~ à qn** to repel *ou* disgust sb; **~ à faire** to be loath *ou* reluctant to do
réputation [ʁepytasjɔ̃] *nf* reputation; **réputé, e** *adj* renowned
requérir [ʁəkeʁiʁ] /21/ *vt* (*nécessiter*) to require, call for
requête [ʁəkɛt] *nf* request
requin [ʁəkɛ̃] *nm* shark
requis, e [ʁəki, -iz] *adj* required
RER *sigle m* (= *Réseau express régional*) *Greater Paris high-speed train service*
rescapé, e [ʁɛskape] *nm/f* survivor
rescousse [ʁɛskus] *nf*: **aller à la ~ de qn** to go to sb's aid *ou* rescue
réseau, x [ʁezo] *nm* network; **~ social** social network
réseautage [ʁezotaʒ] *nm* social networking
réservation [ʁezɛʁvasjɔ̃] *nf* reservation; booking
réserve [ʁezɛʁv] *nf* (*retenue*) reserve; (*entrepôt*) storeroom; (*restriction, aussi: d'Indiens*) reservation; (*de pêche, chasse*) preserve; **de ~** (*provisions etc*) in reserve
réservé, e [ʁezɛʁve] *adj* reserved; (*chasse, pêche*) private
réserver [ʁezɛʁve] /1/ *vt* to reserve; (*chambre, billet etc*) to book, reserve; (*mettre de côté, garder*): **~ qch pour ou à** to keep *ou* save sth for
réservoir [ʁezɛʁvwaʁ] *nm* tank

résidence [Rezidɑ̃s] nf residence; ~ **principale/secondaire** main/ second home; ~ **universitaire** hall of residence (BRIT), dormitory (US); **résidentiel, le** adj residential; **résider** /1/ vi: **résider à** ou **dans** ou **en** to reside in; **résider dans** (fig) to lie in

résidu [Rezidy] nm residue no pl

résigner [Reziɲe] /1/: **se résigner** vi: **se ~ (à qch/à faire)** to resign o.s. (to sth/to doing)

résilier [Rezilje] /7/ vt to terminate

résistance [Rezistɑ̃s] nf resistance; (de réchaud, bouilloire: fil) element

résistant, e [Rezistɑ̃, -ɑ̃t] adj (personne) robust, tough; (matériau) strong, hard-wearing

résister [Reziste] /1/ vi vi to resist; ~ **à** (assaut, tentation) to resist; (matériau, plante) to withstand; (désobéir à) to stand up to, oppose

résolu, e [Rezɔly] pp de **résoudre** ▷ adj: **être ~ à qch/faire** to be set upon sth/doing

résolution [Rezɔlysjɔ̃] nf (fermeté, décision) resolution; (d'un problème) solution

résolvais etc [Rezɔlve] vb voir **résoudre**

résonner [Rezɔne] /1/ vi (cloche, pas) to reverberate, resound; (salle) to be resonant

résorber [RezɔRbe] /1/: **se résorber** vi (Méd) to be resorbed; (fig) to be absorbed

résoudre [RezudR] /51/ vt to solve; **se ~ à faire** to bring o.s. to do

respect [Rεsp̃] nm respect; **tenir en ~** to keep at bay; **présenter ses ~s à qn** to pay one's respects to sb; **respecter** /1/ vt to respect; **respectueux, -euse** adj respectful

respiration [RεspiRasjɔ̃] nf breathing no pl

respirer [RεspiRe] /1/ vi to breathe; (fig: se reposer) to get one's breath; (: être soulagé) to breathe again ▷ vt to

breathe (in), inhale; (manifester: santé, calme etc) to exude

resplendir [Rεsplɑ̃diR] /2/ vi to shine; (fig): ~ **(de)** to be radiant (with)

responsabilité [RεspɔsabiliRe] nf responsibility; (légale) liability

responsable [Rεspɔsabl] adj responsible ▷ nm/f (personne coupable) person responsible; (du ravitaillement etc) person in charge; (de parti, syndicat) official; ~ **de** responsible for

ressaisir [RəseziR] /2/: **se ressaisir** vi to regain one's self-control

ressasser [Rəsase] /1/ vt to keep turning over

ressemblance [Rəsɑ̃blɑ̃s] nf resemblance, similarity, likeness

ressemblant, e [Rəsɑ̃blɑ̃, -ɑ̃t] adj (portrait) lifelike, true to life

ressembler [Rəsɑ̃ble] /1/: ~ **à** vt to be like, resemble; (visuellement) to look like; **se ressembler** vi to be (ou look) alike

ressentiment [Rəsɑ̃timɑ̃] nm resentment

ressentir [RəsɑtiR] /16/ vt to feel; **se ~ de** to feel (ou show) the effects of

resserrer [RəseRe] /1/ vt (nœud, boulon) to tighten (up); (fig: liens) to strengthen

resservir [RəseRviR] /14/ vi to do ou serve again; ~ **qn (d'un plat)** to give sb a second helping (of a dish); **se ~ de** (plat) to take a second helping of; (outil etc) to use again

ressort [RəsɔR] nm (pièce) spring; (force morale) spirit; **en dernier ~** as a last resort; **être du ~ de** to fall within the competence of

ressortir [RəsɔRtiR] /16/ vi to go (ou come) out (again); (contraster) to stand out; ~ **de**: **il ressort de ceci que** it emerges from this that; **faire ~** (fig: souligner) to bring out

ressortissant, e [RəsɔRtisɑ̃, -ɑ̃t] nm/f national

ressources [RəsuRs] nfpl resources

ressusciter [resysite] /1/ vt (fig) to revive, bring back ▷ vi to rise (from the dead)

restant, e [RɛstÃ, -Ãt] adj remaining ▷ nm: **le ~ (de)** the remainder (of); **un ~ de** (de trop) some leftover

restaurant [RɛstoRÃ] nm restaurant

restauration [RɛstoRasjɔ̃] nf restoration; (hôtellerie) catering; **~ rapide** fast food

restaurer [RɛstoRe] /1/ vt to restore; **se restaurer** vi to have something to eat

reste [Rɛst] nm (restant): **le ~ (de)** the rest (of); (de trop): **un ~ (de)** some leftover; **restes** nmpl leftovers; (d'une cité etc, dépouille mortelle) remains; **du ~, au ~** besides, moreover

rester [Rɛste] /1/ vi to stay, remain; (subsister) to remain, be left; (durer) to last, live on ▷ vb impers: **il reste du pain/deux œufs** there's some bread/there are two eggs left (over); **il me reste assez de temps** I have enough time left; **il ne me reste plus qu'à ...** I've just got to ...; **restons-en là** let's leave it at that

restituer [Rɛstitɥe] /1/ vt (objet, somme): **~ qch (à qn)** to return ou restore sth (to sb)

restreindre [RɛstRɛ̃dR] /52/ vt to restrict, limit

restriction [Rɛstriksjɔ̃] nf restriction

résultat [Rezylta] nm result; (d'élection etc) results pl; **résultats** nmpl (d'une enquête) findings

résulter [Rezylte] /1/ vt: **~ de** vt to result from, be the result of

résumé [Rezyme] nm summary, résumé; **en ~** in brief; (pour conclure) to sum up

résumer [Rezyme] /1/ vt (texte) to summarize; (récapituler) to sum up

Attention à ne pas traduire *résumer* par to resume.

résurrection [RezyRɛksjɔ̃] nf resurrection

rétablir [RetabliR] /2/ vt to restore, re-establish; **se rétablir** vi (guérir) to recover; (silence, calme) to return, be restored; **rétablissement** nm restoring; (guérison) recovery

retaper [Rətape] /1/ vt (maison, voiture etc) to do up; (fam: revigorer) to buck up

retard [RətaR] nm (d'une personne attendue) lateness no pl; (sur l'horaire, un programme, une échéance) delay; (fig: scolaire, mental etc) backwardness; **en ~ (de deux heures)** (two hours) late; **désolé d'être en ~** sorry I'm late; **avoir du ~** to be late; (sur un programme) to be behind (schedule); **prendre du ~** (train, avion) to be delayed; **sans ~** without delay

retardataire [Rətardater] nm/f latecomer

retardement [Rətardəmã]: **à ~** adj delayed action cpd; **bombe à ~** time bomb

retarder [Rətarde] /1/ vt to delay; (horloge) to put back; **~ qn (d'une heure)** to delay sb (an hour); (départ, date): **~ qch (de deux jours)** to put sth back (two days) ▷ vi (montre) to be slow

retenir [Rətnir] /22/ vt (garder, retarder) to keep, detain; (maintenir: objet qui glisse, colère, larmes, rire) to hold back; (se rappeler) to retain; (accepter) to accept; (fig: empêcher d'agir): **~ qn (de faire)** to hold sb back (from doing); (prélever): **~ qch (sur)** to deduct sth (from); **se retenir** vi (se raccrocher): **se ~ à** to hold onto; (se contenir): **se ~ de faire** to restrain o.s. from doing; **~ son souffle** ou **haleine** to hold one's breath

retentir [Rətãtir] /2/ vi to ring out; **retentissant, e** adj resounding

retenu, e [Rətny] adj (place) reserved ▷ nf (prélèvement) deduction; (Scol) detention; (modération) (self-)restraint

réticence [ʀetisɑ̃s] *nf* reticence *no pl*; (*réluctance no pl*) **réticent, e** *adj* reticent, reluctant

rétine [ʀetin] *nf* retina

retiré, e [ʀətiʀe] *adj* (*solitaire*) secluded; (*éloigné*) remote

retirer [ʀətiʀe] /1/ *vt* (*argent, plainte*) to withdraw; (*vêtement*) to take off, remove; (*reprendre: billets*) to collect, pick up; **~ qn/qch de** to take sb away from/sth out of, remove sb/ sth from

retomber [ʀətɔ̃be] /1/ *vi* (*à nouveau*) to fall again; (*atterrir: après un saut etc*) to land; (*échoir*) **~ sur qn** to fall on sb

rétorquer [ʀetɔʀke] /1/ *vt*: **~ (à qn) que** to retort (to sb) that

retouche [ʀətuʃ] *nf* (*sur vêtement*) alteration; **retoucher** /1/ *vt* (*photographie, tableau*) to touch up; (*texte, vêtement*) to alter

retour [ʀətuʀ] *nm* return; **au ~** (*en route*) on the way back; **à mon/ton ~** on my/your return; **être de ~ (de)** to be back (from); **quand serons-nous de ~?** when do we get back?; **par ~ du courrier** by return of post

retourner [ʀətuʀne] /1/ *vt* (*dans l'autre sens: matelas, crêpe*) to turn (over); (*: sac, vêtement*) to turn inside out; (*émouvoir*) to shake; (*renvoyer, restituer*): **~ qch à qn** to return sth to sb ▷ *vi* (*aller, revenir*): **~ quelque part/à** to go back ou return somewhere/to; **~ à** (*état, activité*) to return to, go back to; **se retourner** *vi* (*tourner la tête*) to turn round; **se ~ contre** (*fig*) to turn against

retrait [ʀətʀɛ] *nm* (*d'argent*) withdrawal; **en ~** set back; **~ du permis (de conduire)** disqualification from driving (BRIT), revocation of driver's license (US)

retraite [ʀətʀɛt] *nf* (*d'une armée, Rel*) retreat; (*d'un employé*) retirement; (*revenu*) (retirement) pension; **prendre sa ~** to retire; **~ anticipée** early retirement; **retraité, e** *adj* retired ▷ *nm/f* (old age) pensioner

retrancher [ʀətʀɑ̃ʃe] /1/ *vt*: **~ qch de** (*nombre, somme*) to take *ou* deduct sth from; **se ~ derrière/dans** to take refuge behind/in

rétrécir [ʀetʀesiʀ] /2/ *vt* (*vêtement*) to take in ▷ *vi* to shrink; **se rétrécir** (*route, vallée*) to narrow

rétro [ʀetʀo] *adj inv*: **la mode ~** the nostalgia vogue

rétrospectif, -ive [ʀetʀospɛktif, -iv] *adj* retrospective ▷ *nf* (*Art*) retrospective; (*Ciné*) season, retrospective; **rétrospectivement** *adv* in retrospect

retrousser [ʀətʀuse] /1/ *vt* to roll up

retrouvailles [ʀətʀuvaj] *nfpl* reunion *sg*

retrouver [ʀətʀuve] /1/ *vt* (*fugitif, objet perdu*) to find; (*calme, santé*) to regain; (*revoir*) to see again; (*rejoindre*) to meet (again), join; **se retrouver** *vi* to meet; (*s'orienter*) to find one's way; **se ~ quelque part** to find o.s. somewhere; **s'y ~** (*y voir clair*) to make sense of it; (*rentrer dans ses frais*) to break even

rétroviseur [ʀetʀovizœʀ] *nm* (rear-view) mirror

retweeter [ʀətwite] /1/ *vt* (*Inform*: Twitter) to retweet

réunion [ʀeynjɔ̃] *nf* (*séance*) meeting

réunir [ʀeyniʀ] /2/ *vt* (*rassembler*) to gather together; (*inviter: amis, famille*) to have round, have in; (*cumuler: qualités etc*) to combine; (*rapprocher: ennemis*) to bring together (again), reunite; (*rattacher: parties*) to join (together); **se réunir** *vi* (*se rencontrer*) to meet

réussi, e [ʀeysi] *adj* successful

réussir [ʀeysiʀ] /2/ *vi* to succeed, be successful; (*à un examen*) to pass ▷ *vt* to make a success of; **~ à faire** to succeed in doing; **~ à** (*être bénéfique à*) to agree with sb; **réussite** *nf* success; (*Cartes*) patience

revaloir [ʀəvalwaʀ] /29/ vt: **je vous revaudrai cela** I'll repay you some day; (en mal) I'll pay you back for this

revanche [ʀəvɑ̃ʃ] nf revenge; (sport) revenge match; **en ~** on the other hand

rêve [ʀɛv] nm dream; **de ~** dream cpd; **faire un ~** to have a dream

réveil [ʀevej] nm waking up no pl; (fig) awakening; (d'une personne) alarm (clock); **au ~** on waking (up); **réveiller** /1/ vt (personne) to wake up; (fig) to awaken, revive; **se réveiller** vi to wake up

réveillon [ʀevejɔ̃] nm Christmas Eve; (de la Saint-Sylvestre) New Year's Eve; **réveillonner** /1/ vi to celebrate Christmas Eve (ou New Year's Eve)

révélateur, -trice [ʀevelatœʀ, -tʀis] adj: **~ (de qch)** revealing (sth)

révéler [ʀevele] /6/ vt to reveal; **se révéler** vi to be revealed, reveal itself; **se ~ facile/faux** to prove (to be) easy/false

revenant, e [ʀəvnɑ̃, -ɑ̃t] nm/f ghost

revendeur, -euse [ʀəvɑ̃dœʀ, -øz] nm/f (détaillant) retailer; (de drogue) (drug-)dealer

revendication [ʀəvɑ̃dikasjɔ̃] nf claim, demand

revendiquer [ʀəvɑ̃dike] /1/ vt to claim, demand; (responsabilité) to claim

revendre [ʀəvɑ̃dʀ] /41/ vt (d'occasion) to resell; (détailler) to sell; **à ~** (en abondance) to spare

revenir [ʀəvniʀ] /22/ vi to come back; **faire ~** (Culin) to brown; **~ cher/à 100 euros (à qn)** to cost (sb) a lot/100 euros; **~ à** (reprendre: études, projet) to return to, go back to; (équivaloir à) to amount to; **~ à qn** (part, honneur) to go to sb; (souvenir, nom) to come back to sb; **~ sur** (question, sujet) to go back over; (engagement) to go back on; **~ à soi** to come round; **je n'en**

reviens pas I can't get over it; **~ sur ses pas** to retrace one's steps; **cela revient à dire que/au même** it amounts to saying that/to the same thing

revenu [ʀəvny] nm income; **revenus** nmpl income sg

rêver [ʀeve] /1/ vi, vt to dream; **~ de qch/de faire** to dream of sth/of doing; **~ à** to dream of

réverbère [ʀevɛʀbɛʀ] nm street lamp ou light; **réverbérer** /6/ vt to reflect

revers [ʀəvɛʀ] nm (de feuille, main) back; (d'étoffe) wrong side; (de pièce, médaille) back, reverse; (Tennis, Ping-Pong) backhand; (de veston) lapel; (fig: échec) setback

revêtement [ʀəvɛtmɑ̃] nm (des sols) flooring; (de chaussée) surface

revêtir [ʀəvetiʀ] /20/ vt (habit) to don, put on; (prendre: apparence, apparence) to take on; **~ qch de** to cover sth with

rêveur, -euse [ʀevœʀ, -øz] adj dreamy ▷ nm/f dreamer

revient [ʀəvjɛ̃] vb voir **revenir**

revigorer [ʀəvigɔʀe] /1/ vt (air frais) to invigorate, brace up; (repas, boisson) to revive, buck up

revirement [ʀəviʀmɑ̃] nm change of mind; (d'une situation) reversal

réviser [ʀevize] /1/ vt to revise; (machine, installation, moteur) to overhaul, service

révision [ʀevizjɔ̃] nf revision; (de voiture) servicing no pl

revivre [ʀəvivʀ] /46/ vi (reprendre des forces) to come alive again ▷ vt (épreuve, moment) to relive

revoir [ʀəvwaʀ] /30/ vt to see again ▷ nm: **au ~** goodbye

révoltant, e [ʀevɔltɑ̃, -ɑ̃t] adj revolting, appalling

révolte [ʀevɔlt] nf rebellion, revolt

révolter [ʀevɔlte] /1/ vt to revolt; **se révolter** vi: **se ~ (contre)** to rebel (against)

révolu, e [ʀevɔly] *adj* past; (*Admin*): **âgé de 18 ans ou ~s** over 18 years of age

révolution [ʀevɔlysjɔ̃] *nf* revolution; **révolutionnaire** *adj, nm/f* revolutionary

revolver [ʀevɔlvɛʀ] *nm* gun; (*à barillet*) revolver

révoquer [ʀevɔke] /1/ *vt* (*fonctionnaire*) to dismiss; (*arrêt, contrat*) to revoke

revu, e [ʀəvy] *pp de* **revoir** ▷ *nf* review; (*périodique*) review, magazine; (*de music-hall*) variety show; **passer en ~** (*mentalement*) to go through

rez-de-chaussée [ʀedʃose] *nm inv* ground floor

RF *sigle f* = **République française**

Rhin [ʀɛ̃] *nm*: **le ~** the Rhine

rhinocéros [ʀinɔseʀɔs] *nm* rhinoceros

Rhône [ʀon] *nm*: **le ~** the Rhone

rhubarbe [ʀybaʀb] *nf* rhubarb

rhum [ʀɔm] *nm* rum

rhumatisme [ʀymatism] *nm* rheumatism no *pl*

rhume [ʀym] *nm* cold; **~ de cerveau** head cold; **le ~ des foins** hay fever

ricaner [ʀikane] /1/ *vi* (*avec méchanceté*) to snigger; (*bêtement, avec gêne*) to giggle

riche [ʀiʃ] *adj* rich; (*personne, pays*) rich, wealthy; **~ en** rich in; **richesse** *nf* wealth; (*fig: de sol, musée etc*) richness; (*fig: ressources, argent*) wealth *sg*; (*fig: trésors*) treasures

ricochet [ʀikɔʃɛ] *nm*: **faire des ~s** to skip stones

ride [ʀid] *nf* wrinkle

rideau, x [ʀido] *nm* curtain; **~ de fer** (*lit*) metal shutter

rider [ʀide] /1/ *vt* to wrinkle; **se rider** *vi* to become wrinkled

ridicule [ʀidikyl] *adj* ridiculous ▷ *nm*: **le ~** ridicule; **ridiculiser** /1/ *vt* to ridicule; **se ridiculiser** *vi* to make a fool of o.s.

MOT-CLÉ

rien [ʀjɛ̃] *pron* **1** (*ne*) **... rien** nothing; (*tournure négative*) anything; **qu'est-ce que vous avez? — rien** what have you got? — nothing; **il n'a rien dit/fait** he said/did nothing, he hasn't said/done anything; **n'avoir peur de rien** to be afraid *ou* frightened of nothing, not to be afraid *ou* frightened of anything; **il n'a rien** (*n'est pas blessé*) he's all right; **ça ne fait rien** it doesn't matter

2 (*quelque chose*): **a-t-il jamais rien fait pour nous?** has he ever done anything for us?

3: **rien de**: **rien d'intéressant** nothing interesting; **rien d'autre** nothing else; **rien du tout** nothing at all

4: **rien que** just, only; nothing but; **rien que pour lui faire plaisir** only *ou* just to please him; **rien que la vérité** nothing but the truth; **rien que cela** that alone

▶ *excl*: **de rien!** not at all!

▶ *nm*: **un petit rien** (*cadeau*) a little something; **des riens** trivia *pl*; **un rien de** a hint of; **en un rien de temps** in no time at all

rieur, -euse [ʀjœʀ, -øz] *adj* cheerful

rigide [ʀiʒid] *adj* stiff; (*fig*) rigid; (*moralement*) strict

rigoler [ʀigɔle] /1/ *vi* (*rire*) to laugh; (*s'amuser*) to have (some) fun; (*plaisanter*) to be joking *ou* kidding; **rigolo, rigolote** *adj* funny ▷ *nm/f* comic; (*péj*) fraud, phoney

rigoureusement [ʀiguʀøzmɑ̃] *adv* rigorously

rigoureux, -euse [ʀiguʀø, -øz] *adj* rigorous; (*climat, châtiment*) harsh, severe

rigueur [ʀigœʀ] *nf* rigour; **"tenue de soirée de ~"** "evening dress (to be worn)"; **à la ~** at a pinch; **tenir ~ à qn de qch** to hold sth against sb

r

rillettes [Rijɛt] nfpl ≈ potted meat sg (made from pork or goose)

rime [Rim] nf rhyme

rinçage [Rɛ̃saʒ] nm rinsing (out); (opération) rinse

rincer [Rɛ̃se] /3/ vt to rinse; (récipient) to rinse out

ringard, e [Rɛ̃gaR, -aRd] adj old-fashioned

riposter [Riposte] /1/ vi to retaliate ▷ vt: **~ que** to retort that

rire [RiR] /36/ vi to laugh; (se divertir) to have fun ▷ nm laughter; **le ~** laughter; **~ de** to laugh at; **pour ~** (pas sérieusement) for a joke ou a laugh

risible [Rizibl] adj laughable

risque [Risk] nm risk ▷ danger; **à ses ~s et périls** at his own risk; **risqué, e** adj risky; (plaisanterie) risqué, daring; **risquer** /1/ vt to risk; (allusion, question) to venture, hazard; **se risquer** vi: **ça ne risque rien** it's quite safe; **il risque de se tuer** he could get ou risks getting himself killed; **ce qui risque de se produire** what might ou could well happen; **il ne risque pas de recommencer** there's no chance of him doing that again; **se risquer à faire** (tenter) to dare to do

rissoler [Risole] /1/ vi, vt: **(faire) ~** to brown

ristourne [RistuRn] nf discount

rite [Rit] nm rite; (fig) ritual

rivage [Rivaʒ] nm shore

rival, e, -aux [Rival, -o] adj, nm/f rival; **rivaliser** /1/ vi: **rivaliser avec** to rival, vie with; **rivalité** nf rivalry

rive [Riv] nf shore; (de fleuve) bank; **riverain, e** nm/f riverside (ou lakeside) resident; (d'une route) local ou roadside resident

rivière [RivjɛR] nf river

riz [Ri] nm rice; **rizière** nf paddy field

RMI sigle m (= revenu minimum d'insertion) ≈ income support (BRIT), ≈ welfare (US)

RN sigle f = **route nationale**

robe [Rɔb] nf dress; (de juge, d'ecclésiastique) robe; (pelage) coat; **~ de soirée/de mariée** evening/wedding dress; **~ de chambre** dressing gown

robinet [Rɔbinɛ] nm tap (BRIT), faucet (US)

robot [Rɔbo] nm robot; **~ de cuisine** food processor

robuste [Rɔbyst] adj robust, sturdy; **robustesse** nf robustness, sturdiness

roc [Rɔk] nm rock

rocade [Rɔkad] nf bypass

rocaille [Rɔkaj] nf loose stones pl; (jardin) rockery, rock garden

roche [Rɔʃ] nf rock

rocher [Rɔʃe] nm rock

rocheux, -euse [Rɔʃø, -øz] adj rocky

rodage [Rɔdaʒ] nm: **en ~** running ou breaking in

rôder [Rode] /1/ vi to roam ou wander about; (de façon suspecte) to lurk (about ou around); **rôdeur, -euse** nm/f prowler

rogne [Rɔɲ] nf: **être en ~** to be mad ou in a temper

rogner [Rɔɲe] /1/ vt to trim; **~ sur** (fig) to cut down ou back on

rognons [Rɔɲɔ̃] nmpl kidneys

roi [Rwa] nm king; **le jour** ou **la fête des R~s** Twelfth Night

rôle [Rol] nm role; part

rollers [RɔlœR] nmpl Rollerblades®

romain, e [Rɔmɛ̃, -ɛn] adj Roman ▷ nm/f: **R~, e** Roman

roman, e [Rɔmɑ̃, -an] adj (Archit) Romanesque ▷ nm novel; **~ policier** detective novel

romancer [Rɔmɑ̃se] /3/ vt to romanticize; **romancier, -ière** nm/f novelist; **romanesque** adj (amours, aventures) storybook cpd; (sentimental: personne) romantic

roman-feuilleton [Rɔmɑ̃fœjtɔ̃] nm serialized novel

romanichel, le [Rɔmaniʃɛl] nm/f gipsy

romantique [Rɔmɑ̃tik] adj romantic

romarin [ʀɔmaʀɛ̃] nm rosemary

Rome [ʀɔm] n Rome

rompre [ʀɔ̃pʀ] /41/ vt to break; (entretien, fiançailles) to break off ▷ vi (fiancés) to break it off; **se rompre** vi to break; **rompu, e** adj (fourbu) exhausted

ronce [ʀɔ̃s] nf bramble branch; **ronces** nfpl brambles

ronchonner [ʀɔ̃ʃɔne] /1/ vi (fam) to grouse, grouch

rond, e [ʀɔ̃, ʀɔ̃d] adj round; (joues, mollets) well-rounded; (fam: ivre) tight ▷ nm (cercle) ring; (fam: sou): **je n'ai plus un ~** I haven't a penny left ▷ nf (gén: de surveillance) rounds pl, patrol; (danse) round (dance); (Mus) semibreve (BRIT), whole note (US); **en ~** (s'asseoir, danser) in a ring; **à la ~e** (alentour): **à 10 km à la ~e** for 10 km round; **rondelet, te** adj plump

rondelle [ʀɔ̃dɛl] nf (Tech) washer; (tranche) slice, round

rond-point [ʀɔ̃pwɛ̃] nm roundabout

ronflement [ʀɔ̃fləmɑ̃] nm snore

ronfler [ʀɔ̃fle] /1/ vi to snore; (moteur, poêle) to hum

ronger [ʀɔ̃ʒe] /3/ vt to gnaw (at); (vers, rouille) to eat into; **se ~ les sangs** to worry o.s. sick; **se ~ les ongles** to bite one's nails; **rongeur, -euse** [ʀɔ̃ʒœʀ, -øz] nm/f rodent

ronronner [ʀɔ̃ʀɔne] /1/ vi to purr

rosbif [ʀɔsbif] nm: **du ~** roasting beef; (cuit) roast beef

rose [ʀoz] nf rose ▷ adj pink; **~ bonbon** adj inv candy pink

rosé, e [ʀoze] adj pinkish; **(vin) ~** rosé (wine)

roseau, x [ʀozo] nm reed

rosée [ʀoze] nf dew

rosier [ʀozje] nm rosebush, rose tree

rossignol [ʀɔsiɲɔl] nm (Zool) nightingale

rotation [ʀɔtasjɔ̃] nf rotation

roter [ʀɔte] /1/ vi (fam) to burp, belch

rôti [ʀoti] nm: **du ~** roasting meat; (cuit) roast meat; **un ~ de bœuf/porc** a joint of beef/pork

rotin [ʀɔtɛ̃] nm rattan (cane); **fauteuil en ~** cane (arm)chair

rôtir [ʀotiʀ] /2/ vt (aussi: **faire ~**) to roast ▷ vi to roast; **rôtisserie** nf (restaurant) steakhouse; (traiteur) roast meat shop; **rôtissoire** nf (roasting) spit

rotule [ʀɔtyl] nf kneecap

rouage [ʀwaʒ] nm cog(wheel), gearwheel; **les ~s de l'État** the wheels of State

roue [ʀu] nf wheel; **~ de secours** spare wheel

rouer [ʀwe] /1/ vt: **~ qn de coups** to give sb a thrashing

rouge [ʀuʒ] adj, nm/f red ▷ nm red; (vin) ~ red wine; **passer au ~** (signal) to go red; (automobiliste) to go through a red light; **sur la liste ~** ex-directory (BRIT), unlisted (US); **~ à joue** blusher; **~ (à lèvres)** lipstick; **rouge-gorge** nm robin (redbreast)

rougeole [ʀuʒɔl] nf measles sg

rougeoyer [ʀuʒwaje] /8/ vi to glow red

rouget [ʀuʒɛ] nm mullet

rougeur [ʀuʒœʀ] nf redness; **rougeurs** nfpl (Méd) red blotches

rougir [ʀuʒiʀ] /2/ vi to turn red; (de honte, timidité) to blush, flush; (de plaisir, colère) to flush

rouille [ʀuj] nf rust; **rouillé, e** adj rusty; **rouiller** /1/ vt to rust ▷ vi to rust, go rusty

roulant, e [ʀulɑ̃, -ɑ̃t] adj (meuble) on wheels; (surface, trottoir, tapis) moving; **escalier ~** escalator

rouleau, x [ʀulo] nm roll; (à mise en plis, à peinture, vague) roller; **~ à pâtisserie** rolling pin

roulement [ʀulmɑ̃] nm (bruit) rumbling no pl, rumble; (rotation) rotation; **par ~** on a rota (BRIT) ou rotation (US) basis; **~ (à billes)** ball bearings pl; **~ de tambour** drum roll

rouler [ʀule] /1/ vt to roll; (*papier, tapis*) to roll up; (*Culin: pâte*) to roll out; (*fam: duper*) to do, con ▷ vi (*bille, boule*) to roll; (*voiture, train*) to go, run; (*automobiliste*) to drive; (*cycliste*) to ride; (*bateau*) to roll in; **se ~ dans** (*boue*) to roll in; (*couverture*) to roll o.s. (up) in

roulette [ʀulɛt] *nf* (*de table, fauteuil*) castor; (*de dentiste*) drill; (*jeu*): **la ~** roulette; **à ~s** on castors; **ça a marché comme sur des ~s** (*fam*) it went off very smoothly

roulotte [ʀulɔt] *nf* caravan

roumain, e [ʀumɛ̃, -ɛn] *adj* Rumanian ▷ *nm/f*: **R~, e** Rumanian

Roumanie [ʀumani] *nf*: **la ~** Rumania

rouquin, e [ʀukɛ̃, -in] *nm/f* (*péj*) redhead

rouspéter [ʀuspete] /6/ *vi* (*fam*) to moan

rousse [ʀus] *adj f voir* **roux**

roussir [ʀusiʀ] /2/ vt to scorch ▷ vi (*Culin*): **faire ~** to brown

route [ʀut] *nf* road; (*fig: chemin*) way; (*itinéraire, parcours*) route; (*fig: voie*) road, path; **il y a trois heures de ~** it's a three-hour ride *ou* journey; **en ~** on the way; **en ~!** let's go!; **mettre en ~** to start up; **se mettre en ~** to set off; **~ nationale** ≈ A-road (*BRIT*), ≈ state highway (*US*)

routeur [ʀutœʀ] *nm* (*Inform*) router

routier, -ière [ʀutje, -jɛʀ] *adj* road *cpd* ▷ *nm* (*camionneur*) (long-distance) lorry (*BRIT*) *ou* truck (*US*) driver; (*restaurant*) = transport café (*BRIT*) ≈ truck stop (*US*)

routine [ʀutin] *nf* routine; **routinier, -ière** [ʀutinje, -jɛʀ] *adj* (*péj: travail*) humdrum; (: *personne*) addicted to routine

rouvrir [ʀuvʀiʀ] /18/, vt, vi to reopen, open again; **se rouvrir** vi to open up again

roux, rousse [ʀu, ʀus] *adj* red; (*personne*) red-haired ▷ *nm/f* redhead

royal, e, -aux [ʀwajal, -o] *adj* royal; (*fig*) fit for a king

royaume [ʀwajom] *nm* kingdom; (*fig*) realm

Royaume-Uni [ʀwajomyni] *nm*: **le ~** the United Kingdom

royauté [ʀwajote] *nf* (*régime*) monarchy

ruban [ʀybɑ̃] *nm* ribbon; **~ adhésif** adhesive tape

rubéole [ʀybeɔl] *nf* German measles *sg*, rubella

rubis [ʀybi] *nm* ruby

rubrique [ʀybʀik] *nf* (*titre, catégorie*) heading; (*Presse: article*) column

ruche [ʀyʃ] *nf* hive

rude [ʀyd] *adj* (*barbe, toile*) rough; (*métier, tâche*) hard, tough; (*climat*) severe, harsh; (*bourru*) harsh, rough; (*fruste: manières*) rugged, tough; (*fam: fameux*) jolly good; **rudement** *adv* (*très*) terribly

rudimentaire [ʀydimɑ̃tɛʀ] *adj* rudimentary, basic

rudiments [ʀydimɑ̃] *nmpl*: **avoir des ~ d'anglais** to have a smattering of English

rue [ʀy] *nf* street

ruée [ʀye] *nf* rush

ruelle [ʀyɛl] *nf* alley(way)

ruer [ʀye] /1/ *vi* (*cheval*) to kick out; **se ruer** *vi*: **se ~ sur** to pounce on; **se ~ vers/dans/hors de** to rush *ou* dash towards/into/out of

rugby [ʀygbi] *nm* rugby (football)

rugir [ʀyʒiʀ] /2/ *vi* to roar

rugueux, -euse [ʀygø, -øz] *adj* rough

ruine [ʀɥin] *nf* ruin; **ruiner** /1/ vt to ruin; **ruineux, -euse** *adj* ruinous

ruisseau, x [ʀɥiso] *nm* stream, brook

ruisseler [ʀɥisle] /4/ *vi* to stream

rumeur [ʀymœʀ] *nf* (*bruit confus*) rumbling; (*nouvelle*) rumour

ruminer [ʀymine] /1/ vt (*herbe*) to ruminate; (*fig*) to ruminate on *ou* over, chew over

rupture [ʀyptyʀ] *nf* (*de négociations etc*) breakdown; (*de contrat*) breach;

(dans continuité) break; *(séparation, désunion)* break-up, split

rural, e, -aux [ʀyʀal, -o] *adj* rural, country *cpd*

ruse [ʀyz] *nf*: **la ~** cunning, craftiness; *(pour tromper)* trickery; **une ~** a trick, a ruse; **rusé, e** *adj* cunning, crafty

russe [ʀys] *adj* Russian ▷ *nm* (*Ling*) Russian ▷ *nm/f*: **R~** Russian

Russie [ʀysi] *nf*: **la ~** Russia

rustine [ʀystin] *nf* repair patch (for bicycle inner tube)

rustique [ʀystik] *adj* rustic

rythme [ʀitm] *nm* rhythm; *(vitesse)* rate (: *de la vie*) pace, tempo; **rythmé, e** *adj* rhythmic(al)

S

s' [s] *pron voir* **se**

sa [sa] *adj poss voir* **son¹**

sable [sabl] *nm* sand

sablé [sable] *nm* shortbread biscuit

sabler [sable] /1/ *vt (contre le verglas)* to grit; **~ le champagne** to drink champagne

sabot [sabo] *nm* clog; *(de cheval, bœuf)* hoof; **~ de frein** brake shoe

saboter [sabɔte] /1/ *vt (travail, morceau de musique)* to botch, make a mess of; *(machine, installation, négociation etc)* to sabotage

sac [sak] *nm* bag; *(à charbon etc)* sack; **mettre à ~** to sack; **~ à provisions/ de voyage** shopping/travelling bag; **~ de couchage** sleeping bag; **~ à dos** rucksack; **~ à main** handbag

saccadé, e [sakade] *adj* jerky; *(respiration)* spasmodic

saccager [sakaʒe] /3/ *vt (piller)* to sack; *(dévaster)* to create havoc in

saccharine [sakaʀin] *nf* saccharin(e)

sachet [saʃɛ] nm (small) bag; (de lavande, poudre, shampooing) sachet; **~ de thé** tea bag; **du potage en ~** packet soup

sacoche [sakɔʃ] nf (gén) bag; (de bicyclette) saddlebag

sacré, e [sakre] adj sacred; (fam: satané) blasted; (: fameux) **un ~ ...** a heck of a ...

sacrement [sakrəmɑ̃] nm sacrament

sacrifice [sakrifis] nm sacrifice; **sacrifier** /7/ vt to sacrifice

sacristie [sakristi] nf sacristy; (culte protestant) vestry

sadique [sadik] adj sadistic

safran [safrɑ̃] nm saffron

sage [saʒ] adj wise; (enfant) good

sage-femme [saʒfam] nf midwife

sagesse [saʒɛs] nf wisdom

Sagittaire [saʒitɛr] nm: **le ~** Sagittarius

Sahara [saara] nm: **le ~** the Sahara (Desert)

saignant, e [sɛɲɑ̃, -ɑ̃t] adj (viande) rare

saigner [seɲe] /1/ vi to bleed ▷ vt to bleed; (animal) to bleed to death; **~ du nez** to have a nosebleed

saillir [sajir] /13/ vi to project, stick out; (veine, muscle) to bulge

sain, e [sɛ̃, sɛn] adj healthy; **~ et sauf** safe and sound, unharmed; **~ d'esprit** sound in mind, sane

saindoux [sɛ̃du] nm lard

saint, e [sɛ̃, sɛ̃t] adj holy ▷ nm/f saint; **la S~e Vierge** the Blessed Virgin

Saint-Esprit [sɛ̃tɛspri] nm: **le ~** the Holy Spirit ou Ghost

sainteté [sɛ̃tte] nf holiness

Saint-Sylvestre [sɛ̃silvɛstr] nf: **la ~** New Year's Eve

sais etc [sɛ] vb voir **savoir**

saisie [sezi] nf seizure; **~ (de données)** (data) capture

saisir [sezir] /2/ vt to take hold of, grab; (fig: occasion) to seize; (comprendre) to grasp; (entendre) to get, catch; (Inform) to capture; (Culin) to fry quickly; (Jur: biens, publication) to seize; **saisissant, e** adj startling, striking

saison [sezɔ̃] nf season; **haute/ basse/morte ~** high/low/slack season; **saisonnier, -ière** adj seasonal

salade [salad] nf (Bot) lettuce etc (generic term); (Culin) (green) salad; (fam: confusion) tangle, muddle; **~ composée** mixed salad; **~ de fruits** fruit salad; **~ verte** green salad; **saladier** nm (salad) bowl

salaire [salɛr] nm (annuel, mensuel) salary; (hebdomadaire, journalier) pay, wages pl; **~ minimum interprofessionnel de croissance** index-linked guaranteed minimum wage

salarié, e [salarje] nm/f salaried employee; wage-earner

salaud [salo] nm (fam!) sod (!), bastard (!)

sale [sal] adj dirty, filthy; (fig: mauvais) nasty

salé, e [sale] adj (liquide, saveur, mer, goût) salty; (Culin: amandes, beurre etc) salted; (: gâteaux) savoury; (fig: grivois) spicy; (: note, facture) steep

saler [sale] /1/ vt to salt

saleté [salte] nf (état) dirtiness; (crasse) dirt; (tache etc) dirt no pl; (fig: tour) filthy trick; (: chose sans valeur) rubbish no pl; (: obscénité) filth no pl

salière [saljɛr] nf saltcellar

salir [salir] /2/ vt to (make) dirty; (fig) to soil the reputation of; **se salir** vi to get dirty; **salissant, e** adj (tissu) which shows the dirt; (métier) dirty, messy

salle [sal] nf room; (d'hôpital) ward; (de restaurant) dining room; (d'un cinéma) auditorium; (: public) audience; **~ d'attente** waiting room; **~ de bain(s)** bathroom; **~ de classe** classroom; **~ de concert** concert hall; **~ d'eau** shower-room;

~ d'embarquement (à l'aéroport) departure lounge; **~ de jeux** (pour enfants) playroom; **~ à manger** dining room; **~ des professeurs** staffroom; **~ de séjour** living room; **~ des ventes** saleroom

salon [salɔ̃] nm lounge, sitting room; (mobilier) lounge suite; (exposition) exhibition, show; **~ de coiffure** hairdressing salon; **~ de thé** tearoom

salope [salɔp] nf (fam!) bitch (!); **saloperie** nf (fam!: action) dirty trick; (: chose sans valeur) rubbish nf; **salopette** [salɔpɛt] nf dungarees pl; (d'ouvrier) overall(s)

salsifis [salsifi] nm salsify

salubre [salybʀ] adj healthy, salubrious

saluer [salɥe] /1/ vt (pour dire bonjour, fig) to greet; (pour dire au revoir) to take one's leave; (Mil) to salute

salut [saly] nm (sauvegarde) safety; (Rel) salvation; (geste) wave; (parole) greeting; (Mil) salute ▷ excl (fam: pour dire bonjour) hi (there); (: pour dire au revoir) see you, bye!

salutations [salytasjɔ̃] nfpl greetings; **recevez mes ~ distinguées** ou **respectueuses** yours faithfully

samedi [samdi] nm Saturday

SAMU [samy] sigle m (= service d'assistance médicale d'urgence) ≈ ambulance (service) (BRIT), ≈ paramedics (US)

sanction [sɑ̃ksjɔ̃] nf sanction; **sanctionner** /1/ vt (loi, usage) to sanction; (punir) to punish

sandale [sɑ̃dal] nf sandal

sandwich [sɑ̃dwitʃ] nm sandwich

sang [sɑ̃] nm blood; **en ~** covered in blood; **se faire du mauvais ~** to fret, get in a state; **sang-froid** nm calm, sangfroid; **de sang-froid** in cold blood; **sanglant, e** adj bloody

sangle [sɑ̃gl] nf strap

sanglier [sɑ̃glije] nm (wild) boar

sanglot [sɑ̃glo] nm sob; **sangloter** /1/ vi to sob

sangsue [sɑ̃sy] nf leech

sanguin, e [sɑ̃gɛ̃, -in] adj blood cpd

sanitaire [sanitɛʀ] adj health cpd; **sanitaires** nmpl (salle de bain et w.-c.) bathroom sg

sans [sɑ̃] prép without; **~ qu'il s'en aperçoive** without him ou his noticing; **un pull ~ manches** a sleeveless jumper; **~ faute** without fail; **~ arrêt** without a break; **~ ça** (fam) otherwise; **sans-abri** nmpl homeless; **sans-emploi** nm/f inv unemployed person; **les sans-emploi** the unemployed; **sans-gêne** adj inv inconsiderate

santé [sɑ̃te] nf health; **être en bonne ~** to be in good health; **boire à la ~ de qn** to drink (to) sb's health; **à ta** ou **votre ~!** cheers!

saoudien, ne [saudjɛ̃, -ɛn] adj Saudi (Arabian) ▷ nm/f: **S~, ne** Saudi (Arabian)

saoul, e [su, sul] adj = **soûl**

saper [sape] /1/ vt to undermine, sap

sapeur-pompier [sapœʀpɔ̃pje] nm fireman

saphir [safiʀ] nm sapphire

sapin [sapɛ̃] nm fir (tree); (bois) fir; **~ de Noël** Christmas tree

sarcastique [saʀkastik] adj sarcastic

Sardaigne [saʀdɛɲ] nf: **la ~** Sardinia

sardine [saʀdin] nf sardine

SARL [saʀl] sigle f (= société à responsabilité limitée) ≈ plc (BRIT), ≈ Inc. (US)

sarrasin [saʀazɛ̃] nm buckwheat

satané, e [satane] adj (fam) confounded

satellite [satelit] nm satellite

satin [satɛ̃] nm satin

satire [satiʀ] nf satire; **satirique** adj satirical

satisfaction [satisfaksjɔ̃] nf satisfaction

satisfaire [satisfɛʀ] /60/ vt to satisfy; **~ à** (revendications, conditions) to meet; **satisfaisant, e** adj (acceptable) satisfactory; **satisfait, e** adj satisfied; **satisfait de** happy ou satisfied with

saturer [satyʀe] /1/ vt to saturate

sauce [sos] nf sauce; (avec un rôti) gravy; ~ **tomate** tomato sauce; **saucière** nf sauceboat

saucisse [sosis] nf sausage

saucisson [sosisɔ̃] nm (slicing) sausage

sauf¹ [sof] prép except; ~ **si** (à moins que) unless; ~ **avis contraire** unless you hear to the contrary; ~ **erreur** if I'm not mistaken

sauf², sauve [sof, sov] adj unharmed, unhurt; (fig: honneur) intact, saved; **laisser la vie sauve à qn** to spare sb's life

sauge [soʒ] nf sage

saugrenu, e [sogʀəny] adj preposterous

saule [sol] nm willow (tree)

saumon [somɔ̃] nm salmon inv

saupoudrer [sopudʀe] /1/ vt: ~ **qch de** to sprinkle sth with

saur [sɔʀ] adj m: **hareng** ~ smoked ou red herring, kipper

saut [so] nm jump; (discipline sportive) jumping; **faire un** ~ **chez qn** to pop over to sb's (place); ~ **en hauteur/longueur** high/long jump; ~ **à la perche** pole vaulting; ~ **à l'élastique** bungee jumping; ~ **périlleux** somersault

sauter [sote] /1/ vi to jump, leap; (exploser) to blow up, explode; (: fusibles) to blow; (se détacher) to pop out (ou off) ▷ vt to jump (over), leap (over); (fig: omettre) to skip, miss (out); **faire** ~ to blow up; (Culin) to sauté; ~ **à la corde** to skip; ~ **au cou de qn** to fly into sb's arms; ~ **sur une occasion** to jump at an opportunity; ~ **aux yeux** to be quite obvious

sauterelle [sotʀɛl] nf grasshopper

sautiller [sotije] /1/ vi (oiseau) to hop; (enfant) to skip

sauvage [sovaʒ] adj (gén) wild; (peuplade) savage; (farouche) unsociable; (barbare) wild, savage; (non officiel) unauthorized, unofficial; **faire du camping** ~ to camp in the wild ▷ nm/f savage; (timide) unsociable type

sauve [sov] adj f voir **sauf²**

sauvegarde [sovgaʀd] nf safeguard; (Inform) backup; **sauvegarder** /1/ vt to safeguard; (Inform: enregistrer) to save; (: copier) to back up

sauve-qui-peut [sovkipø] excl run for your life!

sauver [sove] /1/ vt to save; (porter secours à) to rescue; (récupérer) to salvage, rescue; **se sauver** vi (s'enfuir) to run away; (fam: partir) to be off; **sauvetage** nm rescue; **sauveteur** nm rescuer; **sauvette**: **à la sauvette** adv (se marier etc) hastily, hurriedly; **sauveur** nm saviour (BRIT), savior (US)

savant, e [savɑ̃, -ɑ̃t] adj scholarly, learned ▷ nm scientist

saveur [savœʀ] nf flavour; (fig) savour

savoir [savwaʀ] /32/ vt to know; (être capable de): **il sait nager** he can swim ▷ nm knowledge; **se savoir** vi (être connu) to be known; **je n'en sais rien** I (really) don't know; ~ **à** ~ **(que)** that is, namely; **faire** ~ **qch à qn** to let sb know sth; **pas que je sache** not as far as I know

savon [savɔ̃] nm (produit) soap; (morceau) bar ou tablet of soap; (fam): **passer un** ~ **à qn** to give sb a good dressing-down; **savonner** /1/ vt to soap; **savonnette** nf bar of soap

savourer [savuʀe] /1/ vt to savour; **savoureux, -euse** adj tasty; (fig: anecdote) spicy, juicy

saxo(phone) [saks(ɔfɔn)] nm sax(ophone)

scabreux, -euse [skabʀø, -øz] adj risky; (indécent) improper, shocking

scandale [skɑ̃dal] nm scandal; **faire un ~** (scène) to make a scene; (Jur) create a disturbance; **faire ~** to scandalize people; **scandaleux, -euse** adj scandalous, outrageous

scandinave [skɑ̃dinav] adj Scandinavian ▷ nm/f: **S~** Scandinavian

Scandinavie [skɑ̃dinavi] nf: **la ~** Scandinavia

scarabée [skaʀabe] nm beetle

scarlatine [skaʀlatin] nf scarlet fever

scarole [skaʀɔl] nf endive

sceau, x [so] nm seal

sceller [sele] /1/ vt to seal

scénario [senaʀjo] nm scenario

scène [sɛn] nf (gén) scene; (estrade, fig: théâtre) stage; **entrer en ~** to come on stage; **mettre en ~** (Théât) to stage; (Ciné) to direct; **faire une ~ (à qn)** to make a scene (with sb); **~ de ménage** domestic fight ou scene

sceptique [sɛptik] adj sceptical

schéma [ʃema] nm (diagramme) diagram, sketch; **schématique** adj diagrammatic(al), schematic; (fig) oversimplified

sciatique [sjatik] nf sciatica

scie [si] nf saw

sciemment [sjamɑ̃] adv knowingly

science [sjɑ̃s] nf science; (savoir) knowledge; **~s humaines/sociales** social sciences; **~s naturelles** (Scol) natural science sg, biology sg; **~s po** political science ou studies pl; **science-fiction** nf science fiction; **scientifique** adj scientific ▷ nm/f scientist; (étudiant) science student

scier [sje] /7/ vt to saw; (retrancher) to saw off; **scierie** nf sawmill

scintiller [sɛ̃tije] /1/ vi to sparkle; (étoile) to twinkle

sciure [sjyʀ] nf: **~ (de bois)** sawdust

sclérose [skleʀoz] nf: **~ en plaques (SEP)** multiple sclerosis (MS)

scolaire [skɔlɛʀ] adj school cpd; **scolariser** /1/ vt to provide with

schooling (ou schools); **scolarité** nf schooling

scooter [skutœʀ] nm (motor) scooter

score [skɔʀ] nm score

scorpion [skɔʀpjɔ̃] nm (signe): **le S~** Scorpio

scotch [skɔtʃ] nm (whisky) scotch, whisky; **Scotch®** (adhésif) Sellotape® (BRIT), Scotch tape® (US)

scout, e [skut] adj, nm scout

script [skʀipt] nm (écriture) printing; (Ciné) (shooting) script

scrupule [skʀypyl] nm scruple

scruter [skʀyte] /1/ vt to scrutinize; (l'obscurité) to peer into

scrutin [skʀytɛ̃] nm (vote) ballot; (ensemble des opérations) poll

sculpter [skylte] /1/ vt to sculpt; (érosion) to carve; **sculpteur** nm sculptor; **sculpture** nf sculpture

SDF sigle m (= sans domicile fixe) homeless person; **les ~** the homeless

○ **MOT-CLÉ**

se, s' [sə, s] pron 1 (emploi réfléchi) oneself; (: masc) himself; (: fém) herself; (: sujet non humain) itself; (: pl) themselves; **se savonner** to soap o.s.

2 (réciproque) one another, each other; **ils s'aiment** they love one another ou each other

3 (passif): **cela se répare facilement** it is easily repaired

4 (possessif): **se casser la jambe/se laver les mains** to break one's leg/ wash one's hands

séance [seɑ̃s] nf (d'assemblée) meeting, session; (de tribunal) sitting, session; (musicale, Ciné, Théât) performance

seau, x [so] nm bucket, pail

sec, sèche [sɛk, sɛʃ] adj dry; (raisins, figues) dried; (insensible: cœur, personne) hard, cold ▷ nm: **tenir au ~** to keep in a dry place ▷ adv hard; **je le**

bois ~ I drink it straight *ou* neat; **à ~** (puits) dried up

sécateur [sekatœʀ] nm secateurs pl (BRIT); shears pl

sèche [sɛʃ] adj f voir **sec**; **sèche-cheveux** nm inv hair-dryer; **sèche-linge** nm inv tumble dryer; **sèchement** adv (répliquer etc) drily

sécher [seʃe] /6/ vt to dry; (dessécher: peau, blé) to dry (out); (: étang) to dry up; (fam: classe, cours) to skip ▷ vi to dry; to dry out; to dry up; (fam: candidat) to be stumped; **se sécher** vi (après le bain) to dry o.s.; **sécheresse** nf dryness; (absence de pluie) drought; **séchoir** nm drier

second, e [s(ə)ɡɔ̃, -ɔ̃d] adj second ▷ nm (assistant) second in command; (Navig) first mate ▷ nf second; (Scol) ≈ tenth grade (US); (Aviat, Rail etc) second class; **voyager en ~e** to travel second-class; **secondaire** adj secondary; **seconder** /1/ vt to assist

secouer [s(ə)kwe] /1/ vt to shake; (passagers) to rock; (traumatiser) to shake (up)

secourir [s(ə)kuʀiʀ] /11/ vt (venir en aide à) to assist; **secourisme** nm first aid; **secouriste** nm/f first-aid worker

secours nm help, aid, assistance ▷ nmpl help; **au ~!** help!; **appeler au ~** to shout for help; **porter ~ à qn** to give sb assistance, help sb; **les premiers ~** first aid sg

- **ÉQUIPES DE SECOURS**

- Emergency phone numbers can
- be dialled free from public phones.
- For the police ('la police') dial 17; for
- medical services ('le SAMU') dial 15;
- for the fire brigade ('les sapeurs-
- pompiers') dial 18.

secousse [s(ə)kus] nf jolt, bump; (électrique) shock; (fig: psychologique) jolt, shock

secret, -ète [səkʀɛ, -ɛt] adj secret; (fig: renfermé) reticent, reserved ▷ nm secret; (discrétion absolue): **le ~** secrecy; **en ~** in secret, secretly; **~ professionnel** professional secrecy

secrétaire [səkʀetɛʀ] nm/f secretary ▷ nm (meuble) writing desk; **~ de direction** private ou personal secretary; **~ d'État** junior minister; **secrétariat** nm (profession) secretarial work; (bureau) (secretary's) office; (: d'organisation internationale) secretariat

secteur [sɛktœʀ] nm sector; (Admin) district; (Élec): **branché sur le ~** plugged into the mains (supply)

section [sɛksjɔ̃] nf section; (de parcours d'autobus) fare stage; (Mil: unité) platoon; **sectionner** /1/ vt to sever

sécu [seky] nf = **sécurité sociale**

sécurité [sekyʀite] nf (absence de troubles) security; (absence de danger) safety; **système de ~** security (ou safety) system; **être en ~** to be safe; **la ~ routière** road safety; **la ~ sociale** ≈ (the) Social Security (BRIT), ≈ (the) Welfare (US)

sédentaire [sedɑ̃tɛʀ] adj sedentary

séduction [sedyksjɔ̃] nf seduction; (charme, attrait) appeal, charm

séduire [sedɥiʀ] /38/ vt to charm; (femme: abuser de) to seduce; **séduisant, e** adj (femme) charming; (homme, offre) very attractive

ségrégation [seɡʀeɡasjɔ̃] nf segregation

seigle [sɛɡl] nm rye

seigneur [sɛɲœʀ] nm lord

sein [sɛ̃] nm breast; (entrailles) womb; **au ~ de** (équipe, institution) within

séisme [seism] nm earthquake

seize [sɛz] num sixteen; **seizième** num sixteenth

séjour [seʒuʀ] nm stay; (pièce) living room; **séjourner** /1/ vi to stay

sel [sɛl] nm salt; (fig: piquant) spice

sélection [seleksjɔ̃] nf selection; **sélectionner** /1/ vt to select

self [sɛlf] nm (fam) self-service

selfie [sɛlfi] nm selfie

self-service [sɛlfsɛʁvis] adj self-service ▷ nm self-service (restaurant)

selle [sɛl] nf saddle; **selles** nfpl (Méd) stools; **seller** /1/ vt to saddle

selon [səlɔ̃] prép according to; (en se conformant à) in accordance with; **~ moi** as I see it; **~ que** according to

semaine [səmɛn] nf week; **en ~** during the week, on weekdays

semblable [sɑ̃blabl] adj similar; (de ce genre): **de ~s mésaventures** such mishaps ▷ nm fellow creature ou man; **~ à** similar to, like

semblant [sɑ̃blɑ̃] nm: **un ~ de vérité** a semblance of truth; **faire ~ (de faire)** to pretend (to do)

sembler [sɑ̃ble] /1/ vb copule to seem ▷ vb impers: **il semble (bien) que/inutile de** it (really) seems ou appears that/useless to; **il me semble (bien) que** it (really) seems to me that; **comme bon lui semble** as he sees fit

semelle [səmɛl] nf sole; (intérieure: insole, inner sole

semer [səme] /5/ vt to sow; (fig: éparpiller) to scatter; (: confusion) to spread; (fam: poursuivants) to lose, shake off; **semé de** (difficultés) riddled with

semestre [səmɛstʁ] nm half-year; (Scol) semester

séminaire [seminɛʁ] nm seminar; **~ en ligne** webinar

semi-remorque [səmiʁəmɔʁk] nm articulated lorry (BRIT), semi(trailer) (US)

semoule [səmul] nf semolina

sénat [sena] nm senate; **sénateur** nm senator

Sénégal [senegal] nm: **le ~** Senegal

montre anticlockwise; **dans le mauvais ~** (aller) the wrong way; in the wrong direction; **bon ~** good sense; **~ dessus dessous** upside down; **~ interdit, ~ unique** one-way street

sensation [sɑ̃sasjɔ̃] nf sensation; **faire ~** to cause a sensation, create a stir; **à ~** (péj) sensational; **sensationnel, le** adj sensational, fantastic

sensé, e [sɑ̃se] adj sensible

sensibiliser [sɑ̃sibilize] /1/ vt: **~ qn (à)** to make sb sensitive (to)

sensibilité [sɑ̃sibilite] nf sensitivity

sensible [sɑ̃sibl] adj sensitive; (aux sens) perceptible; (appréciable: différence, progrès) appreciable, noticeable; **~ à** sensitive to; **sensiblement** adv (à peu près): **ils ont sensiblement le même poids** they weigh approximately the same; **sensiblerie** nf sentimentality

> Attention à ne pas traduire *sensible* par le mot anglais *sensible*.

sensuel, le [sɑ̃sɥɛl] adj (personne) sensual; (musique) sensuous

sentence [sɑ̃tɑ̃s] nf (Jur) sentence

sentier [sɑ̃tje] nm path

sentiment [sɑ̃timɑ̃] nm feeling; **recevez mes ~s respectueux** (personne nommée) yours sincerely; (personne non nommée) yours faithfully; **sentimental, e, -aux** adj sentimental; (vie, aventure) love cpd

sentinelle [sɑ̃tinɛl] nf sentry

sentir [sɑ̃tiʁ] /16/ vt (par l'odorat) to smell; (par le goût) to taste; (au toucher, fig) to feel; (répandre une odeur de) to smell of; (: ressemblance) to smell like ▷ vi to smell; **~ mauvais** to smell bad; **~ bien** to feel good; **se ~ mal** (être indisposé) to feel unwell ou ill; **se ~ le courage/la force de faire** to feel brave/strong enough to do; **il ne peut pas le ~** (fam) he can't stand him; **je ne me sens pas bien** I don't feel well

S

séparation [separasjɔ̃] nf separation; (cloison) division, partition

séparé, e [separe] adj (appartements, pouvoirs) separate; (époux) separated; **séparément** adv separately

séparer [separe] /1/ vt to separate; (désunir) to drive apart; (détacher): **~ qch de** to pull sth (off) from; **se séparer** vi (époux) to separate, part; (prendre congé: amis etc) to part; (se diviser: route, tige etc) to divide; **se ~ de** (époux) to separate ou part from; (employé, objet personnel) to part with

sept [sɛt] num seven; **septante** num (BELGIQUE, SUISSE) seventy

septembre [sɛptɑ̃bʀ] nm September

septicémie [sɛptisemi] nf blood poisoning, septicaemia

septième [sɛtjɛm] num seventh

séquelles [sekɛl] nfpl after-effects; (fig) aftermath sg

serbe [sɛʀb] adj Serbian

Serbie [sɛʀbi] nf: **la ~** Serbia

serein, e [səʀɛ̃, -ɛn] adj serene

sergent [sɛʀʒɑ̃] nm sergeant

série [seʀi] nf series inv; (de clés, casseroles, outils) set; (catégorie: Sport) rank; **en ~** (succession) in quick succession; (Comm) mass cpd; **de ~** (voiture) standard; **hors ~** (Comm) custombuilt; **~ noire** (crime) thriller

sérieusement [seʀjøzmɑ̃] adv seriously

sérieux, -euse [seʀjø, -øz] adj serious; (élève, employé) reliable, responsible; (client, maison) reliable, dependable ▶ nm seriousness; (d'une entreprise) reliability; **garder son ~** to keep a straight face; **prendre qch/ qn au ~** to take sth/sb seriously

serin [səʀɛ̃] nm canary

seringue [səʀɛ̃g] nf syringe

serment [sɛʀmɑ̃] nm (juré) oath; (promesse) pledge, vow

sermon [sɛʀmɔ̃] nm sermon

séropositif, -ive [seʀopozitif, -iv] adj HIV positive

serpent [sɛʀpɑ̃] nm snake; **serpenter** /1/ vi to wind

serpillière [sɛʀpijɛʀ] nf floorcloth

serre [sɛʀ] nf (Agr) greenhouse; **serres** nfpl (griffes) claws, talons

serré, e [seʀe] adj (réseau) dense; (habits) tight; (fig: lutte, match) tight, close-fought; (passagers etc) (tightly) packed; **avoir le cœur ~** to have a heavy heart

serrer [seʀe] /1/ vt (tenir) to grip ou hold tight; (comprimer, coincer) to squeeze; (poings, mâchoires) to clench; (vêtement) to be too tight for; (ceinture, nœud, frein, vis) to tighten ▶ vi: **~ à droite** to keep to the right

serrure [seʀyʀ] nf lock; **serrurier** nm locksmith

sers, sert [sɛʀ] vb voir **servir**

servante [sɛʀvɑ̃t] nf (maid)servant

serveur, -euse [sɛʀvœʀ, -øz] nm/f waiter (waitress)

serviable [sɛʀvjabl] adj obliging, willing to help

service [sɛʀvis] nm service; (série de repas): **premier ~** first sitting; (assortiment de vaisselle) set; service; (bureau: de la vente etc) department, section; **faire le ~** to serve; **rendre ~ à qn** to help sb; **rendre un ~ à qn** to do sb a favour; **être de ~** to be on duty; **être/mettre en ~** to be in/put into service ou operation; **~ compris/ non compris** service included/ not included; **hors ~** out of order; **~ après-vente** after-sales service; **~ militaire** military service; see note **"service militaire"**; **~ d'ordre** police (ou stewards) in charge of maintaining order; **~s secrets** secret service sg

---

SERVICE MILITAIRE

Until 1997, French men over
the age of 18 who were passed
as fit, and who were not in

- full-time higher education,
- were required to do ten months'
- 'service militaire'. Conscientious
- objectors were required to do two
- years' community service. Since
- 1997, military service has been
- suspended in France. However, all
- sixteen-year-olds, both male and
- female, are required to register
- for a compulsory one-day training
- course, the 'JDC' ('journée défense
- et citoyenneté'), which covers
- basic information on the principles
- and organization of defence in
- France, and also advises on career
- opportunities in the military and in
- the voluntary sector. Young people
- must attend the training day
- before their eighteenth birthday.

serviette [sɛʀvjɛt] *nf (de table)* (table) napkin, serviette; *(de toilette)* towel; *(porte-documents)* briefcase; ~ **hygiénique** sanitary towel

servir [sɛʀviʀ] /14/ *vt* to serve; *(au restaurant)* to wait on; *(au magasin)* to serve, attend to ▷ *vi (Tennis)* to serve; *(Cartes)* to deal; **se servir** *vi (prendre d'un plat)* to help o.s.; **vous êtes servi?** are you being served?; **sers-toi** help yourself; **se ~ de** *(plat)* to help o.s. to; *(voiture, outil, relations)* to use; **~ à qn** *(diplôme, livre)* to be of use to sb; **~ à qch/à faire** *(outil etc)* to be used for sth/for doing; **ça ne sert à rien** it's no use; **~ (à qn) de ...** to serve as ... *(for sb)*

serviteur [sɛʀvitœʀ] *nm* servant

ses [se] *adj pos voir* **son¹**

seuil [sœj] *nm* doorstep; *(fig)* threshold

seul, e [sœl] *adj (sans compagnie)* alone; *(unique)*: **un ~ livre** only one book, a single book; **le ~ livre** the only book ▷ *adv (vivre)* alone, on one's own; **faire qch (tout) ~** to do sth (all) on one's own *ou* (all) by oneself ▷ *nm/f:* **il en reste un(e) ~(e)** there's

only one left; **à lui (tout) ~** single-handed, on his own; **se sentir ~** to feel lonely; **parler tout ~** to talk to oneself; **seulement** *adv* only; **non seulement ... mais aussi** *ou* **encore** not only ... but also

sève [sɛv] *nf* sap

sévère [sevɛʀ] *adj* severe

sexe [sɛks] *nm* sex; *(organe mâle)* member; **sexuel, le** *adj* sexual

shampooing [ʃɑ̃pwɛ̃] *nm* shampoo

Shetland [ʃɛtlɑ̃d] *n:* **les îles ~** the Shetland Islands, Shetland

shopping [ʃɔpiŋ] *nm:* **faire du ~** to go shopping

short [ʃɔʀt] *nm (pair of)* shorts *pl*

MOT-CLÉ

si [si] *adv* **1** *(oui)* yes; **"Paul n'est pas venu" — "si!"** "Paul hasn't come" — "Yes he has!"; **je vous assure que si** I assure you he did/has *etc*

2 *(tellement)* so; **si gentil/rapidement** so kind/fast; **(tant et) si bien que** so much so that; **si rapide qu'il soit** however fast he may be

▷ *conj* if; **si tu veux** if you want; **je me demande si** I wonder if *ou* whether; **si seulement** if only

▷ *nm (Mus)* B; *(: en chantant la gamme)* ti

Sicile [sisil] *nf:* **la ~** Sicily

sida [sida] *nm (= syndrome immuno-déficitaire acquis)* AIDS *sg*

sidéré, e [sidere] *adj* staggered

sidérurgie [sideʀyʀʒi] *nf* steel industry

siècle [sjɛkl] *nm* century

siège [sjɛʒ] *nm* seat; *(d'entreprise)* head office; *(d'organisation)* headquarters *pl*; *(Mil)* siege; **~ social** registered office; **siéger** /3, 6/ *vi* to sit

sien, ne [sjɛ̃, sjɛn] *pron:* **le (la) ~(ne), les ~(ne)s** *(d'un homme)* his; *(d'une femme)* hers; *(d'une chose)* its

sieste [sjɛst] *nf* (afternoon) snooze *ou* nap; **faire la ~** to have a snooze *ou* nap

sifflement [sifləmɑ̃] *nm* whistle

siffler [sifle] /1/ *vi* (gén) to whistle; (*en respirant*) to wheeze; (*serpent, vapeur*) to hiss ▷ *vt* (*chanson*) to whistle; (*chien etc*) to whistle for; (*fille*) to whistle at; (*pièce, orateur*) to hiss, boo; (*fin du match, départ*) to blow one's whistle for; (*fam: verre, bouteille*) to guzzle

sifflet [sifle] *nm* whistle; **coup de ~** whistle

siffloter [siflɔte] /1/ *vi, vt* to whistle

sigle [sigl] *nm* acronym

signal, -aux [siɲal, -o] *nm* signal; (*indice, écriteau*) sign; **donner le ~ de** to give the signal for; **~ d'alarme** alarm signal; **signalement** *nm* description, particulars *pl*

signaler [siɲale] /1/ *vt* to indicate; (*vol, perte*) to report; (*personne, faire un signe*) to signal; **~ qch à qn/à qn que** to point out sth to sb/to sb that

signature [siɲatyʀ] *nf* signature; (*action*) signing

signe [siɲ] *nm* sign; (*Typo*) mark; **faire un ~ de la main/tête** to give a sign with one's hand/shake one's head; **faire ~ à qn** (*fig: contacter*) to get in touch with sb; **faire ~ à qn d'entrer** to motion (to) sb to come in; **signer** /1/ *vt* to sign; **se signer** *vi* to cross o.s.

significatif, -ive [siɲifikatif, -iv] *adj* significant

signification [siɲifikasjɔ̃] *nf* meaning

signifier [siɲifje] /7/ *vt* (*vouloir dire*) to mean; (*faire connaître*): **~ qch (à qn)** to make sth known (to sb)

silence [silɑ̃s] *nm* silence; (*Mus*) rest; **garder le ~ (sur qch)** to keep silent (about sth), say nothing (about sth); **silencieux, -euse** *adj* quiet, silent ▷ *nm* silencer

silhouette [silwɛt] *nf* outline, silhouette; (*figure*) figure

sillage [sijaʒ] *nm* wake

sillon [sijɔ̃] *nm* furrow; (*de disque*) groove; **sillonner** /1/ *vt* to criss-cross

simagrées [simagʀe] *nfpl* fuss *sg*

similaire [similɛʀ] *adj* similar; **similicuir** *nm* imitation leather; **similitude** *nf* similarity

simple [sɛ̃pl] *adj* simple; (*non multiple*) single; **~ messieurs/dames** *nm* (*Tennis*) men's/ladies' singles *sg*; **~ d'esprit** *nm/f* simpleton; **~ soldat** private

simplicité [sɛ̃plisite] *nf* simplicity; **en toute ~** quite simply

simplifier [sɛ̃plifje] /7/ *vt* to simplify

simuler [simyle] /1/ *vt* to sham, simulate

simultané, e [simyltane] *adj* simultaneous

sincère [sɛ̃sɛʀ] *adj* sincere; **sincèrement** *adv* sincerely, genuinely; **sincérité** *nf* sincerity

Singapour [sɛ̃gapuʀ] *nm*: Singapore

singe [sɛ̃ʒ] *nm* monkey; (*de grande taille*) ape; **singer** /3/ *vt* to ape, mimic; **singeries** *nfpl* antics

singulariser [sɛ̃gylaʀize] /1/: **se singulariser** *vi* to call attention to o.s.

singularité [sɛ̃gylaʀite] *nf* peculiarity

singulier, -ière [sɛ̃gylje, -jɛʀ] *adj* remarkable, singular ▷ *nm* singular

sinistre [sinistʀ] *adj* sinister ▷ *nm* (*incendie*) blaze; (*catastrophe*) disaster; (*Assurances*) damage (*giving rise to a claim*), disaster; **sinistré, e** *adj* disaster-stricken ▷ *nm/f* disaster victim

sinon [sinɔ̃] *conj* (*autrement, sans quoi*) otherwise, or else; (*sauf*) except, other than; (*si ce n'est*) if not

sinueux, -euse [sinɥø, -øz] *adj* winding

sinus [sinys] *nm* (*Anat*) sinus; (*Géom*) sine; **sinusite** *nf* sinusitis

sirène [siʀɛn] *nf* siren; **~ d'alarme** fire alarm; (*pendant la guerre*) air-raid siren

sirop [siʀo] nm (à diluer: de fruit etc) syrup; (pharmaceutique) syrup, mixture; **~ contre la toux** cough syrup ou mixture

siroter [siʀɔte] /1/ vt to sip

sismique [sismik] adj seismic

site [sit] nm (paysage, environnement) setting; (d'une ville etc: emplacement) site; **~ (pittoresque)** beauty spot; **~s touristiques** places of interest; **~ web** (Inform) website

sitôt [sito] adv: **~ parti** as soon as he etc had left; **pas de ~** not for a long time; **~ (après) que** as soon as

situation [sitɥasjɔ̃] nf situation; (d'un édifice, d'une ville) position; location; **~ de famille** marital status

situé, e [sitɥe] adj: **bien ~** well situated

situer [sitɥe] /1/ vt to site, situate; (en pensée) to place; **se situer** vi: **se ~ à/près de** to be situated at/near

six [sis] num six; **sixième** num sixth ▷ nf (Scol) year 7

skaï® [skaj] nm = Leatherette®

skate [sket], **skate-board** [sketbɔʀd] nm (sport) skateboarding; (planche) skateboard

ski [ski] nm (objet) ski; (sport) skiing; **faire du ~** to ski; **~ de fond** cross-country skiing; **~ nautique** water-skiing; **~ de piste** downhill skiing; **~ de randonnée** cross-country skiing; **skier** /7/ vi to ski; **skieur, -euse** nm/f skier

slip [slip] nm (sous-vêtement) pants pl (BRIT), briefs pl; (de bain: d'homme) trunks pl; (: du bikini) (bikini) briefs pl

slogan [slɔgɑ̃] nm slogan

Slovaquie [slɔvaki] nf: **la ~** Slovakia

SMIC [smik] sigle m = **salaire minimum interprofessionnel de croissance**

smoking [smɔkiŋ] nm dinner ou evening suit

SMS sigle m (= short message service) (service) SMS; (message) text (message)

SNCF sigle f (= Société nationale des chemins de fer français) French railways

snob [snɔb] adj snobbish ▷ nm/f snob; **snobisme** nm snobbery, snobbishness

sobre [sɔbʀ] adj (personne) temperate, abstemious; (élégance, style) sober

sobriquet [sɔbʀikɛ] nm nickname

social, e, -aux [sɔsjal, -o] adj social

socialisme [sɔsjalism] nm socialism; **socialiste** nm/f socialist

société [sɔsjete] nf society; (sportive) club; (Comm) company; **la ~ d'abondance/de consommation** the affluent/consumer society; **~ anonyme** ≈ limited company (BRIT), ≈ incorporated company (US)

sociologie [sɔsjɔlɔʒi] nf sociology

socle [sɔkl] nm (de colonne, statue) plinth, pedestal; (de lampe) base

socquette [sɔkɛt] nf ankle sock

sœur [sœʀ] nf sister; (religieuse) nun, sister

soi [swa] pron oneself; **en ~** (intrinsèquement) in itself; **cela va de ~** that it goes without saying; **soi-disant** adj inv so-called ▷ adv supposedly

soie [swa] nf silk; **soierie** nf (tissu) silk

soif [swaf] nf thirst; **avoir ~** to be thirsty; **donner ~ à qn** to make sb thirsty

soigné, e [swaɲe] adj (tenue) well-groomed, neat; (travail) careful, meticulous

soigner [swaɲe] /1/ vt (malade, maladie: docteur) to treat; (: infirmière, mère) to nurse, look after; (travail, détails) to take care over; (jardin, chevelure, invités) to look after; **soigneux, -euse** adj tidy, neat; (méticuleux) painstaking, careful

soi-même [swamɛm] pron oneself

soin [swɛ̃] nm (application) care; (propreté, ordre) tidiness, neatness; **soins** nmpl (à un malade, blessé) treatment sg, medical attention sg; (hygiène) care sg; **avoir** ou **prendre ~**

de to take care of, look after; **avoir** ou **prendre ~ de faire** to take care to do; **les premiers ~s** first aid sg

soir [swar] *nm* evening; **ce ~** this evening, tonight; **à ce ~!** see you this evening (ou tonight)!; **sept/dix heures du ~** seven in the evening/ten at night; **demain ~** tomorrow evening, tomorrow night; **soirée** *nf* evening; (réception) party

soit [swa] *vb voir* **être** ▷ *conj* (à savoir) namely; (ou): **~ ... ~** either ... or ▷ *adv* so be it, very well; **~ que ... ~ que** ou **ou que** whether ... or whether

soixantaine [swasɑ̃tɛn] *nf:* **une ~ (de)** sixty or so, about sixty; **avoir la ~** (âge) to be around sixty

soixante [swasɑ̃t] *num* sixty; **soixante-dix** *num* seventy

soja [sɔʒa] *nm* soya; (graines) soya beans *pl*; **germes de ~** beansprouts

sol [sɔl] *nm* ground; (de logement) floor; (Agr, Géo) soil; (Mus) G (: en chantant la gamme) so(h)

solaire [sɔlɛʀ] *adj* (énergie etc) solar; (crème etc) sun *cpd*

soldat [sɔlda] *nm* soldier

solde [sɔld] *nf* pay ▷ *nm* (Comm) balance; **soldes** *nmpl* ou *nfpl* (Comm) sales; **en ~** at sale price; **solder** /1/ *vt* (marchandise) to sell at sale price, sell off

sole [sɔl] *nf* sole *inv* (fish)

soleil [sɔlɛj] *nm* sun; (lumière) sun(light); (temps ensoleillé) sun(shine); **il y a** ou **il fait du ~** it's sunny; **au ~** in the sun

solennel, le [sɔlanɛl] *adj* solemn

solfège [sɔlfɛʒ] *nm* rudiments *pl* of music

solidaire [sɔlidɛʀ] *adj:* **être ~s** (personnes) to show solidarity, stand ou stick together; **être ~ de** (collègues) to stand by; **solidarité** *nf* solidarity; **par solidarité (avec)** in sympathy (with)

solide [sɔlid] *adj* solid; (mur, maison, meuble) solid, sturdy; (connaissances,

argument) sound; (personne) robust, sturdy ▷ *nm* solid

soliste [sɔlist] *nm/f* soloist

solitaire [sɔlitɛʀ] *adj (sans compagnie)* solitary, lonely; (lieu) lonely ▷ *nm/f* (ermite) recluse; (fig: ours) loner

solitude [sɔlityd] *nf* loneliness; (paix) solitude

solliciter [sɔlisite] /1/ *vt* (personne) to appeal to; (emploi, faveur) to seek

sollicitude [sɔlisityd] *nf* concern

soluble [sɔlybl] *adj* soluble

solution [sɔlysjɔ̃] *nf* solution; **~ de facilité** easy way out

solvable [sɔlvabl] *adj* solvent

sombre [sɔ̃bʀ] *adj* dark; (fig) gloomy; **sombrer** /1/ *vi* (bateau) to sink; **sombrer dans** (misère, désespoir) to sink into

sommaire [sɔmɛʀ] *adj (simple)* basic; (expéditif) summary ▷ *nm* summary

somme [sɔm] *nf* (Math) sum; (fig) amount; (argent) sum, amount ▷ *nm:* **faire un ~** to have a (short) nap; **en ~**, **~ toute** all in all

sommeil [sɔmɛj] *nm* sleep; **avoir ~** to be sleepy; **sommeiller** /1/ *vi* to doze

sommet [sɔmɛ] *nm* top; (d'une montagne) summit, top; (fig: de la perfection, gloire) height

sommier [sɔmje] *nm* bed base

somnambule [sɔmnɑ̃byl] *nm/f* sleepwalker

somnifère [sɔmnifɛʀ] *nm* sleeping drug; sleeping pill ou tablet

somnoler [sɔmnɔle] /1/ *vi* to doze

somptueux, -euse [sɔ̃ptɥø, -øz] *adj* sumptuous

son¹, sa *(pl ses)* [sɔ̃, sa, se] *adj poss* (antécédent humain: mâle) his; (: femelle) her; (: valeur indéfinie) one's, his (her); (: non humain) its

son² [sɔ̃] *nm* sound; (de blé etc) bran

sondage [sɔ̃daʒ] *nm:* **~ (d'opinion)** (opinion) poll

sonde [sɔ̃d] *nf* (Navig) lead *ou* sounding line; (Méd) probe; (Tech: de forage, sondage) drill

sonder [sɔ̃de] /1/ *vt* (Navig) to sound; (Tech) to bore, drill; (fig: personne) to sound out; **~ le terrain** (fig) to see how the land lies

songe [sɔ̃ʒ] *nm* dream; **songer** /3/ *vi*: **songer à** (rêver à) to think over; (envisager) to contemplate, think of; **songer que** to think that; **songeur, -euse** *adj* pensive

sonnant, e [sɔnɑ̃, -ɑ̃t] *adj*: **à huit heures ~es** on the stroke of eight

sonné, e [sɔne] *adj* (fam) cracked; **il est midi ~** it's gone twelve

sonner [sɔne] /1/ *vi* to ring ▷ *vt* (cloche) to ring; (glas, tocsin) to sound; (portier, infirmière) to ring for; **~ faux** (instrument) to sound out of tune; (rire) to ring false

sonnerie [sɔnʀi] *nf* (son) ringing; (sonnette) bell; (de portable) ringtone; **~ d'alarme** alarm bell

sonnette [sɔnɛt] *nf* bell; **~ d'alarme** alarm bell

sonore [sɔnɔʀ] *adj* (voix) sonorous, ringing; (salle, métal) resonant; (ondes, film, signal) sound *cpd*; **sonorisation** *nf* (équipement: de salle de conférences) public address system, P.A. system; (: de discothèque) sound system; **sonorité** *nf* (de piano, violon) tone; (d'une salle) acoustics *pl*

sophistiqué, e [sɔfistike] *adj* sophisticated

sorbet [sɔʀbɛ] *nm* water ice, sorbet

sorcier, -ière [sɔʀsje, -jɛʀ] *nm/f* sorcerer (witch *ou* sorceress)

sordide [sɔʀdid] *adj* (lieu) squalid; (action) sordid

sort [sɔʀ] *nm* (fortune, destinée) fate; (: condition, situation) lot; (magique): **jeter un ~ à** to cast a spell; **tirer au ~** to draw lots

sorte [sɔʀt] *nf* sort, kind; **de la ~** in that way; **en quelque ~** in a way; **de**

(telle) ~ que so that; **faire en ~ que** to see to it that

sortie [sɔʀti] *nf* (issue) way out, exit; (verbale) outing; (promenade) outing; (le soir, au restaurant etc) night out; (Comm: d'un disque) release; (: d'un livre) publication; (: d'un modèle) launching; **~ de bain** (vêtement) bathrobe; **~ de secours** emergency exit

sortilège [sɔʀtilɛʒ] *nm* (magic) spell

sortir [sɔʀtiʀ] /16/ *vi* (gén) to come out; (partir, se promener, aller au spectacle etc) to go out; (bourgeon, plante, numéro gagnant) to come up ▷ *vt* (gén) to take out; (produit, ouvrage, modèle) to bring out; (fam: dire) to come out with; **~ avec qn** to be going out with sb; **~ de** (endroit) to come ou (come up) out of, leave; (cadre, compétence) to be outside; (provenir de) to come from; **s'en ~** (malade) to pull through; (d'une difficulté etc) to get through

sosie [sɔzi] *nm* double

sot, sotte [so, sɔt] *adj* silly, foolish ▷ *nm/f* fool; **sottise** *nf* silliness *no pl*, foolishness *no pl*; (propos, acte) silly *ou* foolish thing (to do *ou* say)

sou [su] *nm*: **près de ses ~s** tight-fisted; **sans le ~** penniless

soubresaut [subʀəso] *nm* start; (cahot) jolt

souche [suʃ] *nf* (d'arbre) stump; (de carnet) counterfoil (BRIT), stub

souci [susi] *nm* (inquiétude) worry; (préoccupation) concern; (Bot) marigold; **se faire du ~** to worry; **soucier**: **se soucier de** *vt* to care about; **soucieux, -euse** *adj* concerned, worried

soucoupe [sukup] *nf* saucer; **~ volante** flying saucer

soudain, e [sudɛ̃, -ɛn] *adj* (douleur, mort) sudden ▷ *adv* suddenly, all of a sudden

Soudan [sudɑ̃] *nm*: **le ~** Sudan

soude [sud] *nf* soda

souder [sude] /1/ vt (avec fil à souder) to solder; (par soudure autogène) to weld; (fig) to bind ou knit together

soudure [sudyʀ] nf soldering, welding; (joint) soldered joint; weld

souffle [sufl] nm (en expirant) breath; (en soufflant) puff, blow; (respiration) breathing; (d'explosion, de ventilateur) blast; (du vent) blowing; **être à bout de ~** to be out of breath; **un ~ d'air** ou **de vent** a breath of air

soufflé, e [sufle] adj (fam: ahuri, stupéfié) staggered ▷ nm (Culin) soufflé

souffler [sufle] /1/ vi (gén) to blow; (haleter) to puff (and blow) ▷ vt (feu, bougie) to blow out; (chasser: poussière etc) to blow away; (Tech: verre) to blow; (dire): **~ qch à qn** to whisper sth to sb

souffrance [sufʀɑ̃s] nf suffering; **en ~** (affaire) pending

souffrant, e [sufʀɑ̃, -ɑ̃t] adj unwell

souffre-douleur [sufʀədulœʀ] nm inv butt, underdog

souffrir [sufʀiʀ] /18/ vi to suffer; (éprouver des douleurs) to be in pain ▷ vt to suffer, endure; (supporter) to bear, stand; **~ de** (maladie, froid) to suffer from; **elle ne peut pas le ~** she can't stand ou bear him

soufre [sufʀ] nm sulphur

souhait [swɛ] nm wish; **tous nos ~s pour la nouvelle année** (our) best wishes for the New Year; **souhaitable** adj desirable

souhaiter [swete] /1/ vt to wish for; **~ la bonne année à qn** to wish sb a happy New Year; **~ que** to hope that

soûl, e [su, sul] adj drunk ▷ nm: **tout son ~** to one's heart's content

soulagement [sulaʒmɑ̃] nm relief

soulager [sulaʒe] /3/ vt to relieve

soûler [sule] /1/ vt: **~ qn** to make sb drunk; (boisson) to make sb drunk; (fig) to make sb's head spin ou reel; **se soûler** vi to get drunk

soulever [sulve] /5/ vt to lift; (vagues, poussière) to send up; (enthousiasme)

to arouse; (question, débat, protestations, difficultés) to raise; **se soulever** vi (peuple) to rise up; (personne couchée) to lift o.s. up

soulier [sulje] nm shoe

souligner [suliɲe] /1/ vt to underline; (fig) to emphasize, stress

soumettre [sumɛtʀ] /56/ vt (pays) to subject, subjugate; (rebelles) to put down, subdue; **~ qch à qn** to submit sth to sb; **se ~ (à)** (projet etc) to submit sth to sb; **se ~ (à)** (projet etc) to submit (to)

soumis, e [sumi, -iz] adj submissive; **soumission** nf submission

soupçon [supsɔ̃] nm suspicion; (petite quantité): **un ~ de** a hint ou touch of; **soupçonner** /1/ vt to suspect; **soupçonneux, -euse** adj suspicious

soupe [sup] nf soup

souper [supe] /1/ vi to have supper ▷ nm supper

soupeser [supəze] /5/ vt to weigh in one's hand(s); (fig) to weigh up

soupière [supjɛʀ] nf (soup) tureen

soupir [supiʀ] nm sigh; **pousser un ~ de soulagement** to heave a sigh of relief

soupirer [supiʀe] /1/ vi to sigh

souple [supl] adj supple; (fig: règlement, caractère) flexible; (: démarche, taille) lithe, supple; **souplesse** nf suppleness; (de caractère) flexibility

source [suʀs] nf (point d'eau) spring; (d'un cours d'eau, fig) source; **tenir qch de bonne ~/de ~ sûre** to have sth on good authority/from a reliable source

sourcil [suʀsij] nm (eye)brow;

sourciller /1/ vi: **sans sourciller** without turning a hair ou batting an eyelid

sourd, e [suʀ, suʀd] adj deaf; (bruit, voix) muffled; (douleur) dull ▷ nm/f deaf person; **faire la ~e oreille** to turn a deaf ear; **sourdine** nf (Mus) mute; **en sourdine** softly, quietly; **sourd-muet, sourde-muette** adj with a speech and hearing impairment

souriant, e [suʀjɑ̃, -ɑ̃t] adj cheerful

sourire [suʀiʀ] /36/ nm smile ▷ vi to smile; **~ à qn** to smile at sb; (fig: plaire à) to appeal to sb; (chance) to smile on sb; **garder le ~** to keep smiling

souris [suʀi] nf mouse

sournois, e [suʀnwa, -waz] adj deceitful, underhand

sous [su] prép under; **~ la pluie/le soleil** in the rain/sunshine; **~ terre** underground; **~ peu** shortly, before long; **sous-bois** nm inv undergrowth

souscrire [suskʀiʀ] /39/: **~ à** vt to subscribe to

sous: **sous-directeur, -trice** nm/f assistant manager/manageress; **sous-entendre** /41/ vt to imply, infer; **sous-entendu, e** adj implied ▷ nm innuendo, insinuation; **sous-estimer** /1/ vt to underestimate; **sous-jacent, e** adj underlying; **sous-louer** /1/ vt to sublet; **sous-marin, e** adj (flore, volcan) submarine; (navigation, pêche, explosif) underwater ▷ nm submarine; **sous-pull** nm thin poloneck sweater; **sous-sol** nm basement; **sous-titre** [sutitʀ] nm subtitle

soustraction [sustʀaksjɔ̃] nf subtraction

soustraire [sustʀɛʀ] /50/ vt to subtract, take away; (dérober): **~ qch à qn** to remove sth from sb; **se ~ à** (autorité, obligation, devoir) to elude, escape from

sous: **sous-traitant** nm subcontractor; **sous-traiter** /1/ vt, vi to subcontract; **sous-vêtement** nm item of underwear; **sous-vêtements** nmpl underwear sg

soutane [sutan] nf cassock, soutane

soute [sut] nf hold

soutenir [sutniʀ] /22/ vt to support; (assaut, choc, regard) to stand up to, withstand; (intérêt, effort) to keep up; (assurer): **~ que** to maintain that;

soutenu, e adj (efforts) sustained, unflagging; (style) elevated

souterrain, e [suteʀɛ̃, -ɛn] adj underground ▷ nm underground passage

soutien [sutjɛ̃] nm support; **soutien-gorge** nm bra

soutirer [sutiʀe] /1/ vt: **~ qch à qn** to squeeze ou get sth out of sb

souvenir [suvniʀ] /22/ nm (réminiscence) memory; (cadeau) souvenir ▷ vb: **se ~ de** to remember; **se ~ que** to remember that; **en ~ de** in memory ou remembrance of; **avec mes affectueux/meilleurs ~s, ...** with love from, .../regards, ...

souvent [suvɑ̃] adv often; **peu ~** seldom, infrequently

souverain, e [suvʀɛ̃, -ɛn] nm/f sovereign, monarch

soyeux, -euse [swajø, -øz] adj silky

spacieux, -euse [spasjø, -øz] adj spacious; roomy

spaghettis [spageti] nmpl spaghetti sg

sparadrap [spaʀadʀa] nm adhesive ou sticking (BRIT) plaster, bandaid® (US)

spatial, e, -aux [spasjal, -o] adj (Aviat) space cpd

speaker, ine [spikœʀ, -kʀin] nm/f announcer

spécial, e, -aux [spesjal, -o] adj special; (bizarre) peculiar; **spécialement** adv especially, particularly; (tout exprès) specially; **spécialiser** /1/: **se spécialiser** vi to specialize; **spécialiste** nm/f specialist; **spécialité** nf speciality; (Scol) special field

spécifier [spesifje] /7/ vt to specify, state

spécimen [spesimɛn] nm specimen

spectacle [spɛktakl] nm (tableau, scène) sight; (représentation) show; (industrie) show business; **spectaculaire** adj spectacular

spectateur, -trice [spɛktatœʀ, -tʀis] nm/f (Ciné etc) member of the

S

audience; (Sport) spectator; (d'un événement) onlooker, witness

spéculer [spekyle] /1/ vi to speculate

spéléologie [speleɔlɔʒi] nf potholing

sperme [spɛʀm] nm semen, sperm

sphère [sfɛʀ] nf sphere

spirale [spiʀal] nf spiral

spirituel, le [spiʀitɥɛl] adj spiritual; (fin, piquant) witty

splendide [splɑ̃did] adj splendid

spontané, e [spɔ̃tane] adj spontaneous; **spontanéité** nf spontaneity

sport [spɔʀ] nm sport ▷ adj inv (vêtement) casual; **faire du ~** to do sport; **~s d'hiver** winter sports; **sportif, -ive** adj (journal, association, épreuve) sports cpd; (allure, démarche) athletic; (attitude, esprit) sporting

spot [spɔt] nm (lampe) spot(light); (annonce) **~ (publicitaire)** commercial (break)

square [skwaʀ] nm public garden(s)

squelette [skəlɛt] nm skeleton; **squelettique** adj scrawny

SRAS [sʀas] sigle m (= syndrome respiratoire aigu sévère) SARS

Sri Lanka [sʀilɑ̃ka] nm: **le ~** Sri Lanka

stabiliser [stabilize] /1/ vt to stabilize

stable [stabl] adj stable, steady

stade [stad] nm (Sport) stadium; (phase, niveau) stage

stage [staʒ] nm (cours) training course; **~ de formation (professionnelle)** vocational (training) course; **~ de perfectionnement** advanced training course; **stagiaire** [staʒjɛʀ] nm/f, adj trainee

Attention à ne pas traduire stage par le mot anglais stage.

stagner [stagne] /1/ vi to stagnate

stand [stɑ̃d] nm (d'exposition) stand; (de foire) stall; **~ de tir** (à la foire, Sport) shooting range

standard [stɑ̃daʀ] adj inv standard ▷ nm switchboard; **standardiste** nm/f switchboard operator

standing [stɑ̃diŋ] nm standing; **de grand ~** luxury

starter [staʀtɛʀ] nm (Auto) choke

station [stasjɔ̃] nf station; (de bus) stop; (de villégiature) resort; **~ de ski** ski resort; **~ de taxis** taxi rank (BRIT) ou stand (US); **stationnement** nm parking; **stationner** /1/ vi to park; **station-service** nf service station

statistique [statistik] nf (science) statistics sg; (rapport, étude) statistic ▷ adj statistical

statue [staty] nf statue

statu quo [statykwo] nm status quo

statut [staty] nm status; **statuts** nmpl (Jur, Admin) statutes; **statutaire** adj statutory

Sté abr (= société) soc

steak [stɛk] nm steak; **~ haché** hamburger

sténo [steno] nf (aussi: **~graphie**) shorthand

stérile [steʀil] adj sterile

stérilet [steʀilɛ] nm coil, loop

stériliser [steʀilize] /1/ vt to sterilize

stimulant, e [stimylɑ̃, -ɑ̃t] adj stimulating ▷ nm (Méd) stimulant; (fig) stimulus, incentive

stimuler [stimyle] /1/ vt to stimulate

stipuler [stipyle] /1/ vt to stipulate

stock [stɔk] nm stock; **stocker** /1/ vt to stock

stop [stɔp] nm (Auto: écriteau) stop sign; (: signal) brake-light; **faire du ~** (fam) to hitch(hike); **stopper** /1/ vt to stop ▷ vi to stop, halt

store [stɔʀ] nm blind; (de magasin) shade, awning

strabisme [stʀabism] nm squint(ing)

strapontin [stʀapɔ̃tɛ̃] nm jump ou foldaway seat

stratégie [stʀateʒi] nf strategy; **stratégique** adj strategic

stress [strɛs] nm inv stress; **stressant, e** adj stressful; **stresser** /1/ vt: **stresser qn** to make sb (feel) tense

strict, e [strikt] adj strict; (tenue, décor) severe, plain; **le ~ nécessaire/minimum** the bare essentials/minimum

strident, e [stridɑ̃, -ɑ̃t] adj shrill, strident

strophe [strɔf] nf verse, stanza

structure [stryktyr] nf structure; **~s d'accueil/touristiques** reception/tourist facilities

studieux, -euse [stydjø, -øz] adj studious

studio [stydjo] nm (logement) studio flat (brit) ou apartment (us); (d'artiste, TV etc) studio

stupéfait, e [stypefɛ, -ɛt] adj astonished

stupéfiant, e [stypefjɑ̃, -ɑ̃t] adj (étonnant) stunning, astonishing ▷ nm (Méd) drug, narcotic

stupéfier [stypefje] /7/ vt (étonner) to stun, astonish

stupeur [stypœr] nf astonishment

stupide [stypid] adj stupid; **stupidité** nf stupidity no pl; (parole, acte) stupid thing (to say ou do)

style [stil] nm style

stylé, e [stile] adj well-trained

styliste [stilist] nm/f designer

stylo [stilo] nm: **~ (à encre)** (fountain) pen; **~ (à) bille** ballpoint pen

su, e [sy] pp de **savoir** ▷ nm: **au su de** with the knowledge of

suave [sɥav] adj sweet

subalterne [sybaltɛrn] adj (employé, officier) junior; (rôle) subordinate, subsidiary ▷ nm/f subordinate

subconscient [sypkɔ̃sjɑ̃] nm subconscious

subir [sybir] /2/ vt (affront, dégâts, mauvais traitements) to suffer; (traitement, opération, châtiment) to undergo

subit, e [sybi, -it] adj sudden; **subitement** adv suddenly, all of a sudden

subjectif, -ive [sybʒɛktif, -iv] adj subjective

subjonctif [sybʒɔ̃ktif] nm subjunctive

subjuguer [sybʒyge] /1/ vt to subjugate

submerger [sybmɛrʒe] /3/ vt to submerge; (fig) to overwhelm

subordonné, e [sybɔrdɔne] adj, nm/f subordinate

subrepticement [sybrɛptismɑ̃] adv surreptitiously

subside [sypsid] nm grant

subsidiaire [sypsidjɛr] adj: **question ~** deciding question

subsister [sybziste] /1/ vi (rester) to remain, subsist; (survivre) to live on

substance [sypstɑ̃s] nf substance

substituer [sypstitɥe] /1/ vt: **~ qn/qch à** to substitute sb/sth for; **se ~ à qn** (évincer) to substitute o.s. for sb

substitut [sypstity] nm (succédané) substitute

subterfuge [syptɛrfyʒ] nm subterfuge

subtil, e [syptil] adj subtle

subvenir [sybvənir] /22/: **~ à** vt to meet

subvention [sybvɑ̃sjɔ̃] nf subsidy, grant; **subventionner** /1/ vt to subsidize

suc [syk] nm (Bot) sap; (de viande, fruit) juice

succéder [syksede] /6/: **~ à** vt to succeed; **se succéder** vi (accidents, années) to follow one another

succès [syksɛ] nm success; **avoir du ~** to be a success, be successful; **à ~** successful; **~ de librairie** bestseller

successeur [syksesœr] nm successor

successif, -ive [syksesif, -iv] adj successive

succession [syksesjɔ̃] nf (série, Pol) succession; (Jur: patrimoine) estate, inheritance

succomber [sykɔ̃be] /1/ vi to die, succumb; (fig): **~ à** to succumb to

succulent, e [sykylɑ̃, -ɑ̃t] adj delicious

succursale [sykyʀsal] nf branch

sucer [syse] /3/ vt to suck; **sucette** nf (bonbon) lollipop; (de bébé) dummy (BRIT), pacifier (US)

sucre [sykʀ] nm (substance) sugar; (morceau) lump of sugar, sugar lump ou cube; **~ en morceaux/cristallisé/en poudre** lump ou cube/granulated/caster sugar; **~ glace** icing sugar (BRIT), confectioner's sugar (US); **~ d'orge** barley sugar; **sucré, e** adj (produit alimentaire) sweetened; (au goût) sweet; **sucrer** /1/ vt (thé, café) to sweeten, put sugar in; **sucrerie** nf sugar refinery; **sucreries** nfpl (bonbons) sweets, sweet things; **sucrier** nm (récipient) sugar bowl ou basin

sud [syd] nm: **le ~** the south ▷ adj inv south; (côte) south, southern; **au ~** (situation) in the south; (direction) to the south; **au ~ de** (to the south of); **sud-africain, e** adj South African ▷ nm/f: **Sud-Africain, e** South African; **sud-américain, e** adj South American ▷ nm/f: **Sud-Américain, e** South American; **sud-est** nm, adj inv south-east; **sud-ouest** nm, adj inv south-west

Suède [sɥɛd] nf: **la ~** Sweden; **suédois, e** adj Swedish ▷ nm (Ling) Swedish ▷ nm/f: **Suédois, e** Swede

suer [sɥe] /1/ vi to sweat; (suinter) to ooze; **sueur** nf sweat; **en sueur** sweating, in a sweat; **avoir des sueurs froides** to be in a cold sweat

suffire [syfiʀ] /37/ vi (être assez): **~ (à qn/pour qch/pour faire)** to be enough ou sufficient (for sb/for sth/to do); **il suffit d'une négligence/qu'on oublie pour que ...** it only takes one act of carelessness/one only needs to forget for ...; **ça suffit!** that's enough!

suffisamment [syfizamɑ̃] adv sufficiently, enough; **~** sufficient, enough

suffisant, e [syfizɑ̃, -ɑ̃t] adj sufficient; (résultats) satisfactory; (vaniteux) self-important, bumptious

suffixe [syfiks] nm suffix

suffoquer [syfɔke] /1/ vt to choke, suffocate; (stupéfier) to stagger, astound ▷ vi to choke, suffocate

suffrage [syfʀaʒ] nm (Pol: voix) vote

suggérer [sygʒeʀe] /6/ vt to suggest; **suggestion** nf suggestion

suicide [sɥisid] nm suicide; **suicider** /1/: **se suicider** vi to commit suicide

suie [sɥi] nf soot

suisse [sɥis] adj Swiss ▷ nm/f: **S~** Swiss inv ▷ nf: **la S~** Switzerland; **la S~ romande/allemande** French-speaking/German-speaking Switzerland

suite [sɥit] nf (continuation: d'énumération etc) rest, remainder; (: de feuilleton) continuation; (: second film etc sur le même thème) sequel; (série) series, succession; (conséquence) result; (ordre, liaison logique) coherence; (appartement, Mus) suite; (escorte) retinue, suite; **suites** nfpl (d'une maladie etc) effects; **une ~ de** a series ou succession of; **prendre la ~ de** (directeur etc) to succeed, take over from; **donner ~ à** (requête, projet) to follow up; **faire ~ à** to follow; **(faisant) ~ à votre lettre du** further to your letter of the; **de ~** (d'affilée) in succession; (immédiatement) at once; **par la ~** afterwards, subsequently; **à la ~** one after the other; **à la ~ de** (derrière) behind; (en conséquence de) following

suivant, e [sɥivɑ̃, -ɑ̃t] adj next, following ▷ prép (selon) according to; **au ~!** next!

suivi, e [sɥivi] adj (effort, qualité) consistent; (cohérent) coherent; **très/peu ~** (cours) well-/poorly-attended

suivre [sɥivʀ] /40/ vt (gén) to follow; (Scol: cours) to attend; (: programme) to keep up with; (Comm: article) to continue to stock ▷ vi to follow; (élève: assimiler le programme) to keep up; **se suivre** vi (accidents, personnes, voitures etc) to follow one after the other; **faire** ~ (lettre) to forward; "**à** ~" "to be continued"

sujet, te [syʒɛ, -ɛt] adj: **être** ~ **à** (vertige, mal) to be liable ou subject to ▷ nm/f (d'un souverain) subject ▷ nm subject; **au** ~ **de** about; ~ **de conversation** topic ou subject of conversation; ~ **d'examen** (Scol) examination question

super [sypɛʀ] adj inv great, fantastic

superbe [sypɛʀb] adj magnificent, superb

superficie [sypɛʀfisi] nf (surface) area

superficiel, le [sypɛʀfisjɛl] adj superficial

superflu, e [sypɛʀfly] adj superfluous

supérieur, e [sypeʀjœʀ] adj (lèvre, étages, classes) upper; ~ (**à**) (plus élevé: température, niveau) higher (than); (meilleur: qualité, produit) superior (to); (excellent, hautain) superior ▷ nm/f superior; **supériorité** nf superiority

supermarché [sypɛʀmaʀʃe] nm supermarket

superposer [sypɛʀpoze] /1/ vt (faire chevaucher) to superimpose; **lits superposés** bunk beds

superpuissance [sypɛʀpɥisɑ̃s] nf superpower

superstitieux, -euse [sypɛʀstisjø, -øz] adj superstitious

superviser [sypɛʀvize] /1/ vt to supervise

supplanter [syplɑ̃te] /1/ vt to supplant

suppléant, e [sypleɑ̃, -ɑ̃t] adj (juge, fonctionnaire) deputy cpd; (professeur) supply cpd (BRIT), substitute cpd (US) ▷ nm/f (professeur) supply ou substitute teacher

suppléer [syplee] /1/ vt (ajouter: mot manquant etc) to supply, provide; (compenser: lacune) to fill in; ~ **à** to make up for

supplément [syplemɑ̃] nm supplement; **un** ~ **de travail** extra ou additional work; **un** ~ **de frites** etc an extra portion of chips etc; **le vin est en** ~ wine is extra; **payer un** ~ to pay an additional charge; **supplémentaire** adj additional, further; (train, bus) relief cpd, extra

supplication [syplikasjɔ̃] nf supplication; **supplications** nfpl pleas, entreaties

supplice [syplis] nm torture no pl

supplier [syplije] /7/ vt to implore, beseech

support [sypɔʀ] nm support; ~ **audio-visuel** audio-visual aid; ~ **publicitaire** advertising medium

supportable [sypɔʀtabl] adj (douleur, température) bearable

supporter[1] [sypɔʀtɛʀ] nm supporter, fan

supporter[2] [sypɔʀte] vt (conséquences, épreuve) to bear, endure; (défauts, personne) to tolerate, put up with; (chose, chaleur etc) to withstand; (personne, chaleur, vin) to take

⚠ Attention à ne pas traduire supporter par to support.

supposer [sypoze] /1/ vt to suppose; (impliquer) to presuppose; **en supposant** ou **à** ~ **que** supposing (that)

suppositoire [sypozitwaʀ] nm suppository

suppression [sypʀesjɔ̃] nf (voir supprimer) removal; deletion; cancellation

supprimer [sypʀime] /1/ vt (cloison, cause, anxiété) to remove; (clause, mot) to delete; (congés, service d'autobus etc) to cancel; (emplois, privilèges, témoin gênant) to do away with

suprême [sypʀɛm] adj supreme

sur [syʀ] *prép* **1** (*position*) on;
(: *par-dessus*) over; (: *au-dessus*) above;
pose-le sur la table put it on the
table; **je n'ai pas d'argent sur moi** I
haven't any money on me
2 (*direction*) towards; **en allant sur
Paris** going towards Paris; **sur votre
droite** on *ou* to your right
3 (*à propos de*) on, about; **un livre/
une conférence sur Balzac** a book/
lecture on *ou* about Balzac
4 (*proportion, mesure*) out of; **un sur
10** one in 10; (*Scol*) one out of 10; **4 m
sur 2** 4 m by 2; **avoir accident sur
accident** to have one accident after
another

sûr, e [syʀ] *adj* sure, certain; (*digne de
confiance*) reliable; (*sans danger*) safe;
~ **de soi** self-assured, self-confident;
le plus ~ **est de** the safest thing is to

surcharge [syʀʃaʀʒ] *nf* (*de
passagers, marchandises*) excess load;
surcharger /3/ *vt* to overload;
(*décoration*) to overdo

surcroît [syʀkʀwa] *nm*: ~ **de qch**
additional sth; **par** *ou* **de** ~ moreover;
en ~ in addition

surdité [syʀdite] *nf* deafness

sûrement [syʀmɑ̃] *adv* (*sans risques*)
safely; (*certainement*) certainly

surenchère [syʀɑ̃ʃɛʀ] *nf* (*aux
enchères*) higher bid; **surenchérir** /2/
vi to bid higher; (*fig*) to try and outbid
each other

surestimer [syʀɛstime] /1/ *vt* to
overestimate

sûreté [syʀte] *nf* (*exactitude: de
renseignements*) reliability;
(*sécurité*) safety; (*d'un geste*)
steadiness; **mettre en** ~ to put in a
safe place; **pour plus de** ~ as an extra
precaution; to be on the safe side

surf [sœʀf] *nm* surfing

surface [syʀfas] *nf* surface;
(*superficie*) surface area; **une**

grande ~ a supermarket; **faire** ~ to
surface; **en** ~ near the surface; (*fig*)
superficially

surfait, e [syʀfɛ, -ɛt] *adj* overrated

surfer [sœʀfe] /1/ *vi* to surf; ~ **sur
Internet** to surf *ou* browse the
Internet

surgelé, e [syʀʒəle] *adj* (deep-)frozen
▷ *nm*: **les** ~**s** (deep-)frozen food

surgir [syʀʒiʀ] /2/ *vi* to appear
suddenly; (*fig: problème, conflit*)
to arise

sur: surhumain, e *adj* superhuman;
sur-le-champ *adv* immediately;
surlendemain *nm*: **le
surlendemain (soir)** two days later
(in the evening); **le surlendemain
de** two days after; **surmenage**
nm overwork; **surmener /5/: se
surmener** *vi* to overwork

surmonter [syʀmɔ̃te] /1/ *vt* (*vaincre*)
to overcome; (*être au-dessus de*) to top

surnaturel, le [syʀnatyʀɛl] *adj, nm*
supernatural

surnom [syʀnɔ̃] *nm* nickname

surnombre [syʀnɔ̃bʀ] *nm*: **être en** ~
to be too many (*ou* one too many)

surpeuplé, e [syʀpœple] *adj*
overpopulated

surplace [syʀplas] *nm*: **faire du** ~
to mark time

surplomber [syʀplɔ̃be] /1/ *vi* to be
overhanging ▷ *vt* to overhang

surplus [syʀply] *nm* (*Comm*) surplus;
(*reste*): ~ **de bois** wood left over

surprenant, e [syʀpʀənɑ̃, -ɑ̃t] *adj*
amazing

surprendre [syʀpʀɑ̃dʀ] /58/ *vt*
(*étonner, prendre à l'improviste*) to
amaze; (*tomber sur: intrus etc*) to
catch; (*conversation*) to overhear

surpris, e [syʀpʀi, -iz] *adj*: ~ **(de/
que)** amazed *ou* surprised (at/that);
surprise *nf* surprise; **faire une
surprise à qn** to give sb a surprise;
surprise-partie *nf* party

sursaut [syʀso] *nm* start, jump; ~ **de**
(*énergie, indignation*) sudden fit *ou*

burst of; **en ~** with a start; **sursauter** /1/ vi to (give a) start, jump

sursis [syʀsi] nm (Jur: gén) suspended sentence; (aussi fig) reprieve

surtout [syʀtu] adv (avant tout, d'abord) above all; (spécialement, particulièrement) especially; **~, ne dites rien!** whatever you do, don't say anything!; **~ pas!** certainly ou definitely not!; **~ que ...** especially as ...

surveillance [syʀvɛjɑ̃s] nf watch; (Police, Mil) surveillance; **sous ~ médicale** under medical supervision

surveillant, e [syʀvɛjɑ̃, -ɑ̃t] nm/f (de prison) warder; (Scol) monitor

surveiller /1/ vt (enfant, élèves, bagages) to watch, keep an eye on; (prisonnier, suspect) to keep (a) watch on; (territoire, bâtiment) to (keep) watch over; (travaux, cuisson) to supervise; (Scol: examen) to invigilate; **~ son langage/sa ligne** to watch one's language/figure

survenir [syʀvəniʀ] /22/ vi (incident, retards) to occur, arise; (événement) to take place

survêt [syʀvɛt], **survêtement** [syʀvɛtmɑ̃] nm tracksuit

survie [syʀvi] nf survival; **survivant, e** nm/f survivor; **survivre** /46/ vi to survive; **survivre à** (accident etc) to survive

survoler [syʀvɔle] /1/ vt to fly over; (fig: livre) to skim through

survolté, e [syʀvɔlte] adj (fig) worked up

sus [sy(s)]: **en ~ de** prép in addition to, over and above; **en ~** in addition

susceptible [syseptibl] adj touchy, sensitive; **~ de faire** (probabilité) liable to do

susciter /1/ vt (admiration) to arouse; (obstacles, ennuis) to create (for sb)

suspect, e [syspɛ(kt), -ɛkt] adj suspicious; (témoignage, opinions, vin etc) suspect ▷ nm/f suspect

suspecter /1/ vt to suspect; (honnêteté de qn) to question, have one's suspicions about

suspendre [syspɑ̃dʀ] /41/ vt (interrompre, démettre) to suspend; (accrocher: vêtement) **~ qch (à)** to hang sth up (on)

suspendu, e [syspɑ̃dy] adj (accroché): **~ à** hanging on (ou from); (perché): **~ au-dessus de** suspended over

suspens [syspɑ̃]: **en ~** adv (affaire) in abeyance; **tenir en ~** to keep in suspense

suspense [syspɑ̃s] nm suspense

suspension [syspɑ̃sjɔ̃] nf suspension; (lustre) pendant light fitting

suture [sytyʀ] nf: **point de ~** stitch

svelte [svɛlt] adj slender, svelte

SVP abr (= s'il vous plaît) please

sweat [swit] nm (fam) sweatshirt

sweat-shirt [switʃœʀt] nm (pl **sweat-shirts**) sweatshirt

syllabe [silab] nf syllable

symbole [sɛ̃bɔl] nm symbol; **symbolique** adj symbolic; (geste, offrande) token cpd; **symboliser** /1/ vt to symbolize

symétrique [simetʀik] adj symmetrical

sympa [sɛ̃pa] adj inv (fam) nice; **sois ~, prête-le moi** be a pal and lend it to me

sympathie [sɛ̃pati] nf (inclination) liking; (affinité) fellow feeling; (condoléances) sympathy; **avoir de la ~ pour qn** to like sb; **sympathique** adj nice, friendly

> Attention il ne pas traduire sympathique par sympathetic.

sympathisant, e [sɛ̃patizɑ̃, -ɑ̃t] nm/f sympathizer

sympathiser /1/ vi (voisins etc: s'entendre) to get on (BRIT) ou along (US) (well)

symphonie [sɛ̃fɔni] nf symphony

symptôme [sɛ̃ptom] nm symptom

S

synagogue [sinagɔg] nf synagogue

syncope [sɛ̃kɔp] nf (Méd) blackout;
tomber en ~ to faint, pass out

syndic [sɛ̃dik] nm managing agent

syndical, e, -aux [sɛ̃dikal, -o] adj
(trade-)union cpd; **syndicaliste** nm/f
trade unionist

syndicat [sɛ̃dika] nm (d'ouvriers,
employés) (trade(s)) union; **~
d'initiative** tourist office ou bureau;
syndiqué, e adj belonging to a
(trade) union; **syndiquer** /1/: **se
syndiquer** vi to form a trade union;
(adhérer) to join a trade union

synonyme [sinɔnim] adj
synonymous ▷ nm synonym; **~ de**
synonymous with

syntaxe [sɛ̃taks] nf syntax

synthèse [sɛ̃tɛz] nf synthesis

synthétique [sɛ̃tetik] adj synthetic

Syrie [siʁi] nf: **la ~** Syria

systématique [sistematik] adj
systematic

système [sistɛm] nm system; **le ~ D**
resourcefulness

t' [t] pron voir **te**

ta [ta] adj poss voir **ton¹**

tabac [taba] nm tobacco; (aussi: **débit**
ou **bureau de ~**) tobacconist's (shop)

tabagisme [tabaʒism] nm: **~ passif**
passive smoking

table [tabl] nf table; **à ~!** dinner
etc is ready!; **se mettre à ~** to sit
down to eat; **mettre** ou **dresser/
desservir la ~** to lay ou set/clear
the table; **~ à repasser** ironing
board; **~ de cuisson** hob; **~ des
matières** (table of) contents pl; **~
de nuit** ou **de chevet** bedside table;
~ d'orientation viewpoint indicator;
~ roulante (tea) trolley (BRIT), tea
wagon (US)

tableau, x [tablo] nm (Art) painting;
(reproduction, fig) picture; (panneau)
board; (schéma) table, chart;
~ d'affichage notice board; **~ de
bord** dashboard; (Aviat) instrument
panel; **~ noir** blackboard

tablette [tablɛt] nf (planche) shelf; ~ **de chocolat** bar of chocolate; ~ **tactile** (Inform) tablet

tablier [tablije] nm apron

tabou [tabu] nm taboo

tabouret [tyaburɛ] nm stool

tac [tak] nm: **du ~ au ~** tit for tat

tache [taʃ] nf (saleté) stain, mark; (Art, de couleur, lumière) spot; ~ **de rousseur** ou **de son** freckle

tâche [tyaʃ] nf task

tacher [taʃe] /1/ vt to stain, mark

tâcher [tyaʃe] /1/ vi: ~ **de faire** try to do, endeavour (BRIT) ou endeavor (US) to do

tacheté, e [taʃte] adj: ~ **de** speckled ou spotted with

tact [takt] nm tact; **avoir du ~** to be tactful

tactique [taktik] adj tactical ▷ nf (technique) tactics sg; (plan) tactic

taie [tɛ] nf: ~ **(d'oreiller)** pillowslip, pillowcase

taille [taj] nf cutting; (d'arbre) pruning; (milieu du corps) waist; (hauteur) height; (grandeur) size; **de ~ à faire** capable of doing; **de ~** sizeable

taille-crayon(s) [tajkʀɛjɔ̃] nm inv pencil sharpener

tailler [taje] /1/ vt (pierre, diamant) to cut; (arbre, plante) to prune; (vêtement) to cut out; (crayon) to sharpen

tailleur [tajœʀ] nm (couturier) tailor; (vêtement) suit; **en ~** (assis) cross-legged

taillis [taji] nm copse

taire [tɛʀ] /54/ vi: **faire ~ qn** to make sb be quiet; **se taire** vi to be silent ou quiet; **taisez-vous!** be quiet!

Taiwan [tajwan] nf Taiwan

talc [talk] nm talc, talcum powder

talent [talɑ̃] nm talent

talkie-walkie [tɔkiwɔki] nm walkie-talkie

talon [talɔ̃] nm heel; (de chèque, billet) stub, counterfoil (BRIT); ~s **plats/ aiguilles** flat/stiletto heels

talus [taly] nm embankment

tambour [tɑ̃buʀ] nm (Mus, Tech) drum; (musicien) drummer; (porte) revolving door(s pl); **tambourin** nm tambourine

Tamise [tamiz] nf: **la ~** the Thames

tamisé, e [tamize] adj (fig) subdued, soft

tampon [tɑ̃pɔ̃] nm (de coton, d'ouate) pad; (aussi: ~ **hygiénique** ou **périodique**) tampon; (amortisseur, Inform: aussi: **mémoire ~**) buffer; (bouchon) plug, stopper; (cachet, timbre) stamp; **tamponner** /1/ vt (timbres) to stamp; (heurter) to crash ou ram into; **tamponneuse** adj f: **autos tamponneuses** dodgems

tandem [tɑ̃dɛm] nm tandem

tandis [tɑ̃di]: ~ **que** conj while

tanguer [tɑ̃ge] /1/ vi to pitch (and toss)

tant [tɑ̃] adv so much; ~ **de** (sable, eau) so much; (gens, livres) so many; ~ **que** as long as; ~ **que** as much as; ~ **mieux** that's great; (avec une certaine réserve) so much the better; ~ **pis** too bad; (conciliant) never mind; ~ **bien que mal** as well as can be expected

tante [tɑ̃t] nf aunt

tantôt [tɑ̃to] adv (parfois): **tantôt ... tantôt** now ... now; (cet après-midi) this afternoon

taon [tɑ̃] nm horsefly

tapage [tapaʒ] nm uproar, din

tapageur, -euse [tapaʒœʀ, -øz] adj noisy; (voyant) loud, flashy

tape [tap] nf slap

tape-à-l'œil [tapalœj] adj inv flashy, showy

taper [tape] /1/ vt (porte) to bang, slam; (enfant) to slap; (dactylographie) to type (out); (fam: emprunter): ~ **qn de 10 euros** to touch sb for 10 euros ▷ vi (soleil) to beat down; **se taper** vt (fam: travail) to get landed with; (: boire, manger) to down; ~ **sur qn** to thump sb; (fig) to run sb down; ~ **sur qch** (clou etc) to hit sth; (table etc) to bang on sth; **~ à** (*porte etc*) to knock on; **~ dans** (*se servir*) to dig into; **~ des mains/pieds** to clap one's hands/stamp one's feet; **~ (à la machine)** to type

tapi, e [tapi] *adj*: **~ dans/derrière** (*caché*) hidden away in/behind

tapis [tapi] *nm* carpet; (*petit*) rug; **~ roulant** (*pour piétons*) moving walkway; (*pour bagages*) carousel; **~ de sol** (*de tente*) groundsheet; **~ de souris** (*Inform*) mouse mat

tapisser [tapise] /1/ *vt* (*avec du papier peint*) to paper; (*recouvrir*): **~ qch (de)** to cover sth (with); **tapisserie** *nf* (*tenture, broderie*) tapestry; (*papier peint*) wallpaper

tapissier, -ière [tapisje, -jɛʁ] *nm/f*: **~-décorateur** interior decorator

tapoter [tapɔte] /1/ *vt* (*joue, main*) to pat; (*objet*) to tap

taquiner [takine] /1/ *vt* to tease

tard [taʁ] *adv* late ▷ *nm*: **sur le ~** (*dans la vie*) late in life; **plus ~** later (on); **au plus ~** at the latest; **il est trop ~** it's too late

tarder [taʁde] /1/ *vi* (*chose*) to be a long time coming; (*personne*): **~ à faire** to delay doing; **il me tarde d'être** I am longing to be; **sans (plus) ~** without (further) delay

tardif, -ive [taʁdif, -iv] *adj* late

tarif [taʁif] *nm*: **~ des consommations** price list; **~s postaux/douaniers** postal/customs rates; **~ plein/réduit** (*train*) full/reduced fare; (*téléphone*) peak/off-peak rate

tarir [taʁiʁ] /2/ *vi* to dry up, run dry

tarte [taʁt] *nf* tart; **~ aux pommes/à la crème** apple/custard tart; **~ Tatin** = apple upside-down tart

tartine [taʁtin] *nf* slice of bread and butter (*ou* jam); **~ de miel** slice of bread and honey; **tartiner** /1/ *vt* to spread; **fromage à tartiner** cheese spread

tartre [taʁtʁ] *nm* (*des dents*) tartar; (*de chaudière*) fur, scale

tas [tɑ] *nm* heap, pile; **un ~ de** (*fig*) heaps of, lots of; **en ~** in a heap *ou* pile; **formé sur le ~** trained on the job

tasse [tɑs] *nf* cup; **~ à café/thé** coffee/teacup

tassé, e [tɑse] *adj*: **bien ~** (*café etc*) strong

tasser [tɑse] /1/ *vt* (*terre, neige*) to pack down; (*entasser*): **~ qch dans** to cram sth into; **se tasser** *vi* (*se serrer*) to squeeze up; (*s'affaisser*) to settle; (*personne: avec l'âge*) to shrink; (*fig*) to sort itself out, settle down

tâter [tɑte] /1/ *vt* to feel; (*fig*) to try out; **~ de** (*prison etc*) to have a taste of; **se tâter** (*hésiter*) to be in two minds

tatillon, ne [tatijɔ̃, -ɔn] *adj* pernickety

tâtonnement [tɑtɔnmɑ̃] *nm*: **par ~s** (*fig*) by trial and error

tâtonner [tɑtɔne] /1/ *vi* to grope one's way along

tâtons [tɑtɔ̃]: **à ~** *adv*: chercher/avancer à **~** to grope around for/grope one's way forward

tatouage [tatwaʒ] *nm* tattoo

tatouer [tatwe] /1/ *vt* to tattoo

taudis [todi] *nm* hovel, slum

taule [tol] *nf* (*fam*) nick (BRIT); jail

taupe [top] *nf* mole

taureau, x [tɔʁo] *nm* bull; (*signe*): **le T~** Taurus

taux [to] *nm* rate; (*d'alcool*) level; **~ d'intérêt** interest rate

taxe [taks] *nf* tax; (*douanière*) duty; **toutes ~s comprises** inclusive of tax; **la boutique hors ~** the duty-free shop; **~ de séjour** tourist tax; **~ à** *ou* **sur la valeur ajoutée** value added tax

taxer [takse] /1/ *vt* (*personne*) to tax; (*produit*) to put a tax on, tax

taxi [taksi] *nm* taxi; (*chauffeur: fam*) taxi driver

Tchécoslovaquie [tʃekɔslɔvaki] *nf*: **la ~** Czechoslovakia; **tchèque** *adj* Czech ▷ *nm* (*Ling*) Czech ▷ *nm/f*:

Tchèque Czech; **la République tchèque** the Czech Republic

Tchétchénie [tʃetʃeni] nf: **la ~** Chechnya

te, t' [tə] pron you; (réfléchi) yourself

technicien, ne [tɛknisjɛ̃, -ɛn] nm/f technician

technico-commercial, e, -aux [tɛknikokɔmɛʀsjal, -o] adj: **agent ~** sales technician

technique [tɛknik] adj technical ▷ nf technique; **techniquement** adv technically

techno [tɛkno] nf: **la (musique) ~** techno (music)

technologie [tɛknɔlɔʒi] nf technology; **technologique** adj technological

teck [tɛk] nm teak

tee-shirt [tiʃœʀt] nm T-shirt, tee-shirt

teindre [tɛ̃dʀ] /52/ vt to dye; **se ~ (les cheveux)** to dye one's hair; **teint, e** adj dyed ▷ nm (du visage) complexion; (: momentané) colour ▷ nf shade; **grand teint** colourfast

teinté, e [tɛ̃te] adj: **~ de** (fig) tinged with

teinter [tɛ̃te] /1/ vt (verre) to tint; (bois) to stain

teinture [tɛ̃tyʀ] nf dye; **~ d'iode** tincture of iodine; **teinturerie** nf dry cleaner's; **teinturier, -ière** nm/f dry cleaner

tel, telle [tɛl] adj (pareil) such; (comme): **~ un/des ...** like a/like ...; (indéfini) such-and-such; (intensif): **un ~/de ~s ...** such (a)/such ...; **venez ~ jour** come on such-and-such a day; **rien de ~** nothing like it; **~ que** like, such as; **~ quel** as it is ou stands (ou was etc)

télé [tele] nf (fam) TV; **à la ~** on TV ou telly; **télécabine** nf (benne) cable car; **télécarte** nf phonecard; **téléchargeable** adj downloadable; **téléchargement** nm (action) downloading; (fichier) download;

télécharger /3/ vt (recevoir) to download; (transmettre) to upload; **télécommande** nf remote control; **télécopieur** nm fax (machine); **télédistribution** nf cable TV; **télégramme** nm telegram; **télégraphier** /7/ vt to telegraph, cable; **téléguider** /1/ vt to operate by remote control; **télématique** nf telematics sg; **téléobjectif** nm telephoto lens sg; **télépathie** nf telepathy; **téléphérique** nm cable-car

téléphone [telefɔn] nm telephone; **avoir le ~** to be on the (tele)phone; **au ~** on the phone; **~ sans fil** cordless (tele)phone; **téléphoner** /1/ vi to make a phone call; **téléphoner à** to phone, call up; **téléphonique** adj (tele)phone cpd

téléréalité [teleʀealite] nf reality TV

télescope [telɛskɔp] nm telescope

télescoper [telɛskɔpe] /1/ vt to smash up; **se télescoper** (véhicules) to concertina

télé: **téléscripteur** nm teleprinter; **télésiège** nm chairlift; **téléski** nm ski-tow; **téléspectateur, -trice** nm/f (television) viewer; **télétravail** nm telecommuting; **télévente** nf telesales; **téléviseur** nm television set; **télévision** nf television; **à la télévision** on television; **télévision numérique** digital TV; **télévision par câble/satellite** cable/satellite television

télex [telɛks] nm telex

telle [tɛl] adj f voir **tel**; **tellement** adv (tant) so much; (si) so; **tellement de** (sable, eau) so much; (gens, livres) so many; **il s'est endormi tellement il était fatigué** he was so tired (that) he fell asleep; **pas tellement** not really; **pas tellement fort/lentement** not (all) that strong/slowly; **il ne mange pas tellement** he doesn't eat (all that) much

téméraire [temeʀɛʀ] adj reckless, rash

témoignage [temwaɲaʒ] *nm* (Jur: *déclaration*) testimony *no pl*, evidence *no pl*; (*rapport, récit*) account; (fig: *d'affection etc*) token, mark; (*geste*) expression

témoigner [temwaɲe] /1/ *vt* (*intérêt, gratitude*) to show ▷ *vi* (Jur) to testify, give evidence; **~ de** to bear witness to, testify to

témoin [temwɛ̃] *nm* witness ▷ *adj*: **appartement-~** show flat; **être ~ de** to witness; **~ oculaire** eyewitness

tempe [tɑ̃p] *nf* temple

tempérament [tɑ̃peramɑ̃] *nm* temperament, disposition; **à ~** (*vente*) on deferred (payment) terms; (*achat*) by instalments, on hire purchase *(BRIT)*

température [tɑ̃peratyʀ] *nf* temperature; **avoir** *ou* **faire de la ~** to be running *ou* have a temperature

tempête [tɑ̃pɛt] *nf* storm; **~ de sable/neige** sand/snowstorm

temple [tɑ̃pl] *nm* temple; (*protestant*) church

temporaire [tɑ̃pɔʀɛʀ] *adj* temporary

temps [tɑ̃] *nm* (*atmosphérique*) weather; (*durée*) time; (*époque*) time, times *pl*; (Ling) tense; (Mus) beat; (Tech) stroke; **un ~ de chien** (*fam*) rotten weather; **quel ~ fait-il?** what's the weather like?; **il fait beau/ mauvais ~** the weather's fine/ bad; **avoir le ~/tout le ~/juste le ~** to have time/plenty of time/just enough time; **en ~ de paix/guerre** in peacetime/wartime; **en ~ utile** *ou* **voulu** in due time *ou* course; **ces derniers ~** lately; **dans quelque ~** in a (little) while; **de ~ en ~, de ~ à autre** from time to time; **à ~** (*partir, arriver*) in time; **à ~ complet, à ~ plein** *adv, adj* full-time; **à ~ partiel, à mi-~** *adv, adj* part-time; **dans le ~** at one time; **~ d'arrêt** pause, halt; **~ libre** free *ou* spare time; **~ mort** (Comm) slack period

tenable [tənabl] *adj* bearable

tenace [tənas] *adj* persistent

tenant, e [tənɑ̃, -ɑ̃t] *nm/f* (Sport): **~ du titre** title-holder

tendance [tɑ̃dɑ̃s] *nf* (*opinions*) leanings *pl*, sympathies *pl*; (*inclination*) tendency; (*évolution*) trend ▷ *adj inv* trendy; **avoir ~ à** to have a tendency to, tend to

tendeur [tɑ̃dœʀ] *nm* (*attache*) elastic strap

tendre [tɑ̃dʀ] /41/ *adj* tender; (*bois, roche, couleur*) soft ▷ *vt* (*élastique, peau*) to stretch; (*corde*) to tighten; (*muscle*) to tense; (*donner*): **~ qch à qn** to hold sth out to sb; (*offrir*) to offer sb sth; (fig: *piège*) to set, lay; **se tendre** *vi* (*corde*) to tighten; (*relations*) to become strained; **~ à qch/à faire** to tend towards sth/to do; **~ l'oreille** to prick up one's ears; **~ la main/le bras** to hold out one's hand/stretch out one's arm; **tendrement** *adv* tenderly; **tendresse** *nf* tenderness

tendu, e [tɑ̃dy] *pp de* **tendre** ▷ *adj* (*corde*) tight; (*muscles*) tensed; (*relations*) strained

ténèbres [tenɛbʀ] *nfpl* darkness *sg*

teneur [tənœʀ] *nf* content; (*d'une lettre*) terms *pl*, content

tenir [təniʀ] /22/ *vt* to hold; (*magasin, hôtel*) to run; (*promesse*) to keep ▷ *vi* to hold; (*neige, gel*) to last; **se tenir** *vi* (*avoir lieu*) to be held, take place; (*être: personne*) to stand; **se ~ droit** to stand up (*ou* sit up) straight; **bien se ~** to behave well; **se ~ à qch** to hold on to sth; **s'en ~ à qch** to confine o.s. to sth; **~ à** (*personne, objet*) to be attached to, care about (*ou* for); (*réputation*) to care about; **~ à faire** to want to do; (*ressembler à*) to take after; **ça ne tient qu'à lui** it is entirely up to him; **~ qn pour** to take sb for; **~ qch de qn** (*histoire*) to have heard *ou* learnt sth from sb; (*qualité, défaut*) to have inherited *ou* got sth from sb; **~ dans** to fit into; **~ compte de qch** to take sth into account; **~ les**

comptes to keep the books; **~ le coup** to hold out; **~ bon** to stand ou hold fast; **au chaud/à l'abri** to keep hot/under shelter ou cover; **un manteau qui tient chaud** a warm coat; **tiens** (ou **tenez**), **voilà le stylo** there's the pen!; **tiens, voilà Alain!** look, here's Alain!; **tiens?** (surprise) really?

tennis [tenis] *nm* tennis; (aussi: **court de ~**) tennis court ▷ *nmpl, nfpl* (aussi: **chaussures de ~**) tennis ou gym shoes; **~ de table** table tennis; **tennisman** *nm* tennis player

tension [tɑ̃sjɔ̃] *nf* tension; (Méd) blood pressure; **faire** ou **avoir de la ~** to have high blood pressure

tentation [tɑ̃tasjɔ̃] *nf* temptation

tentative [tɑ̃tativ] *nf* attempt

tente [tɑ̃t] *nf* tent

tenter [tɑ̃te] /1/ *vt* (éprouver, attirer) to tempt; (essayer): **~ qch/de faire** to attempt ou try sth/to do; **~ sa chance** to try one's luck

tenture [tɑ̃tyr] *nf* hanging

tenu, e [təny] *pp de* tenir ▷ *adj*: **bien ~** (maison, comptes) well-kept; **~ de faire** (obligé) under an obligation to do ▷ *nf* (vêtements) clothes *pl*; (comportement) manners *pl*, behaviour; (d'une maison) upkeep; **en petite ~e** scantily dressed ou clad

ter [tɛr] *adj*: **16 ~ 16 b** ou **B**

terme [tɛrm] *nm* term; (fin) end; **être en bons/mauvais ~s avec qn** to be on good/bad terms with sb; **à court/long ~** *adj* short-/long-term ou -range; *adv* in the short/long term; **avant ~** (Méd) prematurely; **mettre un ~ à** to put an end ou a stop to

terminaison [tɛrminɛzɔ̃] *nf* (Ling) ending

terminal, e, -aux [tɛrminal, -o] *nm* terminal ▷ *nf* (Scol) ≈ year 13 (BRIT), ≈ twelfth grade (US)

terminer [tɛrmine] /1/ *vt* to finish; **se terminer** *vi* to end

terne [tɛrn] *adj* dull

ternir [tɛrnir] /2/ *vt* to dull; (fig) to sully, tarnish; **se ternir** *vi* to become dull

terrain [tɛrɛ̃] *nm* (sol, fig) ground; (Comm: étendue de terre) land *no pl*; (: parcelle) plot (of land); (: à bâtir) site; **sur le ~** (fig) on the field; **~ de football/rugby** football/rugby pitch (BRIT) ou field (US); **~ d'aviation** airfield; **~ de camping** campsite; **~ de golf** golf course; **~ de jeu** (pour les petits) playground; (Sport) games field; **~ de sport** sports ground; **~ vague** waste ground *no pl*

terrasse [tɛras] *nf* terrace; **à la ~** (café) outside; **terrasser** /1/ *vt* (adversaire) to floor; (maladie etc) to lay low

terre [tɛr] *nf* (gén, aussi Élec) earth; (substance) soil, earth; (opposé à mer) land *no pl*; (contrée) land; **terres** *nfpl* (terrains) lands, land *sg*; **en ~** (pipe, poterie) clay; **à ou par ~** (mettre, être, s'asseoir) on the ground (ou floor); (jeter, tomber) to the ground, down; **~ à ~** *adj inv* down-to-earth; **~ cuite** terracotta; **la ~ ferme** dry land; **~ glaise** clay

terreau [tɛro] *nm* compost

terre-plein [tɛrplɛ̃] *nm* platform; (sur chaussée) central reservation

terrestre [tɛrɛstr] *adj* (surface) earth's, of the earth; (Bot, Zool, Mil) land *cpd*; (Rel) earthly

terreur [tɛrœr] *nf* terror *no pl*

terrible [tɛribl] *adj* terrible, dreadful; (fam) terrific; **pas ~** nothing special

terrien, ne [tɛrjɛ̃, -ɛn] *adj*: **propriétaire ~** landowner ▷ *nm/f* (non martien etc) earthling

terrier [tɛrje] *nm* burrow, hole; (chien) terrier

terrifier [tɛrifje] /7/ *vt* to terrify

terrine [tɛrin] *nf* (récipient) terrine; (Culin) pâté

territoire [tɛritwar] *nm* territory

terroriser [tɛrɔrize] /1/ *vt* to terrorize

terrorisme [terɔrism] nm terrorism;
terroriste [terɔrist] nm/f terrorist

tertiaire [tersjer] adj tertiary ▷ nm
(Écon) service industries pl

tes [te] adj poss voir **ton¹**

test [test] nm test

testament [testamɑ̃] nm (Jur) will;
(fig) legacy; (Rel): **T~** Testament

tester [teste] /1/ vt to test

testicule [testikyl] nm testicle

tétanos [tetanos] nm tetanus

têtard [tetar] nm tadpole

tête [tɛt] nf head; (cheveux) hair no
pl; (visage) face; **de ~** adj (wagon etc)
front cpd ▷ adv (calculer) in one's head,
mentally; **perdre la ~** (fig) (s'affoler) to
lose one's head; (devenir fou) to go off
one's head; **tenir ~ à qn** to stand up
to ou defy sb; **la ~ en bas** with one's
head down; **la ~ la première** (tomber)
head-first; **faire une ~** (Football) to
head the ball; **faire la ~** (fig) to sulk;
en ~ (Sport) in the lead; **à la ~ de** at
the head of; **à ~ reposée** in a more
leisurely moment; **n'en faire qu'à
sa ~** to do as one pleases; **en avoir
par-dessus la ~** to be fed up; **en ~
à ~** in private, together; **de la
~ aux pieds** from head to toe; **~ de
lecture** (playback) head; **~ de liste**
(Pol) chief candidate; **~ de mort**
skull and crossbones; **~ de série**
(Tennis) seeded player, seed; **~ de
Turc** (fig) whipping boy (BRIT), butt;
tête-à-queue nm inv: **faire un tête-
à-queue** to spin round; **tête-à-tête**
nm inv: **en tête-à-tête** in private,
alone together

téter [tete] /6/ vt: **~ (sa mère)** to
suck at one's mother's breast, feed

tétine [tetin] nf teat; (sucette)
dummy (BRIT), pacifier (US)

têtu, e [tety] adj stubborn, pigheaded

texte [tɛkst] nm text; (morceau choisi)
passage

texter [tɛkste] /1/ vi, vt to text

textile [tɛkstil] adj textile cpd ▷ nm
textile; (industrie) textile industry

Texto [tɛksto] nm text (message)

textoter [tɛkstɔte] /1/ vi, vt to text

texture [tɛkstyr] nf texture

TGV sigle m = **train à grande vitesse**

thaïlandais, e [tailɑ̃dɛ, -ɛz] adj Thai
▷ nm/f: **T~, e** Thai

Thaïlande [tailɑ̃d] nf: **la ~** Thailand

thé [te] nm tea; **prendre le ~** to have
tea; **~ au lait/citron** tea with milk/
lemon; **faire le ~** to make the tea

théâtral, e, -aux [teɑtral, -o] adj
theatrical

théâtre [teɑtr] nm theatre; (péj)
playacting; (fig: lieu): **le ~ de** the scene
of; **faire du ~** to act

théière [tejɛr] nf teapot

thème [tɛm] nm theme; (Scol:
traduction) prose (composition)

théologie [teɔlɔʒi] nf theology

théorie [teɔri] nf theory; **théorique**
adj theoretical

thérapie [terapi] nf therapy

thermal, e, -aux [tɛrmal, -o] adj:
station ~ spa; **cure ~** water cure

thermomètre [tɛrmɔmɛtr] nm
thermometer

thermos® [tɛrmos] nm ou f:
(bouteille) ~ vacuum ou Thermos®
flask; BRIT ou bottle (US)

thermostat [tɛrmɔsta] nm
thermostat

thèse [tɛz] nf thesis

thon [tɔ̃] nm tuna (fish)

thym [tɛ̃] nm thyme

Tibet [tibɛ] nm: **le ~** Tibet

tibia [tibja] nm shin; shinbone, tibia

TIC sigle fpl (= technologies de l'information
et de la communication) ICT sg

tic [tik] nm tic, (nervous) twitch; (de
langage etc) mannerism

ticket [tikɛ] nm ticket; **~ de caisse**
till receipt

tiède [tjɛd] adj lukewarm; (vent, air)
mild, warm; **tiédir** /2/ vi (se réchauffer)
to grow warmer; (refroidir) to cool

tien, tienne [tjɛ̃, tjɛn] pron: **le (la)
~(ne)** yours; **les ~(ne)s** yours; **à la
~ne!** cheers!

tiens [tjɛ̃] vb, excl voir **tenir**

tiercé [tjɛʀse] nm system of forecast betting giving first three horses

tiers, tierce [tjɛʀ, tjɛʀs] adj third ▷ nm (Jur) third party; (fraction) third; **le ~ monde** the third world

tige [tiʒ] nf stem; (baguette) rod

tignasse [tiɲas] nf (péj) shock ou mop of hair

tigre [tigʀ] nm tiger; **tigré, e** adj (rayé) striped; (tacheté) spotted; (chat) tabby; **tigresse** nf tigress

tilleul [tijœl] nm lime (tree), linden (tree); (boisson) lime(-blossom) tea

timbre [tɛ̃bʀ] nm (tampon) stamp; (aussi: ~-poste) (postage) stamp; (Mus: de voix, instrument) timbre, tone

timbré, e [tɛ̃bʀe] adj (fam) cracked

timide [timid] adj shy; (timoré) timid; **timidement** adv shyly; timidly; **timidité** nf shyness; timidity

tintamarre [tɛ̃tamaʀ] nm din, uproar

tinter [tɛ̃te] /1/ vi to ring, chime; (argent, clés) to jingle

tique [tik] nf tick (insect)

tir [tiʀ] nm (sport) shooting; (fait ou manière de tirer) firing no pl; (rafale) fire; (stand) shooting gallery; **~ à l'arc** archery

tirage [tiʀaʒ] nm (action) printing; (Photo) print; (de journal) circulation; (de livre) (print-)run; edition; (de loterie) draw; **~ au sort** drawing lots

tire [tiʀ] nf: **vol à la ~** pickpocketing

tiré, e [tiʀe] adj (visage, traits) drawn; **~ par les cheveux** far-fetched

tire-bouchon [tiʀbuʃɔ̃] nm corkscrew

tirelire [tiʀliʀ] nf moneybox

tirer [tiʀe] /1/ vt (gén) to pull; (ligne, trait) to draw; (rideau) to draw; (carte, conclusion, chèque) to draw; (en faisant feu: balle, coup) to shoot; (: animal) to shoot; (journal, livre, photo) to print; (Football: corner etc) to take ▷ vi (faire feu) to fire; (faire du tir, Football) to shoot; **se tirer** vi (fam) to push off;

(aussi: **s'en ~**) (éviter le pire) to get off; (survivre) to pull through; (se débrouiller) to manage; (extraire): **~ qch de** to take ou pull sth out of; **~ sur** (corde, poignée) to pull on ou at; (faire feu sur) to shoot ou fire at; (pipe) to draw on; (fig: avoisiner) to verge ou border on; **~ qn de** (embarras etc) to help ou get sb out of; **~ à l'arc/la carabine** to shoot with a bow and arrow/with a rifle; **~ à sa fin** to be drawing to an end; **~ qch au clair** to clear sth up; **~ au sort** to draw lots; **~ parti de** to take advantage of; **~ profit de** to profit from; **~ les cartes** to read ou tell the cards

tiret [tiʀɛ] nm dash

tireur [tiʀœʀ] nm gunman; **~ d'élite** marksman

tiroir [tiʀwaʀ] nm drawer; **tiroir-caisse** nm till

tisane [tizan] nf herb tea

tisser [tise] /1/ vt to weave

tissu [tisy] nm fabric, material, cloth no pl; (Anat, Bio) tissue; **tissu-éponge** nm (terry) towelling no pl

titre [titʀ] nm (gén) title; (de journal) headline; (diplôme) qualification; (Comm) security; **en ~** (champion, responsable) official; **à juste ~** rightly; **à quel ~?** on what grounds?; **à aucun ~** on no account; **au même ~ (que)** in the same way (as); **à ~ d'information** for (your) information; **à ~ gracieux** free of charge; **à ~ d'essai** on a trial basis; **à ~ privé** in a private capacity; **~ de propriété** title deed; **~ de transport** ticket

tituber [titybe] /1/ vi to stagger ou reel (along)

titulaire [titylɛʀ] adj (Admin) with tenure ▷ nm/f (de permis) holder; **être ~ de** (diplôme, permis) to hold

toast [tost] nm slice ou piece of toast; (de bienvenue) (welcoming) toast; **porter un ~ à qn** to propose ou drink a toast to sb

toboggan [tɔbɔgã] nm slide; (Auto) flyover

toc [tɔk] nm: **en toc** imitation cpd ▷ excl: **toc, toc** knock knock

tocsin [tɔksɛ̃] nm alarm (bell)

tohu-bohu [tɔyboy] nm commotion

toi [twa] pron you

toile [twal] nf (tableau) canvas; **de** ou **en** ~ (pantalon) cotton; (sac) canvas; ~ **d'araignée** cobweb; **la T~** (Internet) the Web; ~ **cirée** oilcloth; ~ **de fond** (fig) backdrop

toilette [twalɛt] nf (habits) outfit; **toilettes** nfpl toilet sg; **faire sa ~** to have a wash, get washed; **articles de** ~ toiletries

toi-même [twamɛm] pron yourself

toit [twa] nm roof; ~ **ouvrant** sun roof

toiture [twatyʀ] nf roof

Tokyo [tɔkjo] n Tokyo

tôle [tol] nf (plaque) steel (ou iron) sheet; ~ **ondulée** corrugated iron

tolérable [tɔleʀabl] adj tolerable

tolérant, e [tɔleʀã, -ãt] adj tolerant

tolérer [tɔleʀe] /6/ vt to tolerate; (Admin: hors taxe etc) to allow

tollé [tɔle] nm: **un ~ (de protestations)** a general outcry

tomate [tɔmat] nf tomato; ~**s farcies** stuffed tomatoes

tombe [tɔ̃b] nf (sépulture) grave; (avec monument) tomb

tombeau, x [tɔ̃bo] nm tomb

tombée [tɔ̃be] nf: **à la ~ du jour** ou **de la nuit** at nightfall

tomber [tɔ̃be] /1/ vi to fall; (fièvre, vent) to drop ▷ vt: **laisser ~** (objet) to drop; (personne) to let down; (activité) to give up; **laisse ~!** forget it!; **faire ~** to knock over; ~ **sur** (rencontrer) to come across; ~ **de fatigue/sommeil** to drop from exhaustion/be falling asleep on one's feet; ~ **à l'eau** (projet etc) to fall through; ~ **en panne** to break down; ~ **en ruine** to fall into ruins; **ça tombe bien/mal** (fig) that's come at the right/wrong time; **il**

est bien/mal tombé (fig) he's been lucky/unlucky

tombola [tɔ̃bɔla] nf raffle

tome [tom] nm volume

ton¹, ta (pl **tes**) [tɔ̃, ta, te] adj poss your

ton² [tɔ̃] nm (gén) tone; (couleur) shade, tone; **de bon** ~ in good taste

tonalité [tɔnalite] nf (au téléphone) dialling tone

tondeuse [tɔ̃døz] nf (à gazon) (lawn)mower; (du coiffeur) clippers pl; (pour la tonte) shears pl

tondre [tɔ̃dʀ] /41/ vt (pelouse, herbe) to mow; (haie) to cut, clip; (mouton, toison) to shear; (cheveux) to crop

tongs [tɔg] nfpl flip-flops

tonifier [tɔnifje] /7/ vt (peau, organisme) to tone up

tonique [tɔnik] adj fortifying ▷ nm tonic

tonne [ton] nf metric ton, tonne

tonneau, x [tɔno] nm (à vin, cidre) barrel; **faire des ~x** (voiture, avion) to roll over

tonnelle [tɔnɛl] nf bower, arbour

tonner [tɔne] /1/ vi to thunder; **il tonne** it is thundering, there's some thunder

tonnerre [tɔnɛʀ] nm thunder

tonus [tɔnys] nm energy

top [tɔp] nm: **au troisième ~** at the third stroke ▷ adj: ~ **secret** top secret

topinambour [tɔpinãbuʀ] nm Jerusalem artichoke

torche [tɔʀʃ] nf torch

torchon [tɔʀʃɔ̃] nm cloth; (à vaisselle) tea towel ou cloth

tordre [tɔʀdʀ] /41/ vt (chiffon) to wring; (barre, fig: visage) to twist; **se tordre** vi; **se ~ le poignet/la cheville** to twist one's wrist/ankle; **se ~ de douleur/rire** to writhe in pain/be doubled up with laughter; **tordu, e** adj (fig) twisted; (fou) crazy

tornade [tɔʀnad] nf tornado

torrent [tɔʀã] nm mountain stream

torsade [tɔʀsad] nf: **un pull à ~s** a cable sweater

torse [tɔʀs] nm chest; (Anat, Sculpture) torso; **~ nu** stripped to the waist

tort [tɔʀ] nm (défaut) fault; **torts** nmpl (Jur) fault sg; **avoir ~** to be wrong; **être dans son ~** to be in the wrong; **donner ~ à qn** to lay the blame on sb; **causer du ~ à** to harm; **à ~** wrongly; **à ~ et à travers** wildly

torticolis [tɔʀtikɔli] nm stiff neck

tortiller [tɔʀtije] /1/ vt to twist; (moustache) to twirl; **se tortiller** vi to wriggle; (en dansant) to wiggle

tortionnaire [tɔʀsjɔnɛʀ] nm torturer

tortue [tɔʀty] nf tortoise; (d'eau douce) terrapin; (d'eau de mer) turtle

tortueux, -euse [tɔʀtɥø, -øz] adj (rue) twisting; (fig) tortuous

torture [tɔʀtyʀ] nf torture; **torturer** /1/ vt to torture; to torment

tôt [to] adv early; **~ ou tard** sooner or later; **si ~** so early; (déjà) so soon; **au plus ~** at the earliest; **plus ~** earlier

total, e, -aux [tɔtal, -o] adj, nm total; **au ~** in total ou all; (fig) on the whole; **faire le ~** to work out the total; **totalement** adv totally; **totaliser** /1/ vt to total (up); **totalitaire** adj totalitarian; **totalité** nf: **la totalité de: la totalité des élèves** all (of) the pupils; **la totalité de la population/classe** the whole population/class; **en totalité** entirely

toubib [tubib] nm (fam) doctor

touchant, e [tuʃɑ̃, -ɑ̃t] adj touching

touche [tuʃ] nf (de piano, de machine à écrire) key; (de téléphone) button; (Peinture etc) stroke, touch; (fig: de couleur, nostalgie) touch; (Football: aussi: **remise en ~**) throw-in; (Escrime) hit; **ligne de ~** touch-line; (Escrime) hit; **~ dièse** (de téléphone, clavier) hash key

toucher [tuʃe] /1/ nm touch ▷ vt to touch; (palper) to feel; (atteindre: d'un coup de feu etc) to hit; (concerner) to concern, affect; (contacter) to reach, contact; (recevoir: récompense) to receive, get; (: salaire) to draw, get; (chèque) to cash; (aborder: problème, sujet) to touch on; **au ~** to the touch; **~ à** to touch; (traiter de, concerner) to have to do with, concern; **je vais lui en ~ un mot** I'll have a word with him about it; **~ au but** (fig) to near one's goal; **~ à sa fin** to be drawing to a close

touffe [tuf] nf tuft

touffu, e [tufy] adj thick, dense

toujours [tuʒuʀ] adv always; (encore) still; (constamment) forever; **essaie ~** (you can) try anyway; **pour ~** forever; **~ est-il que** the fact remains that; **~ plus** more and more

toupie [tupi] nf (spinning) top

tour [tuʀ] nf tower; (immeuble) high-rise block (BRIT) ou building (US); (Échecs) castle, rook ▷ nm (excursion: à pied) stroll, walk; (: en voiture etc) run, ride; (: plus long) trip; (Sport: aussi: **~ de piste**) lap; (d'être servi ou de jouer etc) turn; (de roue etc) revolution; (Pol: aussi: **~ de scrutin**) ballot; (ruse, de prestidigitation, de cartes) trick; (de potier) wheel; (à bois, métaux) lathe; (circonférence): **de 3 m de ~** 3 m round, with a circumference ou girth of 3 m; **faire le ~ de** to go (a)round; (à pied) to walk (a)round; **faire un ~** to go for a walk; **c'est au ~ de Renée** it's Renée's turn; **à ~ de rôle, à ~ de** in turn; **~ de taille/tête** nm waist/head measurement; **~ de chant** nm song recital; **~ de contrôle** nf control tower; **la ~ Eiffel** the Eiffel Tower; **le T~ de France** the Tour de France; **un ~ de main** nm tour de force; **~ de garde** nm spell of duty; **un 33 ~s** an LP; **un 45 ~s** a single; **~ d'horizon** nm (fig) general survey

tourbe [tuʀb] nf peat

tourbillon [tuʀbijɔ̃] nm whirlwind; (d'eau) whirlpool; (fig) whirl, swirl;

tourbillonner /1/ vi to whirl ou twirl round

tourelle [turɛl] nf turret

tourisme [turism] nm tourism; **agence de ~** tourist agency; **faire du ~** to go touring; (en ville) to go sightseeing; **touriste** nm/f tourist; **touristique** adj tourist cpd; (région) touristic (péj)

tourment [turmã] nm torment; **tourmenter** /1/ vt to torment; **se tourmenter** to fret, worry o.s.

tournage [turnaʒ] nm (d'un film) shooting

tournant, e [turnã, -ãt] adj (feu, scène) revolving ▷ nm (de route) bend ; (fig) turning point

tournée [turne] nf (du facteur etc) round; (d'artiste, politicien) tour; (au café) round (of drinks)

tourner [turne] /1/ vt to turn; (sauce, mélange) to stir; (Ciné: faire les prises de vues) to shoot; (: produire) to make ▷ vi to turn; (moteur) to run; (compteur) to tick away; (lait etc) to turn (sour); **se tourner** vi to turn ou turn round; **se ~ vers** to turn to; to turn towards; **mal ~** to go wrong; **~ autour de** to go (a)round; (péj) to hang (a)round; **~ à/en** to turn into; **~ en ridicule** to ridicule; **~ le dos à** (mouvement) to turn one's back on; (position) to have one's back to; **se ~ les pouces** to twiddle one's thumbs; **~ de l'œil** to pass out

tournesol [turnəsɔl] nm sunflower

tournevis [turnəvis] nm screwdriver

tournoi [turnwa] nm tournament

tournure [turnyr] nf (Ling) turn of phrase; **la ~ de qch** (évolution) the way sth is developing; **~ d'esprit** turn ou cast of mind

tourte [turt] nf pie

tourterelle [turtərɛl] nf turtledove

tous [tu, tus] adj, pron voir tout

Toussaint [tusɛ̃] nf: **la ~** All Saints' Day

tousser [tuse] /1/ vi to cough

 MOT-CLÉ

tout, e (mpl **tous**, fpl **toutes**) [tu, tut, tus, tut] adj **1** (avec article singulier) all; **tout le lait** all the milk; **toute la nuit** all night, the whole night; **tout le livre** the whole book; **tout un pain** a whole loaf; **tout le temps** all the time, the whole time; **c'est tout le contraire** it's quite the opposite **2** (avec article pluriel) every; all; **tous les livres** all the books; **toutes les nuits** every night; **toutes les fois** every time; **toutes les trois/ deux semaines** every third/other ou second week, every three/two weeks; **tous les deux** both ou each of us (ou them ou you); **tous les trois** all three of us (ou them ou you) **3** (sans article): **à tout âge** at any age; **pour toute nourriture, il avait ...** his only food was ...
▷ pron everything, all; **il a tout fait** he's done everything; **je les vois tous** I can see them all ou all of them; **nous y sommes tous allés** all of us went, we all went; **c'est tout** that's all; **en tout** in all; **tout ce qu'il sait** all he knows
▷ nm whole; **le tout** all of it (ou them); **le tout est de ...** the main thing is to ...; **pas du tout** not at all
▷ adv **1** (très, complètement) very; **tout près** ou **à côté** very near; **tout premier** the very first; **tout seul** all alone; **le livre tout entier** the whole book; **tout en haut** at the top; **tout droit** straight ahead

2 : tout en while; **tout en travaillant** while working, as he etc works
3 : tout d'abord first of all; **tout à coup** suddenly; **tout à fait** absolutely; **tout à l'heure** a short while ago; (futur) in a short while, shortly; **à tout à l'heure!** see you later!; **tout de même** all the same; **tout le monde** everybody; **tout simplement** quite simply; **tout de suite** immediately, straight away

toutefois [tutfwa] adv however
toutes [tut] adj, pron voir **tout**
tout-terrain [tuterɛ̃] adj: **vélo ~** mountain bike; **véhicule ~** four-wheel drive
toux [tu] nf cough
toxicomane [tɔksikɔman] nm/f drug addict
toxique [tɔksik] adj toxic
trac [trak] nm (aux examens) nerves pl; (Théât) stage fright; **avoir le ~** (aux examens) to get an attack of nerves; (Théât) to have stage fright
tracasser [trakase] /1/ vt to worry, bother; **se tracasser** to worry (o.s.)
trace [tras] nf (empreintes) tracks pl; (marques, fig) mark; (restes, vestige) trace; **~ s de pas** footprints
tracer [trase] /1/ vt to draw; (piste) to open up
tract [trakt] nm tract, pamphlet
tracteur [traktœr] nm tractor
traction [traksjɔ̃] nf: **~ avant/arrière** front-wheel/rear-wheel drive
tradition [tradisjɔ̃] nf tradition;
traditionnel, le adj traditional
traducteur, -trice [tradyktœr, -tris] nm/f translator
traduction [tradyksjɔ̃] nf translation
traduire [traduir] /38/ vt to translate; (exprimer) to convey; **~ en français** to translate into French; **~ en justice** to bring before the courts

trafic [trafik] nm traffic; **~ d'armes** arms dealing; **trafiquant, e** nm/f trafficker; (d'armes) dealer; **trafiquer** /1/ vt (péj: vin) to doctor; (: moteur, document) to tamper with
tragédie [traʒedi] nf tragedy;
tragique [traʒik] adj tragic
trahir [trair] /2/ vt to betray;
trahison nf betrayal; (Jur) treason
train [trɛ̃] nm (Rail) train; (allure) pace; **être en ~ de** faire qch to be doing sth; **~ à grande vitesse** high-speed train; **~ d'atterrissage** undercarriage; **~ électrique** (jouet) (electric) train set; **~ de vie** style of living
traîne [trɛn] nf (de robe) train; **être à la ~** to lag behind
traîneau, x [trɛno] nm sleigh, sledge
traîner [trɛne] /1/ vt (remorque) to pull; (enfant, chien) to drag ou trail along ▷ vi (robe, manteau) to trail; (être en désordre) to be around; (marcher lentement) to dawdle (along); (vagabonder) to hang about; (durer) to drag on; **se traîner** vi: **se ~ par terre** to crawl (on the ground); **~ les pieds** to drag one's feet
train-train [trɛ̃trɛ̃] nm humdrum routine
traire [trɛr] /50/ vt to milk
trait, e [trɛ, -ɛt] nm (ligne) line; (de dessin) stroke; (caractéristique) feature, trait; **traits** nmpl (du visage) features; **d'un ~** (boire) in one gulp; **de ~** (animal) draught; **avoir ~ à** to concern; **~ d'union** hyphen
traitant, e [trɛtɑ̃, -ɑ̃t] adj: **votre médecin ~** your usual ou family doctor; **shampooing ~** medicated shampoo
traite [trɛt] nf (Comm) draft; (Agr) milking; **d'une (seule) ~** without stopping (once)
traité [trɛte] nm treaty
traitement [trɛtmɑ̃] nm treatment; (salaire) salary; **~ de données** ou **de l'information** data processing; **~ de texte** word processing; (logiciel) word processing package

traiter [tʀɛte] /1/ vt to treat;
(qualifier): **~ qn d'idiot** to call sb a fool
▷ vi to deal; **~ de** to deal with

traiteur [tʀɛtœʀ] nm caterer

traître, -esse [tʀɛtʀ, -tʀɛs] adj
(dangereux) treacherous ▷ nm/f
traitor (traitress)

trajectoire [tʀaʒɛktwaʀ] nf path

trajet [tʀaʒɛ] nm (parcours, voyage)
journey; (itinéraire) route; (distance à
parcourir) distance; **il y a une heure
de ~** the journey takes one hour

trampoline [tʀɑ̃pɔlin] nm
trampoline

tramway [tʀamwɛ] nm tram(way);
(voiture) tram(car) (BRIT), streetcar
(US)

tranchant, e [tʀɑ̃ʃɑ̃, -ɑ̃t] adj sharp;
(fig) peremptory ▷ nm (d'un couteau)
cutting edge; (de la main) edge; **à
double ~** double-edged

tranche [tʀɑ̃ʃ] nf (morceau) slice;
(arête) edge; **~ d'âge/de salaires**
age/wage bracket

tranché, e [tʀɑ̃ʃe] adj (couleurs)
distinct; (opinions) clear-cut

trancher [tʀɑ̃ʃe] /1/ vt to cut, sever
▷ vi to be decisive; **~ avec** to contrast
sharply with

tranquille [tʀɑ̃kil] adj quiet; (rassuré)
easy in one's mind, with one's mind
at rest; **se tenir ~** (enfant) to be
quiet; **avoir la conscience ~** to have
an easy conscience; **laisse-moi/
laisse-ça ~** leave me/it alone;
tranquillisant nm tranquillizer;
tranquillité nf peace (and quiet);
tranquillité d'esprit peace of mind

transférer [tʀɑ̃sfeʀe] /6/ vt to
transfer; **transfert** nm transfer

transformation [tʀɑ̃sfɔʀmasjɔ̃]
nf change, alteration; (radicale)
transformation; (Rugby) conversion;
transformations nfpl (travaux)
alterations

transformer [tʀɑ̃sfɔʀme] /1/ vt to
change; (radicalement) to transform;
(vêtement) alter; (matière première,

appartement, Rugby) to convert; **~ en**
to turn into

transfusion [tʀɑ̃sfyzjɔ̃] nf:
~ sanguine blood transfusion

transgénique [tʀɑ̃sʒenik] adj
transgenic

transgresser [tʀɑ̃sgʀese] /1/ vt to
contravene

transi, e [tʀɑ̃zi] adj numb (with
cold), chilled to the bone

transiger [tʀɑ̃ziʒe] /3/ vi to
compromise

transit [tʀɑ̃zit] nm transit; **transiter**
/1/ vi to pass in transit

transition [tʀɑ̃zisjɔ̃] nf transition;
transitoire adj transitional

transmettre [tʀɑ̃smɛtʀ] /56/ vt
(passer): **~ qch à qn** to pass sth on to
sb; (Tech, Tél, Méd) to transmit; (TV,
Radio: retransmettre) to broadcast;
transmission nf transmission

transparent, e [tʀɑ̃spaʀɑ̃, -ɑ̃t] adj
transparent

transpercer [tʀɑ̃spɛʀse] /3/ vt (froid,
pluie) to go through, pierce; (balle) to
go through

transpiration [tʀɑ̃spiʀasjɔ̃] nf
perspiration

transpirer [tʀɑ̃spiʀe] /1/ vi to
perspire

transplanter [tʀɑ̃splɑ̃te] /1/ vt
(Méd, Bot) to transplant

transport [tʀɑ̃spɔʀ] nm transport;
~s en commun public transport
sg; **transporter** /1/ vt to carry,
move; (Comm) to transport,
convey; **transporteur** nm haulage
contractor (BRIT), trucker (US)

transvaser [tʀɑ̃svaze] /1/ vt to
decant

transversal, e, -aux [tʀɑ̃svɛʀsal,
-o] adj (mur, chemin, rue) running at
right angles; **coupe ~e** cross section

trapèze [tʀapɛz] nm (au cirque)
trapeze

trappe [tʀap] nf trap door

trapu, e [tʀapy] adj squat, stocky

traquenard [tʀaknaʀ] nm trap

traquer [tʀake] /1/ vt to track down; (harceler) to hound

traumatiser [tʀomatize] /1/ vt to traumatize

travail, -aux [tʀavaj, -o] nm (gén) work; (tâche, métier) work no pl, job; (Écon, Méd) labour; **travaux** nmpl (de réparation, agricoles etc) work sg; (sur route) roadworks; (de construction) building (work) sg; **être sans ~** (employé) to be out of work; **~ (au) noir** moonlighting; **travaux des champs** farmwork sg; **travaux dirigés** (Scol) supervised practical work sg; **travaux forcés** hard labour sg; **travaux manuels** (Scol) handicrafts; **travaux ménagers** housework sg; **travaux pratiques** (gén) practical work sg; (en laboratoire) lab work sg

travailler [tʀavaje] /1/ vi to work; (bois) to warp ▷ vt (bois, métal) to work; (objet d'art, discipline) to work on; **cela le travaille** it is on his mind; **travailleur, -euse** adj hard-working ▷ nm/f worker; **travailleur social** social worker; **travailliste** adj ≈ Labour cpd

travaux [tʀavo] nmpl voir **travail**

travers [tʀavɛʀ] nm fault, failing; **en ~ (de)** across; **au ~ (de)** through; **de ~** (nez, bouche) crooked; (chapeau) askew; **à ~** through; **regarder de ~** (fig) to look askance at; **comprendre de ~** to misunderstand

traverse [tʀavɛʀs] nf (de voie ferrée) sleeper; **chemin de ~** shortcut

traversée [tʀavɛʀse] nf crossing

traverser [tʀavɛʀse] /1/ vt (gén) to cross; (ville, tunnel, aussi percer, fig) to go through; (ligne, trait) to run across

traversin [tʀavɛʀsɛ̃] nm bolster

travesti [tʀavɛsti] nm transvestite

trébucher [tʀebyʃe] /1/ vi: **~ (sur)** to stumble (over), trip (over)

trèfle [tʀefl] nm (Bot) clover; (Cartes: couleur) clubs pl; (: carte) club; **~ à quatre feuilles** four-leaf clover

treize [tʀɛz] num thirteen; **treizième** num thirteenth

tréma [tʀema] nm diaeresis

tremblement [tʀɑ̃bləmɑ̃] nm: **~ de terre** earthquake

trembler [tʀɑ̃ble] /1/ vi to tremble, shake; **~ de** (froid, fièvre) to shiver ou tremble with; (peur) to shake ou tremble with; **~ pour qn** to fear for sb

trémousser [tʀemuse] /1/: **se trémousser** vi to jig about, wriggle about

trempé, e [tʀɑ̃pe] adj soaking (wet), drenched; (Tech): **acier ~** tempered steel

tremper [tʀɑ̃pe] /1/ vt to soak, drench; (aussi: **faire ~**, **mettre à ~**) to soak ▷ vi to soak; (fig): **~ dans** to be involved ou have a hand in; **se tremper** vi to have a quick dip

tremplin [tʀɑ̃plɛ̃] nm springboard; (Ski) ski jump

trentaine [tʀɑ̃tɛn] nf (âge): **avoir la ~** to be around thirty; **une ~ (de)** thirty or so, about thirty

trente [tʀɑ̃t] num thirty; **être/se mettre sur son ~ et un** to be wearing/put on one's Sunday best; **trentième** num thirtieth

trépidant, e [tʀepidɑ̃, -ɑ̃t] adj (fig: rythme) pulsating; (: vie) hectic

trépigner [tʀepiɲe] /1/ vi to stamp (one's feet)

très [tʀɛ] adv very; **~ beau/bien** very beautiful/well; **~ critiqué** much criticized; **~ industrialisé** highly industrialized

trésor [tʀezɔʀ] nm treasure; **~ (public)** public revenue; **trésorerie** nf (gestion) accounts pl; (bureaux) accounts department; **difficultés de trésorerie** cash problems, shortage of cash ou funds; **trésorier, -ière** nm/f treasurer

tressaillir [tʀesajiʀ] /13/ vi to shiver, shudder

tressauter [tʀesote] /1/ vi to start, jump

tresse [tʀɛs] nf braid, plait; **tresser** /1/ vt (cheveux) to braid, plait; (fil, ficelle) to plait; (corbeille) to weave; (corde) to twist

trêve [tʀɛv] nf (Mil, Pol) truce; (fig) respite; **~ de ...** enough of this ...

tri [tʀi] nm: **faire le ~ (de)** to sort out; **le (bureau de) ~** (Postes) the sorting office

triangle [tʀijɑ̃gl] nm triangle; **triangulaire** adj triangular

tribord [tʀibɔʀ] nm: **à ~** to starboard, on the starboard side

tribu [tʀiby] nf tribe

tribunal, -aux [tʀibynal, -o] nm (Jur) court; (Mil) military court

tribune [tʀibyn] nf (estrade) platform, rostrum; (débat) forum; (d'église, de tribunal) gallery; (de stade) stand

tribut [tʀiby] nm tribute

tributaire [tʀibytɛʀ] adj: **être ~ de** to be dependent on

tricher [tʀiʃe] /1/ vi to cheat; **tricheur, -euse** nm/f cheat

tricolore [tʀikɔlɔʀ] adj three-coloured; (français) red, white and blue

tricot [tʀiko] nm (technique, ouvrage) knitting no pl; (vêtement) jersey, sweater; **~ de corps, ~ de peau** vest; **tricoter** /1/ vt to knit

tricycle [tʀisikl] nm tricycle

trier [tʀije] /7/ vt to sort (out); (Postes, fruits) to sort

trimestre [tʀimɛstʀ] nm (Scol) term; (Comm) quarter; **trimestriel, le** adj quarterly; (Scol) end-of-term

trinquer [tʀɛ̃ke] /1/ vi to clink glasses

triomphe [tʀijɔ̃f] nm triumph; **triompher** /1/ vi to triumph, win; **triompher de** to triumph over, overcome

tripes [tʀip] nfpl (Culin) tripe sg

triple [tʀipl] adj triple ▷ nm: **le ~ (de)** (comparaison) three times as much

(as); **en ~ exemplaire** in triplicate; **tripler** /1/ vi, vt to triple, treble

triplés, -ées [tʀiple] nm/f pl triplets

tripoter [tʀipɔte] /1/ vt to fiddle with

triste [tʀist] adj sad; (couleur, temps, journée) dreary; (péj): **~ personnage/affaire** sorry individual/affair; **tristesse** nf sadness

trivial, e, -aux [tʀivjal, -o] adj coarse, crude; (commun) mundane

troc [tʀɔk] nm barter

trognon [tʀɔɲɔ̃] nm (de fruit) core; (de légume) stalk

trois [tʀwa] num three; **troisième** num third ▷ nf (Scol) year 10 (BRIT), ninth grade (US); **le troisième âge** (période de vie) one's retirement years; (personnes âgées) senior citizens pl

troll [tʀɔl] nm, **trolleur, -euse** [tʀɔlœʀ, -øz] nm/f (Inform) troll

trombe [tʀɔ̃b] nf: **des ~s d'eau** a downpour; **en ~** like a whirlwind

trombone [tʀɔ̃bɔn] nm (Mus) trombone; (de bureau) paper clip

trompe [tʀɔ̃p] nf (d'éléphant) trunk; (Mus) trumpet, horn

tromper [tʀɔ̃pe] /1/ vt to deceive; (vigilance, poursuivants) to elude; **se tromper** vi to make a mistake, be mistaken; **se ~ de voiture/jour** to take the wrong car/get the day wrong; **se ~ de 3 cm/20 euros** to be out by 3 cm/20 euros

trompette [tʀɔ̃pɛt] nf trumpet; **en ~** (nez) turned-up

trompeur, -euse [tʀɔ̃pœʀ, -øz] adj deceptive

tronc [tʀɔ̃] nm (Bot, Anat) trunk; (d'église) collection box

tronçon [tʀɔ̃sɔ̃] nm section; **tronçonner** /1/ vt to saw up; **tronçonneuse** nf chainsaw

trône [tʀon] nm throne

trop [tʀo] adv too; (avec verbe) too much; (aussi: **~ nombreux**) too many; (aussi: **~ souvent**) too often; **~ peu (nombreux)** too few; **~ longtemps** (for) too long; **~ de**

(*nombre*) too many; (*quantité*) too much; **de ~, en ~: des livres en ~** a few books too many; **du lait en ~** too much milk; **trois livres/cinq euros de ~** three books too many/five euros too much; **ça coûte ~ cher** it's too expensive

tropical, e, -aux [tʀɔpikal, -o] *adj* tropical

tropique [tʀɔpik] *nm* tropic

trop-plein [tʀɔplɛ̃] *nm* (*tuyau*) overflow *ou* outlet (pipe); (*liquide*) overflow

troquer [tʀɔke] /1/ *vt*: **~ qch contre** to barter *ou* trade sth for; (*fig*) to swap sth for

trot [tʀo] *nm* trot; **trotter** /1/ *vi* to trot

trottinette [tʀɔtinɛt] *nf* (child's) scooter

trottoir [tʀɔtwaʀ] *nm* pavement (BRIT), sidewalk (US); **faire le ~** (*péj*) to walk the streets; **~ roulant** moving walkway, travelator

trou [tʀu] *nm* hole; (*fig*) gap; (Comm) deficit; **~ d'air** air pocket; **~ de mémoire** blank, lapse of memory

troublant, e [tʀublɑ̃, -ɑ̃t] *adj* disturbing

trouble [tʀubl] *adj* (*liquide*) cloudy; (*image, photo*) blurred; (*affaire*) shady, murky ▷ *adv*: **voir ~** to have blurred vision ▷ *nm* agitation; **troubles** *nmpl* (Pol) disturbances, troubles, unrest *sg*; (Méd) trouble *sg*, disorders; **trouble-fête** *nm/f inv* spoilsport

troubler [tʀuble] /1/ *vt* to disturb; (*liquide*) to make cloudy; (*intriguer*) to bother; **se troubler** *vi* (*personne*) to become flustered *ou* confused

trouer [tʀue] /1/ *vt* to make a hole (*ou* holes) in

trouille [tʀuj] *nf* (*fam*): **avoir la ~** to be scared stiff

troupe [tʀup] *nf* troop; **~ (de théâtre)** (theatrical) company

troupeau, x [tʀupo] *nm* (*de moutons*) flock; (*de vaches*) herd

trousse [tʀus] *nf* case, kit; (*d'écolier*) pencil case; **aux ~s de** (*fig*) on the heels *ou* tail of; **~ à outils** toolkit; **~ de toilette** toilet bag

trousseau, x [tʀuso] *nm* (*de mariée*) trousseau; **~ de clefs** bunch of keys

trouvaille [tʀuvaj] *nf* find

trouver [tʀuve] /1/ *vt* to find; (*rendre visite*): **aller/venir ~ qn** to go/come and see sb; **se trouver** *vi* (*être*) to be; **je trouve que** I find *ou* think that; **~ à boire/critiquer** to find something to drink/criticize; **se ~ mal** to pass out

truand [tʀyɑ̃] *nm* villain; **truander** /1/ *vt*: **se faire truander** to be swindled

truc [tʀyk] *nm* (*astuce*) way; trick, effect; (*de cinéma, prestidigitateur*) trick effect; (*chose*) thing; thingumajig; **avoir le ~** to have the knack; **c'est pas son** (*ou* **mon** *etc*) **~** (*fam*) it's not really his (*ou* my *etc*) thing

truffe [tʀyf] *nf* truffle; (*nez*) nose

truffé, e [tʀyfe] *adj* (Culin) garnished with truffles

truie [tʀɥi] *nf* sow

truite [tʀɥit] *nf* trout *sg* *ou* *inv*

truquage [tʀykaʒ] *nm* special effects *pl*

truquer [tʀyke] /1/ *vt* (*élections, serrure, dés*) to fix

TSVP *abr* (= *tournez s'il vous plaît*) PTO

TTC *abr* (= *toutes taxes comprises*) inclusive of tax

tu¹ [ty] *pron you* ▷ *nm*: **employer le tu** to use the "tu" form

tu², e [ty] *pp de* **taire**

tuba [tyba] *nm* (Mus) tuba; (Sport) snorkel

tube [tyb] *nm* tube; (*chanson, disque*) hit song *ou* record

tuberculose [tybɛʀkyloz] *nf* tuberculosis

tuer [tɥe] /1/ *vt* to kill; **se tuer** (*se suicider*) to kill o.s.; (*dans un accident*) to be killed; **se ~ au travail** (*fig*) to work o.s. to death; **tuerie** *nf* slaughter *no pl*

tue-tête [tytɛt]: **à ~** *adv* at the top of one's voice

tueur [tɥœʀ] *nm* killer; **~ à gages** hired killer

tuile [tɥil] *nf* tile; *(fam)* spot of bad luck, blow

tulipe [tylip] *nf* tulip

tuméfié, e [tymefje] *adj* puffy, swollen

tumeur [tymœʀ] *nf* growth, tumour

tumulte [tymylt] *nm* commotion; **tumultueux, -euse** *adj* stormy, turbulent

tunique [tynik] *nf* tunic

Tunis [tynis] *n* Tunis

Tunisie [tynizi] *nf*: **la ~** Tunisia; **tunisien, ne** *adj* Tunisian ▷ *nm/f*: **Tunisien, ne** Tunisian

tunnel [tynɛl] *nm* tunnel; **le ~ sous la Manche** the Channel Tunnel

turbulent, e [tyʀbylɑ̃, -ɑ̃t] *adj* boisterous, unruly

turc, turque [tyʀk] *adj* Turkish ▷ *nm* *(Ling)* Turkish ▷ *nm/f*: **Turc, Turque** Turk/Turkish woman

turf [tyʀf] *nm* racing; **turfiste** *nm/f* racegoer

Turquie [tyʀki] *nf*: **la ~** Turkey

turquoise [tyʀkwaz] *nf, adj inv* turquoise

tutelle [tytɛl] *nf (Jur)* guardianship; *(Pol)* trusteeship; **sous la ~ de** *(fig)* under the supervision of

tuteur, -trice [tytœʀ, -tʀis] *nm/f (Jur)* guardian; *(de plante)* stake, support

tutoyer [tytwaje] /8/ *vt*: **~ qn** to address sb as "tu"

tuyau, x [tɥijo] *nm* pipe; *(flexible)* tube; *(fam)* tip; **~ d'arrosage** hosepipe; **~ d'échappement** exhaust pipe; **tuyauterie** *nf* piping *no pl*

TVA *sigle f* (= *taxe à ou sur la valeur ajoutée*) VAT

tweet [twit] *nm (aussi Internet: Twitter)* tweet; **tweeter** /1/ *vi (Internet: Twitter)* to tweet

tympan [tɛ̃pɑ̃] *nm (Anat)* eardrum

type [tip] *nm* type; *(fam)* chap, guy ▷ *adj* typical, standard

typé, e [tipe] *adj* ethnic *(euphémisme)*

typique [tipik] *adj* typical

tyran [tiʀɑ̃] *nm* tyrant; **tyrannique** *adj* tyrannical

tzigane [dzigan] *adj* gipsy, tzigane

U

ulcère [ylsɛʀ] nm ulcer
ultérieur, e [ylteʀjœʀ] adj later, subsequent; **remis à une date ~** postponed to a later date; **ultérieurement** adv later, subsequently
ultime [yltim] adj final

MOT-CLÉ

un, une [œ̃, yn] art indéf a; (devant voyelle) an; **un garçon/vieillard** an; **un garçon/vieillard** a boy/an old man; **une fille** a girl
▶ pron one; **l'un des meilleurs** one of the best; **l'un ..., l'autre** (the) one ..., the other; **les uns ..., les autres** some ..., others; **l'un et l'autre** both (of them); **l'un ou l'autre** either (of them); **l'un l'autre, les uns les autres** each other, one another; **pas un seul** not a single one; **un par un** one by one
▶ num one; **une pomme seulement** one apple only, just one apple
▶ nf: **la une** (Presse) the front page

unanime [ynanim] adj unanimous; **unanimité** nf: **à l'unanimité** unanimously
uni, e [yni] adj (ton, tissu) plain; (surface) smooth, even; (famille) close(-knit); (pays) united
unifier [ynifje] /7/ vt to unite, unify
uniforme [ynifɔʀm] adj uniform; (surface, ton) even ▶ nm uniform; **uniformiser** /1/ vt (systèmes) to standardize
union [ynjɔ̃] nf union; **~ de consommateurs** consumers' association; **~ libre: vivre en ~ libre** (en concubinage) to cohabit; **l'U~ européenne** the European Union; **l'U~ soviétique** the Soviet Union
unique [ynik] adj (seul) only; (exceptionnel) unique; **un prix/système ~** a single price/system; **fils/fille ~** only son/daughter, only child; **sens ~** one-way street; **uniquement** adv only, solely; (juste) only, merely
unir [yniʀ] /2/ vt (nations) to unite; (en mariage) to unite, join together; **s'unir** vi to unite; (en mariage) to be joined together
unitaire [yniteʀ] adj: **prix ~** unit price
unité [ynite] nf (harmonie, cohésion) unity; (Math) unit
univers [ynivɛʀ] nm universe; **universel, le** adj universal
universitaire [ynivɛʀsiteʀ] adj university cpd; (diplôme, études) academic, university cpd ▶ nm/f academic
université [ynivɛʀsite] nf university
urbain, e [yʀbɛ̃, -ɛn] adj urban, city cpd; town cpd; **urbanisme** nm town planning
urgence [yʀʒɑ̃s] nf urgency; (Méd etc) emergency; **d'~** adj emergency; ▶ adv as a matter of urgency; **service des ~s** emergency service

urgent, e [yʀʒɑ̃, -ɑ̃t] *adj* urgent
urine [yʀin] *nf* urine; **urinoir** *nm* (public) urinal
urne [yʀn] *nf* (*électorale*) ballot box; (*vase*) urn
urticaire [yʀtikɛʀ] *nf* nettle rash
us [ys] *nmpl*: **us et coutumes** (habits and) customs
usage [yza3] *nm* (*emploi, utilisation*) use; (*coutume*) custom; **à l'~** with use; **à l'~ de** (*pour*) for (use of); **en ~** in use; **hors d'~** out of service; **à ~ interne** (*Méd*) to be taken (internally); **à ~ externe** (*Méd*) for external use only; **usagé, e** *adj* (*usé*) worn; **usager, -ère** *nm/f* user
usé, e [yze] *adj* worn (down ou out ou away); (*banal: argument etc*) hackneyed
user [yze] /1/ *vt* (*outil*) to wear down; (*vêtement*) to wear out; (*matière*) to wear away; (*consommer: charbon etc*) to use; **s'user** *vi* (*tissu, vêtement*) to wear out; **~ de** (*moyen, procédé*) to use, employ; (*droit*) to exercise
usine [yzin] *nf* factory
usité, e [yzite] *adj* common
ustensile [ystɑ̃sil] *nm* implement; **~ de cuisine** kitchen utensil
usuel, le [yzɥɛl] *adj* everyday, common
usure [yzyʀ] *nf* wear
utérus [yteʀys] *nm* uterus, womb
utile [ytil] *adj* useful
utilisation [ytilizasjɔ̃] *nf* use
utiliser [ytilize] /1/ *vt* to use
utilitaire [ytilitɛʀ] *adj* utilitarian
utilité [ytilite] *nf* usefulness *no pl*; **de peu d'~** of little use ou help
utopie [ytɔpi] *nf* utopia

V

va [va] *vb voir* **aller**
vacance [vakɑ̃s] *nf* (*Admin*) vacancy; **vacances** *nfpl* holiday(s) *pl* (*BRIT*), vacation *sg* (*US*); **les grandes ~s** the summer holidays ou vacation; **prendre des/ses ~s** to take a holiday ou vacation/ one's holiday(s) ou vacation; **aller en ~s** to go on holiday ou vacation; **vacancier, -ière** *nm/f* holidaymaker
vacant, e [vakɑ̃, -ɑ̃t] *adj* vacant
vacarme [vakaʀm] *nm* row, din
vaccin [vaksɛ̃] *nm* vaccine; (*opération*) vaccination; **vaccination** *nf* vaccination; **vacciner** /1/ *vt* to vaccinate; **être vacciné** (*fig*) to be immune
vache [vaʃ] *nf* (*Zool*) cow; (*cuir*) cowhide ▷ *adj* (*fam*) rotten, mean; **vachement** *adv* (*fam*) really; **vacherie** *nf* (*action*) dirty trick; (*propos*) nasty remark

vaciller [vasije] /1/ vi to sway, wobble; (bougie, lumière) to flicker; (fig) to be failing, falter

VAE sigle m (= vélo (à assistance électrique) e-bike

va-et-vient [vaevjɛ̃] nm inv comings and goings pl

vagabond, e [vagabɔ̃, -ɔ̃d] adj wandering ▷ nm (rôdeur) tramp, vagrant; (voyageur) wanderer; **vagabonder** /1/ vi to roam, wander

vagin [vaʒɛ̃] nm vagina

vague [vag] nf wave ▷ adj vague; (regard) faraway; (manteau, robe) loose(-fitting); (quelconque): **un ~ bureau/cousin** some office/cousin or other; **~ de froid** cold spell

vaillant, e [vajɑ̃, -ɑ̃t] adj (courageux) gallant; (robuste) hale and hearty

vain, e [vɛ̃, vɛn] adj vain; **en ~** in vain

vaincre [vɛ̃kʀ] /42/ vt to defeat; (fig) to conquer, overcome; **vaincu, e** nm/f defeated party; **vainqueur** nm victor; (Sport) winner

vaisseau, x [veso] nm (Anat) vessel; (Navig) ship, vessel; **~ spatial** spaceship

vaisselier [vesəlje] nm dresser

vaisselle [vesɛl] nf (service) crockery; (plats etc à laver) (dirty) dishes pl; **faire la ~** to do the dishes

valable [valabl] adj valid; (acceptable) decent, worthwhile

valet [valɛ] nm valet; (Cartes) jack

valeur [valœʀ] nf (gén) value; (mérite) worth, merit; (Comm: titre) security; **valeurs** nfpl (morales) values; **mettre en ~** (fig) to highlight; to show off to advantage; **avoir de la ~** to be valuable; **prendre de la ~** to go up ou gain in value; **sans ~** worthless

valide [valid] adj (en bonne santé) fit; (valable) valid; **valider** /1/ vt to validate

valise [valiz] nf (suit)case; **faire sa ~** to pack one's (suit)case

vallée [vale] nf valley

vallon [valɔ̃] nm small valley

valoir [valwaʀ] /29/ vi (être valable) to hold, apply ▷ vt (prix, valeur, effort) to be worth; (causer): **~ qch à qn** to earn sb sth; **se valoir** to be of equal merit; (péj) to be two of a kind; **faire ~** (droits, prérogatives) to assert; **se faire ~** to make the most of o.s.; **à - sur** to be deducted from; **vaille que vaille** somehow or other; **cela ne me dit rien qui vaille** I don't like the look of it at all; **ce climat ne me vaut rien** this climate doesn't suit me; **~ la peine** to be worth the trouble, be worth it; **~ mieux: il vaut mieux se taire** it's better to say nothing; **ça ne vaut rien** it's worthless; **que vaut ce candidat?** how good is this applicant?

valse [vals] nf waltz

vandalisme [vɑ̃dalism] nm vandalism

vanille [vanij] nf vanilla

vanité [vanite] nf vanity; **vaniteux, -euse** adj vain, conceited

vanne [van] nf gate; (fam) dig

vantard, e [vɑ̃taʀ, -aʀd] adj boastful

vanter [vɑ̃te] /1/ vt to speak highly of, praise; **se vanter** vi to boast, brag; **se ~ de** to pride o.s. on; (péj) to boast of

vapeur [vapœʀ] nf steam; (émanation) vapour, fumes pl; **vapeurs** nfpl (bouffées) vapours; **à ~** steam-powered, steam cpd; **cuit à la ~** steamed; **vaporeux, -euse** adj (flou) hazy, misty; (léger) filmy

vaporisateur nm spray; **vaporiser** /1/ vt (parfum etc) to spray

vapoter [vapɔte] /1/ vi to smoke an e-cigarette

varappe [vaʀap] nf rock climbing

vareuse [vaʀøz] nf (blouson) pea jacket; (d'uniforme) tunic

variable [vaʀjabl] adj variable; (temps, humeur) changeable; (divers: résultats) varied, various

varice [vaʀis] nf varicose vein

varicelle [vaʀisɛl] nf chickenpox

V

varié, e [varje] adj varied; (divers) various; **hors-d'œuvre ~s** selection of hors d'œuvres

varier [varje] /7/ vi to vary; (temps, humeur) to change ▷ vt to vary; **variété** nf variety; **spectacle de variétés** variety show

variole [varjɔl] nf smallpox

Varsovie [varsɔvi] n Warsaw

vas [va] vb voir **aller**; **~-y!** go on!

vase [vɑz] nm vase ▷ nf silt, mud; **vaseux, -euse** adj silty, muddy; (fig: confus) woolly, hazy; (: fatigué) peaky

vasistas [vazistas] nm fanlight

vaste [vast] adj vast, immense

vautour [votuʀ] nm vulture

vautrer [votʀe] /1/: **se vautrer** vi: **se ~ dans** to wallow in; **se ~ sur** to sprawl on

va-vite [vavit]: **à la ~** adv in a rush

VDQS sigle m (= vin délimité de qualité supérieure) label guaranteeing quality of wine

veau, x [vo] nm (Zool) calf; (Culin) veal; (peau) calfskin

vécu, e [veky] pp de **vivre**

vedette [vədɛt] nf (artiste etc) star; (canot) patrol boat; (police) launch

végétal, e, -aux [veʒetal, -o] adj vegetable ▷ nm vegetable, plant; **végétalien, ne** adj, nm/f vegan

végétarien, ne [veʒetaʀjɛ̃, -ɛn] adj, nm/f vegetarian

végétation [veʒetasjɔ̃] nf vegetation; **végétations** nfpl (Méd) adenoids

véhicule [veikyl] nm vehicle; **~ utilitaire** commercial vehicle

veille [vɛj] nf (Psych) wakefulness; (jour): **la ~** the day before; **la ~ au soir** the previous evening; **la ~ de** the day before; **la ~ de Noël** Christmas Eve; **la ~ du jour de l'An** New Year's Eve; **à la ~ de** on the eve of

veillée [veje] nf (soirée) evening; (réunion) evening gathering; **~ (funèbre)** wake

veiller [veje] /1/ vi to stay ou sit up ▷ vt (malade, mort) to watch over, sit up with; **~ à** to attend to, see to; **~ à ce que** to make sure that; **~ sur** to keep a watch ou an eye on; **veilleur** nm: **veilleur de nuit** night watchman; **veilleuse** nf (lampe) night light; (Auto) sidelight; (flamme) pilot light

veinard, e [vɛnaʀ, -aʀd] nm/f lucky devil

veine [vɛn] nf (Anat, du bois etc) vein; (filon) vein, seam; **avoir de la ~** (fam) (chance) to be lucky

véliplanchiste [veliplɑ̃ʃist] nm/f windsurfer

vélo [velo] nm bike, cycle; **faire du ~** to go cycling; **vélomoteur** nm moped

velours [v(ə)luʀ] nm velvet; **~ côtelé** corduroy; **velouté, e** adj velvety ▷ nm: **velouté d'asperges/ de tomates** cream of asparagus/ tomato soup

velu, e [vɛly] adj hairy

vendange [vɑ̃dɑ̃ʒ] nf (aussi: ~s) grape harvest; **vendanger** /3/ vi to harvest the grapes

vendeur, -euse [vɑ̃dœʀ, -øz] nm/f shop ou sales assistant ▷ nm (Jur) vendor, seller

vendre [vɑ̃dʀ] /41/ vt to sell; **~ qch à qn** to sell sb sth; **"à ~"** "for sale"

vendredi [vɑ̃dʀədi] nm Friday; **V~ saint** Good Friday

vénéneux, -euse [venenø, -øz] adj poisonous

vénérien, ne [veneʀjɛ̃, -ɛn] adj venereal

vengeance [vɑ̃ʒɑ̃s] nf vengeance no pl, revenge no pl

venger [vɑ̃ʒe] /3/ vt to avenge; **se venger** vi to avenge o.s.; **se ~ de qch** to avenge o.s. for sth; to take one's revenge for sth; **se ~ de qn** to take revenge on sb; **se ~ sur** to take revenge on

venimeux, -euse [vənimø, -øz] adj poisonous, venomous, (fig: haineux) venomous, vicious

venin [vənɛ̃] nm venom, poison

venir [v(ə)niʀ] /22/ vi to come; **~ de** to come from; **~ de faire: je viens d'y aller/de le voir** I've just been there/seen him; **s'il vient à pleuvoir** if it should rain; **où veux-tu en ~** what are you getting at?; **faire ~** (docteur, plombier) to call (out)

vent [vɑ̃] nm wind; **il y a du ~** it's windy; **c'est du ~** it's all hot air; **dans le ~** (fam) trendy

vente [vɑ̃t] nf sale; **la ~** (activité) selling; (secteur) sales pl; **mettre en ~** to put on sale; (objets personnels) to put up for sale; **~ aux enchères** auction sale; **~ de charité** jumble (BRIT) ou rummage (US) sale

venteux, -euse [vɑ̃tø, -øz] adj windy

ventilateur [vɑ̃tilatœʀ] nm fan

ventiler [vɑ̃tile] /1/ vt to ventilate

ventouse [vɑ̃tuz] nf (de caoutchouc) suction pad

ventre [vɑ̃tʀ] nm (Anat) stomach; (fig) belly; **avoir mal au ~** to have (a) stomach ache

venu, e [v(ə)ny] pp de **venir** ▷ adj: **être mal ~ à** ou **de faire** to have no grounds for doing, be in no position to do; **mal ~** ill-timed; **bien ~** timely

ver [vɛʀ] nm worm; (des fruits etc) maggot; (du bois) woodworm no pl; **~ luisant** glow-worm; **~ à soie** silkworm; **~ solitaire** tapeworm; **~ de terre** earthworm

verbe [vɛʀb] nm verb

verdâtre [vɛʀdɑtʀ] adj greenish

verdict [vɛʀdik(t)] nm verdict

verdir [vɛʀdiʀ] /2/ vi, vt to turn green; **verdure** nf greenery

véreux, -euse [veʀø, -øz] adj wormeaten; (malhonnête) shady, corrupt

verge [vɛʀʒ] nf (Anat) penis

verger [vɛʀʒe] nm orchard

verglacé, e [vɛʀglase] adj icy, iced-over

verglas [vɛʀgla] nm (black) ice

véridique [veʀidik] adj truthful

vérification [veʀifikɑsjɔ̃] nf checking no pl, check

vérifier [veʀifje] /7/ vt to check; (corroborer) to confirm, bear out

véritable [veʀitabl] adj real; (ami, amour) true; **un ~ désastre** an absolute disaster

vérité [veʀite] nf truth; **en ~** to tell the truth

verlan [vɛʀlɑ̃] nm (back) slang

vermeil, le [vɛʀmɛj] adj ruby red

vermine [vɛʀmin] nf vermin pl

vermoulu, e [vɛʀmuly] adj wormeaten

verni, e [vɛʀni] adj (fam) lucky; **cuir ~** patent leather

vernir [vɛʀniʀ] /2/ vt (bois, tableau, ongles) to varnish; (poterie) to glaze; **vernis** nm (enduit) varnish; glaze; (fig) veneer; **vernis à ongles** nail varnish (BRIT) ou polish; **vernissage** nm (d'une exposition) preview

vérole [veʀɔl] nf (variole) smallpox

verre [vɛʀ] nm glass; (de lunettes) lens sg; **boire** ou **prendre un ~** to have a drink; **~s de contact** contact lenses; **verrière** nf (grand vitrage) window; (toit vitré) glass roof

verrou [veʀu] nm (targette) bolt; **mettre qn sous les ~s** to put sb behind bars; **verrouillage** nm locking mechanism; **verrouillage central** ou **centralisé** central locking; **verrouiller** /1/ vt to bolt; to lock

verrue [veʀy] nf wart

vers [vɛʀ] nm line ▷ nmpl (poésie) verse sg ▷ prép (en direction de) toward(s); (près de) around (about); (temporel) about, around

versant [vɛʀsɑ̃] nm slopes pl, side

versatile [vɛʀsatil] adj fickle, changeable

verse [vɛʀs]: **à ~** adv: **il pleut à ~** it's pouring (with rain)

Verseau [vɛʀso] nm: le ~ Aquarius

versement [vɛʀsəmɑ̃] nm payment; **en trois ~s** in three instalments

verser [vɛʀse] /1/ vt (liquide, grains) to pour; (larmes, sang) to shed; (argent) to pay; **~ sur un compte** to pay into an account

version [vɛʀsjɔ̃] nf version; (Scol) translation (into the mother tongue); **film en ~ originale** film in the original language

verso [vɛʀso] nm back; **voir au ~** see over(leaf)

vert, e [vɛʀ, vɛʀt] adj green; (vin) young; (vigoureux) sprightly ▷ nm green; **les V~s** (Pol) the Greens

vertèbre [vɛʀtɛbʀ] nf vertebra

vertement [vɛʀtəmɑ̃] adv (réprimander) sharply

vertical, e, -aux [vɛʀtikal, -o] adj vertical; **verticale** nf vertical; **à la verticale** vertically; **verticalement** adv vertically

vertige [vɛʀtiʒ] nm (peur du vide) vertigo; (étourdissement) dizzy spell; (fig) fever; **vertigineux, -euse** adj breathtaking

vertu [vɛʀty] nf virtue; **en ~ de** in accordance with; **vertueux, -euse** adj virtuous

verve [vɛʀv] nf witty eloquence; **être en ~** to be in brilliant form

verveine [vɛʀvɛn] nf (Bot) verbena, vervain; (infusion) verbena tea

vésicule [vezikyl] nf vesicle; **~ biliaire** gall-bladder

vessie [vesi] nf bladder

veste [vɛst] nf jacket; **~ droite/ croisée** single-/double-breasted jacket

vestiaire [vɛstjɛʀ] nm (au théâtre etc) cloakroom; (de stade etc) changing-room (Brit), locker-room (US)

vestibule [vɛstibyl] nm hall

vestige [vɛstiʒ] nm relic; (fig) vestige; **vestiges** nmpl (d'une ville) remains

vestimentaire [vɛstimɑ̃tɛʀ] adj (détail) of dress; (élégance) sartorial; **dépenses ~s** clothing expenditure

veston [vɛstɔ̃] nm jacket

vêtement [vɛtmɑ̃] nm garment, item of clothing; **vêtements** nmpl clothes

vétérinaire [veteʀinɛʀ] nm/f vet, veterinary surgeon

vêtir [vetiʀ] /20/ vt to clothe, dress

vêtu, e [vety] pp de **vêtir** ▷ adj: **~ de** dressed in, wearing

vétuste [vetyst] adj ancient, timeworn

veuf, veuve [vœf, vœv] adj widowed ▷ nm/f widow

vexant, e [vɛksɑ̃, -ɑ̃t] adj (contrariant) annoying; (blessant) upsetting

vexation [vɛksasjɔ̃] nf humiliation

vexer [vɛkse] /1/ vt to hurt; **se vexer** vi to be offended

viable [vjabl] adj viable; (économie, industrie etc) sustainable

viande [vjɑ̃d] nf meat; **je ne mange pas de ~** I don't eat meat

vibrer [vibʀe] /1/ vi to vibrate; (son, voix) to be vibrant; (fig) to be stirred; **faire ~** (to cause to) vibrate; to stir, thrill

vice [vis] nm vice; (défaut) fault; **~ de forme** legal flaw ou irregularity

vicié, e [visje] adj (air) polluted, tainted; (Jur) invalidated

vicieux, -euse [visjø, -øz] adj (pervers) dirty(-minded); (méchant) nasty ▷ nm/f lecher

vicinal, e, -aux [visinal, -o] adj: **chemin ~** byroad, byway

victime [viktim] nf victim; (d'accident) casualty

victoire [viktwaʀ] nf victory

victuailles [viktɥaj] nfpl provisions

vidange [vidɑ̃ʒ] nf (d'un fossé, réservoir) emptying; (Auto) oil change; (de lavabo: bonde) waste outlet; **vidanges** nfpl (matières) sewage sg; **vidanger** /3/ vt to empty

vide [vid] adj empty ▷ nm (Physique) vacuum; (espace) (empty) space, gap; (futilité, néant) void; **emballé sous ~** vacuum-packed; **avoir peur du ~** to be afraid of heights; **à ~** (sans occupants) empty; (sans charge) unladen

vidéo [video] /1/ nf video; **cassette ~** video cassette; **vidéoclip** nm music video; **vidéoconférence** nf videoconference

vide-ordures [vidɔʀdyʀ] nm inv (rubbish) chute

vider [vide] /1/ vt to empty; (Culin: volaille, poisson) to gut, clean out; **se vider** vi to empty; **~ les lieux** to quit ou vacate the premises; **videur** nm (de boîte de nuit) bouncer

vie [vi] nf life; **être en ~** to be alive; **sans ~** lifeless; **à ~** for life; **que faites-vous dans la ~?** what do you do?

vieil [vjɛj] adj m voir **vieux**; **vieillard** nm old man; **vieille** adj f, nf voir **vieux**; **vieilleries** nfpl old things ou stuff sg; **vieillesse** nf old age; **vieillir** /2/ vi (prendre de l'âge) to grow old; (population, vin) to age; (doctrine, auteur) to become dated ▷ vt to age; **se vieillir** to make o.s. older; **vieillissement** nm growing old; ageing

Vienne [vjɛn] n Vienna

viens [vjɛ̃] vb voir **venir**

vierge adj virgin; (page) clean, blank ▷ nf virgin; (signe): **la V~** Virgo

Viêtnam, **Vietnam** [vjɛtnam] nm: **le ~** Vietnam; **vietnamien, ne** adj Vietnamese ▷ nm/f: **V~, ne** Vietnamese

vieux (vieil), **vieille** [vjø, vjɛj] adj old ▷ nm/f old man/woman ▷ nmpl: **les ~** (péj) old people; **un petit ~** a little old man; **mon ~/ ma vieille** (fam) old man/girl; **prendre un coup de ~** to put years on; **~ garçon** bachelor; **~ jeu** adj inv old-fashioned

vif, **vive** [vif, viv] adj (animé) lively; (alerte) sharp; (lumière, couleur) brilliant; (air) crisp; (vent, émotion) keen; (fort: regret, déception) great, deep; (vivant): **brûlé ~** burnt alive; **de vive voix** personally; **avoir l'esprit ~** to be quick-witted; **piquer qn au ~** to cut sb to the quick; **à ~** (plaie) open; **avoir les nerfs à ~** to be on edge

vigne [viɲ] nf (plante) vine; (plantation) vineyard; **vigneron** nm wine grower

vignette [viɲɛt] nf (pour voiture) ≈ (road) tax disc (BRIT), ≈ license plate sticker (US); (sur médicament) price label (on medicines for reimbursement by Social Security)

vignoble [viɲɔbl] nm (plantation) vineyard; (vignes d'une région) vineyards pl

vigoureux, **-euse** [vigurø, -øz] adj vigorous, robust

vigueur [vigœr] nf vigour; **être/ entrer en ~** to be in force/come into force; **en ~** current

vilain, **e** [vilɛ̃, -ɛn] adj (laid) ugly; (affaire, blessure) nasty; (pas sage: enfant) naughty; **~ mot** bad word

villa [vila] nf (détached) house; **~ en multipropriété** time-share villa

village [vilaʒ] nm village; **villageois, e** adj village cpd ▷ nm/f villager

ville [vil] nf town; (importante) city; (administration): **la ~** ≈ the (town) council; **~ d'eaux** spa; **~ nouvelle** new town

vin [vɛ̃] nm wine; **avoir le ~ gai/ triste** to get happy/miserable after a few drinks; **~ d'honneur** reception (with wine and snacks); **~ ordinaire** ou **de table** table wine; **~ de pays** local wine

vinaigre [vinɛgr] nm vinegar; **vinaigrette** nf vinaigrette, French dressing

vindicatif, **-ive** [vɛ̃dikatif, -iv] adj vindictive

V

vingt [vɛ̃, vɛ̃t] (2nd pron used when followed by a vowel) num twenty; **~-quatre heures sur ~-quatre** twenty-four hours a day, round the clock; **vingtaine** nf: **une vingtaine (de)** around twenty, twenty or so; **vingtième** num twentieth

vinicole [vinikɔl] adj wine cpd; wine-growing

vinyle [vinil] nm vinyl

viol [vjɔl] nm (d'une femme) rape; (d'un lieu sacré) violation

violacé, e [vjɔlase] adj purplish, mauvish

violemment [vjɔlamɑ̃] adv violently

violence [vjɔlɑ̃s] nf violence

violent, e [vjɔlɑ̃, -ɑ̃t] adj violent; (remède) drastic

violer [vjɔle] /1/ vt (femme) to rape; (sépulture) to desecrate; (loi, traité) to violate

violet, te [vjɔlɛ, -ɛt] adj, nm purple, mauve ▷ nf (fleur) violet

violon [vjɔlɔ̃] nm violin; (fam: prison) lock-up; **~ d'Ingres** (artistic) hobby; **violoncelle** nm cello; **violoniste** nm/f violinist

virage [viraʒ] nm (d'un véhicule) turn; (d'une route, piste) bend

viral, e, -aux [viral, -o] adj (aussi Inform) viral

virée [vire] nf (fam) run; (à pied) walk; (longue) hike

virement [virmɑ̃] nm (Comm) transfer

virer [vire] /1/ vt (Comm) to transfer; (fam: renvoyer) to sack ▷ vi to turn; (Chimie) to change colour (BRIT) ou color (US); **~ au bleu** to turn blue; **~ de bord** to tack

virevolter [virvɔlte] /1/ vi to twirl around

virgule [virgyl] nf comma; (Math) point

viril, e [viril] adj (propre à l'homme) masculine; (énergique, courageux) manly, virile

virtuel, le [virtɥɛl] adj potential; (théorique) virtual

virtuose [virtɥoz] nm/f (Mus) virtuoso; (gén) master

virus [virys] nm virus

vis vb [vi] voir **voir, vivre** ▷ nf [vis] screw

visa [viza] nm (sceau) stamp; (validation de passeport) visa

visage [vizaʒ] nm face

vis-à-vis [vizavi]: **~ de** prép towards; **en ~** facing ou opposite each other

visée [vize] nf aiming; **visées** nfpl (intentions) designs

viser [vize] /1/ vi to aim ▷ vt to aim at; (concerner) to be aimed ou directed at; (apposer un visa sur) to stamp, visa; **~ à qch/faire** to aim at sth/at doing ou to do

visibilité [vizibilite] nf visibility

visible [vizibl] adj visible; (disponible): **est-il ~?** can he see me?, will he see visitors?

visière [vizjɛr] nf (de casquette) peak; (qui s'attache) eyeshade

vision [vizjɔ̃] nf vision; (sens) (eye)sight, vision; (fait de voir): **la ~ de** the sight of; **visionneuse** nf viewer

visiophone [vizjɔfɔn] nm videophone

visite [vizit] nf visit; **~ médicale** medical examination; **~ accompagnée** ou **guidée** guided tour; **faire une ~ à qn** to call on sb, pay sb a visit; **rendre ~ à qn** to visit sb, pay sb a visit; **être en ~ (chez qn)** to be visiting (sb); **avoir de la ~** to have visitors; **heures de ~** (hôpital, prison) visiting hours

visiter [vizite] /1/ vt to visit; **visiteur, -euse** nm/f visitor

vison [vizɔ̃] nm mink

visser [vise] /1/ vt: **~ qch** (fixer, serrer) to screw sth on

visuel, le [vizɥɛl] adj visual

vital, e, -aux [vital, -o] adj vital

vitamine [vitamin] nf vitamin

vite [vit] adv (rapidement) quickly, fast; (sans délai) quickly; soon; **~!** quick!; **faire ~** to be quick

vitesse [vitɛs] nf speed; (*Auto: dispositif*) gear; **prendre de la ~** to pick up *ou* gather speed; **à toute ~** at full *ou* top speed; **en ~** quickly

LIMITE DE VITESSE

The speed limit in France is 50 km/h in built-up areas, 90 km/h on main roads, and 130 km/h on motorways (110 km/h when it is raining).

viticulteur [vitikyltœr] nm wine grower

vitrage [vitraʒ] nm: **double ~** double glazing

vitrail, -aux [vitraj, -o] nm stained-glass window

vitre [vitr] nf (window) pane; (*de portière, voiture*) window; **vitré, e** adj glass cpd

vitrine [vitrin] nf (shop) window; (*petite armoire*) display cabinet; **en ~** in the window

vivable [vivabl] adj (*personne*) livable-with; (*maison*) fit to live in

vivace [vivas] adj (*arbre, plante*) hardy; (*fig*) enduring

vivacité [vivasite] nf liveliness, vivacity

vivant, e [vivɑ̃, -ɑ̃t] adj (*qui vit*) living, alive; (*animé*) lively; (*preuve, exemple*) living ▷ nm: **du ~ de qn** in sb's lifetime; **les ~s et les morts** the living and the dead

vive [viv] adj f voir **vif** ▷ vb voir **vivre** ▷ excl: **~ le roi!** long live the king!; **vivement** adv sharply ▷ excl: **vivement les vacances!** roll on the holidays!

vivier [vivje] nm (*au restaurant etc*) fish tank; (*étang*) fishpond

vivifiant, e [vivifjɑ̃, -ɑ̃t] adj invigorating

vivoter [vivɔte] /1/ vi (*personne*) to scrape a living, get by; (*fig: affaire etc*) to struggle along

vivre [vivr] /46/ vi, vt to live; **vivres** nmpl provisions, food supplies; **il vit encore** he is still alive; **se laisser ~** to take life as it comes; **ne plus ~** (*être anxieux*) to live on one's nerves; **il a vécu** (*eu une vie aventureuse*) he has seen life; **être facile à ~** to be easy to get on with; **faire ~ qn** (*pourvoir à sa subsistance*) to provide (a living) for sb; **~ de** to live on

vlan [vlɑ̃] excl wham!, bang!

VO sigle f = **version originale**; **voir un film en VO** to see a film in its original language

vocabulaire [vɔkabylɛr] nm vocabulary

vocation [vɔkasjɔ̃] nf vocation, calling

vœu, x [vø] nm wish; (*à Dieu*) vow; **faire ~ de** to take a vow of; **avec tous nos ~x** with every good wish *ou* our best wishes

vogue [vɔg] nf fashion, vogue; **en ~** in fashion, in vogue

voici [vwasi] prép (*pour introduire, désigner*) here is (+ *sg*); here are (+ *pl*); **et ~ que ...** and now it (*ou* he) ...; *voir aussi* **voilà**

voie [vwa] nf way; (*Rail*) track, line; (*Auto*) lane; **par ~ buccale** *ou* **orale** orally; **être en bonne ~** to be shaping *ou* going well; **mettre qn sur la ~** to put sb on the right track; **être en ~ d'achèvement/de rénovation** to be nearing completion/in the process of renovation; **à ~ unique** single-track; **route à deux/trois ~s** two-/three-lane road; **~ express** expressway; **~ ferrée** track; railway line (BRIT), railroad (US); **~ de garage** (*Rail*) siding; **la ~ lactée** the Milky Way; **la ~ publique** the public highway

voilà [vwala] prép (*en désignant*) there is (+ *sg*); there are (+ *pl*); **les ~** *ou* **voici** here *ou* there they are; **en ~** *ou* **voici un** here's one, there's one; **voici mon frère et ~ ma sœur** this is my brother and that's my sister; **~ ou voici deux ans** two years ago; **~ ou voici deux ans que** it's two years since; **et ~!** there we are!; **~ tout** that's all; **~ ou voici!** (en offrant etc) "there ou here you are"; **tiens!** look! there's Paul

voile [vwal] nm vel; (tissu léger) ▷ nf sail; (sport) sailing; **voiler** /1/ vt to veil; (fausser: roue) to buckle; (: bois) to warp; **se voiler** vi (lune, regard) to mist over; (voix) to become husky; (roue, disque) to buckle; (planche) to warp; **voilier** nm sailing ship; (de plaisance) sailing boat; **voilure** nf (de voilier) sails pl

voir [vwar] /30/ vi, vt to see; **se voir**: **cela se voit** (c'est visible) that's obvious, it shows; **faire ~ qch à qn** to show sb sth; **en faire ~ à qn** (fig) to give sb a hard time; **ne pas pouvoir ~ qn** not to be able to stand sb; **voyons!** let's see now; (indignation etc) come (along) now!; **ça n'a rien à ~ avec lui** that has nothing to do with him

voire [vwar] adv or even

voisin, e [vwazɛ̃, -in] adj (proche) neighbouring; next; (ressemblant) connected ▷ nm/f neighbour; **voisinage** nm (proximité) proximity; (environs) vicinity; (quartier, voisins) neighbourhood

voiture [vwatyʀ] nf car; (wagon) coach, carriage; **~ de course** racing car; **~ de sport** sports car

voix [vwa] nf voice; (Pol) vote; **à haute ~** aloud; **à ~ basse** in a low voice; **à deux/quatre ~** (Mus) in two/four parts; **avoir ~ au chapitre** to have a say in the matter

vol [vɔl] nm (trajet, voyage, groupe d'oiseaux) flight; (mode d'appropriation) theft, stealing; (larcin) theft; **à ~ d'oiseau** as the crow flies; **au ~: attraper qch au ~** to catch sth as it flies past; **en ~** in flight; **~ libre** hang-gliding; **~ à main armée** armed

robbery; **~ régulier** scheduled flight; **~ à voile** gliding

volage [vɔlaʒ] adj fickle

volaille [vɔlaj] nf (oiseaux) poultry pl; (viande) poultry no pl; (oiseau) fowl

volant, e [vɔlɑ̃, -ɑ̃t] adj flying ▷ nm (d'automobile) (steering) wheel; (de commande) wheel; (objet lancé) shuttlecock; (bande de tissu) flounce

volcan [vɔlkɑ̃] nm volcano

volée [vɔle] nf (Tennis) volley; **à la ~: rattraper à la ~** to catch in midair; **à toute ~** (sonner les cloches) vigorously; (lancer un projectile) with full force

voler [vɔle] /1/ vi (avion, oiseau, fig) to fly; (voleur) to steal ▷ vt (objet) to steal; (personne) to rob; **~ qch à qn** to steal sth from sb; **on m'a volé mon portefeuille** (BRIT) ou my billfold (US) has been stolen; **il ne l'a pas volé!** he asked for it!

volet [vɔle] nm (de fenêtre) shutter; (Aviat) flap; (de feuillet, document) section; (fig: d'un plan) facet

voleur, -euse [vɔlœʀ, -øz] nm/f thief ▷ adj thieving; **"au ~!"** "stop thief!"

volley [vɔle], **volley-ball** [vɔlebol] nm volleyball

volontaire [vɔlɔ̃tɛʀ] adj (acte, activité) voluntary; (délibéré) deliberate; (caractère, personne: décidé) self-willed ▷ nm/f volunteer

volonté [vɔlɔ̃te] nf (faculté de vouloir) will; (énergie, fermeté) will(power); (souhait, désir) wish; **se servir/boire à ~** to take/drink as much as one likes; **bonne ~** goodwill, willingness; **mauvaise ~** lack of goodwill, unwillingness

volontiers [vɔlɔ̃tje] adv (avec plaisir) willingly, gladly; (habituellement, souvent) readily, willingly; **"~"** "with pleasure"

volt [vɔlt] nm volt

volte-face [vɔltafas] nf inv: **faire ~** to do an about-turn

voltige [vɔltiʒ] nf (Équitation) trick riding; (au cirque) acrobatics sg;

voltiger [vɔltiʒe] /3/ vi to flutter (about)

volubile [vɔlybil] adj voluble

volume [vɔlym] nm volume; (Géom: solide) solid; **volumineux, -euse** adj voluminous, bulky

volupté [vɔlypte] nf sensual delight ou pleasure

vomi [vɔmi] nm vomit; **vomir** /2/ vi to vomit, be sick ▷ vt to vomit, bring up; (fig) to belch out, spew out; (exécrer) to loathe, abhor

vorace [vɔʀas] adj voracious

vos [vo] adj poss voir **votre**

vote [vɔt] nm vote; **~ par correspondance/procuration** postal/proxy vote; **voter** /1/ vi to vote ▷ vt (loi, décision) to vote for

votre [vɔtʀ] (pl **vos**) adj poss your

vôtre [votʀ] pron: **le ~, la ~, les ~s** yours; **les ~s** (fig) your family ou folks; **à la ~** (toast) your (good) health!

vouer [vwe] /1/ vt: **~ sa vie/son temps à** (étude, cause etc) to devote one's life/time to; **~ une haine/ amitié éternelle à qn** to vow undying hatred/friendship to sb

MOT-CLÉ

vouloir [vulwaʀ] /31/ vt **1** (exiger, désirer) to want; **vouloir faire/ que qn fasse** to want to do/sb to do; **voulez-vous du thé?** would you like ou do you want some tea?; **que me veut-il?** what does he want with me?; **sans le vouloir** (involontairement) without meaning to, unintentionally; **je voudrais ceci/faire** I would ou I'd like this/to do; **le hasard a voulu que ...** as fate would have it, ...; **la tradition veut que ...** tradition demands that ...

2 (consentir): **je veux bien** (bonne volonté) I'll be happy to; (concession) fair enough, that's fine; **oui, si on veut** (en quelque sorte) yes, if you like; **veuillez attendre** please

wait; **veuillez agréer ...** (formule épistolaire) yours faithfully

3: **en vouloir à qn** to bear sb a grudge; **s'en vouloir (de)** to be annoyed with o.s. (for); **il en veut à mon argent** he's after my money

4: **vouloir de: l'entreprise ne veut plus de lui** the firm doesn't want him any more; **elle ne veut pas de son aide** she doesn't want his help

5: **vouloir dire** to mean

▷ nm: **le bon vouloir de qn** sb's goodwill; sb's pleasure

voulu, e [vuly] pp de **vouloir** ▷ adj (requis) required, requisite; (délibéré) deliberate, intentional

vous [vu] pron you; (objet indirect) (to) you; (réfléchi: sg) yourself; (: pl) yourselves; (réciproque) each other ▷ nm: **employer le ~** (vouvoyer) to use the "vous" form; **~-même** yourself; **~-mêmes** yourselves

vouvoyer [vuvwaje] /8/ vt: **~ qn** to address sb as "vous"

voyage [vwajaʒ] nm journey, trip; (fait de voyager): **le ~** travel(ling); **partir/être en ~** to go off/be away on a journey ou trip; **faire bon ~** to have a good journey; **~ d'agrément/ d'affaires** pleasure/business trip; **~ de noces** honeymoon; **~ organisé** package tour

voyager [vwajaʒe] /3/ vi to travel; **voyageur, -euse** nm/f traveller; (passager) passenger; **voyageur (de commerce)** commercial traveller

voyant, e [vwajã, -ãt] adj (couleur) loud, gaudy ▷ nm (signal) (warning) light

voyelle [vwajɛl] nf vowel

voyou [vwaju] nm hoodlum

vrac [vʀak]: **en ~** adv loose; (Comm) in bulk

vrai, e [vʀe] adj (véridique: récit, faits) true; (non factice: authentique) real; **à ~ dire** to tell the truth; **vraiment** adv really;

vraisemblable adj likely; (excuse) plausible; **vraisemblablement** adv in all likelihood, very likely; **vraisemblance** nf likelihood; (romanesque) verisimilitude

vrombir [vʀɔ̃biʀ] /2/ vi to hum

VRP sigle m (= voyageur, représentant, placier) (sales) rep (fam)

VTT sigle m (= vélo tout-terrain) mountain bike

vu¹ [vy] prép (en raison de) in view of; **vu que** in view of the fact that

vu², e [vy] pp de **voir** ▷ adj: **bien/mal vu** (personne) well/poorly thought of

vue [vy] nf (sens, faculté) (eye)sight; (panorama, image, photo) view; **la ~ de** (spectacle) the sight of; **vues** nfpl (idées) views; (dessein) designs; **perdre la ~** to lose one's (eye)sight; **perdre de ~** to lose sight of; **hors de ~** out of sight; **à première ~** at first sight; **tirer à ~** to shoot on sight; **à ~ d'œil** visibly; **avoir ~ sur** to have a view of; **en ~** (visible) in sight; (célèbre) in the public eye; **en ~ de faire** with a view to doing; **~ d'ensemble** overall view

vulgaire [vylgɛʀ] adj (grossier) vulgar, coarse; (trivial) commonplace, mundane; (péj: quelconque): **de ~s touristes/chaises de cuisine** common tourists/kitchen chairs; (Bot, Zool: non latin) common; **vulgariser** /1/ vt to popularize

vulnérable [vylneʀabl] adj vulnerable

W

wagon [vagɔ̃] nm (de voyageurs) carriage; (de marchandises) truck, wagon; **wagon-lit** nm sleeper, sleeping car; **wagon-restaurant** nm restaurant ou dining car

wallon, ne [walɔ̃, -ɔn] adj Walloon ▷ nm (Ling) Walloon ▷ nm/f: **W~, ne** Walloon

watt [wat] nm watt

WC [vese] nmpl toilet sg

Web [wɛb] nm inv: **le ~** the (World Wide) Web; **webcam** nf webcam; **webmaster, webmestre** nm/f webmaster

week-end [wikɛnd] nm weekend

western [wɛstɛʀn] nm western

whisky [wiski] (pl **whiskies**) nm whisky

wifi [wifi] nm inv wifi

WWW sigle m (= World Wide Web) WWW

xénophobe [gzenɔfɔb] *adj*
xenophobic ▷ *nm/f* xenophobe
xérès [gzeʀɛs] *nm* sherry
xylophone [gziloʁn] *nm* xylophone

y [i] *adv (à cet endroit)* there; *(dessus)* on
it *(ou* them); *(dedans)* in it *(ou* them)
▷ *pron (about ou on ou of)* it *(vérifier la
syntaxe du verbe employé)*: **j'y pense**
I'm thinking about it; **ça y est!** that's
it!; *voir aussi* **aller, avoir**
yacht [jɔt] *nm* yacht
yaourt [jauʀt] *nm* yogurt; **~ nature/
aux fruits** plain/fruit yogurt
yeux [jø] *nmpl de* **œil**
yoga [jɔga] *nm* yoga
yoghourt [jɔguʀt] *nm* = **yaourt**
yougoslave [jugɔslav] *adj*
Yugoslav(ian) ▷ *nm/f:* **Y~**
Yugoslav(ian)
Yougoslavie [jugɔslavi] *nf:* **la
~** Yugoslavia; **l'ex-~** the former
Yugoslavia

Z

zone [zon] *nf* zone, area;
  (*quartiers pauvres*): **la ~** the slums;
  ~ bleue ≈ restricted parking area;
  ~ industrielle (ZI) industrial estate
zoo [zoo] *nm* zoo
zoologie [zɔɔlɔʒi] *nf* zoology;
  zoologique *adj* zoological
zut [zyt] *excl* dash (it)! (BRIT), nuts!
  (US)

zapper [zape] /1/ *vi* to zap
zapping [zapiŋ] *nm*: **faire du ~** to
  flick through the channels
zèbre [zɛbʀ] *nm* (*Zool*) zebra; **zébré, e**
  adj striped, streaked
zèle [zɛl] *nm* zeal; **faire du ~** (*péj*) to
  be over-zealous; **zélé, e** *adj* zealous
zéro [zero] *nm* zero, nought (BRIT);
  au-dessous de ~ below zero
  (Centigrade), below freezing; **partir
  de ~** to start from scratch; **trois
  (buts) à ~** three (goals to) nil
zeste [zɛst] *nm* peel, zest
zézayer [zezeje] /8/ *vi* to have a lisp
zigzag [zigzag] *nm* zigzag; **zigzaguer**
  /1/ *vi* to zigzag (along)
Zimbabwe [zimbabwe] *nm*: **le ~**
  Zimbabwe
zinc [zɛ̃g] *nm* (*Chimie*) zinc
zipper [zipe] /1/ *vt* (*Inform*) to zip
zizi [zizi] *nm* (*fam*) willy
zodiaque [zɔdjak] *nm* zodiac
zona [zona] *nm* shingles *sg*

Phrasefinder

Phrases utiles

TOPICS | THÈMES

TOPICS | THÈMES

Hello!	Bonjour !
Good evening!	Bonsoir !
Good night!	Bonne nuit !
Goodbye!	Au revoir !
What's your name?	Comment vous appelez-vous ?
My name is ...	Je m'appelle ...
This is ...	Je vous présente ...
my wife.	*ma femme.*
my husband.	*mon mari.*
my partner.	*mon compagnon/*
	ma compagne.
Where are you from?	D'où venez-vous ?
I come from ...	Je suis de ...
How are you?	Comment allez-vous ?
Fine, thanks.	Bien, merci.
And you?	Et vous ?
Do you speak French?	Parlez-vous français ?
I don't understand English.	Je ne comprends pas l'anglais.
Thanks very much!	Merci beaucoup !
Pleasure to meet you.	Enchanté(e) !
I'm French.	Je suis français(e).
What do you do for a living?	Que faites-vous dans la vie ?

Asking the Way | Demander son chemin

Where is the nearest ...?	Où est le/la ... le/la plus proche ?
How do I get to ...?	Comment est-ce qu'on va à/au/à la ... ?
Is it far?	Est-ce que c'est loin ?
How far is it from here?	C'est à combien de minutes/ de mètres d'ici ?
Is this the right way to ...?	C'est la bonne direction pour aller à/au/à la ... ?
I'm lost.	Je suis perdu(e).
Can you show me on the map?	Pouvez-vous me le montrer sur la carte ?
You have to turn round.	Vous devez faire demi-tour.
Go straight on.	Allez tout droit.
Turn left/right.	Tournez à gauche/à droite.
Take the second street on the left/right.	Prenez la deuxième rue à gauche/à droite.

Car Hire | Location de voitures

I want to hire ...	Je voudrais louer ...
a car.	*une voiture.*
a moped.	*une mobylette.*
a motorbike.	*une moto.*
a (motor) scooter.	*un scooter.*
How much is it for ...?	C'est combien pour ... ?
one day	*une journée*
a week	*une semaine*
What is included in the price?	Qu'est-ce qui est inclus dans le prix ?
I'd like a child seat for a ...-year-old child.	Je voudrais un siège-auto pour un enfant de ... ans.
What do I do if I have an accident/if I break down?	Que dois-je faire en cas d'accident/de panne ?

Breakdowns	Pannes
My car has broken down.	Je suis en panne.
Where is the nearest garage?	Où est le garage le plus proche ?
The exhaust	Le pot d'échappement
The gearbox	La boîte de vitesses
The windscreen	Le pare-brise
… is broken.	… est cassé(e).
The brakes	Les freins
The headlights	Les phares
The windscreen wipers	Les essuie-glaces
… are not working.	… ne fonctionnent pas.
The battery is flat.	La batterie est à plat.
The car won't start.	Le moteur ne démarre pas.
The engine is overheating.	Le moteur surchauffe.
I have a flat tyre.	J'ai un pneu à plat.
Can you repair it?	Pouvez-vous le réparer ?
When will the car be ready?	Quand est-ce que la voiture sera prête ?

Parking	Stationnement
Can I park here?	Je peux me garer ici ?
Do I need to buy a parking ticket?	Est-ce qu'il faut acheter un ticket de stationnement ?
Where is the ticket machine?	Où est l'horodateur ?
The ticket machine isn't working.	L'horodateur ne fonctionne pas.

Petrol Station	Station-service
Where is the nearest petrol station?	Où est la station-service la plus proche ?
Fill it up, please.	Le plein, s'il vous plaît.

30 euros' worth of...	30 euros de ...
diesel.	*gazole.*
(unleaded) economy petrol.	*sans plomb.*
premium unleaded.	*super.*
Pump number ..., please.	Pompe numéro ..., s'il vous plaît.
Please check ...	Pouvez-vous vérifier ...
the tyre pressure.	*la pression des pneus ?*
the oil.	*le niveau d'huile ?*
the water.	*le niveau d'eau ?*

Accidents | Accidents

Please call ...	Appelez ..., s'il vous plaît.
the police.	*la police.*
an ambulance.	*une ambulance*
Here are my insurance details.	Voici les références de mon assurance.
Give me your insurance details, please.	Donnez-moi les références de votre assurance , s'il vous plaît.
Can you be a witness for me?	Pouvez-vous me servir de témoin ?
You were driving too fast.	Vous conduisiez trop vite.
It wasn't your right of way.	Vous n'aviez pas la priorité.

Travelling ... by Car | Voyager ... en voiture

What's the best route to ...?	Quel chemin prendre pour aller à ... ?
I'd like a motorway tax sticker ...	Je voudrais un badge de télépéage ...
for a week.	*pour une semaine.*
for a year.	*pour un an.*
Do you have a road map of this area?	Avez-vous une carte de la région ?

By Bike	À vélo
Where is the cycle path to ...?	Où est la piste cyclable pour aller à ... ?
Can I keep my bike here?	Est-ce que je peux laisser mon vélo ici ?
My bike has been stolen.	On m'a volé mon vélo.
Where is the nearest bike repair shop?	Où se trouve le réparateur de vélos le plus proche ?
The brakes	*Les freins*
The gears	*Les vitesses*
... aren't working.	... ne marchent pas.
The chain is broken.	La chaîne est cassée.
I've got a flat tyre.	J'ai une crevaison.
I need a puncture repair kit.	J'ai besoin d'un kit de réparation.

By Train	En train
How much is ...?	Combien coûte ... ?
a single	*l'aller simple*
a return	*l'aller-retour*
A single to ..., please.	Un aller simple pour ..., s'il vous plaît.
I would like to travel first/ second class.	Je voudrais voyager en première/seconde classe.
Two returns to ..., please.	Deux allers-retours pour ..., s'il vous plaît.
Is there a reduction ...?	Est-ce qu'il y a un tarif réduit ... ?
for students	*pour les étudiants*
for pensioners	*pour les seniors*
for children	*pour les enfants*
with this pass	*avec cette carte*
Could I please have a timetable?	Pouvez vous me donner la fiche des horaires ?

I'd like to reserve a seat on the train to ..., please.	Je voudrais faire une réservation pour le train qui va à ..., s'il vous plaît.
Non smoking/Smoking, please.	Non-fumeurs/Fumeurs, s'il vous plaît.
I want to book a sleeper to ...	Je voudrais réserver une couchette pour ...
When is the next train to ...?	À quelle heure part le prochain train pour ... ?
Is there a supplement to pay?	Est-ce qu'il faut payer un supplément ?
Do I need to change?	Est-ce qu'il y a un changement ?
Where do I change?	Où est-ce qu'il faut changer ?
Which platform does the train for ... leave from?	De quel quai part le train pour ... ?
Is this the train for ...?	C'est bien le train pour ... ?
Excuse me, that's my seat.	Excusez-moi, c'est ma place.
I have a reservation.	J'ai réservé.
Is this seat taken/free?	Est-ce que cette place est occupée/libre ?
Please let me know when we get to ...	Pourriez-vous me prévenir lorsqu'on arrivera à ... ?
Where is the buffet car?	Où est le wagon-restaurant ?
Where is coach number ...?	Où est la voiture numéro ... ?

By Ferry | En ferry

Is there a ferry to ...?	Est-ce qu'il y a un ferry pour ... ?
When is the next/first/last ferry to ...?	Quand part le prochain/ premier/dernier ferry pour ... ?
How much is it for a camper/car with ... people?	Combien coûte la traversée pour un camping-car/une voiture avec ... personnes ?
How long does the crossing take?	Combien de temps dure la traversée ?

Where is ...?	Où est ... ?
the restaurant	*le restaurant*
the bar	*le bar*
the duty-free shop	*le magasin hors taxe*
Where is cabin number ...?	Où est la cabine numéro ... ?
Do you have anything for seasickness?	Avez-vous quelque chose contre le mal de mer ?

By Plane | En avion

Where is ...?	Où est ... ?
the taxi rank	*la station de taxis*
the bus stop	*l'arrêt de bus*
the information office	*le bureau de renseignements*
Where do I check in for the flight to ...?	Où a lieu l'enregistrement pour le vol pour ... ?
Which gate for the flight to ...?	À quelle porte faut-il embarquer pour le vol pour ... ?
When is the latest I can check in?	Quelle est l'heure limite d'enregistrement ?
When does boarding begin?	À quelle heure commence l'embarquement ?
Window/aisle, please.	Hublot/couloir, s'il vous plaît.
I've lost my boarding pass/ my ticket.	J'ai perdu mon ticket d'embarquement/mon billet.
My luggage hasn't arrived.	Mes bagages ne sont pas arrivés.
Where is the carousel?	Où est le carrousel à bagages ?
Where are the check-in desks?	Où sont les bornes d'enregistrement ?

Public Transport | Transports en commun

How do I get to ...?	Comment est-ce qu'on va à ... ?
Where is the bus station?	Où est la gare routière ?
Where is the nearest ...?	Où est ... le/la plus proche ?
bus stop	*l'arrêt de bus*

underground station	la station de métro
A ticket to..., please.	Un ticket pour..., s'il vous plaît.
Is there a reduction ...?	Est-ce qu'il y a un tarif réduit ... ?
for students	pour les étudiants
for pensioners	pour les seniors
for children	pour les enfants
for the unemployed	pour les chômeurs
with this pass	avec cette carte
How does the (ticket) machine work?	Comment fonctionne le distributeur de billets ?
Do you have a map of the underground?	Avez-vous un plan de métro ?
Please tell me when to get off.	Pourriez-vous me prévenir quand je dois descendre ?
What is the next stop?	Quel est le prochain arrêt ?
Which line goes to...?	Quelle ligne va à ... ?

Taxi | En taxi

Where can I get a taxi?	Où puis-je trouver un taxi ?
Call me a taxi, please.	Pouvez-vous m'appeler un taxi, s'il vous plaît ?
To the airport/station, please.	À l'aéroport/À la gare, s'il vous plaît.
To this address, please.	À cette adresse, s'il vous plaît.
I'm in a hurry.	Je suis pressé(e).
How much is it?	C'est combien ?
I need a receipt.	Il me faut un reçu.
Keep the change.	Gardez la monnaie.
Stop here, please.	Arrêtez-vous ici, s'il vous plaît.
Would you mind waiting for me?	Pouvez-vous m'attendre ?
Straight ahead/to the left/ to the right.	Tout droit/à gauche/à droite.

Camping | Camping

Is there a campsite here?	Est-ce qu'il y a un camping ici ?
We'd like a site for ...	Nous voudrions un emplacement pour ...
a tent.	*une tente.*
a caravan.	*une caravane.*
We'd like to stay one night/ ... **nights.**	Nous voudrions rester une nuit/... nuits.
How much is it per night?	C'est combien la nuit ?
Where are ...?	Où sont ... ?
the toilets	*les toilettes*
the showers	*les douches*
Where is ...?	Où est ... ?
the site office	*la réception*
Can we camp/park here overnight?	Est-ce qu'on peut camper/ stationner ici pour la nuit ?

Self-Catering | Location de vacances

Where do we get the key for the apartment/house?	Où est-ce qu'il faut aller chercher la clé de l'appartement/la maison ?
Do we have to pay extra for electricity/gas?	Est-ce que l'électricité/le gaz est à payer en plus ?
How does the heating work?	Comment fonctionne le chauffage ?
Who do I contact if there are any problems?	Qui dois-je contacter en cas de problème ?
We need ...	Il nous faut ...
a second key.	*un double de la clé.*
more sheets.	*des draps supplémentaires.*
The gas has run out.	Il n'y a plus de gaz.

There is no electricity.	Il n'y a pas d'électricité.
Do we have to clean the apartment/the house before we leave?	Est-ce qu'on doit nettoyer l'appartement/la maison avant de partir ?

Hotel | Hôtel

Do you have a ... for tonight?	Avez-vous une ... pour ce soir ?
single room	*chambre pour une personne*
double room	*chambre double*
Do you have a room ...?	Avez-vous une chambre ... ?
with a bath	*avec baignoire*
with a shower	*avec douche*
I want to stay for one night/... nights.	Je voudrais rester une nuit/ ... nuits.
I booked a room under the name ...	J'ai réservé une chambre au nom de ...
I'd like another room.	Je voudrais une autre chambre.
What time is breakfast?	À quelle heure est servi le petit déjeuner ?
Can I have breakfast in my room?	Pouvez-vous me servir le petit déjeuner dans ma chambre ?
Where is ...?	Où est ... ?
the gym	*la salle de sport*
the swimming pool/the spa	*la piscine/le spa*
I'd like an alarm call for tomorrow morning at ...	Je voudrais être réveillé(e) demain matin à ...
I'd like to get these things washed/cleaned.	Pourriez-vous faire nettoyer ceci ?
Please bring me ...	S'il vous plaît, apportez-moi ...
The ... doesn't work.	Le/la ... ne marche pas.
Room number ...	Chambre numéro ...
Are there any messages for me?	Est-ce que j'ai reçu des messages ?

SHOPPING | ACHATS

I'd like ...	Je voudrais ...
Do you have ...?	Avez-vous ... ?
Do you have this ...?	Avez-vous ceci ... ?
in another size	*dans une autre taille*
in another colour	*dans une autre couleur*
I take size ...	Je fais du ...
My feet are a size 5½.	Je fais du trente-neuf.
I'll take it.	Je le prends.
Do you have anything else?	Avez-vous autre chose ?
That's too expensive.	C'est trop cher.
I'm just looking.	Je ne fais que regarder.
Do you take credit cards?	Acceptez-vous la carte de crédit ?

Food Shopping | Courses alimentaires

Where is the nearest ...?	Où est ... le/la plus proche ?
supermarket	*le supermarché*
baker's	*la boulangerie*
butcher's	*la boucherie*
Where is the market?	Où est le marché ?
When is the market on?	Quel jour a lieu le marché ?
a kilo/pound of ...	un kilo/une livre de ...
200 grams of ...	deux cents grammes de ...
... slices of ...	... tranches de ...
a litre of ...	un litre de ...
a bottle/packet of ...	une bouteille/un paquet de ...

Post Office | Poste

Where is the nearest post office?	Où est la poste la plus proche ?
When does the post office open?	À quelle heure ouvre la poste ?
Where can I buy stamps?	Où peut-on acheter des timbres ?

I'd like ... stamps for postcards/letters to France/Britain/ the United States.	Je voudrais ... timbres pour des cartes postales/lettres pour la France/la Grande-Bretagne/les États-Unis.
I'd like to send ...	Je voudrais envoyer ...
this letter.	*cette lettre.*
this parcel.	*ce colis.*
by airmail/by express mail/ by registered mail	par avion/en courrier urgent/en recommandé
Is there any mail for me?	Est-ce que j'ai du courrier ?
Where is the nearest postbox?	Où est la boîte aux lettres la plus proche ?

Photography | Photographie

I need passport photos.	J'ai besoin de photos d'identité.
I'm looking for a cable for a digital camera.	Je cherche un câble pour appareil photo numérique.
Do you sell brand-name chargers?	Est-ce que vous vendez des chargeurs de marque ?
I'd like to buy a memory card.	Je voudrais acheter une carte mémoire.
I'd like the photos ...	Je voudrais les photos ...
matt/glossy.	*en mat/en brillant.*
ten by fifteen centimetres.	*en format dix sur quinze.*
Can I print my digital photos here?	Est-ce que je peux imprimer mes photos numériques ici ?
How much do the photos cost?	Combien coûtent les photos ?
Could you take a photo of us, please?	Pourriez-vous nous prendre en photo, s'il vous plaît ?
The photo is blurry.	La photo est floue.

LEISURE | LOISIRS

Sightseeing	Visites touristiques
Where is the tourist office?	Où se trouve l'office de tourisme ?
Do you have any leaflets about ...?	Avez-vous des dépliants sur ... ?
Are there any sightseeing tours of the town?	Est-ce qu'il y a des visites guidées de la ville ?
When is ... open?	À quelle heure ouvre ... ?
the museum	*le musée*
the church	*l'église*
the castle	*le château*
How much does it cost to get in?	Combien coûte l'entrée ?
Are there any reductions ...?	Est-ce qu'il y a un tarif réduit ... ?
for students	*pour les étudiants*
for children	*pour les enfants*
for pensioners	*pour les seniors*
for the unemployed	*pour les chômeurs*
Is there a guided tour in French?	Est-ce qu'il y a une visite guidée en français ?
Can I take (flash) photos here?	Je peux prendre des photos (avec flash) ici ?
Can I film here?	Je peux filmer ici ?

Entertainment	Loisirs
What is there to do here?	Qu'est-ce qu'il y a à faire ici ?
Where can we ...?	Où est-ce qu'on peut ... ?
go dancing	*danser*
hear live music	*écouter de la musique live*
Where is there ...?	Où est-ce qu'il y a ... ?
a nice bar	*un bon bar*
a good club	*une bonne discothèque*

What's on tonight ...?	Qu'est-ce qu'il y a ce soir ... ?
at the cinema	*au cinéma*
at the theatre	*au théâtre*
at the opera	*à l'opéra*
at the concert hall	*à la salle de concert*
Where can I buy tickets for ...?	Où est-ce que je peux acheter des places ... ?
the theatre	*de théâtre*
the concert	*de concert*
the opera	*d'opéra*
the ballet	*pour le spectacle de danse*
How much is it to get in?	Combien coûte l'entrée ?
I'd like a ticket/... tickets for ...	Je voudrais un billet/... billets pour ...
Are there any reductions ...?	Est-ce qu'il y a un tarif réduit ... ?
for children	*pour les enfants*
for pensioners	*pour les seniors*
for students	*pour les étudiants*
for the unemployed	*pour les chômeurs*

At the Beach │ À la plage

Where is the nearest beach?	Où se trouve la plage la plus proche ?
Is it safe to swim here?	Est-ce qu'on peut nager ici sans danger ?
Is the water deep?	L'eau est-elle profonde ?
Is there a lifeguard?	Est-ce qu'il y a un maître-nageur ?
Where can you ...?	Où peut-on ... ?
go surfing	*faire du surf*
go waterskiing	*faire du ski nautique*
go diving	*faire de la plongée*
go paragliding	*faire du parapente*

LEISURE | LOISIRS

I'd like to hire ...	*Je voudrais louer ...*
a deckchair.	*une chaise longue.*
a sunbed.	*un matelas.*
a sunshade.	*un parasol.*
a surfboard.	*une planche de surf.*
a jet-ski.	*un jet-ski.*
a rowing boat.	*une barque.*
a pedal boat.	*un pédalo.*

Sport | Sport

Where can you ...?	*Où peut-on ... ?*
play tennis/golf	*jouer au tennis/golf*
go swimming	*aller nager*
go riding	*faire de l'équitation*
go fishing	*aller pêcher*
How much is it per hour?	*Combien est-ce que ça coûte de l'heure ?*
Where can I book a court?	*Où peut-on réserver un court ?*
Where can I hire rackets?	*Où peut-on louer des raquettes de tennis ?*
Where can I hire a rowing boat/a pedal boat?	*Où peut-on louer une barque/un pédalo ?*
Do you need a fishing permit?	*Est-ce qu'il faut un permis de pêche ?*

Skiing | Ski

Where can I hire skiing equipment?	*Où peut-on louer un équipement de ski ?*
I'd like to hire ...	*Je voudrais louer ...*
downhill skis.	*des skis de piste.*
cross-country skis.	*des skis de fond.*
ski boots.	*des chaussures de ski.*
ski poles.	*des bâtons de ski.*

Can you tighten my bindings, please?	Pourriez-vous resserrer mes fixations, s'il vous plaît ?
Where can I buy a ski pass?	Où est-ce qu'on peut acheter un forfait ?
I'd like a ski pass ...	Je voudrais un forfait ...
for a day.	pour une journée.
for five days.	pour cinq jours.
for a week.	pour une semaine.
How much is a ski pass?	Combien coûte le forfait ?
When does the first/last chair-lift leave?	À quelle heure part le premier/dernier télésiège ?
Do you have a map of the ski runs?	Avez-vous une carte des pistes ?
Where are the beginners' slopes?	Où sont les pistes pour débutants ?
How difficult is this slope?	Quelle est la difficulté de cette piste ?
Is there a ski school?	Y a-t-il une école de ski ?
What's the weather forecast for today?	Quel temps prévoit-on pour aujourd'hui ?
What is the snow like?	Comment est la neige ?
Is there a danger of avalanches?	Est-ce qu'il y a un risque d'avalanche ?

A table for ... people, please.	Une table pour ... personnes, s'il vous plaît.
The ..., please.	La ..., s'il vous plaît.
menu	*carte*
wine list	*carte des vins*
What do you recommend?	Qu'est-ce que vous me conseillez ?
Do you have ...?	Servez-vous ... ?
any vegetarian dishes	*des plats végétariens*
children's portions	*des menus enfants*
Does that contain ...?	Est-ce que cela contient ... ?
peanuts	*des cacahuètes*
alcohol	*de l'alcool*
Could you bring (more) ..., please?	Vous pourriez m'apporter (plus de) ..., s'il vous plaît ?
I'll have ...	Je vais prendre ...
The bill, please.	L'addition, s'il vous plaît.
All together, please.	Une seule addition, s'il vous plaît.
Separate bills, please.	Séparément, s'il vous plaît.
Keep the change.	Gardez la monnaie.
This isn't what I ordered.	Ce n'est pas ce que j'ai commandé.
There's a mistake in the bill.	Il y a une erreur dans l'addition.
It's cold/too salty.	C'est froid/trop salé.
rare/medium/well-done	saignant/à point/bien cuit
A bottle of sparkling/still water.	Une bouteille d'eau gazeuse/plate.

Telephone	Téléphone
Where can I make a phone call?	Où est-ce que je peux téléphoner ?
Hello?	Allô ?
Who's speaking, please?	Qui est à l'appareil ?
This is ...	C'est ...
Can I speak to Mr/Ms ..., please?	Puis-je parler à M./ Mme ..., s'il vous plaît ?
I'll phone back later.	Je rappellerai plus tard.
Can you text me your answer?	Pouvez-vous me répondre par SMS ?
Where can I charge my mobile (phone)?	Où est-ce que je peux recharger mon portable ?
I need a new battery.	Il me faut une batterie neuve.
I can't get a network.	Je n'ai pas de réseau.
I'd like to buy a SIM card with/ without a subscription.	Je voudrais acheter une carte SIM avec/sans abonnement.

Internet	Internet
I'd like to send an email.	Je voudrais envoyer un e-mail.
I'd like to print out a document.	Je voudrais imprimer un document.
How do you change the language of the keyboard?	Comment changer la langue du clavier ?
What's the Wi-Fi password?	Quel est le mot de passe pour le wifi ?

Passport/Customs	Passeport/Douane
Here is ...	Voici ...
my passport.	mon passeport.
my identity card.	ma carte d'identité.
my driving licence.	mon permis de conduire.
Here are my vehicle documents.	Voici les papiers de mon véhicule.
It's a present.	C'est un cadeau.
It's for my own personal use.	C'est pour mon usage personnel.

At the Bank	À la banque
Where can I change money?	Où puis-je changer de l'argent ?
Is there a bank/bureau de change around here?	Est-ce qu'il y a une banque/un bureau de change par ici ?
When does the bank open?	La banque ouvre à quelle heure ?
I'd like ... euros.	Je voudrais ... euros.
I'd like to cash these traveller's cheques.	Je voudrais encaisser ces chèques de voyage.
What's the commission?	Quel est le montant de la commission ?
Can I use my card to get cash?	Est-ce que je peux me servir de ma carte pour retirer de l'argent ?
Is there a cash machine around here?	Est-ce qu'il y a un distributeur par ici ?
The cash machine swallowed my card.	Le distributeur a avalé ma carte.

Repairs	Réparations
Where can I get this repaired?	Où puis-je faire réparer ceci ?
Can you repair ...?	Pouvez-vous réparer ... ?
these shoes	*ces chaussures*
this watch	*cette montre*
How much will the repairs cost?	Combien coûte la réparation ?

Emergency Services	Urgences
Help!	Au secours !
Fire!	Au feu !
Could you please call ...	Pouvez-vous appeler ...
the emergency doctor?	*le SAMU ?*
the fire brigade?	*les pompiers ?*
the police?	*la police ?*
I need to make an urgent phone call.	Je dois téléphoner d'urgence.
I need an interpreter.	J'ai besoin d'un interprète.
Where is the police station?	Où est le commissariat ?
Where is the hospital?	Où est l'hôpital ?
I want to report a theft.	Je voudrais signaler un vol.
... has been stolen.	On m'a volé(e) ...
There's been an accident.	Il y a eu un accident.
There are ... people injured.	Il y a ... blessés.
I've been ...	On m'a ...
robbed.	*volé(e).*
attacked.	*attaqué(e).*
raped.	*violé(e).*
I'd like to phone my embassy.	Je voudrais appeler mon ambassade.

Pharmacy | Pharmacie

Where is the nearest pharmacy?	Où est la pharmacie la plus proche ?
Which pharmacy provides an emergency service?	Quelle est la pharmacie de garde ?
I'd like something ...	Je voudrais quelque chose ...
for diarrhoea.	*contre la diarrhée.*
for a temperature.	*contre la fièvre.*
for travel sickness.	*contre le mal des transports.*
for a headache.	*contre le mal de tête.*
for a cold.	*contre le rhume.*
I'd like ...	Je voudrais ...
plasters.	*des pansements.*
a bandage.	*un bandage.*
some paracetamol.	*du paracétamol.*
I can't take ...	Je suis allergique à ...
aspirin.	*l'aspirine.*
penicillin.	*la pénicilline.*
Is it safe to give to children?	C'est sans danger pour les enfants ?

At the Doctor's | Chez le médecin

I need a doctor.	J'ai besoin de voir un médecin.
Where is casualty?	Où sont les urgences ?
I have a pain here.	J'ai mal ici.
I feel ...	J'ai ...
hot.	*chaud.*
cold.	*froid.*
I feel sick.	Je me sens mal.
I feel dizzy.	J'ai la tête qui tourne.
I have a fever.	J'ai de la fièvre.

I'm ...	Je suis ...
pregnant.	*enceinte.*
diabetic.	*diabétique.*
HIV-positive.	*séropositif(-ive).*
I'm on this medication.	Je prends ces médicaments.
My blood group is ...	Mon groupe sanguin est ...

At the Hospital | À l'hôpital

Which ward is ... in?	Dans quel pavillon se trouve ... ?
When are visiting hours?	Quelles sont les heures de visite ?
I'd like to speak to ...	Je voudrais parler à ...
a doctor.	*un médecin.*
a nurse.	*un infirmier/une infirmière.*
When will I be discharged?	Quand vais-je pouvoir sortir ?

At the Dentist's | Chez le dentiste

I need a dentist.	J'ai besoin de voir un dentiste.
This tooth hurts.	J'ai mal à cette dent.
One of my fillings has fallen out.	J'ai perdu un de mes plombages.
I have an abscess.	J'ai un abcès.
Can you repair my dentures?	Pouvez-vous réparer mon dentier ?
I need a receipt for my insurance.	J'ai besoin d'un reçu pour mon assurance.

Business Travel | Voyages d'affaires

I'd like to arrange a meeting with ...	Je voudrais organiser une réunion avec ...
I have an appointment with Mr/Ms ...	J'ai rendez-vous avec M./Mme ...
Here's my card.	Voici ma carte de visite.
I work for ...	Je travaille pour ...
How do I get to ...?	Comment rejoindre ... ?
your office	*votre bureau*
Mr/Ms ...'s office	*le bureau de M./Mme ...*
I need an interpreter.	J'ai besoin d'un interprète.
May I use ...?	Est-ce que je peux me servir ... ?
your phone/computer/desk	*de votre téléphone/ordinateur/bureau*
Do you have an Internet connection/Wi-Fi?	Y a-t-il une connexion Internet/wifi ?

Disabled Travellers | Voyageurs handicapés

Is it possible to visit ... with a wheelchair?	Est-ce qu'on peut visiter ... en fauteuil roulant ?
Where is the wheelchair-accessible entrance?	Où est l'entrée pour les fauteuils roulants ?
Is your hotel accessible to wheelchairs?	Votre hôtel est-il accessible aux clients en fauteuil roulant ?
I need a room ...	Je voudrais une chambre ...
on the ground floor.	*au rez-de-chaussée.*
with wheelchair access.	*accessible aux fauteuils roulants.*
Do you have a lift for wheelchairs?	Y a-t-il un ascenseur pour fauteuils roulants ?
Where is the disabled toilet?	Où sont les toilettes pour handicapés ?
Can you help me get on/off, please?	Pouvez-vous m'aider à monter/descendre, s'il vous plaît ?

Travelling with children | Voyager avec des enfants

Is it OK to bring children here?	Est-ce que les enfants sont admis ?
Is there a reduction for children?	Est-ce qu'il y a un tarif réduit pour les enfants ?
Do you have children's portions?	Vous avez un menu pour enfant ?
Do you have ...?	Avez-vous ... ?
a high chair	*une chaise pour bébé*
a cot	*un lit de bébé*
a child's seat	*un siège pour enfant*
Where can I change my baby?	Où est-ce que je peux changer mon bébé ?
Where can I breast-feed my baby?	Où est-ce que je peux allaiter mon bébé ?
Can you warm this up, please?	Vous pouvez me réchauffer ceci, s'il vous plaît ?
What is there for children to do?	Qu'est-ce qu'il y a comme activités pour les enfants ?
Where's the nearest playground?	Où est le parc de jeux le plus proche ?
Is there a child-minding service?	Est-ce qu'il y a un service de garderie ?

COMPLAINTS | **RÉCLAMATIONS**

I'd like to make a complaint.	Je voudrais faire une réclamation.
Whom should I speak to in order to make a complaint?	À qui dois-je m'adresser pour faire une réclamation ?
I'd like to speak to the manager, please.	Je voudrais parler au responsable, s'il vous plaît.
The light	*La lumière*
The heating	*Le chauffage*
The shower	*La douche*
... doesn't work.	*... ne marche pas.*
The room is ...	La chambre est ...
dirty.	*sale.*
too small.	*trop petite.*
The room is too cold.	Il fait trop froid dans la chambre.
Could you clean the room, please?	Pourriez-vous nettoyer ma chambre, s'il vous plaît ?
Could you turn down the TV/the radio, please?	Pourriez-vous baisser le son de votre télé/radio, s'il vous plaît ?
I've been robbed.	On m'a volé quelque chose.
We've been waiting for a very long time.	Nous attendons depuis très longtemps.
The bill is wrong.	Il y a une erreur dans l'addition.
I want my money back.	Je veux qu'on me rembourse.
I'd like to exchange this.	Je voudrais échanger ceci.
I'm not satisfied with this.	Je ne suis pas satisfait(e).

bangers and mash saucisses poêlées accompagnées de purée de pommes de terre, d'oignons frits et de sauce au jus de viande

banoffee pie pâte à tarte garnie d'un mélange de bananes, de caramel au beurre et de crème

BLT (sandwich) bacon, salade verte, tomate et mayonnaise entre deux tranches de pain

butternut squash doubeurre

Caesar salad grande salade composée avec de la laitue, des légumes, des œufs, du parmesan et une vinaigrette ; peut être servie en accompagnement ou comme plat principal

chocolate brownie petit gâteau carré au chocolat et aux noix ou noisettes

chowder épaisse soupe de fruits de mer

chicken Kiev blanc de poulet pané garni de beurre, d'ail et de persil et cuit au four

chicken nuggets petits morceaux de poulet pané, frits ou cuits au four et servis dans le menu enfant

club sandwich sandwich sur trois tranches de pain, généralement grillées ; les garnitures les plus courantes sont la viande, le fromage, la salade, les tomates et les oignons

cottage pie viande de bœuf hachée et légumes recouverts de purée de pommes de terre et de fromage et cuits au four

cream tea goûter où l'on sert du thé et des scones accompagnés de crème et de confiture

English breakfast œufs, bacon, saucisses, haricots blancs à la sauce tomate, pain à la poêle et champignons

filo pastry type de pâte feuilletée très fine

ginger ale, ginger beer (Brit) boisson gazeuse au gingembre

haggis plat écossais à base de hachis de cœur et de foie de mouton bouilli avec de l'avoine et des aromates dans une poche faite avec la panse de l'animal

hash browns pommes de terre cuites coupées en dés

puis mélangées à de l'oignon haché et dorées à la poêle. On les sert souvent au petit déjeuner

hotpot ragoût de viande et de légumes servi avec des pommes de terre en lamelles

Irish stew ragoût d'agneau, de pommes de terre et d'oignon

monkfish lotte

oatcake biscuit salé à base d'avoine que l'on mange souvent avec du fromage

pavlova grande meringue recouverte de fruits et de crème fouettée

ploughman's lunch en-cas à base de pain, de fromage et de pickles

purée purée épaisse et onctueuse de fruits ou de légumes cuits et passés

Quorn® protéine végétale employée comme substitut à la viande

savoy cabbage chou frisé de Milan

sea bass bar, loup

Scotch broth soupe chaude à la viande avec des petits légumes et de l'orge

Scotch egg œuf dur enrobé d'un mélange à base de chair à saucisse et recouvert de chapelure avant d'être plongé dans l'huile de friture

spare ribs travers de porc

spring roll nem

Stilton fromage bleu au goût intense

sundae crème glacée recouverte d'un coulis, de noix, de Chantilly etc.

Thousand Island dressing sauce à base de ketchup, de mayonnaise, de sauce Worcester et de jus de citron, souvent servie avec des crevettes

toad in the hole saucisses recouvertes de pâte et passées au four

Welsh rarebit mélange de fromage et d'œufs passé au grill et servi sur du pain grillé

Yorkshire pudding mélange d'œufs, de lait et de farine cuit au four, servi avec du rôti de bœuf

aïoli rich garlic mayonnaise

amuse-bouche nibbles

anchoïade anchovy paste usually served on grilled French bread

assiette du pêcheur assorted fish or seafood

bar sea bass

bavarois moulded cream and custard pudding, usually served with fruit

bisque smooth, rich seafood soup

blanquette white meat stew served with a creamy white sauce

brandade de morue dried salt cod puréed with potatoes and olive oil

brochette, (en) cooked like a kebab (on a skewer)

bulot welks

calamar/calmar squid

cassoulet white bean stew with meat, bacon and sausage

cervelle de Canut savoury dish of fromage frais, goat's cheese, herbs and white wine

charlotte custard and fruit in lining of sponge fingers

clafoutis cherry flan

coq au vin chicken and mushrooms cooked in red wine

coques cockles

crémant sparkling wine

crème pâtissière thick fresh custard used in tarts and desserts

daube meat casserole with wine, herbs, garlic, tomatoes and olives

daurade sea bream

filet mignon small pork fillet steak

fine de claire high-quality oyster

foie gras goose liver

fond d'artichaut artichoke heart

fougasse type of bread with various fillings (olives, anchovies)

gésier gizzard

gratin dauphinois potatoes cooked in cream, garlic and Swiss cheese

homard thermidor lobster grilled in its shell with cream sauce

île flottante soft meringue served with fresh custard

loup de mer sea bass

noisettes d'agneau small round pieces of lamb

onglet cut of beef (steak)

pan-bagnat bread roll with egg, olives, salad, tuna, anchovies and olive oil

parfait rich ice cream

parmentier with potatoes

pignons pine nuts

piperade tomato, pepper and onion omelette

pissaladière a kind of pizza made mainly in the Nice region, topped with onions, anchovies and black olives

pistou garlic, basil and olive oil sauce from Provence – similar to pesto

pommes mousseline creamy mashed potatoes

pot-au-feu beef stew

quenelles poached balls of fish or meat mousse served in a sauce

rascasse scorpion fish

ratatouille tomatoes, aubergines, courgettes and garlic cooked in olive oil

ris de veau calf sweetbread

romaine cos lettuce

rouille spicy version of garlic mayonnaise (aïoli) served with fish stew or soup

salade lyonnaise vegetable salad dressed with eggs, bacon and croutons

salade niçoise many variations on a famous theme: the basic ingredients are green beans, anchovies, black olives and green peppers

suprême de volaille chicken breast cooked in a cream sauce

tapenade paste made of black olives, anchovies, capers and garlic in olive oil

tournedos Rossini thick fillet steak on fried bread topped with goose liver and truffles

English – French

Anglais – Français

A [eɪ] n (Mus) la m

 KEYWORD

a [eɪ, ə] (before vowel and silent h **an**) indef art **1** un(e); **a book** un livre; **an apple** une pomme; **she's a doctor** elle est médecin
2 (instead of the number "one") un(e); **a year ago** il y a un an; **a hundred/thousand** etc **pounds** cent/mille etc livres
3 (in expressing ratios, prices etc): **three a day/week** trois par jour/semaine; **10 km an hour** 10 km à l'heure; **£5 a person** 5£ par personne; **30p a kilo** 30p le kilo

A2 n (BRIT Scol) deuxième partie de l'examen équivalent au baccalauréat
A.A. n abbr (BRIT: = Automobile Association) ≈ ACF m; (= Alcoholics Anonymous) AA

A.A.A. n abbr (= American Automobile Association) ≈ ACF m
aback [ə'bæk] adv: **to be taken ~** être déconcentancé(e)
abandon [ə'bændən] vt abandonner
abattoir ['æbətwɑːʳ] n (BRIT) abattoir m
abbey ['æbɪ] n abbaye f
abbreviation [əbriːvɪ'eɪʃən] n abréviation f
abdomen ['æbdəmən] n abdomen m
abduct [æb'dʌkt] vt enlever
abide [ə'baɪd] vt souffrir, supporter; **I can't ~ it/him** je ne le supporte pas; **abide by** vt fus observer, respecter
ability [ə'bɪlɪtɪ] n compétence f, capacité f; (skill) talent m
able ['eɪbl] adj compétent(e); **to be ~ to do sth** pouvoir faire qch, être capable de faire qch
abnormal [æb'nɔːməl] adj anormal(e)
aboard [ə'bɔːd] adv à bord ▷ prep à bord de; (train) dans
abolish [ə'bɔlɪʃ] vt abolir
abolition [æbə'lɪʃən] n abolition f
abort [ə'bɔːt] vt (Med) faire avorter; (Comput, fig) abandonner; **abortion** [ə'bɔːʃən] n avortement m; **to have an abortion** se faire avorter

 KEYWORD

about [ə'baut] adv **1** (approximately) environ, à peu près; **about a hundred/thousand** etc environ cent/mille etc, une centaine (de)/ un millier (de) etc; **it takes about 10 hours** ça prend environ or à peu près 10 heures; **at 2 o'clock** vers 2 heures; **I've just about finished** j'ai presque fini
2 (referring to place) çà et là, de-ci de-là; **to run about** courir çà et là; **to walk about** se promener, aller et venir; **they left all their things lying about** ils ont laissé traîner toutes leurs affaires

3: **to be about to do sth** être sur le point de faire qch
▷ **prep 1** (*relating to*) au sujet de, à propos de; **a book about London** un livre sur Londres; **what is it about?** de quoi s'agit-il?; **we talked about it** nous en avons parlé; **what or how about doing this?** et si nous faisions ceci?
2 (*referring to place*) dans; **to walk about the town** se promener dans la ville

above [ə'bʌv] adv au-dessus ▷ prep au-dessus de; (*more than*) plus de; **mentioned ~** mentionné ci-dessus; **~ all** par-dessus tout, surtout
abroad [ə'brɔːd] adv à l'étranger
abrupt [ə'brʌpt] adj (*steep, blunt*) abrupt(e); (*sudden, gruff*) brusque
abscess ['æbsɪs] n abcès m
absence ['æbsəns] n absence f
absent ['æbsənt] adj absent(e); **absent-minded** adj distrait(e)
absolute ['æbsəluːt] adj absolu(e); **absolutely** [æbsə'luːtlɪ] adv absolument
absorb [əb'zɔːb] vt absorber; **to be ~ed in a book** être plongé(e) dans un livre; **absorbent cotton** n (us) coton m hydrophile; **absorbing** adj absorbant(e); (*book, film etc*) captivant(e)
abstain [əb'steɪn] vi: **to ~ (from)** s'abstenir (de)
abstract ['æbstrækt] adj abstrait(e)
absurd [əb'sɜːd] adj absurde
abundance [ə'bʌndəns] n abondance f
abundant [ə'bʌndənt] adj abondant(e)
abuse n [ə'bjuːs] (*insults*) insultes fpl, injures fpl; (*ill-treatment*) mauvais traitements mpl; (*of power etc*) abus m ▷ vt [ə'bjuːz] (*insult*) insulter; (*ill-treat*) malmener; (*power etc*) abuser de; **abusive** adj grossier(-ière), injurieux(-euse)

abysmal [ə'bɪzməl] adj exécrable; (*ignorance etc*) sans bornes
academic [ækə'dɛmɪk] adj universitaire; (*person: scholarly*) intellectuel(le); (*pej: issue*) oiseux(-euse), purement théorique ▷ n universitaire m/f; **academic year** n (*University*) année f universitaire; (*Scol*) année scolaire
academy [ə'kædəmɪ] n (*learned body*) académie f; (*school*) collège m; **~ of music** conservatoire m
accelerate [æk'sɛləreɪt] vt, vi accélérer; **acceleration** [æksɛlə'reɪʃən] n accélération f; **accelerator** n (BRIT) accélérateur m
accent ['æksɛnt] n accent m
accept [ək'sɛpt] vt accepter; **acceptable** adj acceptable; **acceptance** n acceptation f
access ['æksɛs] n accès m; **to have ~ to** (*information, library etc*) avoir accès à, pouvoir utiliser ou consulter; (*person*) avoir accès auprès de; **accessible** [æk'sɛsəbl] adj accessible
accessory [æk'sɛsərɪ] n accessoire m; **~ to** (*Law*) accessoire de
accident ['æksɪdənt] n accident m; (*chance*) hasard m; **I've had an ~** j'ai eu un accident; **by ~** (*by chance*) par hasard; (*not deliberately*) accidentellement; **accidental** [æksɪ'dɛntl] adj accidentel(le); **accidentally** [æksɪ'dɛntəlɪ] adv accidentellement; **Accident and Emergency Department** n (BRIT) service m des urgences; **accident insurance** n assurance f accident
acclaim [ə'kleɪm] vt acclamer ▷ n acclamations fpl
accommodate [ə'kɔmədeɪt] vt loger, recevoir; (*oblige, help*) obliger; (*car etc*) contenir
accommodation, (us) **accommodations** [əkɔmə'deɪʃən(z)] n, npl logement m
accompaniment [ə'kʌmpənɪmənt] n accompagnement m

accompany [əˈkʌmpənɪ] vt accompagner

accomplice [əˈkʌmplɪs] n complice m/f

accomplish [əˈkʌmplɪʃ] vt accomplir; **accomplishment** n (skill: gen pl) talent m; (completion) accomplissement m; (achievement) réussite f

accord [əˈkɔːd] n accord m ▷ vt accorder; **of his own** ~ de son plein gré; **accordance** n: **in accordance with** conformément à; **according: according to** prep selon; **accordingly** adv (appropriately) en conséquence; (as a result) par conséquent

account [əˈkaʊnt] n (Comm) compte m; (report) compte rendu, récit m; **accounts** npl (Comm: records) comptabilité f, comptes; **of no** ~ sans importance; **on** ~ en acompte; **to buy sth on** ~ acheter qch à crédit; **on no** ~ en aucun cas; **on** ~ **of** à cause de; **to take into** ~, **take** ~ **of** tenir compte de; **account for** vt fus (explain) expliquer, rendre compte de; (represent) représenter; **accountable** adj: **accountable (for/to)** responsable (de/devant); **accountant** n comptable m/f; **account number** n numéro m de compte

accumulate [əˈkjuːmjʊleɪt] vt accumuler, amasser ▷ vi s'accumuler, s'amasser

accuracy [ˈækjʊrəsɪ] n exactitude f, précision f

accurate [ˈækjʊrɪt] adj exact(e), précis(e); (device) précis; **accurately** adv avec précision

accusation [ækjuˈzeɪʃən] n accusation f

accuse [əˈkjuːz] vt: **to** ~ **sb (of sth)** accuser qn (de qch); **accused** n (Law) accusé(e)

accustomed [əˈkʌstəmd] adj: ~ **to** habitué(e) or accoutumé(e) à

ace [eɪs] n as m

ache [eɪk] n mal m, douleur f ▷ vi (be sore) faire mal, être douloureux(-euse); **my head** ~**s** j'ai mal à la tête

achieve [əˈtʃiːv] vt (aim) atteindre; (victory, success) remporter, obtenir; **achievement** n exploit m, réussite f; (of aims) réalisation f

acid [ˈæsɪd] adj, n acide (m)

acknowledge [əkˈnɒlɪdʒ] vt (also: ~ **receipt of**) accuser réception de; (fact) reconnaître; **acknowledgement** n (of letter) accusé m de réception

acne [ˈæknɪ] n acné m

acorn [ˈeɪkɔːn] n gland m

acoustic [əˈkuːstɪk] adj acoustique

acquaintance [əˈkweɪntəns] n connaissance f

acquire [əˈkwaɪə] vt acquérir; **acquisition** [ækwɪˈzɪʃən] n acquisition f

acquit [əˈkwɪt] vt acquitter; **to** ~ **o.s. well** s'en tirer très honorablement

acre [ˈeɪkə] n acre f (= 4047 m²)

acronym [ˈækrənɪm] n acronyme m

across [əˈkrɒs] prep (on the other side) de l'autre côté de; (crosswise) en travers de ▷ adv de l'autre côté; en travers; **to run/swim** ~ traverser en courant/à la nage; ~ **from** en face de

acrylic [əˈkrɪlɪk] adj, n acrylique (m)

act [ækt] n acte m, action f; (Theat: part of play) acte; (: of performer) numéro m; (Law) loi f ▷ vi (act) agir; (Theat) jouer; (pretend) jouer la comédie ▷ vt (role) jouer, tenir; **to catch sb in the** ~ prendre qn sur le fait or en flagrant délit; **to** ~ **as** servir de; **act up** (inf) vi (person) se conduire mal; (knee, back, injury) jouer des tours; (machine) être capricieux(-ieuse); **acting** adj suppléant(e), par intérim ▷ n (activity): **to do some acting** faire du théâtre (or du cinéma)

action [ˈækʃən] n action f; (Mil) combat m(pl); (Law) procès m, action en justice; **out of** ~ hors de

combat; (*machine etc*) hors d'usage;
to take ~ agir, prendre des mesures;
action replay n (*BRIT TV*) ralenti m

activate ['æktɪveɪt] vt (*mechanism*)
actionner, faire fonctionner

active ['æktɪv] adj actif(-ive);
(*volcano*) en activité; **actively** adv
activement; (*discourage*) vivement

activist ['æktɪvɪst] n activiste m/f

activity [æk'tɪvɪtɪ] n activité f;
activity holiday n vacances actives

actor ['æktə'] n acteur m

actress ['æktrɪs] n actrice f

actual ['æktjuəl] adj réel(le),
véritable; (*emphatic use*) lui-même
(elle-même)

> Be careful not to translate *actual*
> by the French word *actuel*.

actually ['æktjuəlɪ] adv réellement,
véritablement; (*in fact*) en fait

> Be careful not to translate
> *actually* by the French word
> *actuellement*.

acupuncture ['ækjupʌŋktʃə'] n
acupuncture f

acute [ə'kjuːt] adj aigu(ë); (*mind,
observer*) pénétrant(e)

ad [æd] n abbr = **advertisement**

A.D. adv abbr (= *Anno Domini*) ap. J.-C.

adamant ['ædəmənt] adj inflexible

adapt [ə'dæpt] vt adapter ▷ vi: **to ~
(to)** s'adapter (à); **adapter, adaptor**
n (*Elec*) adaptateur m; (*for several
plugs*) prise f multiple

add [æd] vt ajouter; (*figures: also*: ~
up) additionner; **it doesn't ~ up** (*fig*)
cela ne rime à rien; **add up to** (*Math*) s'élever à; (*fig: mean*) signifier

addict ['ædɪkt] n toxicomane
m/f; (*fig*) fanatique m/f; **addicted**
[ə'dɪktɪd] adj: **to be addicted to**
(*drink, drugs*) être adonné(e) à; (*fig:
football etc*) être un(e) fanatique
de; **addiction** [ə'dɪkʃən] n (*Med*)
dépendance f; **addictive** [ə'dɪktɪv]
adj qui crée une dépendance

addition [ə'dɪʃən] n (*adding up*)
addition f; (*thing added*) ajout m; **in ~**

de plus, de surcroît; **in ~ to** en plus de;
additional adj supplémentaire

additive ['ædɪtɪv] n additif m

address [ə'drɛs] n adresse f; (*talk*)
discours m, allocution f ▷ vt adresser;
(*speak to*) s'adresser à; **my ~ is ...** mon
adresse, c'est ...; **address book** n
carnet m d'adresses

adequate ['ædɪkwɪt] adj
(*enough*) suffisant(e); (*satisfactory*)
satisfaisant(e)

adhere [əd'hɪə'] vi: **to ~ to** adhérer à;
(*fig: rule, decision*) se tenir à

adhesive [əd'hiːzɪv] n adhésif m;
adhesive tape n (*BRIT*) ruban m
adhésif; (*us Med*) sparadrap m

adjacent [ə'dʒeɪsənt] adj
adjacent(e), contigu(ë); **~ to**
adjacent à

adjective ['ædʒɛktɪv] n adjectif m

adjoining [ə'dʒɔɪnɪŋ] adj voisin(e),
adjacent(e), attenant(e)

adjourn [ə'dʒəːn] vt ajourner ▷ vi
suspendre la séance; lever la séance;
clore la session

adjust [ə'dʒʌst] vt (*machine*) ajuster,
régler; (*prices, wages*) rajuster ▷ vi:
to ~ (to) s'adapter (à); **adjustable** adj
réglable; **adjustment** n (*of machine*)
ajustage m, réglage m; (*of prices, wages*)
rajustement m; (*of person*) adaptation f

administer [əd'mɪnɪstə'] vt
administrer; **administration**
[ədmɪnɪs'treɪʃən] n (*management*)
administration f; (*government*)
gouvernement m; **administrative**
[əd'mɪnɪstrətɪv] adj
administratif(-ive)

administrator [əd'mɪnɪstreɪtə'] n
administrateur(-trice)

admiral ['ædmərəl] n amiral m

admiration [ædmə'reɪʃən] n
admiration f

admire [əd'maɪə'] vt admirer;
admirer n (*fan*) admirateur(-trice)

admission [əd'mɪʃən] n admission
f; (*to exhibition, night club etc*) entrée f;
(*confession*) aveu m

admit [əd'mɪt] vt laisser entrer;
admettre; (agree) reconnaître,
admettre; (crime) reconnaître avoir
commis; **"children not ~ted"** entrée
interdite aux enfants; **admit to** vt
fus reconnaître, avouer; **admittance**
n admission f, (droit m d')entrée f;
admittedly adv il faut en convenir

adolescent [ædəʊ'lɛsnt] adj, n
adolescent(e)

adopt [ə'dɒpt] vt adopter; **adopted**
adj adoptif(-ive), adopté(e); **adoption**
[ə'dɒpʃən] n adoption f

adore [ə'dɔː'] vt adorer

adorn [ə'dɔːn] vt orner

Adriatic (Sea) [eɪdrɪ'ætɪk-] n: **the
Adriatic (Sea)** la mer Adriatique,
l'Adriatique f

adrift [ə'drɪft] adv à la dérive

ADSL n abbr (= asymmetric digital
subscriber line) ADSL m

adult ['ædʌlt] n adulte m/f ⊳ adj
(grown-up) adulte; (for adults)
pour adultes; **adult education** n
éducation f des adultes

adultery [ə'dʌltərɪ] n adultère m

advance [əd'vɑːns] n avance f
⊳ vt avancer ⊳ vi s'avancer; **in ~** en
avance, d'avance; **to make ~s to
sb** (amorously) faire des avances à
qn; **~ booking** location f; **~ notice,
~ warning** préavis m; (verbal)
avertissement m; **do I need to
book in ~?** est-ce qu'il faut réserver à
l'avance?; **advanced** adj avancé(e);
(Scol: studies) supérieur(e)

advantage [əd'vɑːntɪdʒ] n (also
Tennis) avantage m; **to take ~ of
(person)** exploiter; (opportunity)
profiter de

advent ['ædvənt] n avènement m,
venue f; **A~** (Rel) avent m

adventure [əd'vɛntʃə'] n aventure
f; **adventurous** [əd'vɛntʃərəs] adj
aventureux(-euse)

adverb ['ædvəːb] n adverbe m

adversary ['ædvəsərɪ] n adversaire
m/f

adverse ['ædvəːs] adj adverse; (effect)
négatif(-ive); (weather, publicity)
mauvais(e); (wind) contraire

advert ['ædvəːt] n abbr (BRIT)
= **advertisement**

advertise ['ædvətaɪz] vi faire de la
publicité ou de la réclame; (in classified
ads etc) mettre une annonce ⊳ vt faire
de la publicité ou de la réclame pour; (in
classified ads etc) mettre une annonce
pour vendre; **to ~ for** (staff) recruter
par (voie d')annonce; **advertisement**
[əd'vəːtɪsmənt] n publicité f, réclame
f; (in classified ads etc) annonce
f; **advertiser** n annonceur m;
advertising n publicité f

advice [əd'vaɪs] n conseils mpl;
(notification) avis m; **a piece of ~** un
conseil; **to take legal ~** consulter
un avocat

advisable [əd'vaɪzəbl] adj
recommandable, indiqué(e)

advise [əd'vaɪz] vt conseiller; **to
~ sb of sth** aviser ou informer qn
de qch; **to ~ against sth/doing
sth** déconseiller qch/conseiller de
ne pas faire qch; **adviser, advisor**
n conseiller(-ère); **advisory** adj
consultatif(-ive)

advocate n ['ædvəkɪt] (lawyer)
avocat (plaidant); (upholder)
défenseur m, avocat(e) ⊳ vt
['ædvəkeɪt] recommander, prôner;
to be an ~ of être partisan(e) de

Aegean [iː'dʒiːən] n, adj: **the ~ (Se**
la mer Égée, l'Égée f

aerial ['ɛərɪəl] n antenne f ⊳ adj
aérien(ne)

aerobics [ɛə'rəʊbɪks] n aéro

aeroplane ['ɛərəpleɪn] n (
avion m

aerosol ['ɛərəsɒl] n aéros

affair [ə'fɛə'] n affaire f
liaison f; aventure f

affect [ə'fɛkt] vt affe
disease) atteindre; **a**
affecté(e); **affect**
affectionate

afflict [ə'flɪkt] vt affliger

affluent ['æfluənt] adj aisé(e), riche; **the ~ society** la société d'abondance

afford [ə'fɔːd] vt (behaviour) se permettre; (provide) fournir, procurer; **can we ~ a car?** avons-nous de quoi acheter or les moyens d'acheter une voiture?; **affordable** adj abordable

Afghanistan [æf'gænɪstæn] n Afghanistan m

afraid [ə'freɪd] adj effrayé(e); **to be ~ of** or **to** avoir peur de; **I am ~ that** je crains que + sub; **I'm ~ so/not** oui/ non, malheureusement

Africa ['æfrɪkə] n Afrique f; **African** adj africain(e) ▷ n Africain(e); **African-American** adj afro-américain(e) ▷ n Afro-Américain(e)

after ['ɑːftə*] prep, adv après ▷ conj après que; **it's quarter ~ two** (us) il est deux heures et quart; **~ having done/~ he left** après avoir fait/ après son départ; **to name sb ~ sb** donner le nom de qn; **to ask ~ sb** demander des nouvelles de qn; **what/who are you ~?** que/ qui cherchez-vous?; **~ you!** après vous!; **~ all** après tout; **after-effects** npl (of disaster, radiation, drink) répercussions fpl; (of illness) séquelles fpl, suites fpl; **aftermath** n conséquences fpl; **afternoon** n après-midi m/f; **after-shave (lotion)** n lotion f après-rasage; **aftersun (cream/lotion)** n après-soleil m; **afterwards**, (us) **afterward** ['ɑːftəwəd(z)] adv après

again [ə'gɛn] adv de nouveau, encore (une fois); **to do sth ~** refaire qch; **~ and ~** à plusieurs reprises

against [ə'gɛnst] prep contre; (compared to) par rapport à

age [eɪdʒ] n âge m ▷ vt, vi vieillir; **he is 20 years of ~** il a 20 ans; **to come of ~** atteindre sa majorité; **it's been ~s since I saw you** ça fait une éternité que je ne t'ai pas vu; **aged** adj âgé(e); **~ 10** âgé de 10 ans

age: age group n tranche f d'âge; **age limit** n limite f d'âge

agency ['eɪdʒənsɪ] n agence f

agenda [ə'dʒɛndə] n ordre m du jour

> ⚠ Be careful not to translate agenda by the French word agenda.

agent ['eɪdʒənt] n agent m; (firm) concessionaire m

aggravate ['ægrəveɪt] vt (situation) aggraver; (annoy) exaspérer, agacer

aggression [ə'grɛʃən] n agression f

aggressive [ə'grɛsɪv] adj agressif(-ive)

agile ['ædʒaɪl] adj agile

AGM n abbr (= annual general meeting) AG f

ago [ə'gəu] adv: **two days ~** il y a deux jours; **not long ~** il n'y a pas longtemps; **how long ~?** il y a combien de temps (de cela)?

agony ['ægənɪ] n (pain) douleur f atroce; (distress) angoisse f; **to be in ~** souffrir le martyre

agree [ə'griː] vi convenir de ▷ vi: **to ~ with** (person) être d'accord avec; (statements etc) concorder avec; (Ling) s'accorder avec; **to ~ to do** accepter de or consentir à faire; **to ~ to sth** consentir à qch; **to ~ that** (admit) convenir or reconnaître que; **garlic doesn't ~ with me** je ne supporte pas l'ail; **agreeable** adj (pleasant) agréable; (willing) consentant(e), d'accord; **agreed** adj (time, place) convenu(e); **agreement** n accord m; **in agreement** d'accord

agricultural [ægrɪ'kʌltʃərəl] adj agricole

agriculture ['ægrɪkʌltʃə*] n agriculture f

ahead [ə'hɛd] adv en avant; devant; **go right** or **straight ~** (direction) allez tout droit; **go ~!** (permission) allez-y!; **~ of** devant; (fig: schedule etc) en avance sur; **~ of time** en avance

aid [eɪd] n aide f; (device) appareil m ▷ vt aider; **in ~ of** en faveur de

aide [eɪd] n (person) assistant(e)

admit [əd'mɪt] *vt* laisser entrer; admettre; *(agree)* reconnaître, admettre; *(crime)* reconnaître avoir commis; **"children not ~ed"** "entrée interdite aux enfants"; **admit to** *vt fus* reconnaître, avouer; **admittance** *n* admission *f*, (droit *m* d')entrée *f*; **admittedly** *adv* il faut en convenir

adolescent [ædəʊˈlɛsnt] *adj*, *n* adolescent(e)

adopt [ə'dɔpt] *vt* adopter; **adopted** *adj* adoptif(-ive), adopté(e); **adoption** [ə'dɔpʃən] *n* adoption *f*

adore [ə'dɔː] *vt* adorer

adorn [ə'dɔːn] *vt* orner

Adriatic (Sea) [eɪdrɪˈætɪk-] *n*: **the Adriatic (Sea)** la mer Adriatique, l'Adriatique *f*

adrift [ə'drɪft] *adv* à la dérive

ADSL *n abbr* (= *asymmetric digital subscriber line*) ADSL *m*

adult ['ædʌlt] *n* adulte *m/f* ▷ *adj* *(grown-up)* adulte; *(for adults)* pour adultes; **adult education** *n* éducation *f* des adultes

adultery [ə'dʌltəri] *n* adultère *m*

advance [əd'vɑːns] *n* avance *f* ▷ *vt* avancer ▷ *vi* s'avancer; **in ~** en avance, d'avance; **to make ~s to sb** *(amorously)* faire des avances à qn; **~ booking** location *f*; **~ notice**, **~ warning** préavis *m*; *(verbal)* avertissement *m*; **do I need to book in ~?** est-ce qu'il faut réserver à l'avance?; **advanced** *adj* avancé(e); *(Scol: studies)* supérieur(e)

advantage [əd'vɑːntɪdʒ] *n (also Tennis)* avantage *m*; **to take ~ of** *(person)* exploiter; *(opportunity)* profiter de

advent ['ædvənt] *n* avènement *m*, venue *f*; **A~** *(Rel)* avent *m*

adventure [əd'vɛntʃə] *n* aventure *f*; **adventurous** [əd'vɛntʃərəs] *adj* aventureux(-euse)

adverb ['ædvɜːb] *n* adverbe *m*

adversary ['ædvəsəri] *n* adversaire *m/f*

adverse ['ædvɜːs] *adj* adverse; *(effect)* négatif(-ive); *(weather, publicity)* mauvais(e); *(wind)* contraire

advert ['ædvɜːt] *n abbr* (BRIT) = **advertisement**

advertise ['ædvətaɪz] *vi* faire de la publicité *or* de la réclame; *(in classified ads etc)* mettre une annonce ▷ *vt* faire de la publicité *or* de la réclame pour; *(in classified ads etc)* mettre une annonce pour vendre; **to ~ for** *(staff)* recruter par (voie d')annonce; **advertisement** [əd'vɜːtɪsmənt] *n* publicité *f*, réclame *f*; *(in classified ads etc)* annonce *f*; **advertiser** *n* annonceur *m*; **advertising** *n* publicité *f*

advice [əd'vaɪs] *n* conseils *mpl*; *(notification)* avis *m*; **a piece of ~** un conseil; **to take legal ~** consulter un avocat

advisable [əd'vaɪzəbl] *adj* recommandable, indiqué(e)

advise [əd'vaɪz] *vt* conseiller; **to ~ sb of sth** aviser or informer qn de qch; **to ~ against sth/doing sth** déconseiller qch/conseiller de ne pas faire qch; **adviser, advisor** *n* conseiller(-ère); **advisory** *adj* consultatif(-ive)

advocate *n* ['ædvəkɪt] *(lawyer)* avocat (plaidant); *(upholder)* défenseur *m*, avocat(e) ▷ *vt* ['ædvəkeɪt] recommander, prôner; **to be an ~ of** être partisan(e) de

Aegean [iː'dʒiːən] *n*, *adj*: **the ~ (Sea)** la mer Égée, l'Égée *f*

aerial ['ɛərɪəl] *n* antenne *f* ▷ *adj* aérien(ne)

aerobics [ɛə'rəubɪks] *n* aérobic *m*

aeroplane ['ɛərəpleɪn] *n* (BRIT) avion *m*

aerosol ['ɛərəsɔl] *n* aérosol *m*

affair [ə'fɛə] *n* affaire *f*; *(also: love ~)* liaison *f*, aventure *f*

affect [ə'fɛkt] *vt* affecter; *(subj: disease)* atteindre; **affected** *adj* affecté(e); **affection** *n* affection *f*; **affectionate** *adj* affectueux(-euse)

afflict [əˈflɪkt] vt affliger
affluent [ˈæfluənt] adj aisé(e), riche; **the ~ society** la société d'abondance
afford [əˈfɔːd] vt se permettre; (provide) fournir, procurer; **can we ~ a car?** avons-nous de quoi acheter or les moyens d'acheter une voiture?; **affordable** adj abordable
Afghanistan [æfˈɡænɪstæn] n Afghanistan m
afraid [əˈfreɪd] adj effrayé(e); **to be ~ of** or **to** avoir peur de; **I am ~ that** je crains que + sub; **I'm ~ so/not** oui/ non, malheureusement
Africa [ˈæfrɪkə] n Afrique f; **African** adj africain(e) ▷ n Africain(e); **African-American** adj afro-américain(e) ▷ n Afro-Américain(e)
after [ˈɑːftə*] prep, adv après ▷ conj après que; **it's quarter ~ two** (US) il est deux heures et quart; **~ having done/~ he left** après avoir fait/ après son départ; **to name sb ~ sb** donner à qn le nom de qn; **to ask ~ sb** demander des nouvelles de qn; **what/who are you ~?** que/ qui cherchez-vous?; **~ you!** après vous!; **~ all** après tout; **after-effects** npl (of disaster, radiation, drink etc) répercussions fpl; (of illness) séquelles fpl, suites fpl; (of aftermath n conséquences fpl; **afternoon** n après-midi m/f; **after-shave (lotion)** n lotion f après-rasage; **aftersun (cream/lotion)** n après-soleil m inv; **afterwards** (US) **afterward** [ˈɑːftəwəd(z)] adv après
again [əˈɡen] adv de nouveau, encore (une fois); **to do sth ~** refaire qch; **~ and ~** à plusieurs reprises
against [əˈɡenst] prep contre; (compared to) par rapport à
age [eɪdʒ] n âge m ▷ vt, vi vieillir; **he is 20 years of ~** il a 20 ans; **to come of ~** atteindre sa majorité; **it's been ~s since I saw you** ça fait une éternité que je ne t'ai pas vu

age: age group n tranche f d'âge; **age limit** n limite f d'âge
agency [ˈeɪdʒənsɪ] n agence f
agenda [əˈdʒendə] n ordre m du jour
⚠ Be careful not to translate agenda by the French word agenda.
agent [ˈeɪdʒənt] n agent m; (firm) concessionnaire m
aggravate [ˈæɡrəveɪt] vt (situation) aggraver; (annoy) exaspérer, agacer
aggression [əˈɡreʃən] n agression f
aggressive [əˈɡresɪv] adj agressif(-ive)
agile [ˈædʒaɪl] adj agile
AGM n abbr (= annual general meeting) AG f
ago [əˈɡəu] adv: **two days ~** il y a deux jours; **not long ~** il n'y a pas longtemps; **how long ~?** il y a combien de temps (de cela)?
agony [ˈæɡənɪ] n (pain) douleur f atroce; (distress) angoisse f; **to be in ~** souffrir le martyre
agree [əˈɡriː] vt (price) convenir de ▷ vi: **to ~ with** (person) être d'accord avec; (statements etc) concorder avec; (Ling) s'accorder avec; **to ~ to do** accepter de or consentir à faire; **to ~ to sth** consentir à qch; **to ~ that** (admit) convenir or reconnaître que; **garlic doesn't ~ with me** je ne supporte pas l'ail; **agreeable** adj (pleasant) agréable; (willing) consentant(e), d'accord; **agreed** adj (time, place) convenu(e); **agreement** n accord m; **in agreement** d'accord
agricultural [æɡrɪˈkʌltʃərəl] adj agricole
agriculture [ˈæɡrɪkʌltʃə*] n agriculture f
ahead [əˈhed] adv en avant; devant; **go right** or **straight ~** (direction) allez tout droit; **go ~!** (permission) allez-y!; **~ of** devant; (fig: schedule etc) en avance sur; **~ of time** en avance
aid [eɪd] n aide f; (device) appareil m ▷ vt aider; **in ~ of** en faveur de
aide [eɪd] n (person) assistant(e)

AIDS [eɪdz] n abbr (= acquired immune (or immuno-)deficiency syndrome) SIDA m

ailing ['eɪlɪŋ] adj (person) souffreteux(euse); (economy) malade

ailment ['eɪlmənt] n affection f

aim [eɪm] n (objective) but m; (skill): **his ~ is bad** il vise mal ▷ vi (also: **to take ~**) viser ▷ vt: **to ~ sth (at)** (gun, camera) braquer or pointer qch (sur); (missile) lancer qch (à or contre or en direction de); (remark, blow) destiner or adresser qch (à); **to ~ at** viser; (fig) viser (à); **to ~ to do** avoir l'intention de faire

ain't [eɪnt] (inf) = **am not**; **aren't**; **isn't**

air [ɛəʳ] n air m ▷ vt aérer; (idea, grievance, views) mettre sur le tapis ▷ cpd (currents, attack etc) aérien(ne); **to throw sth into the ~** (ball etc) jeter qch en l'air; **by ~** par avion; **to be on the ~** (Radio, TV: programme) être diffusé(e); (: station) émettre; **airbag** n airbag m; **airbed** n (BRIT) matelas m pneumatique; **airborne** adj (plane) en vol; **as soon as the plane was airborne** dès que l'avion eut décollé; **air-conditioned** adj climatisé(e), à air conditionné; **air conditioning** n climatisation f; **aircraft** n inv avion m; **airfield** n terrain m d'aviation; **Air Force** n Armée f de l'air; **air hostess** n (BRIT) hôtesse f de l'air; **airing cupboard** n (BRIT) placard qui contient la chaudière et dans lequel on met le linge à sécher; **airlift** n pont aérien; **airline** n ligne aérienne, compagnie aérienne; **airliner** n avion m de ligne; **airmail** n: **by airmail** par avion; **airplane** n (US) avion m; **airport** n aéroport m; **air raid** n attaque aérienne; **airsick** adj: **to be airsick** avoir le mal de l'air; **airspace** n espace m aérien; **airstrip** n terrain m d'atterrissage; **air terminal** n aérogare f; **airtight** adj hermétique; **air-traffic controller** n aiguilleur m du ciel; **airy** adj bien aéré(e); (manners) dégagé(e)

aisle [aɪl] n (of church: central) allée f centrale; (: side) nef f latérale, bas-côté m; (in theatre, supermarket) allée; (on plane) couloir m; **aisle seat** n place f côté couloir

ajar [ə'dʒɑ:ʳ] entrouvert(e)

à la carte [æla:'kɑ:t] adv à la carte

alarm [ə'lɑ:m] n alarme f ▷ vt alarmer; **alarm call** n coup m de fil pour réveiller; **could I have an alarm call at 7 am, please?** pouvez-vous me réveiller à 7 heures, s'il vous plaît?; **alarm clock** n réveille-matin m inv, réveil m; **alarmed** adj (frightened) alarmé(e); (protected by an alarm) protégé(e) par un système d'alarme; **alarming** adj alarmant(e)

Albania [æl'beɪnɪə] n Albanie f

albeit [ɔːl'biːɪt] conj bien que + sub, encore que + sub

album ['ælbəm] n album m

alcohol ['ælkəhɒl] n alcool m; **alcohol-free** adj sans alcool; **alcoholic** [ælkə'hɒlɪk] adj, n alcoolique (m/f)

alcove ['ælkəuv] n alcôve f

ale [eɪl] n bière f

alert [ə'lɜːt] adj alerte, vif (vive); (watchful) vigilant(e) ▷ n alerte f ▷ vt alerter; **on the ~** sur le qui-vive; (Mil) en état d'alerte

algebra ['ældʒɪbrə] n algèbre m

Algeria [æl'dʒɪərɪə] n Algérie f

Algerian [æl'dʒɪərɪən] adj algérien(ne) ▷ n Algérien(ne)

Algiers [æl'dʒɪəz] n Alger

alias ['eɪlɪəs] adv alias ▷ n faux nom, nom d'emprunt

alibi ['ælɪbaɪ] n alibi m

alien ['eɪlɪən] n (from abroad) étranger(-ère); (from outer space) extraterrestre ▷ adj: **~ (to)** étranger(-ère) (à); **alienate** vt aliéner; (subj: person) s'aliéner

alight [ə'laɪt] adj en feu ▷ vi mettre pied à terre; (passenger) descendre; (bird) se poser

align [ə'laɪn] vt aligner

alike [ə'laɪk] adj semblable, pareil(le)
▷ adv de même; **to look ~** se
ressembler
alive [ə'laɪv] adj vivant(e); (active)
plein(e) de vie

KEYWORD

all [ɔːl] adj (singular) tout(e); (plural)
tous (toutes); **all day** toute la
journée; **all night** toute la nuit; **all
men** tous les hommes; **all five** tous
les cinq; **all the books** tous les livres;
all his life toute sa vie
▷ pron 1 tout; **I ate it all, I ate all
of it** j'ai tout mangé; **all of us went**
nous y sommes tous allés; **all of the
boys went** tous les garçons y sont
allés; **is that all?** c'est tout?; (in shop)
ce sera tout?
2 (in phrases): **above all** surtout,
par-dessus tout; **after all** après
tout; **at all: not at all** (in answer to
question) pas du tout; (in answer to
thanks) je vous en prie!; **I'm not at all
tired** je ne suis pas du tout fatigué(e);
anything at all will do n'importe
quoi fera l'affaire; **all in all** tout bien
considéré, en fin de compte
▷ adv: **all alone** tout(e) seul(e); **it's
not as hard as all that** ce n'est pas
si difficile que ça; **all the more/
the better** d'autant plus/mieux;
all but presque, pratiquement;
the score is 2 all le score est de 2
partout

Allah [ælə] n Allah m
allegation [ælɪ'ɡeɪʃən] n allégation f
alleged [ə'ledʒd] adj prétendu(e);
allegedly adv à ce que l'on prétend,
paraît-il
allegiance [ə'liːdʒəns] n fidélité f,
obéissance f
allergic [ə'lɜːdʒɪk] adj: **~ to**
allergique à; **I'm ~ to penicillin** je
suis allergique à la pénicilline
allergy [ælədʒɪ] n allergie f

alleviate [ə'liːvɪeɪt] vt soulager,
adoucir
alley [ælɪ] n ruelle f
alliance [ə'laɪəns] n alliance f
allied [ælaɪd] adj allié(e)
alligator [ælɪɡeɪtə] n alligator m
all-in [ɔːlɪn] adj, adv (BRIT: charge)
tout compris
allocate [æləkeɪt] vt (share out)
répartir, distribuer; **to ~ sth to**
(duties) assigner or attribuer qch à;
(sum, time) allouer qch à
allot [ə'lɒt] vt (share out) répartir,
distribuer; **to ~ sth to** (time) allouer
qch à; (duties) assigner qch à
all-out [ɔːlaʊt] adj (effort etc) total(e)
allow [ə'laʊ] vt (practice, behaviour)
permettre, autoriser; (sum to spend
etc) accorder, allouer; (sum, time
estimated) compter, prévoir; (claim,
goal) admettre; (concede): **to ~
that** convenir que; **to ~ sb to do**
permettre à qn de faire, autoriser qn
à faire; **he is ~ed to ...** on lui permet
de ...; **allow for** vt fus tenir compte
de; **allowance** n (money received)
allocation f(: from parent etc) subside
m; (: for expenses) indemnité f; (us:
pocket money) argent m de poche;
(Tax) somme f déductible du revenu
imposable, abattement m; **to make
allowances for** (person) essayer de
comprendre; (thing) tenir compte de
all right adv (feel, work) bien; (as
answer) d'accord
ally [ælaɪ] n allié m ▷ vt [ə'laɪ]: **to ~
o.s. with** s'allier avec
almighty [ɔːl'maɪtɪ] adj tout(e)-
puissant(e); (tremendous) énorme
almond [ɑːmənd] n amande f
almost [ɔːlməʊst] adv presque
alone [ə'ləʊn] adj, adv seul(e); **to
leave sb ~** laisser qn tranquille; **to
leave sth ~** ne pas toucher à qch; **let
~ ...** sans parler de ...; encore moins ...
along [ə'lɒŋ] prep le long de ▷ adv: **is
he coming ~ with us?** vient-il avec
nous?; **he was hopping/limping ~**

among(st) | 308

among(st) [əˈmʌŋ(st)] *prep* parmi, entre

amount [əˈmaʊnt] *n* (*sum of money*) somme *f*; (*total*) montant *m*; (*quantity*) quantité *f*; nombre *m* ▷ *vi*: **to ~ to** (*total*) s'élever à; (*be same as*) équivaloir à, revenir à

amp(ère) [ˈæmp(ɛəʳ)] *n* ampère *m*

ample [ˈæmpl] *adj* ample, spacieux(-euse); (*enough*): **this is ~** c'est largement suffisant; **to have ~ time/room** avoir bien assez de temps/place

amplifier [ˈæmplɪfaɪəʳ] *n* amplificateur *m*

amputate [ˈæmpjuteɪt] *vt* amputer

Amtrak [ˈæmtræk] (*us*) *n* société mixte de transports ferroviaires interurbains pour voyageurs

amuse [əˈmjuːz] *vt* amuser; **amusement** *n* amusement *m*; (*pastime*) distraction *f*; **amusement arcade** *n* salle *f* de jeu; **amusement park** *n* parc *m* d'attractions

amusing [əˈmjuːzɪŋ] *adj* amusant(e), divertissant(e)

an [æn, ən, n] *indef art* see **a**

anaemia, (*us*) **anemia** [əˈniːmɪə] *n* anémie *f*

anaemic, (*us*) **anemic** [əˈniːmɪk] *adj* anémique

anaesthetic, (*us*) **anesthetic** [ænɪsˈθetɪk] *n* anesthésique *m*

analog(ue) [ˈænəlɔg] *adj* (*watch, computer*) analogique

analogy [əˈnælədʒɪ] *n* analogie *f*

analyse [ˈænəlaɪz] *vt* analyser; **analysis** (*pl* **analyses**) [əˈnæləsɪs, -siːz] *n* analyse *f*; **analyst** [ˈænəlɪst] *n* (*political analyst etc*) analyste *m/f*; (*us*) psychanalyste *m/f*

analyze [ˈænəlaɪz] *vt* (*us*) = **analyse**

anarchy [ˈænəkɪ] *n* anarchie *f*

anatomy [əˈnætəmɪ] *n* anatomie *f*

ancestor [ˈænsɪstəʳ] *n* ancêtre *m*, aïeul *m*

anchor [ˈæŋkəʳ] *n* ancre *f* ▷ *vi* (*also:* **to drop ~**) jeter l'ancre, mouiller ▷ *vt*

mettre à l'ancre; (*fig*): **to ~ sth to** fixer qch à

anchovy [ˈæntʃəvɪ] *n* anchois *m*

ancient [ˈeɪnʃənt] *adj* ancien(ne), antique; (*person*) d'un âge vénérable; (*car*) antédiluvien(ne)

and [ænd] *conj* et; **~ so on** et ainsi de suite; **try ~ come** tâchez de venir; **come ~ sit here** venez vous asseoir ici; **he talked ~ talked** il a parlé pendant des heures; **better ~ better** de mieux en mieux; **more ~ more** de plus en plus

Andorra [ænˈdɔːrə] *n* (principauté *f* d')Andorre *f*

anemia *etc* [əˈniːmɪə] *n* (*us*) = **anaemia** *etc*

anesthetic [ænɪsˈθetɪk] *n*, *adj* (*us*) = **anaesthetic** *etc*

angel [ˈeɪndʒəl] *n* ange *m*

anger [ˈæŋgəʳ] *n* colère *f*

angina [ænˈdʒaɪnə] *n* angine *f* de poitrine

angle [ˈæŋgl] *n* angle *m*; **from their ~** de leur point de vue

angler [ˈæŋgləʳ] *n* pêcheur(-euse) à la ligne

Anglican [ˈæŋglɪkən] *adj*, *n* anglican(e)

angling [ˈæŋglɪŋ] *n* pêche *f* à la ligne

angrily [ˈæŋgrɪlɪ] *adv* avec colère

angry [ˈæŋgrɪ] *adj* en colère, furieux(-euse); (*wound*) enflammé(e); **to be ~ with sb/at sth** être furieux contre qn/de qch; **to get ~** se fâcher, se mettre en colère

anguish [ˈæŋgwɪʃ] *n* angoisse *f*

animal [ˈænɪməl] *n* animal *m* ▷ *adj* animal(e)

animated [ˈænɪmeɪtɪd] *adj* animé(e)

animation [ænɪˈmeɪʃən] *n* (*of person*) entrain *m*; (*of street, Cine*) animation *f*

aniseed [ˈænɪsiːd] *n* anis *m*

ankle [ˈæŋkl] *n* cheville *f*

annex [ˈænɛks] *n* (*BRIT: also:* **~e**) annexe *f* ▷ *vt* [æˈnɛks] annexer

anniversary [ænɪˈvɜːsərɪ] *n* anniversaire *m*

il venait or avançait en sautillant/
boitant; **~ with** avec, en plus de;
(person) en compagnie de; **all ~** (all the
time) depuis le début; **alongside** prep
(along) le long de; (beside) à côté de
▷ adv bord à bord; côte à côte

aloof [əˈluːf] adv distant(e) ▷ adv: **to
stand ~** se tenir à l'écart or à distance

aloud [əˈlaud] adv à haute voix

alphabet [ˈælfəbɛt] n alphabet m

Alps [ælps] npl: **the ~** les Alpes fpl

already [ɔːlˈrɛdɪ] adv déjà

alright [ˈɔːlˈraɪt] adv (BRIT) = **all right**

also [ˈɔːlsəu] adv aussi

altar [ˈɔltə⁾] n autel m

alter [ˈɔltə⁾] vt, vi changer; **alteration**
[ɔltəˈreɪʃən] n changement m,
modification f; **alterations** npl
(Sewing) retouches fpl; (Archit)
modifications fpl

alternate adj [ɔlˈtəːnɪt] alterné(e),
alternant(e), alternatif(-ive); (US)
= **alternative** ▷ vi [ˈɔltəːneɪt]
alterner; **to ~ with** alterner avec;
on ~ days un jour sur deux, tous les
deux jours

alternative [ɔlˈtəːnətɪv]
adj (solution, plan) autre, de
remplacement; (lifestyle) parallèle
▷ n (choice) alternative f; (other
possibility) autre possibilité f; **~
medicine** médecine alternative,
médecine douce; **alternatively** adv:
alternatively one could ... une
autre or l'autre solution serait de ...

although [ɔːlˈðəu] conj bien que + sub

altitude [ˈæltɪtjuːd] n altitude f

altogether [ɔːltəˈɡɛðə⁾] adv
entièrement, tout à fait; (on the whole)
tout compte fait; (in all) en tout

aluminium [æljuˈmɪnɪəm],
(US) **aluminum** [əˈluːmɪnəm] n
aluminium m

always [ˈɔːlweɪz] adv toujours

Alzheimer's (disease)
[ˈæltshaɪməz-] n maladie f
d'Alzheimer

am [æm] vb see **be**

a.m. adv abbr (= ante meridiem) du
matin

amalgamate [əˈmælɡəmeɪt] vt,
vi fusionner

amass [əˈmæs] vt amasser

amateur [ˈæmətə⁾] n amateur m

amaze [əˈmeɪz] vt stupéfier; **to be ~d
(at)** être stupéfait(e) (de); **amazed**
adj stupéfait(e); **amazement** n
surprise f, étonnement m; **amazing**
adj étonnant(e), incroyable; (bargain,
offer) exceptionnel(le)

Amazon [ˈæməzən] n (Geo)
Amazone f

ambassador [æmˈbæsədə⁾] n
ambassadeur m

amber [ˈæmbə⁾] n ambre m; **at ~**
(BRIT Aut) à l'orange

ambiguous [æmˈbɪɡjuəs] adj
ambigu(ë)

ambition [æmˈbɪʃən] n ambition
f; **ambitious** [æmˈbɪʃəs] adj
ambitieux(-euse)

ambulance [ˈæmbjuləns] n
ambulance f; **call an ~!** appelez une
ambulance!

ambush [ˈæmbuʃ] n embuscade f
▷ vt tendre une embuscade à

amen [ˈɑːˈmɛn] excl amen

amend [əˈmɛnd] vt (law) amender;
(text) corriger; **to make ~s** réparer
ses torts, faire amende honorable;
amendment n (to law) amendement
m; (to text) correction f

amenities [əˈmiːnɪtɪz] npl
aménagements mpl, équipements
mpl

America [əˈmɛrɪkə] n Amérique
f; **American** adj américain(e) ▷ n
Américain(e); **American football** n
(BRIT) football m américain

amicable [ˈæmɪkəbl] adj amical(e);
(Law) à l'amiable

amid(st) [əˈmɪd(st)] prep parmi, au
milieu de

ammunition [æmjuˈnɪʃən] n
munitions fpl

amnesty [ˈæmnɪstɪ] n amnistie f

announce [əˈnaʊns] vt annoncer; (birth, death) faire part de; **announcement** n annonce f; (for births etc: in newspaper) avis m de faire-part, (: letter, card) faire-part m; **announcer** n (Radio, TV: between programmes) speaker(ine); (: in a programme) présentateur(-trice)

annoy [əˈnɔɪ] vt agacer, ennuyer, contrarier; **don't get ~ed!** ne vous fâchez pas!; **annoying** adj agaçant(e), contrariant(e)

annual [ˈænjuəl] adj annuel(le) ▷ n (Bot) plante annuelle; (book) album m; **annually** adv annuellement

annum [ˈænəm] n see **per**

anonymous [əˈnɒnɪməs] adj anonyme

anorak [ˈænəræk] n anorak m

anorexia [ænəˈrɛksiə] n (also: ~ **nervosa**) anorexie f

anorexic [ænəˈrɛksɪk] adj, n anorexique (m/f)

another [əˈnʌðər] adj: ~ **book** (one more) un autre livre, encore un livre, un livre de plus; (a different one) un autre livre ▷ pron un(e) autre, encore un(e), un(e) de plus; see also **one**

answer [ˈɑːnsər] n réponse f; (to problem) solution f ▷ vi répondre ▷ vt (reply to) répondre à; (problem) résoudre; (prayer) exaucer; **in ~ to your letter** suite à or en réponse à votre lettre; **to ~ the phone** répondre (au téléphone); **to ~ the bell** or **the door** aller or venir ouvrir (la porte); **answer back** vi répondre, répliquer; **answerphone** n (esp BRIT) répondeur m (téléphonique)

ant [ænt] n fourmi f

Antarctic [æntˈɑːktɪk] n: **the ~** l'Antarctique m

antelope [ˈæntɪləʊp] n antilope f

antenatal [ˈæntɪˈneɪtl] adj prénatal(e)

antenna (pl **antennae**) [ænˈtɛnə, -niː] n antenne f

anthem [ˈænθəm] n: **national ~** hymne national

anthology [ænˈθɒlədʒɪ] n anthologie f

anthropology [ænθrəˈpɒlədʒɪ] n anthropologie f

anti [ˈæntɪ] prefix anti-; (all); **antibiotic** [ˈæntɪbaɪˈɒtɪk] n antibiotique m; **antibody** [ˈæntɪbɒdɪ] n anticorps m

anticipate [ænˈtɪsɪpeɪt] vt s'attendre à, prévoir; (wishes, request) aller au devant de, devancer; **anticipation** [æntɪsɪˈpeɪʃən] n attente f

anticlimax [ˈæntɪˈklaɪmæks] n déception f

anticlockwise [ˈæntɪˈklɒkwaɪz] (BRIT) adv dans le sens inverse des aiguilles d'une montre

antics [ˈæntɪks] npl singeries fpl

anti-: **antidote** [ˈæntɪdəʊt] n antidote m, contrepoison m; **antifreeze** [ˈæntɪfriːz] n antigel m; **anti-globalization** n antimondialisation f; **antihistamine** [æntɪˈhɪstəmɪn] n antihistaminique m; **antiperspirant** [æntɪˈpəːspɪrənt] n déodorant m

antique [ænˈtiːk] n (ornament) objet m d'art ancien; (furniture) meuble ancien ▷ adj ancien(ne); **antique shop** n magasin m d'antiquités

antiseptic [ænˈtɪˈsɛptɪk] adj, n antiseptique (m)

antisocial [ˈæntɪˈsəʊʃəl] adj (unfriendly) insociable; (against society) antisocial(e)

antivirus [æntɪˈvaɪrəs] adj (Comput) antivirus inv; **~ software** (logiciel m) antivirus

antlers [ˈæntləz] npl bois mpl, ramure f

anxiety [æŋˈzaɪətɪ] n anxiété f; (keenness): **~ to do** grand désir or impatience f de faire

anxious [ˈæŋkʃəs] adj (très) inquiet(-ète); (always worried) anxieux(-euse); (worrying) angoissant(e); **~ to do/that** (keen

qui tient beaucoup à faire/à ce que
+ sub; impatient(e) de faire/que + sub

○ **KEYWORD**

any ['enɪ] adj **1** (in questions etc:
singular) du, de l', de la; (: plural) des;
**do you have any butter/children/
ink?** avez-vous du beurre/des
enfants/de l'encre?
2 (with negative) de, d'; **I don't have
any money/books** je n'ai pas
d'argent/de livres
3 (no matter which) n'importe quel(le);
(each and every) tout(e), chaque;
choose any book you like vous
pouvez choisir n'importe quel livre;
any teacher you ask will tell you
n'importe quel professeur vous le dira
4 (in phrases): **in any case** de toute
façon; **any day now** d'un jour à
l'autre; **at any moment** à tout
moment, d'un instant à l'autre; **at
any rate** en tout cas; **any time**
n'importe quand; **he might come
(at) any time** il pourrait venir
n'importe quand; **come (at) any
time** venez quand vous voulez
▶ pron **1** (in questions etc) en; **have
you got any?** est-ce que vous en
avez?; **can any of you sing?** est-ce
que parmi vous il y en a qui savent
chanter?
2 (with negative) en; **I can't have
any (of them)** je n'en ai pas, je n'en
ai aucun
3 (no matter which one(s)) n'importe
lequel (or laquelle); (anybody)
n'importe qui; **take any of those
books (you like)** vous pouvez
prendre n'importe lequel de ces livres
▶ adv **1** (in questions etc): **do you
want any more soup/sandwiches?**
voulez-vous encore de la soupe/des
sandwichs?; **are you feeling any
better?** est-ce que vous vous sentez
mieux?
2 (with negative): **I can't hear him**

any more je ne l'entends plus;
don't wait any longer n'attendez
pas plus longtemps; **anybody**
pron n'importe qui; (in interrogative
sentences) quelqu'un; (in negative
sentences): **I don't see anybody** je ne
vois personne; **if anybody should
phone ...** si quelqu'un téléphone
...; **anyhow** adv quoi qu'il en soit;
(haphazardly) n'importe comment;
do it anyhow you like faites-le
comme vous voulez; **she leaves
things just anyhow** elle laisse
tout traîner; **I shall go anyhow**
j'irai de toute façon; **anyone** pron
= **anybody**; **anything** pron (no matter,
what) n'importe quoi; (in questions)
quelque chose; (with negative) ne
... rien; **can you see anything?** tu
vois quelque chose?; **if anything
happens to me** s'il m'arrive quoi
que ce soit ...; **you can say anything
you like** vous pouvez dire ce que vous
voulez; **anything will do** n'importe
quoi fera l'affaire; **he'll eat anything**
il mange de tout; **anytime** adv (at
any moment) d'un moment à l'autre;
(whenever) n'importe quand; **anyway**
adv de toute façon; **anyway, I
couldn't come even if I wanted
to** de toute façon, je ne pouvais pas
venir même si je le voulais; **I shall
go anyway** j'irai quand même; **why
are you phoning anyway?** au
fait, pourquoi tu me téléphones?;
anywhere adv n'importe où; (in
interrogative sentences) quelque part;
(in negative sentences): **I can't see him
anywhere** je ne le vois nulle part;
can you see him anywhere? tu le
vois quelque part?; **put the books
down anywhere** pose les livres
n'importe où; **anywhere in the
world** (no matter where) n'importe où
dans le monde

apart [ə'pɑːt] adv (to one side) à
part; de côté; à l'écart; (separately)

séparément; **to take/pull ~**
démonter; **10 miles/a long way ~** à
10 miles/très éloignés l'un de l'autre;
~ from prep à part, excepté

apartment [ə'pɑːtmənt] n (US)
appartement m, logement m; (room)
chambre f; **apartment building** n
(US) immeuble m; maison divisée en
appartements

apathy ['æpəθɪ] n apathie f,
indifférence f

ape [eɪp] n (grand) singe ▷ vt singer

aperitif [ə'perɪtɪf] n apéritif m

aperture ['æpətjʊə'] n orifice m,
ouverture f; (Phot) ouverture (du
diaphragme)

APEX ['eɪpeks] n abbr (Aviat: = advance
purchase excursion) APEX m

apologize [ə'pɒlədʒaɪz] vi: **to ~ (for
sth to sb)** s'excuser (de qch auprès
de qn), présenter des excuses (à qn
pour qch)

apology [ə'pɒlədʒɪ] n excuses fpl

apostrophe [ə'pɒstrəfɪ] n
apostrophe f

app n abbr (inf: Comput: = application)
appli f

appal, (US) **appall** [ə'pɔːl] vt
consterner, atterrer; horrifier;
appalling adj épouvantable;
(stupidity) consternant(e)

apparatus [æpə'reɪtəs] n appareil m,
dispositif m; (in gymnasium) agrès mpl

apparent [ə'pærənt] adj
apparent(e); **apparently** adv
apparemment

appeal [ə'piːl] vi (Law) faire ou
interjeter appel ▷ n (Law) appel m;
(request) appel; prière f; (charm) attrait
m, charme m; **to ~ for** demander
(instamment); implorer; **to ~ to** (beg)
faire appel à; (be attractive) plaire à;
it doesn't ~ to me cela ne m'attire
pas; **appealing** adj (attractive)
attrayant(e)

appear [ə'pɪə'] vi apparaître,
se montrer; (Law) comparaître;
(publication) paraître, sortir, être

publié(e); (seem) paraître, sembler; **it
would ~ that** il semble que; **to ~ in
Hamlet** jouer dans Hamlet; **to ~ on
TV** passer à la télé; **appearance** n
apparition f; parution f; (look, aspect)
apparence f, aspect m

appendices [ə'pendɪsiːz] npl of
appendix

appendicitis [əpendɪ'saɪtɪs] n
appendicite f

appendix (pl **appendices**)
[ə'pendɪks, -siːz] n appendice m

appetite ['æpɪtaɪt] n appétit m

appetizer ['æpɪtaɪzə'] n (food)
amuse-gueule m; (drink) apéritif m

applaud [ə'plɔːd] vt, vi applaudir

applause [ə'plɔːz] n
applaudissements mpl

apple ['æpl] n pomme f; **apple pie** n
tarte f aux pommes

appliance [ə'plaɪəns] n appareil m

applicable [ə'plɪkəbl] adj applicable;
to be ~ to (relevant) valoir pour

applicant ['æplɪkənt] n: **~ (for)**
candidat(e) (à)

application [æplɪ'keɪʃən] n (also
Comput) application f; (for a job,
grant etc) demande f; candidature f;
application form n formulaire m de
demande

apply [ə'plaɪ] vt: **to ~ (to)** (paint,
ointment) appliquer (sur); (law, etc)
appliquer (à) ▷ vi: **to ~ to** (ask)
s'adresser à; (be suitable for, relevant
to) s'appliquer à; **to ~ for** (permit,
grant) faire une demande (en vue
d'obtenir); (job) poser sa candidature
(pour), faire une demande
d'emploi (concernant); **to ~ o.s. to**
s'appliquer à

appoint [ə'pɔɪnt] vt (to post)
nommer, engager; (date, place)
fixer, désigner; **appointment** n (to
post) nomination f; (job) poste m; (arrangement to meet) rendez-vous
m; **to have an appointment**
avoir un rendez-vous; **to make
an appointment (with)** prendre

rendez-vous (avec); **I'd like to make an appointment** je voudrais prendre rendez-vous

appraisal [əˈpreɪzl] n évaluation f

appreciate [əˈpriːʃɪeɪt] vt (like) apprécier, faire cas de; (be grateful for) être reconnaissant(e) de; (be aware of) comprendre, se rendre compte de ▷ vi (Finance) prendre de la valeur; **appreciation** [əpriːʃɪˈeɪʃən] n appréciation f; (gratitude) reconnaissance f; (Finance) hausse f, valorisation f

apprehension [æprɪˈhɛnʃən] n appréhension f, inquiétude f

apprehensive [æprɪˈhɛnsɪv] adj inquiet(-ète), appréhensif(-ive)

apprentice [əˈprɛntɪs] n apprenti m

approach [əˈprəutʃ] vi approcher ▷ vt (come near) approcher de; (ask, apply to) s'adresser à; (subject, passer-by) aborder ▷ n approche f; accès m, abord m; (intellectual) démarche f

appropriate adj [əˈprəuprɪɪt] (tool etc) qui convient, approprié(e); (moment, remark) opportun(e) ▷ vt [əˈprəuprɪeɪt] (take) s'approprier

approval [əˈpruːvəl] n approbation f; **on ~** (Comm) à l'examen

approve [əˈpruːv] vt approuver; **approve of** vt fus (thing) approuver; (person): **they don't ~ of her** ils n'ont pas bonne opinion d'elle

approximate adj [əˈprɒksɪmɪt] approximatif(-ive); **approximately** adv approximativement

Apr. abbr = April

apricot [ˈeɪprɪkɒt] n abricot m

April [ˈeɪprəl] n avril m; **April Fools' Day** n le premier avril

● APRIL FOOLS' DAY
●
● April Fools' Day est le 1er avril, à
● l'occasion duquel on se fait des farces
● de toutes sortes. Les victimes de
● ces farces sont les "April fools".

● Traditionnellement, on n'est censé
● faire ces farces que jusqu'à midi.

apron [ˈeɪprən] n tablier m

apt [æpt] adj (suitable) approprié(e); **~ to do** (likely) susceptible de faire; ayant tendance à faire

aquarium [əˈkwɛərɪəm] n aquarium m

Aquarius [əˈkwɛərɪəs] n le Verseau

Arab [ˈærəb] n Arabe m/f ▷ adj arabe

Arabia [əˈreɪbɪə] n Arabie f; **Arabian** adj arabe; **Arabic** [ˈærəbɪk] adj, n arabe (m)

arbitrary [ˈɑːbɪtrərɪ] adj arbitraire

arbitration [ɑːbɪˈtreɪʃən] n arbitrage m

arc [ɑːk] n arc m

arcade [ɑːˈkeɪd] n arcade f; (passage with shops) passage m, galerie f; (with games) salle f de jeu

arch [ɑːtʃ] n arche f; (of foot) cambrure f, voûte f plantaire ▷ vt arquer, cambrer

archaeology, (US) **archeology** [ɑːkɪˈɒlədʒɪ] n archéologie f

archbishop [ɑːtʃˈbɪʃəp] n archevêque m

archeology [ɑːkɪˈɒlədʒɪ] (US) n = **archaeology**

architect [ˈɑːkɪtɛkt] n architecte m; **architectural** [ɑːkɪˈtɛktʃərəl] adj architectural(e); **architecture** [ˈɑːkɪtɛktʃə] n architecture f

archive [ˈɑːkaɪv] n (often pl) archives fpl

Arctic [ˈɑːktɪk] adj arctique ▷ n: **the ~** l'Arctique m

are [ɑːʳ] vb see **be**

area [ˈɛərɪə] n (Geom) superficie f; (zone) région f; (: smaller) secteur m; (in room) coin m; (knowledge, research) domaine m; **area code** (US) n (Tel) indicatif m de zone

arena [əˈriːnə] n arène f

aren't [ɑːnt] = **are not**

Argentina [ɑːdʒənˈtiːnə] n Argentine f; **Argentinian**

[ɑ:dʒən'tɪnɪən] adj argentin(e) ▷ n Argentin(e)

arguably ['ɑ:gjuəblɪ] adv: **it is ~ ...** on peut soutenir que c'est ...

argue ['ɑ:gju:] vi (quarrel) se disputer; (reason) argumenter; **to ~ that** objecter or alléguer que, donner comme argument que

argument ['ɑ:gjumənt] n (quarrel) dispute f, discussion f; (reasons) argument m

Aries ['ɛərɪz] n le Bélier

arise (pt arose, pp arisen) [ə'raɪz, ə'rəʊz, ə'rɪzn] vi survenir, se présenter

arithmetic [ə'rɪθmətɪk] n arithmétique f

arm [ɑ:m] n bras m ▷ vt armer; **arms** npl (weapons, Heraldry) armes fpl; **~ in ~** bras dessus bras dessous; **armchair** ['ɑ:mtʃɛə'] n fauteuil m

armed [ɑ:md] adj armé(e); **armed forces** npl: **the armed forces** les forces armées; **armed robbery** n vol m à main armée

armour, (US) **armor** ['ɑ:mə'] n armure f; (Mil: tanks) blindés mpl

armpit ['ɑ:mpɪt] n aisselle f

armrest ['ɑ:mrɛst] n accoudoir m

army ['ɑ:mɪ] n armée f

A road n (BRIT) ≈ route nationale

aroma [ə'rəʊmə] n arôme m; **aromatherapy** n aromathérapie f

arose [ə'rəʊz] pt of **arise**

around [ə'raʊnd] adv (tout) autour; (nearby) dans les parages ▷ prep autour de; (near) près de; (fig: about) environ; (: date, time) vers; **is he ~?** est-il dans les parages or là?

arouse [ə'raʊz] vt (sleeper) éveiller; (curiosity, passions) éveiller, susciter; (anger) exciter

arrange [ə'reɪndʒ] vt arranger; **to ~ to do sth** prévoir de faire qch; **arrangement** n arrangement m; **arrangements** npl (plans etc) arrangements mpl, dispositions fpl

array [ə'reɪ] n (of objects) déploiement m, étalage m

arrears [ə'rɪəz] npl arriéré m; **to be in ~ with one's rent** devoir un arriéré de loyer

arrest [ə'rɛst] vt arrêter; (sb's attention) retenir, attirer ▷ n arrestation f; **under ~** en état d'arrestation

arrival [ə'raɪvl] n arrivée f; **new ~** nouveau venu/nouvelle venue; (baby) nouveau-né(e)

arrive [ə'raɪv] vi arriver; **arrive at** vt fus (decision, solution) parvenir à

arrogance ['ærəgəns] n arrogance f

arrogant ['ærəgənt] adj arrogant(e)

arrow ['ærəʊ] n flèche f

arse [ɑ:s] n (BRIT infl!) cul m (!)

arson ['ɑ:sn] n incendie criminel

art [ɑ:t] n art m; (Scol) les lettres fpl; **art college** n école f des beaux-arts

artery ['ɑ:tərɪ] n artère f

art gallery n musée m d'art; (saleroom) galerie f de peinture

arthritis [ɑ:'θraɪtɪs] n arthrite f

artichoke ['ɑ:tɪtʃəʊk] n artichaut m; **Jerusalem ~** topinambour m

article ['ɑ:tɪkl] n article m

articulate adj [ɑ:'tɪkjʊlɪt] (person) qui s'exprime clairement et aisément; (speech) bien articulé(e), prononcé(e) clairement ▷ vi [ɑ:'tɪkjʊleɪt] parler distinctement ▷ vt articuler, parler distinctement

artificial [ɑ:tɪ'fɪʃəl] adj artificiel(le)

artist ['ɑ:tɪst] n artiste m/f; **artistic** [ɑ:'tɪstɪk] adj artistique

art school n ≈ école f des beaux-arts

KEYWORD

as [æz] conj **1** (time: moment) comme, alors que; à mesure que; **he came in as I was leaving** il est arrivé comme je partais; **as the years went by** à mesure que les années passaient; **as from tomorrow** à partir de demain **2** (because) comme, puisque; **he left early as he had to be home by**

10 comme il or puisqu'il devait être de retour avant 10h, il est parti de bonne heure

3 (referring to manner, way) comme; **do as you wish** faites comme vous voudrez; **as she said** comme elle disait

▶ **adv 1** (in comparisons): **as big as** aussi grand que; **twice as big as** deux fois plus grand que; **as much** or **many as** autant que; **as much money/many books as** autant d'argent/de livres que; **as soon as** dès que

2 (concerning): **as for** or **to that** quant à cela, pour ce qui est de cela

3: **as if** or **though** comme si; **he looked as if he was ill** il avait l'air d'être malade; see also **long; such; well**

▶ **prep** (in the capacity of) en tant que, en qualité de; **he works as a driver** il travaille comme chauffeur; **as chairman of the company, he ...** en tant que président de la société, il ...; **he gave it me as a present** il me l'a offert, il m'en a fait cadeau

a.s.a.p. abbr = **as soon as possible**

asbestos [æz'bɛstɒs] n asbeste m, amiante f

ascent [ə'sɛnt] n (climb) ascension f

ash [æʃ] n (dust) cendre f; (also: ~ **tree**) frêne m

ashamed [ə'ʃeɪmd] adj honteux(-euse), confus(e); **to be ~ of** avoir honte de

ashore [ə'ʃɔː'] adv à terre

ashtray ['æʃtreɪ] n cendrier m

Ash Wednesday n mercredi m des Cendres

Asia ['eɪʃə] n Asie f; **Asian** n (from Asia) Asiatique m/f; (BRIT: from Indian subcontinent) Indo-Pakistanais m ▶ adj asiatique; indo-pakistanais(e)

aside [ə'saɪd] adv de côté; à l'écart ▶ n aparté m

ask [ɑːsk] vt demander; (invite) inviter; **to ~ sb sth/to do sth** demander à

qn qch/de faire qch; **to ~ sb about sth** questionner qn au sujet de qch; se renseigner auprès de qn au sujet de qch; **to ~ (sb) a question** poser une question (à qn); **to ~ sb out to dinner** inviter qn au restaurant; **ask for** vt fus demander; **it's just ~ing for trouble** or **for it** ce serait chercher des ennuis

asleep [ə'sliːp] adj endormi(e); **to fall ~** s'endormir

AS level n abbr (= Advanced Subsidiary level) première partie de l'examen équivalent au baccalauréat

asparagus [əs'pærəgəs] n asperges fpl

aspect ['æspɛkt] n aspect m; (direction in which a building etc faces) orientation f, exposition f

aspire [əs'paɪə'] vi: **to ~ to** aspirer à

aspirin ['æsprɪn] n aspirine f

ass [æs] n âne m; (inf) imbécile m/f; (US infl) cul m (!)

assassin [ə'sæsɪn] n assassin m; **assassinate** vt assassiner

assault [ə'sɔːlt] n (Mil) assaut m; (gen: attack) agression f ▶ vt attaquer; (sexually) violenter

assemble [ə'sɛmbl] vt assembler ▶ vi s'assembler, se rassembler

assembly [ə'sɛmblɪ] n (meeting) rassemblement m; (parliament) assemblée f; (construction) assemblage m

assert [ə'sɜːt] vt affirmer, déclarer; (authority) faire valoir; (innocence) protester de; **assertion** [ə'sɜːʃən] n assertion f, affirmation f

assess [ə'sɛs] vt évaluer, estimer; (tax, damages) établir or fixer le montant de; (person) juger la valeur de; **assessment** n évaluation f, estimation f; (of tax) fixation f

asset ['æsɛt] n avantage m, atout m; (person) atout; **assets** npl (Comm) capital m; avoir(s) m(pl); actif m

assign [ə'saɪn] vt (date) fixer, arrêter; **to ~ sth to** (task) assigner

qch à; *(resources)* affecter qch à;
assignment n *(task)* mission f;
(homework) devoir m

assist [əˈsɪst] vt aider, assister;
assistance n aide f, assistance f;
assistant n assistant(e), adjoint(e);
(BRIT: also: **shop assistant)**
vendeur(-euse)

associate adj, n [əˈsəʊʃɪɪt]
associé(e) ▷ vt [əˈsəʊʃɪeɪt] associer
▷ vi [əˈsəʊʃɪeɪt]: **to ~ with sb**
fréquenter qn

association [əsəʊsɪˈeɪʃən] n
association f

assorted [əˈsɔːtɪd] adj assorti(e)

assortment [əˈsɔːtmənt] n
assortiment m; *(of people)* mélange m

assume [əˈsjuːm] vt supposer;
(responsibilities etc) assumer; *(attitude,
name)* prendre, adopter

assumption [əˈsʌmpʃən] n
supposition f, hypothèse f; *(of power)*
assomption f, prise f

assurance [əˈʃʊərəns] n assurance f

assure [əˈʃʊəʳ] vt assurer

asterisk [ˈæstərɪsk] n astérisque m

asthma [ˈæsmə] n asthme m

astonish [əˈstɔnɪʃ] vt étonner,
stupéfier; **astonished** adj
étonné(e); **to be astonished at**
être étonné(e) de; **astonishing**
adj étonnant(e), stupéfiant(e);
I find it astonishing that ...
je trouve incroyable que ... +
sub; **astonishment** n (grand)
étonnement, stupéfaction f

astound [əˈstaʊnd] vt stupéfier,
sidérer

astray [əˈstreɪ] adv: **to go ~** s'égarer;
(fig) quitter le droit chemin; **to lead ~**
(morally) détourner du droit chemin

astrology [əsˈtrɔlədʒɪ] n astrologie f

astronaut [ˈæstrənɔːt] n
astronaute m/f

astronomer [əsˈtrɔnəməʳ] n
astronome m

astronomical [æstrəˈnɔmɪkl] adj
astronomique

astronomy [əsˈtrɔnəmɪ] n
astronomie f

astute [əsˈtjuːt] adj astucieux(-euse),
malin(-igne)

asylum [əˈsaɪləm] n asile m; **asylum
seeker** [-siːkəʳ] n demandeur(-euse)
d'asile

KEYWORD

at [æt] prep **1** *(referring to position,
direction)* à; **at the top** au sommet;
at home/school à la maison or chez
soi/à l'école; **at the baker's** à la
boulangerie, chez le boulanger; **to
look at sth** regarder qch
2 *(referring to time)*: **at 4 o'clock** à 4
heures; **at Christmas** à Noël; **at night**
la nuit; **at times** par moments, parfois
3 *(referring to rates, speed etc)* à; **at £1
a kilo** une livre le kilo; **two at a time**
deux à la fois; **at 50 km/h** à 50 km/h
4 *(referring to manner)*: **at a stroke**
d'un seul coup; **at peace** en paix
5 *(referring to activity)*: **to be at
work** *(in the office etc)* être au travail;
(working) travailler; **to play at
cowboys** jouer aux cowboys; **to be
good at sth/doing sth** être bon en qch
6 *(referring to cause)*: **shocked/
surprised/annoyed at sth** choqué
par/étonné de/agacé par qch; **I went
at his suggestion** j'y suis allé sur
son conseil

▶ (@ symbol) arobase f

ate [eɪt] pt of **eat**

atheist [ˈeɪθɪɪst] n athée m/f

Athens [ˈæθɪnz] n Athènes

athlete [ˈæθliːt] n athlète m/f

athletic [æθˈletɪk] adj athlétique;
athletics n athlétisme m

Atlantic [ətˈlæntɪk] adj atlantique
▷ n: **the ~ (Ocean)** l'(océan m)
Atlantique m

atlas [ˈætləs] n atlas m

A.T.M. n abbr (= Automated Telling
Machine) guichet m automatique

atmosphere [ˈætməsfɪəʳ] n (air) atmosphère f; (fig: of place etc) atmosphère, ambiance f

atom [ˈætəm] n atome m; **atomic** [əˈtɒmɪk] adj atomique; **atom(ic) bomb** n bombe f atomique

atrocity [əˈtrɒsɪtɪ] n atrocité f

attach [əˈtætʃ] vt (gen) attacher; (document, letter) joindre; **to be ~ed to sb/sth** (to like) être attaché à qn/qch; **to ~ a file to an email** joindre un fichier à un e-mail; **attachment** n (tool) accessoire m; (Comput) fichier m joint; (love): **attachment (to)** affection f (pour), attachement m (à)

attack [əˈtæk] vt attaquer; (task etc) s'attaquer à ▷ n attaque f; **heart ~** crise f cardiaque; **attacker** n attaquant m; agresseur m

attain [əˈteɪn] vt (also: **to ~ to**) parvenir à, atteindre; (knowledge) acquérir

attempt [əˈtɛmpt] n tentative f ▷ vt essayer, tenter

attend [əˈtɛnd] vt (course) suivre; (meeting, talk) assister à; (school, church) aller à, fréquenter; (patient) soigner, s'occuper de; **attend to** vt fus (needs, affairs etc) s'occuper de; (customer) s'occuper de, servir; **attendance** n (being present) présence f; (people present) assistance f; **attendant** n employé(e); gardien(ne) ▷ adj concomitant(e), qui accompagne or s'ensuit

> Be careful not to translate attend by the French word attendre.

attention [əˈtɛnʃən] n attention f ▷ excl (Mil) garde-à-vous!; **for the ~ of** (Admin) à l'attention de

attic [ˈætɪk] n grenier m, combles mpl

attitude [ˈætɪtjuːd] n attitude f

attorney [əˈtɜːnɪ] n (us: lawyer) avocat m; **Attorney General** n (BRIT) ≈ procureur général; (us) = garde m des Sceaux, ministre m de la Justice

attract [əˈtrækt] vt attirer; **attraction** [əˈtrækʃən] n (gen pl: pleasant things) attraction f, attrait m; (Physics) attraction f; (fig: towards sb, sth) attirance f; **attractive** adj séduisant(e), attrayant(e)

attribute n [ˈætrɪbjuːt] attribut m ▷ vt [əˈtrɪbjuːt]: **to ~ sth to** attribuer qch à

aubergine [ˈəʊbəʒiːn] n aubergine f

auburn [ˈɔːbən] adj auburn inv, châtain roux inv

auction [ˈɔːkʃən] n (also: **sale by ~**) vente f aux enchères ▷ vt (also: **to sell by ~**) vendre aux enchères

audible [ˈɔːdɪbl] adj audible

audience [ˈɔːdɪəns] n (people) assistance f, public m; (on radio) auditeurs mpl; (at theatre) spectateurs mpl; (interview) audience f

audit [ˈɔːdɪt] vt vérifier

audition [ɔːˈdɪʃən] n audition f

auditor [ˈɔːdɪtəʳ] n vérificateur m des comptes

auditorium [ɔːdɪˈtɔːrɪəm] n auditorium m, salle f de concert or de spectacle

Aug. abbr = **August**

August [ˈɔːgəst] n août m

aunt [ɑːnt] n tante f; **auntie, aunty** n diminutive of **aunt**

au pair [ˈəʊˈpɛəʳ] n (also: **~ girl**) jeune fille f au pair

aura [ˈɔːrə] n atmosphère f; (of person) aura f

austerity [ɔsˈtɛrɪtɪ] n austérité f

Australia [ɔsˈtreɪlɪə] n Australie f; **Australian** adj australien(ne) ▷ n Australien(ne)

Austria [ˈɔstrɪə] n Autriche f; **Austrian** adj autrichien(ne) ▷ n Autrichien(ne)

authentic [ɔːˈθɛntɪk] adj authentique

author [ˈɔːθəʳ] n auteur m

authority [ɔːˈθɒrɪtɪ] n autorité f; (permission) autorisation (formelle); **the authorities** les autorités fpl, l'administration f

authorize [ˈɔːθəraɪz] vt autoriser

auto ['ɔ:təʊ] n (US) auto f, voiture f; **autobiography** [ɔ:təbaɪ'ɒgrəfɪ] n autobiographie f; **autograph** ['ɔ:təgrɑ:f] n autographe m ▷ vt signer, dédicacer; **automatic** [ɔ:tə'mætɪk] adj automatique ▷ n (gun) automatique m; (car) voiture f à transmission automatique; **automatically** adv automatiquement; **automobile** ['ɔ:təməbi:l] n (US) automobile f; **autonomous** [ɔ:'tɒnəməs] adj autonome; **autonomy** [ɔ:'tɒnəmɪ] n autonomie f

autumn ['ɔ:təm] n automne m

auxiliary [ɔ:g'zɪlɪərɪ] adj, n auxiliaire (m/f)

avail [ə'veɪl] vt: **to ~ o.s. of** user de; profiter de ▷ n: **to no ~** sans résultat, en vain, in pure perte

availability [əveɪlə'bɪlɪtɪ] n disponibilité f

available [ə'veɪləbl] adj disponible

avalanche ['ævəlɑ:nʃ] n avalanche f

Ave. abbr = **avenue**

avenue ['ævənju:] n avenue f; (fig) moyen m

average ['ævərɪdʒ] n moyenne f ▷ adj moyen(ne) ▷ vt (a certain figure) atteindre or faire etc en moyenne; **on ~** en moyenne

avert [ə'vɜ:t] vt (danger) prévenir, écarter; (one's eyes) détourner

avid ['ævɪd] adj avide

avocado [ævə'kɑ:dəʊ] n (BRIT: also: ~ **pear**) avocat m

avoid [ə'vɔɪd] vt éviter

await [ə'weɪt] vt attendre

awake [ə'weɪk] (pt awoke, pp **awoken**) adj éveillé(e) ▷ vt éveiller ▷ vi s'éveiller; **to be ~** être réveillé(e)

award [ə'wɔ:d] n (for bravery) récompense f; (prize) prix m; (Law: damages) dommages-intérêts mpl ▷ vt (prize) décerner; (Law: damages) accorder

aware [ə'wɛə*] adj: **~ of** (conscious) conscient(e) de; (informed) au courant de; **to become ~ of/that** prendre conscience de/que; se rendre compte de/que; **awareness** n conscience f, connaissance f

away [ə'weɪ] adv (au) loin: (movement): **she went ~** elle est partie ▷ adj (not in, not here) absent(e); **far ~** (au) loin; **two kilometres ~** à (une distance de) deux kilomètres, à deux kilomètres de distance; **two hours ~ by car** à deux heures de voiture or de route; **the holiday was two weeks ~** il restait deux semaines jusqu'aux vacances; **to take sth ~ from sb** prendre qch à qn; **to take sth ~ from sth** (subtract) ôter qch de qch; **to work/pedal ~** travailler/pédaler à cœur joie; **to fade ~** (colour) s'estomper; (sound) s'affaiblir

awe [ɔ:] n respect mêlé de crainte, effroi mêlé d'admiration; **awesome** ['ɔ:səm] (US) adj (inf: excellent) génial(e)

awful ['ɔ:fəl] adj affreux(-euse); **an ~ lot of** énormément de; **awfully** adv (very) terriblement, vraiment

awkward ['ɔ:kwəd] adj (clumsy) gauche, maladroit(e); (inconvenient) peu pratique; (embarrassing) gênant

awoke [ə'wəʊk] pt of awake

awoken [ə'wəʊkən] pp of awake

axe, (US) **ax** [æks] n hache f ▷ vt (project etc) abandonner; (jobs) supprimer

axle ['æksl] n essieu m

ay(e) [aɪ] excl (yes) oui

azalea [ə'zeɪlɪə] n azalée f

b

B [biː] n (Mus) si m

B.A. abbr (Scol) = **Bachelor of Arts**

baby ['beɪbɪ] n bébé m; **baby carriage** n (US) voiture f d'enfant; **baby-sit** vi garder les enfants; **baby-sitter** n baby-sitter m/f; **baby wipe** n lingette f (pour bébé)

bachelor ['bætʃələʳ] n célibataire m; **B~ of Arts/Science (BA/BSc)** ≈ licencié(e) ès or en lettres/sciences

back [bæk] n (of person, horse) dos m; (of hand) dos, revers m; (of house) derrière m; (of car, train) arrière m; (of chair) dossier m; (of page) verso m; (Football) arrière m ▷ vt (financially) soutenir (financièrement); (candidate: also: **~ up**) soutenir, appuyer; (horse: at races) parier or miser sur; (car) (faire) reculer ▷ vi reculer; (car etc) faire marche arrière ▷ adv (in compounds) de derrière, à l'arrière ▷ adv (not forward) en arrière; (returned): **he's ~** il est rentré, il est de retour; **can**

the people at the ~ hear me properly? est-ce que les gens du fond m'entendent?; **~ to front** à l'envers; **~ seat/wheel** (Aut) siège m/roue f arrière m; **~ payments/rent** arriéré m de paiements/loyer; **~ garden/ room** jardin/pièce sur l'arrière; **he ran ~** il est revenu en courant; **throw the ball ~** renvoie la balle; **can I have it ~?** puis-je le ravoir?, peux-tu me le rendre?; **he called ~** (again) il a rappelé; **back down** vi rabattre de ses prétentions; **back out** vi (of promise) se dédire; **back up** vt (person) soutenir; (Comput) faire une copie de sauvegarde de; **backache** n mal au dos; **backbencher** n (BRIT) membre du parlement sans portefeuille; **backbone** n colonne vertébrale, épine dorsale; **back door** n porte f de derrière; **backfire** vi (Aut) pétarader; (plans) mal tourner; **backgammon** n trictrac m; **background** n arrière-plan m; (of events) situation f, conjoncture f; (basic knowledge) éléments mpl de base; (experience) formation f; **family background** milieu familial; **backing** n (fig) soutien m, appui m; **backlog** n: **backlog of work** travail m en retard; **backpack** n sac m à dos; **backpacker** n randonneur(-euse); **backslash** n barre oblique inversée; **backstage** adv dans les coulisses; **backstroke** n dos crawlé; **backup** adj (train, plane) supplémentaire, de réserve; (Comput) appui m de sauvegarde ▷ n (support) appui m, soutien m; (Comput: also: **backup file**) sauvegarde f; **backward** adj (movement) en arrière; (person, country) arriéré(e), attardé(e); **backwards** adv (move, go) en arrière; (read a list) à l'envers, à rebours; (fall) à la renverse; (walk) à reculons; **backyard** n arrière-cour f

bacon ['beɪkən] n bacon m, lard m

bacteria [bæk'tɪərɪə] npl bactéries fpl

bad [bæd] adj mauvais(e); (child) vilain(e); (mistake, accident) grave;

(*meat, food*) gâté(e), avarié(e); **his ~ leg** sa jambe malade; **to go ~** (*meat, food*) se gâter; (*milk*) tourner

bade [beɪd] *pt of* **bid**

badge [bædʒ] *n* insigne *m*; (*of policeman*) plaque *f*; (*stick-on, sew-on*) badge *m*

badger ['bædʒə*] *n* blaireau *m*

badly ['bædlɪ] *adv* (*work, dress etc*) mal; **to reflect ~ on sb** donner une mauvaise image de qn; **~ wounded** grièvement blessé; **he needs it ~** il en a absolument besoin; **~ off** *adj, adv* dans la gêne

bad-mannered ['bæd'mænəd] *adj* mal élevé(e)

badminton ['bædmɪntən] *n* badminton *m*

bad-tempered ['bæd'tempəd] *adj* (*by nature*) ayant mauvais caractère; (*on one occasion*) de mauvaise humeur

bag [bæg] *n* sac *m*; **~s of** (*inf: lots of*) des tas de; **baggage** *n* bagages *mpl*; **baggage allowance** *n* franchise *f* de bagages; **baggage reclaim** *n* (*at airport*) livraison *f* des bagages; **baggy** *adj* avachi(e), qui fait des poches; **bagpipes** *npl* cornemuse *f*

bail [beɪl] *n* caution *f* ▷ *vt* (*prisoner: also: **grant ~ to**) mettre en liberté sous caution; (*boat: also: **~ out**) écoper; **to be released on ~** être libéré(e) sous caution; **bail out** *vt* (*prisoner*) payer la caution de

bait [beɪt] *n* appât *m* ▷ *vt* appâter; (*fig: tease*) tourmenter

bake [beɪk] *vt* (faire) cuire au four ▷ *vi* (*bread etc*) cuire (au four); (*make cakes etc*) faire de la pâtisserie; **baked beans** *npl* haricots blancs à la sauce tomate; **baked potato** *n* pomme *f* de terre en robe des champs; **baker** *n* boulanger *m*; **bakery** *n* boulangerie *f*; **baking** *n* (*process*) cuisson *f*; **baking powder** *n* levure *f* (chimique)

balance ['bæləns] *n* équilibre *m*; (*Comm: sum*) solde *m*; (*remainder*) reste

m; (*scales*) balance *f* ▷ *vt* mettre or faire tenir en équilibre; (*pros and cons*) peser; (*budget*) équilibrer; (*account*) balancer; (*compensate*) compenser, contrebalancer; **~ of trade/payments** balance commerciale/des comptes or paiements; **balanced** *adj* (*personality, diet*) équilibré(e); (*report*) objectif(-ive); **balance sheet** *n* bilan *m*

balcony ['bælkənɪ] *n* balcon *m*; **do you have a room with a ~?** avez-vous une chambre avec balcon?

bald [bɔːld] *adj* chauve; (*tyre*) lisse

ball [bɔːl] *n* boule *f*; (*football*) ballon *m*; (*for tennis, golf*) balle *f*; (*dance*) bal *m*; **to play ~** jouer au ballon (or à la balle); (*fig*) coopérer

ballerina [bælə'riːnə] *n* ballerine *f*

ballet ['bæleɪ] *n* ballet *m*; (*art*) danse *f* (classique); **ballet dancer** *n* danseur(-euse) de ballet

balloon [bə'luːn] *n* ballon *m*

ballot ['bælət] *n* scrutin *m*

ballpoint (pen) ['bɔːlpɔɪnt-] *n* stylo *m* à bille

ballroom ['bɔːlrum] *n* salle *f* de bal

Baltic ['bɔːltɪk] *n*: **the ~ (Sea)** la (mer) Baltique

bamboo [bæm'buː] *n* bambou *m*

ban [bæn] *n* interdiction *f* ▷ *vt* interdire

banana [bə'nɑːnə] *n* banane *f*

band [bænd] *n* bande *f*; (*at a dance*) orchestre *m*; (*Mil*) musique *f*, fanfare *f*

bandage ['bændɪdʒ] *n* bandage *m*, pansement *m* ▷ *vt* (*wound, leg*) mettre un pansement or un bandage sur

Band-Aid® ['bændeɪd] *n* (*US*) pansement adhésif

B. & B. *n abbr* = **bed and breakfast**

bandit ['bændɪt] *n* bandit *m*

bang [bæŋ] *n* détonation *f*; (*of door*) claquement *m*; (*blow*) coup (violent) *m* ▷ *vt* frapper (violemment); (*door*) claquer ▷ *vi* détoner, claquer

Bangladesh [bæŋglə'dɛʃ] *n* Bangladesh *m*

Bangladeshi [bæŋgləˈdɛʃɪ] *adj*
du Bangladesh ▷ *n* habitant(e) *m/f* du
Bangladesh
bangle [ˈbæŋgl] *n* bracelet *m*
bangs [bæŋz] *npl* (*us: fringe*) frange *f*
banish [ˈbænɪʃ] *vt* bannir
banister(s) [ˈbænɪstə(z)] *n(pl)*
rampe *f* (d'escalier)
banjo [ˈbændʒəu] (*pl* **banjoes** or
banjos) *n* banjo *m*
bank [bæŋk] *n* banque *f*, (*of river,
lake*) bord *m*, rive *f*, (*of earth*) talus
m, remblai *m* ▷ *vi* (*Aviat*) virer sur
l'aile; **bank on** *vt fus* miser ou tabler
sur; **bank account** *n* compte *m* en
banque; **bank balance** *n* solde *m*
bancaire; **bank card** (*BRIT*) *n* carte
d'identité bancaire; **bank charges**
npl (*BRIT*) frais *mpl* de banque; **banker**
n banquier *m*; **bank holiday** *n* (*BRIT*)
jour férié (*où les banques sont fermées*);
voir article "**bank holiday**"; **banking**
n opérations *fpl* bancaires; profession
f de banquier; **bank manager** *n*
directeur *m* d'agence (bancaire);
banknote *n* billet *m* de banque

● **BANK HOLIDAY**

● Le terme **bank holiday** s'applique
● au Royaume-Uni aux jours fériés
● pendant lesquels banques et
● commerces sont fermés. Les
● principaux **bank holidays** à part Noël
● et Pâques se situent au mois de
● mai et fin août, et contrairement
● aux pays de tradition catholique,
● ne coïncident pas nécessairement
● avec une fête religieuse.

bankrupt [ˈbæŋkrʌpt] *adj* en faillite;
to go ~ faire faillite; **bankruptcy**
n faillite *f*
bank statement *n* relevé *m* de
compte
banner [ˈbænər] *n* bannière *f*
bannister(s) [ˈbænɪstə(z)] *n(pl)*
= **banister(s)**

banquet [ˈbæŋkwɪt] *n* banquet *m*,
festin *m*
baptism [ˈbæptɪzəm] *n* baptême *m*
baptize [bæpˈtaɪz] *vt* baptiser
bar [bɑːʳ] *n* (*in pub*) bar *m*; (*counter*)
comptoir *m*, bar *m*; (*rod: of metal etc*)
barre *f*; (: *of window etc*) barreau
m; (*of chocolate*) tablette *f*, plaque
f, (*fig: obstacle*) obstacle *m*;
(*prohibition*) mesure *f* d'exclusion;
(*Mus*) mesure *f* ▷ *vt* (*road*) barrer;
(*person*) exclure; (*activity*) interdire;
~ of soap savonnette *f*, **behind ~s**
(*prisoner*) derrière les barreaux; **the
B~** (*Law*) le barreau; **~ none** sans
exception
barbaric [bɑːˈbærɪk] *adj* barbare
barbecue [ˈbɑːbɪkjuː] *n* barbecue *m*
barbed wire [ˈbɑːbd-] *n* fil *m* de fer
barbelé
barber [ˈbɑːbəʳ] *n* coiffeur *m* (pour
hommes); **barber's (shop)**, (*US*)
barber shop *n* salon *m* de coiffure
(pour hommes)
bar code *n* code *m* à barres, code-
barre *m*
bare [bɛəʳ] *adj* nu(e) ▷ *vt* mettre à nu,
dénuder; (*teeth*) montrer; **barefoot**
adj, adv nu-pieds, (les) pieds nus;
barely *adv* à peine
bargain [ˈbɑːgɪn] *n* (*transaction*)
marché *m*; (*good buy*) affaire *f*,
occasion *f* ▷ *vi* (*haggle*) marchander;
(*negotiate*) négocier, traiter; **bargain
the ~** par-dessus le marché; **bargain
for** *vt fus* (*inf*): **he got more than he
~ed for** il en a eu pour son argent!
barge [bɑːdʒ] *n* péniche *f*; **barge in**
vi (*walk in*) faire irruption; (*interrupt talk*)
intervenir mal à propos
bark [bɑːk] *n* (*of tree*) écorce *f*; (*of dog*)
aboiement *m* ▷ *vi* aboyer
barley [ˈbɑːlɪ] *n* orge *f*
barmaid [ˈbɑːmeɪd] *n* serveuse *f* (de
bar), barmaid *f*
barman [ˈbɑːmən] (*irreg*) *n* serveur *m*
(de bar), barman *m*
barn [bɑːn] *n* grange *f*

barometer [bə'rɒmɪtə^r] n baromètre m

baron ['bærən] n baron m; **baroness** n baronne f

barracks ['bærəks] npl caserne f

barrage ['bærɑːʒ] n (Mil) tir m de barrage; (dam) barrage m; (of criticism) feu m

barrel ['bærəl] n tonneau m; (of gun) canon m

barren ['bærən] adj stérile

barrette [bə'ret] (US) n barrette f

barricade [bærɪ'keɪd] n barricade f

barrier ['bærɪə^r] n barrière f

barring ['bɑːrɪŋ] prep sauf

barrister ['bærɪstə^r] n (BRIT) avocat (plaidant)

barrow ['bærəʊ] n (cart) charrette f à bras

bartender ['bɑːtendə^r] n (US) serveur m (de bar), barman m

base [beɪs] n base f ▷ vt (opinion, belief): **to ~ sth on** baser or fonder qch sur ▷ adj vil(e), bas(se)

baseball ['beɪsbɔːl] n base-ball m; **baseball cap** n casquette f de base-ball

Basel [bɑːl] n = **Basle**

basement ['beɪsmənt] n sous-sol m

bases ['beɪsiːz] npl of **basis**

bash [bæʃ] vt (inf) frapper, cogner

basic ['beɪsɪk] adj (precautions, rules) élémentaire; (principles, research) fondamental(e); (vocabulary, salary) de base; (minimal) réduit(e) au minimum, rudimentaire; **basically** adv (in fact) en fait; (essentially) fondamentalement; **basics** npl: **the basics** l'essentiel m

basil ['bæzl] n basilic m

basin ['beɪsn] n (vessel, also Geo) cuvette f, bassin m; (BRIT: for food) bol m; (also: **wash~**) lavabo m

basis (pl **bases**) ['beɪsɪs, -siːz] n base f; **on a part-time/trial ~** à temps partiel/à l'essai

basket ['bɑːskɪt] n corbeille f; (with handle) panier m; **basketball** n basket-ball m

Basle [bɑːl] n Bâle

Basque [bæsk] adj basque ▷ n Basque m/f; **the ~ Country** le Pays basque

bass [beɪs] n (Mus) basse f

bastard ['bɑːstəd] n enfant naturel(le), bâtard(e); (inf!) salaud m (!)

bat [bæt] n chauve-souris f; (for baseball etc) batte f; (BRIT: for table tennis) raquette f ▷ vt: **he didn't ~ an eyelid** il n'a pas sourcillé or bronché

batch [bætʃ] n (of bread) fournée f; (of papers) liasse f; (of applicants, letters) paquet m

bath (pl **baths**) [bɑːθ, bɑːðz] n bain m; (bathtub) baignoire f ▷ vt baigner, donner un bain à; **to have a ~** prendre un bain; see also **baths**

bathe [beɪð] vi se baigner ▷ vt baigner; (wound etc) laver

bathing ['beɪðɪŋ] n baignade f; **bathing costume**, (US) **bathing suit** n maillot m (de bain)

bath: **bathrobe** n peignoir m de bain; **bathroom** n salle f de bains; **baths** [bɑːðz] npl (BRIT: also: **swimming baths**) piscine f; **bath towel** n serviette f de bain; **bathtub** n baignoire f

baton ['bætən] n bâton m; (Mus) baguette f; (club) matraque f

batter ['bætə^r] vt battre ▷ n pâte f à frire; **battered** adj (hat, pan) cabossé(e); **battered wife/child** épouse/enfant maltraité(e) or martyr(e)

battery ['bætərɪ] n (for torch, radio) pile f; (Aut, Mil) batterie f; **battery farming** n élevage m en batterie

battle ['bætl] n bataille f, combat m ▷ vi se battre, lutter; **battlefield** n champ m de bataille

bay [beɪ] n (of sea) baie f; (BRIT: for parking) place f de stationnement; (: for loading) aire f de chargement; **B~ of Biscay** golfe m de Gascogne; **to hold sb at ~** tenir qn à distance or en échec

bay leaf n laurier m

bazaar [bəˈzɑːʳ] n (shop, market) bazar m; (sale) vente f de charité

BBC n abbr (= British Broadcasting Corporation) office de la radiodiffusion et télévision britannique

B.C. adv abbr (= before Christ) av. J.-C.

KEYWORD

be [biː] (pt **was**, **were**, pp **been**) aux vb **1** (with present participle, forming continuous tenses): **what are you doing?** que faites-vous?; **they're coming tomorrow** ils viennent demain; **I've been waiting for you for 2 hours** je t'attends depuis 2 heures

2 (with pp, forming passives) être; **to be killed** être tué(e); **the box had been opened** la boîte avait été ouverte; **he was nowhere to be seen** on ne le voyait nulle part

3 (in tag questions): **it was fun, wasn't it?** c'était drôle, n'est-ce pas?; **he's good-looking, isn't he?** il est beau, n'est-ce pas?; **she's back, is she?** elle est rentrée, n'est-ce pas ou alors?

4 (+to + infinitive): **the house is to be sold** (necessity) la maison doit être vendue; (future) la maison va être vendue; **he's not to open it** il ne doit pas l'ouvrir

▶ vb + complement **1** (gen) être; **I'm English** je suis anglais(e); **I'm tired** je suis fatigué(e); **I'm hot/cold** j'ai chaud/froid; **he's a doctor** il est médecin; **be careful/good/quiet!** faites attention/soyez sages/taisez-vous!; **2 and 2 are 4** 2 et 2 font 4

2 (of health) aller; **how are you?** comment allez-vous?; **I'm better now** je vais mieux maintenant; **he's very ill** il est très malade

3 (of age) avoir; **how old are you?** quel âge avez-vous?; **I'm sixteen (years old)** j'ai seize ans

4 (cost) coûter; **how much was the meal?** combien a coûté le repas?; **that'll be £5, please** ça fera 5 livres, s'il vous plaît; **this shirt is £17** cette chemise coûte 17 livres

▶ vi **1** (exist, occur etc) être, exister; **the prettiest girl that ever was** la fille la plus jolie qui ait jamais existé; **is there a God?** y a-t-il un dieu?; **be that as it may** quoi qu'il en soit; **so be it** soit

2 (referring to place) être, se trouver; **I won't be here tomorrow** je ne serai pas là demain

3 (referring to movement) aller; **where have you been?** où êtes-vous allé(s)?

▶ impers vb **1** (referring to time) être; **it's 5 o'clock** il est 5 heures; **it's the 28th of April** c'est le 28 avril

2 (referring to distance): **it's 10 km to the village** le village est à 10 km

3 (referring to the weather) faire; **it's too hot/cold** il fait trop chaud/froid; **it's windy today** il y a du vent aujourd'hui

4 (emphatic): **it's me/the postman** c'est moi/le facteur; **it was Maria who paid the bill** c'est Maria qui a payé la note

beach [biːtʃ] n plage f ▷ vt échouer

beacon [ˈbiːkən] n (lighthouse) fanal m; (marker) balise f

bead [biːd] n perle f; (of dew, sweat) goutte f; **beads** npl (necklace) collier m

beak [biːk] n bec m

beam [biːm] n (Archit) poutre f; (of light) rayon m ▷ vi rayonner

bean [biːn] n haricot m; (of coffee) grain m; **beansprouts** npl pousses fpl or germes mpl de soja

bear [bɛəʳ] n ours m ▷ vt (pt **bore**, pp **borne**) porter; (endure) supporter; (interest) rapporter ▷ vi: **to ~ right/left** obliquer à droite/gauche, se diriger vers la droite/gauche

beard [bɪəd] n barbe f

bearer ['bɛərə'] n porteur m; (of passport etc) titulaire m/f

bearing ['bɛərɪŋ] n maintien m, allure f; (connection) rapport m; **(ball) bearings** npl (Tech) roulement m (à billes)

beast [bi:st] n bête f; (inf: person) brute f

beat [bi:t] n battement m; (Mus) temps m, mesure f; (of policeman) ronde f ▷ vt, vi (pt **beat**, pp **beaten**) battre; **off the ~en track** hors des chemins or sentiers battus; **to ~ it** (inf) ficher le camp; **beat up** vt (inf: person) tabasser; **beating** n raclée f

beautiful ['bju:tɪful] adj beau (belle); **beautifully** adv admirablement

beauty ['bju:tɪ] n beauté f; **beauty parlour**, (us) **beauty parlor** n institut m de beauté; **beauty salon** n institut m de beauté; **beauty spot** n (on skin) grain m de beauté; (BRIT Tourism) site naturel (d'une grande beauté)

beaver ['bi:və'] n castor m

became [bɪ'keɪm] pt of **become**

because [bɪ'kɔz] conj parce que; **~ of** prep à cause de

beckon ['bɛkən] vt (also: **~ to**) faire signe (de venir) à

become [bɪ'kʌm] vi devenir; **to ~ fat/thin** grossir/maigrir; **to ~ angry** se mettre en colère

bed [bɛd] n lit m; (of flowers) parterre m; (of coal, clay) couche f; (of sea, lake) fond m; **to go to ~** aller se coucher; **bed and breakfast** n (terms) chambre et petit déjeuner; (place) ≈ chambre f d'hôte; voir article **"bed and breakfast"; bedclothes** npl couvertures fpl et draps mpl; **bedding** n literie f; **bed linen** n draps mpl de lit (et taies fpl d'oreillers), literie f; **bedroom** n chambre f (à coucher); **bedside** n: **at sb's bedside** au chevet de qn; **bedside lamp** n lampe f de chevet; **bedside table** n table f de chevet; **bedsit(ter)** n (BRIT) chambre

meublée, studio m; **bedspread** n couvre-lit m, dessus-de-lit m

bedtime n: **it's bedtime** c'est l'heure de se coucher

BED AND BREAKFAST

Un bed and breakfast est une petite pension dans une maison particulière ou une ferme où l'on peut louer une chambre avec petit déjeuner compris pour un prix modique par rapport à ce que l'on paierait dans un hôtel. Ces établissements sont communément appelés "B & B", et sont signalés par une pancarte dans le jardin ou au-dessus de la porte.

bee [bi:] n abeille f

beech [bi:tʃ] n hêtre m

beef [bi:f] n bœuf m; **roast ~** rosbif m; **beefburger** n hamburger m

been [bi:n] pp of **be**

beer [bɪə'] n bière f; **beer garden** n (BRIT) jardin m d'un pub (où l'on peut emmener ses consommations)

beet [bi:t] n (vegetable) betterave f; (us: also: **red ~**) betterave (potagère)

beetle ['bi:tl] n scarabée m, coléoptère m

beetroot ['bi:tru:t] n (BRIT) betterave f

before [bɪ'fɔ:'] prep (of time) avant; (of space) devant ▷ conj avant que + sub; avant de ▷ adv avant; **~ going** avant de partir; **~ she goes** avant qu'elle (ne) parte; **the week ~** la semaine précédente or d'avant; **I've never seen it ~** c'est la première fois que je le vois; **beforehand** adv au préalable, à l'avance

beg [bɛg] vi mendier ▷ vt mendier; (forgiveness, mercy etc) demander; (entreat) supplier; **to ~ sb to do sth** supplier qn de faire qch; see also **pardon**

began [bɪˈɡæn] *pt of* begin

beggar [ˈbeɡəʳ] *n* mendiant(e)

begin [bɪˈɡɪn] (*pt* **began**, *pp* **begun**) *vt, vi* commencer; **to ~ doing** or **to do sth** commencer à faire qch; **beginner** *n* débutant(e); **beginning** *n* commencement *m*, début *m*

begun [bɪˈɡʌn] *pp of* begin

behalf [bɪˈhɑːf] *n* **on ~ of**, (us) **in ~ of** (*representing*) de la part de; (*for benefit of*) pour le compte de; **on my/his ~** de ma/sa part

behave [bɪˈheɪv] *vi* se conduire, se comporter; (*well: also:* **~ o.s.**) se conduire bien or comme il faut; **behaviour**, (us) **behavior** *n* comportement *m*, conduite *f*

behind [bɪˈhaɪnd] *prep* derrière; (*time*) en retard sur; (*supporting*) **to be ~ sb** soutenir qn ▷ *adv* derrière; en retard ▷ *n* derrière *m*; **~ the scenes** dans les coulisses; **to be ~ (schedule) with sth** être en retard dans qch

beige [beɪʒ] *adj* beige

Beijing [ˈbeɪˈdʒɪŋ] *n* Pékin

being [ˈbiːɪŋ] *n* être *m*; **to come into ~** prendre naissance

belated [bɪˈleɪtɪd] *adj* tardif(-ive)

belch [bɛltʃ] *vi* avoir un renvoi, roter ▷ *vt* (*smoke etc: also:* **~ out**) vomir, cracher

Belgian [ˈbeldʒən] *adj* belge, de Belgique ▷ *n* Belge *m/f*

Belgium [ˈbeldʒəm] *n* Belgique *f*

belief [bɪˈliːf] *n* (*opinion*) conviction *f*; (*trust, faith*) foi *f*

believe [bɪˈliːv] *vt, vi* croire, estimer; **to ~ in** (*God*) croire en; (*ghosts, method*) croire à; **believer** *n* (*in idea, activity*) partisan(e); (*Rel*) croyant(e)

bell [bɛl] *n* cloche *f*; (*small*) clochette *f*; grelot *m*; (*on door*) sonnette *f*; (*electric*) sonnerie *f*

bellboy [ˈbɛlbɔɪ], (us) **bellhop** [ˈbɛlhɔp] *n* groom *m*, chasseur *m*

bellow [ˈbeləʊ] *vi* (*bull*) meugler; (*person*) brailler

bell pepper *n* (*esp us*) poivron *m*

belly [ˈbɛlɪ] *n* ventre *m*; **belly button** (*inf*) *n* nombril *m*

belong [bɪˈlɔŋ] *vi*: **to ~ to** appartenir à; (*club etc*) faire partie de; **this book ~s here** ce livre va ici, la place de ce livre est ici; **belongings** *npl* affaires *fpl*, possessions *fpl*

beloved [bɪˈlʌvɪd] *adj* (bien-)aimé(e), chéri(e)

below [bɪˈləʊ] *prep* sous, au-dessous de ▷ *adv* en dessous, en contre-bas; **see ~** voir plus bas or plus loin or ci-dessous

belt [bɛlt] *n* ceinture *f*; (*Tech*) courroie *f* ▷ *vt* (*thrash*) donner une raclée à; **beltway** *n* (*us Aut*) route *f* de ceinture; (: *motorway*) périphérique *m*

bemused [bɪˈmjuːzd] *adj* médusé(e)

bench [bɛntʃ] *n* banc *m*; (*in workshop*) établi *m*; **the B~** (*Law: judges*) la magistrature, la Cour

bend [bɛnd] (*pt, pp* **bent**) *vt* courber; (*leg, arm*) plier ▷ *vi* se courber ▷ *n* (*in road*) virage *m*, tournant *m*; (*in pipe, river*) coude *m*; **bend down** *vi* se baisser; **bend over** *vi* se pencher

beneath [bɪˈniːθ] *prep* sous, au-dessous de; (*unworthy of*) indigne de ▷ *adv* dessous, au-dessous

beneficial [bɛnɪˈfɪʃl] *adj*: **~ (to)** salutaire (pour), bénéfique (à)

benefit [ˈbenɪfɪt] *n* avantage *m*, profit *m*; (*allowance of money*) allocation *f* ▷ *vt* faire du bien à, profiter à ▷ *vi*: **he'll ~ from it** cela lui fera du bien, il y gagnera or s'en trouvera bien

Benelux [ˈbenɪlʌks] *n* Bénélux *m*

benign [bɪˈnaɪn] *adj* (*person, smile*) bienveillant(e), affable; (*Med*) bénin(-igne)

bent [bɛnt] *pt, pp of* bend ▷ *n* inclination *f*, penchant *m* ▷ *adj*: **to be ~ on** être résolu(e) à

bereaved [bɪˈriːvd] *n*: **the ~** la famille du disparu

beret [ˈbereɪ] *n* béret *m*

Berlin [bəːˈlɪn] *n* Berlin

Bermuda [bəːˈmjuːdə] n Bermudes fpl

Bern [bəːn] n Berne

berry [ˈberɪ] n baie f

berth [bəːθ] n (bed) couchette f; (for ship) poste m d'amarrage, mouillage m ▷ vi (in harbour) venir à quai; (at anchor) mouiller

beside [bɪˈsaɪd] prep à côté de; (compared with) par rapport à; **that's ~ the point** ça n'a rien à voir; **to be ~ o.s. (with anger)** être hors de soi; **besides** adv en outre, de plus ▷ prep en plus de; (except) excepté

best [best] adj meilleur(e) ▷ adv le mieux; **the ~ part of** (quantity) le plus clair de, la plus grande partie de; **at ~** au mieux; **to make the ~ of sth** s'accommoder de qch (du mieux que l'on peut); **to do one's ~** faire de son mieux; **to the ~ of my knowledge** pour autant que je sache; **to the ~ of my ability** du mieux que je pourrai; **best-before date** n date f de limite d'utilisation or de consommation; **best man** (irreg) n garçon m d'honneur; **bestseller** n best-seller m, succès m de librairie

bet [bet] n pari m ▷ vt, vi (pt, pp **betted**) parier; **to ~ sb sth** parier qch à qn

betray [bɪˈtreɪ] vt trahir

better [ˈbetə*] adj meilleur(e) ▷ adv mieux ▷ vt améliorer ▷ n: **to get the ~ of** triompher de, l'emporter sur; **you had ~ do it** vous feriez mieux de le faire; **he thought ~ of it** il s'est ravisé; **to get ~** (Med) aller mieux; (improve) s'améliorer

betting [ˈbetɪŋ] n paris mpl; **betting shop** n (BRIT) bureau m de paris

between [bɪˈtwiːn] prep entre ▷ adv au milieu, dans l'intervalle

beverage [ˈbevərɪdʒ] n boisson f (gén sans alcool)

beware [bɪˈweə*] vi: **to ~ (of)** prendre garde (à); **"~ of the dog"** (attention) chien méchant"

bewildered [bɪˈwɪldəd] adj dérouté(e), ahuri(e)

beyond [bɪˈjɔnd] prep (in space, time) au-delà de; (exceeding) au-dessus de ▷ adv au-delà; **~ doubt** hors de doute; **~ repair** irréparable

bias [ˈbaɪəs] n (prejudice) préjugé m, parti pris m; (preference) prévention f; **bias(s)ed** adj partial(e), montrant un parti pris

bib [bɪb] n bavoir m

Bible [ˈbaɪbl] n Bible f

bicarbonate of soda [baɪˈkɑːbənɪt-] n bicarbonate m de soude

biceps [ˈbaɪseps] n biceps m

bicycle [ˈbaɪsɪkl] n bicyclette f; **bicycle pump** n pompe f à vélo

bid [bɪd] n offre f; (at auction) enchère f; (attempt) tentative f ▷ vi (pt, pp **bid**) faire une enchère or offre ▷ vt (pt **bade**, pp **bidden**) faire une enchère or offre de; **to ~ sb good day** souhaiter le bonjour à qn; **bidder** n: **the highest bidder** le plus offrant

bidet [ˈbiːdeɪ] n bidet m

big [bɪg] adj (in height: person, building, tree) grand(e); (in bulk, amount: person, parcel, book) gros(se); **Big Apple** n voir article **"Big Apple"**; **bigheaded** adj prétentieux(-euse); **big toe** n gros orteil

BIG APPLE

Si l'on sait que "The Big Apple" désigne la ville de New York ("apple" est en réalité un terme d'argot signifiant "grande ville"), on connaît moins les surnoms donnés aux autres grandes villes américaines. Chicago est surnommée "Windy City" à cause des rafales soufflant du lac Michigan, La Nouvelle-Orléans doit son sobriquet de "Big Easy" à son style de vie décontracté, et l'industrie

● automobile a donné à Detroit son surnom de "Motown".

bike [baɪk] n vélo m; **bike lane** n piste f cyclable

bikini [bɪˈkiːnɪ] n bikini m

bilateral [baɪˈlætərəl] adj bilatéral(e)

bilingual [baɪˈlɪŋɡwəl] adj bilingue

bill [bɪl] n note f, facture f; (in restaurant) addition f, note f; (Pol) projet m de loi; (us: banknote) billet m (de banque); (notice) affiche f; (of bird) bec m; **to put it on my ~** mettez-le sur mon compte; **"post no ~s"** "défense d'afficher"; **to fit** or **fill the ~** (fig) faire l'affaire; **billboard** n (us) panneau m d'affichage; **billfold** [ˈbɪlfəʊld] n (us) portefeuille m

billiards [ˈbɪljədz] n billard m

billion [ˈbɪljən] n (BRIT) billion m (million de millions); (us) milliard m

bin [bɪn] n boîte f; (BRIT: also: **dust~, litter ~**) poubelle f; (for coal) coffre m

bind (pt, pp **bound**) [baɪnd, baʊnd] vt attacher; (book) relier; (oblige) obliger, contraindre ▷ n (inf: nuisance) scie f

binge [bɪndʒ] n (inf): **to go on a ~** faire la bringue

bingo [ˈbɪŋɡəʊ] n sorte de jeu de loto pratiqué dans des établissements publics

binoculars [bɪˈnɔkjʊləz] npl jumelles fpl

bio...: **biochemistry** [baɪəˈkemɪstrɪ] n biochimie f; **biodegradable** [ˈbaɪəʊdɪˈɡreɪdəbl] adj biodégradable; **biodiesel** [ˈbaɪəʊdiːzl] n biogazole m, biodiesel m; **biofuel** [ˈbaɪəʊfjuːəl] n biocarburant; **biography** [baɪˈɒɡrəfɪ] n biographie f; **biological** [baɪəˈlɒdʒɪkl] adj biologique; **biology** [baɪˈɒlədʒɪ] n biologie f; **biometric** [baɪəˈmetrɪk] adj biométrique

bipolar [baɪˈpəʊlə] adj bipolaire

birch [bəːtʃ] n bouleau m

bird [bəːd] n oiseau m; (BRIT inf: girl) nana f; **bird flu** n grippe f aviaire; **bird of prey** n oiseau m de proie; **birdwatching** n ornithologie f (d'amateur)

Biro® [ˈbaɪərəʊ] n stylo m à bille

birth [bəːθ] n naissance f; **to give ~ to** donner naissance à, mettre au monde; (animal) mettre bas; **birth certificate** n acte m de naissance; **birth control** n (policy) limitation f des naissances; (methods) méthode(s) contraceptive(s); **birthday** n anniversaire m ▷ cpd (cake, card etc) d'anniversaire; **birthmark** n envie f, tache f de vin; **birthplace** n lieu m de naissance

biscuit [ˈbɪskɪt] n (BRIT) biscuit m; (us) petit pain au lait

bishop [ˈbɪʃəp] n évêque m; (Chess) fou m

bistro [ˈbiːstrəʊ] n petit restaurant m, bistrot m

bit [bɪt] pt of **bite** ▷ n morceau m; (Comput) bit m, élément m binaire; (of tool) mèche f; (of horse) mors m; **a ~ of** un peu de; **a ~ mad/dangerous** un peu fou/risqué; **~ by ~** petit à petit

bitch [bɪtʃ] n (dog) chienne f; (offensive) salope f (!), garce f

bite [baɪt] vt, vi (pt **bit**, pp **bitten**) mordre; (insect) piquer ▷ n morsure f; (insect bite) piqûre f; (mouthful) bouchée f; **let's have a ~ (to eat)** mangeons un morceau; **to ~ one's nails** se ronger les ongles

bitten [ˈbɪtn] pp of **bite**

bitter [ˈbɪtə] adj amer(-ère); (criticism) cinglant(e); (icy: weather, wind) glacial(e) ▷ n (BRIT: beer) bière f à forte teneur en houblon

bizarre [bɪˈzɑː] adj bizarre

black [blæk] adj noir(e) ▷ n (colour) noir m ▷ vt (BRIT Industry) boycotter; **to give sb a ~ eye** pocher l'œil à qn, faire un œil au beurre noir à qn; **to be in the ~** (in credit) avoir un compte créditeur; **~ and blue** (bruised) couvert(e) de bleus; **black out** vi (faint) s'évanouir; **blackberry** n mûre f; **blackbird** n merle m; **blackboard** n tableau noir; **black coffee** n café noir; **blackcurrant** n cassis m; **black ice** n verglas m; **blackmail** n chantage m ▷ vt faire chanter, soumettre au chantage; **black market** n marché noir; **blackout** n panne f d'électricité; (in wartime) black-out m; (TV) interruption f d'émission; (fainting) syncope f; **black pepper** n poivre noir; **black pudding** n boudin (noir); **Black Sea** n: the Black Sea la mer Noire

bladder ['blædə'] n vessie f

blade [bleɪd] n lame f; (of propeller) pale f; **a ~ of grass** un brin d'herbe

blame [bleɪm] n faute f ▷ vt: **to ~ sb/sth for sth** attribuer à qn/qch la responsabilité de qch; reprocher qch à qn/qch; **I'm not to ~** ce n'est pas ma faute

bland [blænd] adj (taste, food) doux (douce), fade

blank [blæŋk] adj blanc (blanche); (look) sans expression, dénué(e) d'expression ▷ n espace m vide, blanc m; (cartridge) cartouche f à blanc; **his mind was a ~** il avait la tête vide

blanket ['blæŋkɪt] n couverture f; (of snow, cloud) couche f

blast [blɑːst] n explosion f; (shock wave) souffle m; (of air, steam) bouffée f ▷ vt faire sauter or exploser

blatant ['bleɪtənt] adj flagrant(e), criant(e)

blaze [bleɪz] n (fire) incendie m; (fig) flamboiement m ▷ vi (fire) flamber; (fig) flamboyer, resplendir ▷ vt: **to ~ a trail** (fig) montrer la voie; **in a ~ of publicity** à grand renfort de publicité

blazer ['bleɪzə'] n blazer m

bleach [bliːtʃ] n (also: **household ~**) eau f de Javel ▷ vt (linen) blanchir; **bleachers** npl (us Sport) gradins mpl (en plein soleil)

bleak [bliːk] adj morne, triste, maussade; (weather) triste, maussade; (smile) lugubre; (prospect, future) morose

bled [blɛd] pt, pp of **bleed**

bleed (pt, pp **bled**) [bliːd, blɛd] vt saigner; (brakes, radiator) purger ▷ vi saigner; **my nose is ~ing** je saigne du nez

blemish ['blɛmɪʃ] n défaut m; (on reputation) tache f

blend [blɛnd] n mélange m ▷ vt mélanger ▷ vi (colours etc: also: **~ in**) se mélanger, se fondre, s'allier; **blender** n (Culin) mixeur m

bless (pt, pp **blessed** or **blest**) [blɛs, blɛst] vt bénir; **~ you!** (after sneeze) à tes souhaits!; **blessing** n bénédiction f; (godsend) bienfait m

blew [bluː] pt of **blow**

blight [blaɪt] vt (hopes etc) anéantir, briser

blind [blaɪnd] adj aveugle ▷ n (for window) store m ▷ vt aveugler; **~ people** les aveugles mpl; **blind alley** n impasse f; **blindfold** n bandeau m ▷ adj, adv les yeux bandés ▷ vt bander les yeux à

blink [blɪŋk] vi cligner les yeux; (light) clignoter

bliss [blɪs] n félicité f, bonheur m sans mélange

blister ['blɪstə'] n (on skin) ampoule f, cloque f; (on paintwork) boursouflure f ▷ vi (paint) se boursoufler, se cloquer

blizzard ['blɪzəd] n blizzard m, tempête f de neige

bloated ['bləʊtɪd] adj (face) bouffi(e); (stomach, person) gonflé(e)

blob [blɒb] n (drop) goutte f; (stain, spot) tache f

block [blɒk] n bloc m; (in pipes) obstruction f; (toy) cube m; (of buildings) pâté m (de maisons) ▷ vt bloquer; **to put a block on sth** faire obstacle à; **the sink is ~ed** l'évier est bouché; **~ of flats** (BRIT) immeuble (locatif); **mental ~** blocage m; **block up** vt boucher; **blockade** [blɒ'keɪd] n blocus m ▷ vt faire le blocus de; **blockage** n obstruction f; **blockbuster** n (film, book) grand succès; **block capitals** npl majuscules *fpl* d'imprimerie; **block letters** *npl* majuscules *fpl*

blog [blɒg] *n* blog *m* ▷ *vi* bloguer

blogger ['blɒgə^r] *n* blogueur(-euse) *m/f*

blogosphere ['blɒgəsfɪə^r] *n* blogosphère *f*

bloke [bləʊk] *n* (*BRIT inf*) type *m*

blond(e) [blɒnd] *adj, n* blond(e)

blood [blʌd] *n* sang *m*; **blood donor** *n* donneur(-euse) *m/f* de sang; **blood group** *n* groupe sanguin; **blood poisoning** *n* empoisonnement *m* du sang; **blood pressure** *n* tension (artérielle); **bloodshed** *n* effusion *f* de sang, carnage *m*; **bloodshot** *adj*: **bloodshot eyes** yeux injectés de sang; **bloodstream** *n* sang *m*, système sanguin; **blood test** *n* analyse *f* de sang; **blood transfusion** *n* transfusion *f* de sang; **blood type** *n* groupe sanguin; **blood vessel** *n* vaisseau sanguin; **bloody** *adj* sanglant(e); (*BRIT inf!*): **this bloody …** ce foutu …, ce putain de … (*!*) ▷ *adv*: **bloody strong/good** (*BRIT inf!*) vachement or sacrément fort/bon

bloom [bluːm] *n* fleur *f* ▷ *vi* être en fleur

blossom ['blɒsəm] *n* fleur(s) *f(pl)* ▷ *vi* être en fleurs; (*fig*) s'épanouir

blot [blɒt] *n* tache *f* ▷ *vt* tacher; (*ink*) sécher

blouse [blaʊz] *n* (*feminine garment*) chemisier *m*, corsage *m*

blow [bləʊ] (*pt* **blew**, *pp* **blown**) *n* coup *m* ▷ *vi* souffler ▷ *vt* (*instrument*) jouer de; (*fuse*) faire sauter; **to ~ one's nose** se moucher; **blow away** *vi* s'envoler ▷ *vt* chasser, faire s'envoler; **blow out** *vi* (*fire, flame*) s'éteindre; (*tyre*) éclater; (*fuse*) sauter; **blow up** *vi* exploser, sauter ▷ *vt* faire sauter; (*tyre*) gonfler; (*Phot*) agrandir; **blow-dry** *n* (*hairstyle*) brushing *m*

blue [bluː] *adj* bleu(e); (*depressed*) triste; **~ film/joke** film *m*/histoire *f* pornographique; **out of the ~** (*fig*) à l'improviste, sans qu'on s'y attende; **bluebell** *n* jacinthe *f* des bois;

blueberry *n* myrtille *f*, airelle *f*; **blue cheese** *n* (fromage) bleu *m*; **blues** *npl*; **the blues** (*Mus*) le blues; **to have the blues** (*inf: feeling*) avoir le cafard

bluff [blʌf] *vi* bluffer ▷ *n* bluff *m*; **to call sb's ~** mettre qn au défi d'exécuter ses menaces

blunder ['blʌndə^r] *n* gaffe *f*, bévue *f* ▷ *vi* faire une gaffe or une bévue

blunt [blʌnt] *adj* (*knife*) émoussé(e), peu tranchant(e); (*pencil*) mal taillé(e); (*person*) brusque, ne mâchant pas ses mots

blur [blɜː^r] *n* (*shape*): **to become a ~** devenir flou ▷ *vt* brouiller, rendre flou(e); **blurred** *adj* flou(e)

blush [blʌʃ] *vi* rougir ▷ *n* rougeur *f*; **blusher** *n* rouge *m* à joues

board [bɔːd] *n* (*wooden*) planche *f*; (*on wall*) panneau *m*; (*for chess etc*) plateau *m*; (*cardboard*) carton *m*; (*committee*) conseil *m*, comité *m*; (*in firm*) conseil d'administration; (*Naut, Aviat*): **on ~** à bord ▷ *vt* (*ship*) monter à bord de; (*train*) monter dans; **full ~** (*BRIT*) pension complète; **half ~** (*BRIT*) demi-pension *f*; **~ and lodging** *n* chambre *f* avec pension; **to go by the ~** (*hopes, principles*) être abandonné(e); **board game** *n* jeu *m* de société; **boarding card** *n* (*Aviat, Naut*) carte *f* d'embarquement; **boarding pass** *n* (*US*) = **boarding card**; **boarding school** *n* internat *m*, pensionnat *m*; **board room** *n* salle *f* du conseil d'administration

boast [bəʊst] *vi*: **to ~ (about or of)** se vanter (de)

boat [bəʊt] *n* bateau *m*; (*small*) canot *m*; barque *f*

bob [bɒb] *vi* (*boat, cork on water: also:* **~ up and down**) danser, se balancer

bobby pin ['bɒbɪ-] *n* (*US*) pince *f* à cheveux

body ['bɒdɪ] *n* corps *m*; (*of car*) carrosserie *f*; (*fig: society*) organe *m*, organisme *m*; **body-building** *n* body-building *m*, culturisme *m*; **bodyguard**

n garde du corps; **bodywork** *n* carrosserie f

bog [bɒg] *n* tourbière f ▷ *vt*: **to get ~ged down (in)** (*fig*) s'enliser (dans)

bogus ['bəʊgəs] *adj* bidon *inv*; fantôme

boil [bɔɪl] *vt* (*faire*) bouillir ▷ *vi* bouillir ▷ *n* (*Med*) furoncle *m*; **to come to the** *or* (*us*) **a ~** bouillir; **boil down** *vi* (*fig*): **to ~ down to** se réduire *or* ramener à; **boil over** *vi* déborder; **boiled egg** *n* œuf *m* à la coque; **boiler** *n* chaudière f; **boiling** ['bɔɪlɪŋ] *adj*: **I'm boiling (hot)** (*inf*) je crève de chaud; **boiling point** *n* point *m* d'ébullition

bold [bəʊld] *adj* hardi(e), audacieux(-euse); (*pej*) effronté(e); (*outline, colour*) franc (franche), tranché(e), marqué(e)

bollard ['bɒləd] *n* (*BRIT Aut*) borne lumineuse *or* de signalisation

bolt [bəʊlt] *n* verrou *m*; (*with nut*) boulon *m* ▷ *adv*: **~ upright** droit(e) comme un piquet ▷ *vt* (*door*) verrouiller; (*food*) engloutir ▷ *vi* se sauver, filer (comme une flèche); (*horse*) s'emballer

bomb [bɒm] *n* bombe f ▷ *vt* bombarder; **bombard** [bɒm'bɑːd] *vt* bombarder; **bomber** *n* (*Aviat*) bombardier *m*; (*terrorist*) poseur *m* de bombes; **bomb scare** *n* alerte f à la bombe

bond [bɒnd] *n* lien *m*; (*binding promise*) engagement *m*, obligation f; (*Finance*) obligation; **bonds** *npl* (*chains*) chaînes *fpl*; **in ~** (*of goods*) en entrepôt

bone [bəʊn] *n* os *m*; (*of fish*) arête f ▷ *vt* désosser; ôter les arêtes de

bonfire ['bɒnfaɪə'] *n* feu *m* (de joie); (*for rubbish*) feu

bonnet ['bɒnɪt] *n* bonnet *m*; (*BRIT: of car*) capot *m*

bonus ['bəʊnəs] *n* (*money*) prime f; (*advantage*) avantage *m*

boo [buː] *excl* hou!, peuh! ▷ *vt* huer

book [bʊk] *n* livre *m*; (*of stamps, tickets etc*) carnet *m* ▷ *vt* (*ticket*) prendre;

(*seat, room*) réserver; (*football player*) prendre le nom de, donner un carton à; **books** *npl* (*Comm*) comptes *mpl*, comptabilité f; **I ~ed a table in the name of ...** j'ai réservé une table au nom de ...; **book in** *vi* (*BRIT: at hotel*) prendre sa chambre; **book up** *vt* réserver; **the hotel is ~ed up** l'hôtel est complet; **bookcase** *n* bibliothèque f (*meuble*); **booking** *n* (*BRIT*) réservation f; **I confirmed my booking by fax/email** j'ai confirmé ma réservation par fax/e-mail; **booking office** *n* (*BRIT*) bureau *m* de location; **book-keeping** *n* comptabilité f; **booklet** *n* brochure f; **bookmaker** *n* bookmaker *m*; **bookmark** *n* (*for book*) marque-page *m*; (*Comput*) signet *m*; **bookseller** *n* libraire *m*/f; **bookshelf** *n* (*single*) étagère f (à livres); (*bookcase*) bibliothèque f; **bookshop**, **bookstore** *n* librairie f

boom [buːm] *n* (*noise*) grondement *m*; (*in prices, population*) forte augmentation; (*busy period*) boom *m*, vague f de prospérité ▷ *vi* gronder; prospérer

boost [buːst] *n* stimulant *m*, remontant *m* ▷ *vt* stimuler

boot [buːt] *n* botte f; (*for hiking*) chaussure f (de marche); (*ankle boot*) bottine f; (*BRIT: of car*) coffre *m* ▷ *vt* (*Comput*) lancer, mettre en route; **to ~ (in addition)** par-dessus le marché, en plus

booth [buːð] *n* (*at fair*) baraque (*foraine*); (*of telephone etc*) cabine f; (*also: voting ~*) isoloir *m*

booze [buːz] (*inf*) *n* boissons *fpl* alcooliques, alcool *m*

border ['bɔːdə'] *n* bordure f; bord *m*; (*of a country*) frontière f; **borderline** *n* (*fig*) ligne f de démarcation

bore [bɔː'] *pt of* **bear** ▷ *vt* (*person*) ennuyer, raser; (*hole*) percer; (*well, tunnel*) creuser ▷ *n* (*person*) raseur(-euse); (*boring thing*) barbe f;

(of gun) calibre m; **bored** adj: **to be bored** s'ennuyer; **boredom** n ennui m
boring ['bɔːrɪŋ] adj ennuyeux(-euse)
born [bɔːn] adj: **to be ~** naître; **I was ~ in 1960** je suis né en 1960
borne [bɔːn] pp of **bear**
borough ['bʌrə] n municipalité f
borrow ['bɔrəu] vt: **to ~ sth (from sb)** emprunter qch (à qn)
Bosnian ['bɔznɪən] adj bosniaque, bosnien(ne) ▷ n Bosniaque m/f, Bosnien(ne)
bosom ['buzəm] n poitrine f; (fig) sein m
boss [bɔs] n patron(ne); ▷ vt (also: **~ about, ~ around**) mener à la baguette; **bossy** adj autoritaire
both [bəuθ] adj les deux, l'un(e) et l'autre ▷ pron: **~ (of them)** les deux, tous (toutes) les deux, l'un(e) et l'autre; **~ of us went, we ~ went** nous sommes allés tous les deux ▷ adv: **~ A and B** A et B
bother ['bɔðə] vt (worry) tracasser; (needle, bait) importuner, ennuyer; (disturb) déranger ▷ vi (also: **~ o.s.**) se tracasser, se faire du souci ▷ n (trouble) ennuis mpl; **to ~ doing** prendre la peine de faire; **don't ~** ce n'est pas la peine; **it's no ~** aucun problème
bottle ['bɔtl] n bouteille f; (baby's) biberon m; (of perfume, medicine) flacon m ▷ vt mettre en bouteille(s); **bottle bank** n conteneur m (de bouteilles); **bottle-opener** n ouvre-bouteille m
bottom ['bɔtəm] n (of container, sea etc) fond m; (buttocks) derrière m; (of page, list) bas m; (of mountain, tree, hill) pied m ▷ adj (shelf, step) du bas
bought [bɔːt] pt, pp of **buy**
boulder ['bəuldə] n gros rocher (gén lisse, arrondi)
bounce [bauns] vi (ball) rebondir; (cheque) être refusé (étant sans provision) ▷ vt faire rebondir ▷ n (rebound) rebond m; **bouncer** n (inf: at dance, club) videur m

(of gun) calibre m; **bored** adj: **to be**
bound [baund] pt, pp of **bind** ▷ n (gen pl) limite f; (leap) bond m ▷ vi (leap) bondir ▷ vt (limit) borner ▷ adj: **to be ~ to do sth** (obliged) être obligé(e) or avoir obligation de faire qch; **he's ~ to fail** (likely) il est sûr d'échouer, son échec est inévitable or assuré; **~ by** (law, regulation) engagé(e) par; **~ for** à destination de; **out of ~s** dont l'accès est interdit
boundary ['baundrɪ] n frontière f
bouquet ['bukeɪ] n bouquet m
bourbon ['buəbən] n (us: also: **~ whiskey**) bourbon m
bout [baut] n période f; (of malaria etc) accès m, crise f; (Boxing etc) combat m, match m
boutique [buː'tiːk] n boutique f
bow¹ [bəu] n nœud m; (weapon) arc m; (Mus) archet m
bow² [bau] n (with body) révérence f, inclination f (du buste or corps); (Naut: also: **~s**) proue f ▷ vi faire une révérence, s'incliner
bowels [bauəlz] npl intestins mpl; (fig) entrailles fpl
bowl [bəul] n (for eating) bol m; (for washing) cuvette f; (ball) boule f ▷ vi (Cricket) lancer (la balle); **bowler** n (Cricket) lanceur m (de la balle); (BRIT: also: **bowler hat**) (chapeau m) melon m; **bowling** n (game) jeu m de boules, jeu de quilles; **bowling alley** n bowling m; **bowling green** n terrain m de boules (gazonné et carré); **bowls** n (jeu m de) boules fpl
bow tie [bəu-] n nœud m papillon
box [bɔks] n boîte f; (also: **cardboard ~**) carton m; (Theat) loge f ▷ vt mettre en boîte ▷ vi boxer, faire de la boxe; **boxer** n ['bɔksə] n (person) boxeur m; **boxer shorts** npl caleçon m; **boxing** n ['bɔksɪŋ] n (sport) boxe f; **Boxing Day** n (BRIT) le lendemain de Noël; voir article "Boxing Day"; **boxing gloves** npl gants mpl de boxe; **boxing ring** n ring m; **box office** n bureau m de location

◆ **BOXING DAY**

Boxing Day est le lendemain de Noël, férié en Grande-Bretagne. Ce nom vient d'une coutume du XIXe siècle qui consistait à donner des cadeaux de Noël (dans des boîtes) à ses employés etc le 26 décembre.

boy [bɔɪ] n garçon m; **boy band** n boys band m

boycott [ˈbɔɪkɒt] n boycottage m ▷ vt boycotter

boyfriend [ˈbɔɪfrɛnd] n (petit) ami m

bra [brɑː] n soutien-gorge m

brace [breɪs] n (support) attache f, agrafe f; (BRIT: also: ~**s**: on teeth) appareil m (dentaire); (tool) vilebrequin m ▷ vt (support) consolider, soutenir; **braces** npl (BRIT: for trousers) bretelles fpl; **to ~ o.s.** (fig) se préparer mentalement

bracelet [ˈbreɪslɪt] n bracelet m

bracket [ˈbrækɪt] n (Tech) tasseau m, support m; (group) classe f, tranche f; (also: **brace ~**) accolade f; (also: **round ~**) parenthèse f; (also: **square ~**) crochet m ▷ vt mettre entre parenthèses or crochets; **in ~s** entre parenthèses or crochets

brag [bræg] vi se vanter

braid [breɪd] n (trimming) galon m; (of hair) tresse f, natte f

brain [breɪn] n cerveau m; **brains** npl (intellect, food) cervelle f

braise [breɪz] vt braiser

brake [breɪk] n frein m ▷ vt, vi freiner; **brake light** n feu m de stop

bran [bræn] n son m

branch [brɑːntʃ] n branche f; (Comm) succursale f; (of bank) agence f; **branch off** vi (road) bifurquer; **branch out** vi diversifier ses activités

brand [brænd] n marque f (commerciale) ▷ vt (cattle) marquer (au fer rouge); **brand name** n nom m de marque; **brand-new** adj tout(e) neuf (neuve), flambant neuf (neuve)

brandy [ˈbrændɪ] n cognac m

brash [bræʃ] adj effronté(e)

brass [brɑːs] n cuivre m (jaune), laiton m; **the ~** (Mus) les cuivres; **brass band** n fanfare f

brat [bræt] n (pej) mioche m/f, môme m/f

brave [breɪv] adj courageux(-euse), brave ▷ vt braver, affronter; **bravery** n bravoure f, courage m

brawl [brɔːl] n rixe f, bagarre f

Brazil [brəˈzɪl] n Brésil m; **Brazilian** adj brésilien(ne) ▷ n Brésilien(ne)

breach [briːtʃ] vt ouvrir une brèche dans ▷ n (gap) brèche f; (breaking): ~ **of contract** rupture f de contrat; ~ **of the peace** attentat m à l'ordre public

bread [brɛd] n pain m; **breadbin** n (BRIT) boîte f or huche f à pain; **breadbox** n (us) boîte f or huche f à pain; **breadcrumbs** npl miettes fpl de pain; (Culin) chapelure f, panure f

breadth [brɛtθ] n largeur f

break [breɪk] (pt **broke**, pp **broken**) vt casser, briser; (promise) rompre; (law) violer ▷ vi se casser, se briser; (weather) tourner; (storm) éclater; (day) se lever ▷ n (gap) brèche f; (fracture) cassure f; (rest) interruption f, arrêt m; (short) pause f; (: at school) récréation f; (chance) chance f, occasion f favorable; **to ~ one's leg** etc se casser la jambe etc; **to ~ a record** battre un record; **to ~ the news to sb** annoncer la nouvelle à qn; **break down** vt (door etc) enfoncer; (figures, data) décomposer, analyser ▷ vi s'effondrer; (Med) faire une dépression (nerveuse); (Aut) tomber en panne; **my car has broken down** ma voiture est en panne; **break in** vt (horse etc) dresser ▷ vi (burglar) entrer par effraction; (interrupt) interrompre; **break into** vt fus (house) s'introduire or pénétrer par effraction dans; **break off** vi (speaker) s'interrompre; (branch) se rompre ▷ vt (talks, engagement) rompre; **break out** vi éclater, se déclarer; (prisoner) s'évader; **to ~ out in spots** se couvrir de boutons; **break up** vi (partnership) cesser, prendre fin; (marriage) se briser; (crowd, meeting) se séparer; (ship) se disloquer; (Scol: pupils) être en vacances; (line) couper ▷ vt fracasser, casser; (fight etc) interrompre; faire cesser; (marriage) désunir; **the line's** or **you're ~ing up** ça coupe; **breakdown** n (Aut) panne f; (in communications, marriage) rupture f; (Med: also: **nervous breakdown**) dépression (nerveuse); (of figures) ventilation f, répartition f; **breakdown van** n, (us) **breakdown truck** n dépanneuse f

breakfast ['brɛkfəst] n petit déjeuner m; **what time is ~?** le petit déjeuner est à quelle heure?

break: break-in n cambriolage m; **breakthrough** n percée f

breast [brɛst] n (of woman) sein m; (chest) poitrine f; (of chicken, turkey) blanc m; **breast-feed** vt, vi (irreg: like **feed**) allaiter; **breast-stroke** n brasse f

breath [brɛθ] n haleine f, souffle m; **to take a deep ~** respirer à fond; **out of ~** à bout de souffle, essoufflé(e)

Breathalyser® ['brɛθəlaɪzə*] (BRIT) n alcootest m

breathe [briːð] vt, vi respirer; **breathe in** vt inspirer ▷ vt aspirer; **breathe out** vt, vi expirer; **breathing** n respiration f

breath: breathless adj essoufflé(e), haletant(e); **breathtaking** adj stupéfiant(e), à vous couper le souffle; **breath test** n alcootest m

bred [brɛd] pt, pp of **breed**

breed [briːd] (pt, pp **bred**) vt élever, faire l'élevage de ▷ vi se reproduire ▷ n race f, variété f

breeze [briːz] n brise f

breezy ['briːzɪ] adj (day, weather) venteux(-euse); (manner) désinvolte; (person) jovial(e)

brew [bruː] vt (tea) faire infuser; (beer) brasser ▷ vi (fig) se préparer, couver; **brewery** n brasserie f (fabrique)

bribe [braɪb] n pot-de-vin m ▷ vt acheter; soudoyer; **bribery** n corruption f

bric-a-brac ['brɪkəbræk] n bric-à-brac m

brick [brɪk] n brique f; **bricklayer** n maçon m

bride [braɪd] n mariée f, épouse f; **bridegroom** n marié m, époux m; **bridesmaid** n demoiselle f d'honneur

bridge [brɪdʒ] n pont m (Naut) passerelle f (de commandement); (of nose) arête f; (Cards, Dentistry) bridge m ▷ vt (gap) combler

bridle ['braɪdl] n bride f

brief [briːf] adj bref (brève) ▷ n (Law) dossier m, cause f; (gen) tâche f ▷ vt mettre au courant; **briefs** npl slip m; **briefcase** n serviette f, porte-documents m inv; **briefing** n instructions fpl; (Press) briefing m; **briefly** adv brièvement

brigadier [brɪgə'dɪə*] n brigadier général

bright [braɪt] adj brillant(e); (room, weather) clair(e); (person: clever) intelligent(e), doué(e); (: cheerful) gai(e); (idea) génial(e); (colour) vif (vive)

brilliant ['brɪljənt] adj brillant(e); (light, sunshine) éclatant(e); (inf: great) super

brim [brɪm] n bord m

brine [braɪn] n (Culin) saumure f

bring [brɪŋ] (pt, pp **brought**) vt (thing) apporter; (person) amener; **bring about** vt provoquer, entraîner; **bring back** vt rapporter; (person) ramener; **bring down** vt (lower) abaisser; (shoot down) abattre; (government) faire s'effondrer; **bring in** vt (person) faire entrer; (object) rentrer; (Pol: legislation) introduire; (produce: income) rapporter; **bring on** vt (illness, attack) provoquer;

(player, substitute) amener; **bring out**
vt sortir; *(meaning)* faire ressortir,
mettre en relief; **bring up** vt élever;
(carry up) monter; *(question)* soulever;
(food: vomit) vomir, rendre

brink [brɪŋk] n bord m

brisk [brɪsk] adj vif (vive); *(abrupt)*
brusque; *(trade etc)* actif(-ive)

bristle ['brɪsl] n poil m ▷ vi se hérisser

Brit [brɪt] n abbr *(inf: = British person)*
Britannique m/f

Britain ['brɪtən] n *(also:* **Great ~**) la
Grande-Bretagne

British ['brɪtɪʃ] adj britannique ▷ npl:
the ~ les Britanniques mpl; **British
Isles** npl; **the British Isles** les îles fpl
Britanniques

Briton ['brɪtən] n Britannique m/f

Brittany ['brɪtənɪ] n Bretagne f

brittle ['brɪtl] adj cassant(e), fragile

broad [brɔːd] adj large; *(distinction)*
général(e); *(accent)* prononcé(e); **in ~
daylight** en plein jour

B road n abbr *(BRIT)* = route
départementale

broad: broadband n transmission
f à haut débit; **broad bean** n fève
f; **broadcast** *(pt, pp* **broadcast**) n
émission ▷ vt *(Radio)* radiodiffuser;
(TV) téléviser ▷ vi émettre; **broaden**
vt élargir; **to broaden one's mind**
élargir ses horizons ▷ vi s'élargir;
broadly adv en gros, généralement;
broad-minded adj large d'esprit

broccoli ['brɔkəlɪ] n brocoli m

brochure ['brəʊʃjʊər] n
prospectus m, dépliant m

broil [brɔɪl] vt *(us)* rôtir

broke [brəʊk] pt of **break** ▷ adj *(inf)*
fauché(e)

broken ['brəʊkən] pp of **break** ▷ adj
(stick, leg etc) cassé(e); *(machine:
also:* **~ down**) fichu(e); **in ~ French/
English** dans un français/anglais
approximatif ou hésitant

broker ['brəʊkər] n courtier m

bronchitis [brɔŋ'kaɪtɪs] n bronchite f

bronze [brɔnz] n bronze m

brooch [brəʊtʃ] n broche f

brood [bruːd] n couvée f ▷ vi *(person)*
méditer (sombrement), ruminer

broom [brum] n balai m; *(Bot)*
genêt m

Bros. abbr *(Comm: = brothers)* Frères

broth [brɔθ] n bouillon m de viande et
de légumes

brothel ['brɔθl] n maison close,
bordel m

brother ['brʌðər] n frère m; **brother-
in-law** n beau-frère m

brought [brɔːt] pt, pp of **bring**

brow [braʊ] n front m; *(eyebrow)*
sourcil m; *(of hill)* sommet m

brown [braʊn] adj brun(e), marron
inv; *(hair)* châtain inv; *(tanned)*
bronzé(e) ▷ n *(colour)* brun m, marron
m ▷ vt brunir; *(Culin)* faire dorer, faire
roussir; **brown bread** n pain m bis

Brownie ['braʊnɪ] n jeannette f
éclaireuse (cadette)

brown rice n riz m complet

brown sugar n cassonade f

browse [braʊz] vi *(in shop)* regarder
(sans acheter); **to ~ through a
book** feuilleter un livre; **browser** n
(Comput) navigateur m

bruise [bruːz] n bleu m, ecchymose
f, contusion f ▷ vt contusionner,
meurtrir

brunette [bruː'nɛt] n *(femme)* brune

brush [brʌʃ] n brosse f; *(for painting)*
pinceau m; *(for shaving)* blaireau m;
(quarrel) accrochage m, prise f de bec
▷ vt brosser; *(also:* **~ past, ~ against**)
effleurer, frôler

Brussels ['brʌslz] n Bruxelles

Brussels sprout n chou m de
Bruxelles

brutal ['bruːtl] adj brutal(e)

B.Sc. n abbr = **Bachelor of Science**

BSE n abbr (= bovine spongiform
encephalopathy) ESB f, BSE f

bubble ['bʌbl] n bulle f ▷ vi
bouillonner, faire des bulles;
(sparkle, fig) pétiller; **bubble bath**
n bain moussant; **bubble gum**

chewing-gum m; **bubblejet printer** ['bʌbldʒet-] n imprimante f à bulle d'encre

buck [bʌk] n mâle m (d'un lapin, lièvre, daim etc); (us inf) dollar m ▷ vi ruer, lancer une ruade; **to pass the ~ (to sb)** se décharger de la responsabilité (sur qn)

bucket ['bʌkɪt] n seau m; **bucket list** n liste f de choses à faire avant de mourir

buckle ['bʌkl] n boucle f ▷ vt (belt etc) boucler, attacher ▷ vt (warp) tordre, gauchir; (: wheel) se voiler

bud [bʌd] n bourgeon m; (of flower) bouton m ▷ vi bourgeonner; (flower) éclore

Buddhism ['budɪzəm] n bouddhisme m

Buddhist ['budɪst] adj bouddhiste ▷ n Bouddhiste m/f

buddy ['bʌdɪ] n (us) copain m

budge [bʌdʒ] vt faire bouger ▷ vi bouger

budgerigar ['bʌdʒərɪgaːʳ] n perruche f

budget ['bʌdʒɪt] n budget m ▷ vi: **to ~ for sth** inscrire qch au budget

budgie ['bʌdʒɪ] n = **budgerigar**

buff [bʌf] adj (couleur) chamois m ▷ n (inf: enthusiast) mordu(e)

buffalo ['bʌfələu] (pl **buffalo** or **buffaloes** n (BRIT) buffle m; (us) bison m

buffer ['bʌfəʳ] n tampon m; (Comput) mémoire f tampon

buffet n ['bufeɪ] (food, BRIT: bar) buffet m ▷ vt ['bʌfɪt] secouer, ébranler; **buffet car** n (BRIT Rail) voiture-bar f

bug [bʌg] n (bedbug etc) punaise f; (esp us: any insect) insecte m, bestiole f, (fig: germ) virus m, microbe m; (spy device) dispositif m d'écoute (électronique), micro clandestin; (Comput: of program) erreur f ▷ vt (room) poser des micros dans; (inf: annoy) embêter

buggy ['bʌgɪ] n poussette f

build [bɪld] n (of person) carrure f, charpente f ▷ vt (pt, pp **built**)

construire, bâtir; **build up** vt accumuler, amasser; (business) développer; (reputation) bâtir; **builder** n entrepreneur m; **building** n (trade) construction f; (structure) bâtiment m, construction f; (: residential, offices) immeuble m; **building site** n chantier m (de construction); **building society** n (BRIT) société f de crédit immobilier

built [bɪlt] pt, pp of **build**; **built-in** adj (cupboard) encastré(e); (device) incorporé(e); intégré(e); **built-up area** zone urbanisée

bulb [bʌlb] n (Bot) bulbe m, oignon m; (Elec) ampoule f

Bulgaria [bʌlˈgɛərɪə] n Bulgarie f; **Bulgarian** adj bulgare ▷ n Bulgare m/f

bulge [bʌldʒ] n renflement m, gonflement m ▷ vi faire saillie; présenter un renflement; (pocket, file): **to be bulging with** être plein(e) à craquer de

bulimia [bəˈlɪmɪə] n boulimie f

bulimic [bjuːˈlɪmɪk] adj, n boulimique m/f

bulk [bʌlk] n masse f, volume m; **in ~** (Comm) en gros, en vrac; **the ~ of** la plus grande or grosse partie de; **bulky** adj volumineux(-euse), encombrant(e)

bull [bul] n taureau m; (male elephant, whale) mâle m

bulldozer ['buldəuzəʳ] n bulldozer m

bullet ['bulɪt] n balle f (de fusil etc)

bulletin ['bulɪtɪn] n bulletin m, communiqué m; (also: **news ~**) (bulletin d')informations fpl; **bulletin board** n (Comput) messagerie f (électronique)

bullfight ['bulfaɪt] n corrida f, course f de taureaux; **bullfighter** n torero m; **bullfighting** n tauromachie f

bully ['bulɪ] n brute f, tyran m ▷ vt tyranniser, rudoyer

bum [bʌm] n (inf: BRIT: backside) derrière m; (esp us: tramp) vagabond(e), traîne-savates m/f inv; (idler) glandeur m

bumblebee ['bʌmblbi:] n bourdon m

bump [bʌmp] n (blow) coup m, choc m; (jolt) cahot m; (on road etc, on head) bosse f ▷ vt frapper, cogner; (car) emboutir; **bump into** vt fus rentrer dans, tamponner; (inf: meet) tomber sur; **bumper** n pare-chocs m inv ▷ adj: **bumper crop/harvest** récolte/ moisson exceptionnelle; **bumpy** adj (road) cahoteux(-euse); **it was a bumpy flight/ride** on a été secoués dans l'avion/la voiture

bun [bʌn] n (cake) petit gâteau; (bread) petit pain au lait; (of hair) chignon m

bunch [bʌntʃ] n (of flowers) bouquet m; (of keys) trousseau m; (of bananas) régime m; (of people) groupe m; **bunches** npl (in hair) couettes fpl; **~ of grapes** grappe f de raisin

bundle ['bʌndl] n paquet m ▷ vt (also: **~ up**) faire un paquet de; (put): **to ~ sth/sb into** fourrer or enfourner qch/qn dans

bungalow ['bʌŋɡələu] n bungalow m

bungee jumping ['bʌndʒi:'dʒʌmpiŋ] n saut m à l'élastique

bunion ['bʌnjən] n oignon m (au pied)

bunk [bʌŋk] n couchette f; **bunk beds** npl lits superposés

bunker ['bʌŋkəʳ] n (coal store) soute f à charbon; (Mil, Golf) bunker m

bunny ['bʌni] n (also: **~ rabbit**) lapin m

buoy [bɔɪ] n bouée f; **buoyant** adj (ship) flottable; (carefree) gai(e), plein(e) d'entrain; (Comm: market, economy) actif(-ive)

burden ['bə:dn] n fardeau m, charge f ▷ vt charger; (oppress) accabler, surcharger

bureau (pl **bureaux**) ['bjuərəu, -z] n (BRIT: writing desk) bureau m, secrétaire m; (US: chest of drawers) commode f; (office) bureau, office m

bureaucracy [bjuə'rɔkrəsɪ] n bureaucratie f

bureaucrat ['bjuərəkræt] n bureaucrate m/f, rond-de-cuir m

bureau de change [-də'ʃɑ̃ʒ] (pl **bureaux de change**) n bureau m de change

bureaux ['bjuərəuz] npl of **bureau**

burger ['bə:ɡəʳ] n hamburger m

burglar ['bə:ɡləʳ] n cambrioleur m; **burglar alarm** n sonnerie f d'alarme; **burglary** n cambriolage m

Burgundy ['bə:ɡəndɪ] n Bourgogne f

burial ['bɛrɪəl] n enterrement m

burn [bə:n] vt, vi (pt **burned**, pp **burnt**) brûler ▷ n brûlure f; **burn down** vt incendier, détruire par le feu; **burn out** vt (writer etc): **to ~ o.s. out** s'user (à force de travailler); **burning** adj (building, forest) en flammes; (issue, question) brûlant(e); (ambition) dévorant(e)

Burns' Night [bə:nz-] n fête écossaise à la mémoire du poète Robert Burns

◆ **BURNS' NIGHT**

Burns' Night est une fête qui a lieu le 25 janvier, à la mémoire du poète écossais Robert Burns (1759-1796), à l'occasion de laquelle les Écossais partout dans le monde organisent un souper, en général arrosé de whisky. Le plat principal est toujours le haggis, servi avec de la purée de pommes de terre et de la purée de rutabagas. On apporte le haggis au son des cornemuses et au cours du repas on lit des poèmes de Burns et on chante ses chansons.

burnt [bə:nt] pt, pp of **burn**

burp [bə:p] (inf) n rot m ▷ vi roter

burrow ['bʌrəu] n terrier m ▷ vi (rabbit) creuser un terrier; (rummage) fouiller

burst [bə:st] (pt, pp **burst**) vt faire éclater; (river: banks etc) rompre ▷ vi éclater; (tyre) crever ▷ n explosion f; (also: **~ pipe**) fuite f (due à une rupture); **a ~ of enthusiasm/energy** un accès d'enthousiasme/d'énergie; **to ~ into flames** s'enflammer soudainement; **to ~ out laughing** éclater de rire; **to ~ into tears** fondre en larmes; **to ~ open** vi s'ouvrir violemment or soudainement; **to be ~ing with** (container) être plein(e) (à craquer) de, regorger de; (fig) être débordant(e) de; **burst into** vt fus (room etc) faire irruption dans

bury ['bɛrɪ] vt enterrer

bus (pl **buses**) [bʌs, 'bʌsɪz] n (auto) bus m; **bus conductor** n receveur(-euse) m/f de bus

bush [bʊʃ] n buisson m; (scrub land) brousse f; **to beat about the ~** tourner autour du pot

business ['bɪznɪs] n (matter, firm) affaire f; (trading) affaires fpl; (job, duty) travail m; **to be away on ~** être en déplacement d'affaires; **it's none of my ~** cela ne me regarde pas, ce ne sont pas mes affaires; **he means ~** il ne plaisante pas, il est sérieux; **business class** n (on plane) classe f affaires; **businesslike** adj sérieux(-euse), efficace; **businessman** (irreg) n homme m d'affaires; **business trip** n voyage m d'affaires; **businesswoman** (irreg) n femme f d'affaires

busker ['bʌskə'] n (BRIT) artiste m ambulant(e)

bus: bus pass n carte f de bus; **bus shelter** n abribus m; **bus station** n gare routière; **bus stop** n arrêt m d'autobus

bust [bʌst] n buste m; (measurement) tour m de poitrine ▷ adj (inf: broken) fichu(e), fini(e); **to go ~** (inf) faire faillite

bustling ['bʌslɪŋ] adj (town) très animé(e)

busy ['bɪzɪ] adj occupé(e); (shop, street) très fréquenté(e); (us:

telephone, line) occupé ▷ vt: **to ~ o.s.** s'occuper; **busy signal** n (us) tonalité f occupé inv

KEYWORD

but [bʌt] conj mais; **I'd love to come, but I'm busy** j'aimerais venir mais je suis occupé; **he's not English but French** il n'est pas anglais mais français; **but that's far too expensive!** mais c'est bien trop cher!
▶ prep (apart from, except) sauf, excepté; **nothing but** rien d'autre que; **we've had nothing but trouble** nous n'avons eu que des ennuis; **no-one but him can do it** lui seul peut le faire; **who but a lunatic would do such a thing?** qui sinon un fou ferait une chose pareille?; **but for you/your help** sans toi/ton aide; **anything but that** tout sauf ou excepté ça, tout mais pas ça
▶ adv (just, only) ne ... que; **she's but a child** elle n'est qu'une enfant; **had I but known** si seulement j'avais su; **I can but try** je peux toujours essayer; **all but finished** pratiquement terminé

butcher ['bʊtʃə'] n boucher m ▷ vt massacrer; (cattle etc for meat) tuer; **butcher's (shop)** n boucherie f

butler ['bʌtlə'] n maître m d'hôtel

butt [bʌt] n (cask) gros tonneau; (of gun) crosse f; (of cigarette) mégot m; (BRIT fig: target) cible f ▷ vt donner un coup de tête à

butter ['bʌtə'] n beurre m ▷ vt beurrer; **buttercup** n bouton m d'or

butterfly ['bʌtəflaɪ] n papillon m; (Swimming: also: **~ stroke**) brasse f papillon

buttocks ['bʌtəks] npl fesses fpl

button ['bʌtn] n bouton m; (us: badge) pin m ▷ vt (also: **~ up**) boutonner ▷ vi se boutonner

buy [baɪ] (*pt, pp* **bought**) *vt* acheter ▷ *n* achat *m*; **to ~ sb sth/sth from sb** acheter qch à qn; **to ~ sb a drink** offrir un verre or à boire à qn; **can I ~ you a drink?** je vous offre un verre?; **where can I ~ some postcards?** où est-ce que je peux acheter des cartes postales?; **buy out** *vt* (*partner*) désintéresser; **buy up** *vt* acheter en bloc, rafler; **buyer** *n* acheteur(-euse) *m/f*

buzz [bʌz] *n* bourdonnement *m*; (*inf: phone call*) **to give sb a ~** passer un coup de fil à qn ▷ *vi* bourdonner; **buzzer** *n* timbre *m* électrique

KEYWORD

by [baɪ] *prep* **1** (*referring to cause, agent*) par, de; **killed by lightning** tué par la foudre; **surrounded by a fence** entouré d'une barrière; **a painting by Picasso** un tableau de Picasso

2 (*referring to method, manner, means*): **by bus/car** en autobus/voiture; **by train** par le or en train; **to pay by cheque** payer par chèque; **by moonlight/candlelight** à la lueur de la lune/d'une bougie; **by saving hard, he ...** à force d'économiser, il ...

3 (*via, through*) par; **we came by Dover** nous sommes venus par Douvres

4 (*close to, past*) à côté de; **the house by the school** la maison à côté de l'école; **a holiday by the sea** des vacances au bord de la mer; **she went by me** elle est passée à côté de moi; **I go by the post office every day** je passe devant la poste tous les jours

5 (*with time: not later than*) avant; (: *during*): **by daylight** à la lumière du jour; **by night** la nuit, de nuit; **by 4 o'clock** avant 4 heures; **by this time tomorrow** d'ici demain à la même heure; **by the time I got here it was too late** lorsque je suis arrivé il était

déjà trop tard

6 (*amount*) à; **by the kilo/metre** au kilo/au mètre; **paid by the hour** payé à l'heure

7 (*Math: measure*): **to divide/ multiply by 3** diviser/multiplier par 3; **a room 3 metres by 4** une pièce de 3 mètres sur 4; **it's broader by a metre** c'est plus large d'un mètre

8 (*according to*) d'après, selon; **it's 3 o'clock by my watch** il est 3 heures à ma montre; **it's all right by me** je n'ai rien contre

9: **(all) by oneself** *etc* tout(e) seul(e) ▷ *adv* **1** *see* **go**; **pass** *etc*

2: **by and by** un peu plus tard, bientôt; **by and large** dans l'ensemble

bye(-bye) ['baɪ-] *excl* au revoir!, salut!

by-election ['baɪɪlekʃən] *n* (BRIT) élection (législative) partielle

bypass ['baɪpɑːs] *n* rocade *f*; (*Med*) pontage *m* ▷ *vt* éviter

byte [baɪt] *n* (*Comput*) octet *m*

C

C [siː] n (Mus) do m

cab [kæb] n taxi m; (of train, truck) cabine f

cabaret ['kæbəreɪ] n (show) spectacle m de cabaret

cabbage ['kæbɪdʒ] n chou m

cabin ['kæbɪn] n (house) cabane f, hutte f; (on ship) cabine f; (on plane) compartiment m; **cabin crew** n (Aviat) équipage m

cabinet ['kæbɪnɪt] n (Pol) cabinet m; (furniture) petit meuble à tiroirs et rayons; (also: **display ~**) vitrine f, petite armoire vitrée; **cabinet minister** n ministre m (membre du cabinet)

cable ['keɪbl] n câble m ▷ vt câbler, télégraphier; **cable car** n téléphérique m; **cable television** n télévision f par câble

cactus (pl **cacti**) ['kæktəs, -taɪ] n cactus m

café ['kæfeɪ] n ≈ café(-restaurant) m (sans alcool)

cafeteria [kæfɪ'tɪərɪə] n cafétéria f

caffeine ['kæfiːn] n caféine f

cage [keɪdʒ] n cage f

cagoule [kə'guːl] n K-way® m

Cairo ['kaɪərəu] n Le Caire

cake [keɪk] n gâteau m; **~ of soap** savonnette f

calcium ['kælsɪəm] n calcium m

calculate ['kælkjuleɪt] vt calculer; (estimate: chances, effect) évaluer; **calculation** [kælkju'leɪʃən] n calcul m; **calculator** n calculatrice f

calendar ['kæləndə'] n calendrier m

calf (pl **calves**) [kɑːf, kɑːvz] n (of cow) veau m; (of other animals) petit m; (also: **~skin**) veau m, vachette f; (Anat) mollet m

calibre, (us) **caliber** ['kælɪbə'] n calibre m

call [kɔːl] vt appeler; (meeting) convoquer ▷ vi appeler; (visit: also: **~ in, ~ round**) passer ▷ n (shout) appel m, cri m; (also: **telephone ~**) coup m de téléphone; **to be on ~** être de permanence; **to be ~ed** s'appeler; **can I make a ~ from here?** est-ce que je peux téléphoner d'ici?; **call back** vi (return) repasser; (Tel) rappeler ▷ vt (Tel) rappeler; **can you ~ back later?** pouvez-vous rappeler plus tard?; **call for** vt fus (demand) demander; (fetch) passer prendre; **call in** vt (doctor, expert, police) appeler, faire venir; **call off** vt annuler; **call on** vt fus (visit) rendre visite à, passer voir; (request): **to ~ on sb to do** inviter qn à faire; **call out** vi pousser un cri or des cris; **call up** vt (Mil) appeler, mobiliser; (Tel) appeler; **call box** n (BRIT) cabine f téléphonique; **call centre**, (us) **call center** n centre m d'appels; **caller** n (Tel) personne f qui appelle; (visitor) visiteur m

callous ['kæləs] adj dur(e), insensible

calm [kɑːm] adj calme ▷ n calme m ▷ vt calmer, apaiser; **calm down** vi se calmer, s'apaiser ▷ vt calmer, apaiser; **calmly** ['kɑːmlɪ] adv calmement, avec calme

Calor gas® ['kælə-] n (BRIT) butane m, butagaz® m

calorie ['kælərɪ] n calorie f

calves [kɑːvz] npl of **calf**

Cambodia [kæm'bəudɪə] n Cambodge m

camcorder [kæm'kɔːdə'] n caméscope m

came [keɪm] pt of **come**

camel ['kæməl] n chameau m

camera ['kæmərə] n appareil photo m; (Cine, TV) caméra f; **in ~** à huis clos, en privé; **cameraman** (irreg) n caméraman m; **camera phone** n téléphone m avec appareil photo

camouflage ['kæməflɑːʒ] n camouflage m ▷ vt camoufler

camp [kæmp] n camp m ▷ vi camper ▷ adj (man) efféminé(e)

campaign [kæm'peɪn] n (Mil, Pol) campagne f ▷ vi (also fig) faire campagne; **campaigner** n: **campaigner for** partisan(e) de; **campaigner against** opposant(e) à

camp: **camp bed** n (BRIT) lit m de camp; **camper** n campeur(-euse); (vehicle) camping-car m; **camping** n camping m; **to go camping** faire du camping; **campsite** n (terrain m de) camping m

campus ['kæmpəs] n campus m

can¹ [kæn] n (of milk, oil, water) bidon m; (tin) boîte f (de conserve) ▷ vt mettre en conserve

○ **KEYWORD**

can² [kæn] (negative **cannot** or **can't**, conditional, pt **could**) aux vb 1 (be able to) pouvoir; **you can do it if you try** vous pouvez le faire si vous essayez; **I can't hear you** je ne t'entends pas

2 (know how to) savoir; **I can swim/play tennis/drive** je sais nager/jouer au tennis/conduire; **can you speak French?** parlez-vous français?

3 (may) pouvoir; **can I use your phone?** puis-je me servir de votre téléphone?

4 (expressing disbelief, puzzlement etc): **it can't be true!** ce n'est pas possible!; **what can he want?** qu'est-ce qu'il peut bien vouloir?

5 (expressing possibility, suggestion etc): **he could be in the library** il est peut-être dans la bibliothèque; **she could have been delayed** il se peut qu'elle ait été retardée

Canada ['kænədə] n Canada m; **Canadian** [kə'neɪdɪən] adj canadien(ne) ▷ n Canadien(ne)

canal [kə'næl] n canal m

canary [kə'nɛərɪ] n canari m, serin m

cancel ['kænsəl] vt annuler; (train) supprimer; (party, appointment) décommander; (cross out) barrer, rayer; (cheque) faire opposition à; **I would like to ~ my booking** je voudrais annuler ma réservation; **cancellation** [kænsə'leɪʃən] n annulation f; suppression f

Cancer ['kænsə'] n (Astrology) le Cancer

cancer ['kænsə'] n cancer m

candidate ['kændɪdeɪt] n candidat(e)

candle ['kændl] n bougie f; (in church) cierge m; **candlestick** n (also: **candle holder**) bougeoir m; (bigger, ornate) chandelier m

candy ['kændɪ] n sucre candi; (US) bonbon m; **candy bar** (US) n barre f chocolatée; **candyfloss** n (BRIT) barbe f à papa

cane [keɪn] n canne f; (for baskets, chairs etc) rotin m ▷ vt (BRIT Scol) administrer des coups de bâton à

canister ['kænɪstə'] n boîte f (gén en métal); (of gas) bombe f

cannabis ['kænəbɪs] n (drug) cannabis m

canned [kænd] adj (food) en boîte, en conserve; (inf: music) enregistré(e); (BRIT inf: drunk) bourré(e); (US inf: worker) mis(e) à la porte

cannon ['kænən] (pl **cannon** or **cannons**) n (gun) canon m

cannot ['kænɒt] = **can not**

canoe [kə'nu:] n pirogue f; (Sport) canoë m; **canoeing** n (sport) canoë m

canon ['kænən] n (clergyman) chanoine m; (rule) canon m

can-opener [-'əʊpnə'] n ouvre-boîte m

can't [kɑːnt] = **can not**

canteen [kæn'ti:n] n (eating place) cantine f; (BRIT: of cutlery) ménagère f

canter ['kæntə'] vi aller au petit galop

canvas ['kænvəs] n toile f

canvass ['kænvəs] vi (Pol): **to ~ for** faire campagne pour ▷ vt sonder

canyon ['kænjən] n cañon m, gorge f (profonde)

cap [kæp] n casquette f; (for swimming) bonnet m de bain; (of pen) capuchon m; (of bottle) capsule f; (BRIT: contraceptive: also: **Dutch ~**) diaphragme m ▷ vt (outdo) surpasser; (put limit on) plafonner

capability [keɪpə'bɪlɪtɪ] n aptitude f, capacité f

capable ['keɪpəbl] adj capable

capacity [kə'pæsɪtɪ] n (of container) capacité f, contenance f; (ability) aptitude f

cape [keɪp] n (garment) cape f; (Geo) cap m

caper ['keɪpə'] n (Culin: gen pl) câpre f; (prank) farce f

capital ['kæpɪtl] n (also: **~ city**) capitale f; (money) capital m; (also: **~ letter**) majuscule f; **capitalism** n capitalisme m; **capitalist** adj, n capitaliste m/f; **capital punishment** n peine capitale

Capitol ['kæpɪtl] n: **the ~** le Capitole

Capricorn ['kæprɪkɔ:n] n le Capricorne

capsize [kæp'saɪz] vt faire chavirer ▷ vi chavirer

capsule ['kæpsju:l] n capsule f

captain ['kæptɪn] n capitaine m

caption ['kæpʃən] n légende f

captivity [kæp'tɪvɪtɪ] n captivité f

capture ['kæptʃə'] vt (prisoner, animal) capturer; (town) prendre; (attention) capter; (Comput) saisir ▷ n capture f; (of data) saisie f de données

car [kɑ:'] n voiture f, auto f; (US Rail) wagon m, voiture

caramel ['kærəməl] n caramel m

carat ['kærət] n carat m

caravan ['kærəvæn] n caravane f; **caravan site** n (BRIT) camping m pour caravanes

carbohydrate [kɑ:bəʊ'haɪdreɪt] n hydrate m de carbone; (food) féculent m

carbon ['kɑ:bən] n carbone m; **carbon dioxide** [-daɪ'ɒksaɪd] n gaz m carbonique, dioxyde m de carbone; **carbon footprint** n empreinte f carbone; **carbon monoxide** [-mɒ'nɒksaɪd] n oxyde m de carbone; **carbon-neutral** adj neutre en carbone

car boot sale n voir article **"car boot sale"**

⬤ **CAR BOOT SALE**
⬤
⬤ Type de brocante très populaire, où
⬤ chacun vide sa cave ou son grenier.
⬤ Les articles sont présentés dans
⬤ des coffres de voitures, la vente
⬤ a souvent lieu sur un parking ou
⬤ dans un champ. Les brocanteurs
⬤ d'un jour doivent s'acquitter d'une
⬤ petite contribution pour participer
⬤ à la vente.

carburettor, (US) **carburetor** [kɑ:bju'retə'] n carburateur m

card [kɑ:d] n carte f; (material) carton m; **cardboard** n carton m; **card game** n jeu m de cartes

cardigan ['kɑ:dɪgən] n cardigan m

cardinal ['kɑ:dɪnl] adj cardinal(e); (importance) capital(e) ▷ n cardinal m

cardphone ['kɑ:dfəʊn] n téléphone m à carte (magnétique)

care [kɛər] n soin m, attention f; (worry) souci m ▷ vi: **to ~ about** (feel interest for) se soucier de, s'intéresser à; (person: love) être attaché(e) à; **in sb's ~** à la garde de qn, confié à qn; **~ of** (on letter) chez; **to take ~ (to do)** faire attention (à faire); **to take ~ of** vt s'occuper de; **I don't ~** ça m'est bien égal, peu m'importe; **I couldn't ~ less** cela m'est complètement égal, je m'en fiche complètement; **care for** vt fus s'occuper de; (like) aimer

career [kəˈrɪər] n carrière f ▷ vi (also: **~ along**) aller à toute allure

care: carefree adj sans souci, insouciant(e); **careful** adj soigneux(-euse); (cautious) prudent(e); **(be) careful!** (fais) attention!; **carefully** adv avec soin, soigneusement; prudemment; **caregiver** n (us) (professional) travailleur social; (unpaid) personne qui s'occupe d'un proche qui est malade; **careless** adj négligent(e); (heedless) insouciant(e); **carelessness** n manque m de soin, négligence f; insouciance f; **carer** [ˈkɛərər] n (professional) travailleur social; (unpaid) personne qui s'occupe d'un proche qui est malade; **caretaker** n gardien(ne), concierge m/f

car-ferry [ˈkɑːfɛrɪ] n (on sea) ferry m, ferry(-boat) m; (on river) bac m

cargo [ˈkɑːɡəʊ] n (pl **cargoes**) cargaison f, chargement m

car hire n (BRIT) location f de voitures

Caribbean [kærɪˈbiːən] adj, n: **the ~ (Sea)** la mer des Antilles or des Caraïbes

caring [ˈkɛərɪŋ] adj (person) bienveillant(e); (society, organization) humanitaire

carnation [kɑːˈneɪʃən] n œillet m

carnival [ˈkɑːnɪvl] n (public celebration) carnaval m; (us: funfair) fête foraine

carol [ˈkærəl] n: **(Christmas) ~** chant m de Noël

carousel [kærəˈsɛl] n (for luggage) carrousel m; (us) manège m

car park (BRIT) n parking m, parc m de stationnement

carpenter [ˈkɑːpɪntər] n charpentier m; (joiner) menuisier m

carpet [ˈkɑːpɪt] n tapis m ▷ vt recouvrir (d'un tapis); **fitted ~** (BRIT) moquette f

car rental n (us) location f de voitures

carriage [ˈkærɪdʒ] n (BRIT Rail) wagon m; (horse-drawn) voiture f; (of goods) transport m (: cost) port m; **carriageway** n (BRIT: part of road) chaussée f

carrier [ˈkærɪər] n transporteur m, camionneur m; (company) entreprise f de transport; (Med) porteur(-euse); **carrier bag** n (BRIT) sac m en papier or en plastique

carrot [ˈkærət] n carotte f

carry [ˈkærɪ] vt (subj: person) porter; (: vehicle) transporter; (involve: responsibilities etc) comporter, impliquer; (Med: disease) être porteur de ▷ vi (sound) porter; **to get carried away** (fig) s'emballer, s'enthousiasmer; **carry on** vi (continue) continuer ▷ vt (conduct: business) diriger; (: conversation) entretenir; (continue: business, conversation) continuer; **to ~ on with sth/doing** continuer qch/à faire; **carry out** vt (orders) exécuter; (investigation) effectuer

cart [kɑːt] n charrette f ▷ vt (inf) transporter

carton [ˈkɑːtən] n (box) carton m; (of yogurt) pot m (en carton)

cartoon [kɑːˈtuːn] n (Press) dessin m (humoristique); (satirical) caricature f; (comic strip) bande dessinée; (Cine) dessin animé

cartridge [ˈkɑːtrɪdʒ] n (for gun, pen) cartouche f

carve [kɑːv] vt (meat: also: **~ up**) découper; (wood, stone) tailler, sculpter; **carving** n (in wood etc) sculpture f

car wash n station f de lavage (de voitures)

case [keɪs] n cas m; (Law) affaire f, procès m; (box) caisse f, boîte f; (for glasses) étui m; (BRIT: also: **suit~**) valise f; **in ~ of** en cas de; **in ~ he** au cas où il; **just in ~** à tout hasard; **in any ~** en tout cas, de toute façon

cash [kæʃ] n argent m, (Comm) (argent m) liquide m ▷ vt encaisser; **to pay (in) ~** payer (en argent) comptant or en espèces; **~ with order/on delivery** (Comm) payable or paiement à la commande/livraison; **I haven't got any ~** je n'ai pas de liquide; **cashback** n (discount) remise f; (at supermarket etc) retrait m (à la caisse); **cash card** n carte f de retrait; **cash desk** n (BRIT) caisse f; **cash dispenser** n distributeur m automatique de billets

cashew [kæ'ʃuː] n (also: **~ nut**) noix f de cajou

cashier [kæ'ʃɪər] n caissier(-ère)

cashmere ['kæʃmɪər] n cachemire m

cash point n distributeur m automatique de billets

cash register n caisse f enregistreuse

casino [kə'siːnəu] n casino m

casket ['kɑːskɪt] n coffret m; (us: coffin) cercueil m

casserole ['kæsərəul] n (pot) cocotte f; (food) ragoût m (en cocotte)

cassette [kæ'set] n cassette f; **cassette player** n lecteur m de cassettes

cast [kɑːst] (vb: pt, pp **cast**) vt (throw) jeter; (shadow: lit) projeter; (: fig) jeter; (glance) jeter ▷ n (Theat) distribution f; (also: **plaster ~**) plâtre m; **to ~ sb as Hamlet** attribuer à qn le rôle d'Hamlet; **to ~ one's vote** voter, exprimer son suffrage; **to ~ doubt on** jeter un doute sur; **cast off** vi (Naut) larguer les amarres; (Knitting) arrêter les mailles

castanets [kæstə'nets] npl castagnettes fpl

caster sugar ['kɑːstə-] n (BRIT) sucre m semoule

cast-iron ['kɑːstaɪən] adj (lit) de or en fonte, (fig: will) de fer; (alibi) en béton

castle ['kɑːsl] n château m; (fortress) château-fort m; (Chess) tour f

casual ['kæʒjul] adj (by chance) de hasard, fait(e) au hasard, fortuit(e); (irregular: work etc) temporaire; (unconcerned) désinvolte; **~ wear** vêtements mpl sport inv

casualty ['kæʒjultɪ] n accidenté(e), blessé(e); (dead) victime f, mort(e); (BRIT Med: department) urgences fpl

cat [kæt] n chat m

Catalan ['kætəlæn] adj catalan(e)

catalogue, (us) **catalog** ['kætəlɔg] n catalogue m ▷ vt cataloguer

catalytic converter [kætə'lɪtɪkkən'və:tər] n pot m catalytique

cataract ['kætərækt] n (also Med) cataracte f

catarrh [kə'tɑ:r] n rhume m chronique, catarrhe f

catastrophe [kə'tæstrəfɪ] n catastrophe f

catch [kætʃ] (pt, pp **caught**) vt attraper; (person: by surprise) prendre, surprendre; (understand) saisir; (get entangled) accrocher ▷ vi (fire) prendre; (get entangled) s'accrocher ▷ n (fish etc) prise f; (hidden problem) attrape f; (Tech) loquet m; cliquet m; **to ~ sb's attention** or **eye** attirer l'attention de qn; **to ~ fire** prendre feu; **to ~ sight of** apercevoir; **catch up** vi (fig) se rattraper, combler son retard ▷ vt (also: **~ up with**) rattraper; **catching** ['kætʃɪŋ] adj (Med) contagieux(-euse)

category ['kætɪgərɪ] n catégorie f

cater ['keɪtər] vi: **~ for** (BRIT: needs) satisfaire, pourvoir à; (readers, consumers) s'adresser à, pourvoir aux besoins de; (Comm: parties etc) préparer des repas pour

caterpillar ['kætəpɪlə'] n chenille f
cathedral [kə'θi:drəl] n cathédrale f
Catholic ['kæθəlɪk] (Rel) adj
catholique ▷ n catholique m/f
cattle ['kætl] npl bétail m, bestiaux
mpi
catwalk ['kætwɔːk] n passerelle f; (for
models) podium m (de défilé de mode)
caught [kɔːt] pt, pp of **catch**
cauliflower ['kɔlɪflauə'] n chou-
fleur m
cause [kɔːz] n cause f ▷ vt causer
caution ['kɔːʃən] n prudence f;
(warning) avertissement m ▷ vt
avertir, donner un avertissement à;
cautious adj prudent(e)
cave [keɪv] n caverne f, grotte f; **cave
in** vi (roof etc) s'effondrer
caviar(e) ['kævɪɑː'] n caviar m
cavity ['kævɪtɪ] n cavité f; (Med) carie f
cc abbr (= cubic centimetre) cm³; (on
letter etc = carbon copy) cc
CCTV n abbr = **closed-circuit
television**
CD n abbr (= compact disc) CD m; **CD
burner** n graveur m de CD; **CD
player** n platine f laser; **CD-ROM**
[siːdiːˈrɔm] n abbr (= compact disc
read-only memory) CD-ROM m inv; **CD
writer** n graveur m de CD
cease [siːs] vt, vi cesser; **ceasefire** n
cessez-le-feu m
cedar ['siːdə'] n cèdre m
ceilidh ['keɪlɪ] n bal m folklorique
écossais ou irlandais
ceiling ['siːlɪŋ] n (also fig) plafond m
celebrate ['sɛlɪbreɪt] vt, vi célébrer;
celebration [sɛlɪˈbreɪʃən] n
célébration f
celebrity [sɪˈlɛbrɪtɪ] n célébrité f
celery ['sɛlərɪ] n céleri m (en
branches)
cell [sɛl] n (gen) cellule f; (Elec) élément
m (de pile)
cellar ['sɛlə'] n cave f
cello ['tʃɛləu] n violoncelle m
Cellophane® ['sɛləfeɪn] n
cellophane® f

cellphone ['sɛlfəun] n (téléphone m)
portable m, mobile m
Celsius ['sɛlsɪəs] adj Celsius inv
Celtic ['kɛltɪk, 'sɛltɪk] adj celte,
celtique
cement [sə'mɛnt] n ciment m
cemetery ['sɛmɪtrɪ] n cimetière m
censor ['sɛnsə'] n censeur m ▷ vt
censurer; **censorship** n censure f
census ['sɛnsəs] n recensement m
cent [sɛnt] n (unit of dollar, euro) cent
m (= un centième du dollar, de l'euro); see
also **per cent**
centenary [sɛn'tiːnərɪ], (US)
centennial [sɛn'tɛnɪəl] n
centenaire m
center ['sɛntə'] (US) = **centre**
centi... ['sɛntɪ]: **centigrade** adj
centigrade; **centimetre**, (US)
centimeter n centimètre m;
centipede ['sɛntɪpiːd] n mille-
pattes m inv
central ['sɛntrəl] adj central(e);
Central America n Amérique
centrale; **central heating** n
chauffage central; **central
reservation** n (BRIT Aut) terre-plein
central
centre, (US) **center** ['sɛntə'] n centre
m ▷ vt centrer; **centre-forward** n
(Sport) avant-centre m; **centre-half** n
(Sport) demi-centre m
century ['sɛntjurɪ] n siècle m; **in the
twentieth ~** au vingtième siècle
CEO n abbr (US) = **chief executive
officer**
ceramic [sɪˈræmɪk] adj céramique
cereal ['siːrɪəl] n céréale f
ceremony ['sɛrɪmənɪ] n cérémonie f;
to stand on ~ faire des façons
certain ['sɜːtən] adj certain(e);
to make ~ of s'assurer de; **for ~**
certainement, sûrement; **certainly**
adv certainement; **certainty** n
certitude f
certificate [sə'tɪfɪkɪt] n certificat m
certify ['sɜːtɪfaɪ] vt certifier; (award
diploma to) conférer un diplôme à

à; (declare insane) déclarer malade
mental(e)

cf. abbr (= compare) cf., voir

CFC n abbr (= chlorofluorocarbon) CFC m

chain [tʃeɪn] n (gen) chaîne f ▷ vt
(also: ~ up) enchaîner, attacher (avec
une chaîne); **chain-smoke** vi fumer
cigarette sur cigarette

chair [tʃeəʳ] n chaise f; (armchair)
fauteuil m; (of university) chaire f; (of
meeting) présidence f ▷ vt (meeting)
présider; **chairlift** n télésiège m;
chairman (irreg) n président m;
chairperson (irreg) n président(e);
chairwoman (irreg) n présidente f

chalet [ˈʃæleɪ] n chalet m

chalk [tʃɔːk] n craie f

challenge [ˈtʃælɪndʒ] n défi m ▷ vt
défier; (statement, right) mettre
en question, contester; **to ~ sb
to do** mettre qn au défi de faire;
challenging adj (task, career) qui
représente un défi or une gageure;
(tone, look) de défi, provocateur(-trice)

chamber [ˈtʃeɪmbəʳ] n chambre
f; (BRIT Law: gen pl) cabinet m; **~ of
commerce** chambre de commerce;
chambermaid n femme f de
chambre

champagne [ʃæmˈpeɪn] n
champagne m

champion [ˈtʃæmpɪən] n (also of
cause) champion(ne); **championship**
n championnat m

chance [tʃɑːns] n (luck) hasard m;
(opportunity) occasion f, possibilité f;
(hope, likelihood) chance f; (risk) risque
m ▷ vt (risk) risquer ▷ adj fortuit(e),
de hasard; **to take a ~** prendre
un risque; **by ~** par hasard; **to ~ it**
risquer le coup, essayer

chancellor [ˈtʃɑːnsələʳ] n chancelier
m; **Chancellor of the Exchequer**
[-ɪksˈtʃekəʳ] (BRIT) n chancelier m de
l'Échiquier

chandelier [ʃændəˈlɪəʳ] n lustre m

change [tʃeɪndʒ] vt (alter, replace;
Comm: money) changer; (switch,

substitute: hands, trains, clothes,
one's name etc) changer de ▷ vi
(gen) changer; (change clothes) se
changer; (be transformed): **to ~ into**
se changer or transformer en ▷ n
changement m; (money) monnaie f;
to ~ gear (Aut) changer de vitesse;
to ~ one's mind changer d'avis;
a ~ of clothes des vêtements de
rechange; **for a ~** pour changer; **do
you have ~ for £10?** vous avez la
monnaie de 10 livres?; **where can
I ~ some money?** où est-ce que je
peux changer de l'argent?; **keep
the ~!** gardez la monnaie!; **change
over** vi (swap) échanger; (change:
drivers etc) changer; (change sides:
players etc) changer de côté; **to ~ over
from sth to sth** passer de qch à qch;
changeable adj (weather) variable;
change machine n distributeur m de
monnaie; **changing room** n (BRIT:
in shop) salon m d'essayage (: Sport)
vestiaire m

channel [ˈtʃænl] n (TV) chaîne
f; (waveband, groove, fig: medium)
canal m; (of river, sea) chenal m ▷ vt
canaliser; **the (English) C~** la
Manche; **Channel Islands** npl; **the
Channel Islands** les îles fpl Anglo-
Normandes; **Channel Tunnel** n:
the Channel Tunnel le tunnel sous
la Manche

chant [tʃɑːnt] n chant m; (Rel)
psalmodie f ▷ vt chanter; scander

chaos [ˈkeɪɔs] n chaos m

chaotic [keɪˈɔtɪk] adj chaotique

chap [tʃæp] n (BRIT inf: man) type m

chapel [ˈtʃæpl] n chapelle f

chapped [tʃæpt] adj (skin, lips)
gercé(e)

chapter [ˈtʃæptəʳ] n chapitre m

character [ˈkærɪktəʳ] n caractère m;
(in novel, film) personnage m; (eccentric
person) numéro m, phénomène m;
characteristic [kærɪktəˈrɪstɪk] adj,
n caractéristique (f); **characterize**
[ˈkærɪktəraɪz] vt caractériser

charcoal ['tʃɑːkəʊl] n charbon m de bois; (Art) charbon

charge [tʃɑːdʒ] n (accusation) accusation f; (Law) inculpation f; (cost) prix (demandé) m ▷ vt (gun, battery, Mil: enemy) charger; (customer, sum) faire payer ▷ vi foncer; **charges** npl (costs) frais mpl; **to reverse the ~s** (BRIT Tel) téléphoner en PCV; **to take ~ of** se charger de; **to be in ~ of** être responsable de, s'occuper de; **to ~ sb (with)** (Law) inculper qn (de); **charge card** n carte f de client (émise par un grand magasin); **charger** n (also: **battery charger**) chargeur m

charisma [kæˈrɪzmætɪk] adj charismatique

charity ['tʃærɪtɪ] n charité f; (organization) institution f charitable or de bienfaisance, œuvre f (de charité); **charity shop** n (BRIT) boutique vendant des articles d'occasion au profit d'une organisation caritative

charm [tʃɑːm] n charme m; (on bracelet) breloque f ▷ vt charmer, enchanter; **charming** adj charmant(e)

chart [tʃɑːt] n tableau m, diagramme m; graphique m; (map) carte marine f ▷ vt dresser or établir la carte de; (sales, progress) établir la courbe de; **charts** npl (Mus) hit-parade m; **to be in the ~s** (record, pop group) figurer au hit-parade

charter ['tʃɑːtə'] vt (plane) affréter ▷ n (document) charte f; **chartered accountant** n (BRIT) expert-comptable m; **charter flight** n charter m

chase [tʃeɪs] vt poursuivre, pourchasser; (also: **~ away**) chasser ▷ n poursuite f, chasse f

chat [tʃæt] vi (also: **have a ~**) bavarder, causer; (on Internet) chatter ▷ n conversation f; (on Internet) chat m; **chat up** vt (BRIT inf: girl) baratiner; **chat room** n (Internet) salon m de discussion; **chat show** n (BRIT) talk-show m

chatter ['tʃætə'] vi (person) bavarder, papoter ▷ n bavardage m, papotage m; **my teeth are ~ing** je claque des dents

chauffeur ['ʃəʊfə'] n chauffeur m (de maître)

chauvinist ['ʃəʊvɪnɪst] n (also: **male ~**) phallocrate m, macho m; (nationalist) chauvin(e)

cheap [tʃiːp] adj bon marché inv, pas cher (chère); (reduced: ticket) à prix réduit; (: fare) réduit(e); (joke) facile, d'un goût douteux; (poor quality) à bon marché, de qualité médiocre ▷ adv à bon marché, pour pas cher; **can you recommend a ~ hotel/restaurant, please?** pourriez-vous m'indiquer un hôtel/restaurant bon marché?; **cheap day return** n billet m d'aller et retour réduit (valable pour la journée); **cheaply** adv à bon marché, à bon compte

cheat [tʃiːt] vi tricher; (in exam) copier ▷ vt tromper, duper; (rob): **to ~ sb out of sth** escroquer qch à qn ▷ n tricheur(-euse) m/f; escroc m; **cheat on** vt fus tromper

Chechnya [tʃɪtʃˈnjaː] n Tchétchénie f

check [tʃɛk] vt vérifier; (passport, ticket) contrôler; (halt) enrayer; (restrain) maîtriser ▷ vi (official etc) se renseigner ▷ n vérification f; contrôle m; (curb) frein m; (BRIT: bill) addition f; (US) = **cheque**; (pattern: gen pl) carreaux mpl; **to ~ with sb** demander à qn; **check in** vi (in hotel) remplir sa fiche (d'hôtel); (at airport) se présenter à l'enregistrement ▷ vt (luggage) (faire) enregistrer; **check off** vt (tick off) cocher; **check out** vi (in hotel) régler sa note ▷ vt (investigate: story) vérifier; **check up** vi: **to ~ up (on sth)** vérifier (qch); **to ~ up on sb** se renseigner sur le compte de qn; **checkbook** n (US) = **chequebook**; **checked** adj (pattern, cloth) à carreaux; **checkers** n (US) jeu m de dames; **check-in** n (at airport: also:

check-in desk) enregistrement m; **checking account** n (US) compte courant; **checklist** n liste f de contrôle; **checkmate** n échec et mat m; **checkout** n (in supermarket) caisse f; **checkpoint** n contrôle m; **checkroom** (US) n consigne f; **checkup** n (Med) examen médical, check-up m

cheddar ['tʃɛdəʳ] n (also: ~ **cheese**) cheddar m

cheek [tʃiːk] n joue f; (impudence) toupet m, culot m; **what a ~!** quel toupet!; **cheekbone** n pommette f; **cheeky** adj effronté(e), culotté(e)

cheer [tʃɪəʳ] vt acclamer, applaudir; (gladden) réjouir, réconforter ▷ vi applaudir ▷ n (in gen pl) applaudissements mpl; (of crowd) bravos mpl, hourras mpl; ~**s!** à la vôtre!; **cheer up** vi se dérider, reprendre courage ▷ vt remonter le moral à or de, dérider, égayer; **cheerful** adj gai(e), joyeux(-euse)

cheerio [tʃɪərɪˈəʊ] excl salut!, au revoir!

cheerleader ['tʃɪəliːdəʳ] n membre d'un groupe de majorettes qui chantent et dansent pour soutenir leur équipe pendant les matchs de football américain

cheese [tʃiːz] n fromage m; **cheeseburger** n cheeseburger m; **cheesecake** n tarte f au fromage

chef [ʃɛf] n chef (cuisinier)

chemical ['kɛmɪkl] adj chimique ▷ n produit m chimique

chemist ['kɛmɪst] n (BRIT: pharmacist) pharmacien(ne); (scientist) chimiste m/f; **chemistry** n chimie f; **chemist's (shop)** n (BRIT) pharmacie f

cheque, (US) **check** [tʃɛk] n chèque m; **chequebook**, (US) **checkbook** n chéquier m, carnet m de chèques; **cheque card** n (BRIT) carte f (d'identité) bancaire

cherry ['tʃɛrɪ] n cerise f; (also: ~ **tree**) cerisier m

chess [tʃɛs] n échecs mpl

chest [tʃɛst] n poitrine f; (box) coffre m, caisse f

chestnut ['tʃɛsnʌt] n châtaigne f; (also: ~ **tree**) châtaignier m

chest of drawers n commode f

chew [tʃuː] vt mâcher; **chewing gum** n chewing-gum m

chic [ʃiːk] adj chic inv, élégant(e)

chick [tʃɪk] n poussin m; (inf) fille f

chicken ['tʃɪkɪn] n poulet m; (inf: coward) poule mouillée; **chicken out** vi (inf) se dégonfler; **chickenpox** n varicelle f

chickpea ['tʃɪkpiː] n pois m chiche

chief [tʃiːf] n chef m ▷ adj principal(e); **chief executive**, (US) **chief executive officer** n directeur(-trice) général(e); **chiefly** adv principalement, surtout

child (pl **children**) [tʃaɪld, 'tʃɪldrən] n enfant m/f; **child abuse** n maltraitance f d'enfants; (sexual) abus mpl sexuels sur des enfants; **child benefit** n (BRIT) allocations familiales; **childbirth** n accouchement m; **childcare** n (for working parents) garde f des enfants (pour les parents qui travaillent); **childhood** n enfance f; **childish** adj puéril(e), enfantin(e); **child minder** n (BRIT) garde f d'enfants; **children** ['tʃɪldrən] npl of **child**

Chile ['tʃɪlɪ] n Chili m

chill [tʃɪl] n (of water) froid m; (of air) fraîcheur f; (Med) refroidissement m, coup m de froid ▷ vt (person) faire frissonner; (Culin) mettre au frais, rafraîchir; **chill out** vi (inf: esp US) se relaxer

chil(l)i ['tʃɪlɪ] n piment m (rouge)

chilly ['tʃɪlɪ] adj froid(e), glacé(e); (sensitive to cold) frileux(-euse)

chimney ['tʃɪmnɪ] n cheminée f

chimpanzee [tʃɪmpænˈziː] n chimpanzé m

chin [tʃɪn] n menton m

China ['tʃaɪnə] n Chine f

china ['tʃaɪnə] n (material) porcelaine f; (crockery) (vaisselle f en) porcelaine f

Chinese [tʃaɪ'niːz] adj chinois(e) ▷ n (pl inv) Chinois(e); (Ling) chinois m

chip [tʃɪp] n (gen pl: Culin: BRIT) frite f; (: US: also: **potato ~**) chip m; (of wood) copeau m; (of glass, stone) éclat m; (also: **micro~**) puce f; (in gambling) fiche f ▷ vt (cup, plate) ébrécher; **chip shop** n (BRIT) friterie f

> **CHIP SHOP**
>
> Un *chip shop*, que l'on appelle également un "fish-and-chip shop", est un magasin où l'on vend des plats à emporter. Les *chip shops* sont d'ailleurs à l'origine des "takeaways".
> On y achète en particulier du poisson frit et des frites, mais on y trouve également des plats traditionnels britanniques ("steak pies", saucisses, etc). Tous les plats étaient à l'origine emballés dans du papier journal. Dans certains de ces magasins, on peut s'asseoir pour consommer sur place.

chiropodist [kɪ'rɔpədɪst] n (BRIT) pédicure m/f

chisel ['tʃɪzl] n ciseau m

chives [tʃaɪvz] npl ciboulette f, civette f

chlorine ['klɔːriːn] n chlore m

choc-ice ['tʃɒkaɪs] n (BRIT) esquimau® m

chocolate ['tʃɒklɪt] n chocolat m

choice [tʃɔɪs] n choix m ▷ adj de choix

choir ['kwaɪər] n chœur m, chorale f

choke [tʃəʊk] vi étouffer ▷ vt étrangler; étouffer; (block) boucher, obstruer ▷ n (Aut) starter m

cholesterol [kə'lɛstərɔl] n cholestérol m

chook [tʃuk] n (AUST, NZ inf) poule f

choose (pt chose, pp chosen) [tʃuːz, tʃəʊz, 'tʃəʊzn] vt choisir; **to ~ to do** décider de faire, juger bon de faire

chop [tʃɒp] vt (wood) couper (à la hache); (Culin: also: **~ up**) couper (fin), émincer, hacher (en morceaux) ▷ n (Culin) côtelette f; **chop down** vt (tree) abattre; **chop off** vt trancher; **chopsticks** ['tʃɒpstɪks] npl baguettes fpl

chord [kɔːd] n (Mus) accord m

chore [tʃɔːr] n travail m de routine; **household ~s** travaux mpl du ménage

chorus ['kɔːrəs] n chœur m; (repeated part of song, also fig) refrain m

chose [tʃəʊz] pt of **choose**

chosen ['tʃəʊzn] pp of **choose**

Christ [kraɪst] n Christ m

christen ['krɪsn] vt baptiser; **christening** n baptême m

Christian ['krɪstɪən] adj, n chrétien(ne); **Christianity** [krɪstɪ'ænɪtɪ] n christianisme m; **Christian name** n prénom m

Christmas ['krɪsməs] n Noël m or f; **happy** or **merry ~!** joyeux Noël!; **Christmas card** n carte f de Noël; **Christmas carol** n chant m de Noël; **Christmas Day** n le jour de Noël; **Christmas Eve** n la veille de Noël; la nuit de Noël; **Christmas pudding** n (esp BRIT) Christmas m pudding; **Christmas tree** n arbre m de Noël

chrome [krəʊm] n chrome m

chronic ['krɒnɪk] adj chronique

chrysanthemum [krɪ'sænθəməm] n chrysanthème m

chubby ['tʃʌbɪ] adj potelé(e), rondelet(te)

chuck [tʃʌk] vt (inf) lancer, jeter; (job) lâcher; **chuck out** vt (inf: person) flanquer dehors or à la porte; (: rubbish etc) jeter

chuckle ['tʃʌkl] vi glousser

chum [tʃʌm] n copain (copine)

chunk [tʃʌŋk] n gros morceau

church [tʃəːtʃ] n église f; **churchyard** n cimetière m

churn [tʃəːn] n (for butter) baratte f; (also: **milk ~**) (grand) bidon à lait

chute [ʃuːt] n goulotte f; (also: **rubbish ~**) vide-ordures m inv; (BRIT: children's slide) toboggan m

chutney ['tʃʌtnɪ] n chutney m

CIA n abbr (= Central Intelligence Agency) CIA f

CID n abbr (= Criminal Investigation Department) ≈ P.J. f

cider ['saɪdər] n cidre m

cigar [sɪ'ɡɑːr] n cigare m

cigarette [sɪɡə'rɛt] n cigarette f; **cigarette lighter** n briquet m

cinema ['sɪnəmə] n cinéma m

cinnamon ['sɪnəmən] n cannelle f

circle ['səːkl] n cercle m; (in cinema) balcon m ▷ vi faire ou décrire des cercles ▷ vt (surround) entourer, encercler; (move round) faire le tour de, tourner autour de

circuit ['səːkɪt] n circuit m; (lap) tour m

circular ['səːkjʊlər] adj circulaire ▷ n circulaire f; (as advertisement) prospectus m

circulate ['səːkjʊleɪt] vi circuler ▷ vt faire circuler; **circulation** [səːkjʊ'leɪʃən] n circulation f; (of newspaper) tirage m

circumstances ['səːkəmstənsɪz] npl circonstances fpl; (financial condition) moyens mpl, situation financière

circus ['səːkəs] n cirque m

cite [saɪt] vt citer

citizen ['sɪtɪzn] n (Pol) citoyen(ne); (resident): **the ~s of this town** les habitants de cette ville; **citizenship** n citoyenneté f; (BRIT Scol) ≈ éducation f civique

citrus fruits ['sɪtrəs-] npl agrumes mpl

city ['sɪtɪ] n (grande) ville f; **the C~** la Cité de Londres (centre des affaires); **city centre** n centre ville m; **city technology college** n (BRIT) établissement m d'enseignement technologique (situé dans un quartier défavorisé)

civic ['sɪvɪk] adj civique; (authorities) municipal(e)

civil ['sɪvɪl] adj civil(e); (polite) poli(e), civil(e); **civilian** [sɪ'vɪlɪən] adj, n civil(e)

civilization [sɪvɪlaɪ'zeɪʃən] n civilisation f

civilized ['sɪvɪlaɪzd] adj civilisé(e); (fig) où règnent les bonnes manières

civil: civil law n code civil; (study) droit civil; **civil rights** npl droits mpl civiques; **civil servant** n fonctionnaire m/f; **Civil Service** n fonction publique, administration f; **civil war** n guerre civile

CJD n abbr (= Creutzfeldt-Jakob disease) MCJ f

claim [kleɪm] vt (rights etc) revendiquer; (compensation) réclamer; (assert) déclarer, prétendre ▷ vi (for insurance) faire une déclaration de sinistre ▷ n revendication f; prétention f; (right) droit m; **(insurance) ~** demande f d'indemnisation, déclaration f de sinistre; **claim form** n (gen) formulaire m de demande

clam [klæm] n palourde f

clamp [klæmp] n crampon m; (on workbench) valet m; (on car) sabot m de Denver ▷ vt attacher; (car) mettre un sabot à; **clamp down on** vt fus sévir contre, prendre des mesures draconiennes à l'égard de

clan [klæn] n clan m

clap [klæp] vi applaudir

claret ['klærət] n (vin m de) bordeaux m (rouge)

clarify ['klærɪfaɪ] vt clarifier

clarinet [klærɪ'nɛt] n clarinette f

clarity ['klærɪtɪ] n clarté f

clash [klæʃ] n (sound) choc m, fracas m; (with police) affrontement m; (fig) conflit m ▷ vi se heurter; être ou entrer en conflit; (colours) jurer; (dates, events) tomber en même temps

clasp [klɑːsp] n (of necklace, bag) fermoir m ▷ vt serrer, étreindre

class [klɑːs] n (gen) classe f; (group, category) catégorie f ▷ vt classer, classifier

classic ['klæsɪk] adj classique ▷ n (author, work) classique m; **classical** adj classique

classification [klæsɪfɪ'keɪʃən] n classification f

classify ['klæsɪfaɪ] vt classifier, classer

classmate ['klɑːsmeɪt] n camarade m/f de classe

classroom ['klɑːsrum] n (salle f de) classe f; **classroom assistant** n assistant(e) d'éducation

classy ['klɑːsɪ] (inf) adj classe (inf)

clatter ['klætə*] n cliquetis m ▷ vi cliqueter

clause [klɔːz] n clause f; (Ling) proposition f

claustrophobic [klɔːstrə'fəubɪk] adj (person) claustrophobe; (place) où l'on se sent claustrophobe

claw [klɔː] n griffe f; (of bird of prey) serre f; (of lobster) pince f

clay [kleɪ] n argile f

clean [kliːn] adj propre; (clear, smooth) net(te); (record, reputation) sans tache; (joke, story) correct(e) ▷ vt nettoyer; **clean up** vt nettoyer; (fig) remettre de l'ordre dans; **cleaner** n (person) nettoyeur(-euse), femme f de ménage; (product) détachant m; **cleaner's** n (also: **dry cleaner's**) teinturier m; **cleaning** n nettoyage m

cleanser ['klɛnzə*] n (for face) démaquillant m

clear [klɪə*] adj clair(e); (glass, plastic) transparent(e); (road, way) libre, dégagé(e); (profit, majority) net(te); (conscience) tranquille; (skin) frais (fraîche); (sky) dégagé(e) ▷ vt (road) dégager, déblayer; (table) débarrasser; (room etc: of people) faire évacuer; (cheque) compenser; (Law: suspect) innocenter; (obstacle) franchir ou sauter sans heurter ▷ vi (weather) s'éclaircir; (fog) se dissiper

▷ adv: **~ of** à distance de, à l'écart de; **to ~ the table** débarrasser la table, desservir; **clear away** vt (things, clothes etc) enlever, retirer; **to ~ away the dishes** débarrasser la table; **clear up** vt ranger, mettre en ordre; (mystery) éclaircir, résoudre; **clearance** n (removal) déblayage m; (permission) autorisation f; **clear-cut** adj précis(e), nettement défini(e); **clearing** n (in forest) clairière f; **clearly** adv clairement; (obviously) de toute évidence; **clearway** n (BRIT) route f à stationnement interdit

clench [klɛntʃ] vt serrer

clergy ['klɜːdʒɪ] n clergé m

clerk [klɑːk, us klɜːk] n (BRIT) employé(e) de bureau; (us: salesman, woman) vendeur(-euse)

clever ['klɛvə*] adj (intelligent) intelligent(e); (skilful) habile, adroit(e); (device, arrangement) ingénieux(-euse), astucieux(-euse)

cliché ['kliːʃeɪ] n cliché m

click [klɪk] n (Comput) clic m ▷ vi (Comput) cliquer ▷ vt: **to ~ one's tongue** faire claquer sa langue; **to ~ one's heels** claquer des talons; **to ~ on an icon** cliquer sur une icône

client ['klaɪənt] n client(e)

cliff [klɪf] n falaise f

climate ['klaɪmɪt] n climat m; **climate change** n changement m climatique

climax ['klaɪmæks] n apogée m, point culminant; (sexual) orgasme m

climb [klaɪm] vi grimper, monter; (plane) prendre de l'altitude ▷ vt (stairs) monter; (mountain) escalader; (tree) grimper à ▷ n montée f, escalade f; **to ~ over a wall** passer par dessus un mur; **climb down** vi (re)descendre; (BRIT fig) rabattre de ses prétentions; **climber** n (also: **rock climber**) grimpeur(-euse), varappeur(-euse); (plant) plante grimpante; **climbing** n (also: **rock climbing**) escalade f, varappe f

clinch | 350

clinch [klɪntʃ] vt (deal) conclure, sceller

cling (pt, pp **clung**) [klɪŋ, klʌŋ] vi: to **~ (to)** se cramponner (à), s'accrocher (à); (clothes) coller (à); **clingfilm** n film m alimentaire

clinic ['klɪnɪk] n clinique f; centre médical

clip [klɪp] n (for hair) barrette f; (also: **paper ~**) trombone m; (TV, Cine) clip m ▷ vt (also: **~ together**: papers) attacher; (hair, nails) couper; (hedge) tailler; **clipping** n (from newspaper) coupure f de journal

cloak [kləuk] n grande cape ▷ vt (fig) masquer, cacher; **cloakroom** n (for coats etc) vestiaire m; (BRIT: W.C.) toilettes fpl

clock [klɔk] n (large) horloge f; (small) pendule f; **clock in, clock on** (BRIT) vi (with card) pointer (en arrivant); (start work) commencer à travailler; **clock off, clock out** (BRIT) vi (with card) pointer (en partant); (leave work) quitter le travail; **clockwise** adv dans le sens des aiguilles d'une montre; **clockwork** n rouages mpl, mécanisme m; (of clock) mouvement m (d'horlogerie) ▷ adj (toy, train) mécanique

clog [klɔg] n sabot m ▷ vt boucher, encrasser ▷ vi (also: **~ up**) se boucher, s'encrasser

clone [kləun] n clone m ▷ vt cloner

close¹ [kləus] adj (contact, link, watch) étroit(e); (examination) attentif(-ive), minutieux(-euse); (contest) très serré(e); (weather) lourd(e), étouffant(e); (near): **~ (to)** près (de), proche (de) ▷ adv près, à proximité; **~ to** prep près de; **~ by, ~ at hand** adj, adv tout(e) près; **a ~ friend** un ami intime; **to have a ~ shave** (fig) l'échapper belle

close² [kləuz] vt fermer ▷ vi (shop etc) fermer; (lid, door etc) se fermer; (end) se terminer, se conclure ▷ n (end) conclusion f; **what time do you ~?** à quelle heure fermez-vous?; **close**

down vi fermer (définitivement); **closed** adj (shop etc) fermé(e)

close-up ['kləusʌp] n gros plan

closing time n heure f de fermeture

closure ['kləuʒə'] n fermeture f

clot [klɔt] n (of blood, milk) caillot m; (inf: person) ballot m ▷ vi (external bleeding) se coaguler

cloth [klɔθ] n (material) tissu m, étoffe f; (BRIT: also: **tea ~**) torchon m; lavette f; (also: **table~**) nappe f

clothes [kləuðz] npl vêtements mpl, habits mpl; **clothes line** n corde f (à linge); **clothes peg**, (us) **clothes pin** n pince f à linge

clothing ['kləuðɪŋ] n = **clothes**

cloud [klaud] n (also Comput) nuage m; **cloud computing** n (Comput) informatique f en nuage; **cloud over** vi se couvrir; (fig) s'assombrir; **cloudy** adj nuageux(-euse), couvert(e); (liquid) trouble

clove [kləuv] n clou m de girofle; **a ~ of garlic** une gousse d'ail

clown [klaun] n clown m ▷ vi (also: **~ about, ~ around**) faire le clown

club [klʌb] n (society) club m; (weapon) massue f, matraque f; (also: **golf ~**) club m ▷ vt matraquer ▷ vi: to **~ together** s'associer; **clubs** npl (Cards) trèfle m; **club class** n (Aviat) classe f club

clue [kluː] n indice m; (in crosswords) définition f; **I haven't a ~** je n'en ai pas la moindre idée

clump [klʌmp] n: **~ of trees** bouquet m d'arbres

clumsy ['klʌmzɪ] adj (person) gauche, maladroit(e); (object) malcommode, peu maniable

clung [klʌŋ] pt, pp of **cling**

cluster ['klʌstə'] n (petit) groupe; (of flowers) grappe f ▷ vi se rassembler

clutch [klʌtʃ] n (Aut) embrayage m; (grasp): **~es** étreinte f, prise f ▷ vt (grasp) agripper; (hold tightly) serrer fort; (hold on to) se cramponner à

cm abbr (= centimetre) cm

Co. abbr = **company, county**

c/o abbr (= care of) c/o, aux bons soins de

coach [kəʊtʃ] n (bus) autocar m; (horse-drawn) diligence f; (of train) voiture f, wagon m; (Sport: trainer) entraîneur(-euse); (school: tutor) répétiteur(-trice) ▷ vt (Sport) entraîner; (student) donner des leçons particulières à; **coach station** (BRIT) n gare routière; **coach trip** n excursion f en car

coal [kəʊl] n charbon m

coalition [kəʊəˈlɪʃən] n coalition f

coarse [kɔːs] adj grossier(-ère), rude; (vulgar) vulgaire

coast [kəʊst] n côte f ▷ vi (car, cycle) descendre en roue libre; **coastal** adj côtier(-ère); **coastguard** n garde-côte m; **coastline** n côte f, littoral m

coat [kəʊt] n manteau m; (of animal) pelage m, poil m; (of paint) couche f ▷ vt couvrir, enduire; **coat hanger** n cintre m; **coating** n couche f, enduit m

coax [kəʊks] vt persuader par des cajoleries

cob [kɒb] n see **corn**

cobbled ['kɒbld] adj pavé(e)

cobweb ['kɒbweb] n toile f d'araignée

cocaine [kəˈkeɪn] n cocaïne f

cock [kɒk] n (rooster) coq m; (male bird) mâle m ▷ vt (gun) armer; **cockerel** n jeune coq m

cockney ['kɒknɪ] n cockney m/f (habitant des quartiers populaires de l'East End de Londres), ≈ faubourien(ne)

cockpit ['kɒkpɪt] n (in aircraft) poste m de pilotage, cockpit m

cockroach ['kɒkrəʊtʃ] n cafard m, cancrelat m

cocktail ['kɒkteɪl] n cocktail m

cocoa ['kəʊkəʊ] n cacao m

coconut ['kəʊkənʌt] n noix f de coco

cod [kɒd] n morue f fraîche, cabillaud m

C.O.D. abbr = **cash on delivery**

code [kəʊd] n code m; (Tel: area code) indicatif m

coeducational ['kəʊedjuˈkeɪʃənl] adj mixte

coffee ['kɒfɪ] n café m; **coffee bar** n (BRIT) café m; **coffee bean** n grain m de café; **coffee break** n pause-café f; **coffee maker** n cafetière f; **coffeepot** n cafetière f; **coffee shop** n café m; **coffee table** n (petite) table basse

coffin ['kɒfɪn] n cercueil m

cog [kɒg] n (wheel) roue dentée; (tooth) dent f (d'engrenage)

cognac ['kɒnjæk] n cognac m

coherent [kəʊˈhɪərənt] adj cohérent(e)

coil [kɔɪl] n rouleau m, bobine f; (contraceptive) stérilet m ▷ vt enrouler

coin [kɔɪn] n pièce f (de monnaie) ▷ vt (word) inventer

coincide [kəʊɪnˈsaɪd] vi coïncider; **coincidence** [kəʊˈɪnsɪdəns] n coïncidence f

Coke® [kəʊk] n coca m

coke [kəʊk] n (coal) coke m

colander ['kɒləndə] n passoire f (à légumes)

cold [kəʊld] adj froid(e) ▷ n froid m; (Med) rhume m; **it's ~** il fait froid; **to be ~** (person) avoir froid; **to catch a ~** s'enrhumer, attraper un rhume; **in ~ blood** de sang-froid; **cold sore** n bouton m de fièvre

coleslaw ['kəʊlslɔː] n sorte de salade de chou cru

colic ['kɒlɪk] n colique(s) f(pl)

collaborate [kəˈlæbəreɪt] vi collaborer

collapse [kəˈlæps] vi s'effondrer, s'écrouler; (Med) avoir un malaise ▷ n effondrement m, écroulement m; (of government) chute f

collar ['kɒlə] n (of coat, shirt) col m; (for dog) collier m; **collarbone** n clavicule f

colleague ['kɒliːg] n collègue m/f

collect [kə'lɛkt] vt rassembler;
(pick up) ramasser; (as a hobby)
collectionner; (BRIT: call for) (passer)
prendre; (mail) faire la levée de,
ramasser; (money owed) encaisser;
(donations, subscriptions) recueillir
▷ vi (people) se rassembler; (dust,
dirt) s'amasser; **to call ~** (us Tel)
téléphoner en PCV; **collection**
[kə'lɛkʃən] n collection f; (of
mail) levée f; (for money) collecte
f, quête f; **collective** [kə'lɛktɪv]
adj collectif(-ive); **collector** n
collectionneur m

college ['kɔlɪdʒ] n collège m; (of
technology, agriculture etc) institut m

collide [kə'laɪd] vi: **to ~ (with)** entrer
en collision (avec)

collision [kə'lɪʒən] n collision f,
heurt m

cologne [kə'ləun] n (also: **eau de ~**)
eau f de cologne

colon ['kəulən] n (sign) deux-points
mpl; (Med) côlon m

colonel ['kəːnl] n colonel m

colonial [kə'ləunɪəl] adj colonial(e)

colony ['kɔlənɪ] n colonie f

colour, (us) **color** ['kʌlə*] n couleur
f ▷ vt colorer; (dye) teindre; (paint)
peindre; (with crayons) colorier;
(news) fausser, exagérer ▷ vi (blush)
rougir; **I'd like a different ~** je le
voudrais dans un autre coloris;
colour in vt colorier; **colour-blind**,
(us) **color-blind** adj daltonien(ne);
coloured, (us) **colored** adj coloré(e);
(photo) en couleur; **colour film**, (us)
color film n (for camera) pellicule f
(en) couleur; **colourful**, (us) **colorful**
adj coloré(e), vif (vive); (personality)
pittoresque, haut(e) en couleurs;
colouring, (us) **coloring** n colorant
m; (complexion) teint m; **colour
television**, (us) **color television** n
télévision f (en) couleur

column ['kɔləm] n colonne f;
(fashion column, sports column etc)
rubrique f

coma ['kəumə] n coma m

comb [kəum] n peigne m ▷ vt (hair)
peigner; (area) ratisser, passer au
peigne fin

combat ['kɔmbæt] n combat m ▷ vt
combattre, lutter contre

combination [kɔmbɪ'neɪʃən] n (gen)
combinaison f

combine [kəm'baɪn] vt combiner
▷ vi s'associer; (Chem) se combiner
▷ n ['kɔmbaɪn] (Econ) trust m;
(also: **~ harvester**) moissonneuse-
batteuse(-lieuse) f; **to ~ sth with sth**
(one quality with another) joindre ou
allier qch à qch

KEYWORD

come (pt **came**, pp **come**) [kʌm,
keɪm] vi 1 (movement towards) venir;
to come running arriver en courant;
he's come here to work il est venu
ici pour travailler; **come with me**
suivez-moi

2 (arrive) arriver; **to come home**
rentrer (chez soi or à la maison);
we've just come from Paris nous
arrivons de Paris

3 (reach): **to come to** (decision etc)
parvenir à, arriver à; **the bill came to
£40** la note s'est élevée à 40 livres

4 (occur): **an idea came to me** il
m'est venu une idée

5 (be, become): **to come loose/
undone** se défaire/desserrer; **I've
come to like him** j'ai fini par bien
l'aimer

come across vt fus rencontrer par
hasard, tomber sur

come along vi (BRIT: pupil, work) faire
des progrès, avancer

come back vi revenir

come down vi descendre; (prices)
baisser; (buildings) s'écrouler; (: be
demolished) être démoli(e)

come from vt fus (source) venir de;
(place) venir de, être originaire de

come in vi entrer; (train) arriver;

(fashion) entrer en vogue; (on deal etc) participer

come off vi (button) se détacher; (attempt) réussir

come on vi (lights, electricity) s'allumer; (central heating) se mettre en marche; (pupil, work, project) faire des progrès, avancer; **come on!** viens!; allons!, allez!

come out vi sortir; (sun) se montrer; (book) paraître; (stain) s'enlever; (strike) cesser le travail, se mettre en grève

come round vi (after faint, operation) revenir à soi, reprendre connaissance

come to vi revenir à soi

come up vi monter; (sun) se lever; (problem) se poser; (event) survenir; (in conversation) être soulevé

come up with vt fus (money) fournir; **he came up with an idea** a eu une idée, il a proposé quelque chose

comeback ['kʌmbæk] n (Theat) rentrée f

comedian [kə'miːdɪən] n (comic) comique m; (Theat) comédien m

comedy ['kɒmɪdɪ] n comédie f; (humour) comique m

comet ['kɒmɪt] n comète f

comfort ['kʌmfət] n confort m, bien-être m; (solace) consolation f, réconfort m ▷ vt consoler, réconforter; **comfortable** adj confortable; (person) à l'aise; (financially) aisé(e); (patient) dont l'état est stationnaire; **comfort station** n (us) toilettes fpl

comic ['kɒmɪk] adj (also: **-al**) comique ▷ n (person) comique m; (BRIT: magazine: for children) magazine m de bandes dessinées or de BD; (: for adults) illustré m; **comic book** n (us: for children) magazine m de bandes dessinées or de BD; (: for adults) illustré m; **comic strip** n bande dessinée

comma ['kɒmə] n virgule f

command [kə'mɑːnd] n ordre m, commandement m; (Mil: authority) commandement; (mastery) maîtrise f ▷ vt (troops) commander; **to ~ sb to do** donner l'ordre or commander à qn de faire; **commander** n (Mil) commandant m

commemorate [kə'mɛməreɪt] vt commémorer

commence [kə'mɛns] vt, vi commencer

commend [kə'mɛnd] vt louer; (recommend) recommander

comment ['kɒmɛnt] n commentaire m ▷ vi: **to ~ on** faire des remarques sur; **"no ~"** je n'ai rien à déclarer"; **commentary** ['kɒməntəri] n commentaire m; (Sport) reportage m (en direct); **commentator** ['kɒmənteɪtə] n commentateur m; (Sport) reporter m

commerce ['kɒmɜːs] n commerce m

commercial [kə'mɜːʃəl] adj commercial(e) ▷ n (Radio, TV) annonce f publicitaire, spot m (publicitaire); **commercial break** n (Radio, TV) spot m (publicitaire)

commission [kə'mɪʃən] n (committee, fee) commission f ▷ vt (work of art) commander, charger un artiste de l'exécution de; **out of ~** (machine) hors service; **commissioner** n (Police) préfet m (de police)

commit [kə'mɪt] vt (act) commettre; (resources) consacrer; (to sb's care) confier (à); **to ~ o.s. (to do)** s'engager (à faire); **to ~ suicide** se suicider; **commitment** n engagement m; (obligation) responsabilité(s) f(pl)

committee [kə'mɪtɪ] n comité m; commission f

commodity [kə'mɒdɪtɪ] n produit m, marchandise f, article m

common ['kɒmən] adj (gen) commun(e); (usual) courant(e) ▷ n terrain communal; **commonly** adv communément, généralement; couramment; **commonplace** adj banal(e), ordinaire; **Commons**

npl (BRIT Pol): **the (House of) Commons** la chambre des Communes; **common sense** n bon sens; **Commonwealth** n: **the Commonwealth** le Commonwealth

communal ['kɔmjuːnl] adj (life) communautaire; (for common use) commun(e)

commune n ['kɔmjuːn] (group) communauté f ▷ vi [kə'mjuːn]: **to ~ with** (nature) communier avec

communicate [kə'mjuːnɪkeɪt] vt communiquer, transmettre ▷ vi: **to ~ (with)** communiquer (avec)

communication [kəmjuːnɪ'keɪʃən] n communication f

communion [kə'mjuːnɪən] n (also: **Holy C~**) communion f

communism ['kɔmjunɪzəm] n communisme m; **communist** adj, n communiste m/f

community [kə'mjuːnɪtɪ] n communauté f; **community centre**, (US) **community center** n foyer socio-éducatif, centre m de loisirs; **community service** n = travail m d'intérêt général, TIG m

commute [kə'mjuːt] vi faire le trajet journalier (de son domicile à un lieu de travail assez éloigné) ▷ vt (Law) commuer; **commuter** n banlieusard(e) (qui fait un trajet journalier pour se rendre à son travail)

compact adj [kəm'pækt] compact(e) ▷ n ['kɔmpækt] (also: **powder ~**) poudrier m; **compact disc** n disque compact; **compact disc player** n lecteur m de disques compacts

companion [kəm'pænjən] n compagnon (compagne)

company ['kʌmpənɪ] n compagnie f; **to keep sb ~** tenir compagnie à qn; **company car** n voiture f de fonction; **company director** n administrateur(-trice)

comparable ['kɔmpərəbl] adj comparable

comparative [kəm'pærətɪv] adj (study) comparatif(-ive); (relative) relatif(-ive); **comparatively** adv (relatively) relativement

compare [kəm'pεəʳ] vt: **to ~ sth/sb with** or **to** comparer qch/qn avec or à ▷ vi: **to ~ (with)** se comparer (à); être comparable (à); **comparison** [kəm'pærɪsn] n comparaison f

compartment [kəm'pɑːtmənt] n (also Rail) compartiment m; **a non-smoking ~** un compartiment non-fumeurs

compass ['kʌmpəs] n boussole f; **compasses** npl (Math) compas m

compassion [kəm'pæʃən] n compassion f, humanité f

compatible [kəm'pætɪbl] adj compatible

compel [kəm'pεl] vt contraindre, obliger; **compelling** adj (fig: argument) irrésistible

compensate ['kɔmpənseɪt] vt indemniser, dédommager ▷ vi: **to ~ for** compenser; **compensation** [kɔmpən'seɪʃən] n compensation f; (money) dédommagement m, indemnité f

compete [kəm'piːt] vi (take part) concourir; (vie): **to ~ (with)** rivaliser (avec), faire concurrence (à)

competent ['kɔmpɪtənt] adj compétent(e), capable

competition [kɔmpɪ'tɪʃən] n (contest) compétition f, concours m; (Econ) concurrence f

competitive [kəm'petɪtɪv] adj (Econ) concurrentiel(le); (sports) de compétition; (person) qui a l'esprit de compétition

competitor [kəm'petɪtəʳ] n concurrent(e)

complacent [kəm'pleɪsnt] adj (trop) content(e) de soi

complain [kəm'pleɪn] vi: **to ~ (about)** se plaindre (de); (in shop etc) réclamer (au sujet de); **complaint** n

plainte f; (in shop etc) réclamation f; (Med) affection f

complement ['kɒmplɪmənt] n complément m; (esp of ship's crew etc) effectif complet ▷ vt (enhance) compléter; **complementary** [kɒmplɪ'mentərɪ] adj complémentaire

complete [kəm'pli:t] adj complet(-ète); (finished) achevé(e) ▷ vt achever, parachever; (set, group) compléter; (a form) remplir; **completely** adv complètement; **completion** [kəm'pli:ʃən] n achèvement m; (of contract) exécution f

complex ['kɒmpleks] adj complexe ▷ n (Psych, buildings etc) complexe m

complexion [kəm'plekʃən] n (of face) teint m

compliance [kəm'plaɪəns] n (submission) docilité f; (agreement): **~ with** le fait de se conformer à; **in ~ with** en conformité avec, conformément à

complicate ['kɒmplɪkeɪt] vt compliquer; **complicated** adj compliqué(e); **complication** [kɒmplɪ'keɪʃən] n complication f

compliment n ['kɒmplɪmənt] compliment m ▷ vt ['kɒmplɪment] complimenter; **complimentary** [kɒmplɪ'mentərɪ] adj flatteur(-euse); (free) à titre gracieux

comply [kəm'plaɪ] vi: **to ~ with** se soumettre à, se conformer à

component [kəm'pəʊnənt] adj composant(e), constituant(e) ▷ n composant m, élément m

compose [kəm'pəʊz] vt composer; (form): **to be ~d of** se composer de; **to ~ o.s.** se calmer, se maîtriser; **composer** n (Mus) compositeur m; **composition** [kɒmpə'zɪʃən] n composition f

composure [kəm'pəʊʒəʳ] n calme m, maîtrise f de soi

compound n ['kɒmpaʊnd] (Chem, Ling) composé m; (enclosure) enclos m,

enceinte f ▷ adj composé(e); (fracture) compliqué(e)

comprehension [kɒmprɪ'henʃən] n compréhension f

comprehensive [kɒmprɪ'hensɪv] adj (très) complet(-ète); **~ policy** (Insurance) assurance f tous risques; **comprehensive (school)** n (BRIT) école secondaire non sélective avec libre circulation d'une section à l'autre, ≈ CES m

> Be careful not to translate *comprehensive* by the French word *compréhensif*.

compress vt [kəm'pres] comprimer; (text, information) condenser ▷ n ['kɒmpres] (Med) compresse f

comprise [kəm'praɪz] vt (also: **be ~d of**) comprendre; (constitute) constituer, représenter

compromise ['kɒmprəmaɪz] n compromis m ▷ vt compromettre ▷ vi transiger, accepter un compromis

compulsive [kəm'pʌlsɪv] adj (Psych) compulsif(-ive); (book, film etc) captivant(e)

compulsory [kəm'pʌlsərɪ] adj obligatoire

computer [kəm'pju:təʳ] n ordinateur m; **computer game** n jeu m vidéo; **computer-generated** adj de synthèse; **computerize** vt (data) traiter par ordinateur; (system, office) informatiser; **computer programmer** n programmeur(-euse); **computer programming** n programmation f; **computer science** n informatique f; **computer studies** npl informatique f; **computing** [kəm'pju:tɪŋ] n informatique f

con [kɒn] vt duper; (cheat) escroquer ▷ n escroquerie f

conceal [kən'si:l] vt cacher, dissimuler

concede [kən'si:d] vt concéder ▷ vi céder

conceited [kən'si:tɪd] adj vaniteux(-euse), suffisant(e)

conceive [kən'siːv] vt, vi concevoir
concentrate ['kɔnsəntreɪt] vi se
  concentrer ▷ vt concentrer
concentration [kɔnsən'treɪʃən] n
  concentration f
concept ['kɔnsept] n concept m
concern [kən'səːn] n affaire f;
  (Comm) entreprise f, firme f; (anxiety)
  inquiétude f, souci m ▷ vt (worry)
  inquiéter; (involve) concerner;
  (relate to) se rapporter à; **to be
  ~ed (about)** s'inquiéter (de),
  être inquiet(-ète) (au sujet de);
  ~ing prep en ce qui concerne,
  à propos de
concert ['kɔnsət] n concert m;
  concert hall n salle f de concert
concerto [kən'tʃəːtəu] n concerto m
concession [kən'seʃən] n
  (compromise) concession f; (reduced
  price) réduction f; **tax ~** dégrèvement
  fiscal; **"~s"** tarif réduit
concise [kən'saɪs] adj concis(e)
conclude [kən'kluːd] vt conclure;
  conclusion [kən'kluːʒən] n
  conclusion f
concrete ['kɔnkriːt] n béton m ▷ adj
  concret(-ète); (Constr) en béton
concussion [kən'kʌʃən] n (Med)
  commotion (cérébrale)
condemn [kən'dem] vt condamner
condensation [kɔnden'seɪʃən] n
  condensation f
condense [kən'dens] vi se condenser
  ▷ vt condenser
condition [kən'dɪʃən] n condition
  f; (disease) maladie f ▷ vt déterminer,
  conditionner; **on ~ that** à
  condition que + sub, à condition
  de; **conditional** [kən'dɪʃənl] adj
  conditionnel(le); **conditioner** n (for
  hair) baume démêlant; (for fabrics)
  assouplissant m
condo ['kɔndəu] n (US inf)
  = condominium
condom ['kɔndəm] n préservatif m
condominium [kɔndə'mɪnɪəm]
  n (US: building) immeuble m (en

copropriété); (: rooms) appartement
  m (dans un immeuble en copropriété)
condone [kən'dəun] vt fermer les
  yeux sur, approuver (tacitement)
conduct n ['kɔndʌkt] conduite f ▷ vt
  [kən'dʌkt] conduire; (manage) mener,
  diriger; (Mus) diriger; **to ~ o.s.** se
  conduire, se comporter; **conductor**
  n (of orchestra) chef m d'orchestre; (on
  bus) receveur m; (US: on train) chef m
  de train; (Elec) conducteur m
cone [kəun] n cône m; (for ice-cream)
  cornet m; (Bot) pomme f de pin, cône
confectionery [kən'fekʃənrɪ] n
  (sweets) confiserie f
confer [kən'fəː] vt: **to ~ sth
  on** conférer qch à ▷ vi conférer,
  s'entretenir
conference ['kɔnfərns] n
  conférence f
confess [kən'fes] vt confesser,
  avouer ▷ vi (admit sth) avouer; (Rel) se
  confesser; **confession** [kən'feʃən] n
  confession f
confide [kən'faɪd] vi: **to ~ in** s'ouvrir
  à, se confier à
confidence ['kɔnfɪdns] n confiance
  f; (also: **self-~**) assurance f,
  confiance en soi; (secret) confidence
  f; **in ~** (speak, write) en confidence,
  confidentiellement; **confident** adj
  (self-assured) sûr(e) de soi; (sure) sûr;
  confidential [kɔnfɪ'denʃəl] adj
  confidentiel(le)
confine [kən'faɪn] vt limiter,
  borner; (shut up) confiner, enfermer;
  confined adj (space) restreint(e),
  réduit(e)
confirm [kən'fəːm] vt (report, Rel)
  confirmer; (appointment) ratifier;
  confirmation [kɔnfə'meɪʃən] n
  confirmation f; ratification f
confiscate ['kɔnfɪskeɪt] vt confisquer
conflict n ['kɔnflɪkt] conflit m, lutte
  f ▷ vi [kən'flɪkt] (opinions) s'opposer,
  se heurter
conform [kən'fɔːm] vi: **to ~ (to)** se
  conformer (à)

confront [kən'frʌnt] vt (two people) confronter; (enemy, danger) affronter, faire face à; (problem) faire face à; **confrontation** [kɔnfrən'teɪʃən] n confrontation f

confuse [kən'fjuːz] vt (person) troubler; (situation) embrouiller; (one thing with another) confondre; **confused** adj (person) dérouté(e), désorienté(e); (situation) embrouillé(e); **confusing** adj peu clair(e), déroutant(e); **confusion** [kən'fjuːʒən] n confusion f

congestion [kən'dʒestʃən] n (Med) congestion f; (fig: traffic) encombrement m

congratulate [kən'grætjuleɪt] vt: **to ~ sb (on)** féliciter qn (de); **congratulations** [kəngrætjʊ'leɪʃənz] npl; **congratulations (on)** félicitations fpl (pour) ▷ excl: **congratulations!** (toutes mes) félicitations!

congregation [kɔŋgrɪ'geɪʃən] n assemblée f (des fidèles)

congress ['kɔŋgres] n congrès m; (Pol) **C~** Congrès m; **congressman** (irreg) n membre m du Congrès; **congresswoman** (irreg) n membre m du Congrès

conifer ['kɔnɪfəʳ] n conifère m

conjugate ['kɔndʒugeɪt] vt conjuguer

conjugation [kɔndʒə'geɪʃən] n conjugaison f

conjunction [kən'dʒʌŋkʃən] n conjonction f; **in ~ with** (conjointement) avec

conjure ['kʌndʒəʳ] vi faire des tours de passe-passe

connect [kə'nekt] vt joindre, relier; (Elec) connecter; (Tel: caller) mettre en connexion; (: subscriber) brancher; (fig) établir un rapport entre, faire un rapprochement entre ▷ vi (train): **to ~ with** assurer la correspondance avec; **to be ~ed with** avoir un rapport avec; (have dealings with) avoir

des rapports avec, être en relation avec; **connecting flight** n (vol m de) correspondance f; **connection** [kə'nekʃən] n relation f, lien m; (Elec) connexion f; (Tel) communication f; (train etc) correspondance f

conquer ['kɔŋkəʳ] vt conquérir; (feelings) vaincre, surmonter

conquest ['kɔŋkwest] n conquête f

cons [kɔnz] npl see **convenience; pro**

conscience ['kɔnʃəns] n conscience f

conscientious [kɔnʃɪ'enʃəs] adj consciencieux(-euse)

conscious ['kɔnʃəs] adj conscient(e); (deliberate: insult, error) délibéré(e); **consciousness** n conscience f; (Med) connaissance f

consecutive [kən'sekjutɪv] adj consécutif(-ive); **on three ~ occasions** trois fois de suite

consensus [kən'sensəs] n consensus m

consent [kən'sent] n consentement m ▷ vi: **to ~ (to)** consentir (à)

consequence ['kɔnsɪkwəns] n suites fpl, conséquence f; (significance) importance f

consequently ['kɔnsɪkwəntlɪ] adv par conséquent, donc

conservation [kɔnsə'veɪʃən] n préservation f, protection f; (also: **nature ~**) défense f de l'environnement

Conservative [kən'sɜːvətɪv] adj, n (BRIT Pol) conservateur(-trice)

conservative adj conservateur(-trice); (cautious) prudent(e)

conservatory [kən'sɜːvətrɪ] n (room) jardin m d'hiver; (Mus) conservatoire m

consider [kən'sɪdəʳ] vt (study) considérer, réfléchir à; (take into account) penser à, prendre en considération; (regard, judge) considérer, estimer; **to ~ doing sth** envisager de faire qch; **considerable** adj considérable; **considerably** adv nettement; **considerate** adj

prévenant(e), plein(e) d'égards;
consideration [kənsɪdəˈreɪʃən] n
considération f; (reward) rétribution
f, rémunération f; **considering**
prep: **considering (that)** étant
donné (que)

consignment [kənˈsaɪnmənt] n
arrivage m, envoi m

consist [kənˈsɪst] vi: **to ~ of** consister
en, se composer de

consistency [kənˈsɪstənsɪ] n
(thickness) consistance f; (fig)
cohérence f

consistent [kənˈsɪstənt] adj logique,
cohérent(e)

consolation [kɒnsəˈleɪʃən] n
consolation f

console¹ [kənˈsəʊl] vt consoler

console² [ˈkɒnsəʊl] n console f

consonant [ˈkɒnsənənt] n
consonne f

conspicuous [kənˈspɪkjuəs] adj
voyant(e), qui attire l'attention

conspiracy [kənˈspɪrəsɪ] n
conspiration f, complot m

constable [ˈkʌnstəbl] n (BRIT) ≈
agent m de police, gendarme m; **chief
~** ≈ préfet m de police

constant [ˈkɒnstənt] adj
constant(e); incessant(e);
constantly adv constamment,
sans cesse

constipated [ˈkɒnstɪpeɪtɪd]
adj constipé(e); **constipation**
[kɒnstɪˈpeɪʃən] n constipation f

constituency [kənˈstɪtjuənsɪ] n
(Pol: area) circonscription électorale;
(: electors) électorat m

constitute [ˈkɒnstɪtjuːt] vt
constituer

constitution [kɒnstɪˈtjuːʃən] n
constitution f

constraint [kənˈstreɪnt] n
contrainte f

construct [kənˈstrʌkt] vt construire;
construction [kənˈstrʌkʃən] n
construction f; **constructive** adj
constructif(-ive)

consul [ˈkɒnsl] n consul m;
consulate [ˈkɒnsjulɪt] n consulat m

consult [kənˈsʌlt] vt consulter;
consultant n (Med) médecin
consultant; (other specialist)
consultant m, (expert-)conseil m;
consultation [kɒnsəlˈteɪʃən] n
consultation f; **consulting room** n
(BRIT) cabinet m de consultation

consume [kənˈsjuːm] vt
consommer; (subj: flames, hatred,
desire) consumer; **consumer** n
consommateur(-trice)

consumption [kənˈsʌmpʃən] n
consommation f

cont. abbr (= continued) suite

contact [ˈkɒntækt] n contact m;
(person) connaissance f, relation f ▷ vt
se mettre en contact or en rapport
avec; **~ number** numéro m de
téléphone; **contact lenses** npl verres
mpl de contact

contagious [kənˈteɪdʒəs] adj
contagieux(-euse)

contain [kənˈteɪn] vt contenir;
to ~ o.s. se contenir, se maîtriser;
container n récipient m; (for shipping
etc) conteneur m

contaminate [kənˈtæmɪneɪt] vt
contaminer

cont'd abbr (= continued) suite

contemplate [ˈkɒntəmpleɪt] vt
contempler; (consider) envisager

contemporary [kənˈtɛmpərərɪ] adj
contemporain(e); (design, wallpaper)
moderne ▷ n contemporain(e)

contempt [kənˈtɛmpt] n mépris m,
dédain m; **~ of court** (Law) outrage m
à l'autorité de la justice

contend [kənˈtɛnd] vt: **to**
soutenir or prétendre que ▷ vi: **to
~ with** (compete) rivaliser avec;
(struggle) lutter avec

content [kənˈtɛnt] adj content(e),
satisfait(e) vt contenter, satisfaire
▷ n [ˈkɒntɛnt] contenu m; (of fat,
moisture) teneur f; **contents** npl (of
container etc) contenu m; **(table of)**

~ **table** f des matières; **contented**
adj content(e), satisfait(e)

contest n ['kɒntest] combat m,
lutte f; (competition) concours m
▷ vt [kən'test] contester, discuter;
(compete for) disputer; (Law) attaquer;
contestant [kən'testənt] n
concurrent(e); (in fight) adversaire m/f

context ['kɒntekst] n contexte m

continent ['kɒntɪnənt] n
continent m; **the C~** (BRIT) l'Europe
continentale; **continental**
[kɒntɪ'nentl] adj continental(e);
continental breakfast n café (or
thé) complet; **continental quilt** n
(BRIT) couette f

continual [kən'tɪnjuəl] adj
continuel(le); **continually** adv
continuellement, sans cesse

continue [kən'tɪnjuː] vi continuer
▷ vt continuer; (start again) reprendre

continuity [kɒntɪ'njuːɪtɪ] n
continuité f; (TV) enchaînement m

continuous [kən'tɪnjuəs] adj
continu(e), permanent(e); (Ling)
progressif(-ive); **continuous
assessment** (BRIT) n contrôle
continu; **continuously** adv
(repeatedly) continuellement;
(uninterruptedly) sans interruption

contour ['kɒntuə'] n contour m,
profil m; (also: ~ **line**) courbe f de
niveau

contraception [kɒntrə'sepʃən] n
contraception f

contraceptive [kɒntrə'septɪv]
adj contraceptif(-ive),
anticonceptionnel(le) ▷ n
contraceptif m

contract n ['kɒntrækt] contrat
m ▷ vi [kən'trækt] (become smaller)
se contracter, se resserrer ▷ vt
contracter; (Comm): **to ~ to do sth**
s'engager (par contrat) à faire qch;
contractor n entrepreneur m

contradict [kɒntrə'dɪkt] vt
contredire; **contradiction**
[kɒntrə'dɪkʃən] n contradiction f

contrary¹ ['kɒntrərɪ] adj contraire,
opposé(e) ▷ n contraire m; **on the ~**
au contraire; **unless you hear to the
~** sauf avis contraire

contrary² [kən'trɛərɪ] adj (perverse)
contrariant(e), entêté(e)

contrast n ['kɒntrɑːst] contraste
m ▷ vt [kən'trɑːst] mettre en
contraste, contraster; **in ~ to**
or **with** contrairement à, par
opposition à

contribute [kən'trɪbjuːt] vi
contribuer ▷ vt: **to ~ £10/an article
to** donner 10 livres/un article à; **to
~ to** (gen) contribuer à; (newspaper)
collaborer à; (discussion) prendre part
à; **contribution** [kɒntrɪ'bjuːʃən] n
contribution f; (BRIT: for social security)
cotisation f; (to publication) article
m; **contributor** n (to newspaper)
collaborateur(-trice); (of money, goods)
donateur(-trice)

control [kən'trəul] vt (process,
machinery) commander; (temper)
maîtriser; (disease) enrayer ▷ n
maîtrise f; (power) autorité f; **controls
npl** (of machine etc) commandes fpl;
(on radio) boutons mpl de réglage; **to
be in ~ of** être maître de, maîtriser;
(in charge of) être responsable de;
everything is under ~ j'ai (or il a
etc) la situation en main; **the car
went out of ~** (or il a etc) perdu le
contrôle du véhicule; **control tower**
n (Aviat) tour f de contrôle

controversial [kɒntrə'və:ʃl] adj
discutable, controversé(e)

controversy ['kɒntrəvə:sɪ] n
controverse f, polémique f

convenience [kən'viːnɪəns] n
commodité f; **at your ~** quand
or comme cela vous convient; **all
modern ~s, all mod cons** (BRIT)
avec tout le confort moderne, tout
confort

convenient [kən'viːnɪənt] adj
commode

convent ['kɒnvənt] n couvent m

convention [kən'vɛnʃən] *n* convention *f*; (*custom*) usage *m*; **conventional** *adj* conventionnel(le)

conversation [kɒnvə'seɪʃən] *n* conversation *f*

conversely [kɒn'vəːslɪ] *adv* inversement, réciproquement

conversion [kən'vəːʃən] *n* conversion *f*; (*BRIT: of house*) transformation *f*, aménagement *m*; (*Rugby*) transformation *f*

convert *vt* [kən'vəːt] (*Rel, Comm*) convertir; (*alter*) transformer; (*house*) aménager ▷ *n* ['kɒnvəːt] converti(e); **convertible** *adj* convertible ▷ *n* (voiture *f*) décapotable *f*

convey [kən'veɪ] *vt* transporter; (*thanks*) transmettre; (*idea*) communiquer; **conveyor belt** *n* convoyeur *m* tapis roulant

convict *vt* [kən'vɪkt] déclarer (*or* reconnaître) coupable ▷ *n* ['kɒnvɪkt] forçat *m*, convict *m*; **conviction** [kən'vɪkʃən] *n* (*Law*) condamnation *f*; (*belief*) conviction *f*

convince [kən'vɪns] *vt* convaincre, persuader; **convinced** *adj*: **convinced of/that** convaincu(e) de/ que; **convincing** *adj* persuasif(-ive), convaincant(e)

convoy ['kɒnvɔɪ] *n* convoi *m*

cook [kuk] *vt* (faire) cuire ▷ *vi* cuire; (*person*) faire la cuisine ▷ *n* cuisinier(-ière); **cookbook** *n* livre *m* de cuisine; **cooker** *n* cuisinière *f*; **cookery** *n* cuisine *f*; **cookery book** *n* (*BRIT*) = **cookbook**; **cookie** *n* (*US*) biscuit *m*, petit gâteau sec; **cooking** *n* cuisine *f*

cool [kuːl] *adj* frais (fraîche); (*not afraid*) calme; (*unfriendly*) froid(e); (*inf: trendy*) cool *inv* (*inf*); (: *great*) super *inv* (*inf*) ▷ *vt*, *vi* rafraîchir, refroidir; **cool down** *vi* refroidir; (*fig: person, situation*) se calmer; **cool off** *vi* (*become calmer*) se calmer; (*lose enthusiasm*) perdre son enthousiasme

cop [kɒp] *n* (*inf*) flic *m*

cope [kəup] *vi* s'en sortir, tenir le coup; **to ~ with** (*problem*) faire face à

copper ['kɒpə*] *n* cuivre *m*; (*BRIT inf: policeman*) flic *m*

copy ['kɒpɪ] *n* copie *f*; (*book etc*) exemplaire *m* ▷ *vt* copier; (*imitate*) imiter; **copyright** *n* droit *m* d'auteur, copyright *m*

coral ['kɒrəl] *n* corail *m*

cord [kɔːd] *n* corde *f*; (*fabric*) velours côtelé; (*Elec*) cordon *m* (d'alimentation), fil *m* (électrique); **cords** *npl* (*trousers*) pantalon *m* de velours côtelé; **cordless** *adj* sans fil

corduroy ['kɔːdərɔɪ] *n* velours côtelé

core [kɔː*] *n* (*of fruit*) trognon *m*, cœur *m*; (*fig: of problem etc*) cœur ▷ *vt* enlever le trognon *or* le cœur de

coriander [kɒrɪ'ændə*] *n* coriandre *f*

cork [kɔːk] *n* (*material*) liège *m*; (*of bottle*) bouchon *m*; **corkscrew** *n* tire-bouchon *m*

corn [kɔːn] *n* (*BRIT: wheat*) blé *m*; (*US: maize*) maïs *m*; (*on foot*) cor *m*; **~ on the cob** (*Culin*) épi *m* de maïs au naturel

corned beef ['kɔːnd-] *n* corned-beef *m*

corner ['kɔːnə*] *n* coin *m*; (*in road*) tournant *m*, virage *m*; (*Football*) corner *m* ▷ *vt* (*trap: prey*) acculer; (*fig*) coincer; (*Comm: market*) accaparer ▷ *vi* prendre un virage; **corner shop** (*BRIT*) *n* magasin *m* du coin

cornflakes ['kɔːnfleɪks] *npl* cornflakes *mpl*

cornflour ['kɔːnflauə*] *n* (*BRIT*) farine *f* de maïs, maïzena® *f*

cornstarch ['kɔːnstɑːtʃ] *n* (*US*) farine *f* de maïs, maïzena® *f*

Cornwall ['kɔːnwəl] *n* Cornouailles *f*

coronary ['kɒrənərɪ] *n*: **~ (thrombosis)** infarctus *m* (du myocarde), thrombose *f* coronaire

coronation [kɒrə'neɪʃən] *n* couronnement *m*

coroner ['kɒrənə*] *n* coroner *m*, officier de police judiciaire chargé de déterminer les causes d'un décès

corporal ['kɔːpərl] n caporal m, brigadier m ⊳ adj: ~ **punishment** châtiment corporel

corporate ['kɔːpərɪt] adj (action, ownership) en commun; (Comm) de la société

corporation [kɔːpə'reɪʃən] n (of town) municipalité f, conseil municipal; (Comm) société f

corps (pl **corps**) [kɔːr, kɔːz] n corps m; **the diplomatic ~** le corps diplomatique; **the press ~** la presse

corpse [kɔːps] n cadavre m

correct [kə'rekt] adj (accurate) correct(e), exact(e); (proper) correct, convenable ⊳ vt corriger; **correction** [kə'rekʃən] n correction f

correspond [kɔrɪs'pɔnd] vi correspondre; **to ~ to sth** (be equivalent to) correspondre à qch; **correspondence** n correspondance f; **correspondent** n correspondant(e); **corresponding** adj correspondant(e)

corridor ['kɔrɪdɔːr] n couloir m, corridor m

corrode [kə'rəud] vt corroder, ronger ⊳ vi se corroder

corrupt [kə'rʌpt] adj corrompu(e); (Comput) altéré(e) ⊳ vt corrompre; (Comput) altérer; **corruption** n corruption f; (Comput) altération f (de données)

Corsica ['kɔːsɪkə] n Corse f

cosmetic [kɔz'metɪk] n produit m de beauté, cosmétique m ⊳ adj (fig: reforms) symbolique, superficiel(le); **cosmetic surgery** n chirurgie f esthétique

cosmopolitan [kɔzmə'pɔlɪtn] adj cosmopolite

cost [kɔst] (pt, pp **cost**) n coût m ⊳ vi coûter ⊳ vt établir or calculer le prix de revient de; **costs** npl (Comm) frais mpl; (Law) dépens mpl; **how much does it ~?** combien ça coûte?; **to ~ sb time/effort** demander du temps/un effort à qn; **it ~ him his life/job** ça lui

a coûté la vie/son emploi; **at all ~s** coûte que coûte, à tout prix

co-star ['kəustɑːr] n partenaire m/f

costly ['kɔstlɪ] adj coûteux(-euse)

cost of living n coût m de la vie

costume ['kɔstjuːm] n costume m; (BRIT: also: **swimming ~**) maillot m (de bain)

cosy, (US) **cozy** ['kəuzɪ] adj (room, bed) douillet(te); **to be ~** (person) être bien (au chaud)

cot [kɔt] n (BRIT: child's) lit m d'enfant, petit lit; (US: campbed) lit de camp

cottage ['kɔtɪdʒ] n petite maison (à la campagne), cottage m; **cottage cheese** n fromage blanc (maigre)

cotton ['kɔtn] n coton m; (thread) fil m (de coton); **cotton on** vi (inf): **to ~ on (to sth)** piger (qch); **cotton bud** (BRIT) n coton-tige® m; **cotton candy** (US) n barbe f à papa; **cotton wool** n (BRIT) ouate f, coton m hydrophile

couch [kautʃ] n canapé m; divan m

cough [kɔf] vi tousser ⊳ n toux f; **I've got a ~** j'ai la toux; **cough mixture**, **cough syrup** n sirop m pour la toux

could [kud] pt of **can²**; **couldn't = could not**

council ['kaunsl] n conseil m; **city** or **town ~** conseil municipal; **council estate** (BRIT) n (quartier m or zone f de) logements loués à/par la municipalité; **council house** (BRIT) n maison f (à loyer modéré) louée par la municipalité; **councillor**, (US) **councilor** n conseiller(-ère); **council tax** n (BRIT) impôts locaux

counsel ['kaunsl] n conseil m; (lawyer) avocat(e) m ⊳ vt: **to ~ (sb) to do sth** conseiller (à qn de faire qch); **counselling**, (US) **counseling** n (Psych) aide psychosociale; **counsellor**, (US) **counselor** n conseiller(-ère); (US: Law) avocat m

count [kaunt] vi, vt compter ⊳ n compte m; (nobleman) comte m; **count in** vt (inf): **to ~ sb in on sth**

inclure qn dans qch; **count on** vt fus compter sur; **countdown** n compte m à rebours

counter ['kaʊntə'] n comptoir m; (in post office, bank) guichet m; (in game) jeton m ▷ vt aller à l'encontre de, opposer ▷ adv: **~ to** à l'encontre de; contrairement à; **counterclockwise** (us) adv en sens inverse des aiguilles d'une montre

counterfeit ['kaʊntəfɪt] n faux m, contrefaçon f ▷ vt contrefaire ▷ adj faux (fausse)

counterpart ['kaʊntəpɑːt] n (of person) homologue m/f

countess ['kaʊntɪs] n comtesse f

countless ['kaʊntlɪs] adj innombrable

country ['kʌntrɪ] n pays m; (native land) patrie f; (as opposed to town) campagne f; (region) région f, pays; **country and western (music)** n musique f country; **country house** n manoir m, (petit) château; **countryside** n campagne f

county ['kaʊntɪ] n comté m

coup (pl **coups**) [kuː, kuːz] n (achievement) beau coup; (also: **~ d'état**) coup d'État

couple ['kʌpl] n couple m; **a ~ of** (two) deux; (a few) deux ou trois

coupon ['kuːpɔn] n (voucher) bon m de réduction; (detachable form) coupon m détachable, coupon-réponse m

courage ['kʌrɪdʒ] n courage m; **courageous** [kə'reɪdʒəs] adj courageux(-euse)

courgette [kuə'ʒet] n (BRIT) courgette f

courier ['kʊrɪə'] n messager m, courrier m; (for tourists) accompagnateur(-trice)

course [kɔːs] n cours m; (of ship) route f; (for golf) terrain m; (part of meal) plat m; **of ~** adv bien sûr; **(no,) of ~ not!** bien sûr que non!, évidemment que non!; **~ of treatment** (Med) traitement m

court [kɔːt] n cour f; (Law) cour, tribunal m; (Tennis) court m ▷ vt (woman) courtiser, faire la cour à; **to take to ~** actionner or poursuivre en justice

courtesy ['kɜːtəsɪ] n courtoisie f, politesse f; **(by) ~ of** avec l'aimable autorisation de; **courtesy bus, courtesy coach** n navette gratuite

court: court-house ['kɔːthaʊs] n (us) palais m de justice; **courtroom** ['kɔːtrum] n salle f de tribunal; **courtyard** ['kɔːtjɑːd] n cour f

cousin ['kʌzn] n cousin(e); **first ~** cousin(e) germain(e)

cover ['kʌvə'] vt couvrir; (Press: report on) faire un reportage sur; (feelings, mistake) cacher; (include) englober; (discuss) traiter ▷ n (of book, Comm) couverture f; (of pan) couvercle m; (over furniture) housse f; (shelter) abri m; **covers** npl (on bed) couvertures; **to take ~** se mettre à l'abri; **under ~** à l'abri; **under ~ of darkness** à la faveur de la nuit; **under separate ~** (Comm) sous pli séparé; **cover up** vi: **to ~ up for sb** (fig) couvrir qn; **coverage** n (in media) reportage m; **cover charge** n couvert m (supplément à payer); **cover-up** n tentative f pour étouffer une affaire

cow [kaʊ] n vache f ▷ vt effrayer, intimider

coward ['kaʊəd] n lâche m/f; **cowardly** adj lâche

cowboy ['kaʊbɔɪ] n cow-boy m

cozy ['kəʊzɪ] adj (us) = **cosy**

crab [kræb] n crabe m

crack [kræk] n (split) fente f, fissure f; (in cup, bone) fêlure f; (in wall) lézarde f; (noise) craquement m, coup (sec); (Drugs) crack m ▷ vt fendre, fissurer; fêler; lézarder; (whip) faire claquer; (nut) casser; (problem) résoudre; (code) déchiffrer ▷ cpd (athlete) de première classe, d'élite; **crack down on** vt fus (crime) sévir contre, réprimer; **cracked** adj (cup, *bone*) fêlé(e); (*broken*) cassé(e); (*wall*) lézardé(e); (*surface*) craquelé(e); (*inf*) toqué(e), timbré(e); **cracker** n (*also*: **Christmas cracker**) pétard m; (*biscuit*) biscuit m (salé), craquelin m

crackle ['krækl] vi crépiter, grésiller

cradle ['kreidl] n berceau m

craft [krɑ:ft] n métier m (artisanal); (*cunning*) ruse f, astuce f; (*boat*: pl inv) embarcation f, barque f; (*plane*: pl inv) appareil m; **craftsman** (*irreg*) n artisan m, ouvrier m (qualifié); **craftsmanship** n métier m, habileté f

cram [kræm] vt: **to ~ sth with** (*fill*) bourrer qch de; **to ~ sth into** (*put*) fourrer qch dans ▷ vi (*for exams*) bachoter

cramp [kræmp] n crampe f; **I've got ~ in my leg** j'ai une crampe à la jambe; **cramped** adj à l'étroit, très serré(e)

cranberry ['krænbəri] n canneberge f

crane [krein] n grue f

crap [kræp] n (*inf*: *nonsense*) conneries fpl (!); (: *excrement*) merde f(!)

crash [kræʃ] n (*noise*) fracas m; (*of car, plane*) collision f; (*of business*) faillite f ▷ vt (*plane*) écraser ▷ vi (*plane*) s'écraser; (*two cars*) se percuter, s'emboutir; (*business*) s'effondrer; **to ~ into** se jeter or se fracasser contre; **crash course** n cours intensif; **crash helmet** n casque (protecteur)

crate [kreit] n cageot m; (*for bottles*) caisse f

crave [kreiv] vt, vi: **to ~ (for)** avoir une envie irrésistible de

crawl [krɔ:l] vi ramper; (*vehicle*) avancer au pas ▷ n (*Swimming*) crawl m

crayfish ['kreifiʃ] n (pl inv: *freshwater*) écrevisse f; (: *saltwater*) langoustine f

crayon ['kreiən] n crayon m (de couleur)

craze [kreiz] n engouement m

crazy ['kreizi] adj fou (folle); **to be ~ about sb/sth** (*inf*) être fou de qn/qch

creak [kri:k] vi (*hinge*) grincer; (*floor, shoes*) craquer

cream [kri:m] n crème f ▷ adj (*colour*) crème inv; **cream cheese** n fromage m à la crème, fromage blanc; **creamy** adj crémeux(-euse)

crease [kri:s] n pli m ▷ vt froisser, chiffonner ▷ vi se froisser, se chiffonner

create [kri:'eit] vt créer; **creation** [kri:'eiʃən] n création f; **creative** adj créatif(-ive); **creator** n créateur(-trice)

creature ['kri:tʃə] n créature f

crèche [kreʃ] n garderie f, crèche f

credentials [kri'denʃlz] npl (*references*) références fpl; (*identity papers*) pièce f d'identité

credibility [kredi'biliti] n crédibilité f

credible ['kredibl] adj digne de foi, crédible

credit ['kredit] n crédit m; (*recognition*) honneur m; (*Scol*) unité f de valeur ▷ vt (*Comm*) créditer; (*believe*: also: **give ~ to**) ajouter foi à, croire; **credits** npl (*Cine*) générique m; **to be in ~** (*person, bank account*) être créditeur(-trice); **to ~ sb with** (*fig*) prêter or attribuer à qn; **credit card** n carte f de crédit; **do you take credit cards?** acceptez-vous les cartes de crédit?; **credit crunch** n crise f du crédit

creek [kri:k] n (*inlet*) crique f, anse f; (*us*: *stream*) ruisseau m, petit cours d'eau

creep (pt, pp **crept**) [kri:p, krept] vi ramper

cremate [kri'meit] vt incinérer

crematorium (pl **crematoria**) [kremə'tɔ:riəm, -'tɔ:riə] n four m crématoire

crept [krept] pt, pp of **creep**

crescent ['kresnt] n croissant m; (*street*) rue f (en arc de cercle)

cress [kres] n cresson m

crest [krest] n crête f; (*of coat of arms*) timbre m

crew [kru:] n équipage m; (Cine)
équipe f (de tournage); **crew-neck**
n col ras

crib [krɪb] n lit m d'enfant; (for baby)
berceau m ▷ vt (inf) copier

cricket ['krɪkɪt] n (insect) grillon
m, cri-cri m inv; (game) cricket m;
cricketer n joueur m de cricket

crime [kraɪm] n crime m, **criminal**
['krɪmɪnl] adj, n criminel(le)

crimson ['krɪmzn] adj cramoisi(e)

cringe [krɪndʒ] vi avoir un
mouvement de recul

cripple ['krɪpl] n (pej) boiteux(-euse),
infirme m/f ▷ vt (person) estropier,
paralyser; (ship, plane) immobiliser;
(production, exports) paralyser

crisis (pl **crises**) ['kraɪsɪs, -siːz] n crise f

crisp [krɪsp] adj croquant(e);
(weather) vif (vive); (manner etc)
brusque; **crisps** (BRIT) npl (pommes
fpl) chips fpl; **crispy** adj croustillant(e)

criterion (pl **criteria**) [kraɪˈtɪərɪən,
-ˈtɪərɪə] n critère m

critic ['krɪtɪk] n critique m/f, **critical**
adj critique; **criticism** ['krɪtɪsɪzəm]
n critique f; **criticize** ['krɪtɪsaɪz] vt
critiquer

Croat ['krəuæt] adj, n = **Croatian**

Croatia [krəuˈeɪʃə] n Croatie f;
Croatian [krəuˈeɪʃən] adj Croate ▷ n Croate m/f;
(Ling) croate m

crockery ['krɒkərɪ] n vaisselle f

crocodile ['krɒkədaɪl] n crocodile m

crocus ['krəukəs] n crocus m

croissant ['krwɑːsɑ̃] n croissant m

crook [kruk] n (inf) escroc m; (of
shepherd) houlette f; **crooked**
['krukɪd] adj courbé(e), tordu(e);
(action) malhonnête

crop [krɒp] n (produce) culture f;
(amount produced) récolte f; (riding
crop) cravache f ▷ vt (hair) tondre;
crop up vi surgir, se présenter,
survenir

cross [krɒs] n croix f; (Biol) croisement
m ▷ vt (street etc) traverser; (arms,
legs, Biol) croiser; (cheque) barrer

▷ adj en colère, fâché(e); **cross off,
cross out** vt barrer, rayer; **cross
over** vi traverser; **cross-Channel
ferry** ['krɒsˈtʃænl-] n ferry m qui fait
la traversée de la Manche; **cross-
country (race)** n cross(-country) m;
crossing n (sea passage) traversée f;
(also: **pedestrian crossing**) passage
clouté; **how long does the crossing
take?** combien de temps dure la
traversée?; **crossing guard** n (us)
contractuel qui fait traverser la rue aux
enfants; **crossroads** n carrefour m;
crosswalk n (us) passage clouté;
crossword n mots mpl croisés

crotch [krɒtʃ] n (of garment)
entrejambe m; (Anat) entrecuisse m

crouch [krautʃ] vi s'accroupir; (hide)
se tapir; (before springing) se ramasser

crouton ['kruːtɒn] n croûton m

crow [krəu] n (bird) corneille f; (of
cock) chant m du coq, cocorico m ▷ vi
(cock) chanter

crowd [kraud] n foule f ▷ vt bourrer,
remplir ▷ vi affluer, s'attrouper,
s'entasser; **crowded** adj bondé(e)

crown [kraun] n couronne f; (of head)
sommet m de la tête; (of hill) sommet
m ▷ vt (also tooth) couronner; **crown
jewels** npl joyaux mpl de la Couronne

crucial ['kruːʃl] adj crucial(e),
décisif(-ive)

crucifix ['kruːsɪfɪks] n crucifix m

crude [kruːd] adj (materials)
brut(e); non raffiné(e); (basic)
rudimentaire, sommaire; (vulgar)
cru(e), grossier(-ière) ▷ n (also: ~ **oil**)
(pétrole m) brut m

cruel ['kruəl] adj cruel(le); **cruelty**
n cruauté f

cruise [kruːz] n croisière f ▷ vi (ship)
croiser; (car) rouler; (aircraft) voler

crumb [krʌm] n miette f

crumble ['krʌmbl] vt émietter ▷ vi
(plaster etc) s'effriter; (land, earth)
s'ébouler; (building) s'écrouler,
crouler; (fig) s'effondrer

crumpet ['krʌmpɪt] n petite crêpe (épaisse)

crumple ['krʌmpl] vt froisser, friper

crunch [krʌntʃ] vt croquer; (underfoot) faire craquer, écraser; faire crisser ▷ n (fig) instant m or moment m critique, moment de vérité; **crunchy** adj croquant(e), croustillant(e)

crush [krʌʃ] n foule f, cohue f; (love): **to have a ~ on sb** avoir le béguin pour qn; (drink): **lemon ~** citron pressé ▷ vt écraser; (crumple) froisser; (grind, break up: garlic, ice) piler; (: grapes) presser; (hopes) anéantir

crust [krʌst] n croûte f; **crusty** adj (bread) croustillant(e); (inf: person) revêche, bourru(e)

crutch [krʌtʃ] n béquille f; (of garment) entrejambe m; (Anat) entrecuisse m

cry [kraɪ] vi pleurer; (shout: also: ~ **out**) crier ▷ n cri m; **cry out** vi (call out, shout) pousser un cri ▷ vt crier

crystal ['krɪstl] n cristal m

cub [kʌb] n petit m (d'un animal); (also: ~ **scout**) louveteau m

Cuba ['kju:bə] n Cuba m

cube [kju:b] n cube m ▷ vt (Math) élever au cube

cubicle ['kju:bɪkl] n (in hospital) box m; (at pool) cabine f

cuckoo ['kuku:] n coucou m

cucumber ['kju:kʌmbəʳ] n concombre m

cuddle ['kʌdl] vt câliner, caresser ▷ vi se blottir l'un contre l'autre

cue [kju:] n queue f de billard; (Theat etc) signal m

cuff [kʌf] n (BRIT: of shirt, coat etc) poignet m, manchette f; (us: on trousers) revers m; (blow) gifle f; **off the ~** adv à l'improviste; **cufflinks** npl boutons m de manchette

cuisine [kwɪˈziːn] n cuisine f

cul-de-sac ['kʌldəsæk] n cul-de-sac m, impasse f

cull [kʌl] vt sélectionner ▷ n (of animals) abattage sélectif

culminate ['kʌlmɪneɪt] vi: **to ~ in** finir or se terminer par; (lead to) mener à

culprit ['kʌlprɪt] n coupable m/f

cult [kʌlt] n culte m

cultivate ['kʌltɪveɪt] vt cultiver

cultural ['kʌltʃərəl] adj culturel(le)

culture ['kʌltʃəʳ] n culture f

cumin ['kʌmɪn] n (spice) cumin m

cunning ['kʌnɪŋ] n ruse f, astuce f ▷ adj rusé(e), malin(-igne); (clever: device, idea) astucieux(-euse)

cup [kʌp] n tasse f; (prize, event) coupe f; (of bra) bonnet m

cupboard ['kʌbəd] n placard m

cup final n (BRIT Football) finale f de la coupe

curator [kjuəˈreɪtəʳ] n conservateur m (d'un musée etc)

curb [kə:b] vt refréner, mettre un frein à ▷ n (fig) frein m; (us) bord m du trottoir

curdle ['kə:dl] vi (se) cailler

cure [kjuəʳ] vt guérir; (Culin: salt) saler; (: smoke) fumer; (: dry) sécher ▷ n remède m

curfew ['kə:fju:] n couvre-feu m

curiosity [kjuərɪˈɔsɪtɪ] n curiosité f

curious ['kjuərɪəs] adj curieux(-euse); **I'm ~ about him** il m'intrigue

curl [kə:l] n boucle f (de cheveux) ▷ vt, vi boucler; (tightly) friser; **curl up** vi s'enrouler; (person) se pelotonner; **curler** n bigoudi m, rouleau m; **curly** adj bouclé(e); (tightly curled) frisé(e)

currant ['kʌrnt] n raisin m de Corinthe, raisin sec; (fruit) groseille f

currency ['kʌrnsɪ] n monnaie f; **to gain ~** (fig) s'accréditer

current ['kʌrnt] n courant m ▷ adj (common) courant(e); (tendency, price, event) actuel(le); **current account** n (BRIT) compte courant; **current affairs** npl (questions fpl d')actualité f; **currently** adv actuellement

curriculum (pl **curriculums** or **curricula**) ['kʌ'rɪkjuləm, -lə] n programme m d'études; **curriculum vitae** [-'viːtaɪ] n curriculum vitae (CV) m

curry ['kʌrɪ] n curry m ⊳ vt: **to ~ favour with** chercher à gagner la faveur or à s'attirer les bonnes grâces de; **curry powder** n poudre f de curry

curse [kəːs] vi jurer, blasphémer ⊳ vt maudire ⊳ n (spell) malédiction f; (problem, scourge) fléau m; (swearword) juron m

cursor ['kəːsəʳ] n (Comput) curseur m

curt [kəːt] adj brusque, sec (sèche)

curtain ['kəːtn] n rideau m

curve [kəːv] n courbe f; (in the road) tournant m, virage m ⊳ vi se courber; (road) faire une courbe; **curved** adj courbe

cushion ['kuʃən] n coussin m ⊳ vt (fall, shock) amortir

custard ['kʌstəd] n (for pouring) crème anglaise

custody ['kʌstədɪ] n (of child) garde f; (for offenders): **to take sb into ~** placer qn en détention préventive

custom ['kʌstəm] n coutume f, usage m; (Comm) clientèle f

customer ['kʌstəməʳ] n client(e)

customized ['kʌstəmaɪzd] adj personnalisé(e); (car etc) construit(e) sur commande

customs ['kʌstəmz] npl douane f; **customs officer** n douanier m

cut [kʌt] (pt, pp **cut**) vt couper; (meat) découper; (reduce) réduire ⊳ vi couper ⊳ n (gen) coupure f; (of clothes) coupe f; (in salary etc) réduction f; (of meat) morceau m; **to ~ a tooth** percer une dent; **to ~ one's finger** se couper le doigt; **to get one's hair ~** se faire couper les cheveux; **I've ~ myself** je me suis coupé; **cut back** vt (plants) tailler; (production, expenditure) réduire; **cut down** vt (tree) abattre; (reduce) réduire; **cut off** vt couper; (fig) isoler; **cut out** vt (picture etc) découper; (remove) supprimer; **cut up** vt découper; **cutback** n réduction f

cute [kjuːt] adj mignon(ne), adorable

cutlery ['kʌtlərɪ] n couverts mpl

cutlet ['kʌtlɪt] n côtelette f

cut-price ['kʌt'praɪs], (us) **cut-rate** ['kʌt'reɪt] adj au rabais, à prix réduit

cutting ['kʌtɪŋ] adj (fig) cinglant(e) ⊳ n (BRIT: from newspaper) coupure f (de journal); (from plant) bouture f

CV n abbr = **curriculum vitae**

cyberbullying ['saɪbəbulɪɪŋ] n harcèlement m virtuel

cyberspace ['saɪbəspeɪs] n cyberespace m

cycle ['saɪkl] n cycle m; (bicycle) bicyclette f, vélo m ⊳ vi faire de la bicyclette; **cycle hire** n location f de vélos; **cycle lane**, **cycle path** n piste f cyclable; **cycling** n cyclisme m; **cyclist** n cycliste m/f

cyclone ['saɪkləun] n cyclone m

cylinder ['sɪlɪndəʳ] n cylindre m

cymbals ['sɪmblz] npl cymbales fpl

cynical ['sɪnɪkl] adj cynique

Cypriot ['sɪprɪət] adj cypriote, chypriote ⊳ n Cypriote m/f, Chypriote m/f

Cyprus ['saɪprəs] n Chypre f

cyst [sɪst] n kyste m; **cystitis** [sɪs'taɪtɪs] n cystite f

czar [zɑːʳ] n tsar m

Czech [tʃɛk] adj tchèque ⊳ n Tchèque m/f; (Ling) tchèque m; **Czech Republic** n: **the Czech Republic** la République tchèque

d

D [di:] n (Mus) ré m

dab [dæb] vt (eyes, wound) tamponner; (paint, cream) appliquer (par petites touches or rapidement)

dad, daddy [dæd, 'dædɪ] n papa m

daffodil ['dæfədɪl] n jonquille f

daft [dɑːft] adj (inf) idiot(e), stupide

dagger ['dægə'] n poignard m

daily ['deɪlɪ] adj quotidien(ne), journalier(-ière) ▷ n quotidien m ▷ adv tous les jours

dairy ['dɛərɪ] n (shop) crèmerie f, laiterie f; (on farm) laiterie f; **dairy produce** n produits laitiers

daisy ['deɪzɪ] n pâquerette f

dam [dæm] n (wall) barrage m; (water) réservoir m, lac m de retenue ▷ vt endiguer

damage ['dæmɪdʒ] n dégâts mpl, dommages mpl; (fig) tort m ▷ vt endommager, abîmer; (fig) faire du tort à; **damages** npl (Law) dommages-intérêts mpl

damn [dæm] vt condamner; (curse) maudire ▷ n (inf): **I don't give a ~** je

m'en fous ▷ adj (inf: also: **~ed**): **this ~ ...** ce sacré or foutu ...; **~ (it)!** zut!

damp [dæmp] adj humide ▷ n humidité f ▷ vt (also: **~en**: cloth, rag) humecter; (: enthusiasm etc) refroidir

dance [dɑːns] n danse f; (ball) bal m ▷ vi danser; **dance floor** n piste f de danse; **dancer** n danseur(-euse); **dancing** n danse f

dandelion ['dændɪlaɪən] n pissenlit m

dandruff ['dændrəf] n pellicules fpl

D & T n abbr (BRIT Scol) = **design and technology**

Dane [deɪn] n Danois(e)

danger ['deɪndʒə'] n danger m; **~!** (on sign) danger!; **in ~** en danger; **he was in ~ of falling** il risquait de tomber; **dangerous** adj dangereux(-euse)

dangle ['dæŋgl] vt balancer ▷ vi pendre, se balancer

Danish ['deɪnɪʃ] adj danois(e) ▷ n (Ling) danois m

dare [dɛə'] vt: **to ~ sb to do** défier qn or mettre qn au défi de faire ▷ vi: **to ~ (to) do sth** oser faire qch; **I ~ say he'll turn up** il est probable qu'il viendra; **daring** adj hardi(e), audacieux(-euse) ▷ n audace f, hardiesse f

dark [dɑːk] adj (night, room) obscur(e), sombre; (colour, complexion) foncé(e), sombre ▷ n: **in the ~** dans le noir; **to be in the ~ about** (fig) ignorer tout de; **after ~** après la tombée de la nuit; **darken** vt obscurcir, assombrir ▷ vi s'obscurcir, s'assombrir; **darkness** n obscurité f; **darkroom** n chambre noire

darling ['dɑːlɪŋ] adj, n chéri(e)

dart [dɑːt] n fléchette f; (in sewing) pince f ▷ vi: **to ~ towards** se précipiter or s'élancer vers; **dartboard** n cible f (de jeu de fléchettes); **darts** n jeu m de fléchettes

dash [dæʃ] n (sign) tiret m; (small quantity) goutte f, larme f ▷ vt (throw) jeter or lancer violemment; (hopes) anéantir ▷ vi: **to ~ towards** se précipiter or se ruer vers

dashboard ['dæʃbɔːd] n (Aut) tableau m de bord

data ['deɪtə] npl données fpl; **database** n base f de données; **data processing** n traitement m des données

date [deɪt] n date f; (with sb) rendez-vous m; (fruit) datte f ▷ vt dater; (person) sortir avec; **~ of birth** date de naissance; **to ~** adv à ce jour; **out of ~** périmé(e); **up to ~** à la page, moderne; **dated** adj démodé(e)

daughter ['dɔːtə] n fille f; **daughter-in-law** n belle-fille f, bru f

daunting ['dɔːntɪŋ] adj décourageant(e), intimidant(e)

dawn [dɔːn] n aube f, aurore f ▷ vi (day) se lever, poindre; **it ~ed on him that ...** il lui vint à l'esprit que ...

day [deɪ] n jour m; (as duration) journée f; (period of time, age) époque f, temps m; **the ~ before** la veille, le jour précédent; **the ~ after, the following ~** le lendemain, le jour suivant; **the ~ before yesterday** avant-hier; **the ~ after tomorrow** après-demain; **by ~** de jour; **day-care centre** ['deɪkeə-] n (for elderly etc) centre m d'accueil de jour; (for children) garderie f; **daydream** vi rêver (tout éveillé); **daylight** n (lumière f du) jour m; **day return** n (BRIT) billet m d'aller-retour (valable pour la journée); **daytime** n jour m, journée f; **day-to-day** adj (routine, expenses) journalier(-ière); **day trip** n excursion f d'une journée

dazed [deɪzd] adj abruti(e)

dazzle ['dæzl] vt éblouir, aveugler; **dazzling** adj (light) éblouissant(e), aveuglant(e); (fig) éblouissant(e)

DC abbr (Elec) = **direct current**

dead [ded] adj mort(e); (numb) engourdi(e), insensible; (battery) à plat ▷ adv (completely) absolument,

complètement; (exactly) juste; **he was shot ~** il a été tué d'un coup de revolver; **~ tired** éreinté(e), complètement fourbu(e); **to stop ~** s'arrêter pile or net; **the line is ~** (Tel) la ligne est coupée; **dead end** n impasse f; **deadline** n date for heure f limite; **deadly** adj mortel(le); (weapon) meurtrier(-ière); **Dead Sea** n: **the Dead Sea** la mer Morte

deaf [def] adj sourd(e); **deafen** vt rendre sourd(e); **deafening** adj assourdissant(e)

deal [diːl] n affaire f, marché m ▷ vb (pt, pp **dealt**) (blow) porter; (cards) donner, distribuer; **a great ~ of** beaucoup de; **deal with** vt fus (handle) s'occuper or se charger de; (be about) traiter de; **dealer** n (Comm) marchand m; (Cards) donneur m; **dealings** npl (in goods, shares) opérations fpl, transactions fpl; (relations) relations fpl, rapports mpl

dealt [delt] pt, pp of **deal**

dean [diːn] n (Rel, BRIT Scol) doyen m; (US Scol) conseiller principal (conseillère principale) d'éducation

dear [dɪə] adj cher (chère); (expensive) cher, coûteux(-euse) ▷ n: **my ~** mon cher (ma chère) ▷ excl: **~ me!** mon Dieu!; **D~ Sir/Madam** (in letter) Monsieur/Madame; **D~ Mr/Mrs X** Cher Monsieur/Chère Madame X; **dearly** adv (love) tendrement; (pay) cher

death [deθ] n mort f; (Admin) décès m; **death penalty** n peine f de mort; **death sentence** n condamnation f à mort

debate [dɪ'beɪt] n discussion f, débat m ▷ vt discuter, débattre

debit ['debɪt] n débit m ▷ vt: **to ~ a sum to sb** or **to sb's account** porter une somme au débit de qn, débiter qn d'une somme; **debit card** n carte f de paiement

debris ['debriː] n débris mpl, décombres mpl

debt [dɛt] n dette f; **to be in ~** avoir des dettes, être endetté(e)

debug [diːˈbʌg] vt (Comput) déboguer

debut [ˈdeɪbjuː] n début(s) m(pl)

Dec. abbr (= December) déc

decade [ˈdɛkeɪd] n décennie f, décade f

decaffeinated [dɪˈkæfɪneɪtɪd] adj décaféiné(e)

decay [dɪˈkeɪ] n (of tooth, wood etc) décomposition f, pourriture f; (of building) délabrement m; (also: **tooth ~**) carie f (dentaire) ▷ vi (rot) se décomposer, pourrir; (teeth) se carier

deceased [dɪˈsiːst] n: **the ~** le (la) défunt(e)

deceit [dɪˈsiːt] n tromperie f, supercherie f; **deceive** [dɪˈsiːv] vt tromper

December [dɪˈsɛmbəʳ] n décembre m

decency [ˈdiːsənsɪ] n décence f

decent [ˈdiːsənt] adj (proper) décent(e), convenable

deception [dɪˈsɛpʃən] n tromperie f; **deceive** [dɪˈsɛptɪv] adj trompeur(-euse)

decide [dɪˈsaɪd] vt (subj: person) décider; (question, argument) trancher, régler ▷ vi se décider, décider; **to ~ to do/that** décider de faire/que; **to ~ on** décider, se décider pour

decimal [ˈdɛsɪml] adj décimal(e) ▷ n décimale f

decision [dɪˈsɪʒən] n décision f

decisive [dɪˈsaɪsɪv] adj décisif(-ive); (manner, person) décidé(e), catégorique

deck [dɛk] n (Naut) pont m; (of cards) jeu m; (record deck) platine f; (of bus): **top ~** impériale f; **deckchair** n chaise longue

declaration [dɛkləˈreɪʃən] n déclaration f

declare [dɪˈklɛəʳ] vt déclarer

decline [dɪˈklaɪn] n (decay) déclin m; (lessening) baisse f ▷ vt refuser, décliner ▷ vi décliner; (business) baisser

decorate [ˈdɛkəreɪt] vt (adorn, give a medal to) décorer; (paint and paper) peindre et tapisser; **decoration** [dɛkəˈreɪʃən] n (medal etc, adornment) décoration f; **decorator** n peintre m en bâtiment

decrease n [ˈdiːkriːs] diminution f ▷ vt, vi [diːˈkriːs] diminuer

decree [dɪˈkriː] n (Pol, Rel) décret m; (Law) arrêt m, jugement m

dedicate [ˈdɛdɪkeɪt] vt consacrer; (book etc) dédier; **dedicated** adj (person) dévoué(e); (Comput) spécialisé(e), dédié(e); **dedicated word processor** station f de traitement de texte; **dedication** [dɛdɪˈkeɪʃən] n (devotion) dévouement m; (in book) dédicace f

deduce [dɪˈdjuːs] vt déduire, conclure

deduct [dɪˈdʌkt] vt: **to ~ sth (from)** déduire qch (de), retrancher qch (de); **deduction** [dɪˈdʌkʃən] n (deducting, deducing) déduction f; (from wage etc) prélèvement m, retenue f

deed [diːd] n action f, acte m; (Law) acte notarié, contrat m

deem [diːm] vt (formal) juger, estimer

deep [diːp] adj profond(e); (voice) grave ▷ adv profond: **spectators stood 20 ~** il y avait 20 rangs de spectateurs; **4 metres ~** de 4 mètres de profondeur; **how ~ is the water?** l'eau a quelle profondeur?; **deep-fry** vt faire frire (dans une friteuse); **deeply** adv profondément; (regret, interested) vivement

deer [dɪəʳ] n (pl inv): **(red) ~** cerf m; **(fallow) ~** daim m; **(roe) ~** chevreuil m

default [dɪˈfɔːlt] n (Comput: also: **~ value**) valeur f par défaut; **by ~** (Law) par défaut, par contumace; (Sport) par forfait

defeat [dɪˈfiːt] n défaite f ▷ vt (team, opponents) battre

defect n [ˈdiːfɛkt] défaut m ▷ vi [dɪˈfɛkt]: **to ~ to the enemy/the West** passer à l'ennemi/l'Ouest;

d

defective [dɪˈfɛktɪv] *adj*
défectueux(-euse)

defence, (US) **defense** [dɪˈfɛns] *n*
défense *f*

defend [dɪˈfɛnd] *vt* défendre;
defendant *n* défendeur(-deresse); (*in criminal case*) accusé(e), prévenu(e);
defender *n* défenseur *m*

defense [dɪˈfɛns] *n* (US) = **defence**

defensive [dɪˈfɛnsɪv] *adj* défensif(-ive)
▷ *n*: **on the ~** sur la défensive

defer [dɪˈfəːʳ] *vt* (*postpone*) différer,
ajourner

defiance [dɪˈfaɪəns] *n* défi *m*; **in ~ of**
au mépris de; **defiant** [dɪˈfaɪənt] *adj*
provocant(e), de défi; (*person*) rebelle,
intraitable

deficiency [dɪˈfɪʃənsɪ] *n* (*lack*)
insuffisance *f*; (*Med*) carence *f*; (*flaw*)
faiblesse *f*; **deficient** [dɪˈfɪʃənt] *adj*
(*inadequate*) insuffisant(e); **to be**
deficient in manquer de

deficit [ˈdɛfɪsɪt] *n* déficit *m*

define [dɪˈfaɪn] *vt* définir

definite [ˈdɛfɪnɪt] *adj* (*fixed*) défini(e),
(*bien*) déterminé(e); (*clear, obvious*)
net(te), manifeste; (*certain*) sûr(e); **he**
was ~ about it il a été catégorique;
definitely *adv* sans aucun doute

definition [dɛfɪˈnɪʃən] *n* définition *f*;
(*clearness*) netteté *f*

deflate [diːˈfleɪt] *vt* dégonfler

deflect [dɪˈflɛkt] *vt* détourner, faire
dévier

defraud [dɪˈfrɔːd] *vt*: **to ~ sb of sth**
escroquer qch à qn

defriend [dɪˈfrɛnd] *vt* (*Internet*)
supprimer de sa liste d'amis

defrost [diːˈfrɔst] *vt* (*fridge*) dégivrer;
(*frozen food*) décongeler

defuse [diːˈfjuːz] *vt* désamorcer

defy [dɪˈfaɪ] *vt* défier; (*efforts etc*)
résister à; **it defies description** cela
défie toute description

degree [dɪˈɡriː] *n* degré *m*; (*Scol*)
diplôme *m* (universitaire); **a (first)**
~ in maths (BRIT) une licence en
maths; **by ~s** (*gradually*) par degrés;

to some ~ jusqu'à un certain point,
dans une certaine mesure

dehydrated [diːhaɪˈdreɪtɪd] *adj*
déshydraté(e); (*milk, eggs*) en poudre

de-icer [diːˈaɪsəʳ] *n* dégivreur *m*

delay [dɪˈleɪ] *vt* retarder; (*payment*)
différer ▷ *vi* s'attarder ▷ *n* délai *m*,
retard *m*; **to be ~ed** être en retard

delegate *n* [ˈdɛlɪɡɪt] délégué(e) ▷ *vt*
[ˈdɛlɪɡeɪt] déléguer

delete [dɪˈliːt] *vt* rayer, supprimer;
(*Comput*) effacer

deli [ˈdɛlɪ] *n* épicerie fine

deliberate *adj* [dɪˈlɪbərɪt]
(*intentional*) délibéré(e); (*slow*)
mesuré(e) ▷ *vi* [dɪˈlɪbəreɪt] délibérer,
réfléchir; **deliberately** *adv* (*on purpose*) exprès, délibérément

delicacy [ˈdɛlɪkəsɪ] *n* délicatesse
f; (*choice food*) mets fin or délicat,
friandise *f*

delicate [ˈdɛlɪkɪt] *adj* délicat(e)

delicatessen [dɛlɪkəˈtɛsn] *n*
épicerie fine

delicious [dɪˈlɪʃəs] *adj* délicieux(-euse)

delight [dɪˈlaɪt] *n* (grande) joie, grand
plaisir ▷ *vt* enchanter; **she's a ~ to**
work with c'est un plaisir de travailler
avec elle; **to take ~ in** prendre grand
plaisir à; **delighted** *adj*: **delighted**
(at or with sth) ravi(e) (de qch);
to be delighted to do sth/that être
enchanté(e) or ravi(e) de faire qch/
que; **delightful** *adj* (*person*) adorable;
(*meal, evening*) merveilleux(-euse)

delinquent [dɪˈlɪŋkwənt] *adj, n*
délinquant(e)

deliver [dɪˈlɪvəʳ] *vt* (*mail*) distribuer;
(*goods*) livrer; (*message*) remettre;
(*speech*) prononcer; (*Med: baby*)
mettre au monde; **delivery** *n* (*of*
mail) distribution *f*; (*of goods*) livraison
f; (*of speaker*) élocution *f*; (*Med*)
accouchement *m*; **to take delivery of**
prendre livraison de

delusion [dɪˈluːʒən] *n* illusion *f*

de luxe [dəˈlʌks] *adj* de luxe

delve [dɛlv] *vi*: **to ~ into** fouiller dans

demand [dɪˈmɑːnd] vt réclamer, exiger ▷ n exigence f; (claim) revendication f; (Econ) demande f; **in ~** demandé(e), recherché(e); **on ~** sur demande; **demanding** adj (person) exigeant(e); (work) astreignant(e)

⬛ Be careful not to translate to demand by the French word demander.

demise [dɪˈmaɪz] n décès m

demo [ˈdɛməʊ] n abbr (inf: = demonstration) (protest) manif f; (Comput) démonstration f

democracy [dɪˈmɒkrəsɪ] n démocratie f; **democrat** [ˈdɛməkræt] n démocrate m/f; **democratic** [dɛməˈkrætɪk] adj démocratique

demolish [dɪˈmɒlɪʃ] vt démolir; **demolition** [dɛməˈlɪʃən] n démolition f

demon [ˈdiːmən] n démon m

demonstrate [ˈdɛmənstreɪt] vt démontrer, prouver; (show) faire une démonstration de ▷ vi: **to ~ (for/against)** manifester (en faveur de/contre); **demonstration** [dɛmənˈstreɪʃən] n démonstration f; (Pol etc) manifestation f; **demonstrator** n (Pol etc) manifestant(e)

demote [dɪˈməʊt] vt rétrograder

den [dɛn] n (of lion) tanière f; (room) repaire m

denial [dɪˈnaɪəl] n (of accusation) démenti m; (of rights, guilt, truth) dénégation f

denim [ˈdɛnɪm] n jean m; **denims** npl (blue-)jeans mpl

Denmark [ˈdɛnmɑːk] n Danemark m

denomination [dɪnɒmɪˈneɪʃən] n (money) valeur f; (Rel) confession f

denounce [dɪˈnaʊns] vt dénoncer

dense [dɛns] adj dense; (inf: stupid) obtus(e)

density [ˈdɛnsɪtɪ] n densité f

dent [dɛnt] n bosse f ▷ vt (also: **make a ~ in**) cabosser

dental [ˈdɛntl] adj dentaire; **dental floss** [-flɒs] n fil m dentaire; **dental surgery** n cabinet m de dentiste

dentist [ˈdɛntɪst] n dentiste m/f

dentures [ˈdɛntʃəz] npl dentier msg

deny [dɪˈnaɪ] vt nier; (refuse) refuser

deodorant [diːˈəʊdərənt] n déodorant m

depart [dɪˈpɑːt] vi partir; **to ~ from** (fig: differ from) s'écarter de

department [dɪˈpɑːtmənt] n (Comm) rayon m; (Scol) section f; (Pol) ministère m, département m; **department store** n grand magasin

departure [dɪˈpɑːtʃə] n départ m; **a new ~** une nouvelle voie; **departure lounge** n salle f de départ

depend [dɪˈpɛnd] vi: **to ~ (up)on** dépendre de; (rely on) compter sur; **it ~s** cela dépend; **~ing on the result ...** selon le résultat ...; **dependant** n personne f à charge; **dependent** adj: **to be dependent (on)** dépendre (de) ▷ n = **dependant**

depict [dɪˈpɪkt] vt (in picture) représenter; (in words) (dé)peindre, décrire

deport [dɪˈpɔːt] vt déporter, expulser

deposit [dɪˈpɒzɪt] n (Chem, Comm, Geo) dépôt m; (of ore, oil) gisement m; (part payment) acompte m; (on bottle etc) consigne f; (for hired goods etc) cautionnement m, garantie f ▷ vt déposer; **deposit account** n compte m sur livret

depot [ˈdɛpəʊ] n dépôt m; (US Rail) gare f

depreciate [dɪˈpriːʃɪeɪt] vi se déprécier, se dévaloriser

depress [dɪˈprɛs] vt déprimer; (press down) appuyer sur, abaisser; (wages etc) faire baisser; **depressed** adj (person) déprimé(e); (area) en déclin, touché(e) par le sous-emploi; **depressing** adj déprimant(e); **depression** [dɪˈprɛʃən] n dépression f

deprive [dɪˈpraɪv] vt: **to ~ sb of** priver qn de; **deprived** adj déshérité(e)

d

dept. abbr (= department) dép, dépt

depth [dɛpθ] n profondeur f; **to be in the ~s of despair** être au plus profond du désespoir; **to be out of one's ~** (BRIT: swimmer) ne plus avoir pied; (fig) être dépassé(e), nager

deputy ['dɛpjutɪ] n (second in command) adjoint(e); (Pol) député m; (US: also: **~ sheriff**) shérif adjoint ▷ adj: **~ head** (Scol) directeur(-trice) adjoint(e), sous-directeur(-trice)

derail [dɪ'reɪl] vt: **to be ~ed** dérailler

derelict ['dɛrɪlɪkt] adj abandonné(e), à l'abandon

derive [dɪ'raɪv] vt: **to ~ sth from** tirer qch de; trouver qch dans ▷ vi: **to ~ from** provenir de, dériver de

descend [dɪ'sɛnd] vi, vt descendre; **to ~ from** descendre de, être issu(e) de; **to ~ to** s'abaisser à; **descendant** n descendant(e); **descent** n descente f; (origin) origine f

describe [dɪs'kraɪb] vt décrire; **description** [dɪs'krɪpʃən] n description f; (sort) sorte f, espèce f

desert n ['dɛzət] désert m ▷ vt [dɪ'zɜːt] déserter, abandonner ▷ vi (Mil) déserter; **deserted** [dɪ'zɜːtɪd] adj désert(e)

deserve [dɪ'zɜːv] vt mériter

design [dɪ'zaɪn] n (sketch) plan m, dessin m; (layout, shape) conception f, ligne f; (pattern) dessin, motif(s) m(pl); (of dress, car) modèle m; (art) design m, stylisme m; (intention) dessein m ▷ vt dessiner; (plan) concevoir; **design and technology** n (BRIT Scol) technologie f

designate vt ['dɛzɪgneɪt] désigner ▷ adj ['dɛzɪgnɪt] désigné(e)

designer [dɪ'zaɪnər] n (Archit, Art) dessinateur(-trice); (Industry) concepteur m, designer m; (Fashion) styliste m/f

desirable [dɪ'zaɪərəbl] adj (property, location, purchase) attrayant(e)

desire [dɪ'zaɪər] n désir m ▷ vt désirer, vouloir

desk [dɛsk] n (in office) bureau m; (for pupil) pupitre m; (BRIT: in shop, restaurant) caisse f; (in hotel, at airport) réception f; **desktop** ['dɛsktɒp] n bureau m; **desktop publishing** n publication assistée par ordinateur, PAO f

despair [dɪs'pɛər] n désespoir m ▷ vi: **to ~ of** désespérer de

despatch [dɪs'pætʃ] n, vt = **dispatch**

desperate ['dɛsprɪt] adj désespéré(e); (fugitive) prêt(e) à tout; **to be ~ for sth/to do sth** avoir désespérément besoin de qch/de faire qch; **desperately** adv désespérément; (very) terriblement, extrêmement; **desperation** [dɛspə'reɪʃən] n désespoir m; **in (sheer) desperation** en désespoir de cause

despise [dɪs'paɪz] vt mépriser

despite [dɪs'paɪt] prep malgré, en dépit de

dessert [dɪ'zɜːt] n dessert m; **dessertspoon** n cuiller f à dessert

destination [dɛstɪ'neɪʃən] n destination f

destined ['dɛstɪnd] adj: **~ for London** à destination de Londres

destiny ['dɛstɪnɪ] n destinée f, destin m

destroy [dɪs'trɔɪ] vt détruire; (injured horse) abattre; (dog) faire piquer

destruction [dɪs'trʌkʃən] n destruction f

destructive [dɪs'trʌktɪv] adj destructeur(-trice)

detach [dɪ'tætʃ] vt détacher; **detached** adj (attitude) détaché(e); **detached house** n pavillon m, maison(nette) (individuelle)

detail ['diːteɪl] n détail m ▷ vt raconter en détail, énumérer; **in ~** en détail; **detailed** adj détaillé(e)

detain [dɪ'teɪn] vt retenir; (in captivity) détenir

detect [dɪ'tɛkt] vt déceler, percevoir; (Med, Police) dépister; (Mil, Radar, Tech) détecter; **detection** [dɪ'tɛkʃən] n

découverte f; **detective** n policier m;
private detective détective privé;
detective story n roman policier

detention [dɪ'tɛnʃən] n détention f;
(Scol) retenue f, consigne f

deter [dɪ'tə:ʳ] vt dissuader

detergent [dɪ'tə:dʒənt] n détersif m,
détergent m

deteriorate [dɪ'tɪərɪəreɪt] vi se
détériorer, se dégrader

determination [dɪtə:mɪ'neɪʃən] n
détermination f

determine [dɪ'tə:mɪn] vt
déterminer; **to ~ to do** résoudre
de faire, se déterminer à faire;
determined adj (person)
déterminé(e), décidé(e);
determined to do bien décidé à faire

deterrent [dɪ'tɛrənt] n effet m de
dissuasion; force f de dissuasion

detest [dɪ'tɛst] vt détester, avoir
horreur de

detour ['di:tuəʳ] n détour m; (us Aut:
diversion) déviation f

detox ['di:tɔks] n détox f

detract [dɪ'trækt] vt: **to ~ from**
(quality, pleasure) diminuer;
(reputation) porter atteinte à

detrimental [dɛtrɪ'mɛntl] adj: **~ to**
préjudiciable or nuisible à

devastating ['dɛvəsteɪtɪŋ] adj
dévastateur(-trice); (news) accablant(e)

develop [dɪ'vɛləp] vt (gen)
développer; (disease) commencer
à souffrir de; (resources) mettre en
valeur, exploiter; (land) aménager
▷ vi se développer; (situation,
disease: evolve) évoluer; (facts,
symptoms: appear) se manifester,
se produire; **can you ~ this film?**
pouvez-vous développer cette
pellicule?; **developing country** n
pays m en voie de développement;
development n développement m;
(of land) exploitation f; (new fact, event)
rebondissement m, fait(s) nouveau(x)

device [dɪ'vaɪs] n (apparatus) appareil
m, dispositif m

devil ['dɛvl] n diable m; démon m

devious ['di:vɪəs] adj (person)
sournois(e), dissimulé(e)

devise [dɪ'vaɪz] vt imaginer,
concevoir

devote [dɪ'vəut] vt: **to ~ sth to**
consacrer qch à; **to be devoted to**
être dévoué(e); **devoted** adj
dévoué(e); **to be devoted to** être
dévoué(e) or très attaché(e) à; (book
etc) être consacré(e) à; **devotion** n
dévouement m, attachement m; (Rel)
dévotion f, piété f

devour [dɪ'vauəʳ] vt dévorer

devout [dɪ'vaut] adj pieux(-euse)

dew [dju:] n rosée f

diabetes [daɪə'bi:ti:z] n diabète m

diabetic [daɪə'bɛtɪk] n diabétique
m/f ▷ adj (person) diabétique

diagnose [daɪəg'nəuz] vt
diagnostiquer

diagnosis (pl **diagnoses**)
[daɪəg'nəusɪs, -si:z] n diagnostic m

diagonal [daɪ'ægənl] adj diagonal(e)
▷ n diagonale f

diagram ['daɪəgræm] n diagramme
m, schéma m

dial ['daɪəl] n cadran m ▷ vt (number)
faire, composer

dialect ['daɪəlɛkt] n dialecte m

dialling code ['daɪəlɪŋ-], (us) **dial
code** n indicatif m (téléphonique);
what's the ~ for Paris? quel est
l'indicatif de Paris?

dialling tone ['daɪəlɪŋ-], (us) **dial
tone** n tonalité f

dialogue, (us) **dialog** ['daɪəlɔg] n
dialogue m

diameter [daɪ'æmɪtəʳ] n diamètre m

diamond ['daɪəmənd] n diamant
m; (shape) losange m; **diamonds** npl
(Cards) carreau m

diaper ['daɪəpəʳ] n (us) couche f

diarrhoea, (us) **diarrhea** [daɪə'rɪə]
n diarrhée f

diary ['daɪərɪ] n (daily account) journal
m; (book) agenda m

dice [daɪs] n (pl inv) dé m ▷ vt (Culin)
couper en dés or en cubes

dictate vt [dɪk'teɪt] dicter; **dictation** [dɪk'teɪʃən] n dictée f

dictator [dɪk'teɪtə'] n dictateur m

dictionary ['dɪkʃənrɪ] n dictionnaire m

did [dɪd] pt of **do**

didn't [dɪdnt] = **did not**

die [daɪ] vi mourir; **to be dying for sth** avoir une envie folle de qch; **to be dying to do sth** mourir d'envie de faire qch; **die down** vi se calmer, s'apaiser; **die out** vi disparaître, s'éteindre

diesel ['di:zl] n (vehicle) diesel m; (also: ~ **oil**) carburant m diesel, gas-oil m

diet ['daɪət] n alimentation f; (restricted regime) régime m ▷ vi (also: **be on a ~**) suivre un régime

differ ['dɪfə'] vi: **to ~ from sth** (be different) être différent(e) de qch, différer de qch; **to ~ from sb over sth** ne pas être d'accord avec qn au sujet de qch; **difference** n différence f; (quarrel) différend m, désaccord m; **different** adj différent(e); **differentiate** [dɪfə'renʃɪeɪt] vi: **to differentiate between** faire une différence entre; **differently** adv différemment

difficult ['dɪfɪkəlt] adj difficile; **difficulty** n difficulté f

dig [dɪg] vt (pt, pp **dug**) (hole) creuser; (garden) bêcher ▷ n (prod) coup m de coude; (fig: remark) coup de griffe or de patte; (Archaeology) fouille f; **to ~ one's nails into** enfoncer ses ongles dans; **dig up** vt déterrer

digest vt [daɪ'dʒɛst] digérer ▷ n ['daɪdʒɛst] sommaire m, résumé m; **digestion** [dɪ'dʒɛstʃən] n digestion f

digit ['dɪdʒɪt] n (number) chiffre m (de 0 à 9); (finger) doigt m; **digital** adj (system, recording, radio) numérique, digital(e); (watch) à affichage numérique or digital; **digital camera** n appareil m photo numérique; **digital TV** n télévision f numérique

dignified ['dɪgnɪfaɪd] adj digne

dignity ['dɪgnɪtɪ] n dignité f

digs [dɪgz] npl (BRIT inf) piaule f, chambre meublée

dilemma [daɪ'lemə] n dilemme m

dill [dɪl] n aneth m

dilute [daɪ'lu:t] vt diluer

dim [dɪm] adj (light, eyesight) faible; (memory, outline) vague, indécis(e); (room) sombre; (inf: stupid) borné(e), obtus(e) ▷ vt (light) réduire, baisser; (us Aut) mettre en code, baisser

dime [daɪm] n (us) pièce f de 10 cents

dimension [daɪ'menʃən] n dimension f

diminish [dɪ'mɪnɪʃ] vt, vi diminuer

din [dɪn] n vacarme m

dine [daɪn] vi dîner; **diner** n (person) dîneur(-euse); (us: eating place) petit restaurant

dinghy ['dɪŋgɪ] n youyou m; (inflatable) canot m pneumatique; (also: **sailing** ~) voilier m, dériveur m

dingy ['dɪndʒɪ] adj miteux(-euse), minable

dining car ['daɪnɪŋ-] n (BRIT) voiture-restaurant f, wagon-restaurant m

dining room ['daɪnɪŋ-] n salle f à manger

dining table [daɪnɪŋ-] n table f de (la) salle à manger

dinkum ['dɪŋkəm] adj (AUST, NZ inf) vrai(e); **fair** ~ vrai(e)

dinner ['dɪnə'] n (evening meal) dîner m; (lunch) déjeuner m; (public) banquet m; **dinner jacket** n smoking m; **dinner party** n dîner m; **dinner time** n (evening) heure f du dîner; (midday) heure du déjeuner

dinosaur ['daɪnəsɔ:'] n dinosaure m

dip [dɪp] n (slope) déclivité f; (in sea) baignade f, bain m; (Culin) ≈ sauce f ▷ vt tremper, plonger; (BRIT Aut: lights) mettre en code, baisser ▷ vi plonger

diploma [dɪ'pləʊmə] n diplôme m

diplomacy [dɪ'pləʊməsɪ] n diplomatie f

diplomat ['dɪpləmæt] n diplomate m; **diplomatic** [dɪplə'mætɪk] adj diplomatique

dipstick ['dɪpstɪk] n (BRIT Aut) jauge f de niveau d'huile

dire [daɪə*] adj (poverty) extrême; (awful) affreux(-euse)

direct [daɪ'rekt] adj direct(e) ▷ vt (tell way) diriger, orienter; (letter, remark) adresser; (Cine, TV) réaliser; (Theat) mettre en scène; (order): **to ~ sb to do sth** ordonner à qn de faire qch ▷ adv directement; **can you ~ me to ...?** pouvez-vous m'indiquer le chemin de ...?; **direct debit** n (BRIT Banking) prélèvement m automatique

direction [dɪ'rekʃən] n direction f; **directions** npl (to a place) indications fpl; **~s for use** mode m d'emploi; **sense of ~** sens m de l'orientation

directly [dɪ'rektlɪ] adv (in straight line) directement, tout droit; (at once) tout de suite, immédiatement

director [dɪ'rektə*] n directeur m; (Theat) metteur m en scène; (Cine, TV) réalisateur(-trice)

directory [dɪ'rektərɪ] n annuaire m; (Comput) répertoire m; **directory enquiries** (us) **directory assistance** n (Tel: service) renseignements mpl

dirt [dəːt] n saleté f; (mud) boue f; **dirty** adj sale; (joke) cochon(ne) ▷ vt salir

disability [dɪsə'bɪlɪtɪ] n invalidité f, infirmité f

disabled [dɪs'eɪbld] adj handicapé(e); (maimed) mutilé(e)

disadvantage [dɪsəd'vɑːntɪdʒ] n désavantage m, inconvénient m

disagree [dɪsə'griː] vi (differ) ne pas concorder; (be against, think otherwise): **to ~ (with)** ne pas être d'accord (avec); **disagreeable** adj désagréable; **disagreement** n désaccord m, différend m

disappear [dɪsə'pɪə*] vi disparaître; **disappearance** n disparition f

disappoint [dɪsə'pɔɪnt] vt décevoir; **disappointed** adj déçu(e); **disappointing** adj décevant(e); **disappointment** n déception f

disapproval [dɪsə'pruːvəl] n désapprobation f

disapprove [dɪsə'pruːv] vi: **to ~ of** désapprouver

disarm [dɪs'ɑːm] vt désarmer; **disarmament** [dɪs'ɑːməmənt] n désarmement m

disaster [dɪ'zɑːstə*] n catastrophe f, désastre m; **disastrous** adj désastreux(-euse)

disbelief ['dɪsbə'liːf] n incrédulité f

disc [dɪsk] n disque m; (Comput) = **disk**

discard [dɪs'kɑːd] vt (old things) se débarrasser de; (fig) écarter, renoncer à

discharge vt [dɪs'tʃɑːdʒ] (duties) s'acquitter de; (waste etc) déverser, décharger; (patient) renvoyer (chez lui); (employee, soldier) congédier, licencier ▷ n ['dɪstʃɑːdʒ] (Elec, Med) émission f; (dismissal) renvoi m, licenciement m

discipline ['dɪsɪplɪn] n discipline f ▷ vt discipliner; (punish) punir

disc jockey n disque-jockey m (DJ)

disclose [dɪs'kləuz] vt révéler, divulguer

disco ['dɪskəu] n abbr discothèque f

discoloured, (us) **discolored** [dɪs'kʌləd] adj décoloré(e), jauni(e)

discomfort [dɪs'kʌmfət] n malaise m, gêne f; (lack of comfort) manque m de confort

disconnect [dɪskə'nekt] vt (Elec, Radio) débrancher; (gas, water) couper

discontent [dɪskən'tent] n mécontentement m

discontinue [dɪskən'tɪnjuː] vt cesser, interrompre; **"~d"** (Comm) "fin de série"

discount n ['dɪskaunt] remise f, rabais m ▷ vt [dɪs'kaunt] (report etc) ne pas tenir compte de

discourage [dɪsˈkʌrɪdʒ] vt décourager

discover [dɪsˈkʌvəʳ] vt découvrir; **discovery** n découverte f

discredit [dɪsˈkrɛdɪt] vt (idea) mettre en doute; (person) discréditer

discreet [dɪˈskriːt] adj discret(-ète)

discrepancy [dɪˈskrɛpənsɪ] n divergence f, contradiction f

discretion [dɪˈskrɛʃən] n discrétion f; **at the ~ of** à la discrétion de

discriminate [dɪˈskrɪmɪneɪt] vi: **to ~ between** établir une distinction entre, faire la différence entre; **to ~ against** pratiquer une discrimination contre; **discrimination** [dɪskrɪmɪˈneɪʃən] n discrimination f; (judgment) discernement m

discuss [dɪˈskʌs] vt discuter de; (debate) discuter; **discussion** [dɪˈskʌʃən] n discussion f

disease [dɪˈziːz] n maladie f

disembark [dɪsɪmˈbɑːk] vt, vi débarquer

disgrace [dɪsˈɡreɪs] n honte f; (disfavour) disgrâce f ▷ vt déshonorer, couvrir de honte; **disgraceful** adj scandaleux(-euse), honteux(-euse)

disgruntled [dɪsˈɡrʌntld] adj mécontent(e)

disguise [dɪsˈɡaɪz] n déguisement m ▷ vt déguiser; **in ~** déguisé(e)

disgust [dɪsˈɡʌst] n dégoût m, aversion f ▷ vt dégoûter, écœurer; **disgusted** [dɪsˈɡʌstɪd] adj dégoûté(e), écœuré(e); **disgusting** [dɪsˈɡʌstɪŋ] adj dégoûtant(e)

dish [dɪʃ] n plat m; **to do** or **wash the ~es** faire la vaisselle; **dishcloth** n (for drying) torchon m; (for washing) lavette f

dishonest [dɪsˈɔnɪst] adj malhonnête

dishtowel [ˈdɪʃtauəl] n (us) torchon m (à vaisselle)

dishwasher [ˈdɪʃwɔʃəʳ] n lave-vaisselle m

disillusion [dɪsɪˈluːʒən] vt désabuser, désenchanter

disinfectant [dɪsɪnˈfɛktənt] n désinfectant m

disintegrate [dɪsˈɪntɪɡreɪt] vi se désintégrer

disk [dɪsk] n (Comput) disquette f; **single-/double-sided ~** disquette une face/double face; **disk drive** n lecteur m de disquette; **diskette** n (Comput) disquette f

dislike [dɪsˈlaɪk] n aversion f, antipathie f ▷ vt ne pas aimer

dislocate [ˈdɪsləkeɪt] vt disloquer, déboîter

disloyal [dɪsˈlɔɪəl] adj déloyal(e)

dismal [ˈdɪzml] adj (gloomy) lugubre, maussade; (very bad) lamentable

dismantle [dɪsˈmæntl] vt démonter

dismay [dɪsˈmeɪ] n consternation f ▷ vt consterner

dismiss [dɪsˈmɪs] vt congédier, renvoyer; (idea) écarter; (Law) rejeter; **dismissal** n renvoi m

disobedient [dɪsəˈbiːdɪənt] adj désobéissant(e), indiscipliné(e)

disobey [dɪsəˈbeɪ] vt désobéir à

disorder [dɪsˈɔːdəʳ] n désordre m; (rioting) désordres mpl; (Med) troubles mpl

disorganized [dɪsˈɔːɡənaɪzd] adj désorganisé(e)

disown [dɪsˈəun] vt renier

dispatch [dɪsˈpætʃ] vt expédier, envoyer ▷ n envoi m, expédition f; (Mil, Press) dépêche f

dispel [dɪsˈpɛl] vt dissiper, chasser

dispense [dɪsˈpɛns] vt (medicine) préparer (et vendre); **dispense with** vt fus se passer de; **dispenser** n (device) distributeur m

disperse [dɪsˈpəːs] vt disperser ▷ vi se disperser

display [dɪsˈpleɪ] n (of goods) étalage m; affichage m; (Comput: information) visualisation f; (: device) visuel m; (of feeling) manifestation f ▷ vt montrer; (goods) mettre à l'étalage, exposer;

(*results, departure times*) afficher; (*pej*) faire étalage de

displease [dɪsˈpliːz] *vt* mécontenter, contrarier

disposable [dɪsˈpəʊzəbl] *adj* (*pack etc*) jetable; (*income*) disponible

disposal [dɪsˈpəʊzl] *n* (*of rubbish*) évacuation *f*, destruction *f*; (*of property etc: by selling*) vente *f*; (: *by giving away*) cession *f*; **at one's** ~ à sa disposition

dispose [dɪsˈpəʊz] *vi*: **to ~ of** (*unwanted goods*) se débarrasser de, se défaire de; (*problem*) expédier; **disposition** [dɪspəˈzɪʃən] *n* disposition *f*; (*temperament*) naturel *m*

disproportionate [dɪsprəˈpɔːʃənət] *adj* disproportionné(e)

dispute [dɪsˈpjuːt] *n* discussion *f*; (*also*: **industrial** ~) conflit *m* ▷ *vt* (*question*) contester; (*matter*) discuter

disqualify [dɪsˈkwɔlɪfaɪ] *vt* (*Sport*) disqualifier; **to ~ sb for sth/from doing** rendre qn inapte à qch/à faire

disregard [dɪsrɪˈɡɑːd] *vt* ne pas tenir compte de

disrupt [dɪsˈrʌpt] *vt* (*plans, meeting, lesson*) perturber, déranger; **disruption** [dɪsˈrʌpʃən] *n* perturbation *f*, dérangement *m*

dissatisfaction [dɪssætɪsˈfækʃən] *n* mécontentement *m*, insatisfaction *f*

dissatisfied [dɪsˈsætɪsfaɪd] *adj*: **~ (with)** insatisfait(e) (de)

dissect [dɪˈsɛkt] *vt* disséquer

dissent [dɪˈsɛnt] *n* dissentiment *m*, différence *f* d'opinion

dissertation [dɪsəˈteɪʃən] *n* (*Scol*) mémoire *m*

dissolve [dɪˈzɔlv] *vt* dissoudre ▷ *vi* se dissoudre, fondre; **to ~ in(to) tears** fondre en larmes

distance [ˈdɪstns] *n* distance *f*; **in the ~** au loin

distant [ˈdɪstnt] *adj* lointain(e), éloigné(e); (*manner*) distant(e), froid(e)

distil, (*us*) **distill** [dɪsˈtɪl] *vt* distiller; **distillery** *n* distillerie *f*

distinct [dɪsˈtɪŋkt] *adj* distinct(e); (*clear*) marqué(e); **as ~ from** par opposition à, **distinction** [dɪsˈtɪŋkʃən] *n* distinction *f*; (*in exam*) mention *f* très bien; **distinctive** *adj* distinctif(-ive)

distinguish [dɪsˈtɪŋɡwɪʃ] *vt* distinguer; **to ~ o.s.** se distinguer; **distinguished** *adj* (*eminent, refined*) distingué(e)

distort [dɪsˈtɔːt] *vt* déformer

distract [dɪsˈtrækt] *vt* distraire, déranger; **distracted** *adj* (*not concentrating*) distrait(e); (*worried*) affolé(e); **distraction** [dɪsˈtrækʃən] *n* distraction *f*

distraught [dɪsˈtrɔːt] *adj* éperdu(e)

distress [dɪsˈtrɛs] *n* détresse *f* ▷ *vt* affliger; **distressing** *adj* douloureux(-euse), pénible

distribute [dɪsˈtrɪbjuːt] *vt* distribuer; **distribution** [dɪstrɪˈbjuːʃən] *n* distribution *f*; **distributor** *n* (*gen, Tech*) distributeur *m*; (*Comm*) concessionnaire *m/f*

district [ˈdɪstrɪkt] *n* (*of country*) région *f*; (*of town*) quartier *m*; (*Admin*) district *m*; **district attorney** *n* (*us*) ≈ procureur *m* de la République

distrust [dɪsˈtrʌst] *n* méfiance *f*, doute *m* ▷ *vt* se méfier de

disturb [dɪsˈtəːb] *vt* troubler; (*inconvenience*) déranger; **disturbance** *n* dérangement *m*; (*political etc*) troubles *mpl*; **disturbed** *adj* (*worried, upset*) agité(e), troublé(e); **to be emotionally disturbed** avoir des problèmes affectifs; **disturbing** *adj* troublant(e), inquiétant(e)

ditch [dɪtʃ] *n* fossé *m*; (*for irrigation*) rigole *f* ▷ *vt* (*inf*) abandonner; (*person*) plaquer

ditto [ˈdɪtəʊ] *adv* idem

dive [daɪv] *n* plongeon *m*; (*of submarine*) plongée *f* ▷ *vi* plonger; **to ~ into** (*bag etc*) plonger la main dans; (*place*) se précipiter dans; **diver** *n* plongeur *m*

d

diverse [daɪˈvəːs] *adj* divers(e)
diversion [daɪˈvəːʃən] *n* (BRIT
Aut) déviation f; (distraction, Mil)
diversion f
diversity [daɪˈvəːsɪtɪ] *n* diversité
f, variété f
divert [daɪˈvəːt] *vt* (BRIT: traffic)
dévier; (plane) dérouter; (train, river)
détourner
divide [dɪˈvaɪd] *vt* diviser; (separate)
séparer ▷ *vi* se diviser; **divided
highway** *n* (US) route f à quatre voies
divine [dɪˈvaɪn] *adj* divin(e)
diving [ˈdaɪvɪŋ] *n* plongée (sous-
marine); **diving board** *n* plongeoir *m*
division [dɪˈvɪʒən] *n* division f;
(separation) séparation f; (Comm)
service *m*
divorce [dɪˈvɔːs] *n* divorce *m* ▷ *vt*
divorcer d'avec; **divorced** *adj*
divorcé(e); **divorcee** [dɪvɔːˈsiː] *n*
divorcé(e)
DIY *adj, n abbr* (BRIT) = **do-it-yourself**
dizzy [ˈdɪzɪ] *adj*: **I feel ~** la tête me
tourne, j'ai la tête qui tourne
DJ *n abbr* = **disc jockey**
DNA *n abbr* (= deoxyribonucleic acid)
ADN *m*

🔵 **KEYWORD**

do [duː] *n* (inf: party etc) soirée f, fête f
▷ *aux vb* (pt **did**, pp **done**) **1** (in negative
constructions) non traduit: **I don't
understand** je ne comprends pas
2 (to form questions) non traduit:
didn't you know? vous ne le saviez
pas?; **what do you think?** qu'en
pensez-vous?
3 (for emphasis, in polite expressions):
**people do make mistakes
sometimes** on peut toujours se
tromper; **she does seem rather
late** je trouve qu'elle est bien en
retard; **do sit down/help yourself**
asseyez-vous/servez-vous je vous
en prie; **do take care!** faites bien
attention à vous!

4 (used to avoid repeating vb): **she
swims better than I do** elle nage
mieux que moi; **do you agree?**
— **yes, I do/no I don't** vous êtes
d'accord? — oui/non; **she lives
in Glasgow — so do I** elle habite
Glasgow — moi aussi; **he didn't like
it and neither did we** il n'a pas aimé
ça, et nous non plus; **who broke
it?** — **I did** qui l'a cassé? — c'est moi;
he asked me to help him and I did
il m'a demandé de l'aider, et c'est ce
que j'ai fait
5 (in question tags): **you like him,
don't you?** vous l'aimez bien, n'est-ce
pas?; **I don't know him, do I?** je ne
crois pas le connaître
▷ *vt* (pt **did**, pp **done**) **1** (gen: carry out,
perform etc) faire; (visit: city, museum)
faire, visiter; **what are you doing
tonight?** qu'est-ce que vous faites
ce soir?; **what do you do?** (job)
que faites-vous dans la vie?; **what
can I do for you?** que puis-je faire
pour vous?; **to do the cooking/
washing-up** faire la cuisine/la
vaisselle; **to do one's teeth/hair/
nails** se brosser les dents/se coiffer/
se faire les ongles
2 (Aut etc: distance) faire; (: speed) faire
du; **we've done 200 km already**
nous avons déjà fait 200 km; **the
car was doing 100** la voiture faisait
du 100 (à l'heure); **he can do 100 in
that car** il peut faire du 100 (à l'heure)
dans cette voiture-là
▷ *vi* (pt **did**, pp **done**) **1** (act, behave)
faire; **do as I do** faites comme moi
2 (get on, fare) marcher; **the firm
is doing well** l'entreprise marche
bien; **he's doing well/badly at
school** ça marche bien/mal pour lui
à l'école; **how do you do?** comment
allez-vous?; (on being introduced)
enchanté(e)!
3 (suit) aller; **will it do?** est-ce que
ça ira?
4 (be sufficient) suffire, aller; **will £10**

do? est-ce que 10 livres suffiront?; **that'll do** ça suffit, ça ira; **that'll do!** (in annoyance) ça va or suffit comme ça!; **to make do (with)** se contenter (de)

do up vt (laces, dress) attacher; (buttons) boutonner; (zip) fermer; (renovate: room) refaire; (: house) remettre à neuf

do with vt fus (need): **I could do with a drink/some help** quelque chose à boire/un peu d'aide ne serait pas de refus; **it could do with a wash** ça ne lui ferait pas de mal d'être lavé; (be connected with): **that has nothing to do with you** cela ne vous concerne pas; **I won't have anything to do with it** je ne veux pas m'en mêler

do without vi s'en passer; **if you're late for tea then you'll do without** si vous êtes en retard pour le dîner il faudra vous en passer ▷ vt fus se passer de; **I can do without a car** je peux me passer de voiture

dock [dɔk] n dock m; (wharf) quai m; (Law) banc m des accusés ▷ vi se mettre à quai; (Space) s'arrimer; **docks** npl (Naut) docks

doctor ['dɔktə'] n médecin m, docteur m; (PhD etc) docteur m ▷ vt (drink) frelater; **call a ~!** appelez un docteur or un médecin!; **Doctor of Philosophy** n (degree) doctorat m; (person) titulaire m/f d'un doctorat

document ['dɔkjumənt] n document m; **documentary** [dɔkju'mɛntəri] adj, n documentaire m; **documentation** [dɔkjumən'teɪʃən] n documentation f

dodge [dɔdʒ] n truc m; combine f ▷ vt esquiver, éviter

dodgy ['dɔdʒɪ] adj (BRIT inf: uncertain) douteux(-euse); (: shady) louche

does [dʌz] vb see **do**

doesn't ['dʌznt] = **does not**

dog [dɔg] n chien m ▷ vt (follow closely) suivre de près; (fig: memory

etc) poursuivre, harceler; **doggy bag** ['dɔgɪ-] n petit sac pour emporter les restes

do-it-yourself ['duːɪtjɔː'self] n bricolage m

dole [dəul] n (BRIT: payment) allocation f de chômage; **on the ~** au chômage

doll [dɔl] n poupée f

dollar ['dɔlə'] n dollar m

dolphin ['dɔlfɪn] n dauphin m

dome [dəum] n dôme m

domestic [də'mɛstɪk] adj (duty, happiness) familial(e); (policy, affairs, flight) intérieur(e); (animal) domestique

dominant ['dɔmɪnənt] adj dominant(e)

dominate ['dɔmɪneɪt] vt dominer

domino ['dɔmɪnəu] n (pl **dominoes**) n domino m; **dominoes** n (game) dominos mpl

donate [də'neɪt] vt faire don de, donner; **donation** [də'neɪʃən] n donation f, don m

done [dʌn] pp of **do**

dongle ['dɔŋgl] n (Comput) dongle m

donkey ['dɔŋkɪ] n âne m

donor ['dəunə'] n (of blood etc) donneur(-euse); (to charity) donateur(-trice); **donor card** n carte f de don d'organes

don't [dəunt] = **do not**

donut ['dəunʌt] (US) n = **doughnut**

doodle ['duːdl] vi gribouiller

doom [duːm] n (fate) destin m ▷ vt: **to be ~ed to failure** être voué(e) à l'échec

door [dɔː'] n porte f; (Rail, car) portière f; **doorbell** n sonnette f; **door handle** n poignée f de porte; (of car) poignée de portière; **doorknob** n poignée f or bouton m de porte; **doorstep** n pas m de (la) porte, seuil m; **doorway** n (embrasure f de) porte f

dope [dəup] n (inf: drug) drogue f; (: person) andouille f ▷ vt (horse etc) doper

dormitory ['dɔ:mɪtrɪ] n (BRIT) dortoir m; (us: hall of residence) résidence f universitaire

DOS [dɒs] n abbr (= disk operating system) DOS m

dosage ['dəʊsɪdʒ] n dose f; dosage m; (on label) posologie f

dose [dəʊs] n dose f

dot [dɒt] n point m; (on material) pois m ▷ vt: **~ted with** parsemé(e) de; **on the ~** à l'heure tapante; **dotcom** n point com m, pointcom m; **dotted line** ['dɔtɪd-] n ligne pointillée; **to sign on the dotted line** signer à l'endroit indiqué or sur la ligne pointillée

double ['dʌbl] adj double ▷ adv (twice): **to cost ~ (sth)** coûter le double (de qch) or deux fois plus (que qch) ▷ n double m; (Cine) doublure f ▷ vt doubler; (fold) plier en deux ▷ vi doubler; **on the ~, at the ~** au pas de course; **double back** vi (person) revenir sur ses pas; **double bass** n contrebasse f; **double bed** n grand lit; **double-check** vt, vi revérifier; **double-click** vi (Comput) double-cliquer; **double-decker** n autobus m à impériale; **double glazing** n (BRIT) double vitrage m; **double room** n chambre f pour deux; **doubles** n (Tennis) double m; **double yellow lines** npl (BRIT Aut) double bande jaune marquant l'interdiction de stationner

doubt [daʊt] n doute m ▷ vt douter de; **no ~** sans doute; **to ~ that** douter que + sub; **doubtful** adj douteux(-euse); (person) incertain(e); **doubtless** adv sans doute, sûrement

dough [dəʊ] n pâte f; **doughnut**, (us) **donut** n beignet m

dove [dʌv] n colombe f

Dover ['dəʊvəⁿ] n Douvres

down [daʊn] n (fluff) duvet m ▷ adv en bas, vers le bas; (on the ground) par terre ▷ prep en bas de; (along) le long de ▷ vt (inf: drink) siffler; **to walk ~**

a hill descendre une colline; **to run ~ the street** descendre la rue en courant; **~ with X!** à bas X!; **down-and-out** n (tramp) clochard(e); **downfall** n chute f, ruine f; **downhill** adv: **to go downhill** descendre; (business) péricliter

Downing Street ['daʊnɪŋ-] n (BRIT): **10 ~** résidence du Premier ministre

● **DOWNING STREET**

● *Downing Street* est une rue de
● Westminster (à Londres) où se
● trouvent la résidence officielle
● du Premier ministre et celle du
● ministre des Finances. Le nom
● *Downing Street* est souvent utilisé
● pour désigner le gouvernement
● britannique.

down: **download** vt (Comput) télécharger; **downloadable** adj (Comput) téléchargeable; **downright** adj (lie etc) effronté(e); (refusal) catégorique

Down's syndrome [daʊnz-] n trisomie f

down: **downstairs** adv (on or to ground floor) au rez-de-chaussée; (on or to floor below) à l'étage inférieur; **down-to-earth** adj terre à terre inv; **downtown** adv en ville; **down under** adv en Australie ou Nouvelle Zélande; **downward** ['daʊnwəd] adj, adv vers le bas; **downwards** ['daʊnwədz] adv vers le bas

doz. abbr = **dozen**

doze [dəʊz] vi sommeiller

dozen ['dʌzn] n douzaine f; **a ~ books** une douzaine de livres; **~s of** des centaines de

Dr. abbr (= doctor) Dr; (in street names): = **Drive**

drab [dræb] adj terne, morne

draft [drɑ:ft] n (of letter, school work) brouillon m; (of literary work) ébauche f; (Comm) traite f; (us Mil: call-up) conscription f ⊳ vt faire le brouillon de; (Mil: send) détacher; see also **draught**

drag [dræg] vt traîner; (river) draguer ⊳ vi traîner ⊳ n (inf) casse-pieds m/f; (: women's clothing): **in ~** (en) travesti; **to ~ and drop** (Comput) glisser-poser

dragonfly ['drægənflaɪ] n libellule f

drain [dreɪn] n égout m; (on resources) saignée f ⊳ vt (land, marshes) assécher; (vegetables) égoutter; (reservoir etc) vider ⊳ vi (water) s'écouler; **drainage** n (system) système m d'égouts; (act) drainage m; **drainpipe** n tuyau m d'écoulement

drama ['drɑːmə] n (art) théâtre m, art m dramatique; (play) pièce f; (event) drame m; **dramatic** [drə'mætɪk] adj (Theat) dramatique; (impressive) spectaculaire

drank [dræŋk] pt of **drink**

drape [dreɪp] vt draper; **drapes** npl (us) rideaux mpl

drastic ['dræstɪk] adj (measures) d'urgence, énergique; (change) radical(e)

draught, (us) **draft** [drɑːft] n courant m d'air; **on ~** (beer) à la pression; **draught beer** n bière f (à la pression); **draughts** n (BRIT: game) (jeu m de) dames fpl

draw [drɔː] (vb: pt **drew**, pp **drawn**) vt tirer; (picture) dessiner; (attract) attirer; (line, circle) tracer; (money) retirer; (wages) toucher ⊳ vi (Sport) faire match nul ⊳ n match nul; (lottery) loterie f; (picking of ticket) tirage m au sort; **draw out** vi (lengthen) s'allonger ⊳ vt (money) retirer; **draw up** vi (stop) s'arrêter ⊳ vt (document) établir, dresser; (plan) formuler, dessiner; (chair) approcher; **drawback** n inconvénient m, désavantage m

drawer [drɔːʳ] n tiroir m

drawing ['drɔːɪŋ] n dessin m; **drawing pin** n (BRIT) punaise f; **drawing room** n salon m

drawn [drɔːn] pp of **draw**

dread [drɛd] n épouvante f, effroi m ⊳ vt redouter, appréhender; **dreadful** adj épouvantable, affreux(-euse)

dream [driːm] n rêve m ⊳ vt, vi (pt **dreamed**, pp **dreamt**) rêver; **dreamer** n rêveur(-euse)

dreamt [drɛmt] pt, pp of **dream**

dreary ['drɪərɪ] adj triste; monotone

drench [drɛntʃ] vt tremper

dress [drɛs] n robe f; (clothing) habillement m, tenue f ⊳ vt habiller; (wound) panser ⊳ vi: **to get ~ed** s'habiller; **dress up** vi s'habiller; (in fancy dress) se déguiser; **dress circle** n (BRIT) premier balcon; **dresser** n (furniture) vaisselier m (: us) coiffeuse f, commode f; **dressing** n (Med) pansement m; (Culin) sauce f, assaisonnement m; **dressing gown** n (BRIT) robe f de chambre; **dressing room** n (Theat) loge f; (Sport) vestiaire m; **dressing table** n coiffeuse f; **dressmaker** n couturière f

drew [druː] pt of **draw**

dribble ['drɪbl] vi (baby) baver ⊳ vt (ball) dribbler

dried [draɪd] adj (fruit, beans) sec (sèche); (eggs, milk) en poudre

drier ['draɪəʳ] n = **dryer**

drift [drɪft] n (of current etc) force f; direction f; (of snow) rafale f; coulée f (on ground) congère f; (general meaning) sens général m ⊳ vi (boat) aller à la dérive, dériver; (sand, snow) s'amonceler, s'entasser

drill [drɪl] n perceuse f; (bit) foret m; (of dentist) roulette f, fraise f; (Mil) exercice m ⊳ vt percer; (troops) entraîner ⊳ vi (for oil) faire un or des forage(s)

drink [drɪŋk] n boisson f; (alcoholic) verre m ⊳ vt, vi (pt **drank**, pp **drunk**) boire; **to have a ~** boire quelque chose, boire un verre; **a ~ of water** un verre d'eau; **would you like a ~?** tu veux boire quelque chose?; **drink-driving** n conduite f en état d'ivresse;

drinker n buveur(-euse); **drinking water** n eau f potable

drip [drɪp] n (drop) goutte f; (Med: device) goutte-à-goutte m inv; (: liquid) perfusion f ▷ vi tomber goutte à goutte; (tap) goutter

drive [draɪv] (pt **drove**, pp **driven**) n promenade f or trajet m en voiture; (also: ~**way**) allée f; (energy) dynamisme m, énergie f; (push) effort (concerté) campagne f; (Comput: also: disk ~) lecteur m de disquette ▷ vt conduire; (nail) enfoncer; (push) chasser, pousser; (Tech: motor) actionner; entraîner ▷ vi (be at the wheel) conduire; (travel by car) aller en voiture; **left-/right-hand ~** (Aut) conduite f à gauche/droite; **to ~ sb mad** rendre qn fou (folle); **drive out** vt (force out) chasser; **drive-in** adj, n (esp us) drive-in m

driven ['drɪvn] pp of **drive**

driver ['draɪvə'] n conducteur(-trice); (of taxi, bus) chauffeur m; **driver's license** n (us) permis m de conduire

driveway ['draɪvweɪ] n allée f

driving ['draɪvɪŋ] n conduite f; **driving instructor** n moniteur m d'auto-école; **driving lesson** n leçon f de conduite; **driving licence** n (BRIT) permis m de conduire; **driving test** n examen m du permis de conduire

drizzle ['drɪzl] n bruine f, crachin m

droop [dru:p] vi (flower) commencer à se faner; (shoulders, head) s'affaisser

drop [drɔp] n (of liquid) goutte f; (fall) baisse f; (also: **parachute ~**) saut m ▷ vt laisser tomber; (voice, eyes, price) baisser; (passenger) déposer ▷ vi tomber; **drop in** vi (inf: visit): **to ~ in (on)** faire un saut (chez), passer (chez); **drop off** vi (sleep) s'assoupir ▷ vt (passenger) déposer; **drop out** vi (withdraw) se retirer; (student etc) abandonner; décrocher

drought [draut] n sécheresse f

drove [drəuv] pt of **drive**

drown [draun] vt noyer ▷ vi se noyer

drowsy ['drauzɪ] adj somnolent(e)

drug [drʌg] n médicament m; (narcotic) drogue f ▷ vt droguer; **to be on ~s** se droguer; **drug addict** n toxicomane m/f; **drug dealer** n revendeur(-euse) de drogue; **druggist** n (us) pharmacien(ne)-droguiste; **drugstore** n (us) pharmacie-droguerie f, drugstore m

drum [drʌm] n tambour m; (for oil, petrol) bidon m; **drums** npl (Mus) batterie f; **drummer** n (joueur m de) tambour m

drunk [drʌŋk] pp of **drink** ▷ adj ivre, soûl(e) ▷ n (also: ~**ard**) ivrogne m/f; **to get ~** se soûler; **drunken** adj ivre, soûl(e); (rage, stupor) ivrogne, d'ivrogne

dry [draɪ] adj sec (sèche); (day) sans pluie ▷ vt sécher; (clothes) faire sécher ▷ vi sécher; **dry off** vi, vt sécher; **dry up** vi (river, supplies) se tarir; **dry-cleaner's** n teinturerie f; **dry-cleaning** n (process) nettoyage à sec; **dryer** n (tumble-dryer) sèche-linge m inv; (for hair) sèche-cheveux m inv

DSS n abbr (BRIT) = **Department of Social Security**

DTP n abbr (= desktop publishing) PAO f

dual ['djuəl] adj double; **dual carriageway** n (BRIT) route f à quatre voies

dubious ['dju:bɪəs] adj hésitant(e), incertain(e); (reputation, company) douteux(-euse)

duck [dʌk] n canard m ▷ vi se baisser vivement, baisser subitement la tête

due [dju:] adj (money, payment) dû (due); (expected) attendu(e); (fitting) qui convient ▷ adv: ~ **north** droit vers le nord; **~ to** (because of) en raison de; (caused by) dû à; **the train is ~ at 8 a.m.** le train est attendu à 8 h; **she is ~ back tomorrow** elle doit rentrer demain; **he is ~ £10** on lui doit 10 livres; **to give sb his** or **her ~** être juste envers qn

duel ['djuəl] n duel m

duet [dju:'ɛt] n duo m

dug [dʌg] pt, pp of **dig**

duke [dju:k] n duc m

dull [dʌl] adj (boring) ennuyeux(-euse); (not bright) morne, terne; (sound, pain) sourd(e); (weather, day) gris(e), maussade ▷ vt (pain, grief) atténuer; (mind, senses) engourdir

dumb [dʌm] adj (!) muet(te); (stupid) bête

dummy ['dʌmɪ] n (tailor's model) mannequin m; (mock-up) factice m, maquette f; (BRIT: for baby) tétine f ▷ adj faux (fausse), factice

dump [dʌmp] n (also: **rubbish ~**) décharge (publique); (inf: place) trou m ▷ vt (put down) déposer; déverser; (get rid of) se débarrasser de; (Comput) lister

dumpling ['dʌmplɪŋ] n boulette f (de pâte)

dune [dju:n] n dune f

dungarees [dʌngə'ri:z] npl bleu(s) m(pl); (for child, woman) salopette f

dungeon ['dʌndʒən] n cachot m

duplex ['dju:plɛks] n (us: also: ~ **apartment**) duplex m

duplicate n ['dju:plɪkət] double m ▷ vt ['dju:plɪkeɪt] faire un double de; (on machine) polycopier; **in ~** en deux exemplaires, en double

durable ['djuərəbl] adj durable; (clothes, metal) résistant(e), solide

duration [djuə'reɪʃən] n durée f

during ['djuərɪŋ] prep pendant, au cours de

dusk [dʌsk] n crépuscule m

dust [dʌst] n poussière f ▷ vt (furniture) essuyer, épousseter; (cake etc): **to ~ with** saupoudrer de; **dustbin** n (BRIT) poubelle f; **duster** n chiffon m; **dustman** (irreg) n (BRIT) boueux m, éboueur m; **dustpan** n pelle f à poussière; **dusty** adj poussiéreux(-euse)

Dutch [dʌtʃ] adj hollandais(e), néerlandais(e) ▷ n (Ling) hollandais m,

néerlandais m ▷ adv: **to go ~** or **dutch** (inf) partager les frais; **the Dutch** npl les Hollandais, les Néerlandais; **Dutchman** (irreg) n Hollandais m; **Dutchwoman** (irreg) n Hollandaise f

duty ['dju:tɪ] n devoir m; (tax) droit m, taxe f; **on ~** de service; (at night etc) de garde; **off ~** libre, pas de service or de garde; **duty-free** adj exempté(e) de douane, hors-taxe

duvet ['du:veɪ] n (BRIT) couette f

DVD n abbr (= digital versatile or video disc) DVD m; **DVD burner** n graveur m de DVD; **DVD player** n lecteur m de DVD; **DVD writer** n graveur m de DVD

dwarf (pl **dwarves**) [dwɔ:f, dwɔ:vz] n (pej) nain(e) ▷ vt écraser

dwell (pt, pp **dwelt**) [dwɛl, dwɛlt] vi demeurer; **dwell on** vt fus s'étendre sur

dwelt [dwɛlt] pt, pp of **dwell**

dwindle ['dwɪndl] vi diminuer, décroître

dye [daɪ] n teinture f ▷ vt teindre

dying ['daɪɪŋ] adj mourant(e), agonisant(e)

dynamic [daɪ'næmɪk] adj dynamique

dynamite ['daɪnəmaɪt] n dynamite f

dyslexia [dɪs'lɛksɪə] n dyslexie f

dyslexic [dɪs'lɛksɪk] adj, n dyslexique m/f

E [iː] n (Mus) mi m

each [iːtʃ] adj chaque ▷ pron chacun(e); **~ other** l'un l'autre; **they hate ~ other** ils se détestent (mutuellement); **they have 2 books ~** ils ont 2 livres chacun; **they cost £5 ~** ils coûtent 5 livres (la) pièce

eager ['iːgə^r] adj (person, buyer) empressé(e); (keen: pupil, worker) enthousiaste; (impatient) brûler de faire qch; (keen) désirer vivement faire qch; **to be ~ for** (event) désirer vivement; (vengeance, affection, information) être avide de

eagle ['iːgl] n aigle m

ear [ɪə^r] n oreille f; (of corn) épi m; **earache** n mal m aux oreilles; **eardrum** n tympan m

earl [əːl] n comte m

earlier ['əːlɪə^r] adj (date etc) plus rapproché(e); (edition etc) plus ancien(ne), antérieur(e) ▷ adv plus tôt

early ['əːlɪ] adv tôt, de bonne heure; (ahead of time) en avance; (near the beginning) au début ▷ adj précoce, qui se manifeste (or se fait) tôt or de bonne heure; (Christians, settlers) premier(-ière); (reply) rapide; (death) prématuré(e); (work) de jeunesse; **to have an ~ night/start** se coucher/ partir tôt or de bonne heure; **in the ~** or **in the spring/19th century** au début or commencement du printemps/19ème siècle; **early retirement** n retraite anticipée

earmark ['əːmɑːk] vt: **to ~ sth for** réserver or destiner qch à

earn [əːn] vt gagner; (Comm: yield) rapporter; **to ~ one's living** gagner sa vie

earnest ['əːnɪst] adj sérieux(-euse) ▷ n: **in ~** adv sérieusement, pour de bon

earnings ['əːnɪŋz] npl salaire m; gains mpl; (of company etc) profits mpl, bénéfices mpl

ear: earphones npl écouteurs mpl; **earplugs** npl boules fpl Quiès®; (to keep out water) protège-tympans mpl; **earring** n boucle f d'oreille

earth [əːθ] n (gen, also BRIT Elec) terre f ▷ vt (BRIT Elec) relier à la terre; **earthquake** n tremblement m de terre, séisme m

ease [iːz] n facilité f, aisance f; (comfort) bien-être m ▷ vt (soothe: mind) tranquilliser; (reduce: pain, problem) atténuer; (: tension) réduire; (loosen) relâcher, détendre; (help pass): **to ~ sth in/out** faire pénétrer/sortir qch délicatement or avec douceur, faciliter la pénétration/la sortie de qch; **at ~** à l'aise; (Mil) au repos

easily ['iːzɪlɪ] adv facilement; (by far) de loin

east [iːst] n est m ▷ adj (wind) d'est; (side) est inv ▷ adv à l'est, vers l'est; **the E~** l'Orient m; (Pol) les pays mpl de l'Est; **eastbound** adj en direction de l'est; (carriageway) est inv

Easter ['iːstə] fpl Pâques fpl; **Easter egg** n œuf m de Pâques

eastern ['iːstən] adj de l'est, oriental(e)

Easter Sunday n le dimanche de Pâques

easy ['iːzɪ] adj facile; (manner) aisé(e) ▷ adv: **to take it** or **things ~** (rest) ne pas se fatiguer; (not worry) ne pas (trop) s'en faire; **easy-going** adj accommodant(e), facile à vivre

eat (pt **ate**, pp **eaten**) [iːt, eɪt, iːtn] vt, vi manger; **can we have something to ~?** est-ce qu'on peut manger quelque chose?; **eat out** vi manger au restaurant

eavesdrop ['iːvzdrɔp] vi: **to ~ (on)** écouter de façon indiscrète

e-bike ['iːbaɪk] n VAE m

e-book ['iːbuk] n livre m électronique

e-business ['iːbɪznɪs] n (company) entreprise f électronique; (commerce) commerce m électronique

eccentric [ɪkˈsɛntrɪk] adj, n excentrique m/f

echo ['ɛkəʊ] (pl **echoes**) n écho m ▷ vt répéter ▷ vi résonner; faire écho

e-cigarette ['iːsɪgərɛt] n cigarette f électronique

eclipse [ɪˈklɪps] n éclipse f

eco-friendly [iːkəʊˈfrɛndlɪ] adj non nuisible à l'environnement

ecological [iːkəˈlɔdʒɪkəl] adj écologique

ecology [ɪˈkɔlədʒɪ] n écologie f

e-commerce [iːˈkɒməːs] n commerce m électronique

economic [iːkəˈnɒmɪk] adj économique; (profitable) rentable; **economical** adj économique; (person) économe; **economics** n (Scol) économie f politique ▷ npl (of project etc) côté m ou aspect m économique

economist [ɪˈkɒnəmɪst] n économiste m/f

economize [ɪˈkɒnəmaɪz] vi économiser, faire des économies

economy [ɪˈkɒnəmɪ] n économie f; **economy class** n (Aviat) classe f touriste; **economy class syndrome** n syndrome m de la classe économique

ecstasy ['ɛkstəsɪ] n extase f; (Drugs) ecstasy m; **ecstatic** [ɛksˈtætɪk] adj extatique, en extase

eczema ['ɛksɪmə] n eczéma m

edge [ɛdʒ] n bord m; (of knife etc) tranchant m, fil m ▷ vt border; **on ~** (fig) crispé(e), tendu(e)

edgy ['ɛdʒɪ] adj crispé(e), tendu(e)

edible ['ɛdɪbl] adj comestible; (meal) mangeable

Edinburgh ['ɛdɪnbərə] n Édimbourg; voir article **"Edinburgh Festival"**

edit ['ɛdɪt] vt (text, book) éditer; (report) préparer; (film) monter; (magazine) diriger; (newspaper) être le rédacteur ou la rédactrice en chef de; **edition** [ɪˈdɪʃən] n édition f; **editor** n (of newspaper) rédacteur(-trice), rédacteur(-trice) en chef; (of sb's work) éditeur(-trice); (also: **film editor**) monteur(-euse); **political/foreign editor** rédacteur politique/au service étranger; **editorial** [ɛdɪˈtɔːrɪəl] adj de la rédaction ▷ n éditorial m

educate ['ɛdjʊkeɪt] vt (teach) instruire; (bring up) éduquer; **educated** ['ɛdjʊkeɪtɪd] adj (person) cultivé(e)

education [ɛdjʊ'keɪʃən] n éducation f; (studies) études fpl; (teaching) enseignement m, instruction f; **educational** adj pédagogique; (institution) scolaire; (game, toy) éducatif(-ive)

eel [iːl] n anguille f

eerie ['ɪərɪ] adj inquiétant(e), spectral(e), surnaturel(le)

effect [ɪ'fɛkt] n effet m ▷ vt effectuer; **effects** npl (property) effets, affaires fpl; (Law) **to take ~** entrer en vigueur, prendre effet; (drug) agir, faire son effet; **in ~** en fait; **effective** adj efficace; (actual) véritable; **effectively** adv efficacement; (in reality) effectivement, en fait

efficiency [ɪ'fɪʃənsɪ] n efficacité f; (of machine, car) rendement m

efficient [ɪ'fɪʃənt] adj efficace; (machine, car) d'un bon rendement; **efficiently** adv efficacement

effort ['ɛfət] n effort m; **effortless** adj sans effort, aisé(e); (achievement) facile

e.g. adv abbr (= exempli gratia) par exemple, p. ex.

egg [ɛg] n œuf m; **hard-boiled/soft-boiled** ~ œuf dur/à la coque; **eggcup** n coquetier m; **egg plant** (us) n aubergine f; **eggshell** n coquille f d'œuf; **egg white** n blanc m d'œuf; **egg yolk** n jaune m d'œuf

ego ['iːgəʊ] n (self-esteem) amour-propre m; (Psych) moi m

Egypt ['iːdʒɪpt] n Égypte f; **Egyptian** [ɪ'dʒɪpʃən] adj égyptien(ne) ▷ n Égyptien(ne)

Eiffel Tower ['aɪfəl-] n tour f Eiffel

eight [eɪt] num huit; **eighteen** num dix-huit; **eighteenth** num dix-huitième; **eighth** num huitième; **eightieth** [eɪtɪɪθ] num quatre-vingtième

eighty ['eɪtɪ] num quatre-vingt(s)

Eire ['ɛərə] n République f d'Irlande

either ['aɪðə] adj l'un ou l'autre; (both, each) chaque ▷ pron: **~ (of them)** l'un ou l'autre ▷ adv non plus ▷ conj: **~ good or bad** soit bon soit mauvais; **on ~ side** de chaque côté; **I don't like ~** je n'aime ni l'un ni l'autre; **no, I don't ~** moi non plus; **which bike do you want? — ~ will do** quel vélo voulez-vous? — n'importe lequel; **answer with ~ yes or no** répondez par oui ou par non

eject [ɪ'dʒɛkt] vt (tenant etc) expulser; (object) éjecter

elaborate adj [ɪ'læbərɪt] compliqué(e), recherché(e), minutieux(-euse) ▷ vt [ɪ'læbəreɪt] élaborer ▷ vi entrer dans les détails

elastic [ɪ'læstɪk] adj, n élastique (m); **elastic band** (BRIT) élastique m

elbow ['ɛlbəʊ] n coude m

elder ['ɛldə] adj aîné(e) ▷ n (tree) sureau m; **one's ~s** ses aînés; **elderly** adj âgé(e); **~ people** les personnes âgées

eldest ['ɛldɪst] adj, n: **the ~ (child)** l'aîné(e) (des enfants)

elect [ɪ'lɛkt] vt élire; (choose): **to ~ to do** choisir de faire ▷ adj: **the president ~** le président désigné; **election** n élection f; **electoral** adj électoral(e); **electorate** n électorat m

electric [ɪ'lɛktrɪk] adj électrique; **electrical** adj électrique; **electric blanket** n couverture chauffante; **electric fire** (BRIT) radiateur m électrique; **electrician** [ɪlɛk'trɪʃən] n électricien m; **electricity** [ɪlɛk'trɪsɪtɪ] n électricité f; **electric shock** n choc m or décharge f électrique; **electrify** [ɪ'lɛktrɪfaɪ] vt (Rail) électrifier; (audience) électriser

electronic [ɪlɛk'trɔnɪk] adj électronique; **electronic mail** n courrier m électronique; **electronics** n électronique f

elegance ['ɛlɪgəns] n élégance f

elegant ['ɛlɪɡənt] adj élégant(e)

element ['ɛlɪmənt] n (gen) élément m; (of heater, kettle etc) résistance f

elementary [ɛlɪ'mɛntərɪ] adj élémentaire; (school, education) primaire; **elementary school** n (US) école f primaire

elephant ['ɛlɪfənt] n éléphant m

elevate ['ɛlɪveɪt] vt élever

elevator ['ɛlɪveɪtə'] n (in warehouse etc) élévateur m, monte-charge m inv; (US: lift) ascenseur m

eleven [ɪ'lɛvn] num onze; **eleventh** num onzième

eligible ['ɛlɪdʒəbl] adj éligible; (for membership) admissible; **an ~ young man** un beau parti; **to be ~ for sth** remplir les conditions requises pour qch

eliminate [ɪ'lɪmɪneɪt] vt éliminer

elm [ɛlm] n orme m

eloquent ['ɛləkwənt] adj éloquent(e)

else [ɛls] adv: **something ~** quelque chose d'autre, autre chose; **somewhere ~** ailleurs, autre part; **everywhere ~** partout ailleurs; **everyone ~** tous les autres; **nothing ~** rien d'autre; **where ~?** à quel autre endroit?; **little ~** pas grand-chose d'autre; **elsewhere** adv ailleurs, autre part

elusive [ɪ'luːsɪv] adj insaisissable

email ['iːmeɪl] n abbr (= electronic mail) (e-)mail m, courriel m ▷ vt: **to ~ sb** envoyer un (e-)mail or un courriel à qn; **email account** n compte m (e-)mail; **email address** n adresse f (e-)mail or électronique

embankment [ɪm'bæŋkmənt] n (of road, railway) remblai m, talus m; (of river) berge f, quai m; (dyke) digue f

embargo [ɪm'bɑːɡəu] (pl **embargoes**) n (Comm, Naut) embargo m; (prohibition) interdiction f

embark [ɪm'bɑːk] vi ▷ vt embarquer; **to ~ on** (journey etc) commencer, entreprendre; (fig) se lancer or s'embarquer dans

embarrass [ɪm'bærəs] vt embarrasser, gêner; **embarrassed** adj gêné(e); **embarrassing** adj gênant(e), embarrassant(e); **embarrassment** n embarras m, gêne f; (embarrassing thing, person) source f d'embarras

embassy ['ɛmbəsɪ] n ambassade f

embrace [ɪm'breɪs] vt embrasser, étreindre; (include) embrasser ▷ vi s'embrasser, s'étreindre ▷ n étreinte f

embroider [ɪm'brɔɪdə'] vt broder; **embroidery** n broderie f

embryo ['ɛmbrɪəu] n (also fig) embryon m

emerald ['ɛmərəld] n émeraude f

emerge [ɪ'məːdʒ] vi apparaître; (from room, car) surgir; (from sleep, imprisonment) sortir

emergency [ɪ'məːdʒənsɪ] n (crisis) cas m d'urgence; (Med) urgence f; **in an ~** en cas d'urgence; **state of ~** état m d'urgence; **emergency brake** (US) n frein m à main; **emergency exit** n sortie f de secours; **emergency landing** n atterrissage forcé; **emergency room** n (US Med) urgences fpl; **emergency services** npl: **the emergency services** (fire, police, ambulance) les services mpl d'urgence

emigrate ['ɛmɪɡreɪt] vi émigrer; **emigration** [ɛmɪ'ɡreɪʃən] n émigration f

eminent ['ɛmɪnənt] adj éminent(e)

emissions [ɪ'mɪʃənz] npl émissions fpl

emit [ɪ'mɪt] vt émettre

emoticon [ɪ'məutɪkɔn] n (Comput) émoticone m

emotion [ɪ'məuʃən] n sentiment m; **emotional** adj (person) émotif(-ive), très sensible; (needs) affectif(-ive); (scene) émouvant(e); (tone, speech) qui fait appel aux sentiments

emperor ['ɛmpərə'] n empereur m

emphasis (pl **emphases**) ['ɛmfəsɪs, -siːz] n accent m; **to lay** or **place**

~ on sth (fig) mettre l'accent sur, insister sur

emphasize ['emfəsaɪz] vt (syllable, word, point) appuyer or insister sur; (feature) souligner, accentuer

empire ['empaɪər] n empire m

employ [ɪm'plɔɪ] vt employer;
employee [ɪmplɔɪ'iː] n employé(e);
employer n employeur(-euse);
employment n emploi m;
employment agency n agence for bureau m de placement

empower [ɪm'pauər] vt: **to ~ sb to do** autoriser or habiliter qn à faire

empress ['emprɪs] n impératrice f

emptiness ['emptɪnɪs] n vide m; (of area) aspect m désertique

empty ['emptɪ] adj vide; (street, area) désert(e); (threat, promise) en l'air, vain(e) ▷ vt vider ▷ vi se vider; (liquid) s'écouler; **empty-handed** adj les mains vides

EMU n abbr (= European Monetary Union) UME f

emulsion [ɪ'mʌlʃən] n émulsion f; (also: **~ paint**) peinture mate

enable [ɪ'neɪbl] vt: **to ~ sb to do** permettre à qn de faire

enamel [ɪ'næməl] n émail m; (also: **~ paint**) laque f

enchanting [ɪn'tʃɑːntɪŋ] adj ravissant(e), enchanteur(-eresse)

encl. abbr (on letters etc = enclosed) ci-joint(e); (: = enclosure) P.J f

enclose [ɪn'kləuz] vt (land) clôturer; (space, object) entourer; (letter etc): **to ~ (with)** joindre (à); **please find ~d** veuillez trouver ci-joint

enclosure [ɪn'kləuʒər] n enceinte f

encore [ɔŋ'kɔː] excl, n bis (m)

encounter [ɪn'kauntər] n rencontre f ▷ vt rencontrer

encourage [ɪn'kʌrɪdʒ] vt encourager

encouraging [ɪn'kʌrɪdʒɪŋ] adj encourageant(e)

encyclop(a)edia [ɛnsaɪkləu'piːdɪə] n encyclopédie f

end [ɛnd] n fin f; (of table, street, rope etc) bout m, extrémité f ▷ vt terminer; (also: **bring to an ~, put an ~ to**) mettre fin à ▷ vi se terminer, finir; **in the ~** finalement; **on ~** (object) debout, dressé(e); (hair) se dresser sur la tête; **for hours on ~** pendant des heures (et des heures); **end up** vi: **to ~ up in** (condition) finir or se terminer par; (place) finir or aboutir à

endanger [ɪn'deɪndʒər] vt mettre en danger; **an ~ed species** une espèce en voie de disparition

endearing [ɪn'dɪərɪŋ] adj attachant(e)

endeavour, (US) **endeavor** [ɪn'devər] n effort m; (attempt) tentative f ▷ vi: **to ~ to do** tenter or s'efforcer de faire

ending ['ɛndɪŋ] n dénouement m, conclusion f; (Ling) terminaison f

endless ['ɛndlɪs] adj sans fin, interminable

endorse [ɪn'dɔːs] vt (cheque) endosser; (approve) appuyer, approuver, sanctionner;
endorsement n (approval) appui m, aval m; (BRIT: on driving licence) contravention f (portée au permis de conduire)

endurance [ɪn'djuərəns] n endurance f

endure [ɪn'djuər] vt (bear) supporter, endurer ▷ vi (last) durer

enemy ['ɛnəmɪ] adj, n ennemi(e)

energetic [ɛnə'dʒɛtɪk] adj énergique; (activity) très actif(-ive), qui fait se dépenser (physiquement)

energy ['ɛnədʒɪ] n énergie f

enforce [ɪn'fɔːs] vt (law) appliquer, faire respecter

engaged [ɪn'geɪdʒd] adj (BRIT: busy, in use) occupé(e); (betrothed) fiancé(e); **to get ~** se fiancer; **the line's ~** la ligne est occupée;
engaged tone n (BRIT Tel) tonalité f occupé inv

engagement [ɪnˈɡeɪdʒmənt]
n (undertaking) obligation f,
engagement m; (appointment) rendez-
vous m inv; (to marry) fiançailles fpl;
engagement ring n bague f de
fiançailles

engaging [ɪnˈɡeɪdʒɪŋ] adj
engageant(e), attirant(e)

engine [ˈendʒɪn] n (Aut) moteur m;
(Rail) locomotive f

░ Be careful not to translate engine
by the French word engin.

engineer [endʒɪˈnɪəʳ] n ingénieur m;
(BRIT: repairer) dépanneur m; (Navy,
US Rail) mécanicien m; **engineering**
n engineering m, ingénierie f; (of
bridges, ships) génie m; (of machine)
mécanique f

England [ˈɪŋɡlənd] n Angleterre f

English [ˈɪŋɡlɪʃ] adj anglais(e) ▷ n
(Ling) anglais m; **the ~** npl les Anglais;
English Channel n: **the English
Channel** la Manche; **Englishman**
(irreg) n Anglais m; **Englishwoman**
(irreg) n Anglaise f

engrave [ɪnˈɡreɪv] vt graver

engraving [ɪnˈɡreɪvɪŋ] n gravure f

enhance [ɪnˈhɑːns] vt rehausser,
mettre en valeur

enjoy [ɪnˈdʒɔɪ] vt aimer, prendre
plaisir à; (have benefit of: health,
fortune) jouir de; (: success) connaître;
to ~ o.s. s'amuser; **enjoyable** adj
agréable; **enjoyment** n plaisir m

enlarge [ɪnˈlɑːdʒ] vt accroître;
(Phot) agrandir ▷ vi: **to ~ on** (subject)
s'étendre sur; **enlargement** n (Phot)
agrandissement m

enlist [ɪnˈlɪst] vt recruter; (support)
s'assurer ▷ vi s'engager

enormous [ɪˈnɔːməs] adj énorme

enough [ɪˈnʌf] adj: **~ time/
books** assez or suffisamment de
temps/livres ▷ adv: **big ~** assez or
suffisamment grand ▷ pron: **have
you got ~?** (en) avez-vous assez?;
~ to eat assez à manger; **that's
~, thanks** cela suffit or c'est assez,

merci; **I've had ~ of him** j'en ai
assez de lui; **he has not worked
~** il n'a pas assez or suffisamment
travaillé, il n'a pas travaillé assez or
suffisamment; **... which, funnily** or
oddly or **strangely ~ ...** qui, chose
curieuse, ...

enquire [ɪnˈkwaɪəʳ] vt, vi = **inquire**

enquiry [ɪnˈkwaɪərɪ] n = **inquiry**

enrage [ɪnˈreɪdʒ] vt mettre en fureur
or en rage, rendre furieux(-euse)

enrich [ɪnˈrɪtʃ] vt enrichir

enrol, (US) **enroll** [ɪnˈrəul] vt inscrire
▷ vi s'inscrire; **enrolment**, (US)
enrollment n inscription f

en route [ɔnˈruːt] adv en route, en
chemin

en suite [ˈɔnswiːt] adj: **with ~
bathroom** avec salle de bains en
attenante

ensure [ɪnˈʃuəʳ] vt assurer, garantir

entail [ɪnˈteɪl] vt entraîner, nécessiter

enter [ˈentəʳ] vt (room) entrer dans,
pénétrer dans; (club, army) entrer à;
(competition) s'inscrire à or pour; (sb
for a competition) (faire) inscrire; (write
down) inscrire, noter; (Comput) entrer,
introduire ▷ vi entrer

enterprise [ˈentəpraɪz] n
(company, undertaking) entreprise
f; (initiative) (esprit m d')initiative
f; **free ~** libre entreprise; **private
~** entreprise privée; **enterprising**
adj entreprenant(e), dynamique;
(scheme) audacieux(-euse)

entertain [entəˈteɪn] vt amuser,
distraire; (invite) recevoir (à dîner);
(idea, plan) envisager; **entertainer** n
artiste m/f de variétés; **entertaining**
adj amusant(e), distrayant(e);
entertainment n (amusement)
distraction f, divertissement m,
amusement m; (show) spectacle m

enthusiasm [ɪnˈθuːzɪæzəm] n
enthousiasme m

enthusiast [ɪnˈθuːzɪæst] n
enthousiaste m/f; **enthusiastic**
[ɪnθuːzɪˈæstɪk] adj enthousiaste;

to be enthusiastic about être enthousiasmé(e) par

entire [ɪn'taɪəʳ] adj (tout) entier(-ère);
entirely adv entièrement

entitle [ɪn'taɪtl] vt: **to ~ sb to sth** donner droit à qch à qn; **entitled** adj (book) intitulé(e); **to be entitled to do** avoir le droit de faire

entrance n ['ɛntrns] entrée f ▷ vt [ɪn'trɑːns] enchanter, ravir; **where's the ~?** où est l'entrée?; **to gain ~ to** (university etc) être admis à; **entrance examination** n examen m d'entrée or d'admission; **entrance fee** n (to museum etc) prix m d'entrée; (to join club etc) droit m d'inscription; **entrance ramp** n (us Aut) bretelle f d'accès; **entrant** n (in race etc) participant(e), concurrent(e); (BRIT: in exam) candidat(e)

entrepreneur ['ɔntrəprə'nəːʳ] n entrepreneur m

entrust [ɪn'trʌst] vt: **to ~ sth to** confier qch à

entry ['ɛntrɪ] n entrée f; (in register, diary) inscription f; **"no ~"** "défense d'entrer", "entrée interdite"; (Aut) "sens interdit"; **entry phone** n (BRIT) interphone m (à l'entrée d'un immeuble)

envelope ['ɛnvələup] n enveloppe f

envious ['ɛnvɪəs] adj envieux(-euse)

environment [ɪn'vaɪərnmənt] n (social, moral) milieu m; (natural world): **the ~** l'environnement m; **environmental** [ɪnvaɪərn'mɛntl] adj (of surroundings) du milieu; (issue, disaster) écologique; **environmentally** [ɪnvaɪərn'mɛntlɪ] adv: **environmentally sound/ friendly** qui ne nuit pas à l'environnement

envisage [ɪn'vɪzɪdʒ] vt (foresee) prévoir

envoy ['ɛnvɔɪ] n envoyé(e); (diplomat) ministre m plénipotentiaire

envy ['ɛnvɪ] n envie f ▷ vt envier; **to ~ sb sth** envier qch à qn

epic ['ɛpɪk] n épopée f ▷ adj épique

epidemic [ɛpɪ'dɛmɪk] n épidémie f

epilepsy ['ɛpɪlɛpsɪ] n épilepsie f;
epileptic adj, n épileptique m/f;
epileptic fit n crise f d'épilepsie

episode ['ɛpɪsəud] n épisode m

equal ['iːkwl] adj égal(e) ▷ n égal(e);
~ to (task) à la hauteur de; **equality** [iː'kwɔlɪtɪ] n égalité f; **equalize** vt, vi (Sport) égaliser; **equally** adv également; (share) en parts égales; (treat) de la même façon; (pay) autant; (just as) tout aussi

equation [ɪ'kweɪʃən] n (Math) équation f

equator [ɪ'kweɪtəʳ] n équateur m

equip [ɪ'kwɪp] vt équiper, **to ~ sb/ sth with** équiper or munir qn/ qch de; **equipment** n équipement m; (electrical etc) appareillage m, installation f

equivalent [ɪ'kwɪvələnt] adj équivalent(e) ▷ n équivalent m; **to be ~ to** équivaloir à, être équivalent(e) à

ER abbr (BRIT: = Elizabeth Regina) la reine Elisabeth; (us Med: = emergency room) urgences fpl

era ['ɪərə] n ère f, époque f

erase [ɪ'reɪz] vt effacer; **eraser** n gomme f

e-reader ['iːriːdəʳ] n liseuse f

erect [ɪ'rɛkt] adj droit(e) ▷ vt construire; (monument) ériger, élever; (tent etc) dresser; **erection** [ɪ'rɛkʃən] n (Physiol) érection f; (of building) construction f

ERM n abbr (= Exchange Rate Mechanism) mécanisme m des taux de change

erode [ɪ'rəud] vt éroder; (metal) ronger

erosion [ɪ'rəuʒən] n érosion f

erotic [ɪ'rɔtɪk] adj érotique

errand ['ɛrnd] n course f, commission f

erratic [ɪ'rætɪk] adj irrégulier(-ière), inconstant(e)

error ['ɛrəʳ] n erreur f

erupt [ɪ'rʌpt] vi entrer en éruption; (fig) éclater; **eruption** [ɪ'rʌpʃən] n éruption f; (of anger, violence) explosion f

escalate ['ɛskəleɪt] vi s'intensifier; (costs) monter en flèche

escalator ['ɛskəleɪtə*] n escalier roulant

escape [ɪ'skeɪp] n évasion f, fuite f; (of gas etc) fuite f ▷ vi s'échapper, fuir; (from jail) s'évader; (fig) s'en tirer; (leak) s'échapper ▷ vt échapper à; **to ~ from** (person) échapper à; (place) s'échapper de; (fig) fuir; **his name ~s me** son nom m'échappe

escort vt [ɪ'skɔːt] escorter ▷ n ['ɛskɔːt] (Mil) escorte f

especially [ɪ'spɛʃlɪ] adv (particularly) particulièrement; (above all) surtout

espionage ['ɛspɪənɑːʒ] n espionnage m

essay ['ɛseɪ] n (Scol) dissertation f; (Literature) essai m

essence ['ɛsns] n essence f; (Culin) extrait m

essential [ɪ'sɛnʃl] adj essentiel(le); (basic) fondamental(e); **essentials** npl éléments essentiels; **essentially** adv essentiellement

establish [ɪ'stæblɪʃ] vt établir; (business) fonder, créer; (one's power etc) asseoir, affermir; **establishment** n établissement m; (founding) création f; (institution) établissement; **the Establishment** les pouvoirs établis; l'ordre établi

estate [ɪ'steɪt] n (land) domaine m, propriété f; (Law) biens mpl, succession f; (BRIT: also: housing ~) lotissement m; **estate agent** (BRIT) agent immobilier; **estate car** (BRIT) break m

estimate n ['ɛstɪmət] estimation f; (Comm) devis m ▷ vt ['ɛstɪmeɪt] estimer

etc abbr (= et cetera) etc

eternal [ɪ'tɜːnl] adj éternel(le)

eternity [ɪ'tɜːnɪtɪ] n éternité f

ethical ['ɛθɪkl] adj moral(e); **ethics** ['ɛθɪks] n éthique f ▷ npl moralité f

Ethiopia [iːθɪ'əupɪə] n Éthiopie f

ethnic ['ɛθnɪk] adj ethnique; (clothes, food) folklorique, exotique, propre aux minorités ethniques non-occidentales; **ethnic minority** n minorité f ethnique

e-ticket ['iːtɪkɪt] n billet m électronique

etiquette ['ɛtɪkɛt] n convenances fpl, étiquette f

EU n abbr (= European Union) UE f

euro ['juərəu] n (currency) euro m

Europe ['juərəp] n Europe f; **European** [juərə'pɪən] adj européen(ne) ▷ n Européen(ne); **European Community** n Communauté européenne; **European Union** n Union européenne

Eurostar® ['juərəustɑː*] n Eurostar® m

evacuate [ɪ'vækjueɪt] vt évacuer

evade [ɪ'veɪd] vt échapper à; (question etc) éluder; (duties) se dérober à

evaluate [ɪ'væljueɪt] vt évaluer

evaporate [ɪ'væpəreɪt] vi s'évaporer; (fig: hopes, fear) s'envoler; (anger) se dissiper

eve [iːv] n: **on the ~ of** à la veille de

even ['iːvn] adj (level, smooth) régulier(-ière); (equal) égal(e); (number) pair(e) ▷ adv même; **~ if** +indic; **~ though** alors même que +cond; **~ more** encore plus; **~ faster** encore plus vite; **~ so** quand même; **not ~** pas même; **~ he was there** même lui était là; **~ on Sundays** même le dimanche; **to get ~ with sb** prendre sa revanche sur qn

evening ['iːvnɪŋ] n soir m; (as duration, event) soirée f; **in the ~** le soir; **evening class** n cours m du soir; **evening dress** n (man's) tenue f de soirée, smoking m; (woman's) robe f de soirée

e

event [ɪ'vɛnt] n événement m; (Sport) épreuve f; **in ~ of** en cas de; **eventful** adj mouvementé(e)

eventual [ɪ'vɛntʃuəl] adj final(e)

Be careful not to translate *eventual* by the French word *éventuel*.

eventually [ɪ'vɛntʃuəlɪ] adv finalement

Be careful not to translate *eventually* by the French word *éventuellement*.

ever [ɛvə'] adv jamais; (at all times) toujours; **why ~ not?** mais enfin, pourquoi pas?; **the best**; **the best** le meilleur qu'on ait jamais vu; **have you ~ seen it?** l'as-tu déjà vu?, as-tu eu l'occasion or t'est-il arrivé de le voir?; **~ since** (as adv) depuis; (as conj) depuis que; **~ so pretty** si joli; **evergreen** n arbre m à feuilles persistantes

 KEYWORD

every [ɛvrɪ] adj **1** (each) chaque; **every one of them** tous (sans exception); **every shop in town was closed** tous les magasins en ville étaient fermés
2 (all possible) tous (toutes) les; **I gave you every assistance** j'ai fait tout mon possible pour vous aider; **I have every confidence in him** j'ai entièrement or pleinement confiance en lui; **we wish you every success** nous vous souhaitons beaucoup de succès
3 (showing recurrence) tous les; **every day** tous les jours, chaque jour; **every other car** une voiture sur deux; **every other/third day** tous les deux/trois jours; **every now and then** de temps en temps; **everybody** pron = **everyone; everyday** adj (expression) courant(e), d'usage courant; (use) courant(e); (clothes, life) de tous les jours; (occurrence, problem) quotidien(ne); **everyone** pron tout

le monde, tous pl; **everything** pron tout; **everywhere** adv partout; **everywhere you go you meet ...** où qu'on aille on rencontre ...

evict [ɪ'vɪkt] vt expulser

evidence ['ɛvɪdns] n (proof) preuve(s) f(pl); (of witness) témoignage m; (sign): **to show ~ of** donner des signes de; **to give ~** témoigner, déposer

evident ['ɛvɪdnt] adj évident(e); **evidently** adv de toute évidence; (apparently) apparemment

evil ['iːvl] adj mauvais(e) ⊳ n mal m

evoke [ɪ'vəuk] vt évoquer

evolution [iːvə'luːʃən] n évolution f

evolve [ɪ'vɒlv] vt élaborer ⊳ vi évoluer, se transformer

ewe [juː] n brebis f

ex [ɛks] n (inf): **my ex** mon ex

ex- [ɛks] prefix ex-

exact [ɪg'zækt] adj exact(e) ⊳ vt: **to ~ sth (from)** (signature, confession) extorquer qch (à); (apology) exiger qch (de); **exactly** adv exactement

exaggerate [ɪg'zædʒəreɪt] vt, vi exagérer; **exaggeration** [ɪgzædʒə'reɪʃən] n exagération f

exam [ɪg'zæm] n abbr (Scol): = **examination**

examination [ɪgzæmɪ'neɪʃən] n (Scol, Med) examen m; **to take** or **sit an ~** (BRIT) passer un examen

examine [ɪg'zæmɪn] vt (gen) examiner; (Scol, Law: person) interroger; **examiner** n examinateur(-trice)

example [ɪg'zɑːmpl] n exemple m; **for ~** par exemple

exasperated [ɪg'zɑːspəreɪtɪd] adj exaspéré(e)

excavate ['ɛkskəveɪt] vt (site) fouiller, excaver; (object) mettre au jour

exceed [ɪk'siːd] vt dépasser; (one's powers) outrepasser; **exceedingly** adv extrêmement

excel [ɪkˈsɛl] vi exceller ▷ vt
surpasser; **to ~ o.s.** se surpasser
excellence [ˈɛksələns] n excellence f
excellent [ˈɛksələnt] adj excellent(e)
except [ɪkˈsɛpt] prep (also: **~ for,
~ing**) sauf, excepté, à l'exception
de ▷ vt excepter; **~ if/when** sauf
si/quand; **~ that** excepté que, si ce
n'est que; **exception** [ɪkˈsɛpʃən]
n exception f; **to take exception
to** s'offusquer de; **exceptional**
[ɪkˈsɛpʃənl] adj exceptionnel(le);
exceptionally [ɪkˈsɛpʃənəlɪ] adv
exceptionnellement
excerpt [ˈɛksəːpt] n extrait m
excess [ɪkˈsɛs] n excès m; **excess
baggage** n excédent m de bagages;
excessive adj excessif(-ive)
exchange [ɪksˈtʃeɪndʒ] n échange
m; (also: **telephone ~**) central m
▷ vt: **to ~ (for)** échanger (contre);
could I ~ this, please? est-ce que je
peux échanger ceci, s'il vous plaît?;
exchange rate n taux m de change
excite [ɪkˈsaɪt] vt exciter; **excited**
adj (tout) excité(e); **to get excited**
s'exciter; **excitement** n excitation f;
exciting adj passionnant(e)
exclaim [ɪksˈkleɪm] vi s'exclamer;
exclamation [ɛkskləˈmeɪʃən] n
exclamation f; **exclamation mark**,
(US) **exclamation point** n point m
d'exclamation
exclude [ɪksˈkluːd] vt exclure
excluding [ɪksˈkluːdɪŋ] prep: **~ VAT**
la TVA non comprise
exclusion [ɪksˈkluːʒən] n exclusion f
exclusive [ɪksˈkluːsɪv] adj
exclusif(-ive); (club, district) sélect(e);
(item of news) en exclusivité; **~ of VAT**
TVA non comprise; **exclusively** adv
exclusivement
excruciating [ɪksˈkruːʃɪeɪtɪŋ]
adj (pain) atroce, déchirant(e);
(embarrassing) pénible
excursion [ɪksˈkəːʃən] n excursion f
excuse n [ɪksˈkjuːs] excuse f ▷ vt
[ɪksˈkjuːz] (forgive) excuser; **to ~ sb**

from (activity) dispenser qn de; **~
me!** excusez-moi, pardon!; **now if you
will ~ me, ...** maintenant, si vous (le)
permettez ...
ex-directory [ˈɛksdɪˈrɛktərɪ] adj
(BRIT) sur la liste rouge
execute [ˈɛksɪkjuːt] vt exécuter;
execution [ɛksɪˈkjuːʃən] n
exécution f
executive [ɪgˈzɛkjutɪv] n (person)
cadre m; (managing group) bureau m;
(Pol) exécutif m ▷ adj exécutif(-ive);
(position, job) de cadre
exempt [ɪgˈzɛmpt] adj: **~ from**
exempté(e) or dispensé(e) de ▷ vt: **to ~
sb from** exempter or dispenser qn de
exercise [ˈɛksəsaɪz] n exercice m ▷ vt
exercer; (patience etc) faire preuve de;
(dog) promener ▷ vi (also: **to take ~**)
prendre de l'exercice; **exercise book**
n cahier m
exert [ɪgˈzəːt] vt exercer, employer;
to ~ o.s. se dépenser; **exertion**
[ɪgˈzəːʃən] n effort m
exhale [ɛksˈheɪl] vt exhaler ▷ vi
expirer
exhaust [ɪgˈzɔːst] n (also: **~ fumes**)
gaz mpl d'échappement; (also: **~
pipe**) tuyau m d'échappement ▷ vt
épuiser; **exhausted** adj épuisé(e);
exhaustion [ɪgˈzɔːstʃən] n
épuisement m; **nervous exhaustion**
fatigue nerveuse
exhibit [ɪgˈzɪbɪt] n (Art) objet
exposé, pièce exposée; (Law) pièce
à conviction ▷ vt (Art) exposer;
(courage, skill) faire preuve de;
exhibition [ɛksɪˈbɪʃən] n exposition f
exhilarating [ɪgˈzɪləreɪtɪŋ] adj
grisant(e), stimulant(e)
exile [ˈɛksaɪl] n exil m; (person) exilé(e)
▷ vt exiler
exist [ɪgˈzɪst] vi exister; **existence** n
existence f; **existing** adj actuel(le)
exit [ˈɛksɪt] n sortie f ▷ vi (Comput,
Theat) sortir; **where's the ~?** où est la
sortie?; **exit ramp** n (US Aut) bretelle
f d'accès

e

exotic [ɪg'zɒtɪk] adj exotique
expand [ɪk'spænd] vt (area) agrandir; (quantity) accroître ▷ vi (trade, etc) se développer, s'accroître; (gas, metal) se dilater
expansion [ɪk'spænʃən] n (territorial, economic) expansion f; (of trade, influence etc) développement m; (of production) accroissement m; (of population) croissance f; (of gas, metal) expansion, dilatation f
expect [ɪk'spɛkt] vt (anticipate) s'attendre à, s'attendre à ce que + sub; (count on) compter sur, escompter; (require) demander, exiger; (suppose) supposer; (await: also baby) attendre ▷ vi: **to be ~ing** (pregnant woman) être enceinte; **expectation** [ɛkspɛk'teɪʃən] n (hope) attente f, espérance f(pl); (belief) attente
expedition [ɛkspə'dɪʃən] n expédition f
expel [ɪk'spɛl] vt chasser, expulser; (Scol) renvoyer, exclure
expenditure [ɪk'spɛndɪtʃə'] n (act of spending) dépense f; (money spent) dépenses fpl
expense [ɪk'spɛns] n (high cost) coût m; (spending) dépense f, frais mpl; **expenses** npl frais mpl; dépenses; **at the ~ of** (fig) aux dépens de; **expense account** n (note f de) frais mpl
expensive [ɪk'spɛnsɪv] adj cher (chère), coûteux(-euse); **it's too ~** ça coûte trop cher
experience [ɪk'spɪərɪəns] n expérience f ▷ vt connaître; (feeling) éprouver; **experienced** adj expérimenté(e)
experiment [ɪk'spɛrɪmənt] n expérience f ▷ vi faire une expérience; **experimental** [ɪkspɛrɪ'mɛntl] adj expérimental(e)
expert ['ɛkspə:t] adj expert(e) ▷ n expert m; **expertise** [ɛkspə:'ti:z] n (grande) compétence
expire [ɪk'spaɪə'] vi expirer; **expiry** n expiration f; **expiry date** n date

f d'expiration; (on label) à utiliser avant ...
explain [ɪk'spleɪn] vt expliquer; **explanation** [ɛksplə'neɪʃən] n explication f
explicit [ɪk'splɪsɪt] adj explicite; (definite) formel(le)
explode [ɪk'spləʊd] vi exploser
exploit n ['ɛksplɔɪt] exploit m ▷ vt [ɪk'splɔɪt] exploiter; **exploitation** [ɛksplɔɪ'teɪʃən] n exploitation f
explore [ɪk'splɔ:'] vt explorer; (possibilities) étudier, examiner; **explorer** n explorateur(-trice)
explosion [ɪk'spləʊʒən] n explosion f; **explosive** [ɪk'spləʊsɪv] adj explosif(-ive) ▷ n explosif m
export vt [ɛk'spɔ:t] exporter ▷ n ['ɛkspɔ:t] exportation f ▷ cpd ['ɛkspɔ:t] d'exportation; **exporter** n exportateur m
expose [ɪk'spəʊz] vt exposer; (unmask) démasquer, dévoiler; **exposed** adj (land, house) exposé(e); **exposure** [ɪk'spəʊʒə'] n exposition f; (publicity) couverture f; (Phot: speed) (temps m de) pose f; (: shot) pose; **to die of exposure** (Med) mourir de froid
express [ɪk'sprɛs] adj (definite) formel(le), exprès(-esse); (BRIT: letter etc) exprès inv ▷ n (train) rapide m ▷ vt exprimer; **expression** [ɪk'sprɛʃən] n expression f; **expressway** n (US) voie f express (à plusieurs files)
exquisite [ɛk'skwɪzɪt] adj exquis(e)
extend [ɪk'stɛnd] vt (visit, street) prolonger; remettre; (building) agrandir; (offer) présenter, offrir; (hand, arm) tendre ▷ vi (land) s'étendre; **extension** n (of visit, street) prolongation f; (building) annexe f; (telephone: in offices) poste m; (: in private house) téléphone m supplémentaire; **extension cable**, **extension lead** n (Elec) rallonge f; **extensive** adj étendu(e), vaste; (damage, alterations) considérable; (inquiries) approfondi(e)

extent [ɪkˈstɛnt] n étendue f; **to some ~** dans une certaine mesure; **to the ~ of ...** au point de ...; **to what ~?** dans quelle mesure?, jusqu'à quel point?; **to such an ~ that ...** à tel point que ...

exterior [ɛkˈstɪərɪəʳ] adj extérieur(e) ▷ n extérieur m

external [ɛkˈstɜːnl] adj externe

extinct [ɪkˈstɪŋkt] adj (volcano) éteint(e); (species) disparu(e); **extinction** n extinction f

extinguish [ɪkˈstɪŋgwɪʃ] vt éteindre

extra [ˈɛkstrə] adj supplémentaire, de plus ▷ adv (in addition) en plus ▷ n supplément m; (perk) à-côté m; (Cine, Theat) figurant(e)

extract vt [ɪkˈstrækt] extraire; (tooth) arracher; (money, promise) soutirer ▷ n [ˈɛkstrækt] extrait m

extradite [ˈɛkstrədaɪt] vt extrader

extraordinary [ɪkˈstrɔːdnrɪ] adj extraordinaire

extravagance [ɪkˈstrævəgəns] n (excessive spending) prodigalités fpl; (thing bought) folie f, dépense excessive; **extravagant** adj extravagant(e); (in spending: person) prodigue, dépensier(-ière) f; (: tastes) dispendieux(-euse)

extreme [ɪkˈstriːm] adj, n extrême (m); **extremely** adv extrêmement

extremist [ɪkˈstriːmɪst] adj, n extrémiste m/f

extrovert [ˈɛkstrəvɜːt] n extraverti(e)

eye [aɪ] n œil m; (of needle) trou m, chas m ▷ vt examiner; **to keep an ~ on** surveiller; **eyeball** n globe m oculaire; **eyebrow** n sourcil m; **eye drops** npl gouttes fpl pour les yeux; **eyelash** n cil m; **eyelid** n paupière f; **eyeliner** n eye-liner m; **eye shadow** n ombre f à paupières; **eyesight** n vue f; **eye witness** n témoin m oculaire

f

F [ɛf] n (Mus) fa m

fabric [ˈfæbrɪk] n tissu m

fabulous [ˈfæbjuləs] adj fabuleux(-euse); (inf: super) formidable, sensationnel(le)

face [feɪs] n visage m, figure f; (expression) air m; (of clock) cadran m; (of cliff) paroi f; (of mountain) face f; (of building) façade f ▷ vt faire face à; (facts etc) accepter; **~ down** (person) à plat ventre; (card) face en dessous; **to lose/save ~** perdre/sauver la face; **to pull a ~** faire une grimace; **in the ~ of** (difficulties etc) face à, devant; **on the ~ of it** à première vue; **~ to ~** face à face; **face up to** vt fus faire face à, affronter; **face cloth** n (BRIT) gant m de toilette; **face pack** n (BRIT) masque m (de beauté)

facial [ˈfeɪʃl] adj facial(e) ▷ n soin complet du visage

facilitate [fəˈsɪlɪteɪt] vt faciliter

facilities [fəˈsɪlɪtɪz] npl installations fpl, équipement m; **credit ~** facilités de paiement

fact n fait m; **in ~** en fait

faction [ˈfækʃən] n faction f

factor [ˈfæktə*] n facteur m; (of suncream) indice m (de protection); **I'd like a ~ 15 suntan lotion** je voudrais une crème solaire d'indice 15

factory [ˈfæktərɪ] n usine f, fabrique f

factual [ˈfæktjuəl] adj basé(e) sur les faits

faculty [ˈfækəltɪ] n faculté f; (us: teaching staff) corps enseignant

fad [fæd] n (personal) manie f; (craze) engouement m

fade [feɪd] vi se décolorer, passer; (light, sound) s'affaiblir; (flower) se faner; **fade away** (sound) s'affaiblir

fag [fæg] n (BRIT inf: cigarette) clope f

Fahrenheit [ˈfɑːrənhaɪt] n Fahrenheit m inv

fail [feɪl] vt (exam) échouer à; (candidate) recaler; (subj: courage, memory) faire défaut à ▷ vi échouer; (eyesight, health, light: also: **be ~ing**) baisser, s'affaiblir; (brakes) lâcher; **to ~ to do sth** (neglect) négliger de or ne pas faire qch; (be unable) ne pas arriver or parvenir à faire qch; **without ~** à coup sûr; sans faute; **failing** n défaut m ▷ prep faute de; **failing that** à défaut, sinon; **failure** [ˈfeɪljə*] n échec m; (person) raté(e); (mechanical etc) défaillance f

faint [feɪnt] adj faible; (recollection) vague; (mark) à peine visible ▷ n évanouissement m ▷ vi s'évanouir; **to feel ~** défaillir; **faintest** adj: **I haven't the faintest idea** je n'en ai pas la moindre idée; **faintly** adv faiblement; (vaguely) vaguement

fair [fɛə*] adj équitable, juste; (hair) blond(e); (skin, complexion) pâle, blanc (blanche); (weather) beau (belle); (good enough) assez bon(ne); (sizeable) considérable ▷ adv: **to play ~** jouer franc jeu ▷ n foire f; (BRIT: funfair) fête

(foraine); **fairground** n champ m de foire; **fair-haired** adj (person) aux cheveux clairs, blond(e); **fairly** adv (justly) équitablement; (quite) assez; **fair trade** n commerce m équitable; **fairway** n (Golf) fairway m

fairy [ˈfɛərɪ] n fée f; **fairy tale** n conte m de fées

faith [feɪθ] n foi f; (trust) confiance f; (sect) culte m, religion f; **faithful** adj fidèle; **faithfully** adv fidèlement; **yours faithfully** (BRIT: in letters) veuillez agréer l'expression de mes salutations les plus distinguées

fake [feɪk] n (painting etc) faux m; (person) imposteur m ▷ adj faux (fausse) ▷ vt (emotions) simuler; (painting) faire un faux de

falcon [ˈfɔːlkən] n faucon m

fall [fɔːl] n chute f; (decrease) baisse f; (us: autumn) automne m ▷ vi (pt **fell**, pp **fallen**) tomber; (price, temperature, dollar) baisser; **falls** npl (waterfall) chute f d'eau, cascade f; **to ~ flat** vi (on one's face) tomber de tout son long, s'étaler; (joke) tomber à plat; (plan) échouer; **fall apart** vi (object) tomber en morceaux; **fall down** vi (person) tomber; (building) s'effondrer, s'écrouler; **fall for** vt fus (trick) se laisser prendre à; (person) tomber amoureux(-euse) de; **fall off** vi tomber; (diminish) baisser, diminuer; **fall out** vi (friends etc) se brouiller; (hair, teeth) tomber; **fall over** vi tomber (par terre); **fall through** vi (plan, project) tomber à l'eau

fallen [ˈfɔːlən] pp of **fall**

fallout [ˈfɔːlaʊt] n retombées (radioactives)

false [fɔːls] adj faux (fausse); **under ~ pretences** sous un faux prétexte; **false alarm** n fausse alerte; **false teeth** npl (BRIT) fausses dents, dentier m

fame [feɪm] n renommée f, renom m

familiar [fəˈmɪlɪə*] adj familier(-ière); **to be ~ with sth** connaître qch;

familiarize [fəˈmɪljəraɪz] vt: **to familiarize o.s. with** se familiariser avec

family [ˈfæmɪlɪ] n famille f; **family doctor** n médecin m de famille; **family planning** n planning familial

famine [ˈfæmɪn] n famine f

famous [ˈfeɪməs] adj célèbre

fan [fæn] n (folding) éventail m; (Elec) ventilateur m; (person) fan m, admirateur(-trice); (Sport) supporter m/f ▷ vt éventer; (fire, quarrel) attiser

fanatic [fəˈnætɪk] n fanatique m/f

fan belt n courroie f de ventilateur

fan club n fan-club m

fancy [ˈfænsɪ] n (whim) fantaisie f, envie f; (imagination) imagination f ▷ adj (luxury) de luxe; (elaborate: jewellery, packaging) fantaisie inv ▷ vt (feel like, want) avoir envie de; (imagine) imaginer; **to take a ~ to** se prendre d'affection pour, s'enticher de; **he fancies her** elle lui plaît; **fancy dress** n déguisement m, travesti m

fan heater n (BRIT) radiateur m soufflant

fantasize [ˈfæntəsaɪz] vi fantasmer

fantastic [fænˈtæstɪk] adj fantastique

fantasy [ˈfæntəsɪ] n imagination f, fantaisie f; (unreality) fantasme m

fanzine [ˈfænziːn] n fanzine m

FAQ n abbr (= frequently asked question) FAQ f inv, faq f inv

far [fɑː] adj (distant) lointain(e), éloigné(e) ▷ adv loin; **the ~ side/ end** l'autre côté/bout; **it's not ~ (from here)** ce n'est pas loin (d'ici); **~ away, ~ off** au loin, dans le lointain; **~ better** beaucoup mieux; **~ from** loin de; **by ~** de loin, de beaucoup; **go as ~ as the bridge** allez jusqu'au pont; **as ~ as I know** pour autant que je sache; **how ~ is it to ...?** combien y a-t-il jusqu'à ...?; **how ~ have you got with your work?** où en êtes-vous dans votre travail?

farce [fɑːs] n farce f

fare [fɛəˀ] n (on trains, buses) prix m du billet; (in taxi) prix de la course; (food) table f, chère f; **half ~** demi-tarif; **full ~** plein tarif

Far East n: **the ~** l'Extrême-Orient m

farewell [fɛəˈwɛl] excl, n adieu m

farm [fɑːm] n ferme f ▷ vt cultiver; **farmer** n fermier(-ière); **farmhouse** n (maison f de) ferme f; **farming** n agriculture f; (of animals) élevage m; **farmyard** n cour f de ferme

far-reaching [ˈfɑːˈriːtʃɪŋ] adj d'une grande portée

fart [fɑːt] (infl) vi péter

farther [ˈfɑːðəˀ] adv plus loin ▷ adj plus éloigné(e), plus lointain(e)

farthest [ˈfɑːðɪst] superlative of **far**

fascinate [ˈfæsɪneɪt] vt fasciner, captiver

fascinating [ˈfæsɪneɪtɪŋ] adj fascinant(e)

fascination [fæsɪˈneɪʃən] n fascination f

fascist [ˈfæʃɪst] adj, n fasciste m/f

fashion [ˈfæʃən] n mode f; (manner) façon f, manière f ▷ vt façonner; **in ~** à la mode; **out of ~** démodé(e); **fashionable** adj à la mode; **fashion show** n défilé m de mannequins or de mode

fast [fɑːst] adj rapide; (clock): **to be ~** avancer; (dye, colour) grand or bon teint inv ▷ adv vite, rapidement; (stuck, held) solidement ▷ n jeûne m ▷ vi jeûner; **~ asleep** profondément endormi

fasten [ˈfɑːsn] vt attacher, fixer; (coat) attacher, fermer ▷ vi se fermer, s'attacher

fast food n fast food m, restauration f rapide

fat [fæt] adj gros(se) ▷ n graisse f; (on meat) gras m; (for cooking) matière grasse

fatal [ˈfeɪtl] adj (mistake) fatal(e); (injury) mortel(le); **fatality** [fəˈtælɪtɪ] n (road death etc) victime f, décès m;

fatally adv fatalement; (injured) mortellement

fate [feɪt] n destin m; (of person) sort m

father ['fɑ:ðə'] n père m; **Father Christmas** n le Père Noël; **father-in-law** n beau-père m

fatigue [fə'ti:g] n fatigue f

fattening ['fætnɪŋ] adj (food) qui fait grossir

fatty ['fætɪ] adj (food) gras(se) ⊳ n (inf) gros (grosse)

faucet ['fɔ:sɪt] n (us) robinet m

fault [fɔ:lt] n faute f; (defect) défaut m; (Geo) faille f ⊳ vt trouver des défauts à, prendre en défaut; **it's my ~** c'est de ma faute; **to find ~ with** trouver à redire or à critiquer à; **at ~** fautif(-ive), coupable; **faulty** adj défectueux(-euse)

fauna ['fɔ:nə] n faune f

favour, (us) **favor** ['feɪvə'] n faveur f; (help) service m ⊳ vt (proposition) être en faveur de; (pupil etc) favoriser; (team, horse) donner gagnant; **to do sb a ~** rendre un service à qn; **in ~ of** en faveur de; **to find ~ with sb** trouver grâce aux yeux de qn; **favourable**, (us) **favorable** adj favorable; **favourite**, (us) **favorite** ['feɪvrɪt] adj, n favori(te)

fawn [fɔ:n] n (deer) faon m ⊳ adj (also: **~-coloured**) fauve ⊳ vi: **to ~ (up)on** flatter servilement

fax [fæks] n (document) télécopie f; (machine) télécopieur m ⊳ vt envoyer par télécopie

FBI n abbr (us = Federal Bureau of Investigation) FBI m

fear [fɪə'] n crainte f, peur f ⊳ vt craindre; **for ~ of** de peur que + sub or de + infinitive; **fearful** adj craintif(-ive); (sight, noise) affreux(-euse); **fearless** adj intrépide

feasible ['fi:zəbl] adj faisable, réalisable

feast [fi:st] n festin m, banquet m; (Rel: also: **~ day**) fête f ⊳ vi festoyer

feat [fi:t] n exploit m, prouesse f

feather ['feðə'] n plume f

feature ['fi:tʃə'] n caractéristique f; (article) chronique f, rubrique f ⊳ vt (film) avoir pour vedette(s) ⊳ vi figurer (en bonne place); **features** npl (of face) traits mpl; **a (special) ~ on sth/sb** un reportage sur qch/qn; **feature film** n long métrage m

Feb. abbr (= February) fév

February ['februarɪ] n février m

fed [fed] pt, pp of **feed**

federal ['fedərəl] adj fédéral(e)

federation [fedə'reɪʃən] n fédération f

fed up adj: **to be ~ (with)** en avoir marre or plein le dos (de)

fee [fi:] n rémunération f; (of doctor, lawyer) honoraires mpl; (of school, college etc) frais mpl de scolarité; (for examination) droits mpl

feeble ['fi:bl] adj faible; (attempt, excuse) pauvre; (joke) piteux(-euse)

feed [fi:d] n (of animal) nourriture f, pâture f; (on printer) mécanisme m d'alimentation ⊳ vt (pt, pp **fed**) (person) nourrir; (BRIT: baby: breastfeed) allaiter; (: with bottle) donner le biberon à; (horse etc) donner à manger à; (machine) alimenter; (data etc) **to ~ sth into** enregistrer qch dans; **feedback** n (Elec) effet m Larsen; (from person) réactions fpl

feel [fi:l] n (sensation) sensation f; (impression) impression f ⊳ vt (pt, pp **felt**) (touch) toucher; (explore) tâter, palper; (cold, pain) sentir; (grief, anger) ressentir, éprouver; (think, believe): **to ~ (that)** trouver que; **to ~ hungry/cold** avoir faim/froid; **to ~ lonely/better** se sentir seul/mieux; **I don't ~ well** je ne me sens pas bien; **it ~s soft** c'est doux au toucher; **to ~ like** (want) avoir envie de; **feeling** n (physical) sensation f; (emotion, impression) sentiment m; **to hurt sb's feelings** froisser qn

feet [fi:t] npl of **foot**

fell [fɛl] pt of **fall** ⊳ vt (tree) abattre

fellow ['fɛləʊ] n type m; (comrade) compagnon m; (of learned society) membre m ▷ cpd: their **~ prisoners/students** leurs camarades prisonniers/étudiants; **fellow citizen** n concitoyen(ne); **fellow countryman** (irreg) n compatriote m; **fellow men** npl semblables mpl; **fellowship** n (society) association f; (comradeship) amitié f, camaraderie f; (Scol) sorte de bourse universitaire

felony ['fɛlənɪ] n crime m, forfait m

felt [fɛlt] pt, pp of **feel** ▷ n feutre m; **felt-tip** n (also: **felt-tip pen**) stylo-feutre m

female ['fiːmeɪl] n (Zool) femelle f; (pej: woman) bonne femme ▷ adj (Biol) femelle; (sex, character) féminin(e); (vote etc) des femmes

feminine ['fɛmɪnɪn] adj féminin(e)

feminist ['fɛmɪnɪst] n féministe m/f

fence [fɛns] n barrière f ▷ vi (also: **fencing**) faire de l'escrime ▷ vt (also: **fence in**) clôturer; **fencing** n (Sport) escrime m

fend [fɛnd] vi: **to ~ for o.s.** se débrouiller (tout seul); **fend off** vt (attack etc) parer; (questions) éluder

fender ['fɛndə] n garde-feu m inv; (on boat) défense f; (us: of car) aile f

fennel ['fɛnl] n fenouil m

ferment vi [fə'mɛnt] fermenter ▷ n ['fəːmɛnt] (fig) agitation f, effervescence f

fern [fəːn] n fougère f

ferocious [fə'rəʊʃəs] adj féroce

ferret ['fɛrɪt] n furet m

ferry ['fɛrɪ] n (small) bac m; (large: also: **~boat**) ferry(-boat m) m ▷ vt transporter

fertile ['fəːtaɪl] adj fertile; (Biol) fécond(e); **fertilize** ['fəːtɪlaɪz] vt fertiliser; (Biol) féconder; **fertilizer** n engrais m

festival ['fɛstɪvəl] n (Rel) fête f; (Art, Mus) festival m

festive ['fɛstɪv] adj de fête; **the ~ season** (BRIT: Christmas) la période des fêtes

fetch [fɛtʃ] vt aller chercher; (BRIT: sell for) rapporter

fête [feɪt] n fête f, kermesse f

fetus ['fiːtəs] n (US) =**foetus**

feud [fjuːd] n querelle f, dispute f

fever ['fiːvə] n fièvre f; **feverish** adj fiévreux(-euse), fébrile

few [fjuː] adj (not many) peu de ▷ pron peu; **a ~** (as adj) quelques; (as pron) quelques-uns(-unes); **quite a ~ ...** adj un certain nombre de ..., pas mal de ...; **in the past ~ days** ces derniers jours; **fewer** adj moins de; **fewest** adj le moins nombreux

fiancé [fɪ'ɑ̃ːnseɪ] n fiancé m; **fiancée** n fiancée f

fiasco [fɪ'æskəʊ] n fiasco m

fib [fɪb] n bobard m

fibre, (US) **fiber** ['faɪbə] n fibre f; **fibreglass**, (US) **Fiberglass®** n fibre f de verre

fickle ['fɪkl] adj inconstant(e), volage, capricieux(-euse)

fiction ['fɪkʃən] n romans mpl, littérature f romanesque; (invention) fiction f; **fictional** adj fictif(-ive)

fiddle ['fɪdl] n (Mus) violon m; (cheating) combine f; escroquerie f ▷ vt (BRIT: accounts) falsifier, maquiller; **fiddle with** vt fus tripoter

fidelity [fɪ'dɛlɪtɪ] n fidélité f

fidget ['fɪdʒɪt] vi se trémousser, remuer

field [fiːld] n champ m; (fig) domaine m, champ; (Sport: ground) terrain m; **field marshal** n maréchal m

fierce [fɪəs] adj (look, animal) féroce, sauvage; (wind, attack, person) (très) violent(e); (fighting, enemy) acharné(e)

fifteen [fɪf'tiːn] num quinze; **fifteenth** num quinzième

fifth [fɪfθ] num cinquième

fiftieth ['fɪftɪɪθ] num cinquantième

fifty ['fɪftɪ] num cinquante; **fifty-fifty** adv moitié-moitié ▷ adj: **to have a fifty-fifty chance (of success)** avoir une chance sur deux (de réussir)

fig | 400

fig [fɪg] n figue f

fight [faɪt] (pt, pp **fought**) n (between persons) bagarre f; (argument) dispute f; (Mil) combat m; (against cancer etc) lutte f ▷ vt se battre contre; (cancer, alcoholism, emotion) combattre, lutter contre; (election) se présenter à ▷ vi se battre; (argue) se disputer; (fig: against illness) reprendre le dessus ▷ vt (tears) réprimer; **fight off** vt repousser; (disease, sleep, urge) lutter contre; **fighting** n combats mpl; (brawls) bagarres fpl

figure ['fɪgə'] n (Drawing, Geom) figure f; (number) chiffre m; (body, outline) silhouette f; (person's shape) ligne f, formes fpl; (person) personnage m ▷ vt (us: think) supposer ▷ vi (appear) figurer; (us: make sense) s'expliquer; **figure out** vt (understand) arriver à comprendre; (plan) calculer

file [faɪl] n (tool) lime f; (dossier) dossier m; (folder) dossier, chemise f (: binder) classeur m; (Comput) fichier m; (row) file f ▷ vt (nails, wood) limer; (papers) classer; (Law: claim) faire enregistrer; déposer; **filing cabinet** n classeur m (meuble)

Filipino [fɪlɪ'piːnəʊ] adj philippin(e) ▷ n (person) Philippin(e)

fill [fɪl] vt remplir; (vacancy) pourvoir à ▷ n: **to eat one's ~** manger à sa faim; **to ~ with** remplir de; **fill in** vt (hole) boucher; (form) remplir; **fill out** vt (form, receipt) remplir; **fill up** vt remplir ▷ vi (Aut) faire le plein

fillet ['fɪlɪt] n filet m; **fillet steak** n filet m de bœuf, tournedos m

filling ['fɪlɪŋ] n (Culin) garniture f, farce f; (for tooth) plombage m; **filling station** n station-service f, station f d'essence

film [fɪlm] n film m; (Phot) pellicule f, film; (of powder, liquid) couche f, pellicule f ▷ vt (scene) filmer ▷ vi tourner; **I'd like a 36-exposure ~** je

voudrais une pellicule de 36 poses; **film star** n vedette f de cinéma

filter ['fɪltə'] n filtre m ▷ vt filtrer; **filter lane** n (BRIT Aut: at traffic lights) voie f de dégagement; (: on motorway) voie f de sortie

filth [fɪlθ] n saleté f; **filthy** adj sale, dégoûtant(e); (language) ordurier(-ière), grossier(-ière)

fin [fɪn] n (of fish) nageoire f; (of shark) aileron m; (of diver) palme f

final ['faɪnl] adj final(e), dernier(-ière); (decision, answer) définitif(-ive) ▷ n (BRIT Sport) finale f; **finals** npl (US) (Scol) examens mpl de dernière année; (Sport) finale f; **finale** [fɪ'nɑːlɪ] n finale m; **finalist** n (Sport) finaliste m/f; **finalize** vt mettre au point; **finally** adv (eventually) enfin, finalement; (lastly) en dernier lieu

finance [faɪ'næns] n finance f ▷ vt financer; **finances** npl finances fpl; **financial** [faɪ'nænʃəl] adj financier(-ière); **financial year** n année f budgétaire

find [faɪnd] (pt, pp **found**) vt trouver; (lost object) retrouver ▷ n trouvaille f, découverte f; **to ~ sb guilty** (Law) déclarer qn coupable; **find out** vt se renseigner sur; (truth, secret) découvrir; (person) démasquer ▷ vi: **to ~ out about** se renseigner sur; (by chance) apprendre; **findings** npl (Law) conclusions fpl, verdict m; (of report) constatations fpl

fine [faɪn] adj (weather) beau (belle); (excellent) excellent(e); (thin, subtle, not coarse) fin(e); (acceptable) bien inv ▷ adv (well) très bien; (small) fin, finement ▷ n (Law) amende f, contravention f ▷ vt (Law) condamner à une amende; donner une contravention à; **he's ~** il va bien; **the weather is ~** il fait beau; **fine arts** npl beaux-arts mpl

finger ['fɪŋgə'] n doigt m ▷ vt palper, toucher; **index ~** index m; **fingernail** n ongle m (de la main); **fingerprint** n empreinte digitale; **fingertip** n bout m du doigt

finish ['fɪnɪʃ] n fin f; (Sport) arrivée f; (polish etc) finition f ▷ vt finir, terminer ▷ vi finir, se terminer; **to ~ doing sth** finir de faire qch; **to ~ third** arriver or terminer troisième; **when does the show ~?** quand est-ce que le spectacle se termine?; **finish off** vt finir, terminer; (kill) achever; **finish up** vi, vt finir

Finland ['fɪnlənd] n Finlande f; **Finn** n Finnois(e), Finlandais(e); **Finnish** adj finnois(e), finlandais(e) ▷ n (Ling) finnois m

fir [fəːʳ] n sapin m

fire ['faɪəʳ] n feu m; (accidental) incendie m; (heater) radiateur m ▷ vt (discharge): **to ~ a gun** tirer un coup de feu; (fig: interest) enflammer, animer; (inf: dismiss) mettre à la porte, renvoyer ▷ vi (shoot) tirer, faire feu; **~!** au feu!; **on ~** en feu; **to set ~ to sth, set sth on ~** mettre le feu à qch; **fire alarm** n avertisseur m d'incendie; **firearm** n arme f à feu; **fire brigade** n (régiment m de sapeurs-)pompiers mpl; **fire engine** n (BRIT) pompe f à incendie; **fire escape** n escalier m de secours; **fire exit** n issue f or sortie f de secours; **fire extinguisher** n extincteur m; **fireman** (irreg) n pompier m; **fireplace** n cheminée f; **fire station** n caserne f de pompiers; **fire truck** n (US) = **fire engine**; **firewall** n (Internet) pare-feu m; **firewood** n bois m de chauffage; **fireworks** npl (display) feu(x) m(pl) d'artifice

firm [fəːm] adj ferme ▷ n compagnie f, firme f; **firmly** adv fermement

first [fəːst] adj premier(-ière) ▷ adv (before other people) le premier, la première; (before other things) en premier, d'abord; (when listing reasons etc) en premier lieu, premièrement; (in the beginning) au début ▷ n (person: in race)

premier(-ière); (BRIT Scol) mention f très bien; (Aut) première f; **the ~ of January** le premier janvier; **at ~** au commencement, au début; **~ of all** tout d'abord, pour commencer; **first aid** n premiers secours or soins; **first-aid kit** n trousse f à pharmacie; **first-class** (ticket etc) de première classe; (excellent) excellent(e), exceptionnel(le); (post) en tarif prioritaire; **first-hand** adj de première main; **first lady** n (US) femme f du président; **firstly** adv premièrement, en premier lieu; **first name** n prénom m; **first-rate** adj excellent(e)

fiscal ['fɪskl] adj fiscal(e); **fiscal year** n exercice financier

fish [fɪʃ] n (pl inv) poisson m ▷ vt, vi pêcher; **~ and chips** poisson frit et frites; **fisherman** (irreg) n pêcheur m; **fish fingers** npl (BRIT) bâtonnets mpl de poisson (congelés); **fishing** n pêche f; **to go fishing** aller à la pêche; **fishing boat** n barque f de pêche; **fishing line** n ligne f (de pêche); **fishmonger** n (BRIT) marchand m de poisson; **fishmonger's (shop)** n (BRIT) poissonnerie f; **fish sticks** npl (US) = **fish fingers**; **fishy** adj (inf) suspect(e), louche

fist [fɪst] n poing m

fit [fɪt] adj (Med, Sport) en (bonne) forme; (proper) convenable, approprié(e) ▷ vt (subj: clothes) aller à; (put in, attach) installer, poser; (equip) équiper, garnir, munir; (suit) convenir à ▷ vi (clothes) aller; (parts) s'adapter; (in space, gap) entrer, s'adapter ▷ n (Med) accès m, crise f; (of anger) accès; (of hysterics, jealousy) crise; **~ to** (ready to) en état de; **~ for** (worthy) digne de; (capable) apte à; **to keep ~** se maintenir en forme; **this dress is a tight/good ~** cette robe est un peu juste/me va très bien; **a ~ of coughing** une quinte de toux; **by ~s and starts** par à-coups;

fit in vi (add up) cadrer; (integrate) s'intégrer; (to new situation) s'adapter; **fitness** n (Med) forme f physique; **fitted** adj (jacket, shirt) ajusté(e); **fitted carpet** n moquette f; **fitted kitchen** n (BRIT) cuisine f équipée; **fitted sheet** n drap-housse m; **fitting** adj approprié(e) ▷ n (of dress) essayage m; (of piece of equipment) pose f, installation f; **fitting room** n (in shop) cabine f d'essayage; **fittings** npl installations fpl

five [faɪv] num cinq; **fiver** n (inf: US) billet de cinq dollars; (: BRIT) billet de cinq livres

fix [fɪks] vt (date, amount etc) fixer; (sort out) arranger; (mend, repair) réparer; (make ready: meal, drink) préparer ▷ n: **to be in a ~** être dans le pétrin; **fix up** vt (meeting) arranger; **to ~ sb up with sth** faire avoir qch à qn; **fixed** adj (prices etc) fixe; **fixture** n installation f (fixe); (Sport) rencontre f (au programme)

fizzy ['fɪzɪ] adj pétillant(e), gazeux(-euse)

flag [flæg] n drapeau m; (also: **~stone**) dalle f ▷ vi faiblir; fléchir; **flag down** vt héler, faire signe de (s'arrêter) à; **flagpole** n mât m

flair [flɛə] n flair m

flak [flæk] n (Mil) tir antiaérien; (inf: criticism) critiques fpl

flake [fleɪk] n (of rust, paint) écaille f; (of snow, soap powder) flocon m ▷ vi (also: **~ off**) s'écailler

flamboyant [flæm'bɔɪənt] adj flamboyant(e), éclatant(e); (person) haut(e) en couleur

flame [fleɪm] n flamme f

flamingo [flə'mɪŋgəu] n flamant m (rose)

flammable ['flæməbl] adj inflammable

flan [flæn] n (BRIT) tarte f

flank [flæŋk] n flanc m ▷ vt flanquer

flannel ['flænl] n (BRIT: also: **face ~**) gant m de toilette; (fabric) flanelle f

flap [flæp] n (of pocket, envelope) rabat m ▷ vt (wings) battre (de) ▷ vi (sail, flag) claquer

flare [flɛə] n (signal) signal lumineux; (Mil) fusée éclairante; (in skirt etc) évasement m; **flares** npl (trousers) pantalon m à pattes d'éléphant; **flare up** vi s'embraser; (fig: person) se mettre en colère, s'emporter; (: revolt) éclater

flash [flæʃ] n éclair m; (also: **news ~**) flash m (d'information); (Phot) flash m ▷ vt (switch on) allumer (brièvement); (direct): **to ~ sth at** braquer qch sur; (send: message) câbler; (smile) lancer ▷ vi briller; jeter des éclairs; (light on ambulance etc) clignoter; **a ~ of lightning** un éclair; **in a ~** en un clin d'œil; **to ~ one's headlights** faire un appel de phares; **he ~ed by** or **past** il passa (devant nous) comme un éclair; **flashback** n flashback m, retour m en arrière; **flashbulb** n ampoule f de flash; **flashlight** n lampe f de poche

flask [flɑːsk] n flacon m, bouteille f; (also: **vacuum ~**) bouteille f thermos®

flat [flæt] adj plat(e); (tyre) dégonflé(e), à plat; (beer) éventé(e); (battery) à plat; (denial) catégorique; (Mus) bémol inv; (: voice) faux (fausse) ▷ n (BRIT: apartment) appartement m; (Aut) crevaison f, pneu crevé; (Mus) bémol m; **~ out** (work) sans relâche; (race) à fond; **flatten** vt (also: **flatten out**) aplatir; (crop) coucher; (house, city) raser

flatter ['flætə] vt flatter; **flattering** adj flatteur(-euse); (clothes etc) seyant(e)

flaunt [flɔːnt] vt faire étalage de

flavour, (US) **flavor** ['fleɪvə] n goût m, saveur f; (of ice cream etc) parfum m ▷ vt parfumer, aromatiser; **vanilla-~ed** à l'arôme de vanille, vanillé(e); **what ~s do you have?** quels parfums avez-vous?; **flavouring**, (US) **flavoring** n arôme m (synthétique)

flaw [flɔː] n défaut m; **flawless** adj sans défaut

flea [fliː] n puce f; **flea market** n marché m aux puces

fled [flɛd] pt, pp of **flee**

flee (pt, pp **fled**) [fliː, flɛd] vt fuir, s'enfuir de ▷ vi fuir, s'enfuir

fleece [fliːs] n (of sheep) toison f; (top) (laine f) polaire f ▷ vt (inf) voler, filouter

fleet [fliːt] n flotte f; (of lorries, cars etc) parc m; convoi m

fleeting ['fliːtɪŋ] adj fugace, fugitif(-ive); (visit) très bref(brève)

Flemish ['flɛmɪʃ] adj flamand(e) ▷ n (Ling) flamand m; **the ~** npl les Flamands

flesh [flɛʃ] n chair f

flew [fluː] pt of **fly**

flex [flɛks] n fil m or câble m électrique (souple) ▷ vt (knee) fléchir; (muscles) bander; **flexibility** n flexibilité f; **flexible** adj flexible; (person, schedule) souple; **flexitime** ['flɛksɪtaɪm] n horaire m variable or à la carte

flick [flɪk] n petit coup; (with finger) chiquenaude f ▷ vt donner un petit coup à; (switch) appuyer sur; **flick through** vt fus feuilleter

flicker ['flɪkə*] vi (light, flame) vaciller

flies [flaɪz] npl of **fly**

flight [flaɪt] n vol m; (escape) fuite f; (also: **~ of steps**) escalier m; **flight attendant** n steward m, hôtesse f de l'air

flimsy ['flɪmzɪ] adj peu solide; (clothes) trop léger(-ère); (excuse) pauvre, mince

flinch [flɪntʃ] vi tressaillir; **to ~ from** se dérober à, reculer devant

fling [flɪŋ] vt (pt, pp **flung**) jeter, lancer

flint [flɪnt] n silex m; (in lighter) pierre f (à briquet)

flip [flɪp] vt (throw) donner une chiquenaude à; (switch) appuyer sur; (us: pancake) faire sauter; **to ~ sth over** retourner qch

flip-flops ['flɪpflɒps] npl (esp BRIT) tongs fpl

flipper ['flɪpə*] n (of animal) nageoire f; (for swimmer) palme f

flirt [flɜːt] vi flirter ▷ n flirteur(-euse)

float [fləut] n flotteur m; (in procession) char m; (sum of money) réserve f ▷ vi flotter

flock [flɒk] n (of sheep) troupeau m; (of birds) vol m; (of people) foule f

flood [flʌd] n inondation f; (of letters, refugees etc) flot m ▷ vt inonder ▷ vi (place) être inondé; **to ~ into** envahir; **flooding** n inondation f; **floodlight** n projecteur m

floor [flɔː*] n sol m; (storey) étage m; (of sea, valley) fond m ▷ vt (knock down) terrasser; (baffle) désorienter; **ground ~**, (us) **first ~** rez-de-chaussée m; **first ~**, (us) **second ~** premier étage; **what ~ is it on?** c'est à quel étage?; **floorboard** n planche f (du plancher); **flooring** n sol m; (wooden) plancher m; (covering) revêtement m de sol; **floor show** n spectacle m de variétés

flop [flɒp] n fiasco m ▷ vi (fail) faire fiasco; (fall) s'affaler, s'effondrer; **floppy** adj lâche, flottant(e) ▷ n (Comput: also: **floppy disk**) disquette f

flora ['flɔːrə] n flore f

floral ['flɔːrl] adj floral(e); (dress) à fleurs

florist ['flɒrɪst] n fleuriste m/f; **florist's (shop)** n magasin m or boutique f de fleuriste

flotation [fləu'teɪʃən] n (of shares) émission f; (of company) lancement m (en Bourse)

flour ['flauə*] n farine f

flourish ['flʌrɪʃ] vi prospérer ▷ n (gesture) moulinet m

flow [fləu] n (of water, traffic etc) écoulement m; (tide, influx) flux m; (of sea, Elec) circulation f; (of river) courant m ▷ vi couler; (traffic) s'écouler; (robes, hair) flotter

flower ['flauə'] n fleur f ▷ vi fleurir; **flower bed** n plate-bande f; **flowerpot** n pot m (à fleurs)

flown [fləun] pp of **fly**

fl. oz. abbr = **fluid ounce**

flu [fluː] n grippe f

fluctuate ['flʌktjueɪt] vi varier, fluctuer

fluent ['fluːənt] adj (speech, style) coulant(e), aisé(e); **he speaks ~ French, he's ~ in French** il parle le français couramment

fluff [flʌf] n duvet m; (on jacket, carpet) peluche f; **fluffy** adj duveteux(-euse); (toy) en peluche

fluid ['fluːɪd] n fluide m; (in diet) liquide m ▷ adj (liquid); **fluid ounce** n (BRIT) = 0.028 l; 0.05 pints

fluke [fluːk] n coup m de veine

flung [flʌŋ] pt, pp of **fling**

fluorescent [fluə'rɛsnt] adj fluorescent(e)

fluoride ['fluəraɪd] n fluor m

flurry ['flʌrɪ] n (of snow) rafale f, bourrasque f; **a ~ of activity** un affairement soudain

flush [flʌʃ] n (on face) rougeur f; (fig: of youth etc) éclat m ▷ vt nettoyer à grande eau ▷ vi rougir ▷ adj (level); **~ with** au ras de, de niveau avec; **to ~ the toilet** tirer la chasse (d'eau)

flute [fluːt] n flûte f

flutter ['flʌtə'] n (of panic, excitement) agitation f; (of wings) battement m ▷ vi (bird) battre des ailes, voleter

fly [flaɪ] (pt **flew**, pp **flown**) n (insect) mouche f; (on trousers: also: **flies**) braguette f ▷ vt (plane) piloter; (passengers, cargo) transporter (par avion); (distance) parcourir ▷ vi voler; (passengers) aller en avion; (escape) s'enfuir, fuir; (flag) se déployer; **fly away, fly off** vi s'envoler; **fly-drive** n formule f avion plus voiture; **flying** n (activity) aviation f; (action) vol m ▷ adj; **flying visit** visite f éclair inv; **with flying colours** haut la main; **flying saucer** n soucoupe

volante; **flyover** n (BRIT: overpass) pont routier

FM abbr (Radio: = frequency modulation) FM

foal [fəul] n poulain m

foam [fəum] n écume f; (on beer) mousse f; (also: **~ rubber**) caoutchouc m mousse ▷ vi (liquid) écumer; (soapy water) mousser

focus ['fəukəs] n (pl **focuses**) foyer m; (of interest) centre m ▷ vt (field glasses etc) mettre au point ▷ vi; **to ~ (on)** (with lens) régler la mise au point (sur); (with eyes) fixer son regard (sur); (fig: concentrate) se concentrer (sur); **out of/in ~ (picture)** flou(e)/net(te); (camera) pas au point/au point

foetus, (US) **fetus** ['fiːtəs] n fœtus m

fog [fɔg] n brouillard m; **foggy** adj; **it's foggy** il y a du brouillard; **fog lamp**, (US) **fog light** n (Aut) phare m anti-brouillard

foil [fɔɪl] vt déjouer, contrecarrer ▷ n feuille f de métal; (kitchen foil) papier m d'alu(minium); **to act as a ~** (fig) servir de repoussoir à

fold [fəuld] n (bend, crease) pli m; (Agr) parc m à moutons; (fig) bercail m ▷ vt plier; **to ~ one's arms** croiser les bras; **fold up** vi (map etc) se plier, se replier; (business) fermer boutique ▷ vt (map etc) plier, replier; **folder** n (for papers) chemise f; (: binder) classeur m; (Comput) dossier m; **folding** adj (chair, bed) pliant(e)

foliage ['fəulɪɪdʒ] n feuillage m

folk [fəuk] npl gens mpl ▷ cpd folklorique; **folks** npl (inf: parents) famille f, parents mpl; **folklore** ['fəuklɔː'] n folklore m; **folk music** n musique f folklorique; (contemporary) musique folk, folk m; **folk song** n chanson f folklorique; (contemporary) chanson folk inv

follow ['fɔləu] vt suivre; (on Twitter) s'abonner aux tweets de ▷ vi suivre; (result) s'ensuivre; **to ~ suit** (fig) faire

de même; **follow up** vt (letter, offer)
donner suite à; (case) suivre; **follower**
n disciple m/f, partisan(e); **following**
adj suivant(e) ▷ n partisans mpl,
disciples mpl; **follow-up** n suite f; (in
file, case) suivi m

fond [fɒnd] adj (memory, look) tendre,
affectueux(-euse); (hopes, dreams)
un peu fou (folle); **to be ~ of** aimer
beaucoup

food [fuːd] n nourriture f, nourriture;
food mixer n mixeur m; **food
poisoning** n intoxication f alimentaire;
food processor n robot m de cuisine;
food stamp n (us) bon m de nourriture
(pour indigents)

fool [fuːl] n idiot(e); (Culin) mousse
f de fruits ▷ vt berner, duper; **fool
about, fool around** vi (pej: waste
time) traînailler, glandouiller; (: behave
foolishly) faire l'idiot or l'imbécile;
foolish adj idiot(e), stupide; (rash)
imprudent(e); **foolproof** adj (plan
etc) infaillible

foot (pl **feet**) [fut, fiːt] n pied m;
(of animal) patte f; (measure) pied
(= 30.48 cm; 12 inches) ▷ vt (bill)
payer; **on ~** à pied; **footage** n (Cine:
length) ≈ métrage m; (: material)
séquences fpl; **foot-and-mouth
(disease)** [futənd'mauθ-] n fièvre
aphteuse; **football** n (ball) ballon m
(de football); (sport: BRIT) football m;
(: us) football américain; **footballer**
n (BRIT) = **football player**;
football match n (BRIT) match m
de foot(ball); **football player** n
footballeur(-euse), joueur(-euse)
de football; (us) joueur(-euse) de
football américain; **footbridge** n
passerelle f; **foothills** npl contreforts
mpl; **foothold** n prise f (de pied);
footing n (fig) position f; **to lose
one's footing** perdre pied; **footnote**
n note f (en bas de page); **footpath**
n sentier m; **footprint** n trace f (de
pied); **footstep** n pas m; **footwear**
n chaussures fpl

KEYWORD

for [fɔːʳ] prep 1 (indicating destination,
intention, purpose) pour; **the train for
London** le train pour or à destination
de) Londres; **he left for Rome** il est
parti pour Rome; **he went for the
paper** il est allé chercher le journal;
is this for me? c'est pour moi?;
it's time for lunch c'est l'heure du
déjeuner; **what's it for?** ça sert à
quoi?; **what for?** (why?) pourquoi?;
(to what end?) pour quoi faire?, à quoi
bon?; **for sale** à vendre; **to pray for
peace** prier pour la paix

2 (on behalf of, representing) pour; **the
MP for Hove** le député de Hove; **to
work for sb/sth** travailler pour qn/
qch; **I'll ask him for you** je vais lui
demander pour toi; **G for George** G
comme Georges

3 (because of) pour; **for this reason**
pour cette raison; **for fear of being
criticized** de peur d'être critiqué

4 (with regard to) pour; **it's cold for
July** il fait froid pour juillet; **a gift for
languages** un don pour les langues

5 (in exchange for) **I sold it for £5** je l'ai
vendu 5 livres; **to pay 50 pence for a
ticket** payer un billet 50 pence

6 (in favour of) pour; **are you for or
against us?** êtes-vous pour ou contre
nous?; **I'm all for it** je suis tout à fait
pour; **vote for X** votez pour X

7 (referring to distance) pendant, sur;
there are roadworks for 5 km il y a
des travaux sur or pendant 5 km; **we
walked for miles** nous avons marché
pendant des kilomètres

8 (referring to time) pendant; depuis;
pour; **he was away for 2 years**
il a été absent pendant 2 ans; **she
will be away for a month** elle
sera absente pendant un mois; **it
hasn't rained for 3 weeks** ça fait
3 semaines qu'il ne pleut pas, il ne
pleut pas depuis 3 semaines; **I have
known her for years** je la connais

depuis des années; **can you do it for tomorrow?** est-ce que tu peux le faire pour demain?
9 (with infinitive clauses): **it is not for me to decide** ce n'est pas à moi de décider; **it would be best for you to leave** le mieux serait que vous partiez; **there is still time for you to do it** vous avez encore le temps de le faire; **for this to be possible ...** pour que cela soit possible ...
10 (in spite of): **for all that** malgré cela, néanmoins; **for all his work/efforts** malgré tout son travail/tous ses efforts; **for all his complaints, he's very fond of her** il a beau se plaindre, il l'aime beaucoup
▶ conj (since, as: formal) car

forbid (pt **forbad** or **forbade**, pp **forbidden**) [fəˈbɪd, -ˈbæd, -ˈbɪdn] vt défendre, interdire; **to ~ sb to do sth** défendre or interdire à qn de faire; **forbidden** adj défendu(e)
force [fɔːs] n force f ▶ vt forcer; (push) pousser (de force); **to ~ o.s. to do** se forcer à faire; **in ~** (rule, law, prices) en vigueur; (in large numbers) en force; **forced** adj forcé(e); **forceful** adj énergique
ford [fɔːd] n gué m
fore [fɔːr] n: **to the ~** en évidence; **forearm** n avant-bras m inv; **forecast** n prévision f ... (also: **weather forecast**) prévisions fpl météorologiques, météo f ▶ vt (irreg: like **cast**) prévoir; **forecourt** n (of garage) devant m; **forefinger** n index m; **forefront** n: **in the forefront of** au premier rang or plan de; **foreground** n premier plan; **forehead** [ˈfɒrɪd] n front m
foreign [ˈfɒrɪn] adj étranger(-ère); (trade) extérieur(e); (travel) à l'étranger; **foreign currency** n devises étrangères; **foreigner** n étranger(-ère); **foreign exchange** n (system) change m; (money) devises

fpl; **Foreign Office** n (BRIT) ministère m des Affaires étrangères; **Foreign Secretary** n (BRIT) ministre m des Affaires étrangères
fore: foreman (irreg) n (in construction) contremaître m; **foremost** adj le (la) plus en vue, premier(-ière) ▶ adv: **first and foremost** avant tout, tout d'abord; **forename** n prénom m
forensic [fəˈrɛnsɪk] adj: **~ medicine** médecine légale
foresee (pt **foresaw**, pp **foreseen**) [fɔːˈsiː, -ˈsɔː, -ˈsiːn] vt prévoir; **foreseeable** adj prévisible
foreseen [fɔːˈsiːn] pp of **foresee**
forest [ˈfɒrɪst] n forêt f; **forestry** n sylviculture f
forever [fəˈrɛvər] adv pour toujours; (fig: endlessly) continuellement
foreword [ˈfɔːwəːd] n avant-propos m inv
forfeit [ˈfɔːfɪt] vt perdre
forgave [fəˈgeɪv] pt of **forgive**
forge [fɔːdʒ] n forge f ▶ vt (signature) contrefaire; (wrought iron) forger; **to ~ money** (BRIT) fabriquer de la fausse monnaie; **forger** n faussaire m; **forgery** n faux m, contrefaçon f
forget (pt **forgot**, pp **forgotten**) [fəˈgɛt, -ˈgɒt, -ˈgɒtn] vt, vi oublier; **I've forgotten my key/passport** j'ai oublié ma clé/mon passeport; **forgetful** adj distrait(e), étourdi(e)
forgive (pt **forgave**, pp **forgiven**) [fəˈgɪv, -ˈgeɪv, -ˈgɪvn] vt pardonner; **to ~ sb for sth/for doing sth** pardonner qch à qn/à qn de faire qch
forgot [fəˈgɒt] pt of **forget**
forgotten [fəˈgɒtn] pp of **forget**
fork [fɔːk] n (for eating) fourchette f; (for gardening) fourche f; (of roads) bifurcation f ▶ vi (road) bifurquer
forlorn [fəˈlɔːn] adj (deserted) abandonné(e); (hope, attempt) désespéré(e)
form [fɔːm] n forme f; (Scol) classe f; (questionnaire) formulaire m ▶ vt former; (habit) contracter; **to ~ part**

of sth faire partie de qch; **on top ~** en
pleine forme

formal ['fɔːməl] adj (offer, receipt)
en bonne et due forme; (person)
cérémonieux(-euse); (occasion, dinner)
officiel(le); (garden) à la française;
(clothes) de soirée; **formality**
[fɔː'mælɪtɪ] n formalité f

format ['fɔːmæt] n format m ▷ vt
(Comput) formater

formation [fɔː'meɪʃən] n formation f

former ['fɔːmə'] adj ancien(ne);
(before n) précédent(e); **the ~ ... the
latter** le premier ... le second, celui-ci
... celui-là; **formerly** adv autrefois

formidable ['fɔːmɪdəbl] adj
redoutable

formula ['fɔːmjʊlə] n formule f

fort [fɔːt] n fort m

forthcoming [fɔːθ'kʌmɪŋ] adj qui va
paraître or avoir lieu prochainement;
(character) ouvert(e), communicatif(-
ive); (available) disponible

fortieth ['fɔːtɪɪθ] num quarantième

fortify ['fɔːtɪfaɪ] vt (city) fortifier;
(person) remonter

fortnight ['fɔːtnaɪt] n (BRIT)
quinzaine f, quinze jours mpl;
fortnightly adj bimensuel(le) ▷ adv
tous les quinze jours

fortress ['fɔːtrɪs] n forteresse f

fortunate ['fɔːtʃənɪt] adj
heureux(-euse); (person) chanceux(-
euse); **it is ~ that** c'est une chance
que, il est heureux que; **fortunately**
adv heureusement, par bonheur

fortune ['fɔːtʃən] n chance f, (wealth)
fortune f; **fortune-teller** n diseuse f
de bonne aventure

forty ['fɔːtɪ] num quarante

forum ['fɔːrəm] n forum m, tribune f

forward ['fɔːwəd] adj (movement,
position) en avant, vers l'avant;
(not shy) effronté(e); (in time) en
avance ▷ adv (also: **~s**) en avant ▷ n
(Sport) avant m ▷ vt (letter) faire
suivre; (parcel, goods) expédier; (fig)
promouvoir, favoriser; **to move ~**

avancer; **forwarding address** n
adresse f de réexpédition; **forward
slash** n barre f oblique

fossick ['fɔsɪk] vi (AUST, NZ inf)
chercher; **to ~ around for** fouiner
(inf) pour trouver

fossil ['fɔsl] adj, n fossile m

foster ['fɔstə'] vt (encourage)
encourager, favoriser; (child) élever
(sans adopter); **foster child** n enfant
élevé dans une famille d'accueil

fought [fɔːt] pt, pp of **fight**

foul [faʊl] adj (weather, smell, food)
infect(e); (language) ordurier(-ière)
▷ n (Football) faute f ▷ vt (dirty) salir,
encrasser; **he's got a ~ temper** il a
un caractère de chien; **foul play** n
(Law) acte criminel

found [faʊnd] pt, pp of **find** ▷ vt
(establish) fonder; **foundation**
[faʊn'deɪʃən] n (act) fondation
f; (base) fondement m; (also:
foundation cream) fond m de
teint; **foundations** npl (of building)
fondations fpl

founder ['faʊndə'] n fondateur m ▷ vi
couler, sombrer

fountain ['faʊntɪn] n fontaine f;
fountain pen n stylo m (à encre)

four [fɔː'] num quatre; **on all ~s** à
quatre pattes; **four-letter word** n
obscénité f, gros mot; **four-poster**
n (also: **four-poster bed**) lit m à
baldaquin; **fourteen** num quatorze;
fourteenth num quatorzième;
fourth num quatrième ▷ n (Aut:
also: **fourth gear**) quatrième f; **four-
wheel drive** n (Aut: car) voiture f à
quatre roues motrices

fowl [faʊl] n volaille f

fox [fɔks] n renard m ▷ vt mystifier

foyer ['fɔɪeɪ] n (in hotel) vestibule m;
(Theat) foyer m

fracking ['frækɪŋ] n fracturation f
hydraulique

fraction ['frækʃən] n fraction f

fracture ['fræktʃə'] n fracture f ▷ vt
fracturer

fragile ['frædʒaɪl] *adj* fragile
fragment ['frægmənt] *n* fragment *m*
fragrance ['freɪgrəns] *n* parfum *m*
frail [freɪl] *adj* fragile, délicat(e); (*person*) frêle
frame [freɪm] *n* (*of building*) charpente *f*; (*of human, animal*) charpente *f*, ossature *f*; (*of picture*) cadre *m*; (*of door, window*) encadrement *m*, chambranle *m*; (*of spectacles: also:* **~s**) monture *f* ▷ *vt* (*picture*) encadrer; **~ of mind** disposition *f* d'esprit; **framework** *n* structure *f*
France [frɑːns] *n* la France
franchise ['fræntʃaɪz] *n* (*Pol*) droit *m* de vote; (*Comm*) franchise *f*
frank [fræŋk] *adj* franc (franche) ▷ *vt* (*letter*) affranchir; **frankly** *adv* franchement
frantic ['fræntɪk] *adj* (*hectic*) frénétique; (*distraught*) hors de soi
fraud [frɔːd] *n* supercherie *f*, fraude *f*, tromperie *f*; (*person*) imposteur *m*
fraught [frɔːt] *adj* (*tense: situation*) très tendu(e); (~ **with** (*difficulties etc*) chargé(e) de, plein(e) de
fray [freɪ] *vt* effilocher ▷ *vi* s'effilocher
freak [friːk] *n* (*eccentric person*) phénomène *m*; (*unusual event*) hasard *m* extraordinaire; (*pej: fanatic*): **health food ~** fana *m/f* or obsédé(e) de l'alimentation saine ▷ *adj* (*storm*) exceptionnel(le); (*accident*) bizarre
freckle ['frɛkl] *n* tache *f* de rousseur
free [friː] *adj* libre; (*gratis*) gratuit(e) ▷ *vt* (*prisoner etc*) libérer; (*jammed object or person*) dégager; **is this seat ~?** la place est libre?; **~ (of charge)** gratuitement; **freedom** *n* liberté *f*; **Freefone®** *n* numéro vert; **free gift** *n* prime *f*; **free kick** *n* (*Sport*) coup franc; **freelance** *adj* indépendant(e), free-lance *inv* ▷ *adv* en free-lance; **freely** *adv* librement; (*liberally*) libéralement; **Freepost®** *n* (*Brit*) port payé; **free-range** *adj* (*egg*)

de ferme; (*chicken*) fermier; **freeway** *n* (*US*) autoroute *f*; **free will** *n* libre arbitre *m*; **of one's own free will** de son plein gré
freeze [friːz] (*pt* **froze**, *pp* **frozen**) *vi* geler ▷ *vt* geler; (*food*) congeler; (*prices, salaries*) bloquer, geler ▷ *n* gel *m*; (*of prices, salaries*) blocage *m*; **freezer** *n* congélateur *m*; **freezing** *adj*: **freezing (cold)** (*room etc*) glacial(e); (*person, hands*) gelé(e), glacé(e) ▷ *n*: **3 degrees below freezing** 3 degrés au-dessous de zéro; **it's freezing** il fait un froid glacial; **freezing point** *n* point *m* de congélation
freight [freɪt] *n* (*goods*) fret *m*, cargaison *f*; (*money charged*) fret, prix *m* du transport; **freight train** *n* (*US*) train *m* de marchandises
French [frɛntʃ] *adj* français(e) ▷ *n* (*Ling*) français *m*; **the ~** *npl* les Français; **what's the ~ (word) for ...?** comment dit-on ... en français?; **French bean** *n* (*Brit*) haricot vert; **French bread** *n* pain *m* français; **French dressing** *n* (*Culin*) vinaigrette *f*; **French fried potatoes, French fries** (*US*) *npl* (pommes de terre *fpl*) frites *fpl*; **Frenchman** (*irreg*) *n* Français *m*; **French stick** *n* = baguette *f*; **French window** *n* porte-fenêtre *f*; **Frenchwoman** (*irreg*) *n* Française *f*
frenzy ['frɛnzɪ] *n* frénésie *f*
frequency ['friːkwənsɪ] *n* fréquence *f*
frequent *adj* ['friːkwənt] fréquent(e) ▷ *vt* [frɪ'kwɛnt] fréquenter; **frequently** ['friːkwəntlɪ] *adv* fréquemment
fresh [frɛʃ] *adj* frais (fraîche); (*new*) nouveau (nouvelle); (*cheeky*) familier(-ière), culotté(e); **freshen** *vi* (*wind, weather*) fraîchir; **freshen up** *vi* faire un brin de toilette; **fresher** *n* (*Brit University: inf*) bizuth *m*, étudiant(e) de première année; **freshly** *adv*

nouvellement, récemment;
freshman (*irreg*) *n* (us = **fresher**;
freshwater *adj* (fish) d'eau douce
fret [frɛt] *vi* s'agiter, se tracasser
friction [ˈfrɪkʃən] *n* friction *f*,
frottement *m*
Friday [ˈfraɪdɪ] *n* vendredi *m*
fridge [frɪdʒ] *n* (BRIT) frigo *m*,
frigidaire® *m*
fried [fraɪd] *adj* frit(e); **~ egg** œuf *m*
sur le plat
friend [frɛnd] *n* ami(e) ▷ *vt* (Internet)
ajouter comme ami(e); **friendly**
adj amical(e); (kind) sympathique,
gentil(le); (place) accueillant(e); (Pol:
country) ami(e) ▷ *n* (also: **friendly**
match) match amical; **friendship**
n amitié *f*
fries [fraɪz] (esp us) *npl* = **chips**
frigate [ˈfrɪɡɪt] *n* frégate *f*
fright [fraɪt] *n* peur *f*, effroi *m*; **to**
give sb a ~ faire peur à qn; **to take**
~ prendre peur, s'effrayer; **frighten**
vt effrayer, faire peur à; **frightened**
adj: **to be frightened (of)** avoir peur
(de); **frightening** *adj* effrayant(e);
frightful *adj* affreux(-euse)
frill [frɪl] *n* (of dress) volant *m*; (of shirt)
jabot *m*
fringe [frɪndʒ] *n* (BRIT: of hair) frange
f; (edge: of forest etc) bordure *f*
Frisbee® [ˈfrɪzbɪ] *n* Frisbee® *m*
fritter [ˈfrɪtəʳ] *n* beignet *m*
frivolous [ˈfrɪvələs] *adj* frivole
fro [frəu] *adv* see **to**
frock [frɔk] *n* robe *f*
frog [frɔɡ] *n* grenouille *f*; **frogman**
(*irreg*) *n* homme-grenouille *m*

KEYWORD

from [frɔm] *prep* **1** (indicating starting
place, origin etc) de; **where do you**
come from?, **where are you from?**
d'où venez-vous?; **where has he**
come from? d'où arrive-t-il?; **from**
London to Paris de Londres à Paris;
to escape from sb/sth échapper

à qn/qch; **a letter/telephone call**
from my sister une lettre/un appel
de ma sœur; **to drink from the**
bottle boire à (même) la bouteille;
tell him from me that … dites-lui de
ma part que …
2 (indicating time) (à partir) de; **from**
one o'clock to or **until** or **till two**
d'une heure à deux heures; **from**
January (on) à partir de janvier
3 (indicating distance) de; **the hotel**
is one kilometre from the beach
l'hôtel est à un kilomètre de la plage
4 (indicating price, number etc) de;
prices range from £10 to £50 les prix
varient entre 10 livres et 50 livres; **the**
interest rate was increased from
9% to 10% le taux d'intérêt est passé
de 9% à 10%
5 (indicating difference) de; **he can't**
tell red from green il ne peut pas
distinguer le rouge du vert; **to be**
different from sb/sth être différent
de qn/qch
6 (because of, on the basis of): **from**
what he says d'après ce qu'il dit;
weak from hunger affaibli par
la faim

front [frʌnt] *n* (of house, dress)
devant *m*; (of coach, train) avant *m*;
(promenade: also: **sea ~**) bord *m* de
mer; (Mil, Pol, Meteorology) front
m; (fig: appearances) contenance *f*,
façade *f* ▷ *adj* de devant; (seat, wheel)
avant *inv* ▷ *vi*: **in ~ (of)** devant;
front door *n* porte *f* d'entrée; (of car)
portière *f* avant; **frontier** [ˈfrʌntɪəʳ]
n frontière *f*; **front page** *n* première
page; **front-wheel drive** *n* traction
f avant

frost [frɔst] *n* gel *m*, gelée *f*; (also:
hoar~) givre *m*; **frostbite** *n* gelures
fpl; **frosting** *n* (esp us: on cake)
glaçage *m*; **frosty** *adj* (window)
couvert(e) de givre; (weather, welcome)
glacial(e).
froth [frɔθ] *n* mousse *f*; écume *f*

frown [fraun] n froncement m de sourcils ▷ vi froncer les sourcils

froze [frəuz] pt of **freeze**

frozen ['frəuzn] pp of **freeze** ▷ adj (food) congelé(e); (person, also assets) gelé(e)

fruit [fru:t] n (pl inv) fruit m; **fruit juice** n jus m de fruit; **fruit machine** n (BRIT) machine f à sous; **fruit salad** n salade f de fruits

frustrate [frʌs'treɪt] vt frustrer; **frustrated** adj frustré(e)

fry (pt, pp **fried**) [fraɪ, -d] vt (faire) frire ▷ n: **small ~** le menu fretin; **frying pan** n poêle f (à frire)

ft. abbr = **foot; feet**

fudge [fʌdʒ] n (Culin) sorte de confiserie à base de sucre, de beurre et de lait

fuel [fjuəl] n (for heating) combustible m; (for engine) carburant m; **fuel tank** n (in vehicle) réservoir m de or à carburant

fulfil, (us) **fulfill** [ful'fɪl] vt (function, condition) remplir; (order) exécuter; (wish, desire) satisfaire, réaliser

full [ful] adj plein(e); (details, hotel, bus) complet(-ète); (busy: day) chargé(e); (skirt) ample, large ▷ adv: **to know ~ well that** savoir fort bien que; **I'm ~ (up)** j'ai trop mangé; **~ employment/ fare** plein emploi/tarif; **a ~ two hours** deux bonnes heures; **at ~ speed** à toute vitesse; **in ~** (reproduce, quote, pay) intégralement; (write name etc) en toutes lettres; **full-length** adj (portrait) en pied; (coat) long(ue); **full-length film** long métrage; **full moon** n pleine lune; **full-scale** adj (model) grandeur nature inv; (search, retreat) complet(-ète), total(e); **full stop** n point m; **full-time** adj, adv (work) à plein temps; **fully** adv entièrement, complètement

fumble ['fʌmbl] vi fouiller, farfouiller, tâtonner; **fumble with** vt fus tripoter

fume [fju:m] vi (rage) rager; **fumes** [fju:mz] npl vapeurs fpl, émanations fpl, gaz mpl

fun [fʌn] n amusement m, divertissement m; **to have ~** s'amuser; **for ~** pour rire; **to make ~ of** se moquer de

function ['fʌŋkʃən] n fonction f; (reception, dinner) cérémonie f, soirée officielle f ▷ vi fonctionner

fund [fʌnd] n caisse f, fonds m; (source, store) source f, mine f; **funds** npl (money) fonds mpl

fundamental [fʌndə'mentl] adj fondamental(e)

funeral ['fju:nərəl] n enterrement m, obsèques fpl (more formal occasion); **funeral director** n entrepreneur m des pompes funèbres; **funeral parlour** n (BRIT) dépôt m mortuaire

funfair ['fʌnfeə'] n (BRIT) fête (foraine)

fungus (pl **fungi**) ['fʌŋgəs, -gaɪ] n champignon m; (mould) moisissure f

funnel ['fʌnl] n entonnoir m; (of ship) cheminée f

funny ['fʌnɪ] adj amusant(e), drôle; (strange) curieux(-euse), bizarre

fur [fə:'] n fourrure f; (BRIT: in kettle etc) (dépôt m de) tartre m; **fur coat** n manteau m de fourrure

furious ['fjuərɪəs] adj furieux(-euse); (effort) acharné(e)

furnish ['fə:nɪʃ] vt meubler; (supply) fournir; **furnishings** npl mobilier m, articles mpl d'ameublement

furniture ['fə:nɪtʃə'] n meubles mpl, mobilier m; **piece of ~** meuble m

furry ['fə:rɪ] adj (animal) à fourrure; (toy) en peluche

further ['fə:ðə'] adj supplémentaire, autre; nouveau (nouvelle) ▷ adv plus loin; (more) davantage; (moreover) de plus ▷ vt faire avancer or progresser, promouvoir; **further education** n enseignement m postscolaire (recyclage, formation professionnelle); **furthermore** adv de plus, en outre

furthest ['fə:ðɪst] superlative of **far**

fury ['fjuərɪ] n fureur f

fuse, (US) **fuze** [fjuːz] n fusible m;
(for bomb etc) amorce f, détonateur m
▷ vt, vi (metal) fondre; (BRIT Elec): **to
~ the lights** faire sauter les fusibles
or les plombs; **fuse box** n boîte f à
fusibles

fusion ['fjuːʒən] n fusion f

fuss [fʌs] n (anxiety, excitement) chichis
mpl, façons fpl; (commotion) tapage m;
(complaining, trouble) histoire(s) f(pl);
to make a ~ faire des façons (or des
histoires); **to make a ~ of sb** dorloter
qn; **fussy** adj (person) tatillon(ne),
difficile, chichiteux(-euse); (dress,
style) tarabiscoté(e)

future ['fjuːtʃə*] adj futur(e) ▷ n
avenir m; (Ling) futur m; **futures** npl
(Comm) opérations fpl à terme; **in
(the) ~** à l'avenir

fuze [fjuːz] n, vt, vi (US) = **fuse**

fuzzy ['fʌzɪ] adj (Phot) flou(e); (hair)
crépu(e)

FYI abbr = **for your information**

g

G [dʒiː] n (Mus) sol m

g. abbr (= gram) g

gadget ['gædʒɪt] n gadget m

Gaelic ['geɪlɪk] adj, n (Ling) gaélique
(m)

gag [gæg] n (on mouth) bâillon m; (joke)
gag m ▷ vt (prisoner etc) bâillonner

gain [geɪn] n (improvement) gain m;
(profit) gain, profit m ▷ vt gagner
▷ vi (watch) avancer; **to ~ from/by**
gagner de/à; **to ~ on sb** (catch up)
rattraper qn; **to ~ 3lbs (in weight)**
prendre 3 livres; **to ~ ground** gagner
du terrain

gal. abbr = **gallon**

gala ['gɑːlə] n gala m

galaxy ['gæləksɪ] n galaxie f

gale [geɪl] n coup m de vent

gall bladder ['gɔːl-] n vésicule f
biliaire

gallery ['gælərɪ] n (also: **art ~**) musée
m; (private) galerie; (in theatre) dernier
balcon

gallon | 412

gallon ['gælən] n gallon m (Brit = 4.543 l; US = 3.785 l)

gallop ['gæləp] n galop m ▷ vi galoper

gallstone ['gɔːlstəun] n calcul m (biliaire)

gamble ['gæmbl] n pari m, risque calculé ▷ vt, vi jouer; **to ~ on** (fig) miser sur; **gambler** n joueur m; **gambling** n jeu m

game [geɪm] n jeu m; (event) match m; (of tennis, chess, cards) partie f; (Hunting) gibier m ▷ adj (willing): **to be ~ (for)** être prêt(e) (à or pour); **games** npl (Scol) sport m; (sport event) jeux; **big ~** gros gibier; **games console** ['geɪmz-] n console f de jeux vidéo; **game show** n jeu télévisé

gammon ['gæmən] n (bacon) quartier m de lard fumé; (ham) jambon fumé or salé

gang [gæŋ] n bande f; (of workmen) équipe f

gangster ['gæŋstər] n gangster m

gap [gæp] n trou m; (in time) intervalle m; (difference): **~ (between)** écart m (entre)

gape [geɪp] vi (person) être or rester bouche bée; (hole, shirt) être ouvert(e)

gap year n année f que certains étudiants prennent pour voyager ou pour travailler avant d'entrer à l'université

garage ['gærɑːʒ] n garage m; **garage sale** n vide-grenier m

garbage ['gɑːbɪdʒ] n (us: rubbish) ordures fpl, détritus mpl; (inf: nonsense) âneries fpl; **garbage can** n (us) poubelle f, boîte f à ordures; **garbage collector** n (us) éboueur m

garden ['gɑːdn] n jardin m; **gardens** npl (public) jardin public; (private) parc m; **garden centre** n pépinière f, jardinerie f; **gardener** n jardinier m; **gardening** n jardinage m

garlic ['gɑːlɪk] n ail m

garment ['gɑːmənt] n vêtement m

garnish ['gɑːnɪʃ] (Culin) vt garnir ▷ n décoration f

gas [gæs] n gaz m; (us: gasoline) essence f ▷ vt asphyxier; **I can**

smell ~ ça sent le gaz; **gas cooker** n (Brit) cuisinière f à gaz; **gas cylinder** n bouteille f de gaz; **gas fire** n (Brit) radiateur m à gaz

gasket ['gæskɪt] n (Aut) joint m de culasse

gasoline ['gæsəliːn] n (us) essence f

gasp [gɑːsp] n halètement m; (of shock etc): **she gave a small ~ of pain** la douleur lui coupa le souffle ▷ vi haleter; (fig) avoir le souffle coupé

gas: gas pedal n (us) accélérateur m; **gas station** n (us) station-service f; **gas tank** n (us Aut) réservoir m d'essence

gastric band ['gæstrɪk-] n anneau m gastrique

gate [geɪt] n (of garden) portail m; (of field, at level crossing) barrière f; (of building, town, at airport) porte f

gateau (pl **gateaux**) ['gætəu, -z] n gros gâteau à la crème

gatecrash ['geɪtkræʃ] vt s'introduire sans invitation dans

gateway ['geɪtweɪ] n porte f

gather ['gæðər] vt (flowers, fruit) cueillir; (pick up) ramasser; (assemble: objects) rassembler; (: people) réunir; (: information) recueillir; (understand) comprendre; (Sewing) froncer ▷ vi (assemble) se rassembler; **to ~ speed** prendre de la vitesse; **gathering** n rassemblement m

gauge [geɪdʒ] n (instrument) jauge f ▷ vt jauger; (fig) juger de

gave [geɪv] pt of **give**

gay [geɪ] adj homosexuel(le); (colour) gai, vif (vive)

gaze [geɪz] n regard m fixe ▷ vi: **to ~ at** fixer du regard

GB abbr = **Great Britain**

GCSE n abbr (Brit: = General Certificate of Secondary Education) examen passé à l'âge de 16 ans sanctionnant les connaissances de l'élève

gear [gɪər] n matériel m, équipement m; (Tech) engrenage m; (Aut) vitesse f

f ▷ vt (fig: adapt) adapter; **top** or
(US) **high/low~** quatrième (or
cinquième)/première vitesse; **in ~** en
prise; **gear up** vi: **to ~ up (to do)** se
préparer (à faire); **gear box** n boîte
f de vitesse; **gear lever** n levier m de
vitesse; **gear shift** (US), **gear stick**
(BRIT) n = **gear lever**

geese [giːs] n pl of **goose**

gel [dʒel] n gelée f

gem [dʒem] n pierre précieuse

Gemini ['dʒemɪnaɪ] n les Gémeaux
mpl

gender ['dʒendə'] n genre m; (person's
sex) sexe m

gene [dʒiːn] n (Biol) gène m

general ['dʒenərl] n général m
▷ adj général(e); **in ~** en général;
general anaesthetic, (US)
general anesthetic n anesthésie
générale; **general election** n
élection(s) législative(s); **generalize**
vi généraliser; **generally** adv
généralement; **general practitioner**
n généraliste m/f; **general store** n
épicerie f

generate ['dʒenəreɪt] vt engendrer;
(electricity) produire

generation [dʒenə'reɪʃən] n
génération f; (of electricity etc)
production f

generator ['dʒenəreɪtə'] n
générateur m

generosity [dʒenə'rɒsɪtɪ] n
générosité f

generous ['dʒenərəs] adj
généreux(-euse); (copious)
copieux(-euse)

Geneva [dʒɪ'niːvə] n Genève

genitals ['dʒenɪtlz] npl organes
génitaux

genius ['dʒiːnɪəs] n génie m

genome ['dʒiːnəʊm] n génome m

gent [dʒent] n abbr (BRIT inf)
= **gentleman**

gentle ['dʒentl] adj doux (douce);
(breeze, chide) léger(-ère)

gentleman ['dʒentlmən] (irreg)
n monsieur m; (well-bred man)
gentleman m

gently ['dʒentlɪ] adv doucement

gents [dʒents] n W.-C. mpl (pour
hommes)

genuine ['dʒenjuɪn] adj véritable,
authentique; (person, emotion)
sincère; **genuinely** adv sincèrement,
vraiment

geographic(al) [dʒɪə'ɡræfɪk(-l)-] adj
géographique

geography [dʒɪ'ɒɡrəfɪ] n
géographie f

geology [dʒɪ'ɒlədʒɪ] n géologie f

geometry [dʒɪ'ɒmətrɪ] n géométrie f

geranium [dʒɪ'reɪnɪəm] n
géranium m

geriatric [dʒerɪ'ætrɪk] adj
gériatrique ▷ n patient(e) gériatrique

germ [dʒɜːm] n (Med) microbe m

German ['dʒɜːmən] adj allemand(e)
▷ n Allemand(e); (Ling) allemand m;
German measles n rubéole f

Germany ['dʒɜːmənɪ] n Allemagne f

gesture ['dʒestjə'] n geste m

g

○ **KEYWORD**

get [ɡet] (pt, pp **got**, (US) pp **gotten**)
vi **1** (become, be) devenir; **to get old/
tired** devenir vieux/fatigué, vieillir/se
fatiguer; **to get drunk** s'enivrer; **to
get dirty** se salir; **to get married** se
marier; **when do I get paid?** quand
est-ce que je serai payé?; **it's getting
late** il se fait tard

2 (go): **to get to/from** aller à/de;
to get home rentrer chez soi; **how
did you get here?** comment es-tu
arrivé ici?

3 (begin) commencer or se mettre
à; **to get to know sb** apprendre à

connaître qn; **I'm getting to like him** je commence à l'apprécier; **let's get going** or **started** allons-y

4 (modal aux vb): **you've got to do it** il faut que vous le fassiez; **I've got to tell the police** je dois le dire à la police

▶ vt **1**: **to get sth done** (do) faire qch; (have done) faire faire qch; **to get sth/sb ready** préparer qch/qn; **to get one's hair cut** se faire couper les cheveux; **to get the car going** or **to go** (faire) démarrer la voiture; **to get sb to do sth** faire faire qch à qn

2 (obtain: money, permission, results) obtenir, avoir; (buy) acheter; (find: job, flat) trouver; (fetch: person, doctor, object) aller chercher; **to get sth for sb** procurer qch à qn; **get me Mr Jones, please** (on phone) passez-moi Mr Jones, s'il vous plaît; **can I get you a drink?** est-ce que je peux vous servir à boire?

3 (receive: present, letter) recevoir, avoir; (acquire: reputation) obtenir; **what did you get for your birthday?** qu'est-ce que tu as eu pour ton anniversaire?; **how much did you get for the painting?** combien avez-vous vendu le tableau?

4 (catch) prendre, saisir, attraper; (hit: target etc) atteindre; **to get sb by the arm/throat** prendre or saisir or attraper qn par le bras/à la gorge; **get him!** arrête-le!; **the bullet got him in the leg** il a pris la balle dans la jambe

5 (take, move): **to get sth to sb** faire parvenir qch à qn; **do you think we'll get it through the door?** on arrivera à la faire passer par la porte?

6 (catch, take: plane, bus etc) prendre; **where do I get the train for Birmingham?** où prend-on le train pour Birmingham?

7 (understand) comprendre, saisir; (hear) entendre; **I've got it!** j'ai compris!; **I don't get your meaning**

je ne vois or comprends pas ce que vous voulez dire; **I didn't get your name** je n'ai pas entendu votre nom

8 (have, possess): **to have got** avoir; **how many have you got?** vous en avez combien?

9 (illness) avoir? **I've got a cold** j'ai le rhume; **she got pneumonia and died** elle a fait une pneumonie et elle en est morte

get away vi partir, s'en aller; (escape) s'échapper

get away with vt fus (punishment) en être quitte pour; (crime etc) se faire pardonner

get back vi (return) rentrer ▶ vt récupérer, recouvrer; **when do we get back?** quand serons-nous de retour?

get in vi entrer; (arrive home) rentrer; (train) arriver

get into vt fus entrer dans; (car, train etc) monter dans; (clothes) mettre, enfiler, endosser; **to get into bed/a rage** se mettre au lit/en colère

get off vi (from train etc) descendre; (depart: person, car) s'en aller ▶ vt (remove: clothes, stain) enlever ▶ vt fus (train, bus) descendre de; **where do I get off?** où est-ce que je dois descendre?

get on vi (at exam etc) se débrouiller; (agree): **to get on (with)** s'entendre (avec); **how are you getting on?** comment ça va? ▶ vt fus monter dans; (horse) monter sur

get out vi sortir; (of vehicle) descendre ▶ vt sortir

get out of vt fus sortir de; (duty etc) échapper à, se soustraire à

get over vt fus (illness) se remettre de

get through vi (Tel) avoir la communication; **to get through to sb** atteindre qn

get up vi (rise) se lever ▶ vt fus monter

getaway ['gɛtəweɪ] n fuite f

Ghana ['gɑːnə] n Ghana m

ghastly ['gɑːstlɪ] adj atroce, horrible

ghetto ['gɛtəu] n ghetto m

ghost [gəust] n fantôme m, revenant m

giant ['dʒaɪənt] n géant(e) ▷ adj géant(e), énorme

gift [gɪft] n cadeau m; (donation, talent) don m; **gifted** adj doué(e); **gift shop**, (us) **gift store** n boutique f de cadeaux; **gift token**, **gift voucher** n chèque-cadeau m

gig [gɪg] n (inf: concert) concert m

gigabyte ['dʒɪgəbaɪt] n gigaoctet m

gigantic [dʒaɪˈgæntɪk] adj gigantesque

giggle ['gɪgl] vi pouffer, ricaner sottement

gills [gɪlz] npl (of fish) ouïes fpl, branchies fpl

gilt [gɪlt] n dorure f ▷ adj doré(e)

gimmick ['gɪmɪk] n truc m

gin [dʒɪn] n gin m

ginger ['dʒɪndʒə'] n gingembre m

gipsy ['dʒɪpsɪ] n = **gypsy**

giraffe [dʒɪˈrɑːf] n girafe f

girl [gəːl] n fille f, fillette f; (young unmarried woman) jeune fille; (daughter) fille; **an English** ~ une jeune Anglaise; **girl band** n girls band m; **girlfriend** n (of girl) amie f; (of boy) petite amie; **Girl Guide** n (BRIT) éclaireuse f; (Roman Catholic) guide f; **Girl Scout** n (US) = **Girl Guide**

gist [dʒɪst] n essentiel m

give [gɪv] (pt **gave**, pp **given**) vt donner à vi (break) céder; (stretch: fabric) se prêter; **to ~ sb sth**, **~ sth to sb** donner qch à qn; (gift) offrir qch à qn; (message) transmettre qch à qn; **to ~ sb a call/kiss** appeler/embrasser qn; **to ~ a cry/sigh** pousser un cri/un soupir; **give away** vt donner; (give free) faire cadeau de; (betray) donner, trahir; (disclose) révéler; **give back** vt rendre; **give in** vi céder ▷ vt donner; **give out** vt (food etc) distribuer; **give up** vi

renoncer ▷ vt renoncer à; **to ~ up smoking** arrêter de fumer; **to ~ o.s. up** se rendre

given ['gɪvn] pp of **give** ▷ adj (fixed: time, amount) donné(e), déterminé(e) ▷ conj: **~ the circumstances ...** étant donné les circonstances ..., vu les circonstances ...; **~ that ...** étant donné que ...

glacier ['glæsɪə'] n glacier m

glad [glæd] adj content(e); **gladly** ['glædlɪ] adv volontiers

glamorous ['glæmərəs] adj (person) séduisant(e); (job) prestigieux(-euse)

glamour, (US) **glamor** ['glæmə'] n éclat m, prestige m

glance [glɑːns] n coup m d'œil ▷ vi: **to ~** jeter un coup d'œil à

gland [glænd] n glande f

glare [glɛə'] n (of anger) regard furieux; (of light) lumière éblouissante; (of publicity) feux mpl ▷ vi briller d'un éclat aveuglant; **to ~** lancer un regard ardes regards furieux à; **glaring** adj (mistake) criant(e), qui saute aux yeux

glass [glɑːs] n verre m; **glasses** npl (spectacles) lunettes fpl

glaze [gleɪz] vt (door) vitrer; (pottery) vernir ▷ n vernis m

gleam [gliːm] vi luire, briller

glen [glɛn] n vallée f

glide [glaɪd] vi glisser; (Aviat, bird) planer; **glider** n (Aviat) planeur m

glimmer ['glɪmə'] n lueur f

glimpse [glɪmps] n vision passagère, aperçu m ▷ vt entrevoir, apercevoir

glint [glɪnt] vi étinceler

glisten ['glɪsn] vi briller, luire

glitter ['glɪtə'] vi scintiller, briller

global ['gləubl] adj (world-wide) mondial(e); (overall) global(e); **globalization** n mondialisation f; **global warming** n réchauffement m de la planète

globe [gləub] n globe m

gloom [gluːm] n obscurité f; (sadness) tristesse f, mélancolie f; **gloomy**

adj (*person*) morose; (*place, outlook*) sombre

glorious ['glɔːrɪəs] *adj* glorieux(-euse); (*beautiful*) splendide

glory ['glɔːrɪ] *n* gloire *f*; splendeur *f*

gloss [glɒs] *n* (*shine*) brillant *m*, vernis *m*; (*also:* **~ paint**) peinture brillante

glossary ['glɒsərɪ] *n* glossaire *m*, lexique *m*

glossy ['glɒsɪ] *adj* brillant(e), luisant(e) ▷ *n* (*also:* **~ magazine**) revue *f* de luxe

glove [glʌv] *n* gant *m*; **glove compartment** *n* (*Aut*) boîte *f* à gants, vide-poches *m inv*

glow [gləʊ] *vi* rougeoyer; (*face*) rayonner; (*eyes*) briller

glucose ['gluːkəʊs] *n* glucose *m*

glue [gluː] *n* colle *f* ▷ *vt* coller

GM *abbr* (= *genetically modified*) génétiquement modifié(e)

gm *abbr* (= *gram*) g

GM crop *n* culture *f* OGM

GMO *n abbr* (= *genetically modified organism*) OGM *m inv*

GMT *abbr* (= *Greenwich Mean Time*) GMT

gnaw [nɔː] *vt* ronger

go [gəʊ] (*pt* **went**, *pp* **gone**) *vi* aller; (*depart*) partir, s'en aller; (*work*) marcher; (*break*) céder; (*time*) passer; (*be sold*): **to go for £10** se vendre 10 livres; (*become*): **to go pale/mouldy** pâlir/moisir ▷ *n* (*pl* **goes**): **to have a go (at)** essayer (de faire); **to be on the go** être en mouvement; **whose go is it?** à qui est-ce de jouer?; **he's going to do it** il va le faire, il est sur le point de le faire; **to go for a walk** aller se promener; **to go dancing/shopping** aller danser/faire les courses; **to go and see sb, to go to see sb** aller voir qn; **how did it go?** comment est-ce que ça s'est passé?; **to go round the back/by the shop** passer par derrière/devant le magasin; **... to go** (*us: food*) ... à emporter; **go ahead** *vi* (*take place*) avoir lieu; (*get going*) y aller; **go away**

vi partir, s'en aller; **go back** *vi* rentrer; revenir; (*go again*) retourner; **go by** *vi* (*years, time*) passer, s'écouler ▷ *vt fus* s'en tenir à; (*believe*) en croire; **go down** *vi* descendre; (*number, price, amount*) baisser; (*ship*) couler; (*sun*) se coucher ▷ *vt fus* descendre; **go for** *vt fus* (*fetch*) aller chercher; (*like*) aimer; (*attack*) s'en prendre à; attaquer; **go in** *vi* entrer; **go into** *vt fus* entrer dans; (*investigate*) étudier, examiner; (*embark on*) se lancer dans; **go off** *vi* partir, s'en aller; (*food*) se gâter; (*milk*) tourner; (*bomb*) sauter; (*alarm clock*) sonner; (*alarm*) se déclencher; (*lights etc*) s'éteindre; (*event*) se dérouler ▷ *vt fus* ne plus aimer; **the gun went off** le coup est parti; **go on** *vi* continuer; (*happen*) se passer; (*lights*) s'allumer ▷ *vt fus* **to go on doing** continuer à faire; **go out** *vi* sortir; (*fire, light*) s'éteindre; (*tide*) descendre; **go out with sb** sortir avec qn; **go over** *vi, vt fus* (*check*) revoir, vérifier; **go past** *vt fus*: **to go past sth** passer devant qch; **go round** *vi* (*circulate: news, rumour*) circuler; (*revolve*) tourner; (*suffice*) suffire (pour tout le monde); (*visit*): **to go round to sb's** passer chez qn; aller chez qn; (*make a detour*): **to go round (by)** faire un détour (par); **go through** *vt fus* (*town etc*) traverser; (*search through*) fouiller; (*suffer*) subir; **go up** *vi* monter; (*price*) augmenter ▷ *vt fus* gravir; **go with** *vt fus* aller avec; **go without** *vt fus* se passer de

go-ahead ['gəʊəhɛd] *adj* dynamique, entreprenant(e) ▷ *n* feu vert

goal [gəʊl] *n* but *m*; **goalkeeper** *n* gardien *m* de but; **goal-post** *n* poteau *m* de but

goat [gəʊt] *n* chèvre *f*

gobble ['gɒbl] *vt* (*also:* **~ down, ~ up**) engloutir

god [gɒd] *n* dieu *m*; **God** Dieu; **godchild** *n* filleul(e); **goddaughter**

n filleule *f*; **goddess** *n* déesse *f*;
godfather *n* parrain *m*; **godmother**
n marraine *f*; **godson** *n* filleul *m*

going ['gəʊɪŋ] *n* (*conditions*) état *m*
du terrain ▷ *adj*: **the ~ rate** le tarif
(en vigueur)

gold [gəʊld] *n* or *m* ▷ *adj* (*watch*,
(*reserves*) d'or; **golden** *adj* (*made of
gold*) en or; (*in colour*) doré(e);
goldfish *n* poisson *m* rouge;
goldmine *n* mine *f* d'or; **gold-plated**
adj plaqué(e) or *inv*

golf [gɒlf] *n* golf *m*; **golf ball** *n* balle
f de golf; (*on typewriter*) boule *f*; **golf
club** *n* club *m* de golf; (*stick*) club *m*,
crosse *f* de golf; **golf course** *n* terrain
m de golf; **golfer** *n* joueur(-euse)
de golf

gone [gɒn] *pp of* **go**

gong [gɒŋ] *n* gong *m*

good [gʊd] *adj* bon(ne); (*kind*)
gentil(le); (*child*) sage; (*weather*)
beau (belle) ▷ *n* bien *m*; **goods** *npl*
marchandise *f*, articles *mpl*; **~!** bon!,
très bien!; **to be ~ at** être bon en;
to be ~ for être bon pour; **it's no
~ complaining** cela ne sert à rien
de se plaindre; **to make ~** (*deficit*)
combler; (*losses*) compenser; **for ~**
(*for ever*) pour de bon, une fois pour
toutes; **would you be ~ enough to
...?** auriez-vous la bonté or l'amabilité
de ...?; **is this any ~?** (*will it do?*)
est-ce que cela fera l'affaire?, est-ce
que cela peut vous rendre service?;
(*what's it like?*) qu'est-ce que ça vaut?;
a ~ deal (of) beaucoup (de); **a ~
many** beaucoup (de); **~ morning/
afternoon!** bonjour!; **~ evening!**
bonsoir!; **~ night!** bonsoir!; (*on going
to bed*) bonne nuit!; **goodbye** *excl* au
revoir!; **to say goodbye to sb** dire au
revoir à qn; **Good Friday** *n* Vendredi
saint; **good-looking** *adj* beau (belle),
bien *inv*; **good-natured** *adj* (*person*)

qui a un bon naturel; **goodness** *n* (*of
person*) bonté *f*; **for goodness sake!**
je vous en prie!; **goodness gracious!**
mon Dieu!; **goods train** *n* (BRIT)
train *m* de marchandises; **goodwill** *n*
bonne volonté

google ['gu:gl] *vi* faire une recheche
Google® ▷ *vt* googler

goose (*pl* **geese**) [gu:s, gi:s] *n* oie *f*

gooseberry ['gʊzbərɪ] *n* groseille *f*
à maquereau; **to play ~** (BRIT) tenir
la chandelle

goose bumps, goose pimples
npl chair *f* de poule

gorge [gɔ:dʒ] *n* gorge *f* ▷ *vt*: **to ~ o.s.
(on)** se gorger (de)

gorgeous ['gɔ:dʒəs] *adj* splendide,
superbe

gorilla [gə'rɪlə] *n* gorille *m*

gosh [gɒʃ] (*inf*) *excl* mince alors!

gospel ['gɒspl] *n* évangile *m*

gossip ['gɒsɪp] *n* (*chat*) bavardages
mpl; (*malicious*) commérage *m*,
cancans *mpl*; (*person*) commère
f ▷ *vi* bavarder; cancaner, faire des
commérages; **gossip column** *n*
(*Press*) échos *mpl*

got [gɒt] *pt, pp of* **get**

gotten ['gɒtn] (*us*) *pp of* **get**

gourmet ['gʊəmeɪ] *n* gourmet *m*,
gastronome *m/f*

govern ['gʌvən] *vt* gouverner;
(*influence*) déterminer; **government**
n gouvernement *m*; (BRIT: *ministers*)
ministère *m*; **governor** *n* (*of colony,
state, bank*) gouverneur *m*; (*of school,
hospital etc*) administrateur(-trice);
(BRIT: *of prison*) directeur(-trice)

gown [gaʊn] *n* robe *f*; (*of teacher*, BRIT:
of judge) toge *f*

GP *n abbr* (*Med*) = **general
practitioner**

GPS *n abbr* (= *global positioning system*)
GPS *m*

grab [græb] *vt* saisir, empoigner ▷ *vi*:
to ~ at essayer de saisir

grace [greɪs] *n* grâce *f* ▷ *vt* (*honour*)
honorer; (*adorn*) orner; **5 days'**

~ un répit de 5 jours; **graceful** adj
gracieux(-euse), élégant(e); **gracious**
['greɪʃəs] adj bienveillant(e)

grade [greɪd] n (Comm: quality)
qualité f; (: size) calibre m; (: type)
catégorie f; (in hierarchy) grade m,
échelon m; (Scol) note f; (US: school
class) classe f; (: gradient) pente f
▷ vt classer; (by size) calibrer; **grade
crossing** n (US) passage m à niveau;
grade school n (US) école f primaire

gradient ['greɪdɪənt] n inclinaison
f, pente f

gradual ['grædjuəl] adj graduel(le),
progressif(-ive); **gradually** adv peu à
peu, graduellement

graduate n ['grædjuət] diplômé(e)
d'université; (us: of high school)
diplômé(e) de fin d'études ▷ vi
['grædjueɪt] obtenir un diplôme
d'université or de fin d'études);
graduation [grædju'eɪʃən] n
cérémonie f de remise des diplômes

graffiti [grə'fi:tɪ] npl graffiti mpl

graft [grɑ:ft] n (Agr, Med) greffe f;
(bribery) corruption f ▷ vt greffer;
hard ~ (BRIT inf) boulot acharné

grain [greɪn] n (single piece) grain
m; (no pl: cereals) céréales fpl; (us:
corn) blé m

gram [græm] n gramme m

grammar ['græmə'] n grammaire f;
grammar school n (BRIT) ≈ lycée m

gramme [græm] n = **gram**

gran [græn] (inf) (BRIT) mamie f (inf),
mémé f (inf)

grand [grænd] adj magnifique,
splendide; (gesture etc) noble;
grandad n (inf) = **granddad**;
grandchild (pl **grandchildren**)
n petit-fils m, petite-fille f;
grandchildren npl petits-enfants;
granddad n (inf) papy m (inf), papi m
(inf), pépé m (inf); **granddaughter** n
petite-fille f; **grandfather** n grand-
père m; **grandma** n (inf) = **gran**;
grandmother n grand-mère f;
grandpa n (inf) = **granddad**;

grandparents npl grands-parents
mpl; **grand piano** n piano m à queue;
Grand Prix ['grɑ̃'pri:] n (Aut)
grand prix automobile; **grandson** n
petit-fils m

granite ['grænɪt] n granit m

granny ['grænɪ] n (inf) = **gran**

grant [grɑ:nt] vt accorder; (a request)
accéder à; (admit) concéder ▷ n
(Scol) bourse f; (Admin) subside m,
subvention f; **to take sth for ~ed**
considérer qch comme acquis;
to take sb for ~ed considérer qn
comme faisant partie du décor

grape [greɪp] n raisin m

grapefruit ['greɪpfru:t] n
pamplemousse m

graph [grɑ:f] n graphique m, courbe
f; **graphic** ['græfɪk] adj graphique;
(vivid) vivant(e); **graphics** n (art) arts
mpl graphiques; (process) graphisme
m ▷ npl (drawings) illustrations fpl

grasp [grɑ:sp] vt saisir ▷ n (grip)
prise f; (fig) compréhension f,
connaissance f

grass [grɑ:s] n herbe f; (lawn) gazon
m; **grasshopper** n sauterelle f

grate [greɪt] n grille f de cheminée
▷ vi grincer ▷ vt (Culin) râper

grateful ['greɪtful] adj
reconnaissant(e)

grater ['greɪtə'] n râpe f

gratitude ['grætɪtju:d] n gratitude f

grave [greɪv] n tombe f ▷ adj grave,
sérieux(-euse)

gravel ['grævl] n gravier m

gravestone ['greɪvstəun] n pierre
tombale

graveyard ['greɪvjɑ:d] n
cimetière m

gravity ['grævɪtɪ] n (Physics) gravité f,
pesanteur f; (seriousness) gravité

gravy ['greɪvɪ] n jus m (de viande),
sauce f (au jus de viande)

gray [greɪ] adj (US) = **grey**

graze [greɪz] vi paître, brouter ▷ vt
(touch lightly) frôler, effleurer; (scrape)
écorcher ▷ n écorchure f

grease [gri:s] n (fat) graisse f; (lubricant) lubrifiant m ⊳ vt graisser; lubrifier; **greasy** adj gras(se), graisseux(-euse); (hands, clothes) graisseux

great [greɪt] adj grand(e); (heat, pain etc) très fort(e), intense; (inf) formidable; **Great Britain** n Grande-Bretagne f; **great-grandfather** n arrière-grand-père m; **great-grandmother** n arrière-grand-mère f; **greatly** adv très, grandement; (with verbs) beaucoup

Greece [gri:s] n Grèce f

greed [gri:d] n (also: ~iness) avidité f; (for food) gourmandise f; **greedy** adj avide; (for food) gourmand(e)

Greek [gri:k] adj grec (grecque) ⊳ n Grec (Grecque); (Ling) grec m

green [gri:n] adj vert(e); (inexperienced) jeune, naïf(-ïve); (ecological: product etc) écologique ⊳ n (colour) vert m; (on golf course) green m; (stretch of grass) pelouse f; **greens** npl (vegetables) légumes verts; **green card** n (Aut) carte verte; (us: work permit) permis m de travail; **greengage** n (fruit) reine-claude f; **greengrocer** n (BRIT) marchand m de fruits et légumes; **greengrocer's (shop)** n magasin m de fruits et légumes; **greenhouse** n serre f; **the greenhouse effect** l'effet m de serre

Greenland ['gri:nlənd] n Groenland m

green salad n salade verte

green tax n écotaxe f

greet [gri:t] vt accueillir; **greeting** n salutation f; **Christmas/birthday greetings** souhaits mpl de Noël/de bon anniversaire; **greeting(s) card** n carte f de vœux

grew [gru:] pt of **grow**

grey, (us) gray [greɪ] adj gris(e); (dismal) sombre; **grey-haired, (us) gray-haired** adj aux cheveux gris; **greyhound** n lévrier m

grid [grɪd] n grille f; (Elec) réseau m; **gridlock** n (traffic jam) embouteillage m

grief [gri:f] n chagrin m, douleur f

grievance ['gri:vəns] n doléance f, grief m; (cause for complaint) grief

grieve [gri:v] vi avoir du chagrin; se désoler ⊳ vt faire de la peine à, affliger; **to ~ for sb** pleurer qn

grill [grɪl] n (on cooker) gril m; (also: **mixed ~**) grillade(s) f(pl) ⊳ vt (Culin) griller; (inf: question) cuisiner

grille [grɪl] n grillage m; (Aut) calandre f

grim [grɪm] adj sinistre, lugubre; (serious, stern) sévère

grime [graɪm] n crasse f

grin [grɪn] n large sourire m ⊳ vi sourire

grind [graɪnd] (pt, pp **ground**) vt écraser; (coffee, pepper etc) moudre; (us: meat) hacher ⊳ n (work) corvée f

grip [grɪp] n (handclasp) poigne f; (control) prise f; (handle) poignée f; (holdall) sac m de voyage ⊳ vt saisir, empoigner; (viewer, reader) captiver; **to come to ~s with** se colleter avec, en venir aux prises avec; **to ~ the road** (Aut) adhérer à la route; **gripping** adj prenant(e), palpitant(e)

grit [grɪt] n gravillon m; (courage) cran m ⊳ vt (road) sabler; **to ~ one's teeth** serrer les dents

grits [grɪts] npl (us) gruau m de maïs

groan [grəun] n (of pain) gémissement m ⊳ vi gémir

grocer ['grəusə'] n épicier m; **groceries** npl provisions fpl; **grocer's (shop), grocery** n épicerie f

groin [grɔɪn] n aine f

groom [gru:m] n (for horses) palefrenier m; (also: **bride~**) marié m ⊳ vt (horse) panser; (fig): **to ~ sb for** former qn pour

groove [gru:v] n sillon m, rainure f

grope [grəup] vi tâtonner; **to ~ for** chercher à tâtons

gross [grəus] adj grossier(-ière); (Comm) brut(e); **grossly** adv (greatly) très, grandement

grotesque [grə'tɛsk] adj grotesque

ground [graund] pt, pp of **grind** ▷ n sol m, terre f; (land) terrain m, terres fpl; (Sport) terrain m; (reason: gen pl) raison f; (us: also: ~ **wire**) terre f ▷ vt (plane) empêcher de décoller, retenir au sol; (us Elec) équiper d'une prise de terre; **grounds** npl (gardens etc) parc m, domaine m; (of coffee) marc m; **on the ~, to the ~** par terre; **to gain/lose ~** gagner/perdre du terrain; **ground floor** n (BRIT) rez-de-chaussée m; **groundsheet** n (BRIT) tapis m de sol; **groundwork** n préparation f

group [gru:p] n groupe m ▷ vt (also: ~ **together**) grouper ▷ vi (also: ~ **together**) se grouper

grouse [graus] n (pl inv: bird) grouse f (sorte de coq de bruyère) ▷ vi (complain) rouspéter, râler

grovel ['grɔvl] vi (fig): **to ~ (before)** ramper (devant)

grow (pt **grew**, pp **grown**) [grəu, gru:, grəun] vi (plant) pousser, croître; (person) grandir; (increase) augmenter, se développer; (become) devenir; **to ~ rich/weak** s'enrichir/ s'affaiblir ▷ vt cultiver, faire pousser; (hair, beard) laisser pousser; **grow on** vt fus: **that painting is ~ing on me** je finirai par aimer ce tableau; **grow up** vi grandir

growl [graul] vi grogner

grown [grəun] pp of **grow**; **grown-up** n adulte m/f, grande personne

growth [grəuθ] n croissance f, développement m; (what has grown) pousse f, poussée f; (Med) grosseur f, tumeur f

grub [grʌb] n larve f; (inf: food) bouffe f

grubby ['grʌbi] adj crasseux(-euse)

grudge [grʌdʒ] n rancune f ▷ vt: **to ~ sb sth** (in giving) donner qch à qn à contre-cœur; (resent) reprocher

qch à qn; **to bear sb a ~ (for)** garder rancune or en vouloir à qn (de)

gruelling, (us) **grueling** ['gruəlɪŋ] adj exténuant(e)

gruesome ['gru:səm] adj horrible

grumble ['grʌmbl] vi rouspéter, ronchonner

grumpy ['grʌmpɪ] adj grincheux(-euse)

grunt [grʌnt] vi grogner

guarantee [gærən'ti:] n garantie f ▷ vt garantir

guard [gɑ:d] n garde f; (one man) garde m; (BRIT Rail) chef m de train; (safety device: on machine) dispositif m de sûreté; (also: **fire~**) garde-feu m inv ▷ vt garder, surveiller; (protect): **to ~ sb/sth (against** or **from)** protéger qn/qch (contre); **to be on one's ~** (fig) être sur ses gardes; **guardian** n gardien(ne); (of minor) tuteur(-trice)

guerrilla [gə'rɪlə] n guérillero m

guess [gɛs] vi deviner ▷ vt deviner; (estimate) évaluer; (us) croire, penser ▷ n supposition f, hypothèse f; **to take** or **have a ~** essayer de deviner

guest [gɛst] n invité(e); (in hotel) client(e); **guest house** n pension f; **guest room** n chambre f d'amis

guidance ['gaɪdəns] n (advice) conseils mpl

guide [gaɪd] n (person) guide m/f; (book) guide m; (also: **Girl G~**) éclaireuse f; (Roman Catholic) guide f ▷ vt guider; **is there an English-speaking ~?** est-ce que l'un des guides parle anglais?; **guidebook** n guide m; **guide dog** n chien m d'aveugle; **guided tour** n visite guidée; **what time does the guided tour start?** la visite guidée commence à quelle heure?; **guidelines** npl (advice) instructions générales, conseils mpl

guild [gɪld] n (Hist) corporation f; (sharing interests) cercle m, association f

guilt [gɪlt] n culpabilité f; **guilty** adj coupable

guinea pig ['gɪnɪ-] n cobaye m

guitar [gɪ'tɑːʳ] n guitare f; **guitarist** n guitariste m/f

gulf [gʌlf] n golfe m; (abyss) gouffre m

gull [gʌl] n mouette f

gulp [gʌlp] vi avaler sa salive; (from emotion) avoir la gorge serrée, s'étrangler ▷ vt (also: **~ down**) avaler

gum [gʌm] n (Anat) gencive f; (glue) colle f; (also: **chewing-~**) chewing-gum m ▷ vt coller

gun [gʌn] n (small) revolver m, pistolet m; (rifle) fusil m, carabine f; (cannon) canon m; **gunfire** n fusillade f; **gunman** (irreg) n bandit armé; **gunpoint** n: **at gunpoint** sous la menace du pistolet (or fusil); **gunpowder** n poudre f à canon; **gunshot** n coup m de feu

gush [gʌʃ] vi jaillir; (fig) se répandre en effusions

gust [gʌst] n (of wind) rafale f

gut [gʌt] n intestin m, boyau m; **guts** npl (inf: Anat) boyaux mpl; (: courage) cran m

gutter ['gʌtəʳ] n (of roof) gouttière f; (in street) caniveau m

guy [gaɪ] n (inf: man) type m; (also: **~rope**) corde f; (figure) effigie de Guy Fawkes

Guy Fawkes' Night [gaɪ'fɔːks-] n voir article "Guy Fawkes' Night"

- **GUY FAWKES' NIGHT**
-
- Guy Fawkes' Night, que l'on appelle
- également "bonfire night",
- commémore l'échec du complot (le
- "Gunpowder Plot") contre James
- Ier et son parlement le 5 novembre
- 1605. L'un des conspirateurs, Guy
- Fawkes, avait été surpris dans
- les caves du parlement alors
- qu'il s'apprêtait à y mettre le feu.
- Chaque année pour le 5 novembre,
- les enfants préparent à l'avance

- une effigie de Guy Fawkes et ils
- demandent aux passants "un
- penny pour le guy" avec lequel ils
- pourront s'acheter des fusées de
- feu d'artifice. Beaucoup de gens
- font encore un feu dans leur jardin
- sur lequel ils brûlent le "guy".

gym [dʒɪm] n (also: **~nasium**) gymnase m; (also: **~nastics**) gym f; **gymnasium** n gymnase m; **gymnast** n gymnaste m/f; **gymnastics** n, npl gymnastique f; **gym shoes** npl chaussures fpl de gym(nastique)

gynaecologist, (us) **gynecologist** [gaɪnɪ'kɔlədʒɪst] n gynécologue m/f

gypsy ['dʒɪpsɪ] n gitan(e), bohémien(ne)

h

haberdashery [hæbə'dæʃərɪ] n (BRIT) mercerie f

habit ['hæbɪt] n habitude f; (costume: Rel) habit m

habitat ['hæbɪtæt] n habitat m

hack [hæk] vt hacher, tailler ▷ n (pej: writer) nègre m; **hacker** n (Comput) pirate m (informatique)

had [hæd] pt, pp of **have**

haddock ['hædək] n (pl **haddock** or **haddocks**) n églefin m; **smoked ~** haddock m

hadn't ['hædnt] = **had not**

haemorrhage, (US) **hemorrhage** ['hɛmərɪdʒ] n hémorragie f

haemorrhoids, (US) **hemorrhoids** ['hɛmərɔɪdz] npl hémorroïdes fpl

haggle ['hægl] vi marchander

Hague [heɪg] n: **The ~** La Haye

hail [heɪl] n grêle f ▷ vt (call) héler; (greet) acclamer ▷ vi grêler; **hailstone** n grêlon m

hair [hɛə'] n cheveux mpl; (on body) poils mpl; (of animal) pelage m; (single hair: on head) cheveu m; (: on body, of animal) poil m; **to do one's ~** se coiffer; **hairband** n (elasticated) bandeau m; (plastic) serre-tête m; **hairbrush** n brosse f à cheveux; **haircut** n coupe f (de cheveux); **hairdo** n coiffure f; **hairdresser** n coiffeur(-euse); **hairdresser's** n salon m de coiffure, coiffeur m; **hair dryer** n sèche-cheveux m, séchoir m; **hair gel** n gel m pour cheveux; **hair spray** n laque f (pour les cheveux); **hairstyle** n coiffure f; **hairy** adj poilu(e), chevelu(e); (inf: frightening) effrayant(e)

haka ['hɑːkə] n (NZ) haka m

hake [heɪk] n (pl **hake** or **hakes**) n colin m, merlu m

half [hɑːf] n (pl **halves**) moitié f; (of beer: also: **~ pint**) ≈ demi m; (Rail, bus: also: **~ fare**) demi-tarif m; (Sport: of match) mi-temps f ▷ adj demi(e) ▷ adv (à) moitié, à demi; **~ an hour** une demi-heure; **~ a dozen** une demi-douzaine; **~ a pound** une demi-livre, ≈ 250 g; **two and a ~** deux et demi; **to cut sth in ~** couper qch en deux; **half board** n (BRIT: in hotel) demi-pension f; **half-brother** n demi-frère m; **half day** n demi-journée f; **half fare** n demi-tarif m; **half-hearted** adj tiède, sans enthousiasme; **half-hour** n demi-heure f; **half-price** adj à moitié prix ▷ adv (also: **at half-price**) à moitié prix; **half term** n (BRIT Scol) vacances fpl (de demi-trimestre); **half-time** n mi-temps f; **halfway** adv à mi-chemin; **halfway through sth** au milieu de qch

hall [hɔːl] n salle f; (entrance way: big) hall m; (: small) entrée f; (us: corridor) couloir m; (mansion) château m, manoir m

hallmark ['hɔːlmɑːk] n poinçon m; (fig) marque f

hallo [hə'ləu] excl = **hello**

hall of residence n (BRIT) pavillon m or résidence f universitaire

Hallowe'en, Halloween ['hæləu'i:n] n veille f de la Toussaint

● **HALLOWE'EN**

● Selon la tradition, *Hallowe'en* est la nuit des fantômes et des sorcières. En Écosse et aux États-Unis surtout (et de plus en plus en Angleterre), pour fêter *Hallowe'en*, se déguisent ce soir-là et ils vont ainsi de porte en porte en demandant de petits cadeaux (du chocolat, etc).

hallucination [həlu:sı'neıʃən] n hallucination f

hallway ['hɔ:lweı] n (entrance) vestibule m; (corridor) couloir m

halo ['heıləu] n (of saint etc) auréole f

halt [hɔ:lt] n halte f, arrêt m ▷ vt faire arrêter; (progress etc) interrompre ▷ vi faire halte, s'arrêter

halve [hɑ:v] vt (apple etc) partager ou diviser en deux; (reduce by half) réduire de moitié

halves [hɑ:vz] npl of **half**

ham [hæm] n jambon m

hamburger ['hæmbə:gə'] n hamburger m

hamlet ['hæmlıt] n hameau m

hammer ['hæmə'] n marteau m ▷ vt (nail) enfoncer; (fig) éreinter, démolir ▷ vi (at door) frapper à coups redoublés; to ~ a point home to sb faire rentrer qch dans la tête de qn

hammock ['hæmək] n hamac m

hamper ['hæmpə'] vt gêner ▷ n panier m (d'osier)

hamster ['hæmstə'] n hamster m

hamstring ['hæmstrıŋ] n (Anat) tendon m du jarret

hand [hænd] n main f; (of clock) aiguille f; (handwriting) écriture f; (at cards) jeu m; (worker) ouvrier(-ière)

▷ vt passer, donner; **to give sb a ~** donner un coup de main à qn; **at ~** à portée de la main; **in ~** (situation) en main; (work) en cours; **to be on ~** (person) être disponible; (emergency services) se tenir prêt(e) (à intervenir); **to ~** (information etc) sous la main, à portée de la main; **on the one ~ ..., on the other ~ ...**, d'une part ..., d'autre part; **hand down** vt passer; (tradition, heirloom) transmettre; (us: sentence, verdict) prononcer; **hand in** vt remettre; **hand out** vt distribuer; **hand over** vt remettre; (powers etc) transmettre; **handbag** n sac m à main; **hand baggage** n = **hand luggage**; **handbook** n manuel m; **handbrake** n frein m à main; **handcuffs** npl menottes fpl; **handful** n poignée f

handicap ['hændıkæp] n handicap m ▷ vt handicaper

handkerchief ['hæŋkətʃıf] n mouchoir m

handle ['hændl] n (of door etc) poignée f; (of cup etc) anse f; (of knife etc) manche m; (of saucepan) queue f; (for winding) manivelle f ▷ vt toucher, manier; (deal with) s'occuper de; (treat: people) prendre; "~ with care" "fragile"; **to fly off the ~** s'énerver; **handlebar(s)** n(pl) guidon m

hand: hand luggage n bagages mpl à main; **handmade** adj fait(e) à la main; **handout** n (money) aide f, don m; (leaflet) prospectus m; (at lecture) polycopié m; **hands-free** adj mains libres inv ▷ n (also: **hands-free kit**) kit m mains libres inv

handsome ['hænsəm] adj beau (belle); (profit) considérable

handwriting ['hændraıtıŋ] n écriture f

handy ['hændı] adj (person) adroit(e); (close at hand) sous la main; (convenient) pratique

hang (pt, pp **hung**) [hæŋ, hʌŋ] vt accrocher; (criminal) pendre ▷ vi pendre; (hair, drapery) tomber ▷ n: **to get the ~ of (doing) sth** (inf) attraper le coup pour faire qch; **hang about, hang around** vi traîner; **hang down** vi pendre; **hang on** vi (wait) attendre; **hang out** vt (washing) étendre (dehors) ▷ vi (inf: live) habiter, percher; (: spend time) traîner; **hang round** vi = **hang around**; **hang up** vi (Tel) raccrocher ▷ vt (coat, painting etc) accrocher, suspendre

hanger ['hæŋə*] n cintre m, portemanteau m

hang-gliding ['hæŋglaɪdɪŋ] n vol m libre or sur aile delta

hangover ['hæŋəʊvə*] n (after drinking) gueule f de bois

hankie, hanky ['hæŋkɪ] n abbr = **handkerchief**

happen ['hæpən] vi arriver, se passer, se produire; **what's ~ing?** que se passe-t-il?; **she ~ed to be free** il s'est trouvé (or se trouvait) qu'elle était libre; **as it ~s** justement

happily ['hæpɪlɪ] adv heureusement; (cheerfully) joyeusement

happiness ['hæpɪnɪs] n bonheur m

happy ['hæpɪ] adj heureux(-euse); **~ with** (arrangements etc) satisfait(e) de; **to be ~ to do** faire volontiers; **~ birthday!** bon anniversaire!

harass ['hærəs] vt accabler, tourmenter; **harassment** n tracasseries fpl

harbour, (US) **harbor** ['hɑːbə*] n port m ▷ vt héberger, abriter; (hopes, suspicions) entretenir

hard [hɑːd] adj dur(e); (question, problem) difficile; (facts, evidence) concret(-ète) ▷ adv (work) dur; (think, try) sérieusement; **to look ~ at** regarder fixement; (thing) regarder de près; **no ~ feelings!** sans rancune!; **to be ~ of hearing** être dur(e) d'oreille; **to be ~ done by** être traité(e) injustement; **hardback** n livre relié; **hardboard** n Isorel® m; **hard disk** n (Comput) disque dur;

harden vt durcir; (fig) endurcir ▷ vi (substance) durcir

hardly ['hɑːdlɪ] adv (scarcely) à peine; (harshly) durement; **~ anywhere/ever** presque nulle part/jamais

hard: **hardship** n (difficulties) épreuves fpl; (deprivation) privations fpl; **hard shoulder** n (BRIT Aut) accotement stabilisé; **hard-up** adj (inf) fauché(e); **hardware** n quincaillerie f; (Comput, Mil) matériel m; **hardware shop**, (US) **hardware store** n quincaillerie f; **hard-working** adj travailleur(-euse)

hardy ['hɑːdɪ] adj robuste; (plant) résistant(e) au gel

hare [hɛə*] n lièvre m

harm [hɑːm] n mal m; (wrong) tort m ▷ vt (person) faire du mal or du tort à; (thing) endommager; **out of ~'s way** à l'abri du danger, en lieu sûr; **harmful** adj nuisible; **harmless** adj inoffensif(-ive)

harmony ['hɑːmənɪ] n harmonie f

harness ['hɑːnɪs] n harnais m ▷ vt (horse) harnacher; (resources) exploiter

harp [hɑːp] n harpe f ▷ vi: **to ~ on about** revenir toujours sur

harsh [hɑːʃ] adj (hard) dur(e); (severe) sévère; (unpleasant: sound) discordant(e); (: light) cru(e)

harvest ['hɑːvɪst] n (of corn) moisson f; (of fruit) récolte f; (of grapes) vendange f ▷ vt moissonner; récolter; vendanger

has [hæz] vb see **have**

hashtag ['hæʃtæg] n (on Twitter) mot-dièse m, hashtag m

hasn't ['hæznt] = **has not**

hassle ['hæsl] n (inf: fuss) histoire(s) f(pl)

haste [heɪst] n hâte f, précipitation f; **hasten** ['heɪsn] vt hâter, accélérer ▷ vi se hâter, s'empresser; **hastily** adv à la hâte; (leave) précipitamment; **hasty** adj (decision, action) hâtif(-ive); (departure, escape) précipité(e)

hat [hæt] n chapeau m

hatch [hætʃ] n (Naut: also: **~way**) écoutille f; (BRIT: also: **service ~**) passe-plats m inv ▷ vi éclore

hatchback ['hætʃbæk] n (Aut) modèle m avec hayon arrière

hate [heɪt] vt haïr, détester ▷ n haine f; **hatred** ['heɪtrɪd] n haine f

haul [hɔːl] vt traîner, tirer ▷ n (of fish) prise f; (of stolen goods etc) butin m

haunt [hɔːnt] vt (subj: ghost, fear) hanter; (: person) fréquenter ▷ n repaire m; **haunted** adj (castle etc) hanté(e); (look) égaré(e), hagard(e)

🔘 **KEYWORD**

have [hæv] (pt, pp had) aux vb
1 (gen) avoir; être; **to have eaten/slept** avoir mangé/dormi; **to have arrived/gone** être arrivé(e)/allé(e); **having finished** or **when he had finished, he left** quand il a eu fini, il est parti; **we'd already eaten** nous avions déjà mangé
2 (in tag questions): **you've done it, haven't you?** vous l'avez fait, n'est-ce pas?
3 (in short answers and questions): **no I haven't!/yes we have!** mais non!/ mais si!; **so I have!** ah oui!, oui c'est vrai!; **I've been there before, have you?** j'y suis déjà allé, et vous?
▷ modal aux vb (be obliged): **to have (got) to do sth** devoir faire qch, être obligé(e) de faire qch; **she has (got) to do it** elle doit le faire, il faut qu'elle le fasse; **you haven't to tell her** vous n'êtes pas obligé de le lui dire; (must not) ne le lui dites surtout pas; **do you have to book?** il faut réserver?
▷ vt **1** (possess) avoir; **he has (got) blue eyes/dark hair** il a les yeux bleus/les cheveux bruns
2 (referring to meals etc): **to have breakfast** prendre le petit déjeuner; **to have dinner/lunch** dîner/ déjeuner; **to have a drink** prendre un verre; **to have a cigarette** fumer une cigarette
3 (receive) avoir, recevoir; (obtain) avoir; **may I have your address?** puis-je avoir votre adresse?; **you can have it for £5** vous pouvez l'avoir pour 5 livres; **I must have it for tomorrow** il me le faut pour demain; **to have a baby** avoir un bébé
4 (maintain, allow): **I won't have it!** ça ne se passera pas comme ça!; **we can't have that** nous ne tolérerons pas ça
5 (by sb else): **to have sth done** faire faire qch; **to have one's hair cut** se faire couper les cheveux; **to have sb do sth** faire faire qch à qn
6 (experience, suffer) avoir; **to have a cold/flu** avoir un rhume/la grippe; **to have an operation** se faire opérer; **she had her bag stolen** elle s'est fait voler son sac
7 (+noun): **to have a swim/walk** nager/se promener; **to have a bath/shower** prendre un bain/une douche; **let's have a look** regardons; **to have a meeting** se réunir; **to have a party** organiser une fête; **let me have a try** laissez-moi essayer

haven ['heɪvn] n port m; (fig) havre m

haven't ['hævnt] = **have not**

havoc ['hævək] n ravages mpl

Hawaii [hə'waɪi] n (îles fpl) Hawaï m

hawk [hɔːk] n faucon m

hawthorn ['hɔːθɔːn] n aubépine f

hay [heɪ] n foin m; **hay fever** n rhume m des foins; **haystack** n meule f de foin

hazard ['hæzəd] n (risk) danger m, risque m ▷ vt risquer, hasarder; **hazardous** adj hasardeux(-euse), risqué(e); **hazard warning lights** npl (Aut) feux mpl de détresse

haze [heɪz] n brume f

hazel ['heɪzl] n (tree) noisetier m ▷ adj (eyes) noisette inv; **hazelnut** n noisette f

hazy ['heɪzɪ] *adj* brumeux(-euse); (*idea*) vague

he [hiː] *pron* il; **it is who ...** c'est lui qui ...; **here he is** le voici

head [hɛd] *n* tête *f*; (*leader*) chef *m*; (*of school*) directeur(-trice); (*of secondary school*) proviseur *m* ▷ *vt* (*list*) être en tête de; (*group, company*) être à la tête de; **~s or tails** pile ou face; **~ first** la tête la première; **~ over heels in love** follement or éperdument amoureux(-euse); **to ~ the ball** faire une tête; **head for** *vt fus* se diriger vers; (*disaster*) aller à; **head off** *vt* (*threat, danger*) détourner; **headache** *n* mal *m* de tête; **to have a headache** avoir mal à la tête; **heading** *n* titre *m*; (*subject title*) rubrique *f*; **headlamp** (*BRIT*) *n* = **headlight**; **headlight** *n* phare *m*; **headline** *n* titre *m*; **head office** *n* siège *m*, bureau *m* central; **headphones** *npl* casque *m* (à écouteurs); **headquarters** *npl* (*of business*) bureau or siège central; (*Mil*) quartier général; **headroom** *n* (*in car*) hauteur *f* de plafond; (*under bridge*) hauteur limite; **headscarf** *n* foulard *m*; **headset** *n* = **headphones**; **headteacher** *n* directeur(-trice); (*of secondary school*) proviseur *m*; **head waiter** *n* maître *m* d'hôtel

heal [hiːl] *vt, vi* guérir

health [hɛlθ] *n* santé *f*; **health care** *n* services médicaux; **health centre** *n* (*BRIT*) centre *m* de santé; **health food** *n* aliment(s) naturel(s); **Health Service** *n*: **the Health Service** (*BRIT*) ≈ la Sécurité Sociale; **healthy** *adj* (*person*) en bonne santé; (*climate, food, attitude etc*) sain(e)

heap [hiːp] *n* tas *m* ▷ *vt* (*also*: **~ up**) entasser, amonceler; **she ~ed her plate with cakes** elle a chargé son assiette de gâteaux; **~s (of)** (*inf*: *lots*) des tas (de)

hear (*pt, pp* **heard**) [hɪə', hɜːd] *vt* entendre; (*news*) apprendre ▷ *vi* entendre; **to ~ about** entendre

parler de; (*have news of*) avoir des nouvelles de; **to ~ from sb** recevoir des nouvelles de qn

heard [hɜːd] *pt, pp of* **hear**

hearing ['hɪərɪŋ] *n* (*sense*) ouïe *f*; (*of witnesses*) audition *f*; (*of a case*) audience *f*; **hearing aid** *n* appareil *m* acoustique

hearse [hɜːs] *n* corbillard *m*

heart [hɑːt] *n* cœur *m*; **hearts** *npl* (*Cards*) cœur; **at ~** au fond; **by ~** (*learn, know*) par cœur; **to lose/take ~** perdre/prendre courage; **heart attack** *n* crise *f* cardiaque; **heartbeat** *n* battement *m* de cœur; **heartbroken** *adj*: **to be heartbroken** avoir beaucoup de chagrin; **heartburn** *n* brûlures *f pl* d'estomac; **heart disease** *n* maladie *f* cardiaque

hearth [hɑːθ] *n* foyer *m*, cheminée *f*

heartless ['hɑːtlɪs] *adj* (*person*) sans cœur, insensible; (*treatment*) cruel(le)

hearty ['hɑːtɪ] *adj* chaleureux(-euse); (*appetite*) solide; (*dislike*) cordial(e); (*meal*) copieux(-euse)

heat [hiːt] *n* chaleur *f*; (*Sport*: *also*: **qualifying ~**) éliminatoire *f* ▷ *vt* chauffer; **heat up** *vi* (*liquid*) chauffer; (*room*) se réchauffer ▷ *vt* réchauffer; **heated** *adj* chauffé(e); (*fig*) passionné(e), échauffé(e), excité(e); **heater** *n* appareil *m* de chauffage; radiateur *m*; (*in car*) chauffage *m*; (*water heater*) chauffe-eau *m*

heather ['hɛðə'] *n* bruyère *f*

heating ['hiːtɪŋ] *n* chauffage *m*

heatwave ['hiːtweɪv] *n* vague *f* de chaleur

heaven ['hɛvn] *n* ciel *m*, paradis *m*; (*fig*) paradis *m*; **heavenly** *adj* céleste, divin(e)

heavily ['hɛvɪlɪ] *adv* lourdement; (*drink, smoke*) beaucoup; (*sleep, sigh*) profondément

heavy ['hɛvɪ] *adj* lourd(e); (*work, rain, user, eater*) gros(se); (*drinker, smoker*) grand(e); (*schedule, week*) chargé(e)

Hebrew ['hi:bru:] adj hébraïque ▷ n (Ling) hébreu m

Hebrides ['hebrɪdi:z] npl; **the ~** les Hébrides fpl

hectare ['hekta:ʳ] n (BRIT) hectare m

hectic ['hektɪk] adj (schedule) très chargé(e); (day) mouvementé(e); (lifestyle) trépidant(e)

he'd [hi:d] = he would; he had

hedge [hedʒ] n haie f ▷ vi se dérober ▷ vt: **to ~ one's bets** (fig) se couvrir

hedgehog ['hedʒhɒg] n hérisson m

heed [hi:d] vt (also: **take ~ of**) tenir compte de, prendre garde à

heel [hi:l] n talon m ▷ vt retalonner

hefty ['heftɪ] adj (person) costaud(e); (parcel) lourd(e); (piece, price) gros(se)

height [haɪt] n (of person) taille f, grandeur f; (of object) hauteur f; (of plane, mountain) altitude f; (high ground) hauteur, éminence f; (fig: of glory, fame, power) sommet m; (: of luxury, stupidity) comble m; **at the ~ of summer** au cœur de l'été

heighten vt hausser, surélever; (fig) augmenter

heir [ɛəʳ] n héritier m; **heiress** n héritière f

held [held] pt, pp of **hold**

helicopter ['helɪkɒptəʳ] n hélicoptère m

hell [hel] n enfer m; **oh ~!** (inf) merde!

he'll [hi:l] = he will; he shall

hello [hə'ləu] excl bonjour!; (to attract attention) hé!; (surprise) tiens!

helmet ['helmɪt] n casque m

help [help] n aide f; (cleaner etc) femme f de ménage ▷ vt, vi aider; **~!** au secours!; **~ yourself** servez-vous; **can you ~ me?** pouvez-vous m'aider?; **can I ~ you?** (in shop) vous désirez?; **he can't ~ it** il n'y peut rien; **help out** vi aider ▷ vt: **to ~ sb out** aider qn; **helper** n aide m/f, assistant(e); **helpful** adj serviable, obligeant(e); (useful) utile; **helping** n portion f; **helpless** adj impuissant(e); (baby) sans défense; **helpline** n service m

d'assistance téléphonique; (free) ≈ numéro vert

hem [hem] n ourlet m ▷ vt ourler

hemisphere ['hemɪsfɪəʳ] n hémisphère m

hemorrhage ['hemərɪdʒ] n (US) = **haemorrhage**

hemorrhoids ['hemərɔɪdz] npl (US) = **haemorrhoids**

hen [hen] n poule f; (female bird) femelle f

hence [hens] adv (therefore) d'où, de là; **2 years ~** d'ici 2 ans

hen night, hen party n soirée f entre filles (avant le mariage de l'une d'elles)

hepatitis [hepə'taɪtɪs] n hépatite f

her [hə:ʳ] pron (direct) la, l' + vowel or h mute; (indirect) lui; (stressed, after prep) elle ▷ adj son (sa), ses pl; see also **me, my**

herb [hə:b] n herbe f; **herbal** adj à base de plantes; **herbal tea** n tisane f

herd [hə:d] n troupeau m

here [hɪəʳ] adv ici; (time) alors ▷ excl tiens!, tenez!; **~!** (present) présent!; **~ is, ~ are** voici; **~ he/she is** le (la) voici

hereditary [hɪ'redɪtrɪ] adj héréditaire

heritage ['herɪtɪdʒ] n héritage m, patrimoine m

hernia ['hə:nɪə] n hernie f

hero ['hɪərəu] (pl **heroes**) n héros m; **heroic** [hɪ'rəuɪk] adj héroïque

heroin ['herəuɪn] n héroïne f (drogue)

heroine ['herəuɪn] n héroïne f (femme)

heron ['herən] n héron m

herring ['herɪŋ] n hareng m

hers [hə:z] pron le sien (la sienne), les siens (siennes); see also **mine¹**

herself [hə:'self] pron (reflexive) se; (emphatic) elle-même; (after prep) elle; see also **oneself**

he's [hi:z] = he is; he has

hesitant ['hezɪtənt] adj hésitant(e), indécis(e)

hesitate ['hezɪteɪt] vi: **to ~ (about/to do)** hésiter (sur/à faire); **hesitation** [hezɪ'teɪʃən] n hésitation f

heterosexual ['hetərəʊ'seksjʊəl] adj, n hétérosexuel(le)

hexagon ['heksəgən] n hexagone m

hey [heɪ] excl hé!

heyday ['heɪdeɪ] n: **the ~ of** l'âge m d'or de, les beaux jours de

HGV n abbr = **heavy goods vehicle**

hi [haɪ] excl salut!; (to attract attention) hé!

hibernate ['haɪbəneɪt] vi hiberner

hiccough, hiccup ['hɪkʌp] vi hoqueter ▷ n: **to have (the) ~s** avoir le hoquet

hid [hɪd] pt of **hide**

hidden ['hɪdn] pp of **hide** ▷ adj: **~ agenda** intentions non déclarées

hide [haɪd] (pt **hid**, pp **hidden**) n (skin) peau f ▷ vt cacher ▷ vi: **to ~ (from sb)** se cacher (de qn)

hideous ['hɪdɪəs] adj hideux(-euse), atroce

hiding ['haɪdɪŋ] n (beating) correction f, volée f de coups; **to be in ~** (concealed) se tenir caché(e)

hi-fi ['haɪfaɪ] adj, n abbr (= high fidelity) hi-fi f inv

high [haɪ] adj haut(e); (speed, respect, number) grand(e); (price) élevé(e); (wind) fort(e), violent(e); (voice) aigu(ë) ▷ adv haut, en haut; **20 m ~** haut de 20 m; **~ in the air** haut dans le ciel; **highchair** n (child's) chaise haute; **high-class** adj (neighbourhood, hotel) chic inv; (of great standing) **higher education** n études supérieures; **high heels** npl talons hauts, hauts talons; **high jump** n (Sport) saut m en hauteur; **highlands** ['haɪləndz] npl région montagneuse; **the Highlands** (in Scotland) les Highlands mpl; **highlight** n (fig: of event) point culminant ▷ vt (emphasize) faire ressortir, souligner; **highlights** npl

(in hair) reflets mpl; **highlighter** n (pen) surligneur (lumineux); **highly** adv extrêmement, très; (unlikely) fort; (recommended, skilled, qualified) hautement; **to speak highly of** dire beaucoup de bien de; **highness** n: **His/Her Highness** son Altesse f; **high-rise** n (also: **high-rise block, high-rise building**) tour f (d'habitation); **high school** n lycée m; (us) établissement m d'enseignement supérieur; **high season** n (BRIT) haute saison; **high street** n (BRIT) grand-rue f; **high-tech** (inf) adj de pointe; **highway** n (BRIT) route f; (us) route nationale; **Highway Code** n (BRIT) code m de la route

hijack ['haɪdʒæk] vt détourner (par la force); **hijacker** n auteur m d'un détournement d'avion, pirate m de l'air

hike [haɪk] vi faire des excursions à pied ▷ n excursion f à pied, randonnée f; **hiker** n promeneur(-euse), excursionniste m/f; **hiking** n excursions fpl à pied, randonnée f

hilarious [hɪ'leərɪəs] adj (behaviour, event) désopilant(e)

hill [hɪl] n colline f; (fairly high) montagne f; (on road) côte f; **hillside** n (flanc m de) coteau m; **hill walking** n randonnée f de basse montagne; **hilly** adj vallonné(e), montagneux(-euse)

him [hɪm] pron (direct) le, l' + vowel or h mute; (stressed, indirect, after prep) lui; see also **me**; **himself** pron (reflexive) se; (emphatic) lui-même; (after prep) lui; see also **oneself**

hind [haɪnd] adj de derrière

hinder ['hɪndə*] vt gêner, (delay) retarder

hindsight ['haɪndsaɪt] n: **with (the benefit of) ~** avec du recul, rétrospectivement

Hindu ['hɪnduː] n Hindou(e); **Hinduism** n (Rel) hindouisme m

hinge [hɪndʒ] n charnière f ▷ vi (fig):
to ~ on dépendre de

hint [hɪnt] n allusion f; (advice) conseil
m; (clue) indication f ▷ vt: **to ~ that**
insinuer que ▷ vi: **to ~ at** faire une
allusion à

hip [hɪp] n hanche f

hippie, hippy ['hɪpɪ] n hippie m/f

hippo ['hɪpəʊ] (pl **hippos**) n
hippopotame m

hippopotamus (pl
hippopotamuses or **hippopotami**)
[hɪpə'pɒtəməs, hɪpə'pɒtəmaɪ] n
hippopotame m

hippy ['hɪpɪ] n = **hippie**

hire ['haɪə'] vt (BRIT: car, equipment)
louer; (worker) embaucher, engager
▷ n location f; **for ~** à louer; (taxi)
libre; **I'd like to ~ a car** je voudrais
louer une voiture; **hire(d) car** n
(BRIT) voiture f de location; **hire
purchase** n (BRIT) achat m (or vente f)
à tempérament or crédit

his [hɪz] pron le sien(ne), les siens
(siennes) ▷ adj son (sa), ses pl;
mine'; my

Hispanic [hɪs'pænɪk] adj (in US)
hispano-américain(e) ▷ n Hispano-
Américain(e)

hiss [hɪs] vi siffler

historian [hɪ'stɔːrɪən] n
historien(ne)

historic(al) [hɪ'stɔrɪk(l)] adj
historique

history ['hɪstərɪ] n histoire f

hit [hɪt] vt (pt, pp **hit**) frapper; (reach:
target) atteindre, toucher; (collide
with: car) entrer en collision avec,
heurter; (fig: affect) toucher ▷ n coup
m; (success) succès m; (song) tube m;
(to website) visiter f; (on search engine)
résultat m de recherche; **to ~ it off
with sb** bien s'entendre avec qn; **hit
back** vi: **to ~ back at sb** prendre sa
revanche sur qn

hitch [hɪtʃ] vt (fasten) accrocher,
attacher; (also: **~ up**) remonter d'une
saccade ▷ vi faire de l'autostop ▷ n

(difficulty) anicroche f, contretemps
m; **to ~ a lift** faire du stop; **hitch-hike**
vi faire de l'auto-stop; **hitch-hiker**
n auto-stoppeur(-euse); **hitch-hiking**
n auto-stop m, stop m (inf)

hi-tech ['haɪ'tek] adj de pointe

hitman ['hɪtmæn] (irreg) n (inf) tueur
m à gages

HIV n abbr (= human immunodeficiency
virus) HIV m, VIH m; **~-negative**
séronégatif(-ive); **~-positive**
séropositif(-ive)

hive [haɪv] n ruche f

hoard [hɔːd] n (of food) provisions
fpl, réserves fpl; (of money) trésor m
▷ vt amasser

hoarse [hɔːs] adj enroué(e)

hoax [həʊks] n canular m

hob [hɒb] n plaque chauffante

hobble ['hɒbl] vi boitiller

hobby ['hɒbɪ] n passe-temps favori

hobo ['həʊbəʊ] n (us) vagabond m

hockey ['hɒkɪ] n hockey m; **hockey
stick** n crosse f de hockey

hog [hɒg] n porc (châtré) ▷ vt (fig)
accaparer; **to go the whole ~** aller
jusqu'au bout

Hogmanay [hɒgmə'neɪ] n réveillon
m du jour de l'An, Saint-Sylvestre f

- **HOGMANAY**

La Saint-Sylvestre ou "New Year's
Eve" se nomme *Hogmanay* en
Écosse. En cette occasion, la
famille et les amis se réunissent
pour entendre sonner les douze
coups de minuit et pour fêter le
"first-footing", une coutume qui
veut qu'on se rende chez ses amis et
voisins en apportant quelque chose
à boire (du whisky en général) et
un morceau de charbon en gage de
prospérité pour la nouvelle année.

hoist [hɔɪst] n palan m ▷ vt hisser

hold [həʊld] (pt, pp **held**) vt tenir;
(contain) contenir; (meeting)

tenir; (keep back) retenir; (believe) considérer; (possess) avoir ▷ vi (withstand pressure) tenir (bon); (be valid) valoir; (on telephone) attendre ▷ n prise f; (find) influence f; (Naut) cale f; **to catch** or **get (a) ~ of** saisir; **to get ~ of** (find) trouver; **~ the line!** (Tel) ne quittez pas!; **to ~ one's own** (fig) (bien) se défendre; **hold back** vt retenir; (secret) cacher; **hold on** vi tenir bon; (wait) attendre; **~ on!** (Tel) ne quittez pas!; **to ~ on to sth** (grasp) se cramponner à qch; (keep) conserver or garder qch; **hold out** vt offrir ▷ vi (resist): **to ~ out (against)** résister (devant), tenir bon (devant); **hold up** vt (raise) lever; (support) soutenir; (delay) retarder; (: traffic) ralentir; (rob) braquer; **holdall** n (BRIT) fourre-tout m inv; **holder** n (container) support m; (of ticket, record) détenteur(-trice); (of office, title, passport etc) titulaire m/f

hole [həʊl] n trou m

holiday ['hɒlɪdeɪ] n (BRIT: vacation) vacances fpl; (day off) jour m de congé; (public) jour férié; **to be on ~** être en vacances; **I'm here on ~** je suis ici en vacances; **holiday camp** n (also: holiday centre) camp m de vacances; **holiday job** n (BRIT) boulot m (inf) de vacances; **holiday-maker** n (BRIT) vacancier(-ière); **holiday resort** n centre m de villégiature or de vacances

Holland ['hɒlənd] n Hollande f

hollow ['hɒləʊ] adj creux(-euse); (fig) faux (fausse) ▷ n creux m; (in land) dépression f (de terrain), cuvette f ▷ vt: **to ~ out** creuser, évider

holly ['hɒlɪ] n houx m

holocaust ['hɒləkɔːst] n holocauste m

holy ['həʊlɪ] adj saint(e); (bread, water) bénit(e); (ground) sacré(e)

home [həʊm] n foyer m, maison f; (country) pays natal, patrie f; (institution) maison ▷ adj de famille; (Econ, Pol) national(e), intérieur(e);

(Sport: team) qui reçoit; (: match, win) sur leur (or notre) terrain ▷ adv chez soi, à la maison; au pays natal; (right in: nail etc) à fond; **at ~** chez soi, à la maison; **to go** (or **come**) **~** rentrer (chez soi), rentrer à la maison (or au pays); **make yourself at ~** faites comme chez vous; **home address** n domicile permanent; **homeland** n patrie f; **homeless** adj sans foyer, sans abri; **homely** adj (plain) simple, sans prétention; (welcoming) accueillant(e); **home-made** adj fait(e) à la maison; **home match** n match m à domicile; **Home Office** n (BRIT) ministère m de l'Intérieur; **home owner** n propriétaire occupant; **home page** n (Comput) page f d'accueil; **Home Secretary** n (BRIT) ministre m de l'Intérieur; **homesick** adj: **to be homesick** avoir le mal du pays; (missing one's family) s'ennuyer de sa famille; **home town** n ville natale; **homework** n devoirs mpl

homicide ['hɒmɪsaɪd] n (us) homicide m

homoeopathic, (us) homeopathic [həʊmɪəʊˈpæθɪk] adj (medicine) homéopathique; (doctor) homéopathe

homoeopathy, (us) homeopathy [həʊmɪˈɒpəθɪ] n homéopathie f

homosexual [hɒməʊˈsɛksjʊəl] adj, n homosexuel(le)

honest ['ɒnɪst] adj honnête; (sincere) franc (franche); **honestly** adv honnêtement; franchement; **honesty** n honnêteté f

honey ['hʌnɪ] n miel m; **honeymoon** n lune f de miel, voyage m de noces; **we're on honeymoon** nous sommes en voyage de noces; **honeysuckle** n chèvrefeuille m

Hong Kong ['hɒŋ'kɒŋ] n Hong Kong

honorary ['ɒnərərɪ] adj honoraire; (duty, title) honorifique; **~ degree** diplôme m honoris causa

honour, (US) **honor** ['ɒnəʳ] vt
honorer ▷ n honneur m; **to
graduate with ~s** obtenir sa licence
avec mention; **honourable,** (US)
honorable adj honorable; **honours
degree** n (Scol) ≈ licence f avec
mention

hood [hud] n capuchon m; (of cooker)
hotte f; (BRIT Aut) capote f; (US Aut)
capot m; **hoodie** ['hudi] n (top)
sweat m à capuche

hoof (pl **hoofs** or **hooves**) [hu:f,
hu:vz] n sabot m

hook [huk] n crochet m; (on dress)
agrafe f; (for fishing) hameçon m ▷ vt
accrocher; **off the ~** (Tel) décroché

hooligan ['hu:lɪɡən] n voyou m

hoop [hu:p] n cerceau m

hoot [hu:t] vi (BRIT Aut) klaxonner;
(siren) mugir; (owl) hululer

Hoover® ['hu:vəʳ] n aspirateur
m ▷ vt: **to hoover** (room) passer
l'aspirateur dans; (carpet) passer
l'aspirateur sur

hooves [hu:vz] npl of **hoof**

hop [hɒp] vi sauter; (on one foot)
sauter à cloche-pied; (bird) sautiller

hope [həup] vt, vi espérer ▷ n
espoir m; **I ~ so** je l'espère; **I ~
not** j'espère que non; **hopeful**
adj (person) plein(e) d'espoir;
(situation) prometteur(-euse),
encourageant(e); **hopefully** adv
(expectantly) avec espoir; (one hopes)
avec optimisme; (one hopes) avec un
peu de superstition; **hopeless** adj
désespéré(e); (useless) nul(le)

hops [hɒps] npl houblon m

horizon [həˈraɪzn] n horizon
m; **horizontal** [hɒrɪˈzɒntl] adj
horizontal(e)

hormone ['hɔ:məun] n hormone f

horn [hɔ:n] n corne f; (Mus) cor m;
(Aut) klaxon m

horoscope ['hɒrəskəup] n
horoscope m

horrendous [həˈrɛndəs] adj
horrible, affreux(-euse)

horrible ['hɒrɪbl] adj horrible,
affreux(-euse)

horrid ['hɒrɪd] adj (person) détestable;
(weather, place, smell) épouvantable

horrific [hɒˈrɪfɪk] adj horrible

horrifying ['hɒrɪfaɪɪŋ] adj
horrifiant(e)

horror ['hɒrəʳ] n horreur f; **horror
film** n film m d'épouvante

hors d'œuvre [ɔːˈdəːvrə] n hors
d'œuvre m

horse [hɔ:s] n cheval m; **horseback:
on horseback** adj, adv à cheval;
horse chestnut n (nut) marron m
(d'Inde); (tree) marronnier m (d'Inde);
horsepower n puissance f (en
chevaux); (unit) cheval-vapeur m
(CV); **horse-racing** n courses fpl de
chevaux; **horseradish** n raifort m;
horse riding n (BRIT) équitation f

hose [həuz] n tuyau m; (also: **garden
~**) tuyau d'arrosage; **hosepipe** n
tuyau m; (in garden) tuyau d'arrosage

hospital ['hɒspɪtl] n hôpital m; **in ~** à
l'hôpital; **where's the nearest ~?** où
est l'hôpital le plus proche?

hospitality [hɒspɪˈtælɪtɪ] n
hospitalité f

host [həust] n hôte m; (TV, Radio)
présentateur(-trice); (large number): **a
~ of** une foule de; (Rel) hostie f

hostage ['hɒstɪdʒ] n otage m

hostel ['hɒstl] n foyer m; (also: **youth
~**) auberge f de jeunesse

hostess ['həustɪs] n hôtesse f; (BRIT:
also: **air ~**) hôtesse de l'air; (TV, Radio)
présentatrice f

hostile ['hɒstaɪl] adj hostile

hostility [hɒˈstɪlɪtɪ] n hostilité f

hot [hɒt] adj chaud(e); (as opposed
to only warm) très chaud; (spicy)
fort(e); (fig: contest) acharné(e);
(topic) brûlant(e); (temper) violent(e),
passionné(e); **to be ~** (person) avoir
chaud; (thing) être (très) chaud; **it's ~**
(weather) il fait chaud; **hot dog** n
hot-dog m

hotel [həuˈtɛl] n hôtel m

hotspot ['hɒtspɒt] n (Comput: also: **wireless ~**) borne f wifi, hotspot m
hot-water bottle [hɒt'wɔːtə-] n bouillotte f
hound [haund] vt poursuivre avec acharnement ▷ n chien courant
hour ['auə'] n heure f; **hourly** adj toutes les heures; (rate) horaire
house n [haus] maison f; (Pol) chambre f; (Theat) salle f, auditoire m ▷ vt [hauz] (person) loger, héberger; **on the ~** (fig) aux frais de la maison; **household** n (Admin etc) ménage m; (people) famille f, maisonnée f; **householder** n propriétaire m/f; (head of house) chef m de famille; **housekeeper** n gouvernante f; **housekeeping** n (work) ménage m; **housewife** (irreg) n ménagère f; femme f au foyer; **house wine** n cuvée f maison or du patron; **housework** n (travaux mpl du) ménage m
housing ['hauzɪŋ] n logement m; **housing development, housing estate** (BRIT) n (blocks of flats) cité f; (houses) lotissement m
hover ['hɒvə'] vi planer; **hovercraft** n aéroglisseur m, hovercraft m
how [hau] adv comment; **~ are you?** comment allez-vous?; **~ do you do?** bonjour; (on being introduced) enchanté(e); **~ long have you been here?** depuis combien de temps êtes-vous là?; **~ lovely/awful!** que or comme c'est joli/affreux!; **~ much time/many people?** combien de temps/gens?; **~ much does it cost?** ça coûte combien?; **~ old are you?** quel âge avez-vous?; **~ tall is he?** combien mesure-t-il?; **~ is school?** ça va à l'école?; **~ was the film?** comment était le film?
however [hau'ɛvə'] conj pourtant, cependant ▷ adv: **~ I do it** de quelque manière que je m'y prenne; **~ cold it is** même s'il fait très froid; **~ did you do it?** comment y êtes-vous donc arrivé?

howl [haul] n hurlement m ▷ vi hurler; (wind) mugir
H.P. n abbr (BRIT) = **hire purchase**
h.p. abbr (Aut) = **horsepower**
HQ n abbr (= headquarters) QG m
hr abbr (= hour) h
hrs abbr (= hours) h
HTML n abbr (= hypertext markup language) HTML m
hubcap ['hʌbkæp] n (Aut) enjoliveur m
huddle ['hʌdl] vi: **to ~ together** se blottir les uns contre les autres
huff [hʌf] n: **in a ~** fâché(e)
hug [hʌg] vt serrer dans ses bras; (shore, kerb) serrer ▷ n: **to give sb a ~** serrer qn dans ses bras
huge [hjuːdʒ] adj énorme, immense
hull [hʌl] n (of ship) coque f
hum [hʌm] vt (tune) fredonner ▷ vi fredonner; (insect) bourdonner; (plane, tool) vrombir
human ['hjuːmən] adj humain(e) ▷ n (also: **~ being**) être humain
humane [hjuː'meɪn] adj humain(e), humanitaire
humanitarian [hjuːmænɪ'tɛərɪən] adj humanitaire
humanity [hjuː'mænɪtɪ] n humanité f
human rights npl droits mpl de l'homme
humble ['hʌmbl] adj humble, modeste
humid ['hjuːmɪd] adj humide; **humidity** [hjuː'mɪdɪtɪ] n humidité f
humiliate [hjuː'mɪlɪeɪt] vt humilier; **humiliating** [hjuː'mɪlɪeɪtɪŋ] adj humiliant(e); **humiliation** [hjuːmɪlɪ'eɪʃən] n humiliation f
hummus ['huməs] n houm(m)ous m
humorous ['hjuːmərəs] adj humoristique
humour, (US) **humor** ['hjuːmə'] n humeur m; (mood) humeur f ▷ vt (person) faire plaisir à; se prêter aux caprices de

hump [hʌmp] n bosse f
hunch [hʌntʃ] n (premonition) intuition f
hundred ['hʌndrəd] num cent; **~s of** des centaines de; **hundredth** ['hʌndrədɪθ] num centième
hung [hʌŋ] pt, pp of **hang**
Hungarian [hʌŋ'geərɪən] adj hongrois(e) ▷ n Hongrois(e); (Ling) hongrois m
Hungary ['hʌŋgərɪ] n Hongrie f
hunger ['hʌŋgə*] n faim f ▷ vi: **to ~ for** avoir faim de, désirer ardemment
hungry ['hʌŋgrɪ] adj affamé(e); **to be ~** avoir faim; **~ for** (fig) avide de
hunt [hʌnt] vt (seek) chercher; (Sport) chasser ▷ vi (search): **to ~ for** chercher (partout); (Sport) chasser ▷ n (Sport) chasse f; **hunter** n chasseur m; **hunting** n chasse f
hurdle ['hə:dl] n (Sport) haie f; (fig) obstacle m
hurl [hə:l] vt lancer (avec violence); (abuse, insults) lancer
hurrah, hurray [hu'rɑ:, hu'reɪ] excl hourra!
hurricane ['hʌrɪkən] n ouragan m
hurry ['hʌrɪ] n hâte f, précipitation f ▷ vi se presser, se dépêcher ▷ vt (person) faire presser, faire se dépêcher; (work) presser; **to be in a ~** être pressé(e); **to do sth in a ~** faire qch en vitesse; **hurry up** vi se dépêcher
hurt [hə:t] (pt, pp **hurt**) vt (cause pain to) faire mal à; (injure, fig) blesser ▷ vi faire mal ▷ adj blessé(e); **my arm ~s** j'ai mal au bras; **to ~ o.s.** se faire mal
husband ['hʌzbənd] n mari m
hush [hʌʃ] n calme m, silence m ▷ vt faire taire; **~!** chut!
husky ['hʌskɪ] adj (voice) rauque ▷ n chien m esquimau or de traîneau
hut [hʌt] n hutte f; (shed) cabane f
hyacinth ['haɪəsɪnθ] n jacinthe f
hydrofoil ['haɪdrəfoɪl] n hydrofoil m
hydrogen ['haɪdrədʒən] n hydrogène m

hygiene ['haɪdʒi:n] n hygiène f; **hygienic** [haɪ'dʒi:nɪk] adj hygiénique
hymn [hɪm] n hymne m; cantique m
hype [haɪp] n (inf) matraquage m publicitaire or médiatique
hyperlink ['haɪpəlɪŋk] n hyperlien m
hypermarket ['haɪpəmɑ:kɪt] (BRIT) n hypermarché m
hyphen ['haɪfn] n trait m d'union
hypnotize ['hɪpnətaɪz] vt hypnotiser
hypocrite ['hɪpəkrɪt] n hypocrite m/f; **hypocritical** [hɪpə'krɪtɪkl] adj hypocrite
hypothesis (pl **hypotheses**) [haɪ'pɔθɪsɪs, -si:z] n hypothèse f
hysterical [hɪ'sterɪkl] adj hystérique; (funny) hilarant(e)
hysterics [hɪ'sterɪks] npl; **to be in/have ~** (anger, panic) avoir une crise de nerfs; (laughter) attraper un fou rire

I [aɪ] pron je; (before vowel) j'; (stressed) moi

ice [aɪs] n glace f; (on road) verglas m ▷ vt (cake) glacer ▷ vi (also: ~ over) geler; (also: ~ up) se givrer; **iceberg** n iceberg m; **ice cream** n glace f; **ice cube** n glaçon m; **ice hockey** n hockey m sur glace

Iceland ['aɪslənd] n Islande f; **Icelander** n Islandais(e); **Icelandic** [aɪs'lændɪk] adj islandais(e) ▷ n (Ling) islandais m

ice: ice lolly n (BRIT) esquimau m; **ice rink** n patinoire f; **ice skating** n patinage m (sur glace)

icing ['aɪsɪŋ] n (Culin) glaçage m; **icing sugar** n (BRIT) sucre m glace

icon ['aɪkɔn] n icône f

ICT n abbr (BRIT Scol: = information and communications technology) TIC fpl

icy ['aɪsɪ] adj glacé(e); (road) verglacé(e); (weather, temperature) glacial(e)

I'd [aɪd] = **I would; I had**

ID card n carte f d'identité

idea [aɪ'dɪə] n idée f

ideal [aɪ'dɪəl] n idéal m ▷ adj idéal(e); **ideally** [aɪ'dɪəlɪ] adv (preferably) dans l'idéal; (perfectly): **he is ideally suited to the job** il est parfait pour ce poste

identical [aɪ'dɛntɪkl] adj identique

identification [aɪdɛntɪfɪ'keɪʃən] n identification f; **means of ~** pièce f d'identité

identify [aɪ'dɛntɪfaɪ] vt identifier

identity [aɪ'dɛntɪtɪ] n identité f; **identity card** n carte f d'identité; **identity theft** n usurpation f d'identité

ideology [aɪdɪ'ɔlədʒɪ] n idéologie f

idiom ['ɪdɪəm] n (phrase) expression f idiomatique; (style) style m

idiot ['ɪdɪət] n idiot(e), imbécile m/f

idle ['aɪdl] adj (doing nothing) sans occupation, désœuvré(e); (lazy) oisif(-ive), paresseux(-euse); (unemployed) au chômage; (machinery) au repos; (question, pleasures) vain(e), futile ▷ vi (engine) tourner au ralenti

idol ['aɪdl] n idole f

idyllic [ɪ'dɪlɪk] adj idyllique

i.e. abbr (= id est: that is) c. à d., c'est-à-dire

if [ɪf] conj si; **if necessary** si nécessaire, le cas échéant; **if so** si c'est le cas; **if not** sinon; **if only I could!** si seulement je pouvais!; see also **as; even**

ignite [ɪg'naɪt] vt mettre le feu à, enflammer ▷ vi s'enflammer

ignition [ɪg'nɪʃən] n (Aut) allumage m; **to switch on/off the ~** mettre/couper le contact

ignorance ['ɪgnərəns] n ignorance f

ignorant ['ɪgnərənt] adj ignorant(e); **to be ~ of** (subject) ne rien connaître en; (events) ne pas être au courant de

ignore [ɪg'nɔ:] vt ne tenir aucun compte de; (mistake) ne pas relever;

(person: pretend to not see) faire semblant de ne pas reconnaître; (: pay no attention to) ignorer

ill [ɪl] adj (sick) malade; (bad) mauvais(e) ▷ n mal m ▷ adv: **to speak/think ~ of sb** dire/penser du mal de qn; **to be taken ~** tomber malade

I'll [aɪl] = **I will; I shall**

illegal [ɪ'liːgl] adj illégal(e)

illegible [ɪ'lɛdʒɪbl] adj illisible

illegitimate [ɪlɪ'dʒɪtɪmət] adj illégitime

ill health n mauvaise santé

illiterate [ɪ'lɪtərət] adj illettré(e)

illness [ɪlnɪs] n maladie f

illuminate [ɪ'luːmɪneɪt] vt (room, street) éclairer; (for special effect) illuminer

illusion [ɪ'luːʒən] n illusion f

illustrate [ɪləstreɪt] vt illustrer

illustration [ɪlə'streɪʃən] n illustration f

I'm [aɪm] = **I am**

image [ɪmɪdʒ] n image f; (public face) image de marque

imaginary [ɪ'mædʒɪnərɪ] adj imaginaire

imagination [ɪmædʒɪ'neɪʃən] n imagination f

imaginative [ɪ'mædʒɪnətɪv] adj imaginatif(-ive); (person) plein(e) d'imagination

imagine [ɪ'mædʒɪn] vt s'imaginer; (suppose) imaginer, supposer

imam [ɪ'maːm] n imam m

imbalance [ɪm'bæləns] n déséquilibre m

imitate [ɪmɪteɪt] vt imiter; **imitation** [ɪmɪ'teɪʃən] n imitation f

immaculate [ɪ'mækjʊlət] adj impeccable; (Rel) immaculé(e)

immature [ɪmə'tjʊə*] adj (fruit) qui n'est pas mûr(e); (person) qui manque de maturité

immediate [ɪ'miːdɪət] adj immédiat(e); **immediately** adv (at once) immédiatement; **immediately next to** juste à côté de

immense [ɪ'mɛns] adj immense, énorme

immerse [ɪ'məːs] vt immerger, plonger; **to be ~d in** (fig) être plongé dans

immigrant [ɪmɪgrənt] n immigrant(e); (already established) immigré(e); **immigration** [ɪmɪ'greɪʃən] n immigration f

imminent [ɪmɪnənt] adj imminent(e)

immoral [ɪ'mɔrl] adj immoral(e)

immortal [ɪ'mɔːtl] adj, n immortel(le)

immune [ɪ'mjuːn] adj: **~ (to)** immunisé(e) (contre); **immune system** n système m immunitaire

immunize [ɪmjunaɪz] vt immuniser

impact [ɪmpækt] n choc m, impact m; (fig) impact

impair [ɪm'pɛə*] vt détériorer, diminuer

impartial [ɪm'pɑːʃl] adj impartial(e)

impatience [ɪm'peɪʃəns] n impatience f

impatient [ɪm'peɪʃənt] adj impatient(e); **to get** or **grow ~** s'impatienter

impeccable [ɪm'pɛkəbl] adj impeccable, parfait(e)

impending [ɪm'pɛndɪŋ] adj imminent(e)

imperative [ɪm'pɛrətɪv] adj (need) urgent(e), pressant(e); (tone) impérieux(-euse) ▷ n (Ling) impératif m

imperfect [ɪm'pəːfɪkt] adj imparfait(e); (goods etc) défectueux(-euse) ▷ n (Ling: also: **~ tense**) imparfait m

imperial [ɪm'pɪərɪəl] adj impérial(e); (BRIT: measure) légal(e)

impersonal [ɪm'pəːsənl] adj impersonnel(le)

impersonate [ɪm'pəːsəneɪt] vt se faire passer pour; (Theat) imiter

impetus [ɪmpɪtəs] n impulsion f; (of runner) élan m

implant [ɪmˈplɑːnt] vt (Med)
implanter; (fig: idea, principle)
inculquer

implement n [ˈɪmplɪmənt] outil m,
instrument m; (for cooking) ustensile
m ▷ vt [ˈɪmplɪment] exécuter

implicate [ˈɪmplɪkeɪt] vt impliquer,
compromettre

implication [ɪmplɪˈkeɪʃən] n
implication f; **by ~** indirectement

implicit [ɪmˈplɪsɪt] adj implicite;
(complete) absolu(e), sans réserve

imply [ɪmˈplaɪ] vt (hint) suggérer,
laisser entendre; (mean) indiquer,
supposer

impolite [ɪmpəˈlaɪt] adj impoli(e)

import vt [ɪmˈpɔːt] importer ▷ n
[ˈɪmpɔːt] (Comm) importation f;
(meaning) portée f, signification f

importance [ɪmˈpɔːtns] n
importance f

important [ɪmˈpɔːtnt] adj
important(e); **it's not ~** c'est sans
importance, ce n'est pas important

importer [ɪmˈpɔːtə] n
importateur(-trice)

impose [ɪmˈpəuz] vt imposer ▷ vi:
to ~ on sb abuser de la gentillesse
de qn; **imposing** adj imposant(e),
impressionnant(e)

impossible [ɪmˈpɒsɪbl] adj
impossible

impotent [ˈɪmpətnt] adj
impuissant(e)

impoverished [ɪmˈpɒvərɪʃt] adj
pauvre, appauvri(e)

impractical [ɪmˈpræktɪkl] adj pas
pratique; (person) qui manque d'esprit
pratique

impress [ɪmˈpres] vt impressionner,
faire impression sur; (mark) imprimer,
marquer; **to ~ sth on sb** faire bien
comprendre qch à qn

impression [ɪmˈpreʃən] n
impression f; (of stamp, seal)
empreinte f; (imitation) imitation
f; **to be under the ~ that** avoir
l'impression que

impressive [ɪmˈpresɪv] adj
impressionnant(e)

imprison [ɪmˈprɪzn] vt emprisonner,
mettre en prison; **imprisonment**
n emprisonnement m; (period):
**to sentence sb to 10 years'
imprisonment** condamner qn à 10
ans de prison

improbable [ɪmˈprɒbabl] adj
improbable; (excuse) peu plausible

improper [ɪmˈprɒpə] adj (unsuitable)
déplacé(e), de mauvais goût;
(indecent) indécent(e); (dishonest)
malhonnête

improve [ɪmˈpruːv] vt améliorer
▷ vi s'améliorer; (pupil etc) faire
des progrès; **improvement** n
amélioration f; (of pupil etc)
progrès m

improvise [ˈɪmprəvaɪz] vt, vi
improviser

impulse [ˈɪmpʌls] n impulsion f;
on ~ impulsivement, sur un coup
de tête; **impulsive** [ɪmˈpʌlsɪv] adj
impulsif(-ive)

🔵 **KEYWORD**

in [ɪn] prep 1 (indicating place, position)
dans; **in the house/the fridge** dans
la maison/le frigo; **in the garden**
dans le ou au jardin; **in town** en ville;
in the country à la campagne; **in
school** à l'école; **in here/there** ici/là
2 (with place names: of region,
country): **in London** à Londres; **in
England** en Angleterre; **in Japan**
au Japon; **in the United States** aux
États-Unis
3 (indicating time: during): **in spring**
au printemps; **in summer** en été; **in
May/2005** en mai/2005; **in the
afternoon** (dans) l'après-midi; **at 4
o'clock in the afternoon** à 4 heures
de l'après-midi
4 (indicating time: in the space of) en;
(: future) dans; **I did it in 3 hours/
days** je l'ai fait en 3 heures/jours; **I'll**

see you in 2 weeks or in 2 weeks' time je te verrai dans 2 semaines
5 (indicating manner etc): in a loud/soft voice à voix haute/basse; in pencil au crayon; in writing par écrit; in French en français; the boy in the blue shirt le garçon à or avec la chemise bleue
6 (indicating circumstances): in the sun au soleil; in the shade à l'ombre; in the rain sous la pluie; a change in policy un changement de politique
7 (indicating mood, state): in tears en larmes; in anger sous le coup de la colère; in despair au désespoir; in good condition en bon état; to live in luxury vivre dans le luxe
8 (with ratios, numbers): 1 in 10 households, 1 household in 10 1 ménage sur 10; 20 pence in the pound 20 pence par livre sterling; they lined up in twos ils se mirent en rangs (deux) par deux; in hundreds par centaines
9 (referring to people, works): the disease is common in children c'est une maladie courante chez les enfants; in (the works of) Dickens chez Dickens, dans (l'œuvre de) Dickens
10 (indicating profession etc) dans; to be in teaching être dans l'enseignement
11 (after superlative) de; the best pupil in the class le meilleur élève de la classe
12 (with present participle): in saying this en disant ceci
▶ adv: to be in (person: at home, work) être là; (train, ship, plane) être arrivé(e); (in fashion) être à la mode; to ask sb in inviter qn à entrer; to run/limp etc in entrer en courant/boitant etc
▶ n: the ins and outs (of) (of proposal, situation etc) les tenants et aboutissants (de)

inability [ɪnə'bɪlɪtɪ] n incapacité f; ~ to pay incapacité de payer
inaccurate [ɪn'ækjurət] adj inexact(e); (person) qui manque de précision
inadequate [ɪn'ædɪkwət] adj insuffisant(e), inadéquat(e)
inadvertently [ɪnəd'vɜːtntlɪ] adv par mégarde
inappropriate [ɪnə'prəuprɪət] adj inopportun(e), mal à propos; (word, expression) impropre
inaugurate [ɪ'nɔːgjureɪt] vt inaugurer; (president, official) investir de ses fonctions
Inc. abbr = incorporated
incapable [ɪn'keɪpəbl] adj: ~ (of) incapable (de)
incense n [ˈɪnsɛns] encens m ▶ vt [ɪn'sɛns] (anger) mettre en colère
incentive [ɪn'sɛntɪv] n encouragement m, raison f de se donner de la peine
inch [ɪntʃ] n pouce m (= 25 mm; 12 in a foot); within an ~ of à deux doigts de; he wouldn't give an ~ (fig) il n'a pas voulu céder d'un pouce
incidence ['ɪnsɪdns] n (of crime, disease) fréquence f
incident ['ɪnsɪdnt] n incident m
incidentally [ɪnsɪ'dɛntəlɪ] adv (by the way) à propos
inclination [ɪnklɪ'neɪʃən] n inclination f; (desire) envie f
incline [n 'ɪnklaɪn] pente f, plan incliné ▶ vt [ɪn'klaɪn] incliner ▶ vi (surface) s'incliner; to be ~d to do (have a tendency to do) avoir tendance à faire
include [ɪn'kluːd] vt inclure, comprendre; service is/is not ~d le service est compris/n'est pas compris; including prep y compris; inclusion n inclusion f; inclusive adj inclus(e), compris(e); inclusive of tax taxes comprises
income ['ɪnkʌm] n revenu m; (from property etc) rentes fpl; income

support n (BRIT) = revenu m
minimum d'insertion, RMI m;
income tax n impôt m sur le revenu
incoming ['ɪnkʌmɪŋ] adj (passengers,
mail) à l'arrivée; (government, tenant)
nouveau (nouvelle)
incompatible [ɪnkəm'pætɪbl] adj
incompatible
incompetence [ɪn'kɒmpɪtns] n
incompétence f, incapacité f
incompetent [ɪn'kɒmpɪtnt] adj
incompétent(e), incapable
incomplete [ɪnkəm'pli:t] adj
incomplet(-ète)
inconsistent [ɪnkən'sɪstnt] adj
qui manque de constance; (work)
irrégulier(-ière); (statement) peu
cohérent(e); ~ **with** en contradiction
avec
inconvenience [ɪnkən'vi:njəns]
n inconvénient m; (trouble)
dérangement m ▷ vt déranger
inconvenient [ɪnkən'vi:njənt]
adj malcommode; (time, place) mal
choisi(e), qui ne convient pas; (visitor)
importun(e)
incorporate [ɪn'kɔ:pəreɪt] vt
incorporer; (contain) contenir
incorporated [ɪn'kɔ:pəreɪtɪd] adj:
~ **company** (US) = société f anonyme
incorrect [ɪnkə'rɛkt] adj
incorrect(e); (opinion, statement)
inexact(e)
increase n ['ɪnkri:s] augmentation
f ▷ vi, vt [ɪn'kri:s] augmenter;
increasingly adv de plus en plus
incredible [ɪn'krɛdɪbl] adj
incroyable; **incredibly** adv
incroyablement
incur [ɪn'kə:'] vt (expenses) encourir;
(anger, risk) s'exposer à; (debt)
contracter; (loss) subir
indecent [ɪn'di:snt] adj indécent(e),
inconvenant(e)
indeed [ɪn'di:d] adv (confirming,
agreeing) en effet, effectivement; (for
emphasis) vraiment; (furthermore)
d'ailleurs; **yes ~!** certainement!

indefinitely [ɪn'dɛfɪnɪtlɪ] adv (wait)
indéfiniment
independence [ɪndɪ'pɛndns] n
indépendance f; **Independence Day**
n (US) fête de l'Indépendance américaine

independent [ɪndɪ'pɛndnt]
adj indépendant(e); (radio) libre;
independent school (BRIT) école
privée
index ['ɪndɛks] n (pl indexes)
(in book) index m; (in library etc)
catalogue m; (pl indices) (ratio, sign)
indice m
India ['ɪndɪə] n Inde f; **Indian**
adj indien(ne) ▷ n Indien(ne);
(American) Indian Indien(ne)
(d'Amérique)
indicate ['ɪndɪkeɪt] vt indiquer ▷ vi
(BRIT Aut): **to ~ left/right** mettre
son clignotant à gauche/à droite;
indication [ɪndɪ'keɪʃən] n indication
f, signe m; **indicative** [ɪn'dɪkətɪv]
adj: **to be indicative of sth** être
symptomatique de qch ▷ n (Ling)
indicatif m; **indicator** n (sign)
indicateur m; (Aut) clignotant m
indices ['ɪndɪsi:z] npl of **index**
indict [ɪn'daɪt] vt accuser;
indictment n accusation f
indifference [ɪn'dɪfrəns] n
indifférence f
indifferent [ɪn'dɪfrənt] adj
indifférent(e); (poor) médiocre,
quelconque
indigenous [ɪn'dɪdʒɪnəs] adj
indigène

indigestion [ɪndɪˈdʒestʃən] n indigestion f, mauvaise digestion

indignant [ɪnˈdɪɡnənt] adj: **~ (at sth/with sb)** indigné(e) (de qch/contre qn)

indirect [ɪndɪˈrekt] adj indirect(e)

indispensable [ɪndɪˈspensəbl] adj indispensable

individual [ɪndɪˈvɪdjuəl] n individu m ▷ adj individuel(le); (characteristic) particulier(-ière), original(e); **individually** adv individuellement

Indonesia [ɪndəˈniːzɪə] n Indonésie f

indoor [ˈɪndɔː] adj d'intérieur; (plant) d'appartement; (swimming pool) couvert(e); (sport, games) pratiqué(e) en salle; **indoors** [ɪnˈdɔːz] adv à l'intérieur

induce [ɪnˈdjuːs] vt (persuade) persuader; (bring about) provoquer; (labour) déclencher

indulge [ɪnˈdʌldʒ] vt (whim) céder à, satisfaire; (child) gâter ▷ vi: **to ~ in sth** (luxury) s'offrir qch, se permettre qch; (fantasies etc) se livrer à qch; **indulgent** adj indulgent(e)

industrial [ɪnˈdʌstrɪəl] adj industriel(le); (injury) du travail; (dispute) ouvrier(-ière); **industrial estate** n (BRIT) zone industrielle; **industrialist** n industriel m; **industrial park** n (US) zone industrielle

industry [ˈɪndəstrɪ] n industrie f; (diligence) zèle m, application f

inefficient [ɪnɪˈfɪʃənt] adj inefficace

inequality [ɪnɪˈkwɒlɪtɪ] n inégalité f

inevitable [ɪnˈevɪtəbl] adj inévitable; **inevitably** adv inévitablement, fatalement

inexpensive [ɪnɪkˈspensɪv] adj bon marché inv

inexperienced [ɪnɪkˈspɪərɪənst] adj inexpérimenté(e)

inexplicable [ɪnɪkˈsplɪkəbl] adj inexplicable

infamous [ˈɪnfəməs] adj infâme, abominable

infant [ˈɪnfənt] n (baby) nourrisson m; (young child) petit(e) enfant

infantry [ˈɪnfəntrɪ] n infanterie f

infant school n (BRIT) classes fpl préparatoires (entre 5 et 7 ans)

infect [ɪnˈfekt] vt (wound) infecter; (person, blood) contaminer; **infection** [ɪnˈfekʃən] n infection f; (contagion) contagion f; **infectious** [ɪnˈfekʃəs] adj infectieux(-euse); (also fig) contagieux(-euse)

infer [ɪnˈfɜː] vt: **to ~ (from)** conclure (de), déduire (de)

inferior [ɪnˈfɪərɪə] adj inférieur(e); (goods) de qualité inférieure ▷ n inférieur(e); (in rank) subalterne m/f

infertile [ɪnˈfɜːtaɪl] adj stérile

infertility [ɪnfəˈtɪlɪtɪ] n infertilité f, stérilité f

infested [ɪnˈfestɪd] adj: **~ (with)** infesté(e) (de)

infinite [ˈɪnfɪnɪt] adj infini(e); (time, money) illimité(e); **infinitely** adv infiniment

infirmary [ɪnˈfɜːmərɪ] n hôpital m; (in school, factory) infirmerie f

inflamed [ɪnˈfleɪmd] adj enflammé(e)

inflammation [ɪnfləˈmeɪʃən] n inflammation f

inflatable [ɪnˈfleɪtəbl] adj gonflable

inflate [ɪnˈfleɪt] vt (tyre, balloon) gonfler; (fig: exaggerate) grossir; (: increase) gonfler; **inflation** [ɪnˈfleɪʃən] n (Econ) inflation f

inflexible [ɪnˈfleksɪbl] adj inflexible, rigide

inflict [ɪnˈflɪkt] vt: **to ~ on** infliger à

influence [ˈɪnfluəns] n influence f ▷ vt influencer; **under the ~ of alcohol** en état d'ébriété; **influential** [ɪnfluˈenʃl] adj influent(e)

influenza [ɪnfluˈenzə] n grippe f

influx [ˈɪnflʌks] n afflux m

info [ˈɪnfəu] (inf) n (= information) renseignements mpl

inform [ɪnˈfɔːm] vt: **to ~ sb (of)** informer or avertir qn (de) ▷ vi: **to**

~ on sb dénoncer qn, informer contre qn

informal [ɪnˈfɔːməl] *adj* (person, manner, party) simple; (visit, discussion) dénué(e) de formalités; (announcement, invitation) non officiel(le); (colloquial) familier(-ère)

information [ɪnfəˈmeɪʃən] *n* information(s) f(pl); renseignements *mpl*; (knowledge) connaissances *fpl*; **a piece of ~** un renseignement; **information office** *n* bureau *m* de renseignements; **information technology** *n* informatique *f*

informative [ɪnˈfɔːmətɪv] *adj* instructif(-ive)

infra-red [ɪnfrəˈred] *adj* infrarouge

infrastructure [ˈɪnfrəstrʌktʃə*r*] *n* infrastructure *f*

infrequent [ɪnˈfriːkwənt] *adj* peu fréquent(e), rare

infuriate [ɪnˈfjuərɪeɪt] *vt* mettre en fureur

infuriating [ɪnˈfjuərɪeɪtɪŋ] *adj* exaspérant(e)

ingenious [ɪnˈdʒiːnjəs] *adj* ingénieux(-euse)

ingredient [ɪnˈɡriːdɪənt] *n* ingrédient *m*; (fig) élément *m*

inhabit [ɪnˈhæbɪt] *vt* habiter; **inhabitant** *n* habitant(e)

inhale [ɪnˈheɪl] *vt* inhaler; (perfume) respirer; (smoke) avaler ▷ *vi* (breathe in) aspirer; (in smoking) avaler la fumée; **inhaler** *n* inhalateur *m*

inherent [ɪnˈhɪərənt] *adj*: **~ (in or to)** inhérent(e) (à)

inherit [ɪnˈherɪt] *vt* hériter (de); **inheritance** *n* héritage *m*

inhibit [ɪnˈhɪbɪt] *vt* (Psych) inhiber; (growth) freiner; **inhibition** [ɪnhɪˈbɪʃən] *n* inhibition *f*

initial [ɪˈnɪʃl] *adj* initial(e) ▷ *n* initiale *f* ▷ *vt* parafer; **initials** *npl* initiales *fpl*; (as signature) parafe *m*; **initially** *adv* initialement, au début

initiate [ɪˈnɪʃɪeɪt] *vt* (start) entreprendre; amorcer; (enterprise) lancer; (person) initier; **to ~ proceedings against sb** (Law) intenter une action à qn, engager des poursuites contre qn

initiative [ɪˈnɪʃətɪv] *n* initiative *f*

inject [ɪnˈdʒekt] *vt* injecter; (person): **to ~ sb with sth** faire une piqûre de qch à qn; **injection** *n* [ɪnˈdʒekʃən] *n* injection *f*, piqûre *f*

injure [ˈɪndʒə*r*] *vt* blesser; (damage: reputation etc) compromettre; **to ~ o.s.** se blesser; **injured** *adj* (person, leg etc) blessé(e); **injury** *n* blessure *f*; (wrong) tort *m*

injustice [ɪnˈdʒʌstɪs] *n* injustice *f*

ink [ɪŋk] *n* encre *f*; **ink-jet printer** [ˈɪŋkdʒet-] *n* imprimante *f* à jet d'encre

inland *adj* [ˈɪnlənd] intérieur(e) ▷ *adv* [ɪnˈlænd] à l'intérieur, dans les terres; **Inland Revenue** *n* (BRIT) fisc *m*

in-laws [ˈɪnlɔːz] *npl* beaux-parents *mpl*; belle-famille

inmate [ˈɪnmeɪt] *n* (in prison) détenu(e); (in asylum) interné(e)

inn [ɪn] *n* auberge *f*

inner [ˈɪnə*r*] *adj* intérieur(e); **inner-city** *adj* (schools, problems) de quartiers déshérités

inning [ˈɪnɪŋ] *n* (us Baseball) tour *m* de batte; **innings** *npl* (Cricket) tour de batte

innocence [ˈɪnəsns] *n* innocence *f*

innocent [ˈɪnəsnt] *adj* innocent(e)

innovation [ɪnəʊˈveɪʃən] *n* innovation *f*

innovative [ˈɪnəʊˈveɪtɪv] *adj* novateur(-trice); (product) innovant(e)

in-patient [ˈɪnpeɪʃənt] *n* malade hospitalisé(e)

input [ˈɪnput] *n* (contribution) contribution *f*; (resources) ressources *fpl*; (Comput) entrée *f* (de données) (: data) données *fpl* ▷ *vt* (Comput) introduire, entrer

inquest [ˈɪnkwest] *n* enquête (criminelle); (coroner's) enquête judiciaire

inquire [ɪnˈkwaɪər] vi demander ▷ vt demander; **to ~ about** s'informer de, se renseigner sur; **to ~ when/ where/whether** demander quand/ où/si; **inquiry** n demande f de renseignements; enquête f, investigation f; **"inquiries"** "renseignements"

ins. abbr = **inches**

insane [ɪnˈseɪn] adj fou (folle); (Med) aliéné(e)

insanity [ɪnˈsænɪtɪ] n folie f; (Med) aliénation (mentale)

insect [ˈɪnsɛkt] n insecte m; **insect repellent** n crème f anti-insectes

insecure [ɪnsɪˈkjuər] adj (person) anxieux(-euse); (job) précaire; (building etc) peu sûr(e)

insecurity [ɪnsɪˈkjuərɪtɪ] n insécurité f

insensitive [ɪnˈsɛnsɪtɪv] adj insensible

insert vt [ɪnˈsəːt] insérer ▷ n [ˈɪnsəːt] insertion f

inside [ɪnˈsaɪd] n intérieur m ▷ adj intérieur(e) ▷ adv à l'intérieur, dedans ▷ prep à l'intérieur de; (of time): **~ 10 minutes** en moins de 10 minutes; **to go ~** rentrer; **inside lane** n (Aut: in Britain) voie f de gauche; (: in US, Europe) voie f de droite; **inside out** adv à l'envers; (know) à fond; **to turn sth inside out** retourner qch

insight [ˈɪnsaɪt] n perspicacité f; (glimpse, idea) aperçu m

insignificant [ɪnsɪɡˈnɪfɪkənt] adj insignifiant(e)

insincere [ɪnsɪnˈsɪər] adj hypocrite

insist [ɪnˈsɪst] vi insister; **to ~ on doing** insister pour faire; **to ~ that** insister pour que + sub; (claim) maintenir or soutenir que; **insistent** adj insistant(e), pressant(e); (noise, action) ininterrompu(e)

insomnia [ɪnˈsɒmnɪə] n insomnie f

inspect [ɪnˈspɛkt] vt inspecter; (Brit: ticket) contrôler; **inspection**

[ɪnˈspɛkʃən] n inspection f; (Brit: of tickets) contrôle m; **inspector** n inspecteur(-trice); (Brit: on buses, trains) contrôleur(-euse)

inspiration [ɪnspəˈreɪʃən] n inspiration f; **inspire** [ɪnˈspaɪər] vt inspirer; **inspiring** adj inspirant(e)

instability [ɪnstəˈbɪlɪtɪ] n instabilité f

install, (US) **instal** [ɪnˈstɔːl] vt installer; **installation** [ɪnstəˈleɪʃən] n installation f

instalment, (US) **installment** [ɪnˈstɔːlmənt] n (payment) acompte m, versement partiel; (of TV serial etc) épisode m; **in ~s** (pay) à tempérament; (receive) en plusieurs fois

instance [ˈɪnstəns] n exemple m; **for ~** par exemple; **in the first ~** tout d'abord, en premier lieu

instant [ˈɪnstənt] n instant m ▷ adj immédiat(e), urgent(e); (coffee, food) instantané(e), en poudre; **instantly** adv immédiatement, tout de suite; **instant messaging** n messagerie f instantanée

instead [ɪnˈstɛd] adv au lieu de cela; **~ of** au lieu de; **~ of sb** à la place de qn

instinct [ˈɪnstɪŋkt] n instinct m; **instinctive** adj instinctif(-ive)

institute [ˈɪnstɪtjuːt] n institut m ▷ vt instituer, établir; (inquiry) ouvrir; (proceedings) entamer

institution [ɪnstɪˈtjuːʃən] n institution f; (school) établissement m (scolaire); (for care) établissement (psychiatrique etc)

instruct [ɪnˈstrʌkt] vt: **to ~ sb in sth** enseigner qch à qn; **to ~ sb to do** charger qn or ordonner à qn de faire; **instruction** [ɪnˈstrʌkʃən] n instruction f; **instructions** npl (orders) directives fpl; **instructions for use** mode m d'emploi; **instructor** n professeur m; (for skiing, driving) moniteur m

instrument [ˈɪnstrumənt] n instrument m; **instrumental**

~ [ɪnstru'mentl] adj (Mus) instrumental(e); **to be instrumental in sth/in doing sth** contribuer à qch/à faire qch

insufficient [ɪnsə'fɪʃənt] adj insuffisant(e)

insulate ['ɪnsjuleɪt] vt isoler; (against sound) insonoriser; **insulation** [ɪnsju'leɪʃən] n isolation f; (against sound) insonorisation f

insulin ['ɪnsjulɪn] n insuline f

insult n ['ɪnsʌlt] insulte f, affront m ▷ vt [ɪn'sʌlt] insulter, faire un affront à; **insulting** adj insultant(e), injurieux(-euse)

insurance [ɪn'ʃuərəns] n assurance f; **fire/life** ~ assurance-incendie/-vie; **insurance company** n compagnie f or société f d'assurances; **insurance policy** n police f d'assurance

insure [ɪn'ʃuəʳ] vt assurer; **to ~ (o.s.) against** (fig) parer à

intact [ɪn'tækt] adj intact(e)

intake ['ɪnteɪk] n (Tech) admission f; (consumption) consommation f; (BRIT Scol): **an ~ of 200 a year** 200 admissions par an

integral ['ɪntɪɡrəl] adj (whole) intégral(e); (part) intégrant(e)

integrate ['ɪntɪɡreɪt] vt intégrer ▷ vi s'intégrer

integrity [ɪn'teɡrɪtɪ] n intégrité f

intellect ['ɪntəlekt] n intelligence f; **intellectual** [ɪntə'lektjuəl] adj, n intellectuel(le)

intelligence [ɪn'telɪdʒəns] n intelligence f; (Mil) informations fpl, renseignements mpl

intelligent [ɪn'telɪdʒənt] adj intelligent(e)

intend [ɪn'tend] vt (gift etc): **to ~ sth for** destiner à qch; **to ~ to do** avoir l'intention de faire

intense [ɪn'tens] adj intense; (person) véhément(e)

intensify [ɪn'tensɪfaɪ] vt intensifier

intensity [ɪn'tensɪtɪ] n intensité f

intensive [ɪn'tensɪv] adj intensif(-ive); **intensive care** n: **to be in intensive care** être en réanimation; **intensive care unit** n service m de réanimation

intent [ɪn'tent] n intention f ▷ adj attentif(-ive), absorbé(e); **to all ~s and purposes** en fait, pratiquement; **to be ~ on doing sth** être (bien) décidé à faire qch

intention [ɪn'tenʃən] n intention f; **intentional** adj intentionnel(le), délibéré(e)

interact [ɪntər'ækt] vi avoir une action réciproque; (people) communiquer; **interaction** [ɪntər'ækʃən] n interaction f; **interactive** adj (Comput) interactif, conversationnel(le)

intercept [ɪntə'sept] vt intercepter; (person) arrêter au passage

interchange n ['ɪntətʃeɪndʒ] (exchange) échange m; (on motorway) échangeur m

intercourse ['ɪntəkɔːs] n: **sexual ~** rapports sexuels

interest ['ɪntrɪst] n intérêt m; (Comm: stake, share) participation f, intérêts mpl ▷ vt intéresser; **interested** adj intéressé(e); **to be interested in sth** s'intéresser à qch; **I'm interested in going** ça m'intéresse d'y aller; **interesting** adj intéressant(e); **interest rate** n taux m d'intérêt

interface ['ɪntəfeɪs] n (Comput) interface f

interfere [ɪntə'fɪəʳ] vi: **to ~ in** (quarrel) s'immiscer dans; (other people's business) se mêler de; **to ~ with** (object) tripoter, toucher à; (plans) contrecarrer; (duty) être en conflit avec; **interference** n (gen) ingérence f; (Radio, TV) parasites mpl

interim ['ɪntərɪm] adj provisoire; (post) intérimaire ▷ n: **in the ~** dans l'intérim

interior [ɪn'tɪərɪəʳ] n intérieur m ▷ adj intérieur(e); (minister, department) de l'intérieur; **interior design** n architecture f d'intérieur

intermediate [ɪntə'miːdɪət] adj intermédiaire; (*Scol: course, level*) moyen(ne)

intermission [ɪntə'mɪʃən] n pause f; (*Theat, Cine*) entracte m

intern vt [ɪn'təːn] interner ▷ n ['ɪntəːn] (*US*) interne m/f

internal [ɪn'təːnl] adj interne; (*dispute, reform etc*) intérieur(e); **Internal Revenue Service** n (*US*) fisc m

international [ɪntə'næʃənl] adj international(e) ▷ n (*BRIT Sport*) international m

Internet [ɪntə'nɛt] n: **the ~** l'Internet m; **Internet café** n cybercafé m; **Internet Service Provider** n fournisseur m d'accès à Internet; **Internet user** n internaute m/f

interpret [ɪn'təːprɪt] vt interpréter ▷ vi servir d'interprète; **interpretation** [ɪntəːprɪ'teɪʃən] n interprétation f; **interpreter** n interprète m/f; **could you act as an interpreter for us?** pourriez-vous nous servir d'interprète?

interrogate [ɪn'tɛrəugeɪt] vt interroger; (*suspect etc*) soumettre à un interrogatoire; **interrogation** [ɪntɛrəu'geɪʃən] n interrogation f; (*by police*) interrogatoire m

interrogative [ɪntə'rɔgətɪv] adj interrogateur(-trice) ▷ n (*Ling*) interrogatif m

interrupt [ɪntə'rʌpt] vt, vi interrompre; **interruption** [ɪntə'rʌpʃən] n interruption f

intersection [ɪntə'sɛkʃən] n (*of roads*) croisement m

interstate ['ɪntərsteɪt] (*US*) n autoroute f (qui relie plusieurs États)

interval ['ɪntəvl] n intervalle m; (*BRIT: Theat*) entracte m; (*Sport*) mi-temps f; **at ~s** par intervalles

intervene [ɪntə'viːn] vi (*time*) s'écouler (entre-temps); (*event*) survenir; (*person*) intervenir

interview ['ɪntəvjuː] n (*Radio, TV*) interview f; (*for job*) entrevue f ▷ vt interviewer, avoir une entrevue avec; **interviewer** n (*Radio, TV*) interviewer m

intimate adj ['ɪntɪmət] intime; (*friendship*) profond(e); (*knowledge*) approfondi(e) ▷ vt ['ɪntɪmeɪt] suggérer, laisser entendre; (*announce*) faire savoir

intimidate [ɪn'tɪmɪdeɪt] vt intimider

intimidating [ɪn'tɪmɪdeɪtɪŋ] adj intimidant(e)

into ['ɪntu] prep dans; **~ pieces/ French** en morceaux/français

intolerant [ɪn'tɔlərnt] adj: **~ (of)** intolérant(e) (de)

intranet ['ɪntrənɛt] n intranet m

intransitive [ɪn'trænsɪtɪv] adj intransitif(-ive)

intricate ['ɪntrɪkət] adj complexe, compliqué(e)

intrigue [ɪn'triːg] n intrigue f ▷ vt intriguer; **intriguing** adj fascinant(e)

introduce [ɪntrə'djuːs] vt introduire; (*TV show etc*) présenter; **to ~ sb (to sb)** présenter qn (à qn); **to ~ sb to** (*pastime, technique*) initier qn à; **introduction** [ɪntrə'dʌkʃən] n introduction f; (*of person*) présentation f; (*to new experience*) initiation f; **introductory** [ɪntrə'dʌktəri] adj préliminaire, introductif(-ive)

intrude [ɪn'truːd] vi (*person*) être importun(e); **to ~ on** or **into** (*conversation etc*) s'immiscer dans; **intruder** n intrus(e)

intuition [ɪntjuː'ɪʃən] n intuition f

inundate ['ɪnʌndeɪt] vt: **to ~ with** inonder de

invade [ɪn'veɪd] vt envahir

invalid n ['ɪnvəlɪd] malade m/f; (*with disability*) invalide m/f ▷ adj [ɪn'vælɪd] (*not valid*) invalide, non valide

invaluable [ɪn'væljuəbl] adj inestimable, inappréciable

invariably [ɪnˈvɛərɪəblɪ] adv invariablement; **she is ~ late** elle est toujours en retard

invasion [ɪnˈveɪʒən] n invasion f

invent [ɪnˈvɛnt] vt inventer; **invention** [ɪnˈvɛnʃən] n invention f; **inventor** n inventeur(-trice)

inventory [ˈɪnvəntrɪ] n inventaire m

inverted commas [ɪnˈvəːtɪd-] npl (BRIT) guillemets mpl

invest [ɪnˈvɛst] vt investir ▷ vi: **to ~ in** placer de l'argent or investir dans; (fig: acquire) s'offrir, faire l'acquisition de

investigate [ɪnˈvɛstɪɡeɪt] vt étudier, examiner; (crime) faire une enquête sur; **investigation** [ɪnvɛstɪˈɡeɪʃən] n (of crime) enquête f, investigation f

investigator [ɪnˈvɛstɪɡeɪtər] n investigateur(-trice); **private ~** détective privé

investment [ɪnˈvɛstmənt] n investissement m, placement m

investor [ɪnˈvɛstər] n épargnant(e); (shareholder) actionnaire m/f

invisible [ɪnˈvɪzɪbl] adj invisible

invitation [ɪnvɪˈteɪʃən] n invitation f

invite [ɪnˈvaɪt] vt inviter; (opinions etc) demander; **inviting** adj engageant(e), attrayant(e)

invoice [ˈɪnvɔɪs] n facture f ▷ vt facturer

involve [ɪnˈvɔlv] vt (entail) impliquer; (concern) concerner; (require) nécessiter; **to ~ sb in** (theft etc) impliquer qn dans; (activity, meeting) faire participer qn à; **involved** adj (complicated) complexe; **to be involved in** (take part) participer à; **involvement** n (personal role) rôle m; (participation) participation f; (enthusiasm) enthousiasme m

inward [ˈɪnwəd] adj (movement) vers l'intérieur; (thought, feeling) profond(e), intime ▷ adv = **inwards**; **inwards** adv vers l'intérieur

iPod® [ˈaɪpɔd] n iPod® m

IQ n abbr (= intelligence quotient) Q.I. m

IRA n abbr (= Irish Republican Army) IRA f

Iran [ɪˈrɑːn] n Iran m; **Iranian** [ɪˈreɪnɪən] adj iranien(ne) ▷ n Iranien(ne)

Iraq [ɪˈrɑːk] n Irak m; **Iraqi** adj irakien(ne) ▷ n Irakien(ne)

Ireland [ˈaɪələnd] n Irlande f

iris, irises [ˈaɪrɪs, -ɪz] n iris m

Irish [ˈaɪrɪʃ] adj irlandais(e) ▷ npl: **the ~** les Irlandais; **Irishman** (irreg) n Irlandais m; **Irishwoman** (irreg) n Irlandaise f

iron [ˈaɪən] n fer m; (for clothes) fer m à repasser ▷ adj de or en fer ▷ vt (clothes) repasser

ironic(al) [aɪˈrɔnɪk(l)] adj ironique; **ironically** adv ironiquement

ironing [ˈaɪənɪŋ] n (activity) repassage m; (clothes: ironed) linge repassé; (: to be ironed) linge à repasser; **ironing board** n planche f à repasser

irony [ˈaɪrənɪ] n ironie f

irrational [ɪˈræʃənl] adj irrationnel(le); (person) qui n'est pas rationnel

irregular [ɪˈrɛɡjulər] adj irrégulier(-ière); (surface) inégal(e); (action, event) peu orthodoxe

irrelevant [ɪˈrɛləvənt] adj sans rapport, hors de propos

irresistible [ɪrɪˈzɪstɪbl] adj irrésistible

irresponsible [ɪrɪˈspɔnsɪbl] adj (act) irréfléchi(e); (person) qui n'a pas le sens des responsabilités

irrigation [ɪrɪˈɡeɪʃən] n irrigation f

irritable [ˈɪrɪtəbl] adj irritable

irritate [ˈɪrɪteɪt] vt irriter; **irritating** adj irritant(e); **irritation** [ɪrɪˈteɪʃən] n irritation f

IRS n abbr (US) = **Internal Revenue Service**

is [ɪz] vb see **be**

ISDN n abbr (= Integrated Services Digital Network) RNIS m

Islam [ˈɪzlɑːm] n Islam m; **Islamic** [ɪzˈlɑːmɪk] adj islamique

island ['aɪlənd] n île f; (also: **traffic ~**) refuge m (pour piétons); **islander** n habitant(e) d'une île, insulaire m/f
isle [aɪl] n île f
isn't ['ɪznt] = **is not**
isolated ['aɪsəleɪtɪd] adj isolé(e)
isolation [aɪsə'leɪʃən] n isolement m
ISP n abbr = **Internet Service Provider**
Israel ['ɪzreɪl] n Israël m; **Israeli** [ɪz'reɪlɪ] adj israélien(ne) ⊳ n Israélien(ne)
issue ['ɪʃuː] n question f, problème m; (of banknotes) émission f; (of newspaper) numéro m; (of book) publication f, parution f ⊳ vt (rations, equipment) distribuer; (orders) donner; (statement) publier, faire; (certificate, passport) délivrer; (banknotes, cheques, stamps) émettre, mettre en circulation: **at ~** en jeu, en cause; **to take ~ with sb (over sth)** exprimer son désaccord avec qn (sur qch)
IT n abbr = **information technology**

🔘 **KEYWORD**

it [ɪt] pron **1** (specific: subject) il (elle); (: direct object) le (la, l'); (: indirect object) lui; **it's on the table** c'est or il (or elle) est sur la table; **I can't find it** je n'arrive pas à le trouver; **give it to me** donne-le-moi
2 (after prep): **about/from/of it** en; **I spoke to him about it** je lui en ai parlé; **what did you learn from it?** qu'est-ce que vous en avez retiré?; **I'm proud of it** j'en suis fier; **in/to it** y; **put the book in it** mettez-y le livre; **he agreed to it** il y a consenti; **did you go to it?** (party, concert etc) est-ce que vous y êtes allé(s)?
3 (impersonal) il; ce, cela, ça; **it's Friday tomorrow** demain, c'est vendredi or nous sommes vendredi; **it's 6 o'clock** il est 6 heures; **how far is it? — it's 10 miles** c'est loin? — c'est à 10 miles; **who is it? — it's me** qui

est-ce? — c'est moi; **it's raining** il pleut

Italian [ɪ'tæljən] adj italien(ne) ⊳ n Italien(ne); (Ling) italien m
italics [ɪ'tælɪks] npl italique m
Italy ['ɪtəlɪ] n Italie f
itch [ɪtʃ] n démangeaison f ⊳ vi (person) éprouver des démangeaisons; (part of body) démanger; **I m~ing to do** l'envie me démange de faire; **itchy** adj: **my back is itchy** j'ai le dos qui me démange
it'd ['ɪtd] = **it would**; **it had**
item ['aɪtəm] n (gen) article m; (on agenda) question f, point m; (also: **news ~**) nouvelle f
itinerary [aɪ'tɪnərərɪ] n itinéraire m
it'll ['ɪtl] = **it will**; **it shall**
its [ɪts] adj son (sa), ses pl
it's [ɪts] = **it is**; **it has**
itself [ɪt'sɛlf] pron (reflexive) se; (emphatic) lui-même (elle-même)
ITV n abbr (BRIT: = Independent Television) chaîne de télévision commerciale
I've [aɪv] = **I have**
ivory ['aɪvərɪ] n ivoire m
ivy ['aɪvɪ] n lierre m

j

jab [dʒæb] *vt*: **to ~ sth into** enfoncer or planter qch dans ▷ *n* (*Med: inf*) piqûre *f*

jack [dʒæk] *n* (*Aut*) cric *m*; (*Cards*) valet *m*

jacket ['dʒækɪt] *n* veste *f*, veston *m*; (*of book*) couverture *f*, jaquette *f*; **jacket potato** *n* pomme *f* de terre en robe des champs

jackpot ['dʒækpɔt] *n* gros lot

Jacuzzi® [dʒə'ku:zɪ] *n* jacuzzi® *m*

jagged ['dʒægɪd] *adj* dentelé(e)

jail [dʒeɪl] *n* prison *f* ▷ *vt* emprisonner, mettre en prison; **jail sentence** *n* peine *f* de prison

jam [dʒæm] *n* confiture *f*; (*also:* **traffic ~**) embouteillage *m* ▷ *vt* (*passage etc*) encombrer, obstruer; (*mechanism, drawer etc*) bloquer, coincer; (*Radio*) brouiller ▷ *vi* (*mechanism, sliding part*) se coincer, se bloquer; (*gun*) s'enrayer; **to be in a ~** (*inf*) être dans le pétrin; **to ~ sth into** (*stuff*) entasser or comprimer qch dans; (*thrust*) enfoncer qch dans

Jamaica [dʒə'meɪkə] *n* Jamaïque *f*

jammed [dʒæmd] *adj* (*window etc*) coincé(e)

janitor ['dʒænɪtə'] *n* (*caretaker*) concierge *m*

January ['dʒænjuərɪ] *n* janvier *m*

Japan [dʒə'pæn] *n* Japon *m*; **Japanese** [dʒæpə'ni:z] *adj* japonais(e) ▷ *n* (*pl inv*) Japonais(e); (*Ling*) japonais *m*

jar [dʒɑ:'] *n* (*stone, earthenware*) pot *m*; (*glass*) bocal *m* ▷ *vi* (*sound*) produire un son grinçant or discordant; (*colours etc*) détonner, jurer

jargon ['dʒɑ:gən] *n* jargon *m*

javelin ['dʒævlɪn] *n* javelot *m*

jaw [dʒɔ:] *n* mâchoire *f*

jazz [dʒæz] *n* jazz *m*

jealous ['dʒeləs] *adj* jaloux(-ouse); **jealousy** *n* jalousie *f*

jeans [dʒi:nz] *npl* jean *m*

Jello® ['dʒeləu] (*us*) *n* gelée *f*

jelly ['dʒelɪ] *n* (*dessert*) gelée *f*; (*us: jam*) confiture *f*; **jellyfish** *n* méduse *f*

jeopardize ['dʒepədaɪz] *vt* mettre en danger or péril

jerk [dʒə:k] *n* secousse *f*, saccade *f*; (*of muscle*) spasme *m*; (*inf*) pauvre type *m* ▷ *vt* (*shake*) donner une secousse à; (*pull*) tirer brusquement ▷ *vi* (*vehicles*) cahoter

jersey ['dʒə:zɪ] *n* tricot *m*; (*fabric*) jersey *m*

Jesus ['dʒi:zəs] *n* Jésus

jet [dʒet] *n* (*of gas, liquid*) jet *m*; (*Aviat*) avion *m* à réaction, jet *m*; **jet lag** *n* décalage *m* horaire; **jet-ski** *vi* faire du jet-ski or scooter des mers

jetty ['dʒetɪ] *n* jetée *f*, digue *f*

Jew [dʒu:] *n* Juif *m*

jewel ['dʒu:əl] *n* bijou *m*, joyau *m*; (*in watch*) rubis *m*; **jeweller**, (*us*) **jeweler** *n* bijoutier(-ière), joaillier *m*; **jeweller's (shop)** *n* (*BRIT*) bijouterie *f*, joaillerie *f*; **jewellery**, (*us*) **jewelry** *n* bijoux *mpl*

Jewish ['dʒu:ɪʃ] *adj* juif (juive)

jigsaw ['dʒɪgsɔː] n (also: **~ puzzle**) puzzle m

job [dʒɔb] n (chore, task) travail m, tâche f; (employment) emploi m, poste m, place f; **it's a good ~ that ...** c'est heureux or c'est une chance que ... + sub; **just the ~!** (c'est) juste or exactement ce qu'il faut!; **job centre** (BRIT) n ≈ ANPE f, ≈ Agence nationale pour l'emploi; **jobless** adj sans travail, au chômage

jockey ['dʒɔkɪ] n jockey m ▷ vi: **to ~ for position** manœuvrer pour être bien placé

jog [dʒɔg] vt secouer ▷ vi (Sport) faire du jogging; **to ~ sb's memory** rafraîchir la mémoire de qn; **jogging** n jogging m

join [dʒɔɪn] vt (put together) unir, assembler; (become member of) s'inscrire à; (meet) rejoindre, retrouver; (queue) se joindre à ▷ vi (roads, rivers) se rejoindre, se rencontrer ▷ n raccord m; **join in** vi se mettre de la partie ▷ vt fus se mêler à; **join up** vi (meet) se rejoindre; (Mil) s'engager

joiner ['dʒɔɪnə'] (BRIT) n menuisier m

joint [dʒɔɪnt] n (Tech) jointure f, joint m; (Anat) articulation f, jointure; (BRIT Culin) rôti m; (inf: place) boîte f; (of cannabis) joint ▷ adj commun(e); (committee) mixte, paritaire; (winner) ex aequo; **joint account** n compte joint; **jointly** adv ensemble, en commun

joke [dʒəuk] n plaisanterie f; (also: **practical ~**) farce f ▷ vi plaisanter; **to play a ~ on** jouer un tour à, faire une farce à; **joker** n (Cards) joker m

jolly ['dʒɔlɪ] adj gai(e), enjoué(e); (enjoyable) amusant(e), plaisant(e) ▷ adv (BRIT inf) rudement, drôlement

jolt [dʒəult] n cahot m, secousse f; (shock) choc m ▷ vt cahoter, secouer

Jordan ['dʒɔːdən] n (country) Jordanie f

journal ['dʒəːnl] n journal m; **journalism** n journalisme m; **journalist** n journaliste m/f

journey ['dʒəːnɪ] n voyage m; (distance covered) trajet m; **the ~ takes two hours** le trajet dure deux heures; **how was your ~?** votre voyage s'est bien passé?

joy [dʒɔɪ] n joie f; **joyrider** n voleur(-euse) de voiture (qui fait une virée dans le véhicule volé); **joy stick** n (Aviat) manche m à balai; (Comput) manche à balai, manette f (de jeu)

Jr abbr = **junior**

judge [dʒʌdʒ] n juge m ▷ vt juger; (estimate: weight, size etc) apprécier; (consider) estimer

judo ['dʒuːdəu] n judo m

jug [dʒʌg] n pot m, cruche f

juggle ['dʒʌgl] vi jongler; **juggler** n jongleur m

juice [dʒuːs] n jus m; **juicy** adj juteux(-euse)

July [dʒuː'laɪ] n juillet m

jumble ['dʒʌmbl] n fouillis m ▷ vt (also: **~ up, ~ together**) mélanger, brouiller; **jumble sale** n (BRIT) vente f de charité

● **JUMBLE SALE**

● Les jumble sales ont lieu dans les
● églises, salles des fêtes ou halls
● d'écoles, et l'on y vend des articles
● de toutes sortes, en général bon
● marché et surtout d'occasion, pour
● collecter des fonds pour une œuvre
● de charité, une école (par exemple,
● pour acheter des ordinateurs), ou
● encore une église (pour réparer
● un toit etc).

jumbo ['dʒʌmbəu] adj (also: **~ jet**) (avion) gros porteur m (à réaction)

jump [dʒʌmp] vi sauter, bondir; (with fear etc) sursauter; (increase) monter en flèche ▷ vt sauter, franchir ▷ n saut m, bond m; (with fear etc) sursaut m; (fence) obstacle m; **to ~ the queue** (BRIT) passer avant son tour

jumper ['dʒʌmpə'] n (BRIT: pullover) pull-over m; (US: pinafore dress) robe-chasuble f

jump leads, (US) **jumper cables** npl câbles mpl de démarrage

Jun. abbr = **June**; **junior**

junction ['dʒʌŋkʃən] n (BRIT: of roads) carrefour m; (of rails) embranchement m

June [dʒuːn] n juin m

jungle ['dʒʌŋgl] n jungle f

junior ['dʒuːnɪə'] adj, n: **he's ~ to me (by two years), he's my ~** (by two years) il est mon cadet (de deux ans), il est plus jeune que moi (de deux ans); **he's ~ to me** (seniority) il est en dessous de moi (dans la hiérarchie), j'ai plus d'ancienneté que lui; see also **high school**; **junior school** n (BRIT) école f primaire; **junior high school** n (US) ≈ collège m d'enseignement secondaire; see also **high school**; **junior school** n (BRIT) école f primaire

junk [dʒʌŋk] n (rubbish) camelote f; (cheap goods) bric-à-brac m inv; **junk food** n snacks vite prêts (sans valeur nutritive)

junkie ['dʒʌŋkɪ] n (inf) junkie m, drogué(e)

junk mail n prospectus mpl; (Comput) messages mpl publicitaires

Jupiter ['dʒuːpɪtə'] n (planet) Jupiter f

jurisdiction [dʒuərɪs'dɪkʃən] n juridiction f; **it falls or comes within/outside our ~** cela est/n'est pas de notre compétence or ressort

jury ['dʒuərɪ] n jury m

just [dʒʌst] adj juste ▷ adv: **he's ~ done it/left** il vient de le faire/partir; **~ right/two o'clock** exactement or juste ce qu'il faut/deux heures; **we were ~ going** nous partions; **I was ~ about to phone** j'allais téléphoner; **~ as he was leaving** au moment or à l'instant précis où il partait; **~ before/enough/here** juste avant/assez/là; **it's ~ me/a mistake** ce n'est que moi/(rien) qu'une erreur; **~ missed/caught** manqué/attrapé de justesse; **~ listen to this!** écoutez un peu ça!; **she's ~ as clever as you** elle est tout aussi intelligente que vous; **it's ~ as well that you ...** heureusement que vous ...; **~ a minute!, ~ one moment!** un instant (s'il vous plaît)!

justice ['dʒʌstɪs] n justice f; (US: judge) juge m de la Cour suprême

justification [dʒʌstɪfɪ'keɪʃən] n justification f

justify ['dʒʌstɪfaɪ] vt justifier

jut [dʒʌt] vi (also: **~ out**) dépasser, faire saillie

juvenile ['dʒuːvənaɪl] adj juvénile; (court, books) pour enfants ▷ n adolescent(e)

K

K, k [keɪ] abbr (= one thousand) K

kangaroo [kæŋɡəˈruː] n kangourou m

karaoke [kɑːrəˈəʊkɪ] n karaoké m

karate [kəˈrɑːtɪ] n karaté m

kebab [kəˈbæb] n kebab m

keel [kiːl] n quille f; **on an even ~** (fig) à flot

keen [kiːn] adj (eager) plein(e) d'enthousiasme; (interest, desire, competition) vif (vive); (eye, intelligence) pénétrant(e); (edge) effilé(e); **to be ~ to do** or **on doing sth** désirer vivement faire qch, tenir beaucoup à faire qch; **to be ~ on sth/sb** aimer beaucoup qch/qn

keep [kiːp] (pt, pp **kept**) vt (retain, preserve) garder; (hold back) retenir; (shop, accounts, promise, diary) tenir; (support) entretenir; (chickens, bees, pigs etc) élever ▷ vi (food) se conserver; (remain: in a certain state or place) rester ▷ n (of castle) donjon m; (food etc): **enough for his ~** assez pour (assurer) sa subsistance; **to ~ doing sth** (continue) continuer à faire qch; (repeatedly) ne pas arrêter de faire qch; **to ~ sb from doing/sth from happening** empêcher qn de faire or que qn (ne) fasse/que qch (n')arrive; **to ~ sb happy/a place tidy** faire que qn soit content/qu'un endroit reste propre; **to ~ sth to o.s.** garder qch pour soi, tenir qch secret; **to ~ sth from sb** cacher qch à qn; **to ~ time** (clock) être à l'heure, ne pas retarder; **for ~s** (inf) pour de bon, pour toujours; **keep away** vt: **to ~ sth/sb away from sb** éloigner qch/qn ▷ vi: **to ~ away (from)** ne pas s'approcher (de); **keep back** vt (crowds, tears, money) retenir; (conceal: information): **to ~ sth back from sb** cacher qch à qn ▷ vi rester en arrière; **keep off** vt (dog, person) éloigner ▷ vi: **if the rain ~s off** s'il ne pleut pas; **~ your hands off!** pas touché! (inf); **"~ off the grass"** "pelouse interdite"; **keep on** vi continuer; **to ~ on doing** continuer à faire; **don't ~ on about it!** arrête (d'en parler)!; **keep out** vt empêcher d'entrer ▷ vi (stay out) rester en dehors; **"~ out"** "défense d'entrer"; **keep up** vi (in comprehension) suivre ▷ vt tenir, maintenir; **to ~ up with sb** (in work etc) se maintenir au même niveau que qn; (in race etc) aller aussi vite que qn; **keeper** n gardien(ne); **keep-fit** n gymnastique f (d'entretien); **keeping** n (care) garde f; **in keeping with** en harmonie avec

kennel ['kɛnl] n niche f; **kennels** npl (for boarding) chenil m

Kenya ['kɛnjə] n Kenya m

kept [kɛpt] pt, pp of **keep**

kerb [kəːb] n (BRIT) bordure f du trottoir

kerosene ['kɛrəsiːn] n kérosène m

ketchup ['kɛtʃəp] n ketchup m

kettle ['kɛtl] n bouilloire f

key [kiː] n (gen, Mus) clé f; (of piano, typewriter) touche f; (on map) légende f ▷ adj (factor, role, area) clé inv ▷ vt (also: **~ in**) (text) saisir; **can I have my**

~**?** je peux avoir ma clé?; **a ~ issue** un problème fondamental; **keyboard** n clavier m; **keyhole** n trou m de la serrure; **keypad** n pavé m numérique; (of smartphone) clavier m; **keyring** n porte-clés m

kg abbr (= kilogram) K

khaki ['kɑ:kɪ] adj, n kaki m

kick [kɪk] vt donner un coup de pied à ▷ vi (horse) ruer ▷ n coup m de pied; (inf: thrill): **he does it for ~s** il le fait parce que ça l'excite, il le fait pour le plaisir; **to ~ the habit** (inf) arrêter; **kick off** vi (Sport) donner le coup d'envoi; **kick-off** n (Sport) coup m d'envoi

kid [kɪd] n (inf: child) gamin(e), gosse m/f; (animal, leather) chevreau m ▷ vi (inf) plaisanter, blaguer

kidnap ['kɪdnæp] vt enlever, kidnapper; **kidnapping** n enlèvement m

kidney ['kɪdnɪ] n (Anat) rein m; (Culin) rognon m; **kidney bean** n haricot m rouge

kill [kɪl] vt tuer ▷ n mise f à mort; **to ~ time** tuer le temps; **killer** n tueur(-euse); (murderer) meurtrier(-ière); **killing** n meurtre m; (of group of people) tuerie f, massacre m; (inf): **to make a killing** se remplir les poches, réussir un beau coup

kiln [kɪln] n four m

kilo ['ki:ləu] n kilo m; **kilobyte** n (Comput) kilo-octet m; **kilogram(me)** n kilogramme m; **kilometre**, (US) **kilometer** ['kɪləmi:tə'] n kilomètre m; **kilowatt** n kilowatt m

kilt [kɪlt] n kilt m

kin [kɪn] n see **next-of-kin**

kind [kaɪnd] adj gentil(le), aimable ▷ n sorte f, espèce f; (species) genre m; **to be two of a ~** se ressembler; **in ~** (Comm) en nature; **~ of** (inf: rather) plutôt; **a ~ of** une sorte de; **what ~ of ...?** quelle sorte de ...?

kindergarten ['kɪndəgɑ:tn] n jardin m d'enfants

kindly ['kaɪndlɪ] adj bienveillant(e), plein(e) de gentillesse ▷ adv avec

bonté; **will you ~ ...** auriez-vous la bonté or l'obligeance de ...

kindness ['kaɪndnɪs] n (quality) bonté f, gentillesse f

king [kɪŋ] n roi m; **kingdom** n royaume m; **kingfisher** n martin-pêcheur m; **king-size(d) bed** n grand lit (de 1,95 m de large)

kiosk ['ki:ɔsk] n kiosque m; (BRIT: also: **telephone ~**) cabine f (téléphonique)

kipper ['kɪpə'] n hareng fumé et salé

kiss [kɪs] n baiser m ▷ vt embrasser; **to ~ (each other)** s'embrasser; **kiss of life** (BRIT) bouche à bouche m

kit [kɪt] n équipement m, matériel m; (set of tools etc) trousse f; (for assembly) kit m

kitchen ['kɪtʃɪn] n cuisine f

kite [kaɪt] n (toy) cerf-volant m

kitten ['kɪtn] n petit chat, chaton m

kitty ['kɪtɪ] n (money) cagnotte f

kiwi ['ki:wi:] n (also: **~ fruit**) kiwi m

km abbr (= kilometre) km

km/h abbr (= kilometres per hour) km/h

knack [næk] n: **to have the ~ (of doing)** avoir le coup (pour faire)

knee [ni:] n genou m; **kneecap** n rotule f

kneel [ni:l] vt, pp **knelt** [nɛlt, nɛlt] vi (also: **~ down**) s'agenouiller

knelt [nɛlt] pt, pp of **kneel**

knew [nju:] pt of **know**

knickers ['nɪkəz] npl (BRIT) culotte f (de femme)

knife (pl **knives**) [naɪf, naɪvz] n couteau m ▷ vt poignarder, frapper d'un coup de couteau

knight [naɪt] n chevalier m; (Chess) cavalier m

knit [nɪt] vt tricoter ▷ vi tricoter; (broken bones) se ressouder; **to ~ one's brows** froncer les sourcils; **knitting** n tricot m; **knitting needle** n aiguille f à tricoter; **knitwear** n tricots mpl, lainages mpl

knives [naɪvz] npl of **knife**

knob [nɔb] n bouton m; (BRIT): **a ~ of butter** une noix de beurre

knock [nɔk] vt frapper; (bump into) heurter; (inf: fig) dénigrer ▷ vi (at door etc): **to ~ at/on** frapper à/sur ▷ *n* coup *m*; **knock down** *vt* renverser; *(price)* réduire; **knock off** *vi* (*inf*: *finish*) s'arrêter (de travailler) ▷ *vt* (*vase*, *object*) faire tomber; (*inf*: *steal*) piquer; (*fig*: *from price etc*): **to ~ off £10** faire une remise de 10 livres; **knock out** *vt* assommer; (*Boxing*) mettre k.-o.; (*in competition*) éliminer; **knock over** *vt* (*object*) faire tomber; (*pedestrian*) renverser; **knockout** *n* (*Boxing*) knock-out *m*, K.-O. *m*; **knockout competition** *n* (BRIT) compétition *f* avec épreuves éliminatoires

knot [nɔt] *n* (*gen*) nœud *m* ▷ *vt* nouer

know [nəu] (*pt* **knew**, *pp* **known**) *vt* savoir; (*person*, *place*) connaître; **to ~ that** savoir que; **to ~ how to do** savoir faire; **to ~ how to swim** savoir nager; **to ~ about/of sth** (*event*) être au courant de qch; (*subject*) connaître qch; **I don't ~** je ne sais pas; **do you ~ where I can ...?** savez-vous où je peux ...?; **know-all** *n* (BRIT *pej*) je-sais-tout *m/f*; **know-how** *n* savoir-faire *m*, technique *f*, compétence *f*; **knowing** *adj* (*look etc*) entendu(e); **knowingly** *adv* (*on purpose*) sciemment; (*smile*, *look*) d'un air entendu; **know-it-all** *n* (US) = **know-all**

knowledge ['nɔlɪdʒ] *n* connaissance *f*; (*learning*) connaissances, savoir *m*; **without my ~** à mon insu; **knowledgeable** *adj* bien informé(e)

known [nəun] *pp of* **know** ▷ *adj* (*thief*, *facts*) notoire; (*expert*) célèbre

knuckle ['nʌkl] *n* articulation *f* (des phalanges), jointure *f*

koala [kəu'ɑ:lə] *n* (*also*: ~ **bear**) koala *m*

Koran [kɔ'rɑ:n] *n* Coran *m*

Korea [kə'rɪə] *n* Corée *f*; **Korean** *adj* coréen(ne) ▷ *n* Coréen(ne)

kosher ['kəuʃə'] *adj* kascher *inv*

Kosovar, Kosovan ['kɒsəvɑ:', 'kɒsəvən] *adj* kosovar(e)

Kosovo ['kɒsəvəu] *n* Kosovo *m*

Kuwait [ku'weɪt] *n* Koweït *m*

L *abbr* (BRIT Aut: = *learner*) signale un conducteur débutant

l. *abbr* (= *litre*) l

lab [læb] *n abbr* (= *laboratory*) labo *m*

label ['leɪbl] *n* étiquette *f*; (*brand*: *of record*) marque *f* ▷ *vt* étiqueter

labor *etc* ['leɪbə'] (US) *n* = **labour**

laboratory [lə'bɔrətərɪ] *n* laboratoire *m*

Labor Day *n* (US, CANADA) fête *f* du travail (*le premier lundi de septembre*)

● l'occasion de partir pour un long
week-end avant la rentrée des
classes.

labor union n (us) syndicat m

Labour ['leɪbəʳ] n (BRIT Pol: also:
the ~ Party) le parti travailliste, les
travaillistes mpl

labour, (us) **labor** ['leɪbəʳ] n (work)
travail m; (workforce) main d'œuvre f
▷ vi: **to ~ (at)** travailler dur (à), peiner
(sur) ▷ vt: **to ~ a point** insister sur un
point; **in ~** (Med) en travail; **labourer**,
(us) **laborer** n manœuvre m; **farm
labourer** ouvrier m agricole

lace [leɪs] n dentelle f; (of shoe etc)
lacet m ▷ vt (shoe: also: ~ **up**) lacer

lack [læk] n manque m ▷ vt manquer
de; **through** or **for ~ of** faute de, par
manque de; **to be ~ing** manquer,
faire défaut; **to be ~ing in** manque de

lacquer ['lækəʳ] n laque f

lacy ['leɪsɪ] adj (made of lace) en
dentelle; (like lace) comme de la
dentelle

lad [læd] n garçon m, gars m

ladder ['lædəʳ] n échelle f; (BRIT:
in tights) maille filée ▷ vt, vi (BRIT:
tights) filer

ladle ['leɪdl] n louche f

lady ['leɪdɪ] n dame f; "**ladies and
gentlemen …**" "Mesdames (et)
Messieurs …"; **young ~** jeune fille f;
(married) jeune femme f; **the ladies'
(room)** les toilettes fpl des dames;
ladybird, (us) **ladybug** n coccinelle f

lag [læg] n retard m ▷ vi (also: ~
behind) rester en arrière, traîner;
(fig) rester à la traîne ▷ vt (pipes)
calorifuger

lager ['lɑːgəʳ] n bière blonde

lagoon [lə'guːn] n lagune f

laid [leɪd] pt, pp of **lay**; **laid back** adj
(inf) relaxe, décontracté(e)

lain [leɪn] pp of **lie**

lake [leɪk] n lac m

lamb [læm] n agneau m

lame [leɪm] adj (also fig)
boiteux(-euse)

lament [lə'mɛnt] n lamentation f
▷ vt pleurer, se lamenter sur

lamp [læmp] n lampe f; **lamppost**
n (BRIT) réverbère m; **lampshade**
n abat-jour m inv

land [lænd] n (as opposed to sea) terre
f; (farm); (country) pays m; (soil)
terre; (piece of land) terrain m; (estate)
terre(s), domaine(s) m(pl) ▷ vi (from
ship) débarquer; (Aviat) atterrir; (fig:
fall) (re)tomber ▷ vt (passengers,
goods) débarquer; (obtain) décrocher;
to ~ sb with sth (inf) coller qch à qn;
landing n (from ship) débarquement
m; (Aviat) atterrissage m; (of staircase)
palier m; **landing card** n carte f
de débarquement; **landlady** n
propriétaire f, logeuse f; (of pub)
patronne f; **landline** n ligne f fixe;
landlord n propriétaire m, logeur
m; (of pub etc) patron m; **landmark**
n (point m de) repère m; **to be a
landmark** (fig) faire date or époque;
landowner n propriétaire foncier
or terrien; **landscape** n paysage
m; **landslide** n (Geo) glissement
de terrain; (fig: Pol) raz-de-marée
(électoral)

lane [leɪn] n (in country) chemin m;
(Aut: of road) voie f; (: line of traffic) file
f; (in race) couloir m

language ['læŋgwɪdʒ] n langue f;
(way one speaks) langage m; **what ~s
do you speak?** quelles langues parlez-
vous?; **bad ~** grossièretés fpl, langage
grossier; **language laboratory** n
laboratoire m de langues; **language
school** n école f de langue

lantern ['læntn] n lanterne f

lap [læp] n (of track) tour m (de piste);
(of body): **in** or **on one's ~** sur les
genoux ▷ vt (also: ~ **up**) laper ▷ vi
(waves) clapoter

lapel [lə'pɛl] n revers m

lapse [læps] n défaillance f; (in
behaviour) écart m (de conduite)

▷ vi (Law) cesser d'être en vigueur; (contract) expirer; **to ~ into bad habits** prendre de mauvaises habitudes; **~ of time** laps m de temps, intervalle m

laptop (computer) ['læptɔp-] n (ordinateur m) portable m

lard [lɑːd] n saindoux m

larder ['lɑːdə'] n garde-manger m inv

large [lɑːdʒ] adj grand(e); (person, animal) gros (grosse); **at ~** (free) en liberté; (generally) en général; pour la plupart; see also **by**; **largely** adv en grande partie; (principally) surtout; **large-scale** adj (map, drawing etc) à grande échelle; (fig) important(e)

lark [lɑːk] n (bird) alouette f; (joke) blague f, farce f

larrikin ['lærɪkɪn] n (AUST, NZ inf) fripon m (inf)

laryngitis [lærɪn'dʒaɪtɪs] n laryngite f

lasagne [lə'zænjə] n lasagne f

laser ['leɪzə'] n laser m; **laser printer** n imprimante f laser

lash [læʃ] n coup m de fouet; (also: **eye~**) cil m ▷ vt fouetter; (tie) attacher; **lash out** vi: **to ~ out (at or against sb/sth)** attaquer violemment (qn/qch)

lass [læs] (BRIT) n (jeune) fille f

last [lɑːst] adj dernier(-ière) ▷ adv dernier; (most recently) la dernière fois; (finally) finalement ▷ vi durer; **~ week** la semaine dernière; **~ night** (evening) hier soir; (night) la nuit dernière; **at ~** enfin; **~ but one** avant-dernier(-ière); **lastly** adv en dernier lieu, pour finir; **last-minute** adj de dernière minute

latch [lætʃ] n loquet m; **latch onto** vt fus (cling to: person, group) s'accrocher à; (: idea) se mettre en tête

late [leɪt] adj (not on time) en retard; (far in day etc) tardif(-ive); (: edition, delivery) dernier(-ière); (dead) défunt(e) ▷ adv tard; (behind time, schedule) en retard; **to be 10**

minutes ~ avoir 10 minutes de retard; **sorry I'm ~** désolé d'être en retard; **it's too ~** il est trop tard; **of ~** dernièrement; **in ~ May** vers la fin (du mois) de mai, fin mai; **the ~ Mr X** feu M. X; **latecomer** n retardataire m/f; **lately** adv récemment; **later** adj (date etc) ultérieur(e); (version etc) plus récent(e) ▷ adv plus tard; **latest** ['leɪtɪst] adj tout(e) dernier(-ière); **at the latest** au plus tard

lather ['lɑːðə'] n mousse f (de savon) ▷ vt savonner

Latin ['lætɪn] n latin m ▷ adj latin(e); **Latin America** n Amérique latine; **Latin American** adj latino-américain(e), d'Amérique latine ▷ n Latino-Américain(e)

latitude ['lætɪtjuːd] n (also fig) latitude f

latter ['lætə'] adj deuxième, dernier(-ière) ▷ n: **the ~** ce dernier, celui-ci

laugh [lɑːf] n rire m ▷ vi rire; **(to do sth) for a ~** (faire qch) pour rire; **laugh at** vt fus se moquer de; (joke) rire de; **laughter** n rire m; (of several people) rires mpl

launch [lɔːntʃ] n lancement m; (also: **motor~**) vedette f ▷ vt (ship, rocket, plan) lancer; **launch into** vt fus se lancer dans

launder ['lɔːndə'] vt laver; (fig: money) blanchir

Launderette® ['lɔːn'drɛt], (US) **Laundromat®** ['lɔːndrəmæt] n laverie f (automatique)

laundry ['lɔːndrɪ] n (clothes) linge m; (business) blanchisserie f; (room) buanderie f; **to do the ~** faire la lessive

lava ['lɑːvə] n lave f

lavatory ['lævətərɪ] n toilettes fpl

lavender ['lævəndə'] n lavande f

lavish ['lævɪʃ] adj (amount) copieux(-euse); (person: giving freely): **~ with** prodigue de ▷ vt: **to ~ sth on sb** prodiguer qch à qn; (money) dépenser qch sans compter pour qn

law [lɔː] n loi f; (science) droit m; **lawful** adj légal(e), permis(e); **lawless** adj (action) illégal(e); (place) sans loi

lawn [lɔːn] n pelouse f; **lawnmower** n tondeuse f à gazon

lawsuit ['lɔːsuːt] n procès m

lawyer ['lɔːjəʳ] n (consultant, with company) juriste m; (for sales, wills etc) = notaire m; (partner, in court) = avocat m

lax [læks] adj relâché(e)

laxative ['læksətɪv] n laxatif m

lay [leɪ] pt of **lie** ▷ adj laïque, (not expert) profane ▷ vt (pt, pp **laid**) poser, mettre; (eggs) pondre; (trap) tendre; (plans) élaborer; **to ~ the table** mettre la table; **lay down** vt poser; (rules etc) établir; **to ~ down the law** (fig) faire la loi; **lay off** vt (workers) licencier; **lay on** vt (provide: meal etc) fournir; **lay out** vt (design) dessiner, concevoir; (display) disposer; (spend) dépenser; **lay-by** n (BRIT) aire f de stationnement (sur le bas-côté)

layer ['leɪəʳ] n couche f

layman ['leɪmən] (irreg) n (Rel) laïque m; (non-expert) profane m

layout ['leɪaut] n disposition f, plan m, agencement m; (Press) mise f en page

lazy ['leɪzɪ] adj paresseux(-euse)

lb. abbr (weight) = **pound**

lead¹ (pt, pp **led**) [liːd, lɛd] n (front position) tête f; (distance, time ahead) avance f; (clue) piste f; (Elec) fil m; (for dog) laisse f; (Theat) rôle principal ▷ vt (guide) mener, conduire; (be leader of) être à la tête de ▷ vi (Sport) mener, être en tête; **to ~ to** (road, pipe) mener à, conduire à; (result in) conduire à; aboutir à; **to be in the ~** (Sport) (in race) mener, être en tête; (in match) mener (à la marque); **to ~ sb to do sth** amener qn à faire qch; **to ~ the way** montrer le chemin; **lead up to** vt conduire à; (in conversation) en venir à

lead² [lɛd] n (metal) plomb m; (in pencil) mine f

leader ['liːdəʳ] n (of team) chef m; (of party etc) dirigeant(e), leader m; (Sport: in league) leader; (: in race) coureur m de tête; **leadership** n (position) direction f; **under the leadership of ...** sous la direction de ...; **qualities of leadership** qualités fpl de chef or de meneur

lead-free ['lɛdfriː] adj sans plomb

leading ['liːdɪŋ] adj de premier plan; (main) principal(e); (in race) de tête

lead singer [liːd-] n (in pop group) (chanteur m) vedette f

leaf (pl **leaves**) [liːf, liːvz] n feuille f; (of table) rallonge f; **to turn over a new ~** (fig) changer de conduite or d'existence; **leaf through** vt (book) feuilleter

leaflet ['liːflɪt] n prospectus m, brochure f; (Pol, Rel) tract m

league [liːg] n ligue f; (Football) championnat m; **to be in ~ with** avoir partie liée avec, être de mèche avec

leak [liːk] n (lit, fig) fuite f ▷ vi (pipe, liquid etc) fuir; (shoes) prendre l'eau; (ship) faire eau ▷ vt (liquid) répandre; (information) divulguer

lean (pt, pp **leaned** or **leant**) [liːn, lɛnt] adj maigre ▷ vt: **to ~ sth on** appuyer qch sur ▷ vi (slope) pencher; (rest): **to ~ against** s'appuyer contre; être appuyé(e) contre; **to ~ on** s'appuyer sur; **lean forward** vi se pencher en avant; **lean over** vi se pencher; **leaning** n: **leaning (towards)** penchant m (pour)

leant [lɛnt] pt, pp of **lean**

leap (pt, pp **leaped** or **leapt**) [liːp, lɛpt] n bond m, saut m ▷ vi bondir, sauter

leapt [lɛpt] pt, pp of **leap**

leap year n année f bissextile

learn (pt, pp **learned** or **learnt**) [ləːn, ləːnt] vt, vi apprendre; **to ~ (how) to do sth** apprendre à faire qch; **to ~ about sth** (Scol) étudier qch; (hear, read) apprendre qch; **learner** n débutant(e); (BRIT: also: **learner**

driver) (conducteur(-trice)) débutant(e); **learning** n savoir m

learnt [lɑːnt] pp of **learn**

lease [liːs] n bail m ▷ vt louer à bail

leash [liːʃ] n laisse f

least [liːst] adj: **the ~ (+ noun)** le (la) plus petit(e), le (la) moindre; (smallest amount of) le moins de ▷ pron: (the) **~ le moins** ▷ adv (+ verb): **le moins**; (+ adj): **the ~** le (la) moins; **the ~ money** le moins d'argent; **the ~ expensive** le (la) moins cher (chère) **the ~ possible effort** le moins d'effort possible; **at ~** au moins; (or rather) du moins; **you could at ~ have written** tu aurais au moins pu écrire; **not in the ~** pas le moins du monde

leather ['leðəʳ] n cuir m

leave (pt, pp **left**) [liːv, left] vt laisser; (go away from) quitter; (forget) oublier ▷ vi partir, s'en aller ▷ n (time off) congé m; (Mil, also consent) permission f; **what time does the train/bus ~?** le train/le bus part à quelle heure?; **to ~ sth to sb** (money etc) laisser qch à qn; **to be left** rester; **there's some milk left over** il reste du lait; **~ it to me!** laissez-moi faire!, je m'en occupe!; **on ~** en permission; **leave behind** vt (also fig) laisser; (forget) laisser, oublier; **leave out** vt oublier, omettre

leaves [liːvz] npl of **leaf**

Lebanon ['lebənən] n Liban m

lecture ['lektʃəʳ] n conférence f; (Scol) cours (magistral) m ▷ vi donner des cours; enseigner ▷ vt (scold) sermonner, réprimander; **to give a ~ (on)** faire une conférence (sur), faire un cours (sur); **lecture hall** n amphithéâtre m; **lecturer** n (speaker) conférencier(-ière); (BRIT: at university) professeur m (d'université), prof m/f de fac (inf); **lecture theatre** n = **lecture hall**

> Be careful not to translate lecture by the French word lecture.

led [led] pt, pp of **lead¹**

ledge [ledʒ] n (of window, on wall) rebord m; (of mountain) saillie f, corniche f

leek [liːk] n poireau m

left [left] pt, pp of **leave** ▷ adj gauche ▷ adv à gauche ▷ n gauche f; **there are two ~** il en reste deux; **to the ~, to the ~** à gauche; **the L~** (Pol) la gauche; **left-hand** adj: **the left-hand side** la gauche, le côté gauche; **left-hand drive** (vehicle) véhicule m avec la conduite à gauche; **left-handed** adj gaucher(-ère); (scissors etc) pour gauchers; **left-luggage locker** n (BRIT) casier m à consigne f automatique; **left-luggage (office)** n (BRIT) consigne f; **left-overs** npl restes mpl; **left-wing** adj (Pol) de gauche

leg [leg] n jambe f; (of animal) patte f; (of furniture) pied m; (Culin: of chicken) cuisse f; (of journey) étape f; **1st/2nd ~** (Sport) match m aller/retour; **~ of lamb** (Culin) gigot m d'agneau

legacy ['legəsɪ] n (also fig) héritage m, legs m

legal ['liːgl] adj (permitted by law) légal(e); (relating to law) juridique; **legal holiday** (us) n jour férié; **legalize** vt légaliser; **legally** adv légalement

legend ['ledʒənd] n légende f; **legendary** ['ledʒəndərɪ] adj légendaire

leggings ['legɪŋz] npl caleçon m

legible ['ledʒəbl] adj lisible

legislation [ledʒɪs'leɪʃən] n législation f

legislative ['ledʒɪslətɪv] adj législatif(-ive)

legitimate [lɪ'dʒɪtɪmət] adj légitime

leisure ['leʒəʳ] n (free time) temps libre, loisirs mpl; **at ~** (tout) à loisir; **at your ~** (later) à tête reposée; **leisure centre** n (BRIT) centre m de loisirs; **leisurely** adj tranquille, fait(e) sans se presser

lemon ['lɛmən] n citron m;
lemonade n (fizzy) limonade f;
lemon tea n thé m au citron

lend (pt, pp **lent**) [lɛnd, lɛnt] vt: **to ~ sth (to sb)** prêter qch (à qn); **could you ~ me some money?** pourriez-vous me prêter de l'argent?

length [lɛŋθ] n longueur f; (section: of road, pipe etc) morceau m, bout m; **~ of time** durée f; **it is 2 metres in ~** cela fait 2 mètres de long; **at ~** (at last) enfin, à la fin; (lengthily) longuement; **lengthen** vt allonger, prolonger ▷ vi s'allonger; **lengthways** adv dans le sens de la longueur, en long; **lengthy** adj (très) long (longue)

lens [lɛnz] n lentille f; (of spectacles) verre m; (of camera) objectif m

Lent [lɛnt] n carême m

lent [lɛnt] pt, pp of **lend**

lentil ['lɛntl] n lentille f

Leo ['li:əʊ] n le Lion

leopard ['lɛpəd] n léopard m

leotard ['li:əta:d] n justaucorps m

leprosy ['lɛprəsɪ] n lèpre f

lesbian ['lɛzbɪən] n lesbienne f ▷ adj lesbien(ne)

less [lɛs] adj moins de ▷ pron, adv moins ▷ prep: **~ tax/10% discount** avant impôt/moins 10% de remise; **~ than that/you** moins que cela/vous; **~ than half** moins de la moitié; **~ than ever** moins que jamais; **~ and ~** de moins en moins; **the ~ he works ...** moins il travaille ...; **lessen** vi diminuer, s'amoindrir, s'atténuer ▷ vt diminuer, réduire, atténuer; **lesser** ['lɛsə'] adj moindre; **to a lesser extent** or **degree** à un degré moindre

lesson ['lɛsn] n leçon f; **to teach sb a ~** (fig) donner une bonne leçon à qn

let (pt, pp **let**) [lɛt] vt laisser; (BRIT: lease) louer; **to ~ sb do sth** laisser qn faire qch; **to ~ sb know sth** faire savoir qch à qn, prévenir qn de qch; **~ go** lâcher prise; **to ~ go of sth, to ~ sth go** lâcher qch; **~'s go** allons-y; **~ him come** qu'il vienne;

"to ~" (BRIT) "à louer"; **let down** vt (lower) baisser; (BRIT: tyre) dégonfler; (disappoint) décevoir; **let in** vt laisser entrer; (visitor etc) faire entrer; **let off** vt (allow to leave) laisser partir; (not punish) ne pas punir; (firework etc) faire partir; (bomb) faire exploser; **let out** vt laisser sortir; (scream) laisser échapper; (BRIT: rent out) louer

lethal ['li:θl] adj mortel(le), fatal(e); (weapon) meurtrier(-ère)

letter ['lɛtə'] n lettre f; **letterbox** n (BRIT) boîte f aux or à lettres

lettuce ['lɛtɪs] n laitue f, salade f

leukaemia, (us) **leukemia**
[lu:'ki:mɪə] n leucémie f

level ['lɛvl] adj (flat) plat(e), plan(e), uni(e); (horizontal) horizontal(e) ▷ n niveau m ▷ vt niveler, aplanir; **A ~s** npl (BRIT) ≈ baccalauréat m; **to be ~ with** être au même niveau que; **to draw ~ with** (runner, car) arriver à la hauteur de, rattraper; **on the ~** (fig: honest) régulier(-ière); **level crossing** n (BRIT) passage m à niveau

lever ['li:və'] n levier m; **leverage** n (influence): **leverage (on** or **with)** prise f (sur)

levy ['lɛvɪ] n taxe f, impôt m ▷ vt (tax) lever; (fine) infliger

liability [laɪə'bɪlɪtɪ] n responsabilité f; (handicap) handicap m

liable ['laɪəbl] adj (subject): **~ to** sujet(te) à, passible de; (responsible): **~ (for)** responsable (de); (likely): **~ to do** susceptible de faire

liaise [li:'eɪz] vi: **to ~ with** assurer la liaison avec

liar ['laɪə'] n menteur(-euse)

libel ['laɪbl] n diffamation f; (document) écrit m diffamatoire ▷ vt diffamer

liberal ['lɪbərl] adj libéral(e); (generous): **~ with** prodigue de, généreux(-euse) avec ▷ n: **L~** (Pol) libéral(e); **Liberal Democrat** n (BRIT) libéral-démocrate m/f

liberate ['lɪbəreɪt] vt libérer

liberation [lɪbəˈreɪʃən] n libération f
liberty [ˈlɪbətɪ] n liberté f; **to be at ~** (criminal) être en liberté; **at ~ to do** libre de faire; **to take the ~ of** prendre la liberté de, se permettre de
Libra [ˈliːbrə] n la Balance
librarian [laɪˈbrɛərɪən] n bibliothécaire m/f
library [ˈlaɪbrərɪ] n bibliothèque f

Be careful not to translate library by the French word librairie.

Libya [ˈlɪbɪə] n Libye f
lice [laɪs] npl of **louse**
licence, (us) **license** [ˈlaɪsns] n autorisation f, permis m; (Comm) licence f; (Radio, TV) redevance f; **driving ~**, (us) **driver's license** permis m (de conduire)
license [ˈlaɪsns] n (us) = **licence**; **licensed** adj (for alcohol) patenté(e) pour la vente des spiritueux, qui a une patente de débit de boissons; (car) muni(e) de la vignette; **license plate** n (us Aut) plaque f minéralogique; **licensing hours** (BRIT) npl heures fpl d'ouvertures (des pubs)
lick [lɪk] vt lécher; (inf: defeat) écraser, flanquer une piquette or raclée à; **to ~ one's lips** (fig) se frotter les mains
lid [lɪd] n couvercle m; (eyelid) paupière f
lie [laɪ] n mensonge m ▷ vi (pt, pp **lied**) (tell lies) mentir; (pt, **lay**, pp **lain**) (rest) être étendu(e) or allongé(e) or couché(e); (of object: be situated) se trouver, être; **to ~ low** (fig) se cacher, rester caché(e); **to tell ~s** mentir; **lie about, lie around** vi (things) traîner; (BRIT: person) traînasser, flemmarder
Liechtenstein [ˈlɪktənstaɪn] n Liechtenstein m
lie-in [ˈlaɪɪn] n (BRIT): **to have a ~** faire la grasse matinée
lieutenant [lɛfˈtɛnənt, us luːˈtɛnənt] n lieutenant m
life (pl **lives**) [laɪf, laɪvz] n vie f; **to come to ~** (fig) s'animer; **life assurance** n (BRIT) = **life insurance**; **lifeboat** n canot m or chaloupe f de sauvetage; **lifeguard** n surveillant m de baignade; **life insurance** n assurance-vie f; **life jacket** n gilet m or ceinture f de sauvetage; **lifelike** adj qui semble vrai(e) or vivant(e), ressemblant(e); (painting) réaliste; **life preserver** n (us) gilet m or ceinture f de sauvetage; **life sentence** n condamnation f à vie or à perpétuité; **lifestyle** n style m de vie; **lifetime** n: **in his lifetime** de son vivant
lift [lɪft] vt soulever, lever; (end) supprimer, lever ▷ vi (fog) se lever ▷ n (BRIT: elevator) ascenseur m; **to give sb a ~** (BRIT) emmener or prendre qn en voiture; **can you give me a ~ to the station?** pouvez-vous m'emmener à la gare?; **lift up** vt soulever; **lift-off** n décollage m
light [laɪt] n lumière f; (lamp) lampe f; (Aut: rear light) feu m; (: headlamp) phare m; (for cigarette etc): **have you got a ~?** avez-vous du feu? ▷ vt (pt, pp **lit**) (candle, cigarette, fire) allumer; (room) éclairer ▷ adj (room, colour) clair(e); (not heavy, also fig) léger(-ère); (not strenuous) peu fatigant(e); **lights** npl (traffic lights) feux mpl; **to come to ~** être dévoilé(e) or découvert(e); **in the ~ of** à la lumière de; étant donné; **light up** vi s'allumer; (face) s'éclairer; (smoke) allumer une cigarette or une pipe etc ▷ vt (illuminate) éclairer, illuminer; **light bulb** n ampoule f; **lighten** vt (light up) éclairer; (make lighter) éclaircir; (make less heavy) alléger; **lighter** n (also: **cigarette lighter**) briquet m; **light-hearted** adj gai(e), joyeux(-euse), enjoué(e); **lighthouse** n phare m; **lighting** n éclairage m; (in theatre) éclairages; **lightly** adv légèrement; **to get off lightly** s'en tirer à bon compte
lightning [ˈlaɪtnɪŋ] n foudre f; (flash) éclair m

lightweight ['laɪtweɪt] adj (suit) léger(-ère) ▷ n (Boxing) poids léger

like [laɪk] vt aimer (bien) ▷ prep comme ▷ adj semblable, pareil(le) ▷ n: **the ~** (pej) (d')autres du même genre or acabit; **his ~s and dislikes** ses goûts mpl or préférences fpl; **I would ~, I'd ~** je voudrais, j'aimerais; **would you ~ a coffee?** voulez-vous du café?; **to be/look ~ sb/sth** ressembler à qn/qch; **what's he ~?** comment est-il?; **what does it look ~?** de quoi est-ce que ça a l'air?; **what does it taste ~?** quel goût est-ce que ça a?; **that's just ~ him** c'est bien de lui, ça lui ressemble; **do it ~ this** fais-le comme ceci; **it's nothing ~ ...** ce n'est pas du tout comme ...; **likeable** adj sympathique, agréable

likelihood ['laɪklɪhud] n probabilité f

likely ['laɪklɪ] adj (result, outcome) probable; (excuse) plausible; **he's ~ to leave** il va sûrement partir, il risque fort de partir; **not ~!** (inf) pas de danger!

likewise ['laɪkwaɪz] adv de même, pareillement

liking ['laɪkɪŋ] n (for person) affection f; (for thing) penchant m, goût m; **to be to sb's ~** être au goût de qn, plaire à qn

lilac ['laɪlæk] n lilas m

Lilo® ['laɪləu] n matelas m pneumatique

lily ['lɪlɪ] n lis m; **~ of the valley** muguet m

limb [lɪm] n membre m

limbo ['lɪmbəu] n: **to be in ~** (fig) être tombé(e) dans l'oubli

lime [laɪm] n (tree) tilleul m; (fruit) citron vert, lime f; (Geo) chaux f

limelight ['laɪmlaɪt] n: **in the ~** (fig) en vedette, au premier plan

limestone ['laɪmstəun] n pierre f à chaux; (Geo) calcaire m

limit ['lɪmɪt] n limite f ▷ vt limiter; **limited** adj limité(e), restreint(e);

to be limited to se limiter à, ne concerner que

limousine ['lɪməziːn] n limousine f

limp [lɪmp] n: **to have a ~** boiter ▷ vi boiter ▷ adj mou (molle)

line [laɪn] n (gen) ligne f; (stroke) trait m; (wrinkle) ride f; (rope) corde f; (wire) fil m; (of poem) vers m; (row, series) rangée f; (of people) file f, queue f; (railway track) voie f; (Comm: series of goods) article(s) m(pl), ligne de produits; (work) métier m ▷ vt (subj: trees, crowd) border; **to ~ (with)** (clothes) doubler (de); (box) garnir or tapisser (de); **to stand in ~** (us) faire la queue; **in his ~ of business** dans sa partie, dans son rayon; **to be in ~ for sth** (fig) être en lice pour qch; **in ~ with** en accord avec, en conformité avec; **in a ~** aligné(e); **line up** vi s'aligner, se mettre en rang(s); (in queue) faire la queue ▷ vt aligner; (event) préparer; (find) trouver; **to have sb/sth ~d up** avoir qn/qch en vue or de prévu(e)

linear ['lɪnɪə] adj linéaire

linen ['lɪnɪn] n linge m (de corps or de maison); (cloth) lin m

liner ['laɪnə] n (ship) paquebot m de ligne; (for bin) sac-poubelle m

line-up ['laɪnʌp] n (us: queue) file f; (also: **police ~**) parade f d'identification; (Sport) (composition f de l')équipe f

linger ['lɪŋgə] vi s'attarder; traîner; (smell, tradition) persister

lingerie ['lænʒəriː] n lingerie f

linguist ['lɪŋgwɪst] n linguiste m/f; **to be a good ~** être doué(e) pour les langues; **linguistic** adj linguistique

lining ['laɪnɪŋ] n doublure f; (of brakes) garniture f

link [lɪŋk] n (connection) lien m, rapport m; (Internet) lien; (of a chain) maillon m ▷ vt lier, unir, relier; **links** npl (Golf) (terrain m de) golf m; **link up** vt relier ▷ vi (people) se rejoindre; (companies etc) s'associer

lion ['laɪən] n lion m; **lioness** n lionne f
lip [lɪp] n lèvre f; (of cup etc) rebord m;
lip-read vi (irreg: like **read**) lire sur les lèvres; **lip salve** [-sælv] n pommade f pour les lèvres, pommade rosat;
lipstick n rouge m à lèvres
liqueur [lɪ'kjuə^r] n liqueur f
liquid ['lɪkwɪd] n liquide m ▷ adj liquide; **liquidizer** ['lɪkwɪdaɪzə^r] n (BRIT Culin) mixer m
liquor ['lɪkə^r] n spiritueux m, alcool m;
liquor store (US) n magasin m de vins et spiritueux
Lisbon ['lɪzbən] n Lisbonne
lisp [lɪsp] n zézaiement m ▷ vi zézayer
list [lɪst] n liste f ▷ vt (write down) inscrire; (make list of) faire la liste de; (enumerate) énumérer
listen ['lɪsn] vi écouter; **to ~ to** écouter; **listener** n auditeur(-trice)
lit [lɪt] pt, pp of **light**
liter ['liːtə^r] n (US) = **litre**
literacy ['lɪtərəsɪ] n degré m d'alphabétisation, fait m de savoir lire et écrire; (BRIT Scol) enseignement m de la lecture et de l'écriture
literal ['lɪtərl] adj littéral(e); **literally** adv littéralement; (really) réellement
literary ['lɪtərərɪ] adj littéraire
literate ['lɪtərət] adj qui sait lire et écrire; (educated) instruit(e)
literature ['lɪtrɪtʃə^r] n littérature f; (brochures etc) copie f publicitaire, prospectus mpl
litre, (US) **liter** ['liːtə^r] n litre m
litter ['lɪtə^r] n (rubbish) détritus mpl; (dirtier) ordures fpl; (young animals) portée f; **litter bin** n (BRIT) poubelle f
little ['lɪtl] adj (small) petit(e); (not much): ~ **milk** peu de lait ▷ adv peu; **a** ~ un peu (de); **a** ~ **milk** un peu de lait; **a** ~ **bit** un peu; **as** ~ **as possible** le moins possible; ~ **by** ~ petit à petit, peu à peu; **little finger** n auriculaire m, petit doigt
live¹ [laɪv] adj (animal) vivant(e), en vie; (wire) sous tension; (broadcast)

(transmis(e)) en direct; (unexploded) non explosé(e)
live² [lɪv] vi vivre; (reside) vivre, habiter; **to ~ in London** habiter (à) Londres; **where do you ~?** où habitez-vous?; **live together** vi vivre ensemble, cohabiter; **live up to** vt fus se montrer à la hauteur de
livelihood ['laɪvlɪhud] n moyens mpl d'existence
lively ['laɪvlɪ] adj vif (vive), plein(e) d'entrain; (place, book) vivant(e)
liven up ['laɪvn-] vt (room etc) égayer; (discussion, evening) animer ▷ vi s'animer
liver ['lɪvə^r] n foie m
lives [laɪvz] npl of **life**
livestock ['laɪvstɔk] n cheptel m, bétail m
living ['lɪvɪŋ] adj vivant(e), en vie ▷ n: **to earn** or **make a ~** gagner sa vie; **living room** n salle f de séjour
lizard ['lɪzəd] n lézard m
load [ləud] n (weight) poids m; (thing carried) chargement m, charge f; (Elec, Tech) charge f ▷ vt charger; (also: ~ **up**) **to ~ (with)** (lorry, ship) charger (de); (gun, camera) charger (avec); **a ~ of**, ~**s of** (fig) un or des tas de, des masses de; **to talk a ~ of rubbish** (inf) dire des bêtises; **loaded** adj (dice) pipé(e); (question) insidieux(-euse); (inf: rich) bourré(e) de fric
loaf (pl **loaves**) [ləuf, ləuvz] n pain m, miche f ▷ vi (also: ~ **about**, ~ **around**) fainéanter, traîner
loan [ləun] n prêt m ▷ vt prêter; **on ~** prêté(e), en prêt
loathe [ləuð] vt détester, avoir en horreur
loaves [ləuvz] npl of **loaf**
lobby ['lɔbɪ] n hall m, entrée f; (Pol) groupe m de pression, lobby m ▷ vt faire pression sur
lobster ['lɔbstə^r] n homard m
local ['ləukl] adj local(e) ▷ n (BRIT: pub) pub m or café m du coin; **the locals** npl les gens mpl du pays or du

coin; **local anaesthetic**, (us) **local anesthetic** n anesthésie locale; **local authority** n collectivité locale, municipalité f; **local government** n administration locale ou municipale; **locally** ['ləʊkəlɪ] adv localement; dans les environs ou la région

locate [ləʊ'keɪt] vt (find) trouver, repérer; (situate) situer; **to be ~d in** être situé à ou en

location [ləʊ'keɪʃən] n emplacement m; **on ~** (Cine) en extérieur

> Be careful not to translate location by the French word location.

loch [lɔx] n lac m, loch m

lock [lɔk] n (of door, box) serrure f; (of canal) écluse f; (of hair) mèche f, boucle f ▷ vt (with key) fermer à clé ▷ vi (door etc) fermer à clé; (wheels) se bloquer; **lock in** vt enfermer; **lock out** vt enfermer dehors; (on purpose) mettre à la porte; **lock up** vt (person) enfermer; (house) fermer à clé ▷ vi tout fermer (à clé)

locker ['lɔkə'] n casier m; (in station) consigne f automatique; **locker-room** ['lɔkə'ruːm] (us) n (Sport) vestiaire m

locksmith ['lɔksmɪθ] n serrurier m

locomotive [ləʊkə'məʊtɪv] n locomotive f

locum ['ləʊkəm] n (Med) suppléant(e) de médecin etc

lodge [lɔdʒ] n pavillon m (de gardien); (also: hunting ~) pavillon de chasse ▷ vi (person): **to ~ with** être logé(e) chez, être en pension chez; (bullet) se loger ▷ vt (appeal etc) présenter; déposer; **to ~ a complaint** porter plainte; **lodger** n locataire m/f; (with room and meals) pensionnaire m/f

lodging ['lɔdʒɪŋ] n logement m

loft [lɔft] n grenier m; (apartment) grenier aménagé (en appartement) (gén dans ancien entrepôt ou fabrique)

log [lɔg] n (of wood) bûche f; (Naut) livre m or journal m de bord; (of car)

carte grise f ▷ vt enregistrer; **log in**, **log on** vi (Comput) ouvrir une session, entrer dans le système; **log off**, **log out** vi (Comput) clore une session, sortir du système

logic ['lɔdʒɪk] n logique f; **logical** adj logique

login ['lɔgɪn] n (Comput) identifiant m

Loire [lwaː] n: **the ~ (the River)** la Loire

lollipop ['lɔlɪpɔp] n sucette f; **lollipop man/lady** (irreg) (BRIT) n contractuel(le) qui fait traverser la rue aux enfants

lolly ['lɔlɪ] n (inf: ice) esquimau m; (: lollipop) sucette f

London ['lʌndən] n Londres; **Londoner** n Londonien(ne)

lone [ləʊn] adj solitaire

loneliness ['ləʊnlɪnɪs] n solitude f, isolement m

lonely ['ləʊnlɪ] adj seul(e); (childhood etc) solitaire; (place) solitaire, isolé(e)

long [lɔŋ] adj long (longue) ▷ adv longtemps ▷ vi: **to ~ for sth/to do sth** avoir très envie de qch/de faire qch, attendre qch avec impatience/ attendre avec impatience de faire qch; **how ~ is this river/course?** quelle est la longueur de ce fleuve/ la durée de ce cours?; **6 metres ~** (long) de 6 mètres; **6 months ~** qui dure 6 mois, de 6 mois; **all night ~** toute la nuit; **he no ~er comes** il ne vient plus; **I can't stand it any ~er** je ne peux plus le supporter; **~ before** longtemps avant; **before ~** (+future) avant peu, dans peu de temps; (+ past) peu de temps après; **don't be ~!** fais vite!, dépêche-toi!; **I shan't be ~** je n'en ai pas pour longtemps; **at ~ last** enfin; **so ou as ~ as** à condition que + sub; **long-distance** adj (race) de fond; (call) interurbain(e); **long-haul** adj (flight) long-courrier; **longing** n désir m, envie f; (nostalgia) nostalgie f ▷ adj plein(e) d'envie ou de nostalgie

longitude ['lɔŋgɪtjuːd] n longitude f

long: long jump n saut m en longueur; **long-life** adj (batteries etc) longue durée env; (milk) longue conservation; **long-sighted** adj (BRIT) presbyte; (fig) prévoyant(e); **long-standing** adj de longue date; **long-term** adj à long terme

loo [luː] n (BRIT inf) w.-c. mpl, petit coin

look [lʊk] vi regarder; (seem) sembler, paraître, avoir l'air; (building etc): **to ~ south/on to the sea** donner au sud/sur la mer ▷ n regard m; (appearance) air m, allure f, aspect m; (good looks) physique m, beauté f; **to ~ like** ressembler à; **to have a ~** regarder; **to have a ~ at sth** jeter un coup d'œil à qch; **~ (here)!** (annoyance) écoutez!; **look after** vt fus s'occuper de; (luggage etc: watch over) garder, surveiller; **look around** vi regarder autour de soi; **look at** vt fus regarder; (problem etc) examiner; **look back** vi: **to ~ back at sth/sb** se retourner pour regarder qch/qn; **to ~ back on** (event, period) évoquer, repenser à; **look down on** vt fus (fig) regarder de haut, dédaigner; **look for** vt fus chercher; **we're ~ing for a hotel/restaurant** nous cherchons un hôtel/restaurant; **look forward to** vt fus attendre avec impatience; **~ing forward to hearing from you** (in letter) dans l'attente de vous lire; **look into** vt fus (matter, possibility) examiner, étudier; **look out** vi (beware): **to ~ out (for)** prendre garde (à), faire attention (à); **~ out!** attention!; **look out for** vt fus (seek) être à la recherche de; (try to spot) guetter; **look round** vt fus (house, shop) faire le tour de ▷ vi (turn) regarder derrière soi, se retourner; **look through** vt fus (papers, book) examiner (: briefly) parcourir; **look up** vi se lever les yeux; (improve) s'améliorer ▷ vt (word) chercher; **look up to** vt fus avoir du respect pour; **lookout** n (tower etc) poste m de guet; (person)

guetteur m; **to be on the lookout (for)** guetter

loom [luːm] vi (also: **~ up**) surgir; (event) paraître imminent(e); (threaten) menacer

loony ['luːnɪ] adj, n (inf) timbré(e), cinglé(e) m/f

loop [luːp] n boucle f ▷ vt: **to ~ sth round sth** passer qch autour de qch; **loophole** n (fig) porte f de sortie; échappatoire f

loose [luːs] adj (knot, screw) desserré(e); (clothes) vague, ample, lâche; (hair) dénoué(e), épars(e); (not firmly fixed) pas solide; (morals, discipline) relâché(e); (translation) approximatif(-ive) ▷ n: **to be on the ~** être en liberté; **~ connection** (Elec) mauvais contact; **to be at a ~ end** or (US) **at ~ ends** (fig) ne pas trop savoir quoi faire; **loosely** adv sans serrer; (imprecisely) approximativement; **loosen** vt desserrer, relâcher, défaire

loot [luːt] n butin m ▷ vt piller

lop-sided ['lɒp'saɪdɪd] adj de travers, asymétrique

lord [lɔːd] n seigneur m; **L~ Smith** lord Smith; **the L~** (Rel) le Seigneur; **my L~** (to noble) Monsieur le comte/le baron; (to judge) Monsieur le juge; (to bishop) Monseigneur; **good L~!** mon Dieu!; **Lords** npl (BRIT Pol): **the (House of) Lords** la Chambre des Lords

lorry ['lɒrɪ] n (BRIT) camion m; **lorry driver** n (BRIT) camionneur m, routier m

lose (pt, pp **lost**) [luːz, lɒst] vt perdre ▷ vi perdre; **I've lost my wallet/passport** j'ai perdu mon portefeuille/passeport; **to ~ (time)** (clock) retarder; **lose out** vi être perdant(e); **loser** n perdant(e)

loss [lɒs] n perte f; **to make a ~** enregistrer une perte; **to be at a ~** être perplexe or embarrassé(e)

lost [lɒst] pt, pp of **lose** ▷ adj perdu(e); **to get ~** vi se perdre;

I'm ~ je me suis perdu; **~ and found property** n (us) objets trouvés; **~ and found** n (BRIT) (bureau m des) objets trouvés; **lost property** n (BRIT) objets trouvés; **lost property office** or **department** (bureau m des) objets trouvés

lot [lɔt] n (at auctions, set) lot m; (destiny) sort m, destinée f; **the ~** (everything) le tout; (everyone) tous mpl, toutes fpl; **a ~** beaucoup; **a ~ of** beaucoup de; **~s of** des tas de; **to draw ~s (for sth)** tirer (qch) au sort

lotion ['ləʊʃən] n lotion f

lottery ['lɔtərɪ] n loterie f

loud [laʊd] adj bruyant(e), sonore; (voice) fort(e); (condemnation etc) vigoureux(-euse); (gaudy) voyant(e), tapageur(-euse) ▷ adv (speak etc) fort; **out ~** tout haut; **loudly** adv fort, bruyamment; **loudspeaker** n haut-parleur m

lounge [laʊndʒ] n salon m; (of airport) salle f; (BRIT: also: **~ bar**) (salle de) café m or bar m ▷ vi (also: **~ about**, **~ around**) se prélasser, paresser

louse (pl **lice**) [laʊs, laɪs] n pou m

lousy ['laʊzɪ] (inf) adj (bad quality) infect(e), moche; **I feel ~** je suis mal fichu(e)

love [lʌv] n amour m ▷ vt aimer; (caringly, kindly) aimer beaucoup; **I ~ chocolate** j'adore le chocolat; **to ~ to do** aimer beaucoup or adorer faire; **"15 ~"** (Tennis) "15 à rien or zéro"; **to be/fall in ~ with** être/ tomber amoureux(-euse) de; **to make ~** faire l'amour; **~ from Anne, ~, Anne** affectueusement, Anne; **I ~ you** je t'aime; **love affair** n liaison f (amoureuse); **love life** n vie sentimentale

lovely ['lʌvlɪ] adj (pretty) ravissant(e); (friend, wife) charmant(e); (holiday, surprise) très agréable, merveilleux(-euse)

lover ['lʌvə'] n amant m; (person in love) amoureux(-euse); (amateur): **a ~**

of un(e) ami(e) de, un(e) amoureux(-euse) de

loving ['lʌvɪŋ] adj affectueux(-euse), tendre, aimant(e)

low [ləʊ] adj bas (basse); (quality) mauvais(e), inférieur(e) ▷ adv bas ▷ n (Meteorology) dépression f; **to feel ~** se sentir déprimé(e); **he's very ~** (ill) il est bien bas or très affaibli; **to turn (down)** ▷ vt baisser; **to be ~ on** (supplies etc) être à court de; **to reach a new** or **an all-time ~** tomber au niveau le plus bas; **low-alcohol** adj à faible teneur en alcool, peu alcoolisé(e); **low-calorie** adj hypocalorique

lower ['ləʊə'] adj inférieur(e) ▷ vt baisser; (resistance) diminuer; **to ~ o.s. to** s'abaisser à

low-fat ['ləʊ'fæt] adj maigre

loyal ['lɔɪəl] adj loyal(e), fidèle; **loyalty** n loyauté f, fidélité f; **loyalty card** n carte f de fidélité

L-plates ['elpleɪts] npl (BRIT) plaques fpl (obligatoires) d'apprenti conducteur

Lt abbr (= lieutenant) Lt.

Ltd abbr (Comm: = limited) ≈ SA

luck [lʌk] n chance f; **bad ~** malchance f, malheur m; **good ~!** bonne chance!; **bad** or **hard** or **tough ~!** pas de chance!; **luckily** adv heureusement, par bonheur; **lucky** adj (person) qui a de la chance; (coincidence) heureux(-euse); (number etc) qui porte bonheur

lucrative ['luːkrətɪv] adj lucratif(-ive), rentable, qui rapporte

ludicrous ['luːdɪkrəs] adj ridicule, absurde

luggage ['lʌgɪdʒ] n bagages mpl; **our ~ hasn't arrived** nos bagages ne sont pas arrivés; **could you send someone to collect our ~?** pourriez-vous envoyer quelqu'un chercher nos bagages?; **luggage rack** n (in train) porte-bagages m inv; (on car) galerie f

lukewarm ['luːkwɔːm] adj tiède

lull [lʌl] n accalmie f; (in conversation) pause f ▷ vt: **to ~ sb to sleep** bercer qn pour qu'il s'endorme; **to be ~ed into a false sense of security** s'endormir dans une fausse sécurité

lullaby ['lʌləbaɪ] n berceuse f

lumber ['lʌmbə'] n (wood) bois m de charpente; (junk) bric-à-brac m inv ▷ vt (BRIT inf): **to ~ sb with sth/sb** coller or refiler qch/qn à qn

luminous ['lu:mɪnəs] adj lumineux(-euse)

lump [lʌmp] n morceau m; (in sauce) grumeau m; (swelling) grosseur f ▷ vt (also: **~ together**) réunir, mettre en tas; **lump sum** n somme globale or forfaitaire; **lumpy** adj (sauce) qui a des grumeaux; (bed) défoncé(e), peu confortable

lunatic ['lu:nətɪk] n fou (folle), dément(e) ▷ adj fou (folle), dément(e)

lunch [lʌntʃ] n déjeuner m ▷ vi déjeuner; **lunch break, lunch hour** n pause f de midi, heure f du déjeuner; **lunchtime** n: **it's lunchtime** c'est l'heure du déjeuner

lung [lʌŋ] n poumon m

lure [luə'] n (attraction) attrait m, charme m; (in hunting) appât m, leurre m ▷ vt attirer or persuader par la ruse

lurk [lə:k] vi se tapir, se cacher

lush [lʌʃ] adj luxuriant(e)

lust [lʌst] n (sexual) désir m (sexuel); (Rel) luxure f; (fig): **~ for** soif f de

Luxembourg ['lʌksəmbə:g] n Luxembourg m

luxurious [lʌg'zjuərɪəs] adj luxueux(-euse)

luxury ['lʌkʃərɪ] n luxe m ▷ cpd de luxe

Lycra® ['laɪkrə] n Lycra® m

lying ['laɪɪŋ] n mensonge(s) m(pl) ▷ adj (statement, story) mensonger(-ère), faux (fausse); (person) menteur(-euse)

Lyons ['lɪɔ̃] n Lyon m

lyrics ['lɪrɪks] npl (of song) paroles fpl

m. abbr (= metre) m; (= million) M; (= mile) mi

ma [mɑ:] (inf) n maman f

M.A. n abbr (Scol) = Master of Arts

mac [mæk] n (BRIT) imper(méable m) m

macaroni [mækə'rəʊnɪ] n macaronis mpl

Macedonia [mæsɪ'dəʊnɪə] n Macédoine f; **Macedonian** [mæsɪ'dəʊnɪən] adj macédonien(ne) ▷ n Macédonien(ne); (Ling) macédonien m

machine [mə'ʃi:n] n machine f ▷ vt (dress etc) coudre à la machine; (Tech) usiner; **machine gun** n mitrailleuse f; **machinery** n machinerie f, machines fpl; (fig) mécanisme(s) m(pl); **machine washable** adj (garment) lavable en machine

macho ['mætʃəʊ] adj macho inv

mackerel ['mækrl] n (pl inv) maquereau m

mackintosh ['mækɪntɔʃ] n (BRIT) imperméable m

mad [mæd] *adj* fou (folle); (*foolish*)
insensé(e); (*angry*) furieux(-euse);
to be ~ (keen) about or **on sth** (*inf*)
être follement passionné de qch, être
fou de qch
Madagascar [mædə'gæskər] *n*
Madagascar *m*
madam ['mædəm] *n* madame *f*
mad cow disease *n* maladie *f* des
vaches folles
made [meɪd] *pt, pp of* **make**: **made-
to-measure** *adj* (*BRIT*) fait(e) sur
mesure; **made-up** *adj* ['meɪdʌp] (*lip*)
(*story*) inventé(e), fabriqué(e)
madly ['mædlɪ] *adv* follement; **~ in
love** éperdument amoureux(-euse)
madman ['mædmən] (*irreg*) *n* fou
m, aliéné *m*
madness ['mædnɪs] *n* folie *f*
Madrid [mə'drɪd] *n* Madrid *m*
Mafia ['mæfɪə] *n* maf(f)ia *f*
mag [mæg] *n abbr* (*BRIT inf*:
= *magazine*) magazine *m*
magazine [mægə'ziːn] *n* (*Press*)
magazine *m*, revue *f*; (*Radio, TV*)
magazine
maggot ['mægət] *n* ver *m*, asticot *m*
magic ['mædʒɪk] *n* magie *f* ▷ *adj*
magique; **magical** *adj* magique;
(*experience, evening*) merveilleux(-euse);
magician [mə'dʒɪʃən] *n* magicien(ne)
magistrate ['mædʒɪstreɪt] *n*
magistrat *m*; juge *m*
magnet ['mægnɪt] *n* aimant
m; **magnetic** [mæg'nɛtɪk] *adj*
magnétique
magnificent [mæg'nɪfɪsnt] *adj*
superbe, magnifique; (*splendid*):
robe, building) somptueux(-euse),
magnifique
magnify ['mægnɪfaɪ] *vt* grossir;
(*sound*) amplifier; **magnifying glass**
n loupe *f*
magpie ['mægpaɪ] *n* pie *f*
mahogany [mə'hɔgənɪ] *n* acajou *m*
maid [meɪd] *n* bonne *f*; (*in hotel*)
femme *f* de chambre; **old ~** (*pej*)
vieille fille

maiden name *n* nom *m* de jeune fille
mail [meɪl] *n* poste *f*; (*letters*) courrier
m ▷ *vt* envoyer (par la poste); **by ~** par
la poste; **mailbox** *n* (*us, also Comput*)
boîte *f* aux lettres; **mailing list** *n* liste
f d'adresses; **mailman** (*irreg*) *n* (*us*)
facteur *m*; **mail-order** *n* vente *f* par
achat *m* par correspondance
main [meɪn] *adj* principal(e) ▷ *n* (*pipe*)
conduite principale, canalisation
f; **the ~s** (*Elec*) le secteur; **the ~
thing** l'essentiel *m*; **in the ~** dans
l'ensemble; **main course** *n* (*Culin*)
plat *m* de résistance; **mainland**
n continent *m*; **mainly** *adv*
principalement, surtout; **main
road** *n* grand axe, route nationale;
mainstream *n* (*fig*) courant principal;
main street *n* rue *f* principale
maintain [meɪn'teɪn] *vt* entretenir;
(*continue*) maintenir, préserver;
(*affirm*) soutenir; **maintenance**
['meɪntənəns] *n* entretien *m*; (*Law:*
alimony) pension *f* alimentaire
maisonette [meɪzə'nɛt] *n* (*BRIT*)
appartement *m* en duplex
maize [meɪz] *n* (*BRIT*) maïs *m*
majesty ['mædʒɪstɪ] *n* majesté *f*;
(*title*): **Your M~** Votre Majesté
major ['meɪdʒər] *n* (*Mil*) commandant
m ▷ *adj* (*important*) important(e);
(*most important*) principal(e); (*Mus*)
majeur(e) ▷ *vi* (*us Scol*): **to ~ (in)** se
spécialiser (en)
Majorca [mə'jɔːkə] *n* Majorque *f*
majority [mə'dʒɔrɪtɪ] *n* majorité *f*
make [meɪk] *vt* (*pt, pp* **made**) faire;
(*manufacture*) faire, fabriquer; (*earn*)
gagner; (*decision*) prendre; (*friend*)
se faire; (*speech*) faire, prononcer;
(*cause to be*): **to ~ sb sad** *etc* rendre
qn triste *etc*; (*force*): **to ~ sb do sth**
obliger qn à faire qch, faire faire
qch à qn; (*equal*): **2 and 2 ~ 4** 2 et 2
font 4 ▷ *n* (*manufacture*) fabrication
f; (*brand*) marque *f*; **to ~ the bed**
faire le lit; **to ~ a fool of sb** (*ridicule*)
ridiculiser qn; (*trick*) avoir ou duper

qn; **to ~ a profit** faire un or des
bénéfice(s); **to ~ a loss** essuyer une
perte; **to ~ it** (in time etc) y arriver;
(succeed) réussir; **what time do you
~ it?** quelle heure avez-vous? **I ~ it
£249** d'après mes calculs ça fait 249
livres; **to be made of** être en; **to ~ do
with** se contenter de; se débrouiller
avec; **make off** vt filer; **make out**
vt (write out: cheque) faire; (decipher)
déchiffrer; (understand) comprendre;
(see) distinguer; (claim, imply)
prétendre, vouloir faire croire; **make
up** vt (invent) inventer, imaginer;
(constitute) constituer; (parcel,
bed) faire ▷ vi se réconcilier; (with
cosmetics) se maquiller, se farder;
to be made up of se composer
de; **make up for** vt fus compenser;
(lost time) rattraper; **makeover**
['meɪkəʊvə'] n (by beautician) soins
mpl de maquillage; (of image)
changement m d'image; **maker** n
fabricant m; (of film, programme)
réalisateur(-trice); **makeshift** adj
provisoire, improvisé(e); **make-up** n
maquillage m

making ['meɪkɪŋ] n (fig): **in the ~** en
formation or gestation; **to have the
~s of** (actor, athlete) avoir l'étoffe de

malaria [mə'lɛərɪə] n malaria f,
paludisme m

Malaysia [mə'leɪzɪə] n Malaisie f

male [meɪl] n (Biol, Elec) mâle m ▷ adj
(sex, attitude) masculin(e); (animal)
mâle; (child etc) du sexe masculin

malicious [mə'lɪʃəs] adj méchant(e),
malveillant(e)

> Be careful not to translate
> malicious by the French word
> malicieux.

malignant [mə'lɪgnənt] adj (Med)
malin(-igne)

mall [mɔːl] n (also: **shopping ~**)
centre commercial

mallet ['mælɪt] n maillet m

malnutrition [mælnjuː'trɪʃən] n
malnutrition f

malpractice [mæl'præktɪs] n faute
professionnelle; négligence f

malt [mɔːlt] n malt m ▷ cpd (whisky)
pur malt

Malta ['mɔːltə] n Malte f; **Maltese**
[mɔːl'tiːz] adj maltais(e) ▷ n (pl inv)
Maltais(e)

mammal ['mæml] n mammifère m

mammoth ['mæməθ] n mammouth
m ▷ adj géant(e), monstre

man (pl **men**) [mæn, mɛn] n
homme m; (Sport) joueur m; (Chess)
pièce f ▷ vt (Naut: ship) garnir
d'hommes; (machine) assurer le
fonctionnement de; (Mil: gun)
servir; (: post) être de service à; **an
old ~** un vieillard; **~ and wife** mari
et femme

manage ['mænɪdʒ] vi se débrouiller;
(succeed) y arriver, réussir ▷ vt
(business) gérer; (team, operation)
diriger; (control: ship) manier,
manœuvrer; (: person) savoir
s'y prendre avec; **to ~ to do** se
débrouiller pour faire; (succeed)
réussir à faire; **manageable** adj
maniable; (task etc) faisable; (number)
raisonnable; **management** n
(running) administration f, direction
f; (people in charge: of business, firm)
dirigeants mpl, cadres mpl; (: of hotel,
shop, theatre) direction; **manager** n
(of business) directeur m; (of institution
etc) administrateur m; (of department,
unit) responsable m/f, chef m; (of hotel
etc) gérant m; (Sport) manager m; (of
artist) impresario m; **manageress**
n directrice f; (of hotel etc) gérante
f; **managerial** [mænɪ'dʒɪərɪəl]
adj directorial(e); (skills) de cadre,
de gestion; **managing director** n
directeur général

mandarin ['mændərɪn] n (also:
~ orange) mandarine f

mandate ['mændeɪt] n mandat m

mandatory ['mændətərɪ] adj
obligatoire

mane [meɪn] n crinière f

maneuver [mə'nu:vər] (US) n
= **manoeuvre**

mangetout ['mɔnʒ'tu:] n mangetout m inv

mango ['mæŋgəu] (pl **mangoes**) n
mangue f

man: manhole n trou m d'homme;
manhood n (age) âge m d'homme;
(manliness) virilité f

mania ['meɪnɪə] n manie f; **maniac**
['meɪnɪæk] n maniaque m/f; (fig)
fou (folle)

manic ['mænɪk] adj maniaque

manicure ['mænɪkjuər] n manucure f

manifest ['mænɪfest] vt manifester
▷ adj manifeste, évident(e)

manifesto [mænɪ'festəu] n (Pol)
manifeste m

manipulate [mə'nɪpjuleɪt] vt
manipuler; (system, situation)
exploiter

man: mankind [mæn'kaɪnd] n
humanité f, genre humain; **manly** adj
viril(e); **man-made** adj artificiel(le);
(fibre) synthétique

manner ['mænər] n manière f,
façon f; (behaviour) attitude f,
comportement m; **manners** npl:
(good) **~s** (bonnes) manières; **bad ~s**
mauvaises manières; **all ~ of** toutes
sortes de

manoeuvre, (US) **maneuver**
[mə'nu:vər] vt (move) manœuvrer;
(manipulate: person) manipuler;
(: situation) exploiter ▷ n manœuvre f

manpower ['mænpauər] n main-
d'œuvre f

mansion ['mænʃən] n château m,
manoir m

manslaughter ['mænslɔ:tər] n
homicide m involontaire

mantelpiece ['mæntlpi:s] n
cheminée f

manual ['mænjuəl] adj manuel(le)
▷ n manuel m

manufacture [mænju'fæktʃər]
vt fabriquer ▷ n fabrication f;
manufacturer n fabricant m

manure [mə'njuər] n fumier m;
(artificial) engrais m

manuscript ['mænjuskrɪpt] n
manuscrit m

many ['menɪ] adj beaucoup de, de
nombreux(-euses) ▷ pron beaucoup,
un grand nombre; **a great ~** un grand
nombre (de); **~ a ...** bien des ..., plus
d'un(e) ...

map [mæp] n carte f; (of town) plan
m; **can you show it to me on the
~?** pouvez-vous me l'indiquer sur la
carte?; **map out** vt tracer; (fig: task)
planifier

maple ['meɪpl] n érable m

mar [mɑ:] vt gâcher, gâter

marathon ['mærəθən] n
marathon m

marble ['mɑ:bl] n marbre m; (toy)
bille f

March [mɑ:tʃ] n mars m

march [mɑ:tʃ] vi marcher au pas;
(demonstrators) défiler ▷ n marche f;
(demonstration) manifestation f

mare [mɛər] n jument f

margarine [mɑ:dʒə'ri:n] n
margarine f

margin ['mɑ:dʒɪn] n marge f;
marginal adj marginal(e); **marginal
seat** (Pol) siège disputé; **marginally**
adv très légèrement, sensiblement

marigold ['mærɪgəuld] n souci m

marijuana [mærɪ'wɑ:nə] n
marijuana f

marina [mə'ri:nə] n marina f

marinade [mærɪ'neɪd] n marinade f

marinate ['mærɪneɪt] vt (faire)
mariner

marine [mə'ri:n] adj marin(e) ▷ n
fusilier marin; (US) marine m

marital ['mærɪtl] adj matrimonial(e);
marital status n situation f de
famille

maritime ['mærɪtaɪm] adj maritime

marjoram ['mɑ:dʒərəm] n
marjolaine f

mark [mɑ:k] n marque f; (of skid
etc) trace f; (BRIT Scol) note f; (oven

temperature): (**gas**) **~** thermostat m **4** ⊳ vt (*also Sport: player*) marquer; (*stain*) tacher; (BRIT Scol) corriger, noter; **to ~ time** marquer le pas; **marked** adj (*obvious*) marqué(e), net(te); **marker** n (*sign*) jalon m; (*bookmark*) signet m

market ['mɑːkɪt] n marché m ⊳ vt (Comm) commercialiser; **marketing** n marketing m; **marketplace** n place f du marché; (Comm) marché m; **market research** n étude f de marché

marmalade ['mɑːməleɪd] n confiture f d'oranges

maroon [mə'ruːn] vt: **to be ~ed** être abandonné(e); (*fig*) être bloqué(e) ⊳ adj (*colour*) bordeaux inv

marquee [mɑː'kiː] n chapiteau m

marriage ['mærɪdʒ] n mariage m; **marriage certificate** n extrait m d'acte de mariage

married ['mærɪd] adj marié(e); (*life, love*) conjugal(e)

marrow ['mærəʊ] n (*of bone*) moelle f; (*vegetable*) courge f

marry ['mærɪ] vt épouser, se marier avec; (*subj: father, priest etc*) marier ⊳ vi (*also: **get married**) se marier

Mars [mɑːz] n (*planet*) Mars f

Marseilles [mɑː'seɪ] n Marseille

marsh [mɑːʃ] n marais m, marécage m

marshal ['mɑːʃl] n maréchal m; (US: fire, police) ≈ capitaine m; (for demonstration, meeting) membre m du service d'ordre ⊳ vt rassembler

martyr ['mɑːtər] n martyr(e)

marvel ['mɑːvl] n merveille f ⊳ vi: **to ~ (at)** s'émerveiller (de); **marvellous**, (US) **marvelous** adj merveilleux(-euse)

Marxism ['mɑːksɪzəm] n marxisme m

Marxist ['mɑːksɪst] adj, n marxiste (m/f)

marzipan ['mɑːzɪpæn] n pâte f d'amandes

mascara [mæs'kɑːrə] n mascara m

mascot ['mæskət] n mascotte f

masculine ['mæskjulɪn] adj masculin(e) ⊳ n masculin m

mash [mæʃ] vt (Culin) faire une purée de; **mashed potato(es)** n(pl) purée f de pommes de terre

mask [mɑːsk] n masque m ⊳ vt masquer

mason ['meɪsn] n (*also: **stone~**) maçon m; (*also: **free~**) franc-maçon m; **masonry** n maçonnerie f

mass [mæs] n multitude f, masse f; (Physics) masse f; (Rel) messe f ⊳ cpd (communication) de masse; (unemployment) massif(-ive) ⊳ vi se masser; **masses** npl; **the ~es** les masses; **~es of** (inf) des tas de

massacre ['mæsəkər] n massacre m

massage ['mæsɑːʒ] n massage m ⊳ vt masser

massive ['mæsɪv] adj énorme, massif(-ive)

mass media npl mass-media mpl

mass-produce ['mæsprə'djuːs] vt fabriquer en série

mast [mɑːst] n mât m; (Radio, TV) pylône m

master ['mɑːstər] n maître m; (in secondary school) professeur m; (in primary school) instituteur m; (title for boys): **M~ X** Monsieur X ⊳ vt maîtriser; (learn) apprendre à fond; **M~ of Arts/ Science (MA/MSc)** n ≈ titulaire m/f d'une maîtrise (en lettres/science); **M~ of Arts/Science degree (MA/ MSc)** n ≈ maîtrise f; **mastermind** n esprit supérieur ⊳ vt diriger, être le cerveau de; **masterpiece** n chef-d'œuvre m

masturbate ['mæstəbeɪt] vi se masturber

mat [mæt] n petit tapis; (*also: **door~**) paillasson m; (*also: **table~**) set m de table ⊳ adj = **matt**

match [mætʃ] n allumette f; (game) match m, partie f; (*fig*) égal(e) ⊳ vt (*also: **~ up**) assortir; (go well with) aller bien avec, s'assortir à; (equal) égaler, valoir ▷ vi être assorti(e); **to be a good ~** être bien assorti(e); **matchbox** n boîte f d'allumettes; **matching** adj assorti(e)

mate [meɪt] n (inf) copain (copine); (animal) partenaire m/f, mâle (femelle); (in merchant navy) second m ▷ vi s'accoupler

material [məˈtɪərɪəl] n (substance) matière f, matériau m; (cloth) tissu m, étoffe f; (information, data) données fpl ▷ adj matériel(le); (relevant: evidence) pertinent(e); **materials** npl (equipment) matériaux mpl

materialize [məˈtɪərɪəlaɪz] vi se matérialiser, se réaliser

maternal [məˈtəːnl] adj maternel(le)

maternity [məˈtəːnɪtɪ] n maternité f; **maternity hospital** n maternité f; **maternity leave** n congé m de maternité

math [mæθ] n (US: = mathematics) maths fpl

mathematical [mæθəˈmætɪkl] adj mathématique

mathematician [mæθəməˈtɪʃən] n mathématicien(ne)

mathematics [mæθəˈmætɪks] n mathématiques fpl

maths [mæθs] n abbr (BRIT: = mathematics) maths fpl

matinée [ˈmætɪneɪ] n matinée f

matron [ˈmeɪtrən] n (in hospital) infirmière-chef f; (in school) infirmière f

matt [mæt] adj mat(e)

matter [ˈmætəʳ] n question f; (Physics) matière f, substance f; (Med: pus) pus m ▷ vi importer; **matters** npl (affairs, situation) la situation; **it doesn't ~** cela n'a pas d'importance; (I don't mind) cela ne fait rien; **what's the ~?** qu'est-ce qu'il y a?, qu'est-ce qui ne va pas?; **no ~ what** quoi qu'il arrive; **as a ~ of course** tout naturellement; **as a ~ of fact** en fait; **reading** n (BRIT) de quoi lire, de la lecture

mattress [ˈmætrɪs] n matelas m

mature [məˈtjuəʳ] adj mûr(e); (cheese) fait(e); (wine) arrivé(e) à maturité ▷ vi mûrir; (cheese, wine) se faire; **mature student** n étudiant(e) plus âgé(e) que la moyenne; **maturity** n maturité f

maul [mɔːl] vt lacérer

mauve [məuv] adj mauve

max abbr = **maximum**

maximize [ˈmæksɪmaɪz] vt (profits etc, chances) maximiser

maximum (pl **maxima**) [ˈmæksɪməm, -mə] adj maximum ▷ n maximum m

May [meɪ] n mai m

may [meɪ] (conditional **might**) vi (indicating possibility): **he ~ come** il se peut qu'il vienne; (be allowed to): **~ I smoke?** puis-je fumer?; (wishes): **~ God bless you!** (que) Dieu vous bénisse!; **you ~ as well go** vous feriez aussi bien d'y aller

maybe [ˈmeɪbiː] adv peut-être; **~ he'll ...** peut-être qu'il ...

May Day n le Premier mai

mayhem [ˈmeɪhem] n grabuge m

mayonnaise [meɪəˈneɪz] n mayonnaise f

mayor [mεəʳ] n maire m; **mayoress** n (female mayor) maire m; (wife of mayor) épouse f du maire

maze [meɪz] n labyrinthe m, dédale m

MD n abbr (Comm) = **managing director**

me [miː] pron me, m' + vowel or h mute; (stressed, after prep) moi; **it's me** c'est moi; **he heard me** il m'a entendu; **give me a book** donnez-moi un livre; **it's for me** c'est pour moi

meadow [ˈmεdəu] n prairie f, pré m

meagre, (US) **meager** [ˈmiːgəʳ] adj maigre

meal [miːl] n repas m; (flour) farine f; **mealtime** n heure f du repas

mean [miːn] adj (with money) avare, radin(e); (unkind) mesquin(e), méchant(e); (shabby) misérable;

(*average*) moyen(ne) ▷ vt (pt, pp
meant) (*signify*) signifier, vouloir dire;
(*refer to*) faire allusion à, parler de;
(*intend*): **to ~ to do** avoir l'intention de
faire qch; **by ~s of** (*instrument*) au
moyen de; **by all ~s** je vous en prie
meaning ['mi:nɪŋ] n signification
f, sens m; **meaningful** adj
significatif(-ive); (*relationship*)
valable; **meaningless** adj dénué(e)
de sens
meant [mɛnt] pt, pp of **mean**
meantime ['mi:ntaɪm] adv (also: **in
the ~**) pendant ce temps
meanwhile ['mi:nwaɪl] adv
= **meantime**
measles ['mi:zlz] n rougeole f
measure ['mɛʒəʳ] vt, vi mesurer ▷ n
mesure f; (*ruler*) règle (graduée)
measurements ['mɛʒəməntz] npl
mesures fpl; **chest/hip ~** tour m de
poitrine/hanches
meat [mi:t] n viande f; **I don't eat ~**
je ne mange pas de viande; **cold ~s**
(BRIT) viandes froides; **meatball** n
boulette f de viande
Mecca ['mɛkə] n la Mecque
mechanic [mɪ'kænɪk] n mécanicien
m; **can you send a ~?** pouvez-vous
nous envoyer un mécanicien?;
mechanical adj mécanique
mechanism ['mɛkənɪzəm] n
mécanisme m
medal ['mɛdl] n médaille f;
medallist, (US) **medalist** n (Sport)
médaillé(e)
meddle ['mɛdl] vi: **to ~ in** se mêler
de, s'occuper de; **to ~ with** toucher à
media ['mi:dɪə] npl media mpl ▷ npl
of **medium**
mediaeval [mɛdɪ'i:vl] adj
= **medieval**
mediate ['mi:dɪeɪt] vi servir
d'intermédiaire

medical ['mɛdɪkl] adj médical(e)
▷ n (also: **~ examination**) visite
médicale; (*private*) examen médical;
medical certificate n certificat
médical
medicated ['mɛdɪkeɪtɪd] adj
traitant(e), médicamenteux(-euse)
medication [mɛdɪ'keɪʃən] n (drugs
etc) médication f
medicine ['mɛdsɪn] n médecine f;
(*drug*) médicament m
medieval [mɛdɪ'i:vl] adj médiéval(e)
mediocre [mi:dɪ'əukəʳ] adj médiocre
meditate ['mɛdɪteɪt] vi: **to ~ (on)**
méditer (sur)
meditation [mɛdɪ'teɪʃən] n
méditation f
Mediterranean [mɛdɪtə'reɪnɪən]
adj méditerranéen(ne); **the ~ (Sea)** la
(mer) Méditerranée
medium ['mi:dɪəm] adj moyen(ne)
▷ n (pl **media**) (means) moyen m;
(*person*) médium m; **the happy ~**
le juste milieu; **medium-sized** adj
de taille moyenne; **medium wave**
n (Radio) ondes moyennes, petites
ondes

meek [mi:k] adj doux (douce),
humble
meet (pt, pp **met**) [mi:t, mɛt]
vt rencontrer; (by arrangement)
retrouver, rejoindre; (for the first time)
faire la connaissance de; (go and
fetch): **I'll ~ you at the station** j'irai te
chercher à la gare; (*opponent, danger,
problem*) faire face à; (*requirements*)
satisfaire à, répondre à ▷ vi (friends) se
rencontrer; (by arrangement) se
retrouver; (in session) se réunir; (join:
lines, roads) se joindre;
nice ~ing you ravi d'avoir fait votre
connaissance; **meet up** vi: **to ~ up
with sb** rencontrer qn; **meet with** vt
fus (difficulty) rencontrer; **to ~ with
success** être couronné(e) de succès;
meeting n (of group of people) réunion
f; (between individuals) rendez-vous m;
she's at or **in a meeting** (Comm) elle
est en réunion; **meeting place** n lieu

m

m de (la) réunion; *(for appointment)* lieu de rendez-vous

megabyte ['mɛgəbaɪt] *n (Comput)* méga-octet *m*

megaphone ['mɛgəfəʊn] *n* porte-voix *m inv*

megapixel ['mɛgəpɪksl] *n* mégapixel *m*

melancholy ['mɛlənkəlɪ] *n* mélancolie *f* ▷ *adj* mélancolique

melody ['mɛlədɪ] *n* mélodie *f*

melon ['mɛlən] *n* melon *m*

melt [mɛlt] *vi* fondre ▷ *vt* faire fondre

member ['mɛmbəʳ] *n* membre *m*; **M~ of Parliament** eurodéputé *m*; **M~ of Parliament** (BRIT) député *m*; **membership** *n (becoming a member)* adhésion *f*; admission *f*; *(members)* membres *mpl*, adhérents *mpl*; **membership card** *n* carte *f* de membre

memento [mə'mɛntəʊ] *n* souvenir *m*

memo ['mɛməʊ] *n* note *f* (de service)

memorable ['mɛmərəbl] *adj* mémorable

memorandum (*pl* **memoranda**) [mɛmə'rændəm, -də] *n* note *f* (de service)

memorial [mɪ'mɔːrɪəl] *n* mémorial *m* ▷ *adj* commémoratif(-ive)

memorize ['mɛməraɪz] *vt* apprendre *or* retenir par cœur

memory ['mɛmərɪ] *n (also Comput)* mémoire *f*; *(recollection)* souvenir *m*; **in ~ of** à la mémoire de; **memory card** *n (for digital camera)* carte *f* mémoire; **memory stick** *n (Comput: flash pen)* clé *f* USB; *(: card)* carte *f* mémoire

men [mɛn] *npl of* **man**

menace ['mɛnɪs] *n* menace *f*; *(inf: nuisance)* peste *f*, plaie *f* ▷ *vt* menacer

mend [mɛnd] *vt* réparer; *(darn)* raccommoder, repriser ▷ *n*: **on the ~** en voie de guérison; **to ~ one's ways** s'amender

meningitis [mɛnɪn'dʒaɪtɪs] *n* méningite *f*

menopause ['mɛnəʊpɔːz] *n* ménopause *f*

men's room (US) *n*: **the ~** les toilettes *fpl* pour hommes

menstruation [mɛnstru'eɪʃən] *n* menstruation *f*

menswear ['mɛnzwɛəʳ] *n* vêtements *mpl* d'hommes

mental ['mɛntl] *adj* mental(e); **mental hospital** *n (pej)* hôpital *m* psychiatrique; **mentality** [mɛn'tælɪtɪ] *n* mentalité *f*; **mentally** *adv*: **mentally ill people** les malades mentaux

menthol ['mɛnθɔl] *n* menthol *m*

mention ['mɛnʃən] *n* mention *f* ▷ *vt* mentionner, faire mention de; **don't ~ it!** je vous en prie, il n'y a pas de quoi!

menu ['mɛnjuː] *n (set menu, Comput)* menu *m*; *(list of dishes)* carte *f*

MEP *n abbr* = **Member of the European Parliament**

mercenary ['mɜːsɪnərɪ] *adj (person)* intéressé(e), mercenaire ▷ *n* mercenaire *m*

merchandise ['mɜːtʃəndaɪz] *n* marchandises *fpl*

merchant ['mɜːtʃənt] *n* négociant *m*, marchand *m*; **merchant bank** (BRIT) banque *f* d'affaires; **merchant navy**, (US) **merchant marine** *n* marine marchande

merciless ['mɜːsɪlɪs] *adj* impitoyable, sans pitié

mercury ['mɜːkjʊrɪ] *n* mercure *m*

mercy ['mɜːsɪ] *n* pitié *f*, merci *f*; *(Rel)* miséricorde *f*; **at the ~ of** à la merci de

mere [mɪəʳ] *adj* simple; *(chance)* pur(e); **a ~ two hours** seulement deux heures; **merely** *adv* simplement, purement

merge [mɜːdʒ] *vt* unir; *(Comput)* fusionner, interclasser ▷ *vi (colours, shapes, sounds)* se mêler; *(roads)* se joindre; (*Comm*) fusionner; **merger** *n* (*Comm*) fusion *f*

meringue [mə'ræŋ] *n* meringue *f*

merit ['mɛrɪt] *n* mérite *m*, valeur *f* ▷ *vt* mériter

mermaid ['mə:meɪd] *n* sirène *f*

merry ['mɛrɪ] *adj* gai(e); **M~ Christmas!** joyeux Noël!; **merry-go-round** *n* manège *m*

mesh [mɛʃ] *n* mailles *fpl*

mess [mɛs] *n* désordre *m*, fouillis *m*, pagaille *f*; (*muddle: of life*) gâchis *m*; (: *of economy*) pagaille *f*; (*dirt*) saleté *f*; (*Mil*) mess *m*, cantine *f*; **to be (in) a ~** être en désordre; **to be/get o.s. in a ~** (*fig*) être/se mettre dans le pétrin; **mess about, mess around** (*inf*) *vi* perdre son temps; **mess up** *vt* (*inf*: *dirty*) salir; (*spoil*) gâcher; **mess with** (*inf*) *vt fus* (*challenge, confront*) se frotter à; (*interfere with*) toucher à

message ['mɛsɪdʒ] *n* message *m*; **can I leave a ~?** est-ce que je peux laisser un message?; **are there any ~s for me?** est-ce que j'ai des messages?

messenger ['mɛsɪndʒəʳ] *n* messager *m*

Messrs, Messrs. ['mɛsəz] *abbr* (*on letters*: = *messieurs*) MM

messy ['mɛsɪ] *adj* (*dirty*) sale; (*untidy*) en désordre

met [mɛt] *pt, pp of* **meet**

metabolism [mɛ'tæbəlɪzəm] *n* métabolisme *m*

metal ['mɛtl] *n* métal *m* ▷ *cpd* en métal; **metallic** [mɛ'tælɪk] *adj* métallique

metaphor ['mɛtəfəʳ] *n* métaphore *f*

meteor ['mi:tɪəʳ] *n* météore *m*; **meteorite** ['mi:tɪəraɪt] *n* météorite *m* *f*

meteorology [mi:tɪə'rɔlədʒɪ] *n* météorologie *f*

meter ['mi:təʳ] *n* (*instrument*) compteur *m*; (*also*: **parking ~**) parc(o)mètre *m*; (*us: unit*) = **metre** ▷ *vt* (*us Post*) affranchir à la machine

method ['mɛθəd] *n* méthode *f*; **methodical** [mɪ'θɔdɪkl] *adj* méthodique

methylated spirit ['mɛθɪleɪtɪd-] *n* (*BRIT*) alcool *m* à brûler

meticulous [mɛ'tɪkjuləs] *adj* méticuleux(-euse)

metre, (*us*) **meter** ['mi:təʳ] *n* mètre *m*

metric ['mɛtrɪk] *adj* métrique

metro ['mɛtrəu] *n* métro *m*

metropolitan [mɛtrə'pɔlɪtn] *adj* métropolitain(e); **the M~ Police** (*BRIT*) la police londonienne

Mexican ['mɛksɪkən] *adj* mexicain(e) ▷ *n* Mexicain(e)

Mexico ['mɛksɪkəu] *n* Mexique *m*

mg *abbr* (= *milligram*) mg

mice [maɪs] *npl of* **mouse**

micro... [maɪkrəu] *prefix* micro...; **microchip** *n* (*Elec*) puce *f*; **microphone** *n* microphone *m*; **microscope** *n* microscope *m*

mid [mɪd] *adj*: **~ May** la mi-mai; **~ afternoon** le milieu de l'après-midi; **in ~ air** en plein ciel; **he's in his ~ thirties** il a dans les trente-cinq ans; **midday** *n* midi *m*

middle ['mɪdl] *n* milieu *m*; (*waist*) ceinture *f*, taille *f* ▷ *adj* du milieu; (*average*) moyen(ne); **in the ~ of the night** au milieu de la nuit; **middle-aged** *adj* d'un certain âge, ni vieux ni jeune; **Middle Ages** *npl*: **the Middle Ages** le moyen âge; **middle-class(es)** *n(pl)*: **the middle class(es)** ≈ les classes moyennes; **middle-class** *adj* bourgeois(e); **Middle East** *n*: **the Middle East** le Proche-Orient, le Moyen-Orient; **middle name** *n* second prénom; **middle school** *n* (*us*) école pour les enfants de 12 à 14 ans ≈ collège *m*; (*BRIT*) école pour les enfants de 8 à 14 ans

midge [mɪdʒ] *n* moucheron *m*

midget ['mɪdʒɪt] *n* (*pej*) nain(e)

midnight ['mɪdnaɪt] *n* minuit *m*

midst [mɪdst] *n*: **in the ~ of** au milieu de

midsummer [mɪd'sʌmə'] n milieu m de l'été

midway [mɪd'weɪ] adj, adv: ~ (between) à mi-chemin (entre); ~ through ... au milieu de ..., en plein(e) ...

midweek [mɪd'wiːk] adv au milieu de la semaine, en pleine semaine

midwife (pl **midwives**) ['mɪdwaɪf, -vz] n sage-femme f

midwinter [mɪd'wɪntə'] n milieu m de l'hiver

might [maɪt] vb see **may** ⊳ n puissance f, force f; **mighty** adj puissant(e)

migraine ['miːgreɪn] n migraine f

migrant ['maɪgrənt] n (bird, animal) migrateur m; (person) migrant(e) ⊳ adj migrateur(-trice); migrant(e); (worker) saisonnier(-ière)

migrate [maɪ'greɪt] vi migrer

migration [maɪ'greɪʃən] n migration f

mike [maɪk] n abbr (= microphone) micro m

mild [maɪld] adj doux (douce); (reproach, infection) léger(-ère); (illness) bénin(-igne); (interest) modéré(e); (taste) peu relevé(e); **mildly** ['maɪldlɪ] adv doucement; légèrement; **to put it mildly** (inf) c'est le moins qu'on puisse dire

mile [maɪl] n mil(l)e m (= 1609 m); **mileage** n distance f en milles, ≈ kilométrage m; **mileometer** [maɪ'lɒmɪtə'] n compteur m kilométrique; **milestone** n borne f, (fig) jalon m

military ['mɪlɪtərɪ] adj militaire

militia [mɪ'lɪʃə] n milice f

milk [mɪlk] n lait m ⊳ vt (cow) traire; (fig: person) dépouiller, plumer; (: situation) exploiter à fond; **milk chocolate** n chocolat m au lait; **milkman** (irreg) n laitier m; **milky** adj (drink) au lait; (colour) laiteux(-euse)

mill [mɪl] n moulin m; (: factory) usine f, fabrique f; (spinning mill) filature f;

(flour mill) minoterie f ⊳ vt moudre, broyer ⊳ vi (also: ~ **about**) grouiller

millennium (pl **millenniums** or **millennia**) [mɪ'lenɪəm, -'lenɪə] n millénaire m

milli... ['mɪlɪ] prefix milli...; **milligram(me)** n milligramme m; **millilitre**, (us) **milliliter** n millilitre m; **millimetre**, (us) **millimeter** n millimètre m

million ['mɪljən] n million m; **a ~ pounds** un million de livres sterling; **millionaire** [mɪljə'nεə'] n millionnaire m; **millionth** [mɪljə'nθ] num millionième

milometer [maɪ'lɒmɪtə'] n = **mileometer**

mime [maɪm] n mime m ⊳ vt, vi mimer

mimic ['mɪmɪk] n imitateur(-trice) ⊳ vt, vi imiter, contrefaire

min. abbr (= minute(s)) mn.; (= minimum) min.

mince [mɪns] vt hacher ⊳ n (BRIT Culin) viande hachée, hachis m; **mincemeat** n hachis de fruits secs utilisés en pâtisserie; (us) viande hachée, hachis m; **mince pie** n sorte de tarte aux fruits secs

mind [maɪnd] n esprit m ⊳ vt (attend to, look after) s'occuper de; (be careful) faire attention à; (object to): **I don't ~ the noise** je ne crains pas le bruit, le bruit ne me dérange pas; **it is on my ~** cela me préoccupe; **to change one's ~** changer d'avis; **to my ~** à mon avis, selon moi; **to bear sth in ~** tenir compte de qch; **to have sb/sth in ~** avoir qn/qch en tête; **to make up one's ~** se décider; **do you ~ if ...?** est-ce que cela vous gêne si ...?; **I don't ~** cela ne me dérange pas; (don't care) ça m'est égal; **~ you, ...** remarquez, ...; **never ~** peu importe, ça ne fait rien; (don't worry) ne vous en faites pas; **"~ the step"** "attention à la marche"; **mindless** adj irréfléchi(e); (violence, crime) insensé(e); (boring: job) idiot(e)

mine¹ [maɪn] *pron* le (la) mien(ne), les miens (miennes); **a friend of ~** un de mes amis, un ami à moi; **this book is ~** ce livre est à moi

mine² [maɪn] *n* mine *f* ▷ *vt* (coal) extraire; (ship, beach) miner; **minefield** *n* champ de mines; **miner** *n* mineur *m*

mineral ['mɪnərəl] *adj* minéral(e) ▷ *n* minéral *m*; **mineral water** *n* eau minérale

mingle ['mɪŋgl] *vi*: **to ~ with** se mêler à

miniature ['mɪnətʃə²] *adj* (en) miniature ▷ *n* miniature *f*

minibar ['mɪnɪbɑː²] *n* minibar *m*

minibus ['mɪnɪbʌs] *n* minibus *m*

minicab ['mɪnɪkæb] *n* (BRIT) taxi *m* indépendant

minimal ['mɪnɪml] *adj* minimal(e)

minimize ['mɪnɪmaɪz] *vt* (reduce) réduire au minimum; (play down) minimiser

minimum ['mɪnɪməm] *n* (*pl* **minima**) minimum *m* ▷ *adj* minimum

mining ['maɪnɪŋ] *n* exploitation minière

miniskirt ['mɪnɪskəːt] *n* mini-jupe *f*

minister ['mɪnɪstə²] *n* (BRIT Pol) ministre *m*; (Rel) pasteur *m*

ministry ['mɪnɪstrɪ] *n* (BRIT Pol) ministère *m*; (Rel): **to go into the ~** devenir pasteur

minor ['maɪnə²] *adj* petit(e), de peu d'importance; (Mus, poet, problem) mineur(e) ▷ *n* (Law) mineur(e)

minority [maɪ'nɔrɪtɪ] *n* minorité *f*

mint [mɪnt] *n* (plant) menthe *f*; (sweet) bonbon *m* à la menthe ▷ *vt* (coins) battre; **the (Royal) M~**, **the (US) M~** ≈ l'hôtel de la Monnaie; **in ~ condition** à l'état de neuf

minus ['maɪnəs] *n* (also: **~ sign**) signe *m* moins ▷ *prep* moins; **12 ~ 6 equals 6** 12 moins 6 égal 6; **~ 24°C** moins 24°C

minute¹ ['mɪnɪt] *n* minute *f*; **minutes** *npl* (of meeting) procès-verbal *m*, compte rendu; **wait a ~!**

(attendez) un instant!; **at the last ~** à la dernière minute

minute² [maɪ'njuːt] *adj* minuscule; (detailed) minutieux(-euse); **in ~ detail** par le menu

miracle ['mɪrəkl] *n* miracle *m*

miraculous [mɪ'rækjuləs] *adj* miraculeux(-euse)

mirage ['mɪrɑːʒ] *n* mirage *m*

mirror ['mɪrə²] *n* miroir *m*, glace *f*; (in car) rétroviseur *m*

misbehave [mɪsbɪ'heɪv] *vi* mal se conduire

misc. *abbr* = **miscellaneous**

miscarriage ['mɪskærɪdʒ] *n* (Med) fausse couche; **~ of justice** erreur *f* judiciaire

miscellaneous [mɪsɪ'leɪnɪəs] *adj* (items, expenses) divers(es); (selection) varié(e)

mischief ['mɪstʃɪf] *n* (naughtiness) sottises *fpl*; (playfulness) espièglerie *f*; (harm) mal *m*, dommage *m*; (maliciousness) méchanceté *f*; **mischievous** ['mɪstʃɪvəs] *adj* (playful, naughty) coquin(e), espiègle

misconception ['mɪskən'sepʃən] *n* idée fausse

misconduct [mɪs'kɔndʌkt] *n* inconduite *f*; **professional ~** faute professionnelle

miser ['maɪzə²] *n* avare *m/f*

miserable ['mɪzərəbl] *adj* (person, expression) malheureux(-euse); (conditions) misérable; (weather) maussade; (offer, donation) minable; (failure) pitoyable

misery ['mɪzərɪ] *n* (unhappiness) tristesse *f*; (pain) souffrances *fpl*; (wretchedness) misère *f*

misfortune [mɪs'fɔːtʃən] *n* malchance *f*, malheur *m*

misgiving [mɪs'gɪvɪŋ] *n* (apprehension) craintes *fpl*; **to have ~s about sth** avoir des doutes quant à qch

misguided [mɪs'gaɪdɪd] *adj* malavisé(e)

m

mishap ['mɪʃæp] n mésaventure f

misinterpret [mɪsɪn'tɜːprɪt] vt mal interpréter

misjudge [mɪs'dʒʌdʒ] vt méjuger, se méprendre sur le compte de

mislay [mɪs'leɪ] vt (irreg: like **lay**) égarer

mislead [mɪs'liːd] vt (irreg: like **lead¹**) induire en erreur; **misleading** adj trompeur(-euse)

misplace [mɪs'pleɪs] vt égarer; **to be ~d** (trust etc) être mal placé(e)

misprint ['mɪsprɪnt] n faute f d'impression

misrepresent [mɪsreprɪ'zent] vt présenter sous un faux jour

Miss [mɪs] n Mademoiselle

miss [mɪs] vt (fail to get, attend, see) manquer, rater; (regret the absence of): **I ~ him/it** il/cela me manque ▷ vi manquer ▷ n (shot) coup manqué m; **we ~ed our train** nous avons raté notre train; **you can't ~ it** vous ne pouvez pas vous tromper; **miss out** vt (BRIT) oublier; **miss out on** vt fus (fun, party) rater, manquer; (chance, bargain) laisser passer

missile ['mɪsaɪl] n (Aviat) missile m; (object thrown) projectile m

missing ['mɪsɪŋ] adj manquant(e); (after escape, disaster: person) disparu(e); **to go ~** disparaître; **~ in action** (Mil) porté(e) disparu(e)

mission [mɪʃən] n mission f; **on a ~ to sb** en mission auprès de qn; **missionary** n missionnaire m/f

misspell ['mɪs'spel] vt (irreg: like **spell**) mal orthographier

mist [mɪst] n brume f ▷ vi (also: **~ over**, **~ up**) devenir brumeux(-euse); (BRIT: windows) s'embuer

mistake [mɪs'teɪk] n erreur f, faute f ▷ vt (irreg: like **take**) (meaning) mal comprendre; (intentions) se méprendre sur; **by ~** par erreur, par inadvertance; **to make a ~** (in writing) faire une faute; (in calculating

etc) faire une erreur; **there must be some ~** il doit y avoir une erreur, se tromper; **mistaken** pp of **mistake** ▷ adj (idea etc) erroné(e); **to be mistaken** faire erreur, se tromper

mister ['mɪstər] n (inf) Monsieur m; see **Mr**

mistletoe ['mɪsltəu] n gui m

mistook [mɪs'tuk] pt of **mistake**

mistress ['mɪstrɪs] n maîtresse f; (BRIT: in primary school) institutrice f; (: in secondary school) professeur m

mistrust [mɪs'trʌst] vt se méfier de

misty ['mɪstɪ] adj brumeux(-euse); (glasses, window) embué(e)

misunderstand [mɪsʌndə'stænd] vt, vi (irreg: like **understand**) mal comprendre; **misunderstanding** n méprise f, malentendu m; **there's been a misunderstanding** il y a eu un malentendu

misunderstood [mɪsʌndə'stud] pt, pp of **misunderstand** ▷ adj (person) incompris(e)

misuse n [mɪs'juːs] mauvais emploi; (of power) abus m ▷ vt [mɪs'juːz] mal employer; abuser de

mitt(en) ['mɪt(n)] n moufle f; (fingerless) mitaine f

mix [mɪks] vt mélanger; (sauce, drink etc) préparer ▷ vi se mélanger; (socialize): **he doesn't ~ well** il est peu sociable ▷ n mélange m; **to ~ sth with sth** mélanger qch à qch; **cake ~** préparation f pour gâteau; **mix up** vt mélanger; (confuse) confondre; **to be ~ed up in sth** être mêlé(e) à qch or impliqué(e) dans qch; **mixed** adj (feelings, reactions) contradictoire; (school, marriage) mixte; **mixed grill** n (BRIT) assortiment m de grillades; **mixed salad** n salade f de crudités; **mixed-up** adj (person) désorienté(e), embrouillé(e); **mixer** n (for food) batteur m, mixeur m; (drink) boisson gazeuse (servant à couper un alcool); (person): **he is a good mixer** il est très sociable; **mixture** n assortiment

m, mélange *m*; *(Med)* préparation *f*;
mix-up *n*: **there was a mix-up** il y a
eu confusion

ml *abbr* (= *millilitre(s)*) ml

mm *abbr* (= *millimetre*) mm

moan [məʊn] *n* gémissement *m* ▷ *vi*
gémir; *(inf: complain)*: **to ~ (about)** se
plaindre (de)

moat [məʊt] *n* fossé *m*, douves *fpl*

mob [mɒb] *n* foule *f*; *(disorderly)* cohue
f ▷ *vt* assaillir

mobile ['məʊbaɪl] *adj* mobile ▷ *n*
(Art) mobile *m*; *(BRIT inf: phone)*
(téléphone *m*) portable *m*, mobile *m*;
mobile home *n* caravane *f*; **mobile
phone** *n* (téléphone *m*) portable *m*,
mobile *m*

mobility [məʊ'bɪlɪtɪ] *n* mobilité *f*

mobilize ['məʊbɪlaɪz] *vt*, *vi* mobiliser

mock [mɒk] *vt* ridiculiser; *(laugh at)*
se moquer de ▷ *adj* faux (fausse);
mocks *npl* *(BRIT Scol)* examens blancs;
mockery *n* moquerie *f*, raillerie *f*

mod cons *(BRIT)* *npl abbr*
(= *modern conveniences*; *see*
convenience

mode [məʊd] *n* mode *m*; *(of transport)*
moyen *m*

model ['mɒdl] *n* modèle *m*; *(person:
for fashion)* mannequin *m*; *(: for artist)*
modèle *s* ▷ *vt* (*with clay etc*) modeler
▷ *vi* travailler comme mannequin
▷ *adj* *(railway: toy)* modèle réduit *inv*;
(child, factory) modèle; **to ~ clothes**
présenter des vêtements; **to ~ o.s.
on** imiter

modem ['məʊdem] *n* modem *m*

moderate ['mɒdərət] *adj* modéré(e);
(amount, change) peu important(e)
▷ *vi* ['mɒdəreɪt] se modérer, se calmer
▷ *vt* ['mɒdəreɪt] modérer

moderation [mɒdə'reɪʃən] *n*
modération *f*, mesure *f*; **in ~** à dose
raisonnable, pris(e) or pratiqué(e)
modérément

modern ['mɒdən] *adj* moderne;
modernize *vt* moderniser; **modern
languages** *npl* langues vivantes

modest ['mɒdɪst] *adj* modeste;
modesty *n* modestie *f*

modification [mɒdɪfɪ'keɪʃən] *n*
modification *f*

modify ['mɒdɪfaɪ] *vt* modifier

module ['mɒdjuːl] *n* module *m*

mohair ['məʊhɛəʳ] *n* mohair *m*

Mohammed [mə'hæmɛd] *n*
Mahomet *m*

moist [mɔɪst] *adj* humide, moite;
moisture ['mɔɪstʃəʳ] *n* humidité
f; *(on glass)* buée *f*; **moisturizer**
['mɔɪstʃəraɪzəʳ] *n* crème hydratante
f

mold *etc* [məʊld] *(US)* = **mould**

mole [məʊl] *n* *(animal, spy)* taupe *f*;
(spot) grain *m* de beauté

molecule ['mɒlɪkjuːl] *n* molécule *f*

molest [məʊ'lɛst] *vt* *(assault sexually)*
attenter à la pudeur de

molten ['məʊltən] *adj* fondu(e);
(rock) en fusion

mom [mɒm] *n* *(US)* = **mum**

moment ['məʊmənt] *n* moment *m*,
instant *m*; **at the ~** en ce moment;
momentarily *adv* momentanément;
(US: soon) bientôt; **momentary** *adj*
momentané(e), passager(-ère);
momentous [məʊ'mɛntəs] *adj*
important(e), capital(e)

momentum [məʊ'mɛntəm] *n* élan
m, vitesse acquise; *(fig)* dynamique *f*;
to gather ~ prendre de la vitesse; *(fig)*
gagner du terrain

mommy ['mɒmɪ] *n* *(US: mother)*
maman *f*

Monaco ['mɒnəkəʊ] *n* Monaco *f*

monarch ['mɒnək] *n* monarque *m*;
monarchy *n* monarchie *f*

monastery ['mɒnəstərɪ] *n*
monastère *m*

Monday ['mʌndɪ] *n* lundi *m*

monetary ['mʌnɪtərɪ] *adj* monétaire

money ['mʌnɪ] *n* argent *m*; **to
make ~** *(person)* gagner de l'argent;
(business) rapporter; **money belt** *n*
ceinture-portefeuille *f*; **money order**
n mandat *m*

mongrel ['mʌŋgrəl] *n* *(dog)* bâtard *m*

monitor ['mɒnɪtə^r] n (TV, Comput) écran m, moniteur m ▷ vt contrôler; (foreign station) être à l'écoute de; (progress) suivre de près

monk [mʌŋk] n moine m

monkey ['mʌŋkɪ] n singe m

monologue ['mɒnəlɒg] n monologue m

monopoly [mə'nɒpəlɪ] n monopole m

monosodium glutamate [mɒnə'səʊdɪəm 'gluːtəmeɪt] n glutamate m de sodium

monotonous [mə'nɒtənəs] adj monotone

monsoon [mɒn'suːn] n mousson f

monster ['mɒnstə^r] n monstre m

month [mʌnθ] n mois m; **monthly** adj mensuel(le) ▷ adv mensuellement

Montreal [mɒntrɪ'ɔːl] n Montréal

monument ['mɒnjʊmənt] n monument m

mood [muːd] n humeur f, disposition f; **to be in a good/bad ~** être de bonne/mauvaise humeur; **moody** adj (variable) d'humeur changeante, lunatique; (sullen) morose, maussade

moon [muːn] n lune f; **moonlight** n clair m de lune

moor [mʊə^r] n lande f ▷ vt (ship) amarrer ▷ vi mouiller

moose [muːs] n (pl inv) élan m

mop [mɒp] n balai m à laver; (for dishes) lavette f à vaisselle ▷ vt éponger, essuyer; **~ of hair** tignasse f; **mop up** vt éponger

mope [məʊp] vi avoir le cafard, se morfondre

moped ['məʊpɛd] n cyclomoteur m

moral ['mɒrl] adj moral(e) ▷ n morale f; **morals** npl moralité f

morale [mɒ'rɑːl] n moral m

morality [mə'rælɪtɪ] n moralité f

morbid ['mɔːbɪd] adj morbide

KEYWORD

more [mɔː^r] adj 1 (greater in number etc) plus (de), davantage (de); **more**

people/work (than) plus de gens/ de travail (que)

2 (additional) encore (de); **do you want (some) more tea?** voulez-vous encore du thé?; **is there any more wine?** reste-t-il du vin?; **I have no or I don't have any more money** je n'ai plus d'argent; **it'll take a few more weeks** ça prendra encore quelques semaines ▷ pron plus, davantage; **more than 10** plus de 10; **it cost more than we expected** cela a coûté plus que prévu; **I want more** j'en veux plus or davantage; **is there any more?** est-ce qu'il en reste?; **there's no more** il n'y en a plus; **a little more** encore un peu plus; **many/much more** beaucoup plus, bien davantage ▷ adv plus; **more dangerous/easily (than)** plus dangereux/facilement (que); **more and more expensive** de plus en plus cher; **more or less** plus ou moins; **more than ever** plus que jamais; **once more** encore une fois, une fois de plus

moreover [mɔː'rəʊvə^r] adv de plus

morgue [mɔːg] n morgue f

morning ['mɔːnɪŋ] n matin m; (as duration) matinée f ▷ cpd matinal(e); (paper) du matin; **in the ~** le matin; **7 o'clock in the ~** 7 heures du matin; **morning sickness** n nausées matinales

Moroccan [mə'rɒkən] adj marocain(e) ▷ n Marocain(e)

Morocco [mə'rɒkəʊ] n Maroc m

moron ['mɔːrɒn] n (offensive) idiot(e), minus m/f

morphine ['mɔːfiːn] n morphine f

morris dancing ['mɒrɪs-] n (BRIT) danses folkloriques anglaises

● **MORRIS DANCING**

● Le **morris dancing** est une
● danse folklorique anglaise
● traditionnellement réservée aux

hommes. Habillés tout en blanc
et portant des clochettes, ils
exécutent différentes figures avec
des mouchoirs et de longs bâtons.
Cette danse est très populaire dans
les fêtes de village.

Morse [mɔːs] n (also: **~ code**) morse m
mortal ['mɔːtl] adj, n mortel(le)
mortar ['mɔːtər] n mortier m
mortgage ['mɔːgɪdʒ] n hypothèque
f; (loan) prêt m (or crédit m)
hypothécaire ▷ vt hypothéquer
mortician [mɔː'tɪʃən] n (us)
entrepreneur m de pompes funèbres
mortified ['mɔːtɪfaɪd] adj mort(e)
de honte
mortuary ['mɔːtjuəri] n morgue f
mosaic [məʊ'zeɪɪk] n mosaïque f
Moscow ['mɔskəu] n Moscou
Moslem ['mɔzləm] adj, n = **Muslim**
mosque [mɔsk] n mosquée f
mosquito [mɔs'kiːtəu] (pl
mosquitoes) n moustique m
moss [mɔs] n mousse f
most [məʊst] adj (majority of) la
plupart de; (greatest amount of) le plus
de ▷ pron la plupart ▷ adv le plus;
(very) très, extrêmement; **the ~** le
plus; **~ fish** la plupart des poissons;
**the ~ beautiful woman in the
world** la plus belle femme du monde;
~ of (with plural) la plupart de; (with
singular) la plus grande partie de; **~ of
them** la plupart d'entre eux; **~ of
the time** la plupart du temps; **I saw
~** (a lot but not all) j'en ai vu la plupart;
(more than anyone else) c'est moi qui
en ai vu le plus; **at the (very) ~** au
plus; **to make the ~ of** profiter au
maximum de; **mostly** adv (chiefly)
surtout, principalement; (usually)
généralement
MOT n abbr (BRIT) = Ministry of
Transport): **the ~ (test)** visite
technique (annuelle) obligatoire des
véhicules à moteur
motel [məʊ'tɛl] n motel m

moth [mɔθ] n papillon m de nuit; (in
clothes) mite f
mother ['mʌðər] n mère f ▷ vt
(pamper, protect) dorloter;
motherhood n maternité f; **mother-
in-law** n belle-mère f; **mother-of-
pearl** n nacre f; **Mother's Day** n fête
f des Mères; **mother-to-be** n future
maman; **mother tongue** n langue
maternelle
motif [məʊ'tiːf] n motif m
motion ['məʊʃən] n mouvement m;
(gesture) geste m; (at meeting) motion
f ▷ vt, vi: **to ~ (to) sb to do** faire
signe à qn de faire; **motionless** adj
immobile, sans mouvement; **motion
picture** n film m
motivate ['məʊtɪveɪt] vt motiver
motivation [məʊtɪ'veɪʃən] n
motivation f
motive ['məʊtɪv] n motif m, mobile m
motor ['məʊtər] n moteur m; (BRIT
inf: vehicle) auto f; **motorbike** n moto
f; **motorboat** n bateau m à moteur;
motorcar n (BRIT) automobile f;
motorcycle n moto f; **motorcyclist**
n motocycliste m/f; **motoring** (BRIT)
n tourisme automobile; **motorist**
n automobiliste m/f; **motor racing** n
(BRIT) course f automobile;
motorway n (BRIT) autoroute f
motto ['mɔtəʊ] (pl **mottoes**) n
devise f
mould, (us) **mold** [məʊld] n moule
m; (mildew) moisissure f ▷ vt mouler,
modeler; (fig) façonner; **mouldy**, (us)
moldy n moisi(e); (smell) de moisi
mound [maʊnd] n monticule m,
tertre m
mount [maʊnt] n (hill) mont m,
montagne f; (horse) monture f;
(for picture) carton m de montage
▷ vt monter; (horse) monter à;
(bike) monter sur; (picture) monter
sur carton ▷ vi (inflation, tension)
augmenter; **mount up** vi s'élever,
monter; (bills, problems, savings)
s'accumuler

mountain ['mauntɪn] n
montagne f ▷ cpd de (la) montagne;
mountain bike n VTT m, vélo
m tout terrain; **mountaineer** n
alpiniste m/f; **mountaineering** n
alpinisme m; **mountainous** adj
montagneux(-euse); **mountain
range** n chaîne f de montagnes

mourn [mɔːn] vt pleurer ▷ vi: **to
~ for sb** pleurer qn; **to ~ for sth**
se lamenter sur qch; **mourner** n
parent(e) or ami(e) du défunt;
personne f en deuil or venue rendre
hommage au défunt; **mourning** n
deuil m; **in mourning** en deuil

mouse (pl **mice**) [maus, maɪs] n
(also Comput) souris f; **mouse mat** n
(Comput) tapis m de souris

moussaka [mu'saːkə] n moussaka f

mousse [muːs] n mousse f

moustache, (us) **mustache**
[məs'taːʃ] n moustache(s) f(pl)

mouth (pl **mouths**) [mauθ, mauðz] n
bouche f; (of dog, cat) gueule f; (of
river) embouchure f; (of hole, cave)
ouverture f; **mouthful** n bouchée
f; **mouth organ** n harmonica m;
mouthpiece n (of musical instrument)
bec m, embouchure f; (spokesperson)
porte-parole m inv; **mouthwash** n
eau f dentifrice

move [muːv] n (movement)
mouvement m; (in game) coup m
(: turn to play) tour m; (change of
house) déménagement m; (change
of job) changement m d'emploi ▷ vt
déplacer, bouger; (emotionally)
émouvoir; (Pol: resolution etc)
proposer ▷ vi (gen) bouger, remuer;
(traffic) circuler; (also: ~ **house**)
déménager; (in game) jouer; **can you
~ your car, please?** pouvez-vous
déplacer votre voiture, s'il vous
plaît?; **to ~ sb to do sth** pousser
or inciter qn à faire qch; **to get a ~
on** se dépêcher, se remuer; **move
back** vi revenir, retourner; **move in**
vi (to a house) emménager; (police,

soldiers) intervenir; **move off** vi
s'éloigner, s'en aller; **move on** vi
se remettre en route; **move out** vi
(of house) déménager; **move over**
vi se pousser, se déplacer; **move
up** vi avancer; (employee) avoir de
l'avancement; (pupil) passer dans
la classe supérieure; **movement** n
mouvement m

movie ['muːvɪ] n film m; **movies** npl:
the ~s le cinéma; **movie theater** (us)
n cinéma m

moving ['muːvɪŋ] adj en
mouvement; (touching)
émouvant(e)

mow (pt **mowed**, pp **mowed** or
mown) [məu, -d, -n] vt faucher;
(lawn) tondre; **mower** n (also:
lawnmower) tondeuse f à gazon

mown [məun] pp of **mow**

Mozambique [məuzəm'biːk] n
Mozambique m

MP n abbr (BRIT) = **Member of
Parliament**

MP3 n mp3 m; **MP3 player** n baladeur
m numérique, lecteur m mp3

mpg n abbr = **miles per gallon**
(30 mpg = 9,4 l. aux 100 km)

m.p.h. abbr = **miles per hour** (60 mph
= 96 km/h)

Mr, (us) **Mr.** ['mɪstəʳ] n: **~ X** Monsieur
X, M. X

Mrs, (us) **Mrs.** ['mɪsɪz] n: **~ X**
Madame X, Mme X

Ms, (us) **Ms.** [mɪz] n (Miss or Mrs): **~ X**
Madame X, Mme X

MSP n abbr (= Member of the Scottish
Parliament) député m au Parlement
écossais

Mt abbr (Geo: = mount) Mt

much [mʌtʃ] adj beaucoup de ▷ adv,
n, pron beaucoup; **we don't have
~ time** nous n'avons pas beaucoup
de temps; **how ~ is it?** combien
est-ce que ça coûte?; **it's not ~** ce
n'est pas beaucoup; **too ~** trop (de);
so ~ tant (de); **I like it very/so ~**
j'aime beaucoup/tellement; **as ~**

as autant de; **that's ~ better** c'est beaucoup mieux

muck [mʌk] n (mud) boue f; (dirt) ordures fpl; **muck up** vt (inf: ruin) gâcher, esquinter; (dirty) salir; (exam, interview) se planter à; **mucky** adj (dirty) boueux(-euse), sale

mucus ['mjuːkəs] n mucus m

mud [mʌd] n boue f

muddle ['mʌdl] n (mess) pagaille f, fouillis m; (mix-up) confusion f ▷ vt (also: ~ **up**) brouiller, embrouiller; **to get in a ~** (while explaining etc) s'embrouiller

muddy ['mʌdɪ] adj boueux(-euse)

mudguard ['mʌdɡɑːd] n garde-boue m inv

muesli ['mjuːzlɪ] n muesli m

muffin ['mʌfɪn] n (roll) petit pain rond et plat; (cake) petit gâteau au chocolat ou aux fruits

muffled ['mʌfld] adj étouffé(e), voilé(e)

muffler ['mʌflə*] n (scarf) cache-nez m inv; (us Aut) silencieux m

mug [mʌɡ] n (cup) tasse f (sans soucoupe); (: for beer) chope f; (inf: face) bouille f; (: fool) poire f ▷ vt (assault) agresser; **mugger** ['mʌɡə*] n agresseur m; **mugging** n agression f

muggy ['mʌɡɪ] adj lourd(e), moite

mule [mjuːl] n mule f

multicoloured, (us) **multicolored** ['mʌltɪkʌləd] adj multicolore

multimedia [mʌltɪ'miːdɪə] adj multimédia inv

multinational [mʌltɪ'næʃənl] n multinationale f ▷ adj multinational(e)

multiple ['mʌltɪpl] adj multiple ▷ n multiple m; **multiple choice (test)** n QCM m, questionnaire m à choix multiple; **multiple sclerosis** [-sklɪ'rəʊsɪs] n sclérose f en plaques

multiplex (cinema) ['mʌltɪpleks-] n (cinéma m) multisalles m

multiplication [mʌltɪplɪ'keɪʃən] n multiplication f

multiply ['mʌltɪplaɪ] vt multiplier ▷ vi se multiplier

multistorey ['mʌltɪ'stɔːrɪ] adj (BRIT: building) à étages; (: car park) à étages or niveaux multiples

mum [mʌm] n (BRIT) maman f ▷ adj: **to keep ~** ne pas souffler mot

mumble ['mʌmbl] vt, vi marmotter, marmonner

mummy ['mʌmɪ] n (BRIT: mother) maman f; (embalmed) momie f

mumps [mʌmps] n oreillons mpl

munch [mʌntʃ] vt, vi mâcher

municipal [mjuː'nɪsɪpl] adj municipal(e)

mural ['mjuərl] n peinture murale

murder ['məːdə*] n meurtre m, assassinat m ▷ vt assassiner; **murderer** n meurtrier m, assassin m

murky ['məːkɪ] adj sombre, ténébreux(-euse); (water) trouble

murmur ['məːmə*] n murmure m ▷ vt, vi murmurer

muscle ['mʌsl] n muscle m; (fig) force f; **muscular** ['mʌskjulə*] adj musculaire; (person, arm) musclé(e)

museum [mjuː'zɪəm] n musée m

mushroom ['mʌʃrum] n champignon m ▷ vi (fig) pousser comme un (or des) champignon(s)

music ['mjuːzɪk] n musique f; **musical** adj musical(e); (person) musicien(ne) ▷ n (show) comédie musicale; **musical instrument** n instrument m de musique; **musician** [mjuː'zɪʃən] n musicien(ne)

Muslim ['mʊzlɪm] adj, n musulman(e)

muslin ['mʌzlɪn] n mousseline f

mussel ['mʌsl] n moule f

must [mʌst] aux vb (obligation): **I ~ do it** je dois le faire, il faut que je le fasse; (probability): **he ~ be there by now** il doit y être maintenant, il est probablement maintenant; (suggestion, invitation): **you ~ come and see me** il faut que vous veniez me voir ▷ n nécessité f, impératif m;

it's a ~ c'est indispensable; **I ~ have made a mistake** j'ai dû me tromper

mustache ['mʌstæʃ] *n* (US) = **moustache**

mustard ['mʌstəd] *n* moutarde *f*

mustn't ['mʌsnt] = **must not**

mutilate ['mju:tɪleɪt] *vt* mutiler

mutiny ['mju:tɪnɪ] *n* mutinerie *f* ▷ *vi* se mutiner

mutter ['mʌtə'] *vt, vi* marmonner, marmotter

mutton ['mʌtn] *n* mouton *m*

mutual ['mju:tʃuəl] *adj* mutuel(le), réciproque; (*benefit, interest*) commun(e)

muzzle ['mʌzl] *n* museau *m*; (*protective device*) muselière *f*; (*of gun*) gueule *f* ▷ *vt* museler

my [maɪ] *adj* mon (ma), mes *pl*; **my house/car/gloves** ma maison/ma voiture/mes gants; **I've washed my hair/cut my finger** je me suis lavé les cheveux/coupé le doigt; **is this my pen or yours?** c'est mon stylo ou c'est le vôtre?

myself [maɪ'self] *pron* (*reflexive*) me; (*emphatic*) moi-même; (*after prep*) moi; *see also* **oneself**

mysterious [mɪs'tɪərɪəs] *adj* mystérieux(-euse)

mystery ['mɪstərɪ] *n* mystère *m*

mystical ['mɪstɪkl] *adj* mystique

mystify ['mɪstɪfaɪ] *vt* (*deliberately*) mystifier; (*puzzle*) ébahir

myth [mɪθ] *n* mythe *m*; **mythology** [mɪ'θɒlədʒɪ] *n* mythologie *f*

n/a *abbr* (= *not applicable*) n.a.

nag [næg] *vt* (*scold*) être toujours après, reprendre sans arrêt

nail [neɪl] *n* (*human*) ongle *m*; (*metal*) clou *m* ▷ *vt* clouer; **to ~ sth to sth** clouer qch à qch; **to ~ sb down to a date/price** contraindre qn à accepter or donner une date/un prix; **nailbrush** *n* brosse *f* à ongles; **nailfile** *n* lime *f* à ongles; **nail polish** *n* vernis *m* à ongles; **nail polish remover** *n* dissolvant *m*; **nail scissors** *npl* ciseaux *mpl* à ongles; **nail varnish** *n* (BRIT) = **nail polish**

naïve [naɪ'i:v] *adj* naïf(-ïve)

naked ['neɪkɪd] *adj* nu(e)

name [neɪm] *n* nom *m*; (*reputation*) réputation *f* ▷ *vt* nommer; (*identify: accomplice etc*) citer; (*price, date*) fixer, donner; **by ~** par son nom; de nom; **in the ~ of** au nom de; **what's your ~?** comment vous appelez-vous?, quel est votre nom?; **namely** *adv* à savoir

nanny ['nænɪ] *n* bonne *f* d'enfants

nap [næp] n (sleep) (petit) somme

napkin ['næpkɪn] n serviette f (de table)

nappy ['næpɪ] n (BRIT) couche f

narcotics [naːˈkɔtɪkz] npl (illegal drugs) stupéfiants mpl

narrative ['nærətɪv] n récit m ▷ adj narratif(-ive)

narrator [nəˈreɪtəʳ] n narrateur(-trice)

narrow ['nærəʊ] adj étroit(e); (fig) restreint(e), limité(e) ▷ vi (road) devenir plus étroit, se rétrécir; (gap, difference) se réduire; **to have a ~ escape** l'échapper belle; **narrow down** vt restreindre; **narrowly** adv: **he narrowly missed injury/the tree** il a failli se blesser/rentrer dans l'arbre; **he only narrowly missed the target** il a manqué la cible de peu or de justesse; **narrow-minded** adj à l'esprit étroit, borné(e); (attitude) borné(e)

nasal ['neɪzl] adj nasal(e)

nasty ['nɑːstɪ] adj (person: malicious) méchant(e); (: rude) très désagréable; (smell) dégoûtant(e); (wound, situation) mauvais(e), vilain(e)

nation ['neɪʃən] n nation f

national ['næʃənl] adj national(e) ▷ n (abroad) ressortissant(e); (when home) national(e); **national anthem** n hymne national; **national dress** n costume national; **National Health Service** n (BRIT) service national de santé, ≈ Sécurité Sociale; **National Insurance** n (BRIT) ≈ Sécurité Sociale; **nationalist** ['næʃnəlɪst] adj, n nationaliste m/f; **nationality** [næʃəˈnælɪtɪ] n nationalité f; **nationalize** vt nationaliser; **national park** n parc national; **National Trust** n (BRIT) ≈ Caisse f nationale des monuments historiques et des sites

◇ **NATIONAL TRUST**

◦ Le National Trust est un organisme
◦ indépendant, à but non lucratif,
◦ dont la mission est de protéger et

◦ de mettre en valeur les monuments
◦ et les sites britanniques en raison
◦ de leur intérêt historique ou de leur
◦ beauté naturelle.

nationwide ['neɪʃənwaɪd] adj s'étendant à l'ensemble du pays; (problem) à l'échelle du pays entier

native ['neɪtɪv] n habitant(e) du pays, autochtone m/f ▷ adj du pays, indigène; (country) natal(e); (language) maternel(le); (ability) inné(e); **Native American** n Indien(ne) d'Amérique ▷ adj amérindien(ne); **native speaker** n locuteur natif

NATO ['neɪtəʊ] n abbr (= North Atlantic Treaty Organization) OTAN f

natural ['nætʃrəl] adj naturel(le); **natural gas** n gaz naturel; **natural history** n histoire naturelle; **naturally** adv naturellement; **natural resources** npl ressources naturelles

nature ['neɪtʃəʳ] n nature f; **by ~** par tempérament, de nature; **nature reserve** n (BRIT) réserve naturelle

naughty ['nɔːtɪ] adj (child) vilain(e), pas sage

nausea ['nɔːsɪə] n nausée f

naval ['neɪvl] adj naval(e)

navel ['neɪvl] n nombril m

navigate ['nævɪgeɪt] vt (steer) diriger, piloter ▷ vi naviguer; (Aut) indiquer la route à suivre; **navigation** [nævɪˈgeɪʃən] n navigation f

navy ['neɪvɪ] n marine f

navy-blue ['neɪvɪ'bluː] adj bleu marine inv

Nazi ['nɑːtsɪ] n Nazi(e)

NB abbr (= nota bene) NB

near [nɪəʳ] adj proche ▷ adv près ▷ prep (also: **~ to**) près de ▷ vt approcher de; **in the ~ future** dans un proche avenir; **nearby** [nɪəˈbaɪ] adj proche ▷ adv tout près, à proximité; **nearly** adv presque; **I nearly fell** j'ai failli tomber; **it's not**

nearly big enough ce n'est vraiment pas assez grand, c'est loin d'être assez grand; **near-sighted** adj myope

neat [niːt] adj (person, work) soigné(e); (room etc) bien tenu(e) ou rangé(e); (solution, plan) habile; (spirits) pur(e); **neatly** adv avec soin or ordre; (skilfully) habilement

necessarily ['nesɪsərɪlɪ] adv nécessairement; **not ~** pas nécessairement or forcément

necessary ['nesɪsrɪ] adj nécessaire; **if ~** si besoin est, le cas échéant

necessity [nɪ'sesɪtɪ] n nécessité f; chose nécessaire ou essentielle

neck [nɛk] n cou m; (of horse, garment) encolure f; (of bottle) goulot m; **~ and ~** à égalité; **necklace** ['nɛklɪs] n collier m; **necktie** ['nɛktaɪ] n (esp us) cravate f

nectarine ['nɛktərɪn] n brugnon m, nectarine f

need [niːd] n besoin m ▷ vt avoir besoin de; **to ~ to do** devoir faire; avoir besoin de faire; **you don't ~ to go** vous n'avez pas besoin de partir, vous n'êtes pas obligé de partir; **a signature is ~ed** il faut une signature; **there's no ~ to do ....** il n'y a pas lieu de faire ..., il n'est pas nécessaire de faire ...

needle ['niːdl] n aiguille f ▷ vt (inf) asticoter, tourmenter

needless ['niːdlɪs] adj inutile; **~ to say, ...** inutile de dire que ...

needlework ['niːdlwɜːk] n (activity) travaux mpl d'aiguille; (object) ouvrage m

needn't ['niːdnt] = **need not**

needy ['niːdɪ] adj nécessiteux(-euse)

negative ['negətɪv] n (Phot, Elec) négatif m; (Ling) terme m de négation ▷ adj négatif(-ive)

neglect [nɪ'glɛkt] vt négliger; (garden) ne pas entretenir; (duty) manquer à ▷ n (of person, duty, garden) le fait de négliger; (state of) ~ abandon m; **to ~ to do sth** négliger

nett [nɛt] adj = **net**

nettle ['nɛtl] n ortie f

network ['nɛtwɜːk] n réseau m; **there's no ~ coverage here** (Tel) il n'y a pas de réseau ici

or omettre de faire qch; **to ~ one's appearance** se négliger

negotiate [nɪ'gəʊʃɪeɪt] vi négocier ▷ vt négocier; (obstacle) franchir, négocier; **to ~ with sb for sth** négocier avec qn en vue d'obtenir qch

negotiation [nɪgəʊʃɪ'eɪʃən] n négociation f, pourparlers mpl

negotiator [nɪ'gəʊʃɪeɪtər] n négociateur(-trice)

neighbour, (us) **neighbor** ['neɪbər] n voisin(e); **neighbourhood**, (us) **neighborhood** n (place) quartier m; (people) voisinage m; **neighbouring**, (us) **neighboring** adj voisin(e), avoisinant(e)

neither ['naɪðər] adj, pron aucun(e) (des deux), ni l'un(e) ni l'autre ▷ conj: **~ do I** moi non plus ▷ adv: **~ good nor bad** ni bon ni mauvais; **~ of them** ni l'un ni l'autre

neon ['niːɔn] n néon m

Nepal [nɪ'pɔːl] n Népal m

nephew ['nevjuː] n neveu m

nerve [nɜːv] n nerf m; (bravery) sang-froid m, courage m; (cheek) aplomb m, toupet m; **nerves** npl (nervousness) nervosité f; **he gets on my ~s** il m'énerve

nervous ['nɜːvəs] adj nerveux(-euse); (anxious) inquiet(-ète), plein(e) d'appréhension; (timid) intimidé(e); **nervous breakdown** n dépression nerveuse

nest [nɛst] n nid m ▷ vi (se) nicher, faire son nid

Net [nɛt] n (Comput): **the ~** (Internet) le Net

net [nɛt] n filet m; (fabric) tulle f ▷ vt (fish etc) prendre au filet; **netball** n netball m

Netherlands ['nɛðələndz] npl: **the ~** les Pays-Bas mpl

neurotic [njuəˈrɒtɪk] *adj* névrosé(e)

neuter [ˈnjuːtə^r] *adj* neutre ▷ *vt* (*cat etc*) châtrer, couper

neutral [ˈnjuːtrəl] *adj* neutre ▷ *n* (*Aut*) point mort

never [ˈnevə^r] *adv* (ne ...) jamais; **I ~ went** je n'y suis pas allé; **I've ~ been to Spain** je ne suis jamais allé en Espagne; **~ again** plus jamais; **~ in my life** jamais de ma vie; *see also* **mind**; **never-ending** *adj* interminable; **nevertheless** [nevəðəˈles] *adv* néanmoins, malgré tout

new [njuː] *adj* nouveau (nouvelle); (*brand new*) neuf (neuve); **New Age** *n* New Age *m*; **newborn** *adj* nouveau-né(e); **newcomer** [ˈnjuːkʌmə^r] *n* nouveau venu (nouvelle venue); **newly** *adv* nouvellement, récemment

news [njuːz] *n* nouvelle *s* f(pl); (*Radio, TV*) informations *fpl*, actualités *fpl*; **a piece of ~** une nouvelle; **news agency** *n* agence *f* de presse; **newsagent** *n* (*BRIT*) marchand *m* de journaux; **newscaster** *n* (*Radio, TV*) présentateur(-trice); **newsletter** *n* bulletin *m*; **newspaper** *n* journal *m*; **newsreader** *n* = **newscaster**

newt [njuːt] *n* triton *m*

New Year *n* Nouvel An; **Happy ~!** Bonne Année!; **New Year's Day** *n* le jour de l'An; **New Year's Eve** *n* la Saint-Sylvestre

New York [-ˈjɔːk] *n* New York

New Zealand [-ˈziːlənd] *n* Nouvelle-Zélande *f*; **New Zealander** *n* Néo-Zélandais(e)

next [nekst] *adj* (*in time*) prochain(e); (*seat, room*) voisin(e), d'à côté; (*meeting, bus stop*) suivant(e) ▷ *adv* la fois suivante; la prochaine fois; (*afterwards*) ensuite; **~ to** *prep* à côté de; **~ to nothing** presque rien; **~ time** *adv* la prochaine fois; **the ~ day** le lendemain, le jour suivant or d'après; **~ year** l'année prochaine; **~ please!** (*at doctor's etc*) au suivant!;

the week after ~ dans deux semaines; **next door** *adv* à côté ▷ *adj* (*neighbour*) d'à côté; **next-of-kin** *n* parent *m* le plus proche

NHS *n abbr* (*BRIT*) = **National Health Service**

nibble [ˈnɪbl] *vt* grignoter

nice [naɪs] *adj* (*holiday, trip, taste*) agréable; (*flat, picture*) joli(e); (*person*) gentil(le); (*distinction, point*) subtil(e); **nicely** *adv* agréablement; joliment; gentiment; subtilement

niche [niːʃ] *n* (*Archit*) niche *f*

nick [nɪk] *n* (*indentation*) encoche *f*; (*wound*) entaille *f*; (*BRIT inf*): **in good ~** en bon état ▷ *vt* (*cut*): **to ~ o.s.** se couper; (*BRIT inf: steal*) faucher, piquer; **in the ~ of time** juste à temps

nickel [ˈnɪkl] *n* nickel *m*; (*us*) pièce *f* de 5 cents

nickname [ˈnɪkneɪm] *n* surnom *m* ▷ *vt* surnommer

nicotine [ˈnɪkətiːn] *n* nicotine *f*

niece [niːs] *n* nièce *f*

Nigeria [naɪˈdʒɪərɪə] *n* Nigéria *m/f*

night [naɪt] *n* nuit *f*; (*evening*) soir *m*; **at ~** la nuit; **by ~** de nuit; **last ~** (*evening*) hier soir; (*night-time*) la nuit dernière; **night club** *n* boîte *f* de nuit; **nightdress** *n* chemise *f* de nuit; **nightie** [ˈnaɪtɪ] *n* chemise *f* de nuit; **nightlife** *n* vie *f* nocturne; **nightly** *adj* (*news*) du soir; (*by night*) nocturne ▷ *adv* (*every evening*) tous les soirs; (*every night*) toutes les nuits; **nightmare** *n* cauchemar *m*; **night school** *n* cours *mpl* du soir; **night shift** *n* équipe *f* de nuit; **night-time** *n* nuit *f*

nil [nɪl] *n* (*BRIT Sport*) zéro *m*

nine [naɪn] *num* neuf; **nineteen** *num* dix-neuf; **nineteenth** [naɪnˈtiːnθ] *num* dix-neuvième; **ninetieth** [ˈnaɪntɪɪθ] *num* quatre-vingt-dixième; **ninety** *num* quatre-vingt-dix

ninth [naɪnθ] *num* neuvième

nip [nɪp] *vt* pincer ▷ *vi* (*BRIT inf*): **to ~ out/down/up** sortir/descendre/monter en vitesse

nipple ['nɪpl] n (Anat) mamelon m,
bout m du sein
nitrogen ['naɪtrədʒən] n azote m

no [nəʊ] adv (opposite of "yes") non;
are you coming? — no (I'm not)
est-ce que vous venez? — non;
**would you like some more? — no
thank you** vous en voulez encore?
— non merci
▶ adj (not any) (ne …) pas de, (ne
…) aucun(e); **I have no money/
books** je n'ai pas d'argent/de livres;
no student would have done it
aucun étudiant ne l'aurait fait; **"no
smoking"** "défense de fumer"; **"no
dogs"** "les chiens ne sont pas admis"
▶ n (pl **noes**) non m

nobility [nəʊ'bɪlɪtɪ] n noblesse f
noble ['nəʊbl] adj noble
nobody ['nəʊbədɪ] pron (ne …)
personne
nod [nɔd] vi faire un signe de la (la) tête
(affirmatif ou amical), (sleep) somnoler
▶ vt: **to ~ one's head** faire un signe
de (la) tête, (in agreement) faire signe
que oui ▶ n signe m de (la) tête; **nod
off** vi s'assoupir
noise [nɔɪz] n bruit m; **I can't sleep
for the ~** je n'arrive pas à dormir à
cause du bruit; **noisy** adj bruyant(e)
nominal ['nɔmɪnl] adj (rent, fee)
symbolique; (value) nominal(e)
nominate ['nɔmɪneɪt] vt (propose)
proposer; (appoint) nommer;
nomination [nɔmɪ'neɪʃən] n
nomination f; **nominee** [nɔmɪ'niː] n
candidat agréé; personne nommée
none [nʌn] pron aucun(e); **~ of you**
aucun d'entre vous; **I have ~ left** je n'en
ai plus; **he's ~ the worse for it** il ne s'en porte
pas plus mal
nonetheless ['nʌnðə'lɛs] adv
néanmoins

non-fiction [nɔn'fɪkʃən] n
littérature f non romanesque
nonsense ['nɔnsəns] n absurdités fpl,
idioties fpl; **~! ne dites pas d'idioties!**
non: non-smoker n non-fumeur m;
non-smoking adj non-fumeur; **non-
stick** adj qui n'attache pas
noodles ['nuːdlz] npl nouilles fpl
noon [nuːn] n midi m
no-one ['nəʊwʌn] pron = nobody
nor [nɔː] conj = neither ▷ adv see
neither
norm [nɔːm] n norme f
normal ['nɔːml] adj normal(e);
normally adv normalement
Normandy ['nɔːmndɪ] n
Normandie f
north [nɔːθ] n nord m ▷ adj nord
inv; (wind) du nord ▷ adv au or vers
le nord; **North Africa** n Afrique f
du Nord; **North African** adj nord-
africain(e), d'Afrique du Nord ▷ n
Nord-Africain(e); **North America**
n Amérique f du Nord; **North
American** n Nord-Américain(e) ▷ adj
nord-américain(e), d'Amérique du
Nord; **northbound** ['nɔːθbaʊnd]
adj (traffic) en direction du nord;
(carriageway) nord inv; **north-east** n
nord-est m; **northern** ['nɔːðən] adj
du nord, septentrional(e); **Northern
Ireland** n Irlande f du Nord; **North
Korea** n Corée f du Nord; **North
Pole** n: **the North Pole** le pôle Nord;
North Sea n: **the North Sea** la mer
du Nord; **north-west** n nord-ouest m
Norway ['nɔːweɪ] n Norvège f;
Norwegian [nɔː'wiːdʒən] adj
norvégien(ne) ▷ n Norvégien(ne);
(Ling) norvégien m
nose [nəʊz] n nez m; (of dog, cat)
museau m; (fig) flair m; **nose about,
nose around** vi fouiner or fureter
(partout); **nosebleed** n saignement m
de nez; **nosey** adj (inf) curieux(-euse)
nostalgia [nɔs'tældʒɪə] n nostalgie f
nostalgic [nɔs'tældʒɪk] adj
nostalgique

nostril ['nɒstrɪl] n narine f; (of horse) naseau m

nosy ['nəuzɪ] (inf) adj = **nosey**

not [nɒt] adv (ne ...) pas; **he is ~ or isn't here** il n'est pas ici; **you must ~ or mustn't do that** tu ne dois pas faire ça; **I hope ~** j'espère que non; **~ at all** pas du tout; (after thanks) de rien; **it's too late, isn't it?** c'est trop tard, n'est-ce pas?; **~ yet/now** pas encore/maintenant; see also **only**

notable ['nəutəbl] adj notable; **notably** adv (particularly) en particulier; (markedly) spécialement

notch [nɒtʃ] n encoche f

note [nəut] n note f; (letter) mot m; (banknote) billet m ▷ vt (also: **~ down**) noter; (notice) constater; **notebook** n carnet m; (for shorthand etc) bloc-notes m; **noted** ['nəutɪd] adj réputé(e); **notepad** n bloc-notes m; **notepaper** n papier m à lettres

nothing ['nʌθɪŋ] n rien m; **he does ~** il ne fait rien; **~ new** rien de nouveau; **for ~** (free) pour rien, gratuitement; (in vain) pour rien; **~ at all** rien du tout; **~ much** pas grand-chose

notice ['nəutɪs] n (announcement, warning) avis m ▷ vt remarquer, s'apercevoir de; **advance ~** préavis m; **at short ~** dans un délai très court; **until further ~** jusqu'à nouvel ordre; **to give ~, hand in one's ~** (employee) donner sa démission, démissionner; **to take ~ of** prêter attention à; **to bring sth to sb's ~** porter qch à la connaissance de qn; **noticeable** adj visible

notice board n (BRIT) panneau d'affichage

notify ['nəutɪfaɪ] vt: **to ~ sb of sth** avertir qn de qch

notion ['nəuʃən] n idée f; (concept) notion f; **notions** npl (us: haberdashery) mercerie f

notorious [nəu'tɔːriəs] adj notoire (souvent en mal)

notwithstanding [ˌnɒtwɪθ'stændɪŋ] adv néanmoins ▷ prep en dépit de

nought [nɔːt] n zéro m

noun [naun] n nom m

nourish ['nʌrɪʃ] vt nourrir; **nourishment** n nourriture f

Nov. abbr (= November) nov

novel ['nɒvl] n roman m ▷ adj nouveau (nouvelle), original(e); **novelist** n romancier m; **novelty** n nouveauté f

November [nəu'vembər] n novembre m

novice ['nɒvɪs] n novice m/f

now [nau] adv maintenant ▷ conj: **~ (that)** maintenant (que); **right ~** tout de suite; **by ~** à l'heure qu'il est; **that's the fashion just ~** c'est la mode en ce moment or maintenant; **~ and then, ~ and again** de temps en temps; **from ~ on** dorénavant; **nowadays** ['nauədeɪz] adv de nos jours

nowhere ['nəuweər] adv (ne ...) nulle part

nozzle ['nɒzl] n (of hose) jet m, lance f; (of vacuum cleaner) suceur m

nr abbr (BRIT) = **near**

nuclear ['njuːklɪər] adj nucléaire

nucleus (pl **nuclei**) ['njuːklɪəs, 'njuːklɪaɪ] n noyau m

nude [njuːd] adj nu(e) ▷ n (Art) nu m; **in the ~** (tout(e)) nu(e)

nudge [nʌdʒ] vt donner un (petit) coup de coude à

nudist ['njuːdɪst] n nudiste m/f

nudity ['njuːdɪtɪ] n nudité f

nuisance ['njuːsns] n: **it's a ~** c'est (très) ennuyeux or gênant; **he's a ~** il est assommant or casse-pieds; **what a ~!** quelle barbe!

numb [nʌm] adj engourdi(e); (with fear) paralysé(e)

number ['nʌmbər] n nombre m; (numeral) chiffre m; (of page, car, telephone, newspaper) numéro m ▷ vt numéroter; (amount to) compter;

n

a ~ of un certain nombre de; **they were seven in ~** ils étaient (au nombre de) sept; **to be ~ed among** compter parmi; **number plate** *n* (BRIT Aut) plaque *f* minéralogique or d'immatriculation; **Number Ten** *n* (BRIT: 10 Downing Street) résidence du Premier ministre

numerical [njuːˈmɛrɪkl] *adj* numérique

numerous [ˈnjuːmərəs] *adj* nombreux(-euse)

nun [nʌn] *n* religieuse *f*, sœur *f*

nurse [nɜːs] *n* infirmière *f*; (*also*: **~maid**) bonne *f* d'enfants ▷ *vt.* (*patient, cold*) soigner

nursery [ˈnɜːsəri] *n* (*room*) nursery *f*; (*institution*) crèche *f*, garderie *f*; (*for plants*) pépinière *f*; **nursery rhyme** *n* comptine *f*, chansonnette *f* pour enfants; **nursery school** *n* école maternelle; **nursery slope** *n* (BRIT Ski) piste *f* pour débutants

nursing [ˈnɜːsɪŋ] *n* (*profession*) profession *f* d'infirmière; (*care*) soins *mpl*; **nursing home** *n* clinique *f*; (*for convalescence*) maison *f* de convalescence or de repos; (*for old people*) maison de retraite

nurture [ˈnɜːtʃər] *vt* élever

nut [nʌt] *n* (*of metal*) écrou *m*; (*fruit: walnut*) noix *f*; (: *hazelnut*) noisette *f*; (: *peanut*) cacahuète *f* (*terme générique en anglais*)

nutmeg [ˈnʌtmɛg] *n* (*noix f*) muscade *f*

nutrient [ˈnjuːtrɪənt] *n* substance nutritive

nutrition [njuːˈtrɪʃən] *n* nutrition *f*, alimentation *f*

nutritious [njuːˈtrɪʃəs] *adj* nutritif(-ive), nourrissant(e)

nuts [nʌts] (*inf*) *adj* dingue

NVQ *n abbr* (BRIT) = **National Vocational Qualification**

nylon [ˈnaɪlɔn] *n* nylon *m* ▷ *adj* de or en nylon

O

oak [əuk] *n* chêne *m* ▷ *cpd* de or en (bois de) chêne

O.A.P. *n abbr* (BRIT) = **old age pensioner**

oar [ɔːr] *n* aviron *m*, rame *f*

oasis [əuˈeɪsɪs] (*pl* **oases**) [əuˈeɪsiːz, əuˈeɪsiːz] *n* oasis *f*

oath [əuθ] *n* serment *m*; (*swear word*) juron *m*; **on** (BRIT) or **under ~** sous serment; assermenté(e)

oatmeal [ˈəutmiːl] *n* flocons *mpl* d'avoine

oats [əuts] *n* avoine *f*

obedience [əˈbiːdɪəns] *n* obéissance *f*

obedient [əˈbiːdɪənt] *adj* obéissant(e)

obese [əuˈbiːs] *adj* obèse

obesity [əuˈbiːsɪti] *n* obésité *f*

obey [əˈbeɪ] *vt* obéir à; (*instructions, regulations*) se conformer à ▷ *vi* obéir

obituary [əˈbɪtjuərɪ] *n* nécrologie *f*

object *n* [ˈɔbdʒɪkt] objet *m*; (*purpose*) but *m*, objet; (*Ling*) complément *m* d'objet ▷ *vi* [əb'dʒɛkt]: **to ~ to** (*attitude*) désapprouver; (*proposal*) protester contre, élever une objection contre; **I ~!** je proteste!; **he ~ed that ...** il a fait valoir *or* a objecté que ...; **money is no ~** l'argent n'est pas un problème; **objection** [əb'dʒɛkʃən] *n* objection *f*; **if you have no objection** si vous n'y voyez pas d'inconvénient; **objective** *n* objectif *m* ▷ *adj* objectif(-ive)

obligation [ɔblɪ'geɪʃən] *n* obligation *f*, devoir *m*; (*debt*) dette *f* (de reconnaissance)

obligatory [ə'blɪɡətərɪ] *adj* obligatoire

oblige [ə'blaɪdʒ] *vt* (*force*): **to ~ sb to do** obliger *or* forcer qn à faire; (*do a favour*) rendre service à, obliger; **to be ~d to sb for sth** être obligé(e) à qn pour qch

oblique [ə'bliːk] *adj* oblique; (*allusion*) indirect(e)

obliterate [ə'blɪtəreɪt] *vt* effacer

oblivious [ə'blɪvɪəs] *adj*: **~ of** oublieux(-euse) de

oblong ['ɔblɔŋ] *adj* oblong(ue) ▷ *n* rectangle *m*

obnoxious [əb'nɔkʃəs] *adj* odieux(-euse); (*smell*) nauséabond(e)

oboe ['əubəu] *n* hautbois *m*

obscene [əb'siːn] *adj* obscène

obscure [əb'skjuə'] *adj* obscur(e) ▷ *vt* obscurcir; (*hide: sun*) cacher

observant [əb'zɜːvnt] *adj* observateur(-trice)

observation [ɔbzə'veɪʃən] *n* observation *f*; (*by police etc*) surveillance *f*

observatory [əb'zɜːvətrɪ] *n* observatoire *m*

observe [əb'zɜːv] *vt* observer; (*remark*) faire observer *or* remarquer; **observer** *n* observateur(-trice)

obsess [əb'sɛs] *vt* obséder; **obsession** [əb'sɛʃən] *n* obsession *f*; **obsessive** *adj* obsédant(e)

obsolete ['ɔbsəliːt] *adj* dépassé(e), périmé(e)

obstacle ['ɔbstəkl] *n* obstacle *m*

obstinate ['ɔbstɪnɪt] *adj* obstiné(e); (*pain, cold*) persistant(e)

obstruct [əb'strʌkt] *vt* (*block*) boucher, obstruer; (*hinder*) entraver; **obstruction** [əb'strʌkʃən] *n* obstruction *f*; (*to plan, progress*) obstacle *m*

obtain [əb'teɪn] *vt* obtenir

obvious ['ɔbvɪəs] *adj* évident(e), manifeste; **obviously** *adv* manifestement; **obviously!** bien sûr!; **obviously not!** évidemment pas!, bien sûr que non!

occasion [ə'keɪʒən] *n* occasion *f*; (*event*) événement *m*; **occasional** *adj* pris(e) (or fait(e) *etc*) de temps en temps; (*worker, spending*) occasionnel(le); **occasionally** *adv* de temps en temps, quelquefois

occult [ɔ'kʌlt] *adj* occulte ▷ *n*: **the ~** le surnaturel

occupant ['ɔkjupənt] *n* occupant *m*

occupation [ɔkju'peɪʃən] *n* occupation *f*; (*job*) métier *m*, profession *f*

occupy ['ɔkjupaɪ] *vt* occuper; **to ~ o.s. with** *or* **by doing** s'occuper à faire

occur [ə'kəː'] *vi* se produire; (*difficulty, opportunity*) se présenter; (*phenomenon, error*) se rencontrer; **to ~ to sb** venir à l'esprit de qn; **occurrence** [ə'kʌrəns] *n* (*existence*) présence *f*, existence *f*; (*event*) cas *m*, fait *m*

ocean ['əuʃən] *n* océan *m*

o'clock [ə'klɔk] *adv*: **it is 5 ~** il est 5 heures

Oct. *abbr* (= *October*) oct

October [ɔk'təubə'] *n* octobre *m*

octopus ['ɔktəpəs] *n* pieuvre *f*

odd [ɔd] *adj* (*strange*) bizarre, curieux(-euse); (*number*) impair(e); (*not of a set*) dépareillé(e); **60-~** 60 et quelques; **at ~ times** de temps en temps; **the ~ one out** l'exception *f*; **oddly** *adv* bizarrement, curieusement; **odds** npl (in betting) cote f; **it makes no odds** cela n'a pas d'importance; **odds and ends** de petites choses; **at odds** en désaccord

odometer [ɔ'dɔmɪtə'] n (us) odomètre m

odour, (us) **odor** ['əudə'] n odeur f

KEYWORD

of [ɔv, əv] prep **1** (gen) de; **a friend of ours** un de nos amis; **a boy of 10** un garçon de 10 ans; **that was kind of you** c'était gentil de votre part **2** (expressing quantity, amount, dates etc) de; **a kilo of flour** un kilo de farine; **how much of this do you need?** combien vous en faut-il?; **there were three of them** ils étaient 3; (objects) il y en avait 3; **three of us went** 3 d'entre nous y sont allé(e)s; **the 5th of July** le 5 juillet; **a quarter of 4** (us) 4 heures moins le quart
3 (from, out of) en, de; **a statue of marble** une statue de or en marbre; **made of wood** (fait) en bois

off [ɔf] adj, adv (engine) coupé(e); (light, TV) éteint(e); (tap) fermé(e); (BRIT: food) mauvais(e), avancé(e); (: milk) tourné(e); (absent) absent(e); (cancelled) annulé(e); (removed): **the lid was ~** le couvercle était retiré or n'était pas mis; (away): **to run/drive ~** partir en courant/voiture ▷ prep de: **to be ~** (to leave) partir, s'en aller; **to be ~ sick** être absent pour cause de maladie; **a day ~** un jour de congé; **to have an ~ day** n'être pas en forme; **he had his coat ~** il avait enlevé son manteau; **10% ~** (Comm) 10% de rabais; **5 km ~ (the road)** à 5 km (de la route); **~ the coast** au large de la côte; **it's a long way ~** c'est loin (d'ici); **I'm ~ meat** je ne mange plus de viande; je n'aime plus la viande; **on**

the ~ chance à tout hasard; **~ and on, on and ~** de temps à autre

offence, (us) **offense** [ə'fɛns] n (crime) délit m, infraction f; **to take ~ at** se vexer de, s'offenser de

offend [ə'fɛnd] vt (person) offenser, blesser; **offender** n délinquant(e); (against regulations) contrevenant(e)

offense [ə'fɛns] n (us) = **offence**

offensive [ə'fɛnsɪv] adj offensant(e), choquant(e); (smell etc) très déplaisant(e); (weapon) offensif(-ive) ▷ n (Mil) offensive f

offer ['ɔfə'] n offre f, proposition f ▷ vt offrir, proposer; **"on ~"** (Comm) "en promotion"

offhand [ɔf'hænd] adj désinvolte ▷ adv spontanément

office ['ɔfɪs] n (place) bureau m; (position) charge f, fonction f; **doctor's ~** (us) cabinet (médical); **to take ~** entrer en fonctions; **office block**, (us) **office building** n immeuble m de bureaux; **office hours** npl heures fpl de bureau; (us Med) heures de consultation

officer ['ɔfɪsə'] n (Mil etc) officier m; (also: **police ~**) agent m (de police); (of organization) membre m du bureau directeur

office worker n employé m de bureau

official [ə'fɪʃl] adj (authorized) officiel(le) ▷ n officiel m; (civil servant) fonctionnaire m/f; (of railways, post office, town hall) employé m

off-: off-licence (BRIT: shop) débit m de vins et de spiritueux; **off-line** adj (Comput) (en mode) autonome (: switched off) non connecté(e); **off-peak** adj aux heures creuses; (electricity, ticket) au tarif heures creuses; **off-putting** adj (BRIT) (remark) rébarbatif(-ive); (person) rebutant(e), peu engageant(e); **off-season** adj, adv hors-saison inv

offset ['ɔfset] vt (irreg: like set) (counteract) contrebalancer, compenser

offshore [ɒfˈʃɔːʳ] *adj* (breeze) de terre; (island) proche du littoral; (fishing) côtier(-ière)

offside [ˈɒfˈsaɪd] *adj* (Sport) hors-jeu; (Aut: in Britain) de droite; (: in US, Europe) de gauche

offspring [ˈɒfsprɪŋ] *n* progéniture *f*

often [ˈɒfn] *adv* souvent; **how ~ do you go?** vous y allez tous les combien?; **every so ~** de temps en temps, de temps à autre

oh [əʊ] *excl* ô!, oh!, ah!

oil [ɔɪl] *n* huile *f*; (petroleum) pétrole *m*; (for central heating) mazout *m* ▷ *vt* (machine) graisser; **oil filter** *n* (Aut) filtre *m* à huile; **oil painting** *n* peinture *f* à l'huile; **oil refinery** *n* raffinerie *f* de pétrole; **oil rig** *n* derrick *m*; (at sea) plate-forme pétrolière; **oil slick** *n* nappe *f* de mazout; **oil tanker** *n* (ship) pétrolier *m*; (truck) camion-citerne *m*; **oil well** *n* puits *m* de pétrole; **oily** *adj* huileux(-euse); (food) gras(se)

ointment [ˈɔɪntmənt] *n* onguent *m*

O.K., okay [ˈəʊˈkeɪ] (inf) *excl* d'accord! ▷ *vt* approuver, donner son accord à ▷ *adj* (not bad) pas mal; **is it ~?** c'est bon?; **are you ~?** ça va?

old [əʊld] *adj* vieux (vieille); (person) vieux, âgé(e); (former) ancien(ne), vieux; **how ~ are you?** quel âge avez-vous?; **he's 10 years ~** il a 10 ans, il est âgé de 10 ans; **~er brother/sister** frère/sœur aîné(e); **old age** *n* vieillesse *f*; **old-age pensioner** *n* (BRIT) retraité(e); **old-fashioned** *adj* démodé(e); (person) vieux jeu *inv*; **old people's home** *n* (esp BRIT) maison *f* de retraite

olive [ˈɒlɪv] *n* (fruit) olive *f*; (tree) olivier *m* ▷ *adj* (also: **~-green**) (vert) olive *inv*; **olive oil** *n* huile *f* d'olive

Olympic [əʊˈlɪmpɪk] *adj* olympique; **the ~ Games, the ~s** les Jeux *mpl* olympiques

omelet(te) [ˈɒmlɪt] *n* omelette *f*

omen [ˈəʊmən] *n* présage *m*

ominous [ˈɒmɪnəs] *adj* menaçant(e), inquiétant(e); (event) de mauvais augure

omit [əʊˈmɪt] *vt* omettre

KEYWORD

on [ɒn] *prep* **1** (indicating position) sur; **on the table** sur la table; **on the wall** sur le or au mur; **on the left** à gauche

2 (indicating means, method, condition etc): **on foot** à pied; **on the train/plane** (be) dans le train/l'avion; (go) en train/avion; **on the telephone/radio/television** au téléphone/à la radio/à la télévision; **to be on drugs** se droguer; **on holiday**, (us) **on vacation** en vacances

3 (referring to time): **on Friday** vendredi; **on Fridays** le vendredi; **on June 20th** le 20 juin; **a week on Friday** vendredi en huit; **on arrival** à l'arrivée; **on seeing this** en voyant cela

4 (about, concerning) sur, de; **a book on Balzac/physics** un livre sur Balzac/de physique

▷ *adv* **1** (referring to dress): **to have one's coat on** avoir (mis) son manteau; **to put one's coat on** mettre son manteau; **what's she got on?** qu'est-ce qu'elle porte?

2 (referring to covering): **screw the lid on tightly** vissez bien le couvercle

3 (further, continuously): **to walk** *etc* **on** continuer à marcher etc; **from that day on** depuis ce jour

▷ *adj* **1** (in operation: machine) en marche; (: radio, TV, light) allumé(e); (: tap, gas) ouvert(e); (: brakes) mis(e); **is the meeting still on?** (not cancelled) est-ce que la réunion a bien lieu?; **when is this film on?** quand passe ce film?

2 (inf): **that's not on!** (not acceptable) cela ne se fait pas!; (not possible) pas question!

once [wʌns] adv une fois; (formerly) autrefois ▷ conj une fois que + sub; **~ he had left/it was done** une fois qu'il fut parti/ que ce fut terminé; **at ~** tout de suite, immédiatement; (simultaneously) à la fois; **all at ~** adv tout d'un coup; **~ a week** une fois par semaine; **~ more** encore une fois; **~ and for all** une fois pour toutes; **~ upon a time there was …** il y avait une fois …, il était une fois …

oncoming ['ɔnkʌmɪŋ] adj (traffic) venant en sens inverse

KEYWORD

one [wʌn] num une(e); **one hundred and fifty** cent cinquante; **one by one** un(e) à or par un(e); **one day** un jour

▷ adj **1** (sole) seul(e), unique; **the one book** which l'unique or le seul livre qui; **the one man who** le seul (homme) qui

2 (same) même; **they came in the one car** ils sont venus dans la même voiture

▷ pron **1**: **this one** celui-ci (celle-ci); **that one** celui-là (celle-là); **I've already got one/a red one** j'en ai déjà un(e)/un(e) rouge; **which one do you want?** lequel voulez-vous?

2: **another one** l'un(e) l'autre; **to look at one another** se regarder

3 (impersonal) on; **one never knows** on ne sait jamais; **to cut one's finger** se couper le doigt; **one needs to eat** il faut manger

one-off [wʌn'ɔf] n (BRIT inf) exemplaire m unique

oneself [wʌn'sɛlf] pron se; (after prep, also emphatic) soi-même; **to hurt ~** se faire mal; **to keep sth for ~** garder qch pour soi; **to talk to ~** se parler à soi-même; **by ~** tout seul

one: one-shot [wʌn'ʃɔt] (US) n = **one-off**; **one-sided** adj (argument,

decision) unilatéral(e); **one-to-one** adj (relationship) univoque; **one-way** adj (street, traffic) à sens unique

ongoing ['ɔngəʊɪŋ] adj en cours; (relationship) suivi(e)

onion ['ʌnjən] n oignon m

on-line ['ɔnlaɪn] adj (Comput) en ligne (: switched on) connecté(e)

onlooker ['ɔnlʊkə*] n spectateur(-trice)

only ['əʊnlɪ] adv seulement ▷ adj seul(e), unique ▷ conj seulement, mais; **an ~ child** un enfant unique; **not ~ … but also** non seulement … mais aussi; **I ~ took one** j'en ai seulement pris un, je n'en ai pris qu'un

on-screen [ɔn'skriːn] adj à l'écran

onset ['ɔnsɛt] n début m; (of winter, old age) approche f

onto ['ɔntu] prep sur

onward(s) ['ɔnwəd(z)] adv (move) en avant; **from that time ~** à partir de ce moment

oops [ʊps] excl houp!

ooze [uːz] vi suinter

opaque [əʊ'peɪk] adj opaque

open ['əʊpn] adj ouvert(e); (car) découvert(e); (road, view) dégagé(e); (meeting) public(-ique); (admiration) manifeste ▷ vt ouvrir ▷ vi (flower, eyes, door, debate) s'ouvrir; (shop, bank, museum) ouvrir; (book etc: commence) commencer, débuter; **is it ~ to the public?** est-ce ouvert au public?; **what time do you ~?** à quelle heure ouvrez-vous?; **in the ~ (air)** en plein air; **open up** vt ouvrir; (blocked road) dégager ▷ vi s'ouvrir; **open-air** adj en plein air; **opening** n ouverture f; (opportunity) occasion f; (work) débouché m; (job) poste vacant; **opening hours** npl heures fpl d'ouverture; **open learning** n enseignement universitaire à la carte, notamment par correspondance; (distance learning) télé-enseignement m; **openly** adv ouvertement; **open-minded** adj à l'esprit ouvert;

open-necked adj à col ouvert;
open-plan adj sans cloisons; **Open University** n (BRIT) cours universitaires par correspondance

● OPEN UNIVERSITY

● L'*Open University* a été fondée en
● 1969. L'enseignement comprend
● des cours (certaines plages horaires
● sont réservées à cet effet à la
● télévision et à la radio), des devoirs
● qui sont envoyés par l'étudiant
● à son directeur ou sa directrice
● d'études, et un séjour obligatoire en
● université d'été. Il faut préparer un
● certain nombre d'unités de valeur
● pendant une période de temps
● déterminée et obtenir la moyenne
● à un certain nombre d'entre elles
● pour recevoir le diplôme visé.

opera ['ɔpərə] n opéra m; **opera house** n opéra m; **opera singer** n chanteur(-euse) d'opéra
operate ['ɔpəreɪt] vt (machine) faire marcher, faire fonctionner ▷ vi fonctionner; **to ~ on sb (for)** (Med) opérer qn (de)
operating room n (US Med) salle f d'opération
operating theatre n (BRIT Med) salle f d'opération
operation [ɔpə'reɪʃən] n opération f; (of machine) fonctionnement m; **to have an ~** (Med) se faire opérer (de); **to be in ~** (machine) être en service; (system) être en vigueur; **operational** adj opérationnel(le); (ready for use) en état de marche
operative ['ɔpərətɪv] adj (measure) en vigueur ▷ n (in factory) ouvrier(-ière)
operator ['ɔpəreɪtə] n (of machine) opérateur(-trice); (Tel) téléphoniste m/f
opinion [ə'pɪnjən] n opinion f, avis m; **in my ~** à mon avis; **opinion poll** n sondage m d'opinion

opponent [ə'pəunənt] n adversaire m/f
opportunity [ɔpə'tjuːnɪtɪ] n occasion f; **to take the ~ to do** or **of doing** profiter de l'occasion pour faire
oppose [ə'pəuz] vt s'opposer à; **to be ~d to sth** être opposé(e) à qch; **as ~d to** par opposition à
opposite ['ɔpəzɪt] adj opposé(e); (house etc) d'en face ▷ adv en face ▷ prep en face de ▷ n opposé m, contraire m; (of word) contraire
opposition [ɔpə'zɪʃən] n opposition f
oppress [ə'prɛs] vt opprimer
opt [ɔpt] vi: **to ~ for** opter pour; **to ~ to do** choisir de faire; **opt out** vi: **to ~ out of** choisir de ne pas participer à or de ne pas faire
optician [ɔp'tɪʃən] n opticien(ne)
optimism ['ɔptɪmɪzəm] n optimisme m
optimist ['ɔptɪmɪst] n optimiste m/f; **optimistic** [ɔptɪ'mɪstɪk] adj optimiste
optimum ['ɔptɪməm] adj optimum
option ['ɔpʃən] n choix m, option f; (Scol) matière f à option; **optional** adj facultatif(-ive)
or [ɔː] conj ou; (with negative): **he hasn't seen or heard anything** il n'a rien vu ni entendu; **or else** sinon; ou bien
oral ['ɔːrəl] adj oral(e) ▷ n oral m
orange ['ɔrɪndʒ] n (fruit) orange f ▷ adj orange inv; **orange juice** n jus m d'orange
orbit ['ɔːbɪt] n orbite f ▷ vt graviter autour de
orchard ['ɔːtʃəd] n verger m
orchestra ['ɔːkɪstrə] n orchestre m; (US: seating) (fauteuils mpl de l') orchestre
orchid ['ɔːkɪd] n orchidée f
ordeal [ɔː'diːl] n épreuve f
order ['ɔːdə] n ordre m; (Comm) commande f ▷ vt ordonner; (Comm) commander; **in ~** en ordre; (document) en règle; **out of ~** (not in correct order) en désordre;

a

(machine) hors service; (telephone) en dérangement; **a machine in working ~** une machine en état de marche; **in ~ to do/that** pour faire/que + sub; **could I ~ now, please?** je peux commander, s'il vous plaît?; **to be on ~** être en commande; **to ~ sb to do** ordonner à qn de faire; **order form** n bon m de commande; **orderly** n (Mil) ordonnance f; (Med) garçon m de salle ▷ adj (room) en ordre; (mind) méthodique; (person) qui a de l'ordre

ordinary [ˈɔːdnrɪ] adj ordinaire, normal(e); (pej) ordinaire, quelconque; **out of the ~** exceptionnel(le)

ore [ɔːʳ] n minerai m

oregano [ɒrɪˈɡɑːnəʊ] n origan m

organ [ˈɔːɡən] n organe m; (Mus) orgue m, orgues fpl; **organic** [ɔːˈɡænɪk] adj organique; (crops etc) biologique, naturel(le); **organism** n organisme m

organization [ɔːɡənaɪˈzeɪʃən] n organisation f

organize [ˈɔːɡənaɪz] vt organiser; **organized** [ˈɔːɡənaɪzd] adj (planned) organisé(e); (efficient) bien organisé; **organizer** n organisateur(-trice)

orgasm [ˈɔːɡæzəm] n orgasme m

orgy [ˈɔːdʒɪ] n orgie f

oriental [ɔːrɪˈɛntl] adj oriental(e)

orientation [ɔːrɪɛnˈteɪʃən] n (attitudes) tendance f; (in job) orientation f; (of building) orientation, exposition f

origin [ˈɒrɪdʒɪn] n origine f

original [əˈrɪdʒɪnl] adj original(e); (earliest) originel(le) ▷ n original m; **originally** adv (at first) à l'origine

originate [əˈrɪdʒɪneɪt] vi: **to ~ from** être originaire de; (suggestion) provenir de; **to ~ in** (custom) prendre naissance dans, avoir son origine dans

Orkney [ˈɔːknɪ] n (also: **the ~s, the ~ Islands**) les Orcades fpl

ornament [ˈɔːnəmənt] n ornement m; (trinket) bibelot m; **ornamental** [ɔːnəˈmɛntl] adj décoratif(-ive); (garden) d'agrément

ornate [ɔːˈneɪt] adj très orné(e)

orphan [ˈɔːfn] n orphelin(e)

orthodox [ˈɔːθədɒks] adj orthodoxe

orthopaedic, (us) **orthopedic** [ɔːθəˈpiːdɪk] adj orthopédique

osteopath [ˈɒstɪəpæθ] n ostéopathe m/f

ostrich [ˈɒstrɪtʃ] n autruche f

other [ˈʌðəʳ] adj autre ▷ pron: **the ~ (one)** l'autre; **~s** (other people) d'autres ▷ adv: **~ than** autrement que; à part; **the ~ day** l'autre jour; **otherwise** adv, conj autrement

Ottawa [ˈɒtəwə] n Ottawa

otter [ˈɒtəʳ] n loutre f

ouch [autʃ] excl aïe!

ought [ɔːt] aux vb: **I ~ to do it** je devrais le faire, il faudrait que je le fasse; **this ~ to have been corrected** cela aurait dû être corrigé; **he ~ to win** (probability) il devrait gagner

ounce [auns] n once f (28.35g; 16 in a pound)

our [ˈauəʳ] adj notre, nos pl; see also **my**; **ours** pron le (la) nôtre, les nôtres; see also **mine¹**; **ourselves** pl pron (reflexive, after preposition) nous; (emphatic) nous-mêmes; see also **oneself**

oust [aust] vt évincer

out [aut] adv dehors; (published, not at home etc) sorti(e); (light, fire) éteint(e); **~ there** là-bas; **he's ~** (absent) il est sorti; **to be ~ in one's calculations** s'être trompé dans ses calculs; **to run/back** etc **~** sortir en courant/en reculant etc; **~ loud** adv à haute voix; **~ of** prep (outside) en dehors de; (because of: anger etc) par; (from among): **10 ~ of 10** 10 sur 10; (without): **~ of petrol** sans essence, à court d'essence; **~ of order** (machine) en panne; (Tel: line) en dérangement; **outback** n (in Australia) intérieur m; **outbound** adj: **outbound (from/for)** en partance (de/pour); **outbreak** n (of violence) éruption f, explosion f; (of disease) de nombreux cas; **the outbreak of war south of the border** la guerre qui s'est déclarée au sud de la frontière; **outburst** n explosion f, accès m; **outcast** n exilé(e); (socially) paria m; **outcome** n issue f, résultat m; **outcry** n tollé (général); **outdated** adj démodé(e); **outdoor** adj de or en plein air; **outdoors** adv dehors; au grand air

outer ['autə'] adj extérieur(e); **outer space** n espace m cosmique

outfit ['autfit] n (clothes) tenue f

out: outgoing adj (president, tenant) sortant(e); (character) ouvert(e), extraverti(e); **outgoings** npl (BRIT: expenses) dépenses fpl; **outhouse** n appentis m, remise f

outing ['autɪŋ] n sortie f; excursion f

out: outlaw n hors-la-loi m inv ▷ vt (person) mettre hors la loi; (practice) proscrire; **outlay** n dépenses fpl; (investment) mise f de fonds; **outlet** n (for liquid etc) issue f, sortie f; (for emotion) exutoire m; (also: **retail outlet**) point m de vente; (us Elec) prise f de courant; **outline** n (shape) contour m; (summary) esquisse f, grandes lignes ▷ vt (fig: theory, plan) exposer à grands traits; **outlook** n perspective f; (point of view) attitude f; **outnumber** vt surpasser en nombre; **out-of-date** adj (passport, ticket) périmé(e); (theory, idea) dépassé(e); (custom) désuet(-ète); (clothes) démodé(e); **out-of-doors** adv = **outdoors**; **out-of-the-way** adj loin de tout; **out-of-town** adj (shopping centre etc) en périphérie; **outpatient** n malade m/f en consultation externe; **outpost** n avant-poste m; **output** n rendement m, production f; (Comput) sortie f ▷ vt (Comput) sortir

outrage ['autreɪdʒ] n (anger) indignation f; (violent act) atrocité f, acte m de violence; (scandal) scandale m ▷ vt outrager; **outrageous** [aut'reɪdʒəs] adj atroce; (scandalous) scandaleux(-euse)

outright adv complètement; (deny, refuse) catégoriquement; (ask) carrément; (kill) sur le coup ▷ adj ['autraɪt] complet(-ète); catégorique

outset ['autset] n début m

outside ['aut'saɪd] n extérieur m ▷ adj extérieur(e) ▷ adv (au) dehors, à l'extérieur ▷ prep hors de, à l'extérieur de; (in front of) devant; **at the ~** (fig) au plus or maximum; **outside lane** n (Aut: in Britain) voie f de droite; (: in US, Europe) voie de gauche; **outside line** n (Tel) ligne extérieure; **outsider** n (stranger) étranger(-ère)

out: outsize adj énorme; (clothes) grande taille inv; **outskirts** npl faubourgs mpl; **outspoken** adj très franc(franche); **outstanding** adj remarquable, exceptionnel(le); (unfinished: work, business) en suspens, en souffrance; (debt) impayé(e); (problem) non réglé(e)

outward ['autwəd] adj (sign, appearances) extérieur(e); (journey) (d')aller; **outwards** adv (esp BRIT) = **outward**

outweigh [aut'weɪ] vt l'emporter sur

oval ['əuvl] adj, n ovale m

ovary ['əuvərɪ] n ovaire m

oven ['ʌvn] n four m; **oven glove** n gant m de cuisine; **ovenproof** adj allant au four; **oven-ready** adj prêt(e) à cuire

over ['əuvə'] adv (par-)dessus ▷ adj (finished) fini(e), terminé(e); (too much) en plus ▷ prep sur; par-dessus; (above) au-dessus de; (on the other side of) de l'autre côté de; (more than) plus de; (during) pendant; (about, concerning): **they fell out ~ money/her** ils se sont brouillés pour des questions d'argent/à cause d'elle; **~ here** ici; **~ there** là-bas; **all ~** (everywhere) partout; **~ and (again)** à plusieurs reprises; **~ and above** en plus de; **to ask sb ~** inviter qn (à passer); **to fall ~** tomber; **to turn sth ~** retourner qch

overall ['əʊvərɔːl] adj (length) total(e); (study, impression) d'ensemble ▷ n (BRIT) blouse f ▷ adv [əʊvər'ɔːl] dans l'ensemble, en général; **overalls** npl (boiler suit) bleus mpl (de travail)

overboard ['əʊvəbɔːd] adv (Naut) par-dessus bord

overcame [əʊvə'keɪm] pt of **overcome**

overcast ['əʊvəkɑːst] adj couvert(e)

overcharge [əʊvə'tʃɑːdʒ] vt: **to ~ sb for sth** faire payer qch trop cher à qn

overcoat ['əʊvəkəʊt] n pardessus m

overcome [əʊvə'kʌm] vt (irreg: like **come**) (defeat) triompher de; (difficulty) surmonter ▷ adj (emotionally) bouleversé(e); **~ with grief** accablé(e) de douleur

over-: **overcrowded** adj bondé(e); (city, country) surpeuplé(e); **overdo** vt (irreg: like **do**) exagérer; (overcook) trop cuire; **to overdo it, to overdo things** (work too hard) en faire trop, se surmener; **overdone** [əʊvə'dʌn] adj (vegetables, steak) trop cuit(e); (fig) exagéré(e), excessive; **overdraft** n découvert m; **overdrawn** (account) à découvert; **overdue** adj en retard; (bill) impayé(e); (change) qui tarde; **overestimate** vt surestimer

overflow vi [əʊvə'fləʊ] déborder ▷ n ['əʊvəfləʊ] (also: **~ pipe**) tuyau m d'écoulement, trop-plein m

overgrown [əʊvə'grəʊn] adj (garden) envahi(e) par la végétation

overhaul vt [əʊvə'hɔːl] réviser ▷ n ['əʊvəhɔːl] révision f

overhead adv [əʊvə'hɛd] au-dessus ▷ adj ['əʊvəhɛd] aérien(ne); (lighting)

vertical(e) ▷ n ['əʊvəhɛd] (US) = **overheads**; **overhead projector** n rétroprojecteur m; **overheads** npl (BRIT) frais généraux

over-: **overhear** vt (irreg: like **hear**) entendre (par hasard); **overheat** vi (engine) chauffer; **overland** adj, adv par voie de terre; **overlap** vi se chevaucher; **overleaf** adv au verso; **overload** vt surcharger; **overlook** vt (have view of) donner sur; (miss) oublier, négliger; (forgive) fermer les yeux sur

overnight adv [əʊvə'naɪt] (happen) durant la nuit; (fig) soudain ▷ adj ['əʊvənaɪt] d'une (or de) nuit; soudain(e); **to stay ~ (with sb)** passer la nuit (chez qn); **overnight bag** n nécessaire m de voyage

overpass ['əʊvəpɑːs] n (US: for cars) pont autoroutier; (for pedestrians) passerelle f, pont m

overpower [əʊvə'paʊə'] vt vaincre; (fig) accabler; **overpowering** adj irrésistible; (heat, stench) suffocant(e)

over-: **overreact** [əʊvəriː'ækt] vi réagir de façon excessive; **overrule** vt (decision) annuler; (claim) rejeter; (person) rejeter l'avis de; **overrun** vt (irreg: like **run**) (Mil: country etc) occuper; (time limit etc) dépasser ▷ vi dépasser le temps imparti

overseas [əʊvə'siːz] adv outre-mer; (abroad) à l'étranger ▷ adj (trade) extérieur(e); (visitor) étranger(-ère)

oversee [əʊvə'siː] vt (irreg: like **see**) surveiller

overshadow [əʊvə'ʃædəʊ] vt (fig) éclipser

oversight ['əʊvəsaɪt] n omission f, oubli m

oversleep [əʊvə'sliːp] vi (irreg: like **sleep**) se réveiller (trop) tard

overspend [əʊvə'spɛnd] vi (irreg: like **spend**) dépenser de trop

overt [əʊ'vɜːt] adj non dissimulé(e)

overtake [əʊvə'teɪk] vt (irreg: like **take**) dépasser; (BRIT Aut) dépasser, doubler

over: overthrow vt (irreg: like **throw**)
(government) renverser; **overtime**
n heures fpl supplémentaires;
overturn vt renverser; (decision,
plan) annuler ▷ vi se retourner;
overweight adj (person) trop
gros(se); **overwhelm** vt (subj:
emotion) accabler, submerger; (enemy,
opponent) écraser; **overwhelming**
adj (victory, defeat) écrasant(e); (desire)
irrésistible

owe [əu] vt devoir; **to ~ sb sth, to ~**
sth to sb devoir qch à qn; **how much**
do I ~ you? combien est-ce que je
vous dois?; **owing to** prep à cause de,
en raison de

owl [aul] n hibou m

own [əun] vt posséder ▷ adj propre;
a room of my ~ une chambre à moi,
ma propre chambre; **to get one's**
~ back prendre sa revanche; **on**
one's ~ tout(e) seul(e); **own up** vi
avouer; **owner** n propriétaire m/f;
ownership n possession f

ox (pl **oxen**) [ɔks, ˈɔksn] n bœuf m

Oxbridge [ˈɔksbrɪdʒ] n (BRIT) les
universités d'Oxford et de Cambridge

oxen [ˈɔksən] npl of **ox**

oxygen [ˈɔksɪdʒən] n oxygène m

oyster [ˈɔɪstəʳ] n huître f

oz. abbr = **ounce; ounces**

ozone [ˈəuzəun] n ozone m; **ozone**
friendly adj qui n'attaque pas or qui
préserve la couche d'ozone; **ozone**
layer n couche f d'ozone

p

P

p abbr (BRIT) = **penny; pence**

P.A. n abbr = **personal assistant;**
public address system

p.a. abbr = **per annum**

pace [peis] n pas m; (speed) allure f,
vitesse f ▷ vi: **to ~ up and down** faire
les cent pas; **to keep ~ with** aller à
la même vitesse que; (events) se tenir
au courant de; **pacemaker** n (Med)
stimulateur m cardiaque; (Sport: also:
pacesetter) meneur(-euse) de train

Pacific [pəˈsɪfɪk] n: **the ~ (Ocean)** le
Pacifique, l'océan m Pacifique

pacifier [ˈpæsɪfaɪəʳ] n (US: dummy)
tétine f

pack [pæk] n paquet m; (of hounds)
meute f; (of thieves, wolves etc) bande
f; (of cards) jeu m; (US: of cigarettes)
paquet; (back pack) sac m à dos ▷ vt
(goods) empaqueter, emballer; (in
suitcase etc) emballer; (box) remplir;
(cram) entasser ▷ vi: **to ~ (one's**
bags) faire ses bagages; **pack in** (BRIT

inf) vi (*machine*) tomber en panne ▷ vt (*boyfriend*) plaquer; ► **it in!** laisse tomber!; **pack off** vt: **to ~ sb off to** expédier qn à; **pack up** vi (*BRIT inf: machine*) tomber en panne; (*person*) se tirer ▷ vt (*belongings*) ranger; (*goods, presents*) empaqueter, emballer

package ['pækɪdʒ] n paquet m; (*also:* **~ deal**) (*agreement*) marché global; (*purchase*) forfait m; (*Comput*) progiciel m ▷ vt (*goods*) conditionner; **package holiday** n (*BRIT*) vacances organisées; **package tour** n voyage organisé

packaging ['pækɪdʒɪŋ] n (*wrapping materials*) emballage m

packed [pækt] *adj* (*crowded*) bondé(e); **packed lunch** (*BRIT*) n repas froid

packet ['pækɪt] n paquet m

packing ['pækɪŋ] n emballage m

pact [pækt] n pacte m, traité m

pad [pæd] n bloc-notes m; (*to prevent friction*) tampon m ▷ vt rembourrer; **padded** *adj* (*jacket*) matelassé(e); (*bra*) rembourré(e)

paddle ['pædl] n (*oar*) pagaie f; (*us: for table tennis*) raquette f de ping-pong ▷ vi (*with feet*) barboter, faire trempette ▷ vt: **to ~ a canoe** *etc* pagayer; **paddling pool** n petit bassin

paddock ['pædək] n enclos m; (*Racing*) paddock m

padlock ['pædlɒk] n cadenas m

paedophile, (*us*) **pedophile** ['pi:dəufaɪl] n pédophile m

page [peɪdʒ] n (*of book*) page f; (*also:* **~ boy**) groom m, chasseur m; (*at wedding*) garçon m d'honneur ▷ vt (*in hotel etc*) (faire) appeler

pager ['peɪdʒə'] n bip m (*inf*), Alphapage® m

paid [peɪd] *pt, pp of* **pay** ▷ *adj* (*work, official*) rémunéré(e); (*holiday*) payé(e); **to put ~ to** (*BRIT*) mettre fin à, mettre par terre

pain [peɪn] n douleur f; (*inf: nuisance*) plaie f; **to be in ~** souffrir, avoir

mal; **to take ~s to do** se donner du mal pour faire; **painful** *adj* douloureux(-euse); (*difficult*) difficile, pénible; **painkiller** n calmant m, analgésique m; **painstaking** ['peɪnzteɪkɪŋ] *adj* (*person*) soigneux(-euse); (*work*) soigné(e)

paint [peɪnt] n peinture f ▷ vt peindre; **to ~ the door blue** peindre la porte en bleu; **paintbrush** n pinceau m; **painter** n peintre m; **painting** n peinture f; (*picture*) tableau m

pair [pɛə'] n (*of shoes, gloves etc*) paire f; (*of people*) couple m; **~ of scissors** (paire de) ciseaux mpl; **~ of trousers** pantalon m

pajamas [pə'dʒɑːməz] npl (*us*) pyjama m

Pakistan [pɑːkɪ'stɑːn] n Pakistan m; **Pakistani** *adj* pakistanais(e) ▷ n Pakistanais(e)

pal [pæl] n (*inf*) copain (copine)

palace ['pæləs] n palais m

pale [peɪl] *adj* pâle; **~ blue** *adj* bleu pâle *inv*

Palestine ['pælɪstaɪn] n Palestine f; **Palestinian** [pælɪs'tɪnɪən] *adj* palestinien(ne) ▷ n Palestinien(ne)

palm [pɑːm] n (*Anat*) paume f; (*also:* **~ tree**) palmier m ▷ vt: **to ~ sth off on sb** (*inf*) refiler qch à qn

pamper ['pæmpə'] vt gâter, dorloter

pamphlet ['pæmflət] n brochure f

pan [pæn] n (*also:* **sauce~**) casserole f; (*also:* **frying ~**) poêle f

pancake ['pænkeɪk] n crêpe f

panda ['pændə] n panda m

pandemic [pæn'dɛmɪk] n pandémie f

pane [peɪn] n carreau m (de fenêtre), vitre f

panel ['pænl] n (*of wood, cloth etc*) panneau m; (*Radio, TV*) panel m, invités mpl; (*for interview, exams*) jury m

panhandler ['pænhændlə'] n (*us inf*) mendiant(e)

panic ['pænɪk] n panique f, affolement m ▷ vi s'affoler, paniquer

panorama [pænəˈrɑːmə] n
panorama m

pansy ['pænzɪ] n (Bot) pensée f

pant [pænt] vi haleter

panther ['pænθə'] n panthère f

panties ['pæntɪz] npl slip m, culotte f

pantomime ['pæntəmaɪm] n (BRIT)
spectacle m de Noël

○ **PANTOMIME**
○
○ Une *pantomime* (à ne pas confondre
○ avec le mot tel qu'on l'utilise
○ en français), que l'on appelle
○ également de façon familière
○ "panto", est un genre de farce où le
○ personnage principal est souvent
○ un jeune garçon et où il y a toujours
○ une "dame", c'est-à-dire une vieille
○ femme jouée par un homme, et
○ un méchant. La plupart du temps,
○ l'histoire est basée sur un conte de
○ fées comme Cendrillon ou Le Chat
○ botté, et le public est encouragé
○ à participer en prévenant le héros
○ d'un danger imminent. Ce genre
○ de spectacle, qui s'adresse surtout
○ aux enfants, vise également un
○ public d'adultes au travers de
○ nombreuses plaisanteries faisant
○ allusion à des faits d'actualité.

pants [pænts] npl (BRIT: woman's)
culotte f, slip m; (: man's) slip, caleçon
m; (: trousers) pantalon m

pantyhose ['pæntɪhəʊz] npl (US)
collant m

paper ['peɪpə'] n papier m; (also:
wall~) papier peint; (also: **news~**)
journal m; (academic essay) article
m; (exam) épreuve écrite ▷ adj en or
de papier ▷ vt tapisser (de papier
peint); **papers** npl (also: **identity ~s**)
papiers mpl (d'identité); **paperback**
n livre broché or non relié; (small) livre
m de poche; **paper bag** n sac m en
papier; **paper clip** n trombone m;
paper shop n (BRIT) marchand m de

journaux; **paperwork** n papiers mpl;
(pej) paperasserie f

paprika ['pæprɪkə] n paprika m

par [pɑː'] n pair m; (Golf) normale f du
parcours; **on a ~ with** à égalité avec,
au même niveau que

paracetamol [pærə'siːtəmɒl] n
(BRIT) paracétamol m

parachute ['pærəʃuːt] n
parachute m

parade [pə'reɪd] n défilé m ▷ vt (fig)
faire étalage de ▷ vi défiler

paradise ['pærədaɪs] n paradis m

paradox ['pærədɒks] n paradoxe m

paraffin ['pærəfɪn] n (BRIT): **~ (oil)**
pétrole (lampant)

paragraph ['pærəgrɑːf] n
paragraphe m

parallel ['pærəlɛl] adj: **~ (with or to)**
parallèle (à); (fig) analogue (à) ▷ n
(line) parallèle f; (fig, Geo) parallèle m

paralysed ['pærəlaɪzd] adj
paralysé(e)

paralysis (pl **paralyses**) [pə'rælɪsɪs,
-siːz] n paralysie f

paramedic [pærə'mɛdɪk] n
auxiliaire m/f médical(e)

paranoid ['pærənɔɪd] adj (Psych)
paranoïaque; (neurotic) paranoïde

parasite ['pærəsaɪt] n parasite m

parcel ['pɑːsl] n paquet m, colis m ▷ vt
(also: **~ up**) empaqueter

pardon ['pɑːdn] n pardon m; (Law)
grâce f ▷ vt pardonner à; (Law)
gracier; **~ me!** (after
burping etc) excusez-moi!; **I beg your
~!** (I'm sorry) pardon!, je suis désolé(e);
(US): **~ me?** (what did you
say?) pardon?

parent ['pɛərənt] n (father) père
m; (mother) mère f; **parents** npl
parents mpl; **parental** [pə'rɛntl] adj
parental(e), des parents

Paris ['pærɪs] n Paris

parish ['pærɪʃ] n paroisse f; (BRIT: civil)
≈ commune f

Parisian [pə'rɪzɪən] adj parisien(ne),
de Paris ▷ n Parisien(ne)

P

park [paːk] n parc m, jardin public
▷ vt garer ▷ vi se garer; **can I ~ here?** est-ce que je peux me garer ici?

parking ['paːkɪŋ] n stationnement m; **"no ~"** "stationnement interdit"; **parking lot** n (us) parking m, parc m de stationnement; **parking meter** n parc(o)mètre m; **parking ticket** n P.-V. m

⚠ Be careful not to translate *parking* by the French word *parking*.

parkway ['paːkweɪ] n (us) route f express (*en site vert ou aménagé*)

parliament ['paːləmənt] n parlement m; **parliamentary** [paːlə'mɛntərɪ] adj parlementaire

Parmesan [paːmɪ'zæn] n (also: **~ cheese**) Parmesan m

parole [pə'rəʊl] n: **on ~** en liberté conditionnelle

parrot ['pærət] n perroquet m

parsley ['paːslɪ] n persil m

parsnip ['paːsnɪp] n panais m

parson ['paːsn] n ecclésiastique m; (*Church of England*) pasteur m

part [paːt] n partie f; (*of machine*) pièce f; (*Theat*) rôle m; (*of serial*) épisode m; (us: *in hair*) raie f ▷ adv = **partly** ▷ vt séparer ▷ vi (*people*) se séparer; (*crowd*) s'ouvrir; **to take ~ in** participer à, prendre part à; **to take sb's ~** prendre le parti de qn, prendre parti pour qn; **for my ~** en ce qui me concerne; **for the most ~** en grande partie; dans la plupart des cas; **in ~** en partie; **to take sth in good/bad ~** prendre qch du bon/mauvais côté; **part with** vt fus (*person*) se séparer de; (*possessions*) se défaire de

partial ['paːʃl] adj (*incomplete*) partiel(le); **to be ~ to** aimer, avoir un faible pour

participant [paː'tɪsɪpənt] n (*in competition, campaign*) participant(e)

participate [paː'tɪsɪpeɪt] vi: **to ~ (in)** participer (à), prendre part (à)

particle ['paːtɪkl] n particule f; (*of dust*) grain m

particular [pə'tɪkjʊləʳ] adj (*specific*) particulier(-ière); (*special*) spécial(e); (*fussy*) difficile, exigeant(e); (*careful*) méticuleux(-euse); **in ~** en particulier, surtout; **particularly** adv particulièrement; (*in particular*) en particulier; **particulars** npl détails mpl; (*information*) renseignements mpl

parting ['paːtɪŋ] n séparation f; (BRIT: *in hair*) raie f

partition [paː'tɪʃən] n (Pol) partition f, division f; (*wall*) cloison f

partly ['paːtlɪ] adv en partie, partiellement

partner ['paːtnəʳ] n (Comm) associé(e); (Sport) partenaire m/f; (*spouse*) conjoint(e); (*lover*) ami(e); (*at dance*) cavalier(-ière); **partnership** n association f

partridge ['paːtrɪdʒ] n perdrix f

part-time ['paːt'taɪm] adj, adv à mi-temps, à temps partiel

party ['paːtɪ] n (Pol) parti m; (*celebration*) fête f, (C: *formal*) réception f; (: *in evening*) soirée f; (*group*) groupe m; (Law) partie f

pass [paːs] vt (*time, object*) passer; (*place*) passer devant; (*friend*) croiser; (*exam*) être reçu(e) à, réussir; (*overtake*) dépasser; (*approve*) approuver, accepter ▷ vi passer; (*Scol*) être reçu(e) or admis(e), réussir ▷ n (*permit*) laissez-passer m inv; (*membership card*) carte f d'accès or d'abonnement; (*in mountains*) col m; (*Sport*) passe f; (*Scol: also:* **~ mark**); **to get a ~** être reçu(e) (sans mention); **to ~ sb sth** passer qch à qn; **could you ~ the salt/oil, please?** pouvez-vous me passer le sel/l'huile, s'il vous plaît?; **to make a ~ at sb** (*inf*) faire des avances à qn; **pass away** vi mourir; **pass by** vi passer ▷ vt (*ignore*) négliger; **pass on** vt (*hand on*): **to ~ on (to)** transmettre (à); **pass out** vi s'évanouir; **pass over** vt (*ignore*) passer sous silence; **pass up** vt (*opportunity*) laisser passer;

passable adj (road) praticable; (work) acceptable

> Be careful not to translate to pass an exam by the French expression passer un examen.

passage ['pæsɪdʒ] n (also: **~way**) couloir m; (gen, in book) passage m; (by boat) traversée f

passenger ['pæsɪndʒəᵊ] n passager(-ère)

passer-by [pɑːsəˈbaɪ] n passant(e)

passing place n (Aut) aire f de croisement

passion ['pæʃən] n passion f; **passionate** adj passionné(e); **passion fruit** n fruit m de la passion

passive ['pæsɪv] adj (also: Ling) passif(-ive)

passport ['pɑːspɔːt] n passeport m; **passport control** n contrôle m des passeports; **passport office** n bureau m de délivrance des passeports

password ['pɑːswɜːd] n mot m de passe

past [pɑːst] prep (in front of) devant; (further than) au-delà de, plus loin que; après; (later than) après ⊳ adv: **to run ~** passer en courant ⊳ adj passé(e); (president etc) ancien(ne) ⊳ n passé m; **he's ~ forty** il a dépassé la quarantaine, il a plus de or passé quarante ans; **ten/quarter ~ eight** (BRIT) huit heures dix/un or et quart; **for the ~ few/3 days** depuis quelques jours; ces derniers/3 derniers jours

pasta ['pæstə] n pâtes fpl

paste [peɪst] n pâte f; (Culin: meat) pâté m (à tartiner); (: tomato) purée f, concentré m; (glue) colle f (de pâte) ⊳ vt coller

pastel ['pæstl] adj pastel inv ⊳ n (Art: pencil) (crayon m) pastel m; (: drawing) (dessin m au) pastel; (colour) ton m pastel inv

pasteurized ['pæstəraɪzd] adj pasteurisé(e)

pastime ['pɑːstaɪm] n passe-temps m inv, distraction f

pastor ['pɑːstəᵊ] n pasteur m

pastry ['peɪstrɪ] n pâte f; (cake) pâtisserie f

pasture ['pɑːstʃəᵊ] n pâturage m

pasty¹ ['pæstɪ] n petit pâté (en croûte)

pasty² [peɪstɪ] adj (complexion) terreux(-euse)

pat [pæt] vt donner une petite tape à; (dog) caresser

patch [pætʃ] n (of material) pièce f; (eye patch) cache m; (spot) tache f; (of land) parcelle f; (on tyre) rustine f ⊳ vt (clothes) rapiécer; **a bad ~** (BRIT) une période difficile; **patchy** adj inégal(e); (incomplete) fragmentaire

pâté ['pæteɪ] n pâté m, terrine f

patent [peɪtnt, us 'pætnt] n brevet m (d'invention) ⊳ vt faire breveter ⊳ adj patent(e), manifeste

paternal [pəˈtɜːnl] adj paternel(le)

paternity leave [pəˈtɜːnɪtɪ-] n congé m de paternité

path [pɑːθ] n chemin m, sentier m; (in garden) allée f; (of missile) trajectoire f

pathetic [pəˈθetɪk] adj (pitiful) pitoyable; (very bad) lamentable, minable

pathway ['pɑːθweɪ] n chemin m, sentier m; (in garden) allée f

patience ['peɪʃns] n patience f; (BRIT Cards) réussite f

patient ['peɪʃnt] n malade m/f; (of dentist etc) patient(e) ⊳ adj patient(e)

patio ['pætɪəʊ] n patio m

patriotic [pætrɪˈɒtɪk] adj patriotique; (person) patriote

patrol [pəˈtrəʊl] n patrouille f ⊳ vt patrouiller dans; **patrol car** n voiture f de police

patron ['peɪtrən] n (in shop) client(e); (of charity) patron(ne); **~ of the arts** mécène m

patronizing ['pætrənaɪzɪŋ] adj condescendant(e)

P

pattern ['pætən] n (Sewing) patron m; (design) motif m; **patterned** adj à motifs

pause [pɔːz] n pause f, arrêt m ▷ vi faire une pause, s'arrêter

pave [peɪv] vt paver, daller; **to ~ the way for** ouvrir la voie à

pavement ['peɪvmənt] n (BRIT) trottoir m; (us) chaussée f

pavilion [pə'vɪlɪən] n pavillon m; (Sport) stand m

paving ['peɪvɪŋ] n (material) pavé m

paw [pɔː] n patte f

pawn [pɔːn] n (Chess, also fig) pion m ▷ vt mettre en gage; **pawnbroker** n prêteur m sur gages

pay [peɪ] (pt, pp **paid**) n salaire m; (of manual workers) paie f ▷ vt payer ▷ vi payer; (be profitable) être rentable; **can I ~ by credit card?** est-ce que je peux payer par carte de crédit?; **to ~ attention (to)** prêter attention (à); **to ~ sb a visit** rendre visite à qn; **to ~ one's respects to sb** présenter ses respects à qn; **pay back** vt rembourser; **pay for** vt fus payer; **pay in** vt verser; **pay off** vt (debts) régler, acquitter; (person) rembourser ▷ vi (scheme, decision) se révéler payant(e); **pay out** vt (money) payer, sortir de sa poche; **pay up** vt (amount) payer; **payable** adj payable; **to make a cheque payable to sb** établir un chèque à l'ordre de qn; **pay-as-you-go** adj (mobile phone) à carte prépayée; **payday** n jour m de paie; **pay envelope** n (us) paie f; **payment** n paiement m; (of bill) règlement m; (of deposit, cheque) versement m; **monthly payment** mensualité f; **payout** n (from insurance) dédommagement m; (in competition) prix m; **pay packet** n (BRIT) paie f; **pay phone** n cabine f téléphonique, téléphone public; **pay raise** n (us) = **pay rise**; **pay rise** n (BRIT) augmentation f (de salaire); **payroll** n registre m du personnel;

pay slip n (BRIT) bulletin m de paie, feuille f de paie; **pay television** n chaînes fpl payantes; **paywall** n (Comput) mur m (payant)

PC n abbr = **personal computer**; (BRIT) = **police constable** ▷ adj abbr = **politically correct**

p.c. abbr = **per cent**

pcm n abbr (= per calendar month) par mois

PDA n abbr (= personal digital assistant) agenda m électronique

PE n abbr (= physical education) EPS f

pea [piː] n (petit) pois

peace [piːs] n paix f; (calm) calme m, tranquillité f; **peaceful** adj paisible, calme

peach [piːtʃ] n pêche f

peacock ['piːkɔk] n paon m

peak [piːk] n (mountain) pic m, cime f; (of cap) visière f; (fig: highest level) maximum m; (: of career, fame) apogée m; **peak hours** npl heures fpl d'affluence or de pointe

peanut ['piːnʌt] n arachide f, cacahuète f; **peanut butter** n beurre m de cacahuète

pear [pɛər] n poire f

pearl [pəːl] n perle f

peasant ['pɛznt] n paysan(ne)

peat [piːt] n tourbe f

pebble ['pɛbl] n galet m, caillou m

peck [pɛk] vt (also: **~ at**) donner un coup de bec à; (food) picorer ▷ n coup m de bec; (kiss) bécot m; **peckish** adj (BRIT inf): **I feel peckish** je mangerais bien quelque chose, j'ai la dent

peculiar [pɪ'kjuːlɪər] adj (odd) étrange, bizarre, curieux(-euse); (particular) particulier(-ière); **~ to** particulier à

pedal ['pɛdl] n pédale f ▷ vi pédaler

pedestal ['pɛdəstl] n piédestal m

pedestrian [pɪ'dɛstrɪən] n piéton m; **pedestrian crossing** n (BRIT) passage clouté; **pedestrianized** adj: **a pedestrianized street** une rue piétonne; **pedestrian precinct,**

(US) **pedestrian zone** n (BRIT) zone piétonne

pedigree ['pedigri:] n ascendance f; (of animal) pedigree m ▷ cpd (animal) de race

pedophile ['pi:dəʊfaɪl] (US) n = paedophile

pee [pi:] vi (inf) faire pipi, pisser

peek [pi:k] vi jeter un coup d'œil (furtif)

peel [pi:l] n pelure f, épluchure f; (of orange, lemon) écorce f ▷ vt peler, éplucher ▷ vi (paint etc) s'écailler; (wallpaper) se décoller; (skin) peler

peep [pi:p] n (look) coup d'œil furtif; (sound) pépiement m ▷ vi jeter un coup d'œil furtif

peer [pɪə] vi: **to ~ at** regarder attentivement, scruter ▷ n (noble) pair m; (equal) pair, égal(e)

peg [peg] n (for coat etc) patère f; (BRIT: also: **clothes ~**) pince f à linge

pelican ['pelɪkən] n pélican m; **pelican crossing** n (BRIT Aut) feu m à commande manuelle

pelt [pelt] vt: **to ~ sb (with)** bombarder qn (de) ▷ vi (rain) tomber à seaux; (inf: run) courir à toutes jambes ▷ n peau f

pelvis ['pelvɪs] n bassin m

pen [pen] n (for writing) stylo m; (for sheep) parc m

penalty ['penltɪ] n pénalité f, sanction f; (fine) amende f; (Sport) pénalisation f; (Football) penalty m; (Rugby) pénalité f

pence [pens] npl of **penny**

pencil ['pensl] n crayon m; **pencil in** vt noter provisoirement; **pencil case** n trousse f (d'écolier); **pencil sharpener** n taille-crayon(s) m inv

pendant ['pendnt] n pendentif m

pending ['pendɪŋ] prep en attendant ▷ adj en suspens

penetrate ['penɪtreɪt] vt pénétrer dans; (enemy territory) entrer en

pen friend n (BRIT) correspondant(e)

penguin ['pengwɪn] n pingouin m

penicillin [penɪ'sɪlɪn] n pénicilline f

peninsula [pə'nɪnsjulə] n péninsule f

penis ['pi:nɪs] n pénis m, verge f

penitentiary [penɪ'tenʃərɪ] n (US) prison f

penknife ['pennaɪf] n canif m

penniless ['penɪlɪs] adj sans le sou

penny (pl **pennies** or **pence**) ['penɪ, 'peniz, pens] n (BRIT) penny m; (US) cent m

pen pal n correspondant(e)

pension ['penʃən] n (from company) retraite f; **pensioner** n (BRIT) retraité(e)

pentagon ['pentəgən] n: **the P~** (US Pol) le Pentagone

penthouse ['penthaʊs] n appartement m (de luxe) en attique

penultimate [pɪ'nʌltɪmət] adj pénultième, avant-dernier(-ière)

people ['pi:pl] npl gens mpl; personnes fpl; (inhabitants) population f; (Pol) peuple m ▷ n (nation, race) peuple m; **several ~ came** plusieurs personnes sont venues; **~ say that ...** on dit or les gens disent que ...

pepper ['pepə'] n poivre m; (vegetable) poivron m ▷ vt (Culin) poivrer; **peppermint** n (sweet) pastille f de menthe

per [pə:'] prep par; **~ hour** (miles etc) à l'heure; (fee) (de) l'heure; **~ kilo** etc le kilo etc; **~ day/person** par jour/personne; **~ annum** par an

perceive [pə'si:v] vt percevoir; (notice) remarquer, s'apercevoir de

per cent adv pour cent

percentage [pə'sentɪdʒ] n pourcentage m

perception [pə'sepʃən] n perception f; (insight) sensibilité f

perch [pə:tʃ] n (fish) perche f; (for bird) perchoir m ▷ vi (se) percher

percussion [pə'kʌʃən] n percussion f

perennial [pə'renɪəl] n (Bot) plante f vivace f, plante pluriannuelle

P

perfect ['pə:fɪkt] adj parfait(e)
▷ n (also: ~ **tense**) parfait m ▷ vt
[pə'fɛkt] (technique, skill, work of art)
parfaire; (method, plan) mettre au
point; **perfection** f; **perfectly** ['pə:fɪktlɪ]
adv parfaitement

perform [pə'fɔ:m] vt (carry out)
exécuter; (concert etc) jouer,
donner ▷ vi (actor, musician) jouer;
performance n représentation
f, spectacle m; (of an artist)
interprétation f; (Sport: of car,
engine) performance f; (of company,
economy) résultats mpl; **performer** n
artiste m/f

perfume ['pə:fju:m] n parfum m

perhaps [pə'hæps] adv peut-être

perimeter [pə'rɪmɪtə'] n
périmètre m

period ['pɪərɪəd] n période f; (Hist)
époque f; (Scol) cours m; (full stop)
point m; (Med) règles fpl ▷ adj
(costume, furniture) d'époque;
periodical [pɪərɪ'ɔdɪkl] n périodique
m; **periodically** adv périodiquement

perish ['pɛrɪʃ] vi périr, mourir; (decay)
se détériorer

perjury ['pə:dʒərɪ] n (Law: in court)
faux témoignage; (breach of oath)
parjure m

perk [pə:k] n (inf) avantage m,
à-côté m

perm [pə:m] n (for hair) permanente f

permanent ['pə:mənənt] adj
permanent(e); **permanently**
adv de façon permanente; (move
abroad) définitivement; (open, closed)
en permanence; (tired, unhappy)
constamment

permission [pə'mɪʃən] n permission
f, autorisation f

permit [pə'mɪt] n permis m

perplex [pə'plɛks] vt (person) rendre
perplexe

persecute ['pə:sɪkju:t] vt persécuter

persecution [pə:sɪ'kju:ʃən] n
persécution f

persevere [pə:sɪ'vɪə'] vi persévérer

Persian ['pə:ʃən] adj persan(e); **the ~
Gulf** le golfe Persique

persist [pə'sɪst] vi: **to ~ (in doing)**
persister (à faire), s'obstiner (à faire);
persistent adj persistant(e), tenace

person ['pə:sn] n personne f; **in
~** en personne; **personal** adj
personnel(le); **personal assistant** n
secrétaire personnel(le); **personal
computer** n ordinateur individuel,
PC m; **personality** [pə:sə'nælɪtɪ]
n personnalité f; **personally** adv
personnellement; **to take sth
personally** se sentir visé(e) par
qch; **personal organizer** n agenda
(personnel); (electronic) agenda
électronique; **personal stereo** n
Walkman® m, baladeur m

personnel [pə:sə'nel] n personnel m

perspective [pə'spɛktɪv] n
perspective f

perspiration [pə:spɪ'reɪʃən] n
transpiration f

persuade [pə'sweɪd] vt: **to ~ sb to
do sth** persuader qn de faire qch,
amener or décider qn à faire qch

persuasion [pə'sweɪʒən] n
persuasion f; (creed) conviction f

persuasive [pə'sweɪsɪv] adj
persuasif(-ive)

perverse [pə'və:s] adj pervers(e);
(contrary) entêté(e), contrariant(e)

pervert n ['pə:və:t] pervers(e) ▷ vt
[pə'və:t] pervertir; (words) déformer

pessimism ['pɛsɪmɪzəm] n
pessimisme m

pessimist ['pɛsɪmɪst] n pessimiste
m/f; **pessimistic** [pɛsɪ'mɪstɪk] adj
pessimiste

pest [pɛst] n animal m (or insecte m)
nuisible; (fig) fléau m

pester ['pɛstə'] vt importuner,
harceler

pesticide ['pɛstɪsaɪd] n pesticide m

pet [pɛt] n animal familier ▷ cpd
(favourite) favori(e) ▷ vt (stroke)
caresser, câliner; **teacher's ~**

chouchou *m* du professeur; **~ hate**
bête noire

petal ['petl] *n* pétale *m*

petite [pə'tiːt] *adj* menu(e)

petition [pə'tɪʃən] *n* pétition *f*

petrified ['petrɪfaɪd] *adj* (*fig*) mort(e)
de peur

petrol ['petrəl] *n* (BRIT) essence *f*;
I've run out of ~ je suis en panne
d'essence

> Be careful not to translate *petrol*
> by the French word *pétrole*.

petroleum [pə'trəʊliəm] *n* pétrole *m*

petrol: petrol pump *n* (BRIT: *in car,
at garage*) pompe *f* à essence; **petrol
station** *n* (BRIT) station-service *f*;
petrol tank *n* (BRIT) réservoir *m*
d'essence

petticoat ['petɪkəʊt] *n* jupon *m*

petty ['petɪ] *adj* (*mean*) mesquin(e);
(*unimportant*) insignifiant(e), sans
importance

pew [pjuː] *n* banc *m* (d'église)

pewter ['pjuːtə'] *n* étain *m*

phantom ['fæntəm] *n* fantôme *m*

pharmacist ['faːməsɪst] *n*
pharmacien(ne)

pharmacy ['faːməsɪ] *n* pharmacie *f*

phase [feɪz] *n* phase *f*, période
f. **phase in** *vt* introduire
progressivement; **phase out** *vt*
supprimer progressivement

Ph.D. *abbr* = **Doctor of Philosophy**

pheasant ['feznt] *n* faisan *m*

phenomena [fə'nɒmɪnə] *npl of*
phenomenon

phenomenal [fɪ'nɒmɪnl] *adj*
phénoménal(e)

phenomenon (*pl* **phenomena**)
[fə'nɒmɪnən, -nə] *n* phénomène *m*

Philippines ['fɪlɪpiːnz] *npl* (*also:*
Philippine Islands): **the ~** les
Philippines *fpl*

philosopher [fɪ'lɒsəfə'] *n*
philosophe *m*

philosophical [fɪlə'sɒfɪkl] *adj*
philosophique

philosophy [fɪ'lɒsəfɪ] *n* philosophie *f*

phlegm [flem] *n* flegme *m*

phobia ['fəʊbjə] *n* phobie *f*

phone [fəʊn] *n* téléphone *m* ▷ *vt*
téléphoner à ▷ *vi* téléphoner; **to
be on the ~** avoir le téléphone; (*be
calling*) être au téléphone; **phone
back** *vt, vi* rappeler; **phone up**
vt téléphoner à ▷ *vi* téléphoner;
phone book *n* annuaire *m*; **phone
box**, (US) **phone booth** *n* cabine *f*
téléphonique; **phone call** *n* coup *m*
de fil *or* de téléphone; **phonecard** *n*
télécarte *f*; **phone number** *n* numéro
m de téléphone

phonetics [fə'netɪks] *n* phonétique *f*

phoney ['fəʊnɪ] *adj* faux (fausse),
factice; (*person*) pas franc (franche)

photo ['fəʊtəʊ] *n* photo *f*; **photo
album** *n* album *m* de photos;
photocopier *n* copieur *m*;
photocopy *n* photocopie *f* ▷ *vt*
photocopier

photograph ['fəʊtəɡræf] *n*
photographie *f* ▷ *vt* photographier;
photographer [fə'tɒɡrəfə'] *n*
photographe *m/f*; **photography**
[fə'tɒɡrəfɪ] *n* photographie *f*

phrase [freɪz] *n* expression *f*; (*Ling*)
locution *f* ▷ *vt* exprimer; **phrase
book** *n* recueil *m* d'expressions (pour
touristes)

physical ['fɪzɪkl] *adj* physique;
physical education *n* éducation
f physique; **physically** *adv*
physiquement

physician [fɪ'zɪʃən] *n* médecin *m*

physicist ['fɪzɪsɪst] *n* physicien(ne)

physics ['fɪzɪks] *n* physique *f*

physiotherapist [fɪzɪəʊ'θerəpɪst] *n*
kinésithérapeute *m/f*

physiotherapy [fɪzɪəʊ'θerəpɪ] *n*
kinésithérapie *f*

physique [fɪ'ziːk] *n* (*appearance*)
physique *m*; (*health etc*) constitution *f*

pianist ['pɪənɪst] *n* pianiste *m/f*

piano [pɪ'ænəʊ] *n* piano *m*

pick [pɪk] *n* (*tool: also:* **~-axe**) pic *m*,
pioche *f* ▷ *vt* choisir; (*gather*) cueillir;

(*remove*) prendre; (*lock*) forcer; **take your ~** faites votre choix; **the ~ of** le meilleur(e) de; **to ~ one's nose** se mettre les doigts dans le nez; **to ~ one's teeth** se curer les dents; **to ~ a quarrel with sb** chercher noise à qn; **pick on** vt fus harceler; **pick out** vt choisir; (*distinguish*) distinguer; **pick up** vi (*improve*) remonter, s'améliorer ▸ vt ramasser; (*collect*) passer prendre; (*Aut: give lift to*) prendre; (*learn*) apprendre; (*Radio*) capter; **to ~ up speed** prendre de la vitesse; **to ~ o.s. up** se relever

pickle ['pɪkl] n (*also*: **~s**) (*as condiment*) pickles mpl ▸ vt conserver dans du vinaigre ou dans de la saumure; **in a ~** (*fig*) dans le pétrin

pickpocket ['pɪkpɒkɪt] n pickpocket m

pick-up ['pɪkʌp] n (*also*: **~ truck**) pick-up m inv

picnic ['pɪknɪk] n pique-nique m ▸ vi pique-niquer; **picnic area** n aire f de pique-nique

picture ['pɪktʃə'] n (*also TV*) image f; (*painting*) peinture f, tableau m; (*photograph*) photo(graphie) f; (*drawing*) dessin m; (*film*) film m; (*fig: description*) description f ▸ vt (*imagine*) se représenter; **pictures** npl; **the ~s** (*BRIT*) le cinéma; **to take a ~ of sb/sth** prendre qn/qch en photo; **would you take a ~ of us, please?** pourriez-vous nous prendre en photo, s'il vous plaît?; **picture frame** n cadre m; **picture messaging** n picture messaging m, messagerie f d'images

picturesque [pɪktʃə'rɛsk] adj pittoresque

pie [paɪ] n tourte f; (*of fruit*) tarte f; (*of meat*) pâté m en croûte

piece [piːs] n morceau m; (*item*): **a ~ of furniture/advice** un meuble/conseil ▸ vt: **to ~ together** rassembler; **to take to ~s** démonter

pie chart n graphique m à secteurs, camembert m

pier [pɪə'] n jetée f

pierce [pɪəs] vt percer, transpercer; **pierced** adj (*ears*) percé(e)

pig [pɪg] n cochon m, porc m; (*pej: unkind person*) mufle m; (: *greedy person*) goinfre m

pigeon ['pɪdʒən] n pigeon m

piggy bank ['pɪgɪ-] n tirelire f

pigsty ['pɪgstaɪ] n porcherie f

pigtail ['pɪgteɪl] n natte f, tresse f

pike [paɪk] n (*fish*) brochet m

pilchard ['pɪltʃəd] n pilchard m (*sorte de sardine*)

pile [paɪl] n (*pillar, of books*) pile f; (*heap*) tas m; (*of carpet*) épaisseur f; **pile up** vi (*accumulate*) s'entasser, s'accumuler ▸ vt (*put in heap*) empiler, entasser; (*accumulate*) accumuler; **piles** npl hémorroïdes fpl; **pile-up** n (*Aut*) télescopage m, collision f en série

pilgrim ['pɪlgrɪm] n pèlerin m; *voir article* **"Pilgrim Fathers"**

● PILGRIM FATHERS

● Les *Pilgrim Fathers* ("Pères pèlerins") sont un groupe de puritains qui quittèrent l'Angleterre en 1620 pour fuir les persécutions religieuses. Ayant traversé l'Atlantique à bord du "Mayflower", ils fondèrent New Plymouth en Nouvelle-Angleterre, dans ce qui est aujourd'hui le Massachusetts. Ces Pères pèlerins sont considérés comme les fondateurs des États-Unis, et l'on commémore chaque année, le jour de "Thanksgiving", la réussite de leur première récolte.

pilgrimage ['pɪlgrɪmɪdʒ] n pèlerinage m

pill [pɪl] n pilule f; **the ~** la pilule

pillar ['pɪlə'] n pilier m

pillow ['pɪləʊ] n oreiller m; **pillowcase, pillowslip** n taie f d'oreiller

pilot ['paɪlət] n pilote m ▷ cpd (scheme etc) pilote, expérimental(e) ▷ vt piloter; **pilot light** n veilleuse f

pimple ['pɪmpl] n bouton m

PIN n abbr (= personal identification number) code m confidentiel

pin [pɪn] n épingle f; (Tech) cheville f ▷ vt épingler; **~s and needles** fourmis fpl; **to ~ sb down** (fig) coincer qn; **to ~ sth on sb** (fig) mettre qch sur le dos de qn

pinafore ['pɪnəfɔːʳ] n tablier m

pinch [pɪntʃ] n pincement m; (of salt etc) pincée f ▷ vt pincer; (inf: steal) piquer, chiper ▷ vi (shoe) serrer; **at a ~** à la rigueur

pine [paɪn] n (also: **~ tree**) pin m ▷ vi: **to ~ for** aspirer à, désirer ardemment

pineapple ['paɪnæpl] n ananas m

ping [pɪŋ] n (noise) tintement m; **ping-pong®** n ping-pong m

pink [pɪŋk] adj rose ▷ n (colour) rose m

pinpoint ['pɪnpɔɪnt] vt indiquer (avec précision)

pint [paɪnt] n pinte f (Brit = 0,57 l; US = 0,47 l); (Brit: drunk) demi m, ≈ pot m

pioneer [paɪə'nɪəʳ] n pionnier m

pious ['paɪəs] adj pieux(-euse)

pip [pɪp] n (seed) pépin m; **pips** npl; **the ~s** (Brit: time signal on radio) le top

pipe [paɪp] n (for water etc) tuyau m, conduite f; (for smoking) pipe f ▷ vt amener par tuyau; **pipeline** n (for gas) gazoduc m, pipeline m; (for oil) oléoduc m, pipeline; **piper** n (flautist) joueur(-euse) de pipeau; (of bagpipes) joueur(-euse) de cornemuse

pirate ['paɪərət] n pirate m ▷ vt (CD, video, book) pirater

Pisces ['paɪsiːz] n les Poissons mpl

piss [pɪs] vi (inf!) pisser (!); **pissed** adj (inf!: BRIT: drunk) bourré(e); (: US: angry) furieux(-euse)

pistol ['pɪstl] n pistolet m

piston ['pɪstən] n piston m

pit [pɪt] n trou m, fosse f; (also: **coal ~**) puits m de mine; (also: **orchestra ~**) fosse d'orchestre; (US: fruit stone)

noyau m ▷ vt: **to ~ o.s.** or **one's wits against** se mesurer à

pitch [pɪtʃ] n (BRIT Sport) terrain m; (Mus) ton m; (fig: degree) degré m; (tar) poix f ▷ vt (throw) lancer; (tent) dresser ▷ vi (fall): **to ~ into/off** tomber dans/de; **pitch-black** adj noir(e) comme poix

pitfall ['pɪtfɔːl] n piège m

pith [pɪθ] n (of orange etc) intérieur m de l'écorce

pitiful ['pɪtɪful] adj (touching) pitoyable; (contemptible) lamentable

pity ['pɪtɪ] n pitié f ▷ vt plaindre; **what a ~!** quel dommage!

pizza ['piːtsə] n pizza f

placard ['plækɑːd] n affiche f; (in march) pancarte f

place [pleɪs] n endroit m, lieu m; (proper position, job, rank, seat) place f; (home): **at/to his ~** chez lui ▷ vt (position) placer, mettre; (identify) situer; reconnaître; **to take ~** avoir lieu; **to change ~s with sb** changer de place avec qn; **out of ~** (not suitable) déplacé(e), inopportun(e); **in the first ~** d'abord, en premier; **place mat** n set m de table; (in linen studies) stage m

placid ['plæsɪd] adj placide

plague [pleɪg] n (Med) peste f ▷ vt (fig) tourmenter

plaice [pleɪs] n (pl inv) carrelet m

plain [pleɪn] adj (in one colour) uni(e); (clear) clair(e), évident(e); (simple) simple; (not handsome) quelconque, ordinaire ▷ adv franchement, carrément ▷ n plaine f; **plain chocolate** n chocolat m à croquer; **plainly** adv clairement; (frankly) carrément, sans détours

plaintiff ['pleɪntɪf] n plaignant(e)

plait [plæt] n tresse f, natte f

plan [plæn] n plan m; (scheme) projet m ▷ vt (think in advance) projeter; (prepare) organiser ▷ vi faire des projets; **to ~ to do** projeter de faire

plane [pleɪn] n (Aviat) avion m; (also: ~ **tree**) platane m; (tool) rabot m; (Art, Math etc) plan m; (fig) niveau m, plan ▷ vt (with tool) raboter

planet ['plænɪt] n planète f

plank [plæŋk] n planche f

planning ['plænɪŋ] n planification f; **family** ~ planning familial

plant [plɑːnt] n plante f; (machinery) matériel m; (factory) usine f ▷ vt planter; (bomb) déposer, poser; (microphone, evidence) cacher

plantation [plæn'teɪʃən] n plantation f

plaque [plæk] n plaque f

plaster ['plɑːstəʳ] n plâtre m; (also: ~ **of Paris**) plâtre à mouler; (BRIT: also: **sticking** ~) pansement adhésif ▷ vt plâtrer; (cover): **to** ~ **with** couvrir de; **plaster cast** n (Med) plâtre m; (model, statue) moule m

plastic ['plæstɪk] n plastique m ▷ adj (made of plastic) en plastique; **plastic bag** n sac m en plastique; **plastic surgery** n chirurgie f esthétique

plate [pleɪt] n (dish) assiette f; (sheet of metal, on door, Phot) plaque f; (in book) gravure f; (dental) dentier m

plateau (pl **plateaus** or **plateaux**) ['plætəu, -z] n plateau m

platform ['plætfɔːm] n (at meeting) tribune f; (stage) estrade f; (Rail) quai m; (Pol) plateforme f

platinum ['plætɪnəm] n platine m

platoon [plə'tuːn] n peloton m

platter ['plætəʳ] n plat m

plausible ['plɔːzɪbl] adj plausible; (person) convaincant(e)

play [pleɪ] n jeu m; (Theat) pièce f de théâtre ▷ vt (game) jouer à; (team, opponent) jouer contre; (instrument) jouer de; (part, piece of music, note) jouer; (CD etc) passer ▷ vi jouer; **to** ~ **safe** ne prendre aucun risque; **play back** vt repasser, réécouter; **play up** vi (cause trouble) faire des siennes; **player** n joueur(-euse); (Mus) musicien(ne); **playful** adj enjoué(e);

playground n cour f de récréation; (in park) aire f de jeux; **playgroup** n garderie f; **playing card** n carte f à jouer; **playing field** n terrain m de sport; **playschool** n = **playgroup**; **playtime** n (Scol) récréation f; **playwright** n dramaturge m

plc abbr (BRIT: = public limited company) = SARL f

plea [pliː] n (request) appel m; (Law) défense f

plead [pliːd] vt plaider; (give as excuse) invoquer ▷ vi (Law) plaider; (beg): **to** ~ **with sb (for sth)** implorer qn (d'accorder qch); **to** ~ **guilty/not guilty** plaider coupable/non coupable

pleasant ['plɛznt] adj agréable

please [pliːz] excl s'il te (or vous) plaît ▷ vt plaire à ▷ vi (think fit): **do as you** ~ faites comme il vous plaira; ~ **yourself!** (inf) faites comme vous voulez!; **pleased** adj: **pleased (with)** content(e) de); **pleased to meet you** enchanté (de faire votre connaissance)

pleasure ['plɛʒəʳ] n plaisir m; **"it's a** ~**"** je vous en prie"

pleat [pliːt] n pli m

pledge [plɛdʒ] n (promise) promesse f ▷ vt promettre

plentiful ['plɛntɪful] adj abondant(e), copieux(-euse)

plenty ['plɛntɪ] n: ~ **of** beaucoup de; (sufficient) (bien) assez de

pliers ['plaɪəz] npl pinces fpl

plight [plaɪt] n situation f critique

plod [plɒd] vi avancer péniblement; (fig) peiner

plonk [plɒŋk] (inf) n (BRIT: wine) pinard m, piquette f ▷ vt: **to** ~ **sth down** poser brusquement qch

plot [plɒt] n complot m, conspiration f; (of story, play) intrigue f; (of land) lot m de terrain, lopin m ▷ vt (mark out) tracer point par point; (Naut) pointer; (make graph of) faire le graphique de; (conspire) comploter ▷ vi comploter

plough, (us) **plow** [plaʊ] n charrue f ▷ vt (earth) labourer; **to ~ money into** investir dans

ploy [plɔɪ] n stratagème m

pls abbr (= please) SVP m

pluck [plʌk] vt (fruit) cueillir; (musical instrument) pincer; (bird) plumer; **to ~ one's eyebrows** s'épiler les sourcils; **to ~ up courage** prendre son courage à deux mains

plug [plʌg] n (stopper) bouchon m, bonde f; (Elec) prise f de courant; (Aut: also: **spark(ing) ~**) bougie f ▷ vt (hole) boucher; (inf: advertise) faire du battage pour, matraquer; **plug in** vt (Elec) brancher; **plughole** n (BRIT) trou m (d'écoulement)

plum [plʌm] n (fruit) prune f

plumber ['plʌmə'] n plombier m

plumbing ['plʌmɪŋ] n (trade) plomberie f; (piping) tuyauterie f

plummet ['plʌmɪt] vi (person, object) plonger; (sales, prices) dégringoler

plump [plʌmp] adj rondelet(te), dodu(e), bien en chair; **plump for** vt fus (inf: choose) se décider pour

plunge [plʌndʒ] n plongeon m; (fig) chute f ▷ vt plonger ▷ vi (fall) tomber, dégringoler; (dive) plonger; **to take the ~** se jeter à l'eau

pluperfect [pluː'pɜːfɪkt] n (Ling) plus-que-parfait m

plural ['plʊərl] adj pluriel(le) ▷ n pluriel m

plus [plʌs] n (also: **~ sign**) signe m plus; (advantage) atout m ▷ prep plus; **ten/twenty ~** plus de dix/vingt

ply [plaɪ] n (of wool) fil m (a trade) exercer ▷ vi (ship) faire la navette; **to ~ sb with drink** donner continuellement à boire à qn; **plywood** n contreplaqué m

P.M. n abbr (BRIT) = **prime minister**

p.m. adv abbr (= post meridiem) de l'après-midi

PMS n abbr (= premenstrual syndrome) syndrome prémenstruel

PMT n abbr (= premenstrual tension) syndrome prémenstruel

pneumatic drill [njuː'mætɪk-] n marteau-piqueur m

pneumonia [njuː'məʊnɪə] n pneumonie f

poach [pəʊtʃ] vt (cook) pocher; (steal) pêcher (or chasser) sans permis ▷ vi braconner; **poached** adj (egg) poché(e)

P.O. Box n abbr = **post office box**

pocket ['pɔkɪt] n poche f ▷ vt empocher; **to be (£5) out of ~** (BRIT) en être de sa poche (pour 5 livres); **pocketbook** n (us: wallet) portefeuille m; **pocket money** n argent m de poche

pod [pɔd] n cosse f

podcast ['pɔdkɑːst] n podcast m ▷ vi podcaster

podiatrist [pɔ'diːətrɪst] n (us) pédicure m/f

poem ['pəʊɪm] n poème m

poet ['pəʊɪt] n poète m; **poetic** [pəʊ'ɛtɪk] adj poétique; **poetry** n poésie f

poignant ['pɔɪnjənt] adj poignant(e)

point [pɔɪnt] n point m; (tip) pointe f; (in time) moment m; (in space) endroit m; (subject, idea) point m; (purpose) but m; (also: **decimal ~**): **2 ~ 3 (2.3)** 2 virgule 3 (2,3); (BRIT Elec: also: **power ~**) prise f (de courant) ▷ vt (show) montrer; (gun etc) **to ~ sth at** braquer or diriger qch sur ▷ vi: **to ~ at** montrer du doigt; **points** npl (Rail) aiguillage m; **to make a ~ of doing sth** ne pas manquer de faire qch; **to get/miss the ~** comprendre/ne pas comprendre; **to come to the ~** en venir au fait; **there's no ~ (in doing)** cela ne sert à rien (de faire); **to be on the ~ of doing sth** être sur le point de faire qch; **point out** vt (mention) faire remarquer, souligner; **point-blank** adj (fig) catégorique; (also: **at point-blank range**) à bout portant; **pointed** adj (shape) pointu(e); (*remark*) plein(e) de sous-entendus; **pointer** n (*needle*) aiguille f; (*clue*) indication f; (*advice*) tuyau m; **pointless** adj inutile, vain(e); **point of view** n point de vue

poison ['pɔɪzn] n poison m ▷ vt empoisonner; **poisonous** adj (*snake*) venimeux(-euse); (*substance, plant*) vénéneux(-euse); (*fumes*) toxique

poke [pəʊk] vt (*jab with finger, stick etc*) piquer; pousser du doigt; (*put*): **to ~ sth in(to)** fourrer or enfoncer qch dans; **poke about** vi fureter dans; **poke out** vi (*stick out*) sortir

poker ['pəʊkər] n tisonnier m; (*Cards*) poker m

Poland ['pəʊlænd] n Pologne f

polar ['pəʊlər] adj polaire; **polar bear** n ours blanc

Pole [pəʊl] n Polonais(e)

pole [pəʊl] n (*of wood*) mât m, perche f; (*Elec*) poteau m; (*Geo*) pôle m; **pole bean** n (*us*) haricot m (à rames); **pole vault** n saut m à la perche

police [pə'liːs] npl police f ▷ vt maintenir l'ordre dans; **police car** n voiture f de police; **police constable** n (*BRIT*) agent m de police; **police force** n police f, forces fpl de l'ordre; **policeman** (*irreg*) n agent m de police, policier m; **police officer** n agent m de police; **police station** n commissariat m de police; **policewoman** (*irreg*) n femme-agent f

policy ['pɔlɪsɪ] n politique f; (*also*: **insurance ~**) police f (d'assurance)

polio ['pəʊlɪəʊ] n polio f

Polish ['pəʊlɪʃ] adj polonais(e) ▷ n (*Ling*) polonais m

polish ['pɔlɪʃ] n (*for shoes*) cirage m; (*for floor*) cire f, encaustique f; (*for nails*) vernis m; (*shine*) éclat m, poli m; (*fig: refinement*) raffinement m ▷ vt (*put polish on: shoes, wood*) cirer; (*make shiny*) astiquer, faire briller; **polish off** vt (*food*) liquider; **polished** adj (*fig*) raffiné(e)

polite [pə'laɪt] adj poli(e); **politeness** n politesse f

political [pə'lɪtɪkl] adj politique; **politically** adv politiquement; **politically correct** politiquement correct(e)

politician [pɔlɪ'tɪʃən] n homme/femme politique, politicien(ne)

politics ['pɔlɪtɪks] n politique f

poll [pəʊl] n scrutin m, vote m; (*also*: **opinion ~**) sondage m (d'opinion) ▷ vt (*votes*) obtenir

pollen ['pɔlən] n pollen m

polling station n (*BRIT*) bureau m de vote

pollute [pə'luːt] vt polluer

pollution [pə'luːʃən] n pollution f

polo ['pəʊləʊ] n polo m; **polo-neck** adj à col roulé ▷ n (*sweater*) pull m à col roulé; **polo shirt** n polo m

polyester [pɔlɪ'ɛstər] n polyester m

polystyrene [pɔlɪ'staɪriːn] n polystyrène m

polythene ['pɔlɪθiːn] n (*BRIT*) polyéthylène m; **polythene bag** n sac m en plastique

pomegranate ['pɔmɪgrænɪt] n grenade f

pompous ['pɔmpəs] adj pompeux(-euse)

pond [pɔnd] n étang m; (*stagnant*) mare f

ponder ['pɔndər] vt considérer, peser

pony ['pəʊnɪ] n poney m; **ponytail** n queue f de cheval; **pony trekking** n (*BRIT*) randonnée f équestre or à cheval

poodle ['puːdl] n caniche m

pool [puːl] n (*of rain*) flaque f; (*pond*) mare f; (*artificial*) bassin m; (*also*: **swimming ~**) piscine f; (*sth shared*) fonds commun; (*billiards*) poule f ▷ vt mettre en commun; **pools** npl (*football*) = loto sportif

poor [pʊər] adj pauvre; (*mediocre*) médiocre, faible, mauvais(e) ▷ npl: **the ~ les** pauvres mpl ▷ adv; **poorly** adv (badly) mal, médiocrement ▷ adj souffrant(e), malade

pop [pɒp] n (noise) bruit sec; (Mus) musique f pop; (inf: drink) soda m; (us inf: father) papa m ▷ vt (put) fourrer, mettre (rapidement) ▷ vi éclater; (cork) sauter; **pop in** vi entrer en passant; **pop out** vi sortir; **popcorn** n pop-corn m

pope [pəup] n pape m

poplar ['pɒplə'] n peuplier m

popper ['pɒpə'] n (BRIT) bouton-pression m

poppy ['pɒpɪ] n (wild) coquelicot m; (cultivated) pavot m

Popsicle® ['pɒpsɪkl] n (us) esquimau m (glace)

pop star n pop star f

popular ['pɒpjulə'] adj populaire; (fashionable) à la mode; **popularity** [pɒpju'lærɪtɪ] n popularité f

population [pɒpju'leɪʃən] n population f

pop-up adj (Comput: menu, window) pop up inv ▷ n pop up m inv, fenêtre f pop up

porcelain ['pɔ:slɪn] n porcelaine f

porch [pɔ:tʃ] n porche m; (us) véranda f

pore [pɔ:'] n pore m ▷ vi: **to ~ over** s'absorber dans, être plongé(e) dans

pork [pɔ:k] n porc m; **pork chop** n côte f de porc; **pork pie** n pâté m de porc en croûte

porn [pɔ:n] adj (inf) porno ▷ n (inf) porno m; **pornographic** [pɔ:nə'ɡræfɪk] adj pornographique; **pornography** [pɔ:'nɒɡrəfɪ] n pornographie f

porridge ['pɒrɪdʒ] n porridge m

port [pɔ:t] n (harbour) port m; (Naut: left side) bâbord m; (wine) porto m; (Comput) port m, accès m; **~ of call** (port d'escale f

portable ['pɔ:təbl] adj portatif(-ive)

porter ['pɔ:tə'] n (for luggage) porteur m; (doorkeeper) gardien(ne) m/f, portier m

portfolio [pɔ:t'fəuliəu] n portefeuille m; (of artist) portfolio m

portion ['pɔ:ʃən] n portion f, part f

portrait ['pɔ:treɪt] n portrait m

portray [pɔ:'treɪ] vt faire le portrait de; (in writing) dépeindre, représenter; (subj: actor) jouer

Portugal ['pɔ:tjuɡl] n Portugal m

Portuguese [pɔ:tju'ɡi:z] adj portugais(e) ▷ n (pl inv) Portugais(e); (Ling) portugais m

pose [pəuz] n pose f ▷ vi poser; (pretend): **to ~ as** se faire passer pour ▷ vt poser; (problem) créer

posh [pɒʃ] adj (inf) chic inv

position [pə'zɪʃən] n position f; (job, situation) situation f ▷ vt mettre en place or en position

positive ['pɒzɪtɪv] adj positif(-ive); (certain) sûr(e), certain(e); (definite) formel(le), catégorique; **positively** adv (affirmatively, enthusiastically) de façon positive; (inf: really) carrément

possess [pə'zes] vt posséder; **possession** [pə'zeʃən] n possession f; **possessions** npl (belongings) affaires fpl; **possessive** adj possessif(-ive)

possibility [pɒsɪ'bɪlɪtɪ] n possibilité f; (event) éventualité f

possible ['pɒsɪbl] adj possible; **as big as ~** aussi gros que possible; **as big as ~** adv (perhaps) peut-être; **I cannot possibly come** il m'est impossible de venir

post [pəust] n (BRIT: mail) poste f; (: letters, delivery) courrier m; (job, situation) poste m; (pole) poteau m; (Internet) post ▷ vt (Internet) poster; (BRIT: send by post) poster; (appoint): **to ~ to** affecter à; **where can I ~ these cards?** où est-ce que je peux poster ces cartes postales?; **postage** n tarifs mpl d'affranchissement; **postal** adj postal(e); **postal order** n mandat-(poste) m; **postbox** n (BRIT) boîte f aux lettres (publique); **postcard** n carte postale; **postcode** n (BRIT) code postal

poster ['pəʊstə'] n affiche f

postgraduate ['pəʊst'grædjuət] n = étudiant(e) de troisième cycle

postman ['pəʊstmən] (irreg) (BRIT) n facteur m

postmark ['pəʊstmɑːk] n cachet m (de la poste)

post-mortem ['pəʊst'mɔːtəm] n autopsie f

post office n (building) poste f; (organization): **the Post Office** les postes fpl

postpone [pəs'pəʊn] vt remettre (à plus tard), reculer

posture ['pɒstʃə'] n posture f; (fig) attitude f

postwoman ['pəʊst'wʊmən] (irreg) (BRIT) n factrice f

pot [pɒt] n (for cooking) marmite f, casserole f; (teapot) théière f; (for coffee) cafetière f; (for plants, jam) pot m; (inf: marijuana) herbe f ▷ vt (plant) mettre en pot; **to go to ~** (inf) aller à vau-l'eau

potato [pə'teɪtəʊ] (pl **potatoes**) n pomme f de terre; **potato peeler** n épluche-légumes m

potent ['pəʊtnt] adj puissant(e); (drink) fort(e), très alcoolisé(e); (man) viril

potential [pə'tɛnʃl] adj potentiel(le) ▷ n potentiel m

pothole ['pɒthəʊl] n (in road) nid m de poule; (BRIT: underground) gouffre m, caverne f

pot plant n plante f d'appartement

potter ['pɒtə'] n potier m ▷ vi (BRIT): **to ~ around** or **about** bricoler; **pottery** n poterie f

potty ['pɒtɪ] n (child's) pot m

pouch [paʊtʃ] n (Zool) poche f; (for tobacco) blague f; (for money) bourse f

poultry ['pəʊltrɪ] n volaille f

pounce [paʊns] vi: **to ~ (on)** bondir (sur), fondre (sur)

pound [paʊnd] n livre f (weight = 453g, 16 ounces; money = 100 pence); (for dogs, cars) fourrière f ▷ vt (beat)

bourrer de coups, marteler; (crush) piler, pulvériser ▷ vi (heart) battre violemment, taper; **pound sterling** n livre f sterling

pour [pɔː'] vt verser ▷ vi couler à flots; (rain) pleuvoir à verse; **to ~ sb a drink** verser or servir à boire à qn; **pour in** vi (people) affluer, se précipiter; (news, letters) arriver en masse; **pour out** vi (people) sortir en masse ▷ vt vider; (fig) déverser; (serve: a drink) verser; **pouring** adj: **pouring rain** pluie torrentielle

pout [paʊt] vi faire la moue

poverty ['pɒvətɪ] n pauvreté f, misère f

powder ['paʊdə'] n poudre f ▷ vt poudrer; **powdered milk** n lait m en poudre

power ['paʊə'] n (strength, nation) puissance f, force f; (ability, Pol: of party, leader) pouvoir m; (of speech, thought) faculté f; (Elec) courant m; **to be in ~** être au pouvoir; **power cut** n (BRIT) coupure f de courant; **power failure** n panne f de courant; **powerful** adj puissant(e); (performance etc) très fort(e); **powerless** adj impuissant(e); **power point** n (BRIT) prise f de courant; **power station** n centrale f électrique

p.p. abbr (= per procurationem: by proxy) p.p.

PR n abbr = **public relations**

practical ['præktɪkl] adj pratique; **practical joke** n farce f; **practically** adv (almost) pratiquement

practice ['præktɪs] n pratique f; (of profession) exercice m; (at football etc) entraînement m; (business) cabinet m ▷ vt, vi (US) = **practise**; **in ~** (in reality) en pratique; **out of ~** rouillé(e)

practise (US) **practice** ['præktɪs] vt (work at: piano, backhand etc) s'exercer à, travailler; (train for: sport) s'entraîner à; (a sport, religion, method) pratiquer; (profession) exercer ▷ vi s'exercer, travailler; (train) s'entraîner; (lawyer, doctor) exercer; **practising,**

(US) **practicing** adj (Christian etc)
pratiquant(e); (lawyer) en exercice
practitioner [præk'tɪʃənəʳ] n
praticien(ne)
pragmatic [præg'mætɪk] adj
pragmatique
prairie ['prɛərɪ] n savane f
praise [preɪz] n éloge(s) m(pl),
louanges(s) f(pl) ▷ vt louer, faire
l'éloge de
pram [præm] n (BRIT) landau m,
voiture f d'enfant
prank [præŋk] n farce f
prawn [prɔːn] n crevette f (rose);
prawn cocktail n cocktail m de
crevettes
pray [preɪ] vi prier; **prayer** [prɛəʳ]
n prière f
preach [priːtʃ] vi prêcher; **preacher**
n prédicateur m; (US: clergyman)
pasteur m
precarious [prɪ'kɛərɪəs] adj précaire
precaution [prɪ'kɔːʃən] n
précaution f
precede [prɪ'siːd] vt, vi précéder;
precedent ['prɛsɪdənt] n précédent
m; **preceding** [prɪ'siːdɪŋ] adj qui
précède (or précédait)
precinct ['priːsɪŋkt] n (US: district)
circonscription f, arrondissement m;
pedestrian ~ (BRIT) zone piétonnière;
shopping ~ (BRIT) centre commercial
precious ['prɛʃəs] adj précieux(-euse)
precise [prɪ'saɪs] adj précis(e);
precisely adv précisément
precision [prɪ'sɪʒən] n précision f
predator ['prɛdətəʳ] n prédateur m,
rapace m
predecessor ['priːdɪsɛsəʳ] n
prédécesseur m
predicament [prɪ'dɪkəmənt] n
situation difficile
predict [prɪ'dɪkt] vt prédire;
predictable adj prévisible;
prediction [prɪ'dɪkʃən] n prédiction f
predominantly [prɪ'dɔmɪnəntlɪ]
adv en majeure partie; (especially)
surtout

preface ['prɛfəs] n préface f
prefect ['priːfɛkt] n (BRIT: in school)
élève chargé de certaines fonctions de
discipline
prefer [prɪ'fəːʳ] vt préférer;
preferable ['prɛfrəbl] adj préférable;
preferably ['prɛfrəblɪ] adv de
préférence; **preference** ['prɛfrəns]
n préférence f
prefix ['priːfɪks] n préfixe m
pregnancy ['prɛgnənsɪ] n
grossesse f
pregnant ['prɛgnənt] adj enceinte;
(animal) pleine
prehistoric ['priːhɪs'tɔrɪk] adj
préhistorique
prejudice ['prɛdʒudɪs] n préjugé m;
prejudiced adj (person) plein(e) de
préjugés; (in a matter) partial(e)
preliminary [prɪ'lɪmɪnərɪ] adj
préliminaire
prelude ['prɛljuːd] n prélude m
premature ['prɛmətʃuəʳ] adj
prématuré(e)
premier ['prɛmɪəʳ] adj premier(-ière),
principal(e) ▷ n (Pol: Prime Minister)
premier ministre; (Pol: President) chef
m de l'État
premiere ['prɛmɪɛəʳ] n première f
Premier League n première division
premises ['prɛmɪsɪz] npl locaux mpl;
on the ~ sur les lieux; sur place
premium ['priːmɪəm] n prime f; **to
be at a ~** (fig: housing etc) être très
demandé(e), être rarissime
premonition [prɛmə'nɪʃən] n
prémonition f
preoccupied [priː'ɔkjupaɪd] adj
préoccupé(e)
prepaid [priː'peɪd] adj payé(e)
d'avance
preparation [prɛpə'reɪʃən] n
préparation f; **preparations** npl (for
trip, war) préparatifs mpl
preparatory school n (BRIT) école
primaire privée; (US) lycée privé
prepare [prɪ'pɛəʳ] vt préparer ▷ vi: **to
~ for** se préparer à

prepared [prɪ'peəd] *adj:* ~ **for** préparé(e) à; ~ **to** prêt(e) à

preposition [prepə'zɪʃən] *n* préposition *f*

prep school *n* = preparatory school

prerequisite [pri:'rekwɪzɪt] *n* condition *f* préalable

preschool ['pri:'sku:l] *adj* préscolaire; *(child)* d'âge préscolaire

prescribe [prɪ'skraɪb] *vt* prescrire

prescription [prɪ'skrɪpʃən] *n (Med)* ordonnance *f*; *(medicine)* médicament *m* (obtenu sur ordonnance); **could you write me a ~?** pouvez-vous me faire une ordonnance?

presence ['prezns] *n* présence *f*; **in sb's ~** en présence de qn; ~ **of mind** présence d'esprit

present ['preznt] *adj* présent(e); *(current)* présent, actuel(le) ▷ *n* cadeau *m*; *(actuality)* présent *m* ▷ *vt* [prɪ'zent] présenter; *(prize, medal)* remettre; *(give):* **to ~ sb with sth** offrir qch à qn; **at ~** en ce moment; **to give sb a ~** offrir un cadeau à qn; **presentable** [prɪ'zentəbl] *adj* présentable

presentation [prezn'teɪʃən] *n* présentation *f*; *(ceremony)* remise *f* du cadeau *(or* de la médaille *etc)*; **present-day** *adj* contemporain(e), actuel(le); **presenter** [prɪ'zentə*r*] *n (BRIT Radio, TV)* présentateur(-trice); **presently** *adv (soon)* tout à l'heure, bientôt; *(with verb in past)* peu après; *(at present)* en ce moment

preservation [prezə'veɪʃən] *n* préservation *f*, conservation *f*

preservative [prɪ'zə:vətɪv] *n* agent *m* de conservation

preserve [prɪ'zə:v] *vt (keep safe)* préserver, protéger; *(maintain)* conserver, garder; *(food)* mettre en conserve ▷ *n (for game, fish)* réserve *f*; *(often pl: jam)* confiture *f*

preside [prɪ'zaɪd] *vi* présider

president ['prezɪdənt] *n* président(e); **presidential** [prezɪ'denʃl] *adj* présidentiel(le)

press [pres] *n (tool, machine, newspapers)* presse *f*; *(for wine)* pressoir *m* ▷ *vt (push)* appuyer sur; *(squeeze)* presser, serrer; *(clothes: iron)* repasser; *(insist):* **to ~ sth on sb** presser qn d'accepter qch; *(urge, entreat):* **to ~ sb to do** *or* **into doing sth** pousser qn à faire qch ▷ *vi* appuyer; **we are ~ed for time** le temps nous manque; **to ~ for sth** faire pression pour obtenir qch; **press conference** *n* conférence *f* de presse; **pressing** *adj* urgent(e), pressant(e); **press stud** *n (BRIT)* bouton-pression *m*; **press-up** *n (BRIT)* traction *f*

pressure ['preʃə*r*] *n* pression *f*; *(stress)* tension *f*; **to put ~ on sb (to do sth)** faire pression sur qn (pour qu'il fasse qch); **pressure cooker** *n* cocotte-minute® *f*; **pressure group** *n* groupe *m* de pression

prestige [pres'ti:ʒ] *n* prestige *m*

prestigious [pres'tɪdʒəs] *adj* prestigieux(-euse)

presumably [prɪ'zju:məblɪ] *adv* vraisemblablement

presume [prɪ'zju:m] *vt* présumer, supposer

pretence, (*us*) **pretense** [prɪ'tens] *n (claim)* prétention *f*; **under false ~s** sous des prétextes fallacieux

pretend [prɪ'tend] *vt (feign)* feindre, simuler ▷ *vi (feign)* faire semblant

pretense [prɪ'tens] *n (us)* = pretence

pretentious [prɪ'tenʃəs] *adj* prétentieux(-euse)

pretext ['pri:tekst] *n* prétexte *m*

pretty ['prɪtɪ] *adj* joli(e) ▷ *adv* assez

prevail [prɪ'veɪl] *vi (win)* l'emporter, prévaloir; *(be usual)* avoir cours; **prevailing** *adj (widespread)* courant(e), répandu(e); *(wind)* dominant(e)

prevalent ['prevələnt] *adj* répandu(e), courant(e)

prevent [prɪ'vent] *vt:* **to ~ (from doing)** empêcher (de faire); **prevention** [prɪ'venʃən] *n* prévention *f*; **preventive** *adj* préventif(-ive)

preview ['priːvjuː] *n* (of film) avant-première *f*

previous ['priːvɪəs] *adj* (last) précédent(e); (earlier) antérieur(e); **previously** *adv* précédemment, auparavant

prey [preɪ] *n* proie *f* ▷ *vi*: **to ~ on** s'attaquer à; **it was ~ing on his mind** ça le rongeait or minait

price [praɪs] *n* prix *m* ▷ *vt* (goods) fixer le prix de; **priceless** *adj* sans prix, inestimable; **price list** *n* tarif *m*

prick [prɪk] *n* (sting) piqûre *f* ▷ *vt* piquer; **to ~ up one's ears** dresser or tendre l'oreille

prickly ['prɪklɪ] *adj* piquant(e), épineux(-euse); (fig: person) irritable

pride [praɪd] *n* fierté *f*; (pej) orgueil *m* ▷ *vt*: **to ~ o.s. on** se flatter de; s'enorgueillir de

priest [priːst] *n* prêtre *m*

primarily ['praɪmərɪlɪ] *adv* principalement, essentiellement

primary ['praɪmərɪ] *adj* primaire; (first in importance) premier(-ière), primordial(e) ▷ *n* (us: election) (élection *f*) primaire *f*; **primary school** *n* (BRIT) école *f* primaire

prime [praɪm] *adj* primordial(e), fondamental(e); (excellent) excellent(e) ▷ *vt* (fig) mettre au courant ▷ *n*: **in the ~ of life** dans la fleur de l'âge; **Prime Minister** *n* Premier ministre

primitive ['prɪmɪtɪv] *adj* primitif(-ive)

primrose ['prɪmrəuz] *n* primevère *f*

prince [prɪns] *n* prince *m*

princess [prɪn'sɛs] *n* princesse *f*

principal ['prɪnsɪpl] *adj* principal(e) ▷ *n* (head teacher) directeur *m*, principal *m*; **principally** *adv* principalement

principle ['prɪnsɪpl] *n* principe *m*; **in ~** en principe; **on ~** par principe

print [prɪnt] *n* (mark) empreinte *f*; (letters) caractères *mpl*; (fabric)

imprimé *m*; (Art) gravure *f*, estampe *f*; (Phot) épreuve *f* ▷ *vt* imprimer; (publish) publier; (write in capitals) écrire en majuscules; **out of ~** épuisé(e); **print out** *vt* (Comput) imprimer; **printer** *n* (machine) imprimante *f*; (person) imprimeur *m*; **printout** *n* (Comput) sortie *f* imprimante

prior ['praɪə[r]] *adj* antérieur(e), précédent(e); (more important) prioritaire ▷ *adv*: **~ to doing** avant de faire

priority [praɪ'ɔrɪtɪ] *n* priorité *f*; **to have** or **take ~ over sth/sb** avoir la priorité sur qch/qn

prison ['prɪzn] *n* prison *f* ▷ *cpd* pénitentiaire; **prisoner** *n* prisonnier(-ière); **prisoner of war** *n* prisonnier(-ière) de guerre

pristine ['prɪstiːn] *adj* virginal(e)

privacy ['prɪvəsɪ] *n* intimité *f*, solitude *f*

private ['praɪvɪt] *adj* (not public) privé(e); (personal) personnel(le); (house, car, lesson) particulier(-ière); (quiet: place) tranquille ▷ *n* soldat *m* de deuxième classe; **"~"** (on envelope) "personnelle"; (on door) "privé"; **in ~** en privé; **privately** *adv* en privé; (within oneself) intérieurement; **private property** *n* propriété privée; **private school** *n* école privée

privatize ['praɪvɪtaɪz] *vt* privatiser

privilege ['prɪvɪlɪdʒ] *n* privilège *m*

prize [praɪz] *n* prix *m* ▷ *adj* (example, idiot) parfait(e); (bull, novel) primé(e) ▷ *vt* priser, faire grand cas de; **prize-giving** *n* distribution *f* des prix; **prizewinner** *n* gagnant(e)

pro [prəu] *n* (inf: Sport) professionnel(le) ▷ *prep* pro; **pros** *npl*: **the ~s and cons** le pour et le contre

probability [prɔbə'bɪlɪtɪ] *n* probabilité *f*; **in all ~** très probablement

probable ['prɔbəbl] *adj* probable

probably ['prɔbəblɪ] *adv* probablement

probation [prə'beɪʃən] n: **on ~**
(employee) à l'essai; (Law) en liberté
surveillée
probe [prəʊb] n (Med, Space) sonde
f; (enquiry) enquête f, investigation f
▷ vt sonder, explorer
problem ['prɔbləm] n problème m
procedure [prə'siːdʒə'] n (Admin,
Law) procédure f; (method) marche à
suivre, façon f de procéder
proceed [prə'siːd] vi (go forward)
avancer; (act) procéder; (continue):
to ~ (with) continuer, poursuivre;
to ~ to do se mettre à faire;
proceedings npl (measures) mesures
fpl; (Law: against sb) poursuites fpl;
(meeting) réunion f, séance f; (records)
compte rendu; actes mpl; **proceeds**
['prəʊsiːdz] npl produit m, recette f
process ['prəʊsɛs] n processus m;
(method) procédé m ▷ vt traiter
procession [prə'sɛʃən] n défilé
m, cortège m; **funeral ~** (on foot)
cortège funèbre; (in cars) convoi m
mortuaire
proclaim [prə'kleɪm] vt déclarer,
proclamer
prod [prɔd] vt pousser
produce n ['prɔdjuːs] (Agr) produits
mpl ▷ vt [prə'djuːs] produire; (show)
présenter; (cause) provoquer, causer;
(Theat) monter, mettre en scène;
(TV: programme) réaliser; (: play, film)
mettre en scène; (Radio: programme)
réaliser; (: play) mettre en ondes;
producer n (Theat) metteur m en
scène; (Agr, Comm, Cine) producteur
m; (TV: of programme) réalisateur
m; (: of play, film) metteur en scène;
(Radio: of programme) réalisateur; (: of
play) metteur en ondes
product ['prɔdʌkt] n produit
m; **production** [prə'dʌkʃən] n
production f; (Theat) mise f en
scène; **productive** [prə'dʌktɪv]
adj productif(-ive); **productivity** n
[prɔdʌk'tɪvɪtɪ] productivité f
Prof. [prɔf] abbr (= professor) Prof

profession [prə'fɛʃən] n profession
f; **professional** n professionnel(le)
▷ adj professionnel(le); (work) de
professionnel
professor [prə'fɛsə'] n professeur
m (titulaire d'une chaire); (us: teacher)
professeur m
profile ['prəʊfaɪl] n profil m
profit ['prɔfɪt] n (from trading)
bénéfice m; (advantage) profit m
▷ vi: **to ~ (by or from)** profiter (de);
profitable adj lucratif(-ive), rentable
profound [prə'faʊnd] adj profond(e)
programme, (us) **program**
['prəʊgræm] n (Comput)
programme m; (Radio, TV) émission
f ▷ vt programmer; **programmer**
n programmeur(-euse);
programming, (us) **programing** n
programmation f
progress n ['prəʊgrɛs] progrès m(pl)
▷ vi [prə'grɛs] progresser, avancer; **in
~** en cours; **progressive** [prə'grɛsɪv]
adj progressif(-ive); (person)
progressiste
prohibit [prə'hɪbɪt] vt interdire,
défendre
project n ['prɔdʒɛkt] (plan) projet
m, plan m; (venture) opération f,
entreprise f; (Scol: research) étude f,
dossier m ▷ vt [prə'dʒɛkt] projeter
▷ vi [prə'dʒɛkt] (stick out) faire saillie,
s'avancer; **projection** [prə'dʒɛkʃən]
n projection f; (overhang) saillie
f; **projector** [prə'dʒɛktə'] n
projecteur m
prolific [prə'lɪfɪk] adj prolifique
prolong [prə'lɔŋ] vt prolonger
prom [prɔm] n abbr = **promenade**;
(us: ball) bal m d'étudiants; **the P~s**
série de concerts de musique classique

● **PROM**

● En Grande-Bretagne, un promenade
● concert ou prom est un concert de
● musique classique, ainsi appelé
● car, à l'origine, le public restait

- debout et se promenait au lieu
- de rester assis. De nos jours, une
- partie du public reste debout,
- mais il y a également des places
- assises (plus chères). Les Proms
- les plus connus sont les Proms
- londoniens. La dernière séance (le
- "Last Night of the Proms") est un
- grand événement médiatique où
- se jouent des airs traditionnels et
- patriotiques. Aux États-Unis et au
- Canada, le prom ou promenade est
- un bal organisé par le lycée.

promenade [prɒməˈnɑːd] n (by sea) esplanade f, promenade f

prominent [ˈprɒmɪnənt] adj (standing out) proéminent(e); (important) important(e)

promiscuous [prəˈmɪskjuəs] adj (sexually) de mœurs légères

promise [ˈprɒmɪs] n promesse f ⊳ vt, vi promettre; **promising** adj prometteur(-euse)

promote [prəˈməut] vt promouvoir; (new product) lancer; **promotion** [prəˈməuʃən] n promotion f

prompt [prɒmpt] adj rapide ⊳ n (Comput) message m (de guidage) ⊳ vt (cause) entraîner, provoquer; (Theat) souffler (son rôle or ses répliques) à; **at 8 o'clock** = à 8 heures précises; **to ~ sb to do** inciter or pousser qn à faire; **promptly** adv (quickly) rapidement, sans délai; (on time) ponctuellement

prone [prəun] adj (lying) couché(e) (face contre terre); (liable): **to ~ to** enclin(e) à

prong [prɒŋ] n (of fork) dent f

pronoun [ˈprəunaun] n pronom m

pronounce [prəˈnauns] vt prononcer; **how do you ~ it?** comment est-ce que ça se prononce?

pronunciation [prənʌnsɪˈeɪʃən] n prononciation f

proof [pruːf] n preuve f ⊳ adj: **~ against** à l'épreuve de

prop [prɒp] n support m, étai m; (fig) soutien m ⊳ vt (also: ~ **up**) étayer, soutenir; **props** npl accessoires mpl

propaganda [prɒpəˈgændə] n propagande f

propeller [prəˈpɛləʳ] n hélice f

proper [ˈprɒpəʳ] adj (suited, right) approprié(e), bon (bonne); (seemly) correct(e), convenable; (authentic) vrai(e), véritable; (referring to place): **the village** = le village proprement dit; **properly** adv correctement, convenablement; **proper noun** n nom m propre

property [ˈprɒpətɪ] n (possessions) biens mpl; (house etc) propriété f; (land) terres fpl, domaine m

prophecy [ˈprɒfɪsɪ] n prophétie f

prophet [ˈprɒfɪt] n prophète m

proportion [prəˈpɔːʃən] n proportion f; (share) part f, partie f; **proportions** npl (size) dimensions fpl; **proportional, proportionate** adj proportionnel(le)

proposal [prəˈpəuzl] n proposition f, offre f; (plan) projet m; (of marriage) demande f en mariage

propose [prəˈpəuz] vt proposer, suggérer ⊳ vi faire sa demande en mariage; **to ~ to do** avoir l'intention de faire

proposition [prɒpəˈzɪʃən] n proposition f

proprietor [prəˈpraɪətəʳ] n propriétaire m/f

prose [prəuz] n prose f; (Scol: translation) thème m

prosecute [ˈprɒsɪkjuːt] vt poursuivre; **prosecution** [prɒsɪˈkjuːʃən] n poursuites fpl judiciaires; (accusing side: in criminal case) accusation f; (: in civil case) la partie plaignante; **prosecutor** n (lawyer) procureur m; (also: **public prosecutor**) ministère public; (us: plaintiff) plaignant(e)

prospect n [ˈprɒspɛkt] perspective f; (hope) espoir m, chances fpl ⊳ vt, vi

P

[prə'spεkt] prospecter; **prospects** npl (for work etc) possibilités fpl d'avenir, débouchés mpl; **prospective** [prə'spεktɪv] adj (possible) éventuel(le); (future) futur(e)

prospectus [prə'spεktəs] n prospectus m

prosper ['prɒspə*] vi prospérer; **prosperity** [prɒ'spεrɪtɪ] n prospérité f; **prosperous** adj prospère

prostitute ['prɒstɪtju:t] n prostituée f; **male ~** prostitué m

protect [prə'tεkt] vt protéger; **protection** [prə'tεkʃən] n protection f; **protective** adj protecteur(-trice); (clothing) de protection

protein ['prəʊti:n] n protéine f

protest n ['prəʊtεst] protestation f ▷ vi [prə'tεst]: **to ~ against/about** protester contre/à propos de; **to ~ (that)** protester que

Protestant ['prɒtɪstənt] adj, n protestant(e)

protester, protestor [prə'tεstə*] n (in demonstration) manifestant(e)

protractor [prə'træktə*] n (Geom) rapporteur m

proud [praʊd] adj fier(-ère); (pej) orgueilleux(-euse)

prove [pru:v] vt prouver, démontrer ▷ vi: **to ~ correct** etc s'avérer juste etc; **to ~ o.s.** montrer ce dont on est capable

proverb ['prɒvə:b] n proverbe m

provide [prə'vaɪd] vt fournir; **to ~ sb with sth** fournir qch à qn; **provide for** vt fus (person) subvenir aux besoins de; (future event) prévoir; **provided** conj: **provided (that)** à condition que + sub; **providing** [prə'vaɪdɪŋ] conj à condition que + sub

province ['prɒvɪns] n province f; (fig) domaine m; **provincial** [prə'vɪnʃəl] adj provincial(e)

provision [prə'vɪʒən] n (supplying) fourniture f; approvisionnement m; (stipulation) disposition f; **provisions**

npl (food) provisions fpl; **provisional** adj provisoire

provocative [prə'vɒkətɪv] adj provocateur(-trice), provocant(e)

provoke [prə'vəʊk] vt provoquer

prowl [praʊl] vi (also: **~ about, ~ around**) rôder

proximity [prɒk'sɪmɪtɪ] n proximité f

proxy ['prɒksɪ] n: **by ~** par procuration

prudent ['pru:dənt] adj prudent(e)

prune [pru:n] n pruneau m ▷ vt élaguer

pry [praɪ] vi: **to ~ into** fourrer son nez dans

PS n abbr (= postscript) PS m

pseudonym ['sju:dənɪm] n pseudonyme m

PSHE n abbr (BRIT Scol: = personal, social and health education) cours d'éducation personnelle, sanitaire et sociale préparant à la vie adulte

psychiatric [saɪkɪ'ætrɪk] adj psychiatrique

psychiatrist [saɪ'kaɪətrɪst] n psychiatre m/f

psychic ['saɪkɪk] adj (also: **~al**) (méta)psychique; (person) doué(e) de télépathie or d'un sixième sens

psychoanalysis (pl **psychoanalyses**) [saɪkəʊə'nælɪsɪs, -si:z] n psychanalyse f

psychological [saɪkə'lɒdʒɪkl] adj psychologique

psychologist [saɪ'kɒlədʒɪst] n psychologue m/f

psychology [saɪ'kɒlədʒɪ] n psychologie f

psychotherapy [saɪkəʊ'θεrəpɪ] n psychothérapie f

pt abbr = **pint; pints; point; points**

PTO abbr (= please turn over) TSVP

PTV abbr (US) = **pay television**

pub [pʌb] n abbr (= public house) pub m

puberty ['pju:bətɪ] n puberté f

public ['pʌblɪk] adj public(-ique) ▷ n public m; **in ~** en public; **to make ~** rendre public

publication [pʌblɪˈkeɪʃən] n
publication f
public: public company n société
f anonyme; **public convenience** n
(BRIT) toilettes fpl; **public holiday**
n (BRIT) jour férié; **public house**
n (BRIT) pub m
publicity [pʌbˈlɪsɪtɪ] n publicité f
publicize [ˈpʌblɪsaɪz] vt (make
known) faire connaître, rendre
public; (advertise) faire de la publicité
pour
public: public limited company n
≈ société f anonyme (SA) (cotée en
Bourse); **publicly** adv publiquement,
en public; **public opinion** n opinion
publique; **public relations** n or npl
relations publiques (RP); **public
school** n (BRIT) école privée; (US)
école publique; **public transport**,
(US) **public transportation** n
transports mpl en commun
publish [ˈpʌblɪʃ] vt publier; **publisher**
n éditeur m; **publishing** n (industry)
édition f
pub lunch n repas m de bistrot
pudding [ˈpudɪŋ] n (BRIT: dessert)
dessert m, entremets m; (sweet dish)
pudding m, gâteau m
puddle [ˈpʌdl] n flaque f d'eau
puff [pʌf] n bouffée f ▷ vt (also: ~
out: sails, cheeks) gonfler ▷ vi (pant)
haleter; **puff pastry**, (US) **puff paste**
n pâte feuilletée
pull [pul] n (tug): **to give sth a ~** tirer
sur qch ▷ vt tirer; (trigger) presser;
(strain: muscle, tendon) se claquer
▷ vi tirer; **to ~ to pieces** mettre en
morceaux; **to ~ one's punches**
(also fig) ménager son adversaire;
to ~ one's weight y mettre du sien;
to ~ o.s. together se ressaisir; **to
~ sb's leg** (fig) faire marcher qn;
pull apart vt (break) mettre en
pièces, démantibuler; **pull away** vi
(vehicle: move off) partir; (draw back)
s'éloigner; **pull back** vt (lever etc)
tirer sur; (curtains) ouvrir ▷ vi (refrain)

s'abstenir; (Mil: withdraw) se retirer;
pull down vt baisser, abaisser;
(house) démolir; **pull in** vi (Aut) se
ranger; (Rail) entrer en gare; **pull off**
vt enlever, ôter; (deal etc) conclure;
pull out vi démarrer, partir; (Aut:
come out of line) déboîter ▷ vt (from
bag, pocket) sortir; (remove) arracher;
pull over vi (Aut) se ranger; **pull up** vi
(stop) s'arrêter ▷ vt remonter; (uproot)
déraciner, arracher
pulley [ˈpulɪ] n poulie f
pullover [ˈpuləuvər] n pull-over m,
tricot m
pulp [pʌlp] n (of fruit) pulpe f; (for
paper) pâte f à papier
pulpit [ˈpulpɪt] n chaire f
pulse [pʌls] n (of blood) pouls m; (of
heart) battement m; **pulses** npl (Culin)
légumineuses fpl
puma [ˈpjuːmə] n puma m
pump [pʌmp] n pompe f; (shoe)
escarpin m ▷ vt pomper; **pump up**
vt gonfler
pumpkin [ˈpʌmpkɪn] n potiron m,
citrouille f
pun [pʌn] n jeu m de mots,
calembour m
punch [pʌntʃ] n (blow) coup m de
poing; (tool) poinçon m; (drink) punch
m ▷ vt (make a hole in) poinçonner,
perforer; (hit): **to ~ sb/sth** donner un
coup de poing à qn/sur qch; **punch-
up** n (BRIT inf) bagarre f
punctual [ˈpʌŋktjuəl] adj
ponctuel(le)
punctuation [pʌŋktʃuˈeɪʃən] n
ponctuation f
puncture [ˈpʌŋktʃər] n (BRIT)
crevaison f ▷ vt crever
punish [ˈpʌnɪʃ] vt punir; **punishment**
n punition f, châtiment m
punk [pʌŋk] n (person: also: ~ rocker)
punk m/f; (music: also: ~ rock)
punk m; (US inf: hoodlum) voyou m
pup [pʌp] n chiot m
pupil [ˈpjuːpɪl] n élève m/f; (of eye)
pupille f

puppet ['pʌpɪt] n marionnette f, pantin m

puppy ['pʌpɪ] n chiot m, petit chien

purchase ['pɜːtʃɪs] n achat m ▷ vt acheter

pure [pjuəʳ] adj pur(e); **purely** adv purement

purify ['pjuərɪfaɪ] vt purifier, épurer

purity ['pjuərɪtɪ] n pureté f

purple ['pɜːpl] adj violet(te); (face) cramoisi(e)

purpose ['pɜːpəs] n intention f, but m; **on ~** exprès

purr [pɜːʳ] vi ronronner

purse [pɜːs] n (BRIT: for money) porte-monnaie m inv; (us: handbag) sac m (à main) ▷ vt serrer, pincer

pursue [pə'sjuː] vt poursuivre

pursuit [pə'sjuːt] n poursuite f; (occupation) occupation f, activité f

pus [pʌs] n pus m

push [puʃ] n poussée f ▷ vt pousser; (button) appuyer sur; (fig: product) mettre en avant, faire de la publicité pour ▷ vi pousser; **to ~ for** (better pay, conditions) réclamer; **push in** vi s'introduire de force; **push off** vi (inf) filer, ficher le camp; **push on** vi (continue) continuer; **push over** vt renverser; **push through** vi (in crowd) se frayer un chemin; **pushchair** n (BRIT) poussette f; **pusher** n (also: **drug pusher**) revendeur(-euse) (de drogue), ravitailleur(-euse) (en drogue); **push-up** n (us) traction f

putt [pʌt] n putt m; **putting green** n green m

puzzle ['pʌzl] n énigme f, mystère m; (game) jeu m, casse-tête m; (jigsaw) puzzle m; (also: **crossword ~**) mots croisés ▷ vt intriguer, rendre perplexe ▷ vi: **to ~ over** chercher à comprendre; **puzzled** adj perplexe; **puzzling** adj déconcertant(e), inexplicable

pyjamas [pɪ'dʒɑːməz] npl (BRIT) pyjama m

pylon ['paɪlən] n pylône m

pyramid ['pɪrəmɪd] n pyramide f

Pyrenees [pɪrə'niːz] npl Pyrénées fpl

attribuer; (animal) abattre; (cat, dog) faire piquer; **put forward** vt (ideas) avancer, proposer; **put in** vt (complaint) soumettre; (time, effort) consacrer; **put off** vt (postpone) remettre à plus tard, ajourner; (discourage) dissuader; **put on** vt (clothes, lipstick, show) mettre; (light etc) allumer; (play etc) monter; (weight) prendre; (assume: accent, manner) prendre; (assume: accent, manner) prendre; **put out** vt (take outside) mettre dehors; (one's hand) tendre; (light etc) éteindre; (person: inconvenience) déranger, gêner; **put through** vt (Tel: caller) mettre en communication; (: call) passer; (plan) faire accepter; **put together** vt mettre ensemble; (assemble: furniture) monter, assembler; (: meal) préparer; **put up** vt (raise) lever, relever, remonter; (hang) accrocher; (build) construire, ériger; (increase) augmenter; (accommodate) loger; **put up with** vt fus supporter

put [put] (pt, pp **put**) [put] vt (place) poser, placer; (say) dire, exprimer; (a question) poser; (case, view) exposer, présenter; (estimate) estimer; **put aside** vt mettre de côté; **put away** vt (store) ranger; **put back** vt (replace) remettre, replacer; (postpone) remettre; **put by** vt (money) mettre de côté, économiser; **put down** vt (parcel etc) poser, déposer; (in writing) mettre par écrit, inscrire; (suppress: revolt etc) réprimer, écraser; (attribute)

q

quack [kwæk] *n* (*of duck*) coin-coin *m inv*; (*pej: doctor*) charlatan *m*
quadruple [kwɔ'dru:pl] *vt, vi* quadrupler
quail [kweɪl] *n* (*Zool*) caille *f* ▷ *vi*: **to ~ at** *or* **before** reculer devant
quaint [kweɪnt] *adj* bizarre; (*old-fashioned*) désuet(-ète); (*picturesque*) au charme vieillot, pittoresque
quake [kweɪk] *vi* trembler ▷ *n abbr* = **earthquake**
qualification [kwɔlɪfɪ'keɪʃən] *n* (*often pl: degree etc*) diplôme *m*; (*training*) qualification(s) *f(pl)*; (*ability*) compétence(s) *f(pl)*; (*limitation*) réserve *f*, restriction *f*
qualified ['kwɔlɪfaɪd] *adj* (*trained*) qualifié(e); (*professionally*) diplômé(e); (*fit, competent*) compétent(e), qualifié(e); (*limited*) conditionnel(le)
qualify ['kwɔlɪfaɪ] *vt* qualifier; (*modify*) atténuer, nuancer ▷ *vi*: **to ~ (as)** obtenir son diplôme (de); **to ~**

(for) remplir les conditions requises (pour); (*Sport*) se qualifier (pour)
quality ['kwɔlɪtɪ] *n* qualité *f*
qualm [kwɑ:m] *n* doute *m*; scrupule *m*
quantify ['kwɔntɪfaɪ] *vt* quantifier
quantity ['kwɔntɪtɪ] *n* quantité *f*
quarantine ['kwɔrntiːn] *n* quarantaine *f*
quarrel ['kwɔrl] *n* querelle *f*, dispute *f* ▷ *vi* se disputer, se quereller
quarry ['kwɔrɪ] *n* (*for stone*) carrière *f*; (*animal*) proie *f*, gibier *m*
quart [kwɔːt] *n* ≈ litre *m*
quarter ['kwɔːtəʳ] *n* quart *m*; (*of year*) trimestre *m*; (*district*) quartier *m*; (*US, CANADA: 25 cents*) (pièce *f* de) vingt-cinq cents *mpl* ▷ *vt* partager en quartiers *or* en quatre; (*Mil*) caserner, cantonner; **quarters** *npl* logement *m*; (*Mil*) quartiers *mpl*, cantonnement *m*; **a ~ of an hour** un quart d'heure; **quarter final** *n* quart *m* de finale; **quarterly** *adj* trimestriel(le) ▷ *adv* tous les trois mois
quartet(te) [kwɔː'tet] *n* quatuor *m*; (*jazz players*) quartette *m*
quartz [kwɔːts] *n* quartz *m*
quay [kiː] *n* (*also*: **~side**) quai *m*
queasy ['kwiːzɪ] *adj*: **to feel ~** avoir mal au cœur
Quebec ['kwɔlɪbek] *n* (*city*) Québec; (*province*) Québec *m*
queen [kwiːn] *n* (*gen*) reine *f*; (*Cards etc*) dame *f*
queer [kwɪəʳ] *adj* étrange, curieux(-euse); (*suspicious*) louche ▷ *n* (*offensive*) homosexuel *m*
quench [kwentʃ] *vt*: **to ~ one's thirst** se désaltérer
query ['kwɪərɪ] *n* question *f* ▷ *vt* (*disagree with, dispute*) mettre en doute, questionner
quest [kwest] *n* recherche *f*, quête *f*
question ['kwestʃən] *n* question *f* ▷ *vt* (*person*) interroger; (*plan, idea*) mettre en question *or* en doute; **beyond ~** sans aucun doute; **out of the ~** hors de

question; **questionable** adj
discutable; **question mark** n point
m d'interrogation; **questionnaire**
[kwɛstʃəˈnɛəʳ] n questionnaire m
queue [kjuː] (BRIT) n queue f, file f ▷ vi
(also: ~ **up**) faire la queue
quiche [kiːʃ] n quiche f
quick [kwɪk] adj rapide; (mind) vif
(vive); (agile) agile, vif (vive) ▷ n: **cut
to the ~** (fig) touché(e) au vif; **be
~!** dépêche-toi!; **quickly** adv (fast)
vite, rapidement; (immediately) tout
de suite
quid [kwɪd] n (pl inv: BRIT inf) livre f
quiet [ˈkwaɪət] adj tranquille,
calme; (voice) bas(se); (ceremony,
colour) discret(-ète) ▷ n tranquillité
f, calme m; (silence) silence m;
quietly adv tranquillement;
(silently) silencieusement; (discreetly)
discrètement
quilt [kwɪlt] n édredon m; (continental
quilt) couette f
quirky [ˈkwɜːkɪ] adj singulier(-ère)
quit [kwɪt] (pt, pp quit or quitted)
vt quitter ▷ vi (give up) abandonner,
renoncer; (resign) démissionner
quite [kwaɪt] adv (rather) assez,
plutôt; (entirely) complètement,
tout à fait; **~ a few of them** un assez
grand nombre d'entre eux; **that's
not ~ right** ce n'est pas tout à fait
juste; **~ (so)!** exactement!
quits [kwɪts] adj: **~ (with)** quitte
(envers); **let's call it ~** restons-en là
quiver [ˈkwɪvəʳ] vi trembler, frémir
quiz [kwɪz] n (on TV) jeu-concours m
(télévisé); (in magazine etc) test m de
connaissances ▷ vt interroger
quota [ˈkwəʊtə] n quota m
quotation [kwəʊˈteɪʃən] n citation f;
(estimate) devis m; **quotation marks**
npl guillemets mpl
quote [kwəʊt] n citation f; (estimate)
devis m ▷ vt (sentence, author) citer;
(price) donner, soumettre ▷ vi: **to
~ from** citer; **quotes** npl (inverted
commas) guillemets mpl

r

rabbi [ˈræbaɪ] n rabbin m
rabbit [ˈræbɪt] n lapin m
rabies [ˈreɪbiːz] n rage f
RAC n abbr (BRIT: = Royal Automobile
Club) ≈ ACF m
rac(c)oon [rəˈkuːn] n raton m laveur
race [reɪs] n (species) race f;
(competition, rush) course f ▷ vt
(person) faire la course avec ▷ vi
(compete) faire la course, courir;
(pulse) battre très vite; **race car** n (US)
= **racing car**; **racecourse** n champ m
de courses; **racehorse** n cheval m de
course; **racetrack** n piste f
racial [ˈreɪʃl] adj racial(e)
racing [ˈreɪsɪŋ] n courses fpl; **racing
car** n (BRIT) voiture f de course;
racing driver n (BRIT) pilote m de
course
racism [ˈreɪsɪzəm] n racisme m;
racist [ˈreɪsɪst] adj, n raciste m/f
rack [ræk] n (for guns, tools) râtelier
m; (for clothes) portant m; (for bottles)

casier m; (also: **luggage ~**) filet m à bagages; (also: **roof ~**) galerie f; (also: **dish ~**) égouttoir m ▷ vt tourmenter; **to ~ one's brains** se creuser la cervelle

racket ['rækɪt] n (for tennis) raquette f; (noise) tapage m, vacarme m; (swindle) escroquerie f

racquet ['rækɪt] n raquette f

radar ['reɪdɑː'] n radar m

radiation [reɪdɪ'eɪʃən] n rayonnement m; (radioactive) radiation f

radiator ['reɪdɪeɪtə'] n radiateur m

radical ['rædɪkl] adj radical(e)

radio ['reɪdɪəʊ] n radio f ▷ vt (person) appeler par radio; **on the ~** à la radio; **radioactive** adj radioactif(-ive); **radio station** n station f de radio

radish ['rædɪʃ] n radis m

RAF n abbr (BRIT) = **Royal Air Force**

raffle ['ræfl] n tombola f

raft [rɑːft] n (craft: **life ~**) radeau m; (logs) train m de flottage

rag [ræg] n chiffon m, (pej: newspaper) feuille f, torchon m; (for charity) attractions organisées par les étudiants au profit d'œuvres de charité; **rags** npl haillons mpl

rage [reɪdʒ] n (fury) rage f, fureur f ▷ vi (person) être furieux(-euse) (folle) de rage; (storm) faire rage, être déchaîné(e); **it's all the ~** cela fait fureur

ragged ['rægɪd] adj (edge) inégal(e), qui accroche; (clothes) en loques; (appearance) déguenillé(e)

raid [reɪd] n (Mil) raid m; (criminal) hold-up m inv; (by police) descente f, rafle f ▷ vt faire un raid sur or une hold-up dans or une descente dans

rail [reɪl] n (on stair) rampe f; (on bridge, balcony) balustrade f; (of ship) bastingage m; (for train) rail m; **railcard** n (BRIT) carte f de chemin de fer; **railing(s)** n(pl) grille f; **railway**, (us) **railroad** n chemin m de fer; (track) voie f ferrée; **railway line** n (BRIT) ligne f de chemin de fer; (track)

voie ferrée; **railway station** n (BRIT) gare f

rain [reɪn] n pluie f ▷ vi pleuvoir; **in the ~** sous la pluie; **it's ~ing** il pleut; **rainbow** n arc-en-ciel m; **raincoat** n imperméable m; **raindrop** n goutte f de pluie; **rainfall** n chute f de pluie; (measurement) hauteur f des précipitations; **rainforest** n forêt tropicale; **rainy** adj pluvieux(-euse)

raise [reɪz] n augmentation f (lift) lever; hausser; (increase) augmenter; (morale) remonter; (standards) améliorer; (a protest, doubt) provoquer, causer; (a question) soulever; (cattle, family) élever; (crop) faire pousser; (army, funds) rassembler; (loan) obtenir; **to ~ one's voice** élever la voix

raisin ['reɪzn] n raisin sec

rake [reɪk] n (tool) râteau m; (person) débauché m ▷ vt (garden) ratisser

rally ['rælɪ] n (Pol etc) meeting m, rassemblement m; (Aut) rallye m; (Tennis) échange m ▷ vt rassembler, rallier; (support) gagner ▷ vi (sick person) aller mieux; (Stock Exchange) reprendre

RAM [ræm] n abbr (Comput: = random access memory) mémoire vive

ram [ræm] n bélier m ▷ vt (push) enfoncer; (crash into: vehicle) emboutir; (: lamppost etc) percuter

Ramadan [ræmə'dæn] n Ramadan m

ramble ['ræmbl] n randonnée f ▷ vi (walk) se promener, faire une randonnée; (pej: also: **~ on**) discourir, pérorer; **rambler** n promeneur(-euse), randonneur(-euse); **rambling** adj (speech) décousu(e); (house) plein(e) de coins et de recoins; (Bot) grimpant(e)

ramp [ræmp] n (incline) rampe f; (Aut) dénivellation f; (in garage) pont m; **on/off ~** (us Aut) bretelle f d'accès

rampage [ræm'peɪdʒ] n: **to be on the ~** se déchaîner

ran [ræn] *pt of* **run**

ranch [rɑːntʃ] *n* ranch *m*

random ['rændəm] *adj* fait(e) or établi(e) au hasard; (*Comput, Math*) aléatoire ▷ *n*: **at ~** au hasard

rang [ræŋ] *pt of* **ring**

range [reɪndʒ] *n* (*of mountains*) chaîne *f*; (*of missile, voice*) portée *f*; (*of products*) choix *m*, gamme *f*; (also: **shooting ~**) champ *m* de tir; (also: **kitchen ~**) fourneau *m* (de cuisine) ▷ *vt* (*place*) mettre en rang, placer ▷ *vi*: **to ~ over** couvrir; **to ~ from ... to** aller de ... à

ranger ['reɪndʒə'] *n* garde *m* forestier

rank [ræŋk] *n* rang *m*; (*Mil*) grade *m*; (BRIT: *also*: **taxi ~**) station *f* de taxis ▷ *vi*: **to ~ among** compter or se classer parmi ▷ *adj* (*smell*) nauséabond(e); **the ~ and file** (*fig*) la masse, la base

ransom ['rænsəm] *n* rançon *f*; **to hold sb to ~** (*fig*) exercer un chantage sur qn

rant [rænt] *vi* fulminer

rap [ræp] *n* (*music*) rap *m* ▷ *vt* (*door*) frapper sur or à; (*table etc*) taper sur

rape [reɪp] *n* viol *m*; (*Bot*) colza *m* ▷ *vt* violer

rapid ['ræpɪd] *adj* rapide; **rapidly** *adv* rapidement; **rapids** *npl* (*Geo*) rapides *mpl*

rapist ['reɪpɪst] *n* auteur *m* d'un viol

rapport [ræ'pɔː'] *n* entente *f*

rare [rɛə'] *adj* rare; (*Culin: steak*) saignant(e); **rarely** *adv* rarement

rash [ræʃ] *adj* imprudent(e), irréfléchi(e) ▷ *n* (*Med*) rougeur *f*, éruption *f*; (*of events*) série *f* (noire)

rasher ['ræʃə'] *n* fine tranche (de lard)

raspberry ['rɑːzbərɪ] *n* framboise *f*

rat [ræt] *n* rat *m*

rate [reɪt] *n* (*ratio*) taux *m*, pourcentage *m*; (*speed*) vitesse *f*, rythme *m*; (*price*) tarif *m* ▷ *vt* (*price*) évaluer, estimer; (*people*) classer; **rates** *npl* (BRIT: *property tax*) impôts

locaux; **to ~ sb/sth as** considérer qn/qch comme

rather ['rɑːðə'] *adv* (*somewhat*) assez, plutôt; (*to some extent*) un peu; **it's ~ expensive** c'est assez cher; (*too much*) c'est un peu cher; **there's ~ a lot** il y en a beaucoup; **I would** or **I'd ~ go** j'aimerais mieux or je préférerais partir; **or ~** (*more accurately*) ou plutôt

rating ['reɪtɪŋ] *n* (*assessment*) évaluation *f*; (*score*) classement *m*; (*Finance*) cote *f*; **ratings** *npl* (*Radio*) indice(s) *m(pl)* d'écoute; (*TV*) Audimat® *m*

ratio ['reɪʃɪəu] *n* proportion *f*; **in the ~ of 100 to 1** dans la proportion de 100 contre 1

ration ['ræʃən] *n* ration *f* ▷ *vt* rationner; **rations** *npl* (*food*) vivres *mpl*

rational ['ræʃənl] *adj* raisonnable, sensé(e); (*solution, reasoning*) logique; (*Med: person*) lucide

rat race *n* foire *f* d'empoigne

rattle ['rætl] *n* (*of door, window*) battement *m*; (*of coins, chain*) cliquetis *m*; (*of train, engine*) bruit *m* de ferraille; (*for baby*) hochet *m* ▷ *vi* cliqueter; (*car, bus*): **to ~ along** rouler en faisant un bruit de ferraille ▷ *vt* agiter (bruyamment); (*inf: disconcert*) décontenancer

rave [reɪv] *vi* (*in anger*) s'emporter; (*with enthusiasm*) s'extasier; (*Med*) délirer ▷ *n* (*inf: party*) rave *f*, soirée *f* techno

raven ['reɪvən] *n* grand corbeau

ravine [rə'viːn] *n* ravin *m*

raw [rɔː] *adj* (*uncooked*) cru(e); (*not processed*) brut(e); (*sore*) à vif, irrité(e); (*inexperienced*) inexpérimenté(e); **~ materials** matières premières

ray [reɪ] *n* rayon *m*; **~ of hope** lueur *f* d'espoir

razor ['reɪzə'] *n* rasoir *m*; **razor blade** *n* lame *f* de rasoir

Rd *abbr* = **road**

RE n abbr (BRIT. = religious education) instruction religieuse

re [riː] prep concernant

reach [riːtʃ] n portée f, atteinte f; (of river etc) étendue f ▷ vt atteindre, arriver à; (conclusion, decision) parvenir à ▷ vi s'étendre; **out of/ within ~** (object): tenir de/à portée; **reach out** vt tendre ▷ vi: **to ~ out (for)** allonger le bras (pour prendre)

react [riːˈækt] vi réagir; **reaction** [riːˈækʃən] n réaction f; **reactor** [riːˈæktəʳ] n réacteur m

read (pt, pp **read**) [riːd, rɛd] vi lire ▷ vt lire; (understand) comprendre, interpréter; (study) étudier; (meter) relever; (subj: instrument etc) indiquer, marquer; **read out** vt lire à haute voix; **reader** n lecteur(-trice)

readily [ˈrɛdɪlɪ] adv volontiers, avec empressement; (easily) facilement

reading [ˈriːdɪŋ] n lecture f; (understanding) interprétation f; (on instrument) indications fpl

ready [ˈrɛdɪ] adj prêt(e); (willing) prêt, disposé(e); (available) disponible ▷ n: **at the ~** (Mil) prêt à faire feu; **when will my photos be ~?** quand est-ce que mes photos seront prêtes?; **to get ~** (as vi) se préparer; (as vt) préparer; **ready-cooked** adj précuit(e); **ready-made** adj tout(e) fait(e)

real [rɪəl] adj (world, life) réel(le); (genuine) véritable; (proper) vrai(e) ▷ adv (US inf: very) vraiment; **real ale** n bière traditionnelle; **real estate** n biens fonciers ou immobiliers; **realistic** [rɪəˈlɪstɪk] adj réaliste; **reality** [riːˈælɪtɪ] n réalité f; **reality TV** n téléréalité f

realization [rɪəlaɪˈzeɪʃən] n (awareness) prise f de conscience; (fulfilment, also: of asset) réalisation f

realize [ˈrɪəlaɪz] vt (understand) se rendre compte de, prendre conscience de; (a project, Comm: asset) réaliser

really [ˈrɪəlɪ] adv vraiment; **~?** vraiment?, c'est vrai?

realm [rɛlm] n royaume m; (fig) domaine m

realtor [ˈrɪəltɔːʳ] n (US) agent immobilier

reappear [riːəˈpɪəʳ] vi réapparaître, reparaître

rear [rɪəʳ] adj de derrière, arrière inv; (Aut: wheel etc) arrière ▷ n arrière m ▷ vt (cattle, family) élever ▷ vi (also: ~ **up**: animal) se cabrer

rearrange [riːəˈreɪndʒ] vt réarranger

rear: rear-view mirror n (Aut) rétroviseur m; **rear-wheel drive** n (Aut) traction arrière

reason [ˈriːzn] n raison f ▷ vi: **to ~ with sb** raisonner qn, faire entendre raison à qn; **it stands to ~ that** il va sans dire que; **reasonable** adj raisonnable; (not bad) acceptable; **reasonably** adv (behave) raisonnablement; (fairly) assez; **reasoning** n raisonnement m

reassurance [riːəˈʃuərəns] n (factual) assurance f, garantie f; (emotional) réconfort m

reassure [riːəˈʃuəʳ] vt rassurer

rebate [ˈriːbeɪt] n (on tax etc) dégrèvement m

rebel n [ˈrɛbl] rebelle m/f ▷ vi [rɪˈbɛl] se rebeller, se révolter; **rebellion** [rɪˈbɛljən] n rébellion f, révolte f; **rebellious** [rɪˈbɛljəs] adj rebelle

rebuild [riːˈbɪld] vt (irreg: like **build**) reconstruire

recall vt [rɪˈkɔːl] rappeler; (remember) se rappeler, se souvenir de ▷ n [ˈriːkɔl] rappel m; (ability to remember) mémoire f

receipt [rɪˈsiːt] n (document) reçu m; (for parcel etc) accusé m de réception; (act of receiving) réception f; **receipts** npl (Comm) recettes fpl; **can I have a ~, please?** je peux avoir un reçu, s'il vous plaît?

receive [rɪˈsiːv] vt recevoir; (guest) recevoir, accueillir; **receiver** n (Tel) récepteur m, combiné m; (Radio) récepteur m; (of stolen goods) receleur m; (for bankruptcies) administrateur m judiciaire

recent ['ri:snt] adj récent(e); **recently** adv récemment

reception [rɪ'sɛpʃən] n réception f; (welcome) accueil m, réception f; **reception desk** n réception f; **receptionist** n réceptionniste m/f

recession [rɪ'sɛʃən] n (Econ) récession f

recharge [ri:'tʃɑːdʒ] vt (battery) recharger

recipe ['rɛsɪpɪ] n recette f

recipient [rɪ'sɪpɪənt] n (of payment) bénéficiaire m/f; (of letter) destinataire m/f

recital [rɪ'saɪtl] n récital m

recite [rɪ'saɪt] vt (poem) réciter

reckless ['rɛkləs] adj (driver etc) imprudent(e); (spender etc) insouciant(e)

reckon ['rɛkən] vt (count) calculer, compter; (consider) considérer, estimer; (think): **I ~ (that) ...** je pense (que) ..., j'estime que) ...

reclaim [rɪ'kleɪm] vt (land: from sea) assécher; (demand back) réclamer (le remboursement ou la restitution de); (waste materials) récupérer

recline [rɪ'klaɪn] vi être allongé(e) or étendu(e)

recognition [rɛkəg'nɪʃən] n reconnaissance f; **transformed beyond ~** méconnaissable

recognize ['rɛkəgnaɪz] vt: **to ~ (by/ as)** reconnaître (à/comme étant)

recollection [rɛkə'lɛkʃən] n souvenir m

recommend [rɛkə'mɛnd] vt recommander; **can you ~ a good restaurant?** pouvez-vous me conseiller un bon restaurant?; **recommendation** [rɛkəmɛn'deɪʃən] n recommandation f

reconcile ['rɛkənsaɪl] vt (two people) réconcilier; (two facts) concilier, accorder; **to ~ o.s. to** se résigner à

reconsider [ri:kən'sɪdəʳ] vt reconsidérer

reconstruct [ri:kən'strʌkt] vt (building) reconstruire; (crime, system) reconstituer

record n ['rɛkɔːd] rapport m, récit m; (of meeting etc) procès-verbal m; (register) registre m; (file) dossier m; (Comput) article m; (also: **police ~**) casier m judiciaire; (Mus: disc) disque m; (Sport) record m ▷ adj ['rɛkɔːd] record inv ▷ vt [rɪ'kɔːd] (set down) noter; (Mus: song etc) enregistrer; **public ~s** archives fpl; **in ~ time** dans un temps record; **recorded delivery** n (BRIT Post): **to send sth recorded delivery** = envoyer qch en recommandé; **recorder** n (Mus) flûte f à bec; **recording** n (Mus) enregistrement m; **record player** n tourne-disque m

recount [rɪ'kaʊnt] vt raconter

recover [rɪ'kʌvəʳ] vt récupérer ▷ vi (from illness) se rétablir; (from shock) se remettre; **recovery** n récupération f; rétablissement m; (Econ) redressement m

recreate [ri:krɪ'eɪt] vt recréer

recreation [rɛkrɪ'eɪʃən] n (leisure) récréation f, détente f; **recreational drug** n drogue récréative; **recreational vehicle** n (us) camping-car m

recruit [rɪ'kruːt] n recrue f ▷ vt recruter; **recruitment** n recrutement m

rectangle ['rɛktæŋgl] n rectangle m; **rectangular** [rɛk'tæŋgjuləʳ] adj rectangulaire

rectify ['rɛktɪfaɪ] vt (error) rectifier, corriger

rector ['rɛktəʳ] n (Rel) pasteur m

recur [rɪ'kəːʳ] vi se reproduire; (idea, opportunity) se retrouver; (symptoms) réapparaître; **recurring** adj (problem) périodique, fréquent(e); (Math) périodique

recyclable [ri:'saɪkləbl] adj recyclable

recycle [riːˈsaɪkl] vt, vi recycler

recycling [riːˈsaɪklɪŋ] n recyclage m

red [rɛd] n rouge m; (Pol: pej) rouge m/f ▷ adj rouge; (hair) roux (rousse); **in the ~** (account) à découvert; (business) en déficit; **Red Cross** n Croix-Rouge f; **redcurrant** n groseille f

redeem [rɪˈdiːm] vt (debt) rembourser; (sth in pawn) dégager; (fig, also Rel) racheter

red: red-haired adj roux (rousse); **redhead** n roux (rousse); **red-hot** adj chauffé(e) au rouge, brûlant(e); **red light** n: **to go through a red light** (Aut) brûler un feu rouge; **red-light district** n quartier mal famé

red meat n viande f rouge

reduce [rɪˈdjuːs] vt réduire; (lower) abaisser; **"~ speed now"** (Aut) "ralentir"; **to ~ sb to tears** faire pleurer qn; **reduced** adj réduit(e); **"greatly reduced prices"** "gros rabais"; **at a reduced price** (goods) au rabais; (ticket etc) à prix réduit; **reduction** [rɪˈdʌkʃən] n réduction f; (of price) baisse f; (discount) rabais m; réduction; **is there a reduction for children/students?** y a-t-il une réduction pour les enfants/les étudiants?

redundancy [rɪˈdʌndənsɪ] n (BRIT) licenciement m, mise f au chômage

redundant [rɪˈdʌndnt] adj (BRIT: worker) licencié(e), mis(e) au chômage; (detail, object) superflu(e); **to be made ~** (worker) être licencié, être mis au chômage

reed [riːd] n (Bot) roseau m

reef [riːf] n (at sea) récif m, écueil m

reel [riːl] n (of cotton) bobine f; (Fishing) moulinet m; (Cine) bande f; (dance) quadrille écossais ▷ vi (sway) chanceler

ref [rɛf] n abbr (inf: = referee) arbitre m

refectory [rɪˈfɛktərɪ] n réfectoire m

refer [rɪˈfəː] vt: **to ~ sb to** (inquirer, patient) adresser qn à; (reader: to text) renvoyer qn à ▷ vi: **to ~ to** (allude to) parler de, faire allusion à; (consult) se reporter à; (apply to) s'appliquer à

referee [rɛfəˈriː] n arbitre m; (BRIT: for job application) répondant(e) m ▷ vt arbitrer

reference [ˈrɛfrəns] n référence f, renvoi m; (mention) allusion f, mention f; (for job application: letter) références; lettre f de recommandation; **with ~ to** en ce qui concerne; (Comm: in letter) me référant à; **reference number** n (Comm) numéro m de référence

refill vt [riːˈfɪl] remplir à nouveau; (pen, lighter etc) recharger ▷ n [ˈriːfɪl] (for pen etc) recharge f

refine [rɪˈfaɪn] vt (sugar, oil) raffiner; (taste) affiner; (idea, theory) peaufiner; **refined** adj (person, taste) raffiné(e); **refinery** n raffinerie f

reflect [rɪˈflɛkt] vt (light, image) réfléchir, refléter ▷ vi (think) réfléchir, méditer; **it ~s badly on him** cela le discrédite; **it ~s well on him** c'est tout à son honneur; **reflection** [rɪˈflɛkʃən] n réflexion f; (image) reflet m; **on reflection** réflexion faite

reflex [ˈriːflɛks] adj, n réflexe (m)

reform [rɪˈfɔːm] n réforme f ▷ vt réformer

refrain [rɪˈfreɪn] vi: **to ~ from doing** s'abstenir de faire ▷ n refrain m

refresh [rɪˈfrɛʃ] vt rafraîchir; (subj: food, sleep etc) redonner des forces à; **refreshing** adj rafraîchissant(e); (drink) rafraîchissant(e); (sleep) réparateur(-trice); **refreshments** npl rafraîchissements mpl

refrigerator [rɪˈfrɪdʒəreɪtə³] n réfrigérateur m, frigidaire m

refuel [riːˈfjuəl] vi se ravitailler en carburant

refuge [ˈrɛfjuːdʒ] n refuge m; **to take ~ in** se réfugier dans; **refugee** [rɛfjuˈdʒiː] n réfugié(e)

refund n [ˈriːfʌnd] remboursement m ▷ vt [rɪˈfʌnd] rembourser

refurbish [riːˈfəːbɪʃ] vt remettre à neuf

refusal [rɪˈfjuːzəl] n refus m; **to have first - on sth** avoir droit de préemption sur qch

refuse[1] [ˈrefjuːs] n ordures fpl, détritus mpl

refuse[2] [rɪˈfjuːz] vt, vi refuser; **to ~ to do sth** refuser de faire qch

regain [rɪˈgeɪn] vt (lost ground) regagner; (strength) retrouver

regard [rɪˈgɑːd] n respect m, estime f, considération f ▷ vt considérer; **to give one's ~s to** faire ses amitiés à; **"with kindest ~s"** "bien amicalement"; **as ~s, with ~ to** en ce qui concerne; **regarding** prep en ce qui concerne; **regardless** adv quand même; **regardless of** sans se soucier de

regenerate [rɪˈdʒenəreɪt] vt régénérer ▷ vi se régénérer

reggae [ˈregeɪ] n reggae m

regiment [ˈredʒɪmənt] n régiment m

region [ˈriːdʒən] n région f; **in the ~ of** (fig) aux alentours de; **regional** adj régional(e)

register [ˈredʒɪstər] n registre m; (also: **electoral ~**) liste électorale ▷ vt enregistrer, inscrire; (birth) déclarer; (vehicle) immatriculer; (letter) envoyer en recommandé; (subj: instrument) marquer ▷ vi s'inscrire; (at hotel) signer le registre; (make impression) être (bien) compris(e); **registered** adj (BRIT: letter) recommandé(e); **registered trademark** n marque déposée

registrar [ˈredʒɪstrɑːr] n officier m de l'état civil

registration [redʒɪsˈtreɪʃən] n (act) enregistrement m; (of student) inscription f; (BRIT Aut: also: **~ number**) numéro m d'immatriculation

registry office [ˈredʒɪstrɪ-] n (BRIT) bureau m de l'état civil; **to get married in a ~** se marier à la mairie

regret [rɪˈgret] n regret m ▷ vt regretter; **regrettable** adj regrettable, fâcheux(-euse)

regular [ˈregjələr] adj régulier(-ière); (usual) habituel(le), normal(e); (soldier) de métier; (Comm: size) ordinaire ▷ n (client etc) habitué(e); **regularly** adv régulièrement

regulate [ˈregjuleɪt] vt régler; **regulation** [regjuˈleɪʃən] n (rule) règlement m; (adjustment) réglage m

rehabilitation [riːəˌbɪlɪˈteɪʃən] n (of offender) réhabilitation f; (of addict) réadaptation f

rehearsal [rɪˈhəːsəl] n répétition f

rehearse [rɪˈhəːs] vt répéter

reign [reɪn] n règne m ▷ vi régner

reimburse [riːɪmˈbəːs] vt rembourser

rein [reɪn] n (for horse) rêne f

reincarnation [riːɪnkɑːˈneɪʃən] n réincarnation f

reindeer [ˈreɪndɪər] n (pl inv) renne m

reinforce [riːɪnˈfɔːs] vt renforcer; **reinforcements** npl (Mil) renfort(s) m(pl)

reinstate [riːɪnˈsteɪt] vt rétablir, réintégrer

reject n [ˈriːdʒekt] (Comm) article m de rebut ▷ vt [rɪˈdʒekt] refuser; (idea) rejeter; **rejection** [rɪˈdʒekʃən] n rejet m, refus m

rejoice [rɪˈdʒɔɪs] vi: **to ~ (at or over)** se réjouir (de)

relate [rɪˈleɪt] vt (tell) raconter; (connect) établir un rapport entre ▷ vi: **to ~ to** (connect) se rapporter à; **to ~ to sb** (interact) entretenir des rapports avec qn; **related** adj apparenté(e); **related to** (subject) lié(e) à; **relating to** prep concernant

relation [rɪˈleɪʃən] n (person) parent(e); (link) rapport m, lien m; **relations** npl (relatives) famille f; **relationship** n rapport m, lien m; (personal ties) relations fpl, rapports; (also: **family relationship**) lien de parenté; (affair) liaison f

relative ['rɛlətɪv] n parent(e) ▷ adj relatif(-ive); (respective) respectif(-ive); **relatively** adv relativement

relax [rɪ'læks] vi (muscle) se relâcher; (person: unwind) se détendre ▷ vt relâcher; (mind, person) détendre; **relaxation** [riːlæk'seɪʃən] n relâchement m; (of mind) détente f; (recreation) détente, délassement m; **relaxed** adj relâché(e); détendu(e); **relaxing** adj délassant(e)

relay ['riːleɪ] n (Sport) course f de relais ▷ vt (message) retransmettre, relayer

release [rɪ'liːs] n (from prison, obligation) libération f; (of gas etc) émission f; (of film etc) sortie f; (new recording) disque m ▷ vt (prisoner) libérer; (book, film) sortir; (report, news) rendre public, publier; (gas etc) émettre, dégager; (free: from wreckage etc) dégager; (Tech: catch, spring etc) déclencher; (let go: person, animal) relâcher; (: hand, object) lâcher; (: grip, brake) desserrer

relegate ['rɛlɪgeɪt] vt reléguer; (BRIT Sport): **to be ~d** descendre dans une division inférieure

relent [rɪ'lɛnt] vi se laisser fléchir; **relentless** adj implacable; (non-stop) continuel(le)

relevant ['rɛləvənt] adj (question) pertinent(e); (corresponding) approprié(e); (fact) significatif(-ive); (information) utile

reliable [rɪ'laɪəbl] adj (person, firm) sérieux(-euse), fiable; (method, machine) fiable; (news, information) sûr(e)

relic ['rɛlɪk] n (Rel) relique f; (of the past) vestige m

relief [rɪ'liːf] n (from pain, anxiety) soulagement m; (help, supplies) secours m(pl); (Art, Geo) relief m

relieve [rɪ'liːv] vt (pain, patient) soulager; (fear, worry) dissiper; (bring help) secourir; (take over from: gen) relayer; (: guard) relever; **to ~ sb of sth** débarrasser qn de qch; **to ~ o.s.**

(euphemism) se soulager, faire ses besoins; **relieved** adj soulagé(e)

religion [rɪ'lɪdʒən] n religion f

religious [rɪ'lɪdʒəs] adj religieux(-euse); (book) de piété; **religious education** n instruction religieuse

relish ['rɛlɪʃ] n (Culin) condiment m; (enjoyment) délectation f ▷ vt (food etc) savourer; **to ~ doing** se délecter à faire

relocate [riːləu'keɪt] vt (business) transférer ▷ vi se transférer, s'installer or s'établir ailleurs

reluctance [rɪ'lʌktəns] n répugnance f

reluctant [rɪ'lʌktənt] adj peu disposé(e), qui hésite; **reluctantly** adv à contrecœur, sans enthousiasme

rely on [rɪ'laɪ-] vt fus (be dependent on) dépendre de; (trust) compter sur

remain [rɪ'meɪn] vi rester; **remainder** n reste m; (Comm) fin f de série; **remaining** adj qui reste; **remains** npl restes mpl

remand [rɪ'mɑːnd] n: **on ~** en détention préventive ▷ vt: **to be ~ed in custody** être placé(e) en détention préventive

remark [rɪ'mɑːk] n remarque f, observation f ▷ vt (faire) remarquer, dire; **remarkable** adj remarquable

remarry [riː'mærɪ] vi se remarier

remedy ['rɛmədɪ] n: **~ (for)** remède m (contre or à) ▷ vt remédier à

remember [rɪ'mɛmbər] vt se rappeler, se souvenir de; (send greetings): **~ me to him** saluez-le de ma part; **Remembrance Day** [rɪ'mɛmbrəns-] n (BRIT) ≈ (le jour de) l'Armistice, ≈ le 11 novembre

⚫ **REMEMBRANCE DAY**

⚪ Remembrance Day ou Remembrance
⚪ Sunday est le dimanche le plus
⚪ proche du 11 novembre, jour où
⚪ la Première Guerre mondiale

a officiellement pris fin. Il rend
hommage aux victimes des
deux guerres mondiales. À
cette occasion, on observe deux
minutes de silence à 11h, heure de
la signature de l'armistice avec
l'Allemagne en 1918; certaines
membres de la famille royale et
du gouvernement déposent des
gerbes de coquelicots au cénotaphe
de Whitehall, et les couronnes
sont placées sur les monuments
aux morts dans toute la Grande-
Bretagne; par ailleurs, les gens
portent des coquelicots artificiels
fabriqués et vendus par des
membres de la légion britannique
blessés au combat, au profit des
blessés de guerre et de leur famille.

remind [rɪ'maɪnd] vt: **to ~ sb of sth**
rappeler qch à qn; **to ~ sb to do**
penser à qn à faire, rappeler à qn qu'il
doit faire; **reminder** n (Comm: letter)
rappel m; (note etc) pense-bête m;
(souvenir) souvenir m

reminiscent [remɪ'nɪsnt] adj: **~ of**
qui rappelle, qui fait penser à

remnant ['remnənt] n reste m,
restant m; (of cloth) coupon m

remorse [rɪ'mɔːs] n remords m

remote [rɪ'məʊt] adj éloigné(e),
lointain(e); (person) distant(e); (slight:
possibility) vague; **remote control**
n télécommande f; **remotely** adv très
loin; (slightly) très vaguement

removal [rɪ'muːvəl] n (taking away)
enlèvement m; suppression f; (BRIT:
from house) déménagement m;
(from office: dismissal) renvoi m; (of
stain) nettoyage m; (Med) ablation
f; **removal man** n (BRIT)
déménageur m; **removal van** n
(BRIT) camion m de déménagement

remove [rɪ'muːv] vt enlever, retirer;
(employee) renvoyer; (stain) faire
partir; (abuse) supprimer; (doubt)
chasser

Renaissance [rɪ'neɪsɑ̃s] n: **the ~** la
Renaissance

rename [riː'neɪm] vt rebaptiser

render ['rendəʳ] vt rendre

rendezvous ['rɒndɪvuː] n rendez-
vous m inv

renew [rɪ'njuː] vt renouveler;
(negotiations) reprendre;
(acquaintance) renouer; **renewable**
adj (energy) renouvelable

renovate ['renəveɪt] vt rénover;
(work of art) restaurer

renowned [rɪ'naʊnd] adj
renommé(e)

rent [rent] n loyer m ▷ vt louer;
rental n (for television, car) (prix m de)
location f

reorganize [riː'ɔːɡənaɪz] vt
réorganiser

rep [rep] n abbr (Comm)
= **representative**

repair [rɪ'peəʳ] n réparation f ▷ vt
réparer; **in good/bad ~** en bon/
mauvais état; **where can I get
this ~ed?** où est-ce que je peux faire
réparer ceci?; **repair kit** n trousse f de
réparations

repay [riː'peɪ] vt (irreg: like **pay**)
(money, creditor) rembourser; (sb's
efforts) récompenser; **repayment** n
remboursement m

repeat [rɪ'piːt] n (Radio, TV) reprise
f ▷ vt répéter; (promise, attack, also
Comm: order) renouveler; (Scol: a
class) redoubler ▷ vi répéter; **can
you ~ that, please?** pouvez-vous
répéter, s'il vous plaît?; **repeatedly**
adv souvent, à plusieurs reprises;
repeat prescription n (BRIT):
I'd like a repeat prescription
je voudrais renouveler mon
ordonnance

repellent [rɪ'pelənt] adj
repoussant(e) ▷ n: **insect ~**
insectifuge m

repercussions [riːpə'kʌʃənz] npl
répercussions fpl

repetition [repɪ'tɪʃən] n répétition f

repetitive [rɪˈpɛtɪtɪv] *adj* (*movement, work*) répétitif(-ive); (*speech*) plein(e) de redites

replace [rɪˈpleɪs] *vt* (*put back*) remettre, replacer; (*take the place of*) remplacer; **replacement** *n* (*substitution*) remplacement *m*; (*person*) remplaçant(e)

replay [ˈriːpleɪ] *n* (*of match*) match rejoué; (*of tape, film*) répétition *f*

replica [ˈrɛplɪkə] *n* réplique *f*, copie exacte

reply [rɪˈplaɪ] *n* réponse *f* ▷ *vi* répondre

report [rɪˈpɔːt] *n* rapport *m*; (*Press etc*) reportage *m*; (*BRIT: also*: **school ~**) bulletin *m* (scolaire); (*of gun*) détonation *f* ▷ *vt* rapporter, faire un compte rendu de; (*Press etc*) faire un reportage sur; (*notify: accident*) signaler; (*: culprit*) dénoncer ▷ *vi* (*make a report*) faire un rapport; **I'd like to ~ a theft** je voudrais signaler un vol; **to ~ to** (*sb*) (*present o.s.*) se présenter (chez qn); **report card** *n* (*US, SCOTTISH*) bulletin *m* (scolaire); **reportedly** *adv*: **she is reportedly living in Spain** elle habiterait en Espagne; **he reportedly told them to ...** il leur aurait dit de ...; **reporter** *n* reporter *m*

represent [rɛprɪˈzɛnt] *vt* représenter; (*view, belief*) présenter, expliquer; (*describe*): **to ~ sth as** présenter *or* décrire qch comme; **representation** [rɛprɪzɛnˈteɪʃən] *n* représentation *f*; **representative** *n* représentant(e); (*us Pol*) député *m* ▷ *adj* représentatif(-ive), caractéristique

repress [rɪˈprɛs] *vt* réprimer; **repression** [rɪˈprɛʃən] *n* répression *f*

reprimand [ˈrɛprɪmɑːnd] *n* réprimande *f* ▷ *vt* réprimander

reproduce [riːprəˈdjuːs] *vt* reproduire ▷ *vi* se reproduire; **reproduction** [riːprəˈdʌkʃən] *n* reproduction *f*

reptile [ˈrɛptaɪl] *n* reptile *m*

republic [rɪˈpʌblɪk] *n* république *f*; **republican** *adj, n* républicain(e)

reputable [ˈrɛpjutəbl] *adj* de bonne réputation; (*occupation*) honorable

reputation [rɛpjuˈteɪʃən] *n* réputation *f*

request [rɪˈkwɛst] *n* demande *f*; (*formal*) requête *f* ▷ *vt*: **to ~ (of** *or* **from sb)** demander (à qn); **request stop** *n* (*BRIT: for bus*) arrêt facultatif

require [rɪˈkwaɪə²] *vt* (*need: subj: person*) avoir besoin de; (*: thing, situation*) nécessiter, demander; (*want*) exiger; (*order*): **to ~ sb to do sth/sth of sb** exiger que qn fasse qch/qch de qn; **requirement** *n* (*need*) exigence *f*; besoin *m*; (*condition*) condition *f* (requise)

resat [riːˈsæt] *pt, pp of* **resit**

rescue [ˈrɛskjuː] *n* (*from accident*) sauvetage *m*; (*help*) secours *mpl* ▷ *vt* sauver

research [rɪˈsəːtʃ] *n* recherche(s) *f(pl)* ▷ *vt* faire des recherches sur

resemblance [rɪˈzɛmbləns] *n* ressemblance *f*

resemble [rɪˈzɛmbl] *vt* ressembler à

resent [rɪˈzɛnt] *vt* être contrarié(e) par; **resentful** *adj* irrité(e), plein(e) de ressentiment; **resentment** *n* ressentiment *m*

reservation [rɛzəˈveɪʃən] *n* (*booking*) réservation *f*; **to make a ~ (in an hotel/a restaurant/on a plane)** réserver *or* retenir une chambre/une table/une place; **reservation desk** *n* (*us: in hotel*) réception *f*

reserve [rɪˈzəːv] *n* réserve *f*; (*Sport*) remplaçant(e) ▷ *vt* (*seats etc*) réserver, retenir; **reserved** *adj* réservé(e)

reservoir [ˈrɛzəvwɑː²] *n* réservoir *m*

reshuffle [riːˈʃʌfl] *n*: **Cabinet ~** (*Pol*) remaniement ministériel

residence [ˈrɛzɪdəns] *n* résidence *f*; **residence permit** *n* (*BRIT*) permis *m* de séjour

resident ['rɛzɪdənt] n (of country) résident(e); (of area, house) habitant(e); (in hotel) pensionnaire ⊳ adj résidant(e); **residential** [rɛzɪ'dɛnʃəl] adj de résidence; (area) résidentiel(le); (course) avec hébergement sur place

residue ['rɛzɪdjuː] n reste m (Chem, Physics) résidu m

resign [rɪ'zaɪn] vt (one's post) se démettre de ⊳ vi démissionner; **to ~ o.s. to** (endure) se résigner à ; **resignation** [rɛzɪg'neɪʃən] n (from post) démission f; (state of mind) résignation f

resin ['rɛzɪn] n résine f

resist [rɪ'zɪst] vt résister à; **resistance** n résistance f

resit vt [riː'sɪt] (irreg: like **sit**) (BRIT: exam) repasser ⊳ n ['riːsɪt] deuxième session f (d'un examen)

resolution [rɛzə'luːʃən] n résolution f

resolve [rɪ'zɔlv] n résolution f ⊳ vt (problem) résoudre; (decide): **to ~ to do** résoudre or décider de faire

resort [rɪ'zɔːt] n (seaside town) station f balnéaire; (for skiing) station de ski; (recourse) recours m ⊳ vi: **to ~ to** avoir recours à; **in the last ~** en dernier ressort

resource [rɪ'zɔːs] n ressource f; **resourceful** adj ingénieux(-euse), débrouillard(e)

respect [rɪs'pɛkt] n respect m ⊳ vt respecter; **respectable** adj respectable; (quite good: result etc) honorable; **respectful** adj respectueux(-euse); **respective** adj respectif(-ive); **respectively** adv respectivement

respite ['rɛspaɪt] n répit m

respond [rɪs'pɔnd] vi répondre; (react) réagir; **response** [rɪs'pɔns] n réponse f; (reaction) réaction f

responsibility [rɪspɔnsɪ'bɪlɪtɪ] n responsabilité f

responsible [rɪs'pɔnsɪbl] adj (liable): **~ (for)** responsable (de);

(person) digne de confiance; (job) qui comporte des responsabilités; **responsibly** adv avec sérieux

responsive [rɪs'pɔnsɪv] adj (student, audience) réceptif(-ive); (brakes, steering) sensible

rest [rɛst] n repos m; (stop) arrêt m, pause f; (Mus) silence m; (support) support m, appui m; (remainder) reste m, restant m ⊳ vi se reposer; (be supported): **to ~ on** appuyer or reposer sur ⊳ vt (lean): **to ~ sth on/against** appuyer qch sur/contre; **the ~ of them** les autres

restaurant ['rɛstərɔ̃] n restaurant m; **restaurant car** n (BRIT Rail) wagon-restaurant m

restless ['rɛstlɪs] adj agité(e)

restoration [rɛstə'reɪʃən] n (of building) restauration f; (of stolen goods) restitution f

restore [rɪ'stɔː] vt (building) restaurer; (sth stolen) restituer; (peace, health) rétablir; **to ~ to** (former state) ramener à

restrain [rɪs'treɪn] vt (feeling) contenir; (person): **to ~ (from doing)** retenir (de faire); **restraint** n (restriction) contrainte f; (moderation) retenue f; (of style) sobriété f

restrict [rɪs'trɪkt] vt restreindre, limiter; **restriction** [rɪs'trɪkʃən] n restriction f, limitation f

rest room n (US) toilettes fpl

restructure [riː'strʌktʃəʳ] vt restructurer

result [rɪ'zʌlt] n résultat m ⊳ vi: **to ~ in** aboutir à, se terminer par; **as a ~ of** à la suite de

resume [rɪ'zjuːm] vt (work, journey) reprendre ⊳ vi (work etc) reprendre

résumé ['reɪzjuːmeɪ] n (summary) résumé m; (US: curriculum vitae) curriculum vitae m inv

resuscitate [rɪ'sʌsɪteɪt] vt (Med) réanimer

retail ['riːteɪl] adj de or au détail ⊳ adv au détail; **retailer** n détaillant(e)

retain [rɪ'teɪn] vt (keep) garder, conserver

retaliation [rɪtælɪ'eɪʃən] n représailles fpl, vengeance f

retire [rɪ'taɪə*] vi (give up work) prendre sa retraite; (withdraw) se retirer, partir; (go to bed) aller se coucher; **retired** adj (person) retraité(e); **retirement** n retraite f

retort [rɪ'tɔːt] vi riposter

retreat [rɪ'triːt] n retraite f ▷ vi battre en retraite

retrieve [rɪ'triːv] vt (sth lost) récupérer; (situation, honour) sauver; (error, loss) réparer; (Comput) rechercher

retrospect ['retrəspekt] n: **in ~** rétrospectivement, après coup; **retrospective** [retrə'spektɪv] adj rétrospectif(-ive); (law) rétroactif(-ive) ▷ n (Art) rétrospective f

return [rɪ'tɜːn] n (going or coming back) retour m; (of sth stolen etc) restitution f; (Finance: from land, shares) rapport m ▷ cpd (journey) de retour; (BRIT: ticket) aller et retour; (match) retour ▷ vi (person etc: come back) revenir; (: go back) retourner ▷ vt rendre; (bring back) rapporter; (send back) renvoyer; (put back) remettre; (Pol: candidate) élire; **returns** npl (Comm) recettes fpl; **many happy ~s (of the day)!** bon anniversaire!; **by ~ (of post)** par retour (du courrier); **in ~ (for)** en échange (de); **a ~ (ticket) for ...** un billet aller et retour pour ...; **return ticket** n (esp BRIT) billet m aller-retour

retweet [riː'twiːt] vt (on Twitter) retweeter

reunion [riː'juːnɪən] n réunion f

reunite [riːjuː'naɪt] vt réunir

revamp [riː'væmp] vt (house) retaper; (firm) réorganiser

reveal [rɪ'viːl] vt (make known) révéler; (display) laisser voir; **revealing** adj révélateur(-trice); (dress) au décolleté généreux or suggestif

revel ['revl] vi: **to ~ in sth/in doing** se délecter de qch/à faire

revelation [revə'leɪʃən] n révélation f

revenge [rɪ'vendʒ] n vengeance f; (in game etc) revanche f ▷ vt venger; **to take ~ (on)** se venger (sur)

revenue ['revənjuː] n revenu m

Reverend ['revərənd] adj: **the ~ John Smith** (Anglican) le révérend John Smith; (Catholic) l'abbé (John) Smith; (Protestant) le pasteur (John) Smith

reversal [rɪ'vɜːsl] n (of opinion) revirement m; (of order) renversement m; (of direction) changement m

reverse [rɪ'vɜːs] n contraire m, opposé m; (back) dos m, envers m; (of paper) verso m; (of coin) revers m; (Aut: also: **~ gear**) marche f arrière ▷ adj (order, direction) opposé(e), inverse ▷ vt (order, position) changer, inverser; (direction, policy) changer complètement de; (decision) annuler; (roles) renverser ▷ vi (BRIT Aut) faire marche arrière; **reversing lights** npl (BRIT Aut) feux mpl de marche arrière or de recul

revert [rɪ'vɜːt] vi: **to ~ to** revenir à, retourner à

review [rɪ'vjuː] n revue f; (of book, film) critique f; (of situation, policy) examen m, bilan m; (us: examination) examen ▷ vt passer en revue; faire la critique de; examiner

revise [rɪ'vaɪz] vt réviser, modifier; (manuscript) revoir, corriger ▷ vi (study) réviser; **revision** [rɪ'vɪʒən] n révision f

revival [rɪ'vaɪvl] n reprise f; (recovery) rétablissement m; (of faith) renouveau m

revive [rɪ'vaɪv] vt (person) ranimer; (custom) rétablir; (economy) relancer; (hope, courage) raviver, faire renaître; (play, fashion) reprendre ▷ vi (person) reprendre connaissance (: from ill health) se rétablir; (hope etc) renaître; (activity) reprendre

revolt [rɪ'vəʊlt] n révolte f ▷ vi
se révolter, se rebeller ▷ vt
révolter, dégoûter; **revolting** adj
dégoûtant(e)

revolution [rɛvə'lu:ʃən] n révolution
f; (of wheel etc) tour m, révolution;
revolutionary adj, n révolutionnaire
(m/f)

revolve [rɪ'vɒlv] vi tourner

revolver [rɪ'vɒlvə*] n revolver m

reward [rɪ'wɔːd] n récompense f
▷ vt: to ~ (for) récompenser (de);
rewarding adj (fig) qui vaut la
peine, gratifiant(e)

rewind [riː'waɪnd] vt (irreg: like
wind³) (tape) réembobiner

rewritable [riː'raɪtəbl] adj (CD, DVD)
réinscriptible

rewrite [riː'raɪt] (irreg: like **write**)
vt récrire

rheumatism ['ruːmətɪzəm] n
rhumatisme m

Rhine [raɪn] n: **the (River)** ~ le Rhin

rhinoceros [raɪ'nɒsərəs] n
rhinocéros m

rhubarb ['ruːbɑːb] n rhubarbe f

rhyme [raɪm] n rime f; (verse) vers mpl

rhythm ['rɪðm] n rythme m

rib [rɪb] n (Anat) côte f

ribbon ['rɪbən] n ruban m; **in ~s** (torn)
en lambeaux

rice [raɪs] n riz m; **rice pudding** n
riz m au lait

rich [rɪtʃ] adj riche; (gift, clothes)
somptueux(-euse); **to be ~ in sth**
être riche en qch

rid [rɪd] (pt, pp **rid**) vt: **to ~ sb of**
débarrasser qn de; **to get ~ of** se
débarrasser de

ridden ['rɪdn] pp of **ride**

riddle ['rɪdl] n (puzzle) énigme f ▷ vt:
to be ~d with être criblé(e) de; (fig)
être en proie à

ride [raɪd] (pt **rode**, pp **ridden**) n
promenade f, tour m; (distance
covered) trajet m ▷ vi (as sport)
monter (à cheval), faire du cheval;
(go somewhere: on horse, bicycle) aller

(à cheval or bicyclette etc); (travel: on
bicycle, motor cycle, bus) rouler ▷ vt (a
horse) monter; (distance) parcourir,
faire; **to ~ a horse/bicycle** monter à
cheval/à bicyclette; **to take sb for a
~** faire marcher qn; (cheat) rouler
qn; **rider** n cavalier(-ière); (in race)
jockey m; (on bicycle) cycliste m/f; (on
motorcycle) motocycliste m/f

ridge [rɪdʒ] n (of hill) faîte m; (of roof,
mountain) arête f; (on object) strie f

ridicule ['rɪdɪkjuːl] n ridicule m,
dérision f ▷ vt ridiculiser, tourner en
dérision; **ridiculous** [rɪ'dɪkjuləs]
adj ridicule

riding ['raɪdɪŋ] n équitation f;
riding school n manège m, école f
d'équitation

rife [raɪf] adj répandu(e); **~ with**
abondant(e) en

rifle ['raɪfl] n fusil m (à canon rayé)
▷ vt vider, dévaliser

rift [rɪft] n fente f, fissure f; (fig:
disagreement) désaccord m

rig [rɪg] n (also: **oil ~:** on land) derrick
m; (: at sea) plate-forme pétrolière
f ▷ vt (election etc) truquer

right [raɪt] adj (true) juste, exact(e);
(correct) bon (bonne); (suitable)
approprié(e), convenable; (just)
juste, équitable; (morally good) bien,
juste; (not left) droit(e) ▷ n (moral good)
bien m; (title, claim) droit m; (not left)
droite f ▷ adv (answer) correctement;
(treat) bien, comme il faut; (not on
the left) à droite ▷ excl bon!; **do you have the ~ time?**
avez-vous l'heure juste or exacte?; **to
be ~** (person) avoir raison; (answer)
être juste or correct(e); **by ~s** en
toute justice; **on the ~** à droite; **to
be in the ~** avoir raison; **~ in the
middle** en plein milieu; **~ away**
immédiatement; **right angle** n
(Math) angle droit; **rightful** adj (heir)
légitime; **right-hand** adj: **the right-
hand side** la droite; **right-hand
drive** n conduite f à droite; (vehicle)

véhicule m avec la conduite à droite; **right-handed** adj (person) droitier(-ière); **rightly** adv bien, correctement; (with reason) à juste titre; **right of way** n (on path etc) droit m de passage; (Aut) priorité f; **right-wing** adj (Pol) de droite

rigid ['rɪdʒɪd] adj rigide; (principle, control) strict(e)

rigorous ['rɪɡərəs] adj rigoureux(-euse)

rim [rɪm] n bord m; (of spectacles) monture f; (of wheel) jante f

rind [raɪnd] n (of bacon) couenne f; (of lemon etc) écorce f, zeste m; (of cheese) croûte f

ring [rɪŋ] n anneau m; (on finger) bague f; (also: **wedding** ~) alliance f; (of people, objects) cercle m; (of spies) réseau m; (of smoke etc) rond m; (arena) piste f, arène f; (for boxing) ring m; (sound of bell) sonnerie f ▷ vi (pt **rang**, pp **rung**) (telephone, bell) sonner; (person: by telephone) téléphoner; (ears) bourdonner; (also: ~ **out**: voice, words) retentir ▷ vt (also: ~ **up**) (Tel) téléphoner à, appeler; **to ~ the bell** sonner; **to give sb a ~** (Tel) passer un coup de téléphone or de fil à qn; **ring back** vt, vi (BRIT Tel) rappeler; **ring off** vi (BRIT Tel) raccrocher; **ring up** vt (BRIT Tel) téléphoner à, appeler; **ringing tone** n (Tel) tonalité f d'appel; **ringleader** n (of gang) chef m, meneur m; **ring road** n (BRIT) rocade f (motorway) périphérique m; **ringtone** n (on mobile) sonnerie f (de téléphone portable)

rink [rɪŋk] n (also: **ice** ~) patinoire f

rinse [rɪns] n rinçage m ▷ vt rincer

riot ['raɪət] n émeute f, bagarres fpl ▷ vi (demonstrators) manifester avec violence; (population) se soulever, se révolter; **to run** ~ se déchaîner

rip [rɪp] n déchirure f ▷ vt déchirer ▷ vi se déchirer; **rip off** vt (inf: cheat) arnaquer; **rip up** vt déchirer

ripe [raɪp] adj (fruit) mûr(e); (cheese) fait(e)

rip-off ['rɪpɔf] n (inf): **it's a ~!** c'est du vol manifeste!, c'est de l'arnaque!

ripple ['rɪpl] n ride f, ondulation f; (of applause, laughter) cascade f ▷ vi se rider, onduler

rise [raɪz] n (slope) côte f, pente f; (hill) élévation f; (increase: in wages: BRIT) augmentation f; (: in prices, temperature) hausse f, augmentation f; (fig: to power etc) ascension f ▷ vi (pt **rose**, pp **risen**) s'élever, monter; (prices, numbers) augmenter, monter; (waters, river) monter; (sun, wind, person: from chair, bed) se lever; (also: ~ **up**: tower, building) s'élever; (: rebel) se révolter, se rebeller; (in rank) s'élever; **to give ~ to** donner lieu à; **to ~ to the occasion** se montrer à la hauteur; **risen** ['rɪzn] pp of **rise**

rising adj (increasing: number, prices) en hausse; (tide) montant(e); (sun, moon) levant(e)

risk [rɪsk] n risque m ▷ vt risquer; **to take** or **run the ~ of doing** courir le risque de faire; **at ~** en danger; **at one's own ~** à ses risques et périls; **risky** adj risqué(e)

rite [raɪt] n rite m; **the last ~s** les derniers sacrements

ritual ['rɪtjuəl] adj rituel(le) ▷ n rituel m

rival ['raɪvl] n rival(e); (in business) concurrent(e) ▷ adj rival(e); qui fait concurrence ▷ vt (match) égaler; **rivalry** n rivalité f; (in business) concurrence f

river ['rɪvə*] n rivière f; (major: also fig) fleuve m ▷ cpd (port, traffic) fluvial(e); **up/down** ~ en amont/aval; **riverbank** n rive f, berge f

rivet ['rɪvɪt] n rivet m ▷ vt (fig) river, fixer

Riviera [rɪvɪ'eərə] n: **the (French) ~** la Côte d'Azur

road [rəud] n route f; (in town) rue f; (fig) chemin, voie f ▷ cpd (accident) de la route; **major/minor ~** route principale or à priorité/voie secondaire; **which ~ do I take for …?** quelle route dois-je prendre pour aller à …?; **roadblock** n barrage routier; **road map** n carte routière; **road rage** n comportement très agressif de certains usagers de la route; **road safety** n sécurité routière; **roadside** n bord de la route, bas-côté m; **road sign** n panneau m de signalisation; **road tax** n (BRIT Aut) taxe f sur les automobiles; **roadworks** npl travaux mpl (de réfection des routes)

roam [rəʊm] vi errer, vagabonder

roar [rɔːʳ] n rugissement m; (of crowd) hurlements mpl; (of vehicle, thunder, storm) grondement m ▷ vi rugir; hurler; gronder; **to ~ with laughter** rire à gorge déployée

roast [rəʊst] n rôti m ▷ vt (meat) (faire) rôtir; (coffee) griller, torréfier; **roast beef** n rôti m de bœuf, rosbif m

rob [rɔb] vt (person) voler; (bank) dévaliser; **to ~ sb of sth** voler or dérober qch à qn; (fig: deprive) priver qn de qch; **robber** n bandit m, voleur m; **robbery** n vol m

robe [rəʊb] n (for ceremony etc) robe f; (also: **bath~**) peignoir m; (us: rug) couverture f ▷ vt revêtir (d'une robe)

robin ['rɔbɪn] n rouge-gorge m

robot ['rəʊbɔt] n robot m

robust [rəʊ'bʌst] adj robuste; (material, appetite) solide

rock [rɔk] n (substance) roche f, roc m; (boulder) rocher m, roche; (us: small stone) caillou m; (BRIT: sweet) ≈ sucre m d'orge ▷ vt (swing gently: cradle) balancer; (child) bercer; (shake) ébranler, secouer ▷ vi se balancer, être ébranlé(e) or secoué(e); **on the ~s** (drink) avec des glaçons; (marriage etc) en train de craquer; **rock and roll** n rock (and roll) m, rock'n'roll m; **rock climbing** n varappe f

rocket ['rɔkɪt] n fusée f; (Mil) fusée, roquette f; (Culin) roquette

rocking chair ['rɔkɪŋ-] n fauteuil m à bascule

rocky ['rɔkɪ] adj (hill) rocheux(-euse); (path) rocailleux(-euse)

rod [rɔd] n (metallic) tringle f; (Tech) tige f; (wooden) baguette f; (also: **fishing ~**) canne f à pêche

rode [rəʊd] pt of **ride**

rodent ['rəʊdnt] n rongeur m

rogue [rəʊg] n coquin(e)

role [rəʊl] n rôle m; **role-model** n modèle m à émuler

roll [rəʊl] n rouleau m; (of banknotes) liasse f; (also: **bread ~**) petit pain; (register) liste f; (sound: of drums etc) roulement m ▷ vt rouler; (also: **~ up**) (string) enrouler; (also: **~ out**: pastry) étendre au rouleau, abaisser ▷ vi rouler; **roll over** vi se retourner; **roll up** vi (inf: arrive) arriver, s'amener ▷ vt (carpet, cloth, map) rouler; (sleeves) retrousser; **roller** n rouleau m; (wheel) roulette f; (for road) rouleau compresseur; (for hair) bigoudi m; **roller coaster** n montagnes fpl russes; **roller skates** npl patins mpl à roulettes; **roller-skating** n patin m à roulettes; **to go roller-skating** faire du patin à roulettes; **rolling pin** n rouleau m à pâtisserie

ROM [rɔm] n abbr (Comput: = read-only memory) mémoire morte, ROM f

Roman ['rəʊmən] adj romain(e) ▷ n Romain(e); **Roman Catholic** adj, n catholique (m/f)

romance [rə'mæns] n (love affair) idylle f; (charm) poésie f; (novel) roman m à l'eau de rose

Romania [rəʊ'meɪnɪə] n = **Rumania**

Roman numeral n chiffre romain

romantic [rə'mæntɪk] adj romantique; (novel, attachment) sentimental(e)

Rome [rəʊm] n Rome

roof [ruːf] n toit m; (of tunnel, cave) plafond m ▷ vt couvrir (d'un toit); **the ~ of the mouth** la voûte du palais; **roof rack** n (Aut) galerie f

rook [rʊk] n (bird) freux m; (Chess) tour f

room [ruːm] n (in house) pièce f; (also: **bed~**) chambre f (à coucher); (in school etc) salle f; (space) place f; **roommate** n camarade m/f de chambre; **room service** n service des chambres (dans un hôtel); **roomy** adj spacieux(-euse); (garment) ample

rooster ['ruːstə'] n coq m

root [ruːt] n (Bot, Math) racine f; (fig: of problem) origine f, fond m ▷ vi (plant) s'enraciner

rope [rəʊp] n corde f; (Naut) cordage m ▷ vt (tie up or together) attacher; (climbers: also: **~ together**) encorder; (area: also: **~ off**) interdire l'accès de; (: divide off) séparer; **to know the ~s** (fig) être au courant, connaître les ficelles

rort [rɔːt] n (AUST, NZ inf) arnaque f (inf) ▷ vt escroquer

rose [rəʊz] pt of **rise** ▷ n rose f; (also: **~bush**) rosier m

rosé ['rəʊzeɪ] n rosé m

rosemary ['rəʊzmərɪ] n romarin m

rosy ['rəʊzɪ] adj rose; **a ~ future** un bel avenir

rot [rɔt] n (decay) pourri m; (fig: pej: nonsense) idioties fpl, balivernes fpl ▷ vt, vi pourrir

rota ['rəʊtə] n liste f, tableau m de service

rotate [rəʊ'teɪt] vt (revolve) faire tourner; (change round: crops) alterner; (: jobs) faire à tour de rôle ▷ vi (revolve) tourner

rotten ['rɔtn] adj (decayed) pourri(e); (dishonest) corrompu(e); (inf: bad) mauvais(e), moche; **to feel ~** (ill) être mal fichu(e)

rough [rʌf] adj (cloth, skin) rêche, rugueux(-euse); (terrain) accidenté(e); (path) rocailleux(-euse); (voice) rauque, rude; (person, manner: coarse) rude, fruste; (: violent) brutal(e); (district, weather) mauvais(e); (sea) houleux(-euse); (plan) ébauché(e);

(guess) approximatif(-ive) ▷ n (Golf) rough m ▷ vt: **to ~ it** vivre à la dure; **to sleep ~** (BRIT) coucher à la dure; **roughly** adv (handle) rudement, brutalement; (speak) avec brusquerie; (make) grossièrement; (approximately) à peu près, en gros

roulette [ruː'let] n roulette f

round [raʊnd] adj rond(e) ▷ n rond, cercle m; (BRIT: of toast) tranche f; (duty: of policeman, milkman etc) tournée f; (: of doctor) visites fpl; (game: of cards, in competition) partie f; (Boxing) round m; (of talks) série f ▷ vt (corner) tourner ▷ prep autour de ▷ adv: **right~**, **all ~** tout autour; **~ of ammunition** cartouche f; **~ of applause** applaudissements mpl; **~ of drinks** tournée f; **the long way ~** (par) le chemin le plus long; **all (the) year ~** toute l'année; **it's just ~ the corner** (fig) c'est tout près; **to go ~ to sb's (house)** aller chez qn; **go ~ the back** passez par derrière; **enough to go ~** assez pour tout le monde; **she arrived ~ (about) noon** (BRIT) elle est arrivée vers midi; **~ the clock** 24 heures sur 24; **round off** vt (speech etc) terminer; **round up** vt (criminals) effectuer une rafle de; (prices) arrondir (au chiffre supérieur); **roundabout** n (BRIT: Aut) rond-point m (à sens giratoire); (: at fair) manège m (de chevaux de bois) ▷ adj (route, means) détourné(e); **round trip** n (voyage m) aller et retour m; **roundup** n rassemblement m; (of criminals) rafle f

rouse [raʊz] vt (wake up) réveiller; (stir up) susciter, provoquer; (interest) éveiller; (suspicions) susciter, éveiller

route [ruːt] n itinéraire m; (of bus) parcours m; (of trade, shipping) route f

router n (Comput) routeur m

routine [ruː'tiːn] adj (work) ordinaire, courant(e); (procedure) d'usage ▷ n (habits) habitudes fpl; (pej) train-train m; (Theat) numéro m

row¹ ['rəʊ] n (line) rangée f; (of people, seats, Knitting) rang m; (behind one another: of cars, people) file f ▷ vi (in boat) ramer; (as sport) faire de l'aviron ▷ vt (boat) faire aller à la rame or à l'aviron; **in a ~** (fig) d'affilée

row² [raʊ] n (noise) vacarme m; (dispute) dispute f, querelle f; (scolding) réprimande f, savon m ▷ vi (also: **to have a ~**) se disputer, se quereller

rowboat ['rəʊbəʊt] n (US) canot m (à rames)

rowing ['rəʊɪŋ] n canotage m; (as sport) aviron m; **rowing boat** n (BRIT) canot m (à rames)

royal ['rɔɪəl] adj royal(e); **royalty** n (royal persons) (membres mpl de la) famille royale; (payment: to author) droits mpl d'auteur; (: to inventor) royalties fpl

rpm abbr (= revolutions per minute) t/mn (= tours/minute)

R.S.V.P. abbr (= répondez s'il vous plaît) RSVP

Rt. Hon. abbr (BRIT: = Right Honourable) titre donné aux députés de la Chambre des communes

rub [rʌb] n: **to give sth a ~** donner un coup de chiffon or de torchon à qch ▷ vt frotter; (person) frictionner; (hands) se frotter; **to ~ sb up** (BRIT) or **to ~ sb** (US) **the wrong way** prendre qn à rebrousse-poil; **rub in** vt (ointment) faire pénétrer; **rub off** vi partir; **rub out** vt effacer

rubber ['rʌbər] n caoutchouc m; (BRIT: eraser) gomme f (à effacer); **rubber band** n élastique m; **rubber gloves** npl gants mpl en caoutchouc

rubbish ['rʌbɪʃ] n (from household) ordures fpl; (fig: pej) choses fpl sans valeur; camelote f; (nonsense) bêtises fpl, idioties fpl; **rubbish bin** n (BRIT) boîte f à ordures, poubelle f; **rubbish dump** n (BRIT: in town) décharge publique, dépotoir m

rubble ['rʌbl] n décombres mpl; (smaller) gravats mpl; (Constr) blocage m

ruby ['ruːbɪ] n rubis m

rucksack ['rʌksæk] n sac m à dos

rudder ['rʌdər] n gouvernail m

rude [ruːd] adj (impolite: person) impoli(e); (: word, manners) grossier(-ière); (shocking) indécent(e), inconvenant(e)

ruffle ['rʌfl] vt (hair) ébouriffer; (clothes) chiffonner; (fig: person): **to get ~d** s'énerver

rug [rʌg] n petit tapis; (BRIT: blanket) couverture f

rugby ['rʌgbɪ] n (also: **~ football**) rugby m

rugged ['rʌgɪd] adj (landscape) accidenté(e); (features, character) rude

ruin ['ruːɪn] n ruine f ▷ vt ruiner; (spoil: clothes) abîmer; (: event) gâcher; **ruins** npl (of building) ruine(s)

rule [ruːl] n règle f; (regulation) règlement m; (government) autorité f, gouvernement m ▷ vt (country) gouverner; (person) dominer; (decide) décider ▷ vi commander; **as a ~** normalement, en règle générale; **rule out** vt exclure; **ruler** n (sovereign) souverain(e); (leader) chef m d'État; (for measuring) règle f; **ruling** adj (party) au pouvoir; (class) dirigeant(e) ▷ n (Law) décision f

rum [rʌm] n rhum m

Rumania [ruːˈmeɪnɪə] n Roumanie f; **Rumanian** adj roumain(e) ▷ n Roumain(e); (Ling) roumain m

rumble ['rʌmbl] n grondement m; (of stomach, pipe) gargouillement m ▷ vi gronder; (stomach, pipe) gargouiller

rumour, (US) **rumor** ['ruːmər] n rumeur f, bruit m (qui court) ▷ vt: **it is ~d that** le bruit court que

rump steak n romsteck m

run [rʌn] (pt ran, pp run) n (race) course f; (outing) tour m or promenade f (en voiture); (distance travelled) parcours m, trajet m; (series) suite f, série f; (Ski) piste f; (Cricket, Baseball) point m; (in tights, stockings) maille filée, échelle f ▷ vt (business) diriger; (competition, course) organiser; (hotel, house) tenir; (race) participer à; (Comput: program) exécuter; (to pass: hand, finger): **to ~ sth over** promener or passer qch sur; (water, bath) faire couler; (Press: feature) publier ▷ vi courir; (pass: road etc) passer; (work: machine, factory) marcher; (bus, train) circuler; (continue: play) se jouer, être à l'affiche; (: contract) être valide or en vigueur; (flow: river, bath, nose) couler; (colours, washing) déteindre; (in election) être candidat, se présenter; **at a ~** au pas de course; **to go for a ~** aller courir or faire un peu de course à pied; (in car) faire un tour or une promenade (en voiture); **there was a ~ on** (meat, tickets) les gens se sont rués sur; **in the long ~** à la longue; **on the ~** en fuite; **I'll ~ you to the station** je vais vous emmener or conduire à la gare; **to ~ a risk** courir un risque; **run after** vt fus (to catch up) courir après; (chase) poursuivre; **run away** vi s'enfuir; **run down** vt (Aut: knock over) renverser; (BRIT: reduce: production) réduire progressivement; (: factory/shop) réduire progressivement la production/ l'activité de; (criticize) critiquer, dénigrer; **to be ~ down** (tired) être fatigué(e) or à plat; **run into** vt fus (meet: person) rencontrer par hasard; (: trouble) se heurter à; (collide with) heurter; **run off** vi s'enfuir ▷ vt (water) laisser s'écouler; (copies) tirer; **run out** vi (person) sortir en courant; (liquid) couler; (lease) expirer; (money) être épuisé(e); **run out of** vt fus se trouver à court de; **run over** vt (Aut) écraser ▷ vt fus (revise) revoir, reprendre; **run through** vt fus (recap) reprendre, revoir; (play) répéter; **run up** vi: **to ~ up against** (difficulties) se heurter

à; **runaway** adj (horse) emballé(e); (truck) fou (folle); (person) fugitif(-ive); (child) fugueur(-euse)

rung [rʌŋ] pp of **ring** ▷ n (of ladder) barreau m

runner ['rʌnəʳ] n (in race: person) coureur(-euse); (: horse) partant m; (on sledge) patin m; (for drawer etc) coulisseau m; **runner bean** n (BRIT) haricot m (à rames); **runner-up** n second(e)

running ['rʌnɪŋ] n (in race etc) course f; (of business, organization) direction f, gestion f ▷ adj (water) courant(e); (commentary) suivi(e); **6 days ~** 6 jours de suite; **to be in/out of the ~ for sth** être/ne pas être sur les rangs pour qch

runny ['rʌnɪ] adj qui coule

run-up ['rʌnʌp] n (BRIT): **~ to sth** période f précédant qch

runway ['rʌnweɪ] n (Aviat) piste f (d'envol or d'atterrissage)

rupture ['rʌptʃəʳ] n (Med) hernie f

rural ['rʊərl] adj rural(e)

rush [rʌʃ] n (of crowd, Comm: sudden demand) ruée f; (hurry) hâte f; (of anger, joy) accès m; (current) flot m; (Bot) jonc m ▷ vt (hurry) transporter or envoyer d'urgence ▷ vi se précipiter; **to ~ sth off** (do quickly) faire qch à la hâte; **rush hour** n heures fpl de pointe or d'affluence

Russia ['rʌʃə] n Russie f; **Russian** adj russe ▷ n Russe m/f; (Ling) russe m

rust [rʌst] n rouille f ▷ vi rouiller

rusty ['rʌstɪ] adj rouillé(e)

ruthless ['ruːθlɪs] adj sans pitié, impitoyable

RV n abbr (US) = **recreational vehicle**

rye [raɪ] n seigle m

S

Sabbath ['sæbəθ] n (Jewish) sabbat m; (Christian) dimanche m

sabotage ['sæbətɑːʒ] n sabotage m ▷ vt saboter

saccharin(e) ['sækərɪn] n saccharine f

sachet ['sæʃeɪ] n sachet m

sack [sæk] n (bag) sac m ▷ vt (dismiss) renvoyer, mettre à la porte; (plunder) piller, mettre à sac; **to get the ~** être renvoyé(e) or mis(e) à la porte

sacred ['seɪkrɪd] adj sacré(e)

sacrifice ['sækrɪfaɪs] n sacrifice m ▷ vt sacrifier

sad [sæd] adj (unhappy) triste; (deplorable) triste, fâcheux(-euse); (inf: pathetic: thing) triste, lamentable; (: person) minable

saddle ['sædl] n selle f ▷ vt (horse) seller; **to be ~d with sth** (inf) avoir qch sur les bras

sadistic [sə'dɪstɪk] adj sadique

sadly ['sædlɪ] adv tristement; (unfortunately) malheureusement; (seriously) fort

sadness ['sædnɪs] n tristesse f

s.a.e. n abbr (BRIT: = stamped addressed envelope) enveloppe affranchie pour la réponse

safari [sə'fɑːrɪ] n safari m

safe [seɪf] adj (out of danger) hors de danger, en sécurité; (not dangerous) sans danger; (cautious) prudent(e); (sure: bet) assuré(e) ▷ n coffre-fort m; **~ and sound** sain(e) et sauf; **(just) to be on the ~ side** pour plus de sûreté, par précaution; **safely** adv (assume, say) sans risque d'erreur; (drive, arrive) sans accident; **safe sex** n rapports sexuels protégés

safety ['seɪftɪ] n sécurité f; **safety belt** n ceinture f de sécurité; **safety pin** n épingle f de sûreté or de nourrice

saffron ['sæfrən] n safran m

sag [sæg] vi s'affaisser, fléchir; (hem, breasts) pendre

sage [seɪdʒ] n (herb) sauge f; (person) sage m

Sagittarius [sædʒɪ'tɛərɪəs] n le Sagittaire

Sahara [sə'hɑːrə] n: **the ~ (Desert)** le (désert du) Sahara m

said [sed] pt, pp of **say**

sail [seɪl] n (on boat) voile f; (trip): **to go for a ~** faire un tour en bateau ▷ vt (boat) manœuvrer, piloter ▷ vi (travel: ship) avancer, naviguer; (set off) partir, prendre la mer; (Sport) faire de la voile; **they ~ed into Le Havre** ils sont entrés dans le port du Havre; **sailboat** n (US) bateau m à voiles, voilier m; **sailing** n (Sport) voile f; **to go sailing** faire de la voile; **sailing boat** n bateau m à voiles, voilier m; **sailor** n marin m, matelot m

saint [seɪnt] n saint(e)

sake [seɪk] n: **for the ~ of** (out of concern for por) pour (l'amour de), dans l'intérêt de; (out of consideration for) par égard pour

salad ['sæləd] n salade f; **salad cream** n (BRIT) (sorte f de) mayonnaise f; **salad dressing** n vinaigrette f

salami [sə'lɑːmɪ] n salami m

salary ['sælərɪ] n salaire m, traitement m

sale [seɪl] n vente f; (at reduced prices) soldes mpl; **sales** npl (total amount sold) chiffre m de ventes; **"for ~"** "à vendre"; **on ~** en vente; **sales assistant**, (US) **sales clerk** n vendeur(-euse); **salesman** (irreg) n (in shop) vendeur m; **salesperson** (irreg) n (in shop) vendeur(-euse); **sales rep** n (Comm) représentant(e) m/f; **saleswoman** (irreg) n (in shop) vendeuse f

saline ['seɪlaɪn] adj salin(e)

saliva [sə'laɪvə] n salive f

salmon ['sæmən] n (pl inv) saumon m

salon ['sælɔn] n salon m

saloon [sə'luːn] n (US) bar m; (BRIT Aut) berline f; (ship's lounge) salon m

salt [sɔːlt] n sel m ▷ vt saler; **saltwater** adj (fish etc) (d'eau) de mer; **salty** adj salé(e)

salute [sə'luːt] n salut m; (of guns) salve f ▷ vt saluer

salvage ['sælvɪdʒ] n (saving) sauvetage m; (things saved) biens sauvés or récupérés m ▷ vt sauver, récupérer

Salvation Army [sæl'veɪʃən-] n Armée f du Salut

same [seɪm] adj même ▷ pron: le (la) même, les mêmes; **the ~ book as** le même livre que; **at the ~ time** en même temps; (yet) néanmoins; **all** or **just the ~** tout de même, quand même; **to do the ~** faire de même, en faire autant; **to do the ~ as sb** faire comme qn; **and the ~ to you!** et à vous de même!; (after insult) toi-même!

sample ['sɑːmpl] n échantillon m; (Med) prélèvement m ▷ vt (food, wine) goûter

sanction ['sæŋkʃən] n approbation f, sanction f ▷ vt cautionner, sanctionner; **sanctions** npl (Pol) sanctions

sanctuary ['sæŋktjuərɪ] n (holy place) sanctuaire m; (refuge) asile m; (for wildlife) réserve f

sand [sænd] n sable m ▷ vt (also: ~ **down**: wood etc) poncer

sandal ['sændl] n sandale f

sand: sandbox n (US: for children) tas m de sable; **sand castle** n château m de sable; **sand dune** n dune f de sable; **sandpaper** n papier m de verre; **sandpit** n (BRIT: for children) tas m de sable; **sands** npl plage f (de sable); **sandstone** ['sændstəun] n grès m

sandwich ['sændwɪtʃ] n sandwich m ▷ vt (also: ~ **in**) intercaler; **~ed between** pris en sandwich entre; **cheese/ham ~** sandwich au fromage/jambon

sandy ['sændɪ] adj sablonneux(-euse); (colour) sable inv, blond roux inv

sane [seɪn] adj (person) sain(e) d'esprit; (outlook) sensé(e), sain(e)

sang [sæŋ] pt of **sing**

sanitary towel, (US) **sanitary napkin** ['sænɪtərɪ-] n serviette f hygiénique

sanity ['sænɪtɪ] n santé mentale; (common sense) bon sens

sank [sæŋk] pt of **sink**

Santa Claus [sæntə'klɔːz] n le Père Noël

sap [sæp] n (of plants) sève f ▷ vt (strength) saper, miner

sapphire ['sæfaɪə'] n saphir m

sarcasm ['sɑːkæzm] n sarcasme m, raillerie f

sarcastic [sɑː'kæstɪk] adj sarcastique

sardine [sɑː'diːn] n sardine f

SASE n abbr (US: = self-addressed stamped envelope) enveloppe affranchie pour la réponse

sat [sæt] pt, pp of **sit**

Sat. abbr (= Saturday) sa

satchel ['sætʃl] n cartable m

satellite ['sætəlaɪt] n satellite m; **satellite dish** n antenne f parabolique; **satellite navigation system** n système m de navigation par satellite; **satellite television** n télévision f par satellite

satin ['sætɪn] n satin m ▷ adj en or de satin, satiné(e)

satire ['sætaɪə'] n satire f

satisfaction [sætɪs'fækʃən] n satisfaction f

satisfactory [sætɪs'fæktərɪ] adj satisfaisant(e)

satisfied ['sætɪsfaɪd] adj satisfait(e); **to be ~ with sth** être satisfait de qch

satisfy ['sætɪsfaɪ] vt satisfaire, contenter; (convince) convaincre, persuader

Saturday ['sætədɪ] n samedi m

sauce [sɔːs] n sauce f; **saucepan** n casserole f

saucer ['sɔːsə'] n soucoupe f

Saudi Arabia ['saudi-] n Arabie f Saoudite

sauna ['sɔːnə] n sauna m

sausage ['sɔsɪdʒ] n saucisse f; (salami etc) saucisson m; **sausage roll** n friand m

sautéed ['səuteɪd] adj sauté(e)

savage ['sævɪdʒ] adj (cruel, fierce) brutal(e), féroce; (primitive) primitif(-ive), sauvage ▷ n sauvage m/f ▷ vt attaquer férocement

save [seɪv] vt (person, belongings) sauver; (money) mettre de côté, économiser; (time) (faire) gagner; (keep) garder; (Comput) sauvegarder; (Sport: stop) arrêter; (avoid: trouble) éviter ▷ vi (also: **~ up**) mettre de l'argent de côté ▷ n (Sport) arrêt m (du ballon) ▷ prep sauf, à l'exception de

saving ['seɪvɪŋ] n économie f; **savings** npl économies fpl

savings account n compte m d'épargne

savings and loan association (US) n = société f de crédit immobilier

savoury, (US) **savory** ['seɪvərɪ] adj savoureux(-euse); (dish: not sweet) salé(e)

saw [sɔː] pt of **see** ▷ n (tool) scie f ▷ vt (pt sawed, pp sawed or sawn) scier; **sawdust** n sciure f

sawn [sɔːn] pp of **saw**

saxophone ['sæksəfəun] n saxophone m

say [seɪ] vt (pt, pp said) dire ▷ n: **to have one's ~** dire ce qu'on a à dire; **to have a ~** avoir voix au chapitre; **could you ~ that again?** pourriez-vous répéter ce que vous venez de dire?; **to ~ yes/no** dire oui/non; **my watch ~s 3 o'clock** ma montre indique 3 heures, il est 3 heures à ma montre; **that is to ~** c'est-à-dire; **that goes without ~ing** cela va sans dire, cela va de soi; **saying** n dicton m, proverbe m

scab [skæb] n croûte f; (pej) jaune m

scaffolding ['skæfəldɪŋ] n échafaudage m

scald [skɔːld] n brûlure f ▷ vt ébouillanter

scale [skeɪl] n (of fish) écaille f; (Mus) gamme f; (of ruler, thermometer etc) graduation f, échelle (graduée); (of salaries, fees etc) barème m; (of map, also size, extent) échelle f ▷ vt (mountain) escalader; **scales** npl balance f; (larger) bascule f; (also: **bathroom ~s**) pèse-personne m inv; **~ of charges** tableau m des tarifs; **on a large ~** sur une grande échelle, en grand

scallion ['skæljən] n (US: salad onion) ciboule f

scallop ['skɔləp] n coquille f Saint-Jacques; (Sewing) feston m

scalp [skælp] n cuir chevelu ▷ vt scalper

scalpel ['skælpl] n scalpel m

scam [skæm] n (inf) arnaque f

scampi ['skæmpɪ] npl langoustines (frites), scampi mpl

scan [skæn] vt (examine) scruter, examiner; (glance at quickly) parcourir; (TV, Radar) balayer ▷ n (Med) scanographie f

scandal ['skændl] n scandale m; (gossip) ragots mpl

Scandinavia [skændɪ'neɪvɪə] n Scandinavie f; **Scandinavian** adj scandinave ▷ n Scandinave m/f

scanner ['skænə'] n (Radar, Med) scanner m, scanographe m; (Comput) scanner

scapegoat ['skeɪpgəut] n bouc m émissaire

scar [skɑː'] n cicatrice f ▷ vt laisser une cicatrice or une marque sur

scarce [skɛəs] adj rare, peu abondant(e); **to make o.s. ~** (inf) se sauver; **scarcely** adv à peine, presque pas

scare [skɛə'] n peur f, panique f ▷ vt effrayer, faire peur à; **to ~ sb stiff** faire une peur bleue à qn; **bomb ~** alerte f à la bombe; **scarecrow** n épouvantail m; **scared** adj: **to be scared** avoir peur

scarf (pl **scarves**) [skɑːf, skɑːvz] n (long) écharpe f; (square) foulard m

scarlet ['skɑːlɪt] adj écarlate

scarves [skɑːvz] npl of **scarf**

scary ['skɛərɪ] adj (inf) effrayant(e); (film) qui fait peur

scatter ['skætə'] vt éparpiller, répandre; (crowd) disperser ▷ vi se disperser

scenario [sɪ'nɑːrɪəu] n scénario m

scene [siːn] n (Theat, fig etc) scène f; (of crime, accident) lieu(x) m(pl), endroit m; (sight, view) spectacle m, vue f; **scenery** n (Theat) décor(s) m(pl); (landscape) paysage m; **scenic** adj offrant de beaux paysages or panoramas

scent [sɛnt] n parfum m, odeur f; (fig: track) piste f

sceptical, (US) **skeptical** ['skɛptɪkl] adj sceptique

schedule ['ʃɛdjuːl, US 'skɛdjuːl] n programme m, plan m; (of trains) horaire m; (of prices etc) barème m, tarif m ▷ vt prévoir; **on ~** à l'heure (prévue); à la date prévue; **to be ahead of/behind ~** avoir de l'avance/ du retard; **scheduled flight** n vol régulier

scheme [skiːm] n plan m, projet m; (plot) complot m, combine f; (arrangement) arrangement m, classification f; (pension scheme etc) régime m ▷ vt, vi comploter, manigancer

schizophrenic [skɪtsə'frɛnɪk] adj schizophrène

scholar ['skɔlə'] n érudit(e); (pupil) boursier(-ère); **scholarship** n érudition f; (grant) bourse f (d'études)

school [skuːl] n (gen) école f; (secondary school) collège m; lycée m; (in university) faculté f; (us: university) université f ▷ cpd scolaire; **schoolbook** n livre m scolaire or de classe; **schoolboy** n écolier m; (at secondary school) collégien m; lycéen m; **schoolchildren** npl écoliers mpl; (at secondary school) collégiens mpl; lycéens mpl; **schoolgirl** n écolière f; (at secondary school) collégienne f; lycéenne f; **schooling** n instruction f, études fpl; **schoolteacher** n (primary) instituteur(-trice); (secondary) professeur m

science ['saɪəns] n science f; **science fiction** n science-fiction f; **scientific** [saɪən'tɪfɪk] adj scientifique; **scientist** n scientifique m/f; (eminent) savant m

sci-fi ['saɪfaɪ] n abbr (inf: = science fiction) SF f

scissors ['sɪzəz] npl ciseaux mpl; **a pair of ~** une paire de ciseaux

scold [skəuld] vt gronder

scone [skɔn] n sorte de petit pain rond au lait

S

scoop [sku:p] n pelle f (à main); (for ice cream) boule f à glace; (Press) reportage exclusif or à sensation

scooter ['sku:tə'] n (motor cycle) scooter m; (toy) trottinette f

scope [skəup] n (capacity: of plan, undertaking) portée f, envergure f; (: of person) compétence f, capacités fpl; (opportunity) possibilités fpl

scorching ['skɔ:tʃɪŋ] adj torride, brûlant(e)

score [skɔ:'] n score m, décompte m des points; (Mus) partition f ▷ vt (goal, point) marquer; (success) remporter; (cut: leather, wood, card) entailler, inciser ▷ vi marquer des points; (Football) marquer un but; (keep score) compter les points; **on that ~** sur ce chapitre, à cet égard; **a ~ (of)** (twenty) vingt; **~s of** (fig) des tas de; **to ~ 6 out of 10** obtenir 6 sur 10; **score out** vt rayer, barrer, biffer; **scoreboard** n tableau m; **scorer** n (Football) auteur m du but; buteur m; (keeping score) marqueur m

scorn [skɔ:n] n mépris m, dédain m

Scorpio ['skɔ:pɪəu] n le Scorpion

scorpion ['skɔ:pɪən] n scorpion m

Scot [skɔt] n Écossais(e)

Scotch [skɔtʃ] n whisky m, scotch m

Scotch tape® (us) n scotch® m, ruban adhésif

Scotland ['skɔtlənd] n Écosse f

Scots [skɔts] adj écossais(e); **Scotsman** (irreg) n Écossais m; **Scotswoman** (irreg) n Écossaise f; **Scottish** ['skɔtɪʃ] adj écossais(e); **the Scottish Parliament** le Parlement écossais

scout [skaut] n (Mil) éclaireur m; (also: **boy ~**) scout m; **girl ~** (us) guide f

scowl [skaul] vi se renfrogner; **to ~ at** regarder de travers

scramble ['skræmbl] n (rush) bousculade f, ruée f ▷ vi (climb) grimper/ descendre tant bien que mal; **to ~ for** se bousculer ou se disputer pour

(avoir); **to go scrambling** (Sport) faire du trial; **scrambled eggs** npl œufs brouillés

scrap [skræp] n bout m, morceau m; (fight) bagarre f; (also: **~ iron**) ferraille f ▷ vt jeter, mettre au rebut; (fig) abandonner, laisser tomber ▷ vi se bagarrer; **scraps** npl (waste) déchets mpl; **scrapbook** n album m

scrape [skreip] vt, vi gratter, racler ▷ n: **to get into a ~** s'attirer des ennuis; **scrape through** vi (exam etc) réussir de justesse

scrap paper n papier m brouillon

scratch [skrætʃ] n égratignure f, rayure f; (on paint) éraflure f; (from claw) coup m de griffe ▷ vt (rub) (se) gratter; (paint etc) érafler; (with claw, nail) griffer ▷ vi (se) gratter; **to start from ~** partir de zéro; **to be up to ~** être à la hauteur; **scratch card** n carte f à gratter

scream [skri:m] n cri perçant, hurlement m ▷ vi crier, hurler

screen [skri:n] n écran m; (in room) paravent m; (fig) écran, rideau m ▷ vt masquer, cacher; (from the wind etc) abriter, protéger; (film) projeter; (candidates etc) filtrer; **screening** n (of film) projection f; (Med) test m (or tests) de dépistage; **screenplay** n scénario m; **screen saver** n (Comput) économiseur m d'écran; **screenshot** n (Comput) capture f d'écran

screw [skru:] n vis f ▷ vt (also: **~ in**) visser; **screw up** vt (paper etc) froisser; **to ~ up one's eyes** se plisser les yeux; **screwdriver** n tournevis m

scribble ['skrɪbl] n gribouillage m ▷ vt gribouiller, griffonner

script [skrɪpt] n (Cine etc) scénario m, texte m; (writing) écriture f) script m

scroll [skrəul] n rouleau m ▷ vt (Comput) faire défiler (sur l'écran)

scrub [skrʌb] n (land) broussailles fpl ▷ vt (floor) nettoyer à la brosse; (pan) récurer; (washing) frotter

scruffy ['skrʌfɪ] adj débraillé(e)

scrum(mage) ['skrʌm(ɪdʒ)] n mêlée f

scrutiny ['skru:tɪnɪ] n examen minutieux

scuba diving ['sku:bə-] n plongée sous-marine

sculptor ['skʌlptə'] n sculpteur m

sculpture ['skʌlptʃə'] n sculpture f

scum [skʌm] n écume f, mousse f; (pej: people) rebut m, lie f

scurry ['skʌrɪ] vi filer à toute allure; **to ~ off** détaler, se sauver

sea [si:] n mer f ▷ cpd marin(e), de (la) mer, maritime; **by ~ beside the ~** (holiday, town) au bord de la mer; **by ~** par mer, en bateau; **out to ~** au large; **(out) at ~** en mer; **to be all at ~** (fig) nager complètement; **seafood** n fruits mpl de mer; **sea front** n bord m de mer; **seagull** n mouette f

seal [si:l] n (animal) phoque m; (stamp) sceau m, cachet m ▷ vt sceller; (envelope) coller (: with seal) cacheter; **seal off** vt (forbid entry to) interdire l'accès à

sea level n niveau m de la mer

seam [si:m] n couture f; (of coal) veine f, filon m

search [sə:tʃ] n (for person, thing, Comput) recherche(s) f(pl); (of drawer, pockets) fouille f; (Law: at sb's home) perquisition f ▷ vt fouiller; (examine) examiner minutieusement; scruter ▷ vi: **to ~ for** chercher; **in ~ of** à la recherche de; **search engine** n (Comput) moteur m de recherche; **search party** n expédition f de secours

sea: seashore n rivage m, plage f, bord m de (la) mer; **seasick** adj: **to be seasick** avoir le mal de mer; **seaside** n bord m de mer; **seaside resort** n station f balnéaire

season ['si:zn] n saison f ▷ vt assaisonner, relever; **to be in/ out of ~** être/ne pas être de saison; **seasonal** adj saisonnier(-ière); **seasoning** n assaisonnement

m; **season ticket** n carte f d'abonnement

seat [si:t] n siège m; (in bus, train: place) place f; (buttocks) postérieur m; (of trousers) fond m ▷ vt faire asseoir, placer; (have room for) avoir des places assises pour, pouvoir accueillir; **to be ~ed** être assis; **seat belt** n ceinture f de sécurité; **seating** n sièges fpl, places assises

sea: sea water n eau f de mer; **seaweed** n algues fpl

sec. abbr (= second) sec

secluded [sɪ'klu:dɪd] adj retiré(e), à l'écart

second ['sɛkənd] num deuxième, second(e) ▷ adv (in race etc) en seconde position ▷ n (unit of time) seconde f; (Aut: also: ~ **gear**) seconde; (Comm: imperfect) article m de second choix; (BRIT Scol:) licence f avec mention ▷ vt (motion) appuyer; **seconds** npl (inf: food) rab m (inf); **secondary** adj secondaire; **secondary school** n (age 11 to 15) collège m; (age 15 to 18) lycée m; **second-class** adj de deuxième classe; (Rail) de seconde (classe); (Post) au tarif réduit; (pej) de qualité inférieure ▷ adv (Rail) en seconde; (Post) au tarif réduit; **secondhand** adj d'occasion; (information) de seconde main; **secondly** adv deuxièmement; **second-rate** adj de deuxième ordre, de qualité inférieure; **second thoughts** npl: **to have second thoughts** changer d'avis; **on second thoughts** or (US) **thought** à la réflexion

secrecy ['si:krəsɪ] n secret m

secret ['si:krɪt] adj secret(-ète) ▷ n secret m; **in ~** adv en secret, secrètement, en cachette

secretary ['sɛkrətrɪ] n secrétaire m/f; **S~ of State (for)** (Pol) ministre m (de)

secretive ['si:krətɪv] adj réservé(e); (pej) cachottier(-ière), dissimulé(e)

secret service n services secrets

sect [sɛkt] n secte f

section ['sɛkʃən] n section f; (Comm) rayon m; (of document) section, article m, paragraphe m; (cut) coupe f

sector ['sɛktə'] n secteur m

secular ['sɛkjulə'] adj laïque

secure [sɪ'kjuə'] adj (free from anxiety) sans inquiétude, sécurisé(e); (firmly fixed) solide, bien attaché(e) (or fermé(e) etc); (in safe place) en lieu sûr, en sûreté ▷ vt (fix) fixer, attacher; (get) obtenir, se procurer

security [sɪ'kjuərɪtɪ] n sécurité f, mesures fpl de sécurité; (for loan) caution f, garantie f; **securities** npl (Stock Exchange) valeurs fpl, titres mpl; **security guard** n garde chargé de la sécurité; (transporting money) convoyeur m de fonds

sedan [sə'dæn] n (us Aut) berline f

sedate [sɪ'deɪt] adj calme; posé(e) ▷ vt donner des sédatifs à

sedative ['sɛdɪtɪv] n calmant m, sédatif m

seduce [sɪ'djuːs] vt séduire; **seductive** [sɪ'dʌktɪv] adj séduisant(e); (smile) séducteur(-trice); (fig: offer) alléchant(e)

see [siː] (pt **saw**, pp **seen**) vt (gen) voir; (accompany): **to ~ sb to the door** reconduire or raccompagner qn jusqu'à la porte ▷ vi voir; **to ~ that** (ensure) veiller à ce que + sub, faire en sorte que + sub, s'assurer que; **~ you soon/later/tomorrow!** à bientôt/plus tard/demain!; **see off** vt accompagner (à l'aéroport etc); **see out** vt (take to door) raccompagner à la porte; **see through** vt mener à bonne fin ▷ vt fus voir clair dans; **see to** vt fus s'occuper de, se charger de

seed [siːd] n graine f; (fig) germe m; (Tennis) tête f de série; **to go to ~** (plant) monter en graine; (fig) se laisser aller

seeing ['siːɪŋ] conj: **~ (that)** vu que, étant donné que

seek [siːk] (pt, pp **sought**) vt chercher, rechercher

seem [siːm] vi sembler, paraître; **there ~s to be …** il semble qu'il y a …, on dirait qu'il y a …; **seemingly** adv apparemment

seen [siːn] pp of **see**

seesaw ['siːsɔː] n (jeu m de) bascule f

segment ['sɛgmənt] n segment m; (of orange) quartier m

segregate ['sɛgrɪgeɪt] vt séparer, isoler

Seine [seɪn] n: **the (River) ~** la Seine

seize [siːz] vt (grasp) saisir, attraper; (take possession of) s'emparer de; (opportunity) saisir

seizure ['siːʒə'] n (Med) crise f, attaque f; (of power) prise f

seldom ['sɛldəm] adv rarement

select [sɪ'lɛkt] adj choisi(e), d'élite; (hotel, restaurant, club) chic inv, sélect inv ▷ vt sélectionner, choisir; **selection** n sélection f, choix m; **selective** adj sélectif(-ive); (school) à recrutement sélectif

self (pl **selves**) [sɛlf, sɛlvz] n: **the ~** le moi inv ▷ prefix auto-; **self-assured** adj sûr(e) de soi, plein(e) d'assurance; **self-catering** adj (BRIT: flat) avec cuisine, où l'on peut faire sa cuisine; (: holiday) en appartement (or chalet etc) loué; **self-centred**, (us) **self-centered** adj égocentrique; **self-confidence** n confiance f en soi; **self-confident** adj sûr(e) de soi, plein(e) d'assurance; **self-conscious** adj timide, qui manque d'assurance; **self-contained** adj (BRIT: flat) avec entrée particulière, indépendant(e); **self-control** n maîtrise f de soi; **self-defence**, (us) **self-defense** n autodéfense f; (Law) légitime défense f; **self-drive** adj (BRIT): **self-drive car** voiture f de location; **self-employed** adj qui travaille à son compte; **self-esteem** n amour-propre m; **self-harm** vi s'automutiler; **self-indulgent** adj qui ne se refuse rien; **self-interest** n intérêt personnel;

selfish adj égoïste; **self-pity** n apitoiement m sur soi-même; **self-raising** [selfreɪzɪŋ], (US) **self-rising** [selfraɪzɪŋ] adj: **self-raising flour** farine f pour gâteaux (avec levure incorporée); **self-respect** n respect m de soi, amour-propre m; **self-service** adj, n libre-service (m), self-service (m)

selfie [selfi] n selfie m

sell (pt, pp **sold**) [sel, səʊld] vt vendre ▷ vi se vendre; **to ~ at** or **for 10 euros** se vendre 10 euros; **sell off** vt liquider; **sell out** vi: **to ~ out (of sth)** (use up stock) vendre tout son stock (de qch); **sell-by date** n date f limite de vente; **seller** n vendeur(-euse), marchand(e)

Sellotape® [seləʊteɪp] n (BRIT) scotch® m

selves [selvz] npl of **self**

semester [sɪˈmestə] n (esp US) semestre m

semi... [semi] prefix semi-, demi-; à demi, à moitié; **semicircle** n demi-cercle m; **semidetached (house)** n (BRIT) maison jumelée or jumelle; **semi-final** n demi-finale f

seminar [semɪnɑː] n séminaire m

semi-skimmed [semɪskɪmd] adj demi-écrémé(e)

senate [senɪt] n sénat m; (US): **the S~** le Sénat; **senator** n sénateur m

send (pt, pp **sent**) [send, sent] vt envoyer; **to send sb** vt renvoyer; **send for** vt fus (by post) se faire envoyer, commander par correspondance; **send in** vt (report, application, resignation) remettre; **send off** vt (goods) envoyer, expédier; (BRIT Sport: player) expulser or renvoyer du terrain; **send on** vt (BRIT: letter) faire suivre; (luggage etc: in advance) (faire) expédier à l'avance; **send out** vt (invitation) envoyer (par la poste); (emit: light, heat, signal) émettre; **send up** vt (person, price) faire monter; (BRIT: parody) mettre en boîte, parodier; **sender** n expéditeur(-trice); **send-off** n: **a good send-off** des adieux chaleureux

senile [siːnaɪl] adj sénile

senior [siːnɪə] adj (high-ranking) de haut niveau; (of higher rank): **to be ~ to sb** être le supérieur de qn; **senior citizen** n personne f du troisième âge; **senior high school** n (US) ≈ lycée m

sensation [senˈseɪʃən] n sensation f; **sensational** adj qui fait sensation; (marvellous) sensationnel(le)

sense [sens] n sens m; (feeling) sentiment m; (meaning) sens, signification f; (wisdom) bon sens ▷ vt sentir, pressentir; **it makes ~** c'est logique; **senseless** adj insensé(e), stupide; (unconscious) sans connaissance; **sense of humour**, (US) **sense of humor** n sens m de l'humour

sensible [sensɪbl] adj sensé(e), raisonnable; (shoes etc) pratique

> Be careful not to translate sensible by the French word sensible.

sensitive [sensɪtɪv] adj: **~ (to)** sensible (à)

sensual [sensjʊəl] adj sensuel(le)

sensuous [sensjʊəs] adj voluptueux(-euse), sensuel(le)

sent [sent] pt, pp of **send**

sentence [sentns] n (Ling) phrase f; (Law: judgment) condamnation f, sentence f; (: punishment) peine f ▷ vt: **to ~ sb to death/to 5 years** condamner qn à mort/à 5 ans

sentiment [sentɪmənt] n sentiment m; (opinion) opinion f, avis m; **sentimental** [sentɪˈmentl] adj sentimental(e)

separate adj [seprɪt] séparé(e); (organization) indépendant(e); (day, occasion, issue) différent(e) ▷ vt [separeɪt] séparer; (distinguish) distinguer ▷ vi [separeɪt] se séparer; **separately** adv séparément; **separates** npl (clothes) coordonnés mpl; **separation** [sepəˈreɪʃən] n séparation f

September [sɛpˈtɛmbəʳ] n
septembre m

septic [ˈsɛptɪk] adj (wound) infecté(e);
septic tank n fosse f septique

sequel [ˈsiːkwl] n conséquence f;
séquelles fpl; (of story) suite f

sequence [ˈsiːkwəns] n ordre m,
suite f; (in film) séquence f; (dance)
numéro m

sequin [ˈsiːkwɪn] n paillette f

Serb [səːb] adj, n = **Serbian**

Serbia [ˈsəːbɪə] n Serbie f

Serbian [ˈsəːbɪən] adj serbe ▷ n Serbe
m/f; (Ling) serbe m

sergeant [ˈsaːdʒənt] n sergent m;
(Police) brigadier m

serial [ˈsɪərɪəl] n feuilleton m; **serial
killer** n meurtrier m tuant en série;
serial number n numéro m de série

series [ˈsɪərɪz] n série f; (Publishing)
collection f

serious [ˈsɪərɪəs] adj sérieux(-euse);
(accident etc) grave; **seriously** adv
sérieusement; (hurt) gravement

sermon [ˈsəːmən] n sermon m

servant [ˈsəːvənt] n domestique m/f;
(fig) serviteur (servante)

serve [səːv] vt (employer etc) servir,
être au service de; (purpose) servir
à; (customer, food, meal) servir; (subj:
train) desservir; (apprenticeship) faire,
accomplir; (prison term) faire; purger
▷ vi (Tennis) servir; (be useful): **to ~
as/for/to do** servir de/à/à faire ▷ n
(Tennis) service m; **it ~s him right**
c'est bien fait pour lui; **server** n
(Comput) serveur m

service [ˈsəːvɪs] n (gen) service m;
(Aut) révision f; (Rel) office m ▷ vt
(car etc) réviser; **services** npl (Econ:
tertiary sector) (secteur m) tertiaire
m, secteur des services; (BRIT: on
motorway) station-service f; (Mil): **the
S~s** npl les forces armées; **to be of ~
to sb, to do sb a ~** rendre service à
qn; **~ included/not included** service
compris/non compris; **service area**
n (on motorway) aire f de services;

service charge n (BRIT) service m;
serviceman (irreg) n militaire m;
service station n station-service f

serviette [səːvɪˈɛt] n (BRIT) serviette
f (de table)

session [ˈsɛʃən] n (sitting) séance f;
to be in ~ siéger, être en session ou
en séance

set [sɛt] (pt, pp set) n série f,
assortiment m; (of tools etc) jeu m;
(Radio, TV) poste m; (Tennis) set m;
(group of people) cercle m, milieu m;
(Cine) plateau m; (Theat: stage) scène
f; (: scenery) décor m; (Math) ensemble
m; (Hairdressing) mise f en plis ▷ adj
(fixed) fixe, déterminé(e); (ready)
prêt(e) ▷ vt (place) mettre, poser,
placer; (fix, establish) fixer (: record)
établir; (assign: task, homework)
donner; (exam) composer; (adjust)
régler; (decide: rules etc) fixer, choisir
▷ vi (sun) se coucher; (jam, jelly,
concrete) prendre; (bone) se ressouder;
to be ~ on doing être résolu(e)
à faire; **to ~ to music** mettre en
musique; **to ~ on fire** mettre le feu
à; **to ~ free** libérer; **to ~ sth going**
déclencher qch; **to ~ sail** partir,
prendre la mer; **set aside** vt mettre
de côté; (time) garder; **set down** vt
(subj: bus, train) déposer; **set in** vi
(infection, bad weather) s'installer;
(complications) survenir, surgir; **set
off** vi se mettre en route, partir ▷ vt
(bomb) faire exploser; (cause to start)
déclencher; (show up well) mettre en
valeur, faire valoir; **set out** vi: **to ~
out (from)** partir (de) ▷ vt (arrange)
disposer; (state) présenter, exposer;
to ~ out to do entreprendre de
faire; avoir pour but ou intention de
faire; **set up** vt (organization) fonder,
créer; **setback** n (hitch) revers m,
contretemps m; **set menu** n menu m

settee [sɛˈtiː] n canapé m

setting [ˈsɛtɪŋ] n cadre m; (of jewel)
monture f; (position: of controls)
réglage m

settle ['sɛtl] vt (argument, matter, account) régler; (problem) résoudre; (Med: calm) calmer ▸ vi (bird, dust etc) se poser; **to ~ for sth** accepter qch, se contenter de qch; **to ~ on sth** opter or se décider pour qch; **settle down** vi (get comfortable) s'installer; (become calmer) se calmer or se ranger; **settle in** vi s'installer; **settle up** vi: **to ~ up with sb** régler (ce que l'on doit à) qn; **settlement** n (payment) règlement m; (agreement) accord m; (village etc) village m, hameau m

setup ['sɛtʌp] n (arrangement) manière f dont les choses sont organisées; (situation) situation f, allure f des choses

seven ['sɛvn] num sept; **seventeen** num dix-sept; **seventeenth** [sɛvn'tiːnθ] num dix-septième; **seventh** num septième; **seventieth** ['sɛvntiɪθ] num soixante-dixième; **seventy** num soixante-dix

sever ['sɛvəʳ] vt couper, trancher; (relations) rompre

several ['sɛvərl] adj, pron plusieurs pl; **~ of us** plusieurs d'entre nous

severe [sɪ'vɪəʳ] adj (stern) sévère, strict(e); (serious) grave, sérieux(-euse); (plain) sévère, austère

sew (pt sewed, pp sewn) [səʊ, səʊd, səʊn] vt, vi coudre

sewage ['suːdʒ] n vidanges f(pl)

sewer ['suːəʳ] n égout m

sewing ['səʊɪŋ] n couture f; (item(s)) ouvrage m; **sewing machine** n machine f à coudre

sewn [səʊn] pp of **sew**

sex [sɛks] n sexe m; **to have ~ with** avoir des rapports (sexuels) avec; **sexism** ['sɛksɪzəm] n sexisme m; **sexist** adj sexiste; **sexual** ['sɛksjʊəl] adj sexuel(le); **sexual intercourse** n rapports sexuels; **sexuality** [sɛksjʊ'ælɪtɪ] n sexualité f; **sexy** adj sexy inv

shabby ['ʃæbɪ] adj miteux(-euse); (behaviour) mesquin(e), méprisable

shack [ʃæk] n cabane f, hutte f

shade [ʃeɪd] n ombre f; (for lamp) abat-jour m inv; (of colour) nuance f, ton m; (us: window shade) store m; (small quantity): **a ~ of** un soupçon de ▸ vt abriter du soleil, ombrager; **shades** npl (us: sunglasses) lunettes fpl de soleil; **in the ~** à l'ombre; **a ~ smaller** un tout petit peu plus petit

shadow ['ʃædəʊ] n ombre f ▸ vt (follow) filer; **shadow cabinet** n (BRIT Pol) cabinet parallèle formé par le parti qui n'est pas au pouvoir

shady ['ʃeɪdɪ] adj ombragé(e); (fig: dishonest) louche, véreux(-euse)

shaft [ʃɑːft] n (of arrow, spear) hampe f; (Aut, Tech) arbre m; (of mine) puits m; (of lift) cage f; (of light) rayon m, trait m

shake [ʃeɪk] (pt shook, pp shaken) vt secouer; (bottle, cocktail) agiter; (house, confidence) ébranler ▸ vi trembler; **to ~ one's head** (in refusal etc) dire or faire non de la tête; (in dismay) secouer la tête; **to ~ hands with sb** serrer la main à qn; **shake off** vt secouer; (pursuer) se débarrasser de; **shake up** vt secouer; **shaky** adj (hand, voice) tremblant(e); (building) branlant(e), peu solide

shall [ʃæl] aux vb: **I ~ go** j'irai; **~ I open the door?** j'ouvre la porte?; **I'll get the coffee, ~ I?** je vais chercher le café, d'accord?

shallow ['ʃæləʊ] adj peu profond(e); (fig) superficiel(le), qui manque de profondeur

sham [ʃæm] n frime f

shambles ['ʃæmblz] n confusion f, pagaie f, fouillis m

shame [ʃeɪm] n honte f ▸ vt faire honte à; **it is a ~ (that/to do)** c'est dommage (que + sub/de faire); **what a ~!** quel dommage!; **shameful** adj honteux(-euse), scandaleux(-euse); **shameless** adj éhonté(e), effronté(e)

shampoo [ʃæm'puː] n shampooing m ▸ vt faire un shampooing à

shandy ['ʃændɪ] n bière panachée

S

shan't [ʃɑːnt] = **shall not**

shape [ʃeɪp] n forme f ⊳ vt façonner, modeler; (sb's ideas, character) former; (sb's life) déterminer ⊳ vi (also: ~ **up**: events) prendre tournure; (: plans) prendre tournure; (: person) faire des progrès, s'en sortir; **to take ~** prendre forme or tournure

share [ʃɛəʳ] n part f; (Comm) action f ⊳ vt partager; (have in common) avoir en commun; **to ~ out** (among or between) partager (entre); **shareholder** n (BRIT) actionnaire m/f

shark [ʃɑːk] n requin m

sharp [ʃɑːp] adj (razor, knife) tranchant(e), bien aiguisé(e); (point, voice) aigu(ë); (nose, chin) pointu(e); (outline, increase) net(te); (cold, pain) vif (vive); (taste) piquant(e), âcre; (Mus) dièse; (person: quick-witted) vif (vive), éveillé(e); (: unscrupulous) malhonnête ⊳ n (Mus) dièse m ⊳ adv: **at 2 o'clock ~** à 2 heures pile or tapantes; (pencil) tailler; (fig) aviver; **sharpen** vt aiguiser; (pencil) tailler; (fig) aviver; **sharpener** n (also: **pencil sharpener**) taille-crayon m inv; **sharply** adv (turn, stop) brusquement; (stand out) nettement; (criticize, retort) sèchement, vertement

shatter [ˈʃætəʳ] vt briser; (fig: upset) bouleverser; (: ruin) briser, ruiner ⊳ vi voler en éclats, se briser; **shattered** adj (overwhelmed, grief-stricken) bouleversé(e); (inf: exhausted) éreinté(e)

shave [ʃeɪv] vt raser ⊳ vi se raser ⊳ n: **to have a ~** se raser; **shaver** n (also: **electric shaver**) rasoir m électrique

shaving cream n crème f à raser

shaving foam n mousse f à raser

shavings [ˈʃeɪvɪŋz] npl (of wood etc) copeaux mpl

shawl [ʃɔːl] n châle m

she [ʃiː] pron elle

sheath [ʃiːθ] n gaine f, fourreau m, étui m; (contraceptive) préservatif m

shed [ʃɛd] n remise f, resserre f ⊳ vt (pt, pp **shed**) (leaves, fur etc) perdre;

(tears) verser, répandre; (workers) congédier

she'd [ʃiːd] = **she had; she would**

sheep [ʃiːp] n (pl inv) mouton m; **sheepdog** n chien m de berger; **sheepskin** n peau f de mouton

sheer [ʃɪəʳ] adj (utter) pur(e), pur et simple; (steep) à pic, abrupt(e); (almost transparent) extrêmement fin(e) ⊳ adv à pic, abruptement

sheet [ʃiːt] n (on bed) drap m; (of paper) feuille f; (of glass, metal etc) feuille, plaque f

sheikh(h) [ʃeɪk] n cheik m

shelf (pl **shelves**) [ʃɛlf, ʃɛlvz] n étagère f, rayon m

shell [ʃɛl] n (on beach) coquillage m; (of egg, nut etc) coquille f; (explosive) obus m; (of building) carcasse f ⊳ vt (peas) écosser; (Mil) bombarder (d'obus)

she'll [ʃiːl] = **she will; she shall**

shellfish [ˈʃɛlfɪʃ] n (pl inv: crab etc) crustacé m; (: scallop etc) coquillage m ⊳ npl (as food) fruits mpl de mer

shelter [ˈʃɛltəʳ] n abri m, refuge m ⊳ vt abriter, protéger; (give lodging to) donner asile à ⊳ vi s'abriter, se mettre à l'abri; **sheltered** adj (life) retiré(e), à l'abri des soucis; (spot) abrité(e)

shelves [ˈʃɛlvz] npl of **shelf**

shelving [ˈʃɛlvɪŋ] n (shelves) rayonnage(s) m(pl)

shepherd [ˈʃɛpəd] n berger m ⊳ vt (guide) guider, escorter; **shepherd's pie** n ≈ hachis m Parmentier

sheriff [ˈʃɛrɪf] (us) n shérif m

sherry [ˈʃɛrɪ] n xérès m, sherry m

she's [ʃiːz] = **she is; she has**

Shetland [ˈʃɛtlənd] n (also: **the ~s**, **the ~ Isles** or **Islands**) les îles fpl Shetland

shield [ʃiːld] n bouclier m; (protection) écran m de protection ⊳ vt: **to ~ (from)** protéger (de or contre)

shift [ʃɪft] n (change) changement m; (work period) période f de travail; (of workers) équipe f, poste m ⊳ vt

déplacer, changer de place; (remove) enlever ⊳ vi changer de place, bouger
shin [ʃɪn] n tibia m
shine [ʃaɪn] n éclat m, brillant m ⊳ vi (pt, pp **shone**) briller ⊳ vt (pt, pp **shined**) (polish) faire briller or reluire; (torch) braquer qch sur qch
shingles [ˈʃɪŋglz] n (Med) zona m
shiny [ˈʃaɪnɪ] adj brillant(e)
ship [ʃɪp] n bateau m; (large) navire m ⊳ vt transporter (par mer); (send) expédier (par mer); **shipment** n cargaison f; **shipping** n (ships) navires mpl; (traffic) navigation f; (the industry) industrie navale; (transport) transport m; **shipwreck** n épave f; (event) naufrage m ⊳ vt: **to be shipwrecked** faire naufrage; **shipyard** n chantier naval
shirt [ʃəːt] n chemise f; (woman's) chemisier m; **in ~ sleeves** en bras de chemise
shit [ʃɪt] excl (inf!) merde (!)
shiver [ˈʃɪvəʳ] n frisson m ⊳ vi frissonner
shock [ʃɔk] n choc m; (Elec) secousse f, décharge f; (Med) commotion f, choc m ⊳ vt (scandalize) choquer, scandaliser; (upset) bouleverser; **shocking** adj (outrageous) choquant(e), scandaleux(-euse); (awful) épouvantable
shoe [ʃuː] n chaussure f, soulier m; (also: **horse~**) fer m à cheval ⊳ vt (pt, pp **shod**) (horse) ferrer; **shoelace** n lacet m (de soulier); **shoe polish** n cirage m; **shoeshop** n magasin m de chaussures
shone [ʃɔn] pt, pp of **shine**
shonky [ˈʃɔŋkɪ] adj (AUST, NZ inf: untrustworthy) louche
shook [ʃuk] pt of **shake**
shoot [ʃuːt] (pt, pp **shot**) n (on branch, seedling): pousse f ⊳ vt (game: hunt) chasser; (: aim at) tirer; (: kill) abattre; (person) blesser/tuer d'un coup de fusil (or de revolver); (execute) fusiller;

(arrow) tirer; (gun) tirer un coup de; (Cine) tourner ⊳ vi (with gun, bow): **to ~ (at)** tirer (sur); (Football) shooter, tirer; **shoot down** vt (plane) abattre; **shoot up** vi (fig: prices etc) monter en flèche; **shooting** n (shots) coups mpl de feu; (attack) fusillade f; (murder) homicide m (à l'aide d'une arme à feu); (Hunting) chasse f
shop [ʃɔp] n magasin m; (workshop) atelier m ⊳ vi (also: **go ~ping**) faire ses courses or ses achats; **shop assistant** n (BRIT) vendeur(-euse); **shopkeeper** n marchand(e), commerçant(e); **shoplifting** n vol m à l'étalage; **shopping** n (goods) achats mpl, provisions fpl; **shopping bag** n sac m (à provisions); **shopping centre**, (US) **shopping center** n centre commercial; **shopping mall** n centre commercial; **shopping trolley** n (BRIT) Caddie® m; **shop window** n vitrine f
shore [ʃɔːʳ] n (of sea, lake) rivage m, rive f ⊳ vt: **to ~ (up)** étayer; **on ~** à terre
short [ʃɔːt] adj (not long) court(e); (soon finished) court, bref (brève); (person, step) petit(e); (curt) brusque, sec (sèche); (insufficient) insuffisant(e) ⊳ n (also: **~ film**) court métrage; (Elec) court-circuit m; **to be ~ of sth** être à court de or manquer de qch; **in ~** bref; en bref; **~ of doing** à moins de faire; **everything ~ of** tout sauf; **it is ~ for** c'est l'abréviation or le diminutif de; **to cut ~** (speech, visit) abréger, écourter; **to fall ~ of** ne pas être à la hauteur de; **to run ~ of** arriver à court de, venir à manquer de; **to stop ~** s'arrêter net; **to stop ~ of** ne pas aller jusqu'à; **shortage** n manque m, pénurie f; **shortbread** n = sablé m; **shortcoming** n défaut m; **short(crust) pastry** n (BRIT) pâte brisée; **shortcut** n raccourci m; **shorten** vt raccourcir; (text, visit) abréger; **shortfall** n déficit m; **shorthand** n (BRIT) sténo(graphie)

f; **shortlist** n (BRIT: for job) liste f des candidats sélectionnés; **short-lived** adj de courte durée; **shortly** adv bientôt, sous peu; **shorts** npl: **(a pair of) shorts** un short; **short-sighted** adj (BRIT) myope; (fig) qui manque de clairvoyance; **short-sleeved** adj à manches courtes; **short story** n nouvelle f; **short-tempered** adj qui s'emporte facilement; **short-term** adj (effect) à court terme

shot [ʃɔt] pt, pp of **shoot** ▷ n coup m (de feu); (try) coup, essai m; (injection) piqûre f; (Phot) photo f; **to be a good/poor ~** (person) tirer bien/mal; **like a ~** comme une flèche; (very readily) sans hésiter; **shotgun** n fusil m de chasse

should [ʃud] aux vb: **I ~ go now** je devrais partir maintenant; **he ~ be there now** il devrait être arrivé maintenant; **I ~ go if I were you** si j'étais vous j'irais; **I ~ like to** volontiers, j'aimerais bien

shoulder ['ʃəuldə*] n épaule f ▷ vt endosser, se charger de; (fig) **shoulder blade** n omoplate f

shouldn't ['ʃudnt] = **should not**

shout [ʃaut] n cri m ▷ vt crier ▷ vi crier, pousser des cris

shove [ʃʌv] vt pousser; (inf: put): **to ~ sth in** fourrer ou ficher qch dans ▷ n poussée f

shovel ['ʃʌvl] n pelle f ▷ vt pelleter, enlever (ou enfourner) à la pelle

show [ʃəu] (pt **showed**, pp **shown**) n (of emotion) manifestation f, démonstration f; (semblance) semblant m, apparence f; (exhibition) exposition f, salon m; (Theat, TV) spectacle m; (Cine) séance f ▷ vt montrer; (film) passer; (courage etc) faire preuve de, manifester; (exhibit) exposer ▷ vi se voir, être visible; **can you ~ me where it is, please?** pouvez-vous me montrer où c'est?; **to be on ~** être exposé(e); **it's just for ~** c'est juste pour l'effet; **show in**

vt faire entrer; **show off** vi (pej) crâner ▷ vt (display) faire valoir; (pej) faire étalage de; **show out** vt reconduire à la porte; **show up** vi (stand out) ressortir; (inf: turn up) se montrer ▷ vt (unmask) démasquer, dénoncer; (flaw) faire ressortir; **show business** n le monde du spectacle

shower ['ʃauə*] n (for washing) douche f; (rain) averse f; (of stones etc) pluie f, grêle f; (us: party) réunion organisée pour la remise de cadeaux ▷ vi prendre une douche, se doucher ▷ vt: **to ~ sb with** (gifts etc) combler qn de; **to have** ou **take a ~** prendre une douche, se doucher; **shower cap** n bonnet m de douche; **shower gel** n gel m douche

showing ['ʃəuɪŋ] n (of film) projection f

show jumping [-dʒʌmpɪŋ] n concours m hippique

shown [ʃəun] pp of **show**

show: show-off n (inf: person) crâneur(-euse), m'as-tu-vu(e) f; **showroom** n magasin m ou salle f d'exposition

shrank [ʃræŋk] pt of **shrink**

shred [ʃred] n (gen pl) lambeau m, petit morceau; (fig: of truth, evidence) parcelle f ▷ vt mettre en lambeaux, déchirer; (documents) détruire; (Culin: grate) râper; (: lettuce etc) couper en lanières

shrewd [ʃru:d] adj astucieux(-euse), perspicace; (business person) habile

shriek [ʃri:k] n cri perçant ou aigu, hurlement m ▷ vt, vi hurler, crier

shrimp [ʃrɪmp] n crevette grise

shrine [ʃraɪn] n (place) lieu m de pèlerinage

shrink (pt **shrank**, pp **shrunk**) [ʃrɪŋk, ʃræŋk, ʃrʌŋk] vi rétrécir; (fig) diminuer; (also: **~ away**) reculer ▷ vt (wool) (faire) rétrécir ▷ n (inf, pej) psychanalyste m/f; **to ~ from (doing)** sth reculer devant (la pensée de faire) qch

shrivel ['ʃrɪvl], **shrivel up** vt ratatiner, flétrir ▷ vi se ratatiner, se flétrir

shroud [ʃraud] n linceul m ▷ vt: **~ed in mystery** enveloppé(e) de mystère

Shrove Tuesday ['ʃrəuv-] n (le) Mardi gras

shrub [ʃrʌb] n arbuste m

shrug [ʃrʌg] n haussement m d'épaules ▷ vt, vi: **to ~ (one's shoulders)** hausser les épaules; **shrug off** vt faire fi de

shrunk [ʃrʌŋk] pp of **shrink**

shudder ['ʃʌdər] n frisson m, frémissement m ▷ vi frissonner, frémir

shuffle ['ʃʌfl] vt (cards) battre; **to ~ (one's feet)** traîner les pieds

shun [ʃʌn] vt éviter, fuir

shut (pt, pp **shut**) [ʃʌt] vt fermer ▷ vi (se) fermer; **shut down** vt fermer définitivement ▷ vi fermer définitivement; **shut up** vi (inf: keep quiet) se taire ▷ vt (close) fermer; (silence) faire taire; **shutter** n volet m; (Phot) obturateur m

shuttle ['ʃʌtl] n navette f; (also: **~ service**) (service m de) navette f; **shuttlecock** n volant m (de badminton)

shy [ʃaɪ] adj timide

siblings ['sɪblɪŋz] npl (formal) frères et sœurs mpl (de mêmes parents)

Sicily ['sɪsɪlɪ] n Sicile f

sick [sɪk] adj (ill) malade; (BRIT: humour) noir(e), macabre; (vomiting): **to be ~** vomir; **to feel ~** avoir envie de vomir, avoir mal au cœur; **to be ~ of** (fig) en avoir assez de; **sickening** adj (fig) écœurant(e), révoltant(e), répugnant(e); **sick leave** n congé m de maladie; **sickly** adj maladif(-ive), souffreteux(-euse); (causing nausea) écœurant(e); **sickness** n maladie f; (vomiting) vomissement(s) m(pl)

side [saɪd] n côté m; (of lake, road) bord m; (of mountain) versant m; (fig: aspect) côté, aspect m; (team: Sport) équipe

f; (TV: channel) chaîne f ▷ adj (door, entrance) latéral(e) ▷ vi: **to ~ with sb** prendre le parti de qn, se ranger du côté de qn; **by the ~ of** au bord de; **~ by ~** côte à côte; **to rock from ~ to ~** se balancer; **to take ~s (with)** prendre parti (pour); **sideboard** n buffet m; **sideboards**, (US) **sideburns** npl (whiskers) pattes fpl; **side effect** n effet m secondaire; **sidelight** n (Aut) veilleuse f; **sideline** n (Sport) (ligne f de) touche f; (fig) activité f secondaire; **side order** n garniture f; **side road** n petite route, route transversale; **side street** n rue transversale; **sidetrack** vt (fig) faire dévier du sujet; **sidewalk** n (US) trottoir m; **sideways** adv de côté

siege [siːdʒ] n siège m

sieve [sɪv] n tamis m, passoire f ▷ vt tamiser, passer (au tamis)

sift [sɪft] vt passer au tamis ou au crible; (fig) passer au crible

sigh [saɪ] n soupir m ▷ vi soupirer, pousser un soupir

sight [saɪt] n (faculty) vue f; (spectacle) spectacle m ▷ vt apercevoir; **in ~** visible; (fig) en vue; **out of ~** hors de vue; **sightseeing** n tourisme m; **to go sightseeing** faire du tourisme

sign [saɪn] n (gen) signe m; (with hand etc) signe, geste m; (notice) panneau m, écriteau m; (road ~) panneau m de signalisation ▷ vt signer; **where do I ~?** où dois-je signer?; **sign for** vt fus (item) signer le reçu pour; **sign in** vi signer le registre (en arrivant); **sign on** vi (BRIT: as unemployed) s'inscrire au chômage; (enrol) s'inscrire ▷ vt (employee) embaucher; **sign over** vt: **to ~ sth over to sb** céder qch par écrit à qn; **sign up** vi (Mil) s'engager; (for course) s'inscrire

signal ['sɪgnl] n signal m ▷ vi (Aut) mettre son clignotant ▷ vt (person) faire signe à; (message) communiquer par signaux

signature ['sɪgnətʃər] n signature f

significance [sɪɡˈnɪfɪkəns] n
signification f; importance f

significant [sɪɡˈnɪfɪkənt] adj
significatif(-ive); (important)
important(e), considérable

signify [ˈsɪɡnɪfaɪ] vt signifier

sign language n langage m par
signes

signpost [ˈsaɪnpəʊst] n poteau
indicateur

Sikh [siːk] adj, n Sikh m/f

silence [ˈsaɪləns] n silence m ▷ vt faire
taire, réduire au silence

silent [ˈsaɪlnt] adj silencieux(-euse);
(film) muet(te); **to keep** or **remain ~**
garder le silence, ne rien dire

silhouette [sɪluːˈet] n silhouette f

silicon chip [ˈsɪlɪkən-] n puce f
électronique

silk [sɪlk] n soie f ▷ cpd de or en soie

silly [ˈsɪlɪ] adj stupide, sot(te), bête

silver [ˈsɪlvəʳ] n argent m; (money)
monnaie f (en pièces d'argent); (also:
~ware) argenterie f ▷ adj (made
of silver) d'argent, en argent; (in
colour) argenté(e); **silver-plated** adj
plaqué(e) argent

SIM card [ˈsɪm-] n abbr (Tel) carte
f SIM

similar [ˈsɪmɪləʳ] adj: **~ (to)**
semblable (à); **similarity**
[sɪmɪˈlærɪtɪ] n ressemblance f,
similarité f; **similarly** adv de la même
façon, de même

simmer [ˈsɪməʳ] vi cuire à feu doux,
mijoter

simple [ˈsɪmpl] adj simple;
simplicity [sɪmˈplɪsɪtɪ] n simplicité
f; **simplify** [ˈsɪmplɪfaɪ] vt simplifier;
simply adv simplement; (without
fuss) avec simplicité; (absolutely)
absolument

simulate [ˈsɪmjʊleɪt] vt simuler,
feindre

simultaneous [sɪməlˈteɪnɪəs] adj
simultané(e); **simultaneously** adv
simultanément

sin [sɪn] n péché m ▷ vi pécher

since [sɪns] adv, prep depuis ▷ conj
(time) depuis que; (because) puisque,
étant donné que, comme; **~ then,
ever ~** depuis ce moment-là

sincere [sɪnˈsɪəʳ] adj sincère;
sincerely adv sincèrement; **yours
sincerely** (at end of letter) veuillez
agréer, Monsieur (or Madame)
l'expression de mes sentiments
distingués or les meilleurs

Singapore [sɪŋɡəˈpɔːʳ] n
Singapour m

singer [ˈsɪŋəʳ] n chanteur(-euse)

singing [ˈsɪŋɪŋ] n (of person, bird)
chant m

single [ˈsɪŋɡl] adj seul(e), unique;
(unmarried) célibataire; (not double)
simple ▷ n (BRIT: also: **~ ticket**) aller m
(simple); (record) 45 tours m; **singles**
npl (Tennis) simple m; **every ~ day**
chaque jour sans exception; **single
out** vt choisir; (distinguish) distinguer;
single bed n lit m d'une personne or à
une place; **single file** n: **in single file**
en file indienne; **single-handed** adv
tout(e) seul(e), sans (aucune) aide;
single-minded adj résolu(e), tenace;
single parent n parent unique (or
célibataire); **single-parent family**
famille monoparentale; **single
room** n chambre f à un lit or pour une
personne

singular [ˈsɪŋɡjʊləʳ] adj
singulier(-ière); (odd) singulier,
étrange; (outstanding) remarquable;
(Ling) au singulier, du singulier ▷ n
(Ling) singulier m

sinister [ˈsɪnɪstəʳ] adj sinistre

sink [sɪŋk] (pt sank, pp sunk) n
évier m; (washbasin) lavabo m ▷ vt
(ship) (faire) couler, faire sombrer;
(foundations) creuser ▷ vi couler,
sombrer; (ground etc) s'affaisser; **to ~
into sth** (chair) s'enfoncer dans qch;
sink in vi (explanation) rentrer (inf),
être compris

sinus ['saɪnəs] n (Anat) sinus m inv

sip [sɪp] n petite gorgée f ▷ vt boire à petites gorgées

sir [səʳ] n monsieur m; **S~ John Smith** sir John Smith; **yes ~** oui Monsieur

siren ['saɪərn] n sirène f

sirloin ['səːlɔɪn] n (also: **~ steak**) aloyau m

sister ['sɪstəʳ] n sœur f; (nun) religieuse f, (bonne) sœur f; (BRIT: nurse) infirmière f en chef; **sister-in-law** n belle-sœur f

sit (pt, pp **sat**) [sɪt, sæt] vi s'asseoir; (be sitting) être assis(e); (assembly) être en séance, siéger; (for painter) poser ▷ vt (exam) passer, se présenter à; **sit back** vi (in seat) bien s'installer, se carrer; **sit down** vi s'asseoir; **sit on** vt fus (jury, committee) faire partie de; **sit up** vi s'asseoir; (straight) se redresser; (not go to bed) rester debout, ne pas se coucher

sitcom ['sɪtkɒm] n abbr (TV: = situation comedy) sitcom f, comédie f de situation

site [saɪt] n emplacement m, site m; (also: **building ~**) chantier m; (Internet) site m web ▷ vt placer

sitting ['sɪtɪŋ] n (of assembly etc) séance f; (in canteen) service m; **sitting room** n salon m

situated ['sɪtjueɪtɪd] adj situé(e)

situation [sɪtju'eɪʃən] n situation f; **"~s vacant/wanted"** (BRIT) "offres/demandes d'emploi"

six [sɪks] num six m; **sixteen** num seize; **sixteenth** [sɪks'tiːnθ] num seizième; **sixth** [sɪksθ] num sixième; **sixth form** n (BRIT) ≈ classes fpl de première et de terminale; **sixth-form college** n lycée n'ayant que des classes de première et de terminale; **sixtieth** ['sɪkstɪɪθ] num soixantième; **sixty** num soixante

size [saɪz] n dimensions fpl; (of person) taille f; (of clothing) taille f; (of shoes) pointure f; (of problem) ampleur f; (glue) colle f; **sizeable** adj assez

grand(e); (amount, problem, majority) assez important(e)

sizzle ['sɪzl] vi grésiller

skate [skeɪt] n patin m; (fish: pl inv) raie f ▷ vi patiner; **skateboard** n skateboard m, planche f à roulettes; **skateboarding** n skateboard m; **skater** n patineur(-euse); **skating** n patinage m; **skating rink** n patinoire f

skeleton ['skɛlɪtn] n squelette m; (outline) schéma m

skeptical ['skɛptɪkl] (US) adj = **sceptical**

sketch [skɛtʃ] n (drawing) croquis m, esquisse f; (outline plan) aperçu m; (Theat) sketch m, saynète f ▷ vt esquisser, faire un croquis or une esquisse de; (plan etc) esquisser

skewer ['skjuːəʳ] n brochette f

ski [skiː] n ski m ▷ vi skier, faire du ski; **ski boot** n chaussure f de ski

skid [skɪd] n dérapage m ▷ vi déraper

ski: **skier** n skieur(-euse); **skiing** n ski m; **to go skiing** (aller) faire du ski

skilful, (US) **skillful** ['skɪlful] adj habile, adroit(e)

ski lift n remonte-pente m inv

skill [skɪl] n (ability) habileté f, adresse f, talent m; (requiring training) compétences fpl; **skilled** adj habile, adroit(e); (worker) qualifié(e)

skim [skɪm] vt (soup) écumer; (glide over) raser, effleurer ▷ vi: **to ~ through** (fig) parcourir; **skimmed milk**, (US) **skim milk** n lait écrémé

skin [skɪn] n peau f ▷ vt (fruit etc) éplucher; (animal) écorcher; **skinhead** n skinhead m; **skinny** adj maigre, maigrichon(ne)

skip [skɪp] n petit bond or saut; (BRIT: container) benne f ▷ vi gambader, sautiller; (with rope) sauter à la corde ▷ vt (pass over) sauter

ski: **ski pass** n forfait-skieur(s) m; **ski pole** n bâton m de ski

skipper ['skɪpəʳ] n (Naut, Sport) capitaine m; (in race) skipper m

skipping rope ['skɪpɪŋ-], (us) **skip rope** n corde f à sauter

skirt [skɜːt] n jupe f ▷ vt longer, contourner

skirting board ['skɜːtɪŋ-] n (BRIT) plinthe f

ski slope n piste f de ski

ski suit n combinaison f de ski

skull [skʌl] n crâne m

skunk [skʌŋk] n mouffette f

sky [skaɪ] n ciel m; **skyscraper** n gratte-ciel m inv

slab [slæb] n (of stone) dalle f; (of meat, cheese) tranche épaisse

slack [slæk] adj (loose) lâche, desserré(e); (slow) stagnant(e); (careless) négligent(e), peu sérieux(-euse) or conscientieux(-euse); **slacks** npl pantalon m

slain [sleɪn] pp of **slay**

slam [slæm] vt (door) (faire) claquer; (throw) jeter violemment, flanquer; (inf: criticize) éreinter, démolir ▷ vi claquer

slander ['slɑːndər] n calomnie f; (Law) diffamation f

slang [slæŋ] n argot m

slant [slɑːnt] n inclinaison f; (fig) angle m, point m de vue

slap [slæp] n claque f, gifle f; (on the back) tape f ▷ vt donner une claque or une gifle (or une tape) à ▷ adv (directly) tout droit, en plein; **to ~ on** (paint) appliquer rapidement

slash [slæʃ] vt entailler, taillader; (fig: prices) casser

slate [sleɪt] n ardoise f ▷ vt (fig: criticize) éreinter, démolir

slaughter ['slɔːtər] n carnage m, massacre m; (of animals) abattage m ▷ vt (animal) abattre; (people) massacrer; **slaughterhouse** n abattoir m

Slav [slɑːv] adj slave

slave [sleɪv] n esclave m/f ▷ vi (also: **~ away**) trimer, travailler comme un forçat; **slavery** n esclavage m

slay (pt **slew**, pp **slain**) [sleɪ, sluː, sleɪn] vt (literary) tuer

sleazy ['sliːzɪ] adj miteux(-euse), minable

sled [slɛd] (us) n = **sledge**

sledge [slɛdʒ] n luge f

sleek [sliːk] adj (hair, fur) brillant(e), luisant(e); (car, boat) aux lignes pures or élégantes

sleep [sliːp] n sommeil m ▷ vi (pt, pp **slept**) dormir; **to go to ~** s'endormir; **sleep in** vi (oversleep) se réveiller trop tard; (on purpose) faire la grasse matinée; **sleep together** vi (have sex) coucher ensemble; **sleeper** n (person) dormeur(-euse); (BRIT Rail: on track) traverse f; (: train) train-couchettes m; (: berth) couchette f; **sleeping bag** ['sliːpɪŋ-] n sac m de couchage; **sleeping car** n wagon-lits m, voiture-lits f; **sleeping pill** n somnifère m; **sleepover** n nuit f chez un copain or une copine; **we're having a sleepover at Jo's** nous allons passer la nuit chez Jo; **sleepwalk** vi marcher en dormant; **sleepy** adj (fig) endormi(e)

sleet [sliːt] n neige fondue

sleeve [sliːv] n manche f; (of record) pochette f; **sleeveless** adj (garment) sans manches

sleigh [sleɪ] n traîneau m

slender ['slɛndər] adj svelte, mince; (fig) faible, ténu(e)

slept [slɛpt] pt, pp of **sleep**

slew [sluː] pt of **slay**

slice [slaɪs] n tranche f; (round) rondelle f; (utensil) spatule f; (also: **fish ~**) pelle f à poisson ▷ vt couper en tranches or en rondelles

slick [slɪk] adj (skilful) bien ficelé(e); (salesperson) qui a du bagout ▷ n (also: **oil ~**) nappe f de pétrole, marée noire

slide (pt, pp **slid**) [slaɪd, slɪd] n (in playground) toboggan m; (Phot) diapositive f; (BRIT: also: **hair ~**) barrette f; (in prices) chute f, baisse f

▷ vt (faire) glisser ▷ vi glisser; **sliding** adj (door) coulissant(e)

slight [slaɪt] adj (slim) mince, menu(e); (frail) frêle; (trivial) faible, insignifiant(e); (small) petit(e), léger(-ère) before n ▷ n offense f, affront m ▷ vt (offend) blesser, offenser; **not in the ~est** pas le moins du monde, pas du tout; **slightly** adv légèrement, un peu

slim [slɪm] adj mince ▷ vi maigrir; (diet) suivre un régime amaigrissant; **slimming** n amaigrissement m ▷ adj (diet, pills) amaigrissant(e), pour maigrir; (food) qui ne fait pas grossir

slimy ['slaɪmɪ] adj visqueux(-euse), gluant(e)

sling [slɪŋ] n (Med) écharpe f; (for baby) porte-bébé m; (weapon) fronde f, lance-pierre m ▷ vt (pt, pp **slung**) lancer, jeter

slip [slɪp] n faux pas; (mistake) erreur f, bévue f; (underskirt) combinaison f; (of paper) petite feuille, fiche f ▷ vt (slide) glisser ▷ vi (slide) glisser; (decline) baisser; (move smoothly): **to ~ into/ out of** se glisser or se faufiler dans/ hors de; **to ~ sth on/off** enfiler/ enlever qch; **to give sb the ~** fausser compagnie à qn; **a ~ of the tongue** un lapsus; **slip up** vi faire une erreur, gaffer

slipped disc [slɪpt-] n déplacement m de vertèbre

slipper ['slɪpəʳ] n pantoufle f

slippery ['slɪpərɪ] adj glissant(e)

slip road n (BRIT: to motorway) bretelle f d'accès

slit [slɪt] n fente f; (cut) incision f ▷ vt (pt, pp **slit**) fendre; couper, inciser

slog [slɒg] n (BRIT: effort) gros effort; (work) tâche fastidieuse ▷ vi travailler très dur

slogan ['sləʊgən] n slogan m

slope [sləʊp] n pente f, côte f; (side of mountain) versant m; (slant) inclinaison f ▷ vi: **to ~ down** être or descendre en pente; **to ~ up** monter;

sloping adj en pente, incliné(e); (handwriting) penché(e)

sloppy ['slɒpɪ] adj (work) peu soigné(e), bâclé(e); (appearance) négligé(e), débraillé(e)

slot [slɒt] n fente f ▷ vt: encastrer or insérer qch dans; **slot machine** n (BRIT: vending machine) distributeur m, machine f automatique, machine f à sous; (for gambling) appareil m or machine à sous

Slovakia [sləʊˈvækɪə] n Slovaquie f

Slovene [ˈsləʊviːn] adj slovène ▷ n Slovène m/f; (Ling) slovène m

Slovenia [sləʊˈviːnɪə] n Slovénie f; **Slovenian** adj, n = **Slovene**

slow [sləʊ] adj lent(e); (watch): **to be ~** retarder ▷ adv lentement ▷ vt, vi ralentir; **"~"** (road sign) "ralentir"; **slow down** vi ralentir; **slowly** adv lentement; **slow motion** n: **in slow motion** au ralenti

slug [slʌg] n limace f; (bullet) balle f; **sluggish** adj (person) mou (molle), lent(e); (stream, engine, trading) lent(e)

slum [slʌm] n (house) taudis m; **slums** npl (area) quartiers mpl pauvres

slump [slʌmp] n baisse soudaine, effondrement m; (Econ) crise f ▷ vi s'effondrer, s'affaisser

slung [slʌŋ] pt, pp of **sling**

slur [slɜːʳ] n (smear): **~ (on)** atteinte f (à); insinuation f (contre) ▷ vt mal articuler

slush [slʌʃ] n neige fondue

sly [slaɪ] adj (person) rusé(e); (smile, expression, remark) sournois(e)

smack [smæk] n (slap) tape f; (on face) gifle f ▷ vt donner une tape à; (on face) gifler; (on bottom) donner la fessée à ▷ vi: **to ~ of** avoir des relents de, sentir

small [smɔːl] adj petit(e); **small ads** npl (BRIT) petites annonces; **small change** n petite or menue monnaie

smart [smɑːt] adj élégant(e), chic inv; (clever) intelligent(e); (quick) vif (vive), prompt(e) ▷ vi faire mal, brûler;

smart card n carte f à puce; **smart phone** n smartphone m

smash [smæʃ] n (also: ~-**up**) collision f, accident m; (Mus) succès foudroyant ▷ vt casser, briser, fracasser; (opponent) écraser; (Sport: record) pulvériser ▷ vi se briser, se fracasser; s'écraser; **smashing** adj (inf) formidable

smear [smɪə*] n (stain) tache f; (mark) trace f; (Med) frottis m ▷ vt enduire; (make dirty) salir; **smear test** n (BRIT Med) frottis m

smell [smɛl] (pt, pp **smelt** or **smelled**) n odeur f; (sense) odorat m ▷ vt sentir ▷ vi (food etc) sentir mauvais; (pej) sentir ▷ adj qui sent mauvais, malodorant(e)

smelt [smɛlt] pt, pp of **smell**

smile [smaɪl] n sourire m ▷ vi sourire

smirk [sməːk] n petit sourire suffisant or affecté

smog [smɔg] n brouillard mêlé de fumée

smoke [sməuk] n fumée f ▷ vt, vi fumer; **do you mind if I ~?** ça ne vous dérange pas que je fume?; **smoke alarm** n détecteur m de fumée; **smoked** adj (bacon, glass) fumé(e); **smoker** n (person) fumeur(-euse); (Rail) wagon m fumeurs; **smoking** n: **"no smoking"** (sign) "défense de fumer"; **smoky** adj enfumé(e); (taste) fumé(e)

smooth [smuːð] adj lisse; (sauce) onctueux(-euse); (flavour, whisky) moelleux(-euse); (movement) régulier(-ière), sans à-coups or heurts; (flight) sans secousses; (pej: person) doucereux(-euse), mielleux(-euse) ▷ vt (also: ~ **out**) lisser; défroisser; (creases, difficulties) faire disparaître

smother ['smʌðə*] vt étouffer

SMS n abbr (= short message service) SMS m; **SMS message** n (message m) SMS m

smudge [smʌdʒ] n tache f, bavure f ▷ vt salir, maculer

smug [smʌg] adj suffisant(e), content(e) de soi

smuggle ['smʌgl] vt passer en contrebande or en fraude; **smuggling** n contrebande f

snack [snæk] n casse-croûte m inv; **snack bar** n snack(-bar) m

snag [snæg] n inconvénient m, difficulté f

snail [sneɪl] n escargot m

snake [sneɪk] n serpent m

snap [snæp] n (sound) claquement m, bruit sec; (photograph) photo f, instantané m ▷ adj subit(e), fait(e) sans réfléchir ▷ vt (fingers) faire claquer; (break) casser net ▷ vi se casser net or avec un bruit sec; (speak sharply) parler d'un ton brusque; **to ~ open/shut** s'ouvrir/se refermer brusquement; **snap at** vt fus (subj: dog) essayer de mordre; **snap up** vt sauter sur, saisir; **snapshot** n photo f, instantané m

snarl [snɑːl] vi gronder

snatch [snætʃ] n ▷ vt saisir (d'un geste vif); (steal) voler; **to ~ some sleep** arriver à dormir un peu

sneak [sniːk] (US: pt, pp **snuck**) vi: **to ~ in/out** entrer/sortir furtivement or à la dérobée ▷ n (inf: pej: informer) faux jeton; **to ~ up on sb** s'approcher de qn sans faire de bruit; **sneakers** npl tennis mpl, baskets fpl

sneer [snɪə*] vi ricaner; **to ~ at sb/sth** se moquer de qn/qch avec mépris

sneeze [sniːz] vi éternuer

sniff [snɪf] vi renifler ▷ vt renifler, flairer; (glue, drug) sniffer, respirer

snigger ['snɪgə*] vi ricaner

snip [snɪp] n (cut) entaille f; (BRIT inf: bargain) (bonne) occasion or affaire f ▷ vt couper

sniper ['snaɪpə*] n tireur embusqué

snob [snɔb] n snob m/f

snooker ['snuːkə*] n sorte de jeu de billard

snoop [snuːp] vi: **to ~ about** fureter

snooze [snuːz] n petit somme ▷ vi faire un petit somme

snore [snɔːʳ] vi ronfler ▷ n ronflement m

snorkel [ˈsnɔːkl] n (of swimmer) tuba m

snort [snɔːt] n grognement m ▷ vi grogner; (horse) renâcler

snow [snəu] n neige f ▷ vi neiger; **snowball** n boule f de neige; **snowdrift** n congère f; **snowman** (irreg) n bonhomme m de neige; **snowplough**, (us) **snowplow** n chasse-neige m inv; **snowstorm** n tempête f de neige

snub [snʌb] vt repousser, snober ▷ n rebuffade f

snuck [snʌk] pt, pp of **sneak**

snug [snʌg] adj douillet(te), confortable; (person) bien au chaud

⊙ **KEYWORD**

so [səu] adv 1 (thus, likewise) ainsi, de cette façon; **if so** si oui; **so do** or **have I** moi aussi; **it's 5 o'clock — so it is!** il est 5 heures — en effet! or c'est vrai!; **I hope/think so** je l'espère/ le crois; **so far** jusqu'ici, jusqu'à maintenant; (in past) jusque-là

2 (in comparisons etc: to such a degree) si, tellement; **so big (that)** si or tellement grand (que); **she's not so clever as her brother** elle n'est pas aussi intelligente que son frère

3: **so much** adj, adv tant de; **I've got so much work** j'ai tant de travail; **I love you so much** je vous aime tant; **so many** tant de

4 (phrases): **10 or so** à peu près or environ 10; **so long!** (inf: goodbye) au revoir!, à un de ces jours!; **so (what)?** (inf) (bon) et alors?, et après?

▶ conj 1 (expressing purpose): **so as to** do pour faire, afin de faire; **so (that)** pour que or afin que + sub

2 (expressing result) donc, par conséquent; **so that** si bien que; **so**

that's the reason! c'est donc (pour) ça!; **so you see, I could have gone** alors tu vois, j'aurais pu y aller

soak [səuk] vt faire or laisser tremper; (drench) tremper ▷ vi tremper; **soak up** vt absorber; **soaking** adj (also: **soaking wet**) trempé(e)

so-and-so [ˈsəuənsəu] n (somebody) un(e) tel(le)

soap [səup] n savon m; **soap opera** n feuilleton télévisé (quotidienneté réaliste ou embellie); **soap powder** n lessive f, détergent m

soar [sɔːʳ] vi monter (en flèche), s'élancer; (building) s'élancer

sob [sɔb] n sanglot m ▷ vi sangloter

sober [ˈsəubəʳ] adj qui n'est pas (or plus) ivre; (serious) sérieux(-euse), sensé(e); (colour, style) sobre, discret(-ète); **sober up** vi se dégriser

so-called [ˈsəuˈkɔːld] adj soi-disant inv

soccer [ˈsɔkəʳ] n football m

sociable [ˈsəuʃəbl] adj sociable

social [ˈsəuʃl] adj social(e); (sociable) sociable ▷ n (petite) fête; **socialism** n socialisme m; **socialist** adj, n socialiste (m/f); **socialize** vi: **to socialize with** (meet often) fréquenter; (get to know) lier connaissance or parler avec; **social life** n vie sociale; **socially** adv socialement, en société; **social media** npl médias mpl sociaux; **social networking** n réseaux mpl sociaux; **social networking site** n site m de réseautage; **social security** n aide sociale; **social services** npl services sociaux; **social work** n assistance sociale; **social worker** n assistant(e) sociale(e)

society [səˈsaɪətɪ] n société f; (club) société, association f; (also: **high ~**) (haute) société, grand monde

sociology [səusɪˈɔlədʒɪ] n sociologie f

sock [sɔk] n chaussette f

socket ['sɒkɪt] n cavité f; (Elec: also: **wall ~**) prise f de courant

soda ['səʊdə] n (Chem) soude f; (also: **~ water**) eau f de Seltz; (us: also: **~ pop**) soda m

sodium ['səʊdɪəm] n sodium m

sofa ['səʊfə] n sofa m, canapé m; **sofa bed** n canapé-lit m

soft [sɒft] adj (not rough) doux (douce); (not hard) doux, mou (molle); (not loud) doux, léger(-ère); (kind) doux, gentil(le); **soft drink** n boisson non alcoolisée; **soft drugs** npl drogues douces; **soften** ['sɒfn] vt (r)amollir; (fig) adoucir ▷ vi se ramollir; (fig) s'adoucir; **softly** adv doucement; (touch) légèrement; (kiss) tendrement; **software** n (Comput) logiciel m, software m

soggy ['sɒgɪ] adj (clothes) trempé(e); (ground) détrempé(e)

soil [sɔɪl] n (earth) sol m, terre f ▷ vt salir; (fig) souiller

solar ['səʊləʳ] adj solaire; **solar power** n énergie f solaire; **solar system** n système m solaire

sold [səʊld] pt, pp of **sell**

soldier ['səʊldʒəʳ] n soldat m, militaire m

sold out adj (Comm) épuisé(e)

sole [səʊl] n (of foot) plante f; (of shoe) semelle f; (fish: pl inv) sole f ▷ adj seul(e), unique; **solely** adv seulement, uniquement

solemn ['sɒləm] adj solennel(le); (person) sérieux(-euse), grave

solicitor [sə'lɪsɪtəʳ] n (BRIT: for wills etc) ≈ notaire m; (: in court) ≈ avocat m

solid ['sɒlɪd] adj (not liquid) solide; (not hollow: mass) compact(e); (: metal, rock, wood) massif(-ive) ▷ n solide m

solitary ['sɒlɪtərɪ] adj solitaire

solitude ['sɒlɪtjuːd] n solitude f

solo ['səʊləʊ] n solo m ▷ adv (fly) en solitaire; **soloist** n soliste m/f

soluble ['sɒljubl] adj soluble

solution [sə'luːʃən] n solution f

solve [sɒlv] vt résoudre

solvent ['sɒlvənt] adj (Comm) solvable ▷ n (Chem) (dis)solvant m

sombre, (us) **somber** ['sɒmbəʳ] adj sombre, morne

KEYWORD

some [sʌm] adj 1 (a certain amount or number of): **some tea/water/ice cream** du thé/de l'eau/de la glace; **some children/apples** des enfants/pommes; **I've got some money but not much** j'ai de l'argent mais pas beaucoup

2 (certain: in contrasts): **some people say that …** il y a des gens qui disent que …; **some films were excellent, but most were mediocre** certains films étaient excellents, mais la plupart étaient médiocres

3 (unspecified): **some woman was asking for you** il y avait une dame qui vous demandait; **he was asking for some book (or other)** il demandait un livre quelconque; **some day** un de ces jours; **some day next week** un jour la semaine prochaine

▸ pron 1 (a certain number) quelques-un(e)s, certain(e)s; **I've got some** (books etc) j'en ai (quelques-uns); **some of them have been sold** certains ont été vendus

2 (a certain amount) un peu; **I've got some** (money, milk) j'en ai (un peu); **would you like some?** est-ce que vous en voulez?, en voulez-vous?; **could I have some of that cheese?** pourrais-je avoir un peu de ce fromage?; **I've read some of the book** j'ai lu une partie du livre

▸ adv: **some 10 people** quelque 10 personnes, 10 personnes environ; **somebody** ['sʌmbədɪ] pron = **someone**; **somehow** adv d'une façon ou d'une autre; (for some reason) pour une raison ou une autre; **someone** pron quelqu'un; **someplace** adv (us) = **somewhere**;

something pron quelque chose m;
something interesting quelque chose d'intéressant; **something to do** quelque chose à faire; **sometime** adv (in future) un de ces jours, un jour ou l'autre; (in past): **sometime last month** au cours du mois dernier; **sometimes** adv quelquefois, parfois; **somewhat** adv quelque peu, un peu; **somewhere** adv quelque part; **somewhere else** ailleurs, autre part

son [sʌn] n fils m

song [sɒŋ] n chanson f; (of bird) chant m

son-in-law ['sʌnɪnlɔː] n gendre m, beau-fils m

soon [suːn] adv bientôt; (early) tôt; **~ afterwards** peu après; see also **as**; **sooner** adv (time) plus tôt; (preference): **I would sooner do that** j'aimerais autant or je préférerais faire ça; **sooner or later** tôt ou tard

soothe [suːð] vt calmer, apaiser

sophisticated [sə'fɪstɪkeɪtɪd] adj raffiné(e), sophistiqué(e); (machinery) hautement perfectionné(e), très complexe

sophomore ['sɒfəmɔːʳ] n (US) étudiant(e) de seconde année

soprano [sə'prɑːnəu] n (singer) soprano m/f

sorbet ['sɔːbeɪ] n sorbet m

sordid ['sɔːdɪd] adj sordide

sore [sɔːʳ] adj (painful) douloureux(-euse), sensible ▷ n plaie f

sorrow ['sɒrəu] n peine f, chagrin m

sorry ['sɒrɪ] adj désolé(e); (condition, excuse, tale) triste, déplorable; **~!** pardon!, excusez-moi!; **~?** pardon?; **to feel ~ for sb** plaindre qn

sort [sɔːt] n genre m, espèce f, sorte f; (make: of coffee, car etc) marque f ▷ vt (also: **~ out**: select which to keep) trier; (classify) classer; (tidy) ranger; **sort out** vt (problem) résoudre, régler

SOS n SOS m

so-so ['səusəu] adv comme ci comme ça

sought [sɔːt] pt, pp of **seek**

soul [səul] n âme f

sound [saund] adj (healthy) en bonne santé, sain(e); (safe, not damaged) solide, en bon état; (reliable, not superficial) sérieux(-euse), solide; (sensible) sensé(e) ▷ adv: **~ asleep** profondément endormi(e) ▷ n (noise, volume) son m; (louder) bruit m; (Geo) détroit m, bras m de mer ▷ vt (alarm) sonner ▷ vi sonner, retentir; (fig: seem) sembler (être); **to ~ like** ressembler à; **sound bite** n phrase toute faite (pour être citée dans les médias); **soundtrack** n (of film) bande f sonore

soup [suːp] n soupe f, potage m

sour ['sauəʳ] adj aigre; **it's ~ grapes** c'est du dépit

source [sɔːs] n source f

south [sauθ] n sud m ▷ adj sud inv; (wind) du sud ▷ adv au sud, vers le sud; **South Africa** n Afrique f du Sud; **South African** adj sud-africain(e) ▷ n Sud-Africain(e); **South America** n Amérique f du Sud; **South American** adj sud-américain(e) ▷ n Sud-Américain(e); **southbound** adj en direction du sud; (carriageway) sud inv; **south-east** n sud-est m; **southern** ['sʌðən] adj (du) sud; méridional(e); **South Korea** n Corée f du Sud; **South of France** n: **the South of France** le Sud de la France, le Midi; **South Pole** n: **the South Pole** le Pôle Sud; **southward(s)** adv vers le sud; **south-west** n sud-ouest m

souvenir [suːvə'nɪəʳ] n souvenir m (objet)

sovereign ['sɒvrɪn] adj, n souverain(e)

sow[1] (pt **sowed**, pp **sown**) [səu, səud, səun] vt semer

sow[2] n [sau] truie f

soya ['sɔɪə], (US) **soy** [sɔɪ] n: **~ bean** graine f de soja; **~ sauce** sauce f au soja

spa [spɑː] n (town) station thermale; (us: also: **health** ~) établissement m de cure de rajeunissement

space [speɪs] n (gen) espace m; (room) place f; espace; (length of time) laps m de temps ▷ cpd spatial(e) ▷ vt (also: ~ **out**) espacer; **spacecraft** n engin or vaisseau spatial; **spaceship** n = **spacecraft**

spacious ['speɪʃəs] adj spacieux(-euse), grand(e)

spade [speɪd] n (tool) bêche f, pelle f; (child's) pelle; **spades** npl (Cards) pique m

spaghetti [spə'ɡetɪ] n spaghetti mpl

Spain [speɪn] n Espagne f

spam [spæm] n (Comput) pourriel m

span [spæn] n (of bird, plane) envergure f; (of arch) portée f; (in time) espace m de temps, durée f ▷ vt enjamber, franchir; (fig) couvrir, embrasser

Spaniard ['spænjəd] n Espagnol(e)

Spanish ['spænɪʃ] adj espagnol(e), d'Espagne ▷ n (Ling) espagnol m; **the Spanish** npl les Espagnols

spank [spæŋk] vt donner une fessée à

spanner ['spænər] n (BRIT) clé f (de mécanicien)

spare [speər] adj de réserve, de rechange; (surplus) de or en trop, de reste ▷ n (part) pièce f de rechange, pièce détachée ▷ vt (do without) se passer de; (afford to give) donner, accorder, passer; (not hurt) épargner; **to ~** (surplus) en surplus, de trop; **spare part** n pièce f de rechange, pièce détachée; **spare room** n chambre f d'ami; **spare time** n moments mpl de loisir; **spare tyre**, (us) **spare tire** n (Aut) pneu m de rechange; **spare wheel** n (Aut) roue f de secours

spark [spɑːk] n étincelle f

sparkle ['spɑːkl] n scintillement m, étincellement m, éclat m ▷ vi étinceler, scintiller

sparkling ['spɑːklɪŋ] adj (wine) mousseux(-euse), pétillant(e); (water) pétillant(e), gazeux(-euse)

spark plug n bougie f

sparrow ['spærəʊ] n moineau m

sparse [spɑːs] adj clairsemé(e)

spasm ['spæzəm] n (Med) spasme m

spat [spæt] pt, pp of **spit**

spate [speɪt] n (fig): ~ **of** avalanche f or torrent m de

spatula ['spætjʊlə] n spatule f

speak (pt **spoke**, pp **spoken**) [spiːk, spəʊk, 'spəʊkən] vt (language) parler; (truth) dire ▷ vi parler; (make a speech) prendre la parole; **to ~ to sb/of** or **about sth** parler à qn/de qch; **I don't ~ French** je ne parle pas français; **do you ~ English?** parlez-vous anglais?; **can I ~ to ...?** est-ce que je peux parler à ...?; **speaker** n (in public) orateur m; (also: **loudspeaker**) haut-parleur m; (for stereo etc) baffle m, enceinte f; (Pol) **the Speaker** (BRIT) le président de la Chambre des communes or des représentants; (us) le président de la Chambre

spear [spɪər] n lance f ▷ vt transpercer

special ['speʃl] adj spécial(e); **special delivery** n (Post): **by special delivery** en express; **special effects** npl (Cine) effets spéciaux; **specialist** n spécialiste m/f; **speciality** [speʃɪ'ælɪtɪ] n (BRIT) spécialité f; **specialize** vi: **to specialize (in)** se spécialiser (dans); **specially** adv spécialement, particulièrement; **special needs** npl (BRIT) difficultés fpl d'apprentissage scolaire; **special offer** n (Comm) réclame f; **special school** n (BRIT) établissement m d'enseignement spécialisé; **specialty** n (us) = **speciality**

species ['spiːʃiːz] n (pl inv) espèce f

specific [spə'sɪfɪk] adj (not vague) précis(e), explicite; (particular) particulier(-ière); **specifically** adv explicitement, précisément;

(intend, ask, design) expressément, spécialement

specify ['spɛsɪfaɪ] vt spécifier, préciser

specimen ['spɛsɪmən] n spécimen m, échantillon m; (Med: of blood) prélèvement m; (: of urine) échantillon m

speck [spɛk] n petite tache, petit point; (particle) grain m

spectacle ['spɛktəkl] n spectacle m; **spectacles** npl (BRIT) lunettes fpl; **spectacular** [spɛk'tækjələʳ] adj spectaculaire

spectator [spɛk'teɪtəʳ] n spectateur(-trice)

spectrum (pl spectra) ['spɛktrəm, -rə] n spectre m; (fig) gamme f

speculate ['spɛkjuleɪt] vi spéculer; (ponder): **to ~ about** s'interroger sur

sped [spɛd] pt, pp of **speed**

speech [spi:tʃ] n (faculty) parole f; (talk) discours m, allocution f; (manner of speaking) façon f de parler, langage m; (enunciation) élocution f; **speechless** adj muet(te)

speed [spi:d] n vitesse f; (promptness) rapidité f ⊳ vi (pt, pp **sped**) (Aut: exceed speed limit) faire un excès de vitesse; **at full** or **top ~** à toute vitesse or allure; **speed up** (pt, pp **speeded up**) vi aller plus vite, accélérer ⊳ vt accélérer; **speedboat** n vedette f, hors-bord m inv; **speed camera** n (Aut) radar m (automatique); **speeding** n (Aut) excès m de vitesse; **speed limit** n limitation f de vitesse, vitesse maximale permise; **speedometer** [spɪ'dɔmɪtəʳ] n compteur m (de vitesse); **speedy** adj rapide, prompt(e)

spell [spɛl] n (also: **magic ~**) sortilège m, charme m; (period of time) (courte) période f ⊳ vt (pt, pp **spelled** or **spelt**) (in writing) écrire, orthographier; (aloud) épeler; (fig) signifier; **to cast a ~ on sb** jeter un sort à qn; **he can't ~** il fait

des fautes d'orthographe; **spell out** vt (explain): **to ~ sth out for sb** expliquer qch clairement à qn; **spellchecker** ['spɛltʃɛkəʳ] n (Comput) correcteur m or vérificateur m orthographique; **spelling** n orthographe f

spelt [spɛlt] pt, pp of **spell**

spend (pt, pp **spent**) [spɛnd, spɛnt] vt (money) dépenser; (time, life) passer; (devote) consacrer; **spending** n: **government spending** les dépenses publiques

spent [spɛnt] pt, pp of **spend** ⊳ adj (cartridge, bullets) vide

sperm [spə:m] n spermatozoïde m; (semen) sperme m

sphere [sfɪəʳ] n sphère f; (fig) sphère, domaine m

spice [spaɪs] n épice f ⊳ vt épicer

spicy ['spaɪsɪ] adj épicé(e), relevé(e); (fig) piquant(e)

spider ['spaɪdəʳ] n araignée f

spike [spaɪk] n pointe f; (Bot) épi m

spill (pt, pp **spilt** or **spilled**) [spɪl, -t, -d] vt renverser; répandre ⊳ vi se répandre; **spill over** vi déborder

spilt [spɪlt] pt, pp of **spill**

spin [spɪn] (pt, pp **spun**) n (revolution of wheel) tour m; (Aviat) (chute f en) vrille f; (trip in car) petit tour, balade f; (on ball) effet m ⊳ vt (wool etc) filer; (wheel) faire tourner ⊳ vi (turn) tourner, tournoyer

spinach ['spɪnɪtʃ] n épinards mpl

spinal ['spaɪnl] adj vertébral(e), spinal(e); **spinal cord** n moelle épinière

spin doctor n (inf) personne employée pour présenter un parti politique sous un jour favorable

spin-dryer [spɪn'draɪəʳ] n (BRIT) essoreuse f

spine [spaɪn] n colonne vertébrale; (thorn) épine f, piquant m

spiral ['spaɪərl] n spirale f ⊳ vi (fig: prices etc) monter en flèche

spire ['spaɪəʳ] n flèche f, aiguille f

spirit ['spɪrɪt] n (soul) esprit m, âme f; (ghost) esprit, revenant m; (mood) esprit, état m d'esprit; (courage) courage m, énergie f; **spirits** npl (drink) spiritueux mpl, alcool m; **in good ~s** de bonne humeur

spiritual ['spɪrɪtjuəl] adj spirituel(le); (religious) religieux-euse)

spit [spɪt] n (for roasting) broche f; (spittle) crachat m; (saliva) salive f ▷ vi (pt, pp **spat**) cracher; (sound) crépiter; (rain) crachiner

spite [spaɪt] n rancune f, dépit m ▷ vt contrarier, vexer; **in ~ of** en dépit de, malgré; **spiteful** adj malveillant(e), rancunier(-ière)

splash [splæʃ] n (sound) plouf m; (of colour) tache f ▷ vt éclabousser ▷ vi (also: ~ **about**) barboter, patauger; **splash out** vi (BRIT) faire une folie

splendid ['splendɪd] adj splendide, superbe, magnifique

splinter ['splɪntə'] n (wood) écharde f; (metal) éclat m ▷ vi (wood) se fendre; (glass) se briser

split [splɪt] (pt, pp **split**) n fente f, déchirure f; (fig: Pol) scission f ▷ vt fendre, déchirer; (party) diviser; (work, profits) partager, répartir ▷ vi (break) se fendre, se briser; (divide) se diviser; **split up** vi (couple) se séparer, rompre; (meeting) se disperser

spoil (pt, pp **spoiled** or **spoilt**) [spɔɪl, -d, -t] vt (damage) abîmer; (mar) gâcher; (child) gâter

spoilt [spɔɪlt] pt, pp of **spoil** ▷ adj (child) gâté(e); (ballot paper) nul(le)

spoke [spəʊk] pt of **speak** ▷ n rayon m

spoken ['spəʊkn] pp of **speak**

spokesman ['spəʊksmən] (irreg) n porte-parole m inv

spokesperson ['spəʊkspɜːsn] (irreg) n porte-parole m inv

spokeswoman ['spəʊkswʊmən] (irreg) n porte-parole m inv

sponge [spʌndʒ] n éponge f; (Culin: also: ~ **cake**) ≈ biscuit m de Savoie ▷ vt

éponger ▷ vi: **to ~ off** or **on** vivre aux crochets de; **sponge bag** n (BRIT) trousse f de toilette

sponsor ['spɒnsə'] n (Radio, TV, Sport) sponsor m; (for application) parrain m; (BRIT: for fund-raising event) donateur(-trice) ▷ vt sponsoriser; parrainer; (fund-raising event) faire un don à; **sponsorship** n sponsoring m; parrainage m; dons mpl

spontaneous [spɒn'teɪnɪəs] adj spontané(e)

spooky ['spuːkɪ] adj (inf) qui donne la chair de poule

spoon [spuːn] n cuiller f; **spoonful** n cuillerée f

sport [spɔːt] n sport m; (person) chic type m/chic fille f ▷ vt (wear) arborer; **sport jacket** n (us) = **sports jacket**; **sports car** n voiture f de sport; **sports centre** (BRIT) n centre sportif; **sports jacket** (BRIT) n veste f de sport; **sportsman** (irreg) n sportif m; **sports utility vehicle** n véhicule m de loisirs (de type SUV); **sportswear** n vêtements mpl de sport; **sportswoman** (irreg) n sportive f; **sporty** adj sportif(-ive)

spot [spɒt] n tache f; (dot: on pattern) pois m; (pimple) bouton m; (place) endroit m, coin m ▷ vt (notice) apercevoir, repérer; **on the ~** sur place, sur les lieux; (immediately) sur le champ; **spotless** adj immaculé(e); **spotlight** n projecteur m; (Aut) phare m auxiliaire

spouse [spauz] n époux (épouse)

sprain [spreɪn] n entorse f, foulure f ▷ vt: **to ~ one's ankle** se fouler or se tordre la cheville

sprang [spræŋ] pt of **spring**

sprawl [sprɔːl] vi s'étaler

spray [spreɪ] n jet m (en fines gouttelettes); (from sea) embruns mpl; (aerosol) vaporisateur m, bombe f; (for garden) pulvérisateur m; (of flowers) petit bouquet ▷ vt vaporiser, pulvériser; (crops) traiter

spread [sprɛd] (pt, pp **spread**) n (distribution) répartition f; (Culin) pâte f à tartiner; (inf: meal) festin m ▷ vt (paste, contents) étendre, étaler; (rumour, disease) répandre, propager; (wealth) répartir ▷ vi s'étendre; se répandre; se propager; (stain) s'étaler; **spread out** vi (people) se disperser; **spreadsheet** n (Comput) tableur m

spree [spri:] n: **to go on a ~** faire la fête

spring [sprɪŋ] (pt **sprang**, pp **sprung**) n (season) printemps m; (leap) bond m, saut m; (coiled metal) ressort m; (of water) source f ▷ vi bondir, sauter; **spring up** vi (problem) se présenter, surgir; (plant, buildings) surgir de terre; **spring onion** n (BRIT) ciboule f, cive f

sprinkle ['sprɪŋkl] vt: **to ~ water etc on, ~ with water** etc asperger d'eau etc; **to ~ sugar etc on, ~ with sugar** etc saupoudrer de sucre etc

sprint [sprɪnt] n sprint m ▷ vi courir à toute vitesse; (Sport) sprinter

sprung [sprʌŋ] pp of **spring**

spun [spʌn] pt, pp of **spin**

spur [spə:ʳ] n éperon m; (fig) aiguillon m ▷ vt (also: **~ on**) éperonner aiguillonner; **on the ~ of the moment** sous l'impulsion du moment

spurt [spə:t] n jet m; (of blood) jaillissement m; (of energy) regain m, sursaut m ▷ vi jaillir, gicler

spy [spaɪ] n espion(ne) m ▷ vi: **to ~ on** espionner, épier ▷ vt (see) apercevoir

Sq. abbr (in address) = **square**

sq. abbr (Math etc) = **square**

squabble ['skwɔbl] vi se chamailler

squad [skwɔd] n (Mil, Police) escouade f, groupe m; (Football) contingent m

squadron ['skwɔdrn] n (Mil) escadron m; (Aviat, Naut) escadrille f

squander ['skwɔndəʳ] vt gaspiller, dilapider

square [skwɛəʳ] n carré m; (in town) place f ▷ adj carré(e) ▷ vt (arrange)

régler; arranger; (Math) élever au carré; (reconcile) concilier; **all ~** quitte; (à égalité; **a ~ meal** un repas convenable; **2 metres ~** de 2 mètres sur 2; **1 ~ metre** 1 mètre carré; **square root** n racine carrée

squash [skwɔʃ] n (BRIT Sport) squash m; (us: vegetable) courge f; (drink): **lemon/orange ~** citronnade f/orangeade f ▷ vt écraser

squat [skwɔt] adj petit(e) et épais(se), ramassé(e) ▷ vi (also: **~ down**) s'accroupir; **squatter** n squatter m

squeak [skwi:k] vi (hinge, wheel) grincer; (mouse) pousser un petit cri

squeal [skwi:l] vi pousser un ou des cri(s) aigu(s) or perçant(s); (brakes) grincer

squeeze [skwi:z] n pression f ▷ vt presser; (hand, arm) serrer

squid [skwɪd] n calmar m

squint [skwɪnt] vi loucher

squirm [skwə:m] vi se tortiller

squirrel ['skwɪrəl] n écureuil m

squirt [skwə:t] vi jaillir, gicler ▷ vt faire gicler

Sr abbr = **senior**

Sri Lanka [srɪ'læŋkə] n Sri Lanka m

St abbr = **saint**; **street**

stab [stæb] n (with knife etc) coup m (de couteau etc); (of pain) lancée f; (inf: try): **to have a ~ at (doing) sth** s'essayer à (faire) qch ▷ vt poignarder

stability [stə'bɪlɪtɪ] n stabilité f

stable ['steɪbl] n écurie f ▷ adj stable

stack [stæk] n tas m, pile f ▷ vt empiler, entasser

stadium ['steɪdɪəm] n stade m

staff [stɑ:f] n (work force) personnel m; (BRIT Scol: teaching **~**) professeurs mpl, enseignants mpl, personnel enseignant ▷ vt pourvoir en personnel

stag [stæg] n cerf m

stage [steɪdʒ] n scène f; (platform) estrade f; (point) étape f, stade m; (profession): **the ~** le théâtre ▷ vt

S

(play) monter, mettre en scène; (demonstration) organiser; **in ~s** par étapes, par degrés

⚠ Be careful not to translate stage by the French word stage.

stagger ['stægə'] vi chanceler, tituber ▷ vt (person: amaze) stupéfier; (hours, holidays) étaler, échelonner; **staggering** adj (amazing) stupéfiant(e), renversant(e)

stagnant ['stægnənt] adj stagnant(e)

stag night, stag party n enterrement m de vie de garçon

stain [steɪn] n tache f; (colouring) colorant m ▷ vt tacher; (wood) teindre; **stained glass** n (decorative) verre coloré; (in church) vitraux mpl; **stainless steel** n inox m, acier m inoxydable

staircase ['steəkeɪs] n = **stairway**

stairs [steəz] npl escalier m

stairway ['steəweɪ] n escalier m

stake [steɪk] n pieu m, poteau m; (Comm: interest) intérêts mpl; (Betting) enjeu m ▷ vt risquer, jouer; (also: ~ out: area) marquer, délimiter; **to be at ~** être en jeu

stale [steɪl] adj (bread) rassis(e); (food) pas frais (fraîche); (beer) éventé(e); (smell) de renfermé; (air) confiné(e)

stalk [stɔːk] n tige f ▷ vt traquer

stall [stɔːl] n (in street, market etc) éventaire m, étal m; (in stable) stalle f ▷ vt (Aut) caler; (fig: delay) retarder ▷ vi (Aut) caler; (fig) essayer de gagner du temps; **stalls** npl (BRIT: in cinema, theatre) orchestre m

stamina ['stæmɪnə] n vigueur f, endurance f

stammer ['stæmə'] n bégaiement m ▷ vi bégayer

stamp [stæmp] n timbre m; (also: **rubber ~**) tampon m, cachet m; (mark: also fig) empreinte f; (on document) cachet m ▷ vt (also: **~ one's foot**) taper du pied ▷ vt (letter) timbrer; (with rubber stamp) tamponner; **stamp out** vt

(fire) piétiner; (crime) éradiquer; (opposition) éliminer; **stamped addressed envelope** n (BRIT) enveloppe affranchie pour la réponse

stampede [stæm'piːd] n ruée f; (of cattle) débandade f

stance [stæns] n position f

stand [stænd] (pt, pp **stood**) n (position) position f; (for taxis) station f (de taxis); (Comm) étalage m, stand m; (Sport: also: **~s**) tribune f; (also: **music ~**) pupitre m ▷ vi être or se tenir (debout); (rise) se lever, se mettre debout; (be placed) se trouver; (remain: offer etc) rester valable ▷ vt (place) mettre, poser; (tolerate, withstand) supporter; (treat, invite) offrir, payer; **to make a ~** prendre position; **to ~ for parliament** (BRIT) se présenter aux élections (comme candidat à la députation); **I can't ~ him** je ne peux pas le voir; **stand back** vi (move back) reculer, s'écarter; **stand by** vi (be ready) se tenir prêt(e) ▷ vt fus (opinion) s'en tenir à; (person) ne pas abandonner, soutenir; **stand down** vi (withdraw) se retirer; **stand for** vt fus (signify) représenter, signifier; (tolerate) supporter, tolérer; **stand in for** vt fus remplacer; **stand out** vi (be prominent) ressortir; **stand up** vi (rise) se lever, se mettre debout; **stand up for** vt fus défendre; **stand up to** vt fus tenir tête à, résister à

standard ['stændəd] n (norm) norme f, étalon m; (level) niveau m (voulu); (criterion) critère m; (flag) étendard m ▷ adj (size etc) ordinaire, normal(e); (model, feature) standard inv; (practice) courant(e); text: de base; **standards** npl (morals) morale f, principes mpl; **standard of living** n niveau m de vie

stand-by ticket n (Aviat) billet m stand-by

standing ['stændɪŋ] adj debout inv; (permanent) permanent(e) ▷ n (reputation) réputation f, rang m, standing m; **of many years' ~** qui dure or existe depuis longtemps; **standing order** n (BRIT: at bank) virement m automatique, prélèvement m bancaire

stand: standpoint n point m de vue; **standstill** n: **at a standstill** à l'arrêt; (fig) au point mort; **to come to a standstill** s'immobiliser, s'arrêter

stank [stæŋk] pt of **stink**

staple ['steɪpl] n (for papers) agrafe f ▷ adj (food, crop, industry etc) de base principal(e) ▷ vt agrafer

star [staːʳ] n étoile f; (celebrity) vedette f ▷ vt (Cine) avoir pour vedette; **stars** npl: **the ~s** (Astrology) l'horoscope m

starboard ['staːbəd] n tribord m

starch [staːtʃ] n amidon m; (in food) fécule f

stardom ['staːdəm] n célébrité f

stare [stɛəʳ] n regard m fixe ▷ vi: **to ~ at** regarder fixement

stark [staːk] adj (bleak) désolé(e), morne ▷ adv: **~ naked** complètement nu(e)

start [staːt] n commencement m, début m; (of race) départ m; (sudden movement) sursaut m; (advantage) avance f, avantage m ▷ vt commencer; (cause: fight) déclencher; (rumour) donner naissance à; (fashion) lancer; (found: business, newspaper) lancer, créer; (engine) mettre en marche ▷ vi (begin) commencer; (begin journey) partir, se mettre en route; (jump) sursauter; **when does the film ~?** à quelle heure est-ce que le film commence?; **to ~ doing** or **to do sth** se mettre à faire qch; **start off** vi commencer; (leave) partir; **start out** vi (begin) commencer; (set out) partir; **start up** vi commencer; (car) démarrer ▷ vt (fight) déclencher; (business) créer; (car) mettre en marche; **starter** n (Aut) démarreur m; (Sport: official) starter m; (BRIT Culin) entrée f; **starting point** n point m de départ

startle ['staːtl] vt faire sursauter; donner un choc à; **startling** adj surprenant(e), saisissant(e)

starvation [staː'veɪʃən] n faim f, famine f

starve [staːv] vi mourir de faim ▷ vt laisser mourir de faim

state [steɪt] n état m; (Pol) État m ▷ vt (declare) déclarer, affirmer; (specify) indiquer, spécifier; **States** npl: **the S~s** les États-Unis; **to be in a ~** être dans tous ses états; **stately home** ['steɪtlɪ-] n manoir m or château m (ouvert au public); **statement** n déclaration f; (Law) déposition f; **state school** n école publique; **statesman** (irreg) n homme m d'État

static ['stætɪk] n (Radio) parasites mpl; (also: **~ electricity**) électricité f statique ▷ adj fixe

station ['steɪʃən] n gare f; (also: **police ~**) poste m or commissariat m (de police) ▷ vt placer, poster

stationary ['steɪʃnərɪ] adj à l'arrêt, immobile

stationer's (shop) n (BRIT) papeterie f

stationery ['steɪʃnərɪ] n papier m à lettres, petit matériel de bureau

station wagon n (US) break m

statistic [stə'tɪstɪk] n statistique f; **statistics** n (science) statistique f

statue ['stætjuː] n statue f

stature ['stætʃəʳ] n stature f; (fig) envergure f

status ['steɪtəs] n position f, situation f; (prestige) prestige m; (Admin, official position) statut m; **status quo** [-'kwəu] n: **the status quo** le statu quo

statutory ['stætjutrɪ] adj statutaire, prévu(e) par un article de loi

staunch [stɔːntʃ] adj sûr(e), loyal(e)

stay [steɪ] n (period of time) séjour m ▷ vi rester; (reside) loger; (spend some time) séjourner; **to ~ put** ne pas bouger; **to ~ the night** passer la nuit; **stay away** vi (from person, building) ne pas s'approcher; (from event) ne pas venir; **stay behind** vi rester en arrière; **stay in** vi (at home) rester à la maison; **stay on** vi rester; **stay out** vi (of house) ne pas rentrer; (strikers) rester en grève; **stay up** vi (at night) ne pas se coucher

steadily ['stɛdɪlɪ] adv (regularly) progressivement; (firmly) fermement; (walk) d'un pas ferme; (fixedly: look) sans détourner les yeux

steady ['stɛdɪ] adj stable, solide, ferme; (regular) constant(e), régulier(-ière); (person) calme, pondéré(e) ▷ vt assurer, stabiliser; (nerves) calmer; **a ~ boyfriend** un petit ami

steak [steɪk] n (meat) bifteck m, steak m; (fish, pork) tranche f

steal (pt **stole**, pp **stolen**) [stiːl, stəul, 'stəuln] vt, vi voler; (move) se faufiler, se déplacer furtivement; **my wallet has been stolen** on m'a volé mon portefeuille

steam [stiːm] n vapeur f ▷ vt (Culin) cuire à la vapeur ▷ vi fumer; **steam up** vi (window) se couvrir de buée; **to get ~ed up about sth** (fig: inf) s'exciter à propos de qch; **steamy** adj humide; (window) embué(e); (sexy) torride

steel [stiːl] n acier m ▷ cpd d'acier

steep [stiːp] adj raide, escarpé(e); (price) très élevé(e), excessif(-ive) ▷ vt (faire) tremper

steeple ['stiːpl] n clocher m

steer [stɪəʳ] vt diriger; (boat) gouverner; (lead: person) guider, conduire ▷ vi tenir le gouvernail; **steering** n (Aut) conduite f; **steering wheel** n volant m

stem [stɛm] n (of plant) tige f; (of glass) pied m ▷ vt contenir, endiguer; (attack, spread of disease) juguler; **stem** from vt fus découler de, provenir de

step [stɛp] n pas m; (stair) marche f; (action) mesure f, disposition f ▷ vi faire un pas; **to ~ forward/back** faire un pas en avant/arrière, avancer/reculer; **steps** npl (BRIT) = **stepladder**; **to**

be in/out of ~ (with) (fig) aller dans le sens (de)/être déphasé(e) (par rapport à); **step down** vi (fig) se retirer, se désister; **step in** vi (fig) intervenir; **step up** vt (production, sales) augmenter; (campaign, efforts) intensifier; **stepbrother** n demi-frère m; **stepchild** (pl **stepchildren**) n beau-fils m, belle-fille f; **stepdaughter** n belle-fille f; **stepfather** n beau-père m; **stepladder** n (BRIT) escabeau m; **stepmother** n belle-mère f; **stepsister** n demi-sœur f; **stepson** n beau-fils m

stereo ['stɛrɪəu] n (sound) stéréo f; (hi-fi) chaîne f stéréo ▷ adj (also: **~phonic**) stéréo(phonique)

stereotype ['stɪərɪətaɪp] n stéréotype m ▷ vt stéréotyper

sterile ['stɛraɪl] adj stérile; **sterilize** ['stɛrɪlaɪz] vt stériliser

sterling ['stəːlɪŋ] adj (silver) de bon aloi, fin(e) ▷ n (currency) livre f sterling inv

stern [stəːn] adj sévère ▷ n (Naut) arrière m, poupe f

steroid ['stɪərɔɪd] n stéroïde m

stew [stjuː] n ragoût m ▷ vt, vi cuire à la casserole

steward ['stjuːəd] n (Aviat, Naut, Rail) steward m; **stewardess** n hôtesse f

stick [stɪk] (pt, pp **stuck**) n bâton m; (for walking) canne f; (of chalk etc) morceau m ▷ vt (glue) coller; (thrust): **to ~ sth into** piquer or planter or enfoncer qch dans; (inf: put) mettre, fourrer; (: tolerate) supporter ▷ vi (adhere) tenir, coller; (remain) rester; (get jammed: door, lift) se bloquer; **stick out** vi dépasser, sortir; **stick up** vi dépasser, sortir; **stick up for** vt fus défendre; **sticker** n auto-collant m; **sticking plaster** n sparadrap m, pansement adhésif; **stick insect** n phasme m; **stick shift** n (US Aut) levier m de vitesses

sticky ['stɪkɪ] adj poisseux(-euse); (label) adhésif(-ive); (fig: situation) délicat(e)

stiff [stɪf] adj (gen) raide, rigide; (door, brush) dur(e); (difficult) difficile, ardu(e); (cold) froid(e), distant(e); (strong, high) fort(e), élevé(e) ▷ adv: **to be bored/scared/frozen ~** s'ennuyer à mourir/être mort(e) de peur/froid

stifling ['staɪflɪŋ] adj (heat) suffocant(e)

stigma ['stɪgmə] n stigmate m

stiletto [stɪ'lɛtəu] n (BRIT: also: **~ heel**) talon m aiguille

still [stɪl] adj immobile ▷ adv (up to this time) encore, toujours; (even) encore; (nonetheless) quand même, tout de même

stimulate ['stɪmjuleɪt] vt stimuler

stimulus (pl **stimuli**) ['stɪmjuləs, 'stɪmjulaɪ] n stimulant m; (Biol, Psych) stimulus m

sting [stɪŋ] n piqûre f; (organ) dard m ▷ vt, vi (pt, pp **stung**) piquer

stink [stɪŋk] n puanteur f ▷ vi (pt **stank**, pp **stunk**) puer, empester

stir [stəː] n agitation f, sensation f ▷ vt remuer ▷ vi remuer, bouger; **stir up** vt faire lever; **stir-fry** vt faire sauter ▷ n: **vegetable stir-fry** légumes sautés à la poêle

stitch [stɪtʃ] n (Sewing) point m; (Knitting) maille f; (Med) point de suture; (pain) point de côté ▷ vt coudre, piquer; (Med) suturer

stock [stɔk] n réserve f, provision f; (Comm) stock m; (Agr) cheptel m, bétail m; (Culin) bouillon m; (Finance) valeurs fpl, titres mpl; (descent, origin) souche f ▷ adj (fig: reply etc) classique ▷ vt (have in stock) avoir, vendre; **in ~** en stock, en magasin; **out of ~** épuisé(e); **to take ~** (fig) faire le point; **~s and shares** valeurs (mobilières), titres; **stockbroker** ['stɔkbrəukəʳ] n agent m de

change; **stock cube** n (BRIT Culin) bouillon-cube m; **stock exchange** n Bourse f (des valeurs); **stockholder** ['stɔkhəuldəʳ] n (US) actionnaire m/f

stocking ['stɔkɪŋ] n bas m

stock market n Bourse f, marché financier

stole [stəul] pt of **steal** ▷ n étole f

stolen ['stəuln] pp of **steal**

stomach ['stʌmək] n estomac m; (abdomen) ventre m ▷ vt supporter, digérer; **stomachache** n mal à l'estomac or au ventre

stone [stəun] n pierre f; (pebble) caillou m, galet m; (in fruit) noyau m; (Med) calcul m; (BRIT: weight) = 6.348 kg; 14 pounds ▷ cpd de or en pierre ▷ vt (person) lancer des pierres sur, lapider; (fruit) dénoyauter

stood [stud] pt, pp of **stand**

stool [stuːl] n tabouret m

stoop [stuːp] vi (also: **have a ~**) être voûté(e); (also: **~ down**: bend) se baisser, se courber

stop [stɔp] n arrêt m; (in punctuation) point m ▷ vt arrêter; (break off) interrompre; (also: **put a ~ to**) mettre fin à; (prevent) empêcher ▷ vi s'arrêter; (rain, noise etc) cesser, s'arrêter; **to ~ doing sth** cesser or arrêter de faire qch; **to ~ sb (from) doing sth** empêcher qn de faire qch; **~ it!** arrête!; **stop by** vi s'arrêter (au passage); **stop off** vi faire une courte halte; **stopover** n halte f; (Aviat) escale f; **stoppage** n (strike) arrêt m de travail; (obstruction) obstruction f

storage ['stɔːrɪdʒ] n emmagasinage m

store [stɔːʳ] n (stock) provision f, réserve f; (depot) entrepôt m; (BRIT: large shop) grand magasin; (us: shop) magasin m ▷ vt emmagasiner; (information) enregistrer; **stores** npl (food) provisions; **who knows what is in ~ for us?** qui sait ce que l'avenir nous réserve or ce qui nous attend?; **storekeeper** n (US) commerçant(e)

storey, (us) **story** ['stɔːrɪ] n étage m

storm [stɔːm] n tempête f; (thunderstorm) orage m ▷ vi (fig) fulminer ▷ vt prendre d'assaut; **stormy** adj orageux(-euse)

story ['stɔːrɪ] n histoire f; (Press: article) article m; (us) = **storey**

stout [staut] adj (strong) solide; (fat) gros(se), corpulent(e) ▷ n bière brune

stove [stəuv] n (for cooking) fourneau m (: small) réchaud m; (for heating) poêle m

straight [streɪt] adj droit(e); (hair) raide; (frank) honnête, franc (franche); (simple) simple ▷ adv (tout) droit; (drink) sec, sans eau; **to put** or **get ~** mettre en ordre, mettre de l'ordre dans; (fig) mettre au clair; **~ away**, **~ off** (at once) tout de suite; **straighten** vt ajuster; (bed) arranger; **straighten out** vt (fig) débrouiller; **straighten up** vi (stand up) se redresser; **straightforward** adj simple; (frank) honnête, direct(e)

strain [streɪn] n (Tech) tension f; pression f; (physical) effort m; (mental) tension f (nerveuse); (Med) entorse f; (breed: of plants) variété f; (: of animals) race f ▷ vt (fig: resources etc) mettre à rude épreuve, grever; (hurt: back etc) se faire mal à; (vegetables) égoutter; **strains** npl (Mus) accords mpl, accents mpl; **strained** adj (muscle) froissé(e); (laugh etc) forcé(e), contraint(e); (relations) tendu(e); **strainer** n passoire f

strait [streɪt] n (Geo) détroit m; **straits** npl: **to be in dire ~s** (fig) avoir de sérieux ennuis

strand [strænd] n (of thread) fil m, brin m; (of rope) toron m; (of hair) mèche f ▷ vt (boat) échouer; **stranded** adj (person) en rade, en plan

strange [streɪndʒ] adj (not known) inconnu(e); (odd) étrange, bizarre; **strangely** adv étrangement, bizarrement; see also

enough; **stranger** n (unknown) inconnu(e); (from somewhere else) étranger(-ère)

strangle ['stræŋgl] vt étrangler

strap [stræp] n lanière f, courroie f, sangle f; (of slip, dress) bretelle f

strategic [strə'tiːdʒɪk] adj stratégique

strategy ['strætɪdʒɪ] n stratégie f

straw [strɔː] n paille f; **that's the last ~!** ça c'est le comble!

strawberry ['strɔːbərɪ] n fraise f

stray [streɪ] adj (animal) perdu(e), errant(e); (scattered) isolé(e) ▷ vi s'égarer; **~ bullet** balle perdue

streak [striːk] n bande f, filet m; (in hair) raie f ▷ vt zébrer, strier

stream [striːm] n (brook) ruisseau m; (current) courant m, flot m; (of people) défilé m ininterrompu, flot m ▷ vt (Scol) répartir par niveau ▷ vi ruisseler; **to ~ in/out** entrer/sortir à flots

street [striːt] n rue f; **streetcar** n (us) tramway m; **street light** n réverbère m; **street map**, **street plan** n plan m des rues

strength [streŋθ] n force f; (of girder, knot etc) solidité f; **strengthen** vt renforcer; (muscle) fortifier; (building, Econ) consolider

strenuous ['strenjuəs] adj vigoureux(-euse), énergique; (tiring) ardu(e), fatigant(e)

stress [stres] n (force, pressure) pression f; (mental strain) tension f (nerveuse), stress m; (accent) accent m; (emphasis) insistance f ▷ vt insister sur, souligner; (syllable) accentuer; **stressed** adj (tense) stressé(e); (syllable) accentué(e); **stressful** adj (job) stressant(e)

stretch [stretʃ] n (of sand etc) étendue f ▷ vi s'étirer; (extend): **to ~ to** or **as far as** s'étendre jusqu'à ▷ vt tendre, étirer; (fig) pousser (au maximum); **at a ~** d'affilée; **stretch out** vi s'étendre ▷ vt (arm etc) allonger, tendre; (to spread) étendre

stretcher ['strɛtʃər] n brancard m, civière f

strict [strɪkt] adj strict(e); **strictly** adv strictement

stridden ['strɪdn] pp of **stride**

stride [straɪd] n grand pas, enjambée f ▷ vi (pt **strode**, pp **stridden**) marcher à grands pas

strike [straɪk] (pt, pp **struck**) n grève f; (of oil etc) découverte f; (attack) raid m ▷ vt frapper; (oil etc) trouver, découvrir; (make: agreement, deal) conclure ▷ vi faire grève; (attack) attaquer; (clock) sonner; **to go on** or **come out on ~** se mettre en grève, faire grève; **to ~ a match** frotter une allumette; **striker** n gréviste m/f; (Sport) buteur m; **striking** adj frappant(e), saisissant(e); (attractive) éblouissant(e)

string [strɪŋ] n ficelle f, fil m; (row: of beads) rang m; (Mus) corde f ▷ vt (pt, pp **strung**): **to ~ out** échelonner; **to ~ together** enchaîner; **the strings** npl (Mus) les instruments mpl à cordes; **to pull ~s** (fig) faire jouer le piston

strip [strɪp] n bande f; (Sport) tenue f ▷ vt (undress) déshabiller; (paint) décaper; (fig) dégarnir, dépouiller; (also: **~ down**) (machine) démonter ▷ vi se déshabiller; **strip off** vt (paint etc) décaper ▷ vi (person) se déshabiller

stripe [straɪp] n raie f, rayure f; (Mil) galon m; **striped** adj rayé(e), à rayures

stripper ['strɪpər] n strip-teaseuse f

strip-search ['strɪpsɜːtʃ] vt: **to ~ sb** fouiller qn (en le faisant se déshabiller)

strive (pt **strove**, pp **striven**) [straɪv, strəuv, 'strɪvn] vi: **to ~ to do/for sth** s'efforcer de faire/d'obtenir qch

strode [strəud] pt of **stride**

stroke [strəuk] n coup m; (Med) attaque f; (Swimming: style) (sorte de) nage f ▷ vt caresser; **at a ~** d'un (seul) coup

stroll [strəul] n petite promenade ▷ vi flâner, se promener nonchalamment; **stroller** n (us: for child) poussette f

strong [strɔŋ] adj (gen) fort(e); (healthy) vigoureux(-euse); (heart, nerves) solide; **they are 50 ~** ils sont au nombre de 50; **stronghold** n forteresse f, fort m; (fig) bastion m; **strongly** adv fortement, avec force; vigoureusement; solidement

strove [strəuv] pt of **strive**

struck [strʌk] pt, pp of **strike**

structure ['strʌktʃər] n structure f; (building) construction f

struggle ['strʌgl] n lutte f ▷ vi lutter, se battre

strung [strʌŋ] pt, pp of **string**

stub [stʌb] n (of cigarette) bout m, mégot m; (of ticket etc) talon m ▷ vt: **to ~ one's toe (on sth)** se heurter le doigt de pied (contre qch); **stub out** vt écraser

stubble ['stʌbl] n chaume m; (on chin) barbe f de plusieurs jours

stubborn ['stʌbən] adj têtu(e), obstiné(e), opiniâtre

stuck [stʌk] pt, pp of **stick** ▷ adj (jammed) bloqué(e), coincé(e)

stud [stʌd] n (on boots etc) clou m; (collar stud) bouton m de col; (earring) petite boucle d'oreille; (of horses: also: **~ farm**) écurie f, haras m; (also: **~ horse**) étalon m ▷ vt (fig): **~ded with** parsemé(e) or criblé(e) de

student ['stjuːdənt] n étudiant(e) ▷ adj (life) estudiantin(e), étudiant(e), d'étudiant; (residence, restaurant) universitaire; (loan, movement) étudiant; **student driver** n (us) (conducteur(-trice)) débutant(e); **students' union** n (BRIT: association) ≈ union f des étudiants; (: building) ≈ foyer m des étudiants

studio ['stjuːdɪəu] n studio m, atelier m; (TV etc) studio; **studio flat**, (us) **studio apartment** n studio m

study ['stʌdɪ] n étude f; (room) bureau m ▷ vt étudier; (examine) examiner ▷ vi étudier, faire ses études

stuff [stʌf] n (gen) chose(s) f(pl), truc m; (belongings) affaires fpl, trucs; (substance) substance f ▷ vt rembourrer; (Culin) farcir; (inf: push) fourrer; **stuffing** n bourre f, rembourrage m; (Culin) farce f; **stuffy** adj (room) mal ventilé(e) or aéré(e); (ideas) vieux jeu inv

stumble ['stʌmbl] vi trébucher; **to ~ across** or **on** (fig) tomber sur

stump [stʌmp] n souche f; (of limb) moignon m ▷ vt: **to be ~ed** sécher, ne pas savoir que répondre

stun [stʌn] vt (blow) étourdir; (news) abasourdir, stupéfier

stung [stʌŋ] pt, pp of **sting**

stunk [stʌŋk] pp of **stink**

stunned [stʌnd] adj assommé(e); (fig) sidéré(e)

stunning ['stʌnɪŋ] adj (beautiful) étourdissant(e); (news etc) stupéfiant(e)

stunt [stʌnt] n (in film) cascade f, acrobatie f; (publicity) truc m publicitaire ▷ vt retarder, arrêter

stupid ['stju:pɪd] adj stupide, bête; **stupidity** [stju:'pɪdɪtɪ] n stupidité f, bêtise f

sturdy ['stɜ:dɪ] adj (person, plant) robuste, vigoureux(-euse); (object) solide

stutter ['stʌtər] n bégaiement m ▷ vi bégayer

style [staɪl] n style m; (distinction) allure f, cachet m, style; (design) modèle m; **stylish** adj élégant(e), chic inv; **stylist** n (hair stylist) coiffeur(-euse)

sub... [sʌb] prefix sub..., sous-; **subconscious** adj subconscient(e)

subdued [səb'dju:d] adj (light) tamisé(e); (person) qui a perdu de son entrain

subject n ['sʌbdʒɪkt] sujet m; (Scol) matière f ▷ vt [səb'dʒɛkt]: **to ~ to**

soumettre à; **to be ~ to** (law) être soumis(e) à; **subjective** [səb'dʒɛktɪv] adj subjectif(-ive); **subject matter** n (content) contenu m

subjunctive [səb'dʒʌŋktɪv] n subjonctif m

submarine [sʌbmə'ri:n] n sous-marin m

submission [səb'mɪʃən] n soumission f

submit [səb'mɪt] vt soumettre ▷ vi se soumettre

subordinate [sə'bɔ:dɪnət] adj (junior) subalterne; (Grammar) subordonné(e) ▷ n subordonné(e)

subscribe [səb'skraɪb] vi cotiser; **to ~ to** (opinion, fund) souscrire à; (newspaper) s'abonner à; être abonné(e) à

subscription [səb'skrɪpʃən] n (to magazine etc) abonnement m

subsequent ['sʌbsɪkwənt] adj ultérieur(e), suivant(e); **subsequently** adv par la suite

subside [səb'saɪd] vi (land) s'affaisser; (flood) baisser; (wind, feelings) tomber

subsidiary [səb'sɪdɪərɪ] adj subsidiaire; accessoire; (BRIT Scol: subject) complémentaire ▷ n filiale f

subsidize ['sʌbsɪdaɪz] vt subventionner

subsidy ['sʌbsɪdɪ] n subvention f

substance ['sʌbstəns] n substance f

substantial [səb'stænʃl] adj substantiel(le); (fig) important(e)

substitute ['sʌbstɪtju:t] n (person) remplaçant(e); (thing) succédané m ▷ vt: **to ~ sth/sb for** substituer qch/qn à, remplacer par qch/qn; **substitution** n substitution f

subtitles ['sʌbtaɪtlz] npl (Cine) sous-titres mpl

subtle ['sʌtl] adj subtil(e)

subtract [səb'trækt] vt soustraire, retrancher

suburb ['sʌbə:b] n faubourg m; **the ~s** la banlieue; **suburban** [sə'bə:bən] adj de banlieue, suburbain(e)

subway ['sʌbweɪ] n (BRIT: underpass) passage souterrain m; (US: railway) métro m

succeed [sək'siːd] vi réussir ▷ vt succéder à; **to ~ in doing** réussir à faire

success [sək'sɛs] n succès m; réussite f; **successful** adj (business) prospère, qui réussit; (attempt) couronné(e) de succès; **to be successful (in doing)** réussir (à faire); **successfully** adv avec succès

succession [sək'sɛʃən] n succession f

successive [sək'sɛsɪv] adj successif(-ive)

successor [sək'sɛsə'] n successeur m

succumb [sə'kʌm] vi succomber

such [sʌtʃ] adj tel(telle); (of that kind): **~ a book** un livre de ce genre ou pareil, un tel livre; (so much): **~ courage** un tel courage ▷ adv si; **a long trip** un si long voyage; **~ a lot of** tellement ou tant de; **~ as** (like) tel (telle) que, comme; **as ~** adv en tant que tel (telle), à proprement parler; **such-and-such** adj tel ou tel (telle ou telle)

suck [sʌk] vt sucer; (breast, bottle) téter

Sudan [su'dɑːn] n Soudan m

sudden ['sʌdn] adj soudain(e), subit(e); **all of a ~** soudain, tout à coup; **suddenly** adv brusquement, tout à coup, soudain

sudoku [su'dəuku:] n sudoku m

sue [su:] vt poursuivre en justice, intenter un procès à

suede [sweɪd] n daim m, cuir suédé

suffer ['sʌfə'] vt souffrir, subir; (bear) tolérer, supporter, subir ▷ vi souffrir; **to ~ from** (illness) souffrir de, avoir; **suffering** n souffrance(s) f(pl)

suffice [sə'faɪs] vi suffire

sufficient [sə'fɪʃnt] adj suffisant(e)

suffocate ['sʌfəkeɪt] vi suffoquer, étouffer

sugar ['ʃugə'] n sucre m ▷ vt sucrer

suggest [sə'dʒɛst] vt suggérer, proposer; (indicate) sembler indiquer; **suggestion** n suggestion f

suicide ['suɪsaɪd] n suicide m; **~ bombing** attentat m suicide; see also **commit**; **suicide bomber** n kamikaze m/f

suit [su:t] n (man's) costume m, complet m; (woman's) tailleur m, ensemble m; (Cards) couleur f; (lawsuit) procès m ▷ vt (subj: clothes, hairstyle) aller à; (be convenient for) convenir à; (adapt): **to ~ sth to** adapter ou approprier qch à; **well ~ed** (couple) faits l'un pour l'autre, très bien assortis; **suitable** adj qui convient; approprié(e), adéquat(e); **suitcase** n valise f

suite [swiːt] n (of rooms, also Mus) suite f; (furniture): **bedroom/dining room ~** (ensemble m de) chambre f à coucher/salle f à manger; **a three-piece ~** un salon (canapé et deux fauteuils)

sulfur ['sʌlfə'] (US) n = **sulphur**

sulk [sʌlk] vi bouder

sulphur, (US) **sulfur** ['sʌlfə'] n soufre m

sultana [sʌl'tɑːnə] n (fruit) raisin (sec) de Smyrne

sum [sʌm] n somme f; (Scol calc) calcul m; **sum up** vt résumer ▷ vi résumer

summarize ['sʌməraɪz] vt résumer

summary ['sʌmərɪ] n résumé m

summer ['sʌmə'] n été m ▷ cpd d'été, estival(e); **in (the) ~** en été, pendant l'été; **summer holidays** npl grandes vacances; **summertime** n (season) été m

summit ['sʌmɪt] n sommet m; (also: **~ conference**) (conférence f au) sommet m

summon ['sʌmən] vt appeler, convoquer; **to ~ a witness** citer ou assigner un témoin

sun [sʌn] n soleil m

Sun. abbr (= Sunday) dim

sun: **sunbathe** vi prendre un bain de soleil; **sunbed** n lit pliant; (with sun lamp) lit à ultra-violets; **sunblock** n écran m total; **sunburn** n coup m de

soleil; **sunburned, sunburnt** adj
bronzé(e), hâlé(e); (painfully) brûlé(e)
par le soleil

Sunday ['sʌndɪ] n dimanche m

sunflower ['sʌnflauə^r] n
tournesol m

sung [sʌŋ] pp of **sing**

sunglasses ['sʌnglɑːsɪz] npl lunettes
fpl de soleil

sunk [sʌŋk] pp of **sink**

sun: sunlight n (lumière f du) soleil
m; **sun lounger** n chaise longue;
sunny adj ensoleillé(e); **it is sunny** il
fait (du) soleil, il y a du soleil; **sunrise**
n lever m du soleil; **sun roof** n (Aut)
toit ouvrant; **sunscreen** n crème f
solaire; **sunset** n coucher m du soleil;
sunshade n (over table) parasol m;
sunshine n (lumière f du) soleil m;
sunstroke n insolation f, coup m de
soleil; **suntan** n bronzage m; **suntan
lotion** n lotion f or lait m solaire;
suntan oil n huile f solaire

super ['suːpə^r] adj (inf) formidable

superb [suː'pəːb] adj superbe,
magnifique

superficial [suːpə'fɪʃəl] adj
superficiel(le)

superintendent
[suːpərɪn'tendənt] n directeur(-
trice); (Police) ≈ commissaire m

superior [su'pɪərɪə^r] adj supérieur(e);
(smug) condescendant(e),
méprisant(e) ▷ n supérieur(e)

superlative [su'pəːlətɪv] n (Ling)
superlatif m

supermarket ['suːpəmɑːkɪt] n
supermarché m

supernatural [suːpə'nætʃərəl] adj
surnaturel(le) ▷ n: **the** ~ le surnaturel

superpower ['suːpəpauə^r] n (Pol)
superpuissance f

superstition [suːpə'stɪʃən] n
superstition f

superstitious [suːpə'stɪʃəs] adj
superstitieux(-euse)

superstore ['suːpəstɔː^r] n (BRIT)
hypermarché m, grande surface

supervise ['suːpəvaɪz] vt (children
etc) surveiller; (organization, work)
diriger; **supervision** [suːpə'vɪʒən] n
surveillance f; (monitoring) contrôle m;
(management) direction f; **supervisor**
n surveillant(e); (in shop) chef m
de rayon

supper ['sʌpə^r] n dîner m; (late)
souper m

supple ['sʌpl] adj souple

supplement n ['sʌplɪmənt]
supplément m ▷ vt ['sʌplɪ'mɛnt]
ajouter à, compléter

supplier [sə'plaɪə^r] n fournisseur m

supply [sə'plaɪ] vt (provide) fournir;
(equip): **to ~ (with)** approvisionner
ou ravitailler (en); fournir (en) ▷ n
provision f, réserve f; (supplying)
approvisionnement m; **supplies** npl
(food) vivres mpl; (Mil) subsistances fpl

support [sə'pɔːt] n (moral, financial
etc) soutien m, appui m; (Tech)
support m, soutien ▷ vt soutenir,
supporter; (financially) subvenir aux
besoins de; (uphold) être pour, être
partisan de, appuyer; (Sport: team)
être pour; **supporter** n (Pol etc)
partisan(e); (Sport) supporter m

suppose [sə'pəuz] vt, vi supposer;
imaginer; **to be ~d to do/be** être
censé(e) faire/être; **supposedly**
[sə'pəuzɪdlɪ] adv soi-disant;
supposing conj si, à supposer que
+ sub

suppress [sə'prɛs] vt (revolt,
feeling) réprimer; (information) faire
disparaître; (scandal, yawn) étouffer

supreme [su'priːm] adj suprême

surcharge ['səːtʃɑːdʒ] n surcharge f

sure [fuə^r] adj (gen) sûr(e); (definite,
convinced) sûr, certain(e); ~! (of course)
bien sûr!; ~ **enough** effectivement;
to make ~ of sth/that s'assurer de
qch/que, vérifier qch/que; **surely** adv
sûrement; certainement

surf [səːf] n (waves) ressac m ▷ vt: **to
~ the Net** surfer sur Internet, surfer
sur le Net

surface ['sə:fɪs] *n* surface *f* ▷ *vt* (*road*) poser un revêtement sur ▷ *vi* remonter à la surface; (*fig*) faire surface; **by ~ mail** par voie de terre; (*by sea*) par voie maritime

surfboard ['sə:fbɔ:d] *n* planche *f* de surf

surfer ['sə:fə^r] *n* (*in sea*) surfeur(-euse); **web** *or* **Net ~** internaute *m/f*

surfing ['sə:fɪŋ] *n* (*in sea*) surf *m*

surge [sə:dʒ] *n* (*of emotion*) vague *f* ▷ *vi* déferler

surgeon ['sə:dʒən] *n* chirurgien *m*

surgery ['sə:dʒərɪ] *n* chirurgie *f*; (BRIT: *room*) cabinet *m* (de consultation); (*also*: **~ hours**) heures *fpl* de consultation

surname ['sə:neɪm] *n* nom *m* de famille

surpass [sə:'pɑ:s] *vt* surpasser, dépasser

surplus ['sə:pləs] *n* surplus *m*, excédent *m* ▷ *adj* en surplus, de trop; (*Comm*) excédentaire

surprise [sə'praɪz] *n* (*gen*) surprise *f*; (*astonishment*) étonnement *m* ▷ *vt* surprendre, étonner; **surprised** *adj* (*look, smile*) surpris(e), étonné(e); **to be surprised** être surpris; **surprising** *adj* surprenant(e), étonnant(e); **surprisingly** *adv* (*easy, helpful*) étonnamment, étrangement; (**somewhat**) **surprisingly, he agreed** curieusement, il a accepté

surrender [sə'rendə^r] *n* reddition *f*, capitulation *f* ▷ *vi* se rendre, capituler

surround [sə'raund] *vt* entourer; (*Mil etc*) encercler; **surrounding** *adj* environnant(e); **surroundings** *npl* environs *mpl*, alentours *mpl*

surveillance [sə:'veɪləns] *n* surveillance *f*

survey *n* ['sə:veɪ] enquête *f*, étude *f*; (*in house buying etc*) inspection *f*, (*rapport m d'*)expertise *f*; (*of land*) levé *m* ▷ *vt* [sə:'veɪ] (*situation*) passer en revue; (*examine carefully*) inspecter;

(*building*) expertiser; (*land*) faire le levé de; (*look at*) embrasser du regard; **surveyor** *n* (*of building*) expert *m*; (*of land*) (arpenteur *m*) géomètre *m*

survival [sə'vaɪvl] *n* survie *f*

survive [sə'vaɪv] *vi* survivre; (*custom etc*) subsister ▷ *vt* (*accident etc*) survivre à, réchapper de; (*person*) survivre à; **survivor** *n* survivant(e)

suspect *adj, n* ['sʌspekt] suspect(e) ▷ *vt* [səs'pekt] soupçonner, suspecter

suspend [səs'pend] *vt* suspendre; **suspended sentence** *n* (*Law*) condamnation *f* avec sursis; **suspenders** *npl* (BRIT) jarretelles *fpl*; (US) bretelles *fpl*

suspense [səs'pens] *n* attente *f*, incertitude *f*; (*in film etc*) suspense *m*; **to keep sb in ~** tenir qn en suspens, laisser qn dans l'incertitude

suspension [səs'penʃən] *n* (*gen, Aut*) suspension *f*; (*of driving licence*) retrait *m* provisoire; **suspension bridge** *n* pont suspendu

suspicion [səs'pɪʃən] *n* soupçon(s) *m(pl)*; **suspicious** *adj* (*suspecting*) soupçonneux(-euse), méfiant(e); (*causing suspicion*) suspect(e)

sustain [səs'teɪn] *vt* soutenir; (*subj: food*) nourrir, donner des forces à; (*damage*) subir; (*injury*) recevoir

SUV *n abbr* (*esp us*: = *sports utility vehicle*) SUV *m*, véhicule *m* de loisirs

swallow ['swɔləu] *n* (*bird*) hirondelle *f* ▷ *vt* avaler; (*fig: story*) gober

swam [swæm] *pt of* **swim**

swamp [swɔmp] *n* marais *m*, marécage *m* ▷ *vt* submerger

swan [swɔn] *n* cygne *m*

swap [swɔp] *n* échange *m*, troc *m* ▷ *vt*: **to ~ (for)** échanger (contre), troquer (contre)

swarm [swɔ:m] *n* essaim *m* ▷ *vi* (*bees*) essaimer; (*people*) grouiller; **to be ~ing with** grouiller de

sway [sweɪ] *vi* se balancer, osciller ▷ *vt* (*influence*) influencer

S

swear [swɛəʳ] (*pt* **swore**, *pp* **sworn**) *vt, vi* jurer; **swear in** *vt* assermenter; **swearword** *n* gros mot, juron *m*

sweat [swɛt] *n* sueur *f*, transpiration *f* ▷ *vi* suer

sweater ['swɛtəʳ] *n* tricot *m*, pull *m*

sweatshirt ['swɛtʃəːt] *n* sweat-shirt *m*

sweaty ['swɛtɪ] *adj* en sueur, moite or mouillé(e) de sueur

Swede [swiːd] *n* Suédois(e)

swede [swiːd] *n* (BRIT) rutabaga *m*

Sweden ['swiːdn] *n* Suède *f*; **Swedish** ['swiːdɪʃ] *adj* suédois(e) ▷ *n* (Ling) suédois *m*

sweep [swiːp] (*pt, pp* **swept**) *n* (*curve*) grande courbe *f*; (*also*: **chimney ~**) ramoneur *m* ▷ *vt* balayer; (*subj: current*) emporter

sweet [swiːt] *n* (BRIT: *pudding*) dessert *m*; (*candy*) bonbon *m* ▷ *adj* doux (douce); (*not savoury*) sucré(e); (*kind*) gentil(le); (*baby*) mignon(ne); **sweetcorn** *n* maïs doux; **sweetener** ['swiːtnəʳ] *n* (Culin) édulcorant *m*; **sweetheart** *n* amoureux(-euse); **sweetshop** *n* (BRIT) confiserie *f*

swell [swɛl] (*pt* **swelled**, *pp* **swollen** or **swelled**) *n* (*of sea*) houle *f* ▷ *adj* (US *inf*: *excellent*) chouette ▷ *vi* (*increase*) grossir, augmenter ▷ *vi* (*increase*) grossir, augmenter; (*sound*) s'enfler; (*Med: also*: **~ up**) enfler; **swelling** *n* (Med) enflure *f*; (*lump*) tumeur *f*

swept [swɛpt] *pt, pp of* **sweep**

swerve [swəːv] *vi* (*to avoid obstacle*) faire une embardée or un écart; (*off the road*) dévier

swift [swɪft] *n* (*bird*) martinet *m* ▷ *adj* rapide, prompt(e)

swim [swɪm] (*pt* **swam**, *pp* **swum**) *n*: **to go for a ~** aller nager or se baigner ▷ *vi* nager; (Sport) faire de la natation; (*fig: head, room*) tourner ▷ *vt* traverser (à la nage); **to ~ a length** nager une longueur; **swimmer** *n* nageur(-euse); **swimming** *n* nage *f*, natation *f*; **swimming costume** *n*

(BRIT) maillot *m* (de bain); **swimming pool** *n* piscine *f*; **swimming trunks** *npl* maillot *m* de bain; **swimsuit** *n* maillot *m* (de bain)

swine flu [swaɪn-] *n* grippe *f* A

swing [swɪŋ] (*pt, pp* **swung**) *n* (*in playground*) balançoire *f*; (*movement*) balancement *m*, oscillations *fpl*; (*change in opinion etc*) revirement *m* ▷ *vt* balancer, faire osciller; (*also*: **~ round**) tourner, faire virer ▷ *vi* se balancer, osciller; (*also*: **~ round**) virer, tourner; **to be in full ~** battre son plein

swipe card ['swaɪp-] *n* carte *f* magnétique

swirl [swəːl] *vi* tourbillonner, tournoyer

Swiss [swɪs] *adj* suisse ▷ *n* (*pl inv*) Suisse(-esse)

switch [swɪtʃ] *n* (*for light, radio etc*) bouton *m*; (*change*) changement *m*, revirement *m* ▷ *vt* (*change*) changer; **switch off** *vt* éteindre; (*engine, machine*) arrêter; **could you ~ off the light?** pouvez-vous éteindre la lumière?; **switch on** *vt* allumer; (*engine, machine*) mettre en marche; **switchboard** *n* (Tel) standard *m*

Switzerland ['swɪtsələnd] *n* Suisse *f*

swivel ['swɪvl] *vi* (*also*: **~ round**) pivoter, tourner

swollen ['swəulən] *pp of* **swell**

swoop [swuːp] *n* (*by police etc*) rafle *f*, descente *f* ▷ *vi* (*bird: also*: **~ down**) descendre en piqué, piquer

swop [swɔp] *n, vt* = **swap**

sword [sɔːd] *n* épée *f*; **swordfish** *n* espadon *m*

swore [swɔːʳ] *pt of* **swear**

sworn [swɔːn] *pp of* **swear** ▷ *adj* (*statement, evidence*) donné(e) sous serment; (*enemy*) juré(e)n

swum [swʌm] *pp of* **swim**

swung [swʌŋ] *pt, pp of* **swing**

syllable ['sɪləbl] *n* syllabe *f*

syllabus ['sɪləbəs] *n* programme *m*

symbol ['sɪmbl] n symbole m;
symbolic(al) [sɪm'bɔlɪk(l)] adj
symbolique

symmetrical [sɪ'metrɪkl] adj
symétrique

symmetry ['sɪmɪtrɪ] n symétrie f

sympathetic [sɪmpə'θɛtɪk] adj
(showing pity) compatissant(e);
(understanding) bienveillant(e),
compréhensif(-ive); **~ towards** bien
disposé(e) envers

> Be careful not to translate
> sympathetic by the French word
> sympathique.

sympathize ['sɪmpəθaɪz] vi: **to
~ with sb** plaindre qn; (in grief)
s'associer à la douleur de qn; **to ~
with sth** comprendre qch

sympathy ['sɪmpəθɪ] n (pity)
compassion f

symphony ['sɪmfənɪ] n symphonie f

symptom ['sɪmptəm] n symptôme
m; indice m

synagogue ['sɪnəgɔg] n synagogue f

syndicate ['sɪndɪkɪt] n syndicat
m, coopérative f; (Press) agence f
de presse

syndrome ['sɪndrəum] n
syndrome m

synonym ['sɪnənɪm] n synonyme m

synthetic [sɪn'θɛtɪk] adj synthétique

Syria ['sɪrɪə] n Syrie f

syringe [sɪ'rɪndʒ] n seringue f

syrup ['sɪrəp] n sirop m; (BRIT: also:
golden ~) mélasse raffinée

system ['sɪstəm] n système m;
(Anat) organisme m; **systematic**
[sɪstə'mætɪk] adj systématique;
méthodique; **systems analyst** n
analyste-programmeur m/f

ta [tɑː] excl (BRIT inf) merci!

tab [tæb] n (label) étiquette f; (on
drinks can etc) languette f; **to keep ~s
on** (fig) surveiller

table ['teɪbl] n table f ▷ vt (BRIT:
motion etc) présenter; **to lay** or
set the ~ mettre le couvert or la
table; **tablecloth** n nappe f; **table
d'hôte** [tɑːbl'dəut] adj (meal)
à prix fixe; **table lamp** n lampe
décorative or de table; **tablemat** n
(for plate) napperon m, set m; (for
hot dish) dessous-de-plat m inv;
tablespoon n cuiller f de service;
(also: **tablespoonful**: as measurement)
cuillerée f à soupe

tablet ['tæblɪt] n (Med) comprimé m;
(Comput) tablette f (tactile); (of stone)
plaque f

table tennis n ping-pong m

tabloid ['tæblɔɪd] n (newspaper)
quotidien m populaire

taboo [tə'buː] adj, n tabou (m)

tack [tæk] n (nail) petit clou m; (fig) direction f ▷ vt (nail) clouer; (sew) bâtir ▷ vi (Naut) tirer un ou des bord(s); **to ~ sth on to (the end of) sth** (of letter, book) rajouter qch à la fin de qch

tackle ['tækl] n matériel m, équipement m; (for lifting) appareil m de levage; (Football, Rugby) plaquage m ▷ vt (difficulty, animal, burglar) s'attaquer à; (person: challenge) s'expliquer avec; (Football, Rugby) plaquer

tacky ['tækɪ] adj collant(e); (paint) pas sec (sèche); (pej: poor-quality) minable; (: showing bad taste) ringard(e)

tact [tækt] n tact m; **tactful** adj plein(e) de tact

tactics ['tæktɪks] npl tactique f

tactless ['tæktlɪs] adj qui manque de tact

tadpole ['tædpəʊl] n têtard m

taffy ['tæfɪ] n (us) (bonbon m au) caramel m

tag [tæg] n étiquette f

tail [teɪl] n queue f; (of shirt) pan m ▷ vt (follow) suivre, filer; **tails** npl (suit) habit m; see also **head**

tailor ['teɪlə'] n tailleur m (artisan)

Taiwan ['taɪ'wɑ:n] n Taïwan (no article); **Taiwanese** [taɪwə'niːz] adj taïwanais(e) ▷ n inv Taïwanais(e)

take [teɪk] (pt **took**, pp **taken**) vt prendre; (gain: prize) remporter; (require: effort, courage) demander; (tolerate) accepter, supporter; (hold: passengers etc) contenir; (accompany) emmener, accompagner; (bring, carry) apporter, emporter; (exam) passer, se présenter à; **to ~ sth from** (drawer etc) prendre qch dans; (person) prendre qch à; **I ~ it that** je suppose que; **to be ~n ill** tomber malade; **it won't ~ long** ça ne prendra pas longtemps; **I was quite ~n with her/it** elle/cela m'a beaucoup plu; **take after** vt fus ressembler à; **take apart** vt démonter; **take away** vt

(carry off) emporter; (remove) enlever; (subtract) soustraire; **take back** vt (return) rendre, rapporter; (one's words) retirer; **take down** vt (building) démolir; (letter etc) prendre, écrire; **take in** vt (deceive) tromper, rouler; (understand) comprendre, saisir; (include) couvrir, inclure; (lodger) prendre; (dress, waistband) reprendre; **take off** vi (Aviat) décoller ▷ vt (remove) enlever; **take on** vt (work) accepter, se charger de; (employee) prendre, embaucher; (opponent) accepter de se battre contre; **take out** vt (remove) enlever; (invite) sortir avec; **to ~ sth out of** (out of drawer etc) prendre qch dans; **to ~ sb out to a restaurant** emmener qn au restaurant; **take over** vt (business) reprendre ▷ vi: **to ~ over from sb** prendre la relève de qn; **take up** vt (one's story) reprendre; (dress) raccourcir; (occupy: time, space) prendre, occuper; (engage in: hobby etc) se mettre à; (accept: offer, challenge) accepter; **takeaway** (BRIT) adj (food) à emporter ▷ n (shop, restaurant) ≈ magasin m qui vend des plats à emporter; **taken** pp of **take**; **takeoff** n (Aviat) décollage m; **takeout** adj, n (us) = **takeaway**; **takeover** n (Comm) rachat m; **takings** npl (Comm) recette f

talc [tælk] n (also: **~um powder**) talc m

tale [teɪl] n (story) conte m, histoire f; (account) récit m; **to tell ~s** (fig) rapporter

talent ['tælnt] n talent m, don m; **talented** adj doué(e), plein(e) de talent

talk [tɔːk] n (a speech) causerie f, exposé m; (conversation) discussion f; (interview) entretien m; (gossip) racontars mpl (pej) ▷ vi parler; (chatter) bavarder; **talks** npl (Pol etc) entretiens mpl; **to ~ about** parler de; **to ~ sb out of/into doing** persuader qn de ne pas faire/de faire; **to ~ shop** parler métier or affaires; **talk over** vt discuter (de); **talk show** n (TV, Radio) émission-débat f

tall [tɔ:l] adj (person) grand(e); (building, tree) haut(e); **to be 6 feet ~** = mesurer 1 mètre 80

tambourine [tæmbə'ri:n] n tambourin m

tame [teɪm] adj apprivoisé(e); (fig: story, style) insipide

tamper ['tæmpə*] vi: **to ~ with** toucher à (en cachette ou sans permission)

tampon ['tæmpən] n tampon m hygiénique or périodique

tan [tæn] n (also: **sun~**) bronzage m ▷ vt, vi bronzer, brunir ▷ adj (colour) marron clair inv

tandem ['tændəm] n tandem m

tangerine [tændʒə'ri:n] n mandarine f

tangle ['tæŋgl] n enchevêtrement m; **to get in(to) a ~** s'emmêler

tank [tæŋk] n réservoir m; (for fish) aquarium m; (Mil) char m d'assaut, tank m

tanker ['tæŋkə*] n (ship) pétrolier m, tanker m; (truck) camion-citerne m

tanned [tænd] adj bronzé(e)

tantrum ['tæntrəm] n accès m de colère

Tanzania [tænzə'nɪə] n Tanzanie f

tap [tæp] n (on sink etc) robinet m; (gentle blow) petite tape f ▷ vt (hit gently) taper légèrement; (resources) exploiter, utiliser; (telephone) mettre sur écoute; **on ~** (fig: resources) disponible; **tap dancing** n claquettes fpl

tape [teɪp] n (for tying) ruban m; (also: **magnetic ~**) bande f (magnétique); (cassette) cassette f; (sticky) Scotch® m ▷ vt (record) enregistrer (au magnétoscope ou sur cassette); (stick) coller avec du Scotch®; **tape measure** n mètre m à ruban; **tape recorder** n magnétophone m

tapestry ['tæpɪstrɪ] n tapisserie f

tar [tɑ:] n goudron m

target ['tɑ:gɪt] n cible f; (fig: objective) objectif m

tariff ['tærɪf] n (Comm) tarif m; (taxes) tarif douanier

tarmac ['tɑ:mæk] n (BRIT: on road) macadam m; (Aviat) aire f d'envol

tarpaulin [tɑ:'pɔ:lɪn] n bâche goudronnée

tarragon ['tærəgən] n estragon m

tart [tɑ:t] n (Culin) tarte f; (BRIT inf: pej: prostitute) poule f ▷ adj (flavour) âpre, aigrelet(te)

tartan ['tɑ:tn] n tartan m ▷ adj écossais(e)

tartar(e) sauce ['tɑ:tə-] n sauce f tartare

task [tɑ:sk] n tâche f; **to take to ~** prendre à partie

taste [teɪst] n goût m; (fig: glimpse, idea) idée f, aperçu m ▷ vt goûter ▷ vi: **to ~ of** (fish etc) avoir le or un goût de; **you can ~ the garlic (in it)** on sent bien l'ail; **to have a ~ of sth** goûter (à) qch; **can I have a ~?** je peux goûter?; **to be in good/bad** or **poor ~** être de bon/mauvais goût; **tasteful** adj de bon goût; **tasteless** adj (food) insipide; (remark) de mauvais goût; **tasty** adj savoureux(-euse), délicieux(-euse)

tatters ['tætəz] npl: **in ~** (also: **tattered**) en lambeaux

tattoo [tə'tu:] n tatouage m; (spectacle) parade f militaire ▷ vt tatouer

taught [tɔ:t] pt, pp of **teach**

taunt [tɔ:nt] n raillerie f ▷ vt railler

Taurus ['tɔ:rəs] n le Taureau

taut [tɔ:t] adj tendu(e)

tax [tæks] n (on goods etc) taxe f; (on income) impôts mpl, contributions fpl ▷ vt taxer; imposer; (fig: patience etc) mettre à l'épreuve; **tax disc** n (BRIT Aut) vignette f (automobile); **tax-free** adj exempt(e) d'impôts

taxi ['tæksɪ] n taxi m ▷ vi (Aviat) rouler (lentement) au sol; **taxi driver** n

tax payer | 578

chauffeur m de taxi; **taxi rank**, (US) **taxi stand** n station f de taxis

tax payer [-peɪəʳ] n contribuable m/f

tax return n déclaration f d'impôts or de revenus

TB n abbr = **tuberculosis**

tbc abbr = **to be confirmed**

tea [tiː] n thé m; (BRIT: snack: for children) goûter m; **high ~** (BRIT) collation combinant goûter et dîner; **tea bag** n sachet m de thé; **tea break** n (BRIT) pause-thé f

teach (pt, pp **taught**) [tiːtʃ, tɔːt] vt: **to ~ sb sth, to ~ sth to sb** apprendre qch à qn; (in school etc) enseigner qch à qn ▷ vi enseigner; **teacher** n (in secondary school) professeur m; (in primary school) instituteur(-trice); **teaching** n enseignement m; **teaching assistant** n aide-éducateur(-trice)

tea: teacup n tasse f à thé; **tea leaves** npl feuilles fpl de thé

team [tiːm] n équipe f; (of animals) attelage m; **team up** vi: **to ~ up (with)** faire équipe (avec)

teapot [tiːpɔt] n théière f

tear¹ [tɪəʳ] n larme f; **in ~s** en larmes

tear² [tɛəʳ] (pt **tore**, pp **torn**) n déchirure f ▷ vt déchirer ▷ vi se déchirer; **tear apart** vt (also fig) déchirer; **tear down** vt (building, statue) démolir; (poster, flag) arracher; **tear off** vt (sheet of paper etc) arracher; (one's clothes) enlever à toute vitesse; **tear up** vt (sheet of paper etc) déchirer, mettre en morceaux or pièces

tearful [tɪəful] adj larmoyant(e)

tear gas [tɪə-] n gaz m lacrymogène

tearoom [tiːruːm] n salon m de thé

tease [tiːz] vt taquiner; (unkindly) tourmenter

tea: teaspoon n petite cuiller; (also: **teaspoonful**: as measurement) ≈ cuillerée f à café; **teatime** n l'heure f du thé; **tea towel** n (BRIT) torchon m (à vaisselle)

technical [tɛknɪkl] adj technique

technician [tɛkˈnɪʃən] n technicien(ne)

technique [tɛkˈniːk] n technique f

technology [tɛkˈnɔlədʒɪ] n technologie f

teddy (bear) [tɛdɪ-] n ours m (en peluche)

tedious [tiːdɪəs] adj fastidieux(-euse)

tee [tiː] n (Golf) tee m

teen [tiːn] adj = **teenage** ▷ n (US) = **teenager**

teenage [tiːneɪdʒ] adj (fashions etc) pour jeunes, pour adolescents; (child) qui est adolescent(e); **teenager** n adolescent(e)

teens [tiːnz] npl: **to be in one's ~** être adolescent(e)

teeth [tiːθ] npl of **tooth**

teetotal [tiːˈtəutl] adj (person) qui ne boit jamais d'alcool

telecommunications [tɛlɪkəmjuːnɪˈkeɪʃənz] n télécommunications fpl

telegram [tɛlɪgræm] n télégramme m

telegraph pole [tɛlɪgrɑːf-] n poteau m télégraphique

telephone [tɛlɪfəun] n téléphone m ▷ vt (person) téléphoner à; (message) téléphoner; **to be on the ~** (be speaking) être au téléphone; **telephone book** n = **telephone directory**; **telephone box**, (US) **telephone booth** n cabine f téléphonique; **telephone call** n appel m téléphonique; **telephone directory** n annuaire m (du téléphone); **telephone number** n numéro m de téléphone

telesales [tɛlɪseɪlz] npl télévente f

telescope [tɛlɪskəup] n télescope m

televise [tɛlɪvaɪz] vt téléviser

television [tɛlɪvɪʒən] n télévision f; **on ~** à la télévision; **television programme** n (BRIT) émission f de télévision

tell (pt, pp **told**) [tɛl, təʊld] vt dire; (relate: story) raconter; (distinguish): **to ~ sth from** distinguer qch de ▷ vi (talk): **to ~ of** parler de; (have effect) se faire sentir, se voir; **to ~ sb to do** dire à qn de faire; **to ~ the time** (know how to) savoir lire l'heure; **tell off** vt réprimander, gronder; **teller** n (in bank) caissier(-ière)

telly ['tɛlɪ] n abbr (BRIT inf: = television) télé f

temp [tɛmp] n (BRIT: = temporary worker) intérimaire m/f ▷ vi travailler comme intérimaire

temper ['tɛmpə^r] n (nature) caractère m; (mood) humeur f; (fit of anger) colère f ▷ vt (moderate) tempérer, adoucir; **to be in a ~** être en colère; **to lose one's ~** se mettre en colère

temperament ['tɛmprəmənt] n (nature) tempérament n; **temperamental** [tɛmprə'mɛntl] adj capricieux(-euse)

temperature ['tɛmprətʃə^r] n température f; **to have** or **run a ~** avoir de la fièvre

temple ['tɛmpl] n (building) temple m; (Anat) tempe f

temporary ['tɛmpərərɪ] adj temporaire, provisoire; (job, worker) temporaire

tempt [tɛmpt] vt tenter; **to ~ sb into doing** induire qn à faire; **temptation** n tentation f; **tempting** adj tentant(e); (food) appétissant(e)

ten [tɛn] num dix

tenant ['tɛnənt] n locataire m/f

tend [tɛnd] vt s'occuper de ▷ vi: **to ~ to do** avoir tendance à faire; **tendency** ['tɛndənsɪ] n tendance f

tender ['tɛndə^r] adj tendre; (delicate) délicat(e); (sore) sensible ▷ n (Comm: offer) soumission f; (money): **legal ~** cours légal ▷ vt offrir

tendon ['tɛndən] n tendon m

tenner ['tɛnə^r] n (BRIT inf) billet m de dix livres

tennis ['tɛnɪs] n tennis m; **tennis ball** n balle f de tennis; **tennis court** n (court m de) tennis m; **tennis match** n match m de tennis; **tennis player** n joueur(-euse) de tennis; **tennis racket** n raquette f de tennis

tenor ['tɛnə^r] n (Mus) ténor m

tenpin bowling ['tɛnpɪn-] n (BRIT) bowling m (à 10 quilles)

tense [tɛns] adj tendu(e) ▷ n (Ling) temps m

tension ['tɛnʃən] n tension f

tent [tɛnt] n tente f

tentative ['tɛntətɪv] adj timide, hésitant(e); (conclusion) provisoire

tenth [tɛnθ] num dixième

tent: tent peg n piquet m de tente; **tent pole** n montant m de tente

tepid ['tɛpɪd] adj tiède

term [tə:m] n terme m; (Scol) trimestre m ▷ vt appeler; **terms** npl (conditions) conditions fpl; (Comm) tarif m; **in the short/long ~** à court/ long terme; **to come to ~s with** (problem) faire face à; **to be on good ~s with** bien s'entendre avec, être en bons termes avec

terminal ['tə:mɪnl] adj (disease) dans sa phase terminale; (patient) incurable ▷ n (Elec) borne f; (for oil, ore etc: also Comput) terminal m; (also: **air ~**) aérogare f; (BRIT: also: **coach ~**) gare routière

terminate ['tə:mɪneɪt] vt mettre fin à; (pregnancy) interrompre

termini ['tə:mɪnaɪ] npl of **terminus**

terminology [tə:mɪ'nɔlədʒɪ] n terminologie f

terminus (pl **termini**) ['tə:mɪnəs, 'tə:mɪnaɪ] n terminus m inv

terrace ['tɛrəs] n terrasse f; (BRIT: row of houses) rangée f de maisons (attenantes les unes aux autres); **the ~s** (BRIT Sport) les gradins mpl; **terraced** adj (garden) en terrasses; (in a row: house) attenant(e) aux maisons voisines

terrain [tɛ'reɪn] n terrain m (sol)

terrestrial [tɪˈrestrɪəl] adj terrestre
terrible [ˈterɪbl] adj terrible, atroce; (weather, work) affreux(-euse), épouvantable; **terribly** adv terriblement; (very badly) affreusement mal
terrier [ˈterɪə] n terrier m (chien)
terrific [təˈrɪfɪk] adj (very great) fantastique, incroyable, terrible; (wonderful) formidable, sensationnel(le)
terrified [ˈterɪfaɪd] adj terrifié(e); **to be ~ of sth** avoir très peur de qch
terrify [ˈterɪfaɪ] vt terrifier; **terrifying** adj terrifiant(e)
territorial [terɪˈtɔːrɪəl] adj territorial(e)
territory [ˈterɪtərɪ] n territoire m
terror [ˈterə] n terreur f; **terrorism** n terrorisme m; **terrorist** n terroriste m/f; **terrorist attack** n attentat m terroriste
test [test] n (trial, check) essai m; (of courage etc) épreuve f; (Med) examen m; (Chem) analyse f; (Scol) interrogation f de contrôle; (also: **driving ~**) (examen du) permis de conduire ▷ vt essayer; mettre à l'épreuve; examiner; analyser; faire subir une interrogation à
testicle [ˈtestɪkl] n testicule m
testify [ˈtestɪfaɪ] vi (Law) témoigner, déposer; **to ~ to sth** (Law) attester qch
testimony [ˈtestɪmənɪ] n (Law) témoignage m, déposition f
test: test match n (Cricket, Rugby) match international; **test tube** n éprouvette f
tetanus [ˈtetənəs] n tétanos m
text [tekst] n texte m; (on mobile phone) SMS m inv, texto® m ▷ vt (inf) envoyer un SMS or texto® à; **textbook** n manuel m
textile [ˈtekstaɪl] n textile m
text message n SMS m inv, texto® m
text messaging [-ˈmesɪdʒɪŋ] n messagerie textuelle

texture [ˈtekstʃə] n texture f; (of skin, paper etc) grain m
Thai [taɪ] adj thaïlandais(e) ▷ n Thaïlandais(e)
Thailand [ˈtaɪlænd] n Thaïlande f
Thames [temz] n: **the (River) ~** la Tamise
than [ðæn, ðən] conj que; (with numerals): **more ~ 10/once** plus de 10/d'une fois; **I have more/less ~ you** j'en ai plus/moins que toi; **she has more apples ~ pears** elle a plus de pommes que de poires; **it is better to phone ~ to write** il vaut mieux téléphoner (plutôt) qu'écrire; **she is older ~ you think** elle est plus âgée que tu le crois
thank [θæŋk] vt remercier, dire merci à; **thanks** npl remerciements mpl; **~s!** merci!; **~ you (very much)** merci (beaucoup); **~ God** Dieu merci; **~s to** prep grâce à; **thankfully** adv (fortunately) heureusement; **Thanksgiving (Day)** n jour m d'action de grâce

THANKSGIVING (DAY)

Thanksgiving (Day) est un jour de congé aux États-Unis, le quatrième jeudi du mois de novembre, commémorant la bonne récolte que les Pèlerins venus de Grande-Bretagne ont eue en 1621; traditionnellement, c'était un jour où l'on remerciait Dieu et où l'on organisait un grand festin. Une fête semblable, mais qui n'a aucun rapport avec les Pères Pèlerins, a lieu au Canada le deuxième lundi d'octobre.

KEYWORD

that [ðæt] adj (demonstrative) ce, cet + vowel or h mute, cette f; **that man/woman/book** cet homme/cette femme/ce livre; (not this) cet

homme-là/cette femme-là/ce livre-là; **that one** celui-là (celle-là)
▶ **pron 1** (demonstrative): (: not this one) cela, ça; (: that one) celui (celle); **who's that?** qui est-ce?; **what's that?** qu'est-ce que c'est?; **is that you?** c'est toi?; **I prefer this to that** je préfère ceci à cela or ça; **that's what he said** c'est or voilà ce qu'il a dit; **will you eat all that?** tu vas manger tout ça?; **that is (to say)** c'est-à-dire, à savoir
2 (relative: subject) qui; (: object) que; (: after prep) lequel (laquelle), lesquels (lesquelles) pl; **the book that I read** le livre que j'ai lu; **the books that are in the library** les livres qui sont dans la bibliothèque; **all that I have** tout ce que j'ai; **the box that I put it in** la boîte dans laquelle je l'ai mis; **the people that I spoke to** les gens auxquels or à qui j'ai parlé
3 (relative, of time) où; **the day that he came** le jour où il est venu
▶ **conj** que; **he thought that I was ill** il pensait que j'étais malade
▶ **adv** (demonstrative): **I don't like it that much** ça ne me plaît pas tant que ça; **I didn't know it was that bad** je ne savais pas que c'était si or aussi mauvais; **it's about that high** c'est à peu près de cette hauteur

thatched [θætʃt] *adj* (roof) de chaume; **~ cottage** chaumière f

thaw [θɔː] *n* dégel *m* ▶ *v* (ice) fondre; (food) dégeler ▶ *vt* (food) (faire) dégeler

⊙ **KEYWORD**

the [ðiː, ðə] *def art* **1** (gen) le, la f, l' + vowel or h mute, les pl (NB: à + le(s) = **au(x)**; de + le = **du**; de + les = **des**); **the boy/girl/ink** le garçon, la fille/l'encre; **the children** les enfants; **the history of the world** l'histoire du monde; **give it to the postman** donne-la au facteur; **to**

play the piano/flute jouer du piano/de la flûte
2 (+ adj to form n) le, la f, l' + vowel or h mute, les pl; **the rich and the poor** les riches et les pauvres; **to attempt the impossible** tenter l'impossible
3 (in titles): **Elizabeth the First** Elisabeth première; **Peter the Great** Pierre le Grand
4 (in comparisons): **the more he works, the more he earns** plus il travaille, plus il gagne de l'argent

theatre, (US) **theater** [ˈθɪətəʳ] *n* théâtre *m*; (Med: also: **operating ~**) salle f d'opération

theft [θɛft] *n* vol *m* (larcin)

their [ðɛəʳ] *adj* leur, leurs pl; *see also* **my**; **theirs** *pron* le (la) leur, les leurs; *see also* **mine¹**

them [ðɛm, ðəm] *pron* (direct) les; (indirect) leur; (stressed, after prep) eux (elles); **give me a few of ~** donnez m'en quelques uns (or quelques unes); *see also* **me**

theme [θiːm] *n* thème *m*; **theme park** *n* parc *m* à thème

themselves [ðəmˈsɛlvz] *pl pron* (reflexive) se; (emphatic, after prep) eux-mêmes (elles-mêmes); **between ~** entre eux (elles); *see also* **oneself**

then [ðɛn] *adv* (at that time) alors, à ce moment-là; (next) puis, ensuite; (and also) et puis ▶ *conj* (therefore) alors, dans ce cas ▶ *adj*: **the ~ president** le président d'alors or de l'époque; **by ~** (past) à ce moment-là; (future) d'ici là; **from ~ on** dès lors; **until ~** jusqu'à ce moment-là, jusque-là

theology [θɪˈɒlədʒɪ] *n* théologie f

theory [ˈθɪərɪ] *n* théorie f

therapist [ˈθɛrəpɪst] *n* thérapeute m/f

therapy [ˈθɛrəpɪ] *n* thérapie f

⊙ **KEYWORD**

there [ðɛəʳ] *adv* **1**: **there is, there are** il y a; **there are 3 of them**

(*people, things*) il y a en a 3; **there is no-one here/no bread left** il n'y a personne/il n'y a plus de pain; **there has been an accident** il y a eu un accident

2 (*referring to place*) là, là-bas; **it's there** c'est là(-bas); **in/on/up/down there** là-dedans/là-dessus/là-haut/en bas; **he went there on Friday** il y est allé vendredi; **I want that book there** je veux ce livre-là; **there he is!** le voilà!

3: **there, there!** (*esp to child*) allons, allons!

there: **thereabouts** *adv* (*place*) par là, près de là; (*amount*) environ, à peu près; **thereafter** *adv* par la suite; **thereby** *adv* ainsi; **therefore** *adv* donc, par conséquent

there's ['ðɛəz] = **there is**; **there has**

thermal ['θəːml] *adj* thermique; **~ underwear** sous-vêtements *mpl* en Thermolactyl®

thermometer [θə'mɒmɪtəʳ] *n* thermomètre *m*

thermostat ['θəːməustæt] *n* thermostat *m*

these [ðiːz] *pl pron* ceux-ci (celles-ci) ▷ *pl adj* ces; (*not those*): **~ books** ces livres-ci

thesis (*pl* **theses**) ['θiːsɪs, 'θiːsiːz] *n* thèse *f*

they [ðeɪ] *pl pron* ils (elles); (*stressed*) eux (elles); **~ say that ...** (*it is said that*) on dit que ...; **they'd** = **they had; they would; they'll** = **they shall; they will; they're** = **they are; they've** = **they have**

thick [θɪk] *adj* épais(se); (*stupid*) bête, borné(e) ▷ *n*: **in the ~ of** au beau milieu de, en plein cœur de; **it's 20 cm ~** ça a 20 cm d'épaisseur; **thicken** *vi* s'épaissir ▷ *vt* (*sauce etc*) épaissir; **thickness** *n* épaisseur *f*

thief (*pl* **thieves**) [θiːf, θiːvz] *n* voleur(-euse)

thigh [θaɪ] *n* cuisse *f*

thin [θɪn] *adj* mince; (*skinny*) maigre; (*soup*) peu épais(se); (*hair, crowd*) clairsemé(e) ▷ *vt* (*also*: **~ down**: *sauce, paint*) délayer

thing [θɪŋ] *n* chose *f*; (*object*) objet *m*; (*contraption*) truc *m*; **things** *npl* (*belongings*) affaires *fpl*; **the ~ is ...** c'est que ...; **the best ~ would be to** le mieux serait de; **how are ~s?** comment ça va?; **to have a ~ about** (*be obsessed by*) être obsédé(e) par; (*hate*) détester; **poor ~!** le (or la) pauvre!

think (*pt, pp* **thought**) [θɪŋk, θɔːt] *vi* penser, réfléchir ▷ *vt* penser, croire; (*imagine*) s'imaginer; **what did you ~ of them?** qu'avez-vous pensé d'eux?; **to ~ about sth/sb** penser à qch/qn; **I'll ~ about it** je vais y réfléchir; **to ~ of doing** avoir l'idée de faire; **I ~ so/not** je crois *or* pense que oui/non; **to ~ well of** avoir une haute opinion de; **think over** *vt* bien réfléchir à; **think up** *vt* inventer, trouver

third [θəːd] *num* troisième ▷ *n* (*fraction*) tiers *m*; (*Aut*) troisième (*vitesse*) *f*; (*BRIT Scol: degree*) ≈ licence *f* avec mention passable; **thirdly** *adv* troisièmement; **third party insurance** *n* (*BRIT*) assurance *f* au tiers; **Third World** *n*: **the Third World** le Tiers-Monde

thirst [θəːst] *n* soif *f*; **thirsty** *adj* qui a soif, assoiffé(e); (*work*) qui donne soif; **to be thirsty** avoir soif

thirteen [θəː'tiːn] *num* treize; **thirteenth** [θəː'tiːnθ] *num* treizième

thirtieth ['θəːtɪɪθ] *num* trentième

thirty ['θəːtɪ] *num* trente

KEYWORD

this [ðɪs] *adj* (*demonstrative*) ce, cet + *vowel or h mute*, cette *f*; **this man/woman/book** cet homme/cette femme/ce livre; (*not that*) cet homme-ci/cette femme-ci/ce livre-ci; **this one** celui-ci (celle-ci)

▶ pron (demonstrative) ce (: not that one) celui-ci (celle-ci), ceci; **who's this?** qui est-ce?; **what's this?** qu'est-ce que c'est?; **I prefer this to that** je préfère ceci à cela; **this is where I live** c'est ici que j'habite; **this is what he said** voici ce qu'il a dit; **this is Mr Brown** (in introductions) je vous présente Mr Brown; (in photo) c'est Mr Brown; (on telephone) c'est Mr Brown ▶ adv (demonstrative): **it was about this big** c'était à peu près de cette grandeur or grand comme ça; **I didn't know it was this bad** je ne savais pas que c'était si or aussi mauvais

thistle ['θɪsl] n chardon m

thorn [θɔːn] n épine f

thorough ['θʌrə] adj (search) minutieux(-euse); (knowledge, research) approfondi(e); (work, person) consciencieux(-euse); (cleaning) à fond; **thoroughly** adv (search) minutieusement; (study) en profondeur; (clean) à fond; (very) tout à fait

those [ðəuz] pl pron ceux-là (celles-là) ▶ pl adj ces; (not these): **~ books** ces livres-là

though [ðəu] conj bien que + sub, quoique + sub ▶ adv pourtant

thought [θɔːt] pt, pp of **think** ▶ n pensée f; (idea) idée f; (opinion) avis m; **thoughtful** adj (deep in thought) pensif(-ive); (serious) réfléchi(e); (considerate) prévenant(e); **thoughtless** adj qui manque de considération

thousand ['θauzənd] num mille; **one ~** mille; **two ~** deux mille; **~s of** des milliers de; **thousandth** num millième

thrash [θræʃ] vt rouer de coups; (inf: defeat) donner une raclée à (inf)

thread [θred] n fil m; (of screw) pas m, filetage m ▶ vt (needle) enfiler

threat [θret] n menace f; **threaten** vi (storm) menacer ▶ vt: **to threaten sb with sth/to do** menacer qn de qch/de faire; **threatening** adj menaçant(e)

three [θriː] num trois; **three-dimensional** adj à trois dimensions; **three-piece suite** n salon m (canapé et deux fauteuils); **three-quarters** npl trois-quarts mpl; **three-quarters full** aux trois-quarts plein

threshold ['θreʃhəuld] n seuil m

threw [θruː] pt of **throw**

thrill [θrɪl] n (excitement) émotion f, sensation forte; (shudder) frisson m ▶ vt (audience) électriser; **thrilled** adj: **thrilled (with)** ravi(e) de; **thriller** n film m (or roman m or pièce f) à suspense; **thrilling** adj (book, play etc) saisissant(e); (news, discovery) excitant(e)

thriving ['θraɪvɪŋ] adj (business, community) prospère

throat [θrəut] n gorge f; **to have a sore ~** avoir mal à la gorge

throb [θrɔb] vi (heart) palpiter; (engine) vibrer; **my head is ~bing** j'ai des élancements dans la tête

throne [θrəun] n trône m

through [θruː] prep à travers; (time) pendant, durant; (by means of) par, par l'intermédiaire de; (owing to) à cause de ▶ adj (ticket, train, passage) direct(e) ▶ adv à travers; **(from) Monday ~ Friday** (us) de lundi à vendredi; **to put sb ~ to sb** (Tel) passer qn à qn; **to be ~** (BRIT Tel) avoir la communication; (esp us: have finished) avoir fini; **"no ~ traffic"** (us) "passage interdit"; **"no ~ road"** (BRIT) "impasse"; **throughout** prep (place) partout dans; (time) durant tout(e) le ▶ adv partout

throw [θrəu] n jet m; (Sport) lancer m ▶ vt (pt **threw**, pp **thrown**) lancer, jeter; (Sport) lancer; (rider) désarçonner; (fig) déconcerter; **to ~ a party** donner une réception; **throw away** vt jeter; (money) gaspiller; **throw in** vt (Sport: ball) remettre en jeu; (include) ajouter; **throw off** vt se débarrasser de; **throw out** vt (reject) rejeter; (person) mettre à la porte; **throw up** vi vomir

thrown [θrəʊn] pp of **throw**

thru [θruː] (US) prep = **through**

thrush [θrʌʃ] n (Zool) grive f

thrust [θrʌst] vt (pt, pp **thrust**) pousser brusquement; (push in) enfoncer

thud [θʌd] n bruit sourd

thug [θʌɡ] n voyou m

thumb [θʌm] n (Anat) pouce m ▷ vt: **to ~ a lift** faire de l'auto-stop, arrêter une voiture; **thumbtack** n (US) punaise f (clou)

thump [θʌmp] n grand coup; (sound) bruit sourd ▷ vt cogner sur ▷ vi cogner, frapper

thunder [ˈθʌndəʳ] n tonnerre m ▷ vi tonner; (train etc): **to ~ past** passer dans un grondement or un bruit de tonnerre; **thunderstorm** n orage m

Thursday [ˈθɜːzdɪ] n jeudi m

thus [ðʌs] adv ainsi

thwart [θwɔːt] vt contrecarrer

thyme [taɪm] n thym m

Tibet [tɪˈbɛt] n Tibet m

tick [tɪk] n (sound: of clock) tic-tac m; (mark) coche f; (Zool) tique f ▷ vi faire tic-tac ▷ vt (item on list) cocher; **in a ~** (BRIT inf) dans un instant; **tick off** vt (item on list) cocher; (person) réprimander, attraper

ticket [ˈtɪkɪt] n billet m; (for bus, tube) ticket m; (in shop, on goods) étiquette f; (for library) carte f; (also: **parking ~**) contravention f, p.-v. m; **ticket barrier** n (BRIT Rail) portillon m automatique; **ticket collector** n contrôleur(-euse); **ticket inspector** n contrôleur(-euse); **ticket machine** n billetterie f automatique; **ticket office** n guichet m, bureau m de vente des billets

tickle [ˈtɪkl] vi chatouiller ▷ vt chatouiller; **ticklish** adj (person)

chatouilleux(-euse); (problem) épineux(-euse)

tide [taɪd] n marée f; (fig: of events) cours m

tidy [ˈtaɪdɪ] adj (room) bien rangé(e); (dress, work) net (nette), soigné(e); (person) ordonné(e), qui a de l'ordre ▷ vt (also: **~ up**) ranger

tie [taɪ] n (string etc) cordon m; (BRIT: also: **neck~**) cravate f; (fig: link) lien m; (Sport: draw) égalité f de points match nul à vt (parcel) attacher; (ribbon) nouer ▷ vi (Sport) faire match nul; finir à égalité de points; **to ~ sth in a bow** faire un nœud or avec qch; **to ~ a knot in sth** faire un nœud à qch; **tie down** vt: **to ~ sb down to** (fig) contraindre qn à accepter; **to feel ~d down** (by relationship) se sentir coincé(e); **tie up** vt (parcel) ficeler; (dog, boat) attacher; (prisoner) ligoter; (arrangements) conclure; **to be ~d up** (busy) être pris(e) or occupé(e)

tier [tɪəʳ] n gradin m; (of cake) étage m

tiger [ˈtaɪɡəʳ] n tigre m

tight [taɪt] adj (rope) tendu(e), raide; (clothes) étroit(e), très juste; (budget, programme, bend) serré(e); (control) strict(e), sévère; (inf: drunk) ivre, rond(e) ▷ adv (squeeze) très fort; (shut) à bloc, hermétiquement; **hold ~!** accrochez-vous bien!; **tighten** vt (rope) tendre; (screw) resserrer; (control) renforcer ▷ vi se tendre; se resserrer; **tightly** adv (grasp) bien, très fort; **tights** npl (BRIT) collant m

tile [taɪl] n (on roof) tuile f; (on wall or floor) carreau m

till [tɪl] n caisse (enregistreuse) ▷ prep, conj = **until**

tilt [tɪlt] vt pencher, incliner ▷ vi pencher, être incliné(e)

timber [ˈtɪmbəʳ] n (material) bois m de construction

time [taɪm] n temps m; (epoch: often pl) époque f, temps; (by clock) heure f; (moment) moment m; (occasion, also Math) fois f; (Mus) mesure f ▷ vt (race) chronométrer; (programme) minuter; (visit) fixer; (remark etc) choisir le moment de; **a long ~** un long moment, longtemps; **four at a ~** quatre à la fois; (be free) pour le moment; **from ~ to ~** de temps en temps; **at ~s** parfois; **in ~** (soon enough) à temps; (after some time) avec le temps, à la longue; (Mus) en mesure; **in a week's ~** dans une semaine; **in ~ no** en un rien de temps; **any ~** n'importe quand; **on ~** à l'heure; **5 ~s 5** 5 fois 5; **what ~ is it?** quelle heure est-il?; **what ~ is the museum/shop open?** à quelle heure ouvre le musée/magasin?; **to have a good ~** bien s'amuser; **time limit** n limite f de temps, délai m; **timely** adj opportun(e); **timer** n (in kitchen) compte-minutes m inv; (Tech) minuteur m; **time-share** n maison f/appartement m en multipropriété; **timetable** n (Rail) (indicateur m) horaire m; (Scol) emploi m du temps; **time zone** n fuseau m horaire

timid ['tɪmɪd] adj timide; (easily scared) peureux(-euse)

timing ['taɪmɪŋ] n (Sport) chronométrage m; **the ~ of his resignation** le moment choisi pour sa démission

tin [tɪn] n étain m; (also: **~ plate**) fer-blanc m; (BRIT: can) boîte f (de conserve); (for baking) moule à (à gâteau); (for storage) boîte f; **tinfoil** n papier m d'étain ou d'aluminium

tingle ['tɪŋgl] vi picoter; (person) avoir des picotements

tinker ['tɪŋkər]: **tinker with** vt fus bricoler, rafistoler

tinned [tɪnd] adj (BRIT: food) en boîte, en conserve

tin opener [-'əʊpnər] n (BRIT) ouvre-boîte(s) m

tinsel ['tɪnsl] n guirlandes fpl de Noël (argentées)

tint [tɪnt] n teinte f; (for hair) shampooing colorant; **tinted** adj (hair) teint(e); (spectacles, glass) teinté(e)

tiny ['taɪnɪ] adj minuscule

tip [tɪp] n (end) bout m; (gratuity) pourboire m; (BRIT: for rubbish) décharge f; (advice) tuyau m ▷ vt (waiter) donner un pourboire à; (tilt) incliner; (overturn: also: **~ over**) renverser; (empty: also: **~ out**) déverser; **how much should I ~?** combien de pourboire est-ce qu'il faut laisser?; **tip off** vt prévenir, avertir

tiptoe ['tɪptəʊ] n: **on ~** sur la pointe des pieds

tire ['taɪər] n (US) = **tyre** ▷ vt fatiguer ▷ vi se fatiguer; **tired** adj fatigué(e); **to be tired of** en avoir assez de, être las (lasse) de; **tire pressure** (US) n = **tyre pressure**; **tiring** adj fatigant(e)

tissue ['tɪʃu:] n tissu m; (paper handkerchief) mouchoir m en papier, kleenex® m; **tissue paper** n papier m de soie

tit [tɪt] n (bird) mésange f; **to give ~ for tat** rendre coup pour coup

title ['taɪtl] n titre m

T-junction ['tiː'dʒʌŋkʃən] n croisement m en T

TM n abbr = **trademark**

KEYWORD

to [tu:, tə] prep (with noun/pronoun) **1** (direction) à; (: towards) vers; envers; **to go to France/Portugal/London/school** aller en France/au Portugal/à Londres/à l'école; **to go to Claude's/the doctor's** aller chez Claude/le docteur; **the road to Edinburgh** la route d'Édimbourg **2** (as far as) (jusqu')à; **to count to 10** compter jusqu'à 10; **from 40 to 50 people** de 40 à 50 personnes **3** (with expressions of time): **a quarter to 5** 5 heures moins le quart; **it's twenty to 3** il est 3 heures moins vingt

4 (for, of) de; **the key to the front door** la clé de la porte d'entrée; **a letter to his wife** une lettre (adressée) à sa femme

5 (expressing indirect object) à; **to give sth to sb** donner qch à qn; **to talk to sb** parler à qn; **to be a danger to sb** être dangereux(-euse) pour qn

6 (in relation to) à; **3 goals to 2** 3 (buts) à 2; **30 miles to the gallon** ≈ 9,4 litres aux cent (km)

7 (purpose, result): **to come to sb's aid** venir au secours de qn, porter secours à qn; **to sentence sb to death** condamner qn à mort; **to my surprise** à ma grande surprise

▶ prep (with vb) **1** (simple infinitive): **to go/eat** aller/manger

2 (following another vb): **to want/ try/start to do** vouloir/essayer de/ commencer à faire

3 (with vb omitted): **I don't want to** je ne veux pas

4 (purpose, result) pour; **I did it to help you** je l'ai fait pour vous aider

5 (equivalent to relative clause): **I have things to do** j'ai des choses à faire; **the main thing is to try** l'important est d'essayer

6 (after adjective etc): **ready to go** prêt(e) à partir; **too old/young to ...** trop vieux/jeune pour ...

▶ adv: **push/pull the door to** tirez/ poussez la porte

toad [təud] n crapaud m; **toadstool** n champignon (vénéneux)

toast [təust] n (Culin) pain grillé, toast m; (drink, speech) toast ▶ vt (Culin) faire griller; (drink to) porter un toast à; **toaster** n grille-pain m inv

tobacco [tə'bækəu] n tabac m

toboggan [tə'bɔgən] n toboggan m; (child's) luge f

today [tə'deɪ] adv, n (also fig) aujourd'hui (m)

toddler ['tɔdlə*] n enfant m/f qui commence à marcher, bambin m

toe [təu] n doigt m de pied, orteil m; (of shoe) bout m ▶ vt: **to ~ the line** (fig) obéir, se conformer; **toenail** n ongle m de l'orteil

toffee ['tɔfɪ] n caramel m

together [tə'geðə*] adv ensemble; (at same time) en même temps; **~ with** prep avec

toilet ['tɔɪlət] n (BRIT: lavatory) toilettes fpl, cabinets mpl; **to go to the ~** aller aux toilettes; **where's the ~?** où sont les toilettes?; **toilet bag** (BRIT) nécessaire m de toilette; **toilet paper** n papier m hygiénique; **toiletries** npl articles mpl de toilette; **toilet roll** n rouleau m de papier hygiénique

token ['təukən] n (sign) marque f, témoignage m; (metal disc) jeton m ▶ adj (fee, strike) symbolique; **book/ record ~** (BRIT) chèque-livre/ -disque m

Tokyo ['təukjəu] n Tokyo

told [təuld] pt, pp of **tell**

tolerant ['tɔlərnt] adj: **~ (of)** tolérant(e) (à l'égard de)

tolerate ['tɔləreɪt] vt supporter

toll [təul] n (tax, charge) péage m ▶ vi (bell) sonner; **the accident ~ on the roads** le nombre des victimes de la route; **toll call** n (US Tel) appel m (à) longue distance; **toll-free** adj (US) gratuit(e) ▶ adv gratuitement

tomato [tə'mɑːtəu] (pl **tomatoes**) n tomate f; **tomato sauce** n sauce f tomate

tomb [tuːm] n tombe f; **tombstone** n pierre tombale

tomorrow [tə'mɔrəu] adv, n (also fig) demain (m); **the day after ~** après-demain; **a week ~** demain en huit; **~ morning** demain matin

ton [tʌn] n tonne f (Brit: = 1016 kg; US = 907 kg; metric = 1000 kg); **~s of** (inf) des tas de

tone [təun] n ton m; (of radio, BRIT Tel) tonalité f ▶ vi (also: **~ in**) s'harmoniser; **tone down** vt (colour, criticism) adoucir

tongs [tɒŋz] npl pinces fpl; (for coal) pincettes fpl; (for hair) fer m à friser

tongue [tʌŋ] n langue f; **~ in cheek** adv ironiquement

tonic [ˈtɒnɪk] n (Med) tonique m; (also: **~ water**) Schweppes® m

tonight [təˈnaɪt] adv, n cette nuit; (this evening) ce soir

tonne [tʌn] n (BRIT: metric ton) tonne f

tonsil [ˈtɒnsl] n amygdale f; **tonsillitis** [tɒnsɪˈlaɪtɪs] n: **to have tonsillitis** avoir une angine ou une amygdalite

too [tuː] adv (excessively) trop; (also) aussi; **~ much** (as adv) trop; (as adj) trop de; **~ many** adj trop de

took [tʊk] pt of **take**

tool [tuːl] n outil m; **tool box** n boîte f à outils; **tool kit** n trousse f à outils

tooth (pl **teeth**) [tuːθ, tiːθ] n (Anat, Tech) dent f; **to brush one's teeth** se laver les dents; **toothache** n mal m de dents; **to have toothache** avoir mal aux dents; **toothbrush** n brosse f à dents; **toothpaste** n (pâte f) dentifrice m; **toothpick** n cure-dent m

top [tɒp] n (of mountain, head) sommet m; (of page, ladder) haut m; (of box, cupboard, table) dessus m; (lid: of box, jar) couvercle m; (: of bottle) bouchon m; (toy) toupie f; (Dress: blouse etc) haut; (: of pyjamas) veste f ▷ adj du haut; (in rank) premier(-ière); (best) meilleur(e) ▷ vt (exceed) dépasser; (be first in) être en tête de; **from ~ to bottom** de fond en comble; **on ~ of** sur; (in addition to) en plus de; **over the ~** (inf) (behaviour etc) qui dépasse les limites; **top up**, (US) **top off** vt (bottle) remplir; (salary) compléter; **to ~ up one's mobile (phone)** recharger son compte; **top floor** n dernier étage; **top hat** n haut-de-forme m

topic [ˈtɒpɪk] n sujet m, thème m; **topical** adj d'actualité

topless [ˈtɒplɪs] adj (bather etc) aux seins nus

topping [ˈtɒpɪŋ] n (Culin) couche de crème, fromage etc qui recouvre un plat

topple [ˈtɒpl] vt renverser, faire tomber ▷ vi basculer; tomber

top-up [ˈtɒpʌp] n (for mobile phone) recharge f, minutes fpl; **top-up card** n (for mobile phone) recharge f

torch [tɔːtʃ] n torche f; (BRIT: electric) lampe f de poche

tore [tɔːʳ] pt of **tear²**

torment n [ˈtɔːment] tourment m ▷ vt [tɔːˈment] tourmenter; (fig: annoy) agacer

torn [tɔːn] pp of **tear²**

tornado [tɔːˈneɪdəu] (pl **tornadoes**) n tornade f

torpedo [tɔːˈpiːdəu] (pl **torpedoes**) n torpille f

torrent [ˈtɒrnt] n torrent m; **torrential** [tɒˈrenʃl] adj torrentiel(le)

tortoise [ˈtɔːtəs] n tortue f

torture [ˈtɔːtʃəʳ] n torture f ▷ vt torturer

Tory [ˈtɔːrɪ] adj, n (BRIT Pol) tory m/f, conservateur(-trice)

toss [tɒs] vt lancer, jeter; (BRIT: pancake) faire sauter; (head) rejeter en arrière ▷ vi: **to ~ up for sth** jouer qch à pile ou face; **to ~ a coin** jouer à pile ou face; **to ~ and turn** (in bed) se tourner et se retourner

total [ˈtəutl] adj total(e) ▷ n total m ▷ vt (add up) faire le total de, additionner; (amount to) s'élever à

totalitarian [təutælɪˈtɛərɪən] adj totalitaire

totally [ˈtəutəlɪ] adv totalement

touch [tʌtʃ] n contact m, toucher m; (sense, skill: of pianist etc) toucher ▷ vt (gen) toucher; (tamper with) toucher à; **a ~ of** (fig) un petit peu de; une touche de; **to get in ~ with** prendre contact avec; **to lose ~** (friends) se perdre de vue; **touch down** vi (Aviat) atterrir; (on sea) amerrir; **touchdown** n (Aviat) atterrissage m; (on sea) amerrissage m; (US Football) essai m; **touched** adj (moved) touché(e); **touching**

touchline n (Sport) (ligne f de) touche f; **touch-sensitive** adj (keypad) à effleurement; (screen) tactile

tough [tʌf] adj dur(e); (resistant) résistant(e), solide; (meat) dur, coriace; (firm) inflexible; (task, problem, situation) difficile

tour ['tʊər] n voyage m; (also: **package ~**) voyage organisé; (of town, museum) tour m, visite f; (by band) tournée f ▷ vt visiter; **tour guide** n (person) guide m/f

tourism ['tʊərɪzəm] n tourisme m

tourist ['tʊərɪst] n touriste m/f ▷ cpd touristique; **tourist office** n syndicat m d'initiative

tournament ['tʊənəmənt] n tournoi m

tour operator n (BRIT) organisateur m de voyages, tour-opérateur m

tow [təʊ] vt remorquer; (caravan, trailer) tracter; **"on ~"**, (US) **"in ~"** (Aut) "véhicule en remorque"; **tow away** vt (subj: police) emmener à la fourrière; (breakdown service) remorquer

toward(s) [tə'wɔːd(z)] prep vers; (of attitude) envers, à l'égard de; (of purpose) pour

towel ['taʊəl] n serviette f (de toilette); **towelling** n (fabric) tissu-éponge m

tower ['taʊər] n tour f; **tower block** n (BRIT) tour f (d'habitation)

town [taʊn] n ville f; **to go to ~** aller en ville; (fig) y mettre le paquet; **town centre** n (BRIT) centre m de la ville, centre-ville m; **town hall** n ≈ mairie f

tow truck n (US) dépanneuse f

toxic ['tɔksɪk] adj toxique

toy [tɔɪ] n jouet m; **toy with** vt fus jouer avec; (idea) caresser; **toyshop** n magasin m de jouets

trace [treɪs] n trace f ▷ vt (draw) tracer, dessiner; (follow) suivre la trace de; (locate) retrouver

tracing paper ['treɪsɪŋ-] n papier-calque m

track [træk] n (mark) trace f; (path: gen) chemin m, piste f; (: of bullet etc) trajectoire f; (: of suspect, animal) piste f; (Rail) voie ferrée, rails mpl; (Comput, Sport) piste f; (on CD) piste f; (on record) plage f ▷ vt suivre la trace ou la piste de; **to keep ~ of** suivre; **track down** vt (prey) trouver et capturer; (sth lost) finir par retrouver; **tracksuit** n survêtement m

tractor ['træktər] n tracteur m

trade [treɪd] n commerce m; (skill, job) métier m ▷ vi faire du commerce ▷ vt (exchange): **to ~ sth (for sth)** échanger qch (contre qch); **to ~ with/in** faire du commerce avec/le commerce de; **trade in** vt (old car etc) faire reprendre; **trademark** n marque f de fabrique; **trader** n commerçant(e), négociant(e); **tradesman** (irreg) n (shopkeeper) commerçant m; **trade union** n syndicat m

trading ['treɪdɪŋ] n affaires fpl, commerce m

tradition [trə'dɪʃən] n tradition f; **traditional** adj traditionnel(le)

traffic ['træfɪk] n trafic m; (cars) circulation f ▷ vi: **to ~ in** (pej: liquor, drugs) faire le trafic de; **traffic circle** n (US) rond-point m; **traffic island** n refuge m (pour piétons); **traffic jam** n embouteillage m; **traffic lights** npl feux mpl (de signalisation); **traffic warden** n contractuel(le)

tragedy ['trædʒədɪ] n tragédie f

tragic ['trædʒɪk] adj tragique

trail [treɪl] n (tracks) trace f, piste f; (path) chemin m, piste f; (of smoke etc) traînée f ▷ vt (drag) traîner, tirer; (follow) suivre ▷ vi traîner; (in game, contest) être en retard; **trailer** n (Aut) remorque f; (US: caravan) caravane f; (Cine) bande-annonce f

train [treɪn] n train m; (in underground) rame f; (of dress) traîne f; (BRIT: series):

~ of events série f d'événements ▷ vt (apprentice, doctor etc) former; (Sport) entraîner; (dog) dresser; (memory) exercer; (point: gun etc) **to ~ sth on** braquer qch sur ▷ vi recevoir sa formation; (Sport) s'entraîner; **one's ~ of thought** le fil de sa pensée; **what time does the ~ from Paris get in?** à quelle heure arrive le train de Paris?; **is this the ~ for ...?** c'est bien le train pour ...?; **trainee** ['treɪˈniː] n stagiaire m/f; (in trade) apprenti(e); **trainer** n (Sport) entraîneur(-euse); (of dogs etc) dresseur(-euse); **trainers** npl (shoes) chaussures fpl de sport; **training** n formation f; (Sport) entraînement m; (of dog etc) dressage m; **in training** (Sport) à l'entraînement; (fit) en forme; **training course** n cours m de formation professionnelle; **training shoes** npl chaussures fpl de sport

trait [treɪt] n trait m (de caractère)

traitor ['treɪtə'] n traître m

tram [træm] n (BRIT: also: **~car**) tram(way) m

tramp [træmp] n (person) vagabond(e), clochard(e); (inf, pej: woman) **to be a ~** être coureuse

trample ['træmpl] vt: **to ~ (underfoot)** piétiner

trampoline ['træmpəliːn] n trampoline m

tranquil ['træŋkwɪl] adj tranquille; **tranquillizer**, (US) **tranquilizer** n (Med) tranquillisant m

transaction [trænˈzækʃən] n transaction f

transatlantic ['trænzətˈlæntɪk] adj transatlantique

transcript ['trænskrɪpt] n transcription f (texte)

transfer n ['trænsfə'] (gen, also Sport) transfert m; (Pol: of power) passation f; (of money) virement m; (picture, design) décalcomanie f; (: stick-on) autocollant m ▷ vt ['trænsˈfəː] transférer; passer; virer; **to ~ the**

charges (BRIT Tel) téléphoner en P.C.V.

transform [trænsˈfɔːm] vt transformer; **transformation** n transformation f

transfusion [trænsˈfjuːʒən] n transfusion f

transit ['trænzɪt] n: **in ~** en transit

transition [trænˈzɪʃən] n transition f

transitive ['trænzɪtɪv] adj (Ling) transitif(-ive)

translate [trænzˈleɪt] vt: **to ~ (from/into)** traduire (du/en); **can you ~ this for me?** pouvez-vous me traduire ceci?; **translation** [trænzˈleɪʃən] n traduction f; (Scol: as opposed to prose) version f; **translator** n traducteur(-trice)

transmission [trænzˈmɪʃən] n transmission f

transmit [trænzˈmɪt] vt transmettre; (Radio, TV) émettre; **transmitter** n émetteur m

transparent [trænsˈpærnt] adj transparent(e)

transplant ['trænsplɑːnt] n (Med) transplantation f

transport n ['trænspɔːt] transport m ▷ vt [trænsˈpɔːt] transporter; **transportation** [trænspɔːˈteɪʃən] n (moyen m de) transport m

transvestite [trænzˈvestaɪt] n travesti(e)

trap [træp] n (snare, trick) piège m; (carriage) cabriolet m ▷ vt prendre au piège; (confine) coincer

trash [træʃ] n (inf: pej: goods) camelote f; (: nonsense) sottises fpl; (US: rubbish) ordures fpl; **trash can** n (US) poubelle f

trauma ['trɔːmə] n traumatisme m; **traumatic** [trɔːˈmætɪk] adj traumatisant(e)

travel ['trævl] n voyage(s) m(pl) ▷ vi voyager; (news, sound) se propager ▷ vt (distance) parcourir; **travel agency** n agence f de voyages; **travel agent** n agent m de voyages; **travel insurance**

t

n assurance-voyage f; **traveller**, (us) **traveler** n voyageur(-euse); **traveller's cheque**, (us) **traveler's check** n chèque m de voyage; **travelling**, (us) **traveling** n voyage(s) m(pl); **travel-sick** adj: **to get travel-sick** avoir le mal de la route (or de mer or de l'air); **travel sickness** n mal m de la route (or de mer or de l'air)

tray [treɪ] n (for carrying) plateau m; (on desk) corbeille f

treacherous ['trɛtʃərəs] adj traître(sse); (ground, tide) dont il faut se méfier

treacle ['triːkl] n mélasse f

tread [trɛd] n (step) pas m; (sound) bruit m de pas; (of tyre) chape f, bande f de roulement ▷ vi (pt **trod**, pp **trodden**) marcher; **tread on** vt fus marcher sur

treasure ['trɛʒəʳ] n trésor m ▷ vt (value) tenir beaucoup à; **treasurer** n trésorier(-ière)

treasury ['trɛʒərɪ] n: **the T~**, (us) **the T~ Department** ≈ le ministère des Finances

treat [triːt] n petit cadeau, petite surprise ▷ vt traiter; **to ~ sb to sth** offrir qch à qn; **treatment** n traitement m

treaty ['triːtɪ] n traité m

treble ['trɛbl] adj triple ▷ vt, vi tripler

tree [triː] n arbre m

trek [trɛk] n (long walk) randonnée f; (tiring walk) longue marche, trotte f

tremble ['trɛmbl] vi trembler

tremendous [trɪ'mɛndəs] adj (enormous) énorme; (excellent) formidable, fantastique

trench [trɛntʃ] n tranchée f

trend [trɛnd] n (tendency) tendance f; (of events) cours m; (fashion) mode f; **trendy** adj (idea, person) dans le vent; (clothes) dernier cri inv

trespass ['trɛspəs] vi: **to ~ on** s'introduire sans permission dans; **"no ~ing"** "propriété privée", "défense d'entrer"

trial ['traɪəl] n (Law) procès m, jugement m; (test: of machine etc) essai m; **trials** npl (unpleasant experiences) épreuves fpl; **trial period** n période d'essai

triangle ['traɪæŋgl] n (Math, Mus) triangle m

triangular [traɪ'æŋgjuləʳ] adj triangulaire

tribe [traɪb] n tribu f

tribunal [traɪ'bjuːnl] n tribunal m

tribute ['trɪbjuːt] n tribut m, hommage m; **to pay ~ to** rendre hommage à

trick [trɪk] n (magic) tour m; (joke, prank) tour, farce f; (skill, knack) astuce f; (Cards) levée f ▷ vt attraper, rouler; **to play a ~ on sb** jouer un tour à qn; **that should do the ~** (inf) ça devrait faire l'affaire

trickle ['trɪkl] n (of water etc) filet m ▷ vi couler en filet or goutte à goutte

tricky ['trɪkɪ] adj difficile, délicat(e)

tricycle ['traɪsɪkl] n tricycle m

trifle ['traɪfl] n bagatelle f; (Culin) ≈ diplomate m ▷ adv: **a ~ long** un peu long

trigger ['trɪgəʳ] n (of gun) gâchette f

trim [trɪm] adj (house, garden) bien tenu(e); (figure) svelte ▷ n (haircut etc) légère coupe; (on car) garnitures fpl ▷ vt (cut) couper légèrement; (Naut: a sail) gréer; (decorate) **to ~ (with)** décorer (de)

trio ['triːəu] n trio m

trip [trɪp] n voyage m; (excursion) excursion f; (stumble) faux pas ▷ vi faire un faux pas, trébucher; **trip up** vi trébucher ▷ vt faire un croc-en-jambe à

triple ['trɪpl] adj triple

triplets ['trɪplɪts] npl triplés(-ées)

tripod ['traɪpɔd] n trépied m

triumph ['traɪʌmf] n triomphe m ▷ vi: **to ~ (over)** triompher (de); **triumphant** [traɪ'ʌmfənt] adj triomphant(e)

trivial ['trɪvɪəl] adj insignifiant(e); (commonplace) banal(e)

trod [trɒd] pt of **tread**

trodden ['trɒdn] pp of **tread**

troll [trɒl] n (Comput) troll m, trolleur(-euse) m/f

trolley ['trɒlɪ] n chariot m

trombone [trɒm'bəun] n trombone m

troop [tru:p] n bande f, groupe m; **troops** npl (Mil) troupes fpl (: men) hommes mpl, soldats mpl

trophy ['trəufɪ] n trophée m

tropical ['trɒpɪkl] adj tropical(e)

trot [trɒt] n trot m ▷ vi trotter; **on the ~** (BRIT fig) d'affilée

trouble ['trʌbl] n difficulté(s) f(pl), problème(s) m(pl); (worry) ennuis mpl, soucis mpl; (bother, effort) peine f; (Pol) conflit(s) m(pl), troubles mpl; (Med): **stomach** etc ~ ennuis mpl gastriques etc ▷ vt (disturb) déranger, gêner; (worry) inquiéter ▷ vi: **to ~ to do** se donner la peine de faire; **troubles** npl (Pol etc) troubles; (personal) ennuis, soucis; **to be in ~** avoir des ennuis; (ship, climber etc) être en difficulté; **to have ~ doing sth** avoir du mal à faire qch; **it's no ~!** je vous en prie!; **the ~ is ...** le problème, c'est que ...; **what's the ~?** qu'est-ce qui ne va pas?; **troubled** adj (person) inquiet(-ète); (epoch, life) agité(e); **troublemaker** n élément perturbateur, fauteur m de troubles; **troublesome** adj (child) fatigant(e), difficile; (cough) gênant(e)

trough [trɒf] n (also: **drinking ~**) abreuvoir m; (also: **feeding ~**) auge f; (depression) creux m

trousers ['trauzəz] npl pantalon m; **short ~** (BRIT) culottes courtes

trout [traut] n (pl inv) truite f

truant ['truənt] n: **to play ~** (BRIT) faire l'école buissonnière

truce [tru:s] n trêve f

truck [trʌk] n camion m; (Rail) wagon m à plate-forme; **truck driver** n camionneur m

true [tru:] adj vrai(e); (accurate) exact(e); (genuine) vrai, véritable; (faithful) fidèle; **to come ~** se réaliser

truly ['tru:lɪ] adv vraiment, réellement; (truthfully) vraiment; **yours ~** (in letter) je vous prie d'agréer, Monsieur (or Madame etc), l'expression de mes sentiments respectueux

trumpet ['trʌmpɪt] n trompette f

trunk [trʌŋk] n (of tree, person) tronc m; (of elephant) trompe f; (case) malle f; (US Aut) coffre m; **trunks** npl (also: **swimming ~**) maillot m or slip m de bain

trust [trʌst] n confiance f; (responsibility): **to place sth in sb's ~** confier la responsabilité de qch à qn; (Law) fidéicommis m ▷ vt (rely on) avoir confiance en; (entrust): **to ~ sth to sb** confier qch à qn; (hope): **to ~ (that)** espérer (que); **to take sth on ~** accepter qch les yeux fermés; **trusted** adj en qui l'on a confiance; **trustworthy** adj digne de confiance

truth [tru:θ, tru:ðz] n vérité f; **truthful** adj (person) qui dit la vérité; (answer) sincère

try [traɪ] n essai m, tentative f; (Rugby) essai ▷ vt (attempt) essayer, tenter; (test: sth new also: ~ **out**) essayer, tester; (Law: person) juger; (strain) éprouver ▷ vi essayer; **to ~ to do** essayer de faire; (seek) chercher à faire; **try on** vt (clothes) essayer; **trying** adj pénible

T-shirt ['ti:ʃə:t] n tee-shirt m

tub [tʌb] n cuve f; (for washing clothes) baquet m; (bath) baignoire f

tube [tju:b] n tube m; (BRIT: underground) métro m; (for tyre) chambre f à air

tuberculosis [tjubə:kju'ləusɪs] n tuberculose f

tube station n (BRIT) station f de métro

tuck [tʌk] vt (put) mettre; **tuck away** vt cacher, ranger; (money) mettre de côté; (building): **to be ~ed away** être caché(e); **tuck in** vt rentrer; (child) border ▷ vi (eat) manger de bon appétit; attaquer le repas

tucker ['tʌkə'] n (AUST, NZ inf) bouffe f(inf)

tuck shop n (BRIT Scol) boutique f à provisions

Tuesday ['tjuːzdɪ] n mardi m

tug [tʌg] n (ship) remorqueur m ▷ vt tirer (sur)

tuition [tjuː'ɪʃən] n (BRIT: lessons) leçons fpl; (: private) cours particuliers; (US: fees) frais mpl de scolarité

tulip ['tjuːlɪp] n tulipe f

tumble ['tʌmbl] n (fall) chute f, culbute f ▷ vi tomber, dégringoler; **to ~ to sth** (inf) réaliser qch; **tumble dryer** n (BRIT) séchoir m (à linge) à air chaud

tumbler ['tʌmblə'] n verre (droit), gobelet m

tummy ['tʌmɪ] n (inf) ventre m

tumour, (US) **tumor** ['tjuːmə'] n tumeur f

tuna ['tjuːnə] n (pl inv also: ~ **fish**) thon m

tune [tjuːn] n (melody) air m ▷ vt (Mus) accorder; (Radio, TV, Aut) régler, mettre au point; **to be in/ out of ~** (instrument) être accordé/ désaccordé; (singer) chanter juste/ faux; **tune in** vi (Radio, TV): **to ~ in (to)** se mettre à l'écoute (de); **tune up** vi (musician) accorder son instrument

tunic ['tjuːnɪk] n tunique f

Tunis ['tjuːnɪs] n Tunis

Tunisia [tjuː'nɪzɪə] n Tunisie f

Tunisian [tjuː'nɪzɪən] adj tunisien(ne) ▷ n Tunisien(ne)

tunnel ['tʌnl] n tunnel m; (in mine) galerie f ▷ vi creuser un tunnel (or une galerie)

turbulence ['təːbjuləns] n (Aviat) turbulence f

turf [təːf] n gazon m; (clod) motte f (de gazon) ▷ vt gazonner

Turk [təːk] n Turc (Turque)

Turkey ['təːkɪ] n Turquie f

turkey ['təːkɪ] n dindon m, dinde f

Turkish ['təːkɪʃ] adj turc (turque) ▷ n (Ling) turc m

turmoil ['təːmɔɪl] n trouble m, bouleversement m

turn [təːn] n tour m; (in road) tournant m; (tendency: of mind, events) tournure f; (performance) numéro m; (Med) crise f, attaque f ▷ vt tourner; (collar, steak) retourner; (age) atteindre; (change): **to ~ sth into** changer qch en ▷ vi (object, wind, milk) tourner; (person: look back) se (re)tourner; (reverse direction) faire demi-tour; (become) devenir; **to ~ into** se changer en, se transformer en; **a good ~** un service; **it gave me quite a ~** ça m'a fait un coup; **"no left ~"** (Aut) "défense de tourner à gauche"; **~ left/right at the next junction** tournez à gauche/droite au prochain carrefour; **it's your ~** c'est (à) votre tour; **in ~** à son tour; à tour de rôle; **to take ~s** se relayer; **turn around** vi (person) se retourner ▷ vt (object) tourner; **turn away** vi se détourner, tourner la tête ▷ vt (reject: person) renvoyer; (: business) refuser; **turn back** vi revenir, faire demi-tour; **turn down** vt (refuse) rejeter, refuser; (reduce) baisser; (person) renvoyer; **turn in** vi (inf: go to bed) aller se coucher ▷ vt (fold) rentrer; **turn off** vi (from road) tourner ▷ vt (light, radio etc) éteindre; (tap) fermer; (engine) arrêter; **I can't ~ the heating off** je n'arrive pas à éteindre le chauffage; **turn on** vt (light, radio etc) allumer; (tap) ouvrir; (engine) mettre en marche; **I can't ~ the heating on** je n'arrive pas à allumer le chauffage; **turn out** vt (light, gas) éteindre; (produce) produire ▷ vi (voters, troops) se présenter; **to ~ out to be ...** s'avérer ..., se révéler ...; **turn over** vi (person) se retourner ▷ vt (object) retourner; (page) tourner; **turn round** vi faire demi-tour;

(rotate) tourner; **turn to** vt fus: **to ~ to sb** s'adresser à qn; **turn up** vi (person) arriver, se pointer (inf); (lost object) être retrouvé(e) ▷ vt (collar) remonter; (radio, heater) mettre plus fort; **turning** n (in road) tournant m; **turning point** n (fig) tournant m, moment décisif

turnip ['təːnɪp] n navet m

turn: turnout n (of voters) taux m de participation; **turnover** n (Comm: amount of money) chiffre m d'affaires; (: of goods) roulement m; (of staff) renouvellement m, changement m; **turnstile** n tourniquet m (d'entrée); **turn-up** n (BRIT: on trousers) revers m

turquoise ['təːkwɔɪz] n (stone) turquoise f ▷ adj turquoise inv

turtle ['təːtl] n tortue marine; **turtleneck (sweater)** n pullover m à col montant

tusk [tʌsk] n défense f (d'éléphant)

tutor ['tjuːtəʳ] n (BRIT Scol: in college) directeur(-trice) d'études; (private teacher) précepteur(-trice); **tutorial** [tjuː'tɔːrɪəl] n (Scol) (séance f de) travaux mpl pratiques

tuxedo [tʌk'siːdəu] n (US) smoking m

TV [tiː'viː] n abbr (= television) télé f, TV f

tweed [twiːd] n tweed m

tweet [twiːt] (on Twitter) n tweet m ▷ vt, vi tweeter

tweezers ['twiːzəz] npl pince f à épiler

twelfth [twelfθ] num douzième

twelve [twelv] num douze; **at ~ (o'clock)** à midi; (midnight) à minuit

twentieth ['twentɪɪθ] num vingtième

twenty ['twentɪ] num vingt; **in ~ fourteen** en deux mille quatorze

twice [twaɪs] adv deux fois; **~ as much** deux fois plus

twig [twɪg] n brindille f ▷ vt, vi (inf) piger

twilight ['twaɪlaɪt] n crépuscule m

twin [twɪn] adj, n jumeau(-elle) ▷ vt jumeler; **twin-bedded room** n

= **twin room**; **twin beds** npl lits mpl jumeaux

twinkle ['twɪŋkl] vi scintiller; (eyes) pétiller

twin room n chambre f à deux lits

twist [twɪst] n torsion f, tour m; (in wire, flex) tortillon m; (bend: in road) tournant m; (in story) coup m de théâtre ▷ vt tordre; (weave) entortiller; (roll around) enrouler; (fig) déformer ▷ vi (road, river) serpenter; **to ~ one's ankle/wrist** (Med) se tordre la cheville/le poignet

twit [twɪt] n (inf) crétin(e)

twitch [twɪtʃ] n (pull) coup sec, saccade f; (nervous) tic m ▷ vi se convulser; avoir un tic

two [tuː] num deux; **to put ~ and ~ together** (fig) faire le rapprochement

type [taɪp] n (category) genre m, espèce f; (model) modèle m; (example) type m; (Typ) type, caractère m ▷ vt (letter etc) taper (à la machine); **typewriter** n machine f à écrire

typhoid ['taɪfɔɪd] n typhoïde f

typhoon [taɪ'fuːn] n typhon m

typical ['tɪpɪkl] adj typique, caractéristique; **typically** ['tɪpɪklɪ] adv (as usual) comme d'habitude; (characteristically) typiquement

typing ['taɪpɪŋ] n dactylo(graphie) f

typist ['taɪpɪst] n dactylo m/f

tyre, (US) **tire** ['taɪəʳ] n pneu m; **tyre pressure** n (BRIT) pression f (de gonflage)

t

U

UFO ['ju:fəu] n abbr (= unidentified flying object) ovni m

Uganda [ju:'gændə] n Ouganda m

ugly ['ʌglɪ] adj laid(e), vilain(e); (fig) répugnant(e)

UHT adj abbr (= ultra-heat treated): ~ **milk** lait m UHT or longue conservation

UK n abbr = **United Kingdom**

ulcer ['ʌlsə'] n ulcère m; **mouth ~** aphte f

ultimate ['ʌltɪmət] adj ultime, final(e); (authority) suprême; **ultimately** adv (at last) en fin de compte; (fundamentally) finalement; (eventually) par la suite

ultimatum (pl **ultimatums** or **ultimata**) [ʌltɪ'meɪtəm, -tə] n ultimatum m

ultrasound ['ʌltrəsaund] n (Med) ultrason m

ultraviolet ['ʌltrə'vaɪəlɪt] adj ultraviolet(te)

umbrella [ʌm'brɛlə] n parapluie m; (for sun) parasol m

umpire ['ʌmpaɪə'] n arbitre m; (Tennis) juge m de chaise

UN n abbr = **United Nations**

unable [ʌn'eɪbl] adj: **to be ~ to** ne (pas) pouvoir, être dans l'impossibilité de; (not capable) être incapable de

unacceptable [ʌnək'sɛptəbl] adj (behaviour) inadmissible; (price, proposal) inacceptable

unanimous [ju:'nænɪməs] adj unanime

unarmed [ʌn'ɑ:md] adj (person) non armé(e); (combat) sans armes

unattended [ʌnə'tɛndɪd] adj (car, child, luggage) sans surveillance

unattractive [ʌnə'træktɪv] adj peu attrayant(e); (character) peu sympathique

unavailable [ʌnə'veɪləbl] adj (article, room, book) (qui n'est) pas disponible; (person) (qui n'est) pas libre

unavoidable [ʌnə'vɔɪdəbl] adj inévitable

unaware [ʌnə'wɛə'] adj: **to be ~ of** ignorer, ne pas savoir, être inconscient(e) de; **unawares** adv à l'improviste, au dépourvu

unbearable [ʌn'bɛərəbl] adj insupportable

unbeatable [ʌn'bi:təbl] adj imbattable

unbelievable [ʌnbɪ'li:vəbl] adj incroyable

unborn [ʌn'bɔ:n] adj à naître

unbutton [ʌn'bʌtn] vt déboutonner

uncalled-for [ʌn'kɔ:ldfɔ:'] adj déplacé(e), injustifié(e)

uncanny [ʌn'kænɪ] adj étrange, troublant(e)

uncertain [ʌn'sə:tn] adj incertain(e); (hesitant) hésitant(e); **uncertainty** n incertitude f, doutes mpl

unchanged [ʌn'tʃeɪndʒd] adj inchangé(e)

uncle ['ʌŋkl] n oncle m

unclear [ʌnˈklɪəʳ] *adj* (qui n'est pas clair(e) ou évident(e)); **I'm still ~ about what I'm supposed to do** je ne sais pas encore exactement ce que je dois faire

uncomfortable [ʌnˈkʌmfətəbl] *adj* inconfortable, peu confortable; (*uneasy*) mal à l'aise, gêné(e); (*situation*) désagréable

uncommon [ʌnˈkɔmən] *adj* rare, singulier(-ière), peu commun(e)

unconditional [ʌnkənˈdɪʃənl] *adj* sans conditions

unconscious [ʌnˈkɔnʃəs] *adj* sans connaissance, évanoui(e); (*unaware*) **~ (of)** inconscient(e) (de) ▷ *n*: **the ~** l'inconscient *m*

uncontrollable [ʌnkənˈtrəʊləbl] *adj* (*child, dog*) indiscipliné(e); (*temper, laughter*) irrépressible

unconventional [ʌnkənˈvɛnʃənl] *adj* peu conventionnel(le)

uncover [ʌnˈkʌvəʳ] *vt* découvrir

undecided [ʌndɪˈsaɪdɪd] *adj* indécis(e), irrésolu(e)

undeniable [ʌndɪˈnaɪəbl] *adj* indéniable, incontestable

under [ˈʌndəʳ] *prep* sous; (*less than*) (de) moins de; au-dessous de; (*according to*) selon, en vertu de ▷ *adv* au-dessous; en dessous; **~ there** là-dessous; **~ the circumstances** étant donné les circonstances; **~ repair** en (cours de) réparation; **undercover** *adj* secret(-ète), clandestin(e); **underdone** *adj* (Culin) saignant(e); (: *pej*) pas assez cuit(e); **underestimate** *vt* sous-estimer, mésestimer; **undergo** *vt* (*irreg: like* **go**) subir; (*treatment*) suivre; **undergraduate** *n* étudiant(e) (qui prépare la licence); **underground** *adj* souterrain(e); (*fig*) clandestin(e) ▷ *n* (BRIT: *railway*) métro *m*; (*Pol*) clandestinité *f*; **undergrowth** *n* broussailles *fpl*, sous-bois *m*; **underline** *vt* souligner; **undermine** *vt* saper, miner; **underneath**

[ʌndəˈniːθ] *adv* (en) dessous ▷ *prep* sous, au-dessous de; **underpants** *npl* caleçon *m*, slip *m*; **underpass** *n* (BRIT: *for pedestrians*) passage souterrain; (: *for cars*) passage inférieur; **underprivileged** *adj* défavorisé(e); **underscore** *vt* souligner; **undershirt** *n* (US) tricot *m* de corps; **underskirt** *n* (BRIT) jupon *m*

understand [ʌndəˈstænd] *vt, vi* (*irreg: like* **stand**) comprendre; **I don't ~** je ne comprends pas; **understandable** *adj* compréhensible; **understanding** *adj* compréhensif(-ive) ▷ *n* compréhension *f*; (*agreement*) accord *m*

understatement [ˈʌndəsteɪtmənt] *n*: **that's an ~** c'est (bien) peu dire, le terme est faible

understood [ʌndəˈstud] *pt, pp of* **understand** ▷ *adj* entendu(e); (*implied*) sous-entendu(e)

undertake [ʌndəˈteɪk] *vt* (*irreg: like* **take**) (*job, task*) entreprendre; (*duty*) se charger de; **to ~ to do sth** s'engager à faire qch

undertaker [ˈʌndəteɪkəʳ] *n* (BRIT) entrepreneur *m* des pompes funèbres, croque-mort *m*

undertaking [ˈʌndəteɪkɪŋ] *n* entreprise *f*; (*promise*) promesse *f*

under: **underwater** *adv* sous l'eau ▷ *adj* sous-marin(e); **underway** *adj*: **to be underway** (*meeting, investigation*) être en cours; **underwear** *n* sous-vêtements *mpl*; (*women's only*) dessous *mpl*; **underwent** *pt of* **undergo**; **underworld** *n* (*of crime*) milieu *m*, pègre *f*

undesirable [ʌndɪˈzaɪərəbl] *adj* peu souhaitable; (*person, effect*) indésirable

undisputed [ʌndɪsˈpjuːtɪd] *adj* incontesté(e)

undo [ʌnˈduː] *vt* (*irreg: like* **do**) défaire

undone [ʌnˈdʌn] *pp of* **undo** ▷ *adj*: **to come ~** se défaire

undoubtedly [ʌnˈdautɪdlɪ] *adv* sans aucun doute

undress [ʌnˈdrɛs] *vi* se déshabiller

unearth [ʌnˈəːθ] *vt* déterrer; (*fig*) dénicher

uneasy [ʌnˈiːzɪ] *adj* mal à l'aise, gêné(e); (*worried*) inquiet(-ète); (*feeling*) désagréable; (*peace, truce*) fragile

unemployed [ʌnɪmˈplɔɪd] *adj* sans travail, au chômage ▷ *n*: **the ~** les chômeurs *mpl*

unemployment [ʌnɪmˈplɔɪmənt] *n* chômage *m*; **unemployment benefit**, (*us*) **unemployment compensation** *n* allocation *f* de chômage

unequal [ʌnˈiːkwəl] *adj* inégal(e)

uneven [ʌnˈiːvn] *adj* inégal(e); (*quality, work*) irrégulier(-ière)

unexpected [ʌnɪkˈspɛktɪd] *adj* inattendu(e), imprévu(e); **unexpectedly** *adv* (*succeed*) contre toute attente; (*arrive*) à l'improviste

unfair [ʌnˈfɛəʳ] *adj*: **~ (to)** injuste (envers)

unfaithful [ʌnˈfeɪθful] *adj* infidèle

unfamiliar [ʌnfəˈmɪlɪəʳ] *adj* étrange, inconnu(e); **to be ~ with sth** mal connaître qch

unfashionable [ʌnˈfæʃnəbl] *adj* (*clothes*) démodé(e); (*place*) peu chic *inv*

unfasten [ʌnˈfɑːsn] *vt* défaire; (*belt, necklace*) détacher; (*open*) ouvrir

unfavourable, (*us*) **unfavorable** [ʌnˈfeɪvrəbl] *adj* défavorable

unfinished [ʌnˈfɪnɪʃt] *adj* inachevé(e)

unfit [ʌnˈfɪt] *adj* (*physically: ill*) en mauvaise santé; (: *out of condition*) pas en forme; (*incompetent*): **~ (for)** impropre (à); (*work, service*) inapte (à)

unfold [ʌnˈfəuld] *vt* déplier ▷ *vi* se dérouler

unforgettable [ʌnfəˈgɛtəbl] *adj* inoubliable

unfortunate [ʌnˈfɔːtʃnət] *adj* malheureux(-euse); (*event, remark*) malencontreux(-euse); **unfortunately** *adv* malheureusement

unfriend [ʌnˈfrɛnd] *vt* (*Internet*) supprimer de sa liste d'amis

unfriendly [ʌnˈfrɛndlɪ] *adj* peu aimable, froid(e)

unfurnished [ʌnˈfəːnɪʃt] *adj* non meublé(e)

unhappiness [ʌnˈhæpɪnɪs] *n* tristesse *f*, peine *f*

unhappy [ʌnˈhæpɪ] *adj* triste, malheureux(-euse); (*unfortunate: remark etc*) malheureux(-euse); (*not pleased*): **~ with** mécontent(e) de, peu satisfait(e) de

unhealthy [ʌnˈhɛlθɪ] *adj* (*gen*) malsain(e); (*person*) maladif(-ive)

unheard-of [ʌnˈhəːdɔv] *adj* inouï(e), sans précédent

unhelpful [ʌnˈhɛlpful] *adj* (*person*) peu serviable; (*advice*) peu utile

unhurt [ʌnˈhəːt] *adj* indemne, sain(e) et sauf

unidentified [ʌnaɪˈdɛntɪfaɪd] *adj* non identifié(e); *see also* **UFO**

uniform [ˈjuːnɪfɔːm] *n* uniforme *m* ▷ *adj* uniforme

unify [ˈjuːnɪfaɪ] *vt* unifier

unimportant [ʌnɪmˈpɔːtənt] *adj* sans importance

uninhabited [ʌnɪnˈhæbɪtɪd] *adj* inhabité(e)

unintentional [ʌnɪnˈtɛnʃənəl] *adj* involontaire

union [ˈjuːnjən] *n* union *f*; (*also*: **trade ~**) syndicat *m* ▷ *cpd* du syndicat, syndical(e); **Union Jack** *n* drapeau du Royaume-Uni

unique [juːˈniːk] *adj* unique

unisex [ˈjuːnɪsɛks] *adj* unisexe

unit [ˈjuːnɪt] *n* unité *f*; (*section: of furniture etc*) élément *m*, bloc *m*; (*team, squad*) groupe *m*, service *m*; **kitchen ~** élément de cuisine

unite [juːˈnaɪt] *vt* unir ▷ *vi* s'unir; **united** *adj* uni(e); (*country, party*)

unifié(e); (*efforts*) conjugué(e);
United Kingdom n Royaume-Uni
m; **United Nations (Organization)**
n (Organisation f des) Nations unies;
United States (of America) n
États-Unis mpl

unity ['ju:nɪtɪ] n unité f

universal [ju:nɪ'vɜːsl] adj
universel(le)

universe ['ju:nɪvɜːs] n univers m

university [ju:nɪ'vɜːsɪtɪ] n
université f ▷ cpd (student, professor)
d'université; (education, year, degree)
universitaire

unjust [ʌn'dʒʌst] adj injuste

unkind [ʌn'kaɪnd] adj peu gentil(le),
méchant(e)

unknown [ʌn'nəʊn] adj inconnu(e)

unlawful [ʌn'lɔːful] adj illégal(e)

unleaded [ʌn'ledɪd] n (also: ~ **petrol**)
essence f sans plomb

unleash [ʌn'liːʃ] vt (fig) déchaîner,
déclencher

unless [ʌn'lɛs] conj: ~ **he leaves** à
moins qu'il (ne) parte; ~ **otherwise
stated** sauf indication contraire

unlike [ʌn'laɪk] adj dissemblable,
différent(e) ▷ prep à la différence de,
contrairement à

unlikely [ʌn'laɪklɪ] adj (result,
event) improbable; (explanation)
invraisemblable

unlimited [ʌn'lɪmɪtɪd] adj illimité(e)

unlisted ['ʌn'lɪstɪd] adj (US Tel) sur
la liste rouge

unload [ʌn'ləʊd] vt décharger

unlock [ʌn'lɔk] vt ouvrir

unlucky [ʌn'lʌkɪ] adj (person)
malchanceux(-euse); (object, number)
qui porte malheur; **to be ~** (person) ne
pas avoir de chance

unmarried [ʌn'mærɪd] adj
célibataire

unmistak(e)able [ʌnmɪs'teɪkəbl]
adj indubitable; qu'on ne peut pas ne
pas reconnaître

unnatural [ʌn'nætʃrəl] adj non
naturel(le); (perversion) contre nature

unnecessary [ʌn'nɛsəsərɪ] adj
inutile, superflu(e)

UNO ['juːnəʊ] n abbr = **United
Nations Organization**

unofficial [ʌnə'fɪʃl] adj (news)
officieux(-euse), non officiel(le);
(strike) ≈ sauvage

unpack [ʌn'pæk] vi défaire sa valise
▷ vt (suitcase) défaire; (belongings)
déballer

unpaid [ʌn'peɪd] adj (bill) non payé(e);
(holiday) non-payé(e), sans salaire;
(work) non rétribué(e)

unpleasant [ʌn'plɛznt] adj
déplaisant(e), désagréable

unplug [ʌn'plʌg] vt débrancher

unpopular [ʌn'pɔpjulər] adj
impopulaire

unprecedented [ʌn'prɛsɪdɛntɪd]
adj sans précédent

unpredictable [ʌnprɪ'dɪktəbl] adj
imprévisible

unprotected ['ʌnprə'tɛktɪd] adj
(sex) non protégé(e)

unqualified [ʌn'kwɔlɪfaɪd] adj
(teacher) non diplômé(e), sans titres;
(success) sans réserve, total(e);
(disaster) total(e)

unravel [ʌn'rævl] vt démêler

unreal [ʌn'rɪəl] adj irréel(le);
(extraordinary) incroyable

unrealistic ['ʌnrɪə'lɪstɪk] adj (idea)
irréaliste; (estimate) peu réaliste

unreasonable [ʌn'riːznəbl] adj qui
n'est pas raisonnable

unrelated [ʌnrɪ'leɪtɪd] adj sans
rapport; (people) sans lien de parenté

unreliable [ʌnrɪ'laɪəbl] adj sur qui
(or quoi) on ne peut pas compter,
peu fiable

unrest [ʌn'rɛst] n agitation f,
troubles mpl

unroll [ʌn'rəʊl] vt dérouler

unruly [ʌn'ruːlɪ] adj indiscipliné(e)

unsafe [ʌn'seɪf] adj (in danger) en
danger; (journey, car) dangereux(-euse)

unsatisfactory ['ʌnsætɪs'fæktərɪ]
adj peu satisfaisant(e)

u

unscrew [ʌnˈskruː] vt dévisser

unsettled [ʌnˈsɛtld] adj (restless) perturbé(e); (unpredictable) instable; incertain(e); (not finalized) non résolu(e)

unsettling [ʌnˈsɛtlɪŋ] adj qui a un effet perturbateur

unsightly [ʌnˈsaɪtlɪ] adj disgracieux(-euse), laid(e)

unskilled [ʌnˈskɪld] adj: ~ **worker** manœuvre m

unspoiled [ʌnˈspɔɪld], **unspoilt** [ʌnˈspɔɪlt] adj (place) non dégradé(e)

unstable [ʌnˈsteɪbl] adj instable

unsteady [ʌnˈstɛdɪ] adj mal assuré(e), chancelant(e), instable

unsuccessful [ʌnsəkˈsɛsful] adj (attempt) infructueux(-euse); (writer, proposal) qui n'a pas de succès; **to be** ~ (in attempting sth) ne pas réussir; ne pas avoir de succès; (application) ne pas être retenu(e)

unsuitable [ʌnˈsuːtəbl] adj qui ne convient pas, peu approprié(e); (time) inopportun(e)

unsure [ʌnˈʃuə] adj pas sûr(e); **to be** ~ **of o.s.** ne pas être sûr de soi, manquer de confiance en soi

untidy [ʌnˈtaɪdɪ] adj (room) en désordre; (appearance, dress) débraillé(e); (person: in character) sans ordre, désordonné(e); (work) peu soigné(e)

untie [ʌnˈtaɪ] vt (knot, parcel) défaire; (prisoner, dog) détacher

until [ənˈtɪl] prep jusqu'à; (after negative) avant ▷ conj jusqu'à ce que + sub; (in past, after negative) avant que + sub; ~ **he comes** jusqu'à ce qu'il vienne, jusqu'à son arrivée; ~ **now** jusqu'à présent, jusqu'ici; ~ **then** jusque-là

untrue [ʌnˈtruː] adj (statement) faux (fausse)

unused¹ [ʌnˈjuːzd] adj (new) neuf (neuve)

unused² [ʌnˈjuːst] adj: **to be** ~ **to sth/to doing sth** ne pas avoir l'habitude de qch/de faire qch

unusual [ʌnˈjuːʒuəl] adj insolite, exceptionnel(le), rare; **unusually** adv exceptionnellement, particulièrement

unveil [ʌnˈveɪl] vt dévoiler

unwanted [ʌnˈwɒntɪd] adj (child, pregnancy) non désiré(e); (clothes etc) à donner

unwell [ʌnˈwɛl] adj souffrant(e); **to feel** ~ ne pas se sentir bien

unwilling [ʌnˈwɪlɪŋ] adj: **to be** ~ **to do** ne pas vouloir faire

unwind [ʌnˈwaɪnd] vt (irreg: like **wind²**) dérouler ▷ vi (relax) se détendre

unwise [ʌnˈwaɪz] adj imprudent(e), peu judicieux(-euse)

unwittingly [ʌnˈwɪtɪŋlɪ] adv involontairement

unwrap [ʌnˈræp] vt défaire; ouvrir

unzip [ʌnˈzɪp] vt ouvrir (la fermeture éclair de); (Comput) dézipper

KEYWORD

up [ʌp] prep: **he went up the stairs/ the hill** il a monté l'escalier/la colline; **the cat was up a tree** le chat était dans un arbre; **they live further up the street** ils habitent plus haut dans la rue; **go up that road and turn left** remontez la rue et tournez à gauche

▶ adv 1 en haut; en l'air; (upwards, higher): **up in the sky/in the mountains** (là-haut) dans le ciel/les montagnes; **put it a bit higher up** mettez-le un peu plus haut; **to stand up** (get up) se lever, se mettre debout; (be standing) être debout; **up there** là-haut; **up above** au-dessus

2: **to be up** (out of bed) être levé(e); (prices) avoir augmenté or monté; (finished): **when the year was up** à la fin de l'année

3: **up to** (as far as) jusqu'à; **up to now** jusqu'à présent

4: **to be up to** (depending on): **it's up**

to you c'est à vous de décider; (*equal to*): **he's not up to it** (*job, task etc*) il n'en est pas capable; (*inf: being*): **what is he up to?** qu'est-ce qu'il peut bien faire?
▷ *n*: **ups and downs** hauts et bas *mpl*

up-and-coming [ʌpənd'kʌmɪŋ] *adj* plein(e) d'avenir ou de promesses

upbringing ['ʌpbrɪŋɪŋ] *n* éducation *f*

update [ʌp'deɪt] *vt* mettre à jour

upfront [ʌp'frʌnt] *adj* (*open*) franc (franche) ▷ *adv* (*pay*) d'avance; **to be ~ about sth** ne rien cacher de qch

upgrade [ʌp'greɪd] *vt* (*person*) promouvoir; (*job*) revaloriser; (*property, equipment*) moderniser

upheaval [ʌp'hi:vl] *n* bouleversement *m*; (*in room*) branle-bas *m*; (*event*) crise *f*

uphill [ʌp'hɪl] *adj* qui monte; (*fig: task*) difficile, pénible ▷ *adv* (*face, look*) en amont, vers l'amont; **to go ~** monter

upholstery [ʌp'həʊlstərɪ] *n* rembourrage *m*; (*cover*) tissu *m* d'ameublement; (*of car*) garniture *f*

upload ['ʌpləʊd] *vt* (*Comput*) télécharger

upmarket [ʌp'mɑ:kɪt] *adj* (*product*) haut de gamme *inv*; (*area*) chic *inv*

upon [ə'pɔn] *prep* sur

upper ['ʌpə'] *adj* supérieur(e); du dessus ▷ *n* (*of shoe*) empeigne *f*; **upper-class** *adj* de la haute société, aristocratique; (*district*) élégant(e), huppé(e); (*accent, attitude*) caractéristique des classes supérieures

upright ['ʌpraɪt] *adj* droit(e); (*fig*) droit, honnête

uprising ['ʌpraɪzɪŋ] *n* soulèvement *m*, insurrection *f*

uproar ['ʌprɔ:'] *n* tumulte *m*, vacarme *m*; (*protests*) protestations *fpl*

upset *n* ['ʌpset] dérangement *m* ▷ *vt* [ʌp'set] (*irreg: like* **set**) (*glass etc*) renverser; (*plan*) déranger;

(*person: offend*) contrarier; (*: grieve*) faire de la peine à; bouleverser ▷ *adj* [ʌp'set] contrarié(e); peiné(e); **to have a stomach ~** (BRIT) avoir une indigestion

upside down ['ʌpsaɪd-] *adv* à l'envers; **to turn sth ~** (*fig: place*) mettre sens dessus dessous

upstairs [ʌp'stɛəz] *adv* en haut ▷ *adj* (*room*) du dessus, d'en haut ▷ *n*: **the ~** l'étage *m*

up-to-date ['ʌptə'deɪt] *adj* moderne; (*information*) très récent(e)

upward ['ʌpwəd] *adj* ascendant(e); vers le haut ▷ *adv* = **upwards**

upwards *adv* vers le haut; (*more than*): **~ of** plus de

uranium [juə'reɪnɪəm] *n* uranium *m*

Uranus [juə'reɪnəs] *n* Uranus *f*

urban ['ə:bən] *adj* urbain(e)

urge [ə:dʒ] *n* besoin (impératif), envie (pressante) ▷ *vt* (*person*): **to ~ sb to do** exhorter qn à faire, pousser qn à faire, recommander vivement à qn de faire

urgency ['ə:dʒənsɪ] *n* urgence *f*; (*of tone*) insistance *f*

urgent ['ə:dʒənt] *adj* urgent(e); (*plea, tone*) pressant(e)

urinal ['jʊərɪnl] *n* (BRIT: *place*) urinoir *m*

urinate ['jʊərɪneɪt] *vi* uriner

urine ['jʊərɪn] *n* urine *f*

URL *abbr* (= *uniform resource locator*) URL *f*

US *n abbr* = **United States**

us [ʌs] *pron* nous; *see also* **me**

USA *n abbr* = **United States of America**

USB stick *n* clé *f* USB

use *n* [ju:s] emploi *m*, utilisation *f*; (*usefulness*) utilité *f* ▷ *vt* [ju:z] se servir de, utiliser, employer; **in ~** en usage; **out of ~** hors d'usage; **to be of ~** servir, être utile; **it's no ~** ça ne sert à rien; **to have the ~ of** avoir l'usage de; **she ~d to do it** elle le faisait (autrefois), elle avait coutume de le faire; **to be ~d to** avoir l'habitude de, être habitué(e) à; **use up** vt finir, épuiser; (food) consommer; **used** [juːzd] adj (car) d'occasion; **useful** adj utile; **useless** adj inutile; (inf: person) nul(le); **user** n utilisateur(-trice), usager m; **user-friendly** adj convivial(e), facile d'emploi; **username** n (Comput) nom m d'utilisateur

usual ['juːʒuəl] adj habituel(le); **as ~** comme d'habitude; **usually** adv d'habitude, d'ordinaire

ute [juːt] n (AUST, NZ) pick-up m inv

utensil [juːˈtɛnsl] n ustensile m; **kitchen ~s** batterie f de cuisine

utility [juːˈtɪlɪtɪ] n utilité f; (also: **public ~**) service public

utilize ['juːtɪlaɪz] vt utiliser; (make good use of) exploiter

utmost ['ʌtməust] adj extrême, le plus grand(e) ▷ n: **to do one's ~** faire tout son possible

utter ['ʌtə'] adj total(e), complet(-ète) ▷ vt prononcer, proférer; (sounds) émettre; **utterly** adv complètement, totalement

U-turn ['juːˈtəːn] n demi-tour m; (fig) volte-face f inv

v. abbr = **verse**; (= vide) v.; (= versus) vs; (= volt) V

vacancy ['veɪkənsɪ] n (job) poste vacant; (room) chambre f disponible; **"no vacancies"** "complet"

vacant ['veɪkənt] adj (post) vacant(e); (seat etc) libre, disponible; (expression) distrait(e)

vacate [vəˈkeɪt] vt quitter

vacation [vəˈkeɪʃən] n (esp us) vacances fpl; **on ~** en vacances; **vacationer, vacationist** (us) n vacancier(-ière)

vaccination [væksɪˈneɪʃən] n vaccination f

vaccine ['væksiːn] n vaccin m

vacuum ['vækjum] n vide m; **vacuum cleaner** n aspirateur m

vagina [vəˈdʒaɪnə] n vagin m

vague [veɪg] adj vague, imprécis(e); (blurred: photo, memory) flou(e)

vain [veɪn] adj (useless) vain(e); (conceited) vaniteux(-euse); **in ~** en vain

Valentine's Day ['væləntaɪnz-] *n* Saint-Valentin *f*

valid ['vælɪd] *adj* (document) valide, valable; (excuse) valable

valley ['vælɪ] *n* vallée *f*

valuable ['væljuəbl] *adj* (jewel) de grande valeur; (time, help) précieux(-euse); **valuables** *npl* objets *mpl* de valeur

value ['vælju:] *n* valeur *f* ▷ *vt* (fix price) évaluer, expertiser; (appreciate) apprécier; **values** *npl* (principles) valeurs *fpl*

valve [vælv] *n* (in machine) soupape *f*; (on tyre) valve *f*; (Med) valve, valvule *f*

vampire ['væmpaɪə*ʳ*] *n* vampire *m*

van [væn] *n* (Aut) camionnette *f*

vandal ['vændl] *n* vandale *m/f*; **vandalism** *n* vandalisme *m*; **vandalize** *vt* saccager

vanilla [və'nɪlə] *n* vanille *f*

vanish ['vænɪʃ] *vi* disparaître

vanity ['vænɪtɪ] *n* vanité *f*

vapour, (US) **vapor** ['veɪpə*ʳ*] *n* vapeur *f*; (on window) buée *f*

variable ['vεəriəbl] *adj* variable; (mood) changeant(e)

variant ['vεəriənt] *n* variante *f*

variation [vεəri'eɪʃən] *n* variation *f*; (in opinion) changement *m*

varied ['vεərid] *adj* varié(e), divers(e)

variety [və'raɪətɪ] *n* variété *f*; (quantity) nombre *m*, quantité *f*

various ['vεəriəs] *adj* divers(e), différent(e); (several) divers, plusieurs

varnish ['vɑ:nɪʃ] *n* vernis *m* ▷ *vt* vernir

vary ['vεəri] *vt, vi* varier, changer

vase [vɑ:z] *n* vase *m*

Vaseline® ['væsɪli:n] *n* vaseline *f*

vast [vɑ:st] *adj* vaste, immense; (amount, success) énorme

VAT [væt] *n abbr* (BRIT: = value added tax) TVA *f*

vault [vɔ:lt] *n* (of roof) voûte *f*; (tomb) caveau *m*; (in bank) salle *f* des coffres, chambre forte *f* ▷ *vt* (also: ~ over) sauter (d'un bond)

VCR *n abbr* = **video cassette recorder**

VDU *n abbr* = **visual display unit**

veal [vi:l] *n* veau *m*

veer [vɪə*ʳ*] *vi* tourner; (car, ship) virer

vegan ['vi:gən] *n* végétalien(ne)

vegetable ['vεdʒtəbl] *n* légume *m* ▷ *adj* végétal(e)

vegetarian [vεdʒɪ'tεəriən] *adj*, *n* végétarien(ne); **do you have any ~ dishes?** avez-vous des plats végétariens?

vegetation [vεdʒɪ'teɪʃən] *n* végétation *f*

vehicle ['vi:ɪkl] *n* véhicule *m*

veil [veɪl] *n* voile *m*

vein [veɪn] *n* veine *f*; (on leaf) nervure *f*

Velcro® ['vεlkrəu] *n* velcro® *m*

velvet ['vεlvɪt] *n* velours *m*

vending machine ['vεndɪŋ-] *n* distributeur *m* automatique

vendor ['vεndə*ʳ*] *n* vendeur(-euse); **street ~** marchand ambulant

Venetian blind [vɪ'ni:ʃən-] *n* store vénitien

vengeance ['vεndʒəns] *n* vengeance *f*; **with a ~** (fig) vraiment, pour de bon

venison ['vεnɪsn] *n* venaison *f*

venom ['vεnəm] *n* venin *m*

vent [vεnt] *n* conduit *m* d'aération; (in dress, jacket) fente *f* ▷ *vt* (fig: one's feelings) donner libre cours à

ventilation [vεntɪ'leɪʃən] *n* ventilation *f*, aération *f*

venture ['vεntʃə*ʳ*] *n* entreprise *f* ▷ *vt* risquer, hasarder ▷ *vi* s'aventurer, se risquer; **a business ~** une entreprise commerciale

venue ['vεnju:] *n* lieu *m*

Venus ['vi:nəs] *n* (planet) Vénus *f*

verb [və:b] *n* verbe *m*; **verbal** *adj* verbal(e)

verdict ['və:dɪkt] *n* verdict *m*

verge [və:dʒ] *n* bord *m*; **"soft ~s"** (BRIT) "accotements non stabilisés"; **on the ~ of doing** sur le point de faire

verify ['vεrɪfaɪ] *vt* vérifier

versatile ['və:sətaɪl] *adj* polyvalent(e)

verse [vəːs] n vers mpl; (stanza) strophe f; (in Bible) verset m

version ['vəːʃən] n version f

versus ['vəːsəs] prep contre

vertical ['vəːtɪkl] adj vertical(e)

very ['vɛrɪ] adv très ▷ adj: **the ~ book which** le livre même que; **the ~ last** le tout dernier; **at the ~ least** au moins; **~ much** beaucoup

vessel ['vɛsl] n (Anat, Naut) vaisseau m; (container) récipient m; see also **blood vessel**

vest [vɛst] n (BRIT: underwear) tricot m de corps; (US: waistcoat) gilet m

vet [vɛt] n abbr (BRIT: = veterinary surgeon) vétérinaire m/f; (US: = veteran) ancien(ne) combattant(e) ▷ vt examiner minutieusement

veteran ['vɛtərn] n vétéran m; (also: **war ~**) ancien combattant

veterinary surgeon ['vɛtrɪnərɪ-] (BRIT) n vétérinaire m/f

veto ['viːtəu] n (pl **vetoes**) veto m ▷ vt opposer son veto à

via ['vaɪə] prep par, via

viable ['vaɪəbl] adj viable

vibrate [vaɪ'breɪt] vi: **to ~ (with)** vibrer (de)

vibration [vaɪ'breɪʃən] n vibration f

vicar ['vɪkə*] n pasteur m (de l'Église anglicane)

vice [vaɪs] n (evil) vice m; (Tech) étau m; **vice-chairman** (irreg) n vice-président m

vice versa ['vaɪsɪ'vəːsə] adv vice versa

vicinity [vɪ'sɪnɪtɪ] n environs mpl, alentours mpl

vicious ['vɪʃəs] adj (remark) cruel(le), méchant(e); (blow) brutal(e); (dog) méchant(e), dangereux(-euse); **a ~ circle** un cercle vicieux

victim ['vɪktɪm] n victime f

victor ['vɪktə*] n vainqueur m

Victorian [vɪk'tɔːrɪən] adj victorien(ne)

victorious [vɪk'tɔːrɪəs] adj victorieux(-euse)

victory ['vɪktərɪ] n victoire f

video ['vɪdɪəu] n (video film) vidéo f; (also: **~ cassette**) vidéocassette f; (also: **~ cassette recorder**) magnétoscope m ▷ vt (with recorder) enregistrer; (with camera) filmer; **video camera** n caméra f vidéo inv; **video game** n jeu m vidéo inv; **videophone** n vidéophone m; **video recorder** n magnétoscope m; **video shop** n vidéoclub m; **video tape** n bande f vidéo inv; (cassette) vidéocassette f

vie [vaɪ] vi: **to ~ with** lutter avec, rivaliser avec

Vienna [vɪ'ɛnə] n Vienne

Vietnam, Viet Nam ['vjɛt'næm] n Viêt-nam or Vietnam m; **Vietnamese** [vjɛtnə'miːz] adj vietnamien(ne) ▷ n (pl inv) Vietnamien(ne)

view [vjuː] n vue f; (opinion) avis m, vue f ▷ vt voir, regarder; (situation) considérer; (house) visiter; **in full ~ of sb** sous les yeux de qn; **in my ~** à mon avis; **in ~ of the fact that** étant donné que; **viewer** n (TV) téléspectateur(-trice); **viewpoint** n point m de vue

vigilant ['vɪdʒɪlənt] adj vigilant(e)

vigorous ['vɪgərəs] adj vigoureux(-euse)

vile [vaɪl] adj (action) vil(e); (smell, food) abominable; (temper) massacrant(e)

villa ['vɪlə] n villa f

village ['vɪlɪdʒ] n village m; **villager** n villageois(e)

villain ['vɪlən] n (scoundrel) scélérat m; (BRIT: criminal) bandit m; (in novel etc) traître m

vinaigrette [vɪneɪ'grɛt] n vinaigrette f

vine [vaɪn] n vigne f

vinegar ['vɪnɪgə*] n vinaigre m

vineyard ['vɪnjɑːd] n vignoble m

vintage ['vɪntɪdʒ] n (year) année f, millésime m ▷ cpd (car) d'époque; (wine) de grand cru

vinyl ['vaɪnl] n vinyle m

viola [vɪ'əʊlə] n alto m

violate ['vaɪəleɪt] vt violer

violation [vaɪə'leɪʃən] n violation f; **in ~ of** (rule, law) en infraction à, en violation de

violence ['vaɪələns] n violence f

violent ['vaɪələnt] adj violent(e)

violet ['vaɪələt] adj (colour) violet(te) ▷ n (plant) violette f

violin [vaɪə'lɪn] n violon m

VIP n abbr (= very important person) VIP m

viral ['vaɪərəl] adj (also Comput) viral(e)

virgin ['vəːdʒɪn] n vierge f

Virgo ['vəːgəʊ] n la Vierge

virtual ['vəːtjuəl] adj (Comput, Physics) virtuel(le); (in effect): **it's a ~ impossibility** c'est quasiment impossible; **virtually** adv (almost) pratiquement; **virtual reality** n (Comput) réalité virtuelle

virtue ['vəːtju:] n vertu f; (advantage) mérite m, avantage m; **by ~ of** en vertu or raison de

virus ['vaɪərəs] n virus m

visa ['vi:zə] n visa m

vise [vaɪs] n (us Tech) = **vice**

visibility [vɪzɪ'bɪlɪtɪ] n visibilité f

visible ['vɪzəbl] adj visible

vision ['vɪʒən] n (sight) vue f, vision f; (foresight, in dream) vision f

visit ['vɪzɪt] n visite f; (stay) séjour m ▷ vt (person: us: also: ~ **with**) rendre visite à; (place) visiter; **visiting hours** npl heures fpl de visite; **visitor** n visiteur(-euse); (to one's house) invité(e); **visitor centre**, (us) **visitor center** n hall m or centre m d'accueil

visual ['vɪzjuəl] adj visuel(le); **visualize** vt se représenter

vital ['vaɪtl] adj vital(e); **of ~ importance (to sb/sth)** d'une importance capitale (pour qn/qch)

vitality [vaɪ'tælɪtɪ] n vitalité f

vitamin ['vɪtəmɪn] n vitamine f

vivid ['vɪvɪd] adj (account) frappant(e), vivant(e); (light, imagination) vif (vive)

V-neck ['viːnɛk] n décolleté m en V

vocabulary [vəʊ'kæbjʊlərɪ] n vocabulaire m

vocal ['vəʊkl] adj vocal(e); (articulate) qui n'hésite pas à s'exprimer, qui sait faire entendre ses opinions

vocational [vəʊ'keɪʃənl] adj professionnel(le)

vodka ['vɔdkə] n vodka f

vogue [vəʊg] n: **to be in ~** être en vogue or à la mode

voice [vɔɪs] n voix f ▷ vt (opinion) exprimer, formuler; **voice mail** n (system) messagerie f vocale, boîte f vocale; (device) répondeur m

void [vɔɪd] n vide m ▷ adj (invalid) nul(le); (empty): **~ of** vide de, dépourvu(e) de

volatile ['vɔlətaɪl] adj volatil(e); (fig: person) versatile; (: situation) explosif(-ive)

volcano [vɔl'keɪnəʊ] (pl **volcanoes**) n volcan m

volleyball ['vɔlɪbɔːl] n volley(-ball) m

volt [vəʊlt] n volt m; **voltage** n tension f, voltage m

volume ['vɔljuːm] n volume m; (of tank) capacité f

voluntarily ['vɔləntrɪlɪ] adv volontairement

voluntary ['vɔləntərɪ] adj volontaire; (unpaid) bénévole

volunteer [vɔlən'tɪə] n volontaire m/f ▷ vt (information) donner spontanément ▷ vi (Mil) s'engager comme volontaire; **to ~ to do** se proposer pour faire

vomit ['vɔmɪt] n vomissure f ▷ vt, vi vomir

vote [vəʊt] n vote m, suffrage m; (votes cast) voix f, vote; (franchise) droit m de vote ▷ vt (chairman) élire; (propose): **to ~ that** proposer que + sub ▷ vi voter; **~ of thanks** discours m de remerciement;

voter n électeur(-trice); **voting** n
scrutin m, vote m

voucher ['vautʃər] n (for meal, petrol,
gift) bon m

vow [vau] n vœu m, serment m
▷ vi jurer

vowel ['vauəl] n voyelle f

voyage ['vɔɪɪdʒ] n voyage m par mer,
traversée f

vulgar ['vʌlgər] adj vulgaire

vulnerable ['vʌlnərəbl] adj
vulnérable

vulture ['vʌltʃər] n vautour m

waddle ['wɔdl] vi se dandiner

wade [weɪd] vi: **to ~ through**
marcher dans, patauger dans; (fig:
book) venir à bout de

wafer ['weɪfər] n (Culin) gaufrette f

waffle ['wɔfl] n (Culin) gaufre f ▷ vi
parler pour ne rien dire; faire du
remplissage

wag [wæg] vt agiter, remuer ▷ vi
remuer

wage [weɪdʒ] n (also: **~s**) salaire m,
paye f ▷ vt: **to ~ war** faire la guerre

wag(g)on ['wægən] n (horse-drawn)
chariot m; (BRIT Rail) wagon m (de
marchandises)

wail [weɪl] n gémissement m; (of siren)
hurlement m ▷ vi gémir; (siren) hurler

waist [weɪst] n taille f, ceinture f;
waistcoat n (BRIT) gilet m

wait [weɪt] n attente f ▷ vi attendre;
to ~ for sb/sth attendre qn/qch; **to
keep sb ~ing** faire attendre qn; **~ for
me, please** attendez-moi, s'il vous

plaît; **I can't ~ to ...** (fig) je meurs d'envie de ...; **to lie in ~ for** guetter; **wait on** vt fus servir; **waiter** n garçon m (de café), serveur m; **waiting list** n liste f d'attente; **waiting room** n salle f d'attente; **waitress** ['weitris] n serveuse f

waive [weiv] vt renoncer à, abandonner

wake [weik] (pt **woke** or **waked**, pp **woken** or **waked**) vt (also: **~ up**) réveiller ▷ vi (also: **~ up**) se réveiller ▷ n (for dead person) veillée f mortuaire; (Naut) sillage m

Wales [weilz] n pays m de Galles; **the Prince of ~** le prince de Galles

walk [wɔːk] n promenade f; (short) petit tour; (gait) démarche f; (path) chemin m; (in park etc) allée f ▷ vi marcher; (for pleasure, exercise) se promener ▷ vt (distance) faire à pied; (dog) promener; **10 minutes' ~ from** à 10 minutes de marche de; **to go for a ~** se promener; faire un tour; **from all ~s of life** de toutes conditions sociales; **walk out** vi (go out) sortir; (as protest) partir (en signe de protestation); (strike) se mettre en grève; **to ~ out on sb** quitter qn; **walker** n (person) marcheur(-euse); **walkie-talkie** ['wɔːki'tɔːki] n talkie-walkie m; **walking** n marche f à pied; **walking shoes** npl chaussures fpl de marche; **walking stick** n canne f; **Walkman®** n Walkman® m; **walkway** n promenade f, cheminement piéton

wall [wɔːl] n mur m, (of tunnel, cave) paroi f

wallet ['wɔlit] n portefeuille m; **I can't find my ~** je ne retrouve plus mon portefeuille

wallpaper ['wɔːlpeipə'] n papier peint ▷ vt tapisser

walnut ['wɔːlnʌt] n noix f, (tree, wood) noyer m

walrus ['wɔːlrəs] (pl **walrus** or **walruses**) n morse m

waltz [wɔːlts] n valse f ▷ vi valser

wand [wɔnd] n (also: **magic ~**) baguette f (magique)

wander ['wɔndə'] vi (person) errer, aller sans but; (thoughts) vagabonder ▷ vt errer dans

want [wɔnt] vt vouloir; (need) avoir besoin de ▷ n: **for ~ of** par manque de, faute de; **to ~ to do** vouloir faire; **to ~ sb to do** vouloir que qn fasse; **wanted** adj (criminal) recherché(e) par la police

war [wɔː'] n guerre f, **to make ~ (on)** faire la guerre (à)

ward [wɔːd] n (in hospital) salle f, (Pol) section électorale; (Law: child: also: **~ of court**) pupille m/f

warden ['wɔːdn] n (BRIT: of institution) directeur(-trice); (of park, game reserve) gardien(ne); (BRIT: also: **traffic ~**) contractuel(le)

wardrobe ['wɔːdrəub] n (cupboard) armoire f, (clothes) garde-robe f

warehouse ['weəhaus] n entrepôt m

warfare ['wɔːfeə'] n guerre f

warhead ['wɔːhed] n (in Mil) ogive f

warm [wɔːm] adj chaud(e); (person, thanks, welcome, applause) chaleureux(-euse); **it's ~** il fait chaud; **I'm ~** j'ai chaud; **warm up** vi (person, room) se réchauffer; (athlete, discussion) s'échauffer ▷ vt (food) (faire) réchauffer; (water) (faire) chauffer; (engine) faire chauffer; **warmly** adv (dress) chaudement; (thank, welcome) chaleureusement; **warmth** n chaleur f

warn [wɔːn] vt avertir, prévenir; **to ~ sb (not) to do** conseiller à qn de (ne pas) faire; **warning** n avertissement m; (notice) avis m; **warning light** n avertisseur lumineux

warrant ['wɔrnt] n (guarantee) garantie f, (Law: to arrest) mandat m d'arrêt; (: to search) mandat de perquisition ▷ vt (justify, merit) justifier

warranty ['wɔrənti] n garantie f

warrior ['wɒrɪə'] n guerrier(-ière)
Warsaw ['wɔːsɔː] n Varsovie
warship ['wɔːʃɪp] n navire m de guerre
wart [wɔːt] n verrue f
wartime ['wɔːtaɪm] n: **in ~** en temps de guerre
wary ['wɛərɪ] adj prudent(e)
was [wɒz] pt of **be**
wash [wɒʃ] vt laver ▷ vi se laver; (sea): **to ~ over/against sth** inonder/baigner qch ▷ n (clothes) lessive f; (washing programme) lavage m; (of ship) sillage m; **to have a ~** se laver, faire sa toilette; **wash up** vi (BRIT) faire la vaisselle; (US: have a wash) se débarbouiller; **washbasin** n lavabo m; **washer** n (Tech) rondelle f, joint m; **washing** n (BRIT: linen etc: dirty) linge m; (: clean) lessive f; **washing line** n (BRIT) corde f à linge; **washing machine** n machine f à laver; **washing powder** n (BRIT) lessive f (en poudre)
Washington ['wɒʃɪŋtən] n Washington m
wash: washing-up n (BRIT) vaisselle f, **washing-up liquid** n (BRIT) produit m pour la vaisselle; **washroom** n (US) toilettes fpl
wasn't ['wɒznt] = **was not**
wasp [wɒsp] n guêpe f
waste [weɪst] n gaspillage m; (of time) perte f; (rubbish) déchets mpl; (also: **household ~**) ordures fpl ▷ adj (land, ground: in city) à l'abandon; (leftover): **~ material** déchets ▷ vt gaspiller; (time, opportunity) perdre; **waste ground** n (BRIT) terrain m vague; **wastepaper basket** n corbeille f à papier
watch [wɒtʃ] n montre f; (act of watching) surveillance f; (guard: Mil) sentinelle f; (: Naut) homme m de quart; (Naut: spell of duty) quart m ▷ vt (look at) observer (: match, programme) regarder; (spy on, guard) surveiller; (be careful with) faire attention à ▷ vi regarder; (keep guard) monter la

garde; **to keep ~** faire le guet; **watch out** vi faire attention; **watchdog** n chien m de garde; (fig) gardien(ne); **watch strap** n bracelet m de montre
water ['wɔːtə'] n eau f ▷ vt (plant, garden) arroser ▷ vi (eyes) pleurer; **in British ~s** dans les eaux territoriales Britanniques; **to make sb's mouth ~** mettre l'eau à la bouche de qn; **water down** vt (milk etc) couper avec de l'eau; (fig: story) édulcorer; **watercolour**, (us) **watercolor** n aquarelle f; **watercress** n cresson m (de fontaine); **waterfall** n chute f d'eau; **watering can** n arrosoir m; **watermelon** n pastèque f; **waterproof** adj imperméable; **water-skiing** n ski m nautique
watt [wɒt] n watt m
wave [weɪv] n vague f; (of hand) geste m, signe m; (Radio) onde f; (in hair) ondulation f; (fig) vague ▷ vi faire signe de la main; (flag) flotter au vent; (grass) ondoyer ▷ vt (handkerchief) agiter; (stick) brandir; **wavelength** n longueur f d'ondes
waver ['weɪvə'] vi vaciller; (voice) trembler; (person) hésiter
wavy ['weɪvɪ] adj (hair, surface) ondulé(e); (line) onduleux(-euse)
wax [wæks] n cire f; (for skis) fart m ▷ vt cirer; (car) lustrer; (skis) farter ▷ vi (moon) croître
way [weɪ] n chemin m, voie f; (distance) distance f; (direction) chemin m, direction f; (manner) façon f, manière f; (habit) habitude f, façon f; **which ~? – this ~/that ~** par où ? or de quel côté? – par ici/par là; **to lose one's ~** perdre son chemin; **on the ~ (to)** en route (pour); **to be on one's ~** être en route; **to be in the ~** bloquer le passage; (fig) gêner; **it's a long ~ away** c'est loin d'ici; **to go out of one's ~ to do** (fig) se donner beaucoup de mal pour faire; **to be under ~** (work, project) être en cours; **in a ~** dans un sens; **by the ~** à

propos; "~ **in**" (BRIT) "entrée"; "~ **out**" (BRIT) "sortie"; **the ~ back** le chemin du retour; "**give ~**" (BRIT Aut) "cédez la priorité"; **no ~!** (inf) pas question!

W.C. n abbr (BRIT: = water closet) w.-c. mpl, waters mpl

we [wi:] pl pron nous

weak [wi:k] adj faible; (health) fragile; (beam etc) peu solide; (tea, coffee) léger(-ère); **weaken** vi faiblir ▷ vt affaiblir; **weakness** n faiblesse f; (fault) point m faible

wealth [wɛlθ] n (money, resources) richesse(s) f(pl); (of details) profusion f; **wealthy** adj riche

weapon ['wɛpən] n arme f; ~s **of mass destruction** armes fpl de destruction massive

wear [wɛə^r] (pt wore, pp worn) n (use) usage m; (deterioration through use) usure f ▷ vt (clothes) porter; (put on) mettre; (damage: through use) user ▷ vi (last) faire de l'usage; (rub etc: through use) s'user; **sports/baby~** vêtements mpl de sport/pour bébés; **evening ~** tenue f de soirée; **wear off** vt user; (person, strength) épuiser

weary ['wɪərɪ] adj (tired) épuisé(e); (dispirited) las (lasse); abattu(e) ▷ vi: **to ~ of** se lasser de

weasel ['wi:zl] n (Zool) belette f

weather ['wɛðə^r] n temps m ▷ vt (storm: lit, fig) essuyer; (crisis) survivre à; **under the ~** (fig: ill) mal fichu(e); **weather forecast** n prévisions fpl météorologiques, météo f

weave [wi:v] (pt wove, pp woven) vt (cloth) tisser; (basket) tresser

web [wɛb] n (of spider) toile f; (on duck's foot) palmure f; (fig) tissu m; (Comput): **the (World-Wide) W~** le Web; **web address** n adresse f Web; **webcam** n webcam f; **webinar** ['wɛbɪnɑ:^r] n (Comput) séminaire m en ligne; **web page** n (Comput) page f Web; **website** n (Comput) site m Web

wed [wɛd] (pt, pp wedded) vt épouser ▷ vi se marier

we'd [wi:d] = **we had**; **we would**

wedding ['wɛdɪŋ] n mariage m; **wedding anniversary** n anniversaire m de mariage; **silver/golden wedding anniversary** noces fpl d'argent/d'or; **wedding day** n jour m du mariage; **wedding dress** n robe f de mariée; **wedding ring** n alliance f

wedge [wɛdʒ] n (of wood etc) coin m; (under door etc) cale f; (of cake) part f ▷ vt (fix) caler; (push) enfoncer, coincer

Wednesday ['wɛdnzdɪ] n mercredi m

wee [wi:] adj (SCOTTISH) petit(e); tout(e) petit(e)

weed [wi:d] n mauvaise herbe ▷ vt désherber; **weedkiller** n désherbant m

week [wi:k] n semaine f; **a ~ today/on Tuesday** aujourd'hui/mardi en huit; **weekday** n jour m de semaine; (Comm) jour ouvrable; **weekend** n week-end m; **weekly** adv une fois par semaine, chaque semaine ▷ adj, n hebdomadaire m

weep [wi:p] (pt, pp wept) vi (person) pleurer

weigh [weɪ] vt, vi peser; **to ~ anchor** lever l'ancre; **weigh up** vt examiner

weight [weɪt] n poids m; **to put on/lose ~** grossir/maigrir; **weightlifting** n haltérophilie f

weir [wɪə^r] n barrage m

weird [wɪəd] adj bizarre; (eerie) surnaturel(le)

welcome ['wɛlkəm] adj bienvenu(e) ▷ n accueil m ▷ vt accueillir; (also: **bid ~**) souhaiter la bienvenue à; (be glad of) se réjouir de; **you're ~!** (after thanks) de rien, il n'y a pas de quoi

weld [wɛld] vt souder

welfare ['wɛlfɛə^r] n (wellbeing) bien-être m; (social aid) assistance sociale; **welfare state** n État-providence m

well [wɛl] n puits m ▷ adv bien ▷ adj: **to be ~** aller bien ▷ excl eh bien!; (relief also) bon!; (resignation) enfin!; **~ done!** bravo!; **get ~ soon!** remets-toi vite!; **to do ~** bien réussir; (business) prospérer; **as ~** (in addition) aussi, également; **as ~ as** aussi bien que or de; en plus de

we'll [wi:l] = we will; we shall

well: **well-behaved** adj sage, obéissant(e); **well-built** adj (person) bien bâti(e); **well-dressed** adj bien habillé(e), bien vêtu(e); **well-groomed** [-'gru:md] adj très soigné(e)

wellies ['weliz] npl (BRIT inf) = **wellingtons**

wellingtons ['weliŋtənz] npl (also: **wellington boots**) bottes fpl en caoutchouc

well: **well-known** adj (person) bien connu(e); **well-off** adj aisé(e), assez riche; **well-paid** [wel'peid] adj bien payé(e)

Welsh [welʃ] adj gallois(e) ▷ n (Ling) gallois m; **the Welsh** npl (people) les Gallois; **Welshman** (irreg) n Gallois m; **Welshwoman** (irreg) n Galloise f

went [wɛnt] pt of **go**

wept [wɛpt] pt, pp of **weep**

were [wəː] pt of **be**

we're [wɪə] = we are

weren't [wəːnt] = were not

west [wɛst] n ouest m ▷ adj (wind) d'ouest; (side) ouest inv ▷ adv à or vers l'ouest; **the W~** l'Occident m, l'Ouest; **westbound** ['wɛstbaund] adj en direction de l'ouest; (carriageway) ouest inv; **western** adj occidental(e), de or à l'ouest ▷ n (Cine) western m; **West Indian** adj antillais(e) ▷ n Antillais(e); **West Indies** [-'ɪndɪz] npl Antilles fpl

wet [wɛt] adj mouillé(e); (damp) humide; (soaked: also: **~ through**) trempé(e); (rainy) pluvieux(-euse); **to get ~** se mouiller; **"~ paint"** "attention peinture fraîche"; **wetsuit** n combinaison f de plongée

we've [wi:v] = we have

whack [wæk] vt donner un grand coup à

whale [weɪl] n (Zool) baleine f

wharf (pl **wharves**) [wɔːf, wɔːvz] n quai m

what [wɔt] adj **1** (in questions) quel(le); **what size is he?** quelle taille fait-il?; **what colour is it?** de quelle couleur est-ce?; **what books do you need?** quels livres vous faut-il?

2 (in exclamations): **what a mess!** quel désordre!; **what a fool I am!** que je suis bête!

▷ pron **1** (interrogative) que; de/à/en etc quoi; **what are you doing?** que faites-vous?, qu'est-ce que vous faites?; **what is happening?** qu'est-ce qui se passe?, que se passe-t-il?; **what are you talking about?** de quoi parlez-vous?; **what are you thinking about?** à quoi pensez-vous?; **what is it called?** comment est-ce que ça s'appelle?; **what about me?** et moi?; **what about doing ...?** et si on faisait ...?

2 (relative: subject) ce qui; (: direct object) ce que; (: indirect object) ce à quoi, ce dont; **I saw what you did/was on the table** j'ai vu ce que vous avez fait/ce qui était sur la table; **tell me what you remember** dites-moi ce dont vous vous souvenez; **what I want is a cup of tea** ce que je veux, c'est une tasse de thé

▷ excl (disbelieving) quoi!, comment!

whatever [wɔt'ɛvə] adj: **take ~ book you prefer** prenez le livre que vous préférez, n'importe lequel; **~ book you take** quel que soit le livre que vous preniez ▷ pron: **do ~ is necessary** faites (tout) ce qui est nécessaire; **~ happens** quoi qu'il arrive; **no reason ~** or **whatsoever** pas la moindre raison; **nothing ~** or **whatsoever** rien du tout

whatsoever [wɒtsəʊˈevəʳ] adj see whatever

wheat [wiːt] n blé m, froment m

wheel [wiːl] n roue f; (Aut: also: **steering ~**) volant m; (Naut) gouvernail m ▷ vt (pram etc) pousser, rouler ▷ vi (birds) tournoyer; (also: **~ round**: person) se retourner, faire volte-face; **wheelbarrow** n brouette f; **wheelchair** n fauteuil roulant; **wheel clamp** n (Aut) sabot m (de Denver)

wheeze [wiːz] vi respirer bruyamment

KEYWORD

when [wɛn] adv quand; **when did he go?** quand est-ce qu'il est parti?
▶ conj **1** (at, during, after the time that) quand, lorsque; **she was reading when I came in** elle lisait quand or lorsque je suis entré
2 (on, at which): **on the day when I met him** le jour où je l'ai rencontré
3 (whereas) alors que; **I thought I was wrong when in fact I was right** j'ai cru que j'avais tort alors qu'en fait j'avais raison

whenever [wɛnˈevəʳ] adv quand donc ▷ conj quand; (every time that) chaque fois que

where [wɛəʳ] adv, conj où; **this is ~** c'est là que; **whereabouts** adv où donc ▷ n: **nobody knows his whereabouts** personne ne sait où il se trouve; **whereas** conj alors que; **whereby** adv (formal) par lequel (or laquelle etc); **wherever** adv où donc ▷ conj où que + sub; **sit wherever you like** asseyez-vous (là) où vous voulez

whether [ˈwɛðəʳ] conj si; **I don't know ~ to accept or not** je ne sais pas si je dois accepter ou non; **it's doubtful ~** il est peu probable que + sub; **~ you go or not** que vous y alliez ou non

KEYWORD

which [wɪtʃ] adj **1** (interrogative, direct, indirect) quel(le); **which picture do you want?** quel tableau voulez-vous?; **which one?** lequel (laquelle)?
2: **in which case** auquel cas; **we got there at 8pm, by which time the cinema was full** quand nous sommes arrivés à 20h, le cinéma était complet

▶ pron **1** (interrogative) lequel (laquelle), lesquels (lesquelles) pl; **I don't mind which** peu importe lequel; **which (of these) are yours?** lesquels sont à vous?; **tell me which you want** dites-moi lesquels or ceux que vous voulez
2 (relative: subject) qui; (: object) que; sur/vers etc lequel (laquelle) (NB: à + lequel = **auquel**; de + lequel = **duquel**); **the apple which you ate/which is on the table** la pomme que vous avez mangée/qui est sur la table; **the chair on which you are sitting** la chaise sur laquelle vous êtes assis; **the book of which you spoke** le livre dont vous avez parlé; **he said he knew, which is true/I was afraid of** il a dit qu'il le savait, ce qui est vrai/ce que je craignais; **after which** après quoi

whichever [wɪtʃˈevəʳ] adj: **take ~ book you prefer** prenez le livre que vous préférez, peu importe lequel; **~ book you take** quel que soit le livre que vous preniez

while [waɪl] n moment m ▷ conj pendant que; (as long as) tant que; (as, whereas) alors que; (though) bien que + sub, quoique + sub; **for a ~** pendant quelque temps; **in a ~** dans un moment

whilst [waɪlst] conj = **while**

whim [wɪm] n caprice m

whine [waɪn] n gémissement m; (of engine, siren) plainte stridente ▷ vi

W

gémir, geindre, pleurnicher; (dog, engine, siren) gémir

whip [wɪp] n fouet m; (for riding) cravache f; (Pol: person) chef m de file (assurant la discipline dans son groupe parlementaire) ▷ vt fouetter; (snatch) enlever (or sortir) brusquement; **whipped cream** n crème fouettée

whirl [wə:l] n tourbillon m; (dancers) tournoyer ▷ vt faire tourbillonner; faire tournoyer

whisk [wɪsk] n (Culin) fouet m ▷ vt (eggs) fouetter, battre; **to ~ sb away or off** emmener qn rapidement

whiskers ['wɪskəz] npl (of animal) moustaches fpl; (of man) favoris mpl

whisky, (IRISH, US) **whiskey** ['wɪski] n whisky m

whisper ['wɪspə'] n chuchotement m ▷ vt, vi chuchoter

whistle ['wɪsl] n (sound) sifflement m; (object) sifflet m ▷ vi siffler ▷ vt siffler, siffloter

white [waɪt] adj blanc (blanche); (with fear) blême ▷ n blanc m; (person) blanc (blanche); **White House** n (US): **the White House** la Maison-Blanche; **whitewash** n (paint) lait m de chaux ▷ vt blanchir à la chaux; (fig) blanchir

whiting ['waɪtɪŋ] n (pl inv: fish) merlan m

Whitsun ['wɪtsn] n la Pentecôte

whittle ['wɪtl] vt: **to ~ away, to ~ down** (costs) réduire, rogner

whizz [wɪz] vi aller (or passer) à toute vitesse

who [hu:] pron qui

whoever [hu:ˈɛvə'] pron: **~ finds it** celui (celle) qui le trouve (, qui que ce soit), quiconque le trouve; **ask ~ you like** demandez à qui vous voulez; **~ he marries** qui que ce soit or quelle que soit la personne qu'il épouse; **~ told you that?** qui a bien pu vous dire ça?, qui donc vous a dit ça?

whole [həul] adj (complete) entier(-ière), tout(e); (not broken) intact(e), complet(-ète) ▷ n (entire unit) tout

m; (all): **the ~ of** la totalité de, tout(e) le; **the ~ of the town** la ville tout entière; **on the ~, as a ~** dans l'ensemble; **wholefood(s)** n(pl) aliments complets; **wholeheartedly** [həulˈhɑːtɪdlɪ] adv sans réserve; **to agree wholeheartedly** être entièrement d'accord; **wholemeal** adj (BRIT: flour, bread) complet(-ète); **wholesale** n (vente f en) gros m ▷ adj (price) de gros; (destruction) systématique; **wholewheat** adj = **wholemeal**; **wholly** adv entièrement, tout à fait

KEYWORD

whom [hu:m] pron **1** (interrogative) qui; **whom did you see?** qui avez-vous vu?; **to whom did you give it?** à qui l'avez-vous donné?
2 (relative) que à/de/etc qui; **the man whom I saw/to whom I spoke** l'homme que j'ai vu/à qui j'ai parlé

whore [hɔ:'] n (inf: pej) putain f

KEYWORD

whose [hu:z] adj **1** (possessive, interrogative): **whose book is this?, whose is this book?** à qui est ce livre?; **whose pencil have you taken?** à qui est le crayon que vous avez pris?, c'est le crayon de qui que vous avez pris?; **whose daughter are you?** de qui êtes-vous la fille?
2 (possessive, relative): **the man whose son you rescued** l'homme dont or de qui vous avez sauvé le fils; **the girl whose sister you were speaking to** la fille à la sœur de qui or de laquelle vous parliez; **the woman whose car was stolen** la femme dont la voiture a été volée
▷ pron à qui; **whose is this?** à qui est ceci?; **I know whose it is** je sais à qui c'est

KEYWORD

why [waɪ] *adv* pourquoi; **why not?** pourquoi pas?
▶ *conj*: **I wonder why he said that** je me demande pourquoi il a dit ça; **that's not why I'm here** ce n'est pas pour ça que je suis là; **the reason why** la raison pour laquelle
▶ *excl* eh bien!, tiens!; **why, it's you!** tiens, c'est vous!; **why, that's impossible!** voyons, c'est impossible!

wicked ['wɪkɪd] *adj* méchant(e); *(mischievous: grin, look)* espiègle, malicieux(-euse); *(crime)* pervers(e); *(inf: very good)* génial(e) *(inf)*

wicket ['wɪkɪt] *n* (Cricket: stumps) guichet *m*; (: *grass area*) espace compris entre les deux guichets

wide [waɪd] *adj* large; *(area, knowledge)* vaste, très étendu(e); *(choice)* grand(e) ▷ *adv*: **to open ~** ouvrir tout grand; **to shoot ~** tirer à côté; **it is 3 metres ~** cela fait 3 mètres de large; **widely** *adv (different)* radicalement; *(spaced)* sur une grande étendue; *(believed)* généralement; *(travel)* beaucoup; **widen** *vt* élargir ▷ *vi* s'élargir; **wide open** *adj* grand(e) ouvert(e); **widespread** *adj (belief etc)* très répandu(e)

widow ['wɪdəu] *n* veuve *f*; **widower** *n* veuf *m*

width [wɪdθ] *n* largeur *f*

wield [wiːld] *vt (sword)* manier; *(power)* exercer

wife [waɪf] *(pl* **wives**) [waɪf, waɪvz] *n* femme *f*, épouse *f*

Wi-Fi ['waɪfaɪ] *n* wifi *m*

wig [wɪg] *n* perruque *f*

wild [waɪld] *adj* sauvage; *(sea)* déchaîné(e); *(idea, life)* fou (folle); *(behaviour)* déchaîné(e), extravagant(e); *(inf: angry)* hors de soi, furieux(-euse) ▷ *n*: **the ~** la nature; **wilderness** ['wɪldənɪs] *n*

désert *m*, région *f* sauvage; **wildlife** *n* faune *f*(et flore *f*); **wildly** *adv (behave)* de manière déchaînée; *(applaud)* frénétiquement; *(hit, guess)* au hasard; *(happy)* follement

KEYWORD

will [wɪl] *aux vb* **1** *(forming future tense)*: **I will finish it tomorrow** je le finirai demain; **I will have finished it by tomorrow** je l'aurai fini d'ici demain; **will you do it? — yes I will/ no I won't** le ferez-vous? — oui/non
2 *(in conjectures, predictions)*: **he will** or **he'll be there by now** il doit être arrivé à l'heure qu'il est; **that will be the postman** ça doit être le facteur
3 *(in commands, requests, offers)*: **will you be quiet!** voulez-vous bien vous taire!; **will you help me?** est-ce que vous pouvez m'aider?; **will you have a cup of tea?** voulez-vous une tasse de thé?; **I won't put up with it!** je ne le tolérerai pas!
▶ *vt (pt, pp* **willed**): **to will sb to do** souhaiter ardemment que qn fasse; **he willed himself to go on** par un suprême effort de volonté, il continua
▶ *n* **1** volonté *f*; **against one's will** à contre-cœur
2 *(document)* testament *m*

willing ['wɪlɪŋ] *adj* de bonne volonté, serviable; **he's ~ to do it** il est disposé à le faire, il veut bien le faire; **willingly** *adv* volontiers

willow ['wɪləu] *n* saule *m*

willpower ['wɪl'pauə⁸] *n* volonté *f*

wilt [wɪlt] *vi* dépérir

win [wɪn] *(pt, pp* **won**) *n (in sports etc)* victoire *f* ▷ *vt (battle, money)* gagner; *(prize, contract)* remporter; *(popularity)* acquérir ▷ *vi* gagner; **win over** *vt* convaincre

wince [wɪns] *vi* tressaillir

wind¹ [wɪnd] *n (also Med)* vent *m*; *(breath)* souffle *m* ▷ *vt (take breath*

W

away) couper le souffle à; **the ~(s)** *(Mus)* les instruments *mpl* à vent

wind² *(pt, pp* **wound)** *(waind, waund) vt* enrouler; *(wrap)* envelopper; *(clock, toy)* remonter ▷ *vi (road, river)* serpenter; **wind down** *vt (car window)* baisser; *(fig: production, business)* réduire progressivement; **wind up** *vt (clock)* remonter; *(debate)* terminer, clôturer

windfall ['wɪndfɔːl] *n* coup *m* de chance

wind farm *n* ferme *f* éolienne

winding ['waɪndɪŋ] *adj (road)* sinueux(-euse); *(staircase)* tournant(e)

windmill ['wɪndmɪl] *n* moulin *m* à vent

window ['wɪndəʊ] *n* fenêtre *f; (in car, train: also:* **~pane)** vitre *f; (in shop etc)* vitrine *f; (window box)* n jardinière *f;* **window cleaner** *n (person)* laveur(-euse) de vitres; **window pane** *n* vitre *f,* carreau *m;* **window seat** *n (on plane)* place *f* côté hublot; **windowsill** *n (inside)* appui *m* de la fenêtre; *(outside)* rebord *m* de la fenêtre

windscreen ['wɪndskriːn] *n* parebrise *m inv;* **windscreen wiper** *n* essuie-glace *m inv*

windshield ['wɪndʃiːld] *(us) n* = **windscreen**

windsurfing ['wɪndsəːfɪŋ] *n* planche *f* à voile

wind turbine [-təːbaɪn] *n* éolienne *f*

windy ['wɪndɪ] *adj (day)* de vent, venteux(-euse); *(weather)* venteux; **it's ~** il y a du vent

wine [waɪn] *n* vin *m;* **wine bar** *n* bar *m* à vin; **wine glass** *n* verre *m* à vin; **wine list** *n* carte *f* des vins; **wine tasting** *n* dégustation *f* (de vins)

wing [wɪŋ] *n* aile *f,* **wings** *npl (Theat)* coulisses *fpl;* **wing mirror** *n (BRIT)* rétroviseur latéral

wink [wɪŋk] *n* clin *m* d'œil ▷ *vi* faire un clin d'œil; *(blink)* cligner des yeux

winner ['wɪnəʳ] *n* gagnant(e)

winning ['wɪnɪŋ] *adj (team)* gagnant(e); *(goal)* décisif(-ive); *(charming)* charmeur(-euse)

winter ['wɪntəʳ] *n* hiver *m* ▷ *vi* hiverner; **in ~** en hiver; **winter sports** *npl* sports *mpl* d'hiver; **wintertime** *n* hiver *m*

wipe [waɪp] *n:* **to give sth a ~** donner un coup de torchon/de chiffon/d'éponge à qch ▷ *vt* essuyer; *(erase: tape)* effacer; **to ~ one's nose** se moucher; **wipe out** *vt (debt)* éteindre, amortir; *(memory)* effacer; *(destroy)* anéantir; **wipe up** *vt* essuyer

wire ['waɪəʳ] *n* fil *m* (de fer); *(Elec)* fil électrique; *(Tel)* télégramme *m* ▷ *vt (house)* faire l'installation électrique de; *(also:* **~ up)** brancher; *(person: send telegram to)* télégraphier à

wireless ['waɪəlɪs] *adj* sans fil; **wireless technology** *n* technologie *f* sans fil

wiring ['waɪərɪŋ] *n (Elec)* installation *f* électrique

wisdom ['wɪzdəm] *n* sagesse *f; (of action)* prudence *f;* **wisdom tooth** *n* dent *f* de sagesse

wise [waɪz] *adj* sage, prudent(e); *(remark)* judicieux(-euse)

wish [wɪʃ] *n (desire)* désir *m; (specific desire)* souhait *m,* vœu *m* ▷ *vt* souhaiter, désirer, vouloir; **best ~es** *(on birthday etc)* meilleurs vœux; **with best ~es** *(in letter)* bien amicalement; **to ~ sb goodbye** dire au revoir à qn; **he ~ed me well** il m'a souhaité bonne chance; **to ~ to do/sb to do** désirer or vouloir faire/que qn fasse; **to ~ for** souhaiter

wistful ['wɪstfʊl] *adj* mélancolique

wit [wɪt] *n (also:* **~s: intelligence)** intelligence *f,* esprit *m; (presence of mind)* présence *f* d'esprit; *(wittiness)* esprit; *(person)* homme/femme d'esprit

witch [wɪtʃ] *n* sorcière *f*

KEYWORD

with [wɪð, wɪθ] prep 1 (in the company of) avec; (: at the home of) chez; **we stayed with friends** nous avons logé chez des amis; **I'll be with you in a minute** je suis à vous dans un instant **2** (descriptive): **a room with a view** une chambre avec vue; **the man with the grey hat/blue eyes** l'homme au chapeau gris/aux yeux bleus **3** (indicating manner, means, cause): **with tears in her eyes** les larmes aux yeux; **to walk with a stick** marcher avec une canne; **red with anger** rouge de colère; **to shake with fear** trembler de peur; **to fill sth with water** remplir qch d'eau **4** (in phrases): **I'm with you** (I understand) je vous suis; **to be with it** (inf: up-to-date) être dans le vent

withdraw [wɪðˈdrɔː] vt (irreg: like draw) retirer ▷ vi se retirer; **withdrawal** n retrait m; (Med) état m de manque; **withdrawn** pp of **withdraw** ▷ adj (person) renfermé(e)

withdrew [wɪðˈdruː] pt of **withdraw**

wither [ˈwɪðəʳ] vi se faner

withhold [wɪðˈhəʊld] vt (irreg: like **hold**) (money) retenir; (decision) remettre; **to ~ (from)** (permission) refuser (à); (information) cacher (à)

within [wɪðˈɪn] prep à l'intérieur de ▷ adv à l'intérieur; **~ his reach** à sa portée; **~ sight of** en vue de; **~ a mile of** à moins d'un mille de; **~ the week** avant la fin de la semaine

without [wɪðˈaʊt] prep sans; **~ a coat** sans manteau; **~ speaking** sans parler; **to go or do ~ sth** se passer de qch

withstand [wɪðˈstænd] vt (irreg: like **stand**) résister à

witness [ˈwɪtnɪs] n (person) témoin m ▷ vt (event) être témoin de; (document)

attester l'authenticité de; **to bear ~ to sth** témoigner de qch

witty [ˈwɪtɪ] adj spirituel(le), plein(e) d'esprit

wives [waɪvz] npl of **wife**

wizard [ˈwɪzəd] n magicien m

wk abbr = **week**

wobble [ˈwɔbl] vi trembler; (chair) branler

woe [wəʊ] n malheur m

woke [wəʊk] pt of **wake**

woken [ˈwəʊkn] pp of **wake**

wolf (pl **wolves**) [wulf, wulvz] n loup m

woman (pl **women**) [ˈwʊmən, ˈwɪmɪn] n femme f ▷ cpd: **~ doctor** femme f médecin; **~ teacher** professeur m femme

womb [wuːm] n (Anat) utérus m

women [ˈwɪmɪn] npl of **woman**

won [wʌn] pt, pp of **win**

wonder [ˈwʌndəʳ] n merveille f, miracle m; (feeling) émerveillement m ▷ vi: **to ~ whether/why** se demander si/pourquoi; **to ~ at** (surprise) s'étonner de; (admiration) s'émerveiller de; **to ~ about** songer à; **it's no ~ that** il n'est pas étonnant que + sub; **wonderful** adj merveilleux(-euse)

won't [wəʊnt] = **will not**

wood [wud] n (timber, forest) bois m; **wooden** adj en bois; (fig: actor) raide; (: performance) qui manque de naturel; **woodwind** n: **the woodwind** les bois mpl; **woodwork** n menuiserie f

wool [wul] n laine f; **to pull the ~ over sb's eyes** (fig) en faire accroire à qn; **woollen**, (US) **woolen** adj de or en laine; **woolly**, (US) **wooly** adj laineux(-euse); (fig: ideas) confus(e)

word [wəːd] n mot m; (spoken) parole f; (promise) parole; (news) nouvelles fpl ▷ vt (letter, report) rédiger, formuler; **in other ~s** en d'autres termes; **to have a ~ with sb** toucher un mot à qn; **to break/keep one's ~** manquer à sa parole/tenir (sa) parole;

W

wording n termes mpl, langage m; (of document) libellé m; **word processing** n traitement m de texte; **word processor** n machine f de traitement de texte

wore [wɔːʳ] pt of **wear**

work [wəːk] n travail m; (Art, Literature) œuvre f ▷ vi travailler; (mechanism) marcher, fonctionner; (plan etc) marcher; (medicine) agir ▷ vt (clay, wood etc) travailler; (mine etc) exploiter; (machine) faire marcher or fonctionner; (miracles etc) faire; **works** n (BRIT: factory) usine f; **how does this ~?** comment est-ce que ça marche?; **the TV isn't ~ing** la télévision est en panne or ne marche pas; **to be out of ~** être au chômage or sans emploi; **to ~ loose** se défaire, se desserrer; **work out** vi (plans etc) marcher; (Sport) s'entraîner ▷ vt (problem) résoudre; (plan) élaborer; **it ~s out at £100** ça fait 100 livres; **worker** n travailleur(-euse), ouvrier(-ière); **work experience** n stage m; **workforce** n main-d'œuvre f; **working class** n classe ouvrière ▷ adj: **working-class** ouvrier(-ière), de la classe ouvrière; **working week** n semaine f de travail; **workman** (irreg) n ouvrier m; **work of art** n œuvre f d'art; **workout** n (Sport) séance f d'entraînement; **work permit** n permis m de travail; **workplace** n lieu m de travail; **worksheet** n (Scol) feuille f d'exercices; **workshop** n atelier m; **work station** n poste m de travail; **work surface** n plan m de travail; **worktop** n plan m de travail

world [wəːld] n monde m ▷ cpd (champion) du monde; (power, war) mondial(e); **to think the ~ of sb** (fig) ne jurer que par qn; **World Cup** n: **the World Cup** (Football) la Coupe du monde; **world-wide** adj universel(le); **World-Wide Web** n: **the World-Wide Web** le Web

worm [wəːm] n (also: **earth~**) ver m

worn [wɔːn] pp of **wear** ▷ adj usé(e); **worn-out** adj (object) complètement usé(e); (person) épuisé(e)

worried [ˈwʌrɪd] adj inquiet(-ète); **to be ~ about sth** être inquiet au sujet de qch

worry [ˈwʌrɪ] n souci m ▷ vt inquiéter ▷ vi s'inquiéter, se faire du souci; **worrying** adj inquiétant(e)

worse [wəːs] adj pire, plus mauvais(e) ▷ adv plus mal ▷ n pire m; **to get ~** (condition, situation) empirer, se dégrader; **a change for the ~** une détérioration; **worsen** vt, vi empirer; **worse off** adj moins à l'aise financièrement; (fig): **you'll be worse off this way** ça ira moins bien de cette façon

worship [ˈwəːʃɪp] n culte m ▷ vt (God) rendre un culte à; (person) adorer

worst [wəːst] adj (le, la) pire, le (la) plus mauvais(e) ▷ adv le plus mal ▷ n pire m; **at ~** au pis aller

worth [wəːθ] n valeur f ▷ adj: **to be ~** valoir; **it's ~ it** cela en vaut la peine, ça vaut la peine; **it is ~ one's while (to do)** ça vaut le coup (inf) (de faire); **worthless** adj qui ne vaut rien; **worthwhile** adj (activity) qui en vaut la peine; (cause) louable

worthy [ˈwəːðɪ] adj (person) digne; (motive) louable; **~ of** digne de

KEYWORD

would [wud] aux vb **1** (conditional tense): **if you asked him he would do it** si vous le lui demandiez, il le ferait; **if you had asked him he would have done it** si vous le lui aviez demandé, il l'aurait fait
2 (in offers, invitations, requests): **would you like a biscuit?** voulez-vous un biscuit?; **would you close the door please?** voulez-vous fermer la porte, s'il vous plaît?
3 (in indirect speech): **I said I would do**

it j'ai dit que je le ferais
4 (emphatic): **it WOULD have to snow today!** naturellement il neige aujourd'hui, il fallait qu'il neige aujourd'hui!
5 (insistence): **she wouldn't do it** elle n'a pas voulu or elle a refusé de le faire
6 (conjecture): **it WOULD have been midnight** il devait être minuit; **it would seem so** on dirait bien
7 (indicating habit): **he would go there on Mondays** il y allait le lundi

wouldn't ['wʊdnt] = **would not**
wound¹ [wuːnd] n blessure f ▷ vt blesser
wound² [waʊnd] pt, pp of **wind²**
wove [wəʊv] pt of **weave**
woven ['wəʊvn] pp of **weave**
wrap [ræp] vt (also: ~ **up**) envelopper; (parcel) emballer; (wind) enrouler; **wrapper** n (on chocolate etc) papier m; (BRIT: of book) couverture f; **wrapping paper** n (of sweet, chocolate) papier m; (of parcel) emballage m; **wrapping paper** n papier m d'emballage; (for gift) papier cadeau
wreath [riːθ] n couronne f
wreck [rɛk] n (sea disaster) naufrage m; (ship) épave f; (vehicle) véhicule accidenté; (pej: person) loque (humaine) f ▷ vt démolir; ruiner; **wreckage** n débris mpl; (of building) décombres mpl; (of ship) naufrage m
wren [rɛn] n (Zool) troglodyte m
wrench [rɛntʃ] n (Tech) clé f (à écrous); (tug) violent mouvement de torsion; (fig) déchirement m ▷ vt tirer violemment sur, tordre; **to ~ sth from** arracher qch (violemment) à or de
wrestle ['rɛsl] vi: **to ~ (with sb)** lutter (avec qn); **wrestler** n lutteur(-euse); **wrestling** n lutte f; (BRIT: also: **all-in wrestling**) catch m
wretched ['rɛtʃɪd] adj misérable
wriggle ['rɪgl] vi (also: ~ **about**) se tortiller

wring (pt, pp **wrung**) [rɪŋ, rʌŋ] vt tordre; (wet clothes) essorer; (fig): **to ~ sth out of** arracher qch à
wrinkle ['rɪŋkl] n (on skin) ride f; (on paper etc) pli m ▷ vt rider, plisser ▷ vi se plisser
wrist [rɪst] n poignet m
write (pt **wrote**, pp **written**) [raɪt, rəʊt, 'rɪtn] vt, vi écrire; (prescription) rédiger; **write down** vt noter; (put in writing) mettre par écrit; **write off** vt (debt) passer aux profits et pertes; (project) mettre une croix sur; (smash up: car etc) démolir complètement; **write out** vt écrire; (copy) recopier; **write-off** n perte totale; **the car is a write-off** la voiture est bonne pour la casse; **writer** n auteur m, écrivain m
writing ['raɪtɪŋ] n écriture f; (of author) œuvres fpl; **in ~** par écrit; **writing paper** n papier m à lettres
written ['rɪtn] pp of **write**
wrong [rɒŋ] adj (bad) incorrect) faux (fausse); (incorrectly chosen: number, road etc) mauvais(e); (not suitable) qui ne convient pas; (wicked) mal; (unfair) injuste ▷ adv mal ▷ n tort m ▷ vt faire du tort à, léser; **you are ~ to do it** tu as tort de le faire; **you are ~ about that, you've got it ~** tu te trompes; **what's ~?** qu'est-ce qui ne va pas?; **what's ~ with the car?** qu'est-ce qu'elle a, la voiture?; **to go ~** (person) se tromper; (plan) mal tourner; (machine) se détraquer; **I took a ~ turning** je me suis trompé de route; **wrongly** adv à tort; (answer, do, count) mal, incorrectement; **wrong number** n (Tel): **you have the wrong number** vous vous êtes trompé de numéro
wrote [rəʊt] pt of **write**
wrung [rʌŋ] pt, pp of **wring**
WWW n abbr = **World-Wide Web**

XL *abbr* (= *extra large*) XL
Xmas ['ɛksməs] *n abbr* = **Christmas**
X-ray ['ɛksreɪ] *n* (*ray*) rayon m X;
(*photograph*) radio(graphie) f ▷ *vt*
radiographier
xylophone ['zaɪləfəun] *n*
xylophone m

yacht [jɔt] *n* voilier m; (*motor, luxury yacht*) yacht m; **yachting** *n* yachting m, navigation f de plaisance
yard [jɑːd] *n* (*of house etc*) cour f; (*us: garden*) jardin m; (*measure*) yard m
(= 914 mm; 3 feet); **yard sale** *n* (*us*)
brocante f (dans son propre jardin)
yarn [jɑːn] *n* fil m; (*tale*) longue
histoire
yawn [jɔːn] *n* bâillement m ▷ *vi* bâiller
yd. *abbr* = **yard; yards**
yeah [jɛə] *adv* (*inf*) ouais
year [jɪə'] *n* an m, année f; (*Scol etc*)
année; **to be 8 ~s old** avoir 8 ans;
an eight-~-old child un enfant de
huit ans; **yearly** *adj* annuel(le) ▷ *adv*
annuellement; **twice yearly** deux
fois par an
yearn [jəːn] *vi*: **to ~ for sth/to do**
aspirer à qch/à faire
yeast [jiːst] *n* levure f
yell [jɛl] *n* hurlement m, cri m ▷ *vi*
hurler

yellow ['jɛləʊ] adj, n jaune (m);
Yellow Pages® npl (Tel) pages fpl
jaunes

yes [jɛs] adv oui; (answering negative
question) si ▷ n oui m: **to say ~ (to)**
dire oui (à)

yesterday ['jɛstədɪ] adv, n hier (m);
~ morning/evening hier matin/soir;
all day ~ toute la journée d'hier

yet [jɛt] adv encore; (in questions) déjà
▷ conj pourtant, néanmoins; **it is not
finished** ~ ce n'est pas encore fini or
toujours pas fini; **have you eaten ~?**
vous avez déjà mangé?; **the best** ~
le meilleur jusqu'ici or jusque-là; **as** ~
jusqu'ici, encore

yew [ju:] n if m

Yiddish ['jɪdɪʃ] n yiddish m

yield [ji:ld] n production f, rendement
m; (Finance) rapport m ▷ vt produire,
rendre, rapporter; (surrender) céder
▷ vi céder; (us Aut) céder la priorité

yob(bo) ['jɔb(əʊ)] n (BRIT inf)
loubar(d) m

yoga ['jəʊɡə] n yoga m

yog(h)urt ['jəʊɡət] n yaourt m

yolk [jəʊk] n jaune m (d'œuf)

○ **KEYWORD**

you [ju:] pron 1 (subject) tu; (: polite
form) vous; (: plural) vous; **you are
very kind** vous êtes très gentil; **you
French enjoy your food** vous autres
Français, vous aimez bien manger;
you and I will go toi et moi or vous
et moi, nous irons; **there you are!**
vous voilà!

2 (object: direct, indirect) te, t' + vowel;
vous; **I know you** je te or vous
connais; **I gave it to you** je te l'ai
donné, je vous l'ai donné

3 (stressed) toi; vous; **I told you to do
it** c'est à toi or vous que j'ai dit de le faire

4 (after prep, in comparisons) toi; vous;
it's for you c'est pour toi or vous;
she's younger than you elle est plus
jeune que toi or vous

5 (impersonal: one) on; **fresh air does
you good** l'air frais fait du bien; **you
never know** on ne sait jamais; **you
can't do that!** ça ne se fait pas!

you'd [ju:d] = **you had; you would**

you'll [ju:l] = **you will; you shall**

young [jʌŋ] adj jeune ▷ npl (of animal)
petits mpl; **the** ~ (people) les jeunes, la
jeunesse; **my ~er brother** mon frère
cadet; **youngster** n jeune m/f; (child)
enfant m/f

your [jɔ:ʳ] adj ton (ta), tes pl; (polite
form, pl) votre, vos pl; see also **my**

you're [jʊəʳ] = **you are**

yours [jɔ:z] pron le (la) tien(ne), les
tiens (tiennes); (polite form, pl) le (la)
vôtre, les vôtres; **is it ~?** c'est à toi (or
à vous)?; **a friend of ~** un(e) de tes
(or de vos) amis; see also **faithfully;
mine!; sincerely**

yourself [jɔ:'sɛlf] pron (reflexive) te;
(: polite form) vous; (after prep) toi;
vous; (emphatic) toi-même; vous-
même; see also **oneself; yourselves**
pl pron vous; (emphatic) vous-mêmes;
see also **oneself**

youth [ju:θ] n jeunesse f; (young man)
jeune homme m; **youth club** n centre
m de jeunes; **youthful** adj jeune;
(enthusiasm etc) juvénile; **youth
hostel** n auberge f de jeunesse

you've [ju:v] = **you have**

Yugoslav ['ju:ɡəʊslɑ:v] adj (Hist)
yougoslave ▷ n Yougoslave m/f

Yugoslavia [ju:ɡəʊ'slɑ:vɪə] n (Hist)
Yougoslavie f

Z

zoology [zuːˈɒlədʒɪ] n zoologie f
zoom [zuːm] vi: **to ~ past** passer en
trombe; **zoom lens** n zoom m
zucchini [zuːˈkiːnɪ] n (us) courgette f

zeal [ziːl] n (revolutionary etc) ferveur f,
(keenness) ardeur f, zèle m
zebra [ˈziːbrə] n zèbre m; **zebra
crossing** n (BRIT) passage clouté or
pour piétons
zero [ˈzɪərəʊ] n zéro m
zest [zest] n entrain m, élan m; (of
lemon etc) zeste m
zigzag [ˈzɪɡzæɡ] n zigzag m ▷ vi
zigzaguer, faire des zigzags
Zimbabwe [zɪmˈbɑːbwɪ] n
Zimbabwe m
zinc [zɪŋk] n zinc m
zip [zɪp] n (also: ~ **fastener**) fermeture
f éclair® or à glissière ▷ vt (file)
zipper; (also: ~ **up**) fermer (avec une
fermeture éclair®); **zip code** n (us)
code postal; **zip file** n (Comput) fichier
m zip inv; **zipper** n (us) = **zip**
zit [zɪt] (inf) n bouton m
zodiac [ˈzəʊdɪæk] n zodiaque m
zone [zəʊn] n zone f
zoo [zuː] n zoo m

Collins

easy learning French

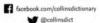

Collins

easy learning German

Easy Learning German Dictionary
978-0-00-753095-3 £9.99

Easy Learning German Grammar
978-0-00-814200-1 £7.99

Easy Learning German Verbs
978-0-00-815842-2 £7.99

**Easy Learning Complete German Grammar,
Verbs and Vocabulary**
(3 books in 1) 978-0-00-814178-3 £12.99

Easy Learning German Grammar & Practice
978-0-00-814165-3 £10.99

Available to buy from all good booksellers and online.
Many titles are also available as ebooks.
www.collins.co.uk/languagesupport

facebook.com/collinsdictionary

@collinsdict

Collins

easy learning Italian

Easy Learning Italian Dictionary
978-0-00-753093-9   £10.99

Easy Learning Italian Grammar
978-0-00-814202-5   £7.99

Easy Learning Italian Verbs
978-0-00-815844-6   £7.99

Easy Learning Complete Italian Grammar,
Verbs and Vocabulary
(3 books in 1) 978-0-00-814175-2   £12.99

Easy Learning Italian Grammar & Practice
978-0-00-814166-0   £10.99

Available to buy from all good booksellers and online.
Many titles are also available as ebooks.
www.collins.co.uk/languagesupport

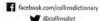

facebook.com/collinsdictionary

@collinsdict